Praise for Previous Editions of *A Practical Guide to Linux® Commands, Editors, and Shell Programming*

"This book is a very useful tool for anyone who wants to 'look under the hood' so to speak, and really start putting the power of Linux to work. What I find particularly frustrating about man pages is that they never include examples. Sobell, on the other hand, outlines very clearly what the command does and then gives several common, easy-to-understand examples that make it a breeze to start shell programming on one's own. As with Sobell's other works, this is simple, straight-forward, and easy to read. It's a great book and will stay on the shelf at easy arm's reach for a long time."

—*Ray Bartlett*
Travel Writer

"Overall I found this book to be quite excellent, and it has earned a spot on the very front of my bookshelf. It covers the real 'guts' of Linux— the command line and its utilities—and does so very well. Its strongest points are the outstanding use of examples, and the Command Reference section. Highly recommended for Linux users of all skill levels. Well done to Mark Sobell and Prentice Hall for this outstanding book!"

—*Dan Clough*
Electronics Engineer and
Slackware Linux User

"Totally unlike most Linux books, this book avoids discussing everything via GUI and jumps right into making the power of the command line your friend."

—*Bjorn Tipling*
Software Engineer
ask.com

"This book is the best distro-agnostic, foundational Linux reference I've ever seen, out of dozens of Linux-related books I've read. Finding this book was a real stroke of luck. If you want to really understand how to get things done at the command line, where the power and flexibility of free UNIX-like OSes really live, this book is among the best tools you'll find toward that end."

—*Chad Perrin*
Writer, TechRepublic

"I moved to Linux from Windows XP a couple of years ago, and after some distro hopping settled on Linux Mint. At age 69 I thought I might be biting off more than I could chew, but thanks to much reading and the help of a local LUG I am now quite at home with Linux at the GUI level.

"Now I want to learn more about the CLI and a few months ago bought your book: *A Practical Guide to Linux® Commands, Editors, and Shell Programming, Second Edition.*

"For me, this book is proving to be the foundation upon which my understanding of the CLI is being built. As a comparative 'newbie' to the Linux world, I find your book a wonderful, easy-to-follow guide that I highly recommend to other Linux users."

—*John Nawell*
CQLUG (Central Queensland Linux User Group)

"I have the second edition of *A Practical Guide to Linux® Commands, Editors, and Shell Programming* and am a big fan. I used it while working as a Cisco support engineer. I plan to get the third edition as soon as it is released. We will be doing a ton of command-line work on literally 1000 boxes (IMS core nodes). I feel you have already given me a lot of tools with the second edition. I want to get your new book as soon as possible. The way you write works very well for my style of learning."

—*Robert Lingenfelter*
Support Engineer, VoIP/IMS

Praise for Other Books by Mark G. Sobell

"Since I'm in an educational environment, I found the content of Sobell's book to be right on target and very helpful for anyone managing Linux in the enterprise. His style of writing is very clear. He builds up to the chapter exercises, which I find to be relevant to real-world scenarios a user or admin would encounter. An IT/IS student would find this book a valuable complement to their education. The vast amount of information is extremely well balanced and Sobell manages to present the content without complicated asides and meandering prose. This is a 'must have' for anyone managing Linux systems in a networked environment or anyone running a Linux server. I would also highly recommend it to an experienced computer user who is moving to the Linux platform."

—*Mary Norbury*
IT Director
Barbara Davis Center
University of Colorado at Denver
from a review posted on slashdot.org

"I had the chance to use your UNIX books when I when was in college years ago at Cal Poly, San Luis Obispo, CA. I have to say that your books are among the best! They're quality books that teach the theoretical aspects and applications of the operating system."

—*Benton Chan*
IS Engineer

"The book has more than lived up to my expectations from the many reviews I read, even though it targets FC2. I have found something very rare with your book: It doesn't read like the standard technical text, it reads more like a story. It's a pleasure to read and hard to put down. Did I say that?! :-)"

—*David Hopkins*
Business Process Architect

"Thanks for your work and for the book you wrote. There are really few books that can help people to become more efficient administrators of different workstations. We hope (in Russia) that you will continue bringing us a new level of understanding of Linux/UNIX systems."

—*Anton Petukhov*

"Mark Sobell has written a book as approachable as it is authoritative."

—*Jeffrey Bianchine*
Advocate, Author, Journalist

"Excellent reference book, well suited for the sysadmin of a Linux cluster, or the owner of a PC contemplating installing a recent stable Linux. Don't be put off by the daunting heft of the book. Sobell has striven to be as inclusive as possible, in trying to anticipate your system administration needs."

—*Wes Boudville*
Inventor

"*A Practical Guide to Red Hat® Linux®* is a brilliant book. Thank you Mark Sobell."

—*C. Pozrikidis*
University of California at San Diego

"This book presents the best overview of the Linux operating system that I have found. . . . [It] should be very helpful and understandable no matter what the reader's background: traditional UNIX user, new Linux devotee, or even Windows user. Each topic is presented in a clear, complete fashion and very few assumptions are made about what the reader knows. . . . The book is extremely useful as a reference, as it contains a 70-page glossary of terms and is very well indexed. It is organized in such a way that the reader can focus on simple tasks without having to wade through more advanced topics until they are ready."

—*Cam Marshall*
Marshall Information Service LLC
Member of Front Range UNIX
Users Group [FRUUG]
Boulder, Colorado

"Conclusively, this is THE book to get if you are a new Linux user and you just got into RH/Fedora world. There's no other book that discusses so many different topics and in such depth."

—*Eugenia Loli-Queru*
Editor in Chief
OSNews.com

"I currently own one of your books, *A Practical Guide to Linux®*. I believe this book is one of the most comprehensive and, as the title says, practical guides to Linux I have ever read. I consider myself a novice and I come back to this book over and over again."

—*Albert J. Nguyen*

"Thank you for writing a book to help me get away from Windows XP and to never touch Windows Vista. The book is great; I am learning a lot of new concepts and commands. Linux is definitely getting easier to use."

—*James Moritz*

"I am so impressed by how Mark Sobell can approach a complex topic in such an understandable manner. His command examples are especially useful in providing a novice (or even an advanced) administrator with a cookbook on how to accomplish real-world tasks on Linux. He is truly an inspired technical writer!"

—*George Vish II*
Senior Education Consultant
Hewlett-Packard Company

"Overall, I think it's a great, comprehensive Ubuntu book that'll be a valuable resource for people of all technical levels."

—*John Dong*
Ubuntu Forum Council Member
Backports Team Leader

"The JumpStart sections really offer a quick way to get things up and running, allowing you to dig into the details of the book later."

—*Scott Mann*
Aztek Networks

"I would so love to be able to use this book to teach a class about not just Ubuntu or Linux but about computers in general. It is thorough and well written with good illustrations that explain important concepts for computer usage."

—*Nathan Eckenrode*
New York Local Community Team

"Ubuntu is gaining popularity at the rate alcohol did during Prohibition, and it's great to see a well-known author write a book on the latest and greatest version. Not only does it contain Ubuntu-specific information, but it also touches on general computer-related topics, which will help the average computer user to better understand what's going on in the background. Great work, Mark!"

—*Daniel R. Arfsten*
Pro/ENGINEER Drafter/Designer

"I read a lot of Linux technical information every day, but I'm rarely impressed by tech books. I usually prefer online information sources instead. Mark Sobell's books are a notable exception. They're clearly written, technically accurate, comprehensive, and actually enjoyable to read."

—*Matthew Miller*
Senior Systems Analyst/Administrator
BU Linux Project
Boston University Office
of Information Technology

"This is well-written, clear, comprehensive information for the Linux user of any type, whether trying Ubuntu on for the first time and wanting to know a little about it, or using the book as a very good reference when doing something more complicated like setting up a server. This book's value goes well beyond its purchase price and it'll make a great addition to the Linux section of your bookshelf."

—*Linc Fessenden*
Host of The LinuxLink TechShow
tllts.org

"The author has done a very good job at clarifying such a detail-oriented operating system. I have extensive Unix and Windows experience and this text does an excellent job at bridging the gaps between Linux, Windows, and Unix. I highly recommend this book to both 'newbs' and experienced users. Great job!"

—*Mark Polczynski*
Information Technology Consultant

"Your text, *A Practical Guide to Ubuntu Linux®, Third Edition*, is a well constructed, informative, superbly written text. You deserve an award for outstanding talent; unfortunately my name is not Pulitzer."

—*Harrison Donnelly*
Physician

"When I first started working with Linux just a short ten years or so ago, it was a little more difficult than now to get going. . . . Now, someone new to the community has a vast array of resources available on the web, or if they are inclined to begin with Ubuntu, they can literally find almost every single thing they will need in the single volume of Mark Sobell's *A Practical Guide to Ubuntu Linux®*.

"I'm sure this sounds a bit like hyperbole. Everything a person would need to know? Obviously not everything, but this book, weighing in at just under 1200 pages, covers so much so thoroughly that there won't be much left out. From install to admin, networking, security, shell scripting, package management, and a host of other topics, it is all there. GUI and command-line tools are covered. There is not really any wasted space or fluff, just a huge amount of information. There are screen shots when appropriate but they do not take up an inordinate amount of space. This book is information-dense."

—*JR Peck*
Editor
GeekBook.org

"I have been wanting to make the jump to Linux but did not have the guts to do so—until I saw your familiarly titled *A Practical Guide to Red Hat® Linux®* at the bookstore. I picked up a copy and am eagerly looking forward to regaining my freedom."

—*Carmine Stoffo*
Machine and Process Designer
to pharmaceutical industry

"I am currently reading *A Practical Guide to Red Hat® Linux®* and am finally understanding the true power of the command line. I am new to Linux and your book is a treasure."

—*Juan Gonzalez*

"Overall, *A Practical Guide to Ubuntu Linux®* by Mark G. Sobell provides all of the information a beginner to intermediate user of Linux would need to be productive. The inclusion of the Live DVD of the Gutsy Gibbon release of Ubuntu makes it easy for the user to test-drive Linux without affecting his installed OS. I have no doubts that you will consider this book money well spent."

—*Ray Lodato*
Slashdot contributor
www.slashdot.org

A Practical Guide to Linux® Commands, Editors, and Shell Programming

FOURTH EDITION

Mark G. Sobell

coauthored by **Matthew Helmke**

Addison-Wesley

Boston • Colombus • Indianapolis • New York • San Francisco • Amsterdam • Cape Town
Dubai • London • Madrid • Milan • Munich • Paris • Montreal • Toronto • Delhi • Mexico City
São Paulo• Sydney • Hong Kong • Seoul • Singapore • Taipei • Tokyo

For information about buying this title in bulk quantities, or for special sales opportunities (which may include electronic versions; custom cover designs; and content particular to your business, training goals, marketing focus, or branding interests), please contact our corporate sales department at corpsales@pearsoned.com or (800) 382-3419.

For government sales inquiries, please contact governmentsales@pearsoned.com.

For questions about sales outside the U.S., please contact intlcs@pearson.com.

Visit us on the Web: informit.com/aw

Library of Congress Control Number: 201795249

ISBN-13: 978-0-13-477460-2
ISBN-10: 0-13-477460-4

6 2021

For Sandra,
Sage, Sedona, Philip, and Evan.
Love you tons!

—Matthew Helmke

Brief Contents

Contents

PART I THE LINUX AND MACOS OPERATING SYSTEMS 21

CHAPTER 2: GETTING STARTED 23

CHAPTER 3: THE UTILITIES 49

PART II THE EDITORS 163

CHAPTER 6: THE vim EDITOR 165

PART III THE SHELLS 283

CHAPTER 8: THE BOURNE AGAIN SHELL (bash) 285

CHAPTER 14: THE AWK PATTERN PROCESSING LANGUAGE 635

CHAPTER 15: THE sed EDITOR 669

PART VI Command Reference 729

PREFACE

Linux *A Practical Guide to Linux® Commands, Editors, and Shell Programming, Fourth Edition,* explains how to work with the Linux operating system from the command line. The first few chapters of this book build a foundation for learning about Linux. The rest of the book covers more advanced topics and goes into more detail. This book does not describe a particular release or distribution of Linux but rather pertains to all recent versions of Linux.

macOS This book also explains how to work with the UNIX/Linux foundation of macOS. It looks "under the hood," past the traditional GUI (graphical user interface) that most people associate with the Macintosh, and explains how to use the powerful command-line interface (CLI) that connects you directly to macOS. Where this book refers to Linux, it implicitly refers to macOS as well and makes note of differences between the two operating systems.

Command-line interface (CLI) In the beginning there was the command-line (textual) interface, which enabled a user to give Linux commands from the command line. There was no mouse to point with or icons to drag and drop. Some programs, such as emacs, implemented rudimentary windows using the very minimal graphics available in the ASCII character set. Reverse video helped separate areas of the screen.

Linux was born and raised in this environment, so naturally all the original Linux tools were invoked from the command line. The real power of Linux still lies in this environment, which explains why many Linux professionals work *exclusively* from the command line. Using clear descriptions and many examples, this book shows you how to get the most out of your Linux system using the command-line interface.

Linux distributions A Linux distribution comprises the Linux kernel, utilities, and application programs. Many distributions are available, including Ubuntu, Fedora, openSUSE, Red Hat, Debian, Mageia, Arch, CentOS, Solus, and Mint. Although the distributions differer from one another in various ways, all of them rely on the Linux kernel, utilities, and applications. This book is based on the code that is common to most distributions. As a consequence you can use it regardless of which distribution you are running.

Overlap If you read one of Mark Sobell's other books, *A Practical Guide to Fedora™ and Red Hat® Enterprise Linux,* or *A Practical Guide to Ubuntu Linux®,* or Matthew Helmke's *Ubuntu Unleashed* or *The Official Ubuntu Book,* you will notice some overlap between those books and the one you are reading now. The books cover similar information, presented from different perspectives and at different levels of depth depending on the intended audience for each book.

Audience This book is designed for a wide range of readers. It does not require programming experience, although some experience using a computer is helpful. It is appropriate for the following readers:

- **Students** taking a class in which they use Linux or macOS
- **Power users** who want to explore the power of Linux or macOS from the command line
- **Professionals** who use Linux or macOS at work
- **Beginning Macintosh users** who want to know what UNIX/Linux is, why everyone keeps saying it is important, and how to take advantage of it
- **Experienced Macintosh users** who want to know how to take advantage of the power of UNIX/Linux that underlies macOS
- **UNIX users** who want to adapt their UNIX skills to the Linux or macOS environment
- **System administrators** who need a deeper understanding of Linux or macOS and the tools that are available to them, including the bash, Perl, and Python scripting languages
- **Web developers** who need to understand Linux inside and out, including Perl and Python
- **Computer science students** who are studying the Linux or macOS operating system
- **Programmers** who need to understand the Linux or macOS programming environment
- **Technical executives** who want to get a grounding in Linux or macOS

Benefits *A Practical Guide to Linux® Commands, Editors, and Shell Programming, Fourth Edition,* gives you a broad understanding of how to use Linux and macOS from the command line. Regardless of your background, it offers the knowledge you need to get on with your work: You will come away from this book with an understanding of how to use Linux/macOS, and this text will remain a valuable reference for years to come.

A large amount of free software has always been available for Macintosh systems. In addition, the Macintosh shareware community is very active. By introducing the UNIX/Linux aspects of macOS, this book throws open to Macintosh users the vast store of free and low-cost software available for Linux and other UNIX-like systems.

In this book, *Linux* refers to *Linux* and *macOS*

tip The UNIX operating system is the common ancestor of Linux and macOS. Although the GUIs (graphical user interfaces) of these two operating systems differ significantly, the command-line interfaces (CLIs) are very similar and in many cases identical. This book describes the CLIs of both Linux and macOS. To make the content more readable, this book uses the term *Linux* to refer to both *Linux* and *macOS.* It makes explicit note of where the two operating systems differ.

FEATURES OF THIS BOOK

This book is organized for ease of use in different situations. For example, you can read it from cover to cover to learn command-line Linux from the ground up. Alternatively, once you are comfortable using Linux, you can use this book as a reference: Look up a topic of interest in the table of contents or index and read about it. Or refer to one of the utilities covered in Part VI, "Command Reference." You can also think of this book as a catalog of Linux topics: Flip through the pages until a topic catches your eye. The book also includes many pointers to Web sites where you can obtain additional information: Consider the Internet to be an extension of this book.

A Practical Guide to Linux® Commands, Editors, and Shell Programming, Fourth Edition, offers the following features:

- **Optional sections** allow you to read the book at different levels, returning to more difficult material when you are ready to tackle it.
- **Caution boxes** highlight procedures that can easily go wrong, giving you guidance *before* you run into trouble.
- **Tip boxes** highlight places in the text where you can save time by doing something differently or when it might be useful or just interesting to have additional information.
- **Security boxes** point out ways you can make a system more secure.
- Each chapter starts with a list of **chapter objectives**—a list of important tasks you should be able to perform after reading the chapter.
- Concepts are illustrated by **practical examples** found throughout the book.
- The many useful **URLs** (Internet addresses) identify sites where you can obtain software and information.
- **Main, File Tree, and Utility indexes** help you find what you are looking for quickly; for easy access, the Utility index is reproduced on the insides of the front and back covers.

- **Chapter summaries** review the important points covered in each chapter.
- **Review exercises** are included at the end of each chapter for readers who want to hone their skills. Answers to even-numbered exercises are posted at www.sobell.com.
- Important **GNU tools**, including gcc, GNU Configure and Build System, make, gzip, and many others, are described in detail.
- Pointers throughout the book provide help in obtaining **online documentation** from many sources, including the local system and the Internet.
- Important command-line utilities that were developed by Apple specifically for macOS are covered in detail, including diskutil, ditto, dscl, GetFileInfo, launchctl, otool, plutil, and SetFile.
- Descriptions of macOS **extended attributes** include **file forks, file attributes, attribute flags**, and **Access Control Lists (ACLs)**.
- Appendix D, "macOS Notes," lists some differences between macOS and Linux.

CONTENTS

This section describes the information that each chapter covers and explains how that information can help you take advantage of the power of Linux. You might want to review the table of contents for more detail.

- **Chapter 1—Welcome to Linux and macOS**
  Presents background information on Linux and macOS. This chapter covers the **history of Linux**, profiles the macOS **Mach kernel**, explains how the GNU Project helped Linux get started, and discusses some of the **important features of Linux** that distinguish it from other operating systems.

PART I: THE LINUX AND MACOS OPERATING SYSTEMS

Experienced users might want to skim Part I

tip If you have used a UNIX/Linux system before, you might want to skim or skip some or all of the chapters in Part I. All readers should take a look at "Conventions Used in This Book" (page 24), which explains the typographic conventions that this book uses, and "Where to Find Documentation" (page 33), which points you toward both local and remote sources of Linux documentation.

Part I introduces Linux and gets you started using it.

- **Chapter 2—Getting Started**
  Explains the **typographic conventions** this book uses to make explanations clearer and easier to read. This chapter provides basic information and

explains how to log in, **change your password**, give Linux commands using the shell, and **find system documentation.**

- Chapter 3—The Utilities
Explains the **command-line interface** (CLI) and briefly introduces **more than 30 command-line utilities.** Working through this chapter gives you a feel for Linux and introduces some of the tools you will use day in, day out. Deeper discussion of utilities is reserved for Part VI. The utilities covered in this chapter include
    - grep, which **searches through files** for strings of characters;
    - unix2dos, which **converts Linux text files** to Windows format;
    - tar, which **creates archive files** that can hold many other files;
    - bzip2 and gzip, which **compress files** so that they take up less space on disk and allow you to transfer them over a network more quickly; and
    - diff, which **displays the differences** between two text files.
- Chapter 4—The Filesystem
Discusses the Linux hierarchical filesystem, covering files, filenames, **pathnames**, working with directories, **access permissions**, and hard and **symbolic links.** Understanding the filesystem allows you to **organize your data** so that you can find information quickly. It also enables you to **share some of your files** with other users while **keeping other files private.**
- Chapter 5—The Shell
Explains how to use shell features to make your work faster and easier. All of the features covered in this chapter work with both bash and tcsh. This chapter discusses
    - Using **command-line options** to modify the way a command works;
    - Making minor changes in a command line to **redirect input** to a command so that it comes from a file instead of the keyboard;
    - **Redirecting output** from a command to go to a file instead of the screen;
    - Using **pipelines** to send the output of one utility directly to another utility so you can solve problems right on the command line;
    - Running programs in the **background** so you can work on one task while Linux is working on a different one; and
    - Using the shell to **generate filenames** to save time spent on typing and help you when you do not remember the exact name of a file.

PART II: THE EDITORS

Part II covers two classic, powerful Linux command-line text editors. Most Linux distributions include the vim text editor, an "improved" version of the widely used vi editor, as well as the popular GNU emacs editor. Text editors enable you to create and modify text files that can hold programs, shell scripts, memos, and input to text formatting programs. Because Linux system administration involves editing text-based configuration files, skilled Linux administrators are adept at using text editors.

- **Chapter 6—The vim Editor**
  Starts with a **tutorial** on vim and then explains how to use many of the **advanced features** of vim, including special characters in search strings, the General-Purpose and Named buffers, parameters, markers, and execution of commands from within vim. The chapter concludes with a **summary of vim commands.**

- **Chapter 7—The emacs Editor**
  Opens with a **tutorial** and then explains many of the features of the emacs editor, as well as how to use the META, ALT, and ESCAPE keys. In addition, this chapter covers key bindings, buffers, and **incremental and complete searching** for both character strings and regular expressions. It details the relationship between Point, the cursor, Mark, and Region. It also explains how to take advantage of the extensive **online help** facilities available from emacs. Other topics covered include cutting and pasting, using multiple windows and frames, and working with emacs modes—specifically **C mode**, which aids programmers in writing and debugging C code. Chapter 7 concludes with a **summary of emacs commands.**

PART III: THE SHELLS

Part III goes into more detail about bash and introduces the TC Shell (tcsh).

- **Chapter 8—The Bourne Again Shell** (bash)
  Picks up where Chapter 5 left off, covering more advanced aspects of working with a shell. For examples it uses the Bourne Again Shell—bash, the shell used almost exclusively for system shell scripts. Chapter 8 describes how to

  - Use shell **startup files**, shell options, and shell features to **customize the shell;**
  - Use **job control** to stop jobs and move jobs from the foreground to the background, and vice versa;
  - Modify and reexecute commands using the **shell history** list;
  - Create **aliases** to customize commands;
  - Work with **user-created and keyword variables** in shell scripts;
  - Implement localization including discussions of the locale utility, the LC_ variables, and internationalization;
  - Set up **functions**, which are similar to shell scripts but are executed more quickly;

- Write and execute simple **shell scripts**; and
- **Redirect error messages** so they go to a file instead of the screen.

- **Chapter 9—The TC Shell** (tcsh)
  Describes tcsh and covers features common to and different between bash and tcsh. This chapter explains how to
  - Run tcsh and **change your default shell** to tcsh;
  - **Redirect error messages** so they go to files instead of the screen;
  - Use **control structures** to alter the flow of control within shell scripts;
  - Work with tcsh **array and numeric variables**; and
  - Use shell **builtin commands**.

PART IV: PROGRAMMING TOOLS

Part IV covers important programming tools that are used extensively in Linux and macOS system administration and general-purpose programming.

- **Chapter 10—Programming the Bourne Again Shell** (bash)
  Continues where Chapter 8 left off, going into greater depth about advanced shell programming using bash, with the discussion enhanced by extensive examples. This chapter discusses
  - **Control structures** including **if...then...else** and **case**;
  - **Variables**, with discussions of attributes, expanding null and unset variables, array variables, and variables in functions;
  - **Environment**, including environment versus local variables, inheritance, and process locality;
  - **Arithmetic and logical** (**Boolean**) **expressions**; and
  - Some of the most useful **shell builtin commands**, including exec, trap, and getopts.

  Once you have mastered the basics of Linux, you can use your knowledge to build more complex and specialized programs, using the shell as a programming language.

  Chapter 10 poses two complete **shell programming problems** and then shows you how to solve them step by step. The first problem uses **recursion** to create a hierarchy of directories. The second problem develops a quiz program, shows you how to set up a shell script that **interacts with a user**, and explains how the script processes data. (The examples in Part VI also demonstrate many features of the utilities you can use in shell scripts.)

- **Chapter 11—The Perl Scripting Language**
  Introduces the popular, feature-rich Perl programming language. This chapter covers
  - Perl **help tools,** including perldoc;
  - Perl **variables** and **control structures;**
  - **File handling;**
  - **Regular expressions;** and
  - Installation and use of **CPAN modules.**

  Many Linux administration scripts are written in Perl. After reading Chapter 11 you will be able to better understand these scripts and start writing your own. This chapter includes many examples of Perl scripts.

- **Chapter 12—The Python Programming Language**
  Introduces the flexible and friendly Python programming language. This chapter covers
  - Python **lists** and **dictionaries;**
  - Python functions and methods you can use to **write to and read from files;**
  - Using **pickle** to store an object on disk;
  - Importing and using **libraries;**
  - Defining and using **functions,** including regular and **Lambda functions;**
  - **Regular expressions;** and
  - Using **list comprehensions.**

  Many Linux tools are written in Python. Chapter 12 introduces Python, including some basic object-oriented concepts, so you can read and understand Python programs and write your own. This chapter includes many examples of Python programs.

- **Chapter 13—The MariaDB SQL Database Management System**
  Introduces the widely used MariaDB/MySQL relational database management system (RDBMS). This chapter covers
  - Relational database **terminology;**
  - **Installing** the MariaDB client and server;
  - **Creating a database;**
  - **Adding a user;**
  - Creating and modifying **tables;**
  - **Adding data** to a database; and
  - **Backing up** and restoring a database.

- **Chapter 14—The AWK Pattern Processing Language**
  Explains how to use the powerful AWK language to write programs that filter data, **write reports**, and **retrieve data from the Internet**. The advanced programming section describes how to set up **two-way communication** with another program using a **coprocess** and how to obtain input over a network instead of from a local file.
- **Chapter 15—The sed Editor**
  Describes sed, the **noninteractive stream editor** that finds many applications as a filter within shell scripts. This chapter discusses how to use sed's buffers to write **simple yet powerful programs** and includes many examples.

PART V: SECURE NETWORK UTILITIES

Part V describes two utilities you can use to work on a remote system and copy files across a network securely.

- **Chapter 16—The rsync Secure Copy Utility**
  Covers rsync, a secure utility that **copies** an ordinary file or **directory hierarchy** locally or between the local system and **a remote system**. As you write programs, you can use this utility to back them up to another system.
- **Chapter 17—The OpenSSH Secure Communication Utilities**
  Explains how to use the ssh, scp, and sftp utilities to communicate securely over the Internet. This chapter covers the use of authorized keys that allow you to log in on a remote system securely without a password, ssh-agent that can hold your **private keys** while you are working, and **forwarding X11** so you can run graphical programs remotely.

PART VI: COMMAND REFERENCE

Linux includes hundreds of utilities. Chapters 14, 15, 16, and 17 as well as Part VI provide extensive examples of the use of over 100 of the **most important utilities** with which you can solve problems without resorting to programming in C. If you are already familiar with UNIX/Linux, this part of the book will be a valuable, **easy-to-use reference**. If you are not an experienced user, it will serve as a useful supplement while you are mastering the earlier sections of the book.

Although the descriptions of the utilities in Chapters 14, 15, 16, and 17 and Part VI are presented in a format similar to that used by the Linux manual (man) pages, they are much easier to read and understand. These utilities are included because you will work with them **day in, day out** (for example, ls and cp), because they are **powerful tools** that are especially useful in shell scripts (sort, paste, and test), because they help you **work with a Linux system** (ps, kill, and fsck), or because they enable you to **communicate with other systems** (ssh, scp, and ftp). Each utility description includes complete explanations of its most useful options, differentiating between options supported under macOS and those supported under Linux. The "Discussion" and "Notes" sections present **tips and tricks** for taking full advantage of the utility's power. The "**Examples**" **sections** demonstrate how to use these utilities in real life, alone and together with other utilities, to generate reports, summarize data, and extract information. Take a look at the "Examples" sections for find (page 826), ftp (page 841), and sort (page 971) to see how extensive these sections are. Some utilities, such as Midnight Commander (mc; page 902) and screen (page 958), include extensive discussion sections and tutorials.

PART VII: APPENDIXES

Part VII includes the appendixes, the glossary, and three indexes.

- **Appendix A—Regular Expressions**
  Explains how to use **regular expressions** to take advantage of the **hidden power of Linux.** Many utilities, including grep, sed, vim, AWK, Perl, and Python, accept regular expressions in place of simple strings of characters. A single regular expression can match many simple strings.
- **Appendix B—Help**
  Details the steps typically used to **solve the problems** you might encounter when using a Linux system.
- **Appendix C—Keeping the System Up-to-Date**
  Describes how to use tools to download software and **keep a system current.** This appendix includes information on
  - dnf—Downloads software from the Internet, keeping a system up-to-date and **resolving dependencies** as it goes.
  - apt-get—An alternative to dnf for keeping a system current.
  - **BitTorrent**—Good for distributing large amounts of data such as Linux installation CDs and DVDs.
- **Appendix D—macOS Notes**
  A brief guide to macOS features and quirks that might be unfamiliar to users who have been using Linux or other UNIX-like systems.
- **Glossary**
  Defines more than 500 terms that pertain to the use of Linux and macOS.
- **Indexes**
  Three indexes that make it easier to find what you are looking for quickly. These indexes indicate where you can locate tables (page numbers followed by the letter t) and definitions (*italic* page numbers). They also differentiate between light and comprehensive coverage (page numbers in light and standard fonts, respectively).
  - **File Tree Index**—Lists, in hierarchical fashion, most files mentioned in this book. These files are also listed in the Main index.
  - **Utility Index**—Locates all utilities mentioned in this book. A page number in a light font indicates a brief mention of the utility; use of

the regular font indicates more substantial coverage. The Utility index is reproduced on the insides of the front and back covers.

- **Main Index**—Helps you find the information you want quickly.

SUPPLEMENTS

The author's home page (www.sobell.com) contains downloadable listings of the longer programs from this book as well as pointers to many interesting and useful Linux- and macOS-related sites on the World Wide Web; a list of corrections to the book; answers to even numbered exercises; and a solicitation for corrections, comments, and suggestions.

Register your copy of *A Practical Guide to Linux® Commands, Editors, and Shell Programming, Fourth Edition*, at informit.com/register for convenient access to downloads, updates, and/or corrections as they become available (you must log in or create a new account). Enter the product ISBN (9780134774602) and click Submit. Once the process is complete, you will find any available bonus content under Registered Products. If you would like to be notified of exclusive offers on new editions and updates, please check the box to receive email from us.

THANKS

As this is my (Matthew's) first edition of this book, I would like to begin by thanking Mark Sobell for trusting me with his creation. You have gifted me an excellent foundation and I am truly grateful. Enjoy your well-deserved retirement! I also want to thank Debra Williams Cauley and Mark Taub for approaching both me and Mark Sobell when he decided it was time to hand the book to someone else. Your trust in me is appreciated and not taken lightly.

I take responsibility for any errors and omissions in this book. If you find one or just have a comment, let me know (matthew@matthewhelmke.com), and I will fix it in the next printing. I inherited a fabulous amount of well-vetted content, and I have tested what is here while updating the text for this edition, but it is possible I have not done so perfectly and am happy to receive your kind assistance and corrections where needed.

The rest of this section is from Mark's previous edition. I share his gratitude to and appreciation of all who are mentioned here, many of whom have also worked with me on this edition.

Matthew Helmke
North Liberty, Iowa

(From the Third Edition, 2013)

First and foremost, I want to thank Mark L. Taub, Editor-in-Chief of the IT Professional Group at Pearson, who provided encouragement and support through the hard parts of this project. Mark is unique in my 30 years of book writing experience: an editor who works with the tools I write about. Because Mark runs Linux on his home computer, we shared experiences as I wrote this book. Mark, your comments and direction are invaluable; this book would not exist without your help. Thank you, Mark T.

The production people at Pearson are wonderful to work with.: Julie Nahil, Full-Service Production Manager, worked with me day-by-day during production of this book, providing help and keeping everything on track, while John Fuller, Managing Editor, kept the large view in focus. Thanks to Jill Hobbs, Copyeditor; and Audrey Doyle, Proofreader, who made each page sparkle and found the mistakes I left behind.

Thanks also to the folks at Pearson who helped bring this book to life, especially Kim Boedigheimer, Editorial Assistant, who attended to the many details involved in publishing this book; Heather Fox, Publicist; Stephane Nakib, Marketing Manager; Cheryl Lenser, Senior Indexer; Sandra Schroeder, Design Manager; Chuti Prasertsith, Cover Designer; and everyone else who worked behind the scenes to make this book come into being.

I am also indebted to Denis Howe, Editor of *The Free On-Line Dictionary of Computing* (FOLDOC). Denis has graciously permitted me to use entries from his compilation; visit www.foldoc.org to look at this dictionary.

Special thanks go to Max Sobell, Intrepidus Group, for his extensive help writing the Python chapter; Doug Hellmann, Senior Developer, DreamHost, for his careful and insightful reviews of the Python chapter; and Angjoo Kanazawa, Graduate Student, University of Maryland, College Park, for her helpful comments on this chapter.

Thanks to Graham Lee, Mobile App Developer and Software Security Consultant, Agant, Ltd., and David Chisnall, University of Cambridge, for their reviews and comments on the Mac-related sections of this book.

In his reviews, Jeffrey S. Haemer taught me many tricks of the bash trade. I had no idea how many ways you could get bash to do your bidding. Jeffrey, you are a master; thank you for your help.

In addition to her insightful comments on many sections, Jennifer Davis, Yahoo! Sherpa Service Engineering Team Lead, used her thorough understanding of MySQL to cause me to change many aspects of that chapter.

A big "thank you" to the folks who read through the drafts of the book and made comments that caused me to refocus parts of the book where things were not clear or were left out altogether: Michael Karpeles; Robert P. J. Day, Candy Strategies; Gavin Knight, Noisebridge; Susan Lauber, Lauber System Solutions, Inc.; William Skiba; Carlton "Cobolt" Sue; Rickard Körkkö, Bolero AB; and Benjamin Schupak.

Thanks also to the following people who helped with my previous Linux books, which provided a foundation for this book:

Doug Hughes; Richard Woodbury, Site Reliability Engineer, Google; Max Sobell, Intrepidus Group; Lennart Poettering, Red Hat, Inc.; George Vish II, Senior Education Consultant, Hewlett-Packard; Matthew Miller, Senior Systems Analyst/Administrator, BU Linux Project, Boston University Office of Information Technology; Garth Snyder; Nathan Handler; Dick Seabrook, Emeritus Professor, Anne Arundel Community College; Chris Karr, Audacious Software; Scott McCrea, Instructor, ITT Technical Schools; John Dong, Ubuntu Developer, Forums Council Member; Andy Lester, author of *Land the Tech Job You Love: Why Skill and Luck Are Not Enough;* Scott James Remnant, Ubuntu Development Manager and Desktop Team Leader; David Chisnall, Swansea University; Scott Mann, Aztek Networks; Thomas Achtemichuk, Mansueto Ventures; Daniel R. Arfsten, Pro/Engineer Drafter/Designer; Chris Cooper, Senior Education Consultant, Hewlett-Packard Education Services; Sameer Verma, Associate Professor of Information Systems, San Francisco State University; Valerie Chau, Palomar College and Programmers Guild; James Kratzer; Sean McAllister; Nathan Eckenrode, New York Ubuntu Local Community Team; Christer Edwards; Nicolas Merline; Michael Price; Mike Basinger, Ubuntu Community and Forums Council Member; Joe Barker, Ubuntu Forums Staff Member; James Stockford, Systemateka, Inc.; Stephanie Troeth, Book Oven; Doug Sheppard; Bryan Helvey, IT Director, OpenGeoSolutions; and Vann Scott, Baker College of Flint.

Also, thanks to Jesse Keating, Fedora Project; Carsten Pfeiffer, Software Engineer and KDE Developer; Aaron Weber, Ximian; Cristof Falk, Software Developer, CritterDesign; Steve Elgersma, Computer Science Department, Princeton University; Scott Dier, University of Minnesota; Robert Haskins, Computer Net Works; Lars Kellogg-Stedman, Harvard University; Jim A. Lola, Principal Systems Consultant, Privateer Systems; Eric S. Raymond, Cofounder, Open Source Initiative; Scott Mann; Randall Lechlitner, Independent Computer Consultant; Jason Wertz, Computer Science Instructor, Montgomery County Community College; Justin Howell, Solano Community College; Ed Sawicki, The Accelerated Learning Center; David Mercer; Jeffrey Bianchine, Advocate, Author, Journalist; John Kennedy; and Jim Dennis, Starshine Technical Services.

Thanks also to Dustin Puryear, Puryear Information Technology; Gabor Liptak, Independent Consultant; Bart Schaefer, Chief Technical Officer, iPost; Michael J. Jordan, Web Developer, Linux Online; Steven Gibson, Owner, SuperAnt.com; John Viega, Founder and Chief Scientist, Secure Software; K. Rachael Treu, Internet Security Analyst, Global Crossing; Kara Pritchard, K & S Pritchard Enterprises; Glen Wiley, Capital One Finances; Karel Baloun, Senior Software Engineer, Looksmart; Matthew Whitworth; Dameon D. Welch-Abernathy, Nokia Systems; Josh Simon, Consultant; Stan Isaacs; and Dr. Eric H. Herrin II, Vice President, Herrin Software Development.

More thanks go to consultants Lorraine Callahan and Steve Wampler; Ronald Hiller, Graburn Technology; Charles A. Plater, Wayne State University; Bob Palowoda; Tom Bialaski, Sun Microsystems; Roger Hartmuller, TIS Labs at Network Associates; Kaowen Liu; Andy Spitzer; Rik Schneider; Jesse St. Laurent; Steve Bellenot; Ray W. Hiltbrand; Jennifer Witham; Gert-Jan Hagenaars; and Casper Dik.

A Practical Guide to Linux® Commands, Editors, and Shell Programming, Fourth Edition, is based in part on two of my previous UNIX books: *UNIX System V: A Practical Guide* and *A Practical Guide to the UNIX System.* Many people helped me with those books, and thanks here go to Pat Parseghian; Dr. Kathleen Hemenway; Brian LaRose; Byron A. Jeff, Clark Atlanta University; Charles Stross; Jeff Gitlin, Lucent Technologies; Kurt Hockenbury; Maury Bach, Intel Israel; Peter H. Salus; Rahul Dave, University of Pennsylvania; Sean Walton, Intelligent Algorithmic Solutions; Tim Segall, Computer Sciences Corporation; Behrouz Forouzan, DeAnza College; Mike Keenan, Virginia Polytechnic Institute and State University; Mike Johnson, Oregon State University; Jandelyn Plane, University of Maryland; Arnold Robbins and Sathis Menon, Georgia Institute of Technology; Cliff Shaffer, Virginia Polytechnic Institute and State University; and Steven Stepanek, California State University, Northridge, for reviewing this book.

I continue to be grateful to the many people who helped with the early editions of my UNIX books. Special thanks are due to Roger Sippl, Laura King, and Roy Harrington for introducing me to the UNIX system. My mother, Dr. Helen Sobell, provided invaluable comments on the original manuscript at several junctures. Also, thanks go to Isaac Rabinovitch, Professor Raphael Finkel, Professor Randolph Bentson, Bob Greenberg, Professor Udo Pooch, Judy Ross, Dr. Robert Veroff, Dr. Mike Denny, Joe DiMartino, Dr. John Mashey, Diane Schulz, Robert Jung, Charles Whitaker, Don Cragun, Brian Dougherty, Dr. Robert Fish, Guy Harris, Ping Liao, Gary Lindgren, Dr. Jarrett Rosenberg, Dr. Peter Smith, Bill Weber, Mike Bianchi, Scooter Morris, Clarke Echols, Oliver Grillmeyer, Dr. David Korn, Dr. Scott Weikart, and Dr. Richard Curtis.

I take responsibility for any errors and omissions in this book. If you find one or just have a comment, let me know (mgs@sobell.com), and I will fix it in the next printing. My home page (www.sobell.com) contains a list of errors and credits those who found them. It also offers copies of the longer scripts from the book and pointers to interesting Linux pages on the Internet. You can follow me on Twitter at twitter.com/marksobell.

Mark G. Sobell
San Francisco, California

1

Welcome to Linux and macOS

In This Chapter

Objectives

After reading this chapter you should be able to:

- Discuss the history of UNIX, Linux, and the GNU project
- Explain what is meant by "free software" and list characteristics of the GNU General Public License
- List characteristics of Linux and reasons the Linux operating system is so popular
- Discuss three benefits of virtual machines over single physical machines

An *operating system* is the low-level software that schedules tasks, allocates storage, and handles the interfaces to peripheral hardware, such as printers, disk drives, the screen, keyboard, and mouse. An operating system has two main parts: the *kernel* and the *system programs*. The kernel allocates machine resources—including memory, disk space, and *CPU* (page 1092) cycles—to all other programs that run on the computer. The system programs include device drivers, libraries, utility programs, shells (command interpreters), configuration scripts and files, application programs, servers, and documentation. They perform higher-level housekeeping tasks, often acting as servers in a client/server relationship. For Linux and macOS, many of the libraries, servers, and utility programs were written by the GNU Project, which is discussed shortly.

Linux kernel The Linux *kernel* was developed by Finnish undergraduate student Linus Torvalds, who used the Internet to make the source code immediately available to others for free. Torvalds released Linux version 0.01 in September 1991.

The new operating system came together through a lot of hard work. Programmers around the world were quick to extend the kernel and develop other tools, adding functionality to match that already found in both BSD UNIX and System V UNIX (SVR4) as well as new functionality. The name *Linux* is a combination of *Linus* and *UNIX*.

The Linux operating system, which was developed through the cooperation of numerous people around the world, is a product of the Internet and is a *free* (*open source;* page 1113) operating system. In other words, all the source code is free. You are free to study it, redistribute it, and modify it. As a result, the code is available free of cost—no charge for the software, source, documentation, or support (via newsgroups, mailing lists, and other Internet resources). As the GNU Free Software Definition (www.gnu.org/philosophy/free-sw.html) puts it:

Free beer

> "Free software" is a matter of liberty, not price. To understand the concept, you should think of "free" as in "free speech," not as in "free beer."

Mach kernel macOS runs the Mach kernel, which was developed at Carnegie Mellon University (CMU) and is free software. CMU concluded its work on the project in 1994, although other groups have continued this line of research. Much of the macOS software is open source: The macOS kernel is based on Mach and FreeBSD code; utilities come from BSD and the GNU project; and system programs come mostly from BSD code, although Apple has developed a number of new programs.

Linux, macOS, and UNIX

tip Linux and macOS are closely related to the UNIX operating system. This book describes Linux and macOS. To make reading easier, this book talks about Linux when it means macOS and Linux, and points out where macOS behaves differently from Linux. For the same reason, this chapter frequently uses the term Linux to describe both Linux and macOS features.

The History of UNIX and GNU–Linux

This section presents some background on the relationships between UNIX and Linux and between GNU and Linux. Visit www.levenez.com/unix for an extensive history of UNIX.

The Heritage of Linux: UNIX

The UNIX system was developed by researchers who needed a set of modern computing tools to help them with their projects. The system allowed a group of people working together on a project to share selected data and programs while keeping other information private.

Universities and colleges played a major role in furthering the popularity of the UNIX operating system through the "four-year effect." When the UNIX operating system became widely available in 1975, Bell Labs offered it to educational institutions at nominal cost. The schools, in turn, used it in their computer science programs, ensuring that computer science students became familiar with it. Because UNIX was such an advanced development system, the students became acclimated to a sophisticated programming environment. As these students graduated and went into industry, they expected to work in a similarly advanced environment. As more of them worked their way up the ladder in the commercial world, the UNIX operating system found its way into industry.

Berkeley UNIX (BSD)

In addition to introducing students to the UNIX operating system, the Computer Systems Research Group (CSRG) at the University of California at Berkeley made significant additions and changes to it. In fact, it made so many popular changes that one version of the system is called the Berkeley Software Distribution (BSD) of the UNIX system, or just *Berkeley UNIX*. The other major version is UNIX System V (SVR4), which descended from versions developed and maintained by AT&T and UNIX System Laboratories. macOS inherits much more strongly from the BSD branch of the tree.

Fade to 1983

Richard Stallman (www.stallman.org) announced[1] the GNU Project for creating an operating system, both kernel and system programs, and presented the GNU Manifesto,[2] which begins as follows:

> GNU, which stands for Gnu's Not UNIX, is the name for the complete UNIX-compatible software system which I am writing so that I can give it away free to everyone who can use it.

1. www.gnu.org/gnu/initial-announcement.html
2. www.gnu.org/gnu/manifesto.html

Some years later, Stallman added a footnote to the preceding sentence when he realized that it was creating confusion:

> The wording here was careless. The intention was that nobody would have to pay for *permission* to use the GNU system. But the words don't make this clear, and people often interpret them as saying that copies of GNU should always be distributed at little or no charge. That was never the intent; later on, the manifesto mentions the possibility of companies providing the service of distribution for a profit. Subsequently I have learned to distinguish carefully between "free" in the sense of freedom and "free" in the sense of price. Free software is software that users have the freedom to distribute and change. Some users may obtain copies at no charge, while others pay to obtain copies—and if the funds help support improving the software, so much the better. The important thing is that everyone who has a copy has the freedom to cooperate with others in using it.

In the manifesto, after explaining a little about the project and what has been accomplished so far, Stallman continues:

> **Why I Must Write GNU**
> I consider that the golden rule requires that if I like a program I must share it with other people who like it. Software sellers want to divide the users and conquer them, making each user agree not to share with others. I refuse to break solidarity with other users in this way. I cannot in good conscience sign a nondisclosure agreement or a software license agreement. For years I worked within the Artificial Intelligence Lab to resist such tendencies and other inhospitalities, but eventually they had gone too far: I could not remain in an institution where such things are done for me against my will.
>
> So that I can continue to use computers without dishonor, I have decided to put together a sufficient body of free software so that I will be able to get along without any software that is not free. I have resigned from the AI Lab to deny MIT any legal excuse to prevent me from giving GNU away.

NEXT SCENE, 1991

The GNU Project has moved well along toward its goal. Much of the GNU operating system, except for the kernel, is complete. Richard Stallman later writes:

> By the early '90s we had put together the whole system aside from the kernel (and we were also working on a kernel, the GNU Hurd,[3]

3. www.gnu.org/software/hurd/hurd.html

> which runs on top of Mach[4]). Developing this kernel has been a lot harder than we expected, and we are still working on finishing it.[5]
>
> ...[M]any believe that once Linus Torvalds finished writing the kernel, his friends looked around for other free software, and for no particular reason most everything necessary to make a UNIX-like system was already available.
>
> What they found was no accident—it was the GNU system. The available free software[6] added up to a complete system because the GNU Project had been working since 1984 to make one. The GNU Manifesto had set forth the goal of developing a free UNIX-like system, called GNU. The Initial Announcement of the GNU Project also outlines some of the original plans for the GNU system. By the time Linux was written, the [GNU] system was almost finished.[7]

Today the GNU "operating system" runs on top of the FreeBSD (www.freebsd.org) and NetBSD (www.netbsd.org) kernels with complete Linux binary compatibility and on top of Hurd pre-releases and Darwin (developer.apple.com/opensource) without this compatibility.

THE CODE IS FREE

The tradition of free software dates back to the days when UNIX was released to universities at nominal cost, which contributed to its portability and success. This tradition eventually died as UNIX was commercialized and manufacturers came to regard the source code as proprietary, making it effectively unavailable. Another problem with the commercial versions of UNIX related to their complexity. As each manufacturer tuned UNIX for a specific architecture, the operating system became less portable and too unwieldy for teaching and experimentation.

MINIX Two professors created their own stripped-down UNIX look-alikes for educational purposes: Doug Comer created XINU, and Andrew Tanenbaum created MINIX. Linus Torvalds created Linux to counteract the shortcomings in MINIX. Every time there was a choice between code simplicity and efficiency/features, Tanenbaum chose simplicity (to make it easy to teach with MINIX), which meant this system lacked many features people wanted. Linux went in the opposite direction.

You can obtain Linux at no cost over the Internet. You can also obtain the GNU code via the U.S. mail at a modest cost for materials and shipping. You can support the Free Software Foundation (www.fsf.org) by buying the same (GNU) code in higher-priced packages, and you can buy commercial packaged releases of Linux (called

4. www.gnu.org/software/hurd/microkernel/machgnumach.html
5. www.gnu.org/software/hurd/hurd-and-linux.html
6. www.gnu.org/philosophy/free-sw.html
7. www.gnu.org/gnu/linux-and-gnu.html

distributions), such as Fedora/Red Hat Enterprise Linux, openSUSE, Debian, and Ubuntu, that include installation instructions, software, and support.

GPL Linux and GNU software are distributed under the terms of the GNU General Public License (GPL; www.gnu.org/licenses/licenses.html). The GPL says you have the right to copy, modify, and redistribute the code covered by the agreement. When you redistribute the code, however, you must also distribute the same license with the code, thereby making the code and the license inseparable. If you download source code from the Internet for an accounting program that is under the GPL and then modify that code and redistribute an executable version of the program, you must also distribute the modified source code and the GPL agreement with it. Because this arrangement is the reverse of the way a normal copyright works (it *gives* rights instead of *limiting* them), it has been termed a *copyleft*. (This paragraph is not a legal interpretation of the GPL; it is intended merely to give you an idea of how it works. Refer to the GPL itself when you want to make use of it.)

HAVE FUN!

Two key words for Linux are "Have Fun!" These words pop up in prompts and documentation. The UNIX—now Linux—culture is steeped in humor that can be seen throughout the system. For example, less is more—GNU has replaced the UNIX paging utility named more with an improved utility named less. The utility to view PostScript documents is named ghostscript, and one of several replacements for the vi editor is named elvis. While machines with Intel processors have "Intel Inside" logos on their outside, some Linux machines sport "Linux Inside" logos. And Torvalds himself has been seen wearing a T-shirt bearing a "Linus Inside" logo.

WHAT IS SO GOOD ABOUT LINUX?

In recent years Linux has emerged as a powerful and innovative UNIX work-alike. Its popularity has surpassed that of its UNIX predecessors. Although it mimics UNIX in many ways, the Linux operating system departs from UNIX in several significant ways: The Linux kernel is implemented independently of both BSD and System V, the continuing development of Linux is taking place through the combined efforts of many capable individuals throughout the world, and Linux puts the power of UNIX within easy reach of both business and personal computer users. Using the Internet, today's skilled programmers submit additions and improvements to the operating system to Linus Torvalds, GNU, or one of the other authors of Linux.

Standards In 1985, individuals from companies throughout the computer industry joined together to develop the POSIX (Portable Operating System Interface for Computer Environments) standard, which is based largely on the UNIX System V Interface Definition (SVID) and other earlier standardization efforts. These efforts were spurred by the U.S. government, which needed a standard computing environment to minimize its training and procurement costs. Released in 1988, POSIX is a group of IEEE standards that define the API (application programming interface), shell, and utility interfaces for an operating system. Although aimed at UNIX-like systems, the standards can apply to any compatible operating system. Now that these standards have gained acceptance, software developers are able to develop applications that run on all conforming versions of UNIX, Linux, and other operating systems.

Applications A rich selection of applications is available for Linux—both free and commercial—as well as a wide variety of tools: graphical, word processing, networking, security, administration, Web server, and many others. Large software companies have recently seen the benefit in supporting Linux and now have on-staff programmers whose job it is to design and code the Linux kernel, GNU, KDE, or other software that runs on Linux. For example, IBM (www.ibm.com/linux) is a major Linux supporter. Linux conforms increasingly more closely to POSIX standards, and some distributions and parts of others meet this standard. These developments indicate that Linux is becoming mainstream and is respected as an attractive alternative to other popular operating systems.

Peripherals Another aspect of Linux that appeals to users is the amazing range of peripherals that is supported and the speed with which support for new peripherals emerges. Linux often supports a peripheral or interface card before any company does. Unfortunately some types of peripherals—particularly proprietary graphics cards—lag in their support because the manufacturers do not release specifications or source code for drivers in a timely manner, if at all.

Software Also important to users is the amount of software that is available—not just source code (which needs to be compiled) but also prebuilt binaries that are easy to install and ready to run. These programs include more than free software. Netscape, for example, was available for Linux from the start and included Java support before it was available from many commercial vendors. Its sibling Mozilla/Thunderbird/ Firefox is now a viable browser, mail client, and newsreader, performing many other functions as well.

Platforms Linux is not just for Intel-based platforms (which now include Apple computers): It has been ported to and runs on the Power PC, including older Apple computers (ppclinux), Compaq's (née Digital Equipment Corporation) Alpha-based machines, MIPS-based machines, Motorola's 68K-based machines, various 64-bit systems, and IBM's S/390. Nor is Linux just for single-processor machines: As of version 2.0, it runs on multiple-processor machines (*SMPs;* page 1124). It also includes an O(1) scheduler, which dramatically increases scalability on SMP systems.

Emulators Linux supports programs, called *emulators,* that run code intended for other operating systems. By using emulators you can run some DOS, Windows, and Macintosh programs under Linux. For example, Wine (www.winehq.com) is an open-source implementation of the Windows API that runs on top of the X Window System and UNIX/Linux.

Virtual machines A *virtual machine* (VM or guest) appears to the user and to the software running on it as a complete physical machine. It is, however, one of potentially many such VMs running on a single physical machine (the host). The software that provides the virtualization is called a *virtual machine monitor* (VMM) or *hypervisor*. Each VM can run a different operating system from the other VMs. For example, on a single host you could have VMs running Windows 7, Ubuntu 12.10, Ubuntu 13.04, and Fedora 17.

A multitasking operating system allows you to run many programs on a single physical system. Similarly, a hypervisor allows you to run many operating systems (VMs) on a single physical system.

VMs provide many advantages over single, dedicated machines:

- **Isolation**—Each VM is isolated from the other VMs running on the same host. Thus, if one VM crashes or is compromised, the others are not affected.
- **Security**—When a single server system running several servers is compromised, all servers are compromised. If each server is running on its own VM, only the compromised server is affected; other servers remain secure.
- **Power consumption**—Using VMs, a single powerful machine can replace many less powerful machines, thereby cutting power consumption.
- **Development and support**—Multiple VMs, each running a different version of an operating system and/or different operating systems, can facilitate development and support of software designed to run in many environments. With this organization you can easily test a product in different environments before releasing it. Similarly, when a user submits a bug, you can reproduce the bug in the same environment it occurred in.
- **Servers**—In some cases, different servers require different versions of system libraries. In this instance, you can run each server on its own VM, all on a single piece of hardware.
- **Testing**—Using VMs, you can experiment with cutting-edge releases of operating systems and applications without concern for the base (stable) system, all on a single machine.
- **Networks**—You can set up and test networks of systems on a single machine.
- **Sandboxes**—A VM presents a sandbox—an area (system) that you can work in without regard for the results of your work or for the need to clean up.
- **Snapshots**—You can take snapshots of a VM and return the VM to the state it was in when you took the snapshot simply by reloading the VM from the snapshot.

Xen

Xen, which was created at the University of Cambridge and is now being developed in the open-source community, is an open-source virtual machine monitor (VMM). A VMM enables several virtual machines (VMs), each running an instance of a separate operating system, to run on a single computer. Xen introduces minimal performance overhead when compared with running each of the operating systems natively. For more information on Xen, refer to the Xen home page at www.cl.cam.ac.uk/research/srg/netos/xen and wiki.xen.org.

VMware VMware, Inc. (www.vmware.com) offers VMware Server, a free, downloadable, proprietary product you can install and run as an application under Linux. VMware Server enables you to install several VMs, each running a different operating system, including Windows and Linux. VMware also offers a free VMware player that enables you to run VMs you create using VMware Server.

KVM The Kernel-based Virtual Machine (KVM; www.linux-kvm.org and libvirt.org) is an open-source VM and runs as part of the Linux kernel.

Qemu Qemu (wiki.qemu.org), written by Fabrice Bellard, is an open-source VMM that runs as a user application with no CPU requirements. It can run code written for a different CPU from that of the host machine.

VirtualBox VirtualBox (www.virtualbox.org) is a VM developed by Sun Microsystems. If you want to run a virtual instance of Windows, you might want to investigate VirtualBox.

Why Linux Is Popular with Hardware Companies and Developers

Two trends in the computer industry set the stage for the growing popularity of UNIX and Linux. First, advances in hardware technology created the need for an operating system that could take advantage of available hardware power. In the mid-1970s, minicomputers began challenging the large mainframe computers because, in many applications, minicomputers could perform the same functions less expensively. More recently, powerful 64-bit processor chips, plentiful and inexpensive memory, and lower-priced hard disk storage have allowed hardware companies to install multiuser operating systems on desktop computers.

Proprietary operating systems Second, with the cost of hardware continually dropping, hardware manufacturers could no longer afford to develop and support proprietary operating systems. A *proprietary* operating system is one that is written and owned by the manufacturer of the hardware (for example, DEC/Compaq owns VMS). Today's manufacturers need a generic operating system they can easily adapt to their machines.

Generic operating systems A *generic* operating system is written outside of the company manufacturing the hardware and is sold (UNIX, macOS, Windows) or given (Linux) to the manufacturer. Linux is a generic operating system because it runs on different types of hardware produced by different manufacturers. Of course, if manufacturers can pay only for development and avoid per-unit costs (which they have to pay to Microsoft for each copy of Windows they sell), they are much better off. In turn, software developers need to keep the prices of their products down; they cannot afford to create new versions of their products to run under many different proprietary operating systems. Like hardware manufacturers, software developers need a generic operating system.

Although the UNIX system once met the needs of hardware companies and researchers for a generic operating system, over time it has become more proprietary as manufacturers added support for their own specialized features and introduced new software libraries and utilities. Linux emerged to serve both needs: It is a generic operating system that takes advantage of available hardware power.

Linux Is Portable

A *portable* operating system is one that can run on many different machines. More than 95 percent of the Linux operating system is written in the C programming language, and C is portable because it is written in a higher-level, machine-independent language. (The C compiler is written in C.)

Because Linux is portable, it can be adapted (ported) to different machines and can meet special requirements. For example, Linux is used in embedded computers, such as the ones found in cellphones, PDAs, and the cable boxes on top of many TVs. The file structure takes full advantage of large, fast hard disks. Equally important, Linux was originally designed as a multiuser operating system; it was not modified to serve several users as an afterthought. Sharing the computer's power among many users and giving them the ability to share data and programs are central features of the system.

Because it is adaptable and takes advantage of available hardware, Linux runs on many different microprocessor-based systems as well as mainframes. The popularity of the microprocessor-based hardware drives Linux; these microcomputers are getting faster all the time at about the same price point. This widespread acceptance benefits both users, who do not like having to learn a new operating system for each vendor's hardware, and system administrators, who like having a consistent software environment.

The advent of a standard operating system has given a boost to the development of the software industry. Now software manufacturers can afford to make one version of a product available on machines from different manufacturers.

The C Programming Language

Ken Thompson wrote the UNIX operating system in 1969 in PDP-7 assembly language. Assembly language is machine-dependent: Programs written in assembly language work on only one machine or, at best, on one family of machines. For this reason, the original UNIX operating system could not easily be transported to run on other machines: It was not portable.

To make UNIX portable, Thompson developed the B programming language, a machine-independent language, from the BCPL language. Dennis Ritchie developed the C programming language by modifying B and, with Thompson, rewrote UNIX in C in 1973. Originally, C was touted as a "portable assembler." The revised operating system could be transported more easily to run on other machines.

That development marked the start of C. Its roots reveal some of the reasons why it is such a powerful tool. C can be used to write machine-independent programs. A programmer who designs a program to be portable can easily move it to any computer that has a C compiler. C is also designed to compile into very efficient code. With the advent of C, a programmer no longer had to resort to assembly language to produce code that would run well (that is, quickly—although an assembler will always generate more efficient code than a high-level language).

C is a good systems language. You can write a compiler or an operating system in C. It is a highly structured but not necessarily a high-level language. C allows a programmer to manipulate bits and bytes, as is necessary when writing an operating system. At the same time, it has high-level constructs that allow for efficient, modular programming.

In the late 1980s the American National Standards Institute (ANSI) defined a standard version of the C language, commonly referred to as *ANSI C* or *C89* (for the year the standard was published). Ten years later the C99 standard was published; it is mostly supported by the GNU Project's C compiler (named gcc). The original version of the language is often referred to as *Kernighan & Ritchie* (or *K&R*) C, named for the authors of the book that first described the C language.

Another researcher at Bell Labs, Bjarne Stroustrup, created an object-oriented programming language named *C++*, which is built on the foundation of C. Because object-oriented programming is desired by many employers today, C++ is preferred over C in many environments. Another language of choice is Objective-C, which was used to write the first Web browser. The GNU Project's C compiler supports C, C++, and Objective-C.

OVERVIEW OF LINUX

The Linux operating system has many unique and powerful features. Like other operating systems, it is a control program for computers. But like UNIX, it is also a well-thought-out family of utility programs (Figure 1-1) and a set of tools that allow users to connect and use these utilities to build systems and applications.

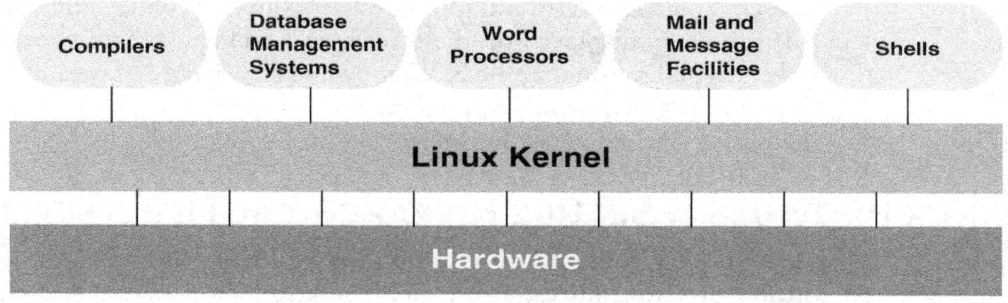

Figure 1-1 A layered view of the Linux operating system

Linux Has a Kernel Programming Interface

The Linux kernel—the heart of the Linux operating system—is responsible for allocating the computer's resources and scheduling user jobs so each one gets its fair share of system resources, including access to the CPU; peripheral devices, such as hard disk, DVD, and tape storage; and printers. Programs interact with the kernel through *system calls,* special functions with well-known names. A programmer can use a single system call to interact with many kinds of devices. For example, there is one **write**() system call, rather than many device-specific ones. When a program issues a **write**() request, the kernel interprets the context and passes the request to the appropriate device. This flexibility allows old utilities to work with devices that did not exist when the utilities were written. It also makes it possible to move programs to new versions of the operating system without rewriting them (provided the new version recognizes the same system calls).

Linux Can Support Many Users

Depending on the hardware and the types of tasks the computer performs, a Linux system can support from 1 to more than 1,000 users, each concurrently running a different set of programs. The per-user cost of a computer that can be used by many people at the same time is less than that of a computer that can be used by only a single person at a time. It is less because one person cannot generally take advantage of all the resources a computer has to offer. That is, no one can keep all the printers going constantly, keep all the system memory in use, keep all the disks busy reading and writing, keep the Internet connection in use, and keep all the terminals busy at the same time. By contrast, a multiuser operating system allows many people to use all of the system resources almost simultaneously. The use of costly resources can be maximized, and the cost per user can be minimized—the primary objectives of a multiuser operating system.

Linux Can Run Many Tasks

Linux is a fully protected multitasking operating system, allowing each user to run more than one job at a time. Processes can communicate with one another but remain fully protected from one another, just as the kernel remains protected from all processes. You can run several jobs in the background while giving all your attention to the job being displayed on the screen, and you can switch back and forth between jobs. If you are running the X Window System (page 16), you can run different programs in different windows on the same screen and watch all of them. This capability helps users be more productive.

Linux Provides a Secure Hierarchical Filesystem

A *file* is a collection of information, such as text for a memo or report, an accumulation of sales figures, an image, a song, or an executable program. Each file is stored under a unique identifier on a storage device, such as a hard disk. The Linux filesystem provides a structure whereby files are arranged under *directories,* which are like folders or boxes. Each directory has a name and can hold other files and directories. Directories, in turn, are arranged under other directories and so forth in a treelike organization. This structure helps users keep track of large numbers of files by grouping related files in directories. Each user has one primary directory and as many subdirectories as required (Figure 1-2).

Standards With the idea of making life easier for system administrators and software developers, a group got together over the Internet and developed the Linux Filesystem Standard (FSSTND), which has since evolved into the Linux Filesystem Hierarchy Standard (FHS). Before this standard was adopted, key programs were located in different places in different Linux distributions. Today you can sit down at a Linux system and expect to find any given standard program at a consistent location (page 98).

Links A *link* allows a given file to be accessed by means of two or more names. The alternative names can be located in the same directory as the original file or in another directory. Links can make the same file appear in several users' directories, enabling those users to share the file easily. Windows uses the term *shortcut* in place of *link* to describe this capability. Macintosh users will be more familiar with the term *alias.* Under Linux, an *alias* is different from a *link;* it is a command macro feature provided by the shell (page 352).

Security Like most multiuser operating systems, Linux allows users to protect their data from access by other users. It also allows users to share selected data and programs with certain other users by means of a simple but effective protection scheme. This level of security is provided by file access permissions, which limit the users who can read from, write to, or execute a file. Linux also implements ACLs (Access Control Lists), which give users and administrators finer-grained control over file access permissions.

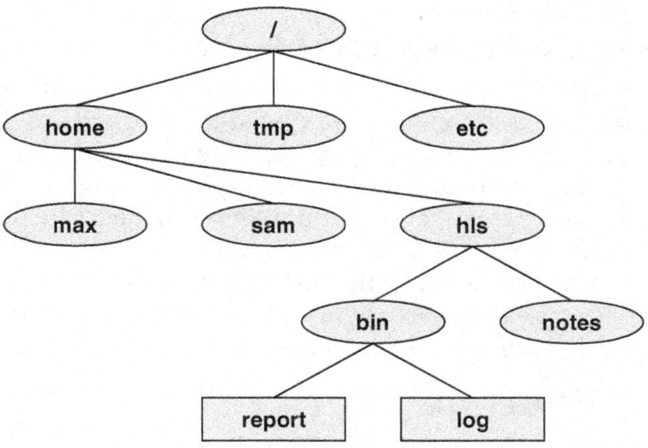

Figure 1-2 The Linux filesystem structure

THE SHELL: COMMAND INTERPRETER AND PROGRAMMING LANGUAGE

In a textual environment, the shell—the command interpreter—acts as an interface between you and the operating system. When you enter a command on the screen, the shell interprets the command and calls the program you want. A number of shells are available for Linux. The four most popular shells are

- The Bourne Again Shell (bash), an enhanced version of the original Bourne Shell (an original UNIX shell).
- The Debian Almquist Shell (dash; page 287), a smaller version of bash with fewer features. Many startup shell scripts call dash in place of bash to speed the boot process.
- The TC Shell (tcsh; Chapter 9), an enhanced version of the C Shell, developed as part of BSD UNIX.
- The Z Shell (zsh), which incorporates features from a number of shells, including the Korn Shell.

Because different users might prefer different shells, multiuser systems can have several different shells in use at any given time. The choice of shells demonstrates one of the advantages of the Linux operating system: the ability to provide a customized interface for each user.

Shell scripts

Besides performing its function of interpreting commands from a keyboard and sending those commands to the operating system, the shell is a high-level programming language. Shell commands can be arranged in a file for later execution. (Linux calls these files *shell scripts;* Windows calls them *batch files.*) This flexibility allows users to perform complex operations with relative ease, often by issuing short commands, or to build with surprisingly little effort elaborate programs that perform highly complex operations.

FILENAME GENERATION

Wildcards and ambiguous file references

When you type commands to be processed by the shell, you can construct patterns using characters that have special meanings to the shell. These characters are called *wildcard* characters. The patterns, which are called *ambiguous file references,* are a kind of shorthand: Rather than typing in complete filenames, you can type patterns; the shell expands these patterns into matching filenames. An ambiguous file reference can save you the effort of typing in a long filename or a long series of similar filenames. For example, the shell might expand the pattern **mak*** to **make-3.80.tar.gz.** Patterns can also be useful when you know only part of a filename or cannot remember the exact spelling of a filename.

COMPLETION

In conjunction with the Readline library, the shell performs command, filename, pathname, and variable completion: You type a prefix and press TAB, and the shell lists the items that begin with that prefix or completes the item if the prefix specifies a unique item.

Device-Independent Input and Output

Redirection Devices (such as a printer or a terminal) and disk files appear as files to Linux programs. When you give a command to the Linux operating system, you can instruct it to send the output to any one of several devices or files. This diversion is called output *redirection.*

Device independence In a similar manner, a program's input, which normally comes from a keyboard, can be redirected so that it comes from a disk file instead. Input and output are *device independent;* that is, they can be redirected to or from any appropriate device.

As an example, the cat utility normally displays the contents of a file on the screen. When you run a cat command, you can easily cause its output to go to a disk file instead of the screen.

Shell Functions

One of the most important features of the shell is that users can use it as a programming language. Because the shell is an interpreter, it does not compile programs written for it but rather interprets programs each time they are loaded from the disk. Loading and interpreting programs can be time-consuming.

Many shells, including the Bourne Again Shell, support shell functions that the shell holds in memory so it does not have to read them from the disk each time you execute them. The shell also keeps functions in an internal format so it does not have to spend as much time interpreting them.

Job Control

Job control is a shell feature that allows users to work on several jobs at once, switching back and forth between them as desired. When you start a job, it is frequently run in the foreground so it is connected to the terminal. Using job control, you can move the job you are working with to the background and continue running it there while working on or observing another job in the foreground. If a background job then needs your attention, you can move it to the foreground so it is once again attached to the terminal. The concept of job control originated with BSD UNIX, where it appeared in the C Shell.

A Large Collection of Useful Utilities

Linux includes a family of several hundred utility programs, often referred to as *commands.* These utilities perform functions that are universally required by users. The sort utility, for example, puts lists (or groups of lists) in alphabetical or numerical order and can be used to sort lists by part number, last name, city, ZIP code, telephone number, age, size, cost, and so forth. The sort utility is an important programming tool that is part of the standard Linux system. Other utilities allow users to create, display, print, copy, search, and delete files as well as to edit, format, and typeset text. The man (for manual) and info utilities provide online documentation for Linux.

Interprocess Communication

Pipelines and filters

Linux enables users to establish both pipelines and filters on the command line. A *pipeline* passes the output of one program to another program as input. A *filter* is a special kind of pipeline that processes a stream of input data to yield a stream of output data. A filter processes another program's output, altering it as a result. The filter's output then becomes input to another program.

Pipelines and filters frequently join utilities to perform a specific task. For example, you can use a pipeline to send the output of the sort utility to head (a filter that lists the first ten lines of its input); you can then use another pipeline to send the output of head to a third utility, lpr, that sends the data to a printer. Thus, in one command line, you can use three utilities together to sort and print part of a file.

System Administration

On a Linux system the system administrator is frequently the owner and only user of the system. This person has many responsibilities. The first responsibility might be to set up the system, install the software, and possibly edit configuration files. Once the system is up and running, the system administrator is responsible for downloading and installing software (including upgrading the operating system); backing up and restoring files; and managing such system facilities as printers, terminals, servers, and a local network. The system administrator is also responsible for setting up accounts for new users on a multiuser system, bringing the system up and down as needed, monitoring the system, and taking care of any problems that arise.

Additional Features of Linux

The developers of Linux included features from BSD, System V, and Sun Microsystems' Solaris, as well as new features, in their operating system. Although most of the tools found on UNIX exist for Linux, in some cases these tools have been replaced by more modern counterparts. This section describes some of the popular tools and features available under Linux.

GUIs: Graphical User Interfaces

The X Window System (also called X or X11) was developed in part by researchers at MIT (Massachusetts Institute of Technology) and provides the foundation for the GUIs available with Linux. Given a terminal or workstation screen that supports X, a user can interact with the computer through multiple windows on the screen; display graphical information; or use special-purpose applications to draw pictures, monitor processes, or preview formatted output. X is an across-the-network protocol that allows a user to open a window on a workstation or computer system that is remote from the CPU generating the window.

Aqua Most Macintosh users are familiar with Aqua, the standard macOS graphical interface. Aqua is based on a rendering technology named Quartz and has a standard look and feel for applications. By default, X11 is not installed on a Macintosh; you can use XQuartz in its place (xquartz.macosforge.org/trac/wiki).

Desktop manager Usually two layers run on top of X: a desktop manager and a window manager. A *desktop manager* is a picture-oriented user interface that enables you to interact with system programs by manipulating icons instead of typing the corresponding commands to a shell. Many Linux distributions run the GNOME desktop manager (www.gnome.org) by default, but X can also run KDE (www.kde.org) and a number of other desktop managers. macOS handles the desktop in Aqua, not in X11, so there is no desktop manager under X11.

Window manager A *window manager* is a program that runs under the desktop manager and allows you to open and close windows, run programs, and set up a mouse so it has different effects depending on how and where you click it. The window manager also gives the screen its personality. Whereas Microsoft Windows allows you to change the color of key elements in a window, a window manager under X allows you to customize the overall look and feel of the screen: You can change the way a window looks and works (by giving it different borders, buttons, and scrollbars), set up virtual desktops, create menus, and more. When you are working from the command line, you can approximate a window manager by using Midnight Commander (mc; page 902).

Several popular window managers run under X and Linux. Many Linux distributions provide both Metacity (the default under GNOME 2) and kwin (the default under KDE). In addition to KDE, Fedora provides Mutter (the default under GNOME 3). *Mutter* is short for Metacity Clutter (the graphics library is named Clutter). Other window managers, such as Sawfish and WindowMaker, are also available.

Under macOS, most windows are managed by a Quartz layer, which applies the Apple Aqua look and feel. For X11 applications only, this task is performed by quartz-wm, which mimics the Apple Aqua look and feel so X11 applications on the Mac desktop have the same appearance as native macOS applications.

(Inter)Networking Utilities

Linux network support includes many utilities that enable you to access remote systems over a variety of networks. In addition to sending email to users on other systems, you can access files on disks mounted on other computers as if they were located on the local system, make your files available to other systems in a similar manner, copy files back and forth, run programs on remote systems while displaying the results on the local system, and perform many other operations across local area networks (LANs) and wide area networks (WANs), including the Internet.

Layered on top of this network access is a wide range of application programs that extend the computer's resources around the globe. You can carry on conversations with people throughout the world, gather information on a wide variety of subjects, and download new software over the Internet quickly and reliably.

SOFTWARE DEVELOPMENT

One of Linux's most impressive strengths is its rich software development environment. Linux supports compilers and interpreters for many computer languages. Besides C and C++, languages available for Linux include Ada, Fortran, Java, Lisp, Pascal, Perl, and Python. The bison utility generates parsing code that makes it easier to write programs to build *compilers* (tools that parse files containing structured information). The flex utility generates scanners (code that recognizes lexical patterns in text). The make utility and the GNU Configure and Build System make it easier to manage complex development projects. Source code management systems, such as CVS, simplify version control. Several debuggers, including ups and gdb, can help you track down and repair software defects. The GNU C compiler (gcc) works with the gprof profiling utility to help programmers identify potential bottlenecks in a program's performance. The C compiler includes options to perform extensive checking of C code, thereby making the code more portable and reducing debugging time. Under macOS, Apple's Xcode development environment provides a unified graphical front end to most of these tools as well as other options and features.

CHAPTER SUMMARY

The Linux operating system grew out of the UNIX heritage to become a popular alternative to traditional systems (that is, Windows) available for microcomputer (PC) hardware. UNIX users will find a familiar environment in Linux. Distributions of Linux contain the expected complement of UNIX utilities, contributed by programmers around the world, including the set of tools developed as part of the GNU Project. The Linux community is committed to the continued development of this system. Support for new microcomputer devices and features is added soon after the hardware becomes available, and the tools available on Linux continue to be refined. Given the many commercial software packages available to run on Linux platforms and the many hardware manufacturers offering Linux on their systems, it is clear that the system has evolved well beyond its origin as an undergraduate project to become an operating system of choice for academic, commercial, professional, and personal use.

EXERCISES

1. What is free software? List three characteristics of free software.
2. Why is Linux popular? Why is it popular in academia?
3. What are multiuser systems? Why are they successful?

4. What is the Free Software Foundation/GNU? What is Linux? Which parts of the Linux operating system did each provide? Who else has helped build and refine this operating system?
5. In which language is Linux written? What does the language have to do with the success of Linux?
6. What is a utility program?
7. What is a shell? How does it work with the kernel? With the user?
8. How can you use utility programs and a shell to create your own applications?
9. Why is the Linux filesystem referred to as *hierarchical*?
10. What is the difference between a multiuser and a multitasking system?
11. Give an example of when you would want to use a multitasking system.
12. Approximately how many people wrote Linux? Why is this project unique?
13. What are the key terms of the GNU General Public License?

PART I

The Linux and macOS Operating Systems

2

GETTING STARTED

IN THIS CHAPTER

OBJECTIVES

After reading this chapter you should be able to:

- Log in on a Linux system using the textual interface
- Describe the advantages of the textual interface
- Correct typing mistakes on the command line
- Use kill to abort program execution using the termination signal
- Repeat and edit previous command lines
- Understand the need to be careful when working with **root** privileges
- Use man and info to display information about utilities
- Use the **--help** option to display information about a utility
- Change your password from the command line

One way or another you are sitting in front of a screen that is connected to a computer running Linux. You might be working with a graphical user interface (GUI) or a textual interface. This book is about the textual interface, also called the command-line interface (CLI). If you are working with a GUI, you will need to use a terminal emulator such as xterm, Konsole, GNOME Terminal, Terminal (under macOS), or a virtual console (page 44) to follow the examples in this book.

This chapter starts with a discussion of the typographical conventions used in this book, followed by a section about logging in on the system. The next section introduces the shell and explains how to fix mistakes on the command line and repeat previous command lines. Next come a brief reminder about the powers of working with **root** privileges and suggestions about how to avoid making mistakes that will make your system inoperable or hard to work with. The chapter continues with a discussion about where to find more information about Linux. It concludes with additional information on logging in, including how to change your password.

Be sure to read the warning on page 32 about the dangers of misusing the powers of working with **root** privileges. While heeding that warning, feel free to experiment with the system: Give commands, create files, follow the examples in this book, and have fun.

Conventions Used in This Book

This book uses conventions to make its explanations shorter and clearer. The following paragraphs describe these conventions.

macOS versions — References to **macOS** refer to version **10.12** (Sierra). Because the book focuses on the underlying operating system, which changes little from one release of macOS to the next, the text will remain relevant through several future releases.

Text and examples — The text is set in this type, whereas examples are shown in a `monospaced font` (also called a *fixed-width* font):

```
$ cat practice
This is a small file I created
with a text editor.
```

Items you enter — Everything you enter at the keyboard is shown in a bold typeface. Within the text, **this bold typeface** is used; within examples and screens, **`this one`** is used. In the previous example, the dollar sign (`$`) on the first line is a prompt that Linux displays, so it is not bold; the remainder of the first line is entered by a user, so it is bold.

Utility names — Names of utilities are printed in this sans serif typeface. This book references the emacs text editor and the ls utility or ls command (or just ls) but instructs you to enter **ls –a** on the command line. In this way the text distinguishes between utilities, which are programs, and the instructions you enter on the command line to invoke the utilities.

Filenames Filenames appear in a bold typeface. Examples are **memo5**, **letter.1283**, and **reports**. Filenames might include uppercase and lowercase letters; however, Linux is *case sensitive* (page 1088), so **memo5**, **MEMO5**, and **Memo5** name three different files.

The default macOS filesystem, HFS+, is not case sensitive; under macOS, **memo5**, **MEMO5**, and **Memo5** refer to the same file. For more information refer to "Case Sensitivity" on page 1070.

Character strings Within the text, characters and character strings are marked by putting them in a bold typeface. This convention avoids the need for quotation marks or other delimiters before and after a string. An example is the following string, which is displayed by the passwd utility: **Sorry, passwords do not match.**

Keys and characters This book uses SMALL CAPS for three kinds of items:

- Keyboard keys, such as the SPACE bar and the RETURN,[1] ESCAPE, and TAB keys.
- The characters that keys generate, such as the SPACEs generated by the SPACE bar.
- Keyboard keys that you press simultaneously with the CONTROL key, such as CONTROL-D. (Even though D is shown as an uppercase letter, you do not have to press the SHIFT key; enter CONTROL-D by holding the CONTROL key down and pressing **d**.)

Prompts and RETURNS Most examples include the *shell prompt*—the signal that Linux is waiting for a command—as a dollar sign (**$**), a hashmark (**#**), or sometimes a percent sign (**%**). The prompt does not appear in a bold typeface in this book because you do not enter it. Do not type the prompt on the keyboard when you are experimenting with examples from this book. If you do, the examples will not work.

Examples *omit* the RETURN keystroke that you must use to execute them. An example of a command line is

```
$ vim memo.1204
```

To use this example as a model for running the vim text editor, enter the command **vim memo.1204** (some systems use **vim.tiny** in place of **vim**) and press the RETURN key. (Press ESCAPE **ZZ** to exit from vim; see page 167 for a vim tutorial.) This method of displaying commands makes the examples in the book correspond to what appears on the screen.

Definitions All glossary entries marked with FOLDOC are courtesy of Denis Howe, editor of the Free Online Dictionary of Computing (foldoc.org), and are used with permission. This site is an ongoing work containing definitions, anecdotes, and trivia.

---

1. Different keyboards use different keys to move the *cursor* (page 1093) to the beginning of the next line. This book always refers to the key that ends a line as the RETURN key. The keyboard you are using might have a RET, NEWLINE, ENTER, RETURN, or some other key. Use the corresponding key on your keyboard each time this book asks you to press RETURN.

optional

Optional Information

Passages marked as optional appear in a gray box. This material is not central to the ideas presented in the chapter and often involves more challenging concepts. A good strategy when reading a chapter is to skip the optional sections and then return to them when you are comfortable with the main ideas presented in the chapter. This is an optional paragraph.

URLs (Web addresses) Web addresses, or URLs, have an implicit **http://** prefix, unless **ftp://** or **https://** is shown. You do not normally need to specify a prefix when the prefix is **http://**, but you must use a prefix in a browser when you specify an FTP or secure HTTP site. Thus you can specify a URL in a browser exactly as it is shown in this book.

ls output This book uses the output of **ls –l** commands, such as produced by including the option **––time-style=iso**. This option produces shorter lines, making the examples more readable.

Tip, caution, and security boxes The following boxes highlight information that might be helpful while you are using or administrating a Linux system.

This is a tip box

tip A tip box might help you avoid repeating a common mistake or might point toward additional information.

This box warns you about something

caution A caution box warns you about a potential pitfall.

This box marks a security note

security A security box highlights a potential security issue. These notes are usually intended for system administrators, but some apply to all users.

Logging In from a Terminal (Emulator)

Above the login prompt on a terminal, terminal emulator, or other textual device, many systems display a message called *issue* (stored in the **/etc/issue** file). This message usually identifies the version of Linux running on the system, the name of the system, and the device you are logging in on. A sample issue message follows:

```
Fedora release 16 (Verne)
Kernel 3.3.2-6.fc16.i686 on an i686 (tty4)
```

The issue message is followed by a prompt to log in. Enter your username and password in response to the system prompts. Make sure you enter your username and password as they were specified when your account was set up; the routine that verifies the username and password is case sensitive. Like most systems, Linux does not display your password when you enter it. By default macOS does not allow remote logins (page 1076).

The following example shows Max logging in on the system named **tiny**:

```
tiny login: max
Password:
Last login: Wed Mar 13 19:50:38 from plum
[max@tiny max]$
```

If you are using a *terminal* (page 1128) and the screen does not display the **login:** prompt, check whether the terminal is plugged in and turned on, and then press the RETURN key a few times. If **login:** still does not appear, try pressing CONTROL-Q (Xon).

Did you log in last?

security As you are logging in to a textual environment, after you enter your username and password, the system displays information about the last login on this account, showing when it took place and where it originated. You can use this information to determine whether anyone has accessed the account since you last used it. If someone has, perhaps an unauthorized user has learned your password and logged in as you. In the interest of maintaining security, advise the system administrator of any circumstances that make you suspicious and change your password.

If you are using a Mac, PC, another Linux system, or a *workstation* (page 1133), open the program that runs ssh (secure; page 980), telnet (not secure; page 1001), or whichever communications/emulation software you use to log in on the system, and give it the name or IP address (page 1104) of the system you want to log in on.

telnet is not secure

security One of the reasons telnet is not secure is that it sends your username and password over the network in *cleartext* (page 1090) when you log in, allowing someone to capture your login information and log in on your account. The ssh utility encrypts all information it sends over the network and, if available, is a better choice than telnet. The ssh program has been implemented on many operating systems, not just Linux. Many user interfaces to ssh include a terminal emulator.

Following is an example of logging in using ssh from a Linux system:

```
$ ssh max@tiny
max@tiny's password:
Permission denied, please try again.
max@tiny's password:
Last login: Wed Mar 13 21:21:49 2005 from plum
[max@tiny max]$
```

In the example Max mistyped his password, received an error message and another prompt, and then retyped the password correctly. If your username is the same on the system you are logging in from and the system you are logging in on, you can omit your username and the following at sign (@). In the example, Max could have given the command **ssh tiny**.

After you log in, the *shell prompt* (or just *prompt*) appears, indicating you have successfully logged in; it shows the system is ready for you to give a command. The first shell prompt might be preceded by a short message called the *message of the day*, or **motd**, which is stored in the **/etc/motd** file.

The usual prompt is a dollar sign (**$**). Do not be concerned if you have a different prompt; the examples in this book will work regardless of which prompt the system displays. In the previous example, the **$** prompt (last line) is preceded by the username (**max**), an at sign (**@**), the system name (**tiny**), and the name of the directory Max is working in (**max**). For information on how to change the prompt, refer to page 319 (bash) or page 403 (tcsh).

Make sure TERM is set correctly

tip The **TERM** shell variable establishes the pseudographical characteristics of a character-based terminal or terminal emulator. Typically **TERM** is set for you—you do not have to set it manually. If things on the screen do not look right, refer to "Specifying a Terminal" on page 1050.

WORKING FROM THE COMMAND LINE

Before the introduction of the graphical user interface, UNIX and then Linux provided only a textual (command-line) interface. Today, a textual interface is available when you log in from a terminal, a terminal emulator, or a textual virtual console, or when you use ssh or telnet to log in on a system.

Advantages of the textual interface Although the concept might seem antiquated, the textual interface has a place in modern computing. In some cases an administrator might use a command-line tool either because a graphical equivalent does not exist or because the graphical tool is not as powerful or flexible as the textual one. For example, chmod (pages 102 and 759) is more powerful and flexible than its GUI counterpart. Frequently, on a server system, a graphical interface might not even be installed. The first reason for this omission is that a GUI consumes a lot of system resources; on a server, those resources are better dedicated to the main task of the server. Additionally, security considerations mandate that a server system run as few tasks as possible because each additional task can make the system more vulnerable to attack.

You can also write scripts using the textual interface. Using scripts, you can easily reproduce tasks on multiple systems, enabling you to scale the tasks to larger environments. When you are the administrator of only a single system, using a GUI is often the easiest way to configure the system. When you act as administrator for many systems, all of which need the same configuration installed or updated, a script can make the task go more quickly. Writing a script using command-line tools is frequently easy, whereas the same task can be difficult to impossible using graphical tools.

Pseudographical interface Before the introduction of GUIs, resourceful programmers created textual interfaces that included graphical elements such as boxes, borders outlining rudimentary windows, highlights, and, more recently, color. These textual interfaces, called pseudographical interfaces, bridge the gap between textual and graphical interfaces. The Midnight Commander file management utility (mc; page 902) is a good example of a utility with a well-designed pseudographical interface.

WHICH SHELL ARE YOU RUNNING?

This book discusses both the Bourne Again Shell (bash) and the TC Shell (tcsh). You are probably running bash, but you might be running tcsh or another shell such as the Z Shell (zsh). When you enter **echo $0** and press RETURN in response to a shell prompt (usually $ or %), the shell displays the name of the shell you are working with. This command works because the shell expands $0 to the name of the program you are running (page 470). This command might display output like this:

```
$ echo $0
-bash
```

Or the local system might display output like this:

```
$ echo $0
/bin/bash
```

Either way, this output shows you are running bash. If you are running a different shell, the shell will display appropriate output.

CORRECTING MISTAKES

This section explains how to correct typographical and other errors you might make while you are logged in on a textual display. Because the shell and most other utilities do not interpret the command line or other text you enter until you press RETURN, you can readily correct a typing mistake before you press RETURN.

You can correct such mistakes in several ways: Erase one character at a time, back up a word at a time, or back up to the beginning of the line in one step. After you press RETURN, it is too late to correct a mistake: At that point, you must either wait for the command to run to completion or abort execution of the program (next page).

ERASING A CHARACTER

While entering characters from the keyboard, you can back up and erase a mistake by pressing the *erase key* once for each character you want to delete. The erase key backs over as many characters as you wish. It does not, in general, back up past the beginning of the line.

The default erase key is BACKSPACE. If this key does not work, try pressing DEL or CONTROL-H. If these keys do not work, give the following stty[2] command to set the erase and line kill (see "Deleting a Line") keys to their default values:

```
$ stty ek
```

2. The command stty is an abbreviation for *set teletypewriter,* the first terminal UNIX ran on. Today stty is commonly thought of as meaning *set terminal.*

Alternatively, you can give the next command to reset most terminal parameters to a sane value. If the RETURN key does not move the cursor to the next line, press CONTROL-J instead.

```
$ stty sane
```

See page 989 for more examples of using stty.

Deleting a Word

You can delete a word you entered by pressing CONTROL-W. A *word* is any sequence of characters that does not contain a SPACE or TAB. When you press CONTROL-W, the cursor moves left to the beginning of the current word (as you are entering a word) or the previous word (when you have just entered a SPACE or TAB), removing the word.

CONTROL-Z **suspends a program**

tip Although it is not a way of correcting a mistake, you might press the suspend key (typically CONTROL-Z) by mistake and wonder what happened. If you see a message containing the word **Stopped**, you have just stopped your job using job control (page 151). If you give the command **fg** to continue your job in the foreground, you should return to where you were before you pressed the suspend key. For more information refer to "bg: Sends a Job to the Background" on page 306.

Deleting a Line

Any time before you press RETURN, you can delete the line you are entering by pressing the (*line*) *kill key*. When you press this key, the cursor moves to the left, erasing characters as it goes, back to the beginning of the line. The default line kill key is CONTROL-U. If this key does not work, try CONTROL-X. If these keys do not work, give the stty command described under "Erasing a Character."

Aborting Execution

Sometimes you might want to terminate a running program. For example, you might want to stop a program that is performing a lengthy task such as displaying the contents of a file that is several hundred pages long or copying a large file that is not the one you meant to copy.

To terminate a program from a textual display, press the *interrupt key* (CONTROL-C or sometimes DELETE or DEL). When you press this key, the Linux operating system sends a TERM (termination) signal to the program you are running and to the shell. Exactly what effect this signal has depends on the program. Some programs stop execution immediately, some ignore the signal, and some take other actions. When the shell receives a TERM signal, it displays a prompt and waits for another command.

If these methods do not terminate the program, try sending the program a QUIT signal (CONTROL-\). If all else fails, try pressing the suspend key (typically CONTROL-Z), giving a **jobs** command to verify the number of the job running the program, and using kill to abort the job. The job number is the number within the brackets at the left end of the line displayed by **jobs** ([1]). In the next example, the **kill** command (pages 152 and 866) uses **–TERM** to send a TERM signal to the job specified by the job number, which is preceded by a percent sign (**%1**). You can omit **–TERM** from the command, as kill sends a TERM signal by default. Table 10-5 on page 496 lists some signals.

Use the KILL signal as a last resort

caution When the termination signal does not work, use the KILL signal (specify **–KILL** in place of **–TERM** in the example). A running program cannot ignore a KILL signal; it is sure to abort the program.

Because a program receiving a KILL signal has no chance to clean up its open files before being terminated, using KILL can corrupt application data. Use the KILL signal as a last resort. Before using KILL, give a termination (TERM) or quit (QUIT) signal a full ten seconds to take effect.

```
$ bigjob
^Z
[1]+  Stopped                 bigjob
$ jobs
[1]+  Stopped                 bigjob
$ kill -TERM %1
[1]+  Killed                  bigjob
```

The **kill** command returns a prompt; you might need to press RETURN again to see the confirmation message. For more information refer to "Running a Command in the Background" on page 150.

REPEATING/EDITING COMMAND LINES

To repeat a previous command, press the UP ARROW key. Each time you press this key, the shell displays an earlier command line. Press the DOWN ARROW key to browse through the command lines in the other direction. To reexecute the displayed command line, press RETURN.

The RIGHT ARROW and LEFT ARROW keys move the cursor back and forth along the displayed command line. At any point along the command line, you can add characters by typing them. Use the erase key (page 29) to remove characters from the command line. Press RETURN to execute the modified command.

You can also repeat the previous command using **!!**. This technique is useful if you forgot to use su (next page) to prefix a command. In this case, if you type **su –c "!!"**, the shell will run the previous command with **root** privileges. Or, if the local system is set up to use sudo (next page), you can type **sudo !!** and the shell will run the previous command with **root** privileges.

The command **^old^new^** reruns the previous command, substituting the first occurrence of the string **old** with **new**. Also, on a command line, the shell replaces the characters **!$** with the last token (word) on the previous command line. The following example shows the user correcting the filename **meno** to **memo** using **^n^m^** and then printing the file named **memo** by giving the command **lpr !$**. The shell replaces **!$** with **memo**, the last token on the previous command line.

```
$ cat meno
cat: meno: No such file or directory
$ ^n^m^
cat memo
This is the memo file.
$ lpr !$
lpr memo
```

For information about more complex command-line editing, see page 338.

su/sudo: CURBING YOUR POWER (root PRIVILEGES)

UNIX and Linux systems have always had a privileged user named **root**. When you are working as the **root** user ("working with *root privileges*"), you have extraordinary systemwide powers. A user working with **root** privileges is sometimes referred to as *Superuser* or *administrator*. When working with **root** privileges, you can read from or write to almost any file on the system, execute programs that ordinary users cannot, and more. On a multiuser system you might not be permitted to gain **root** privileges and so might not be able to run certain programs. Nevertheless, someone—the *system administrator*—can, and that person maintains the system.

Do not experiment while you are working with root privileges

caution Feel free to experiment when you are *not* working with **root** privileges. When you *are* working with **root** privileges, do only what you have to do and make sure you know exactly what you are doing. After you have completed the task at hand, revert to working as yourself. When working with **root** privileges, you can damage the system to such an extent that you will need to reinstall Linux to get it working again.

With a conventional setup, you can gain **root** privileges in one of two ways. First, you can log in as the user named **root**; when you do so you are working with **root** privileges until you log out. Alternatively, while you are working as yourself, you can use the su (substitute user) utility to execute a single command with **root** privileges or to gain **root** privileges temporarily so you can execute several commands. Logging in as **root** and running su to gain **root** privileges require you to enter the **root** password. The following example shows how to use su to execute a single command:

```
$ ls -l /lost+found
ls: cannot open directory /lost+found: Permission denied
$ su -c 'ls -l /lost+found'
Password:                       Enter the root password
total 0
$
```

The first command in the preceding example shows that a user who is not working with **root** privileges is not permitted to list the files in the **/lost+found** directory: ls displays an error message. The second command uses su with the **–c** (command) option to execute the same command with **root** privileges. Single quotation marks enclose the command to ensure the shell interprets the command properly. When the command finishes executing (ls shows there are no files in the directory), the user no longer has **root** privileges.

Without any arguments, su spawns a new shell running with **root** privileges. Typically the shell displays a hashmark (#) prompt when you are working with **root** privileges. Give an **exit** command to return to the normal prompt and nonroot privileges.

```
$ su
Password:                          Enter the root password
# ls -l /lost+found
total 0
# exit
exit
$
```

Some distributions (e.g., Ubuntu) ship with the **root** account locked—there is no **root** password—and rely on the sudo (www.sudo.ws) utility to allow users to work with **root** privileges. The sudo utility requires you to enter *your* password (not the **root** password) to gain **root** privileges. The following example allows the user to gain **root** privileges to view the contents of the **/lost+found** directory:

```
$ sudo ls -l /lost+found
[sudo] password for sam:           Enter your password
total 0
$
```

With an argument of **–s**, sudo spawns a new shell running with **root** privileges. Typically the shell displays a hashmark (#) prompt when you are working with **root** privileges. Give an **exit** command to return to the normal prompt and nonroot privileges.

```
$ sudo -s
[sudo] password for sam:           Enter your password
# ls -l /lost+found
total 0
# exit
logout
$
```

Where to Find Documentation

Distributions of Linux typically do not come with hardcopy reference manuals. However, its online documentation has always been one of Linux's strengths. The man (or manual) and info pages have been available via the man and info utilities since early releases of the operating system. Not surprisingly, with the ongoing growth of Linux and the Internet, the sources of documentation have expanded as well. This section discusses some of the places you can look for information on Linux. See also Appendix B.

man: Displays the System Manual

The textual man (manual) utility displays (man) pages from the system documentation. This documentation is helpful when you know which utility you want to use but have forgotten exactly how to use it. You can also refer to the man pages to get more information about specific topics or to determine which features are available with Linux. Because the descriptions in the system documentation are often terse, they are most helpful if you already understand the basic

To find out more about a utility, give the command **man**, followed by the name of the utility. Figure 2-1 shows man displaying information about itself; the user entered a **man man** command.

less (pager) The man utility sends its output through a *pager*—usually less (page 53), which displays one screen of information at a time. When you display a manual page using man, less displays a prompt [e.g., **Manual page man(1) line 1**] at the bottom of the screen after it displays each screen of text and waits for you to take one of the following steps:

- Press the SPACE bar to display another screen of text.
- Press PAGE UP, PAGE DOWN, UP ARROW, or DOWN ARROW to navigate the text.
- Press **h** (help) to display a list of less commands.
- Press **q** (quit) to stop less and cause the shell to display a prompt.

You can search for topics covered by man pages using the apropos utility (next page).

Manual sections Based on the FHS (Filesystem Hierarchy Standard; page 98), the Linux system manual and the man pages are divided into ten sections, where each section describes related tools:

1. User Commands
2. System Calls
3. Subroutines
4. Devices
5. File Formats
6. Games
7. Miscellaneous
8. System Administration
9. Kernel
10. New

```
MAN(1)                        Manual pager utils                        MAN(1)

NAME
       man - an interface to the on-line reference manuals

SYNOPSIS
       man  [-C  file]  [-d]  [-D]  [--warnings[=warnings]]  [-R encoding] [-L
       locale] [-m system[,...]] [-M path] [-S list]  [-e  extension]  [-i|-I]
       [--regex|--wildcard]   [--names-only]  [-a]  [-u]  [--no-subpages]  [-P
       pager] [-r prompt] [-7] [-E encoding] [--no-hyphenation] [--no-justifi-
       cation]  [-p  string]  [-t]  [-T[device]]  [-H[browser]] [-X[dpi]] [-Z]
       [[section] page ...] ...
       man -k [apropos options] regexp ...
       man -K [-w|-W] [-S list] [-i|-I] [--regex] [section] term ...
       man -f [whatis options] page ...
       man -l [-C file] [-d] [-D] [--warnings[=warnings]]  [-R  encoding]  [-L
       locale]  [-P  pager]  [-r  prompt]  [-7] [-E encoding] [-p string] [-t]
       [-T[device]] [-H[browser]] [-X[dpi]] [-Z] file ...
       man -w|-W [-C file] [-d] [-D] page ...
       man -c [-C file] [-d] [-D] page ...
       man [-hV]

DESCRIPTION
 Manual page man(1) line 1 (press h for help or q to quit)
```

Figure 2-1 The man utility displaying information about itself

This layout closely mimics the way the set of UNIX manuals has always been divided. Unless you specify a manual section, man displays the earliest occurrence in the manual of the word you specify on the command line. Most users find the information they need in sections 1, 6, and 7; programmers and system administrators frequently need to consult the other sections.

In some cases the manual contains entries for different tools with the same name. For example, the following command displays the man page for the passwd utility from section 1 of the system manual:

```
$ man passwd
```

To see the man page for the **passwd** file from section 5, enter this command:

```
$ man 5 passwd
```

The preceding command instructs man to look only in section 5 for the man page. In documentation you might see this man page referred to as **passwd(5)**. Use the **–a** option (see the adjacent tip) to view all man pages for a given subject (press qRETURN to display each subsequent man page). For example, give the command **man –a passwd** to view all man pages for **passwd**.

Options

tip An option modifies the way a utility works. Options are usually specified as one or more letters that are preceded by one or two hyphens. An option typically appears following the name of the utility you are calling and a SPACE. Other *arguments* (page 1083) to the command follow the option and a SPACE. For more information refer to "Options" on page 131.

apropos: SEARCHES FOR A KEYWORD

When you do not know the name of the command required to carry out a particular task, you can use apropos with a keyword to search for it. This utility searches for the keyword in the short description line of all man pages and displays those that contain a match. The man utility, when called with the **–k** (keyword) option, provides the same output as apropos.

The database apropos uses, named **mandb** or **makewhatis**, is not available when a system is first installed but is built automatically by **cron** or **crond** (see crontab on page 781 for a discussion of **cron/crond**).

The following example shows the output of apropos when you call it with the **who** keyword. The output includes the name of each command, the section of the manual that contains it, and the short description from the man page. This list includes the utility you need (who) and identifies other, related tools you might find useful.

```
$ apropos who
at.allow (5)         - determine who can submit jobs via at or batch
jwhois (1)           - client for the whois service
w (1)                - show who is logged on and what they are doing
who (1)              - show who is logged on
who (1p)             - display who is on the system
whoami (1)           - print effective userid
```

```
whois (1)            - client for the whois service
whois.jwhois (1)     - client for the whois service
```

whatis The whatis utility is similar to apropos but finds only complete word matches for the name of the utility:

```
$ whatis who
who (1p)             - display who is on the system
who (1)              - show who is logged on
```

info: Displays Information About Utilities

The textual info utility (www.gnu.org/software/texinfo) is a menu-based hypertext system developed by the GNU project (page 3) and distributed with Linux. It includes a tutorial on itself (give the command **info info**) and documentation on many Linux shells, utilities, and programs developed by the GNU project. Figure 2-2 shows the screen that info displays when you give the command **info coreutils** (the **coreutils** software package holds the Linux core utilities).

man and info display different information

tip The info utility displays more complete and up-to-date information on GNU utilities than does man. When a man page displays abbreviated information on a utility that is covered by info, the man page refers to info. The man utility frequently displays the only information available on non-GNU utilities. When info displays information on non-GNU utilities, it is frequently a copy of the man page.

Because the information on this screen is drawn from an editable file, your display might differ from the screens shown in this section. You can press any of the following keys while the initial info screen is displayed:

- h or ? to list info commands
- SPACE to scroll through the display

```
File: coreutils.info,  Node: Top,  Next: Introduction,  Up: (dir)

GNU Coreutils
*************

This manual documents version 8.12 of the GNU core utilities, including
the standard programs for text and file manipulation.

   Copyright (C) 1994-1996, 2000-2011 Free Software Foundation, Inc.

     Permission is granted to copy, distribute and/or modify this
     document under the terms of the GNU Free Documentation License,
     Version 1.3 or any later version published by the Free Software
     Foundation; with no Invariant Sections, with no Front-Cover Texts,
     and with no Back-Cover Texts.  A copy of the license is included
     in the section entitled "GNU Free Documentation License".

* Menu:

* Introduction::                    Caveats, overview, and authors
* Common options::                  Common options
* Output of entire files::          cat tac nl od base64
--zz-Info: (coreutils.info.gz)Top, 334 lines --Top------------------------
Welcome to Info version 4.13. Type h for help, m for menu item.
```

Figure 2-2 The initial screen displayed by the command **info coreutils**

- **m** followed by the name of the menu you want to display or a SPACE to display a list of menus
- q or CONTROL-C to quit

The notation **info** uses to describe keyboard keys is the same notation **emacs** uses and might not be familiar to you. For example, the notation **C-h** is the same as CONTROL-H. Similarly, **M-x** means hold down the META or ALT key and press **x**. (On some systems you need to press ESCAPE and then **x** to duplicate the function of META-X.) For more information refer to "Keys: Notation and Use" on page 231.

After giving the command **info coreutils**, press the SPACE bar a few times to scroll through the display. Type **/sleep**RETURN to search for the string **sleep**. When you type **/**, the cursor moves to the bottom line of the window and displays **Regexp search [*string*]:**, where ***string*** is the last string you searched for. Press RETURN to search for ***string*** or enter the string you want to search for. Typing **sleep** displays **sleep** on that line, and pressing RETURN displays the next occurrence of **sleep**.

You might find pinfo easier to use than info

tip The **pinfo** utility is similar to **info** but is more intuitive if you are not familiar with **emacs** editor commands. This utility runs in a textual environment, as does **info**. When it is available, **pinfo** uses color to make its interface easier to use. If **pinfo** is not installed on the system, install the **pinfo** package as explained in Appendix C.

Now type **/**RETURN (or **/sleep**RETURN) to search for the next occurrence of **sleep** as shown in Figure 2-3. The asterisk at the left end of the line indicates that this entry is a menu item. Following the asterisk is the name of the menu item and a description of the item.

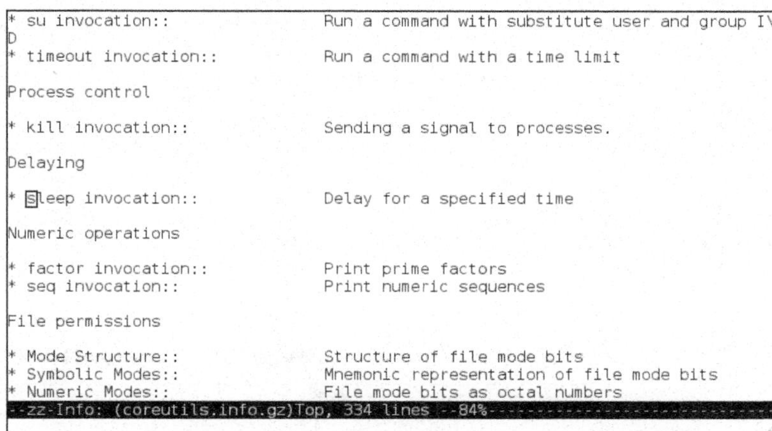

```
* su invocation::                Run a command with substitute user and group I\
D
* timeout invocation::           Run a command with a time limit

Process control

* kill invocation::              Sending a signal to processes.

Delaying

* sleep invocation::             Delay for a specified time

Numeric operations

* factor invocation::            Print prime factors
* seq invocation::               Print numeric sequences

File permissions

* Mode Structure::               Structure of file mode bits
* Symbolic Modes::               Mnemonic representation of file mode bits
* Numeric Modes::                File mode bits as octal numbers
--zz-Info: (coreutils.info.gz)Top, 334 lines --84%------------------------------
```

Figure 2-3 The screen displayed by the command **info coreutils** after you type **/sleep**RETURN twice

Each menu item is a link to the info page that describes the item. To jump to that page, search for or use the ARROW keys to move the cursor to the line containing the menu item and press RETURN. With the cursor positioned as it is in Figure 2-3, press RETURN to display information on sleep. Alternatively, you can type the name of the menu item in a menu command to view the information: To display information on sleep, for example, you can give the command **m sleep**, followed by RETURN. When you type **m** (for *menu*), the cursor moves to the bottom line of the window (as it did when you typed **/**) and displays **Menu item:**. Typing **sleep** displays **sleep** on that line, and pressing RETURN displays information about the menu item you specified.

Figure 2-5 shows the *top node* of information on sleep. A node groups a set of information you can scroll through by pressing the SPACE bar. To display the next node, press **n**. Press **p** to display the previous node.

As you read through this book and learn about new utilities, you can use man or info to find out more about those utilities. If the local system can print PostScript documents, you can print a manual page by using the man utility with the **–t** option. For example, **man –t cat | lpr** prints information about the cat utility. You can also use a Web browser to display the documentation at one of the sites listed in Appendix B and then print the desired information from the browser.

THE --help OPTION

Another tool you can use in a textual environment is the **--help** option. Most GNU utilities provide a **--help** option that displays information about the utility. A non-GNU utility might use a **–h** or **–help** option to display information about itself.

```
File: coreutils.info,  Node: sleep invocation,  Up: Delaying

25.1 `sleep': Delay for a specified time
========================================

`sleep' pauses for an amount of time specified by the sum of the values
of the command line arguments.  Synopsis:

     sleep NUMBER[smhd]...

   Each argument is a number followed by an optional unit; the default
is seconds.  The units are:

`s'
     seconds

`m'
     minutes

`h'
     hours

--zz-Info: (coreutils.info.gz)sleep invocation, 41 lines --Top-----------
```

Figure 2-4 The info page on the sleep utility

```
$ cat --help
Usage: cat [OPTION] [FILE]...
Concatenate FILE(s), or standard input, to standard output.

  -A, --show-all           equivalent to -vET
  -b, --number-nonblank    number nonempty output lines, overrides -n
  -e                       equivalent to -vE
  -E, --show-ends          display $ at end of each line
...
```

If the information that **--help** displays runs off the screen, send the output through the less pager (page 34) using a pipeline (page 60):

```
$ ls --help | less
```

THE bash help COMMAND

The bash **help** command displays information about bash commands, control structures, and other features. From the bash prompt, give the command **help** followed by the keyword you are interested in. Following are some examples:

```
$ help help
help: help [-dms] [pattern ...]
    Display information about builtin commands.

    Displays brief summaries of builtin commands.  If PATTERN is
    specified, gives detailed help on all commands matching PATTERN,
    otherwise the list of help topics is printed.
...

$ help echo
echo: echo [-neE] [arg ...]
    Write arguments to the standard output.

    Display the ARGs on the standard output followed by a newline.

    Options:
      -n        do not append a newline
...

$ help while
while: while COMMANDS; do COMMANDS; done
    Execute commands as long as a test succeeds.
...
```

GETTING HELP

This section describes several methods you can use to get help with a Linux system and lists some helpful Web sites. See also Appendix B.

FINDING HELP LOCALLY

/usr/share/doc The **/usr/src/linux/Documentation** (present only if you install the kernel source code) and **/usr/share/doc** directories often contain more detailed and different information about a utility than either man or info provides. Frequently this information is meant for people who will be compiling and modifying the utility, not just using it. These directories hold thousands of files, each containing information on a separate topic. As the following example shows, the names of most directories in **/usr/share/doc** end in version numbers:

```
$ ls /usr/share/doc
abrt-2.0.7                 iwl100-firmware-39.31.5.1       openldap-2.4.26
accountsservice-0.6.15 iwl3945-firmware-15.32.2.9      openobex-1.5
acl-2.2.51                 iwl4965-firmware-228.61.2.24    openssh-5.8p2
aic94xx-firmware-30        iwl5000-firmware-8.83.5.1_1     openssl-1.0.0g
aisleriot-3.2.1            iwl5150-firmware-8.24.2.2       openvpn-2.2.1
alsa-firmware-1.0.25       iwl6000-firmware-9.221.4.1      orc-0.4.16
alsa-lib-1.0.25            iwl6000g2a-firmware-17.168.5.3 orca-3.2.1
```

Most of these directories hold a **README** file, which is a good place to start reading about the utility or file the directory describes. Use an asterisk (*; page 154) in place of the version number to make it easier to type the filename. The following **README** file for bzip2 (pages 64 and 750) explains how to compile the source code:

```
$ cat /usr/share/doc/bzip2*/README
This is the README for bzip2/libzip2.
This version is fully compatible with the previous public releases.
...
Complete documentation is available in Postscript form (manual.ps),
PDF (manual.pdf) or html (manual.html).  A plain-text version of the
manual page is available as bzip2.txt.

HOW TO BUILD -- UNIX

Type 'make'.  This builds the library libbz2.a and then the programs
bzip2 and bzip2recover.  Six self-tests are run.  If the self-tests
complete ok, carry on to installation:

To install in /usr/local/bin, /usr/local/lib, /usr/local/man and
/usr/local/include, type

   make install
...
```

USING THE INTERNET TO GET HELP

The Internet provides many helpful sites related to Linux and macOS. Aside from sites that offer various forms of documentation, you can enter an error message from a program you are having a problem with in a search engine such as Google (www.google.com). The search will likely yield a post concerning your problem and suggestions about how to solve it. See Figure 2-5.

GNU GNU manuals are available at www.gnu.org/manual. In addition, you can visit the GNU home page (www.gnu.org) to obtain other documentation and GNU resources. Many of the GNU pages and resources are available in a variety of languages.

Figure 2-5 Google reporting on an error message

The Linux Documentation Project

The Linux Documentation Project (www.tldp.org; Figure 2-6), which has been around for almost as long as Linux, houses a complete collection of guides, HOWTOs, FAQs, man pages, and Linux magazines. The home page is available in English, Portuguese (Brazilian), Spanish, Italian, Korean, and French. It is easy to use and supports local text searches. This site also provides a complete set of links you can use to find almost anything you want related to Linux (click **Links** in the Search box or go to www.tldp.org/links). The links page includes sections on general information, events, getting started, user groups, mailing lists, and newsgroups, with each section containing many subsections.

HOWTOs

A HOWTO document explains in detail how to do something related to Linux—from setting up a specialized piece of hardware to performing a system administration task to setting up specific networking software. Mini-HOWTOs offer shorter explanations.

Figure 2-6 The Linux Documentation Project home page

The Linux Documentation Project site houses most HOWTO and mini-HOWTO documents. Use a Web browser to visit www.tldp.org, click **HOWTOs**, and pick the index you want to use to find a HOWTO or mini-HOWTO. You can also use the LDP search feature on its home page to find HOWTOs and other documents.

More About Logging In and Passwords

Refer to "Logging In from a Terminal (Emulator)" on page 26 for information about logging in. This section covers solutions to common login problems, logging in remotely, virtual consoles, and changing your password.

Always use a password

security

Unless you are the only user of a system; the system is not connected to any other systems, the Internet, or a modem; and you are the only one with physical access to the system, it is poor practice to maintain a user account without a password.

What to Do If You Cannot Log In

If you enter either your username or your password incorrectly, the system displays an error message after you enter *both* your username *and* your password. This message indicates that you have entered either the username or the password incorrectly or that they are not valid. It does not differentiate between an unacceptable username and an unacceptable password—a strategy meant to discourage unauthorized people from guessing names and passwords to gain access to the system.

Following are some common reasons why logins fail:

- **The username and password are case sensitive.** Make sure the CAPS LOCK key is off and enter your username and password exactly as specified or as you set them up.
- **You are not logging in on the right machine.** The login/password combination might not be valid if you are trying to log in on the wrong machine. On a larger, networked system, you might have to specify the machine you want to connect to before you can log in.
- **Your username is not valid.** The login/password combination might not be valid if you have not been set up as a user.
- **A filesystem is full.** When a filesystem critical to the login process is full, it might appear as though you have logged in successfully, but after a moment the login prompt reappears. In this situation you must boot the system in rescue/recovery mode and delete some files.
- **The account is disabled.** On some systems, the **root** account is disabled by default. An administrator might disable other accounts. Often the **root** account is not allowed to log in over a network: In this case, log in as yourself and then gain root privileges using su/sudo.

Refer to "Changing Your Password" on page 44 if you want to change your password.

Logging In Remotely: Terminal Emulators, ssh, and Dial-Up Connections

When you are not using a console, terminal, or other device connected directly to the Linux system you are logging in on, you are probably connected to the Linux system using terminal emulation software on another system. Running on the local system, this software connects to the remote Linux system via a network (Ethernet, asynchronous phone line, PPP, or other type) and allows you to log in.

Make sure TERM is set correctly

tip No matter how you connect, make sure the **TERM** variable is set to the type of terminal your emulator is emulating. For more information refer to "Specifying a Terminal" on page 1050.

When you log in via a dial-up line, the connection is straightforward: You instruct the local emulator program to contact the remote Linux system, it dials the phone, and the remote system displays a login prompt. When you log in via a directly connected network, you use either ssh (secure; page 703) or telnet (not secure; page 1001) to connect to the remote system. The ssh program has been implemented on many operating systems, not just Linux. Many user interfaces to ssh include a terminal emulator. From an Apple, Windows, or UNIX machine, open the program that runs ssh and give it the name or IP address of the system you want to log in on.

USING VIRTUAL CONSOLES

When running Linux on a personal computer, you will frequently work with the display and keyboard attached to the computer. Using this physical console, you can access as many as 63 *virtual consoles* (also called *virtual terminals*). Some are set up to allow logins; others act as graphical displays. To switch between virtual consoles, hold the CONTROL and ALT keys down and press the function key that corresponds to the console you want to view. For example, CONTROL-ALT-F5 displays the fifth virtual console.

By default, five or six virtual consoles are active and have textual login sessions running. When you want to use both textual and graphical interfaces, you can set up a textual session on one virtual console and a graphical session on another.

LOGGING OUT

To log out from a character-based interface, press CONTROL-D in response to the shell prompt. This action sends the shell an EOF (end of file). Alternatively, you can give the command **exit**. Exiting from a shell does not end a graphical session; it just exits from the shell you are working with. For example, exiting from the shell that GNOME terminal provides closes the GNOME terminal window.

CHANGING YOUR PASSWORD

If someone else assigned you a password, it is a good idea to give yourself a new one. For security reasons, passwords you enter are not displayed by any utility.

Protect your password

security Do not allow someone to find out your password: *Do not* put your password in a file that is not encrypted, allow someone to watch you type your password, or give your password to someone you do not know (a system administrator never needs to know your password). You can always write your password down and keep it in a safe, private place.

Choose a password that is difficult to guess

security Do not use phone numbers, names of pets or kids, birthdays, words from a dictionary (not even a foreign language), and so forth. Do not use permutations of these items or a l33t-speak variation of a word: Modern dictionary crackers might also try these permutations.

Include nonalphanumeric characters in your password

security Automated password cracking tools first try using alphabetic and numeric characters when they try to guess your password. Including at least one character such as @ or # in a password increases the amount of time it takes for one of these tools to crack your password.

Differentiate between important and less important passwords

security It is a good idea to differentiate between important and less important passwords. For example, Web site passwords for blogs or download access are not very important; it is acceptable to use the same password for these types of sites. However, your login, mail server, and bank account Web site passwords are critical: Never use these passwords for an unimportant Web site and use a different password for each of these accounts.

Secure passwords

To be relatively secure, a password should contain a combination of numbers, uppercase and lowercase letters, and punctuation characters. It should also meet the following criteria:

- Must be at least six characters long (or longer if the system administrator sets it up that way). Seven or eight characters is a good compromise between being easy to remember and being secure.
- Should not be a word in a dictionary of any language, no matter how seemingly obscure.
- Should not be the name of a person, place, pet, or other thing that might be discovered easily.
- Should contain at least two letters and one digit or punctuation character.
- Should not be your username, the reverse of your username, or your username shifted by one or more characters.

Only the first item is mandatory. Avoid using control characters (such as CONTROL-H) because they might have a special meaning to the system, making it impossible for you to log in. If you are changing your password, the new password should differ from the old one by at least three characters. Changing the case of a character does not make it count as a different character.

pwgen helps you pick a password

security The pwgen utility (install the **pwgen** package as explained in Appendix C) generates a list of almost random passwords. With a little imagination, you can pronounce, and therefore remember, some of these passwords.

To change your password, give the command **passwd**. The first item passwd asks for is your current (old) password. This password is verified to ensure that an unauthorized user is not trying to alter your password. Then the system requests a new password.

```
$ passwd
Changing password for user sam.
Changing password for sam.
(current) UNIX password:
New password:
Retype new password:
passwd: all authentication tokens updated successfully.
```

After you enter your new password, the system asks you to retype it to make sure you did not make a mistake when you entered it the first time. If the new password is the same both times you enter it, your password is changed. If the passwords differ, it means that you made an error in one of them, and the system displays this error message:

```
Sorry, passwords do not match
```

If your password is not long enough, the system displays the following message:

```
BAD PASSWORD: it is too short
```

When it is too simple, the system displays this message:

```
BAD PASSWORD: it is too simplistic/systematic
```

After several failures, the system displays an error message and displays a prompt. At this point you need to run passwd again.

macOS: passwd does not change your Keychain password

tip Under macOS, the passwd utility changes your login password, but does not change your Keychain password. The Keychain password is used by various graphical applications. You can change the Keychain password using the Keychain Access application.

When you successfully change your password, you change the way you log in. If you forget your password, someone working with **root** privileges can run passwd to change it and tell you your new password.

Working with **root** privileges (use su/sudo [page 32]) you can assign a new password to any user on the system without knowing the user's old password. Use this technique when a user forgets his password:

```
# passwd sam
Changing password for user sam.
New password:
...
```

CHAPTER SUMMARY

As with many operating systems, your access to a Linux system is authorized when you log in. You enter your username in response to the **login:** prompt, followed by a password. You can use passwd to change your password while you are logged in.

Choose a password that is difficult to guess and that conforms to the criteria imposed by the system administrator.

The system administrator is responsible for maintaining the system. On a single-user system, you are the system administrator. On a small, multiuser system, you or another user will act as the system administrator, or this job might be shared. On a large, multiuser system or network of systems, there is frequently a full-time system administrator. When extra privileges are required to perform certain system tasks, the system administrator gains **root** privileges by logging in as **root** or by running su or sudo. On a multiuser system, several trusted users might be allowed to gain **root** privileges.

Do not work with **root** privileges as a matter of course. When you have to do something that requires **root** privileges, work with **root** privileges for only as long as you need to; revert to working as yourself as soon as possible.

The man utility provides online documentation on system utilities. This utility is helpful both to new Linux users and to experienced users who must often delve into the system documentation for information on the fine points of a utility's behavior. The apropos utility can help you search for utilities. The info utility helps the beginner and the expert alike. It includes documentation on many Linux utilities. Some utilities, when called with the **--help** option, provide brief documentation on themselves.

EXERCISES

1. The following message is displayed when you attempt to log in with an incorrect username *or* an incorrect password:

   ```
   Login incorrect
   ```

   This message does not indicate whether your username, your password, or both are invalid. Why does it not tell you this information?
2. Give three examples of poor password choices. What is wrong with each? Include one that is too short. Give the error message the system displays.
3. Is **fido** an acceptable password? Give several reasons why or why not.
4. What would you do if you could not log in?
5. Try to change your password to **dog**. What happens? Now change it to a more secure password. What makes that password relatively secure?
6. How would you display a list of utilities that compress files?
7. How would you repeat the second preceding command line, edit it, and then execute it?
8. Briefly, what information does the **--help** option display for the tar utility? How would you display this information one screen at a time?

ADVANCED EXERCISES

9. How would you display the man page for **shadow** in section 5 of the system manual?
10. How would you change your login shell to tcsh without using **root** privileges?
11. How many man pages are in the **Devices** subsection of the system manual? (*Hint:* **Devices** is a subsection of **Special Files.**)
12. The example on page 35 shows that man pages for **passwd** appear in sections 1 and 5 of the system manual. Explain how you can use man to determine which sections of the system manual contain a manual page with a given name.
13. How would you find out which Linux utilities create and work with archive files?

3

The Utilities

In This Chapter

Objectives

After reading this chapter you should be able to:

- List special characters and methods of preventing the shell from interpreting these characters
- Use basic utilities to list files and display text files
- Copy, move, and remove files
- Search, sort, print, and compare text files
- String commands together using a pipeline
- Compress, decompress, and archive files
- Locate utilities on the system
- Display information about users
- Communicate with other users

When Linus Torvalds introduced Linux and for a long time thereafter, Linux did not have a graphical user interface (GUI): It ran on character-based terminals only, using a command-line interface (CLI), also referred to as a textual interface. All the tools ran from a command line. Today the Linux GUI is important, but many people—especially system administrators—run many command-line utilities. Command-line utilities are often faster, more powerful, or more complete than their GUI counterparts. Sometimes there is no GUI counterpart to a textual utility; some people just prefer the hands-on feeling of the command line.

When you work with a command-line interface, you are working with a shell (Chapters 5, 8, and 10). Before you start working with a shell, it is important that you understand something about the characters that are special to the shell, so this chapter starts with a discussion of special characters. The chapter then describes five basic utilities: ls, cat, rm, less, and hostname. It continues by describing several other file manipulation utilities as well as utilities that compress and decompress files, pack and unpack archive files, locate utilities, display system information, communicate with other users, and print files.

SPECIAL CHARACTERS

Special characters, which have a special meaning to the shell, are discussed in "Filename Generation/Pathname Expansion" on page 152. These characters are mentioned here so you can avoid accidentally using them as regular characters until you understand how the shell interprets them. Avoid using any of the following characters in a filename (even though emacs and some other programs do) because they make the file harder to reference on the command line:

```
& ; | * ? ' " ` [ ] ( ) $ < > { } # / \ ! ~
```

Whitespace Although not considered special characters, RETURN, SPACE, and TAB have special meanings to the shell. RETURN usually ends a command line and initiates execution of a command. The SPACE and TAB characters separate tokens (elements) on the command line and are collectively known as *whitespace* or *blanks.*

Quoting special characters If you need to use a character that has a special meaning to the shell as a regular character, you can *quote* (or *escape*) it. When you quote a special character, you prevent the shell from giving it special meaning. The shell treats a quoted special character as a regular character. However, a slash (/) is always a separator in a pathname, even when you quote it.

Backslash To quote a character, precede it with a backslash (\). When two or more special characters appear together, you must precede each with a backslash (for example, you would enter ** as **). You can quote a backslash just as you would quote any other special character—by preceding it with a backslash (\\).

Single quotation marks Another way of quoting special characters is to enclose them between single quotation marks: '**'. You can quote many special and regular characters between a pair of single quotation marks: '**This is a special character: >**'. The regular characters are interpreted as usual, and the shell also interprets the special characters as regular characters.

The only way to quote the erase character (CONTROL-H), the line kill character (CONTROL-U), and other control characters (try CONTROL-M) is by preceding each with a CONTROL-V. Single quotation marks and backslashes do not work. Try the following:

```
$ echo 'xxxxxxCONTROL-U'
$ echo xxxxxxCONTROL-V CONTROL-U
```

optional Although you cannot see the CONTROL-U displayed by the second of the preceding pair of commands, it is there. The following command sends the output of echo (page 61) through a pipeline (page 60) to od (octal display; page 921) to display CONTROL-U as octal 25 (025):

```
$ echo xxxxxxCONTROL-V CONTROL-U | od -c
0000000   x   x   x   x   x   x 025  \n
0000010
```

The **\n** is the NEWLINE character that echo sends at the end of its output.

BASIC UTILITIES

One of the advantages of Linux is that it comes with thousands of utilities that perform myriad functions. You will use utilities whenever you work with Linux, whether you use them directly by name from the command line or indirectly from a menu or icon. The following sections discuss some of the most basic and important utilities; these utilities are available from a CLI. Some of the more important utilities are also available from a GUI; others are available only from a GUI.

Run these utilities from a command line

tip This chapter describes command-line, or textual, utilities. You can experiment with these utilities from a terminal, a terminal emulator within a GUI, or a virtual console.

Folder/directory The term *directory* is used extensively in the next sections. A directory is a resource that can hold files. On other operating systems, including Windows and macOS, and frequently when speaking about a Linux GUI, a directory is referred to as a *folder*. That is a good analogy: A traditional manila folder holds files just as a directory does.

In this chapter you work in your home directory

tip When you log in on the system, you are working in your *home directory*. In this chapter that is the only directory you use: All the files you create in this chapter are in your home directory. Chapter 4 goes into more detail about directories.

ls: LISTS THE NAMES OF FILES

Using the editor of your choice, create a small file named **practice.** (A tutorial on the vim editor appears on page 167 and a tutorial on emacs appears on page 224.) After exiting from the editor, you can use the ls (list) utility to display a list of the names of the files in your home directory. In the first command in Figure 3-1, ls lists the name of the **practice** file. (You might also see files that the system or a program created automatically.) Subsequent commands in Figure 3-1 display the contents of the file and remove the file. These commands are described next.

cat: DISPLAYS A TEXT FILE

The cat utility displays the contents of a text file. The name of the command is derived from *catenate,* which means to join together, one after the other. (Figure 5-8 on page 141 shows how to use cat to string together the contents of three files.)

A convenient way to display the contents of a file on the screen is by giving the command **cat**, followed by a SPACE and the name of the file. Figure 3-1 shows cat displaying the contents of **practice**. This figure shows the difference between the ls and cat utilities: The ls utility displays the *name* of a file, whereas cat displays the *contents* of a file.

rm: DELETES A FILE

The rm (remove) utility deletes a file. Figure 3-1 shows rm deleting the file named **practice**. After rm deletes the file, ls and cat show that **practice** is no longer in the directory.

A safer way of removing files

tip You can use the interactive form of rm to make sure you delete only the file(s) you intend to delete. When you follow rm with the **–i** option (see page 35 for a tip on options) and the name of the file you want to delete, rm prompts you with the name of the file and waits for you to respond with **y** (yes) before it deletes the file. It does not delete the file if you respond with a string that begins with a character other than **y**. Under some distributions, the **–i** option is set up by default for the **root** user:

```
$ rm -i toollist
rm: remove regular file 'toollist'? y
```

Optional: You can create an alias (page 352) for **rm –i** and put it in your startup file (page 89) so rm always runs in interactive mode.

```
$ ls
practice
$ cat practice
This is a small file that I created
with a text editor.
$ rm practice
$ ls
$ cat practice
cat: practice: No such file or directory
$
```

Figure 3-1 Using ls, cat, and rm on the file named **practice**

The ls utility does not list its filename, and cat says that no such file exists. Use rm carefully. Refer to page 953 or give the command **info coreutils 'rm invocation'** for more information. If you are running macOS, see "Many Utilities Do Not Respect Apple Human Interface Guidelines" on page 1076.

less Is more: Display a Text File One Screen at a Time

Pagers When you want to view a file that is longer than one screen, you can use either the less utility or the more utility. Each of these utilities pauses after displaying a screen of text; press the SPACE bar to display the next screen of text. Because these utilities show one page at a time, they are called *pagers*. Although less and more are very similar, they have subtle differences. At the end of the file, for example, less displays an **END** message and waits for you to press **q** before returning you to the shell. In contrast, more returns you directly to the shell. While using both utilities you can press **h** to display a Help screen that lists commands you can use while paging through a file. Give the commands **less practice** and **more practice** in place of the **cat** command in Figure 3-1 to see how these commands work. Use the command **less /etc/services** instead if you want to experiment with a longer file. Refer to page 873 for more information on less.

hostname: Displays the System Name

The hostname utility displays the name of the system you are working on. Use this utility if you are not sure that you are logged in on the correct machine.

```
$ hostname
guava
```

Working with Files

This section describes utilities that copy, move, print, search through, display, sort, compare, and identify files. If you are running macOS, see "Resource forks" on page 1071.

Filename completion

tip After you enter one or more letters of a filename (following a command) on a command line, press TAB, and the shell will complete as much of the filename as it can. When only one filename starts with the characters you entered, the shell completes the filename and places a SPACE after it. You can keep typing or you can press RETURN to execute the command at this point. When the characters you entered do not uniquely identify a filename, the shell completes what it can and waits for more input. If pressing TAB does not change the display, press TAB again (bash; page 348) or CONTROL-D (tcsh; "Word Completion" on page 391) to display a list of possible completions.

cp: Copies a File

The cp (copy) utility (Figure 3-2, next page) makes a copy of a file. This utility can copy any file, including text and executable program (binary) files. You can use cp to make a backup copy of a file or a copy to experiment with.

The cp command line uses the following syntax to specify source and destination files:

cp source-file destination-file

The ***source-file*** is the name of the file that cp will copy. The ***destination-file*** is the name cp assigns to the resulting (new) copy of the file.

The cp command line in Figure 3-2 copies the file named **memo** to **memo.copy**. The period is part of the filename—just another character. The initial ls command shows that **memo** is the only file in the directory. After the cp command, a second ls shows two files in the directory, **memo** and **memo.copy**.

Sometimes it is useful to incorporate the date into the name of a copy of a file. The following example includes the date January 30 (**0130**) in the copied file:

```
$ cp memo memo.0130
```

Although it has no significance to Linux, including the date in this way can help you find a version of a file you created on a certain date. Including the date can also help you avoid overwriting existing files by providing a unique filename each day. For more information refer to "Filenames" on page 86.

Use scp (page 713) or ftp (page 838) when you need to copy a file from one system to another on a network.

cp can destroy a file

caution If the ***destination-file*** exists *before* you give a cp command, cp overwrites it. Because cp overwrites (and destroys the contents of) an existing ***destination-file*** without warning, you must take care not to cause cp to overwrite a file that you need. The cp **–i** (interactive) option prompts you before it overwrites a file. See page 35 for a tip on options.

The following example assumes the file named **orange.2** exists before you give the cp command. The user answers **y** to overwrite the file.

```
$ cp -i orange orange.2
cp: overwrite 'orange.2'? y
```

mv: Changes the Name of a File

The mv (move) utility can rename a file without making a copy of it. The mv command line specifies an existing file and a new filename using the same syntax as cp:

```
$ ls
memo
$ mv memo memo.0130
$ ls
memo.0130
```

Figure 3-2 mv renames a file

mv existing-filename new-filename

The command line in Figure 3-2 changes the name of the file **memo** to **memo.0130**. The initial ls command shows that **memo** is the only file in the directory. After you give the mv command, **memo.0130** is the only file in the directory. Compare this result to that of the cp example in Figure 3-2.

The mv utility can be used for more than changing the name of a file; refer to "mv, cp: Move or Copy Files" on page 97 and to the mv info page.

mv **can destroy a file**

caution Just as cp can destroy a file, so can mv. Also like cp, mv has a **–i** (interactive) option. See the caution box labeled "cp can destroy a file."

lpr: PRINTS A FILE

The lpr (line printer) utility places one or more files in a print queue for printing. Linux provides print queues so only one job is printed on a given printer at a time. A queue allows several people or jobs to send output simultaneously to a single printer with the expected results. For systems that have access to more than one printer, you can use **lpstat –p** to display a list of available printers. Use the **–P** option to instruct lpr to place the file in the queue for a specific printer—even one that is connected to another system on the network. The following command prints the file named **report**:

```
$ lpr report
```

Because this command does not specify a printer, the output goes to the default printer, which is *the* printer when you have only one printer.

The next command line prints the same file on the printer named **mailroom**:

```
$ lpr -P mailroom report
```

You can send more than one file to the printer with a single command. The following command line prints three files on the printer named **laser1**:

```
$ lpr -P laser1 05.txt 108.txt 12.txt
```

```
$ ls
memo
$ cp memo memo.copy
$ ls
memo memo.copy
```

Figure 3-3 cp copies a file

lpq You can see which jobs are in the print queue by giving an **lpstat –o** command or by using the lpq utility:

```
$ lpq
lp is ready and printing
Rank   Owner    Job Files                          Total Size
active max       86 (standard input)                 954061 bytes
```

lprm In this example, Max has one job that is being printed; no other jobs are in the queue. You can use the job number (86 in this case) with the lprm utility to remove the job from the print queue and stop it from printing:

```
$ lprm 86
```

grep: SEARCHES FOR A STRING

The grep[1] utility searches through one or more files to see whether any contain a specified string of characters. This utility does not change the file it searches but simply displays each line that contains the string.

The grep command in Figure 3-4 searches through the **memo** file for lines that contain the string **credit** and displays the single line that meets this criterion. If **memo** contained such words as **discredit**, **creditor**, or **accreditation**, grep would have displayed those lines as well because they contain the string it was searching for. The **–w** (words) option causes grep to match only whole words. Although you do not need to enclose the string you are searching for in single quotation marks, doing so allows you to put SPACEs and special characters in the search string.

```
$ cat memo

Helen:

In our meeting on June 6 we
discussed the issue of credit.
Have you had any further thoughts
about it?

             Max

$ grep 'credit' memo
discussed the issue of credit.
```

Figure 3-4 grep searches for a string

1. Originally the name grep was a play on an ed (an original UNIX editor, available on most distributions) command: **g/re/p**. In this command **g** stands for global, **re** is a regular expression delimited by slashes, and **p** means print.

The grep utility can do much more than search for a simple string in a single file. Refer to page 853 and Appendix A for more information.

head: Displays the Beginning of a File

By default the head utility displays the first ten lines of a file. You can use head to help you remember what a particular file contains. For example, if you have a file named **months** that lists the 12 months of the year in calendar order, one to a line, then head displays **Jan** through **Oct** (Figure 3-5).

This utility can display any number of lines, so you can use it to look at only the first line of a file, at a full screen, or even more. To specify the number of lines displayed, include a hyphen followed by the number of lines you want head to display. For example, the following command displays only the first line of **months**:

```
$ head -1 months
Jan
```

The head utility can also display parts of a file based on a count of blocks or characters rather than lines. Refer to page 861 for more information on head.

tail: Displays the End of a File

The tail utility is similar to head but by default displays the *last* ten lines of a file. Depending on how you invoke it, this utility can display fewer or more than ten lines. Alternatively, you can use a count of blocks or characters rather than lines to display

```
$ head months
Jan
Feb
Mar
Apr
May
Jun
Jul
Aug
Sep
Oct

$ tail -5 months
Aug
Sep
Oct
Nov
Dec
```

Figure 3-5 head displays the first ten lines of a file

parts of a file. The tail command in Figure 3-5 displays the last five lines (**Aug** through **Dec**) of the **months** file.

You can monitor lines as they are added to the end of the growing file named **logfile** by using the following command:

```
$ tail -f logfile
```

Press the interrupt key (usually CONTROL-C) to stop tail and display the shell prompt. Refer to page 992 for more information on tail.

sort: DISPLAYS A FILE IN ORDER

The sort utility displays the contents of a file in order by lines; it does not change the original file.

Figure 3-6 shows cat displaying the file named **days**, which contains the name of each day of the week on a separate line in calendar order. The sort utility then displays the file in alphabetical order.

The sort utility is useful for putting lists in order. The **–u** option generates a sorted list in which each line is unique (no duplicates). The **–n** option puts a list of numbers in numerical order. Refer to page 969 for more information on sort.

uniq: REMOVES DUPLICATE LINES FROM A FILE

The uniq (unique) utility displays a file, skipping adjacent duplicate lines; it does not change the original file. If a file contains a list of names and has two successive entries for the same person, uniq skips the extra line (Figure 3-7).

Figure 3-6 sort displays the lines of a file in order

If a file is sorted before it is processed by uniq, this utility ensures that no two lines in the file are the same. (Of course, sort can do that all by itself with the **–u** option.) Refer to page 1023 for more information on uniq.

diff: Compares Two Files

The diff (difference) utility compares two files and displays a list of the differences between them. This utility does not change either file; it is useful when you want to compare two versions of a letter or a report, or two versions of the source code for a program.

The diff utility with the **–u** (unified output format) option first displays two lines indicating which of the files you are comparing will be denoted by a plus sign (**+**) and which by a minus sign (**–**). In Figure 3-8, a minus sign indicates the **colors.1** file; a plus sign indicates the **colors.2** file.

```
$ cat dups
Cathy
Fred
Joe
John
Mary
Mary
Paula

$ uniq dups
Cathy
Fred
Joe
John
Mary
Paula
```

Figure 3-7 uniq removes duplicate lines

```
$ diff -u colors.1 colors.2
--- colors.1    2018-04-05 10:12:12.322528610 -0700
+++ colors.2    2018-04-05 10:12:18.420531033 -0700
@@ -1,6 +1,5 @@
 red
+blue
 green
 yellow
-pink
-purple
 orange
```

Figure 3-8 diff displaying the unified output format

The **diff –u** command breaks long, multiline text into *hunks*. Each hunk is preceded by a line starting and ending with two at signs (@@). This hunk identifier indicates the starting line number and the number of lines from each file for this hunk. In Figure 3-8, the hunk covers the section of the **colors.1** file (indicated by a minus sign) from the first line through the sixth line. The **+1,5** then indicates the hunk covers **colors.2** from the first line through the fifth line.

Following these header lines, **diff –u** displays each line of text with a leading minus sign, a leading plus sign, or a SPACE. A leading minus sign indicates the line occurs only in the file denoted by the minus sign. A leading plus sign indicates the line occurs only in the file denoted by the plus sign. A line that begins with a SPACE (neither a plus sign nor a minus sign) occurs in both files in the same location. Refer to page 795 for more information on diff.

file: Identifies the Contents of a File

You can use the file utility to learn about the contents of any file on a Linux system without having to open and examine the file yourself. In the following example, file reports that **letter_e.bz2** contains data that was compressed using the bzip2 utility (page 64):

```
$ file letter_e.bz2
letter_e.bz2: bzip2 compressed data, block size = 900k
```

Next, file reports on two more files:

```
$ file memo zach.jpg
memo:      ASCII text
zach.jpg: JPEG image data, ... resolution (DPI), 72 x 72
```

Refer to page 820 for more information on file.

| (Pipeline): Communicates Between Processes

Because pipelines are integral to the functioning of a Linux system, this chapter introduces them for use in examples. Pipelines are covered in detail beginning on page 145. Pipelines do not work with macOS resource forks; they work with data forks only.

A *pipeline* (denoted by a pipe symbol that is written as a vertical bar [|] on the command line and appears as a solid or broken vertical line on a keyboard) takes the output of one utility and sends that output as input to another utility. More accurately, a pipeline takes standard output of one process and redirects it to become standard input of another process. See page 137 for more information on standard output and standard input.

Some utilities, such as head, can accept input from a file named on the command line or, via a pipeline, from standard input. In the following command line, sort processes the **months** file (Figure 3-5, page 57); using a pipeline, the shell sends the output from sort to the input of head, which displays the first four months of the sorted list:

```
$ sort months | head -4
Apr
Aug
Dec
Feb
```

wc The next command line displays the number of files in a directory. The wc (word count) utility with the **–w** (words) option displays the number of words in its standard input or in a file you specify on the command line:

```
$ ls | wc -w
14
```

You can also use a pipeline to send output of a program to the printer:

```
$ tail months | lpr
```

Four More Utilities

The echo and date utilities are two of the most frequently used members of the large collection of Linux utilities. The script utility records part of a session in a file, and unix2dos makes a copy of a Linux text file that can be read on a machine running either Windows or macOS.

echo: Displays Text

The echo utility copies the characters you type on the command line following **echo** to the screen. Figure 3-9 shows some echo commands. The last command shows what the shell does with an unquoted asterisk (*) on the command line: It expands the asterisk into a list of filenames in the directory.

```
$ ls
memo  memo.0714  practice
$ echo Hi
Hi
$ echo This is a sentence.
This is a sentence.
$ echo star: *
star: memo memo.0714 practice
$
```

Figure 3-9 echo copies the command line (but not the word **echo**) to the screen

The echo utility is a good tool for learning about the shell and other Linux utilities. Some examples on page 154 use echo to illustrate how special characters, such as the asterisk, work. Throughout Chapters 5, 8, and 10, echo helps explain how shell variables work and how you can send messages from shell scripts to the screen. Refer to page 812 for more information on echo.

optional You can use echo to create a simple file by redirecting its output to a file:

```
$ echo 'My new file.' > myfile
$ cat myfile
My new file.
```

The greater than (>) sign tells the shell to redirect the output of echo to the file named **myfile** instead of to the screen. For more information refer to "Redirecting Standard Output" on page 140.

date: Displays the Time and Date

The date utility displays the current date and time:

```
$ date
Tue Apr  3 10:14:41 PDT 2018
```

The following example shows how you can specify the format and contents of the output of date:

```
$ date +"%A %B %d"
Tuesday April 03
```

Refer to page 787 for more information on date.

script: Records a Shell Session

The script utility records all or part of a login session, including your input and the system's responses. This utility is useful only from character-based devices, such as a terminal or a terminal emulator. It does capture a session with vim; however, because vim uses control characters to position the cursor and display different typefaces, such as bold, the output will be difficult to read and might not be useful. When you cat a file that has captured a vim session, the session quickly passes before your eyes.

By default script captures the session in a file named **typescript**. To specify a different filename, follow the script command with a SPACE and the filename. To append to a file, use the **–a** option after **script** but before the filename; otherwise, script overwrites an existing file. Following is a session being recorded by script:

```
$ script
Script started, file is typescript
$ ls -l /bin | head -5
-rwxr-xr-x. 1 root root     123 02-07 17:32 alsaunmute
-rwxr-xr-x. 1 root root   25948 02-08 03:46 arch
lrwxrwxrwx. 1 root root       4 02-25 16:52 awk -> gawk
```

```
-rwxr-xr-x. 1 root root   25088 02-08 03:46 basename
$ exit
exit
Script done, file is typescript
```

Use the exit command to terminate a script session. You can then view the file you created using cat, less, more, or an editor. Following is the file created by the preceding script command:

```
$ cat typescript
Script started on Tue 03 Apr 2018 10:16:36 AM PDT
$ ls -l /bin | head -5
-rwxr-xr-x. 1 root root     123 02-07 17:32 alsaunmute
-rwxr-xr-x. 1 root root   25948 02-08 03:46 arch
lrwxrwxrwx. 1 root root       4 02-25 16:52 awk -> gawk
-rwxr-xr-x. 1 root root   25088 02-08 03:46 basename
$ exit
exit

Script done on Tue 03 Apr 2018 10:16:50 AM PDT
```

If you will be editing the file, you can use dos2unix (next) to eliminate from the **typescript** file the ^M characters that appear at the ends of the lines. Refer to the script man page for more information.

unix2dos: Converts Linux Files to Windows and macOS Format

unix2dos, unix2mac If you want to share a text file you created on a Linux system with someone on a Windows or macOS system, you need to convert the file for the person on the other system to read it easily. The unix2dos utility converts a Linux text file so it can be read on a Windows machine; use unix2mac to convert a Linux file so it can be read on a Macintosh system. This utility is part of the **dos2unix** software package. Some distributions use todos in place of unix2dos; todos is part of the **tofrodos** software package and has no Macintosh-specific conversion utility. If you are using unix2dos, enter the following command to convert a file named **memo.txt** (created with a text editor) to a DOS-format file (use unix2mac to convert to a Macintosh-format file):

```
$ unix2dos memo.txt
```

You can now email the file as an attachment to someone on a Windows or macOS system. This utility overwrites the original file.

dos2unix, mac2unix The dos2unix (or fromdos) utility converts Windows files so they can be read on a Linux system (use mac2unix to convert from a Macintosh system):

```
$ dos2unix memo.txt
```

See the dos2unix man page for more information.

tr You can also use tr (translate; page 1014) to change a Windows or macOS text file into a Linux text file. In the following example, the **–d** (delete) option causes tr to remove RETURNs (represented by **\r**) as it makes a copy of the file:

```
$ cat memo | tr -d '\r' > memo.txt
```

The greater than (**>**) symbol redirects the standard output of tr to the file named **memo.txt**. For more information refer to "Redirecting Standard Output" on page 140. Converting a file the other way without using unix2dos is not as easy.

COMPRESSING AND ARCHIVING FILES

Large files use more disk space and take longer to transfer over a network than smaller files. To reduce these factors you can compress a file without losing any of the information it holds. Similarly, a single archive of several files packed into a larger file is easier to manipulate, upload, download, and email than multiple files. You might frequently download compressed, archived files from the Internet. The utilities described in this section compress and decompress files, and pack and unpack archives.

bzip2: COMPRESSES A FILE

The bzip2 utility compresses a file by analyzing it and recoding it more efficiently. The new version of the file looks completely different. In fact, because the new file contains many nonprinting characters, you cannot view it directly. The bzip2 utility works particularly well on files that contain a lot of repeated information, such as text and image data, although most image data is already in a compressed format.

The following example shows a boring file. Each of the 8,000 lines of the **letter_e** file contains 72 e's and a NEWLINE character that marks the end of the line. The file occupies more than half a megabyte of disk storage.

```
$ ls -l
-rw-rw-r--. 1 sam pubs 584000 03-01 22:31 letter_e
```

The **–l** (long) option causes ls to display more information about a file. Here it shows that **letter_e** is 584,000 bytes long. The **–v** (verbose) option causes bzip2 to report how much it was able to reduce the size of the file. In this case it shrank the file by 99.99 percent:

```
$ bzip2 -v letter_e
letter_e: 11680.00:1, 0.001 bits/byte, 99.99% saved, 584000 in, 50 out.
$ ls -l
-rw-rw-r--. 1 sam pubs 50 03-01 22:31 letter_e.bz2
```

.bz2 filename extension Now the file is only 50 bytes long. The bzip2 utility also renamed the file, appending **.bz2** to its name. This naming convention reminds you that the file is compressed; you would not want to display or print it, for example, without first decompressing it.

The bzip2 utility does not change the modification date associated with the file, even though it completely changes the file's contents.

Keep the original file by using the –k option

tip The bzip2 utility and its counterpart, bunzip2, remove the original file when they compress or decompress a file. Use the **–k** (keep) option to keep the original file.

In the following, more realistic example, the file **zach.jpg** contains a computer graphics image:

```
$ ls -l
-rw-r--r--. 1 sam pubs 33287 03-01 22:40 zach.jpg
```

The bzip2 utility can reduce the size of the file by only 28 percent because the image is already in a compressed format:

```
$ bzip2 -v zach.jpg
zach.jpg:  1.391:1,  5.749 bits/byte, 28.13% saved, 33287 in, 23922 out.

$ ls -l
-rw-r--r--. 1 sam pubs 23922 03-01 22:40 zach.jpg.bz2
```

Refer to page 750, www.bzip.org, and the *Bzip2 mini-HOWTO* (see page 41 for instructions on obtaining this document) for more information.

bzcat AND bunzip2: DECOMPRESS A FILE

bzcat The bzcat utility displays a file that has been compressed with bzip2. The equivalent of cat for **.bz2** files, bzcat decompresses the compressed data and displays the decompressed data. Like cat, bzcat does not change the source file. The pipe symbol in the following example redirects the output of bzcat so that instead of being displayed on the screen it becomes the input to head, which displays the first two lines of the file:

```
$ bzcat letter_e.bz2 | head -2
eeeeeeeeeeeeeeeeeeeeeeeeeeeeeeeeeeeeeeeeeeeeeeeeeeeeeeeeeeeeeeeeeeee
eeeeeeeeeeeeeeeeeeeeeeeeeeeeeeeeeeeeeeeeeeeeeeeeeeeeeeeeeeeeeeeeeeee
```

After bzcat is run, the contents of **letter_e.bz2** is unchanged; the file is still stored on the disk in compressed form.

bunzip The bunzip2 utility restores a file that has been compressed with bzip2:

```
$ bunzip2 letter_e.bz2
$ ls -l
-rw-rw-r--. 1 sam pubs 584000 03-01 22:31 letter_e
$ bunzip2 zach.jpg.bz2
$ ls -l
-rw-r--r--. 1 sam pubs 33287 03-01 22:40 zach.jpg
```

bzip2recover The bzip2recover utility supports limited data recovery from media errors. Give the command **bzip2recover** followed by the name of the compressed, corrupted file from which you want to try to recover data.

gzip: Compresses a File

gunzip and zcat The gzip (GNU zip) utility is older and less efficient than bzip2. Its flags and operation are very similar to those of bzip2. A file compressed by gzip is marked with a **.gz** filename extension. Linux stores manual pages in gzip format to save disk space; likewise, files you download from the Internet are frequently in gzip format. Use gzip, gunzip, and zcat just as you would use bzip2, bunzip2, and bzcat, respectively. Refer to page 858 for more information on gzip.

compress The compress utility can also compress files, albeit not as well as gzip. This utility marks a file it has compressed by adding **.Z** to its name.

gzip versus zip

tip Do not confuse gzip and gunzip with the zip and unzip utilities. These last two are used to pack and unpack zip archives containing several files compressed into a single file that has been imported from or is being exported to a Windows system. The zip utility constructs a zip archive, whereas unzip unpacks zip archives. The zip and unzip utilities are compatible with PKZIP, a Windows program that compresses and archives files.

tar: Packs and Unpacks Archives

The tar utility performs many functions. Its name is short for *tape archive,* as its original function was to create and read archive and backup tapes. Today it is used to create a single file (called a *tar file, archive,* or *tarball*) from multiple files or directory hierarchies and to extract files from a tar file. The cpio (page 776) and pax (page 932) utilities perform a similar function.

In the following example, the first ls shows the sizes of the files **g**, **b**, and **d**. Next, tar uses the **–c** (create), **–v** (verbose), and **–f** (write to or read from a file) options to create an archive named **all.tar** from these files. Each line of output displays the name of the file tar is appending to the archive it is creating.

The tar utility adds overhead when it creates an archive. The next command shows that the archive file **all.tar** occupies more than 9,700 bytes, whereas the sum of the sizes of the three files is about 6,000 bytes. This overhead is more appreciable on smaller files, such as the ones in this example:

```
$ ls -l g b d
-rw-r--r--. 1 zach other 1178 08-20 14:16 b
-rw-r--r--. 1 zach zach  3783 08-20 14:17 d
-rw-r--r--. 1 zach zach  1302 08-20 14:16 g

$ tar -cvf all.tar g b d
g
b
d

$ ls -l all.tar
-rw-r--r--. 1 zach zach 9728 08-20 14:17 all.tar
```

```
$ tar -tvf all.tar
-rw-r--r-- zach /zach     1302 2018-08-20 14:16 g
-rw-r--r-- zach /other    1178 2018-08-20 14:16 b
-rw-r--r-- zach /zach     3783 2018-08-20 14:17 d
```

The final command in the preceding example uses the **–t** option to display a table of contents for the archive. Use **–x** in place of **–t** to extract files from a tar archive. Omit the **–v** option if you want tar to do its work silently.[2]

You can use bzip2, compress, or gzip to compress tar files, making them easier to store and handle. Many files you download from the Internet will already be in one of these formats. Files that have been processed by tar and compressed by bzip2 frequently have a filename extension of **.tar.bz2** or **.tbz**. Those processed by tar and gzip have an extension of **.tar.gz** or **.tgz**, whereas files processed by tar and compress use **.tar.Z** as the extension.

You can unpack a tarred and gzipped file in two steps. (Follow the same procedure if the file was compressed by bzip2, but use bunzip2 instead of gunzip.) The next example shows how to unpack the GNU make utility after it has been downloaded (ftp.gnu.org/pub/gnu/make/make-3.82.tar.gz):

```
$ ls -l mak*
-rw-r--r--. 1 sam pubs 1712747 04-05 10:43 make-3.82.tar.gz

$ gunzip mak*
$ ls -l mak*
-rw-r--r--. 1 sam pubs 6338560 04-05 10:43 make-3.82.tar

$ tar -xvf mak*
make-3.82/
make-3.82/vmsfunctions.c
make-3.82/getopt.h
make-3.82/make.1
...
make-3.82/README.OS2
make-3.82/remote-cstms.c
```

The first command lists the downloaded tarred and gzipped file: **make-3.82.tar.gz** (about 1.7 megabytes). The asterisk (*) in the filename matches any characters in any filenames (page 154), so ls displays a list of files whose names begin with **mak**; in this case there is only one. Using an asterisk saves typing and can improve accuracy with long filenames. The gunzip command decompresses the file and yields **make-3.82.tar** (no **.gz** extension), which is about 6.3 megabytes. The tar command creates the **make-3.82** directory in the working directory and unpacks the files into it.

2. Although the original UNIX tar did not use a leading hyphen to indicate an option on the command line, the GNU/Linux version accepts hyphens but works as well without them. This book precedes tar options with a hyphen for consistency with most other utilities.

```
$ ls -ld mak*
drwxr-xr-x. 8 sam pubs    4096 2018-07-27  make-3.82
-rw-r--r--. 1 sam pubs 6338560 04-05 10:43 make-3.82.tar

$ ls -l make-3.82
-rw-r--r--. 1 sam pubs  53838 2018-07-27  ABOUT-NLS
-rw-r--r--. 1 sam pubs   4783 2018-07-12  acinclude.m4
-rw-r--r--. 1 sam pubs  36990 2018-07-27  aclocal.m4
-rw-r--r--. 1 sam pubs  14231 2002-10-14  alloca.c
...
-rw-r--r--. 1 sam pubs  18391 2018-07-12  vmsjobs.c
-rw-r--r--. 1 sam pubs  17905 2018-07-19  vpath.c
drwxr-xr-x. 6 sam pubs   4096 2018-07-27  w32
```

After tar extracts the files from the archive, the working directory contains two files whose names start with **mak**: **make-3.82.tar** and **make-3.82**. The **–d** (directory) option causes ls to display only file and directory names, not the contents of directories as it normally does. The final ls command shows the files and directories in the **make-3.82** directory. Refer to page 995 for more information on tar.

tar: the –x option might extract a lot of files

caution Some tar archives contain many files. To list the files in the archive without unpacking them, run tar with the **–tf** options followed by the name of the tar file. In some cases you might want to create a new directory (mkdir [page 93]), move the tar file into that directory, and expand it there. That way the unpacked files will not mingle with existing files, and no confusion will occur. This strategy also makes it easier to delete the extracted files. Depending on how they were created, some tar files automatically create a new directory and put the files into it; the **–t** option indicates where tar will place the files you extract.

tar: the –x option can overwrite files

caution The **–x** option to tar overwrites a file that has the same filename as a file you are extracting. Follow the suggestion in the preceding caution box to avoid overwriting files.

optional You can combine the gunzip and tar commands on one command line using a pipe symbol (|), which redirects the output of gunzip so it becomes the input to tar:

```
$ gunzip -c make-3.82.tar.gz | tar -xvf -
```

The **–c** option causes gunzip to send its output through the pipeline instead of creating a file. The final hyphen (–) causes tar to read from standard input. Refer to "Pipelines" (page 145), gzip (pages 66 and 858), and tar (page 995) for more information about how this command line works.

A simpler solution is to use the **–z** option to tar. This option causes tar to call gunzip (or gzip when you are creating an archive) directly and simplifies the preceding command line to

```
$ tar -xvzf make-3.82.tar.gz
```

In a similar manner, the **–j** option calls bzip2 or bunzip2.

LOCATING UTILITIES

The whereis and locate utilities can help you find a command whose name you have forgotten or whose location you do not know. When multiple copies of a utility or program are present, which tells you which copy you will run. The locate utility searches for files on the local system.

which AND whereis: LOCATE A UTILITY

When you give Linux a command, the shell searches a list of directories for a program with that name. This list of directories is called a *search path*. For information on how to change the search path, refer to "PATH: Where the Shell Looks for Programs" on page 318. If you do not change the search path, the shell searches only a standard set of directories and then stops searching. However, other directories on the system might also contain useful utilities.

which The which utility locates utilities by displaying the full pathname of the file for the utility. (Chapter 4 contains more information on pathnames and the structure of the Linux filesystem.) The local system might include several utilities that have the same name. When you type the name of a utility, the shell searches for the utility in your search path and runs the first one it finds. You can find out which copy of the utility the shell will run by using which. In the following example, which reports the location of the tar utility:

```
$ which tar
/bin/tar
```

The which utility can be helpful when a utility seems to be working in unexpected ways. By running which, you might discover that you are running a nonstandard version of a tool or a different one from the one you expected. ("Important Standard Directories and Files" on page 98 provides a list of standard locations for executable files.) For example, if tar is not working properly and you find that you are running **/usr/local/bin/tar** instead of **/bin/tar**, you might suspect the local version is broken.

whereis The whereis utility searches for files related to a utility by looking in standard locations instead of using your search path. For example, you can find the locations for files related to tar:

```
$ whereis tar
tar: /bin/tar /usr/share/man/man1/tar.1.gz
```

In this example whereis finds two references to tar: the tar utility file and the (compressed) tar man page.

which versus whereis

tip Given the name of a utility, which looks through the directories in your *search path* (page 318) in order and locates the utility. If your search path includes more than one utility with the specified name, which displays the name of only the first one (the one you would run).

The whereis utility looks through a list of *standard directories* and works independently of your search path. Use whereis to locate a binary (executable) file, any manual pages, and source code for a program you specify; whereis displays all the files it finds.

which, whereis, and builtin commands

caution Both the which and whereis utilities report only the names for utilities as they are found on the disk; they do not report shell builtins (utilities that are built into a shell; page 157). When you use whereis to try to find where the echo command (which exists as both a utility program and a shell builtin) is kept, it displays the following information:

```
$ whereis echo
echo: /bin/echo /usr/share/man/man1/echo.1.gz
```

The whereis utility does not display the echo builtin. Even the which utility reports the wrong information:

```
$ which echo
/bin/echo
```

Under bash you can use the type builtin (page 489) to determine whether a command is a builtin:

```
$ type echo
echo is a shell builtin
```

locate: SEARCHES FOR A FILE

The locate utility (locate package; some distributions use mlocate) searches for files on the local system:

```
$ locate init
/boot/initramfs-2.6.38-0.rc5.git1.1.fc15.i686.img
/boot/initrd-plymouth.img
/etc/gdbinit
/etc/gdbinit.d
/etc/init
/etc/init.d
...
```

Before you can use locate (mlocate), the updatedb utility must build or update the locate (mlocate) database. Typically the database is updated once a day by a cron script (page 781).

Displaying User and System Information

This section covers utilities that provide information about who is using the system, what those users are doing, and how the system is running.

To find out who is using the local system, you can employ one of several utilities that vary in the details they provide and the options they support. The oldest utility, who, produces a list of users who are logged in on the local system, the device each person is using, and the time each person logged in.

The w and finger utilities show more detail, such as each user's full name and the command line each user is running. The finger utility can retrieve information about users on remote systems. Table 3-1 on page 74 summarizes the output of these utilities.

who: Lists Users on the System

The who utility displays a list of users who are logged in on the local system. In Figure 3-10 the first column who displays shows that Sam, Max, and Zach are logged in. (Max is logged in from two locations.) The second column shows the name of the device that each user's terminal, workstation, or terminal emulator is connected to. The third column shows the date and time the user logged in. An optional fourth column shows (in parentheses) the name of the system a remote user logged in from.

The information who displays is useful when you want to communicate with a user on the local system. When the user is logged in, you can use write (page 75) to establish communication immediately. If who does not list the user or if you do not need to communicate immediately, you can send email to that person (page 77).

If the output of who scrolls off the screen, you can redirect the output using a pipe symbol (|; page 60) so it becomes the input to less, which displays the output one screen at a time. You can also use a pipe symbol to redirect the output through grep to look for a specific name.

If you need to find out which terminal you are using or what time you logged in, you can use the command **who am i**:

```
$ who am i
max       pts/4         2018-07-25 17:27 (guava)
```

```
$ who
sam       tty4          2018-07-25 17:18
max       tty2          2018-07-25 16:42
zach      tty1          2018-07-25 16:39
max       pts/4         2018-07-25 17:27 (guava)
```

Figure 3-10 who lists who is logged in

finger: LISTS USERS ON THE SYSTEM

The finger utility displays a list of users who are logged in on the local system and, in some cases, information about remote systems and users. In addition to usernames, finger supplies each user's full name along with information about which device the user's terminal is connected to, how recently the user typed something on the keyboard, when the user logged in, and contact information. If the user has logged in over the network, the name of the remote system is shown as the user's office. For example, in Figure 3-11 Max is logged in from the remote system named **guava**. The asterisks (*) in front of the device names in the **Tty** column indicate the user has blocked messages sent directly to his terminal (refer to "mesg: Denies or Accepts Messages" on page 76).

finger can be a security risk

security On systems where security is a concern, the system administrator might disable finger because it can reveal information that can help a malicious user break into a system. macOS disables remote finger support by default.

You can also use finger to learn more about an individual by specifying a username on the command line. In Figure 3-12 on the next page, finger displays detailed information about Max: He is logged in and actively using one of his terminals (**tty2**), and he has not typed at his other terminal (**pts/4**) for 3 minutes and 7 seconds. You also learn from finger that if you want to set up a meeting with Max, you should contact Sam at extension 1693.

```
$ finger
Login     Name            Tty      Idle  Login Time   Office ...
max       Max Wild        *tty2          Jul 25 16:42
max       Max Wild         pts/4      3  Jul 25 17:27 (guava)
sam       Sam the Great   *tty4      29  Jul 25 17:18
zach      Zach Brill      *tty1    1:07  Jul 25 16:39
```

Figure 3-11 finger I: lists who is logged in

```
$ finger max
Login: max                              Name: Max Wild
Directory: /home/max                    Shell: /bin/tcsh
On since Wed Jul 25 16:42 (PDT) on tty2 (messages off)
On since Wed Jul 25 17:27 (PDT) on pts/4 from guava
   3 minutes 7 seconds idle
New mail received Wed Jul 25 17:16 2018 (PDT)
     Unread since Wed Jul 25 16:44 2018 (PDT)
Plan:
I will be at a conference in Hawaii next week.
If you need to see me, contact Sam, x1693.
```

Figure 3-12 finger II: lists details about one user

.plan and .project Most of the information in Figure 3-12 was collected by finger from system files. The information shown after the heading **Plan:**, however, was supplied by Max. The finger utility searched for a file named **.plan** in Max's home directory and displayed its contents. (Filenames that begin with a period, such as **.plan**, are not normally listed by ls and are called hidden filenames [page 88].)

You might find it helpful to create a **.plan** file for yourself; it can contain any information you choose, such as your schedule, interests, phone number, or address. In a similar manner, finger displays the contents of the **.project** and **.pgpkey** files in your home directory. If Max had not been logged in, finger would have reported only his user information, the last time he logged in, the last time he read his email, and his plan.

You can also use finger to display a user's username. For example, on a system with a user named Helen Simpson, you might know that Helen's last name is Simpson but might not guess her username is **hls**. The finger utility, which is not case sensitive, can search for information on Helen using her first or last name. The following commands find the information you seek as well as information on other users whose names are Helen or Simpson:

```
$ finger HELEN
Login: hls                              Name: Helen Simpson.
...
$ finger simpson
Login: hls                              Name: Helen Simpson.
...
```

uptime: DISPLAYS SYSTEM LOAD AND DURATION INFORMATION

The uptime utility displays a single line that includes the time of day, the period of time the computer has been running (in days, hours, and minutes), the number of users logged in, and the load average (how busy the system is). The three load average numbers represent the number of jobs waiting to run, averaged over the past 1, 5, and 15 minutes.

```
$ uptime
09:49:14 up 2 days, 23:13,  3 users,  load average: 0.00, 0.01, 0.05
```

w: LISTS USERS ON THE SYSTEM

The first line the w utility displays is the same as the output of uptime (above). Following that line, w displays a list of the users who are logged in. As discussed in the section on who, the information that w displays is useful when you want to communicate with someone at your installation.

The first column in Figure 3-13 shows that Max, Zach, and Sam are logged in. The second column shows the name of the device file each user's terminal is connected to. The third column shows the system that a remote user is logged in from. The fourth column shows the time each user logged in. The fifth column indicates how long each user has been idle (how much time has elapsed since the user pressed a key on the keyboard). The next two columns identify how much computer processor time each user has used during this login session and on the task that user is running. The last column shows the command each user is running. Table 3-1 compares the w, who, and finger utilities.

```
$ w
 17:47:35 up 1 day,  8:10,  6 users,  load average: 0.34, 0.23, 0.26
USER     TTY      FROM             LOGIN@   IDLE   JCPU   PCPU WHAT
sam      tty4     -               17:18   29:14m  0.20s  0.00s vi memo
max      tty2     -               16:42    0.00s  0.20s  0.07s w
zach     tty1     -               16:39    1:07   0.05s  0.00s run_bdgt
max      pts/4    guava           17:27    3:10m  0.24s  0.24s -bash
```

Figure 3-13 The w utility

Table 3-1 Comparison of w, who, and finger

Information displayed	w	who	finger
Username	x	x	x
Terminal-line identification (tty)	x	x	x
Login time (and day for old logins)	x		
Login date and time		x	x
Idle time	x		x
Program the user is executing	x		
Location the user logged in from			x
CPU time used	x		
Full name (or other information from **/etc/passwd**)			x
User-supplied vanity information			x
System uptime and load average	x		

free: Displays Memory Usage Information

The free utility displays the amount of physical (RAM) and swap (swap space on the disk; page 1127) memory in the local system. It displays columns for total, used, and free memory as well as for kernel buffers. The column labeled **shared** is obsolete. This utility is not available under macOS; vm_stat performs a similar function.

In the following example, the **–m** option causes free to display memory sizes in megabytes and the **–t** option adds the line labeled **Total** to the end of the output. You can cause free to display memory sizes in gigabytes (**–g**), megabytes (**–m**), kilobytes (**–k**; the default), or bytes (**–b**). See the free man page for additional options.

```
$ free -mt
             total       used       free     shared    buffers     cached
Mem:          2013        748       1264          0        110        383
-/+ buffers/cache:        254       1759
Swap:         2044          0       2044
Total:        4058        748       3309
```

One of the ways Linux takes advantage of free memory is to allocate memory it is not otherwise using to *buffers* (page 1087) and *cache* (page 1088). Thus, the value on the **Mem** line in the **free** column will be small and is not representative of the total available memory when the kernel is working properly. As the kernel needs more memory, it reallocates memory it had allocated to buffers and cache.

The **–/+ buffers/cache** line gives values assuming memory used for buffers and cache is free memory. The value in the **used** column on this line assumes buffers and cache (110 + 383 = 493 on the **Mem** line) are freed; thus, the value in the **used** column is 254 (~748 – 493) while the value in the **free** column value increases to 1759 (~1,264 + 493). Unlike the value in the **free** column on the **Mem** line, as the value in the **free** column on the **–/+ buffers/cache** line approaches zero, the system is truly running out of memory.

The **Swap** line displays the total, used, and free amounts of swap space.

Communicating with Other Users

The utilities discussed in this section enable you to exchange messages and files with other users either interactively or through email.

write: Sends a Message

The write utility sends a message to another user who is logged in. When you and another user use write to send messages to each other, you establish two-way communication. Initially a write command (Figure 3-14) displays a banner on the other user's terminal, saying that you are about to send a message.

The syntax of a write command line is

write ***username [terminal]***

The ***username*** is the username of the user you want to communicate with. The ***terminal*** is an optional device name that is useful if the user is logged in more than once. You can display the usernames and device names of all users who are logged in on the local system by using who, w, or finger.

```
$ write max
Hi Max, are you there? o
```

Figure 3-14 The write utility I

To establish two-way communication with another user, you and the other user must each execute write, specifying the other's username as the ***username***. The write utility then copies text, line by line, from one keyboard/display to the other (Figure 3-15). Sometimes it helps to establish a convention, such as typing **o** (for "over") when you are ready for the other person to type and typing **oo** (for "over and out") when you are ready to end the conversation. When you want to stop communicating with the other user, press CONTROL-D at the beginning of a line. Pressing CONTROL-D tells write to quit, displays **EOF** (end of file) on the other user's terminal, and returns you to the shell. The other user must do the same.

If the **Message from** banner appears on your screen and obscures something you are working on, press CONTROL-L or CONTROL-R to refresh the screen and remove the banner. Then you can clean up, exit from your work, and respond to the person who is writing to you. You have to remember who is writing to you, however, because the banner will no longer appear on the screen.

mesg: Denies or Accepts Messages

If messages to your screen are blocked, give the following mesg command to allow other users to send you messages:

```
$ mesg y
```

If Max had not given this command before Zach tried to send him a message, Zach might have seen the following message:

```
$ write max
write: max has messages disabled
```

You can block messages by entering **mesg n**. Give the command **mesg** by itself to display **is y** (for "yes, messages are allowed") or **is n** (for "no, messages are not allowed").

If you have messages blocked and you write to another user, write displays the following message because even if you are allowed to write to another user, the user will not be able to respond to you:

```
$ write max
write: you have write permission turned off.
```

```
$ write max
Hi Max, are you there? o

Message from max@guava on pts/4 at 18:23 ...
Yes Zach, I'm here. o
```

Figure 3-15 The write utility II

EMAIL

Email enables you to communicate with users on the local system as well as those on the network. If you are connected to the Internet, you can communicate electronically with users around the world.

Email utilities differ from write in that they can send a message when the recipient is not logged in. In this case the email is stored until the recipient reads it. These utilities can also send the same message to more than one user at a time.

Many email programs are available for Linux, including the original character-based mail program, Mozilla/Thunderbird, pine, mail through emacs, KMail, and evolution. Another popular graphical email program is sylpheed (sylpheed.sraoss.jp/en).

Two programs are available that can make any email program easier to use and more secure. The procmail program (www.procmail.org) creates and maintains email servers and mailing lists; preprocesses email by sorting it into appropriate files and directories; starts various programs depending on the characteristics of incoming email; forwards email; and so on. The GNU Privacy Guard (GPG or GNUpg) encrypts and decrypts email making it almost impossible for an unauthorized person to read.

Network addresses If the local system is part of a LAN, you can generally send email to and receive email from users on other systems on the LAN by using their usernames. Someone sending Max email on the Internet would need to specify his *domain name* (page 1095) along with his username. Use this address to send email to the author of this book: **mgs@sobell.com**.

CHAPTER SUMMARY

The utilities introduced in this chapter are a small but powerful subset of the many utilities available on a typical system. Because you will use them frequently and because they are integral to the following chapters, it is important that you become comfortable using them.

The utilities listed in Table 3-2 manipulate, display, compare, and print files.

Table 3-2 File utilities

Utility	Function
cp	Copies one or more files (page 53)
diff	Displays the differences between two files (page 59)
file	Displays information about the contents of a file (page 60)
grep	Searches file(s) for a string (page 56)

Table 3-2 File utilities (continued)

Utility	Function
head	Displays the lines at the beginning of a file (page 57)
lpq	Displays a list of jobs in the print queue (page 56)
lpr	Places file(s) in the print queue (page 55)
lprm	Removes a job from the print queue (page 56)
mv	Renames a file or moves file(s) to another directory (page 54)
sort	Puts a file in order by lines (page 58)
tail	Displays the lines at the end of a file (page 57)
uniq	Displays the contents of a file, skipping adjacent duplicate lines (page 58)

To reduce the amount of disk space a file occupies, you can compress it using the bzip2 utility. Compression works especially well on files that contain patterns, as do most text files, but reduces the size of almost all files. The inverse of bzip2—bunzip2—restores a file to its original, decompressed form. Table 3-3 lists utilities that compress and decompress files. The bzip2 utility is the most efficient of these.

Table 3-3 (De)compression utilities

Utility	Function
bunzip2	Returns a file compressed with bzip2 to its original size and format (page 65)
bzcat	Displays a file compressed with bzip2 (page 65)
bzip2	Compresses a file (page 64)
compress	Compresses a file (not as well as bzip2 or gzip; page 66)
gunzip	Returns a file compressed with gzip or compress to its original size and format (page 66)
gzip	Compresses a file (not as well as bzip2; page 66)
unzip	Unpacks zip archives, which are compatible with Windows PKZIP
zcat	Displays a file compressed with gzip (page 66)
zip	Constructs zip archives, which are compatible with Windows PKZIP

An archive is a file, frequently compressed, that contains a group of files. The tar utility (Table 3-4) packs and unpacks archives. The filename extensions **.tar.bz2**, **.tar.gz**, and **.tgz** identify compressed tar archive files and are often seen on software packages obtained over the Internet.

Table 3-4 Archive utility

Utility	Function
tar	Creates or extracts files from an archive file (page 66)

The utilities listed in Table 3-5 determine the location of a utility on the local system. For example, they can display the pathname of a utility or a list of C++ compilers available on the local system.

Table 3-5 Location utilities

Utility	Function
locate/mlocate	Searches for files on the local system (page 70)
whereis	Displays the full pathnames of a utility, source code, or man page (page 69)
which	Displays the full pathname of a command you can run (page 69)

Table 3-6 lists utilities that display information about the local system and other users. You can easily learn a user's full name, login status, login shell, and other information maintained by the system.

Table 3-6 User and system information utilities

Utility	Function
finger	Displays detailed information about users, including their full names (page 72)
free	Displays memory usage information (page 74)
hostname	Displays the name of the local system (page 53)
uptime	Displays system load and duration information (page 73)
w	Displays detailed information about users who are logged in on the local system (page 73)
who	Displays information about users who are logged in on the local system (page 71)

The utilities shown in Table 3-7 can help you stay in touch with other users on the local network.

Table 3-7 User communication utilities

Utility	Function
mesg	Permits or denies messages sent by write (page 76)
write	Sends a message to another user who is logged in (page 75)

Table 3-8 lists miscellaneous utilities.

Table 3-8 Miscellaneous utilities

Utility	Function
date	Displays the current date and time (page 62)
echo	Copies its *arguments* (page 1083) to the screen (page 61)

EXERCISES

1. Which commands can you use to determine who is logged in on a specific terminal?
2. How can you keep other users from using write to communicate with you? Why would you want to?
3. What happens when you give the following commands if the file named **done** already exists?

```
$ cp to_do done
$ mv to_do done
```

4. How can you find out which utilities are available on your system for editing files? Which utilities are available for editing on your system?
5. How can you find the phone number for **Ace Electronics** in a file named **phone** that contains a list of names and phone numbers? Which command can you use to display the entire file in alphabetical order? How can you display the file without any adjacent duplicate lines? How can you display the file without any duplicate lines?
6. What happens when you use diff to compare two binary files that are not identical? (You can use gzip to create the binary files.) Explain why the diff output for binary files is different from the diff output for ASCII files.
7. Create a **.plan** file in your home directory. Does finger display the contents of your **.plan** file?

8. What is the result of giving the which utility the name of a command that resides in a directory that is *not* in your search path?
9. Are any of the utilities discussed in this chapter located in more than one directory on the local system? If so, which ones?
10. Experiment by calling the file utility with the names of files in **/usr/bin**. How many different types of files are there?
11. Which command can you use to look at the first few lines of a file named **status.report**? Which command can you use to look at the end of the file?

ADVANCED EXERCISES

12. Re-create the **colors.1** and **colors.2** files used in Figure 3-8 on page 59. Test your files by running **diff –u** on them. Does diff display the same results as in the figure?
13. Try giving these two commands:

```
$ echo cat
$ cat echo
```

Explain the differences between the output of each command.

14. Repeat exercise 5 using the file **phone.gz**, a compressed version of the list of names and phone numbers. Consider more than one approach to answer each question and explain how you made your choices.
15. Find or create files that
    a. gzip compresses by more than 80 percent.
    b. gzip compresses by less than 10 percent.
    c. Get larger when compressed with gzip.
    d. Use **ls –l** to determine the sizes of the files in question. Can you characterize the files in a, b, and c?
16. Older email programs were not able to handle binary files. Suppose you are emailing a file that has been compressed with gzip, which produces a binary file, and the recipient is using an old email program. Refer to the man page on uuencode, which converts a binary file to ASCII. Learn about the utility and how to use it.
    a. Convert a compressed file to ASCII using uuencode. Is the encoded file larger or smaller than the compressed file? Explain. (If uuencode is not on the local system, you can install it using one of the tools described in Appendix C; it is part of the **sharutils** package.)
    b. Would it ever make sense to use uuencode on a file before compressing it? Explain.

4

The Filesystem

In This Chapter

Objectives

After reading this chapter you should be able to:

- Define hierarchical filesystem, ordinary file, directory file, home directory, working directory, and parent directory
- List best practices for filenames
- Determine the name of the working directory
- Explain the difference between absolute and relative pathnames
- Create and remove directories
- List files in a directory, remove files from a directory, and copy and move files between directories
- List and describe the uses of standard Linux directories and files
- Display and interpret file and directory ownership and permissions
- Modify file and directory permissions
- Expand access control using ACLs
- Describe the uses, differences, and methods of creating hard links and symbolic links

A *filesystem* is a set of *data structures* (page 1093) that usually resides on part of a disk and holds directories of files. Filesystems store user and system data that are the basis of users' work on the system and the system's existence. This chapter discusses the organization and terminology of the Linux filesystem, defines ordinary and directory files, and explains the rules for naming them. It also shows how to create and delete directories, move through the filesystem, and use absolute and relative pathnames to access files in various directories. It includes a discussion of important files and directories as well as file access permissions and ACLs (Access Control Lists), which allow you to share selected files with specified users. It concludes with a discussion of hard and symbolic links, which can make a single file appear in more than one directory.

In addition to reading this chapter, you can refer to the df, fsck, mkfs, and tune2fs utilities in Part VII for more information on filesystems. If you are running macOS, see "Filesystems" on page 1069.

THE HIERARCHICAL FILESYSTEM

Family tree A *hierarchical* (page 1101) structure frequently takes the shape of a pyramid. One example of this type of structure is found by tracing a family's lineage: A couple has a child, who might in turn have several children, each of whom might have more children. This hierarchical structure is called a *family tree* (Figure 4-1).

Directory tree Like the family tree it resembles, the Linux filesystem is called a *tree*. It consists of a set of connected files. This structure allows you to organize files so you can easily find any particular one. On a standard Linux system, each user starts with one directory,

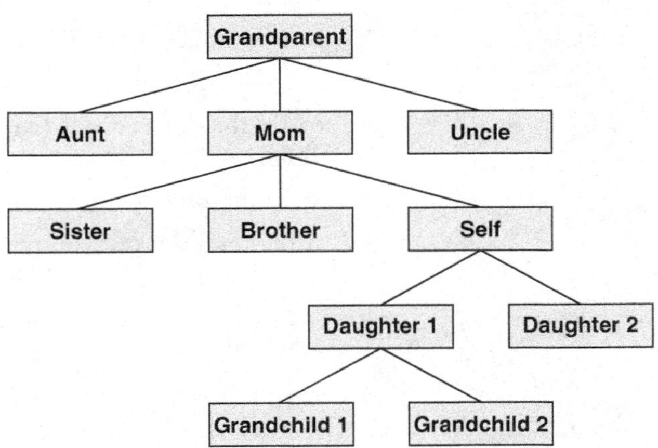

Figure 4-1 A secretary's directories

to which the user can add subdirectories to any desired level. By creating multiple levels of subdirectories, a user can expand the structure as needed.

Subdirectories Typically each subdirectory is dedicated to a single subject, such as a person, project, or event. The subject dictates whether a subdirectory should be subdivided further. For example, Figure 4-2 shows a secretary's subdirectory named **correspond**. This directory contains three subdirectories: **business**, **memos**, and **personal**. The **business** directory contains files that store each letter the secretary types. If you expect many letters to go to one client, as is the case with **milk_co**, you can dedicate a subdirectory to that client.

One major strength of the Linux filesystem is its ability to adapt to users' needs. You can take advantage of this strength by strategically organizing your files so they are most convenient and useful for you.

Directory Files and Ordinary Files

Like a family tree, the tree representing the filesystem is usually pictured upside down with its *root* at the top. Figures 4-2 and 4-3 (on the next page) show that the tree "grows" downward from the root with paths connecting the root to each of the other files. At the end of each path is either an ordinary file or a directory file. Special files, which can also appear at the ends of paths, provide access to operating system features. *Ordinary files,* or simply *files,* appear at the ends of paths that cannot support other paths. *Directory files,* also referred to as *directories* or *folders,* are the points that other paths can branch off from. (Figures 4-2 and 4-3 show some empty directories.) When you refer to the tree, *up* is toward the root and *down* is away from the root. Directories directly connected by a path are called *parents* (closer to the root) and *children* (fartherlar one. On a standard Linux system, each user starts from the root). A *pathname*

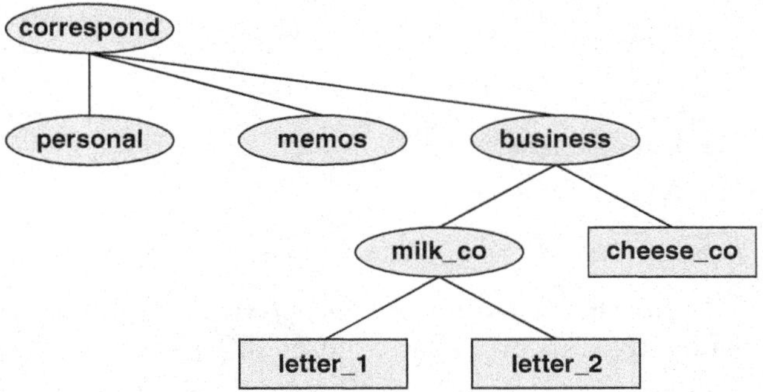

Figure 4-2 A secretary's directories

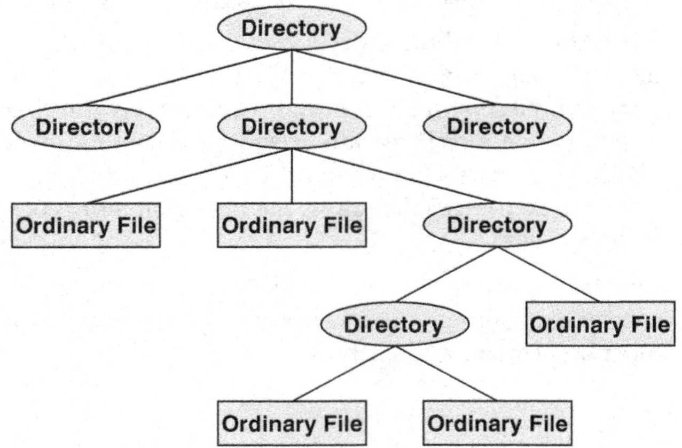

Figure 4-3 Directories and ordinary files

is a series of names that trace a path along branches from one file to another. See page 90 for more information about pathnames.

FILENAMES

Every file has a *filename*. The maximum length of a filename varies with the type of filesystem; Linux supports several types of filesystems. Most modern filesystems allow files with names up to 255 characters long; however, some filesystems restrict filenames to fewer characters. Although you can use almost any character in a filename, you will avoid confusion if you choose characters from the following list:

- Uppercase letters (A–Z)
- Lowercase letters (a–z)
- Numbers (0–9)
- Underscore (_)
- Period (.)
- Comma (,)

Like the children of one parent, no two files in the same directory can have the same name. (Parents give their children different names because it makes good sense, but Linux requires it.) Files in different directories, like the children of different parents, can have the same name.

The filenames you choose should mean something. Too often a directory is filled with important files with such unhelpful names as **hold1**, **wombat**, and **junk**, not to mention **foo** and **foobar**. Such names are poor choices because they do not help you recall what you stored in a file. The following filenames conform to the suggested syntax *and* convey information about the contents of the file:

- correspond
- january
- davis
- reports
- 2001
- acct_payable

Filename length When you share your files with users on other systems, you might need to make long filenames differ within the first few characters. Systems running DOS or older versions of Windows have an 8-character filename body length limit and a 3-character filename extension length limit. Some UNIX systems have a 14-character limit, and older Macintosh systems have a 31-character limit. If you keep filenames short, they are easy to type; later you can add extensions to them without exceeding the shorter limits imposed by some filesystems. The disadvantage of short filenames is that they are typically less descriptive than long filenames.

Long filenames enable you to assign descriptive names to files. To help you select among files without typing entire filenames, shells support filename completion. For more information about this feature, see the "Filename completion" tip on page 53.

Case sensitivity You can use uppercase and/or lowercase letters within filenames, but be careful: Many filesystems are case sensitive. For example, the popular **ext** family of filesystems and the UFS filesystem are case sensitive, so files named **JANUARY**, **January**, and **january** refer to three distinct files. The FAT family of filesystems (used mostly for removable media) is not case sensitive, so those three filenames represent the same file. The HFS+ filesystem, which is the default macOS filesystem, is case preserving but not case sensitive; refer to "Case Sensitivity" on page 1070 for more information.

Do not use SPACEs within filenames

caution Although Linux allows you to use SPACEs within filenames, it is a poor idea. Because a SPACE is a special character, you must quote it on a command line. Quoting a character on a command line can be difficult for a novice user and cumbersome for an experienced user. Use periods or underscores instead of SPACEs: **joe.05.04.26**, **new_stuff**.

If you are working with a filename that includes a SPACE, such as a file from another operating system, you must quote the SPACE on the command line by preceding it with a backslash or by placing quotation marks on either side of the filename. The two following commands send the file named **my file** to the printer:

```
$ lpr my\ file
$ lpr "my file"
```

FILENAME EXTENSIONS

A *filename extension* is the part of the filename that follows an embedded period. In the filenames listed in Table 4-1 on the next page, filename extensions help describe the contents of the file. Some programs, such as the C programming language compiler, default to specific filename extensions; in most cases, however, filename extensions are optional. Use extensions freely to make filenames easy to understand. If you like, you can use several periods within the same filename—for example, **notes.4.10.54** or **files.tar.gz**. Under macOS, some applications use filename extensions to identify files, but many use type codes and creator codes (page 1073).

Table 4-1 Filename extensions

Filename with extension	Meaning of extension
compute.c	A C programming language source file
compute.o	The object code file for **compute.c**
compute	The executable file for **compute.c**
memo.0410.txt	A text file
memo.pdf	A PDF file; view with xpdf or kpdf under a GUI
memo.ps	A PostScript file; view with ghostscript or kpdf under a GUI
memo.Z	A file compressed with compress (page 66); use uncompress or gunzip (page 66) to decompress
memo.gz	A file compressed with gzip (page 66); view with zcat or decompress with gunzip (both on page 66)
memo.tgz or **memo.tar.gz**	A tar (page 66) archive of files compressed with gzip (page 66)
memo.bz2	A file compressed with bzip2 (page 64); view with bzcat or decompress with bunzip2 (both on page 65)
memo.html	A file meant to be viewed using a Web browser, such as Firefox
photo.gif, **photo.jpg**, **photo.jpeg**, **photo.bmp**, **photo.tif**, or **photo.tiff**	A file containing graphical information, such as a picture

HIDDEN FILENAMES

A filename that begins with a period is called a *hidden filename* (or a *hidden file* or sometimes an *invisible file*) because ls does not normally display it. Use the command ls –a to display *all* filenames, including hidden ones. Names of startup files (next page) usually begin with a period so they are hidden and do not clutter a directory listing. Two special hidden entries—single and double periods (. and ..)—appear in every directory (page 95).

The Working Directory

pwd While you are logged in on a character-based interface to a Linux system, you are always associated with a directory. The directory you are associated with is called the *working directory* or *current directory*. Sometimes this association is referred to in a physical sense: "You are *in* (or *working in*) the **zach** directory." The pwd (print working directory) builtin displays the pathname of the working directory.

Your Home Directory

When you first log in on a system or start a terminal emulator window, the working directory is your *home directory*. To display the pathname of your home directory, use pwd just after you log in (Figure 4-4). Linux home directories are typically located in **/home** while macOS home directories are located in **/Users**.

When called without arguments, the ls utility displays a list of the files in the working directory. Because your home directory has been the only working directory you have used so far, ls has always displayed a list of files in your home directory. (All the files you have created up to this point were created in your home directory.)

Startup Files

Startup files, which appear in your home directory, give the shell and other programs information about you and your preferences. Under macOS these files are called *configuration files* or *preference files* (page 1076). Frequently one of these files tells the shell what kind of terminal you are using (page 1050) and executes the stty (set terminal) utility to establish the erase (page 29) and line kill (page 30) keys.

Either you or the system administrator can put a shell startup file containing shell commands in your home directory. The shell executes the commands in this file each time you log in. Because the startup files have hidden filenames (filenames that begin with a period; page 88), you must use the **ls –a** command to see whether one is in your home directory. See page 288 (bash) and page 382 (tcsh) for more information about startup files.

```
login: max
Password:
Last login: Wed Oct 20 11:14:21 from 172.16.192.150
$ pwd
/home/max
```

Figure 4-4 Logging in and displaying the pathname of your home directory

PATHNAMES

Every file has a *pathname,* which is a trail from a directory through part of the directory hierarchy to an ordinary file or a directory. Within a pathname, a slash (**/**) following (to the right of) a filename indicates that the file is a directory file. The file following (to the right of) the slash can be an ordinary file or a directory file. The simplest pathname is a simple filename, which points to a file in the working directory. This section discusses absolute and relative pathnames and explains how to use each.

ABSOLUTE PATHNAMES

/ (root) The root directory of the filesystem hierarchy does not have a name; it is referred to as the *root directory* and is represented by a slash (**/**) standing alone or at the left end of a pathname.

An *absolute pathname* starts with a slash (**/**), which represents the root directory. The slash is followed by the name of a file located in the root directory. An absolute pathname can continue, tracing a path through all intermediate directories, to the file identified by the pathname. String all the filenames in the path together, following each directory with a slash (**/**). This string of filenames is called an absolute pathname because it locates a file absolutely by tracing a path from the root directory to the file. Typically the absolute pathname of a directory does not include the trailing slash, although that format can be used to emphasize that the pathname specifies a directory (e.g., **/home/zach/**). The part of a pathname following the final slash is called a *simple filename, filename,* or *basename.* Figure 4-5 shows the absolute pathnames of directories and ordinary files in part of a filesystem hierarchy.

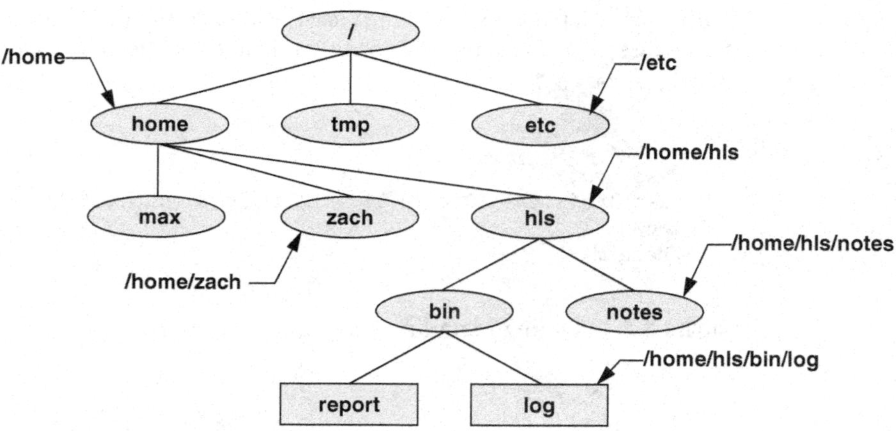

Figure 4-5 Absolute pathnames

Using an absolute pathname, you can list or otherwise work with any file on the local system, assuming you have permission to do so, regardless of the working directory at the time you give the command. For example, Sam can give the following command while working in his home directory to list the files in the **/etc/ssh** directory:

```
$ pwd
/home/sam
$ ls /etc/ssh
moduli        ssh_host_dsa_key       ssh_host_key.pub
ssh_config    ssh_host_dsa_key.pub   ssh_host_rsa_key
sshd_config   ssh_host_key           ssh_host_rsa_key.pub
```

~ (TILDE) IN PATHNAMES

In another form of absolute pathname, the shell expands the characters **~/** (a tilde followed by a slash) at the start of a pathname into the pathname of your home directory. Using this shortcut, you can display your **.bashrc** startup file (page 289) by using the following command no matter which directory is the working directory:

```
$ less ~/.bashrc
```

A tilde quickly references paths that start with your or someone else's home directory. The shell expands a tilde followed by a username at the beginning of a pathname into the pathname of that user's home directory. For example, assuming he has permission to do so, Max can examine Sam's **.bashrc** file by using the following command:

```
$ less ~sam/.bashrc
```

Refer to "Tilde Expansion" on page 368 for more information.

RELATIVE PATHNAMES

A *relative pathname* traces a path from the working directory to a file. The pathname is *relative* to the working directory. Any pathname that does not begin with the root directory (represented by **/**) or a tilde (**~**) is a relative pathname. Like absolute pathnames, relative pathnames can trace a path through many directories. The simplest relative pathname is a simple filename, which identifies a file in the working directory. The examples in the next sections use absolute and relative pathnames.

SIGNIFICANCE OF THE WORKING DIRECTORY

To access any file in the working directory, you need only a simple filename. To access a file in another directory, you *must* use a pathname. Typing a long pathname is tedious and increases the chance of making a mistake. This possibility is less likely under a GUI, where you click filenames or icons. You can choose a working directory for any particular task to reduce the need for long pathnames. Your choice of a working directory does not allow you to do anything you could not do otherwise; it just makes some operations easier.Refer to Figure 4-6 as you read this paragraph. Files

When using a relative pathname, know which directory is the working directory

caution The location of the file you are accessing with a relative pathname is dependent on (is relative to) the working directory. Always make sure you know which directory is the working directory before you use a relative pathname. Use pwd to verify the name of the directory. If you are creating a file using vim and you are not where you think you are in the file hierarchy, the new file will end up in an unexpected location.

It does not matter which directory is the working directory when you use an absolute pathname. Thus, the following command always edits a file named **goals** in your home directory:

```
$ vim ~/goals
```

that are children of the working directory can be referenced by simple filenames. Grandchildren of the working directory can be referenced by short relative pathnames: two filenames separated by a slash. When you manipulate files in a large directory structure, using short relative pathnames can save you time and aggravation. If you choose a working directory that contains the files used most often for a particular task, you need to use fewer long, cumbersome pathnames.

WORKING WITH DIRECTORIES

This section discusses how to create directories (mkdir), switch between directories (cd), remove directories (rmdir), use pathnames to make your work easier, and move and copy files and directories between directories. It concludes with brief descriptions of important standard directories and files in the Linux filesystem.

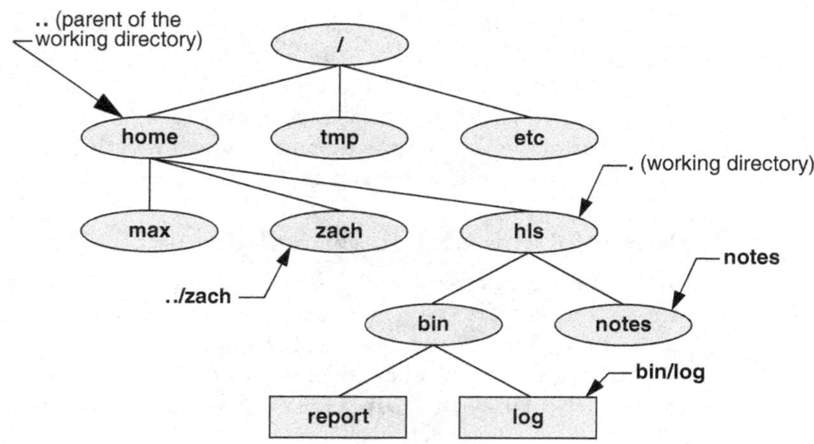

Figure 4-6 Relative pathnames

mkdir: CREATES A DIRECTORY

The mkdir utility creates a directory. The *argument* (page 1083) to mkdir is the pathname of the new directory. The following examples develop the directory structure shown in Figure 4-7. In the figure, the directories that are added appear lighter than the others and are connected by dashes.

In Figure 4-8, pwd shows that Max is working in his home directory (**/home/max**), and ls shows the names of the files in his home directory: **demo**, **names**, and **temp**. Using mkdir, Max creates a directory named **literature** as a child of his home directory. He uses a relative pathname (a simple filename) because he wants the **literature** directory to be a child of the working directory. Max could have used an absolute pathname to create the same directory: **mkdir /home/max/literature**, **mkdir ~max/literature**, or **mkdir ~/literature**.

The second ls in Figure 4-8 verifies the presence of the new directory. The **–F** option to ls displays a slash after the name of each directory and an asterisk after each executable file (shell script, utility, or application). When you call it with an argument that is the name of a directory, ls lists the contents of that directory. The final ls displays nothing because there are no files in the **literature** directory.

The following commands show two ways for Max to create the **promo** directory as a child of the newly created **literature** directory. The first way checks that **/home/max** is the working directory and uses a relative pathname:

```
$ pwd
/home/max
$ mkdir literature/promo
```

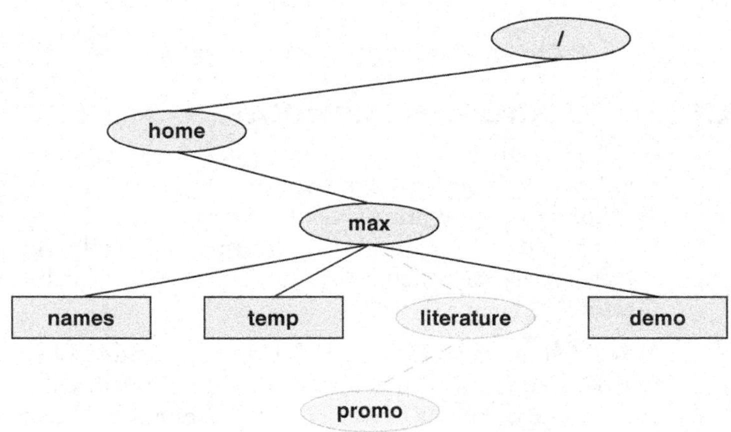

Figure 4-7 The file structure developed in the examples

```
$ pwd
/home/max
$ ls
demo  names  temp
$ mkdir literature
$ ls
demo  literature  names  temp
$ ls -F
demo  literature/  names  temp
$ ls literature
$
```

Figure 4-8 The mkdir utility

The second way uses an absolute pathname:

```
$ mkdir /home/max/literature/promo
```

Use the **–p** (parents) option to mkdir to create both the **literature** and **promo** directories using one command:

```
$ pwd
/home/max
$ ls
demo  names  temp
$ mkdir -p literature/promo
```

or

```
$ mkdir -p /home/max/literature/promo
```

cd: Changes to Another Working Directory

Using cd (change directory) makes another directory the working directory; it does not *change* the contents of the working directory. Figure 4-9 shows two ways to make the **/home/max/literature** directory the working directory, as verified by pwd. First, Max uses cd with an absolute pathname to make **literature** his working directory—it does not matter which is the working directory when you give a command with an absolute pathname.

A pwd command confirms the change Max made. When used without an argument, cd makes your home directory the working directory, as it was when you logged in. The second cd command in Figure 4-9 does not have an argument, so it makes Max's home directory the working directory. Finally, knowing that he is working in his home directory, Max uses a simple filename to make the **literature** directory his working directory (**cd literature**) and confirms the change using pwd.

```
$ cd /home/max/literature
$ pwd
/home/max/literature
$ cd
$ pwd
/home/max
$ cd literature
$ pwd
/home/max/literature
```

Figure 4-9 cd changes the working directory

THE . AND .. DIRECTORY ENTRIES

The mkdir utility automatically puts two entries in each directory it creates: a single period (.) and a double period (..). The . is synonymous with the pathname of the working directory and can be used in its place; the .. is synonymous with the pathname of the parent of the working directory. These entries are hidden because their filenames begin with a period.

With the **literature** directory as the working directory, the following example uses .. three times: first to list the contents of the parent directory (**/home/max**), second to copy the **memoA** file to the parent directory, and third to list the contents of the parent directory again.

```
$ pwd
/home/max/literature
$ ls ..
demo  literature  names  temp
$ cp memoA ..
$ ls ..
demo  literature  memoA  names  temp
```

After using cd to make **promo** (a subdirectory of **literature**) his working directory, Max can use a relative pathname to call vim to edit a file in his home directory.

```
$ cd promo
$ vim ../../names
```

You can use an absolute or relative pathname or a simple filename virtually anywhere a utility or program requires a filename or pathname. This usage holds true for ls, vim, mkdir, rm, and most other utilities.

The working directory versus your home directory

tip The working directory is not the same as your home directory. Your home directory remains the same for the duration of your session and usually from session to session. Immediately after you log in, you are always working in the same directory: your home directory.

Unlike your home directory, the working directory can change as often as you like. You have no set working directory, which explains why some people refer to it as the *current directory*. When you log in and until you change directories using cd, your home directory is the working directory. If you were to change directories to Sam's home directory, then Sam's home directory would be the working directory.

rmdir: Deletes a Directory

The rmdir (remove directory) utility deletes a directory. You cannot delete the working directory or a directory that contains files other than the . and .. entries. If you need to delete a directory that has files in it, first use rm to delete the files and then delete the directory. You do not have to (nor can you) delete the . and .. entries; rmdir removes them automatically. The following command deletes the **promo** directory:

```
$ rmdir /home/max/literature/promo
```

The rm utility has a –r option (**rm –r *filename***) that recursively deletes files, including directories, within a directory and also deletes the directory itself.

Use rm –r carefully, if at all

caution Although **rm –r** is a handy command, you must use it carefully. Do not use it with an ambiguous file reference such as *. It is frighteningly easy to wipe out the contents of your entire home directory with a single short command.

Using Pathnames

touch Use a text editor to create a file named **letter** if you want to experiment with the examples that follow. Alternatively, you can use touch (page 1012) to create an empty file:

```
$ cd
$ pwd
/home/max
$ touch letter
```

With **/home/max** as the working directory, the following example uses cp with a relative pathname to copy the file named **letter** to the **/home/max/literature/promo** directory. (You will need to create **promo** again if you deleted it earlier.) The copy of the file has the simple filename **letter.0210**:

```
$ cp letter literature/promo/letter.0210
```

If Max does not change to another directory, he can use vim as shown to edit the copy of the file he just made:

```
$ vim literature/promo/letter.0210
```

If Max does not want to use a long pathname to specify the file, he can use cd to make **promo** the working directory before using vim:

```
$ cd literature/promo
$ pwd
/home/max/literature/promo
$ vim letter.0210
```

To make the parent of the working directory the new working directory, Max can give the following command, which takes advantage of the .. directory entry:

```
$ cd ..
$ pwd
/home/max/literature
```

mv, cp: MOVE OR COPY FILES

Chapter 3 discussed the use of mv to rename files. However, mv works even more generally: You can use this utility to move files from one directory to another (change the pathname of a file) as well as to change a simple filename. When used to move one or more files to a new directory, the mv command has this syntax:

mv existing-file-list directory

If the working directory is **/home/max**, Max can use the following command to move the files **names** and **temp** from the working directory to the **literature** directory:

```
$ mv names temp literature
```

This command changes the absolute pathnames of the **names** and **temp** files from **/home/max/names** and **/home/max/temp** to **/home/max/literature/names** and **/home/max/literature/temp**, respectively (Figure 4-10). Like most utilities, mv accepts either absolute or relative pathnames.

As you create more files, you will need to create new directories using mkdir to keep the files organized. The mv utility is a useful tool for moving files from one directory to another as you extend your directory hierarchy.

The cp utility works in the same way mv does, except it makes copies of the ***existing-file-list*** in the specified ***directory***.

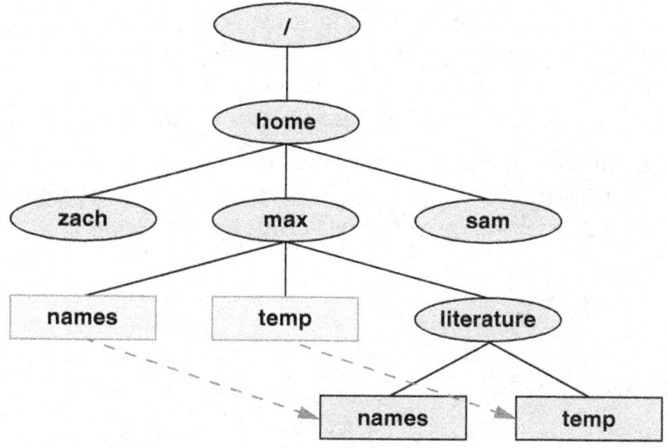

Figure 4-10 Using mv to move **names** and **temp**

mv: Moves a Directory

Just as it moves ordinary files from one directory to another, so mv can move directories. The syntax is similar except you specify one or more directories, not ordinary files, to move:

mv existing-directory-list new-directory

If ***new-directory*** does not exist, the ***existing-directory-list*** must contain just one directory name, which mv changes to ***new-directory*** (mv renames the directory). Although you can rename directories using mv, you cannot copy their contents with cp unless you use the **–r** (recursive) option. Refer to the explanations of cpio (page 776), pax (page 932), and tar (page 995) for other ways to copy and move directories.

Important Standard Directories and Files

Originally files on a Linux system were not located in standard places within the directory hierarchy. The scattered files made it difficult to document and maintain a Linux system and just about impossible for someone to release a software package that would compile and run on all Linux systems. The first standard for the Linux filesystem, the FSSTND (Linux Filesystem Standard), was released early in 1994. In early 1995 work was started on a broader standard covering many UNIX-like systems: FHS (Linux Filesystem Hierarchy Standard; www.pathname.com/fhs). More recently FHS has been incorporated in LSB (Linux Standard Base; wiki.linuxfoundation.org/lsb/start), a workgroup of FSG (Free Standards Group). Finally, FSG combined with Open Source Development Labs (OSDL) to form the Linux Foundation (www.linuxfoundation.org). Figure 4-11 shows the locations of some important directories and files as specified by FHS. The significance of many of these directories will become clear as you continue reading.

The following list describes the directories shown in Figure 4-11, some of the directories specified by FHS, and some other directories. Most distributions do not use all the directories specified by FHS. Be aware that you cannot always determine the function of a directory by its name. For example, although **/opt** stores add-on software, **/etc/opt** stores configuration files for the software in **/opt**.

/ **Root** The root directory, present in all Linux filesystem structures, is the ancestor of all files in the filesystem. It does not have a name and is represented by a slash (**/**) standing alone or at the left end of a pathname.

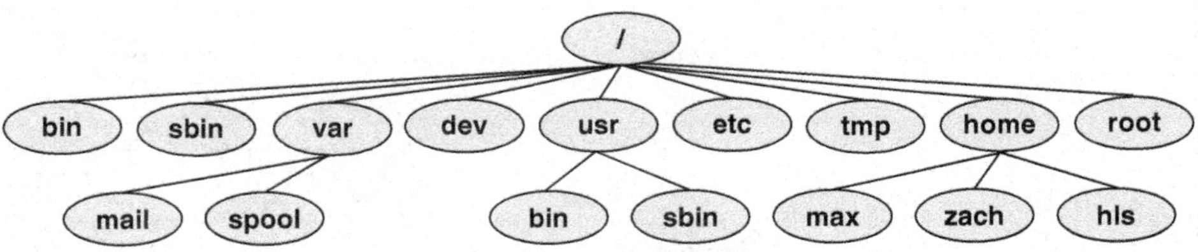

Figure 4-11 A typical FHS-based Linux filesystem structure

/bin **Essential command binaries** Holds the files needed to bring the system up and run it when it first comes up in single-user/recovery mode.

/boot **Static files of the boot loader** Contains all the files needed to boot the system.

/dev **Device files** Contains all the files that represent peripheral devices, such as disk drives, terminals, and printers. Previously this directory was filled with all possible devices. The udev utility provides a dynamic device directory that enables **/dev** to contain only devices that are present on the system.

/etc **Machine-local system configuration files** Holds administrative, configuration, and other system files. macOS uses Open Directory (page 1068) in place of **/etc/passwd**.

/etc/opt **Configuration files for add-on software packages kept in /opt**

/etc/X11 **Machine-local configuration files for the X Window System**

/home **User home directories** Each user's home directory is typically one of many subdirectories of the **/home** directory. As an example, assuming that users' directories are under **/home**, the absolute pathname of Zach's home directory is **/home/zach**. Under macOS, user home directories are typically located in **/Users**.

/lib **Shared libraries**

/lib/modules **Loadable kernel modules**

/mnt **Mount point for temporarily mounting filesystems**

/opt **Add-on (optional) software packages**

/proc **Kernel and process information virtual filesystem**

/root **Home directory for the root account**

/run **Runtime data** A **tmpfs** filesystem (mounted, but stored in RAM) that holds startup files previously hidden in **/dev** and other directories. For more information see lists.fedoraproject.org/pipermail/devel/2011-March/150031.html.

/sbin **Essential system binaries** Utilities used for system administration are stored in **/sbin** and **/usr/sbin**. The **/sbin** directory includes utilities needed during the booting process, and **/usr/sbin** holds utilities used after the system is up and running.

/sys **Device pseudofilesystem**

/tmp **Temporary files**

/Users **User home directories** Under macOS, each user's home directory is typically one of many subdirectories of the **/Users** directory. Linux typically stores home directories in **/home**.

/usr **Second major hierarchy** Traditionally includes subdirectories that contain information used by the system. Files in **/usr** subdirectories do not change often and can be shared by several systems.

/usr/bin **Most user commands** Contains the standard Linux utility programs—that is, binaries that are not needed in single-user/recovery mode.

/usr/games **Games and educational programs**

/usr/include **Header files included by C programs**

/usr/lib **Libraries**

/usr/local **Local hierarchy** Holds locally important files and directories that are added to the system. Subdirectories can include **bin, games, include, lib, sbin, share,** and **src.**

/usr/sbin **Nonvital system administration binaries** See **/sbin.**

/usr/share **Architecture-independent data** Subdirectories can include **dict, doc, games, info, locale, man, misc, terminfo,** and **zoneinfo.**

/usr/share/doc **Documentation**

/usr/share/info **GNU info system's primary directory**

/usr/share/man **Online manuals**

/usr/src **Source code**

/var **Variable data** Files with contents that vary as the system runs are kept in subdirectories under **/var**. The most common examples are temporary files, system log files, spooled files, and user mailbox files. Subdirectories can include **cache, lib, lock, log, mail, opt, run, spool, tmp,** and **yp.**

/var/log **Log files** Contains **lastlog** (a record of the last login by each user), **messages** (system messages from **syslogd**), and **wtmp** (a record of all logins/logouts), among other log files.

/var/spool **Spooled application data** Contains **anacron, at, cron, lpd, mail, mqueue, samba,** and other directories. The file **/var/mail** is typically a link to **/var/spool/mail.**

ACCESS PERMISSIONS

Most distributions support two methods of controlling who can access a file and how they can access it: traditional access permissions and ACLs (Access Control Lists). This section describes traditional access permissions. See page 106 for a discussion of ACLs, which provide finer-grained control of access permissions than do traditional access permissions.

Three types of users can access a file: the owner of the file (*owner*), a member of a group that the file is associated with (*group*), and everyone else (*other*). A user can attempt to access an ordinary file in three ways: by trying to *read from, write to,* or *execute* it.

ls –l: DISPLAYS PERMISSIONS

When you call ls with the –l option and the name of one or more ordinary files, ls displays a line of information about the file(s). See "ls output" on page 26 for information about the format of the display this book uses. The following example displays information for two files. The file **letter.0210** contains the text of a letter, and

check_spell contains a shell script, a program written in a high-level shell programming language:

```
$ ls -l check_spell letter.0210
-rwxr-xr-x. 1 sam pubs  766 03-21 14:02 check_spell
-rw-r--r--. 1 sam pubs 6193 02-10 14:22 letter.0210
```

From left to right, the lines that an **ls –l** command displays contain the following information (refer to Figure 4-12):

- The type of file (first character)
- The file's access permissions (the next nine characters)
- The ACL flag (present if the file has an ACL; page 106)
- The number of links to the file (page 112)
- The name of the owner of the file (usually the person who created the file)
- The name of the group the file is associated with
- The size of the file in characters (bytes)
- The date and time the file was created or last modified
- The name of the file

The type of file (first column) for **letter.0210** is a hyphen (–) because it is an ordinary file (directory files have a **d** in this column; see Table VI-21 on page 887).

The next three characters shown specify the access permissions for the *owner* of the file: **r** indicates read permission, **w** indicates write permission, and **x** indicates execute permission. A **–** in a column indicates that the owner does *not* have the permission that could have appeared in that position.

In a similar manner the next three characters represent permissions for the *group*, and the final three characters represent permissions for *other* (everyone else). In the preceding example, Sam, the owner of **letter.0210**, can read from and write to the file, whereas the group and others can only read from the file, and no one is allowed to execute it. Although execute permission can be allowed for any file, it does not make sense to assign execute permission to a file that contains a document such as a letter.

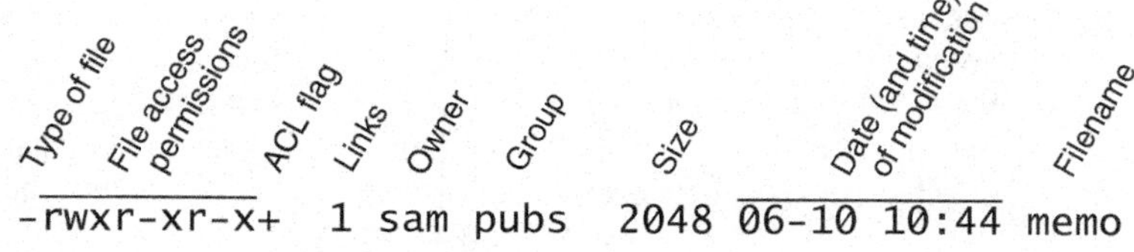

Figure 4-12 The columns displayed by the ls –l command

The **check_spell** file is an executable shell script, so execute permission is appropriate for it. (The owner, group, and others have execute permission.) For more information refer to "Discussion" on page 887.

chmod: Changes Access Permissions

The Linux file access permission scheme lets you give other users access to the files you want to share yet keep your private files confidential. You can allow other users to read from *and* write to a file (handy if you are one of several people working on a joint project). You can allow others only to read from a file (perhaps a project specification you are proposing). Or you can allow others only to write to a file (similar to an inbox or mailbox, where you want others to be able to send you mail but do not want them to read your mail). Similarly, you can protect entire directories from being scanned (covered shortly).

A user with root privileges can access any file on the system

security There is an exception to the access permissions described in this section. Anyone who can gain **root** privileges has full access to *all* files, regardless of the file's owner or access permissions. Of course, if the file is encrypted, read access does not mean the person reading the file can understand what is in the file.

The owner of a file controls which users have permission to access the file and how those users can access it. When you own a file, you can use the chmod (change mode) utility to change access permissions for that file. You can specify symbolic (relative) or numeric (absolute) arguments to chmod.

Symbolic Arguments to chmod

The following example, which uses symbolic arguments to chmod, adds (**+**) read and write permissions (**rw**) for all (**a**) users:

```
$ ls -l letter.0210
-rw-r-----. 1 sam pubs 6193 02-10 14:22 letter.0210
$ chmod a+rw letter.0210
$ ls -l letter.0210
-rw-rw-rw-. 1 sam pubs 6193 02-10 14:22 letter.0210
```

You must have read permission to execute a shell script

tip Because a shell needs to read a shell script (a text file containing shell commands) before it can execute the commands within that script, you must have read permission for the file containing the script to execute it. You also need execute permission to execute a shell script directly from the command line. In contrast, binary (program) files do not need to be read; they are executed directly. You need only execute permission to run a binary program.

Using symbolic arguments with chmod modifies existing permissions; the change a given argument makes depends on (is relative to) the existing permissions. In the next example, chmod removes (–) read (**r**) and execute (**x**) permissions for other (**o**) users. The owner and group permissions are not affected.

```
$ ls -l check_spell
-rwxr-xr-x. 1 sam pubs 766 03-21 14:02 check_spell
$ chmod o-rx check_spell
$ ls -l check_spell
-rwxr-x---. 1 sam pubs 766 03-21 14:02 check_spell
```

In addition to **a** (all) and **o** (other), you can use **g** (group) and **u** (user, although *user* refers to the *owner* of the file who might or might not be the user of the file at any given time) in the argument to chmod. For example, **chmod a+x** adds execute permission for all users (other, group, and owner), and **chmod go–rwx** removes all permissions for all but the owner of the file.

chmod: o for other, u for owner

tip When using chmod, many people assume that the **o** stands for *owner;* it does not. The **o** stands for *other,* whereas **u** stands for *owner* (*user*). The acronym UGO (user-group-other) might help you remember how permissions are named.

NUMERIC ARGUMENTS TO chmod

You can also use numeric arguments to specify permissions with chmod. In place of the letters and symbols specifying permissions used in the previous examples, numeric arguments comprise three octal digits. (A fourth, leading digit controls setuid and setgid permissions and is discussed next.) The first digit specifies permissions for the owner, the second for the group, and the third for other users. A **1** gives the specified user(s) execute permission, a **2** gives write permission, and a **4** gives read permission. Construct the digit representing the permissions for the owner, group, or others by ORing (adding) the appropriate values as shown in the following examples. Using numeric arguments sets file permissions absolutely; it does not modify existing permissions as symbolic arguments do.

In the following example, chmod changes permissions so only the owner of the file can read from and write to the file, regardless of how permissions were previously set. The 6 in the first position gives the owner read (4) and write (2) permissions. The 0s remove all permissions for the group and other users.

```
$ chmod 600 letter.0210
$ ls -l letter.0210
-rw-------. 1 sam pubs 6193 02-10 14:22 letter.0210
```

Next, 7 (4 + 2 + 1) gives the owner read, write, and execute permissions. The 5 (4 + 1) gives the group and other users read and execute permissions:

```
$ chmod 755 check_spell
$ ls -l check_spell
-rwxr-xr-x. 1 sam pubs 766 03-21 14:02 check_spell
```

Refer to Table 4-2 for more examples of numeric permissions.

Table 4-2 Examples of numeric permission specifications

Mode	Meaning
777	Owner, group, and others can read, write, and execute file
755	Owner can read, write, and execute file; group and others can read and execute file
711	Owner can read, write, and execute file; group and others can execute file
644	Owner can read and write file; group and others can read file
640	Owner can read and write file; group can read file; others cannot access file

Refer to page 295 for more information on using chmod to make a file executable and to page 759 for more information on absolute arguments and chmod in general.

Setuid and Setgid Permissions

When you execute a file that has setuid (set user ID) permission, the process executing the file takes on the privileges of the file's owner. For example, if you run a setuid program that removes all files in a directory, you can remove files in any of the file owner's directories, even if you do not normally have permission to do so. In a similar manner, setgid (set group ID) permission gives the process executing the file the privileges of the group the file is associated with.

Minimize use of setuid and setgid programs owned by root

security Executable files that are setuid and owned by **root** have **root** privileges when they run, even if they are not run by **root**. This type of program is very powerful because it can do anything that **root** can do (and that the program is designed to do). Similarly, executable files that are setgid and belong to the group **root** have extensive privileges.

Because of the power they hold and their potential for destruction, it is wise to avoid indiscriminately creating and using setuid programs owned by **root** and setgid programs belonging to the group **root**. Because of their inherent dangers, many sites minimize the use of these programs on their systems. One necessary setuid program is passwd.

The following example shows a user working with **root** privileges and using symbolic arguments to chmod to give one program setuid privileges and another program setgid privileges. The **ls –l** output (page 100) shows thesetuid permission by displaying an s in the owner's executable position and setgid permission by displaying an s in the group's executable position:

```
# ls -l myprog*
-rwxr-xr-x. 1 root pubs 362804 03-21 15:38 myprog1
-rwxr-xr-x. 1 root pubs 189960 03-21 15:38 myprog2

# chmod u+s myprog1
# chmod g+s myprog2

# ls -l myprog*
-rwsr-xr-x. 1 root pubs 362804 03-21 15:38 myprog1
-rwxr-sr-x. 1 root pubs 189960 03-21 15:38 myprog2
```

The next example uses numeric arguments to chmod to make the same changes. When you use four digits to specify permissions, setting the first digit to **1** sets the *sticky bit* (page 1126), setting it to **2** specifies setgid permissions, and setting it to **4** specifies setuid permissions:

```
# ls -l myprog*
-rwxr-xr-x. 1 root pubs 362804 03-21 15:38 myprog1
-rwxr-xr-x. 1 root pubs 189960 03-21 15:38 myprog2

# chmod 4755 myprog1
# chmod 2755 myprog2

# ls -l myprog*
-rwsr-xr-x. 1 root pubs 362804 03-21 15:38 myprog1
-rwxr-sr-x. 1 root pubs 189960 03-21 15:38 myprog2
```

Do not give shell scripts setuid/setgid permission

security Never give shell scripts setuid or setgid permission. Several techniques for subverting files with these permissions are well known.

DIRECTORY ACCESS PERMISSIONS

Access permissions have slightly different meanings when they are applied to directories. Although the three types of users can read from or write to a directory, the directory cannot be executed. Execute permission is redefined for a directory: It means that you can cd into the directory and/or examine files that you have permission to read from in the directory. It has nothing to do with executing a file.

When you have only execute permission for a directory, you can use ls to list a file in the directory if you know its name. You cannot use ls to list the contents of the directory. In the following exchange, Zach first verifies that he is logged in as himself. He then checks the permissions on Max's **info** directory. You can view the access permissions associated with a directory by running ls with the **–d** (directory) and the **–l** (long) options:

```
$ who am i
zach      pts/7   Aug 21 10:02
$ ls -ld /home/max/info
drwx-----x. 2 max pubs 4096 08-21 09:31 /home/max/info
```

```
$ ls -l /home/max/info
ls: /home/max/info: Permission denied
```

The **d** at the left end of the line that ls displays indicates **/home/max/info** is a directory. Max has read, write, and execute permissions; members of the **pubs** group have no access permissions; and other users have execute permission only, indicated by the **x** at the right end of the permissions. Because Zach does not have read permission for the directory, the **ls –l** command returns an error.

When Zach specifies the names of the files he wants information about, he is not reading new directory information but rather searching for specific information, which he is allowed to do with execute access to the directory. He has read permission for **notes** so he has no problem using cat to display the file. He cannot display **financial** because he does not have read permission for it:

```
$ ls -l /home/max/info/financial /home/max/info/notes
-rw-------. 1 max pubs 34 08-21 09:31 /home/max/info/financial
-rw-r--r--. 1 max pubs 30 08-21 09:32 /home/max/info/notes
$ cat /home/max/info/notes
This is the file named notes.
$ cat /home/max/info/financial
cat: /home/max/info/financial: Permission denied
```

Next, Max gives others read access to his **info** directory:

```
$ chmod o+r /home/max/info
```

When Zach checks his access permissions on **info**, he finds he has both read and execute access to the directory. Now **ls –l** displays the contents of the **info** directory, but he still cannot read **financial**. (This restriction is an issue of file permissions, not directory permissions.) Finally, Zach tries to create a file named **newfile** using touch (page 1012). If Max were to give him write permission to the **info** directory, Zach would be able to create new files in it:

```
$ ls -ld /home/max/info
drwx---r-x. 2 max pubs 4096 08-21 09:31 /home/max/info
$ ls -l /home/max/info
-rw-------. 1 max pubs 34 08-21 09:31 financial
-rw-r--r--. 1 max pubs 30 08-21 09:32 notes
$ cat /home/max/info/financial
cat: financial: Permission denied
$ touch /home/max/info/newfile
touch: cannot touch '/home/max/info/newfile': Permission denied
```

ACLs: Access Control Lists

ACLs (Access Control Lists) provide finer-grained control over which users can access specific directories and files than do traditional permissions (page 100). Using ACLs you can specify the ways in which each of several users can access a directory or file. Because ACLs can reduce performance, do not enable them on filesystems that hold system files, where the traditional Linux permissions are sufficient. Also, be careful when moving, copying, or archiving files: Not all utilities preserve ACLs. In addition, you cannot copy ACLs to filesystems that do not support ACLs.

An ACL comprises a set of rules. A rule specifies how a specific user or group can access the file that the ACL is associated with. There are two kinds of rules: *access rules* and *default rules*. (The documentation refers to *access ACLs* and *default ACLs*, even though there is only one type of ACL: There is one type of list [ACL] and there are two types of rules an ACL can contain.)

An access rule specifies access information for a single file or directory. A default ACL pertains to a directory only; it specifies default access information (an ACL) for any file in the directory that is not given an explicit ACL.

Most utilities do not preserve ACLs

caution When used with the **–p** (preserve) or **–a** (archive) option, cp preserves ACLs when it copies files. The mv utility also preserves ACLs. When you use cp with the **–p** or **–a** option and it is not able to copy ACLs, and in the case where mv is unable to preserve ACLs, the utility performs the operation and issues an error message:

```
$ mv report /tmp
mv: preserving permissions for '/tmp/report': Operation not supported
```

Other utilities, such as tar, cpio, and dump, do not support ACLs. You can use cp with the **–a** option to copy directory hierarchies, including ACLs.

You can never copy ACLs to a filesystem that does not support ACLs or to a filesystem that does not have ACL support turned on.

Enabling ACLs

The following explanation of how to enable ACLs pertains to Linux. See page 1074 if you are running macOS.

The **acl** package must be installed before you can use ACLs. Most Linux distributions officially support ACLs on **ext2**, **ext3**, and **ext4** filesystems only, although informal support for ACLs is available on other filesystems. To use ACLs on an **ext2/ext3/ext4** filesystem, you must mount the device with the **acl** option (**no_acl** is the default). For example, if you want to mount the device represented by **/home** so you can use ACLs on files in **/home**, you can add **acl** to its options list in **/etc/fstab**:

```
$ grep home /etc/fstab
LABEL=/home             /home              ext4    defaults,acl          1 2
```

remount option After changing **fstab**, you need to remount **/home** before you can use ACLs. If no one else is using the system, you can unmount it and mount it again (working with **root** privileges) as long as the working directory is not in the **/home** hierarchy. Alternatively, you can use the **remount** option to mount to remount **/home** while the device is in use:

```
# mount -v -o remount /home
/dev/sda3 on /home type ext4 (rw,acl)
```

WORKING WITH ACCESS RULES

The setfacl utility modifies a file's ACL and getfacl displays a file's ACL. These utilities are available under Linux only. If you are running macOS you must use chmod as explained on page 1074. When you use getfacl to obtain information about a file that does not have an ACL, it displays some of the same information as an **ls –l** command, albeit in a different format:

```
$ ls -l report
-rw-r--r--. 1 max pubs 9537 01-12 23:17 report

$ getfacl report
# file: report
# owner: max
# group: pubs
user::rw-
group::r--
other::r--
```

The first three lines of the getfacl output comprise the header; they specify the name of the file, the owner of the file, and the group the file is associated with. For more information refer to "**ls –l**: Displays Permissions" on page 100. The **––omit-header** (or just **––omit**) option causes getfacl not to display the header:

```
$ getfacl --omit-header report
user::rw-
group::r--
other::r--
```

In the line that starts with **user**, the two colons (**::**) with no name between them indicate that the line specifies the permissions for the owner of the file. Similarly, the two adjacent colons in the **group** line indicate the line specifies permissions for the group the file is associated with. The two colons following **other** are for consistency: No name can be associated with **other**.

The setfacl **––modify** (or **–m**) option adds or modifies one or more rules in a file's ACL using the following syntax:

setfacl ––modify ***ugo:name:permissions file-list***

where ***ugo*** can be either **u**, **g**, or **o** to indicate that the command sets file permissions for a user, a group, or all other users, respectively; ***name*** is the name of the user or group that permissions are being set for; ***permissions*** is the permissions in either symbolic or absolute format; and ***file-list*** is the list of files the permissions are to be applied to. You must omit ***name*** when you specify permissions for other users (**o**). Symbolic permissions use letters to represent file permissions (**rwx**, **r–x**, and so on), whereas absolute permissions use an octal number. While chmod uses three sets of permissions or three octal numbers (one each for the owner, group, and other users), setfacl uses a single set of permissions or a single octal number to represent the permissions being granted to the user or group represented by ***ugo*** and ***name***. See the discussion of chmod on pages 102 and 759 for more information about symbolic and absolute representations of file permissions.

For example, both of the following commands add a rule to the ACL for the **report** file that gives Sam read and write permission to that file:

```
$ setfacl --modify u:sam:rw- report
```

or

```
$ setfacl --modify u:sam:6 report

$ getfacl report
# file: report
# owner: max
# group: pubs
user::rw-
user:sam:rw-
group::r--
mask::rw-
other::r--
```

The line containing **user:sam:rw–** shows that the user named **sam** has read and write access (**rw–**) to the file. See page 100 for an explanation of how to read access permissions. See the following optional section for a description of the line that starts with **mask**.

When a file has an ACL, **ls –l** displays a plus sign (**+**) following the permissions, even if the ACL is empty:

```
$ ls -l report
-rw-rw-r--+ 1 max pubs 9537 01-12 23:17 report
```

optional

Effective Rights Mask

The line in the output of getfacl that starts with **mask** specifies the *effective rights mask*. This mask limits the effective permissions granted to ACL groups and users. It does not affect the owner of the file or the group the file is associated with. In other words, it does not affect traditional Linux permissions. However, because setfacl always sets the effective rights mask to the least restrictive ACL permissions for the file, the mask has no effect unless you set it explicitly after you set up an ACL for the file. You can set the mask by specifying **mask** in place of ***ugo*** and by not specifying a ***name*** in a setfacl command.

The following example sets the effective rights mask to **read** for the **report** file:

```
$ setfacl -m mask::r-- report
```

The **mask** line in the following getfacl output shows the effective rights mask set to read (**r––**). The line that displays Sam's file access permissions shows them still set to read and write. However, the comment at the right end of the line shows that his effective permission is read.

```
$ getfacl report
# file: report
# owner: max
# group: pubs
```

```
user::rw-
user:sam:rw-                        #effective:r--
group::r--
mask::r--
other::r--
```

As the next example shows, setfacl can modify ACL rules and can set more than one ACL rule at a time:

```
$ setfacl -m u:sam:r--,u:zach:rw- report

$ getfacl --omit-header report
user::rw-
user:sam:r--
user:zach:rw-
group::r--
mask::rw-
other::r--
```

The **–x** option removes ACL rules for a user or a group. It has no effect on permissions for the owner of the file or the group that the file is associated with. The next example shows setfacl removing the rule that gives Sam permission to access the file:

```
$ setfacl -x u:sam report

$ getfacl --omit-header report
user::rw-
user:zach:rw-
group::r--
mask::rw-
other::r--
```

You must not specify ***permissions*** when you use the **–x** option. Instead, specify only the ***ugo*** and ***name***. The **–b** option, followed by a filename only, removes all ACL rules and the ACL itself from the file or directory you specify.

Both setfacl and getfacl have many options. Use the **––help** option to display brief lists of options or refer to the man pages for details.

Setting Default Rules for a Directory

The following example shows that the **dir** directory initially has no ACL. The setfacl command uses the **–d** (default) option to add two default rules to the ACL for **dir**. These rules apply to all files in the **dir** directory that do not have explicit ACLs. The rules give members of the **pubs** group read and execute permissions and give members of the **adm** group read, write, and execute permissions.

```
$ ls -ld dir
drwx------. 2 max pubs 4096 02-12 23:15 dir
$ getfacl dir
# file: dir
# owner: max
# group: pubs
user::rwx
group::---
```

```
other::---

$ setfacl -d -m g:pubs:r-x,g:adm:rwx dir
```

The following **ls** command shows that the **dir** directory now has an ACL, as indicated by the + to the right of the permissions. Each of the default rules that **getfacl** displays starts with **default:**. The first two default rules and the last default rule specify the permissions for the owner of the file, the group that the file is associated with, and all other users. These three rules specify the traditional Linux permissions and take precedence over other ACL rules. The third and fourth rules specify the permissions for the **pubs** and **adm** groups. Next is the default effective rights mask.

```
$ ls -ld dir
drwx------+ 2 max pubs 4096 02-12 23:15 dir
$ getfacl dir
# file: dir
# owner: max
# group: pubs
user::rwx
group::---
other::---
default:user::rwx
default:group::---
default:group:pubs:r-x
default:group:adm:rwx
default:mask::rwx
default:other::---
```

Remember that the default rules pertain to files held in the directory that are not assigned ACLs explicitly. You can also specify access rules for the directory itself.

When you create a file within a directory that has default rules in its ACL, the effective rights mask for that file is created based on the file's permissions. In some cases the mask can override default ACL rules.

In the next example, **touch** creates a file named **new** in the **dir** directory. The **ls** command shows this file has an ACL. Based on the value of **umask** (page 1021), both the owner and the group that the file is associated with have read and write permissions for the file. The effective rights mask is set to read and write so that the effective permission for **pubs** is read and the effective permissions for **adm** are read and write. Neither group has execute permission.

```
$ cd dir
$ touch new
$ ls -l new
-rw-rw----+ 1 max pubs 0 02-13 00:39 new
$ getfacl --omit new
user::rw-
group::---
group:pubs:r-x                  #effective:r--
group:adm:rwx                   #effective:rw-
mask::rw-
other::---
```

If you change the file's traditional permissions to read, write, and execute for the owner and the group, the effective rights mask changes to read, write, and execute, and the groups specified by the default rules gain execute access to the file.

```
$ chmod 770 new
$ ls -l new
-rwxrwx---+ 1 max pubs 0 02-13 00:39 new
$ getfacl --omit new
user::rwx
group::---
group:pubs:r-x
group:adm:rwx
mask::rwx
other::---
```

LINKS

A *link* is a pointer to a file. Each time you create a file using vim, touch, cp, or by some other means, you are putting a pointer in a directory. This pointer associates a filename with a place on the disk. When you specify a filename in a command, you are indirectly pointing to the place on the disk that holds the information you want.

Sharing files can be useful when two or more people are working on the same project and need to share some information. You can make it easy for other users to access one of your files by creating additional links to the file.

To share a file with another user, first give the user permission to read from and write to the file (page 102). You might also have to change the access permissions of the parent directory of the file to give the user read, write, or execute permission (page 105). When the permissions are appropriately set, the user can create a link to the file so each of you can access the file from your separate directory hierarchies.

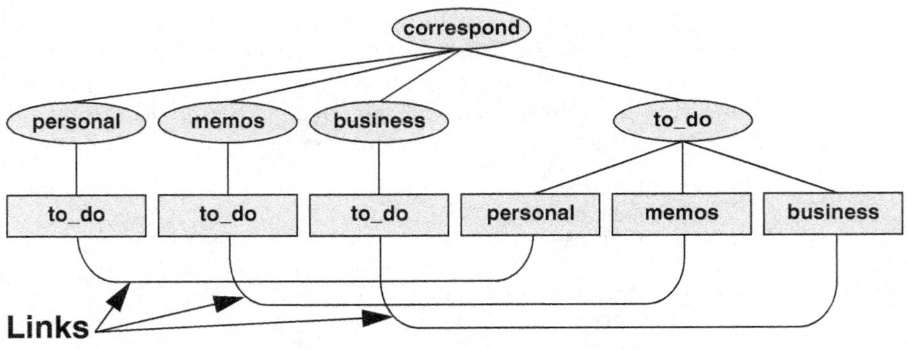

Figure 4-13 Using links to cross-classify files

A link can also be useful to a single user with a large directory hierarchy. You can create links to cross-classify files in your directory hierarchy, using different classifications for different tasks. For example, if you have the file layout depicted in Figure 4-2 on page 85, a file named **to_do** might appear in each subdirectory of the **correspond** directory—that is, in **personal, memos,** and **business.** If you find it difficult to keep track of everything you need to do, you can create a separate directory named **to_do** in the **correspond** directory. You can then link each subdirectory's to-do list into that directory. For example, you could link the file named **to_do** in the **memos** directory to a file named **memos** in the **to_do** directory. This set of links is shown in Figure 4-13.

Although it might sound complicated, this technique keeps all your to-do lists conveniently in one place. The appropriate list is easily accessible in the task-related directory when you are busy composing letters, writing memos, or handling personal business.

About the discussion of hard links

tip Two kinds of links exist: hard links and symbolic (soft) links. Hard links are older and becoming outdated. The section on hard links is marked as optional; you can skip it, although it discusses inodes and gives you insight into the structure of the filesystem.

optional

HARD LINKS

A hard link to a file appears as another file. If the file appears in the same directory as the linked-to file, the links must have different filenames because two files in the same directory cannot have the same name. You can create a hard link to a file only from within the filesystem that holds the file.

ln: CREATES A HARD LINK

The ln (link) utility (without the **–s** or **––symbolic** option) creates a hard link to an existing file using the following syntax:

ln existing-file new-link

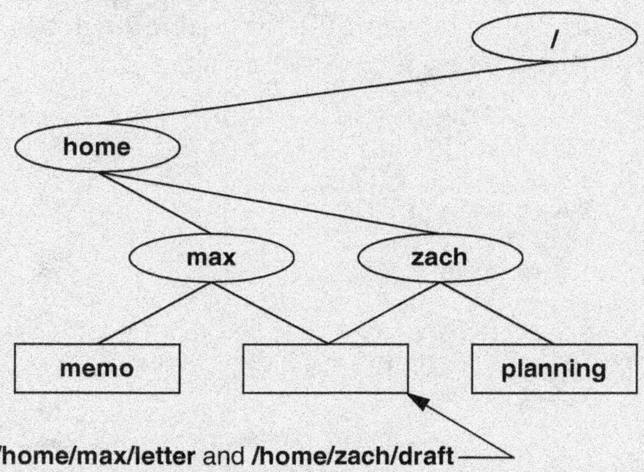

Figure 4-14 Two links to the same file: **/home/max/letter** and **/home/zach/draft**

The next command shows Zach making the link shown in Figure 4-14 by creating a new link named **/home/max/letter** to an existing file named **draft** in Zach's home directory:

```
$ pwd
/home/zach
$ ln draft /home/max/letter
```

The new link appears in the **/home/max** directory with the filename **letter**. In practice, Max might need to change directory permissions so Zach will be able to create the link. Even though **/home/max/letter** appears in Max's directory, Zach is the owner of the file because he created it.

The ln utility creates an additional pointer to an existing file, but it does *not* make another copy of the file. Because there is only one file, the file status information—such as access permissions, owner, and the time the file was last modified—is the same for all links; only the filenames differ. When Zach modifies **/home/zach/draft**, for example, Max sees the changes in **/home/max/letter**.

cp Versus ln

The following commands verify that ln does not make an additional copy of a file. Create a file, use ln to make an additional link to the file, change the contents of the file through one link, and verify the change through the other link:

```
$ cat file_a
This is file A.
$ ln file_a file_b
$ cat file_b
This is file A.
$ vim file_b
...
$ cat file_b
This is file B after the change.
$ cat file_a
This is file B after the change.
```

If you try the same experiment using cp instead of ln and change a *copy* of the file, the difference between the two utilities will become clearer. After you change a *copy* of a file, the two files are different:

```
$ cat file_c
This is file C.
$ cp file_c file_d
$ cat file_d
This is file C.
$ vim file_d
...
$ cat file_d
This is file D after the change.
$ cat file_c
This is file C.
```

ls and link counts You can use **ls** with the **–l** option, followed by the names of the files you want to compare, to confirm that the status information is the same for two links to the same file and is different for files that are not linked. In the following example, the **2** in the links field (just to the left of **max**) shows there are two links to **file_a** and **file_b** (from the previous example):

```
$ ls -l file_a file_b file_c file_d
-rw-r--r--. 2 max pubs 33 05-24 10:52 file_a
-rw-r--r--. 2 max pubs 33 05-24 10:52 file_b
-rw-r--r--. 1 max pubs 16 05-24 10:55 file_c
-rw-r--r--. 1 max pubs 33 05-24 10:57 file_d
```

Although it is easy to guess which files are linked to one another in this example, **ls** does not explicitly tell you.

ls and inodes Use **ls** with the **–i** option to determine without a doubt which files are linked. Use the **–i** option to list the *inode* (page 1103) number for each file. An inode is the control structure for a file. (HFS+, the default filesystem under macOS, does not have inodes but, through an elaborate scheme, appears to have inodes.) If the two filenames have the same inode number, they share the same control structure and are links to the same file. Conversely, when two filenames have different inode numbers, they are different files. The following example shows that **file_a** and **file_b** have the same inode number and that **file_c** and **file_d** have different inode numbers:

```
$ ls -i file_a file_b file_c file_d
3534 file_a  3534 file_b  5800 file_c  7328 file_d
```

All links to a file are of equal value: The operating system cannot distinguish the order in which multiple links were created. When a file has two links, you can remove either one and still access the file through the remaining link. You can remove the link used to create the file, for example, and as long as one link remains, still access the file through that link.

SYMBOLIC LINKS

In addition to hard links, Linux supports *symbolic links,* also called *soft links* or *symlinks.* A hard link is a pointer to a file (the directory entry points to the inode), whereas a symbolic link is an *indirect* pointer to a file (the directory entry contains the pathname of the pointed-to file—a pointer to the hard link to the file).

Dereferencing symbolic links To *dereference* a symbolic link means to follow the link to the target file rather than work with the link itself. See page 118 for information on dereferencing symbolic links.

Advantages of symbolic links Symbolic links were developed because of the limitations inherent in hard links. You cannot create a hard link to a directory, but you can create a symbolic link to a directory.

In many cases the Linux file hierarchy encompasses several filesystems. Because each filesystem keeps separate control information (that is, separate inode tables or filesystem structures) for the files it holds, it is not possible to create hard links between files in different filesystems. A symbolic link can point to any file, regardless of where it is located in the file structure, but a hard link to a file must be in the same filesystem as the other hard link(s) to the file. When you create links only among files in your home directory, you will not notice this limitation.

A major advantage of a symbolic link is that it can point to a nonexistent file. This ability is useful if you need a link to a file that is periodically removed and re-created. A hard link keeps pointing to a "removed" file, which the link keeps alive even after a new file is created. In contrast, a symbolic link always points to the newly created file and does not interfere when you delete the old file. For example, a symbolic link could point to a file that gets checked in and out under a source code control system, a **.o** file that is re-created by the C compiler each time you run make, or a log file that is repeatedly archived.

Although they are more general than hard links, symbolic links have some disadvantages. Whereas all hard links to a file have equal status, symbolic links do not have the same status as hard links. When a file has multiple hard links, it is analogous to a person having multiple full legal names, as many married women do. In contrast, symbolic links are analogous to nicknames. Anyone can have one or more nicknames, but these nicknames have a lesser status than legal names. The following sections describe some of the peculiarities of symbolic links.

ln: CREATES SYMBOLIC LINKS

The ln utility with the **––symbolic** (or **–s**) option creates a symbolic link. The following example creates a symbolic link **/tmp/s3** to the file **sum** in Max's home directory. When you use an **ls –l** command to look at the symbolic link, ls displays the name of the link and the name of the file it points to. The first character of the listing is **l** (for link). The size of a symbolic link is the number of characters in the target pathname.

```
$ ln --symbolic /home/max/sum /tmp/s3
$ ls -l /home/max/sum /tmp/s3
-rw-rw-r--. 1 max pubs 38 06-12 09:51 /home/max/sum
lrwxrwxrwx. 1 max pubs 13 06-12 09:52 /tmp/s3 -> /home/max/sum
$ cat /tmp/s3
This is sum.
```

The sizes and times of the last modifications of the two files are different. Unlike a hard link, a symbolic link to a file does not have the same status information as the file itself.

You can also use ln to create a symbolic link to a directory. When you use the **--symbolic** option, ln works as expected whether the file you are creating a link to is an ordinary file or a directory.

Use absolute pathnames with symbolic links

caution Symbolic links are literal and are not aware of directories. A link that points to a relative pathname, which includes simple filenames, assumes the relative pathname is relative to the directory that the link was created *in* (not the directory the link was created *from*). In the following example, the link points to the file named **sum** in the **/tmp** directory. Because no such file exists, cat gives an error message:

```
$ pwd
/home/max
$ ln --symbolic sum /tmp/s4
$ ls -l /home/max/sum /tmp/s4
lrwxrwxrwx. 1 max pubs 3 06-12 10:13 /tmp/s4 -> sum
-rw-rw-r--. 1 max pubs 38 06-12 09:51 /home/max/sum
$ cat /tmp/s4
cat: /tmp/s4: No such file or directory
```

optional

cd AND SYMBOLIC LINKS

When you use a symbolic link as an argument to cd to change directories, the results can be confusing, particularly if you did not realize that you were using a symbolic link.

If you use cd to change to a directory that is represented by a symbolic link, the pwd shell builtin (page 157) lists the name of the symbolic link. The pwd utility (**/bin/pwd**) lists the name of the linked-to directory, not the link, regardless of how you got there. You can also use the pwd builtin with the **–P** (physical) option to display the linked-to directory. This option displays a pathname that does not contain symbolic links.

```
$ ln -s /home/max/grades /tmp/grades.old
$ pwd
/home/max
$ cd /tmp/grades.old
$ pwd
/tmp/grades.old
$ /bin/pwd
/home/max/grades
$ pwd -P
/home/max/grades
```

When you change directories back to the parent, you end up in the directory holding the symbolic link (unless you use the **–P** option to cd):

```
$ cd ..
$ pwd
/tmp
$ /bin/pwd
/tmp
```

Under macOS, **/tmp** is a symbolic link to **/private/tmp**. When you are running macOS, after you give the **cd ..** command in the previous example, the working directory is **/private/tmp**.

rm: Removes a Link

When you create a file, there is one hard link to it. You can then delete the file or, using more accurate terminology, remove the link using the rm utility. When you remove the last hard link to a file, you can no longer access the information stored there, and the operating system releases the space the file occupied on the disk for use by other files. This space is released even if symbolic links to the file remain. When there is more than one hard link to a file, you can remove a hard link and still access the file from any remaining link. Unlike DOS and Windows, Linux does not provide an easy way to undelete a file once you have removed it. A skilled hacker, however, can sometimes piece the file together with time and effort.

When you remove all hard links to a file, you will not be able to access the file through a symbolic link. In the following example, cat reports that the file **total** does not exist because it is a symbolic link to a file that has been removed:

```
$ ls -l sum
-rw-r--r--. 1 max pubs 981 05-24 11:05 sum
$ ln -s sum total
$ rm sum
$ cat total
cat: total: No such file or directory
$ ls -l total
lrwxrwxrwx. 1 max pubs 6 05-24 11:09 total -> sum
```

When you remove a file, be sure to remove all symbolic links to it. Remove a symbolic link in the same way you remove other files:

```
$ rm total
```

Dereferencing Symbolic Links

A filename points at a file. A *symbolic link* is a file whose name refers to another file (a target file) without pointing directly at the target file: It is a reference to the target file. See page 115 for more information on symbolic links.

To *dereference* a symbolic link means to follow the link to the target file rather than work with the link itself. When you dereference a symbolic link, you end up with a pointer to the file (the filename of the target file). The term *no-dereference* is a double negative: It means reference. To no-dereference a symbolic link means to work with the link itself (do not dereference the symbolic link).

Many utilities have dereference and no-dereference options, usually invoked by the –L (**––dereference**) option and the **–P** (**––no-dereference**) option, respectively. Some utilities, such as chgrp, cp, and ls, also have a partial dereference option that is usually invoked by –H. With a –H option, a utility dereferences files listed on the command line only, not files found by traversing the hierarchy of a directory listed on the command line.

This section explains the **–L** (**––dereference**) and **–H** (partial dereference) options twice, once using ls and then using chgrp. It also covers the chgrp **–P** (**––no-dereference**) option.

DEREFERENCING SYMBOLIC LINKS USING ls

No options Most utilities default to no-dereference, although many do not have an explicit no-dereference option. For example, the GNU ls utility, which is used in most Linux distributions, does not have a **–P** (**––no-dereference**) option, although the BSD ls utility, which is used in macOS, does.

In the following example, ls with the **–l** option displays information about the files in the working directory and does not dereference the **sam.memo** symbolic link; it displays the symbolic link including the pathname of the file the link points to (the target file). The first character of the **sam.memo** line is an **l**, indicating the line describes a symbolic link; Max created the symbolic link and owns it.

```
$ ls -l
-rw-r--r--. 1 max pubs  1129 04-10 15:53 memoD
-rw-r--r--. 1 max pubs 14198 04-10 15:56 memoE
lrwxrwxrwx. 1 max pubs    19 04-10 15:57 sam.memo -> /home/max/sam/memoA
```

The next command specifies on the command line the file the symbolic link points to (the target file) and displays information about that file. The file type, permissions, owner, and time for the file are different from that of the link. Sam created the file and owns it.

```
$ ls -l /home/max/sam/memoA
-rw-r--r--. 1 sam sam 2126 04-10 15:54 /home/max/sam/memoA
```

–L (––dereference) Next, the **–L** (**––dereference**) option to ls displays information about the files in the working directory and dereferences the **sam.memo** symbolic link; it displays the file the link points to (the target file). The first character of the **sam.memo** line is a –, indicating the line describes a regular file. The command displays the same information about **memoA** as the preceding command, except it displays the name of the link (**sam.memo**), not that of the target file (**memoA**).

```
$ ls -lL
-rw-r--r--. 1 max pubs  1129 04-10 15:53 memoD
-rw-r--r--. 1 max pubs 14198 04-10 15:56 memoE
-rw-r--r--. 1 sam sam   2126 04-10 15:54 sam.memo
```

–H When you do not specify a symbolic link as an argument to ls, the **–H** (partial dereference; this short option has no long version) option displays the same information as the **–l** option.

```
$ ls -lH
-rw-r--r--. 1 max pubs  1129 04-10 15:53 memoD
-rw-r--r--. 1 max pubs 14198 04-10 15:56 memoE
lrwxrwxrwx. 1 max pubs    19 04-10 15:57 sam.memo -> /home/max/sam/memoA
```

When you specify a symbolic link as an argument to ls, the **–H** option causes ls to dereference the symbolic link; it displays information about the file the link points to (the target file; **memoA** in the example). As with **–L**, it refers to the file by the name of the symbolic link.

```
$ ls -lH sam.memo
-rw-r--r--. 1 sam sam 2126 04-10 15:54 sam.memo
```

In the next example, the shell expands the * to a list of the names of the files in the working directory and passes that list to ls. Specifying an ambiguous file reference that expands to a symbolic link produces the same results as explicitly specifying the symbolic link (because ls does not know it was called with an ambiguous file reference, it just sees the list of files the shell passes to it).

```
$ ls -lH *
-rw-r--r--. 1 max pubs  1129 04-10 15:53 memoD
-rw-r--r--. 1 max pubs 14198 04-10 15:56 memoE
-rw-r--r--. 1 sam sam   2126 04-10 15:54 sam.memo
```

optional

readlink The readlink utility displays the absolute pathname of a file, dereferencing symbolic links when needed. With the **–f** (**––canonicalize**) option, readlink follows nested symbolic links; all links except the last must exist. Following is an example:

```
$ ls -l /etc/alternatives/mta-mailq
lrwxrwxrwx. 1 root root 23 01-11 15:35 /etc/alternatives/mta-mailq ->
/usr/bin/mailq.sendmail
$ ls -l /usr/bin/mailq.sendmail
lrwxrwxrwx. 1 root root 25 01-11 15:32 /usr/bin/mailq.sendmail ->
../sbin/sendmail.sendmail

$ readlink -f /etc/alternatives/mta-mailq
/usr/sbin/sendmail.sendmail
```

DEREFERENCING SYMBOLIC LINKS USING chgrp

No options The following examples demonstrate the difference between the **–H** and **–L** options, this time using chgrp. Initially all files and directories in the working directory are associated with the **zach** group:

```
$ ls -lR
.:
-rw-r--r-- 1 zach zach  102 07-02 12:31 bb
drwxr-xr-x 2 zach zach 4096 07-02 15:34 dir1
drwxr-xr-x 2 zach zach 4096 07-02 15:33 dir4

./dir1:
-rw-r--r-- 1 zach zach 102 07-02 12:32 dd
lrwxrwxrwx 1 zach zach   7 07-02 15:33 dir4.link -> ../dir4

./dir4:
```

```
-rw-r--r-- 1 zach zach 125 07-02 15:33 gg
-rw-r--r-- 1 zach zach 375 07-02 15:33 hh
```

–H When you call chgrp with the –R and –H options (when used with chrgp, –H does not work without –R), chgrp dereferences only symbolic links you list on the command line and those in directories you list on the command line. The chgrp utility changes the group association of the files these links point to. It does not dereference symbolic links it finds as it descends directory hierarchies, nor does it change symbolic links themselves. While descending the **dir1** hierarchy, chgrp does not change **dir4.link**, but it does change **dir4**, the directory **dir4.link** points to.

```
$ chgrp -RH pubs bb dir1
$ ls -lR
.:
-rw-r--r-- 1 zach pubs  102 07-02 12:31 bb
drwxr-xr-x 2 zach pubs 4096 07-02 15:34 dir1
drwxr-xr-x 2 zach pubs 4096 07-02 15:33 dir4

./dir1:
-rw-r--r-- 1 zach pubs 102 07-02 12:32 dd
lrwxrwxrwx 1 zach zach   7 07-02 15:33 dir4.link -> ../dir4

./dir4:
-rw-r--r-- 1 zach zach 125 07-02 15:33 gg
-rw-r--r-- 1 zach zach 375 07-02 15:33 hh
```

The –H option under macOS

caution The chgrp **–H** option works slightly differently under macOS than it does under Linux. Under macOS, chgrp **–RH** changes the group of the symbolic link it finds in a directory listed on the command line and does not change the file the link points to. (It does not dereference the symbolic link.) When you run the preceding example under macOS, the group association of **dir4** is not changed, but the group association of **dir4.link** is.

If your program depends on how the **–H** option functions with a utility under macOS, test the option with that utility to determine exactly how it works.

–L When you call chgrp with the –R and –L options (when used with chgrp, –L does not work without –R), chgrp dereferences all symbolic links: those you list on the command line and those it finds as it descends the directory hierarchy. It does not change the symbolic links themselves. This command changes the files in the directory **dir4.link** points to:

```
$ chgrp -RL pubs bb dir1

$ ls -lR
.:
-rw-r--r-- 1 zach pubs  102 07-02 12:31 bb
drwxr-xr-x 2 zach pubs 4096 07-02 15:34 dir1
drwxr-xr-x 2 zach pubs 4096 07-02 15:33 dir4

./dir1:
```

```
-rw-r--r-- 1 zach pubs 102 07-02 12:32 dd
lrwxrwxrwx 1 zach zach   7 07-02 15:33 dir4.link -> ../dir4

./dir4:
-rw-r--r-- 1 zach pubs 125 07-02 15:33 gg
-rw-r--r-- 1 zach pubs 375 07-02 15:33 hh
```

–P When you call chgrp with the **–R** and **–P** options (when used with chgrp, **–P** does not work without **–R**), chgrp does not dereference symbolic links. It does change the group of the symbolic link itself.

```
$ ls -l bb*
-rw-r--r-- 1 zach zach 102 07-02 12:31 bb
lrwxrwxrwx 1 zach zach   2 07-02 16:02 bb.link -> bb

$ chgrp -PR pubs bb.link

$ ls -l bb*
-rw-r--r-- 1 zach zach 102 07-02 12:31 bb
lrwxrwxrwx 1 zach pubs   2 07-02 16:02 bb.link -> bb
```

CHAPTER SUMMARY

Linux has a hierarchical, or treelike, file structure that makes it possible to organize files so you can find them quickly and easily. The file structure contains directory files and ordinary files. Directories contain other files, including other directories; ordinary files generally contain text, programs, or images. The ancestor of all files is the root directory and is represented by / standing alone or at the left end of a pathname.

Most Linux filesystems support 255-character filenames. Nonetheless, it is a good idea to keep filenames simple and intuitive. Filename extensions can help make filenames more meaningful.

When you are logged in, you are always associated with a working directory. Your home directory is the working directory from the time you log in until you use cd to change directories.

An absolute pathname starts with the root directory and contains all the filenames that trace a path to a given file. The pathname starts with a slash, representing the root directory, and contains additional slashes following each of the directories in the path, except for the last directory in the case of a path that points to a directory file.

A relative pathname is similar to an absolute pathname but traces the path starting from the working directory. A simple filename is the last element of a pathname and is a form of a relative pathname; it represents a file in the working directory.

A Linux filesystem contains many important directories, including **/usr/bin**, which stores most of the Linux utilities, and **/dev**, which stores device files, many of which represent physical pieces of hardware. An important standard Linux file is **/etc/passwd**; it contains information about users, such as a user's ID and full name.

Among the attributes associated with each file are access permissions. They determine who can access the file and how the file may be accessed. Three groups of users can potentially access the file: the owner, the members of a group, and all other users. An ordinary file can be accessed in three ways: read, write, and execute. The ls utility with the –l option displays these permissions. For directories, execute access is redefined to mean that the directory can be searched.

The owner of a file or a user working with **root** privileges can use the chmod utility to change the access permissions of a file. This utility specifies read, write, and execute permissions for the file's owner, the group, and all other users on the system.

ACLs (Access Control Lists) provide finer-grained control over which users can access specific directories and files than do traditional permissions. Using ACLs you can specify the ways in which each of several users can access a directory or file. Few utilities preserve ACLs when working with files.

An ordinary file stores user data, such as textual information, programs, or images. A directory is a standard-format disk file that stores information, including names, about ordinary files and other directory files. An inode is a data structure, stored on disk, that defines a file's existence and is identified by an inode number. A directory relates each of the filenames it stores to an inode.

A link is a pointer to a file. You can have several links to a file so you can share the file with other users or have the file appear in more than one directory. Because only one copy of a file with multiple links exists, changing the file through any one link causes the changes to appear in all the links. Hard links cannot link directories or span filesystems, whereas symbolic links can.

Table 4-3 summarizes the utilities introduced in this chapter.

Table 4-3 Utilities introduced in Chapter 4

Utility	Function
cd	Associates you with another working directory (page 94)
chmod	Changes access permissions on a file (page 102)
getfacl	Displays a file's ACL (page 108)
ln	Makes a link to an existing file (page 113)
mkdir	Creates a directory (page 93)
pwd	Displays the pathname of the working directory (page 89)
rmdir	Deletes a directory (page 96)
setfacl	Modifies a file's ACL (page 108)

EXERCISES

1. Is each of the following an absolute pathname, a relative pathname, or a simple filename?

   a. **milk_co**

   b. **correspond/business/milk_co**

   c. **/home/max**

   d. **/home/max/literature/promo**

   e. **..**

   f. **letter.0210**

2. List the commands you can use to perform these operations:

   a. Make your home directory the working directory

   b. Identify the working directory

3. If the working directory is **/home/max** with a subdirectory named **literature**, give three sets of commands you can use to create a subdirectory named **classics** under **literature**. Also give several sets of commands you can use to remove the **classics** directory and its contents.

4. The df utility displays all mounted filesystems along with information about each. Use the df utility with the **–h** (human-readable) option to answer the following questions:

   a. How many filesystems are mounted on the local system?

   b. Which filesystem stores your home directory?

   c. Assuming your answer to exercise 4a is two or more, attempt to create a hard link to a file on another filesystem. What error message is displayed? What happens when you attempt to create a symbolic link to the file instead?

5. Suppose you have a file that is linked to a file owned by another user. How can you ensure that changes to the file are no longer shared?

6. You should have read permission for the **/etc/passwd** file. To answer the following questions, use cat or less to display **/etc/passwd**. Look at the fields of information in **/etc/passwd** for the users on the local system.

   a. Which character is used to separate fields in **/etc/passwd**?

   b. How many fields are used to describe each user?

   c. How many users are on the local system?

d. How many different login shells are in use on your system? (*Hint:* Look at the last field.)

e. The second field of **/etc/passwd** stores user passwords in encoded form. If the password field contains an **x**, your system uses shadow passwords and stores the encoded passwords elsewhere. Does your system use shadow passwords?

7. If **/home/zach/draft** and **/home/max/letter** are links to the same file and the following sequence of events occurs, what will be the date in the opening of the letter?

   a. Max gives the command **vim letter**.

   b. Zach gives the command **vim draft**.

   c. Zach changes the date in the opening of the letter to January 31, writes the file, and exits from vim.

   d. Max changes the date to February 1, writes the file, and exits from vim.

8. Suppose a user belongs to a group that has all permissions on a file named **jobs_list**, but the user, as the owner of the file, has no permissions. Describe which operations, if any, the user/owner can perform on **jobs_list**. Which command can the user/owner give that will grant the user/owner all permissions on the file?

9. Does the root directory have any subdirectories you cannot search as an ordinary user? Does the root directory have any subdirectories you cannot read as a regular user? Explain.

10. Assume you are given the directory structure shown in Figure 4-2 on page 85 and the following directory permissions:

```
d--x--x---   3 zach pubs 512 2018-03-10 15:16 business
drwxr-xr-x   2 zach pubs 512 2018-03-10 15:16 business/milk_co
```

    For each category of permissions—owner, group, and other—what happens when you run each of the following commands? Assume the working directory is the parent of **correspond** and that the file **cheese_co** is readable by everyone.

   a. **cd correspond/business/milk_co**

   b. **ls –l correspond/business**

   c. **cat correspond/business/cheese_co**

Advanced Exercises

11. What is an inode? What happens to the inode when you move a file within a filesystem?

12. What does the .. entry in a directory point to? What does this entry point to in the root (/) directory?

13. How can you create a file named –i? Which techniques do not work, and why do they not work? How can you remove the file named –i?

14. Suppose the working directory contains a single file named **andor**. What error message is displayed when you run the following command line?

    ```
    $ mv andor and\/or
    ```

    Under what circumstances is it possible to run the command without producing an error?

15. The **ls –i** command displays a filename preceded by the inode number of the file (page 115). Write a command to output inode/filename pairs for the files in the working directory, sorted by inode number. (*Hint:* Use a pipeline.)

16. Do you think the system administrator has access to a program that can decode user passwords? Why or why not? (See exercise 6.)

17. Is it possible to distinguish a file from a hard link to a file? That is, given a filename, can you tell whether it was created using an **ln** command? Explain.

18. Explain the error messages displayed in the following sequence of commands:

    ```
    $ ls -l
    drwxrwxr-x. 2 max pubs 1024 03-02 17:57 dirtmp
    $ ls dirtmp
    $ rmdir dirtmp
    rmdir: dirtmp: Directory not empty
    $ rm dirtmp/*
    rm: No match.
    ```

5

The Shell

In This Chapter

Objectives

After reading this chapter you should be able to:

- List special characters and methods of preventing the shell from interpreting these characters
- Describe a simple command
- Understand command-line syntax and run commands that include options and arguments
- Explain how the shell interprets the command line
- Redirect output of a command to a file, overwriting the file or appending to it
- Redirect input for a command so it comes from a file
- Connect commands using a pipeline
- Run commands in the background
- Use special characters as wildcards to generate filenames
- Explain the difference between a stand-alone utility and a shell builtin

This chapter takes a close look at the shell and explains how to use some of its features. It discusses command-line syntax and describes how the shell processes a command line and initiates execution of a program. This chapter also explains how to redirect input to and output from a command, construct pipelines and filters on the command line, and run a command in the background. The final section covers filename expansion and explains how you can use this feature in your everyday work.

Except as noted, everything in this chapter applies to the Bourne Again (bash) and TC (tcsh) Shells. The exact wording of the shell output differs from shell to shell: What the shell you are using displays might differ slightly from what appears in this book. For shell-specific information, refer to Chapters 8 (bash) and 9 (tcsh). Chapter 10 covers writing and executing bash shell scripts.

SPECIAL CHARACTERS

Special characters, which have a special meaning to the shell, are discussed in "Filename Generation/Pathname Expansion" on page 152. These characters are mentioned here so you can avoid accidentally using them as regular characters until you understand how the shell interprets them. Avoid using any of the following characters in a filename (even though emacs and some other programs do) because they make the file harder to reference on the command line:

```
& ; | * ? ' " ` [ ] ( ) $ < > { } # / \ ! ~
```

Whitespace Although not considered special characters, RETURN, SPACE, and TAB have special meanings to the shell. RETURN usually ends a command line and initiates execution of a command. The SPACE and TAB characters separate tokens (elements) on the command line and are collectively known as *whitespace* or *blanks.*

Quoting special characters If you need to use a character that has a special meaning to the shell as a regular character, you can *quote* (or *escape*) it. When you quote a special character, you prevent the shell from giving it special meaning. The shell treats a quoted special character as a regular character. However, a slash (/) is always a separator in a pathname, even when you quote it.

Backslash To quote a character, precede it with a backslash (\). When two or more special characters appear together, you must precede each with a backslash (e.g., you would enter ** as **). You can quote a backslash just as you would quote any other special character—by preceding it with a backslash (\\).

Single quotation marks Another way of quoting special characters is to enclose them between single quotation marks: '**'. You can quote many special and regular characters between a pair of single quotation marks: **'This is a special character: >'**. The regular characters are interpreted as usual, and the shell also interprets the special characters as regular characters.

The only way to quote the erase character (CONTROL-H), the line kill character (CONTROL-U), and other control characters (try CONTROL-M) is by preceding each with a CONTROL-V. Single quotation marks and backslashes do not work. Try the following:

```
$ echo 'xxxxxxCONTROL-U'
$ echo xxxxxxCONTROL-V CONTROL-U
```

optional Although you cannot see the CONTROL-U displayed by the second of the preceding pair of commands, it is there. The following command sends the output of echo (page 812) through a pipeline (page 145) to od (octal display; page 921) to display CONTROL-U as octal 25 (025):

```
$ echo xxxxxxCONTROL-V CONTROL-U | od -c
0000000   x   x   x   x   x   x 025  \n
0000010
```

The \n is the NEWLINE character that echo sends at the end of its output.

Ordinary Files and Directory Files

Ordinary files, or simply *files,* are files that can hold documents, pictures, programs, and other kinds of data. *Directory files,* also referred to as *directories* or *folders,* can hold ordinary files and other directory files.

The Working Directory

pwd While you are logged in on a character-based interface to a Linux system, you are always associated with a directory. The directory you are associated with is called the *working directory* or *current directory.* Sometimes this association is referred to in a physical sense: "You are *in* (or *working in*) the **zach** directory." The pwd (print working directory) builtin displays the pathname of the working directory.

```
login: max
Password:
Last login: Wed Oct 20 11:14:21 from 172.16.192.150
$ pwd
/home/max
```

Your Home Directory

When you first log in on a Linux system or start a terminal emulator window, the working directory is your *home directory.* To display the pathname of your home directory, use pwd just after you log in.

THE COMMAND LINE

Command This book uses the term *command* to refer to both the characters you type on the command line and the program that action invokes.

Command line A *command line* comprises a simple command (below), a pipeline (page 145), or a list (page 149).

A SIMPLE COMMAND

The shell executes a program when you enter a command in response to its prompt. For example, when you give an ls command, the shell executes the utility program named ls. You can cause the shell to execute other types of programs—such as shell scripts, application programs, and programs you have written—in the same way. The line that contains the command, including any arguments, is called a *simple command*. The following sections discuss simple commands; see page 133 for a more technical and complete description of a simple command.

SYNTAX

Command-line syntax dictates the ordering and separation of the elements on a command line. When you press the RETURN key after entering a command, the shell scans the command line for proper syntax. The syntax for a simple command is

***command** [arg1] [arg2] ... [argn]* RETURN

Whitespace (any combination of SPACEs and/or TABs) must separate elements on the command line. The ***command*** is the name of the command, ***arg1*** through ***argn*** are arguments, and RETURN is the keystroke that terminates the command line. The brackets in the command-line syntax indicate that the arguments they enclose are optional. Not all commands require arguments: Some commands do not allow arguments; other commands allow a variable number of arguments; and still others require a specific number of arguments. Options, a special kind of argument, are usually preceded by one or two hyphens (–).

COMMAND NAME

Usage message Some useful Linux command lines consist of only the name of the command without any arguments. For example, ls by itself lists the contents of the working directory. Commands that require arguments typically give a short error message, called a *usage message,* when you use them without arguments, with incorrect arguments, or with the wrong number of arguments.

For example, the mkdir (make directory) utility requires an argument that specifies the name of the directory you want it to create. Without this argument, it displays a usage message (*operand* is another term for "argument"):

```
$ mkdir
mkdir: missing operand
Try 'mkdir --help' for more information.
```

ARGUMENTS

Token On the command line each sequence of nonblank characters is called a *token* or *word*. An *argument* is a token that a command acts on (e.g., a filename, a string of characters, a number). For example, the argument to a vim or emacs command is the name of the file you want to edit.

The following command line uses cp to copy the file named **temp** to **tempcopy**:

```
$ cp temp tempcopy
```

Arguments are numbered starting with the command itself, which is argument zero. In this example, **cp** is argument zero, **temp** is argument one, and **tempcopy** is argument two. The cp utility requires at least two arguments on the command line. Argument one is the name of an existing file. In this case, argument two is the name of the file that cp is creating or overwriting. Here, the arguments are not optional; both arguments must be present for the command to work. When you do not supply the right number or kind of arguments, cp displays a usage message. Try typing **cp** and then pressing RETURN.

OPTIONS

An *option* is an argument that modifies the effects of a command. These arguments are called options because they are usually optional. You can frequently specify more than one option, modifying the command in several ways. Options are specific to and interpreted by the program that the command line calls, not the shell.

By convention, options are separate arguments that follow the name of the command and usually precede other arguments, such as filenames. Many utilities require options to be prefixed with a single hyphen. However, this requirement is specific to the utility and not the shell. GNU long (multicharacter) program options are frequently prefixed with two hyphens. For example, **--help** generates a (sometimes extensive) usage message.

The first command in Figure 5-1 shows the output of an ls command without any options. By default, ls lists the contents of the working directory in alphabetical order, vertically sorted in columns. Next, the **–r** (reverse order; because this is a GNU utility, you can also specify **--reverse**) option causes the ls utility to display the list of files in reverse alphabetical order, still sorted in columns. The **–x** option causes ls to display the list of files in horizontally sorted rows.

Combining options When you need to use several options, you can usually group multiple single-letter options into one argument that starts with a single hyphen; do not put SPACEs between the options. You cannot combine options that are preceded by two hyphens in this way. Specific rules for combining options depend on the program you are running.

Figure 5-1 shows both the **–r** and **–x** options with the **ls** utility. Together these options generate a list of filenames in horizontally sorted rows in reverse alphabetical order. Most utilities allow you to list options in any order; thus, **ls –xr** produces the same results as **ls –rx**. The command **ls –x –r** also generates the same list.

The --help option

tip Many utilities display a (sometimes extensive) help message when you call them with an argument of **--help**. All utilities developed by the GNU Project (page 3) accept this option. Following is the help message displayed by the **bzip2** compression utility (page 64):

```
$ bzip2 --help
bzip2, a block-sorting file compressor.  Version 1.0.6, 6-Sept-2010.

   usage: bunzip2 [flags and input files in any order]

   -h --help           print this message
   -d --decompress     force decompression
   -z --compress       force compression
   -k --keep           keep (don't delete) input files
   -f --force          overwrite existing output files
...
   If invoked as 'bzip2', default action is to compress.
              as 'bunzip2',  default action is to decompress.
              as 'bzcat', default action is to decompress to stdout.
...
```

Option arguments Some utilities have options that require arguments. These arguments are not optional. For example, the **gcc** utility (C compiler) has a **–o** (output) option that must be followed by the name you want to give the executable file that **gcc** generates. Typically, an argument to an option is separated from its option letter by a SPACE:

```
$ gcc -o prog prog.c
```

Some utilities sometimes require an equal sign between an option and its argument. For example, you can specify the width of output from **diff** in two ways:

```
$ ls
hold   mark  names   oldstuff  temp  zach
house  max   office  personal  test
$ ls -r
zach  temp      oldstuff  names  mark   hold
test  personal  office    max    house
$ ls -x
hold      house     mark  max   names  office
oldstuff  personal  temp  test  zach
$ ls -rx
zach   test  temp  personal  oldstuff  office
names  max   mark  house     hold
```

Figure 5-1 Using options

```
$ diff -W 60 filea fileb
```

or

```
$ diff --width=60 filea fileb
```

Displaying readable file sizes: the –h option

tip Most utilities that report on file sizes specify the size of a file in bytes. Bytes work well when you are dealing with smaller files, but the numbers can be difficult to read when you are working with file sizes that are measured in gigabytes or terabytes. Use the **–h** (or **––human-readable**) option to display file sizes in kilobytes, megabytes, gigabytes, and terabytes. Experiment with the **df –h** (disk free) and **ls –lh** commands.

Arguments that start with a hyphen Another convention allows utilities to work with arguments, such as filenames, that start with a hyphen. If a file named –l is in the working directory, the following command is ambiguous:

```
$ ls -l
```

This command could be a request to display a long listing of all files in the working directory (–l option) or a request for a listing of the file named –l. The ls utility interprets it as the former. Avoid creating a file whose name begins with a hyphen. If you do create such a file, many utilities follow the convention that a –– argument (two consecutive hyphens) indicates the end of the options (and the beginning of the arguments). To disambiguate the preceding command, you can type

```
$ ls -- -l
```

Using two consecutive hyphens to indicate the end of the options is a convention, not a hard-and-fast rule, and a number of utilities do not follow it (e.g., find). Following this convention makes it easier for users to work with a program you write.

For utilities that do not follow this convention, there are other ways to specify a filename that begins with a hyphen. You can use a period to refer to the working directory and a slash to indicate the following filename refers to a file in the working directory:

```
$ ls ./-l
```

You can also specify the absolute pathname of the file:

```
$ ls /home/max/-l
```

optional

Simple Commands

This section expands on the discussion of command-line syntax starting on page 130.

A simple command comprises zero or more variable assignments followed by a command line. It is terminated by a control operator (e.g., &, ;, |, NEWLINE; page 299). A simple command has the following syntax:

[name=value ...] command-line

The shell assigns a ***value*** to each ***name*** and places it in the environment (page 480) of the program that ***command-line*** calls so it is available to the called program and its children as a variable. The shell evaluates the ***name=value*** pairs from left to right, so if ***name*** appears more than once in this list, the rightmost ***value*** takes precedence. The ***command-line*** might include redirection operators such as **>** and **<** (page 140). The exit status (page 477) of a simple command is its return value. Under tcsh you must use env (page 483) to place variables in the environment of a called program without declaring them in the calling shell.

Placing a variable in the environment of a child

The following commands demonstrate how you can assign a value to a name (variable) and place that name in the environment of a child program; the variable is not available to the interactive shell you are running (the parent program). The script named **echo_ee** displays the value of the variable named **ee**. The first call to **echo_ee** shows **ee** is not set in the child shell running the script. When the call to **echo_ee** is preceded by assigning a value to **ee**, the script displays the value of **ee** in the child shell. The final command shows **ee** has not been set in the interactive shell.

```
$ cat echo_ee
echo "The value of the ee variable is: $ee"

$ ./echo_ee
The value of the ee variable is:
$ ee=88 ./echo_ee
The value of the ee variable is: 88
$ echo $ee

$
```

Processing the Command Line

As you enter a command line, the tty device driver (part of the Linux kernel) examines each character to see whether it must take immediate action. When you press CONTROL-H (to erase a character) or CONTROL-U (to kill a line), the device driver immediately adjusts the command line as required; the shell never sees the character(s) you erased or the line you killed. Often a similar adjustment occurs when you press CONTROL-W (to erase a word). When the character you entered does not require immediate action, the device driver stores the character in a buffer and waits for additional characters. When you press RETURN, the device driver passes the command line to the shell for processing.

Parsing the command line

When the shell processes a command line, it looks at the line as a whole and *parses* (breaks) it into its component parts (Figure 5-2). Next, the shell looks for the name of the command. Usually the name of the command is the first item on the command line after the prompt (argument zero). The shell takes the first characters on the command line up to the first blank (TAB or SPACE) and then looks for a command with that name. The command name (the first token) can be specified on the command line either as a simple filename or as a pathname. For example, you can call the **ls** command in either of the following ways:

```
$ ls
```

or

```
$ /bin/ls
```

optional The shell does not require the name of the program to appear first on the command line. Thus, you can structure a command line as follows:

```
$ >bb <aa cat
```

This command runs cat with standard input coming from the file named **aa** and standard output going to the file named **bb**. When the shell recognizes the redirect symbols (page 140), it processes them and their arguments before finding the name of the program that the command line is calling. This is a properly structured—albeit rarely encountered and possibly confusing—command line.

Absolute versus relative pathnames

From the command line, there are three ways you can specify the name of a file you want the shell to execute: as an absolute pathname (starts with a slash [/]; page 90), as a relative pathname (includes a slash but does not start with a slash; page 91), or as a simple filename (no slash). When you specify the name of a file for the shell to execute in either of the first two ways (the pathname includes a slash), the shell looks in the specified directory for a file with the specified name that you have permission

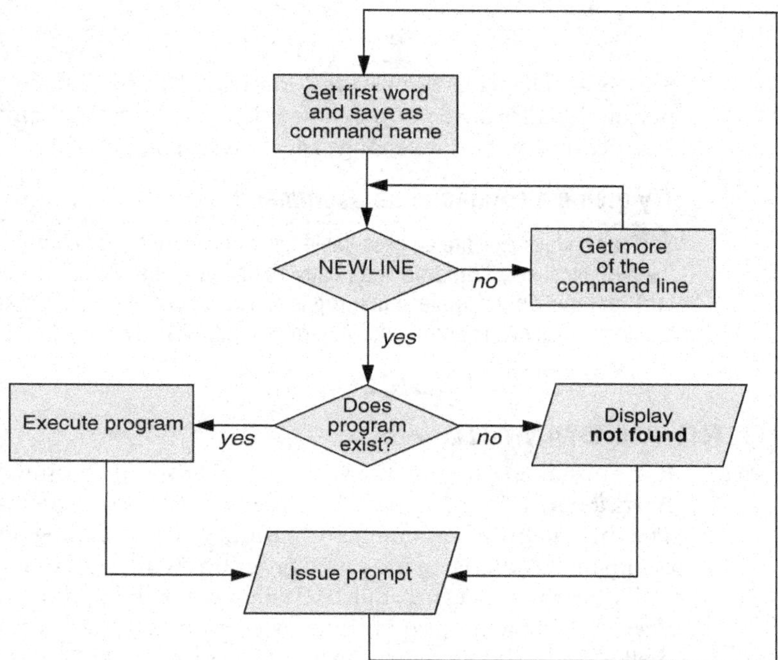

Figure 5-2 Processing the command line

to execute. When you specify a simple filename (no slash), the shell searches through a list of directories for a filename that matches the specified name and for which you have execute permission. The shell does not look through all directories but only the ones specified by the variable named **PATH**. Refer to page 318 (bash) or page 403 (tcsh) for more information on **PATH**. Also refer to the discussion of the which and whereis utilities on page 69.

When it cannot find the file, bash displays the following message:

```
$ abc
bash: abc: command not found...
```

Some systems are set up to suggest where you might be able to find the program you tried to run. One reason the shell might not be able to find the executable file is that it is not in a directory listed in the **PATH** variable. Under bash the following command temporarily adds the working directory (.) to **PATH**:

```
$ PATH=$PATH:.
```

For security reasons, it is poor practice to add the working directory to **PATH** permanently; see the following tip and the one on page 319.

When the shell finds the file but cannot execute it (i.e., because you do not have execute permission for the file), it displays a message similar to

```
$ def
bash: ./def: Permission denied
```

See "ls –l: Displays Permissions" on page 100 for information on displaying access permissions for a file and "chmod: Changes Access Permissions" on page 102 for instructions on how to change file access permissions.

Try giving a command as ./*command*

tip You can always execute an executable file in the working directory by prepending **./** to the name of the file. Because **./filename** is a relative pathname, the shell does not consult **PATH** when looking for **filename**. For example, if **myprog** is an executable file in the working directory, you can execute it using the following command (regardless of how **PATH** is set):

```
$ ./myprog
```

EXECUTING A COMMAND

Process If it finds an executable file with the name specified on the command line, the shell starts a new process. A *process* is the execution of a command by Linux (page 333). The shell makes each command-line argument, including options and the name of the command, available to the called program. While the command is executing, the shell waits for the process to finish. At this point the shell is in an inactive state named *sleep*. When the program finishes execution, it passes its exit status (page 477) to the shell. The shell then returns to an active state (wakes up), issues a prompt, and waits for another command.

The shell does not process arguments Because the shell does not process command-line arguments but merely passes them to the called program, the shell has no way of knowing whether a particular option or other argument is valid for a given program. Any error or usage messages about options or arguments come from the program itself. Some utilities ignore bad options.

EDITING THE COMMAND LINE

You can repeat and edit previous commands and edit the current command line. See page 31, page 338 (bash), and page 393 (tcsh) for more information.

STANDARD INPUT AND STANDARD OUTPUT

Standard output is a place to which a program can send information (e.g., text). The program never "knows" where the information it sends to standard output is going (Figure 5-3). The information can go to a printer, an ordinary file, or the screen. The following sections show that by default the shell directs standard output from a command to the screen[1] and describe how you can cause the shell to redirect this output to another file.

Standard input is a place a program gets information from; by default, the shell directs standard input from the keyboard. As with standard output, the program never "knows" where the information comes from. The following sections explain how to redirect standard input to a command so it comes from an ordinary file instead of from the keyboard.

In addition to standard input and standard output, a running program has a place to send error messages: *standard error*. By default, the shell directs standard error to the screen. Refer to page 292 (bash) and page 389 (tcsh) for more information on redirecting standard error.

optional By convention, a process expects that the program that called it (frequently the shell) has set up standard input, standard output, and standard error so the process can use them immediately. The called process does not *have* to know which files or devices are connected to standard input, standard output, or standard error.

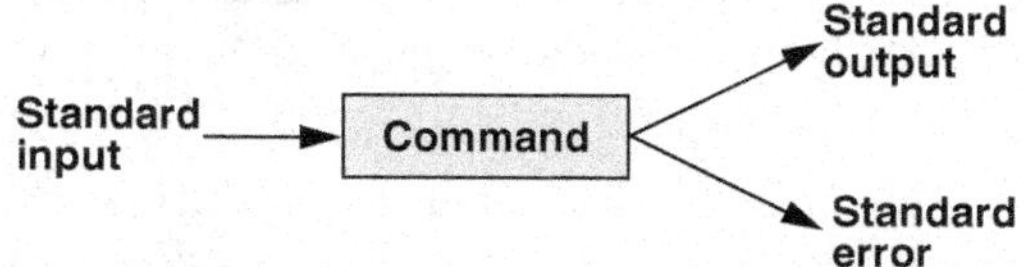

Figure 5-3 The command does not know where standard input comes from or where standard output and standard error go

1. This book uses the term *screen* to refer to a screen, terminal emulator window, or workstation—in other words, to the device that the shell displays its prompt and messages on.

However, a process *can* query the kernel to get information about the device that standard input, standard output, or standard error is connected to. For example, the ls utility displays output in multiple columns when the output goes to the screen, but generates a single column of output when the output is redirected to a file or another program. The ls utility uses the **isatty()** system call to determine if output is going to the screen (a tty). In addition, ls can use another system call to determine the width of the screen it is sending output to; with this information it can modify its output to fit the screen. Compare the output of ls by itself and when you send it through a pipeline to less. See page 468 for information on how you can determine if standard input and standard output of shell scripts is going to/coming from the terminal.

THE SCREEN AS A FILE

Device file Chapter 4 introduced ordinary files, directory files, and hard and soft links. Linux has an additional type of file: a device file. A *device file* resides in the file structure, usually in the **/dev** directory, and represents a peripheral device, such as a terminal, printer, or disk drive.

The device name the who utility displays following a username is the filename of the terminal that user is working on. For example, when who displays the device name **pts/4**, the pathname of the terminal is **/dev/pts/4**. When you work with multiple windows, each window has its own device name. You can also use the tty utility to display the name of the device that you give the command from. Although you would not normally have occasion to do so, you can read from and write to this file as though it were a text file. Reading from the device file that represents the terminal you are using reads what you enter on the keyboard; writing to it displays what you write on the screen.

THE KEYBOARD AND SCREEN AS STANDARD INPUT AND STANDARD OUTPUT

After you log in, the shell directs standard output of commands you enter to the device file that represents the terminal (Figure 5-4). Directing output in this manner causes it to appear on the screen. The shell also directs standard input to come from the same file, so commands receive as input anything you type on the keyboard.

cat The cat utility provides a good example of the way the keyboard and screen function as standard input and standard output, respectively. When you run cat, it copies a file to standard output. Because the shell directs standard output to the screen, cat displays the file on the screen.

Up to this point cat has taken its input from the filename (argument) you specify on the command line. When you do not give cat an argument (that is, when you give the command cat followed immediately by RETURN), cat takes its input from standard input. Thus, when called without an argument, cat copies standard input to standard output, one line at a time.

To see how cat works, type **cat** and press RETURN in response to the shell prompt. Nothing happens. Enter a line of text and press RETURN. The same line appears just under the one you entered. The cat utility is working. Because the shell associates cat's standard input with the keyboard and cat's standard output with the screen, when you type a line of text cat copies the text from standard input (the keyboard) to standard output (the screen). Figure 5-5 shows this exchange.

CONTROL-D signals EOF

The cat utility keeps copying text until you enter CONTROL-D on a line by itself. Pressing CONTROL-D causes the tty device driver to send an EOF (end of file) signal to cat. This signal indicates to cat that it has reached the end of standard input and there is no more text for it to copy. The cat utility then finishes execution and returns control to the shell, which displays a prompt.

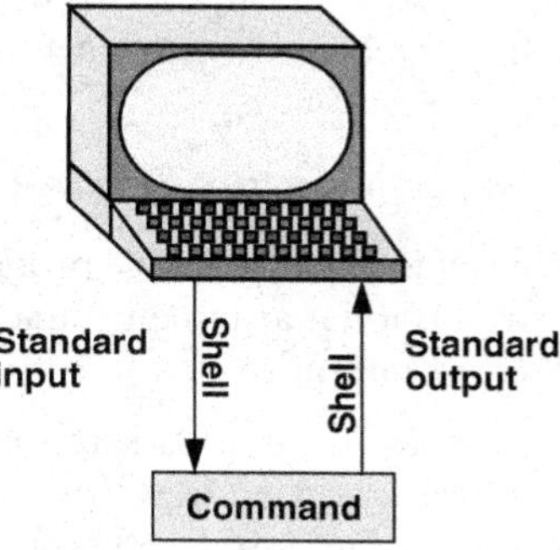

Figure 5-4 By default, standard input comes from the keyboard, and standard output goes to the screen

```
$ cat
This is a line of text.
This is a line of text.
Cat keeps copying lines of text
Cat keeps copying lines of text
until you press CONTROL-D at the beginning
until you press CONTROL-D at the beginning
of a line.
of a line.
CONTROL-D
$
```

Figure 5-5 The cat utility copies standard input to standard output

REDIRECTION

The term *redirection* encompasses the various ways you can cause the shell to alter where standard input of a command comes from and where standard output goes to. By default, the shell associates standard input and standard output of a command with the keyboard and the screen. You can cause the shell to redirect standard input or standard output of any command by associating the input or output with a command or file other than the device file representing the keyboard or the screen. This section demonstrates how to redirect input/output from/to text files and utilities.

REDIRECTING STANDARD OUTPUT

The *redirect output symbol* (**>**) instructs the shell to redirect the output of a command to the specified file instead of to the screen (Figure 5-6). The syntax of a command line that redirects output is

command [arguments] > *filename*

where ***command*** is any executable program (e.g., an application program or a utility), ***arguments*** are optional arguments, and ***filename*** is the name of the ordinary file the shell redirects the output to.

Figure 5-7 uses cat to demonstrate output redirection. This figure contrasts with Figure 5-5, where standard input *and* standard output are associated with the keyboard and screen. The input in Figure 5-7 comes from the keyboard. The redirect output symbol on the command line causes the shell to associate cat's standard output with the **sample.txt** file specified following this symbol.

Redirecting output can destroy a file I

caution Use caution when you redirect output to a file. If the file exists, the shell will overwrite it and destroy its contents. For more information see the tip "Redirecting output can destroy a file II" on page 143.

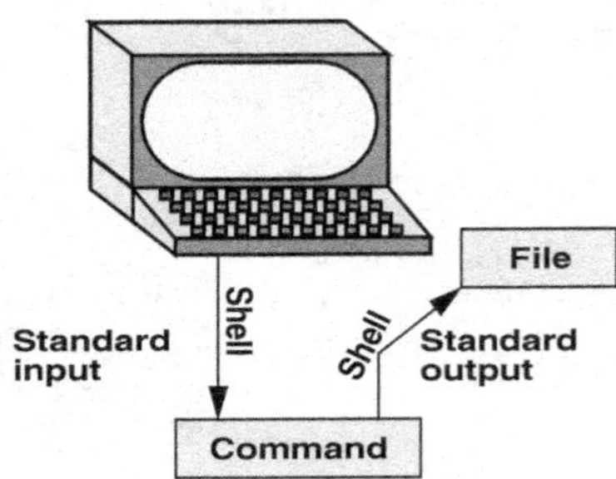

Figure 5-6 Redirecting standard output

After giving the command and typing the text shown in Figure 5-7, the **sample.txt** file contains the text you entered. You can use cat with an argument of **sample.txt** to display this file. The next section shows another way to use cat to display the file.

Figure 5-7 shows that redirecting standard output from cat is a handy way to create a file without using an editor. The drawback is that once you enter a line and press RETURN, you cannot edit the text until after you finish creating the file. While you are entering a line, the erase and kill keys work to delete text on that line. This procedure is useful for creating short, simple files.

Figure 5-8 shows how to run cat and use the redirect output symbol to *catenate* (join one after the other—the derivation of the name of the cat utility) several files into one larger file. The first three commands display the contents of three files: **stationery**, **tape**, and **pens**. The next command shows cat with three filenames as arguments. When you call it with more than one filename, cat copies the files, one at a time, to standard output. This command redirects standard output to the file **supply_orders**. The final cat command shows that **supply_orders** contains the contents of the three original files.

```
$ cat > sample.txt
This text is being entered at the keyboard and
cat is copying it to a file.
Press CONTROL-D to indicate the
end of file.
CONTROL-D
$
```

Figure 5-7 cat with its output redirected

```
$ cat stationery
2,000 sheets letterhead ordered:   October 7
$ cat tape
1 box masking tape ordered:        October 14
5 boxes filament tape ordered:     October 28
$ cat pens
12 doz. black pens ordered:        October 4

$ cat stationery tape pens > supply_orders

$ cat supply_orders
2,000 sheets letterhead ordered:   October 7
1 box masking tape ordered:        October 14
5 boxes filament tape ordered:     October 28
12 doz. black pens ordered:        October 4
```

Figure 5-8 Using cat to catenate files

REDIRECTING STANDARD INPUT

Just as you can redirect standard output, so you can redirect standard input. The *redirect input symbol* (**<**) instructs the shell to redirect a command's input to come from the specified file instead of from the keyboard (Figure 5-9). The syntax of a command line that redirects input is

command [arguments] < filename

where ***command*** is any executable program (such as an application program or a utility), ***arguments*** are optional arguments, and ***filename*** is the name of the ordinary file the shell redirects the input from.

Figure 5-10 shows cat with its input redirected from the **supply_orders** file created in Figure 5-8 and standard output going to the screen. This setup causes cat to display the **supply_orders** file on the screen. The system automatically supplies an EOF signal at the end of an ordinary file.

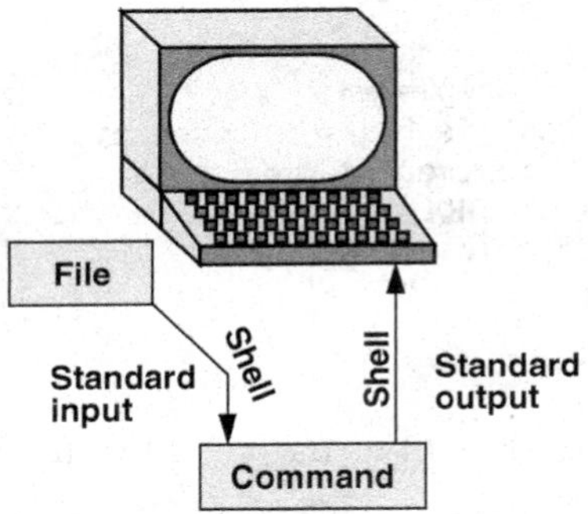

Figure 5-9 Redirecting standard input

```
$ date > whoson
$ cat whoson
Tues Mar 27 14:31:18 PST 2018
$ who >> whoson
$ cat whoson
Tues Mar 27 14:31:18 PST 2018
sam          tty1          2018-03-27 05:00(:0)
max          pts/4         2018-03-27 12:23(:0.0)
max          pts/5         2018-03-27 12:33(:0.0)
zach         pts/7         2018-03-26 08:45 (172.16.192.1)
```

Figure 5-10 Redirecting and appending output

Utilities that take input from a file or standard input

Giving a cat command with input redirected from a file yields the same result as giving a cat command with the filename as an argument. The cat utility is a member of a class of utilities that function in this manner. Other members of this class of utilities include lpr, sort, grep, and Perl. These utilities first examine the command line that called them. If the command line includes a filename as an argument, the utility takes its input from the specified file. If no filename argument is present, the utility takes its input from standard input. It is the utility or program—not the shell or operating system—that functions in this manner.

Redirecting output can destroy a file II

caution Depending on which shell you are using and how the environment is set up, a command such as the following can yield undesired results:

```
$ cat orange pear > orange
cat: orange: input file is output file
```

Although cat displays an error message, the shell destroys the contents of the existing **orange** file. The new **orange** file will have the same contents as **pear** because the first action the shell takes when it sees the redirection symbol (**>**) is to remove the contents of the original **orange** file. If you want to catenate two files into one, use cat to put the two files into a temporary file and then use mv to rename the temporary file:

```
$ cat orange pear > temp
$ mv temp orange
```

What happens in the next example can be even worse. The user giving the command wants to search through files **a**, **b**, and **c** for the word **apple** and redirect the output from grep (page 56) to the file **a.output**. Unfortunately, the user enters the filename as **a output**, omitting the period and inserting a SPACE in its place:

```
$ grep apple a b c > a output
grep: output: No such file or directory
```

The shell obediently removes the contents of **a** and then calls grep. The error message could take a moment to appear, giving you a sense that the command is running correctly. Even after you see the error message, it might take a while to realize that you have destroyed the contents of **a**.

noclobber: PREVENTS OVERWRITING FILES

The shell provides the **noclobber** feature, which prevents you from overwriting a file using redirection. Enable this feature by setting **noclobber** using the command **set –o noclobber**. The same command with **+o** unsets **noclobber**. Under tcsh use **set noclobber** and **unset noclobber**. With **noclobber** set, if you redirect output to an existing file, theshell displays an error message and does not execute the command. Run under bash and tcsh, the following examples create a file using touch, set **noclobber**, attempt to redirect the output from echo to the newly created file, unset **noclobber**, and perform the same redirection:

bash

```
$ touch tmp
$ set -o noclobber
$ echo "hi there" > tmp
-bash: tmp: cannot overwrite existing file
$ set +o noclobber
$ echo "hi there" > tmp
```

tcsh

```
tcsh $ touch tmp
tcsh $ set noclobber
tcsh $ echo "hi there" > tmp
tmp: File exists.
tcsh $ unset noclobber
tcsh $ echo "hi there" > tmp
```

You can override **noclobber** by putting a pipe symbol (tcsh uses an exclamation point) after the redirect symbol (>|). In the following example, the user creates a file by redirecting the output of date. Next, the user sets the **noclobber** variable and redirects output to the same file again. The shell displays an error message. Then the user places a pipe symbol after the redirect symbol, and the shell allows the user to overwrite the file.

```
$ date > tmp2
$ set -o noclobber
$ date > tmp2
-bash: tmp2: cannot overwrite existing file
$ date >| tmp2
```

For more information on using **noclobber** under tcsh, refer to page 407.

Do not trust noclobber

caution Appending output is simpler than the two-step procedure described in the preceding caution box but you must be careful to include both greater than signs. If you accidentally use only one greater than sign and the **noclobber** feature is not set, the shell will overwrite the **orange** file. Even if you have the **noclobber** feature turned on, it is a good idea to keep backup copies of the files you are manipulating in case you make a mistake.

Although it protects you from overwriting a file using redirection, **noclobber** does not stop you from overwriting a file using cp or mv. These utilities include the **–i** (interactive) option that helps protect you from this type of mistake by verifying your intentions when you try to overwrite a file. For more information see the tip "cp can destroy a file" on page 54.

APPENDING STANDARD OUTPUT TO A FILE

The *append output symbol* (>>) causes the shell to add new information to the end of a file, leaving existing information intact. This symbol provides a convenient way of catenating two files into one. The following commands demonstrate the action of the append output symbol. The second command accomplishes the catenation described in the preceding caution box:

```
$ cat orange
this is orange
$ cat pear >> orange
$ cat orange
this is orange
this is pear
```

The first command displays the contents of the **orange** file. The second command appends the contents of the **pear** file to the **orange** file. The final command displays the result.

Figure 5-10 shows how to create a file that contains the date and time (the output from date), followed by a list of who is logged in (the output from who). The first command in the example redirects the output from date to the file named **whoson**. Then cat displays the file. The next command appends the output from who to the **whoson** file. Finally, cat displays the file containing the output of both utilities.

/dev/null: MAKING DATA DISAPPEAR

The **/dev/null** device is a *data sink*, commonly referred to as a *bit bucket*. You can redirect output you do not want to keep or see to **/dev/null**, and the output will disappear without a trace:

```
$ echo "hi there" > /dev/null
$
```

Reading from **/dev/null** yields a null string. The following command truncates the file named **messages** to zero length while preserving the ownership and permissions of the file:

```
$ ls -lh messages
-rw-rw-r--. 1 sam pubs 125K 03-16 14:30 messages
$ cat /dev/null > messages
$ ls -lh messages
-rw-rw-r--. 1 sam pubs 0 03-16 14:32 messages
```

PIPELINES

A *pipeline* consists of one or more commands separated by a pipe symbol (|). The shell connects standard output (and optionally standard error) of the command preceding the pipe symbol to standard input of the command following the pipe symbol. A pipeline has the same effect as redirecting standard output of one command to a file and then using that file as standard input to another command. A pipeline does away with separate commands and the intermediate file. The syntax of a pipeline is

command_a [arguments] | command_b [arguments]

The preceding command line uses a pipeline to effect the same result as the following three commands:

command_a [arguments] > temp
command_b [arguments] < temp
rm temp

```
$ cat < supply_orders
2,000 sheets letterhead ordered:    October 7
1 box masking tape ordered:         October 14
5 boxes filament tape ordered:      October 28
12 doz. black pens ordered:         October 4
```

Figure 5-11 cat with its input redirected

In the preceding sequence of commands, the first line redirects standard output from ***command_a*** to an intermediate file named ***temp***. The second line redirects standard input for ***command_b*** to come from ***temp***. The final line deletes ***temp***. The pipeline syntax is not only easier to type but also is more efficient because it does not create a temporary file.

optional More precisely, a bash pipeline comprises one or more simple commands (page 133) separated by a | or |& control operator. A pipeline has the syntax:

[time] [!] ***command1*** *[| | |&* ***command2 ...*** *]*

where *time* is an optional utility that summarizes the system resources used by the pipeline, *!* logically negates the exit status returned by the pipeline, and the ***commands*** are simple commands (page 133) separated by | or |&. The | control operator sends standard output of ***command1*** to standard input of ***command2***. The |& control operator is short for **2>&1 |** (see "Sending errors through a pipeline" on page 293) and sends standard output and standard error of ***command1*** to standard input of ***command2***. The exit status of a pipeline is the exit status of the last simple command unless **pipefail** (page 363) is set, in which case the exit status is the rightmost simple command that failed (returned a nonzero exit status) or zero if all simple commands completed successfully.

EXAMPLES OF PIPELINES

tr You can include in a pipeline any utility that accepts input either from a file specified on the command line or from standard input. You can also include utilities that accept input only from standard input. For example, the tr (translate; page 1014) utility takes its input from standard input only. In its simplest usage tr has the syntax:

tr ***string1 string2***

The tr utility accepts input from standard input and looks for characters that match one of the characters in ***string1***. Upon finding a match, it translates the matched character in ***string1*** to the corresponding character in ***string2***. That is, the first character in ***string1*** translates into the first character in ***string2***, and so forth. The tr utility sends its output to standard output. In both of the following tr commands, tr displays the contents of the **abstract** file with the letters **a**, **b**, and **c** translated into **A**, **B**, and **C**, respectively:

```
$ cat abstract
I took a cab today!

$ cat abstract | tr abc ABC
I took A CAB todAy!
$ tr abc ABC < abstract
I took A CAB todAy!
```

The tr utility does not change the contents of the original file; it cannot change the original file because it does not "know" the source of its input.

lpr The lpr (line printer) utility accepts input from either a file or standard input. When you type the name of a file following lpr on the command line, it places that file in the print queue. When you do not specify a filename on the command line, lpr takes input from standard input. This feature enables you to use a pipeline to redirect input to lpr. The first set of commands in Figure 5-12 shows how you can use ls and lpr with an intermediate file (**temp**) to send a list of the files in the working directory to the printer. If the **temp** file exists, the first command overwrites its contents. The second set of commands uses a pipeline to send the same list (with the exception of **temp**) to the printer.

sort The commands in Figure 5-13 redirect the output from the who utility to **temp** and then display this file in sorted order. The sort utility (page 58) takes its input from the file specified on the command line or, when a file is not specified, from standard input; it sends its output to standard output. The sort command line in Figure 5-13 takes its input from standard input, which is redirected (**<**) to come from **temp**. The output sort sends to the screen lists the users in sorted (alphabetical) order. Because sort can take its input from standard input or from a file named on the command line, omitting the **<** symbol from Figure 5-13 yields the same result.

```
$ ls > temp
$ lpr temp
$ rm temp

or

$ ls | lpr
```

Figure 5-12 A pipeline

```
$ who > temp
$ sort < temp
max          pts/4        2018-03-24 12:23
max          pts/5        2018-03-24 12:33
sam          tty1         2018-03-24 05:00
zach         pts/7        2018-03-23 08:45
$ rm temp
```

Figure 5-13 Using a temporary file to store intermediate results

Figure 5-14 achieves the same result without creating the **temp** file. Using a pipeline, the shell redirects the output from who to the input of sort. The sort utility takes input from standard input because no filename follows it on the command line.

grep When many people are using the system and you want information about only one of them, you can send the output from who to grep (pages 56 and 853) using a pipeline. The grep utility displays the line containing the string you specify—**sam** in the following example.

```
$ who | grep sam
sam        tty1         2018-03-24 05:00
```

less and more Another way of handling output that is too long to fit on the screen, such as a list of files in a crowded directory, is to use a pipeline to send the output through less or more (both on page 53).

```
$ ls | less
```

The less utility displays text one screen at a time. To view another screen of text, press the SPACE bar. To view one more line, press RETURN. Press **h** for help and **q** to quit.

optional The pipe symbol (|) implies continuation. Thus, the following command line

```
$ who | grep 'sam'
sam        tty1         2018-03-24 05:00
```

is the same as these command lines:

```
$ who |
> grep 'sam'
sam        tty1         2018-03-24 05:00
```

When the shell parses a line that ends with a pipe symbol, it requires more input before it can execute the command line. In an interactive environment, it issues a secondary prompt (>; page 321) as shown above. Within a shell script, it processes the next line as a continuation of the line that ends with the pipe symbol. See page 512 for information about control operators and implicit command-line continuation.

```
$ who | sort
max        pts/4        2018-03-24 12:23
max        pts/5        2018-03-24 12:33
sam        tty1         2018-03-24 05:00
zach       pts/7        2018-03-23 08:45
```

Figure 5-14 A pipeline doing the work of a temporary file

```
$ who | tee who.out | grep sam
sam          tty1          2018-03-24 05:00
$ cat who.out
sam          tty1          2018-03-24 05:00
max          pts/4         2018-03-24 12:23
max          pts/5         2018-03-24 12:33
zach         pts/7         2018 -03-23 08:45
```

Figure 5-15 tee sends its output to a file and to standard output

Filters

A *filter* is a command that processes an input stream of data to produce an output stream of data. A command line that includes a filter uses a pipe symbol to connect standard output of one command to standard input of the filter. Another pipe symbol connects standard output of the filter to standard input of another command. Not all utilities can be used as filters.

In the following example, sort is a filter, taking standard input from standard output of who and using a pipe symbol to redirect standard output to standard input of lpr. This command line sends the sorted output of who to the printer:

```
$ who | sort | lpr
```

The preceding example demonstrates the power of the shell combined with the versatility of Linux utilities. The three utilities who, sort, and lpr were not designed to work with one another, but they all use standard input and standard output in the conventional way. By using the shell to handle input and output, you can piece standard utilities together on the command line to achieve the results you want.

tee The tee utility copies its standard input both to a file and to standard output. This utility is aptly named: It takes a single stream of input and sends the output in two directions. In Figure 5-15 the output of who is sent via a pipeline to standard input of tee. The tee utility saves a copy of standard input in a file named **who.out** and also sends a copy to standard output. Standard output of tee goes via a pipeline to standard input of grep, which displays only those lines containing the string **sam**. Use tee with the **–a** (append) option to cause it to append to a file instead of overwriting it.

optional

Lists

A *list* is one or more pipelines (including simple commands), each separated from the next by one of the following control operators: ;, &, &&, or ||. The && and || control operators have equal precedence; they are followed by ; and &, which have equal precedence. The ; control operator is covered on page 300 and & on page 300. See page 512 for information about control operators and implicit command-line continuation.

An AND list has the syntax:

pipeline1 && *pipeline2*

where *pipeline2* is executed if and only if *pipeline1* returns a *true* (zero) exit status. In the following example, the first command in the list fails (and displays an error message) so the shell does not execute the second command (**cd /newdir**; because it is not executed, it does not display an error message):

```
$ mkdir /newdir && cd /newdir
mkdir: cannot create directory '/newdir': Permission denied
```

The exit status of AND and OR lists is the exit status of the last command in the list that is executed. The exit status of the preceding list is *false* because mkdir was the last command executed and it failed.

An OR list has the syntax:

pipeline1 || *pipeline2*

where *pipeline2* is executed if and only if *pipeline1* returns a *false* (nonzero) exit status. In the next example, the first command (ping tests the connection to a remote machine and sends standard output and standard error to **/dev/null**) in the list fails so the shell executes the second command (it displays a message). If the first command had completed successfully, the shell would not have executed the second command (and would not have displayed the message). The list returns an exit status of *true*.

```
$ ping -c1 station &>/dev/null || echo "station is down"
station is down
```

For more information refer to "&& and || Boolean Control Operators" on page 301.

RUNNING A COMMAND IN THE BACKGROUND

Foreground All commands up to this point have been run in the foreground. When you run a command in the *foreground*, the shell waits for it to finish before displaying another prompt and allowing you to continue. When you run a command in the *background*, you do not have to wait for the command to finish before running another command.

Jobs A *job* is another name for a process running a pipeline (which can be a simple command). You can have only one foreground job on a screen, but you can have many background jobs. By running more than one job at a time, you are using one of Linux's features: multitasking. Running a command in the background can be useful when the command will run for a long time and does not need supervision. It leaves the screen free so you can use it for other work.

Job number, PID number To run a command in the background, type an ampersand (&; a control operator) just before the RETURN that ends the command line. The shell assigns a small number to the job and displays this *job number* between brackets. Following the job number, the shell displays the *process identification (PID) number*—a larger number assigned by the operating system. Each of these numbers identifies the command running in the background. The shell then displays another prompt, and you can enter another command. When the background job finishes, the shell displays a message giving both the job number and the command line used to run the command.

The following example runs in the background; it is a pipeline that sends the output of ls to lpr, which sends it to the printer.

```
$ ls -l | lpr &
[1] 22092
$
```

The [1] following the command line indicates that the shell has assigned job number 1 to this job. The **22092** is the PID number of the first command in the job. (The TC Shell shows PID numbers for all commands in a job.) When this background job completes execution, you see the message

```
[1]+ Done              ls -l | lpr
```

(In place of **ls –l**, the shell might display something similar to **ls ––color=auto –l**. This difference is due to the fact that ls is aliased [page 352] to **ls ––color=auto**.)

Moving a Job from the Foreground to the Background

CONTROL-Z and bg You can suspend a foreground job (stop it from running) by pressing the suspend key, usually CONTROL-Z. The shell then stops the process and disconnects standard input from the keyboard. It does, however, still send standard output and standard error to the screen. You can put a suspended job in the background and restart it by using the bg command followed by the job number. You do not need to specify the job number when there is only one suspended job.

Redirect the output of a job you run in the background to keep it from interfering with whatever you are working on in the foreground (on the screen). Refer to "Control Operators: Separate and Group Commands" on page 299 for more detail about background tasks.

fg Only the foreground job can take input from the keyboard. To connect the keyboard to a program running in the background, you must bring the program to the foreground. To do so, type **fg** without any arguments when only one job is in the background. When more than one job is in the background, type **fg**, or a percent sign (%), followed by the number of the job you want to bring to the foreground. The shell displays the command you used to start the job (**promptme** in the following example), and you can enter input the program requires to continue.

```
$ fg 1
promptme
```

kill: Aborting a Background Job

The interrupt key (usually CONTROL-C) cannot abort a background process because the keyboard is not attached to the job; you must use kill (page 866) for this purpose. Follow **kill** on the command line with either the PID number of the process you want to abort or a percent sign (%) followed by the job number.

Determining the PID of a process using ps If you forget a PID number, you can use the ps (process status) utility (page 334) to display it. The following example runs a find command in the background, uses ps to display the PID number of the process, and aborts the job using kill:

```
$ find / -name memo55 > mem.out &
[1] 18228
$ ps | grep find
18228 pts/10   00:00:01 find
$ kill 18228
[1]+  Terminated              find / -name memo55 > mem.out
$
```

Determining the number of a job using jobs If you forget a job number, you can use the jobs command to display a list of jobs that includes job numbers. The next example is similar to the previous one except it uses the job number instead of the PID number to identify the job to be killed. Sometimes the message saying the job is terminated does not appear until you press RETURN after the RETURN that executes the kill command.

```
$ find / -name memo55 > mem.out &
[1] 18236

$ bigjob &
[2] 18237

$ jobs
[1]-  Running                 find / -name memo55 > mem.out &
[2]+  Running                 bigjob &
$ kill %1
$ RETURN
[1]-  Terminated              find / -name memo55 > mem.out
$
```

Filename Generation/Pathname Expansion

Wildcards, globbing When you specify an abbreviated filename that contains *special characters,* also called *metacharacters,* the shell can generate filenames that match the names of existing files. These special characters are also referred to as *wildcards* because they act much as the jokers do in a deck of cards. When one of these characters appears in an argument on the command line, the shell expands that argument in sorted order into a list of filenames and passes the list to the program called by the command line. Filenames that contain these special characters are called *ambiguous file references* because they do not refer to one specific file. The process the shell performs on these filenames is called *pathname expansion* or *globbing*.

Ambiguous file references can quickly refer to a group of files with similar names, saving the effort of typing the names individually. They can also help find a file whose name you do not remember in its entirety. If no filename matches the ambiguous file reference, the shell generally passes the unexpanded reference—special characters and all—to the command. See "Brace Expansion" on page 366 for a technique that generates strings that do not necessarily match filenames.

The ? Special Character

The question mark (?) is a special character that causes the shell to generate filenames. It matches any single character in the name of an existing file. The following command uses this special character in an argument to the lpr utility:

```
$ lpr memo?
```

The shell expands the **memo?** argument and generates a list of files in the working directory that have names composed of **memo** followed by any single character. The shell then passes this list to lpr. The lpr utility never "knows" the shell generated the filenames it was called with. If no filename matches the ambiguous file reference, the shell passes the string itself (**memo?**) to lpr or, if it is set up to do so, passes a null string (see **nullglob** on page 363).

The following example uses ls first to display the names of all files in the working directory and then to display the filenames that **memo?** matches:

```
$ ls
mem    memo12  memo9  memomax    newmemo5
memo   memo5   memoa  memos

$ ls memo?
memo5  memo9  memoa  memos
```

The **memo?** ambiguous file reference does not match **mem**, **memo**, **memo12**, **memomax**, or **newmemo5**. You can also use a question mark in the middle of an ambiguous file reference:

```
$ ls
7may4report  may4report     mayqreport  may_report
may14report  may4report.79  mayreport   may.report

$ ls may?report
may4report  mayqreport  may_report  may.report
```

echo You can use echo and ls to practice generating filenames. The echo utility displays the arguments the shell passes to it:

```
$ echo may?report
may4report mayqreport may_report may.report
```

The shell first expands the ambiguous file reference into a list of files in the working directory that match the string **may?report**. It then passes this list to echo, as though you had entered the list of filenames as arguments to echo. The echo utility displays the list of filenames.

A question mark does not match a leading period (one that indicates a hidden filename; page 88). When you want to match filenames that begin with a period, you must explicitly include the period in the ambiguous file reference.

THE * SPECIAL CHARACTER

The asterisk (*) performs a function similar to that of the question mark but matches any number of characters, *including zero characters,* in a filename. The following example first shows all files in the working directory and then shows commands that display all the filenames that begin with the string **memo**, end with the string **mo**, and contain the string **alx**:

```
$ ls
amemo   memalx   memo.0612   memoalx.0620   memorandum   sallymemo
mem     memo     memoa       memoalx.keep   memosally    user.memo

$ echo memo*
memo memo.0612 memoa memoalx.0620 memoalx.keep memorandum memosally

$ echo *mo
amemo memo sallymemo user.memo

$ echo *alx*
memalx memoalx.0620 memoalx.keep
```

The ambiguous file reference **memo*** does not match **amemo, mem, sallymemo,** or **user.memo.** Like the question mark, an asterisk does *not* match a leading period in a filename.

The **–a** option causes ls to display hidden filenames (page 88). The command **echo *** does not display **.** (the working directory), **..** (the parent of the working directory), **.aaa**, or **.profile**. In contrast, the command **echo .*** displays only those four names:

```
$ ls
aaa  memo.0612  memo.sally  report  sally.0612  saturday  thurs

$ ls -a
.   aaa   memo.0612   .profile  sally.0612  thurs
..  .aaa  memo.sally  report    saturday

$ echo *
```

```
aaa memo.0612 memo.sally report sally.0612 saturday thurs

$ echo .*
. .. .aaa .profile
```

In the following example, **.p*** does not match **memo.0612, private, reminder**, or **report**. The **ls .*** command causes ls to list **.private** and **.profile** in addition to the contents of the **.** directory (the working directory) and the **..** directory (the parent of the working directory). When called with the same argument, echo displays the names of files (including directories) in the working directory that begin with a dot (.) but not the contents of directories.

```
$ ls -a
.  ..  memo.0612  private  .private  .profile  reminder  report

$ echo .p*
.private .profile

$ ls .*
.private .profile
.:
memo.0612  private   reminder   report
..:
...

$ echo .*
. .. .private .profile
```

You can plan to take advantage of ambiguous file references when you establish conventions for naming files. For example, when you end the names of all text files with **.txt**, you can reference that group of files with ***.txt**. The next command uses this convention to send all text files in the working directory to the printer. The ampersand causes lpr to run in the background.

```
$ lpr *.txt &
```

The shell expands ambiguous file references

tip *The shell does the expansion* when it processes an ambiguous file reference, not the program that the shell runs. In the examples in this section, *the utilities* (ls, cat, echo, lpr) *never see the ambiguous file references.* The shell expands the ambiguous file references and passes a list of ordinary filenames to the utility. In the previous examples, echo demonstrates this fact because it simply displays its arguments; it never displays the ambiguous file reference.

THE [ ] SPECIAL CHARACTERS

A pair of brackets surrounding one or more characters causes the shell to match filenames containing the individual characters within the brackets. Whereas **memo?** matches **memo** followed by any character, **memo[17a]** is more restrictive: It matches only **memo1, memo7**, and **memoa**. The brackets define a *character class* that includes all the characters within the brackets. (GNU calls this a *character list;* a

GNU character class is something different.) The shell expands an argument that includes a character-class definition by substituting each member of the character class, *one at a time,* in place of the brackets and their contents. The shell then passes the list of matching filenames to the program it is calling.

Each character-class definition can replace only a single character within a filename. The brackets and their contents are like a question mark that substitutes only the members of the character class.

The first of the following commands lists the names of all files in the working directory that begin with **a**, **e**, **i**, **o**, or **u**. The second command displays the contents of the files named **page2.txt**, **page4.txt**, **page6.txt**, and **page8.txt**.

```
$ echo [aeiou]*
...

$ less page[2468].txt
...
```

A hyphen within brackets defines a range of characters within a character-class definition. For example, [6–9] represents [6789], [a–z] represents all lowercase letters in English, and [a–zA–Z] represents all letters, both uppercase and lowercase, in English.

The following command lines show three ways to print the files named **part0**, **part1**, **part2**, **part3**, and **part5**. Each of these command lines causes the shell to call lpr with five filenames:

```
$ lpr part0 part1 part2 part3 part5

$ lpr part[01235]

$ lpr part[0-35]
```

The first command line explicitly specifies the five filenames. The second and third command lines use ambiguous file references, incorporating character-class definitions. The shell expands the argument on the second command line to include all files that have names beginning with **part** and ending with any of the characters in the character class. The character class is explicitly defined as 0, 1, 2, 3, and 5. The third command line also uses a character-class definition but defines the character class to be all characters in the range 0–3 plus 5.

The following command line prints 39 files, **part0** through **part38**:

```
$ lpr part[0-9] part[12][0-9] part3[0-8]
```

The first of the following commands lists the files in the working directory whose names start with **a** through **m**. The second lists files whose names end with **x**, **y**, or **z**.

```
$ echo [a-m]*
...
```

```
$ echo *[x-z]
...
```

optional When an exclamation point (!) or a caret (^) immediately follows the opening bracket ([) that starts a character-class definition, the character class matches any character *not* between the brackets. Thus [^tsq]* matches any filename that does *not* begin with **t**, **s**, or **q**.

The following examples show that *[^ab] matches filenames that do not end with the letter **a** or **b** and that [^b-d]* matches filenames that do not begin with **b**, **c**, or **d**.

```
$ ls
aa  ab  ac  ad  ba  bb  bc  bd  cc  dd

$ ls *[^ab]
ac  ad  bc  bd  cc  dd

$ ls [^b-d]*
aa  ab  ac  ad
```

You can cause a character class to match a hyphen (–) or a closing bracket (]) by placing it immediately before the final (closing) bracket.

The next example demonstrates that the ls utility cannot interpret ambiguous file references. First, ls is called with an argument of **?old**. The shell expands **?old** into a matching filename, **hold**, and passes that name to ls. The second command is the same as the first, except the **?** is quoted (by preceding it with a backslash [\]; refer to "Special Characters" on page 50). Because the **?** is quoted, the shell does not recognize it as a special character and passes it to ls. The ls utility generates an error message saying that it cannot find a file named **?old** (because there is no file named **?old**).

```
$ ls ?old
hold

$ ls \?old
ls: ?old: No such file or directory
```

Like most utilities and programs, ls cannot interpret ambiguous file references; that work is left to the shell.

BUILTINS

A *builtin* is a utility (also called a *command*) that is built into a shell. Each of the shells has its own set of builtins. When it runs a builtin, the shell does not fork a new process. Consequently, builtins run more quickly and can affect the environment of the current shell. Because builtins are used in the same way as utilities, you will not typically be aware of whether a utility is built into the shell or is a stand-alone utility.

For example, echo is a shell builtin. It is also a stand-alone utility. The shell always executes a shell builtin before trying to find a command or utility with the same name. See page 489 for an in-depth discussion of builtin commands, page 503 for a list of bash builtins, and page 418 for a list of tcsh builtins.

Listing bash builtins To display a list of bash builtins, give the command **info bash shell builtin**. To display a page with information on each builtin, move the cursor to the **Bash Builtins** line and press RETURN. Alternatively, you can view the **builtins** man page.

Getting help with bash builtins You can use the bash **help** command to display information about bash builtins. See page 39 for more information.

Listing tcsh builtins To list tcsh builtins, give the command **man tcsh** to display the tcsh man page and then search for the second occurrence of **Builtin commands** by using the following two commands: **/Builtin commands** (search for the string) and **n** (search for the next occurrence of the string).

Chapter Summary

The shell is the Linux command interpreter. It scans the command line for proper syntax, picking out the command name and arguments. The name of the command is argument zero. The first argument is argument one, the second is argument two, and so on. Many programs use options to modify the effects of a command. Most Linux utilities identify an option by its leading one or two hyphens.

When you give it a command, the shell tries to find an executable program with the same name as the command. When it does, the shell executes the program. When it does not, the shell tells you it cannot find or execute the program. If the command is a simple filename, the shell searches the directories listed in the **PATH** variable to locate the command.

When it executes a command, the shell assigns one file or device to the command's standard input and another file to its standard output. By default, the shell causes a command's standard input to come from the keyboard and its standard output to go to the screen. You can instruct the shell to redirect a command's standard input from or standard output to any file or device. You can also connect standard output of one command to standard input of another command to form a pipeline. A filter is a command that reads its standard input from standard output of one command and writes its standard output to standard input of another command.

When a command runs in the foreground, the shell waits for the command to finish before it displays a prompt and allows you to continue. When you put an ampersand (&) at the end of a command line, the shell executes the command in the background and displays another prompt immediately. Run slow commands in the background when you want to enter other commands at the shell prompt. The jobs builtin displays a list of suspended jobs and jobs running in the background and includes the job number of each.

The shell interprets special characters on a command line to generate filenames. A reference that uses special characters (wildcards) to abbreviate a list of one or more filenames is called an ambiguous file reference. A question mark represents any single character, and an asterisk represents zero or more characters. A single character might also be represented by a character class: a list of characters within brackets.

A builtin is a utility that is built into a shell. Each shell has its own set of builtins. When it runs a builtin, the shell does not fork a new process. Consequently builtins run more quickly and can affect the environment of the current shell.

Utilities and Builtins Introduced in This Chapter

Table 5-1 lists the utilities introduced in this chapter.

Table 5-1 New utilities

Utility	Function
tr	Maps one string of characters to another (page 146)
tee	Sends standard input to both a file and standard output (page 149)
bg	Moves a process to the background (page 151)
fg	Moves a process to the foreground (page 151)
jobs	Displays a list of suspended jobs and jobs running in the background (page 152)

Exercises

1. What does the shell ordinarily do while a command is executing? What should you do if you do not want to wait for a command to finish before running another command?
2. Using sort as a filter, rewrite the following sequence of commands:

```
$ sort list > temp
$ lpr temp
$ rm temp
```

3. What is a PID number? Why are these numbers useful when you run processes in the background? Which utility displays the PID numbers of the commands you are running?
4. Assume the following files are in the working directory:

```
$ ls
intro       notesb      ref2        section1    section3    section4b
notesa      ref1        ref3        section2    section4a   sentrev
```

Give commands for each of the following, using wildcards to express filenames with as few characters as possible.

a. List all files that begin with **section**.

b. List the **section1**, **section2**, and **section3** files only.

c. List the **intro** file only.

   d. List the **section1**, **section3**, **ref1**, and **ref3** files.

5. Refer to Part VII or the info or man pages to determine which command will
   a. Display the number of lines in its standard input that contain the *word* **a** or **A**.
   b. Display only the names of the files in the working directory that contain the pattern **$(**.
   c. List the files in the working directory in reverse alphabetical order.
   d. Send a list of files in the working directory to the printer, sorted by size.

6. Give a command to
   a. Redirect standard output from a sort command to a file named **phone_list**. Assume the input file is named **numbers**.
   b. Translate all occurrences of the characters [and { to the character (, and all occurrences of the characters] and } to the character), in the file **permdemos.c**. (*Hint:* Refer to tr on page 1014.)
   c. Create a file named **book** that contains the contents of two other files: **part1** and **part2**.

7. The lpr and sort utilities accept input either from a file named on the command line or from standard input.
   a. Name two other utilities that function in a similar manner.
   b. Name a utility that accepts its input only from standard input.

8. Give an example of a command that uses grep
   a. With both input and output redirected.
   b. With only input redirected.
   c. With only output redirected.
   d. Within a pipeline.

   In which of the preceding cases is grep used as a filter?

9. Explain the following error message. Which filenames would a subsequent ls command display?

```
$ ls
abc  abd  abe  abf  abg  abh
$ rm abc ab*
rm: cannot remove 'abc': No such file or directory
```

ADVANCED EXERCISES

10. When you use the redirect output symbol (>) on a command line, the shell creates the output file immediately, before the command is executed. Demonstrate that this is true.

11. In experimenting with variables, Max accidentally deletes his **PATH** variable. He decides he does not need the **PATH** variable. Discuss some of the problems he could soon encounter and explain the reasons for these problems. How could he *easily* return **PATH** to its original value?
12. Assume permissions on a file allow you to write to the file but not to delete it.
    a. Give a command to empty the file without invoking an editor.
    b. Explain how you might have permission to modify a file that you cannot delete.
13. If you accidentally create a filename that contains a nonprinting character, such as a CONTROL character, how can you remove the file?
14. Why does the **noclobber** variable *not* protect you from overwriting an existing file with cp or mv?
15. Why do command names and filenames usually not have embedded SPACEs? How would you create a filename containing a SPACE? How would you remove it? (This is a thought exercise, not recommended practice. If you want to experiment, create a file and work in a directory that contains only your experimental file.)
16. Create a file named **answer** and give the following command:

```
$ > answers.0102 < answer cat
```

    Explain what the command does and why. What is a more conventional way of expressing this command?

PART II

THE EDITORS

6

THE vim EDITOR

IN THIS CHAPTER

OBJECTIVES

After reading this chapter you should be able to:

- Use vim to create and edit a file
- View vim online help
- Explain the difference between Command and Input modes
- Explain the purpose of the Work buffer
- List the commands that open a line above the cursor, append text to the end of a line, move the cursor to the first line of the file, and move the cursor to the middle line of the screen
- Describe Last Line mode and list some commands that use this mode
- Describe how to set and move the cursor to a marker
- List the commands that move the cursor backward and forward by characters and words
- Describe how to read a file into the Work buffer
- Explain how to search backward and forward for text and how to repeat that search

This chapter begins with a history and description of vi, the original, powerful, sometimes cryptic, interactive, visually oriented text editor. The chapter continues with a tutorial that explains how to use vim (vi improved—a vi clone supplied with or available for most Linux distributions) to create and edit a file. Much of the tutorial and the balance of the chapter apply to vi and other vi clones. Following the tutorial, the chapter delves into the details of many vim commands and explains how to use parameters to customize vim to meet your needs. It concludes with a quick reference/summary of vim commands.

HISTORY

Before vi was developed, the standard UNIX system editor was ed (available on most Linux systems), a line-oriented editor that made it difficult to see the context of your editing. Next came ex,[1] a superset of ed. The most notable advantage that ex has over ed is a display-editing facility that allows you to work with a full screen of text instead of just a line. While using ex, you can bring up the display-editing facility by giving a **vi** (Visual mode) command. People used this display-editing facility so extensively that the developers of ex made it possible to start the editor with the display-editing facility already running, rather than having to start ex and then give a **vi** command. Appropriately, they named the program vi. You can call the Visual mode from ex, and you can go back to ex while you are using vi. Start by running ex; give a **vi** command to switch to Visual mode, and give a **Q** command while in Visual mode to use ex. The **quit** command exits from ex.

vi clones Linux offers a number of versions, or *clones,* of vi. The most popular of these clones are elvis (elvis.the-little-red-haired-girl.org), nvi (an implementation of the original vi editor by Keith Bostic), vile (invisible-island.net/vile/vile.html), and vim (www.vim.org). Each clone offers additional features beyond those provided by the original vi.

The examples in this book are based on vim. Several Linux distributions support multiple versions of vim. For example, Fedora provides **/bin/vi**, a minimal build of vim that is compact and faster to load but offers fewer features, and **/usr/bin/vim**, a full-featured version of vim.

If you use one of the clones other than vim, or vi itself, you might notice slight differences from the examples presented in this chapter. The vim editor is compatible with almost all vi commands and runs on many platforms, including Windows, Macintosh, OS/2, UNIX, and Linux. Refer to the vim home page (www.vim.org) for more information and a very useful Tips section.

1. The ex program is usually a link to vi, which is a version of vim on some systems.

What vim is not The vim editor is not a text formatting program. It does not justify margins or provide the output formatting features of a sophisticated word processing system such as LibreOffice Writer (www.libreoffice.org). Rather, vim is a sophisticated text editor meant to be used to write code (C, HTML, Java, and so on), short notes, and input to a text formatting system, such as groff or troff. You can use fmt (page 831) to minimally format a text file you create with vim.

Reading this chapter Because vim is so large and powerful, this chapter describes only some of its features. Nonetheless, if vim is completely new to you, you might find even this limited set of commands overwhelming. The vim editor provides a variety of ways to accomplish most editing tasks. A useful strategy for learning vim is to begin by learning a subset of commands to accomplish basic editing tasks. Then, as you become more comfortable with the editor, you can learn other commands that enable you to edit a file more quickly and efficiently. The following tutorial section introduces a basic, useful set of vim commands and features that will enable you to create and edit a file.

TUTORIAL: USING vim TO CREATE AND EDIT A FILE

This section explains how to start vim, enter text, move the cursor, correct text, save the file to the disk, and exit from vim. The tutorial discusses three of the modes of operation of vim and explains how to switch from one mode to another.

vimtutor In addition to working with this tutorial, you might want to try vim's instructional program, vimtutor. Enter its name as a command to run it.

vimtutor **and** vim **help files are not installed by default**

tip To run vimtutor and to get help as described on page 171, you must install the **vim-enhanced** or **vim-runtime** package. See Appendix C for instructions.

Specifying a terminal Because vim takes advantage of features that are specific to various kinds of terminals, you must tell it what type of terminal or terminal emulator you are using. On many systems, and usually when you work on a terminal emulator, your terminal type is set automatically. If you need to specify your terminal type explicitly, refer to "Specifying a Terminal" on page 1050.

STARTING vim

Start vim with the following command to create and edit a file named **practice** (you might need to use the command **vi** or **vim.tiny** in place of **vim**):

```
$ vim practice
```

When you press RETURN, the command line disappears, and the screen looks similar to the one shown in Figure 6-1.

The tildes (~) at the left of the screen indicate the file is empty. They disappear as you add lines of text to the file. If the screen looks like a distorted version of the one shown in Figure 6-1, the terminal type is probably not set correctly (see "Problem," next).

The vi command might run vim

tip On some systems the command **vi** runs vim in vi-compatible mode (page 174).

The **practice** file is new, so it contains no text. The vim editor displays a message similar to the one shown in Figure 6-1 on the status (bottom) line of the terminal to indicate you are creating and editing a new file. When you edit an existing file, vim displays the first few lines of the file and gives status information about the file on the status line.

Problem If you start vim with a terminal type that is not in the **terminfo** database, vim displays an error message and waits for you to press RETURN or sets the terminal type to **ansi**, which works on many terminals.

Emergency exit To reset the terminal type, press ESCAPE and then give the following command to exit from vim and display the shell prompt:

```
:q!
```

When you enter the colon (**:**), vim moves the cursor to the bottom line of the screen. The characters **q!** tell vim to quit without saving your work. (You will not ordinarily exit from vim this way because you typically want to save your work.) You must press RETURN after you give this command. When the shell displays its prompt, refer to "Specifying a Terminal" on page 1050 and start vim again. If you start vim without a filename, it displays information about itself (Figure 6-2).

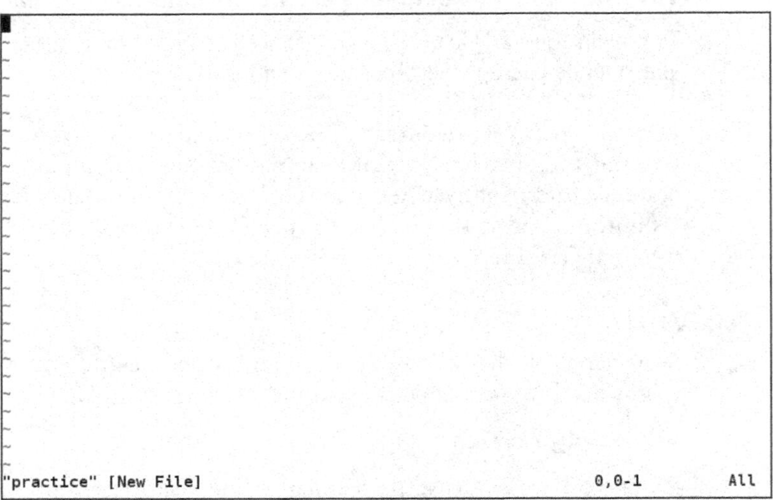

Figure 6-1 Starting vim

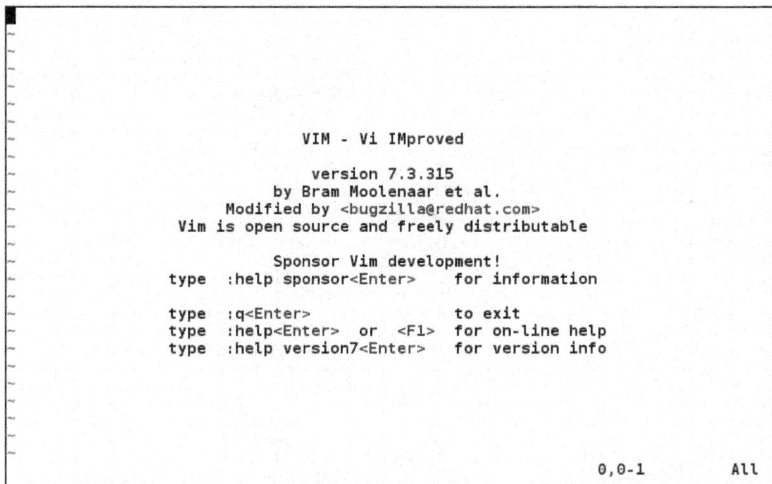

Figure 6-2 Starting vim without a filename

COMMAND AND INPUT MODES

Two of vim's modes of operation are *Command mode* (also called *Normal mode*) and *Input mode* (Figure 6-3). While vim is in Command mode, you can give vim commands. For example, you can delete text or exit from vim. You can also command vim to enter Input mode. In Input mode, vim accepts anything you enter as text and displays it on the screen. Press ESCAPE to return vim to Command mode. By default the vim editor keeps you informed about which mode it is in: It displays **INSERT** at the lower-left corner of the screen while it is in Insert mode.

The following command causes vim to display line numbers next to the text you are editing:

```
:set number RETURN
```

Last Line mode

The colon (:) in the preceding command puts vim into another mode, *Last Line mode*. While in this mode, vim keeps the cursor on the bottom line of the screen. When you finish entering the command by pressing RETURN, vim restores the cursor to its place in the text. Give the command **:set nonumber** RETURN to turn off line numbering.

vim is case sensitive

When you give vim a command, remember that the editor is case sensitive. In other words, vim interprets the same letter as two different commands, depending on whether you enter an uppercase or lowercase character. Beware of the CAPS LOCK (SHIFT-LOCK) key. If you set this key to enter uppercase text while you are in Input mode and then exit to Command mode, vim interprets your commands as uppercase letters. It can be confusing when this happens because vim does not appear to be executing the commands you are entering.

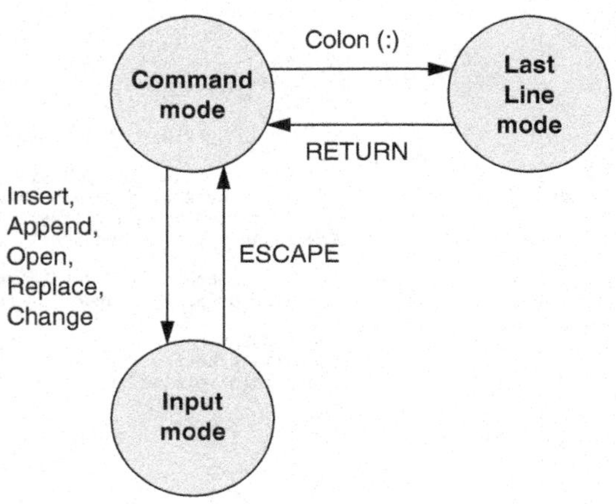

Figure 6-3 Modes in vim

ENTERING TEXT

i/a (Input mode) When you start vim, you must put it in Input mode before you can enter text. To put vim in Input mode, press the **i** (insert before cursor) key or the **a** (append after cursor) key.

If you are not sure whether vim is in Input mode, press the ESCAPE key; vim returns to Command mode if it is in Input mode or beeps, flashes, or does nothing if it is already in Command mode. You can put vim back in Input mode by pressing the **i** or **a** key again.

While vim is in Input mode, you can enter text by typing on the keyboard. If the text does not appear on the screen as you type, vim is not in Input mode.

To continue with this tutorial, enter the sample paragraph shown in Figure 6-4, pressing the RETURN key at the end of each line. If you do not press RETURN before the cursor reaches the right side of the screen or window, vim wraps the text so that it appears to start a new line. Physical lines will not correspond to programmatic (logical) lines in this situation, so editing will be more difficult. While you are using vim, you can correct typing mistakes. If you notice a mistake on the line you are entering, you can correct it before you continue (page 172). You can correct other mistakes later. When you finish entering the paragraph, press ESCAPE to return vim to Command mode.

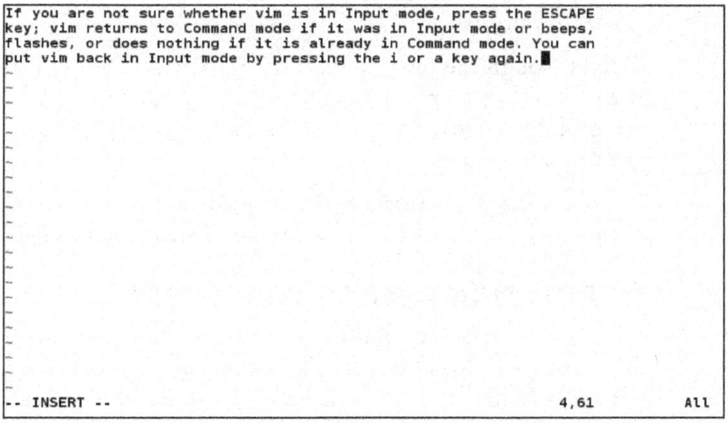

```
If you are not sure whether vim is in Input mode, press the ESCAPE
key; vim returns to Command mode if it was in Input mode or beeps,
flashes, or does nothing if it is already in Command mode. You can
put vim back in Input mode by pressing the i or a key again.
~
~
~
~
~
~
~
~
~
~
~
~
~
~
~
~
~
~
~
~
~
-- INSERT --                                             4,61          All
```

Figure 6-4 Entering text with vim

GETTING HELP

You must have the **vim-runtime** package installed to use vim's help system; see Appendix C.

To get help while you are using vim, enter the command **:help** [*feature*] followed by RETURN. The editor must be in Command mode when you enter this command. The colon moves the cursor to the last line of the screen. If you type **:help**, vim displays an introduction to vim Help (Figure 6-5). Each dark band near the bottom of the screen names the file that is displayed above it. (Each area of the screen that displays a file, such as the two areas shown in Figure 6-5, is a vim "window.") The **help.txt** file occupies most of the screen (the upper window) in Figure 6-5. The file that is

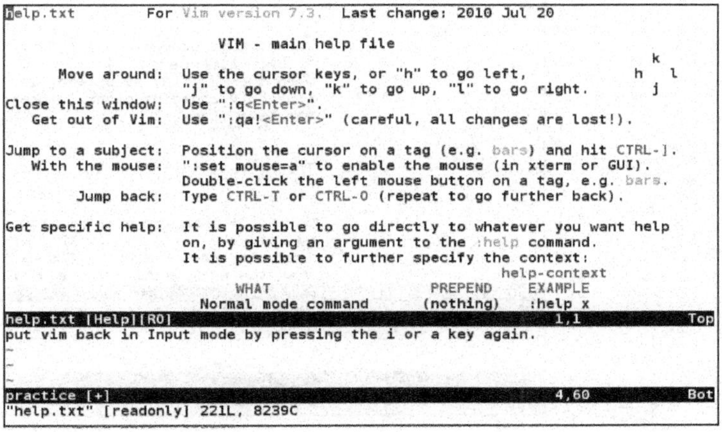

```
help.txt        For Vim version 7.3.  Last change: 2010 Jul 20

                     VIM - main help file
                                                                   k
      Move around:  Use the cursor keys, or "h" to go left,      h   l
                    "j" to go down, "k" to go up, "l" to go right.   j
Close this window:  Use ":q<Enter>".
   Get out of Vim:  Use ":qa!<Enter>" (careful, all changes are lost!).

Jump to a subject:  Position the cursor on a tag (e.g. bars) and hit CTRL-].
   With the mouse:  ":set mouse=a" to enable the mouse (in xterm or GUI).
                    Double-click the left mouse button on a tag, e.g. bars.
        Jump back:  Type CTRL-T or CTRL-O (repeat to go further back).

Get specific help:  It is possible to go directly to whatever you want help
                    on, by giving an argument to the :help command.
                    It is possible to further specify the context:
                                                      help-context
                          WHAT                  PREPEND    EXAMPLE
                      Normal mode command       (nothing)   :help x
help.txt [Help][RO]                                      1,1          Top
put vim back in Input mode by pressing the i or a key again.
~
~
practice [+]                                             4,60         Bot
"help.txt" [readonly] 221L, 8239C
```

Figure 6-5 The main vim Help screen

being edited (**practice**) occupies a few lines in the lower portion of the screen (the lower window).

Read through the introduction to Help by scrolling the text as you read. Press **j** or the DOWN ARROW key to move the cursor down one line at a time; press CONTROL-D or CONTROL-U to scroll the cursor down or up half a window at a time. Give the command **:q** to close the Help window.

You can display information about the insert commands by giving the command **:help insert** while vim is in Command mode (Figure 6-6).

Correcting Text as You Insert It

The keys that back up and correct a shell command line serve the same functions when vim is in Input mode. These keys include the erase, line kill, and word kill keys (usually CONTROL-H, CONTROL-U, and CONTROL-W, respectively). Although vim might not remove deleted text from the screen as you back up over it using one of these keys, the editor does remove it when you type over the text or press RETURN.

Moving the Cursor

You need to be able to move the cursor on the screen so you can delete, insert, and correct text. While vim is in Command mode, the RETURN key, the SPACE bar, and the ARROW keys move the cursor. If you prefer to keep your hand closer to the center of the keyboard, if your terminal does not have ARROW keys, or if the emulator you are using does not support them, you can use the **h**, **j**, **k**, and **l** (lowercase "l") keys to move the cursor left, down, up, and right, respectively.

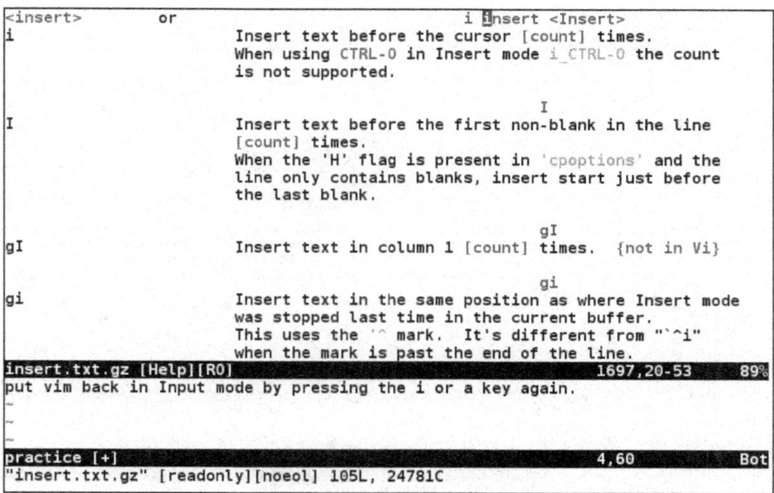

Figure 6-6 Help with insert commands

DELETING TEXT

x (Delete character) **dw** (Delete word) **dd** (Delete line)

You can delete a single character by moving the cursor until it is over the character you want to delete and then giving the command **x**. You can delete a word by positioning the cursor on the first letter of the word and then giving the command **dw** (Delete word). You can delete a line of text by moving the cursor until it is anywhere on the line and then giving the command **dd**.

UNDOING MISTAKES

u (Undo)

If you delete a character, line, or word by mistake or give any command you want to reverse, give the command **u** (Undo) immediately after the command you want to undo. The vim editor will restore the text to the way it was before you gave the last command. If you give the **u** command again, vim will undo the command you gave before the one it just undid. You can use this technique to back up over many of your actions. With the **compatible** parameter (page 174) set, however, vim can undo only the most recent change.

:redo (Redo)

If you undo a command you did not mean to undo, give a Redo command: CONTROL-R or **:redo** (followed by a RETURN). The vim editor will redo the undone command. As with the Undo command, you can give the Redo command many times in a row.

ENTERING ADDITIONAL TEXT

i (Insert) **a** (Append)

When you want to insert new text within existing text, move the cursor so it is on the character that follows the new text you plan to enter. Then give the **i** (Insert) command to put vim in Input mode, enter the new text, and press ESCAPE to return vim to Command mode. Alternatively, you can position the cursor on the character that precedes the new text and use the **a** (Append) command.

o/O (Open)

To enter one or more lines, position the cursor on the line above where you want the new text to go. Give the command **o** (Open). The vim editor opens a blank line below the line the cursor was on, puts the cursor on the new, empty line, and goes into Input mode. Enter the new text, ending each line with a RETURN. When you are finished entering text, press ESCAPE to return vim to Command mode. The **O** command works in the same way **o** works, except it opens a blank line *above* the line the cursor is on.

CORRECTING TEXT

To correct text, use **dd**, **dw**, or **x** to remove the incorrect text. Then, use either **i**, **a**, **o**, or **O** to insert the correct text.

For example, to change the word **pressing** to **hitting** in Figure 6-4 on page 171, you might use the ARROW keys to move the cursor until it is on top of the **p** in **pressing**. Then give the command **dw** to delete the word **pressing**. Put vim in Input mode by giving an **i** command, enter the word **hitting** followed by a SPACE, and press ESCAPE. The word is changed, and vim is in Command mode, waiting for another command. A shorthand for the two commands **dw** followed by the **i** command is **cw** (Change word). The command **cw** puts vim into Input mode.

Page breaks for the printer

tip CONTROL-L tells the printer to skip to the top of the next page. You can enter this character anywhere in a document by pressing CONTROL-L while you are in Input mode. If **^L** does not appear, press CONTROL-V before CONTROL-L.

ENDING THE EDITING SESSION

While you are editing, vim keeps the edited text in an area named the *Work buffer*. When you finish editing, you must write out the contents of the Work buffer to a disk file so the edited text is saved and available when you next want it.

Make sure vim is in Command mode and use the **ZZ** command (you must use uppercase Zs) to write the newly entered text to the disk and end the editing session. After you give the **ZZ** command, vim returns control to the shell. You can exit with **:q!** if you do not want to save your work.

Do not confuse ZZ with CONTROL-Z

caution When you exit from vim with **ZZ**, make sure that you type **ZZ** and not CONTROL-Z (typically the suspend key). When you press CONTROL-Z, vim disappears from your screen, almost as though you had exited from it. In fact, vim will continue running in the background with your work unsaved. Refer to "Job Control" on page 304. If you try to start editing the same file with a new **vim** command, vim displays a message about a swap file.

THE compatible PARAMETER

The **compatible** parameter makes vim more compatible with vi. By default this parameter is not set. To get started with vim, you can ignore this parameter.

Setting the **compatible** parameter changes many aspects of how vim works. For example, when the **compatible** parameter is set, the Undo command (page 173) can undo only the most recent change; in contrast, with the **compatible** parameter unset, you can call Undo repeatedly to undo many changes. This chapter notes when the **compatible** parameter affects a command. To obtain more details on the **compatible** parameter, give the command **:help compatible** RETURN. To display a complete list of vim's differences from the original vi, use **:help vi-diff** RETURN. See page 171 for a discussion of the **help** command.

From the command line use the **–C** option to set the **compatible** parameter and the **–N** option to unset it.

INTRODUCTION TO vim FEATURES

This section covers online help, modes of operation, the Work buffer, emergency procedures, and other vim features. To see which features are incorporated in a particular build, give a **vim** command followed by the **--version** option.

ONLINE HELP

As covered briefly earlier, vim provides help while you are using it. Give the command **:help** ***feature*** to display information about ***feature***. As you scroll through the various help texts, you will see words with a bar on either side, such as **|tutor|**. These words are *active links:* Move the cursor on top of an active link and press CONTROL-] to jump to the linked text. Use CONTROL-o (lowercase "o") to jump back to where you were in the help text. You can also use the active link words in place of ***feature***. For example, you might see the reference **|credits|**; you could enter **:help credits** RETURN to read more about credits. Enter **:q!** to close a help window.

Some common ***features*** that you might want to investigate by using the help system are **insert**, **delete**, and **opening-window**. Although *opening-window* is not intuitive, you will get to know the names of ***features*** as you spend more time with vim. You can also give the command **:help doc-file-list** to view a complete list of the help files. Although vim is a free program, the author requests that you donate the money you would have spent on similar software to help the children in Uganda (give the command **:help iccf** for more information).

TERMINOLOGY

This chapter uses the following terms:

Current character — The character the cursor is on.

Current line — The line the cursor is on.

Status line — The last or bottom line of the screen. This line is reserved for Last Line mode and status information. Text you are editing does not appear on this line.

MODES OF OPERATION

The vim editor is part of the ex editor, which has five modes of operation:

- ex Command mode
- ex Input mode
- vim Command mode
- vim Input mode
- vim Last Line mode

While in Command mode, vim accepts keystrokes as commands, responding to each command as you enter it. It does not display the characters you type in this mode. While in Input mode, vim accepts and displays keystrokes as text that it eventually puts into the file you are editing. All commands that start with a colon (:) put vim in Last Line mode. The colon moves the cursor to the status line of the screen, where you enter the rest of the command.

In addition to the position of the cursor, there is another important difference between Last Line mode and Command mode. When you give a command in Command mode, you do not terminate the command with a RETURN. In contrast, you must terminate all Last Line mode commands with a RETURN.

You do not normally use the ex modes. When this chapter refers to Input and Command modes, it means the vim modes, not the ex modes.

When an editing session begins, vim is in Command mode. Several commands, including Insert and Append, put vim in Input mode. When you press the ESCAPE key, vim always reverts to Command mode.

The Change and Replace commands combine the Command and Input modes. The Change command deletes the text you want to change and puts vim in Input mode so you can insert new text. The Replace command deletes the character(s) you overwrite and inserts the new one(s) you enter. Figure 6-3 on page 170 shows the modes and the methods for changing between them.

Watch the mode and the CAPS LOCK key

tip Almost anything you type in Command mode means something to vim. If you think vim is in Input mode when it is in Command mode, typing in text can produce confusing results. When you are learning to use vim, make sure the **showmode** parameter (page 205) is set (it is by default) to remind you which mode you are using. You might also find it useful to turn on the status line by giving a **:set laststatus=2** command (page 204).

Also keep your eye on the CAPS LOCK key. In Command mode, typing uppercase letters produces different results than typing lowercase ones. It can be disorienting to give commands and have vim give the "wrong" responses.

THE DISPLAY

The vim editor uses the status line and several symbols to give information about what is happening during an editing session.

STATUS LINE

The vim editor displays status information on the bottom line of the display area. This information includes error messages, information about the deletion or addition of blocks of text, and file status information. In addition, vim displays Last Line mode commands on the status line.

REDRAWING THE SCREEN

Sometimes the screen might become garbled or overwritten. When vim puts characters on the screen, it sometimes leaves @ on a line instead of deleting the line. When output from a program becomes intermixed with the display of the Work buffer, things can get even more confusing. The output *does not* become part of the Work buffer but affects only the display. If the screen gets overwritten, press ESCAPE to make sure vim is in Command mode, and press CONTROL-L to redraw (refresh) the screen.

TILDE (~) SYMBOL

If the end of the file is displayed on the screen, vim marks lines that would appear past the end of the file with a tilde (~) at the left of the screen. When you start editing a new file, the vim editor marks each line on the screen (except the first line) with this symbol.

CORRECTING TEXT AS YOU INSERT IT

While vim is in Input mode, you can use the erase and line kill keys to back up over text so you can correct it. You can also use CONTROL-W to back up over words.

WORK BUFFER

The vim editor does all its work in the Work buffer. At the beginning of an editing session, vim reads the file you are editing from the disk into the Work buffer. During the editing session, it makes all changes to this copy of the file but does not change the file on the disk until you write the contents of the Work buffer back to the disk. Normally when you end an editing session, you tell vim to write the contents of the Work buffer, which makes the changes to the text final. When you edit a new file, vim creates the file when it writes the contents of the Work buffer to the disk, usually at the end of the editing session.

Storing the text you are editing in the Work buffer has both advantages and disadvantages. If you accidentally end an editing session without writing out the contents of the Work buffer, your work is lost. However, if you unintentionally make some major changes (such as deleting the entire contents of the Work buffer), you can end the editing session without implementing the changes.

To look at a file but not to change it while you are working with vim, you can use the view utility:

```
$ view filename
```

Calling the view utility is the same as calling the vim editor with the **–R** (readonly) option. Once you have invoked the editor in this way, you cannot write the contents of the Work buffer back to the file whose name appeared on the command line. You can always write the Work buffer out to a file with a different name. If you have installed mc (Midnight Commander; page 902), the **view** command calls mcview and not vim.

LINE LENGTH AND FILE SIZE

The vim editor operates on files of any format, provided the length of a single line (that is, the characters between two NEWLINE characters) can fit into available memory. The total length of the file is limited only by available disk space and memory.

WINDOWS

The vim editor allows you to open, close, and hide multiple windows, each of which allows you to edit a different file. Most of the window commands consist of CONTROL-W followed by another letter. For example, CONTROL-W **s** opens another window (splits the screen) that is editing the same file. CONTROL-W **n** opens a second window that is editing an empty file. CONTROL-W **w** moves the cursor between windows, and CONTROL-W **q** (or **:q**) quits (closes) a window. Give the command **:help windows** to display a complete list of windows commands.

FILE LOCKS

When you edit an existing file, vim displays the first few lines of the file, gives status information about the file on the status line, and locks the file. When you try to open a locked file with vim, you will see a message similar to the one shown in Figure 6-7. You will see this type of message in two scenarios: when you try to edit a file that someone is already editing (perhaps you are editing it in another window, in the background, or on another terminal) and when you try to edit a file that you were editing when vim or the system crashed.

Although it is advisable to follow the instructions that vim displays, a second user can edit a file and write it out with a different filename. Refer to the next sections for more information.

```
E325: ATTENTION
Found a swap file by the name ".practice.swp"
          owned by: sam   dated: Tue May  1 16:56:40 2012
         file name: ~sam/practice
          modified: YES
         user name: sam   host name: guava
        process ID: 3721 (still running)
While opening file "practice"
             dated: Thu May 10 17:19:27 2012
      NEWER than swap file!

(1) Another program may be editing the same file.  If this is the case,
    be careful not to end up with two different instances of the same
    file when making changes.  Quit, or continue with caution.
(2) An edit session for this file crashed.
    If this is the case, use ":recover" or "vim -r practice"
    to recover the changes (see ":help recovery").
    If you did this already, delete the swap file ".practice.swp"
    to avoid this message.

Swap file ".practice.swp" already exists!
[O]pen Read-Only, (E)dit anyway, (R)ecover, (Q)uit, (A)bort:
```

Figure 6-7 Attempting to open a locked file

ABNORMAL TERMINATION OF AN EDITING SESSION

You can end an editing session in one of two ways: When you exit from vim, you can save the changes you made during the editing session or you can abandon those changes. You can use the **ZZ** or **:wq** command from Command mode to save the changes and exit from vim (see "Ending the Editing Session" on page 174).

To end an editing session without writing out the contents of the Work buffer, give the following command:

```
:q!
```

Use the **:q!** command cautiously. When you use this command to end an editing session, vim does not preserve the contents of the Work buffer, so you will lose any work you did since the last time you wrote the Work buffer to disk. The next time you edit or use the file, it will appear as it did the last time you wrote the Work buffer to disk.

Sometimes you might find that you created or edited a file but vim will not let you exit. For example, if you forgot to specify a filename when you first called vim, you will get a message saying **No file name** when you give a **ZZ** command. If vim does not let you exit normally, you can use the Write command (**:w**) to name the file and write it to disk before you quit vim. Give the following command, substituting the name of the file for ***filename*** (remember to follow the command with a RETURN):

:w ***filename***

After you give the Write command, you can use **:q** to quit using vim. You do not need to include the exclamation point (as in **q!**); it is necessary only when you have made changes since the last time you wrote the Work buffer to disk. Refer to page 200 for more information about the Write command.

When you cannot write to a file

tip It might be necessary to write a file using **:w *filename*** if you do not have write permission for the file you are editing. If you give a **ZZ** command and see the message **"*filename*" is read only**, you do not have write permission for the file. Use the Write command with a temporary filename to write the file to disk under a different filename. If you do not have write permission for the working directory, however, vim might not be able to write the file to the disk. Give the command again, using an absolute pathname of a dummy (nonexistent) file in your home directory in place of the filename. (For example, Max might give the command **:w /home/max/temp** or **:w ~/temp**.)

If vim reports **File exists**, you will need to use **:w! *filename*** to overwrite the existing file (make sure you want to overwrite the file). Refer to page 201.

RECOVERING TEXT AFTER A CRASH

The vim editor temporarily stores the file you are working on in a *swap file*. If the system crashes while you are editing a file with vim, you can often recover its text from the swap file. When you attempt to edit a file that has a swap file, you will see a message similar to the one shown in Figure 6-7 on page 178. If someone else is editing the file, quit or open the file as a readonly file.

In the following example, Max uses the **–r** option to check whether the swap file exists for a file named **memo**, which he was editing when the system crashed:

```
$ vim -r
Swap files found:
   In current directory:
1.     .party.swp
           owned by: max   dated: Fri Jan 26 11:36:44 2018
          file name: ~max/party
           modified: YES
          user name: max   host name: coffee
         process ID: 18439
2.     .memo.swp
           owned by: max   dated: Fri Mar 23 17:14:05 2018
          file name: ~max/memo
           modified: no
          user name: max   host name: coffee
         process ID: 27733 (still running)
   In directory ~/tmp:
      -- none --
   In directory /var/tmp:
      -- none --
   In directory /tmp:
-- none --
```

With the **–r** option, vim displays a list of swap files it has saved (some might be old). If your work was saved, give the same command followed by a SPACE and the name of the file. You will then be editing a recent copy of your Work buffer. Give the command **:w** ***filename*** immediately to save the salvaged copy of the Work buffer to disk under a name different from the original file; then check the recovered file to make sure it is OK. Following is Max's exchange with vim as he recovers **memo**. Subsequently, he deletes the swap file:

```
$ vim -r memo
Using swap file ".memo.swp"
Original file "~/memo"
Recovery completed. You should check if everything is OK.
(You might want to write out this file under another name
and run diff with the original file to check for changes)
Delete the .swp file afterwards.

Hit ENTER or type command to continue
:w memo2
:q
$ rm .memo.swp
```

You must recover files on the system you were using

tip The recovery feature of vim is specific to the system you were using when the crash occurred. If you are running on a cluster, you must log in on the system you were using before the crash to use the **–r** option successfully.

COMMAND MODE: MOVING THE CURSOR

While vim is in Command mode, you can position the cursor over any character on the screen. You can also display a different portion of the Work buffer on the screen. By manipulating the screen and cursor position, you can place the cursor on any character in the Work buffer.

You can move the cursor forward or backward through the text. As illustrated in Figure 6-8, *forward* means toward the right and bottom of the screen and the end of the file. *Backward* means toward the left and top of the screen and the beginning of the file. When you use a command that moves the cursor forward past the end (right) of a line, the cursor generally moves to the beginning (left) of the next line. When you move it backward past the beginning of a line, the cursor generally moves to the end of the previous line.

Long lines Sometimes a line in the Work buffer might be too long to appear as a single line on the screen. In such a case vim wraps the current line onto the next line (unless you set the **nowrap** option [page 204]).

You can move the cursor through the text by any *Unit of Measure* (that is, character, word, line, sentence, paragraph, or screen). If you precede a cursor-movement command with a number, called a *Repeat Factor,* the cursor moves that number of units through the text. Refer to pages 210 through page 213 for precise definitions of these terms.

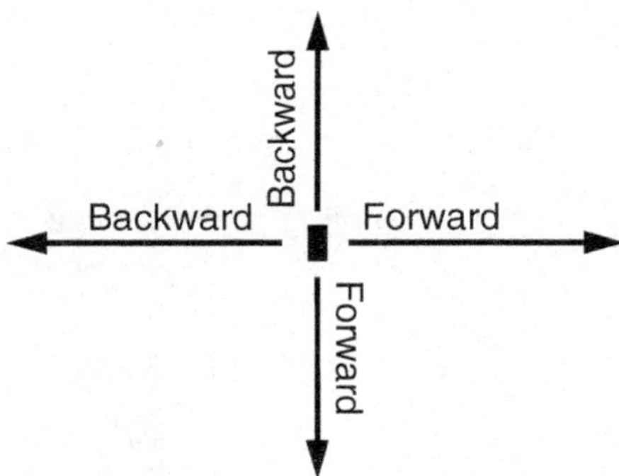

Figure 6-8 Forward and backward

MOVING THE CURSOR BY CHARACTERS

l/h The SPACE bar moves the cursor forward, one character at a time, toward the right side of the screen. The **l** (lowercase "l") key and the RIGHT ARROW key (Figure 6-9) do the same thing. For example, the command **7** SPACE or **7l** moves the cursor seven characters to the right. These keys cannot move the cursor past the end of the current line to the beginning of the next line. The **h** and LEFT ARROW keys are similar to the **l** and RIGHT ARROW keys but work in the opposite direction.

MOVING THE CURSOR TO A SPECIFIC CHARACTER

f/F You can move the cursor to the next occurrence of a specified character on the current line by using the Find command. For example, the following command moves the cursor from its current position to the next occurrence of the character **a**, if one appears on the same line:

```
fa
```

You can also find the previous occurrence by using a capital **F**. The following command moves the cursor to the position of the closest previous **a** in the current line:

```
Fa
```

A semicolon (;) repeats the last Find command.

MOVING THE CURSOR BY WORDS

w/W The **w** (word) key moves the cursor forward to the first letter of the next word (Figure 6-10). Groups of punctuation count as words. This command goes to the next line if the next word is located there. The command **15w** moves the cursor to the first character of the fifteenth subsequent word.

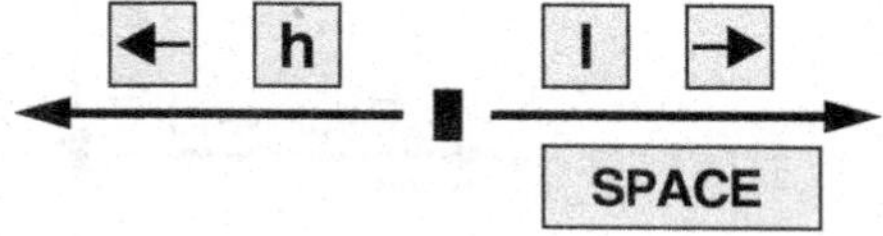

Figure 6-9 Moving the cursor by characters

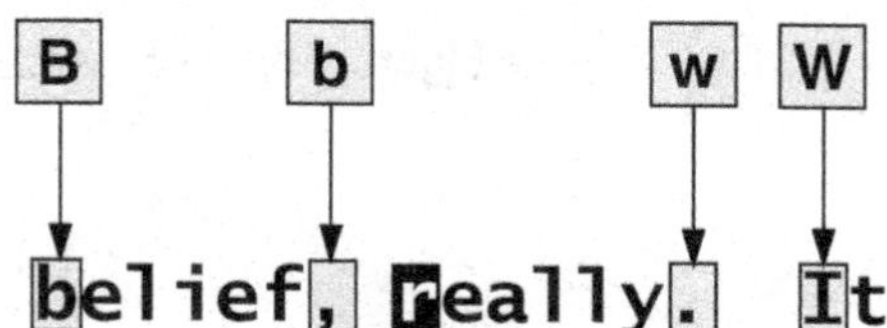

Figure 6-10 Moving the cursor by words

The W key is similar to the w key but moves the cursor by blank-delimited words, including punctuation, as it skips forward. (Refer to "Blank-Delimited Word" on page 211.)

b/B The b (back) key moves the cursor backward to the first letter of the previous word.
e/E The B key moves the cursor backward by blank-delimited words. Similarly, the e key moves the cursor to the end of the next word; E moves it to the end of the next blank-delimited word.

Moving the Cursor by Lines

j/k The RETURN key moves the cursor to the beginning of the next line; the j and DOWN ARROW keys move the cursor down one line to the character just below the current character (Figure 6-11). If no character appears immediately below the current character, the cursor moves to the end of the next line. The cursor will not move past the last line of text in the work buffer.

The k and UP ARROW keys are similar to the j and DOWN ARROW keys but work in the opposite direction. The minus (–) key is similar to the RETURN key but works in the opposite direction.

Moving the Cursor by Sentences and Paragraphs

)/(
}/{ The) and } keys move the cursor forward to the beginning of the next sentence or the next paragraph, respectively (Figure 6-12). The (and { keys move the cursor backward to the beginning of the current sentence or paragraph, respectively. You can find more information on sentences and paragraphs starting on page 211.

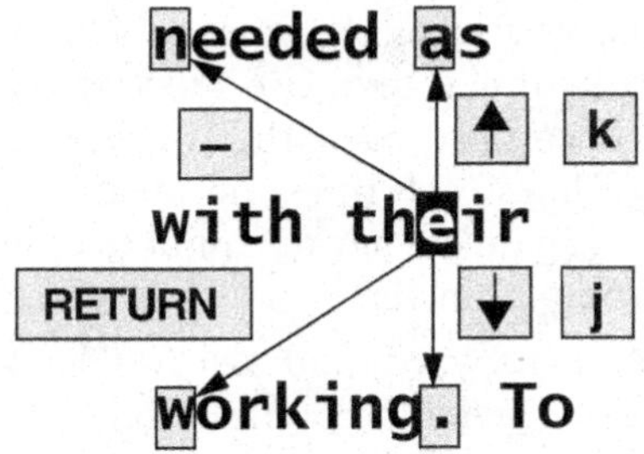

Figure 6-11 Moving the cursor by lines

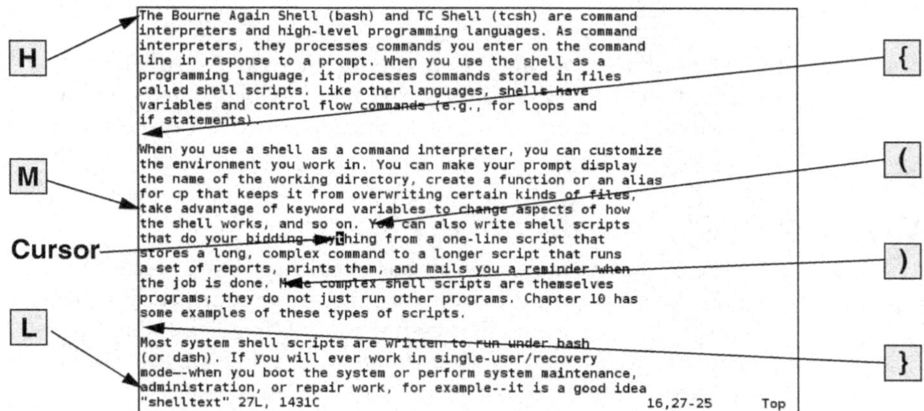


```
The Bourne Again Shell (bash) and TC Shell (tcsh) are command
interpreters and high-level programming languages. As command
interpreters, they processes commands you enter on the command
line in response to a prompt. When you use the shell as a
programming language, it processes commands stored in files
called shell scripts. Like other languages, shells have
variables and control flow commands (e.g., for loops and
if statements).

When you use a shell as a command interpreter, you can customize
the environment you work in. You can make your prompt display
the name of the working directory, create a function or an alias
for cp that keeps it from overwriting certain kinds of files,
take advantage of keyword variables to change aspects of how
the shell works, and so on. You can also write shell scripts
that do your bidding--anything from a one-line script that
stores a long, complex command to a longer script that runs
a set of reports, prints them, and mails you a reminder when
the job is done. More complex shell scripts are themselves
programs; they do not just run other programs. Chapter 10 has
some examples of these types of scripts.

Most system shell scripts are written to run under bash
(or dash). If you will ever work in single-user/recovery
mode--when you boot the system or perform system maintenance,
administration, or repair work, for example--it is a good idea
"shelltext" 27L, 1431C                          16,27-25      Top
```

Figure 6-12 Moving the cursor by sentences, paragraphs, **H**, **M**, and **L**

Moving the Cursor Within the Screen

H/M/L The **H** (home) key positions the cursor at the left end of the top line of the screen, the **M** (middle) key moves the cursor to the middle line, and the **L** (lower) key moves it to the bottom line (Figure 6-12).

Viewing Different Parts of the Work Buffer

The screen displays a portion of the text that is in the Work buffer. You can display the text preceding or following the text on the screen by *scrolling* the display. You can also display a portion of the Work buffer based on a line number.

CONTROL-D CONTROL-U Press CONTROL-D to scroll the screen down (forward) through the file so that vim displays half a screen of new text. Use CONTROL-U to scroll the screen up (backward) by the same amount. If you precede either of these commands with a number, vim scrolls that number of lines each time you press CONTROL-D or CONTROL-U for the rest of the session (unless you again change the number of lines to scroll). See page 205 for a discussion of the **scroll** parameter.

CONTROL-F CONTROL-B The CONTROL-F (forward) and CONTROL-B (backward) keys display almost a *whole* screen of new text, leaving a couple of lines from the previous screen for continuity. On many keyboards you can use the PAGE DOWN and PAGE UP keys in place of CONTROL-F and CONTROL-B, respectively.

Line numbers (**G**) When you enter a line number followed by **G** (goto), vim positions the cursor on that line in the Work buffer. If you press **G** without a number, vim positions the cursor on the last line in the Work buffer. Line numbers are implicit; the file does not need to have actual line numbers for this command to work. Refer to "Line numbers" on page 204 if you want vim to display line numbers.

INPUT MODE

The Insert, Append, Open, Change, and Replace commands put vim in Input mode. While vim is in this mode, you can put new text into the Work buffer. To return vim to Command mode when you finish entering text, press the ESCAPE key. Refer to "Show mode" on page 205 if you want vim to remind you when it is in Input mode (it does by default).

INSERTING TEXT

Insert (**i**/**I**) The **i** (Insert) command puts vim in Input mode and places the text you enter before the current character. The **I** command places text at the beginning of the current line (Figure 6-13). Although the **i** and **I** commands sometimes overwrite text on the screen, the characters in the Work buffer are not changed; only the display is affected. The overwritten text is redisplayed when you press ESCAPE and vim returns to Command mode. Use **i** or **I** to insert a few characters or words into existing text or to insert text in a new file.

APPENDING TEXT

Append (**a**/**A**) The **a** (Append) command is similar to the **i** command, except that it places the text you enter after the current character (Figure 6-13). The **A** command places the text after the last character on the current line.

OPENING A LINE FOR TEXT

Open (**o**/**O**) The **o** (Open) and **O** commands open a blank line within existing text, place the cursor at the beginning of the new (blank) line, and put vim in Input mode. The **O** command opens a line above the current line; the **o** command opens one below the current line. Use these commands when you are entering several new lines within existing text.

REPLACING TEXT

Replace (**r**/**R**) The **r** and **R** (Replace) commands cause the new text you enter to overwrite (replace) existing text. The single character you enter following an **r** command overwrites the current character. After you enter that character, vim returns to Command mode—you do not need to press the ESCAPE key.

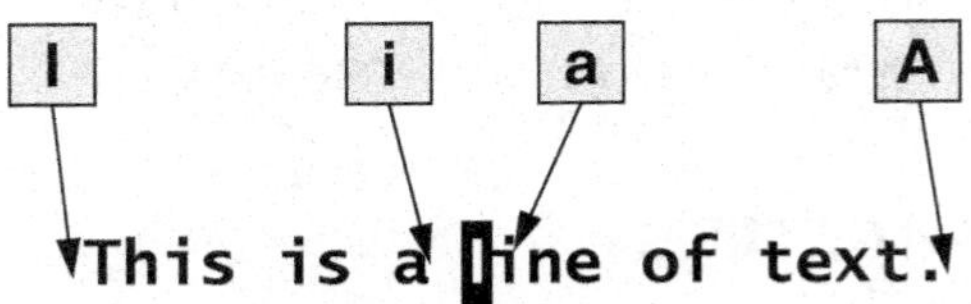

Figure 6-13 The I, i, a, and A commands

The **R** command causes *all* subsequent characters to overwrite existing text until you press ESCAPE to return vim to Command mode.

Replacing TABs

tip The Replace commands might appear to behave strangely when you replace TAB characters. TAB characters can appear as several SPACEs—until you try to replace them. A TAB is one character and is replaced by a single character. Refer to "Invisible characters" on page 204 for information on displaying TABs as visible characters.

Quoting Special Characters in Input Mode

CONTROL-V While you are in Input mode, you can use the Quote command, CONTROL-V, to enter any character into the text, including characters that normally have special meaning to vim. Among these characters are CONTROL-L (or CONTROL-R), which redraws the screen; CONTROL-W, which backs the cursor up a word to the left; CONTROL-M, which enters a NEWLINE; and ESCAPE, which ends Input mode.

To insert one of these characters into the text, type CONTROL-V followed by the character. CONTROL-V quotes the single character that follows it. For example, to insert the sequence ESCAPE[2J into a file you are creating in vim, you would type the character sequence CONTROL-V ESCAPE[2J. This character sequence clears the screen of a DEC VT-100 and other similar terminals. Although you would not ordinarily want to type this sequence into a document, you might want to use it or another ESCAPE sequence in a shell script you are creating in vim. Refer to Chapter 10 for information about writing shell scripts.

Command Mode: Deleting and Changing Text

This section describes the commands to delete and replace, or change, text in the document you are editing. The Undo command is covered here because it allows you to restore deleted or changed text.

Undoing Changes

Undo (**u**/**U**) The **u** command (Undo) restores text that you just deleted or changed by mistake. A single Undo command restores only the most recently deleted text. If you delete a line and then change a word, the first Undo restores only the changed word; you have to give a second Undo command to restore the deleted line. With the **compatible** parameter (page 174) set, vim can undo only the most recent change. The **U** command restores the last line you changed to the way it was before you started changing it, even after several changes.

Deleting Characters

Delete character (**x**/**X**) The **x** command deletes the current character. You can precede the **x** command by a Repeat Factor (page 213) to delete several characters on the current line, starting with the current character. The **X** command deletes the character to the left of the cursor.

DELETING TEXT

Delete (**d/D**) The **d** (Delete) command removes text from the Work buffer. The amount of text that **d** removes depends on the Repeat Factor and the Unit of Measure (page 210). After the text is deleted, vim is still in Command mode.

Use dd to delete a single line

tip The command **d** RETURN deletes two lines: the current line and the following one. Use **dd** to delete just the current line, or precede **dd** by a Repeat Factor (page 213) to delete several lines.

You can delete from the current cursor position up to a specific character on the same line. To delete up to the next semicolon (;), give the command **dt;** (see page 190 for more information on the **t** command). To delete the remainder of the current line, use **D** or **d$**. Table 6-1 lists some Delete commands. Each command, except the last group that starts with **dd**, deletes *from/to* the current character.

Exchange characters and lines

tip If two characters are out of order, position the cursor on the first character and give the commands **xp**.

If two lines are out of order, position the cursor on the first line and give the commands **ddp**.

See page 198 for more information on the Put commands.

Table 6-1 Delete command examples

Command	Result
dl	Deletes current character (same as the **x** command)
d0	Deletes from beginning of line
d^	Deletes from first character of line (not including leading SPACEs or TABs)
dw	Deletes to end of word
d3w	Deletes to end of third word
db	Deletes from beginning of word
dW	Deletes to end of blank-delimited word
dB	Deletes from beginning of blank-delimited word
d7B	Deletes from seventh previous beginning of blank-delimited word
d4)	Deletes to end of fourth sentence
d(	Deletes from beginning of sentence

Table 6-1 Delete command examples (continued)

Command	Result
d}	Deletes to end of paragraph
d{	Deletes from beginning of paragraph
d7{	Deletes from seventh paragraph preceding beginning of paragraph
d/*text*	Deletes up to next occurrence of word ***text***
df*c*	Deletes on current line up to and including next occurrence of character ***c***
dt*c*	Deletes on current line up to next occurrence of ***c***
D	Deletes to end of line
d$	Deletes to end of line
dd	Deletes current line
5dd	Deletes five lines starting with current line
dL	Deletes through last line on screen
dH	Deletes from first line on screen
dG	Deletes through end of Work buffer
d1G	Deletes from beginning of Work buffer

CHANGING TEXT

Change (**c**/**C**) The **c** (Change) command replaces existing text with new text. The new text does not have to occupy the same space as the existing text. You can change a word to several words, a line to several lines, or a paragraph to a single character. The **C** command replaces the text from the cursor position to the end of the line.

The **c** command deletes the amount of text specified by the Repeat Factor and the Unit of Measure (page 210) and puts vim in Input mode. When you finish entering the new text and press ESCAPE, the old word, line, sentence, or paragraph is changed to the new one. Pressing ESCAPE without entering new text deletes the specified text (that is, it replaces the specified text with nothing).

Table 6-2 lists some Change commands. Except for the last two, each command changes text *from/to* the current character.

dw works differently from cw

tip The **dw** command deletes all characters through (including) the SPACE at the end of a word. The **cw** command changes only the characters in the word, leaving the trailing SPACE intact.

Table 6-2 Change command examples

Command	Result
cl	Changes current character
cw	Changes to end of word
c3w	Changes to end of third word
cb	Changes from beginning of word
cW	Changes to end of blank-delimited word
cB	Changes from beginning of blank-delimited word
c7B	Changes from beginning of seventh previous blank-delimited word
c$	Changes to end of line
c0	Changes from beginning of line
c)	Changes to end of sentence
c4)	Changes to end of fourth sentence
c(	Changes from beginning of sentence
c}	Changes to end of paragraph
c{	Changes from beginning of paragraph
c7{	Changes from beginning of seventh preceding paragraph
ct*c*	Changes on current line up to next occurrence of ***c***
C	Changes to end of line
cc	Changes current line
5cc	Changes five lines starting with current line

REPLACING TEXT

Substitute (**s**/**S**) The **s** and **S** (Substitute) commands also replace existing text with new text (Table 6-3). The **s** command deletes the current character and puts vim into Input mode. It has the effect of replacing the current character with whatever you type until you press ESCAPE. The **S** command does the same thing as the **cc** command: It changes the current line. The **s** command replaces characters only on the current line. If you specify a Repeat Factor before an **s** command and this action would replace more characters than are present on the current line, **s** changes characters only to the end of the line (same as **C**).

Table 6-3 Substitute command examples

Command	Result
s	Substitutes one or more characters for current character
S	Substitutes one or more characters for current line
5s	Substitutes one or more characters for five characters, starting with current character

CHANGING CASE

The tilde (~) character changes the case of the current character from uppercase to lowercase, or vice versa. You can precede the tilde with a number to specify the number of characters you want the command to affect. For example, the command 5~ transposes the next five characters starting with the character under the cursor, but will not transpose characters past the end of the current line.

SEARCHING AND SUBSTITUTING

Searching for and replacing a character, a string of text, or a string that is matched by a regular expression is a key feature of any editor. The vim editor provides simple commands for searching for a character on the current line. It also provides more complex commands for searching for—and optionally substituting for—single and multiple occurrences of strings or regular expressions anywhere in the Work buffer.

SEARCHING FOR A CHARACTER

Find (**f**/**F**) You can search for and move the cursor to the next occurrence of a specified character on the current line using the **f** (Find) command. Refer to "Moving the Cursor to a Specific Character" on page 182.

Find (**t**/**T**) The next two commands are used in the same manner as the Find commands. The lowercase **t** command places the cursor on the character before the next occurrence of the specified character. The **T** command places the cursor on the character after the previous occurrence of the specified character.

A semicolon (**;**) repeats the last **f**, **F**, **t**, or **T** command.

You can combine these search commands with other commands. For example, the command **d2fq** deletes the text from the current character to the second occurrence of the letter **q** on the current line.

SEARCHING FOR A STRING

Search (**/**/**?**) The vim editor can search backward or forward through the Work buffer to find a string of text or a string that matches a regular expression (Appendix A). To find the next occurrence of a string (forward), press the forward slash (**/**) key, enter the text you want to find (called the *search string*), and press RETURN. When you press the slash key, vim displays a slash on the status line. As you enter the string of text, it is also displayed on the status line. When you press RETURN, vim searches for the string. If this search is successful, vim positions the cursor on the first character of the string. If you use a question mark (?) in place of the forward slash, vim searches for the previous occurrence of the string. If you need to include a forward slash in a forward search or a question mark in a backward search, you must quote it by preceding it with a backslash (\).

Two distinct ways of quoting characters

tip You use CONTROL-V to quote special characters in text that you are entering into a file (page 186). This section discusses the use of a backslash (\) to quote special characters in a search string. The two techniques of quoting characters are not interchangeable.

Next (**n**/**N**) The **N** and **n** keys repeat the last search but do not require you to reenter the search string. The **n** key repeats the original search exactly, and the **N** key repeats the search in the opposite direction of the original search.

If you are searching forward and vim does not find the search string before it gets to the end of the Work buffer, the editor typically *wraps around* and continues the search at the beginning of the Work buffer. During a backward search, vim wraps around from the beginning of the Work buffer to the end. Also, vim normally performs case-sensitive searches. Refer to "Wrap scan" (page 206) and "Ignore case in searches" (page 204) for information about how to change these search parameters.

NORMAL VERSUS INCREMENTAL SEARCHES

When vim performs a normal search (its default behavior), you enter a slash or question mark followed by the search string and press RETURN. The vim editor then moves the cursor to the next or previous occurrence of the string you are searching for.

When vim performs an incremental search, you enter a slash or question mark. As you enter each character of the search string, vim moves the highlight to the next or previous occurrence of the string you have entered so far. When the highlight is on the string you are searching for, you must press RETURN to move the cursor to the highlighted string. If the string you enter does not match any text, vim does not highlight anything.

The type of search that vim performs depends on the **incsearch** parameter (page 204). Give the command **:set incsearch** to turn on incremental searching; use **noincsearch** to turn it off. When you set the **compatible** parameter (page 174), vim turns off incremental searching.

SPECIAL CHARACTERS IN SEARCH STRINGS

Because the search string is a regular expression, some characters take on a special meaning within the search string. The following paragraphs list some of these characters. See also "Extended Regular Expressions" on page 1043.

The first two items in the following list (^ and $) always have their special meanings within a search string unless you quote them by preceding them with a backslash (\). You can turn off the special meanings within a search string for the rest of the items in the list by setting the **nomagic** parameter. For more information refer to "Allow special characters in searches" on page 203.

^ Beginning-of-Line Indicator

When the first character in a search string is a caret (also called a circumflex), it matches the beginning of a line. For example, the command **/^the** finds the next line that begins with the string **the**.

$ End-of-Line Indicator

A dollar sign matches the end of a line. For example, the command **/!$** finds the next line that ends with an exclamation point and **/ $** matches the next line that ends with a SPACE.

. Any-Character Indicator

A period matches *any* character, anywhere in the search string. For example, the command **/l..e** finds **line, followed, like, included, all memory,** or any other word or character string that contains an **l** followed by any two characters and an **e**. To search for a period, use a backslash to quote the period (**\.**).

\> End-of-Word Indicator

This pair of characters matches the end of a word. For example, the command **/s\>** finds the next word that ends with an **s**. Whereas a backslash (\) is typically used to *turn off* the special meaning of a character, the character sequence **\>** has a special meaning, while **>** alone does not.

\< Beginning-of-Word Indicator

This pair of characters matches the beginning of a word. For example, the command **/\<The** finds the next word that begins with the string **The**. The beginning-of-word indicator uses the backslash in the same, atypical way as the end-of-word indicator.

* Zero or More Occurrences

This character is a modifier that will match zero or more occurrences of the character immediately preceding it. For example, the command **/dis*m** will match the string **di** followed by zero or more s characters followed by an **m**. Examples of successful matches would include **dim**, or **dism**, and **dissm**.

[ ] Character-Class Definition

Brackets surrounding two or more characters match any *single* character located between the brackets. For example, the command **/dis[ck]** finds the next occurrence of *either* **disk** or **disc**.

There are two special characters you can use within a character-class definition. Using a caret (^) as the first character following the left bracket defines the character class to be *any except the following characters*. A hyphen between two characters indicates a range of characters. Refer to the examples in Table 6-4.

Table 6-4 Search examples

Search string	What it finds
/and	Finds the next occurrence of the string **and** **Examples: sand and standard slander andiron**
/\<and\>	Finds the next occurrence of the word **and** **Example: and**
/^The	Finds the next line that starts with **The** **Examples:** **The . . .** **There . . .**
/^[0-9][0-9])	Finds the next line that starts with a two-digit number followed by a right parenthesis **Examples:** **77)...** **01)...** **15)...**
/\<[adr]	Finds the next word that starts with **a**, **d**, or **r** **Examples: apple drive road argument right**
/^[A-Za-z]	Finds the next line that starts with an uppercase or lowercase letter **Examples:** **will not find a line starting with the number 7 . . .** **Dear Mr. Jones . . .** **in the middle of a sentence like this . . .**

SUBSTITUTING ONE STRING FOR ANOTHER

A Substitute command combines the effects of a Search command and a Change command. That is, it searches for a string (regular expression) just as the **/** command does, allowing the same special characters discussed in the previous section. When it finds the string or matches the regular expression, the Substitute command changes the string or regular expression it matches. The syntax of the Substitute command is

:[g][address]s/search-string/replacement-string[/option]

As with all commands that begin with a colon, vim executes a Substitute command from the status line.

THE SUBSTITUTE ADDRESS

If you do not specify an *address,* Substitute searches only the current line. If you use a single line number as the *address,* Substitute searches that line. If the *address* is two line numbers separated by a comma, Substitute searches those lines and the lines between them. Refer to "Line numbers" on page 204 if you want vim to display line numbers. Wherever a line number is allowed in the *address,* you might also use an *address* string enclosed between slashes. The vim editor operates on the next line that the *address* string matches. When you precede the first slash of the *address* string with the letter **g** (for global), vim operates on all lines in the file that the *address* string matches. (This **g** is not the same as the one that goes at the end of the Substitute command to cause multiple replacements on a single line; see "Searching for and Replacing Strings").

Within the *address,* a period represents the current line, a dollar sign represents the last line in the Work buffer, and a percent sign represents the entire Work buffer. You can perform *address* arithmetic using plus and minus signs. Table 6-5 shows some examples of *addresses*.

Table 6-5 Addresses

Address	Portion of Work buffer addressed
5	Line 5
77,100	Lines 77 through 100 inclusive
1,.	Beginning of Work buffer through current line
.,$	Current line through end of Work buffer
1,$	Entire Work buffer
%	Entire Work buffer
/pine/	The next line containing the word **pine**
g/pine/	All lines containing the word **pine**
.,.+10	Current line through tenth following line (11 lines in all)

SEARCHING FOR AND REPLACING STRINGS

An s comes after the *address* in the command syntax, indicating that this is a Substitute command. A delimiter follows the s, marking the beginning of the *search-string.*

Although the examples in this book use a forward slash, you can use as a delimiter any character that is not a letter, number, blank, or backslash. You must use the same delimiter at the end of the *search-string*.

Next comes the *search-string*. It has the same format as the search string in the **/** command and can include the same special characters (page 191). (The *search-string* is a regular expression; refer to Appendix A for more information.) Another delimiter marks the end of the *search-string* and the beginning of the *replacement-string*.

The *replacement-string* replaces the text matched by the *search-string* and is typically followed by the delimiter character. You can omit the final delimiter when no option follows the *replacement-string;* a final delimiter is required if an option is present.

Several characters have special meanings in the *search-string*, and other characters have special meanings in the *replacement-string*. For example, an ampersand (&) in the *replacement-string* represents the text that was matched by the *search-string*. A backslash in the *replacement-string* quotes the character that follows it. Refer to Table 6-6 and Appendix A.

Table 6-6 Search and replace examples

Command	Result
:s/bigger/biggest/	Replaces the first occurrence of the string **bigger** on the current line with **biggest** **Example:** **bigger ⇨ biggest**
:1,.s/Ch 1/Ch 2/g	Replaces every occurrence of the string **Ch 1**, before or on the current line, with the string **Ch 2** **Examples:** **Ch 1 ⇨ Ch 2** **Ch 12 ⇨ Ch 22**
:1,$s/ten/10/g	Replaces every occurrence of the string **ten** with the string **10** **Examples:** **ten ⇨ 10** **often ⇨ of10** **tenant ⇨ 10ant**
:g/chapter/s/ten/10/	Replaces the first occurrence of the string **ten** with the string **10** on all lines containing the word **chapter** **Examples:** **chapter ten ⇨ chapter 10** **chapters will often ⇨ chapters will of10**

Table 6-6 Search and replace examples (continued)

Command	Result
:%s/\<ten\>/10/g	Replaces every occurrence of the word **ten** with the string **10** **Example:** **ten ⇨ 10**
:.,.+10s/every/each/g	Replaces every occurrence of the string **every** with the string **each** on the current line through the tenth following line **Examples:** **every ⇨ each** **everything ⇨ eachthing**
:s/\<short\>/"&"/	Replaces the word **short** on the current line with **"short"** (enclosed within quotation marks) **Example:** **the shortest of the short ⇨ the shortest of the "short"**

Normally, the Substitute command replaces only the first occurrence of any text that matches the ***search-string*** on a line. If you want a global substitution—that is, if you want to replace all matching occurrences of text on a line—append the **g** (global) option after the delimiter that ends the ***replacement-string***. A useful option, **c** (check), causes vim to ask whether you would like to make the change each time it finds text that matches the ***search-string***. Pressing **y** replaces the ***search-string***, **q** terminates the command, **l** (last) makes the replacement and quits, **a** (all) makes all remaining replacements, and **n** continues the search without making that replacement.

The ***address*** string need not be the same as the ***search-string***. For example,

```
:/candle/s/wick/flame/
```

substitutes **flame** for the first occurrence of **wick** on the next line that contains the string **candle**. Similarly,

```
:g/candle/s/wick/flame/
```

performs the same substitution for the first occurrence of **wick** on each line of the file containing the string **candle** and

```
:g/candle/s/wick/flame/g
```

performs the same substitution for all occurrences of **wick** on each line that contains the string **candle**.

If the ***search-string*** is the same as the ***address***, you can leave the ***search-string*** blank. For example, the command **:/candle/s//lamp/** is equivalent to the command **:/candle/s/candle/lamp/**.

Miscellaneous Commands

This section describes three commands that do not fit naturally into any other groups.

Join

Join (J)

The J (Join) command joins the line below the current line to the end of the current line, inserting a SPACE between what was previously two lines and leaving the cursor on this SPACE. If the current line ends with a period, vim inserts two SPACEs.

You can always "unjoin" (break) a line into two lines by replacing the SPACE or SPACEs where you want to break the line with a RETURN.

Status

Status (CONTROL-G)

The Status command, CONTROL-G, displays the name of the file you are editing, information about whether the file has been modified or is a readonly file, the number of the current line, the total number of lines in the Work buffer, and the percentage of the Work buffer preceding the current line. You can also use **:f** to display status information. Following is a sample status line:

```
"/usr/share/dict/words" [readonly] line 28501 of 98569 --28%-- col 1
```

. (Period)

Repeat last command (.)

The **.** (period) command repeats the most recent command that made a change. If you had just given a **d2w** command (delete the next two words), for example, the **.** command would delete the next two words. If you had just inserted text, the **.** command would repeat the insertion of the same text. This command is useful if you want to change some occurrences of a word or phrase in the Work buffer. Search for the first occurrence of the word (use **/**) and then make the change you want (use **cw**). You can then use **n** to search for the next occurrence of the word and **.** to make the same change to it. If you do not want to make the change, give the **n** command again to find the next occurrence.

Copying, Moving, and Deleting Text

The vim editor has a General-Purpose buffer and 26 Named buffers that can hold text during an editing session. These buffers are useful if you want to move or copy a portion of text to another location in the Work buffer. A combination of the Delete and Put commands removes text from one location in the Work buffer and places it in another location in the Work buffer. The Yank and Put commands copy text to another location in the Work buffer without changing the original text.

THE GENERAL-PURPOSE BUFFER

The vim editor stores the text that you most recently changed, deleted, or yanked (covered below) in the General-Purpose buffer. The Undo command retrieves text from the General-Purpose buffer when it restores text.

COPYING TEXT TO THE BUFFER

Yank (**y**/**Y**) The Yank command (**y**) is identical to the Delete (**d**) command except that it does not delete text from the Work buffer. The vim editor places a *copy* of the yanked text in the General-Purpose buffer. You can then use a Put command to place another copy of it elsewhere in the Work buffer. Use the Yank command just as you use the Delete command. The uppercase **Y** command yanks an entire line into the General-Purpose buffer.

Use yy to yank one line

tip Just as **d** RETURN deletes two lines, so **y** RETURN yanks two lines. Use the **yy** command to yank and **dd** to delete the current line.

D works differently from Y

tip The **D** command (page 187) does not work in the same manner as the **Y** command. Whereas the **D** deletes to the end of the line, **Y** yanks the entire line regardless of the cursor position.

COPYING TEXT FROM THE BUFFER

Put (**p**/**P**) The Put commands, **p** and **P**, copy text from the General-Purpose buffer to the Work buffer. When you delete or yank characters or words into the General-Purpose buffer, **p** inserts them after the current *character,* and **P** inserts them before this character. If you delete or yank lines, sentences, or paragraphs, **P** inserts the contents of the General-Purpose buffer before the current *line,* and **p** inserts them after the current line.

Put commands do not destroy the contents of the General-Purpose buffer. Thus you can place the same text at several points within the file by giving one Delete or Yank command and several Put commands.

DELETING TEXT COPIES IT INTO THE BUFFER

Any of the Delete commands described earlier in this chapter (page 186) place the deleted text in the General-Purpose buffer. Just as you can use the Undo command to put the deleted text back where it came from, so you can use a Put command to put the deleted text at another location in the Work buffer.

Suppose you delete a word from the middle of a sentence by giving the **dw** command and then move the cursor to a SPACE between two words and give a **p** command; vim places the word you just deleted at the new location. If you delete a line using the **dd** command and then move the cursor to the line *below* the line where you want the deleted line to appear and give a **P** command, vim places the line at the new location.

optional

Named Buffers

You can use a Named buffer with any of the Delete, Yank, or Put commands. Each of the 26 Named buffers is named by a letter of the alphabet. Each Named buffer can store a different block of text and you can recall each block as needed. Unlike the General-Purpose buffer, vim does not change the contents of a Named buffer unless you issue a command that specifically overwrites that buffer. The vim editor maintains the contents of the Named buffers throughout an editing session.

The vim editor stores text in a Named buffer if you precede a Delete or Yank command with a double quotation mark (") and a buffer name (for example, **"kyy** yanks a copy of the current line into buffer **k**). You can put information from the Work buffer into a Named buffer in two ways. First, if you give the name of the buffer as a lowercase letter, vim overwrites the contents of the buffer when it deletes or yanks text into the buffer. Second, if you use an uppercase letter for the buffer name, vim appends the newly deleted or yanked text to the end of the buffer. This feature enables you to collect blocks of text from various sections of a file and deposit them at one place in the file with a single command. Named buffers are also useful when you are moving a section of a file and do not want to give a Put command immediately after the corresponding Delete command, and when you want to insert a paragraph, sentence, or phrase repeatedly in a document.

If you have one sentence you use throughout a document, you can yank that sentence into a Named buffer and put it wherever you need it by using the following procedure: After entering the first occurrence of the sentence and pressing ESCAPE to return to Command mode, leave the cursor on the line containing the sentence. (The sentence must appear on a line or lines by itself for this procedure to work.) Then yank the sentence into Named buffer **a** by giving the **"ayy** command (or **"a2yy** if the sentence takes up two lines). Now anytime you need the sentence, you can return to Command mode and give the command **"ap** to put a copy of the sentence below the current line.

This technique provides a quick and easy way to insert text that you use frequently in a document. For example, if you were editing a legal document, you might store the phrase **The Plaintiff alleges that the Defendant** in a Named buffer to save yourself the trouble of typing it every time you want to use it. Similarly, if you were creating a letter that frequently used a long company name, such as **National Standards Institute**, you might put it into a Named buffer.

Numbered Buffers

In addition to the 26 Named buffers and 1 General-Purpose buffer, 9 Numbered buffers are available. They are, in one sense, readonly buffers. The vim editor fills them with the nine most recently deleted chunks of text that are at least one line long. The most recently deleted text is held in **"1**, the next most recent in **"2**, and so on. If you delete a block of text and then give other vim commands so that you cannot reclaim the deleted text with an Undo command, you can use **"1p** to paste the most recently deleted chunk of text below the location of the cursor. If you have deleted several blocks of text and want to reclaim a specific one, proceed as follows: Paste the contents of the first buffer with **"1p**. If the first buffer does not hold the text you are looking for, undo the paste operation with **u** and then give the period (**.**) command to repeat the previous command. The Numbered buffers work in a unique way with the period command: Instead of pasting the contents of buffer **"1**, the period command pastes the contents of the next buffer (**"2**). Another **u** and period would replace the contents of buffer **"2** with that of buffer **"3**, and so on through the nine buffers.

READING AND WRITING FILES

Exit (**ZZ**) The vim editor reads a disk file into the Work buffer when you specify a filename on the command line you use to call vim. A ZZ command that terminates an editing session writes the contents of the Work buffer back to the disk file. This section discusses other ways of reading text into the Work buffer and writing it to a file.

READING FILES

Read (**:r**) The Read command reads a file into the Work buffer. The new file does not overwrite any text in the Work buffer but rather is positioned following the single address you specify (or the current line if you do not specify an address). You can use an address of 0 to read the file into the beginning of the Work buffer. The Read command has the following syntax:

*:[address]r [**filename**]*

As with other commands that begin with a colon, when you enter the colon it appears on the status line. The ***filename*** is the pathname of the file that you want to read and must be terminated by RETURN. If you omit the ***filename***, vim reads from the disk the file you are editing.

WRITING FILES

Write (**:w**) The Write command writes part or all of the Work buffer to a file. You can specify an address to write part of the Work buffer and a filename to specify a file to receive the text. If you do not specify an address or filename, vim writes the entire contents of the Work buffer to the file you are editing, updating the file on the disk.

During a long editing session, it is a good idea to use the Write command occasionally. If a problem develops later, a recent copy of the Work buffer is then safe on the disk. If you use a **:q!** command to exit from vim, the disk file reflects the version of the Work buffer at the time you last used a Write command.

The Write command has two syntaxes:

:[address]w[!] [filename]
:[address]w>> filename

The second syntax appends text to an existing file. The ***address*** specifies the portion of the Work buffer vim will write to the file. The ***address*** follows the form of the ***address*** that the Substitute command uses (page 194). If you do not specify an ***address,*** vim writes the entire contents of the Work buffer. The optional ***filename*** is the pathname of the file you are writing to. If you do not specify a ***filename,*** vim writes to the file you are editing.

w! Because the Write command can quickly destroy a large amount of work, vim demands that you enter an exclamation point (**!**) following the **w** as a safeguard against accidentally overwriting a file. The only times you do not need an exclamation point are when you are writing out the entire contents of the Work buffer to the file being edited (using no ***address*** and no ***filename***) and when you are writing part or all of the Work buffer to a new file. When you are writing part of the file to the file being edited or when you are overwriting another file, you must use an exclamation point.

IDENTIFYING THE CURRENT FILE

The File command (**:f**) provides the same information as the Status command (CONTROL-G; page 197). The filename the File command displays is the one the Write command uses if you give a **:w** command without a filename.

SETTING PARAMETERS

You can tailor the vim editor to your needs and habits by setting vim parameters. Parameters perform such functions as displaying line numbers, automatically inserting RETURNs, and establishing incremental and nonstandard searches.

You can set parameters in several ways. For example, you can set them to establish the environment for the current editing session while you are using vim. Alternatively, you can set the parameters in your **~/.bash_profile** (bash) or **~/.tcshrc** (tcsh) shell startup file or in the vim startup file, **~/.vimrc**. When you set the parameters in any of these files, the same customized environment will be available each time vim starts and you can begin editing immediately.

SETTING PARAMETERS FROM WITHIN vim

To set a parameter while you are using vim, enter a colon (**:**), the word **set**, a SPACE, and the parameter (refer to "Parameters" on the next page). The command appears on the status line as you type it and takes effect when you press RETURN. The following command establishes incremental searches for the current editing session:

```
:set incsearch
```

SETTING PARAMETERS IN A STARTUP FILE

VIMINIT If you are using bash, you can put a line with the following syntax in your **~/.bash_profile** startup file (page 288):

*export VIMINIT='set **param1 param2** ...'*

Replace ***param1*** and ***param2*** with parameters selected from Table 6-7. **VIMINIT** is a shell variable that vim reads. The following statement causes vim to ignore the case of characters in searches, display line numbers, use the TC Shell to execute Linux commands, and wrap text 15 characters from the right edge of the screen:

```
export VIMINIT='set ignorecase number shell=/bin/tcsh wrapmargin=15'
```

If you use the parameter abbreviations, it looks like this:

```
export VIMINIT='set ic nu sh=/bin/tcsh wm=15'
```

If you are using tcsh, put the following line in your **~/.tcshrc** startup file (page 382):

*setenv VIMINIT 'set **param1 param2** ...'*

Again, replace ***param1*** and ***param2*** with parameters from Table 6-7. The values between the single quotation marks are the same as those shown in the preceding examples.

THE .vimrc STARTUP FILE

Instead of setting vim parameters in your shell startup file, you can create a **~/.vimrc** file in your home directory and set the parameters there. Creating a **.vimrc** file causes vim to start with the **compatible** parameter unset (page 174). Lines in a **.vimrc** file follow this syntax:

*set **param1 param2** ...*

Following are examples of **.vimrc** files that perform the same function as **VIMINIT** described previously:

```
$ cat ~/.vimrc
set ignorecase
set number
set shell=/bin/tcsh
set wrapmargin=15

$ cat ~/.vimrc
set ic nu sh=/bin/tcsh wm=15
```

Parameters set by the **VIMINIT** variable take precedence over those set in the **.vimrc** file.

PARAMETERS

Table 6-7 lists some of the most useful vim parameters. The vim editor displays a complete list of parameters and indicates how they are currently set when you give the command **:set all** followed by a RETURN. The command **:set** RETURN displays a list of options that are set to values other than their default values. Two classes of parameters exist: those that contain an equal sign (and can take on a value) and those that are optionally prefixed with **no** (switches that are on or off). You can change the sense of a switch parameter by giving the command **:set** [**no**]***param***. For example, give the command **:set number** (or **:set nonumber**) to turn on (or off) line numbering. To change the value of a parameter that takes on a value (and uses an equal sign), give a command such as **:set shiftwidth=15**.

Most parameters have abbreviations—for example, **nu** for **number**, **nonu** for **nonumber**, and **sw** for **shiftwidth**. The abbreviations are listed in the left column of Table 6-7, following the name of the parameter.

Table 6-7 Parameters

Parameter	Effect
Allow special characters in searches **magic**	Refer to "Special Characters in Search Strings" on page 191. By default the following characters have special meanings when used in a search string: **. [ ] *** When you set the **nomagic** parameter, these characters no longer have special meanings. The **magic** parameter restores their special meanings. The **^** and **$** characters always have special meanings within search strings, regardless of how you set this parameter.
Automatic indention **autoindent**, **ai**	The automatic indention feature works with the **shiftwidth** parameter to provide a regular set of indentions for programs or tabular material. This feature is off by default. You can turn it on by setting **autoindent** and turn it off by setting **noautoindent**. When automatic indention is on and vim is in Input mode, pressing CONTROL-T moves the cursor from the left margin (or an indention) to the next indention position, pressing RETURN moves the cursor to the left side of the next line under the first character of the previous line, and pressing CONTROL-D backs up over indention positions. The CONTROL-T and CONTROL-D keys work only before text is placed on a line.
Automatic write **autowrite**, **aw**	By default vim asks you before writing out the Work buffer when you have not explicitly told it to do so (as when you give a **:n** command to edit the next file). The **autowrite** option causes vim to write the Work buffer automatically when you use commands, such as **:n**, to edit to another file. You can disable this parameter by setting the **noautowrite** or **noaw** option.
Flash **flash**, **fl**	The vim editor normally causes the terminal to beep when you give an invalid command or press ESCAPE when it is in Command mode. Setting the parameter **flash** causes the terminal to flash instead of beep. Set **noflash** to cause it to beep. Not all terminals and emulators support this parameter.

Table 6-7 Parameters (continued)

Parameter	Effect
Ignore case in searches **ignorecase**, **ic**	The vim editor normally performs case-sensitive searches, differentiating between uppercase and lowercase letters. It performs case-insensitive searches when you set the **ignorecase** parameter. Set **noignorecase** to restore case-sensitive searches.
Incremental search **incsearch**, **is**	Refer to "Normal Versus Incremental Searches" on page 191. By default vim does not perform incremental searches. To cause vim to perform incremental searches, set the parameter **incsearch**. To cause vim not to perform incremental searches, set the parameter **noincsearch**.
Invisible characters **list**	To cause vim to display each TAB as **^I** and to mark the end of each line with a **$**, set the **list** parameter. To display TABs as whitespace and not mark ends of lines, set **nolist**.
Status line **laststatus=*n***, **ls=*n***	This parameter displays a status line that shows the name of the file you are editing, a **[+]** if the file has been changed since it was last written out, and the position of the cursor. When setting the parameter **laststatus=*n***, ***n*** equal to **0** (zero) turns off the status line, **1** displays the status line when at least two vim windows are displayed, and **2** always displays the status line.
Line numbers **number**, **nu**	The vim editor does not normally display the line number associated with each line. To display line numbers, set the parameter **number**. To cause line numbers not to be displayed, set the parameter **nonumber**. Line numbers are not part of the file, are not stored with the file, and are not displayed when the file is printed. They appear on the screen only while you are using vim.
Line wrap **wrap**	The line wrap controls how vim displays lines that are too long to fit on the screen. To cause vim to wrap long lines and continue them on the next line, set **wrap** (set by default). If you set **nowrap**, vim truncates long lines at the right edge of the screen.
Line wrap margin **wrapmargin=*nn***, **wm=*nn***	The line wrap margin causes vim to break the text that you are inserting at approximately the specified number of characters from the right margin. The vim editor breaks the text by inserting a NEWLINE character at the closest blank-delimited word boundary. Setting the line wrap margin is handy if you want all the text lines to be approximately the same length. This feature relieves you of the need to remember to press RETURN to end each line of input. When setting the parameter **wrapmargin=*nn***, ***nn*** is the number of characters *from the right side of the screen* where you want vim to break the text. This number is not the column width of the text but rather the distance from the end of the text to the right edge of the screen. Setting the wrap margin to **0** (zero) turns this feature off. By default the line wrap margin is off (set to **0**).

Table 6-7 Parameters (continued)

Parameter	Effect
Report **report=*nn***	This parameter causes vim to display a report on the status line whenever you make a change that affects at least ***nn*** lines. For example, if **report** is set to **7** and you delete seven lines, vim displays the message **7 lines deleted**. When you delete six or fewer lines, vim does not display a message. The default for **report** is **5**.
Scroll **scroll=*nn*, scr=*nn***	This parameter controls the number of lines that CONTROL-D and CONTROL-U (page 184) scroll text on the screen. By default **scroll** is set to half the window height. There are two ways to change the value of **scroll**. First you can enter a number before pressing CONTROL-D or CONTROL-U; vim sets **scroll** to that number. Alternatively, you can set **scroll** explicitly with **scroll=*nn***, where ***nn*** is the number of lines you want to scroll with each CONTROL-D or CONTROL-U command.
Shell **shell=*path*, sh=*path***	While you are using vim, you can cause it to spawn a new shell. You can either create an interactive shell (if you want to run several commands) or run a single command. The **shell** parameter determines which shell vim invokes. By default vim sets the **shell** parameter to your login shell. To change it, set the parameter **shell=*path***, where ***path*** is the absolute pathname of the shell you want to use.
Shift width **shiftwidth=*nn*, sw=*nn***	This parameter controls the functioning of CONTROL-T and CONTROL-D in Input mode when automatic indention is on (see "Automatic indention" in this table). When setting the parameter **shiftwidth=*nn***, ***nn*** is the spacing of the indention positions (**8** by default). Setting the shift width is similar to setting the TAB stops on a typewriter; with **shiftwidth**, however, the distance between TAB stops remains constant.
Show match **showmatch**, **sm**	This parameter is useful for programmers who are working in languages that use braces (**{ }**) or parentheses as expression delimiters (Lisp, C, Tcl, and so on). When **showmatch** is set and you are entering code (in Input mode) and type a closing brace or parenthesis, the cursor jumps briefly to the matching opening brace or parenthesis (that is, the preceding corresponding element at the same nesting level). After it highlights the matching element, the cursor resumes its previous position. When you type a right brace or parenthesis that does not have a match, vim beeps. Use **noshowmatch** to turn off automatic matching.
Show mode **showmode**, **smd**	Set the parameter **showmode** to display the mode in the lower-right corner of the screen when vim is in Input mode (default). Set **noshowmode** to cause vim not to display the mode.

Table 6-7 Parameters (continued)

Parameter	Effect
vi compatibility **compatible**, **cp**	Refer to "The compatible Parameter" on page 174. By default, vim does not attempt to be compatible with vi. To cause vim to be compatible with vi, set the parameter **compatible**. To cause vim not to be compatible with vi, set the parameter **nocompatible**.
Wrap scan **wrapscan**, **ws**	By default, when a search for the next occurrence of a search string reaches the end of the Work buffer, vim continues the search at the beginning of the Work buffer. The reverse is true with a search for the previous occurrence of a search string. The **nowrapscan** parameter stops the search at either end of the Work buffer. Set the **wrapscan** parameter if you want searches to wrap around the ends of the Work buffer.

ADVANCED EDITING TECHNIQUES

This section presents several commands you might find useful once you have become comfortable using vim.

optional

USING MARKERS

While you are using vim, you can set and use markers to make addressing more convenient. Set a marker by giving the command **m*c***, where *c* is any character. (Letters are preferred because some characters, such as a single quotation mark, have special meanings when used as markers.) The vim editor does not preserve markers when you exit from vim.

Once you have set a marker, you can use it in a manner similar to a line number. You can move the cursor to the beginning of a line that contains a marker by preceding the marker name with a single quotation mark. For example, to set marker **t**, position the cursor on the line you want to mark and give the command **mt**. During the remainder of this editing session, unless you reset marker **t** or delete the line it marks, you can return to the beginning of the line you marked by giving the command **'t**.

You can delete all text from the current line through the line containing marker **r** with the following command:

```
d'r
```

You can use a back tick (**`**, also called a grave accent or reverse single quotation mark) to go to the exact position of the marker on the line. After setting marker **t**, you can move the cursor to the location of this marker (not the beginning of the line that holds the marker) with the command **`t**. The following command deletes all the text from the current line up to the character where the marker **r** was placed; the rest of the line containing the marker remains intact:

```
d`r
```

You can use markers in addresses of commands instead of line numbers. The following command replaces all occurrences of **The** with **THE** on all lines starting from marker **m** to the current line (marker **m** must precede the current line):

```
:'m,.s/The/THE/g
```

EDITING OTHER FILES

The following command causes vim to edit the file you specify with ***filename***:

*:e[!] [**filename**]*

If you want to save the contents of the Work buffer, you must write it out (using **:w**) before you give this command. If you do not want to save the contents of the Work buffer, vim insists you use an exclamation point to acknowledge that you will lose the work you did since the last time you wrote out the Work buffer. If you do not supply a ***filename***, vim edits the file you are working on.

:e! The command **:e!** starts an editing session over again. This command returns the Work buffer to the state it was in the last time you wrote it out or, if you have not written it out, the state it was in when you started editing the file. It is useful when you make mistakes while editing a file and decide that it would be easier to start over than to fix the mistakes.

Because the **:e** command does not destroy the contents of the General-Purpose or Named buffers, you can store text from one file in a buffer, use a **:e** command to edit a second file, and put text from the buffer in the second file.

:e# The command **:e#** closes the current file and opens the last file you were editing, placing the cursor on the line that it was on when you last closed the file. If you do not save the file you are working on before you give this command, vim prompts you to do so. Setting the **autowrite** parameter (page 203) will not stop vim from prompting you.

:n
:rew The **:e#** command can help you copy blocks of text from one file to another. When you call vim with the names of several files as arguments, you can use **:n** to edit the next file, **:e#** to edit the file you just edited, and **:rew** to rewind the sequence of files so that you are editing the first file again. As you move between files, you can copy text from one file into a buffer and paste that text into another file. You can use **:n!** to force vim to close a file without writing out changes before it opens the next file.

MACROS AND SHORTCUTS

:map The vim editor allows you to create both macros and shortcuts. The **:map** command defines a key or sequence of keys that perform some action in Command mode. The following command maps CONTROL-X to the commands that will find the next left bracket on the current line (**f[**), delete all characters from that bracket to the next right bracket (**df]**) on the same line, delete the next character (**x**), move the cursor down two lines (**2j**), and finally move the cursor to the beginning of the line (**0**):

```
:map ^X f[df]x2j0
```

Although you can use ESCAPE and CONTROL sequences, it is a good idea to avoid remapping characters or sequences that are vim commands. Type **:map** by itself to see a list of the current mappings. You might need to use CONTROL-V (page 186) to quote some of the characters you want to enter into the **:map** string.

:abbrev The **:abbrev** command is similar to **:map** but creates abbreviations you can use while in Input mode. When you are in Input mode and type a string you have defined with **:abbrev**, followed by a SPACE, vim replaces the string and the SPACE with the characters you specified when you defined the string. For ease of use, avoid common sequences of characters when creating abbreviations. The following command defines **ZZ** as an abbreviation for **Sam the Great**:

```
:abbrev ZZ Sam the Great
```

Even though **ZZ** is a vim command, it is used only in Command mode. It has no special meaning in Input mode, where you use abbreviations.

EXECUTING SHELL COMMANDS FROM WITHIN vim

:sh You can execute shell commands in several ways while you are using vim. For instance, you can spawn a new interactive shell by giving the following command and pressing RETURN:

```
:sh
```

The vim **shell** parameter (page 205) determines which shell is spawned (usually bash or tcsh). By default **shell** is the same as your login shell.

After you have finished your work in the shell, you can return to vim by exiting from the shell (press CONTROL-D or give an **exit** command).

If :sh does not work correctly

tip The **:sh** command might behave strangely depending on how the shell has been configured. You might get warnings with the **:sh** command or it might even hang. Experiment with the **:sh** command to be sure it works correctly with your configuration. If it does not, you might want to set the vim **shell** parameter to another shell before using **:sh**. For example, the following command causes vim to use tcsh with the **:sh** command:

```
:set shell=/bin/tcsh
```

You might need to change the **SHELL** environment variable after starting **:sh** to show the correct shell.

Edit only one copy of a file

caution When you create a new shell by giving the command **:sh**, remember you are still using vim. A common mistake is to try to edit the same file from the new shell, forgetting that vim is already editing the file from a different shell. Because you can lose information by editing the same file from two instances of an editor, vim warns you when you make this mistake. Refer to "File Locks" on page 178 to see an example of the message that vim displays.

:!*command* You can execute a shell command line from vim by giving the following command, replacing ***command*** with the command line you want to execute and terminating the command with a RETURN:

> :!*command*

The vim editor spawns a new shell that executes the ***command***. When the ***command*** runs to completion, the newly spawned shell returns control to the editor.

:!!*command* You can execute a command from vim and have it replace the current line with the output from the command. If you do not want to replace any text, put the cursor on a blank line before giving the following command:

> !!*command*

Nothing happens when you enter the first exclamation point. When you enter the second one, vim moves the cursor to the status line and allows you to enter the command you want to execute. Because this command puts vim in Last Line mode, you must end the command with a RETURN (as you would end most shell commands).

You can also execute a command from vim with standard input to the command coming from all or part of the file you are editing and standard output from the command replacing the input in the file you are editing. This type of command is handy for sorting a list in place within a file.

To specify the block of text that will become standard input for the command, move the cursor to one end of the block of text. Then enter an exclamation point followed by a command that would normally move the cursor to the other end of the block of text. For example, if the cursor is at the beginning of the file and you want to specify the whole file, give the command **!G**. If you want to specify the part of the file between the cursor and marker **b**, give the command **!'b**. After you give the cursor-movement command, vim displays an exclamation point on the status line and waits for you to enter a shell command.

To sort a list of names in a file, move the cursor to the beginning of the list and set marker **q** with an **mq** command. Then move the cursor to the end of the list and give the following command:

```
!'qsort
```

Press RETURN and wait. After a few seconds, the sorted list should replace the original list on the screen. If the command did not behave as expected, you can usually undo the change with a **u** command. Refer to page 969 for more information on sort.

! can destroy a file

caution If you enter the wrong command or mistype a command, you can destroy a file (for example, if the command hangs or stops vim from working). For this reason it is a good idea to save your file before using this command. The Undo command (page 186) can be a lifesaver. A **:e!** command (page 207) will get rid of the changes, returning the buffer to the state it was in last time you saved it.

As with the **:sh** command, the default shell might not work properly with the **!** command. You might want to test the shell with a sample file before executing this command with your real work. If the default shell does not work properly, change the **shell** parameter.

UNITS OF MEASURE

Many vim commands operate on a block of text—ranging from one character to many paragraphs. You specify the size of a block of text with a *Unit of Measure*. You can specify multiple Units of Measure by preceding a Unit of Measure with a Repeat Factor (page 213). This section defines the various Units of Measure.

CHARACTER

A character is one character—visible or not, printable or not—including SPACEs and TABs. Some examples of characters are

```
a  q  A  .  5  R  -  >  TAB SPACE
```

WORD

A word, similar to a word in the English language, is a string of one or more characters bounded on both sides by any combination of one or more of the following elements: a punctuation mark, SPACE, TAB, numeral, or NEWLINE. In addition, vim considers each group of punctuation marks to be a word (Table 6-8).

Table 6-8 Words

Word count	Text
1	`pear`
2	`pear!`
2	`pear!)`
3	`pear!) The`
4	`pear!) "The`
11	`This is a short, concise line (no frills).`

BLANK-DELIMITED WORD

A blank-delimited word is the same as a word but includes adjacent punctuation. Blank-delimited words are separated by one or more of the following elements: either a SPACE, TAB, or NEWLINE (Table 6-9).

Table 6-9 Blank-delimited words

Word count	Text
1	`pear`
1	`pear!`
1	`pear!)`
2	`pear!) The`
2	`pear!) "The`
8	`This is a short, concise line (no frills).`

LINE

A line is a string of characters bounded by NEWLINEs that is not necessarily displayed as a single physical line on the screen. You can enter a very long single (logical) line that wraps around (continues on the next physical line) several times or disappears off the right edge of the display. It is a good idea to avoid creating long logical lines; ideally, you would terminate lines with a RETURN before they reach the right side of the screen. Terminating lines in this manner ensures that each physical line contains one logical line and avoids confusion when you edit and format text. Some commands do not *appear* to work properly on physical lines that are longer than the width of the screen. For example, with the cursor on a long logical line that wraps around several physical lines, pressing RETURN once appears to move the cursor down more than one line. You can use fmt (page 831) to break long logical lines into shorter ones.

SENTENCE

A sentence is an English sentence or the equivalent. A sentence starts at the end of the previous sentence and ends with a period, exclamation point, or question mark, followed by two SPACEs or a NEWLINE (Table 6-10).

Table 6-10 Sentences

Sentence count	Text
One: only one SPACE after the first period and a NEWLINE after the second period	`That's it. This is one sentence.`

Table 6-10 Sentences (continued)

Sentence count	Text
Two: two SPACEs after the first period and a NEWLINE after the second period	`That's it.  This is two sentences.`
Three: two SPACEs after the first two question marks and a NEWLINE after the exclamation point	`What?  Three sentences?  One line!`

One: NEWLINE after the period	`This sentence takes`
	`up a total of`
	`three lines.`

PARAGRAPH

A paragraph is preceded and followed by one or more blank lines. A blank line is composed of two NEWLINE characters in a row (Table 6-11).

Table 6-11 Paragraphs

Paragraph count	Text
One: blank line before and after text	 `One paragraph`

One: blank line before and after text	
	`        This might appear to be`
	`more than one paragraph.`
	`        Just because there are`
	`two indentions does not mean`
	`it qualifies as two paragraphs.`

Three: three blocks of text separated by blank lines	
	`Even though in`
	
	`English this is only`
	`one sentence,`
	
	`vim considers it to be`
	`three paragraphs.`

Screen (Window)

Under vim, a screen or terminal emulator window can display one or more logical windows of information. A window displays all or part of a Work buffer. Figure 6-5 on page 171 shows a screen with two windows.

Repeat Factor

A number that precedes a Unit of Measure (page 210) is a Repeat Factor. Just as the 5 in *5 inches* causes you to consider *5 inches* as a single Unit of Measure, so a Repeat Factor causes vim to group more than one Unit of Measure and consider it as a single Unit of Measure. For example, the command **w** moves the cursor forward 1 word, the command **5w** moves it forward 5 words, and the command **250w** moves it forward 250 words. If you do not specify a Repeat Factor, vim assumes a Repeat Factor of 1. If the Repeat Factor would move the cursor past the end of the file, the cursor is left at the end of the file.

Chapter Summary

This summary of vim includes all the commands covered in this chapter, plus a few more. Table 6-12 lists some of the ways you can call vim from the command line.

Table 6-12 Calling vim

Command	Result
vim *filename*	Edits ***filename*** starting at line 1
vim +*n filename*	Edits ***filename*** starting at line ***n***
vim + *filename*	Edits ***filename*** starting at the last line
vim +/*pattern filename*	Edits ***filename*** starting at the first line containing ***pattern***
vim –r *filename*	Recovers ***filename*** after a system crash
vim –R *filename*	Edits ***filename*** readonly (same as opening the file with view)

You must be in Command mode to use commands that move the cursor by Units of Measure (Table 6-13). You can use these Units of Measure with Change, Delete, and Yank commands. Each of these commands can be preceded by a Repeat Factor.

Table 6-13 Moving the cursor by Units of Measure

Command	Moves the cursor
SPACE, **l** (ell), *or* RIGHT ARROW	Space to the right
h *or* LEFT ARROW	Space to the left
w	Word to the right

Table 6-13 Moving the cursor by Units of Measure (continued)

Command	Moves the cursor
W	Blank-delimited word to the right
b	Word to the left
B	Blank-delimited word to the left
$	End of line
e	End of word to the right
E	End of blank-delimited word to the right
0 (zero)	Beginning of line (cannot be used with a Repeat Factor)
RETURN	Beginning of next line
j *or* DOWN ARROW	Down one line
–	Beginning of previous line
k *or* UP ARROW	Up one line
)	End of sentence
(	Beginning of sentence
}	End of paragraph
{	Beginning of paragraph
%	Move to matching brace of same type at same nesting level

Table 6-14 shows the commands that enable you to view different parts of the Work buffer.

Table 6-14 Viewing the Work buffer

Command	Moves the cursor
CONTROL-D	Forward one-half window
CONTROL-U	Backward one-half window
CONTROL-F *or* PAGE DOWN	Forward one window
CONTROL-B *or* PAGE UP	Backward one window
***n*G**	To line ***n*** (without ***n***, to the last line)
H	To top of window
M	To middle of window
L	To bottom of window

The commands in Table 6-15 enable you to add text to the buffer. All these commands, except r, leave vim in Input mode. You must press ESCAPE to return to Command mode.

Table 6-15 Adding text

Command	Adds text
i	Before cursor
I	Before first nonblank character on line
a	After cursor
A	At end of line
o	Opens a line below current line
O	Opens a line above current line
r	Replaces current character (no ESCAPE needed)
R	Replaces characters, starting with current character (overwrite until ESCAPE)

Table 6-16 lists commands that delete and change text. In this table *M* is a Unit of Measure that you can precede with a Repeat Factor, *n* is an optional Repeat Factor, and *c* is any character.

Table 6-16 Deleting and changing text

Command	Result
*n*x	Deletes the number of characters specified by *n*, starting with the current character
*n*X	Deletes *n* characters before the current character, starting with the character preceding the current character
d*M*	Deletes text specified by *M*
*n*dd	Deletes *n* lines
dt*c*	Deletes to the next character *c* on the current line
D	Deletes to end of the line
n~	Changes case of the next *n* characters
The following commands leave vim in Input mode. You must press ESCAPE to return to Command mode.	
*n*s	Substitutes *n* characters
S	Substitutes for the entire line

Table 6-16 Deleting and changing text (continued)

Command	Result
c*M*	Changes text specified by ***M***
***n*cc**	Changes ***n*** lines
ct*c*	Changes to the next character ***c*** on the current line
C	Changes to end of line

Table 6-17 lists search commands. Here, *rexp* is a regular expression that can be a simple string of characters.

Table 6-17 Searching

Command	Result
/*rexp*RETURN	Searches forward for ***rexp***
?*rexp* RETURN	Searches backward for ***rexp***
n	Repeats original search exactly
N	Repeats original search, in the opposite direction
/RETURN	Repeats original search forward
?RETURN	Repeats original search backward
f*c*	Positions the cursor on the next character ***c*** on the current line
F*c*	Positions the cursor on the previous character ***c*** on the current line
t*c*	Positions the cursor on the character before (to the left of) the next character ***c*** on the current line
T*c*	Positions the cursor on the character after (to the right of) the previous character ***c*** on the current line
;	Repeats the last **f**, **F**, **t**, or **T** command

The syntax of a Substitute command is

:[address]s/search-string/replacement-string[/g]

where ***address*** is one line number or two line numbers separated by a comma. A . (period) represents the current line, $ represents the last line, and % represents the entire file. You can use a marker or a search string in place of a line number. The ***search-string*** is a regular expression that can be a simple string of characters. The ***replacement-string*** is the replacement string. A **g** indicates a global replacement (more than one replacement per line).

Table 6-18 lists miscellaneous vim commands.

Table 6-18 Miscellaneous commands

Command	Result
J	Joins the current line and the following line
.	Repeats the most recent command that made a change
:w ***filename***	Writes the contents of the Work buffer to ***filename*** (or to the current file if there is no ***filename***)
:q	Quits vim
ZZ	Writes the contents of the Work buffer to the current file and quits vim
:f *or* CONTROL-G	Displays the filename, status, current line number, number of lines in the Work buffer, and percentage of the Work buffer preceding the current line
CONTROL-V	Inserts the next character literally even if it is a vim command (use in Input mode)

Table 6-19 lists commands that yank and put text. In this table *M* is a Unit of Measure that you can precede with a Repeat Factor and *n* is a Repeat Factor. You can precede any of these commands with the name of a buffer using the form **"***x*, where *x* is the name of the buffer (**a–z**).

Table 6-19 Yanking and putting text

Command	Result
y*M*	Yanks text specified by ***M***
***n*yy**	Yanks ***n*** lines
Y	Yanks to end of line
P	Puts text before or above
p	Puts text after or below

Table 6-20 lists advanced vim commands.

Table 6-20 Advanced commands

Command	Result
m*x*	Sets marker ***x***, where ***x*** is a letter from **a** to **z**.
' ' (two single quotation marks)	Moves cursor back to its previous location.
'*x*	Moves cursor to line with marker ***x***.
\`*x*	Moves cursor to character with marker ***x***.

Table 6-20 Advanced commands (continued)

Command	Result
:e *filename*	Edits ***filename***, requiring you to write changes to the current file (with **:w** or **autowrite**) before editing the new file. Use **:e!** ***filename*** to discard changes to the current file. Use **:e!** without a filename to discard changes to the current file and start editing the saved version of the current file.
:n	Edits the next file when vim is started with multiple filename arguments. Requires you to write changes to the current file (with **:w** or **autowrite**) before editing the next file. Use **:n!** to discard changes to the current file and edit the next file.
:rew	Rewinds the filename list when vim is started with multiple filename arguments and starts editing with the first file. Requires you to write changes to the current file (with **:w** or **autowrite**) before editing the first file. Use **:rew!** to discard changes to the current file and edit the first file.
:sh	Starts a shell. Exit from the shell to return to vim.
:!*command*	Starts a shell and executes ***command***.
!!*command*	Starts a shell, executes ***command***, and places output in the Work buffer, replacing the current line.

EXERCISES

1. How can you cause vim to enter Input mode? How can you make vim revert to Command mode?
2. What is the Work buffer? Name two ways of writing the contents of the Work buffer to the disk.
3. Suppose that you are editing a file that contains the following paragraph and the cursor is on the second tilde (~):

```
The vim editor has a command, tilde (~),
that changes lowercase letters to
uppercase, and vice versa.
The ~ command works with a Unit of Measure or
a Repeat Factor, so you can change
the case of more than one character at a time.
```

How can you

a. Move the cursor to the end of the paragraph?

b. Move the cursor to the beginning of the word **Unit**?

c. Change the word **character** to **letter**?

4. While working in vim, with the cursor positioned on the first letter of a word, you give the command **x** followed by **p**. Explain what happens.
5. What are the differences between the following commands?

   a. **i** and **I**

   b. **a** and **A**

   c. **o** and **O**

   d. **r** and **R**

   e. **u** and **U**
6. Which command would you use to search backward through the Work buffer for lines that start with the word **it**?
7. Which command substitutes all occurrences of the phrase **this week** with the phrase **next week**?
8. Consider the following scenario: You start vim to edit an existing file. You make many changes to the file and then realize that you deleted a critical section of the file early in your editing session. You want to get that section back but do not want to lose all the other changes you made. What would you do?
9. How can you move the current line to the beginning of the file?
10. Use vim to create the **letter_e** file of e's used on page 64. Use as few vim commands as possible. Which vim commands did you use?

ADVANCED EXERCISES

11. Which commands can you use to take a paragraph from one file and insert it in a second file?
12. Create a file that contains the following list, and then execute commands from within vim to sort the list and display it in two columns. (*Hint:* Refer to page 940 for more information on pr.)

```
Command mode
Input mode
Last Line mode
Work buffer
General-Purpose buffer
Named buffer
Regular Expression
Search String
Replacement String
Startup File
Repeat Factor
```

13. How do the Named buffers differ from the General-Purpose buffer?
14. Assume that your version of vim does not support multiple Undo commands. If you delete a line of text, then delete a second line, and then a third line, which commands would you use to recover the first two lines that you deleted?
15. Which command would you use to swap the words **hither** and **yon** on any line with any number of words between them? (You need not worry about special punctuation, just uppercase and lowercase letters and spaces.)

7

The emacs Editor

In This Chapter

Objectives

After reading this chapter you should be able to:

- Use emacs to create and edit a file
- Save and retrieve the buffer
- Use emacs online help
- Describe how to move the cursor by characters, words, lines, and paragraphs
- List the commands that move the cursor backward and forward by characters and words
- Explain how to search backward and forward for text and what an incremental search is
- Describe emacs key notation
- Split a window
- Describe the process of undoing changes

HISTORY

In 1956, the Lisp (List processing) language was developed at MIT by John McCarthy. In its original conception, Lisp had only a few scalar (*atomic*) data types and only one *data structure* (page 1093): a list. Lists could contain atomic data or other lists. Lisp supported recursion and nonnumeric data (exciting concepts in those Fortran and COBOL days) and, in the Cambridge culture at least, was once the favored implementation language. Richard Stallman and Guy Steele were part of this MIT Lisp culture. In 1975 they collaborated on emacs, which Stallman maintained by himself for a long time. This chapter discusses the emacs editor as implemented by the Free Software Foundation (GNU), version 23. The emacs home page is www.gnu.org/software/emacs.

The emacs editor was prototyped as a series of extension commands or macros for the late 1960s text editor TECO (Text Editor and COrrector). Its acronymic name, Editor MACroS, reflects this origin, although there have been many humorous reinterpretations, including ESCAPE META ALT CONTROL SHIFT, Emacs Makes All Computing Simple, and the unkind translation Eight Megabytes And Constantly Swapping.

EVOLUTION

Over time emacs has grown and evolved through more than 20 major revisions to the mainstream GNU version. The emacs editor, which is coded in C, contains a complete Lisp interpreter and fully supports the X Window System and mouse interaction. The original TECO macros are long gone, but emacs is still very much a work in progress. Over the years, Emacs has received significant internationalization upgrades: an extended UTF-8 internal character set four times bigger than Unicode, along with fonts and keyboard input methods for more than 30 languages. Also, the user interface is moving in the direction of a WYSIWYG (what you see is what you get) word processor, which makes it easier for beginners to use the editor.

The emacs editor has always been considerably more than a text editor. Not having been developed originally in a UNIX environment, it does not adhere to the UNIX/Linux philosophy. Whereas a UNIX/Linux utility is typically designed to do one thing and to be used in conjunction with other utilities, emacs is designed to "do it all." Taking advantage of the underlying programming language (Lisp), emacs users tend to customize and extend the editor rather than to use existing utilities or create new general-purpose tools. Instead, they share their ~/.emacs (customization) files.

Well before the emergence of the X Window System, Stallman put a great deal of thought and effort into designing a window-oriented work environment, and he used emacs as his research vehicle. Over time he built facilities within emacs for reading and composing email messages, reading and posting netnews, giving shell commands, compiling programs and analyzing error messages, running and debugging these programs, and playing games. Eventually it became possible to enter the emacs environment and not come out all day, switching from window to window and from file to file. If you had only an ordinary serial, character-based terminal, emacs gave you tremendous leverage.

In an X Window System environment, emacs does not need to control the whole display. Instead, it usually operates only one or two windows. The original, character-based work environment is still available and is covered in this chapter.

As a *language-sensitive* editor, emacs has special features that you can turn on to help edit text, nroff, TeX, Lisp, C, Fortran, and so on. These feature sets are called *modes*, but they are not related to the Command and Input modes found in vi, vim, and other editors. Because you never need to switch emacs between Input and Command modes, emacs is a *modeless* editor.

emacs VERSUS vim

See en.wikipedia.org/wiki/Editor_war for an interesting discussion of the ongoing editor wars; or search the Web for **emacs vs vi**.

Like vim, emacs is a display editor: It displays on the screen the text you are editing and changes the display as you type each command or insert new text. Unlike vim, emacs does not require you to keep track of whether you are in Command mode or Insert mode: Commands always use CONTROL or other special keys. The emacs editor inserts ordinary characters into the text you are editing (as opposed to using ordinary characters as commands), another trait of modeless editing. For many people this approach is convenient and natural.

As with vim, you use emacs to edit a file in a work area, or *buffer*, and have the option of writing this buffer back to the file on the disk when you are finished. With emacs, however, you can have many work buffers and switch among them without having to write the buffer out and read it back in. Furthermore, you can display multiple buffers at one time, each in its own window within emacs. This way of displaying files is often helpful when you are cutting and pasting text or when you want C declarations visible while editing related code in another part of a file.

Like vim, emacs has a rich, extensive command set for moving about in the buffer and altering text. This command set is not "cast in concrete"—you can change or customize commands at any time. Any key can be coupled (*bound*) to any command to match a particular keyboard better or to fulfill a personal whim. Usually key bindings are set in the **~/.emacs** startup file, but they can also be changed interactively during a session. All the key bindings described in this chapter are standard on the current versions of GNU emacs.

Too many key bindings

caution If you change too many key bindings, you might produce a command set that you will not remember or that will make it impossible for you to return to the standard bindings in the same session.

Finally, and very unlike vim, emacs allows you to use Lisp to write new commands or override old ones. Stallman calls this feature *online extensibility*, but it would take a gutsy Lisp guru to write and debug a new command while editing text. It is much more common to add debugged commands to the **.emacs** file, where they are loaded when you start emacs. Experienced emacs users often write modes, or environments, that are conditionally loaded by emacs for specific tasks. For more information on the **.emacs** file, see page 266.

The screen and emacs windows

tip In this chapter, the term *screen* denotes a character-based terminal screen or a terminal emulator window in a graphical environment. The term *window* refers to an emacs window within a screen.

emacs and the X Window System

tip Since version 19, GNU emacs has fully embraced the X Window System environment. If you start emacs from a terminal emulator window running in a graphical environment, you will bring up the X interface (GUI) to emacs. This book does not cover the graphical interface; use the **–nw** option when you start emacs to bring up the textual interface in any environment. See "Starting emacs" below.

TUTORIAL: GETTING STARTED WITH emacs

The emacs editor has many, many features, and there are many ways to use it. Its complete manual includes more than 35 chapters. Nevertheless, you can do a considerable amount of meaningful work with a relatively small subset of the commands. This section describes a simple editing session, explaining how to start and exit from emacs and how to move the cursor and delete text. Coverage of some issues is postponed or simplified in the interest of clarity.

emacs online tutorial

tip The emacs editor provides an online tutorial. After starting emacs, press CONTROL-H **t** to start the tutorial. Press CONTROL-X CONTROL-C to exit from emacs. If you have more than one emacs window open, see the tip "Closing the help window" on page 238.

STARTING emacs

To edit a file named **sample** using emacs as a text-based editor, enter the following command:

```
$ emacs -nw -q sample
```

The **–nw** option, which must be the first option on the emacs command line, tells emacs not to use its X interface (GUI). The **–q** option tells emacs *not* to read the **~/.emacs** startup file. Not reading this file guarantees that emacs will behave in a standard manner and can be useful for beginners or for other users who want to bypass a **.emacs** file.

The preceding command starts emacs, reads the file named **sample** into a buffer, and displays its contents on the screen or window. If no file has this name, emacs displays a blank screen with (**New File**) at the bottom (Figure 7-1). If the file exists, emacs displays the file and a different message (Figure 7-2 , page 226). If you start emacs without naming a file on the command line, it displays a welcome screen that includes usage information and a list of basic commands.

Initially, emacs displays a single window. At the top of the window is a reverse-video menubar that you can access using a mouse or keyboard. From the keyboard, F10, META-` (back tick), or META-x **tmm-menubar** RETURN displays the Menubar Completion List window. For more information refer to "Using the Menubar from the Keyboard" on page 237.

At the bottom of the emacs window is a reverse-video titlebar called the *Mode Line*. At a minimum, the Mode Line shows which buffer the window is viewing, whether the buffer has been changed, which major and minor modes are in effect, and how far down the buffer the window is positioned. When multiple windows appear on the screen, one Mode Line appears in each window. At the bottom of the screen, emacs leaves a single line open. This *Echo Area* and *Minibuffer* line (they coexist on one line) is used for messages and special one-line commands.

The emacs manual

tip The emacs manual is available from within emacs. While you are running emacs, give the command CONTROL-H **r**. Then use the ARROW keys to scroll to the section you want to view and press RETURN. Alternatively, type **m** (which moves the cursor to the Minibuffer) followed by the name of the section (menu) you want to view. Type TAB to cause emacs to complete the menu name; menu completion works similarly to pathname completion (page 248). See page 238 for a tip on closing the help window and for more information about online help.

For example, to view the Minibuffer section of the online manual, give the command CONTROL-H **r m minibuffer** RETURN. You can also give the command CONTROL-H **r m min** TAB RETURN.

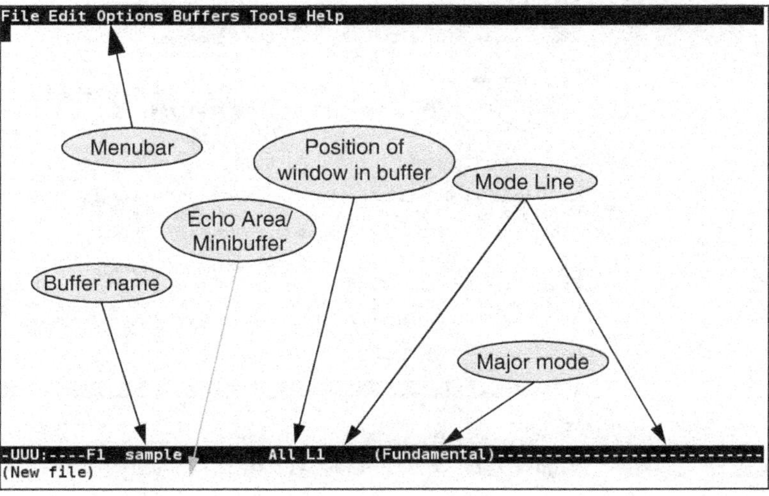

Figure 7-1 The emacs new file screen

If you make an error while you are typing in the Minibuffer, emacs displays the error message in the Echo Area. The error message overwrites the command you were typing, but emacs restores the command in a few seconds. The brief display of the error messages gives you time to read it before you continue typing the command from where you left off. More detailed information is available from the Minibuffer menu of the emacs online manual (see the preceding tip).

A cursor is either in the window or in the Minibuffer. All input and nearly all editing take place at the cursor. As you type ordinary characters, emacs inserts them at the cursor position. If characters are under the cursor or to its right, they are pushed to the right as you type, so no characters are lost.

EXITING

The command to exit from emacs is CONTROL-X CONTROL-C. You can give this command at almost any time (in some modes you might have to press CONTROL-G first). It stops emacs gracefully, asking if you want to keep the changes you made during the editing session.

If you want to cancel a half-typed command or stop a running command before it is done, press CONTROL-G. The emacs editor displays **Quit** in the Echo Area and waits for another command.

INSERTING TEXT

Typing an ordinary (printing) character pushes the cursor and any characters to the right of the cursor one position to the right and inserts the new character in the space opened by moving the characters.

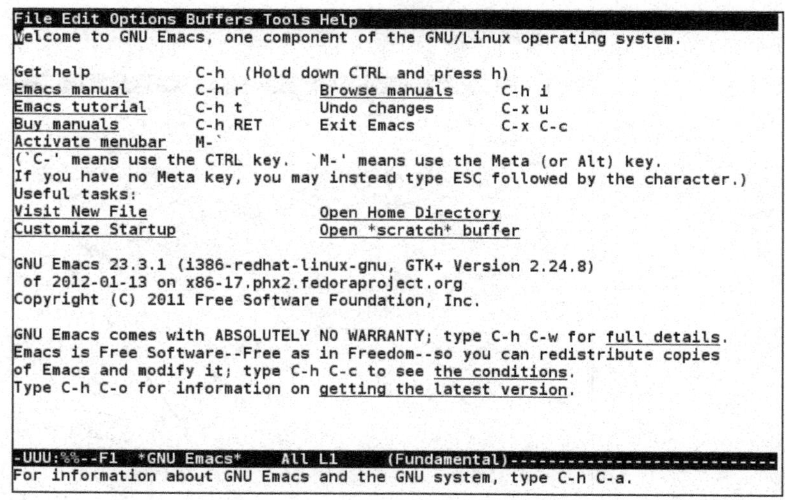

Figure 7-2 The emacs welcome screen

DELETING CHARACTERS

Depending on the keyboard and the **emacs** startup file, different keys might delete characters in different ways. CONTROL-D typically deletes the character under the cursor, as do DELETE and DEL. BACKSPACE typically deletes the character to the left of the cursor. Try each of these keys and see what it does.

More about deleting characters

tip If the instructions described in this section do not work, read the **emacs info** section on **deletion**. Give this command from a shell prompt:

```
$ info emacs
```

From **info** give the command **m deletion** to display a document that describes in detail how to delete small amounts of text. Use the SPACE bar to scroll through the document. Type **q** to exit from **info**. You can read the same information in the **emacs** online manual (CONTROL-H **r**; page 225)

Start **emacs** and type a few lines of text. If you make a mistake, correct the error using the deletion characters discussed previously. The RETURN key inserts an invisible end-of-line character in the buffer and returns the cursor to the left margin, one line down. It is possible to back up past the start of a line and up to the end of the previous line. Figure shows a sample buffer.

Use the ARROW keys

tip Sometimes the easiest way to move the cursor is by using the LEFT ARROW, RIGHT ARROW, UP ARROW, and DOWN ARROW keys.

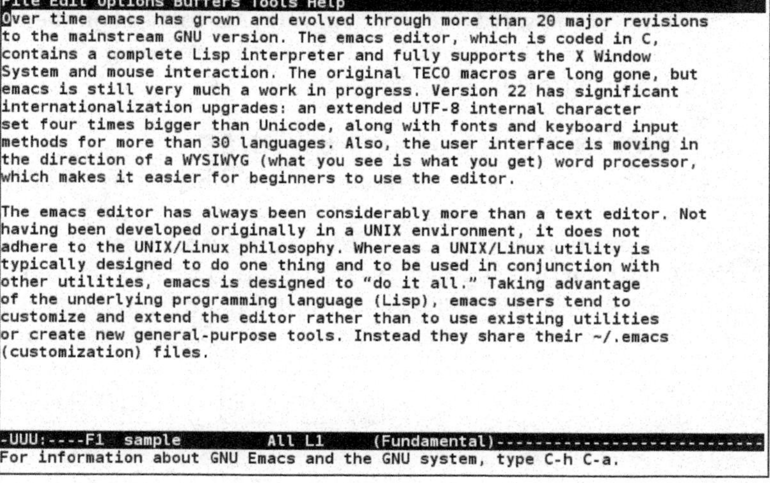

Figure 7-3 Sample buffer

MOVING THE CURSOR

You can position the cursor over any character in the emacs window and move the window so it displays any portion of the buffer. You can move the cursor forward or backward through the text (Figure 6-8, page 181) by various textual units—for example, characters, words, sentences, lines, and paragraphs. Any of the cursor-movement commands can be preceded by a repetition count (CONTROL-U followed by a numeric argument), which causes the cursor to move that number of textual units through the text. Refer to page 233 for a discussion of numeric arguments.

MOVING THE CURSOR BY CHARACTERS

CONTROL-F Pressing the RIGHT ARROW key or CONTROL-F moves the cursor forward (to the right) one character. If the cursor is at the end of a line, these commands wrap it to the beginning of the next line. For example, the command CONTROL-U 7 CONTROL-F moves the cursor seven characters forward.

CONTROL-B Pressing the LEFT ARROW key or CONTROL-B moves the cursor backward (to the left) one character. For example, the command CONTROL-U 7 CONTROL-B moves the cursor seven characters backward. The command CONTROL-B works in a manner similar to CONTROL-F (Figure 7-4).

MOVING THE CURSOR BY WORDS

META-f Pressing META-f moves the cursor forward one word. To invoke this command, hold down the META or ALT key while you press f. If the keyboard you are using does not have either of these keys, press ESCAPE, release it, and then press f. This command leaves the cursor on the first character that is not part of the word the cursor started on. The command CONTROL-U 4 META-f moves the cursor forward one space past the end of the fourth word. For more information refer to "Keys: Notation and Use" on page 231.

META-b Pressing META-b moves the cursor backward one word, leaving the cursor on the first letter of the word it started on. If the cursor was on the first letter of a word, META-b moves the cursor to the first letter of the preceding word. The command META-b works in a manner similar to META-f (Figure 7-5).

MOVING THE CURSOR BY LINES

CONTROL-A CONTROL-E CONTROL-P CONTROL-N Pressing CONTROL-A moves the cursor to the beginning of the line it is on; CONTROL-E moves it to the end. Pressing the UP ARROW key or CONTROL-P moves the cursor up one line to the position directly above where the cursor started; pressing the DOWN ARROW key or CONTROL-N moves it down. As with the other cursor-movement keys, you can precede CONTROL-P and CONTROL-N with CONTROL-U and a numeric argument to move the cursor up or down multiple lines. You can also use pairs of these commands to move the cursor

Figure 7-4 Moving the cursor by characters

up to the beginning of the previous line, down to the end of the following line, and so on (Figure 7-6).

Moving the Cursor by Sentences, Paragraphs, and Window Position

META-a, META-e META-{, META-} Pressing META-a moves the cursor to the beginning of the sentence the cursor is on; META-e moves the cursor to the end. META-{ moves the cursor to the beginning of the paragraph the cursor is on; META-} moves it to the end. (Sentences and paragraphs are defined starting on page 257.) You can precede any of these commands with a repetition count (CONTROL-U followed by a numeric argument) to move the cursor by that many sentences or paragraphs.

META-r Pressing META-r moves the cursor to the beginning of the middle line of the window. You can precede this command with CONTROL-U and a line number (here CONTROL-U does not indicate a repetition count but rather a screen line number). The command CONTROL-U 0 META-r moves the cursor to the beginning of the top line (line zero) in the window. The command CONTROL-U – (minus sign) moves the cursor to the beginning of the last line of the window (Figure 7-7, next page).

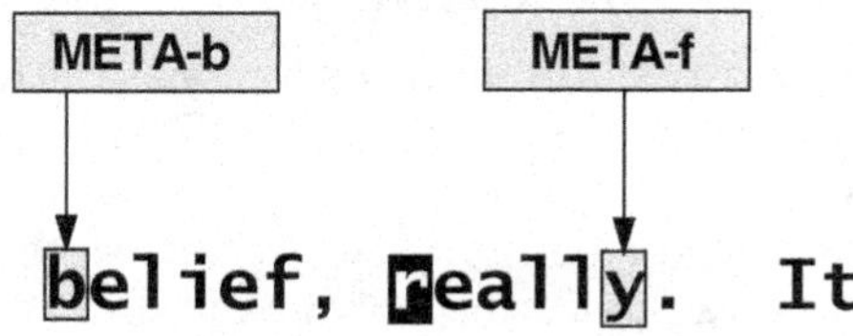

Figure 7-5 Moving the cursor by words

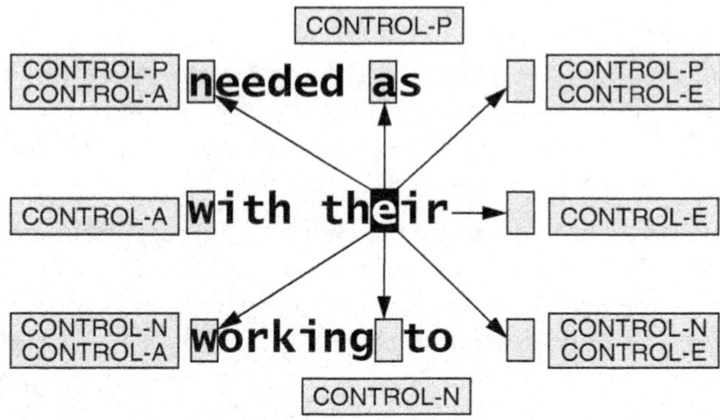

Figure 7-6 Moving the cursor by lines

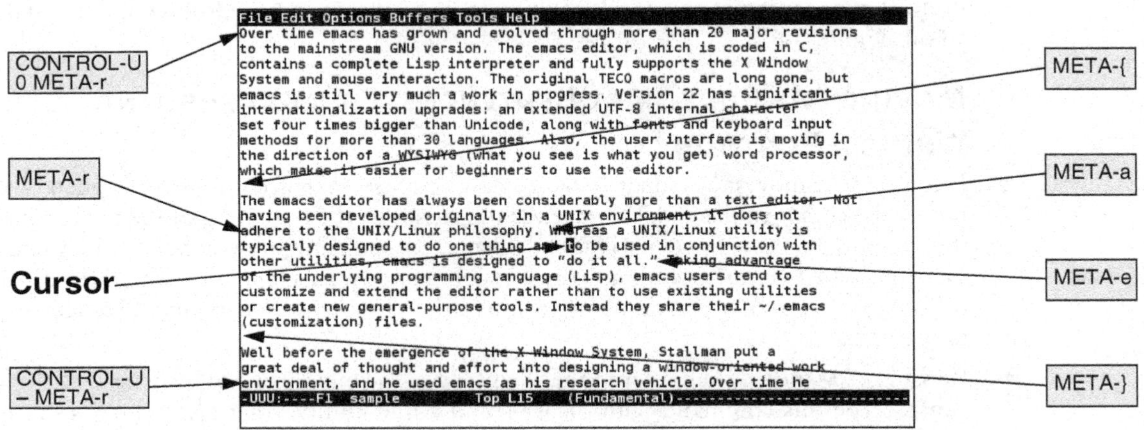

Figure 7-7 Moving the cursor by sentences, paragraphs, and window position

EDITING AT THE CURSOR POSITION

Entering text requires no commands once you position the cursor in the window at the location you want to enter text. When you type text, emacs displays that text at the position of the cursor. Any text under or to the right of the cursor is pushed to the right. If you type enough characters so the text would extend past the right edge of the window, emacs displays a backslash (\) near the right edge of the window and wraps the text to the next line. The backslash appears on the screen but is not saved as part of the file and is never printed. Although you can create an arbitrarily long line, some Linux tools have problems with text files containing such lines. To split a line into two lines, position the cursor at the location you want to split the line and press RETURN.

Deleting text Pressing BACKSPACE removes characters to the left of the cursor. The cursor and the remainder of the text on this line both move to the left each time you press BACKSPACE. To join a line with the line above it, position the cursor on the first character of the second line and press BACKSPACE.

Press CONTROL-D to delete the character under the cursor. The cursor remains stationary, but the remainder of the text on the line moves left to replace the deleted character. See the tip "More about deleting characters" on page 227 if either of these keys does not work as described here.

SAVING AND RETRIEVING THE BUFFER

No matter what changes you make to a buffer during an emacs session, the associated file does not change until you save the buffer. If you leave emacs without saving the buffer (emacs allows you to do so if you are persistent), the file is not changed and emacs discards the work you did during the session.

Backups As it writes a buffer's edited contents back to the file, emacs might optionally first make a backup of the original file. You can choose to make no backups, one level of backup (default), or an arbitrary number of levels of backups. The level one backup filenames are formed by appending a tilde (~) to the original filename. The multilevel backups have **.~*n*~** appended to the filename, where ***n*** is the sequential backup number, starting with 1. The **version-control** variable dictates how emacs saves backups. See page 266 for instructions on assigning a value to an emacs variable.

Saving the buffer The command CONTROL-X CONTROL-S saves the current buffer in its associated file. The emacs editor confirms a successful save by displaying an appropriate message in the Echo Area.

Visiting another file When you are editing a file with emacs and want to edit another file (emacs documentation refers to editing a file as *visiting* a file), you can copy the new file into a new emacs buffer by giving the command CONTROL-X CONTROL-F. The emacs editor prompts for a filename, reads that file into a new buffer, and displays that buffer in the current window. Having two files open in one editing session is more convenient than exiting from emacs, returning to the shell, and then starting a new copy of emacs to edit a second file.

Visiting a file with CONTROL-X CONTROL-F

tip When you give the command CONTROL-X CONTROL-F to visit a file, emacs displays the pathname of the directory in which it assumes the file is located. Normally it displays the pathname of the working directory, but in some situations emacs displays a different pathname, such as the pathname of your home directory. Edit this pathname if it is not pointing to the correct directory. This command provides pathname completion (page 248).

BASIC EDITING COMMANDS

This section takes a more detailed look at the fundamental emacs editing commands. It covers editing a single file in a single emacs window.

KEYS: NOTATION AND USE

Although emacs has been internationalized, its keyboard input is still an evolved and extended ASCII code, usually with one keystroke producing one byte. ASCII keyboards have a typewriter-style SHIFT key and a CONTROL key. Some keyboards also have a META (diamond or ALT) key that controls the eighth bit. It takes seven bits to describe an ASCII character; the eighth bit of an eight-bit byte can be used to communicate additional information. Because so much of the emacs command set is in the nonprinting CONTROL or META case, Stallman was one of the first to develop a nonnumeric notation for describing keystrokes.

His solution, which is still used in the emacs community, is clear and unambiguous (Table 7-1). It uses the capital letters **C** and **M** to denote holding down the CONTROL and META (or ALT) keys, respectively, and a few simple acronyms for the most common special characters, such as RET (this book uses RETURN), LFD (LINEFEED), DEL (DELETE), ESC (ESCAPE),

SPC (SPACE), and TAB. Most emacs documentation, including the online help, uses this notation.

Table 7-1 emacs key notation

Character	Classic emacs notation
(lowercase) a	a
(uppercase) SHIFT-a	A
CONTROL-a	C-a
CONTROL-A	C-a (do *not* use SHIFT), equivalent to CONTROL-a
META-a	M-a
META-A	M-A (*do* use SHIFT), different from M-a
CONTROL-META-a	C-M-a
META-CONTROL-a	M-C-a (not used frequently)

The emacs use of keys had some problems. Many keyboards had no META key, and some operating systems discarded the META bit. In addition, the emacs command set clashes with the increasingly outdated XON-XOFF flow control, which also uses CONTROL-S and CONTROL-Q.

Under macOS, most keyboards do not have a META or ALT key. See page 1076 for an explanation of how to set up the OPTION key to perform the same functions as the META key on a Macintosh.

The missing META key issue was resolved by making an optional two-key sequence starting with ESCAPE equate to a META character. If the keyboard you are using does not have a META or ALT key, you can use the two-key ESCAPE sequence by pressing the ESCAPE key, releasing it, and then pressing the key following the META key in this book. For example, you can type ESCAPE **a** instead of META-a or type ESCAPE CONTROL-A instead of CONTROL-META-a.

Stallman considers XON-XOFF flow control to be a historical issue, and has no plans to change the emacs command set. However, the online help emacs FAQ offers several workarounds for this issue.

The notation used in this book

tip This book uses an uppercase letter following the CONTROL key and a lowercase letter following the META key. In either case *you do not have to hold down the* SHIFT *key while entering a* CONTROL *or* META *character.* Although the META uppercase character (that is, META-A) is a different character, it is usually set up to cause no action or to have the same effect as its lowercase counterpart.

Key Sequences and Commands

In emacs the relationship between key sequences (one or more keys that you press together or in sequence to issue an emacs command) and commands is very flexible, and there is considerable opportunity for exercising your personal preference. You can translate and remap key sequences to other commands and replace or reprogram commands.

Although most emacs documentation glosses over the details and talks about keystrokes as though they were the commands, it is important to recognize that the underlying machinery remains separate from the key sequences and to understand that you can change the behavior of the key sequences and the commands. For more information refer to "Customizing emacs" on page 265.

META-x: Running a Command Without a Key Binding

The emacs keymaps (the tables, or vectors, that emacs uses to translate key sequences into commands [page 267]) are very crowded, and often it is not possible to bind every command to a key sequence. You can execute any command by name by preceding it with META-x. When you press META-x, the emacs editor prompts you for a command in the Echo Area. After you enter the command name and press RETURN, it executes the command.

Smart completion When a command has no common key sequence, it is sometimes described as META-x ***command-name***. The emacs editor provides *smart completion* for most answers it prompts for. After you type part of a response to a prompt, press SPACE or TAB to cause emacs to complete, if possible, to the end of the current word or the whole command, respectively. Forcing a completion past the last unambiguous point or typing a question mark (?) opens a Completion List window that displays a list of alternatives. Smart completion works in a manner similar to pathname completion (page 248).

Numeric Arguments

Some of the emacs editing commands accept a numeric argument as a repetition count. Place this argument immediately before the key sequence for the command. The absence of an argument almost always means a count of 1. Even an ordinary alphabetic character can have a numeric argument, which means "insert this many times." Use either of the following techniques to give a numeric argument to a command:

- Press META with each digit (0–9) or the minus sign (–). For example, to insert 10 **z** characters, type META-1 META-0 **z**.
- Use CONTROL-U to begin a string of digits, including the minus sign. For example, to move the cursor forward 20 words, type CONTROL-U 20 META-f.

CONTROL-U For convenience, CONTROL-U defaults to *multiply by 4* when you do not follow it with a string of one or more digits. For example, entering CONTROL-U **r** means insert **rrrr** (4 * 1), whereas CONTROL-U CONTROL-U **r** means insert **rrrrrrrrrrrrrrrr** (4 * 4 * 1). For quick partial scrolling of a tall window, you might find it convenient to use repeated sequences of CONTROL-U CONTROL-V to scroll down 4 lines, CONTROL-U META-v to scroll up 4 lines, CONTROL-U CONTROL-U CONTROL-V to scroll down 16 lines, or CONTROL-U CONTROL-U META-v to scroll up 16 lines.

POINT AND THE CURSOR

Point is the place in a buffer where editing takes place and is where the cursor is positioned. Strictly speaking, Point is at the left edge of the cursor—think of it as lying *between* two characters.

Each window has its own Point, but there is only one cursor. When the cursor is in a window, moving the cursor also moves Point. Switching the cursor out of a window does not change that window's Point; it is in the same place when you switch the cursor back to that window.

All of the cursor-movement commands described previously also move Point.

SCROLLING THROUGH A BUFFER

CONTROL-V
META-v
CONTROL-L

A buffer is likely to be much larger than the window through which it is viewed, so you need a way of moving the display of the buffer contents up or down so as to position the interesting part in the window. *Scrolling forward* refers to moving the text upward, with new lines entering at the bottom of the window. Press CONTROL-V or the PAGE DOWN key to scroll forward one window (minus two lines for context). *Scrolling backward* refers to moving the text downward, with new lines entering at the top of the window. Press META-v or the PAGE UP key to scroll backward one window (again leaving two lines for context). Pressing CONTROL-L clears the screen and repaints it, moving the line the cursor is on to the middle line of the window. This command is useful if the screen becomes garbled.

A numeric argument to CONTROL-V or META-v means "scroll that many lines"; for example, CONTROL-U 10 CONTROL-V means scroll forward ten lines. A numeric argument to CONTROL-L means "scroll the text so the cursor is on that line of the window," where 0 means the top line and –1 means the bottom line, just above the Mode Line. Scrolling occurs automatically if you exceed the window limits when pressing CONTROL-P or CONTROL-N.

META-<
META->

You can move the cursor to the beginning of the buffer with META-< or to the end of the buffer with META->.

ERASING TEXT

Delete versus kill

When you erase text you can discard it or move it into a holding area and optionally bring it back later. The term *delete* means *permanently discard,* and the term *kill* means *move to a holding area.* The holding area, called the *Kill Ring,* can hold several pieces of killed text. You can use the text in the Kill Ring in many ways (refer to "Cut and Paste: Yanking Killed Text" on page 243).

META-d
CONTROL-K

The META-d command kills from the cursor forward to the end of the current word.Similarly, CONTROL-K kills from the cursor forward to the end of the current line. It does *not* delete the line-ending LINEFEED character unless Point and the cursor are just to the left of the LINEFEED. This setup allows you to reach the left end of a line with CONTROL-A, kill the whole line with CONTROL-K, and then immediately type a replacement line without having to reopen a hole for the new line. Another consequence is that, from the beginning of the line, it takes the command CONTROL-K CONTROL-K (or CONTROL-U 2 CONTROL-K) to kill the text and close the hole.

Searching for Text

The emacs editor allows you to search for text in the following ways:

- Incrementally for a character string
- Incrementally for a regular expression (possible but uncommon)
- For a complete character string
- For a complete regular expression (Appendix A)

You can run each of the four types of searches either forward or backward in the buffer.

The *complete* searches behave in the same manner as searches carried out in other editors. Searching begins only when the search string is complete. In contrast, an *incremental* search begins when you type the first character of the search string and keeps going as you enter additional characters. Initially, this approach might sound confusing, but it is surprisingly useful.

Incremental Searches

CONTROL-S
CONTROL-R

A single command selects the direction of and starts an incremental search. CONTROL-S starts a forward incremental search and CONTROL-R starts a reverse incremental search.

When you start an incremental search, emacs prompts you with **I-search:** in the Echo Area. When you enter a character, it immediately searches for that character in the buffer. If it finds that character, emacs moves Point and cursor to that position so you can see the search progress. If the search fails, emacs tells you so.

After you enter each character of the search string, you can take one of several actions depending on the result of the search to that point. The following paragraphs list results and corresponding actions:

- The search finds the string you are looking for, leaving the cursor positioned just to its right. You can stop the search and leave the cursor in its new position by pressing RETURN. (Any emacs command not related to searching will also stop the search but remembering exactly which ones apply can be difficult. For a new user, RETURN is safer.)
- The search finds a string but it is not the one you are looking for. You can refine the search string by adding another letter, press CONTROL-R or CONTROL-S to look for the next occurrence of this search string, or press RETURN to stop the search and leave the cursor where it is.

- The search hits the beginning or end of the buffer and reports **Failing I-Search**. You can proceed in one of the following ways:
  - If you mistyped the search string, press BACKSPACE as needed to remove characters from the search string. The text and cursor in the window jump backward in step as you remove characters.
  - If you want to wrap past the beginning or end of the buffer and continue searching, you can force a wrap by pressing CONTROL-R or CONTROL-S.
  - If the search has not found the string you are looking for but you want to leave the cursor at its current position, press RETURN to stop the search.
  - If the search has gone wrong and you just want to get back to where you started, press CONTROL-G (the quit character). From an unsuccessful search, a single CONTROL-G backs out all the characters in the search string that could not be found. If this action returns you to a place you wish to continue searching from, you can add characters to the search string again. If you do not want to continue the search from that position, pressing CONTROL-G a second time stops the search and leaves the cursor where it was initially.

NONINCREMENTAL SEARCHES

CONTROL-S RETURN
CONTROL-R RETURN

If you prefer that your searches succeed or fail without showing all the intermediate results, you can give the nonincremental command CONTROL-S RETURN to search forward or CONTROL-R RETURN to search backward. Searching does not begin until you enter a search string in response to the emacs prompt and press RETURN again. Neither of these commands wraps past the end of the buffer.

REGULAR EXPRESSION SEARCHES

You can perform both incremental and nonincremental regular expression searching in emacs. Use the commands listed in Table 7-2 to begin a regular expression search.

Table 7-2 Searching for regular expressions

Command	Result
META-CONTROL-s	Incrementally searches forward for a regular expression; prompts for a regular expression one character at a time
META-CONTROL-r	Incrementally searches backward for a regular expression; prompts for a regular expression one character at a time
META-CONTROL-s RETURN	Prompts for and then searches forward for a complete regular expression
META-CONTROL-r RETURN	Prompts for and then searches backward for a complete regular expression

USING THE MENUBAR FROM THE KEYBOARD

This section describes how to use the keyboard to make selections from the emacs menubar (Figure 7-1, page 225). In a graphical environment you can also use a mouse for this purpose. The menubar selections are appropriate to the Major mode emacs is in (see "Major Modes: Language-Sensitive Editing" on page 255). For example, when you are editing a C program, the menubar includes a C menu that holds commands specific to editing and indenting C programs.

To make a selection from the menubar, first press the F10 function key, META-` (back tick), or META-x **tmm-menubar** RETURN. The emacs editor displays the Menubar Completion List window populated with the top-level menubar selections (File, Edit, Options, and so on), with the current selection displayed in the Minibuffer. Figure 7-8 shows the Menubar Completion List window with **File** as the current selection in the Minibuffer.

With the Menubar Completion List window open, you can perform any of the following actions:

- Cancel the menu selection by pressing CONTROL-G or ESCAPE ESCAPE ESCAPE. The display returns to the state it was in before you opened the Menubar Completion List window.
- Use the UP ARROW and DOWN ARROW keys to display successive menu selections in the Minibuffer. Press RETURN to choose the displayed selection.

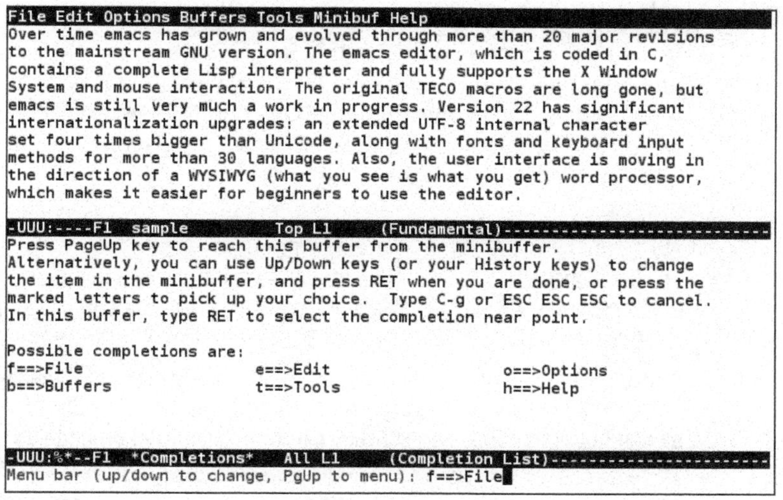

Figure 7-8 The top-level Menubar Completion List window

- Type the one-character abbreviation of a selection as shown in the Menubar Completion List window to choose the selection. You do not need to press RETURN.
- Press PAGE UP or META-v to move the cursor to the Menubar Completion List window. Use the ARROW keys to move the cursor between selections. Press RETURN to choose the selection the cursor is on. You can type ESCAPE ESCAPE ESCAPE to back out of this window and return the cursor to the Minibuffer.

When you make a choice from the top-level menu, emacs displays the corresponding second-level menu in the Menubar Completion List window. Repeat one of the preceding actions to make a selection from this menu. When you make a final selection, emacs closes the Menubar Completion List window and takes the action you selected. More information is available from the Menu Bar menu of the emacs online manual (see the tip on page 225).

ONLINE HELP

CONTROL-H The emacs help system is always available. With the default key bindings, you can start it with CONTROL-H. The help system then prompts you for a one-letter help command. If you do not know which help command you want, type ? or CONTROL-H to switch the current window to a list of help commands, each with a one-line description; emacs again requests a one-letter help command. If you decide you do not want help after all, type CONTROL-G to cancel the help request and return to the former buffer.

If the help output is only a single line, it appears in the Echo Area. If it is more than one line, the output appears in its own window. Use CONTROL-V and META-v to scroll forward and backward through the buffer (page 234). You can move the cursor between windows with CONTROL-X o (lowercase "o"). See page 252 for a discussion of working with multiple windows.

Closing the help window

tip To delete the help window while the cursor is in the window that holds the text you are editing, type CONTROL-X **1** (one). Alternatively, you can move the cursor to the help window (CONTROL-X **o** [lowercase "o"]) and type CONTROL-X **0** (zero) to delete the current window.

If help displays a window that occupies the entire screen, as is the case with CONTROL-H **n** (emacs news) and CONTROL-H **t** (emacs tutorial), you can kill the help buffer by pressing CONTROL-X **k** or switch buffers by pressing CONTROL-X **b** (both discussed on page 251).

On many terminals the BACKSPACE or LEFT ARROW key generates CONTROL-H. If you forget that you are using emacs and try to back over a few characters, you might unintentionally enter the help system. This action does not pose a danger to the buffer you are editing, but it can be unsettling to lose the window contents and not have a clear picture of how to restore it. While you are being prompted for the type of help you want, you can type CONTROL-G to remove the prompt and return to editing the buffer. Some users elect to put help on a different key (page 267). Table 7-3 lists some of the help commands.

Table 7-3 Help commands

Command	Type of help offered
CONTROL-H a	Prompts for a string and displays a list of commands whose names contain that string.
CONTROL-H b	Displays a long table of the key bindings in effect.
CONTROL-H c ***key-sequence***	Displays the name of the command bound to ***key-sequence***. Multiple key sequences are allowed. For a long key sequence where only the first part is recognized, the command describes the first part and quietly inserts the unrecognized part into the buffer. This can happen with three-character function keys (F1, F2, and so on, on the keyboard) that generate character sequences such as ESCAPE [SHIFT.
CONTROL-H f	Prompts for the name of a Lisp function and displays the documentation for it. Because commands are Lisp functions, you can use a command name with this command.
CONTROL-H i	Displays the top info (page 225) menu where you can browse for emacs or other documentation.
CONTROL-H k ***key-sequence***	Displays the name and documentation of the command bound to ***key-sequence***. (See the notes on CONTROL-H **c**.)
CONTROL-H l (lowercase "l")	Displays the last 100 characters typed. The record is kept *after* the first-stage keyboard translation. If you have customized the keyboard translation table, you must make a mental reverse translation.
CONTROL-H m	Displays the documentation and special key bindings for the current Major mode (Text, C, Fundamental, and so on, [page 256]).
CONTROL-H n	Displays the emacs news file, which lists recent changes to emacs, ordered with the most recent changes first.
CONTROL-H r	Displays the emacs manual.
CONTROL-H t	Runs an emacs tutorial session.
CONTROL-H v	Prompts for a Lisp variable name and displays the documentation for that variable.
CONTROL-H w	Prompts for a command name and identifies any key sequence bound to that command. Multiple key sequences are allowed. (See the notes on CONTROL-H **c**.)

optional As this abridged presentation makes clear, you can use the help system to browse through the emacs internal Lisp system. For the curious, following is Stallman's list of strings that match many names in the Lisp system. To get a view of the internal functionality of emacs, you can use any of these strings with CONTROL-H **a** (help system list of commands) or META-x **apropos** (prompts for a string and lists variables whose names contain that string).

backward	dir	insert	previous	view
beginning	down	kill	region	what
buffer	end	line	register	window
case	file	list	screen	word
change	fill	mark	search	yank
char	find	mode	sentence	
defun	forward	next	set	
delete	goto	page	sexp	
describe	indent	paragraph	up	

ADVANCED EDITING

The basic emacs commands suffice for many editing tasks but the serious user will quickly discover the need for more power. This section presents some of the more advanced emacs capabilities.

UNDOING CHANGES

An editing session begins when you read a file into an emacs buffer. At that point the buffer content matches the file exactly. As you insert text and give editing commands, the buffer content becomes increasingly more different from the file. If you are satisfied with the changes, you can write the altered buffer back out to the file and end the session.

Near the left end of the Mode Line (Figure 7-1, page 225) is an indicator that shows the modification state of the buffer displayed in the window. The three possible states are -- (not modified), ** (modified), and %% (readonly).

The emacs editor keeps a record of all keys you have pressed (text and commands) since the beginning of the editing session, up to a limit currently set at 20,000 characters. If you are within this limit, it is possible to undo the entire session for this buffer, one change at a time. If you have multiple buffers (page 251), each buffer has its own undo record.

Undoing is considered so important that it has a backup key sequence, in case a keyboard cannot easily handle the primary sequence. The two sequences are CONTROL-_ (underscore, which on old ASR-33 TTY keyboards was LEFT ARROW) and CONTROL-X **u**. When you type CONTROL-_, **emacs** undoes the last command and moves the cursor to the position of the change in the buffer so you can see what happened. If you type CONTROL-_ a second time, the next-to-last command is undone, and so on. If you keep typing CONTROL-_, eventually the buffer will be returned to its original unmodified state and the ** Mode Line indicator will change to --.

When you break the string of Undo commands by typing text or giving any command except Undo, all reverse changes you made during the string of undos become a part of the change record and can themselves be undone. This strategy offers a way to redo some or all of the undo operations. If you decide you backed up too far, type a command (something innocuous that does not change the buffer, such as CONTROL-F), and begin undoing your changes in reverse. Table 7-4 lists some examples of Undo commands.

Table 7-4 Undo commands

Commands	Result
CONTROL-_	Undoes the last change
CONTROL-_ CONTROL-F CONTROL-_	Undoes the last change and changes it back again
CONTROL-_ CONTROL-_	Undoes the last two changes
CONTROL-_ CONTROL-_ CONTROL-F CONTROL-_ CONTROL-_	Undoes two changes and changes them both back again
CONTROL-_ CONTROL-_ CONTROL-F CONTROL-_	Undoes two changes and changes the most recent one back again

If you do not remember the last change you made, you can type CONTROL-_ and undo it. If you wanted to make this change, type CONTROL-F CONTROL-_ to make the change again. If you modified a buffer by accident, you can keep typing CONTROL-_ until the Mode Line indicator shows -- once more.

If the buffer is completely ruined and you want to start over, issue the command META-x **revert-buffer** to discard the current buffer contents and reread the associated file. The **emacs** editor asks you to confirm your intentions.

POINT, MARK, AND REGION

Point is the current editing position in a buffer. You can move Point anywhere within the buffer by moving the cursor. It is also possible to set a marker called *Mark* in the buffer. The contiguous characters between Point and Mark (either one might come first) are called *Region*. Many commands operate on a buffer's Region, not just on the characters near Point.

MOVING MARK AND ESTABLISHING REGION

CONTROL-@
CONTROL-SPACE
CONTROL-X CONTROL-X

Mark is not as easy to move as Point. Once set, Mark can be moved only by setting it somewhere else. Each buffer has only one Mark. The CONTROL-@ (or CONTROL-SPACE) command explicitly sets Mark at the current cursor (and Point) position. Some keyboards generate CONTROL-@ when you type CONTROL-Q. Although this is not really a backup key binding, it is occasionally a convenient alternative. You can use CONTROL-X CONTROL-X to exchange Point and Mark (and move the cursor to the new Point).

To establish Region, you usually position the cursor (and Point) at one end of the desired Region, set Mark with CONTROL-@, and then move the cursor (and Point) to the other end of Region. If you forget where you left Mark, you can move the cursor back to it again by giving the command CONTROL-X CONTROL-X. You can move the cursor back and forth with repeated CONTROL-X CONTROL-X commands to show Region more clearly.

If a Region boundary is not to your liking, you can swap Point and Mark using CONTROL-X CONTROL-X to move the cursor from one end of Region to the other and then move Point. Continue until you are satisfied with Region.

OPERATING ON REGION

Table 7-5 lists selected commands that operate on Region. Give the command CONTROL-H **a region** to see a complete list of these commands.

Table 7-5 Operating on Region

Command	Result
META-w	Copies Region nondestructively (without killing it) to the Kill Ring
CONTROL-W	Kills Region
META-x print-region	Sends Region to the printer
META-x append-to-buffer	Prompts for a buffer and appends Region to that buffer
META-x append-to-file	Prompts for a filename and appends Region to that file
META-x capitalize-region	Converts Region to uppercase
CONTROL-X CONTROL-L	Converts Region to lowercase

The Mark Ring

Each time you set Mark in a buffer, you are also pushing Mark's former location onto the buffer's *Mark Ring*. The Mark Ring is organized as a FIFO (first in, first out) list and holds the 16 most recent locations where Mark was set. Each buffer has its own Mark Ring. This record of recent Mark history is useful because it often holds locations that you want to jump back to quickly. Jumping to a location pointed to by the Mark Ring can be faster and easier than scrolling or searching your way through the buffer to find the site of a previous change.

CONTROL-U CONTROL-@ To work your way backward along the trail of former Mark locations, use the command CONTROL-U CONTROL-@ one or more times. Each time you give the command, emacs

- Moves Point (and the cursor) to the current Mark location
- Saves the current Mark location at the *oldest* end of the Mark Ring
- Pops off the *youngest* (most recent) Mark Ring entry and sets Mark

Each additional CONTROL-U CONTROL-@ command causes emacs to move Point and the cursor to the previous entry on the Mark Ring.

Although this process might seem complex, it really just makes a safe jump to a previous Mark location. It is safe because each jump's starting point is recirculated through the Mark Ring, where it is easy to find again. You can jump to all previous locations on the Mark Ring (it might be fewer than 16) by giving the command CONTROL-U CONTROL-@ repeatedly. You can go around the ring as many times as you like and stop whenever you want.

Setting Mark Automatically

Some commands set Mark automatically: The idea is to leave a bookmark before moving Point a long distance. For example, META-> sets Mark before jumping to the end of the buffer. You can then return to your starting position with CONTROL-U CONTROL-@. Searches behave similarly. To help you avoid surprises the message **Mark Set** appears in the Echo Area whenever Mark is set, either explicitly or implicitly.

Cut and Paste: Yanking Killed Text

Recall that killed text is not discarded but rather is kept in the Kill Ring. The Kill Ring holds the last 30 pieces of killed text and is visible from all buffers.

Retrieving text from the Kill Ring is called *yanking*. The meaning of this term in emacs is the opposite of that used in vim: In vim *yanking* pulls text from the buffer, and *putting* puts text into the buffer. Killing and yanking—which are roughly analogous to cutting and pasting—are emacs's primary mechanisms for moving and copying text. Table 7-6 lists the most common kill and yank commands.

Table 7-6 Common kill and yank commands

Command	Result
META-d	Kills to end of current word
META-D	Kills from beginning of previous word
CONTROL-K	Kills to end of line, not including LINEFEED
CONTROL-U 1 CONTROL-K	Kills to end of line, including LINEFEED
CONTROL-U 0 CONTROL-K	Kills from beginning of line
META-w	Copies Region to the Kill Ring but does *not* erase Region from the buffer
CONTROL-W	Kills Region
META-z ***char***	Kills up to next occurrence of ***char***
CONTROL-Y	Yanks the most recently killed text into the current buffer at Point, sets Mark at the beginning of this text, and positions Point and the cursor at the end; follow with CONTROL-Y to swap Point and Mark
META-y	Erases the just-yanked text, rotates the Kill Ring, and yanks the next item (only after CONTROL-Y or META-y)

To move two lines of text, move Point to the beginning of the first line and then enter CONTROL-U 2 CONTROL-K to kill two lines. Move Point to the destination position and then enter CONTROL-Y.

To copy two lines of text, move Point to the beginning of the first line and give the commands CONTROL-U 2 CONTROL-K CONTROL-Y to kill the lines and then yank them back immediately. Move Point to the destination position and type CONTROL-Y.

To copy a larger piece of the buffer, set Region to cover this piece and type CONTROL-W CONTROL-Y to kill Region and yank it back. Next move Point to the destination and type CONTROL-Y. You can also set Region and use META-w to copy Region to the Kill Ring.

The Kill Ring is organized as a fixed-length FIFO list, with each new entry causing the eldest to be discarded (once you build up to 30 entries). Simple cut-and-paste operations generally use only the newest entry. The older entries are retained to give you time to change your mind about a deletion. If you do change your mind, you can "mine" the Kill Ring like an archaeological dig, working backward through time and down through the strata of killed material to copy a specific item back into the buffer.

To view every entry in the Kill Ring, begin a yanking session by pressing CONTROL-Y. This action copies the youngest entry in the Kill Ring to the buffer at the current cursor position. If this entry is not the item you want, continue the yanking session by pressing META-y. This action erases the previous yank and copies the next youngest entry to the buffer at the current cursor position. If this still is not the item you wanted, press META-y again to erase it and retrieve a copy of the next entry, and so on. You can continue giving META-y commands all the way back to the oldest entry. If you continue to press META-y, you will eventually wrap back to the youngest entry again. In this manner you can examine each entry as many times as you wish.

The sequence used in a yanking session consists of CONTROL-Y followed by any mixture of CONTROL-Y and META-y. If you type any other command after META-y, the sequence is broken and you must give the CONTROL-Y command again to start another yanking session.

As you work backward in the Kill Ring, it is useful to think of this process as advancing a Last Yank pointer back through history to increasingly older entries. This pointer is *not* reset to the youngest entry until you give a new kill command. Using this technique, you can work backward partway through the Kill Ring with CONTROL-Y and a few META-y commands, give some commands that do not kill, and then pick up where you left off with another CONTROL-Y and a succession of META-y commands.

It is also possible to position the Last Yank pointer with positive or negative numeric arguments to META-y. Refer to the online documentation for more information.

INSERTING SPECIAL CHARACTERS

As stated earlier, emacs inserts everything that is not a command into the buffer at the position of the cursor. To insert characters that would ordinarily be emacs commands, you can use the emacs escape character: CONTROL-Q. There are two ways of using this escape character:

- CONTROL-Q followed by any other character inserts that character in the buffer, no matter which command interpretation it was supposed to have.
- CONTROL-Q followed by three octal digits inserts a byte with that value in the buffer.

CONTROL-Q

tip Depending on the way your terminal is set up, CONTROL-Q might clash with software flow control. If CONTROL-Q seems to have no effect, it is most likely being used for flow control. In that case you must bind another key to the command **quoted-insert** (page 267).

GLOBAL BUFFER COMMANDS

The vim editor and its predecessors have global commands for bufferwide search and replace operations. They operate on the entire buffer. The emacs editor has a similar family of commands. They operate on the portion of the buffer between Point and the end of the buffer. If you wish to operate on the entire buffer, use META-< to move Point to the beginning of the buffer before issuing the command.

LINE-ORIENTED OPERATIONS

The commands listed in Table 7-7 take a regular expression and apply it to the lines between Point and the end of the buffer.

Table 7-7 Line-oriented operations

Command	Result
META-x occur	Prompts for a regular expression and copies each line with a match for the expression to a buffer named ***Occur***
META-x delete-matching-lines	Prompts for a regular expression and deletes each line with a match for the expression
META-x delete-non-matching-lines	Prompts for a regular expression and deletes each line that does *not* have a match for that expression

The META-x **occur** command puts its output in a special buffer named ***Occur***, which you can peruse and discard or use as a jump menu to reach each line quickly. To use the ***Occur*** buffer as a jump menu, switch to it (CONTROL-X **o** [lowercase "o"]), move the cursor to the copy of the desired destination line, and give the command CONTROL-C CONTROL-C. This command moves the cursor to the buffer that was searched and positions it on the line that the regular expression matched.

As with any buffer change, you can undo the effect of the delete commands.

UNCONDITIONAL AND INTERACTIVE REPLACEMENT

The commands listed in Table 7-8 operate on the characters between Point and the end of the buffer, changing every string match or regular expression match. An unconditional replacement makes all replacements automatically. An interactive replacement gives you the opportunity to see and approve each replacement before it is made.

Table 7-8 Replacement commands

Command	Result
META-x replace-string	Prompts for ***string*** and ***newstring*** and replaces every instance of ***string*** with ***newstring***. Point is left at the site of the last replacement, but Mark is set when you give the command, so you can return to it with CONTROL-U CONTROL-@.
META-x replace-regexp	Prompts for ***regexp*** and ***newstring*** and replaces every match for ***regexp*** with ***newstring***. Point is left at the site of the last replacement, but Mark is set when you give the command, so you can return to it with CONTROL-U CONTROL-@.

Table 7-8 Replacement commands

META-% ***string*** *or* META-x query-replace	The first form uses ***string;*** the second form prompts for ***string.*** Both forms prompt for ***newstring,*** query each instance of ***string,*** and, depending on your response, replace it with ***newstring.*** Point is left at the site of the last replacement, but Mark is set when you give the command, so you can return to it with CONTROL-U CONTROL-@.
META-x query-replace-regexp	Prompts for ***regexp*** and ***newstring,*** queries each match for ***regexp***, and, depending on your response, replaces it with ***newstring.*** Point is left at the site of the last replacement, but Mark is set when you give the command, so you can return to it with CONTROL-U CONTROL-@.

If you perform an interactive replacement, emacs displays each instance of *string* or match for *regexp* and prompts you for an action to take. Table 7-9 lists some of the possible responses.

Table 7-9 Responses to interactive replacement prompts

Response	**Meaning**
RETURN	Do not do any more replacements; quit now.
SPACE	Make this replacement and go on.
DELETE	Do *not* make this replacement. Skip it and go on.
, (comma)	Make this replacement, display the result, and ask for another command. Any command is legal except DELETE is treated like SPACE and does not undo the change.
. (period)	Make this replacement and quit searching.
! (exclamation point)	Replace this and all remaining instances without asking any more questions.

VISITING AND SAVING FILES

When you *visit* (emacs terminology for "call up") a file, emacs reads it into a buffer (page 251), allows you to edit the buffer, and eventually usually saves the buffer back to the file. The commands discussed here relate to visiting and saving files.

META-x **pwd**
META-x **cd**

Each emacs buffer keeps a record of its default directory (the directory the file was read from or the working directory, if it is a new file) that is prepended to any relative pathname you specify. This convenience is meant to save some typing. Enter META-x **pwd** to print the default directory for the current buffer or META-x **cd** to prompt for a new default directory and assign it to this buffer. The next section discusses pathname completion, which you can use when emacs prompts for a pathname.

VISITING FILES

The emacs editor works well when you visit a file that has already been called up and whose image is now in a buffer. After a check of the modification time to ensure that the file has not been changed since it was last called up, emacs simply switches to that buffer. Table 7-10 lists commands used to visit files.

Table 7-10 Visiting files

Command	Result
CONTROL-X CONTROL-F	Prompts for a filename and reads its contents into a new buffer. Assigns the file's simple filename as the buffer name. Other buffers are unaffected. It is common practice and often useful to have several files open simultaneously for editing.
CONTROL-X CONTROL-V	Prompts for a filename and replaces the current buffer with a buffer containing the contents of the requested file. The current buffer is destroyed.
CONTROL-X 4 CONTROL-F	Prompts for a filename and reads its contents into a new buffer. Assigns the file's simple filename as the buffer name. Creates a new window for this buffer and selects that window. The window selected before the command still displays the buffer it was showing before this operation, although the new window might cover up part of the old window.

To create a new file, simply call it up. An empty buffer is created and properly named so you can eventually save it. The message (**New File**) appears in the Echo Area, reflecting emacs's understanding of the situation. If this new file grew out of a typographical error, you can give the command CONTROL-X CONTROL-V and enter the correct name.

PATHNAME COMPLETION

When you are prompted for the pathname of a file in the Minibuffer, you can type the pathname followed by a RETURN. Alternatively, you can use pathname completion, which is similar to bash filename completion (page 348), to help you enter a pathname.

While you are entering a pathname in the Minibuffer, press TAB and emacs will complete the pathname as far as possible. If the completed pathname is satisfactory, press RETURN. In some cases, emacs cannot complete a pathname. For example, a directory in the pathname you entered might not exist or you might not have permission to read it. If emacs cannot complete a pathname, it displays a message in the Echo Area. If the characters following the rightmost slash (/) in the pathname you are typing match more than one filename, when you press TAB emacs displays [**Complete, but not unique**]. If you press TAB a second time, emacs opens a Pathname Completion List window that displays a list of possible completions (Figure 7-9). You can open this window manually while you are entering a pathname by typing a question mark (?).

With the Pathname Completion List window open, you can

- Cancel the selection by pressing CONTROL-G or ESCAPE ESCAPE ESCAPE. The display returns to the state it was in before you opened the Pathname Completion List window.
- Type more characters in the Minibuffer to finish the pathname. Press RETURN to select the pathname; emacs closes the completion window.
- Type more characters in the Minibuffer to make the completion unambiguous and press TAB again.

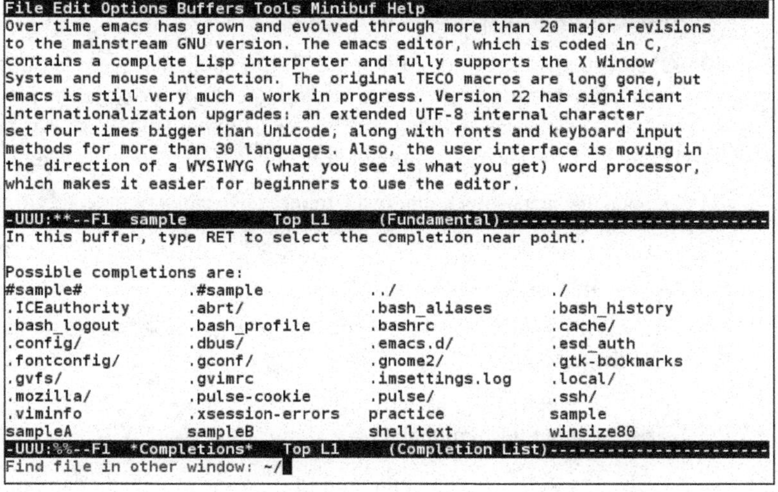

Figure 7-9 A Pathname Completion List window

- Press META-v or PAGE UP to move the cursor into the Pathname Completion List window. Use the ARROW keys to move the cursor between selections. Press RETURN to choose the selection the cursor is on. You can press CONTROL-G or ESCAPE ESCAPE ESCAPE to back out of this window and return the cursor to the Minibuffer.

When you press RETURN, emacs closes the Pathname Completion List window, adds the filename you selected to the end of the pathname you were typing, and moves the cursor to the end of the pathname you were typing in the Minibuffer. You can continue typing in the Minibuffer and perform more completions before you press RETURN to accept the pathname. More information is available from the Completion and Completion Commands menus of the Minibuffer menu of the emacs online manual (see the tip on page 225).

SAVING FILES

You save a buffer by copying its contents back to the original file you called up. Table 7-11 (next page) lists the relevant commands.

You can exit without first getting a warning

caution Clearing the modified flag (META-~) allows you to exit without saving a modified buffer with no warning. Make sure you know what you are doing when you use META-~.

Did you modify a buffer by mistake?

caution When you give a CONTROL-X **s** command, you might discover files whose buffers were modified by mistake as emacs tries to save the wrong changes back to the file. When emacs prompts you to confirm the save, *do not* answer **y** if you are not sure. First, exit from the CONTROL-X **s** dialog by typing **n** to any saves you are not sure about. You then have several options:

- Save the suspicious buffer to a temporary file with CONTROL-X CONTROL-W and analyze it later.
- Undo the changes with a string of CONTROL-_ commands until the ** indicator disappears from the buffer's Mode Line.
- If you are sure that all the changes are wrong, use META-x **revert-buffer** to get a fresh copy of the file.
- Kill the buffer outright. Because it is modified, emacs asks whether you are sure before carrying out this command.
- Give the META-~ (tilde) command to clear the modified condition and ** indicator. A subsequent CONTROL-X **s** then believes that the buffer does not need to be written.

Table 7-11 Saving files

Command	Result
CONTROL-X CONTROL-S	This workhorse file-saving command saves the current buffer into its original file. If the current buffer is not modified, emacs displays the message **(No changes need to be saved)**.
CONTROL-X s	For each modified buffer, you are asked whether you wish to save it. Answer **y** or **n**. This command is given automatically as you exit from emacs and allows you to save any buffers that have been modified but not yet written out. Give this command to save intermediate copies of your work.
META-x set-visited-file-name	Prompts for a filename and sets this name as the "original" name for the current buffer.
CONTROL-X CONTROL-W	Prompts for a filename, sets this name as the "original" name for the current buffer, and saves the current buffer into that file. Equivalent to META-x **set-visited-file-name** followed by CONTROL-X CONTROL-S.
META-~ (tilde)	Clears the modified flag from the current buffer. If you mistakenly type META-~ against a buffer with changes you want to keep, you need to make sure the modified condition and its ** indicator are turned back on before leaving emacs, or all the changes you made will be lost. One easy way to mark a buffer as modified is to insert a SPACE and then remove it using DELETE.

BUFFERS

An emacs *buffer* is a storage object that you can edit. It often holds the contents of a file but can also exist without being associated with a file. You can select only one buffer at a time, designated as the *current buffer*. Most commands operate only on the current buffer, even when windows show multiple buffers on the screen. For the most part each buffer is its own world: It has its own name, its own modes, its own file associations, its own modified state, and perhaps its own special key bindings. You can use the commands shown in Table 7-12 to create, select, list, and manipulate buffers.

Table 7-12 Working with buffers

Command	Result
CONTROL-X b	Prompts for a buffer name and selects it. If the buffer you name does not exist, this command creates it.
CONTROL-X 4 b	Prompts for a buffer name and selects it in another window. The existing window is not disturbed, although the new window might overlap it.

Table 7-12 Working with buffers (continued)

Command	Result
CONTROL-X CONTROL-B	Creates a buffer named ***Buffer List*** and displays it in another window. The existing window is not disturbed, although the new window might overlap it. The new buffer is not selected. In the ***Buffer List*** buffer, each buffer's data is shown along with the name, size, mode(s), and original filename. A % appears for a readonly buffer, a * indicates a modified buffer, and **.** appears for the selected buffer.
META-x rename-buffer	Prompts for a new buffer name and gives this new name to the current buffer.
CONTROL-X CONTROL-Q	Toggles the current buffer's readonly status and the associated **%%** Mode Line indicator. This command can prevent you from accidentally modifying a buffer or allow you to modify a buffer when visiting a readonly file.
META-x append-to-buffer	Prompts for a buffer name and appends Region to the end of that buffer.
META-x prepend-to-buffer	Prompts for a buffer name and prepends Region to the beginning of that buffer.
META-x copy-to-buffer	Prompts for a buffer name and deletes the contents of the buffer before copying Region to that buffer.
META-x insert-buffer	Prompts for a buffer name and inserts the contents of that buffer in the current buffer at Point.
CONTROL-X k	Prompts for a buffer name and deletes that buffer. If the buffer has been modified but not saved, emacs asks you to confirm the operation.
META-x kill-some-buffers	Goes through the list of buffers and offers the chance to delete each buffer. As with CONTROL-X **k**, emacs asks you to confirm the kill command if a modified buffer has not been saved.

WINDOWS

An emacs *window* is a viewport that looks into a buffer. The emacs screen begins by displaying a single window, but this screen space can later be divided among two or more windows. On the screen the *current window* holds the cursor and views the *current buffer*. For a tip on terminology, see "The screen and emacs windows" on page 224.

CONTROL-X **b** ***buffer-name*** A window displays one buffer at a time. The command CONTROL-X **b** ***buffer-name*** switches the buffer that the current window displays. Multiple windows can display the same buffer with each window displaying a different part of the buffer. Any change to a buffer is reflected in all windows displaying that buffer. Also, a buffer can exist without a window open on it.

SPLITTING A WINDOW

One way to divide the screen is to split the starting window explicitly into two or more pieces. The command CONTROL-X **2** splits the current window in two, with one new window appearing above the other. A numeric argument is taken as the size of the upper window in lines. The command CONTROL-X **3** splits the current window in two, with the new windows being arranged side by side (Figure 7-10). A numeric argument is taken as the number of columns to give the left window. For example, CONTROL-U CONTROL-X **2** splits the current window in two; because of the special "times 4" interpretation of CONTROL-U standing alone, the upper window is given four lines (barely enough to be useful).

Although these commands split the current window, both windows continue to view the same buffer. You can select a new buffer in either or both new windows, or you can scroll each window to show different portions of the same buffer.

MANIPULATING WINDOWS

CONTROL-X **o**
META-CONTROL-V

You can use CONTROL-X **o** (lowercase "o") to select the other window. If more than two windows appear on the screen, a sequence of CONTROL-X **o** commands cycles through them in top-to-bottom, left-to-right order. The META-CONTROL-V command scrolls the other window. If more than two windows are visible, the command scrolls the window that CONTROL-X **o** would select next. You can use either a positive or negative scrolling argument, just as with CONTROL-V scrolling in the current window.

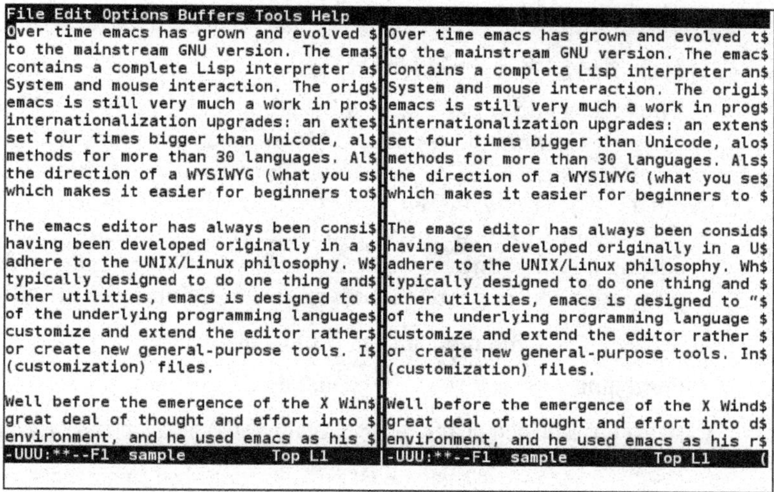

Figure 7-10 Splitting a window horizontally

OTHER-WINDOW DISPLAY

CONTROL-X 4b
CONTROL-X 4f

In normal emacs operation, explicit window splitting is not nearly as common as the implicit splitting done by the family of CONTROL-X 4 commands. The CONTROL-X 4b command, for example, prompts for a *buffer name* and selects it in the other window. If no other window exists, this command begins with a half-and-half split that arranges the windows one above the other. The CONTROL-X 4f command prompts for a *filename,* calls the file up in the other window, and selects the other window. If no other window exists, this command begins with a half-and-half split that arranges the windows one above the other.

ADJUSTING AND DELETING WINDOWS

CONTROL-X 0
CONTROL-X 1

Windows might be destroyed when they get in the way. No data is lost in the window's associated buffer with this operation, and you can make another window whenever you like. The CONTROL-X 0 (zero) command deletes the current window and gives its space to its neighbors; CONTROL-X 1 deletes all windows except the current window.

META-x **shrink-window**
CONTROL-X ^
CONTROL-X }
CONTROL-X {

You can also adjust the dimensions of the current window at the expense of its neighbors. To make a window shorter, give the command META-x **shrink-window**. Press CONTROL-X ^ to increase the height of a window, CONTROL-X } to make the window wider, and CONTROL-X { to make the window narrower. Each of these commands adds or subtracts one line or column to or from the window, unless you precede the command with a numeric argument.

The emacs editor has its own guidelines for a window's minimum useful size and might destroy a window before you force one of its dimensions to zero. Although the window might disappear, the buffer remains intact.

FOREGROUND SHELL COMMANDS

The emacs editor can run a subshell (a shell that is a child of emacs—refer to "Executing a Command" on page 335) to execute a single command line, optionally with standard input coming from Region of the current buffer and optionally with standard output replacing Region (Table 7-13). This process is analogous to executing a shell command from the vim editor and having the input come from the file you are editing and the output go back to the same file (page 209). As with vim, how well this process works depends in part on the capabilities of the shell.

Table 7-13 Foreground shell commands

Command	Result
META-! (exclamation point)	Prompts for a shell command, executes it, and displays the output
CONTROL-U META-! (exclamation point)	Prompts for a shell command, executes it, and inserts the output at Point
META-| (vertical bar)	Prompts for a shell command, gives Region as input, filters it through the command, and displays the output

Table 7-13 Foreground shell commands (continued)

CONTROL-U META-| (vertical bar)	Prompts for a shell command, gives Region as input, filters it through the command, deletes the old Region, and inserts the output in that position

The emacs editor can also start an interactive subshell that runs continuously in its own buffer. See "Shell Mode" on page 264 for more information.

BACKGROUND SHELL COMMANDS

The emacs editor can run processes in the background, with their output being fed into a growing emacs buffer that does not have to remain in view. You can continue editing while the background process runs and look at its output later. Any shell command can be run in this way.

The growing output buffer is always named ***compilation***. You can read it, copy from it, or edit it in any way, without waiting for the background process to finish. Most commonly this buffer is used to review the output of program compilation and to correct any syntax errors found by the compiler.

META-x **compile** To run a process in the background, give the command META-x **compile** to prompt for a shell command and begin executing it as a background process. The screen splits in half to show the ***compilation*** buffer.

You can switch to the ***compilation*** buffer and watch the execution, if you wish. To make the display scroll as you watch, position the cursor at the very end of the text with a META-> command. If you are not interested in this display, just remove the window with CONTROL-X 0 (zero) if you are in it or CONTROL-X 1 otherwise and keep working. You can switch back to the ***compilation*** buffer later with CONTROL-X **b**.

To kill the background process give the command META-x **kill-compilation**. The emacs editor asks for confirmation and then kills the background process.

If standard format error messages appear in ***compilation***, you can automatically visit the line in the file where each error occurred. Give the command CONTROL-X ` (back tick) to split the screen into two windows and visit the file and line of the next error message. Scroll the **\*compilation\*** buffer until this error message appears at the top of its window. Use CONTROL-U CONTROL-X ` to start over with the first error message and visit that file and line.

MAJOR MODES: LANGUAGE-SENSITIVE EDITING

The emacs editor has a large collection of feature sets, each specific to a certain variety of text. The feature sets are called *Major modes*. A buffer can have only one Major mode at a time.

A buffer's Major mode is private to the buffer and does not affect editing in any other buffer. If you switch to a new buffer having a different mode, rules for the new mode take effect immediately. To avoid confusion, the name of a buffer's Major mode appears in the Mode Line of any window viewing that buffer (Figure 7-1 on page 225).

The three classes of Major modes are used for the following tasks:

- Editing human languages (for example, text, nroff, TeX)
- Editing programming languages (for example, C, Fortran, Lisp)
- Special purposes (for example, shell, mail, dired, ftp)

In addition, one Major mode—Fundamental—does nothing special. A Major mode usually sets up the following:

- Special commands unique to the mode, possibly with their own key bindings. Whereas languages might have just a few special commands, special-purpose modes might have dozens.
- Mode-specific character syntax and regular expressions defining word-constituent characters, delimiters, comments, whitespace, and so on. This setup conditions the behavior of commands oriented to syntactic units, such as words, sentences, comments, or parenthesized expressions.

SELECTING A MAJOR MODE

META-x ***modename***

The emacs editor chooses and sets a mode when a file is called up by matching the filename against a set of regular expression patterns describing the filename and filename extension. The explicit command to enter a Major mode is META-x ***modename***. This command is used mostly to correct the Major mode when emacs guesses wrong.

To have a file define its own mode, include the text **–*– modename –*–** somewhere in the first nonblank line of the file, possibly inside a comment suitable for the programming language the file is written in.

HUMAN-LANGUAGE MODES

A *human* language is meant eventually to be used by humans, possibly after being formatted by a text-formatting program. Human languages share many conventions about the structure of words, sentences, and paragraphs. With regard to these textual units, the major human language modes all behave in the same way.

Beyond this area of commonality, each mode offers additional functionality oriented to a specific text formatter, such as TeX, LaTeX, or nroff/troff. Text-formatter extensions are beyond the scope of this chapter; the focus here is on the commands relating to human textual units.

WORDS

As mnemonic aids, the bindings for words are defined parallel to the character-oriented bindings CONTROL-F, CONTROL-B, CONTROL-D, DELETE, and CONTROL-T.

META-f META-b Just as CONTROL-F and CONTROL-B move forward and backward over characters, so META-f and META-b move forward and backward over words. They might start from a position inside or outside the word to be traversed, but in all cases Point finishes just beyond the word, adjacent to the last character skipped over. Both commands accept a numeric argument specifying the number of words to be traversed.

META-d META-DELETE Just as CONTROL-D and DELETE delete characters forward and backward, so the keys META-d and META-DELETE kill words forward and backward. They leave Point in exactly the same finishing position as META-f and META-b do, but they kill the words they pass over. They also accept a numeric argument.

META-t META-t transposes the word before Point with the word after Point.

SENTENCES

META-a META-e CONTROL-X DELETE META-k As mnemonic aids, three of the bindings for sentences are defined parallel to the line-oriented bindings: CONTROL-A, CONTROL-E, and CONTROL-K. The META-a command moves backward to the beginning of a sentence; META-e moves forward to the end of a sentence. In addition, CONTROL-X DELETE kills backward to the beginning of a sentence; META-k kills forward to the end of a sentence.

The emacs editor recognizes the ends of sentences by referring to a regular expression that is kept in a variable named **sentence-end**. Briefly, emacs looks for the characters **.**, **?**, or **!** followed by two SPACEs or an end-of-line marker, possibly with close quotation marks or close braces. Give the command CONTROL-H **v sentence-end** RETURN to display the value of this variable.

The META-a and META-e commands leave Point adjacent to the first or last nonblank character in the sentence. They accept a numeric argument specifying the number of sentences to traverse; a negative argument runs them in reverse.

The META-k and CONTROL-X DELETE commands kill sentences forward and backward, in a manner analogous to CONTROL-K line kill. They leave Point in the same position as META-a and META-e do, but they kill the sentences they pass over. They also accept a numeric argument. CONTROL-X DELETE is useful for quickly backing out of a half-finished sentence.

PARAGRAPHS

META-{ META-} META-h The META-{ command moves backward to the most recent paragraph beginning; META-} moves forward to the next paragraph ending. The META-h command marks the paragraph the cursor is on as Region (that is, it puts Point at the beginning and Mark at the end), or marks the next paragraph if the cursor is between paragraphs.

The META-} and META-{ commands leave Point at the beginning of a line, adjacent to the first character or last character, respectively, of the paragraph. They accept a numeric argument specifying the number of paragraphs to traverse and run in reverse if given a negative argument.

In human-language modes, paragraphs are separated by blank lines and text-formatter command lines, and an indented line starts a paragraph. Recognition is based on the regular expressions stored in the variables **paragraph-separate** and **paragraph-start**. A paragraph is composed of complete lines, including the final line terminator. If a paragraph starts following one or more blank lines, the last blank line before the paragraph belongs to the paragraph.

FILL

The emacs editor can *fill* a paragraph to fit a specified width, breaking lines and rearranging them as necessary. It breaks lines between words and does not hyphenate words. The emacs editor can fill automatically as you type or in response to an explicit command.

META-x **auto-fill-mode**

The META-x **auto-fill-mode** command toggles Auto Fill mode on and off. When this mode is on, emacs automatically breaks lines when you press SPACE or RETURN and are currently beyond the specified line width. This feature is useful when you are entering new text.

META-q
META-x **fill-region**

Auto Fill mode does not automatically refill the entire paragraph you are currently working on. If you add new text in the middle of a paragraph, Auto Fill mode breaks the new text as you type but does not refill the complete paragraph. To refill a complete paragraph or Region of paragraphs, use either META-q to refill the current paragraph or META-x **fill-region** to refill each paragraph in Region (between Point and Mark).

You can change the filling width from its default value of 70 by setting the **fill-column** variable. Give the command CONTROL-X **f** to set **fill-column** to the current cursor position and the command CONTROL-U ***nnn*** CONTROL-X **f** to set **fill-column** to ***nnn***, where 0 is the left margin.

CASE CONVERSION

The emacs editor can force words or Regions to all uppercase, all lowercase, or initial caps (the first letter of each word uppercase, the rest lowercase) characters. Refer to Table 7-14.

Table 7-14 Case conversion

Command	Result
META-l (lowercase "l")	Converts word to the right of Point to lowercase
META-u	Converts word to the right of Point to uppercase
META-c	Converts word to the right of Point to initial caps
CONTROL-X CONTROL-L	Converts Region to lowercase
CONTROL-X CONTROL-U	Converts Region to uppercase

The word-oriented conversions move Point over the word just converted (just as META-f does), allowing you to walk through text and convert each word with META-l, META-u, or META-c, or skip over words to be left alone with META-f. A positive numeric argument converts that number of words to the right of Point, moving Point as it goes. A negative numeric argument converts that number of words to the left of Point but leaves Point stationary. This feature is useful for quickly changing the case of words you have just typed. Table 7-15 shows some examples.

Table 7-15 Examples of case conversion

Characters and commands	Result
HELLOMETA-–META-l (lowercase "l")	**hello**
helloMETA-–META-u	**HELLO**
helloMETA-–META-c	**Hello**

When the cursor (Point) is in the middle of a word, the case conversion commands convert the characters to the left of the cursor.

TEXT MODE

META-x **text-mode**

With very few exceptions, the commands for human-language textual units are always turned on and available, even when the programming-language modes are activated. Text mode adds very little to these basic commands but is still worth turning on just to activate the TAB key function (next). Use the command META-x **text-mode** to activate Text mode.

META-x **edit-tab-stops**

In Text mode, pressing TAB runs the function **tab-to-tab-stop**. By default TAB stops are set every eight columns. You can adjust them with META-x **edit-tab-stops**, which switches to a special ***Tab Stops*** buffer. The current TAB stops are laid out in this buffer on a scale for you to edit. The new stops are installed when or if you type CONTROL-C CONTROL-C. You can kill this buffer (CONTROL-X**k**) or switch away from it (CONTROL-X**b**) without changing the TAB stops.

The TAB stops you set with the META-x **edit-tab-stops** command affect only the interpretation of TAB characters arriving from the keyboard. The emacs editor automatically inserts enough spaces to reach the TAB stop. This command does not affect the interpretation of TAB characters already in the buffer or the underlying file. If you edit the TAB stops and then use them, when you print the file the hard copy will look the same as the text on the screen.

C MODE

Programming languages are read by humans but are interpreted by machines. Besides continuing to handle some of the human-language text units (for example, words and sentences), the major programming-language modes address several additional issues:

- Handling *balanced expressions* enclosed by parentheses, brackets, or braces as textual units
- Handling comments as textual units
- Indention

The emacs editor includes Major modes to support C, Fortran, and several variants of Lisp. In addition, many users have contributed modes for their favorite languages. In these modes the commands for human textual units are still available, with occasional redefinitions. For example, a paragraph is bounded only by blank lines and indention does not signal a paragraph start. In addition, each mode has custom code to handle the language-specific conventions for balanced expressions, comments, and indention. This chapter discusses only C mode.

EXPRESSIONS

The emacs Major modes are limited to lexical analysis. They can recognize most tokens (for example, symbols, strings, and numbers) and all matched sets of parentheses, brackets, and braces. This is enough for Lisp but not for C, since the C mode lacks a full-function syntax analyzer and is not prepared to recognize all of C's possible expressions.[1]

Table 7-16 lists the emacs commands applicable to parenthesized expressions and some tokens. By design the bindings run parallel to the CONTROL commands for characters and the META commands for words. All of these commands accept a numeric argument and run in reverse if that argument is negative.

Table 7-16 Commands for expressions and tokens

Command	Result
CONTROL-META-f	Moves forward over an expression. The exact behavior depends on which character lies to the right of Point (or left of Point, depending on which direction you are moving Point): • If the first nonwhitespace is an opening delimiter (parenthesis, bracket, or brace), Point is moved just past the matching closing delimiter. • If the first nonwhitespace is a token, Point is moved just past the end of this token.
CONTROL-META-b	Moves backward over an expression.

1. In the emacs documentation the recurring term *sexp* refers to the Lisp term *S-expression*. Unfortunately, it is sometimes used interchangeably with *expression*, even though the language might not be Lisp.

Table 7-16 Commands for expressions and tokens

CONTROL-META-k	Kills an expression forward. This command leaves Point at the same finishing position as CONTROL-META-f but kills the expression it traverses.
CONTROL-META-@	Sets Mark at the position CONTROL-META-f would move to but does not change Point. To see the marked Region clearly, give a pair of CONTROL-X CONTROL-X commands to exchange Point and Mark.

FUNCTION DEFINITIONS

In emacs a balanced expression at the outermost level is considered to be a function definition and is often called a *defun,* even though that term is specific to Lisp. More generally it is understood to be a function definition in the language at hand.

In C mode a function definition includes the return data type, the function name, and the argument declarations appearing before the { character. Table 7-17 shows the commands for operating on function definitions.

Function indention style

caution The emacs editor assumes an opening brace at the left margin is part of a function definition. This heuristic speeds up the reverse scan for a definition's leading edge. If your code has an indention style that puts the opening brace elsewhere, you might get unexpected results.

Table 7-17 Function definition commands

Command	Result
CONTROL-META-a	Moves to the beginning of the most recent function definition. Use this command to scan backward through a buffer one function at a time.
CONTROL-META-e	Moves to the end of the next function definition. Use this command to scan forward through a buffer one function at a time.
CONTROL-META-h	Marks as Region the current function definition (or next function definition, if the cursor is between two functions). This command sets up an entire function definition for a Region-oriented operation such as kill.

INDENTION

The emacs C mode has extensive logic to control the indention of C programs. You can adjust this logic for many different styles of C indention (Table 7-18).

Table 7-18 Indention commands

Command	Result
TAB	Adjusts the indention of the current line. TAB inserts or deletes whitespace at the beginning of the line until the indention conforms to the current context and rules in effect. Point is not moved unless it lies in the whitespace area; in that case it is moved to the end of the whitespace. TAB inserts leading SPACEs; you can press TAB with the cursor at any position on the line. If you want to insert a TAB in the text, use META-i or CONTROL-Q TAB.
LINEFEED	Shorthand for RETURN followed by TAB. The LINEFEED key is a convenience for entering new code, giving you an autoindent as you begin each line.
The next two commands indent multiple lines with a single command.	
CONTROL-META-q	Reindents all lines inside the next pair of matched braces. CONTROL-META-q assumes the left brace is correctly indented and drives the indention from there. If you need to adjust the left brace, type TAB just to the left of the brace before giving this command. All lines up to the matching brace are indented as if you had typed TAB on each one.
CONTROL-META-\	Reindents all lines in Region. Put Point just to the left of a left brace and then give the command. All lines up to the matching brace are indented as if you had typed TAB on each one.

Customizing Indention

Many styles of C programming have evolved, and emacs does its best to support automatic indention for all of them. The indention coding was completely rewritten for emacs version 19; it supports C, C++, Objective-C, and Java. The new emacs syntactic analysis is much more precise and can classify each syntactic element of each line of a program into a single syntactic category (out of about 50), such as *statement, string,* or *else-clause.* Based on that analysis, emacs refers to the offset table named **c-offsets-alist** to look up how much each line should be indented from the preceding line.

To customize indention, you must change the offset table. Although you can define a completely new offset table for each customized style, it is typically more convenient to feed in a short list of exceptions to the standard rules. Each mainstream style (GNU, K&R [Kernighan and Ritchie], BSD, and so on) has such an exception list; all are collected in **c-style-alist**. Here is one entry from **c-style-alist**:

```
("gnu"
(c-basic-offset . 2)
(c-comment-only-line-offset . (0 . 0))
(c-offsets-alist . ((statement-block-intro . +)
    (knr-argdecl-intro . 5)
    (substatement-open . +)
    (label . 0)
```

```
        (statement-case-open . +)
        (statement-cont . +)
        (arglist-intro . c-lineup-arglist-intro-after-paren)
        (arglist-close . c-lineup-arglist)
        ))
    )
```

Constructing a custom style is beyond the scope of this book. If you are curious, the long story is available in emacs info beginning at "Customizing C Indentation." The sample **.emacs** file given in this chapter (page 269) adds a very simple custom style and arranges to use it on every **.c** file that is edited.

COMMENTS

Each buffer has its own **comment-column** variable, which you can view with the CONTROL-H **v comment-column** RETURN help command. Table 7-19 lists commands that facilitate working with comments.

Table 7-19 Comment commands

Command	Result
META-;	Inserts a comment on the current line or aligns an existing comment. This command's behavior differs according to the situation. • If no comment is on this line, META-; creates an empty comment at the value of **comment-column**. • If text already on this line overlaps the position of **comment-column**, META-; creates an empty comment one SPACE after the end of the text. • If a comment is already on this line but not at the current value of **comment-column**, META-; realigns the comment at that column. If text is in the way, it places the comment one SPACE after the end of the text. Once an aligned (possibly empty) comment exists on the line, Point moves to the start of the comment text.
CONTROL-X ;	Sets **comment-column** to the column after Point. The left margin is column 0.
CONTROL-U – CONTROL-X ;	Kills the comment on the current line. This command sets **comment-column** from the first comment found above this line and then performs a META-; command to insert or align a comment at that position.
CONTROL-U CONTROL-X ;	Sets **comment-column** to the position of the first comment found above this line and then executes a META-; command to insert or align a comment on this line.

SPECIAL-PURPOSE MODES

The emacs editor includes a third family of Major modes that are not oriented toward a particular language or toward ordinary editing. Instead, these modes perform some special function. The following modes might define their own key bindings and commands to accomplish that function:

- Rmail: reads, archives, and composes email
- Dired: moves around an ls –l display and operates on files
- VIP: simulates a complete vi environment
- VC: allows you to drive version-control systems (including RCS, CVS, and Subversion) from within emacs
- GUD (Grand Unified Debugger): allows you to run and debug C (and other) programs from within emacs
- Tramp: allows you to edit files on any remote system you can reach with ftp or scp
- Shell: runs an interactive subshell from inside an emacs buffer

This book discusses only Shell mode.

SHELL MODE

One-time shell commands and Region filtering were discussed earlier under "Foreground Shell Commands" on page 254. Each emacs buffer in Shell mode has an underlying interactive shell permanently associated with it. This shell takes its input from the last line of the buffer and sends its output back to the buffer, advancing Point as it goes. If you do not edit the buffer, it holds a record of the complete shell session.

The shell runs asynchronously, whether or not you have its buffer in view. The emacs editor uses idle time to read the shell's output and add it to the buffer.

META-x **shell**

Type META-x **shell** to create a buffer named ***shell*** and start a subshell. If a buffer named ***shell*** already exists, emacs just switches to that buffer. The shell that this command runs is taken from one of the following sources:

- The Lisp variable **explicit-shell-file-name**
- The environment variable **ESHELL**
- The environment variable **SHELL**

To start a second shell, first give the command META-x **rename-buffer** to change the name of the existing shell's buffer, and then give the command META-x **shell** to start another shell. You can create as many subshells and buffers as you like, all running in parallel.

A special set of commands is defined in Shell mode (Table 7-20). These commands are bound mostly to two-key sequences starting with CONTROL-C. Each sequence is similar to the ordinary control characters found in Linux but uses a leading CONTROL-C.

Table 7-20 Shell mode commands

Command	Result
RETURN	If Point is at the end of the buffer, emacs inserts the RETURN and sends this (the last) line to the shell. If Point is elsewhere, it copies this line to the end of the buffer, peeling off the old shell prompt (see the regular expression **shell-prompt-pattern**), if one existed. Then this copied line—now the last in the buffer—is sent to the shell.
CONTROL-C CONTROL-D	Sends CONTROL-D to the shell or its subshell.
CONTROL-C CONTROL-C	Sends CONTROL-C to the shell or its subshell.
CONTROL-C CONTROL-\	Sends a quit signal to the shell or its subshell.
CONTROL-C CONTROL-U	Kills the text on the current line not yet completed.
CONTROL-C CONTROL-R	Scrolls back to the beginning of the last shell output, putting the first line of output at the top of the window.
CONTROL-C CONTROL-O	Deletes the last batch of shell output.

optional

CUSTOMIZING emacs

At the heart of emacs is a Lisp interpreter written in C. This version of Lisp is significantly extended and includes many special editing commands. The interpreter's main task is to execute the Lisp-coded system that implements the look-and-feel of emacs.

Reduced to its essentials, this system implements a continuous loop that watches keystrokes arrive, parses them into commands, executes those commands, and updates the screen. This behavior can be customized in a number of ways:

- As single keystrokes arrive, they are mapped immediately through a keyboard translation table. By changing the entries in this table, it is possible to swap keys. If you are used to vi or vim, for example, you might want to swap DELETE and CONTROL-H. Then CONTROL-H backspaces as it does in vim, and DELETE (which is not used by vim) is the help key. If you use DELETE as an interrupt key, you might want to choose another key to swap with CONTROL-H.
- The mapped keystrokes are gathered into small groups called *key sequences*. A key sequence might be only a single key, such as CONTROL-N, or might include two or more keys, such as CONTROL-X CONTROL-F. Once gathered, the key sequences are used to select a particular procedure to be executed. The rules for gathering each key sequence and the specific procedure name

to be executed when that sequence comes in are codified in a series of tables called *keymaps*. By altering the keymaps, you can change the gathering rules or change which procedure is associated with which sequence. For example, if you are used to vi's or vim's use of CONTROL-W to back up over the word you are entering, you might want to change emacs's CONTROL-W binding from the standard **kill-region** to **delete-word-backward**.

- The command behavior is often conditioned by one or more environment variables or options. It might be possible to get the behavior you want by setting some of these variables.
- The command itself is usually a Lisp program that can be reprogrammed to make it behave as desired. Although this task is not appropriate for beginners, the Lisp source to nearly all commands is available and the internal Lisp system is fully documented. As mentioned earlier, it is common practice to load customized Lisp code at startup time, even if you did not write the code yourself.

Most emacs documentation glosses over the translation, gathering, and procedure selection steps and talks about keystrokes as though they were commands. However, it is important to know that the underlying machinery exists and to understand that you can change its behavior.

THE .emacs STARTUP FILE

Each time you start emacs, it loads the file of Lisp code named **~/.emacs**. Using this file is the most common way to customize emacs. Two command-line options control the use of the **.emacs** file. The **–q** option ignores the **.emacs** file so emacs starts without it; this is one way to get past a bad **.emacs** file. The **–u** ***user*** option uses the **~*user*/.emacs** file (the **.emacs** file from the home directory of ***user***).

The **.emacs** startup file is generally concerned only with key bindings and option settings; it is possible to write the Lisp statements for this file in a straightforward style. Each parenthesized Lisp statement is a Lisp function call. Inside the parentheses the first symbol is the function name; the rest of the SPACE-separated tokens are arguments to that function.

Assigning a value to a variable

The most common function in the **.emacs** file, **setq**, is a simple assignment to a global variable. The first argument is the name of the variable to set and the second argument is its value. The following example sets the variable named **c-indent-level** to **8**:

```
(setq c-indent-level 8)
```

Displaying the value of a variable

While you are running emacs, the command CONTROL-H **v** prompts for the name of a variable. When you enter the name of a variable and press RETURN, emacs displays the value of the variable.

Setting the default value of a variable

You can set the default value for a variable that is buffer-private by using the function named **setq-default**. To set a specific element of a vector, use the function name **aset**.

The first argument is the name of the vector, the second is the offset, and the third is the value of the target entry. In the startup file the new values are usually constants. Table 7-21 shows the formats of these constants.

Table 7-21 Formats of constants in **.emacs**

Command	Result
Numbers	Decimal integers, with an optional minus sign
Strings	Similar to C strings but with extensions for CONTROL and META characters: **\C-s** yields CONTROL-S, **\M-s** yields META-s, and **\M-\C-s** yields CONTROL-META-s
Characters	*Not* like C characters; start with **?** and continue with a printing character or with a backslash escape sequence (for example, **?a**, **?\C-i**, **?\033**)
Booleans	*Not* **1** and **0**; use **t** for *true* and **nil** for *false*
Other Lisp objects	Begin with a single quotation mark and continue with the object's name

REMAPPING KEYS

The emacs command loop begins each cycle by translating incoming keystrokes into the name of the command to be executed. The basic translation operation uses the ASCII value of the incoming character to index a 128-element vector called a *keymap*.

Sometimes a character's eighth bit is interpreted as the META *case*, but this cannot always be relied on. At the point of translation all META characters appear with the ESCAPE prefix, whether or not they were typed that way.

Each position in this vector is one of the following:

- Not defined: No translation possible in this map.
- The name of another keymap: Switches to that keymap and waits for the next character to arrive.
- The name of a Lisp function to be called: Translation process is done; call this command.

Because keymaps can reference other keymaps, an arbitrarily complex recognition tree can be set up. The mainstream emacs bindings use at most three keys, with a very small group of well-known *prefix keys*, each with its well-known keymap name.

Each buffer can have a *local keymap* that is used first for any keystrokes arriving while a window into that buffer is selected. The local keymap allows the regular mapping to be extended or overridden on a per-buffer basis and is most often used to add bindings for a Major mode.

The basic translation flow runs as follows:

- Map the first character through the buffer's local keymap. If it is defined as a Lisp function name, translation is done and **emacs** executes that function. If it is not defined, use this same character to index the global top-level keymap.
- Map the first character through the top-level global keymap **global-map**. At this and each following stage, the following conditions hold:
  - If the entry for this character is not defined, it is an error. Send a bell to the terminal and discard all the characters entered in this key sequence.
  - If the entry for this character is defined as a Lisp function name, translation is done and the function is executed.
  - If the entry for this character is defined as the name of another keymap, switch to that keymap and wait for another character to select one of its elements.

Everything input during the remapping process must be either a command or an error. Ordinary characters that are to be inserted in the buffer are usually bound to the command **self-insert-command**. Each of the well-known prefix characters is each associated with a keymap (Table 7-22).

Table 7-22 Keymap prefixes

Keymap prefix	Applies to
ctl-x-map	For characters following CONTROL-X
ctl-x-4-map	For characters following CONTROL-X **4**
esc-map	For characters following ESCAPE (including META characters)
help-map	For characters following CONTROL-H
mode-specific-map	For characters following CONTROL-C

To see the current state of the keymaps, type CONTROL-H **b**. They appear in the following order: local, global, and shorter maps for each prefix key. Each line specifies the name of the Lisp function to be called; the documentation for that function can be retrieved with the command CONTROL-H **f** ***function-name*** or CONTROL-H **k** ***key-sequence***.

The most common type of keymap customization is making small changes to the global command assignments without creating any new keymaps or commands. This type of customization is most easily done in the **.emacs** file using the Lisp function **define-key**. The **define-key** function takes three arguments:

- The keymap name
- A single character defining a position in that map
- The command to be executed when this character appears

For instance, to bind the command **backward-kill-word** to CONTROL-W, use the statement

```
(define-key global-map "\C-w" 'backward-kill-word)
```

The \ character causes **C-w** to be interpreted as CONTROL-W instead of three letters (equivalent to **\^w**). The unmatched single quotation mark in front of the command name is correct. This Lisp escape character keeps the name from being evaluated too soon. To bind the command **kill-region** to CONTROL-X CONTROL-K, use the statement

```
(define-key ctl-x-map "\C-k" 'kill-region)
```

A SAMPLE .emacs FILE

The following **~/.emacs** file produces a plain editing environment that minimizes surprises for vi and vim users. If any section or any line is not appropriate for your situation, you can edit it or make it a comment by placing one or more semicolons (;) beginning in column 1.

```
;;; Preference Variables

(setq make-backup-files nil)          ;Do not make backup files
(setq backup-by-copying t)            ;If you do, at least do not destroy links
(setq delete-auto-save-files t)       ;Delete autosave files when writing orig
(setq blink-matching-paren nil)       ;Do not blink opening delim
(setq require-final-newline 'ask)     ;Ask about missing final newline

;; Reverse mappings for C-h and DEL.
;; Sometimes useful to get DEL character from the Backspace key,
;; and online help from the Delete key.
;; NB: F1 is always bound to online help.
(keyboard-translate ?\C-h ?\177)
(keyboard-translate ?\177 ?\C-h)

;; Some vi sugar: emulate the CR command
;; that positions us to first non-blank on next line.
(defun forward-line-1-skipws ()
  "Position to first nonwhitespace character on next line."
  (interactive)
  (if (= (forward-line) 0)            ;if moved OK to start of next line
      (skip-chars-forward " \t")))    ;skip over horizontal whitespace

;; Bind this to M-n. ("enhanced next-line")
;; C-M-n is arguably more "correct" but (1) it takes three fingers
;; and (2) C-M-n is already bound to forward-list.
(define-key esc-map "n" 'forward-line-1-skipws)
```

```
;; C mode customization: set vanilla (8-space bsd) indention style

(require 'cc-mode)                    ;kiss: be sure it's here

(setq c-default-style
  '(
    (java-mode . "java")
    (awk-mode . "awk")
    (c-mode . "bsd")
    (other . "gnu")
  ))

;; See also CC Mode in online help for more style setup examples.

;; end of c mode style setup
```

MORE INFORMATION

A lot of emacs documentation is available in both paper and electronic form. The emacs info page and emacs help functions (page 238) provide an abundance of information. See also the GNU emacs Web page at www.gnu.org/software/emacs.

The comp.emacs and gnu.emacs.help newsgroups offer support for and a general discussion about emacs.

ACCESS TO emacs

The emacs editor is included in the repositories of most Linux distributions. You can download and install emacs with apt-get (page 1060) or yum (page 1054). You can download the latest version of the source code from www.gnu.org.

The Free Software Foundation can be reached at these addresses:

Mail Free Software Foundation, Inc.
51 Franklin Street, Fifth Floor
Boston, MA 02110-1301, USA

Email gnu@gnu.org

Phone +1 617-542-5942

Fax +1 617 542 2652

Web www.gnu.org

CHAPTER SUMMARY

You can precede many of the commands in the following tables with a numeric argument to make the command repeat the number of times specified by the argument.

Precede a numeric argument with CONTROL-U to keep emacs from entering the argument as text.

Table 7-23 lists commands that move the cursor.

Table 7-23 Moving the cursor

Command	Result
CONTROL-F	Forward by characters
CONTROL-B	Backward by characters
META-f	Forward by words
META-b	Backward by words
META-e	To end of sentence
META-a	To beginning of sentence
META-}	To end of paragraph
META-{	To beginning of paragraph
META->	Forward to end of buffer
META-<	Backward to beginning of buffer
CONTROL-ESCAPE	To end of line
CONTROL-A	To beginning of line
CONTROL-N	Forward (down) one line
CONTROL-P	Backward (up) one line
CONTROL-V	Scroll forward (down) one window
META-v	Scroll backward (up) one window
CONTROL-L	Clear and repaint screen, and scroll current line to center of window
META-r	To beginning of middle line
CONTROL-U ***num*** META-r	To beginning of line number ***num*** (0 = top, – = bottom)

Table 7-24 lists commands that kill and delete text.

Table 7-24 Killing and deleting text

Command	Result
CONTROL-DELETE	Deletes character under cursor
DELETE	Deletes character to left of cursor
META-d	Kills forward to end of current word

Table 7-24 Killing and deleting text (continued)

Command	Result
META-DELETE	Kills backward to beginning of previous word
META-k	Kills forward to end of sentence
CONTROL-X DELETE	Kills backward to beginning of sentence
CONTROL-K	Kills forward to, but not including, line-ending LINEFEED; if there is no text between the cursor and the LINEFEED, kills the LINEFEED
CONTROL-U 1 CONTROL-K	Kills from cursor forward to and including LINEFEED
CONTROL-U 0 CONTROL-K	Kills from cursor backward to beginning of line
META-z ***char***	Kills forward to, but not including, next occurrence of ***char***
META-w	Copies Region to Kill Ring (does not delete Region from buffer)
CONTROL-W	Kills Region (deletes Region from buffer)
CONTROL-Y	Yanks most recently killed text into current buffer at Point; sets Mark at beginning of this text, with Point and cursor at the end
META-y	Erases just-yanked text, rotates Kill Ring, and yanks next item (only after CONTROL-Y or META-y)

Table 7-25 lists commands that search for strings and regular expressions.

Table 7-25 Search commands

Command	Result
CONTROL-S	Prompts incrementally for a string and searches forward
CONTROL-S RETURN	Prompts for a complete string and searches forward
CONTROL-R	Prompts incrementally for a string and searches backward
CONTROL-R RETURN	Prompts for a complete string and searches backward
META-CONTROL-S	Prompts incrementally for a regular expression and searches forward
META- CONTROL-S RETURN	Prompts for a complete regular expression and searches forward
META-CONTROL-R	Prompts incrementally for a regular expression and searches backward
META- CONTROL-R RETURN	Prompts for a complete regular expression and searches backward

Table 7-26 lists commands that provide online help.

Table 7-26 Online help

Command	Result
CONTROL-H a	Prompts for ***string*** and displays a list of commands whose names contain ***string***
CONTROL-H b	Displays a (long) table of all key bindings now in effect
CONTROL-H c ***key-sequence***	Displays the name of the command bound to ***key-sequence***
CONTROL-H k ***key-sequence***	Displays the name of and documentation for the command bound to ***key-sequence***
CONTROL-H f	Prompts for the name of a Lisp function and displays the documentation for that function
CONTROL-H i (lowercase "i")	Displays the top menu of info (page 225)
CONTROL-H l (lowercase "l")	Displays the last 100 characters typed
CONTROL-H m	Displays the documentation and special key bindings for the current Major mode
CONTROL-H n	Displays the emacs news file
CONTROL-H t	Starts an emacs tutorial session
CONTROL-H v	Prompts for a Lisp variable name and displays the documentation for that variable
CONTROL-H w	Prompts for a command name and displays the key sequence, if any, bound to that command

Table 7-27 lists commands that work with a Region.

Table 7-27 Working with a Region

Command	Result
META-W	Copies Region nondestructively to the Kill Ring
CONTROL-W	Kills (deletes) Region
META-x print-region	Copies Region to the print spooler
META-x append-to-buffer	Prompts for buffer name and appends Region to that buffer
META-x append-to-file	Prompts for filename and appends Region to that file
CONTROL-X CONTROL-U	Converts Region to uppercase
CONTROL-X CONTROL-L	Converts Region to lowercase

Table 7-28 lists commands that work with lines.

Table 7-28 Working with lines

Command	Result
META-x occur	Prompts for a regular expression and lists each line containing a match for the expression in a buffer named ***Occur***
META-x delete-matching-lines	Prompts for a regular expression and deletes lines from Point forward that have a match for the regular expression
META-x delete-non-matching-lines	Prompts for a regular expression and deletes lines from Point forward that do *not* have a match for the regular expression

Table 7-29 lists commands that replace strings and regular expressions unconditionally and interactively.

Table 7-29 Commands that replace text

Command	Result
META-x replace-string	Prompts for two strings and replaces each instance of the first string with the second string from Mark forward; sets Mark at the start of the command
META-% *or* META-x query-replace	As above but queries for each replacement (see Table 7-30 for a list of responses)
META-x replace-regexp	Prompts for a regular expression and a string, and replaces each match for the regular expression with the string; sets Mark at the start of the command
META-x query-replace-regexp	As above but queries for each replacement (see Table 7-30 for a list of responses)

Table 7-30 lists responses to replacement queries.

Table 7-30 Responses to replacement queries

Command	Result
RETURN	Quits searching (does not make or query for any more replacements)
SPACE	Makes this replacement and continues querying
DELETE	Does *not* make this replacement and continues querying
, (comma)	Makes this replacement, displays the result, and asks for another command

Table 7-30 Responses to replacement queries (continued)

Command	Result
. (period)	Makes this replacement and does not make or query for any more replacements
! (exclamation point)	Replaces this and all remaining instances without querying

Table 7-31 lists commands that work with windows.

Table 7-31 Working with windows

Command	Result
CONTROL-X b	Prompts for and displays a different buffer in current window
CONTROL-X 2	Splits current window vertically into two
CONTROL-X 3	Splits current window horizontally into two
CONTROL-X o (lowercase "o")	Selects other window
META-CONTROL-V	Scrolls other window
CONTROL-X 4b	Prompts for buffer name and selects it in other window
CONTROL-X 4f	Prompts for filename and selects it in other window
CONTROL-X 0 (zero)	Deletes current window
CONTROL-X 1 (one)	Deletes all windows except current window
META-x shrink-window	Makes current window one line shorter
CONTROL-X ^	Makes current window one line taller
CONTROL-X }	Makes current window one character wider
CONTROL-X {	Makes current window one character narrower

Table 7-32 lists commands that work with files.

Table 7-32 Working with files

Command	Result
CONTROL-X CONTROL-F	Prompts for a filename and reads its contents into a new buffer; assigns the file's simple filename as the buffer name.
CONTROL-X CONTROL-V	Prompts for a filename and reads its contents into the current buffer (overwriting the contents of the current buffer).

Table 7-32 Working with files (continued)

Command	Result
CONTROL-X 4 CONTROL-F	Prompts for a filename and reads its contents into a new buffer; assigns the file's simple filename as the buffer name. Creates a new window for the new buffer and selects that window. This command splits the screen in half if you begin with only one window.
CONTROL-X CONTROL-S	Saves the current buffer to the original file.
CONTROL-X s	Prompts for whether to save each modified buffer (**y**/**n**).
META-x set-visited-file-name	Prompts for a filename and sets the current buffer's "original" name to that filename.
CONTROL-X CONTROL-W	Prompts for a filename, sets the current buffer's "original" name to that filename, and saves the current buffer in that file.
META-~ (tilde)	Clears modified flag from the current buffer. Use with caution.

Table 7-33 lists commands that work with buffers.

Table 7-33 Working with buffers

Command	Result
CONTROL-X CONTROL-S	Saves current buffer in its associated file.
CONTROL-X CONTROL-F	Prompts for filename and visits (opens) that file.
CONTROL-X b	Prompts for buffer name and selects it. If that buffer does not exist, creates it.
CONTROL-X 4b	Prompts for buffer name and displays that buffer in another window. The existing window is not disturbed, although the new window might overlap it.
CONTROL-X CONTROL-B	Creates a buffer named ***Buffer List*** and displays it in another window. The existing window is not disturbed, although the new window might overlap it. The new buffer is not selected. In the ***Buffer List*** buffer, each buffer's data is displayed with its name, size, mode(s), and original filename.
META-x rename-buffer	Prompts for a new buffer name and assigns this new name to the current buffer.
CONTROL-X CONTROL-Q	Toggles the current buffer's readonly status and the associated **%%** Mode Line indicator.
META-x append-to-buffer	Prompts for buffer name and appends Region to the end of that buffer.

Table 7-33 Working with buffers (continued)

Command	Result
META-x prepend-to-buffer	Prompts for buffer name and prepends Region to the beginning of that buffer.
META-x copy-to-buffer	Prompts for buffer name, deletes contents of that buffer, and copies Region to that buffer.
META-x insert-buffer	Prompts for buffer name and inserts entire contents of that buffer in current buffer at Point.
CONTROL-X k	Prompts for buffer name and deletes that buffer.
META-x kill-some-buffers	Goes through the entire buffer list and offers the chance to delete each buffer.

Table 7-34 lists commands that run shell commands in the foreground. These commands might not work with all shells.

Table 7-34 Foreground shell commands

Command	Result
META-! (exclamation point)	Prompts for shell command, executes it, and displays the output
CONTROL-U META-! (exclamation point)	Prompts for shell command, executes it, and inserts the output at Point
META-| (vertical bar)	Prompts for shell command, supplies Region as input to that command, and displays output of command
CONTROL-U META-| (vertical bar)	Prompts for shell command, supplies Region as input to that command, deletes old Region, and inserts output of command in place of Region

Table 7-35 lists commands that run shell commands in the background.

Table 7-35 Background shell commands

Command	Result
META-x compile	Prompts for shell command and runs that command in the background, with output going to the buffer named ***compilation***
META-x kill-compilation	Kills background process

Table 7-36 lists commands that convert text from uppercase to lowercase, and vice versa.

Table 7-36 Case conversion commands

Command	Result
META-l (lowercase "l")	Converts word to right of Point to lowercase
META-u	Converts word to right of Point to uppercase
META-c	Converts word to right of Point to initial caps
CONTROL-X CONTROL-L	Converts Region to lowercase
CONTROL-X CONTROL-U	Converts Region to uppercase

Table 7-37 lists commands that work in C mode.

Table 7-37 C mode commands

Command	Result
CONTROL-META-f	Moves forward over expression
CONTROL-META-b	Moves backward over expression
CONTROL-META-k	Moves forward over expression and kills it
CONTROL-META-@	Sets Mark at the position CONTROL-META-f would move to, without changing Point
CONTROL-META-a	Moves to beginning of the most recent function definition
CONTROL-META-e	Moves to end of the next function definition
CONTROL-META-h	Moves Point to beginning and Mark to end of current (or next, if between) function definition

Type META-x **shell** to create a buffer named ***shell*** and start a subshell. Table 7-38 lists commands that work on this buffer.

Table 7-38 Shell mode commands

Command	Result
RETURN	Sends current line to the shell
CONTROL-C CONTROL-D	Sends CONTROL-D to shell or its subshell
CONTROL-C CONTROL-C	Sends CONTROL-C to shell or its subshell
CONTROL-C CONTROL-\	Sends quit signal to shell or its subshell
CONTROL-C CONTROL-U	Kills text on the current line not yet completed
CONTROL-C CONTROL-R	Scrolls back to beginning of last shell output, putting first line of output at the top of the window
CONTROL-C CONTROL-O (uppercase "O")	Deletes last batch of shell output

EXERCISES

1. Given a buffer full of English text, answer the following questions:

   a. How would you change every instance of **his** to **hers**?

   b. How would you make this change only in the final paragraph?

   c. Is there a way to look at every usage in context before changing it?

   d. How would you deal with the possibility that **His** might begin a sentence?

2. Which command moves the cursor to the end of the current paragraph? Can you use this command to skip through the buffer in one-paragraph steps?

3. Suppose that you are lost in the middle of typing a long sentence.

   a. Is there an easy way to kill the botched sentence and start over?

   b. What if only one word is incorrect? Is there an alternative to backspacing one letter at a time?

4. After you have been working on a paragraph for a while, most likely some lines will have become too short and others too long. Is there a command to "neaten up" the paragraph without rebreaking all the lines by hand?

5. Is there a way to change the entire contents of the buffer to capital letters? Can you think of a way to change just one paragraph?

6. How would you reverse the order of two paragraphs?

7. How would you reverse two words?

8. Imagine that you saw a Usenet posting with something particularly funny in it and saved the posting to a file. How would you incorporate this file into your own buffer? What if you wanted to use only a couple of paragraphs from the posting? How would you add **>** to the beginning of each included line?

9. On the keyboard alone **emacs** has always offered a full set of editing possibilities. Generally, several techniques will accomplish the same goal for any editing task. In the X environment the choice is enlarged still further with a new group of mouse-oriented visual alternatives. From these options you must select the way that you like to solve a given editing puzzle best.

   Consider this Shakespearean fragment:

```
Full fathom five thy father lies;
  Of his bones are coral made;
Those are pearls that were his eyes:
  Nothing of him that doth fade,
But doth suffer a sea-change
```

```
6. Into something rich and strange.
7. Sea-nymphs hourly ring his knell:
8.       Ding-dong.
9. Hark! now I hear them--
10.  Ding-dong, bell!
```

The following fragment has been typed with some errors:

```
1. Full fathiom five tyy father lies;
2. These are pearls that were his eyes:
3.   Of his bones are coral made;
4.   Nothin of him that doth fade,
5. But doth susffer a sea-change
6. Into something rich and strange.
7. Sea-nymphs hourly ring his knell:
8.       Ding=dong.
9. Hard! now I hear them--
10.  Ding-dong, bell!
```

Use only the keyboard to answer the following:

a. How many ways can you think of to move the cursor to the spelling errors?

b. Once the cursor is on or near the errors, how many ways can you think of to fix them?

c. Are there ways to fix errors without explicitly navigating to or searching for them? How many can you think of?

d. Lines 2 and 3 in the retyped material are transposed. How many ways can you think of to correct this situation?

ADVANCED EXERCISES

10. Assume that your buffer contains the C code shown here, with the Major mode set for C and the cursor positioned at the end of the **while** line as shown by the black square:

```
/*
 * Copy string s2 to s1.  s1 must be large enough
 * return s1
 */
char *strcpy(char *s1, char *s2)
{
        char *os1;

        os1 = s1;
        while (*s1++ = *s2++)
                ;
        return os1;
}
```

```
/*
 * Copy source into dest, stopping after '\0' is copied, and
 * return a pointer to the '\0' at the end of dest. Then our
caller
 * can catenate to the dest  * string without another strlen call.
 */
char *stpcpy (char *dest, char *source)
{
        while ((*dest++ = *source++) != '\0') ■
                ; /* void loop body */
        return (dest - 1);
}
```

a. Which command moves the cursor to the opening brace of **strcpy**? Which command moves the cursor past the closing brace? Can you use these commands to skip through the buffer in one-procedure steps?

b. Assume the cursor is just past the closing parenthesis of the **while** condition. How do you move to the matching opening parenthesis? How do you move back to the matching close parenthesis again? Does the same command set work for matched [] (square brackets) and {} (braces)? How does this differ from the vim % command?

c. One procedure is indented in the Berkeley indention style; the other is indented in the GNU style. Which command reindents a line in accordance with the current indention style you have set up? How would you reindent an entire procedure?

d. Suppose that you want to write five string procedures and intend to use **strcpy** as a starting point for further editing. How would you make five copies of the **strcpy** procedure?

e. How would you compile the code without leaving emacs?

PART III

THE SHELLS

8

The Bourne Again Shell (bash)

In This Chapter

Objectives

After reading this chapter you should be able to:

- Describe the purpose and history of bash
- List the startup files bash runs
- Use three different methods to run a shell script
- Understand the purpose of the PATH variable
- Manage multiple processes using job control
- Redirect error messages to a file
- Use control operators to separate and group commands
- Create variables and display the values of variables and parameters
- List and describe common variables found on the system
- Reference, repeat, and modify previous commands using history
- Use control characters to edit the command line
- Create, display, and remove aliases and functions
- Customize the bash environment using the set and shopt builtins
- List the order of command-line expansion

This chapter picks up where Chapter 5 left off by focusing on the Bourne Again Shell (bash). It notes where tcsh implementation of a feature differs from that of bash; if appropriate, you are directed to the page where the alternative implementation is discussed. Chapter 10 expands on this chapter, exploring control flow commands and more advanced aspects of programming the Bourne Again Shell. The bash home page is at www.gnu.org/software/bash. The bash info page is a complete Bourne Again Shell reference.

The Bourne Again Shell (bash) and the TC Shell (tcsh) are command interpreters and high-level programming languages. As command interpreters, they process commands you enter on the command line in response to a prompt. When you use the shell as a programming language, it processes commands stored in files called *shell scripts*. Like other languages, shells have variables and control flow commands (e.g., **for** loops and **if** statements).

When you use a shell as a command interpreter, you can customize the environment you work in. You can make the prompt display the name of the working directory, create a function or an alias for cp that keeps it from overwriting certain kinds of files, take advantage of keyword variables to change aspects of how the shell works, and so on. You can also write shell scripts that do your bidding—anything from a one-line script that stores a long, complex command to a longer script that runs a set of reports, prints them, and mails you a reminder when the job is done. More complex shell scripts are themselves programs; they do not just run other programs. Chapter 10 has some examples of these types of scripts.

Most system shell scripts are written to run under bash (or dash; next page). If you will ever work in single-user/recovery mode—when you boot the system or perform system maintenance, administration, or repair work, for example—it is a good idea to become familiar with this shell.

This chapter expands on the interactive features of the shell described in Chapter 5, explains how to create and run simple shell scripts, discusses job control, talks about locale, introduces the basic aspects of shell programming, talks about history and aliases, and describes command-line expansion. Chapter 9 covers interactive use of the TC Shell and TC Shell programming, and Chapter 10 presents some more challenging shell programming problems.

BACKGROUND

bash Shell

The Bourne Again Shell is based on the Bourne Shell (an early UNIX shell; this book refers to it as the *original Bourne Shell* to avoid confusion), which was written by Steve Bourne of AT&T's Bell Laboratories. Over the years the original Bourne Shell has been expanded, but it remains the basic shell provided with many commercial versions of UNIX.

sh Shell Because of its long and successful history, the original Bourne Shell has been used to write many of the shell scripts that help manage UNIX systems. Some of these scripts appear in Linux as Bourne Again Shell scripts. Although the Bourne Again Shell includes many extensions and features not found in the original Bourne Shell, bash maintains compatibility with the original Bourne Shell so you can run Bourne Shell scripts under bash. On UNIX systems the original Bourne Shell is named sh.

On many Linux systems sh is a symbolic link to bash or dash, ensuring scripts that require the presence of the Bourne Shell still run. When called as sh, bash does its best to emulate the original Bourne Shell. Under macOS, sh is a copy of bash.

dash Shell The bash executable file is almost 900 kilobytes, has many features, and is well suited as a user login shell. The dash (Debian Almquist) shell is about 100 kilobytes, offers Bourne Shell compatibility for shell scripts (noninteractive use), and because of its size, can load and execute shell scripts much more quickly than bash.

Korn Shell The Korn Shell (ksh), written by David Korn, ran on System V UNIX. This shell extended many features of the original Bourne Shell and added many new features. Some features of the Bourne Again Shell, such as command aliases and command-line editing, are based on similar features from the Korn Shell.

POSIX The POSIX (Portable Operating System Interface) family of related standards is being developed by PASC (IEEE's Portable Application Standards Committee; standards.ieee.org/develop/wg/PASC_WG.html). A comprehensive FAQ on POSIX, including many links, appears at www.opengroup.org/austin/papers/posix_faq.html.

POSIX standard 1003.2 describes shell functionality. The Bourne Again Shell provides the features that match the requirements of this standard. Efforts are under way to make the Bourne Again Shell fully comply with the POSIX standard. In the meantime, if you invoke bash with the **--posix** option, the behavior of the Bourne Again Shell will closely match the POSIX requirements.

chsh: changes your login shell

tip The person who sets up your account determines which shell you use when you first log in on the system or when you open a terminal emulator window in a GUI environment. Under most Linux systems, bash is the default shell. You can run any shell you like after you are logged in. Enter the name of the shell you want to use (bash, tcsh, or another shell) and press RETURN; the next prompt will be that of the new shell. Give an **exit** command to return to the previous shell. Because shells you call in this manner are nested (one runs on top of the other), you will be able to log out only from your original shell. When you have nested several shells, keep giving **exit** commands until you reach your original shell. You will then be able to log out.

The chsh utility changes your login shell more permanently. First give the command **chsh**. In response to the prompts, enter your password and the absolute pathname of the shell you want to use (**/bin/bash**, **/bin/tcsh**, or the pathname of another shell). When you change your login shell in this manner using a terminal emulator under a GUI, subsequent terminal emulator windows might not reflect the change until you log out of the system and log back in. See page 381 for an example of how to use chsh.

Startup Files

When a shell starts, it runs startup files to initialize itself. Which files the shell runs depends on whether it is a login shell, an interactive shell that is not a login shell (give the command **bash** to run one of these shells), or a noninteractive shell (one used to execute a shell script). You must have read access to a startup file to execute the commands in it. Typically, Linux distributions put appropriate commands in some of these files. This section covers bash startup files. See page 382 for information on tcsh startup files and page 1076 for information on startup files under macOS.

Login Shells

A *login shell* is the first shell that displays a prompt when you log in on a system from the system console or a virtual console, remotely using ssh or another program, or by another means. When you are running a GUI and open a terminal emulator such as gnome-terminal, you are not logging in on the system (you do not provide your username and password), so the shell the emulator displays is (usually) not a login shell; it is an interactive nonlogin shell (next page). Login shells are, by their nature, interactive. See "**bash** versus **–bash**" on page 471 for a way to tell which type of shell you are running.

This section describes the startup files that are executed by login shells and shells that you start with the bash **––login** option.

/etc/profile The shell first executes the commands in **/etc/profile**, establishing systemwide default characteristics for users running bash. In addition to executing the commands it holds, some versions of **profile** execute the commands within each of the files with a **.sh** filename extension in the **/etc/profile.d** directory. This setup allows a user working with **root** privileges to modify the commands **profile** runs without changing the **profile** file itself. Because **profile** can be replaced when the system is updated, making changes to files in the **profile.d** directory ensures the changes will remain when the system is updated.

Set environment variables for all users in /etc/profile or in a *.sh file in /etc/profile.d

tip Setting and exporting a variable in **/etc/profile** or in a file with a **.sh** filename extension in the **/etc/profile.d** directory makes that variable available to every user's login shell. Variables that are exported (placed in the environment) are also available to all interactive and noninteractive subshells of the login shell.

.bash_profile, .bash_login, and .profile Next, the shell looks for **~/.bash_profile**, **~/.bash_login**, or **~/.profile** (**~/** is shorthand for your home directory), in that order, executing the commands in the first of these files it finds. You can put commands in one of these files to override the defaults set in **/etc/profile**.

By default, a typical Linux distribution sets up new accounts with **~/.bash_profile** and **~/.bashrc** files. The default **~/.bash_profile** file calls **~/.bashrc**, which calls **/etc/bashrc**.

.bash_logout When you log out, bash executes commands in the **~/.bash_logout** file. This file often holds commands that clean up after a session, such as those that remove temporary files.

INTERACTIVE NONLOGIN SHELLS

The commands in the preceding startup files are not executed by interactive, nonlogin shells. However, these shells inherit from the login shell variables that are declared and exported in these startup files.

.bashrc An interactive nonlogin shell executes commands in the **~/.bashrc** file. The default **~/.bashrc** file calls **/etc/bashrc**.

/etc/bashrc Although not called by bash directly, many **~/.bashrc** files call **/etc/bashrc**.

NONINTERACTIVE SHELLS

The commands in the previously described startup files are not executed by noninteractive shells, such as those that run shell scripts. However, if these shells are forked by a login shell, they inherit variables that are declared and exported in these startup files. Specifically, crontab files (page 781) do not inherit variables from startup files.

BASH_ENV Noninteractive shells look for the environment variable **BASH_ENV** (or **ENV** if the shell is called as sh) and execute commands in the file named by this variable.

SETTING UP STARTUP FILES

Although many startup files and types of shells exist, usually all you need are the **.bash_profile** and **.bashrc** files in your home directory. Commands similar to the following in **.bash_profile** run commands from **.bashrc** for login shells (when **.bashrc** exists). With this setup, the commands in **.bashrc** are executed by login and nonlogin shells.

```
if [ -f ~/.bashrc ]; then . ~/.bashrc; fi
```

The [**–f ~/.bashrc**] tests whether the file named **.bashrc** in your home directory exists. See pages 431, 434, and 1005 for more information on test and its synonym [ ]. See page 290 for information on the . (dot) builtin.

Set PATH in .bash_profile

tip Because commands in **.bashrc** might be executed many times, and because subshells inherit environment (exported) variables, it is a good idea to put commands that add to existing variables in the **.bash_profile** file. For example, the following command adds the **bin** subdirectory of the **home** directory to **PATH** (page 318) and should go in **.bash_profile**:

```
PATH=$PATH:$HOME/bin
```

When you put this command in **.bash_profile** and not in **.bashrc**, the string is added to the **PATH** variable only once, when you log in.

Modifying a variable in **.bash_profile** causes changes you make in an interactive session to propagate to subshells. In contrast, modifying a variable in **.bashrc** overrides changes inherited from a parent shell.

Sample **.bash_profile** and **.bashrc** files follow. Some commands used in these files are not covered until later in this chapter. In any startup file, you must place in the environment (export) those variables and functions that you want to be available to child processes. For more information refer to "Environment, Environment Variables, and Inheritance" on page 480.

```
$ cat ~/.bash_profile
if [ -f ~/.bashrc ]; then
    . ~/.bashrc                    # Read local startup file if it exists
fi
PATH=$PATH:/usr/local/bin          # Add /usr/local/bin to PATH
export PS1='[\h \W \!]\$ '         # Set prompt
```

The first command in the preceding **.bash_profile** file executes the commands in the user's **.bashrc** file if it exists. The next command adds to the **PATH** variable (page 318). Typically, **PATH** is set and exported in **/etc/profile**, so it does not need to be exported in a user's startup file. The final command sets and exports **PS1** (page 319), which controls the user's prompt.

The first command in the **.bashrc** file shown below executes the commands in the **/etc/bashrc** file if it exists. Next, the file sets **noclobber** (page 143), unsets **MAILCHECK** (page 319), exports **LANG** (page 324) and **VIMINIT** (for vim initialization; page 202), and defines several aliases. The final command defines a function (page 356) that swaps the names of two files.

```
$ cat ~/.bashrc
if [ -f /etc/bashrc ]; then
    source /etc/bashrc             # read global startup file if it exists
fi

set -o noclobber                   # prevent overwriting files
unset MAILCHECK                    # turn off "you have new mail" notice
export LANG=C                      # set LANG variable
export VIMINIT='set ai aw'         # set vim options
alias df='df -h'                   # set up aliases
alias rm='rm -i'                   # always do interactive rm's
alias lt='ls -ltrh | tail'
alias h='history | tail'
alias ch='chmod 755 '

function switch() {                # a function to exchange
    local tmp=$$switch             # the names of two files
    mv "$1" $tmp
    mv "$2" "$1"
    mv $tmp "$2"
}
```

. (DOT) OR source: RUNS A STARTUP FILE IN THE CURRENT SHELL

After you edit a startup file such as **.bashrc**, you do not have to log out and log in again to put the changes into effect. Instead, you can run the startup file using the

. (dot) or source builtin (they are the same command under bash; only source is available under tcsh [page 421]). As with other commands, the . must be followed by a SPACE on the command line. Using . or source is similar to running a shell script, except these commands run the script as part of the current process. Consequently, when you use . or source to run a script, changes you make to variables from within the script affect the shell you run the script from. If you ran a startup file as a regular shell script and did not use the . or source builtin, the variables created in the startup file would remain in effect only in the subshell running the script—not in the shell you ran the script from. You can use the . or source command to run any shell script—not just a startup file—but undesirable side effects (such as changes in the values of shell variables you rely on) might occur. For more information refer to "Environment, Environment Variables, and Inheritance" on page 480.

In the following example, **.bashrc** sets several variables and sets **PS1**, the bash prompt, to the name of the host. The . builtin puts the new values into effect.

```
$ cat ~/.bashrc
export TERM=xterm                    # set the terminal type
export PS1="$(hostname -f): "        # set the prompt string
export CDPATH=:$HOME                 # add HOME to CDPATH string
stty kill '^u'                       # set kill line to control-u

$ . ~/.bashrc
guava:
```

COMMANDS THAT ARE SYMBOLS

The Bourne Again Shell uses the symbols (,), [,], and $ in a variety of ways. To minimize confusion, Table 8-1 lists the most common use of each of these symbols and the page on which it is discussed.

Table 8-1 Builtin commands that are symbols

Symbol	Command
( )	Subshell (page 302)
$( )	Command substitution (page 371)
(( ))	Arithmetic evaluation; a synonym for let (use when the enclosed value contains an equal sign; page 505)
$(( ))	Arithmetic expansion (not for use with an enclosed equal sign; page 369)
[ ]	The test command (pages 431, 434, and 1005)
[[ ]]	Conditional expression; similar to [ ] but adds string comparisons (page 506)

REDIRECTING STANDARD ERROR

Chapter 5 covered the concept of standard output and explained how to redirect standard output of a command. In addition to standard output, commands can send output to *standard error*. A command might send error messages to standard error to keep them from getting mixed up with the information it sends to standard output.

Just as it does with standard output, by default the shell directs standard error to the screen. Unless you redirect one or the other, you might not know the difference between the output a command sends to standard output and the output it sends to standard error. One difference is that the system buffers standard output but does not buffer standard error. This section describes the syntax used by bash to redirect standard error and to distinguish between standard output and standard error. See page 389 if you are using tcsh.

File descriptors A *file descriptor* is the place a program sends its output to and gets its input from. When you execute a program, the shell opens three file descriptors for the program: 0 (standard input), 1 (standard output), and 2 (standard error). The redirect output symbol (**>** [page 140]) is shorthand for **1>**, which tells the shell to redirect standard output. Similarly **<** (page 142) is short for **0<**, which redirects standard input. The symbols **2>** redirect standard error. For more information refer to "File Descriptors" on page 464.

The following examples demonstrate how to redirect standard output and standard error to different files and to the same file. When you run the cat utility with the name of a file that does not exist and the name of a file that does exist, cat sends an error message to standard error and copies the file that does exist to standard output. Unless you redirect them, both messages appear on the screen.

```
$ cat y
This is y.
$ cat x
cat: x: No such file or directory

$ cat x y
cat: x: No such file or directory
This is y.
```

When you redirect standard output of a command, output sent to standard error is not affected and still appears on the screen.

```
$ cat x y > hold
cat: x: No such file or directory
$ cat hold
This is y.
```

Similarly, when you send standard output through a pipeline, standard error is not affected. The following example sends standard output of cat through a pipeline to tr (page 1014), which in this example converts lowercase characters to uppercase.

The text that cat sends to standard error is not translated because it goes directly to the screen rather than through the pipeline.

```
$ cat x y | tr "[a-z]" "[A-Z]"
cat: x: No such file or directory
THIS IS Y.
```

The following example redirects standard output and standard error to different files. The shell redirects standard output (file descriptor 1) to the filename following **1>**. You can specify **>** in place of **1>**. The shell redirects standard error (file descriptor 2) to the filename following **2>**.

```
$ cat x y 1> hold1 2> hold2
$ cat hold1
This is y.
$ cat hold2
cat: x: No such file or directory
```

Combining standard output and standard error

In the next example, the **&>** token redirects standard output and standard error to a single file. The **>&** token performs the same function under tcsh (page 389).

```
$ cat x y &> hold
$ cat hold
cat: x: No such file or directory
This is y.
```

Duplicating a file descriptor

In the next example, first **1>** redirects standard output to **hold**, and then **2>&1** declares file descriptor 2 to be a duplicate of file descriptor 1. As a result, both standard output and standard error are redirected to **hold**.

```
$ cat x y 1> hold 2>&1
$ cat hold
cat: x: No such file or directory
This is y.
```

In this case, **1> hold** precedes **2>&1**. If they had appeared in the opposite order, standard error would have been made a duplicate of standard output before standard output was redirected to **hold**. Only standard output would have been redirected to **hold** in that case.

Sending errors through a pipeline

The next example declares file descriptor 2 to be a duplicate of file descriptor 1 and sends the output for file descriptor 1 (as well as file descriptor 2) through a pipeline to the tr command.

```
$ cat x y 2>&1 | tr "[a-z]" "[A-Z]"
CAT: X: NO SUCH FILE OR DIRECTORY
THIS IS Y.
```

The token **|&** is shorthand for **2>&1 |**:

```
$ cat x y |& tr "[a-z]" "[A-Z]"
CAT: X: NO SUCH FILE OR DIRECTORY
THIS IS Y.
```

Sending errors to standard error

You can use **1>&2** (or simply **>&2**; the **1** is not required) to redirect standard output of a command to standard error. Shell scripts use this technique to send the output of echo to standard error. In the following script, standard output of the first echo is redirected to standard error:

```
$ cat message_demo
echo This is an error message. 1>&2
echo This is not an error message.
```

If you redirect standard output of **message_demo**, error messages such as the one produced by the first echo appear on the screen because you have not redirected standard error. Because standard output of a shell script is frequently redirected to a file, you can use this technique to display on the screen any error messages generated by the script. The **lnks** script (page 439) uses this technique. You can use the exec builtin to create additional file descriptors and to redirect standard input, standard output, and standard error of a shell script from within the script (page 494).

The Bourne Again Shell supports the redirection operators shown in Table 8-2.

Table 8-2 Redirection operators

Operator	Meaning
< ***filename***	Redirects standard input from ***filename***.
> ***filename***	Redirects standard output to ***filename*** unless ***filename*** exists and **noclobber** (page 143) is set. If **noclobber** is not set, this redirection creates ***filename*** if it does not exist and overwrites it if it does exist.
>! ***filename***	Redirects standard output to ***filename***, even if the file exists and **noclobber** (page 143) is set.
>> ***filename***	Redirects and appends standard output to ***filename***; creates ***filename*** if it does not exist.
&> ***filename***	Redirects standard output and standard error to ***filename***.
<&***m***	Duplicates standard input from file descriptor ***m*** (page 465).
[n]>&***m***	Duplicates standard output or file descriptor ***n*** if specified from file descriptor ***m*** (page 465).
[n]<&–	Closes standard input or file descriptor ***n*** if specified (page 465).
[n]>&–	Closes standard output or file descriptor ***n*** if specified.

WRITING AND EXECUTING A SIMPLE SHELL SCRIPT

A *shell script* is a file that holds commands the shell can execute. The commands in a shell script can be any commands you can enter in response to a shell prompt. For example, a command in a shell script might run a utility, a compiled program, or another shell script. Like the commands you give on the command line, a command in a shell script can use ambiguous file references and can have its input or output redirected from or to a file or sent through a pipeline. You can also use pipelines and redirection with the input and output of the script itself.

In addition to the commands you would ordinarily use on the command line, *control flow* commands (also called *control structures*) find most of their use in shell scripts. This group of commands enables you to alter the order of execution of commands in a script in the same way you would alter the order of execution of statements using a structured programming language. Refer to "Control Structures" on page 430 (bash) and page 408 (tcsh) for specifics.

The shell interprets and executes the commands in a shell script, one after another. Thus, a shell script enables you to simply and quickly initiate a complex series of tasks or a repetitive procedure.

chmod: Makes a File Executable

To execute a shell script by giving its name as a command, you must have permission to read and execute the file that contains the script (refer to "Access Permissions" on page 100). Read permission enables you to read the file that holds the script. Execute permission tells the system that the owner, group, and/or public has permission to execute the file; it implies the content of the file is executable.

When you create a shell script using an editor, the file does not typically have its execute permission set. The following example shows a file named **whoson** that contains a shell script:

```
$ cat whoson
date
echo "Users Currently Logged In"
who

$ ./whoson
bash: ./whoson: Permission denied
```

You cannot execute **whoson** by giving its name as a command because you do not have execute permission for the file. The system does not recognize **whoson** as an executable file and issues the error message **Permission denied** when you try to execute it. (See the tip on the next page if the shell issues a **command not found** error message.) When you give the filename as an argument to bash (**bash whoson**), bash assumes the argument is a shell script and executes it. In this case **bash** is executable, and **whoson** is an argument that bash executes, so you do not need execute permission to **whoson**. You must have read permission.

The chmod utility changes the access privileges associated with a file. Figure 8-1 shows ls with the –l option displaying the access privileges of **whoson** before and after chmod gives execute permission to the file's owner.

The first ls displays a hyphen (–) as the fourth character, indicating the owner does not have permission to execute the file. Next, chmod gives the owner execute permission: **u+x** causes chmod to add (**+**) execute permission (**x**) for the owner (**u**). (The **u** stands for *user*, although it means the owner of the file.) The second argument is the name of the file. The second ls shows an **x** in the fourth position, indicating the owner has execute permission.

Command not found?

tip If you give the name of a shell script as a command without including the leading ./, the shell typically displays the following error message:

```
$ whoson
bash: whoson: command not found
```

This message indicates the shell is not set up to search for executable files in the working directory. Enter this command instead:

```
$ ./whoson
```

The ./ tells the shell explicitly to look for an executable file in the working directory. Although not recommended for security reasons, you can change the **PATH** variable so the shell searches the working directory automatically; see **PATH** on page 318.

If other users will execute the file, you must also change group and/or public access permissions for the file. Any user must have execute access to use the file's name as a command. If the file is a shell script, the user trying to execute the file must have read access to the file as well. You do not need read access to execute a binary executable (compiled program).

The final command in Figure 8-1 shows the shell executing the file when its name is given as a command. For more information refer to "Access Permissions" on page 100 as well as the discussions of ls and chmod in Part VII.

```
$ ls -l whoson
-rw-rw-r--. 1 max pubs 40 05-24 11:30 whoson

$ chmod u+x whoson
$ ls -l whoson
-rwxrw-r--. 1 max pubs 40 05-24 11:30 whoson

$ ./whoson
Fri May 25 11:40:49 PDT 2018
Users Currently Logged In
zach     pts/7    2018-05-23 18:17
hls      pts/1    2018-05-24 09:59
sam      pts/12   2018-05-24 06:29 (guava)
max      pts/4    2018-05-24 09:08
```

Figure 8-1 Using chmod to make a shell script executable

#! SPECIFIES A SHELL

You can put a special sequence of characters on the first line of a shell script to tell the operating system which shell (or other program) should execute the file and which options you want to include. Because the operating system checks the initial characters of a program before attempting to execute it using **exec**, these characters save the system from making an unsuccessful attempt. If **#!** (sometimes said out loud as *hashbang* or *shebang*) are the first two characters of a script, the system interprets the characters that follow as the absolute pathname of the program that is to execute the script. This pathname can point to any program, not just a shell, and can be useful if you have a script you want to run with a shell other than the shell you are running the script from. The following example specifies that bash should run the script:

```
$ cat bash_script
#!/bin/bash
echo "This is a Bourne Again Shell script."
```

The bash –e and –u options can make your programs less fractious

tip The bash **–e** (errexit) option causes bash to exit when a simple command (e.g., not a control structure) fails. The bash **–u** (nounset) option causes bash to display a message and exit when it tries to expand an unset variable. See Table 8-13 on page 361 for details. It is easy to turn these options on in the **!#** line of a bash script:

```
#!/bin/bash -eu
```

These options can prevent disaster when you mistype lines like this in a script:

```
MYDIR=/tmp/$$
cd $MYDIr; rm -rf .
```

During development, you can also specify the **–x** option in the **!#** line to turn on debugging (page 442).

The next example runs under Perl and can be run directly from the shell without explicitly calling Perl on the command line:

```
$ cat ./perl_script.pl
#!/usr/bin/perl -w
print "This is a Perl script.\n";

$ ./perl_script.pl
This is a Perl script.
```

The next example shows a script that should be executed by tcsh:

```
$ cat tcsh_script
#!/bin/tcsh
echo "This is a tcsh script."
set person = zach
echo "person is $person"
```

Because of the #! line, the operating system ensures that tcsh executes the script no matter which shell you run it from.

You can use **ps –f** within a shell script to display the name of the program that is executing the script. The three lines that ps displays in the following example show the process running the parent bash shell, the process running the tcsh script, and the process running the ps command:

```
$ cat tcsh_script2
#!/bin/tcsh
ps -f

$ ./tcsh_script2
UID        PID  PPID  C STIME TTY          TIME CMD
max       3031  3030  0 Nov16 pts/4    00:00:00 -bash
max       9358  3031  0 21:13 pts/4    00:00:00 /bin/tcsh ./tcsh_script2
max       9375  9358  0 21:13 pts/4    00:00:00 ps -f
```

If you do not follow **#!** with the name of an executable program, the shell reports it cannot find the program you asked it to run. You can optionally follow **#!** with SPACEs before the name of the program. If you omit the **#!** line and try to run, for example, a tcsh script from bash, the script will run under bash and might generate error messages or not run properly. See page 682 for an example of a stand-alone sed script that uses **#!**.

Begins a Comment

Comments make shell scripts and all code easier to read and maintain by you and others. The comment syntax is common to both the Bourne Again Shell and the TC Shell.

If a hashmark (**#**) in the first character position of the first line of a script is not immediately followed by an exclamation point (**!**) or if a hashmark occurs in any other location in a script, the shell interprets it as the beginning of a comment. The shell then ignores everything between the hashmark and the end of the line (the next NEWLINE character).

Executing a Shell Script

fork and **exec** system calls

As discussed earlier, you can execute commands in a shell script file that you do not have execute permission for by using a bash command to **exec** a shell that runs the script directly. In the following example, bash creates a new shell that takes its input from the file named **whoson**:

```
$ bash whoson
```

Because the bash command expects to read a file containing commands, you do not need execute permission for **whoson**. (You do need read permission.) Even though bash reads and executes the commands in **whoson**, standard input, standard output, and standard error remain directed from/to the terminal. Alternatively, you can supply commands to bash using standard input:

```
$ bash < whoson
```

Although you can use bash to execute a shell script, these techniques cause the script to run more slowly than if you give yourself execute permission and directly invoke the script. Users typically prefer to make the file executable and run the script by typing its name on the command line. It is also easier to type the name, and this practice is consistent with the way other kinds of programs are invoked (so you do not need to know whether you are running a shell script or an executable file). However, if bash is not your interactive shell or if you want to see how the script runs with different shells, you might want to run a script as an argument to **bash** or **tcsh**.

sh does not call the original Bourne Shell

caution The original Bourne Shell was invoked with the command **sh**. Although you can call bash or, on some systems dash, with an **sh** command, it is not the original Bourne Shell. The **sh** command (**/bin/sh**) is a symbolic link to **/bin/bash** or **/bin/dash**, so it is simply another name for the **bash** or **dash** command. When you call bash using the command **sh**, bash tries to mimic the behavior of the original Bourne Shell as closely as possible—but it does not always succeed.

CONTROL OPERATORS: SEPARATE AND GROUP COMMANDS

Whether you give the shell commands interactively or write a shell script, you must separate commands from one another. This section, which applies to the Bourne Again and TC Shells, reviews the ways to separate commands that were covered in Chapter 5 and introduces a few new ones.

The tokens that separate, terminate, and group commands are called *control operators*. Each of the control operators implies line continuation as explained on page 512. Following is a list of the control operators and the page each is discussed on.

- ; Command separator (next page)
- NEWLINE Command initiator (next page)
- & Background task (next page)
- | Pipeline (next page)
- |& Standard error pipeline (page 293)
- () Groups commands (page 302)
- || Boolean OR (page 302)
- && Boolean AND (page 302)
- ;; Case terminator (page 454)

; AND NEWLINE SEPARATE COMMANDS

The NEWLINE character is a unique control operator because it initiates execution of the command preceding it. You have seen this behavior throughout this book each time you press the RETURN key at the end of a command line.

The semicolon (;) is a control operator that *does not* initiate execution of a command and *does not* change any aspect of how the command functions. You can execute a series of commands sequentially by entering them on a single command line and separating each from the next using a semicolon (;). You initiate execution of the sequence of commands by pressing RETURN:

```
$ x ; y ; z
```

If **x**, **y**, and **z** are commands, the preceding command line yields the same results as the next three commands. The difference is that in the next example the shell issues a prompt after each of the commands finishes executing, whereas the preceding command line causes the shell to issue a prompt only after **z** is complete:

```
$ x
$ y
$ z
```

Whitespace Although the whitespace (SPACEs and/or TABs) around the semicolons in the previous example makes the command line easier to read, it is not necessary. None of the control operators needs to be surrounded by whitespace.

| AND & SEPARATE COMMANDS AND DO SOMETHING ELSE

The pipe symbol (|) and the background task symbol (&) are also control operators. They *do not* start execution of a command but *do* change some aspect of how the command functions. The pipe symbol alters the source of standard input or the destination of standard output. The background task symbol causes the shell to execute the task in the background and display a prompt immediately so you can continue working on other tasks.

Each of the following command lines initiates a pipeline (page 145) comprising three simple commands:

```
$ x | y | z
$ ls -l | grep tmp | less
```

In the first pipeline, the shell redirects standard output of **x** to standard input of **y** and redirects **y**'s standard output to **z**'s standard input. Because it runs the entire pipeline in the foreground, the shell does not display a prompt until task **z** runs to completion: **z** does not finish until **y** finishes, and **y** does not finish until **x** finishes. In the second pipeline, **x** is an **ls –l** command, **y** is **grep tmp**, and **z** is the pager **less**. The shell displays a long (wide) listing of the files in the working directory that contain the string **tmp**, sent via a pipeline through **less**.

The next command line executes a list (page 149) by running the simple commands **d** and **e** in the background and the simple command **f** in the foreground:

```
$ d & e & f
[1] 14271
[2] 14272
```

The shell displays the job number between brackets and the PID number for each process running in the background. It displays a prompt as soon as **f** finishes, which might be before **d** or **e** finishes.

Before displaying a prompt for a new command, the shell checks whether any background jobs have completed. For each completed job, the shell displays its job number, the word **Done**, and the command line that invoked the job; the shell then displays a prompt. When the job numbers are listed, the number of the last job started is followed by a + character, and the job number of the previous job is followed by a – character. Other job numbers are followed by a SPACE character. After running the last command, the shell displays the following lines before issuing a prompt:

```
[1]-  Done                          d
[2]+  Done                          e
```

The next command line executes a list that runs three commands as background jobs. The shell displays a shell prompt immediately:

```
$ d & e & f &
[1] 14290
[2] 14291
[3] 14292
```

The next example uses a pipe symbol to send the output from one command to the next command and an ampersand (&) to run the entire pipeline in the background. Again, the shell displays the prompt immediately. The shell commands that are part of a pipeline form a single job. That is, the shell treats a pipeline as a single job, no matter how many commands are connected using pipe (|) symbols or how complex they are. The Bourne Again Shell reports only one process in the background (although there are three):

```
$ d | e | f &
[1] 14295
```

The TC Shell shows three processes (all belonging to job 1) in the background:

```
tcsh $ d | e | f &
[1] 14302 14304 14306
```

&& AND || BOOLEAN CONTROL OPERATORS

The && (AND) and || (OR) Boolean operators are called *short-circuiting* control operators. If the result of using one of these operators can be decided by looking only at the left operand, the right operand is not evaluated. The result of a Boolean operation is either 0 (*true*) or 1 (*false*).

&& The && operator causes the shell to test the exit status of the command preceding it. If the command succeeds, bash executes the next command; otherwise, it skips the next command. You can use this construct to execute commands conditionally.

```
$ mkdir bkup && cp -r src bkup
```

This compound command creates the directory **bkup**. If mkdir succeeds, the content of directory **src** is copied recursively to **bkup**.

|| The || control operator also causes bash to test the exit status of the first command but has the opposite effect: The remaining command(s) are executed only if the first command failed (that is, exited with nonzero status).

```
$ mkdir bkup || echo "mkdir of bkup failed" >> /tmp/log
```

The exit status of a command list is the exit status of the last command in the list. You can group lists with parentheses. For example, you could combine the previous two examples as

```
$ (mkdir bkup && cp -r src bkup) || echo "mkdir failed" >> /tmp/log
```

In the absence of parentheses, && and || have equal precedence and are grouped from left to right. The following examples use the true and false utilities. These utilities do nothing and return *true* (0) and *false* (1) exit statuses, respectively:

```
$ false; echo $?
1
```

The $? variable holds the exit status of the preceding command (page 477). The next two commands yield an exit status of 1 (*false*):

```
$ true || false && false
$ echo $?
1
$ (true || false) && false
$ echo $?
1
```

Similarly, the next two commands yield an exit status of 0 (*true*):

```
$ false && false || true
$ echo $?
0
$ (false && false) || true
$ echo $?
0
```

See "Lists" on page 149 for more examples.

optional

() GROUPS COMMANDS

You can use the parentheses control operator to group commands. When you use this technique, the shell creates a copy of itself, called a *subshell*, for each group. It treats each group of commands as a list and creates a new process to execute each command (refer to "Process Structure" on page 333 for more information on creating subshells). Each subshell has its own environment, meaning it has its own set of variables whose values can differ from those in other subshells.

The following command line executes commands **a** and **b** sequentially in the background while executing **c** in the background. The shell displays a prompt immediately.

```
$ (a ; b) & c &
[1] 15520
[2] 15521
```

The preceding example differs from the earlier example **d & e & f &** in that tasks **a** and **b** are initiated sequentially, not concurrently.

Similarly the following command line executes **a** and **b** sequentially in the background and, at the same time, executes **c** and **d** sequentially in the background. The subshell running **a** and **b** and the subshell running **c** and **d** run concurrently. The shell displays a prompt immediately.

```
$ (a ; b) & (c ; d) &
[1] 15528
[2] 15529
```

The next script copies one directory to another. The second pair of parentheses creates a subshell to run the commands following the pipe symbol. Because of these parentheses, the output of the first tar command is available for the second tar command, despite the intervening cd command. Without the parentheses, the output of the first tar command would be sent to cd and lost because cd does not process standard input. The shell variables **$1** and **$2** hold the first and second command-line arguments (page 471), respectively. The first pair of parentheses, which creates a subshell to run the first two commands, allows users to call **cpdir** with relative pathnames. Without them, the first cd command would change the working directory of the script (and consequently the working directory of the second cd command). With them, only the working directory of the subshell is changed.

```
$ cat cpdir
(cd $1 ; tar -cf - . ) | (cd $2 ; tar -xvf - )
$ ./cpdir /home/max/sources /home/max/memo/biblio
```

The **cpdir** command line copies the files and directories in the **/home/max/sources** directory to the directory named **/home/max/memo/biblio**. Running this shell script is the same as using cp with the **–r** option. See page 772 for more information on cp.

\ Continues a Command

Although it is not a control operator, you can use a backslash (\) character in the middle of commands. When you enter a long command line and the cursor reaches the right side of the screen, you can use a backslash to continue the command on the next line. The backslash quotes, or escapes, the NEWLINE character that follows it so the shell does not treat the NEWLINE as a control operator. Enclosing a backslash within single quotation marks or preceding it with another backslash turns off the power of a backslash to quote special characters such as NEWLINE (not tcsh; see **prompt2** on page 404). Enclosing a backslash within double quotation marks has no effect on the power of the backslash (not tcsh).

Although you can break a line in the middle of a word (token), it is typically simpler, and makes code easier to read, if you break a line immediately before or after whitespace.

optional You can enter a RETURN in the middle of a quoted string on a command line without using a backslash. (See **prompt2** on page 404 for tcsh behavior.) The NEWLINE (RETURN) you enter will then be part of the string:

```
$ echo "Please enter the three values
> required to complete the transaction."
Please enter the three values
required to complete the transaction.
```

In the three examples in this section, the shell does not interpret RETURN as a control operator because it occurs within a quoted string. The greater than sign (>) is a secondary prompt (**PS2**; page 321) indicating the shell is waiting for you to continue the unfinished command. In the next example, the first RETURN is quoted (escaped) so the shell treats it as a separator and does not interpret it literally.

```
$ echo "Please enter the three values \
> required to complete the transaction."
Please enter the three values required to complete the transaction.
```

Single quotation marks cause the shell to interpret a backslash literally:

```
$ echo 'Please enter the three values \
> required to complete the transaction.'
Please enter the three values \
required to complete the transaction.
```

JOB CONTROL

As explained on page 150, a *job* is another name for a process running a pipeline (which can be a simple command). You run one or more jobs whenever you give the shell a command. For example, if you type **date** on the command line and press RETURN, you have run a job. You can also create several jobs on a single command line by entering several simple commands separated by control operators (& in the following example):

```
$ find . -print | sort | lpr & grep -l max /tmp/* > maxfiles &
[1] 18839
[2] 18876
```

The portion of the command line up to the first & is one job—a pipeline comprising three simple commands connected by pipe symbols: find, sort, and lpr. The second job is a pipeline that is a simple command (grep). The & characters following each pipeline put each job in the background, so bash does not wait for them to complete before displaying a prompt.

Using job control you can move jobs from the foreground to the background, and vice versa; temporarily stop jobs; and list jobs that are running in the background or stopped.

jobs: Lists Jobs

The jobs builtin lists all background jobs. In the following example, the sleep command runs in the background and creates a background job that jobs reports on:

```
$ sleep 60 &
[1] 7809
$ jobs
[1] + Running                          sleep 60 &
```

fg: Brings a Job to the Foreground

The shell assigns a job number to each job you run in the background. For each job run in the background, the shell lists the job number and PID number immediately, just before it issues a prompt:

```
$ gnome-calculator &
[1] 1246
$ date &
[2] 1247
$ Fri Dec 7 11:44:40 PST 2018
[2]+ Done           date
$ find /usr -name ace -print > findout &
[2] 1269
$ jobs
[1]- Running            gnome-calculator &
[2]+ Running            find /usr -name ace -print > findout &
```

The shell discards job numbers when a job is finished and reuses discarded job numbers. When you start or put a job in the background, the shell assigns a job number that is one more than the highest job number in use.

In the preceding example, the jobs command lists the first job, gnome-calculator, as job 1. The date command does not appear in the jobs list because it finished before jobs was run. Because the date command was completed before find was run, the find command became job 2.

To move a background job to the foreground, use the fg builtin followed by the job number. Alternatively, you can give a percent sign (%) followed by the job number as a command. Either of the following commands moves job 2 to the foreground.

When you move a job to the foreground, the shell displays the command it is now executing in the foreground.

```
$ fg 2
find /usr -name ace -print > findout
```

or

```
$ %2
find /usr -name ace -print > findout
```

You can also refer to a job by following the percent sign with a string that uniquely identifies the beginning of the command line used to start the job. Instead of the preceding command, you could have used either **fg %find** or **fg %f** because both uniquely identify job 2. If you follow the percent sign with a question mark and a string, the string can match any part of the command line. In the preceding example, **fg %?ace** would also bring job 2 to the foreground.

Often, the job you wish to bring to the foreground is the only job running in the background or is the job that jobs lists with a plus (+). In these cases, calling fg without an argument brings the job to the foreground.

Suspending a Job

Pressing the suspend key (usually CONTROL-Z) immediately suspends (temporarily stops) the job in the foreground and displays a message that includes the word **Stopped**.

```
CONTROL-Z
[2]+  Stopped                  find /usr -name ace -print > findout
```

For more information refer to "Moving a Job from the Foreground to the Background" on page 151.

bg: Sends a Job to the Background

To move the foreground job to the background, you must first suspend the job (above). You can then use the bg builtin to resume execution of the job in the background.

```
$ bg
[2]+ find /usr -name ace -print > findout &
```

If a background job attempts to read from the terminal, the shell stops the job and displays a message saying the job has been stopped. You must then move the job to the foreground so it can read from the terminal.

```
$ (sleep 5; cat > mytext) &
[1] 1343
$ date
Fri Dec  7 11:58:20 PST 2018
```

```
[1]+ Stopped                    ( sleep 5; cat >mytext )
$ fg
( sleep 5; cat >mytext )
Remember to let the cat out!
CONTROL-D
$
```

In the preceding example, the shell displays the job number and PID number of the background job as soon as it starts, followed by a prompt. Demonstrating that you can give a command at this point, the user gives the command date, and its output appears on the screen. The shell waits until just before it issues a prompt (after date has finished) to notify you that job 1 is stopped. When you give an fg command, the shell puts the job in the foreground, and you can enter the data the command is waiting for. In this case the input needs to be terminated using CONTROL-D, which sends an EOF (end of file) signal to cat. The shell then displays another prompt.

The shell keeps you informed about changes in the status of a job, notifying you when a background job starts, completes, or stops, perhaps because it is waiting for input from the terminal. The shell also lets you know when a foreground job is suspended. Because notices about a job being run in the background can disrupt your work, the shell delays displaying these notices until just before it displays a prompt. You can set **notify** (page 363) to cause the shell to display these notices without delay.

If you try to exit from a nonlogin shell while jobs are stopped, the shell issues a warning and does not allow you to exit. If you then use jobs to review the list of jobs or you immediately try to exit from the shell again, the shell allows you to exit. If **huponexit** (page 362) is not set (it is not set by default), stopped jobs remain stopped and background jobs keep running in the background. If it is set, the shell terminates these jobs.

MANIPULATING THE DIRECTORY STACK

Both the Bourne Again Shell and the TC Shell allow you to store a list of directories you are working with, enabling you to move easily among them. This list is referred to as a *stack*. It is analogous to a stack of dinner plates: You typically add plates to and remove plates from the top of the stack, so this type of stack is named a LIFO (last in, first out) stack.

dirs: DISPLAYS THE STACK

The dirs builtin displays the contents of the directory stack. If you call dirs when the directory stack is empty, it displays the name of the working directory:

```
$ dirs
~/literature
```

The dirs builtin uses a tilde (~) to represent the name of a user's home directory. The examples in the next several sections assume you are referring to the directory structure shown in Figure 8-2.

pushd: Pushes a Directory on the Stack

When you supply the pushd (push directory) builtin with one argument, it pushes the directory specified by the argument on the stack, changes directories to the specified directory, and displays the stack. The following example is illustrated in Figure 8-3:

```
$ pushd ../demo
~/demo ~/literature
$ pwd
/home/sam/demo
$ pushd ../names
~/names ~/demo ~/literature
$ pwd
/home/sam/names
```

When you call pushd without an argument, it swaps the top two directories on the stack, makes the new top directory (which was the second directory) the new working directory, and displays the stack (Figure 8-4).

```
$ pushd
~/demo ~/names ~/literature
$ pwd
/home/sam/demo
```

Using pushd in this way, you can easily move back and forth between two directories. You can also use **cd –** to change to the previous directory, whether or not you have explicitly created a directory stack. To access another directory in the stack, call pushd with a numeric argument preceded by a plus sign. The directories in the stack are numbered starting with the top directory, which is number 0. The following pushd command continues with the previous example, changing the working directory to **literature** and moving **literature** to the top of the stack:

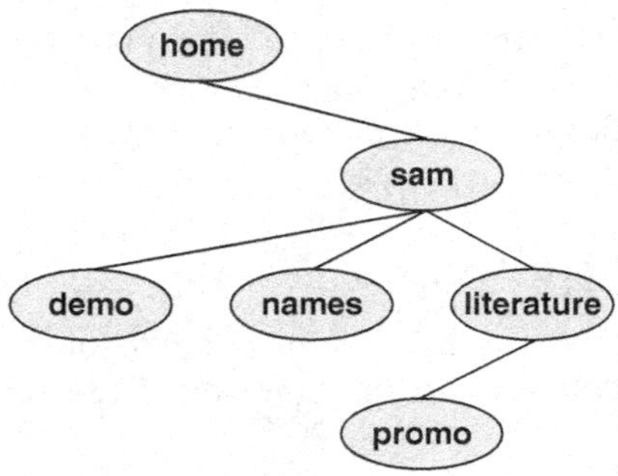

Figure 8-2 The directory structure used in the examples

```
$ pushd +2
~/literature ~/demo ~/names
$ pwd
/home/sam/literature
```

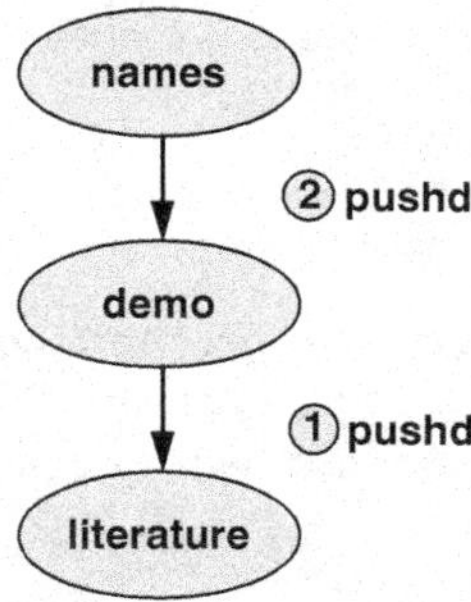

Figure 8-3 Creating a directory stack

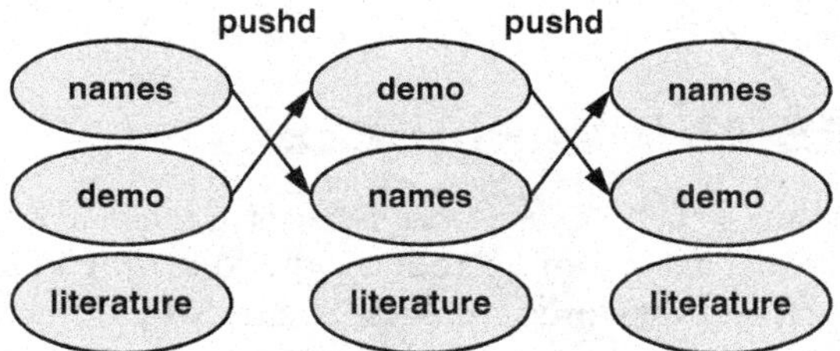

Figure 8-4 Using pushd to change working directories

popd: Pops a Directory Off the Stack

To remove a directory from the stack, use the popd (pop directory) builtin. As the following example and Figure 8-5 show, without an argument, popd removes the

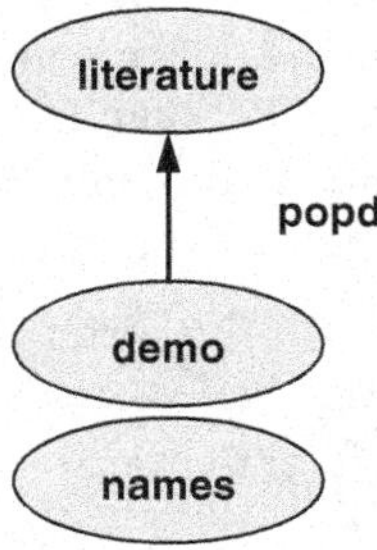

Figure 8-5 Using popd to remove a directory from the stack

top directory from the stack and changes the working directory to the new top directory:

```
$ dirs
~/literature ~/demo ~/names
$ popd
~/demo ~/names
$ pwd
/home/sam/demo
```

To remove a directory other than the top one from the stack, use popd with a numeric argument preceded by a plus sign. The following example removes directory number 1, **demo**. Removing a directory other than directory number 0 does not change the working directory.

```
$ dirs
~/literature ~/demo ~/names
$ popd +1
~/literature ~/names
```

Parameters and Variables

Shell parameter Within a shell, a *shell parameter* is associated with a value you or a shell script can access. This section introduces the following kinds of shell parameters: user-created variables, keyword variables, positional parameters, and special parameters.

Variables Parameters whose names consist of letters, digits, and underscores are referred to as *variables*. A variable name must start with a letter or underscore, not with a number. Thus, **A76**, **MY_CAT**, and **___X___** are valid variable names, whereas **69TH_STREET** (starts with a digit) and **MY-NAME** (contains a hyphen) are not.

User-created variables Variables that you name and assign values to are *user-created variables*. You can change the values of user-created variables at any time, or you can make them *readonly* so that their values cannot be changed.

Shell variables and environment variables By default, a variable is available only in the shell it was created in (i.e., local); this type of variable is called a *shell variable*. You can use export to make a variable available in shells spawned from the shell it was created in (i.e., global); this type of variable is called an *environment variable*. One naming convention is to use mixed-case or lowercase letters for shell variables and only uppercase letters for environment variables. Refer to "Variables" on page 479 for more information on shell variables and environment variables.

To declare and initialize a variable in bash, use the following syntax:

VARIABLE=value

There can be no whitespace on either side of the equal sign (=). An example follows:

```
$ myvar=abc
```

Under tcsh the assignment must be preceded by the word **set** and the SPACEs on either side of the equal sign are optional:

```
$ set myvar = abc
```

Declaring and initializing a variable for a script

The Bourne Again Shell permits you to put variable assignments at the beginning of a command line. This type of assignment places variables in the environment of the command shell—that is, the variable is accessible only from the program (and the children of the program) the command runs. It is not available from the shell running the command. The **my_script** shell script displays the value of **TEMPDIR**. The following command runs **my_script** with **TEMPDIR** set to **/home/sam/temp**. The echo builtin shows that the interactive shell has no value for **TEMPDIR** after running **my_script**. If **TEMPDIR** had been set in the interactive shell, running **my_script** in this manner would have had no effect on its value.

```
$ cat my_script
echo $TEMPDIR
$ TEMPDIR=/home/sam/temp ./my_script
/home/sam/temp
$ echo $TEMPDIR

$
```

Keyword variables

Keyword variables have special meaning to the shell and usually have short, mnemonic names. When you start a shell (by logging in, for example), the shell inherits several keyword variables from the environment. Among these variables are **HOME**, which identifies your home directory, and **PATH**, which determines which directories the shell searches and in which order to locate commands you give the shell. The shell creates and initializes (with default values) other keyword variables when you start it. Still other variables do not exist until you set them.

You can change the values of most keyword shell variables. It is usually not necessary to change the values of keyword variables initialized in the **/etc/profile** or **/etc/csh.cshrc** systemwide startup files. If you need to change the value of a bash keyword variable, do so in one of your startup files (for bash see page 288; for tcsh see page 382). Just as you can make user-created variables environment variables, so you can make keyword variables environment variables—a task usually done automatically in startup files. You can also make a keyword variable readonly. See page 317 for a discussion of keyword variables.

Positional and special parameters

The names of positional and special parameters do not resemble variable names. Most of these parameters have one-character names (for example, **1**, **?**, and **#**) and are referenced (as are all variables) by preceding the name with a dollar sign (**$1**, **$?**, and **$#**). The values of these parameters reflect different aspects of your ongoing interaction with the shell.

Whenever you run a command, each argument on the command line becomes the value of a *positional parameter* (page 470). Positional parameters enable you to access command-line arguments, a capability you will often require when you write shell scripts. The **set** builtin (page 472) enables you to assign values to positional parameters.

Other frequently needed shell script values, such as the name of the last command executed, the number of positional parameters, and the status of the most recently executed command, are available as *special parameters* (page 475). You cannot assign values to special parameters.

USER-CREATED VARIABLES

The first line in the following example declares the variable named **person** and initializes it with the value **max**:

```
$ person=max
$ echo person
person
$ echo $person
max
```

Parameter substitution Because the **echo** builtin copies its arguments to standard output, you can use it to display the values of variables. The second line of the preceding example shows that **person** does not represent **max**. Instead, the string **person** is echoed as **person**. The shell substitutes the value of a variable only when you precede the name of the variable with a dollar sign (**$**). Thus, the command **echo $person** displays the value of the variable **person**; it does not display **$person** because the shell does not pass **$person** to **echo** as an argument. Because of the leading **$**, the shell recognizes that **$person** is the name of a variable, *substitutes* the value of the variable, and passes that value to **echo**. The **echo** builtin displays the value of the variable (not its name), never "knowing" you called it with the name of a variable.

Quoting the $** You can prevent the shell from substituting the value of a variable by quoting the leading **$. Double quotation marks do not prevent the substitution; single quotation marks or a backslash (****) do.

```
$ echo $person
max
$ echo "$person"
max
$ echo '$person'
$person
$ echo \$person
$person
```

SPACES Because they do not prevent variable substitution but do turn off the special meanings of most other characters, double quotation marks are useful when you assign values to variables and when you use those values. To assign a value that contains SPACEs or

TABs to a variable, use double quotation marks around the value. Although double quotation marks are not required in all cases, using them is a good habit.

```
$ person="max and zach"
$ echo $person
max and zach
$ person=max and zach
bash: and: command not found
```

When you reference a variable whose value contains TABs or multiple adjacent SPACEs, you must use quotation marks to preserve the spacing. If you do not quote the variable, the shell collapses each string of blank characters into a single SPACE before passing the variable to the utility:

```
$ person="max    and    zach"
$ echo $person
max and zach
$ echo "$person"
max    and    zach
```

Pathname expansion in assignments

When you execute a command with a variable as an argument, the shell replaces the name of the variable with the value of the variable and passes that value to the program being executed. If the value of the variable contains a special character, such as * or ?, the shell *might* expand that variable.

The first line in the following sequence of commands assigns the string **max*** to the variable **memo**. All shells interpret special characters as special when you reference a variable that contains an unquoted special character. In the following example, the shell expands the value of the **memo** variable because it is not quoted:

```
$ memo=max*
$ ls
max.report
max.summary
$ echo $memo
max.report max.summary
```

Above, the shell expands the **$memo** variable to **max***, expands **max*** to **max.report** and **max.summary**, and passes these two values to echo. In the next example, the Bourne Again Shell *does not expand the string* because bash does not perform pathname expansion (page 152) when it assigns a value to a variable.

```
$ echo "$memo"
max*
```

All shells process a command line in a specific order. Within this order bash (but not tcsh) expands variables before it interprets commands. In the preceding echo command line, the double quotation marks quote the asterisk (*) in the expanded value of **$memo** and prevent bash from performing pathname expansion on the expanded **memo** variable before passing its value to the echo command.

optional

Braces around variables

The *$VARIABLE* syntax is a special case of the more general syntax *${VARIABLE}*, in which the variable name is enclosed by ${}. The braces insulate the variable name from adjacent characters. Braces are necessary when catenating a variable value with a string:

```
$ PREF=counter
$ WAY=$PREFclockwise
$ FAKE=$PREFfeit
$ echo $WAY $FAKE

$
```

The preceding example does not work as expected. Only a blank line is output because although **PREFclockwise** and **PREFfeit** are valid variable names, they are not initialized. By default the shell evaluates an unset variable as an empty (null) string and displays this value (bash) or generates an error message (tcsh). To achieve the intent of these statements, refer to the **PREF** variable using braces:

```
$ PREF=counter
$ WAY=${PREF}clockwise
$ FAKE=${PREF}feit
$ echo $WAY $FAKE
counterclockwise counterfeit
```

The Bourne Again Shell refers to command-line arguments using the positional parameters **$1**, **$2**, **$3**, and so forth up to **$9**. You must use braces to refer to arguments past the ninth argument: **${10}**. The name of the command is held in **$0** (page 470).

unset: REMOVES A VARIABLE

Unless you remove a variable, it exists as long as the shell in which it was created exists. To remove the *value* of a variable but not the variable itself, assign a null value to the variable. In the following example, set (page 472) displays a list of all variables and their values; grep extracts the line that shows the value of **person**.

```
$ echo $person
zach
$ person=
$ echo $person

$ set | grep person
person=
```

You can remove a variable using the unset builtin. The following command removes the variable **person**:

```
$ unset person
$ echo $person

$ set | grep person
$
```

VARIABLE ATTRIBUTES

This section discusses attributes and explains how to assign attributes to variables.

readonly: MAKES THE VALUE OF A VARIABLE PERMANENT

You can use the readonly builtin (not in tcsh) to ensure the value of a variable cannot be changed. The next example declares the variable **person** to be readonly. You must assign a value to a variable *before* you declare it to be readonly; you cannot change its value after the declaration. When you attempt to change the value of or unset a readonly variable, the shell displays an error message:

```
$ person=zach
$ echo $person
zach
$ readonly person
$ person=helen
bash: person: readonly variable
$ unset person
bash: unset: person: cannot unset: readonly variable
```

If you use the readonly builtin without an argument, it displays a list of all readonly shell variables. This list includes keyword variables that are automatically set as readonly as well as keyword or user-created variables that you have declared as readonly. See the next page for an example (**readonly** and **declare –r** produce the same output).

declare: LISTS AND ASSIGNS ATTRIBUTES TO VARIABLES

The declare builtin (not in tcsh) lists and sets attributes and values for shell variables. The typeset builtin (another name for declare) performs the same function but is deprecated. Table 8-3 lists five of these attributes.

Table 8-3 Variable attributes (declare)

Attribute	Meaning
–a	Declares a variable as an array (page 486)
–f	Declares a variable to be a function name (page 356)
–i	Declares a variable to be of type integer (page 316)
–r	Makes a variable readonly; also readonly (above)
–x	Makes a variable an environment variable; also export (page 480)

The following commands declare several variables and set some attributes. The first line declares **person1** and initializes it to **max**. This command has the same effect with or without the word **declare**.

```
$ declare person1=max
$ declare -r person2=zach
$ declare -rx person3=helen
$ declare -x person4
```

readonly and export

The readonly and export builtins are synonyms for the commands **declare –r** and **declare –x**, respectively. You can declare a variable without initializing it, as the preceding declaration of the variable **person4** illustrates. This declaration makes **person4** an environment variable so it is available to all subshells. Until **person4** is initialized, it has a null value.

You can list the options to declare separately in any order. The following is equivalent to the preceding declaration of **person3**:

```
$ declare -x -r person3=helen
```

Use the + character in place of – when you want to remove an attribute from a variable. You cannot remove the readonly attribute. After the following command is given, the variable **person3** is no longer exported, but it is still readonly:

```
$ declare +x person3
```

See page 481 for more information on exporting variables.

Listing variable attributes

Without any arguments or options, declare lists all shell variables. The same list is output when you run set (page 473) without any arguments.

If you call declare with options but no variable names, the command lists all shell variables that have the specified attributes set. The command **declare –r** displays a list of all readonly variables. This list is the same as that produced by the **readonly** command without any arguments. After the declarations in the preceding example have been given, the results are as follows:

```
$ declare -r
declare -r BASHOPTS="checkwinsize:cmdhist:expand_aliases: ... "
declare -ir BASHPID
declare -ar BASH_VERSINFO='([0]="4" [1]="2" [2]="24" [3]="1" ... '
declare -ir EUID="500"
declare -ir PPID="1936"
declare -r SHELLOPTS="braceexpand:emacs:hashall:histexpand: ... "
declare -ir UID="500"
declare -r person2="zach"
declare -rx person3="helen"
```

The first seven entries are keyword variables that are automatically declared as readonly. Some of these variables are stored as integers (**–i**). The **–a** option indicates that **BASH_VERSINFO** is an array variable; the value of each element of the array is listed to the right of an equal sign.

Integer

By default, the values of variables are stored as strings. When you perform arithmetic on a string variable, the shell converts the variable into a number, manipulates it, and then converts it back to a string. A variable with the integer attribute is stored as an integer. Assign the integer attribute as follows:

```
$ declare -i COUNT
```

You can use declare to display integer variables:

```
$ declare -i
declare -ir BASHPID
declare -i COUNT
declare -ir EUID="1000"
declare -i HISTCMD
declare -i LINENO
declare -i MAILCHECK="60"
declare -i OPTIND="1"
...
```

KEYWORD VARIABLES

Keyword variables are either inherited or declared and initialized by the shell when it starts. You can assign values to these variables from the command line or from a startup file. Typically, these variables are environment variables (exported) so they are available to subshells you start as well as your login shell.

HOME: YOUR HOME DIRECTORY

By default, your home directory is the working directory when you log in. Your home directory is established when your account is set up; under Linux its name is stored in the **/etc/passwd** file. macOS uses Open Directory (page 1068) to store this information.

```
$ grep sam /etc/passwd
sam:x:500:500:Sam the Great:/home/sam:/bin/bash
```

When you log in, the shell inherits the pathname of your home directory and assigns it to the environment variable **HOME** (tcsh uses **home**). When you give a **cd** command without an argument, cd makes the directory whose name is stored in **HOME** the working directory:

```
$ pwd
/home/max/laptop
$ echo $HOME
/home/max
$ cd
$ pwd
/home/max
```

This example shows the value of the **HOME** variable and the effect of the cd builtin. After you execute cd without an argument, the pathname of the working directory is the same as the value of **HOME**: your home directory.

Tilde (~) The shell uses the value of **HOME** to expand pathnames that use the shorthand tilde (~) notation (page 91) to denote a user's home directory. The following example uses echo to display the value of this shortcut and then uses ls to list the files in Max's **laptop** directory, which is a subdirectory of his home directory:

```
$ echo ~
/home/max
$ ls ~/laptop
tester      count       lineup
```

PATH: WHERE THE SHELL LOOKS FOR PROGRAMS

When you give the shell an absolute or relative pathname as a command, it looks in the specified directory for an executable file with the specified filename. If the file with the pathname you specified does not exist, the shell reports **No such file or directory**. If the file exists as specified but you do not have execute permission for it, or in the case of a shell script you do not have read and execute permission for it, the shell reports **Permission denied.**

When you give a simple filename as a command, the shell searches through certain directories (your search path) for the program you want to execute. It looks in several directories for a file that has the same name as the command and that you have execute permission for (a compiled program) or read and execute permission for (a shell script). The **PATH** (tcsh uses **path**) variable controls this search.

The default value of **PATH** is determined when bash is compiled. It is not set in a startup file, although it might be modified there. Normally, the default specifies that the shell search several system directories used to hold common commands. These system directories include **/bin** and **/usr/bin** and other directories appropriate to the local system. When you give a command, if the shell does not find the executable—and, in the case of a shell script, readable—file named by the command in any of the directories listed in **PATH**, the shell generates one of the aforementioned error messages.

Working directory

The **PATH** variable specifies the directories in the order the shell should search them. Each directory must be separated from the next by a colon. The following command sets **PATH** so a search for an executable file starts with the **/usr/local/bin** directory. If it does not find the file in this directory, the shell looks next in **/bin** and then in **/usr/bin**. If the search fails in those directories, the shell looks in the **~/bin** directory, a subdirectory of the user's home directory. Finally, the shell looks in the working directory. Exporting **PATH** makes sure it is an environment variable so it is available to subshells, although it is typically exported when it is declared so exporting it again is not necessary:

```
$ export PATH=/usr/local/bin:/bin:/usr/bin:~/bin:
```

A null value in the string indicates the working directory. In the preceding example, a null value (nothing between the colon and the end of the line) appears as the last element of the string. The working directory is represented by a leading colon (not recommended; see the following security tip), a trailing colon (as in the example), or two colons next to each other anywhere in the string. You can also represent the working directory explicitly using a period (.).

Because Linux stores many executable files in directories named **bin** (*binary*), users typically put their executable files in their own **~/bin** directories. If you put your own **bin** directory toward the end of **PATH**, as in the preceding example, the shell looks there for any commands it cannot find in directories listed earlier in **PATH**.

If you want to add directories to **PATH**, you can reference the old value of the **PATH** variable in setting **PATH** to a new value (but see the preceding security tip). The following command adds **/usr/local/bin** to the beginning of the current **PATH** and the **bin** directory in the user's home directory (**~/bin**) to the end:

```
$ PATH=/usr/local/bin:$PATH:~/bin
```

Set PATH in ~/.bash_profile; see the tip on page 289.

PATH and security

security Do not put the working directory first in **PATH** when security is a concern. If you are working as **root**, you should *never* put the working directory first in **PATH**. It is common for **root**'s **PATH** to omit the working directory entirely. You can always execute a file in the working directory by prepending **./** to the name: **./myprog**.

Putting the working directory first in **PATH** can create a security hole. Most people type **ls** as the first command when entering a directory. If the owner of a directory places an executable file named **ls** in the directory, and the working directory appears first in a user's **PATH**, the user giving an **ls** command from the directory executes the ls program in the working directory instead of the system ls utility, possibly with undesirable results.

MAIL: Where Your Mail Is Kept

The **MAIL** variable (**mail** under tcsh) usually contains the pathname of the file that holds your mail (your *mailbox*, usually **/var/mail/*name*,** where ***name*** is your username). However, you can use **MAIL** to watch any file (including a directory): Set **MAIL** to the name of the file you want to watch.

If **MAIL** is set and **MAILPATH** (below) is not set, the shell informs you when the file specified by **MAIL** is modified (such as when mail arrives). In a graphical environment you can unset **MAIL** so the shell does not display mail reminders in a terminal emulator window (assuming you are using a graphical mail program).

Most macOS systems do not use local files for incoming mail. Instead, mail is typically kept on a remote mail server. The **MAIL** variable and other mail-related shell variables have no effect unless you have a local mail server.

The **MAILPATH** variable (not in tcsh) contains a list of filenames separated by colons. If this variable is set, the shell informs you when any one of the files is modified (for example, when mail arrives). You can follow any of the filenames in the list with a question mark (?) and a message. The message replaces the **you have mail** message when you receive mail while you are logged in.

The **MAILCHECK** variable (not in tcsh) specifies how often, in seconds, the shell checks the directories specified by **MAIL** or **MAILPATH**. The default is 60 seconds. If you set this variable to zero, the shell checks before it issues each prompt.

PS1: User Prompt (Primary)

The default Bourne Again Shell prompt is a dollar sign ($). When you run bash with **root** privileges, bash typically displays a hashmark (#) prompt. The **PS1** variable (**prompt** under tcsh; page 403) holds the prompt string the shell uses to let you know it is waiting for a command. When you change the value of **PS1**, you change the appearance of your prompt.

You can customize the prompt displayed by **PS1**. For example, the assignment

```
$ PS1="[\u@\h \W \!]$ "
```

displays the prompt

[user@host directory event]$

where ***user*** is the username, ***host*** is the hostname up to the first period, ***directory*** is the basename of the working directory, and ***event*** is the event number (page 337) of the current command.

If you are working on more than one system, it can be helpful to incorporate the system name into your prompt. The first example that follows changes the prompt to the name of the local host, a SPACE, and a dollar sign (or, if the user is running with **root** privileges, a hashmark), followed by a SPACE. A SPACE at the end of the prompt makes commands you enter following the prompt easier to read. The second example changes the prompt to the time followed by the name of the user. The third example changes the prompt to the one used in this book (a hashmark for a user running with **root** privileges and a dollar sign otherwise):

```
$ PS1='\h \$ '
guava $

$ PS1='\@ \u $ '
09:44 PM max $

$ PS1='\$ '
$
```

Table 8-4 describes some of the symbols you can use in **PS1**. See Table 9-4 on page 403 for the corresponding tcsh symbols. For a complete list of special characters you can use in the prompt strings, open the bash man page and search for the third occurrence of **PROMPTING** (enter the command **/PROMPTING** followed by a RETURN and then press **n** two times).

Table 8-4 **PS1** symbols

Symbol	Display in prompt
\$	# if the user is running with **root** privileges; otherwise, **$**
\w	Pathname of the working directory
\W	Basename of the working directory
\!	Current event (history) number (page 341)
\d	Date in Weekday Month Date format
\h	Machine hostname, without the domain
\H	Full machine hostname, including the domain
\u	Username of the current user

Table 8-4 **PS1** symbols (continued)

Symbol	Display in prompt
\@	Current time of day in 12-hour, AM/PM format
\T	Current time of day in 12-hour HH:MM:SS format
\A	Current time of day in 24-hour HH:MM format
\t	Current time of day in 24-hour HH:MM:SS format

PS2: USER PROMPT (SECONDARY)

The **PS2** variable holds the secondary prompt (**prompt2** under tcsh). On the first line of the next example, an unclosed quoted string follows echo. The shell assumes the command is not finished and on the second line displays the default secondary prompt (>). This prompt indicates the shell is waiting for the user to continue the command line. The shell waits until it receives the quotation mark that closes the string and then executes the command:

```
$ echo "demonstration of prompt string
> 2"
demonstration of prompt string
2
```

The next command changes the secondary prompt to **Input =>** followed by a SPACE. On the line with who, a pipe symbol (|) implies the command line is continued (page 512) and causes bash to display the new secondary prompt. The command **grep sam** (followed by a RETURN) completes the command; grep displays its output.

```
$ PS2="Input => "
$ who |
Input => grep sam
sam      tty1        2018-05-01 10:37 (:0)
```

PS3: MENU PROMPT

The **PS3** variable holds the menu prompt (**prompt3** in tcsh) for the **select** control structure (page 461).

PS4: DEBUGGING PROMPT

The **PS4** variable holds the bash debugging symbol (page 443; not in tcsh).

IFS: SEPARATES INPUT FIELDS (WORD SPLITTING)

The **IFS** (Internal Field Separator) shell variable (not in tcsh) specifies the characters you can use to separate arguments on a command line. It has the default value of SPACE-TAB-NEWLINE. Regardless of the value of **IFS**, you can always use one or more SPACE or TAB characters to separate arguments on the command line, provided these characters are not quoted or escaped. When you assign character values to **IFS**, these characters can also separate fields—but only if they undergo expansion. This type of interpretation of the command line is called *word splitting* and is discussed on page 372.

Be careful when changing IFS

caution Changing **IFS** has a variety of side effects, so work cautiously. You might find it useful to save the value of **IFS** before changing it. You can then easily restore the original value if a change yields unexpected results. Alternatively, you can fork a new shell using a **bash** command before experimenting with **IFS**; if you run into trouble, you can **exit** back to the old shell, where **IFS** is working properly.

The following example demonstrates how setting **IFS** can affect the interpretation of a command line:

```
$ a=w:x:y:z

$ cat $a
cat: w:x:y:z: No such file or directory
$ IFS=":"

$ cat $a
cat: w: No such file or directory
cat: x: No such file or directory
cat: y: No such file or directory
cat: z: No such file or directory
```

The first time cat is called, the shell expands the variable **a**, interpreting the string **w:x:y:z** as a single word to be used as the argument to cat. The cat utility cannot find a file named **w:x:y:z** and reports an error for that filename. After **IFS** is set to a colon (**:**), the shell expands the variable **a** into four words, each of which is an argument to cat. Now cat reports errors for four files: **w**, **x**, **y**, and **z**. Word splitting based on the colon (**:**) takes place only *after* the variable **a** is expanded.

The shell splits all *expanded* words on a command line according to the separating characters found in **IFS**. When there is no expansion, there is no splitting. Consider the following commands:

```
$ IFS="p"
$ export VAR
```

Although **IFS** is set to **p**, the **p** on the **export** command line is not expanded, so the word **export** is not split.

The following example uses variable expansion in an attempt to produce an **export** command:

```
$ IFS="p"
$ aa=export
$ echo $aa
ex ort
```

This time expansion occurs, so the **p** in the token **export** is interpreted as a separator (as the echo command shows). Next, when you try to use the value of the **aa** variable to export the **VAR** variable, the shell parses the **$aa VAR** command line as **ex ort VAR**. The effect is that the command line starts the ex editor with two filenames: **ort** and **VAR**.

```
$ $aa VAR
2 files to edit
"ort" [New File]
Entering Ex mode.  Type "visual" to go to Normal mode.
:q
E173: 1 more file to edit
:q
$
```

If **IFS** is unset, bash uses its default value (SPACE-TAB-NEWLINE). If **IFS** is null, bash does not split words.

Multiple separator characters

tip Although the shell treats sequences of multiple SPACE or TAB characters as a single separator, it treats *each occurrence* of another field-separator character as a separator.

CDPATH: Broadens the Scope of cd

The **CDPATH** variable (**cdpath** under tcsh) allows you to use a simple filename as an argument to the cd builtin to change the working directory to a directory other than a child of the working directory. If you typically work in several directories, this variable can speed things up and save you the tedium of using cd with longer pathnames to switch among them.

When **CDPATH** is not set and you specify a simple filename as an argument to cd, cd searches the working directory for a subdirectory with the same name as the argument. If the subdirectory does not exist, cd displays an error message. When **CDPATH** is set, cd searches for an appropriately named subdirectory in the directories in the **CDPATH** list. If it finds one, that directory becomes the working directory. With **CDPATH** set, you can use cd and a simple filename to change the working directory to a child of any of the directories listed in **CDPATH**.

The **CDPATH** variable takes on the value of a colon-separated list of directory pathnames (similar to the **PATH** variable). It is usually set in the **~/.bash_profile** startup file with a command line such as the following:

```
export CDPATH=$HOME:$HOME/literature
```

This command causes cd to search your home directory, the **literature** directory, and then the working directory when you give a cd command. If you do not include the working directory in **CDPATH**, cd searches the working directory if the search of all the other directories in **CDPATH** fails. If you want cd to search the working directory first, include a colon (:) as the first entry in **CDPATH**:

```
export CDPATH=:$HOME:$HOME/literature
```

If the argument to the cd builtin is anything other than a simple filename (i.e., if the argument contains a slash [/]), the shell does not consult **CDPATH**.

Keyword Variables: A Summary

Table 8-5 lists the bash keyword variables. See page 402 for information on tcsh variables.

Table 8-5 bash keyword variables

Variable	Value
BASH_ENV	The pathname of the startup file for noninteractive shells (page 289)
CDPATH	The cd search path (page 323)
COLUMNS	The width of the display used by **select** (page 460)
HISTFILE	The pathname of the file that holds the history list (default: **~/.bash_history**; page 336)
HISTFILESIZE	The maximum number of entries saved in **HISTFILE** (default: 1,000–2,000; page 336)
HISTSIZE	The maximum number of entries saved in the history list (default: 1,000; page 336)
HOME	The pathname of the user's home directory (page 317); used as the default argument for cd and in tilde expansion (page 91)
IFS	Internal Field Separator (page 321); used for word splitting (page 372)
INPUTRC	The pathname of the Readline startup file (default: **~/.inputrc**; page 349)
LANG	The locale category when that category is not specifically set using one of the **LC_** variables (page 327)
LC_	A group of variables that specify locale categories including **LC_ALL**, **LC_COLLATE**, **LC_CTYPE**, **LC_MESSAGES**, and **LC_NUMERIC**; use the locale builtin (page 328) to display a more complete list including values
LINES	The height of the display used by **select** (page 460)
MAIL	The pathname of the file that holds a user's mail (page 319)
MAILCHECK	How often, in seconds, bash checks for mail (default: 60; page 319)
MAILPATH	A colon-separated list of file pathnames that bash checks for mail in (page 319)
OLDPWD	The pathname of the previous working directory
PATH	A colon-separated list of directory pathnames that bash looks for commands in (page 318)
PROMPT_COMMAND	A command that bash executes just before it displays the primary prompt

Table 8-5 bash keyword variables (continued)

Variable	Value
PS1	Prompt String 1; the primary prompt (page 319)
PS2	Prompt String 2; the secondary prompt (page 321)
PS3	The prompt issued by **select** (page 460)
PS4	The bash debugging symbol (page 443)
PWD	The pathname of the working directory
REPLY	Holds the line that read accepts (page 490); also used by **select** (page 460)

Special Characters

Table 8-6 lists most of the characters that are special to the bash and tcsh shells.

Table 8-6 Shell special characters

Character	Use
NEWLINE	A control operator that initiates execution of a command (page 300)
;	A control operator that separates commands (page 300)
( )	A control operator that groups commands (page 302) for execution by a subshell; these characters are also used to identify a function (page 356)
(( ))	Evaluates an arithmetic expression (page 505)
&	A control operator that executes a command in the background (pages 150 and 300)
|	A control operator that sends standard output of the preceding command to standard input of the following command (pipeline; page 300)
|&	A control operator that sends standard output and standard error of the preceding command to standard input of the following command (page 293)
>	Redirects standard output (page 140)
>>	Appends standard output (page 144)
<	Redirects standard input (page 142)
<<	Here document (page 462)
*	Matches any string of zero or more characters in an ambiguous file reference (page 154)

Table 8-6 Shell special characters (continued)

Character	Use
?	Matches any single character in an ambiguous file reference (page 153)
\	Quotes the following character (page 50)
'	Quotes a string, preventing all substitution (page 50)
"	Quotes a string, allowing only variable and command substitution (pages 50 and 312)
`...`	Performs command substitution [deprecated, see **$()**]
[ ]	Character class in an ambiguous file reference (page 155)
$(( ))	Evaluates an arithmetic expression (page 369)
$	References a variable (page 310)
. (dot builtin)	Executes a command in the current shell (page 290)
#	Begins a comment (page 298)
{ }	Surrounds the contents of a function (page 356)
: (null builtin)	Returns *true* (page 498)
&& (Boolean AND)	A control operator that executes the command on the right only if the command on the left succeeds (returns a zero exit status; page 302)
|| (Boolean OR)	A control operator that executes the command on the right only if the command on the left fails (returns a nonzero exit status; page 302)
! (Boolean NOT)	Reverses the exit status of a command
$() (not in tcsh)	Performs command substitution (preferred form; page 371)

LOCALE

In conversational English, a *locale* is a place or location. When working with Linux, a locale specifies the way locale-aware programs display certain kinds of data such as times and dates, money and other numeric values, telephone numbers, and measurements. It can also specify collating sequence and printer paper size.

Localization and internationalization

Localization and internationalization go hand in hand: Internationalization is the process of making software portable to multiple locales while localization is the process of adapting software so that it meets the language, cultural, and other requirements of a specific locale. Linux is well internationalized so you can easily specify a locale for a given system or user. Linux uses variables to specify a locale.

i18n The term i18n is an abbreviation of the word *internationalization:* the letter *i* followed by 18 letters (*nternationalizatio*) followed by the letter *n.*

l10n The term l10n is an abbreviation of the word *localization:* the letter *l* followed by 10 letters (*ocalizatio*) followed by the letter *n.*

LC_: Locale Variables

The bash man page lists the following locale variables; other programs use additional locale variables. See the locale man pages (sections 1, 5, and 7) or use locale **--help** for more information.

- **LANG**—Specifies the locale category for categories not specified by an **LC_** variable (except see **LC_ALL**). Many setups use only this locale variable and do not specify any of the **LC_** variables.
- **LC_ALL**—Overrides the value of **LANG** and all other **LC_** variables.
- **LC_COLLATE**—Specifies the collating sequence for the sort utility (page 969) and for sorting the results of pathname expansion (page 313).
- **LC_CTYPE**—Specifies how characters are interpreted and how character classes within pathname expansion and pattern matching behave. Also affects the sort utility (page 969) when you specify the **–d** (**--dictionary-order**) or the **–i** (**--ignore-nonprinting**) options.
- **LC_MESSAGES**—Specifies how affirmative and negative answers appear and the language messages are displayed in.
- **LC_NUMERIC**—Specifies how numbers are formatted (e.g., are thousands separated by a comma or a period?).

Internationalized C programs call setlocale()

tip Internationalized C programs call **setlocale**(). Other languages have analogous facilities. Shell scripts are typically internationalized to the degree that the routines they call are. Without a call to **setlocale**(), the **hello, world** program will always display **hello, world**, regardless of how you set **LANG**.

You can set one or more of the **LC_** variables to a value using the syntax

xx_YY.CHARSET

where *xx* is the ISO-639 language code (e.g., **en** = English, **fr** = French, **zu** = Zulu), *YY* is the ISO-3166 country code (e.g., **FR** = France, **GF** = French Guiana, **PF** = French Polynesia), and *CHARSET* is the name of the character set (e.g., **UTF-8** [page 1131], **ASCII** [page 1083], **ISO-8859-1** [Western Europe], also called the *character map* or *charmap*). On some systems you can specify *CHARSET* using lowercase letters. For example, **en_GB.UTF-8** can specify English as written in Great Britain, **en_US.UTF-8** can specify English as written in the United States, and **fr_FR.UTF-8** can specify French as written in France.

The C locale

tip Setting the locale to C forces a program to process and display strings as the program was written (i.e., without translating input or output), which frequently means the program works in English. Many system scripts set **LANG** to **C** so they run in a known environment. Some text processing utilities run slightly faster when you set **LANG** to **C**. Setting **LANG** to **C** before you run sort can help ensure you get the results you expect.

If you want to make sure your shell script will work properly, put the following line near the top of the file:

```
export LANG=C
```

Following is an example of a difference that setting **LANG** can cause. It shows that having **LANG** set to different values can cause commands to behave differently, especially with regard to sorting.

```
$ echo $LANG
en_US.UTF-8
$ ls
m666  Makefile  merry
$ ls [l-n]*
m666  Makefile  merry

$ export LANG=C
$ ls
Makefile  m666  merry
$ ls [l-n]*
m666  merry
```

locale: Displays Locale Information

The locale utility displays information about the current and available locales. Without options, locale displays the value of the locale variables. In the following example, only the LANG variable is set, although you cannot determine this fact from the output. Unless explicitly set, each of the LC_ variables derives its value from LANG.

```
$ locale
LANG=en_US.UTF-8
LC_CTYPE="en_US.UTF-8"
LC_NUMERIC="en_US.UTF-8"
LC_TIME="en_US.UTF-8"
LC_COLLATE="en_US.UTF-8"
LC_MONETARY="en_US.UTF-8"
LC_MESSAGES="en_US.UTF-8"
LC_PAPER="en_US.UTF-8"
LC_NAME="en_US.UTF-8"
LC_ADDRESS="en_US.UTF-8"
LC_TELEPHONE="en_US.UTF-8"
LC_MEASUREMENT="en_US.UTF-8"
LC_IDENTIFICATION="en_US.UTF-8"
LC_ALL=
```

Typically, you will want all locale variables to have the same value. However, in some cases you might want to change the value of one or more locale variables. For example, if you are using paper size A4 but working in English, you could change the value of **LC_PAPER** to **nl_NL.utf8**.

The **–a** (all) option causes locale to display the names of available locales; **–v** (verbose; not in macOS) displays more complete information.

```
$ locale -av
locale: aa_DJ           archive: /usr/lib/locale/locale-archive
-------------------------------------------------------------------------------
    title | Afar language locale for Djibouti (CaduLaaqo Dialects).
   source | Ge'ez Frontier Foundation
  address | 7802 Solomon Seal Dr., Springfield, VA 22152, USA
    email | locales@geez.org
 language | aa
territory | DJ
 revision | 0.20
     date | 2003-07-05
  codeset | ISO-8859-1
...
```

The **–m** (maps) option causes locale to display the names of available character maps. On Linux systems, locale definition files are kept in the **/usr/share/i18n/locales** directory; on macOS systems, they are kept in **/usr/share/locale**.

Following are some examples of how some **LC_** variables change displayed values. Each of these command lines sets an **LC_** variable and places it in the environment of the utility it calls. The **+%x** format causes date to display the locale's date representation. The last example does not work under macOS.

```
$ LC_TIME=en_GB.UTF-8 date +%x
24/01/18
$ LC_TIME=en_US.UTF-8 date +%x
01/24/2018

$ ls xx
ls: impossible d'accéder à xx: Aucun fichier ou dossier de ce type
$ LC_MESSAGES=en_US.UTF-8 ls xx
ls: cannot access xx: No such file or directory
```

SETTING THE LOCALE

You might have to install a language package for a locale before you can specify a locale. If you are working in a GUI, it is usually easiest to change the locale using the GUI.

For all Linux distributions and macOS, put locale variable assignments in **~/.profile** or **~/.bash_profile** to affect both GUI and bash command-line logins for a single user. Remember to export the variables. The following line in one of these files will set all **LC_** variables for the given user to French as spoken in France:

```
export LANG=fr_FR.UTF-8
```

Under tcsh, put the following line in **~/.tcshrc** or **~/.cshrc** to have the same effect:

```
setenv LANG fr_FR.UTF-8
```

The following paragraphs explain how to use the command-line interface to change the locale for all users; the technique varies by distribution.

Fedora/RHEL Put locale variable assignments (previous page) in **/etc/profile.d/zlang.sh** (you will need to create this file; the filename was chosen to be executed after **lang.sh**) to affect both GUI and command-line logins for all users. Under tcsh, put the variable assignment in **/etc/profile.d/zlang.csh**.

Debian/Ubuntu/Mint Put locale variable assignments (previous page) in **/etc/default/locale** to affect both GUI and command-line logins for all users.

openSUSE Put locale variable assignments (previous page) in **/etc/profile.local** (you might need to create this file) to affect both GUI and command-line logins for all users. The **/etc/sysconfig/language** file controls the locale of GUI logins; see the file for instructions.

macOS Put locale variable assignments (previous page) in **/etc/profile** to affect both GUI and command-line logins for all users.

TIME

UTC On networks with systems in different time zones it can be helpful to set all systems to the *UTC* (page 1131) time zone. Among other benefits, doing so can make it easier for an administrator to compare logged events on different systems over time. Each user account can be set to the local time for that user.

Time zone The time zone for a user is specified by an environment variable or, if one is not set, by the time zone for the system.

TZ The **TZ** variable gives a program access to information about the local time zone. This variable is typically set in a startup file (pages 288 and 382) and placed in the environment (page 480) so called programs have access to it. It has two syntaxes.

The first syntax of the **TZ** variable is

nam±val[nam2]

where ***nam*** is a string comprising three or more letters that typically name the time zone (e.g., PST; its value is not significant) and ***±val*** is the offset of the time zone from UTC, with positive values indicating the local time zone is west of the prime meridian and negative values indicating the local time zone is east of the prime meridian. If the ***nam2*** is present, it indicates the time zone observes daylight savings time; it is the name of the daylight savings time zone (e.g., PDT).

In the following example, date is called twice, once without setting the **TZ** variable and then with the **TZ** variable set in the environment in which date is called:

```
$ date
Wed May  3 10:08:06 PDT 2017

$ TZ=EST+5EDT date
Wed May  3 13:08:08 EDT 2017
```

The second syntax of the **TZ** variable is

continent/country

where ***continent*** is the name of the continent or ocean and ***country*** is the name of the country that includes the desired time zone. This syntax points to a file in the **/usr/share/zoneinfo** hierarchy (next page). See tzselect (below) if you need help determining these values.

In the next example, date is called twice, once without setting the **TZ** variable and then with the **TZ** variable set in the environment in which date is called:

```
$ date
Wed May  3 10:09:27 PDT 2017

$ TZ=America/New_York date
Wed May  3 13:09:28 EDT 2017
```

See www.gnu.org/software/libc/manual/html_node/TZ-Variable.html for extensive documentation on the **TZ** variable.

tzconfig The tzconfig utility was available under Debian/Ubuntu and is now deprecated; use **dpkg-reconfigure tzdata** in its place.

tzselect The tzselect utility can help you determine the name of a time zone by asking you first to name the continent or ocean and then the country the time zone is in. If necessary, it asks for a time zone region (e.g., Pacific Time). This utility does not change system settings but rather displays a line telling you the name of the time zone. In the following example, the time zone is named **Europe/Paris**. Newer releases keep time zone information in **/usr/share/zoneinfo** (next page). Specifications such as **Europe/Paris** refer to the file in that directory (**/usr/share/zoneinfo/Europe/Paris**).

```
$ tzselect
Please identify a location so that time zone rules can be set correctly.
Please select a continent or ocean.
 1) Africa
...
 8) Europe
 9) Indian Ocean
10) Pacific Ocean
11) none - I want to specify the time zone using the Posix TZ format.
#? 8
Please select a country.
 1) Aaland Islands          18) Greece                    35) Norway
...
15) France                  32) Monaco                    49) Vatican City
16) Germany                 33) Montenegro
17) Gibraltar               34) Netherlands
#? 15
...
Here is that TZ value again, this time on standard output so that you
can use the /usr/bin/tzselect command in shell scripts:
Europe/Paris
```

/etc/timezone Under some distributions, including Debian/Ubuntu/Mint, the **/etc/timezone** file holds the name of the local time zone.

```
$ cat /etc/timezone
America/Los_Angeles
```

/usr/share/zoneinfo The **/usr/share/zoneinfo** directory hierarchy holds time zone data files. Some time zones are held in regular files in the **zoneinfo** directory (e.g., Japan and GB) while others are held in subdirectories (e.g., Azores and Pacific). The following example shows a small part of the **/usr/share/zoneinfo** directory hierarchy and illustrates how file (page 820) reports on a time zone file.

```
$ find /usr/share/zoneinfo
/usr/share/zoneinfo
/usr/share/zoneinfo/Atlantic
/usr/share/zoneinfo/Atlantic/Azores
/usr/share/zoneinfo/Atlantic/Madeira
/usr/share/zoneinfo/Atlantic/Jan_Mayen
...
/usr/share/zoneinfo/Japan
/usr/share/zoneinfo/GB
/usr/share/zoneinfo/US
/usr/share/zoneinfo/US/Pacific
/usr/share/zoneinfo/US/Arizona
/usr/share/zoneinfo/US/Michigan
...

$ file /usr/share/zoneinfo/Atlantic/Azores
/usr/share/zoneinfo/Atlantic/Azores: timezone data, version 2, 12 gmt
time flags, 12 std time flags, no leap seconds, 220 transition times, 12
abbreviation chars
```

/etc/localtime Some Linux distributions use a link at **/etc/localtime** to a file in **/usr/share/zoneinfo** to specify the local time zone. Others copy the file from the **zoneinfo** directory to **localtime**. Following is an example of setting up this link; to create this link you must work with **root** privileges.

```
# date
Wed Tue Jan 24 13:55:00 PST 2018
# cd /etc
# ln -sf /usr/share/zoneinfo/Europe/Paris localtime
# date
Wed Jan 24 22:55:38 CET 2018
```

On some of these systems, the **/etc/systemconfig/clock** file sets the **ZONE** variable to the name of the time zone:

```
$ cat /etc/sysconfig/clock
# The time zone of the system is defined by the contents of /etc/localtime.
# This file is only for evaluation by system-config-date, do not rely on its
# contents elsewhere.
ZONE="Europe/Paris"
```

macOS On macOS, you can use systemsetup to work with the time zone.

```
$ systemsetup -gettimezone
Time Zone: America/Los_Angeles

$ systemsetup -listtimezones
Time Zones:
 Africa/Abidjan
 Africa/Accra
 Africa/Addis_Ababa
...

$ systemsetup -settimezone America/Los_Angeles
Set TimeZone: America/Los_Angeles
```

PROCESSES

A *process* is the execution of a command by the Linux kernel. The shell that starts when you log in is a process, like any other. When you specify the name of a utility as a command, you initiate a process. When you run a shell script, another shell process is started, and additional processes are created for each command in the script. Depending on how you invoke the shell script, the script is run either by the current shell or, more typically, by a subshell (child) of the current shell. Running a shell builtin, such as cd, does not start a new process.

PROCESS STRUCTURE

fork() system call Like the file structure, the process structure is hierarchical, with parents, children, and a *root.* A parent process *forks* (or *spawns*) a child process, which in turn can fork other processes. The term *fork* indicates that, as with a fork in the road, one process turns into two. Initially the two forks are identical except that one is identified as the parent and one as the child. The operating system routine, or *system call,* that creates a new process is named **fork**().

init daemon A Linux system begins execution by starting the **init** daemon, a single process called a *spontaneous process,* with PID number 1. This process holds the same position in the process structure as the root directory does in the file structure: It is the ancestor of all processes the system and users work with. When a command-line system is in multiuser mode, init runs getty or mingetty processes, which display **login:** prompts on terminals and virtual consoles. When a user responds to the prompt and presses RETURN, getty or mingetty passes control to a utility named login, which checks the username and password combination. After the user logs in, the login process becomes the user's shell process.

When you enter the name of a program on the command line, the shell **forks** a new process, creating a duplicate of the shell process (a subshell). The new process attempts to **exec** (execute) the program. Like **fork**(), **exec**() is a system call. If the program is a binary executable, such as a compiled C program, **exec**() succeeds, and the system overlays the newly created subshell with the executable program. If the command is a shell script, **exec**() fails. When **exec** fails, the program is assumed to be a shell script, and the subshell runs the commands in the script. Unlike a login shell, which expects input from the command line, the subshell takes its input from a file—namely, the shell script.

PROCESS IDENTIFICATION

PID numbers Linux assigns a unique PID (process identification) number at the inception of each process. As long as a process exists, it keeps the same PID number. During one session the same process is always executing the login shell (page 288). When you fork a new process—for example, when you use an editor—the PID number of the new (child) process is different from that of its parent process. When you return to the login shell, it is still being executed by the same process and has the same PID number as when you logged in.

The following example shows that the process running the shell forked (is the parent of) the process running ps. When you call it with the –f option, ps displays a full listing of information about each process. The line of the ps display with **bash** in the **CMD** column refers to the process running the shell. The column headed by **PID** identifies the PID number. The column headed by **PPID** identifies the PID number of the *parent* of the process. From the PID and PPID columns you can see that the process running the shell (PID 21341) is the parent of the processes running sleep (PID 22789) and ps (PID 22790).

```
$ sleep 10 &
[1] 22789
$ ps -f
UID        PID  PPID  C STIME TTY          TIME CMD
max      21341 21340  0 10:42 pts/16   00:00:00 bash
max      22789 21341  0 17:30 pts/16   00:00:00 sleep 10
max      22790 21341  0 17:30 pts/16   00:00:00 ps -f
```

Refer to page 946 for more information on ps and the columns it displays when you specify the –f option. A second pair of **sleep** and **ps –f** commands shows that the shell is still being run by the same process but that it forked another process to run sleep:

```
$ sleep 10 &
[1] 22791
$ ps -f
UID        PID  PPID  C STIME TTY          TIME CMD
max      21341 21340  0 10:42 pts/16   00:00:00 bash
max      22791 21341  0 17:31 pts/16   00:00:00 sleep 10
max      22792 21341  0 17:31 pts/16   00:00:00 ps -f
```

You can also use pstree (or **ps ––forest**, with or without the **–e** option) to see the parent–child relationship of processes. The next example shows the **–p** option to pstree, which causes it to display PID numbers:

```
$ pstree -p
systemd(1)-+-NetworkManager(655)---{NetworkManager}(702)
           |-abrtd(657)---abrt-dump-oops(696)
```

```
                |-accounts-daemon(1204)---{accounts-daemo}(1206)
                |-agetty(979)
...
                |-login(984)---bash(2071)-+-pstree(2095)
                |                         `-sleep(2094)
...
```

The preceding output is abbreviated. The first line shows the PID 1 (**systemd init**) and a few of the processes it is running. The line that starts with **–login** shows a textual user running sleep in the background and pstree in the foreground. The tree for a user running a GUI is much more complex. Refer to "$$: PID Number" on page 476 for a description of how to instruct the shell to report on PID numbers.

EXECUTING A COMMAND

fork() and **sleep**() When you give the shell a command, it usually forks [spawns using the **fork**() system call] a child process to execute the command. While the child process is executing the command, the parent process (running the shell) *sleeps* [implemented as the **sleep**() system call]. While a process is sleeping, it does not use any computer time; it remains inactive, waiting to wake up. When the child process finishes executing the command, it tells its parent of its success or failure via its exit status and then dies. The parent process (which is running the shell) wakes up and prompts for another command.

Background process When you run a process in the background by ending a command with the ampersand control operator (&), the shell forks a child process without going to sleep and without waiting for the child process to run to completion. The parent process, which is executing the shell, reports the job number and PID number of the child process and prompts for another command. The child process runs in the background, independent of its parent.

Builtins Although the shell forks a process to run most commands, some commands are built into the shell (e.g., cd, alias, jobs, pwd). The shell does not fork a process to run builtins. For more information refer to "Builtins" on page 157.

Variables Within a given process, such as a login shell or subshell, you can declare, initialize, read, and change variables. Some variables, called shell variables, are local to a process. Other variables, called environment variables, are available to child processes. For more information refer to "Variables" on page 479.

Hash table The first time you specify a command as a simple filename (and not a relative or absolute pathname), the shell looks in the directories specified by the **PATH** (bash; page 318) or **path** (tcsh; page 403) variable to find that file. When it finds the file, the shell records the absolute pathname of the file in its hash table. When you give the command again, the shell finds it in its hash table, saving the time needed to search through the directories in **PATH**. The shell deletes the hash table when you log out and starts a new hash table when you start a session. This section shows some of the ways you can use the bash hash builtin; tcsh uses different commands for working with its hash table.

When you call the hash builtin without any arguments, it displays the hash table. When you first log in, the hash table is empty:

```
$ hash
hash: hash table empty
$ who am i
sam        pts/2         2017-03-09 14:24 (plum)
$ hash
hits    command
   1    /usr/bin/who
```

The hash –r option causes bash to empty the hash table, as though you had just logged in; tcsh uses rehash for a similar purpose.

```
$ hash -r
$ hash
hash: hash table empty
```

Having bash empty its hash table is useful when you move a program to a different directory in PATH and bash cannot find the program in its new location, or when you have two programs with the same name and bash is calling the wrong one. Refer to the bash info page for more information on the hash builtin.

History

The history mechanism, a feature adapted from the C Shell, maintains a list of recently issued command lines, called *events,* that provides a quick way to reexecute any events in the list. This mechanism also enables you to edit and then execute previous commands and to reuse arguments from them. You can use the history list to replicate complicated commands and arguments that you used previously and to enter a series of commands that differ from one another in minor ways. The history list also serves as a record of what you have done. It can prove helpful when you have made a mistake and are not sure what you did or when you want to keep a record of a procedure that involved a series of commands.

history **can help track down mistakes**

tip When you have made a mistake on a command line (not an error within a script or program) and are not sure what you did wrong, look at the history list to review your recent commands. Sometimes this list can help you figure out what went wrong and how to fix things.

The history builtin displays the history list. If it does not, read the next section, which describes the variables you might need to set.

Variables That Control History

The TC Shell's history mechanism is similar to bash's but uses different variables and has some other differences. See page 384 for more information.

The value of the **HISTSIZE** variable determines the number of events preserved in the history list during a session. A value in the range of 100 to 1,000 is normal.

When you exit from the shell, the most recently executed commands are saved in the file whose name is stored in the **HISTFILE** variable (default is **~/.bash_history**). The next time you start the shell, this file initializes the history list. The value of the **HISTFILESIZE** variable determines the number of lines of history saved in **HISTFILE** (see Table 8-7).

Table 8-7 History variables

Variable	Default	Function
HISTSIZE	1,000 events	Maximum number of events saved during a session
HISTFILE	**~/.bash_history**	Location of the history file
HISTFILESIZE	1,000–2,000 events	Maximum number of events saved between sessions

Event number The Bourne Again Shell assigns a sequential *event number* to each command line. You can display this event number as part of the bash prompt by including **\!** in **PS1** (page 319). Examples in this section show numbered prompts when they help to illustrate the behavior of a command.

Enter the following command manually to establish a history list of the 100 most recent events; place it in **~/.bash_profile** to affect future sessions:

```
$ HISTSIZE=100
```

The following command causes bash to save the 100 most recent events across login sessions:

```
$ HISTFILESIZE=100
```

After you set **HISTFILESIZE**, you can log out and log in again, and the 100 most recent events from the previous login session will appear in your history list.

Enter the command **history** to display the events in the history list. This list is ordered with the oldest events at the top. A tcsh history list includes the time the command was executed. The following history list includes a command to modify the bash prompt so it displays the history event number. The last event in the history list is the **history** command that displayed the list.

```
32 $ history | tail
   23  PS1="\! bash$ "
   24  ls -l
   25  cat temp
   26  rm temp
   27  vim memo
   28  lpr memo
   29  vim memo
   30  lpr memo
   31  rm memo
   32  history | tail
```

As you run commands and your history list becomes longer, it might run off the top of the screen when you use the history builtin. Send the output of history through a pipeline to less to browse through it or give the command **history 10** or **history | tail** to look at the ten most recent commands.

Handy history aliases

tip Creating the following aliases makes working with history easier. The first allows you to give the command **h** to display the ten most recent events. The second alias causes the command **hg *string*** to display all events in the history list that contain ***string***. Put these aliases in your **~/.bashrc** file to make them available each time you log in. See page 352 for more information on aliases.

```
$ alias 'h=history | tail'
$ alias 'hg=history | grep'
```

REEXECUTING AND EDITING COMMANDS

You can reexecute any event in the history list. Not having to reenter long command lines allows you to reexecute events more easily, quickly, and accurately than you could if you had to retype the command line in its entirety. You can recall, modify, and reexecute previously executed events in three ways: You can use the fc builtin (next), the exclamation point commands (page 341), or the Readline Library, which uses a one-line vi- or emacs-like editor to edit and execute events (page 345).

Which method to use?

tip If you are more familiar with vi or emacs and less familiar with the C or TC Shell, use fc or the Readline Library. If you are more familiar with the C or TC Shell, use the exclamation point commands. If it is a toss-up, try the Readline Library; it will benefit you in other areas of Linux more than learning the exclamation point commands will.

fc: DISPLAYS, EDITS, AND REEXECUTES COMMANDS

The fc (fix command) builtin (not in tcsh) enables you to display the history list and to edit and reexecute previous commands. It provides many of the same capabilities as the command-line editors.

VIEWING THE HISTORY LIST

When you call fc with the –l option, it displays commands from the history list. Without any arguments, fc –l lists the 16 most recent commands in a list that includes event numbers, with the oldest appearing first:

```
$ fc -l
1024     cd
1025     view calendar
1026     vim letter.adams01
1027     aspell -c letter.adams01
1028     vim letter.adams01
1029     lpr letter.adams01
1030     cd ../memos
1031     ls
```

```
1032     rm *0405
1033     fc -l
1034     cd
1035     whereis aspell
1036     man aspell
1037     cd /usr/share/doc/*aspell*
1038     pwd
1039     ls
1040     ls man-html
```

The fc builtin can take zero, one, or two arguments with the –l option. The arguments specify the part of the history list to be displayed:

*fc –l [**first** [**last**]]*

The fc builtin lists commands beginning with the most recent event that matches ***first***. The argument can be an event number, the first few characters of the command line, or a negative number, which specifies the ***n***th previous command. Without ***last***, fc displays events through the most recent. If you include ***last***, fc displays commands from the most recent event that matches ***first*** through the most recent event that matches ***last***.

The next command displays the history list from event 1030 through event 1035:

```
$ fc -l 1030 1035
1030     cd ../memos
1031     ls
1032     rm *0405
1033     fc -l
1034     cd
1035     whereis aspell
```

The following command lists the most recent event that begins with **view** through the most recent command line that begins with **whereis**:

```
$ fc -l view whereis
1025     view calendar
1026     vim letter.adams01
1027     aspell -c letter.adams01
1028     vim letter.adams01
1029     lpr letter.adams01
1030     cd ../memos
1031     ls
1032     rm *0405
1033     fc -l
1034     cd
1035     whereis aspell
```

To list a single command from the history list, use the same identifier for the first and second arguments. The following command lists event 1027:

```
$ fc -l 1027 1027
1027     aspell -c letter.adams01
```

Editing and Reexecuting Previous Commands

You can use fc to edit and reexecute previous commands.

*fc [–e **editor**] [**first** [**last**]]*

When you call fc with the **–e** option followed by the name of an editor, fc calls the editor with event(s) in the Work buffer. By default, fc invokes the vi(m) or nano editor. Without *first* and *last,* it defaults to the most recent command. The next example invokes the vim editor (Chapter 6) to edit the most recent command. When you exit from the editor, the shell executes the command.

```
$ fc -e vi
```

The fc builtin uses the stand-alone vim editor. If you set the **EDITOR** variable, you do not need to use the **–e** option to specify an editor on the command line. Because the value of **EDITOR** has been changed to **/usr/bin/emacs** and fc has no arguments, the following command edits the most recent command using the emacs editor (Chapter 7):

```
$ export EDITOR=/usr/bin/emacs
$ fc
```

If you call it with a single argument, fc invokes the editor on the specified command. The following example starts the editor with event 1029 in the Work buffer:

```
$ fc 1029
```

As described earlier, you can identify commands either by using numbers or by specifying the first few characters of the command name. The following example calls the editor to work on events from the most recent event that begins with the letters **vim** through event 1030:

```
$ fc vim 1030
```

Clean up the fc buffer

caution When you execute an fc command, the shell executes whatever you leave in the editor buffer, possibly with unwanted results. If you decide you do not want to execute a command, delete everything from the buffer before you exit from the editor.

Reexecuting Commands Without Calling the Editor

You can also reexecute previous commands without using an editor. If you call fc with the –s option, it skips the editing phase and reexecutes the command. The following example reexecutes event 1029:

```
$ fc -s 1029
lpr letter.adams01
```

The next example reexecutes the previous command:

```
$ fc -s
```

When you reexecute a command, you can tell fc to substitute one string for another. The next example substitutes the string **john** for the string **adams** in event 1029 and executes the modified event:

```
$ fc -s adams=john 1029
lpr letter.john01
```

USING AN EXCLAMATION POINT (!) TO REFERENCE EVENTS

The C Shell history mechanism uses an exclamation point to reference events. This technique, which is available under bash and tcsh, is frequently more cumbersome to use than fc but nevertheless has some useful features. For example, the !! command reexecutes the previous event, and the shell replaces the !$ token with the last word from the previous command line.

You can reference an event by using its absolute event number, its relative event number, or the text it contains. All references to events, called event designators, begin with an exclamation point (!). One or more characters follow the exclamation point to specify an event.

You can put history events anywhere on a command line. To escape an exclamation point so the shell interprets it literally instead of as the start of a history event, precede it with a backslash (\) or enclose it within single quotation marks.

EVENT DESIGNATORS

An event designator specifies a command in the history list. Table 8-8 lists event designators.

Table 8-8 Event designators

Designator	**Meaning**
!	Starts a history event unless followed immediately by SPACE, NEWLINE, =, or (.
!!	The previous command.
!*n*	Command number ***n*** in the history list.
!–*n*	The ***n***th preceding command.
!*string*	The most recent command line that started with ***string***.
!?*string*[?]	The most recent command that contained ***string***. The last **?** is optional.
!#	The current command (as you have it typed so far).

!! reexecutes the previous event

You can reexecute the previous event by giving a !! command. In the following example, event 45 reexecutes event 44:

```
44 $ ls -l text
-rw-rw-r--. 1 max pubs 45 04-30 14:53 text
45 $ !!
ls -l text
-rw-rw-r--. 1 max pubs 45 04-30 14:53 text
```

The !! command works whether or not your prompt displays an event number. As this example shows, when you use the history mechanism to reexecute an event, the shell displays the command it is reexecuting.

!*n* event number A number following an exclamation point refers to an event. If that event is in the history list, the shell executes it. Otherwise, the shell displays an error message. A negative number following an exclamation point references an event relative to the current event. For example, the command **!–3** refers to the third preceding event. After you issue a command, the relative event number of a given event changes (event –3 becomes event –4). Both of the following commands reexecute event 44:

```
51 $ !44
ls -l text
-rw-rw-r--. 1 max pubs 45 04-30 14:53 text
52 $ !-8
ls -l text
-rw-rw-r--. 1 max pubs 45 04-30 14:53 text
```

!*string* event text When a string of text follows an exclamation point, the shell searches for and executes the most recent event that *began* with that string. If you enclose the string within question marks, the shell executes the most recent event that *contained* that string. The final question mark is optional if a RETURN would immediately follow it.

```
68 $ history 10
   59  ls -l text*
   60  tail text5
   61  cat text1 text5 > letter
   62  vim letter
   63  cat letter
   64  cat memo
   65  lpr memo
   66  pine zach
   67  ls -l
   68  history
69 $ !l
ls -l
...
70 $ !lpr
lpr memo
71 $ !?letter?
cat letter
...
```

optional

WORD DESIGNATORS

A *word designator* specifies a word (token) or series of words from an event (a command line). Table 8-9 on page 344 lists word designators. The words on a command line are numbered starting with 0 (the first word, usually the command), continuing with 1 (the first word following the command), and ending with ***n*** (the last word on the command line).

To specify a particular word from a previous event, follow the event designator (such as **!14**) with a colon and the number of the word in the previous event. For example,

!14:3 specifies the third word following the command from event 14. You can specify the first word following the command (word number 1) using a caret (^) and the last word using a dollar sign ($). You can specify a range of words by separating two word designators with a hyphen.

```
72 $ echo apple grape orange pear
apple grape orange pear
73 $ echo !72:2
echo grape
grape
74 $ echo !72:^
echo apple
apple
75 $ !72:0 !72:$
echo pear
pear
76 $ echo !72:2-4
echo grape orange pear
grape orange pear
77 $ !72:0-$
echo apple grape orange pear
apple grape orange pear
```

As the next example shows, **!$** refers to the last word of the previous event. You can use this shorthand to edit, for example, a file you just displayed using cat:

```
$ cat report.718
...
$ vim !$
vim report.718
...
```

If an event contains a single command, the word numbers correspond to the argument numbers. If an event contains more than one command, this correspondence does not hold for commands after the first. In the next example, event 78 contains two commands separated by a semicolon so the shell executes them sequentially; the semicolon is word number 5.

```
78 $ !72 ; echo helen zach barbara
echo apple grape orange pear ; echo helen zach barbara
apple grape orange pear
helen zach barbara
79 $ echo !78:7
echo helen
helen
80 $ echo !78:4-7
echo pear ; echo helen
pear
helen
```

Table 8-9 Word designators

Designator	Meaning
n	The *n*th word. Word 0 is normally the command name.
^	The first word (after the command name).
$	The last word.
m–*n*	All words from word number *m* through word number *n*; *m* defaults to 0 if you omit it (0–*n*).
*n**	All words from word number *n* through the last word.
*	All words except the command name. The same as **1***.
%	The word matched by the most recent **?*string*?** search.

MODIFIERS

On occasion you might want to change an aspect of an event you are reexecuting. Perhaps you entered a complex command line with a typo or incorrect pathname or you want to specify a different argument. You can modify an event or a word of an event by putting one or more modifiers after the word designator or after the event designator if there is no word designator. Each modifier must be preceded by a colon (:).

Substitute modifier

The following example shows the *substitute modifier* correcting a typo in the previous event:

```
$ car /home/zach/memo.0507 /home/max/letter.0507
bash: car: command not found
$ !!:s/car/cat
cat /home/zach/memo.0507 /home/max/letter.0507
...
```

The substitute modifier has the syntax

*[g]s/**old**/**new**/*

where ***old*** is the original string (not a regular expression) and ***new*** is the string that replaces ***old***. The substitute modifier substitutes the first occurrence of ***old*** with ***new***. Placing a **g** before the **s** causes a global substitution, replacing all occurrences of ***old***. Although / is the delimiter in the examples, you can use any character that is not in either ***old*** or ***new***. The final delimiter is optional if a RETURN would immediately follow it. As with the vim Substitute command, the history mechanism replaces an ampersand (&) in ***new*** with ***old***. The shell replaces a null old string (*s//**new**/*) with the previous old string or the string within a command you searched for using *?**string**?*.

Quick substitution

An abbreviated form of the substitute modifier is *quick substitution*. Use it to reexecute the most recent event while changing some of the event text. The quick substitution character is the caret (^). For example, the command

```
$ ^old^new^
```

produces the same results as

```
$ !!:s/old/new/
```

Thus, substituting **cat** for **car** in the previous event could have been entered as

```
$ ^car^cat
cat /home/zach/memo.0507 /home/max/letter.0507
. . .
```

You can omit the final caret if it would be followed immediately by a RETURN. As with other command-line substitutions, the shell displays the command line as it appears after the substitution.

Other modifiers Modifiers (other than the substitute modifier) perform simple edits on the part of the event that has been selected by the event designator and the optional word designators. You can use multiple modifiers, each preceded by a colon (**:**).

The following series of commands uses ls to list the name of a file, repeats the command without executing it (**p** modifier), and repeats the last command, removing the last part of the pathname (**h** modifier) again without executing it:

```
$ ls /etc/ssh/ssh_config
/etc/ssh/ssh_config
$ !!:p
ls /etc/ssh/ssh_config
$ !!:h:p
ls /etc/ssh
```

Table 8-10 lists event modifiers other than the substitute modifier.

Table 8-10 Event modifiers

Modifier	Function
e (extension)	Removes all but the filename extension
h (head)	Removes the last part of a pathname
p (print)	Displays the command but does not execute it
q (quote)	Quotes the substitution to prevent further substitutions on it
r (root)	Removes the filename extension
t (tail)	Removes all elements of a pathname except the last
x	Like **q** but quotes each word in the substitution individually

THE READLINE LIBRARY

Command-line editing under the Bourne Again Shell is implemented through the *Readline Library*, which is available to any application written in C. Any application that uses the Readline Library supports line editing that is consistent with that provided by bash. Programs that use the Readline Library, including bash, read **~/.inputrc** (page 349) for key binding information and configuration settings. The **––noediting** command-line option turns off command-line editing in bash.

vi mode You can choose one of two editing modes when using the Readline Library in bash: emacs or vi(m). Both modes provide many of the commands available in the stand-alone versions of the emacs and vim editors. You can also use the ARROW keys to move around. Up and down movements move you backward and forward through the history list. In addition, Readline provides several types of interactive word completion (page 348). The default mode is emacs; you can switch to vi mode using the following command:

```
$ set -o vi
```

emacs mode The next command switches back to emacs mode:

```
$ set -o emacs
```

vi Editing Mode

Before you start, make sure the shell is in vi mode.

When you enter bash commands while in vi editing mode, you are in Input mode (page 169). As you enter a command, if you discover an error before you press RETURN, you can press ESCAPE to switch to vim Command mode. This setup is different from the stand-alone vim editor's initial mode. While in Command mode you can use many vim commands to edit the command line. It is as though you were using vim to edit a copy of the history file with a screen that has room for only one command. When you use the **k** command or the UP ARROW to move up a line, you access the previous command. If you then use the **j** command or the DOWN ARROW to move down a line, you return to the original command. To use the **k** and **j** keys to move between commands, you must be in Command mode; you can use the ARROW keys in both Command and Input modes.

The command-line vim editor starts in Input mode

tip The stand-alone vim editor starts in Command mode, whereas the command-line vim editor starts in Input mode. If commands display characters and do not work properly, you are in Input mode. Press ESCAPE and enter the command again.

In addition to cursor-positioning commands, you can use the search-backward (**?**) command followed by a search string to look *back* through the history list for the most recent command containing a string. If you have moved back in the history list, use a forward slash (**/**) to search *forward* toward the most recent command. Unlike the search strings in the stand-alone vim editor, these search strings cannot contain regular expressions. You can, however, start the search string with a caret (**^**) to force the shell to locate commands that start with the search string. As in vim, pressing **n** after a successful search looks for the next occurrence of the same string.

You can also use event numbers to access events in the history list. While you are in Command mode (press ESCAPE), enter the event number followed by a **G** to go to the command with that event number.

When you use /, ?, or **G** to move to a command line, you are in Command mode, not Input mode: You can edit the command or press RETURN to execute it.

When the command you want to edit is displayed, you can modify the command line using vim Command mode editing commands such as **x** (delete character), **r** (replace character), ~ (change case), and **.** (repeat last change). To switch to Input mode, use an Insert (**i**, **I**), Append (**a**, **A**), Replace (**R**), or Change (**c**, **C**) command. You do not have to return to Command mode to execute a command; simply press RETURN, even if the cursor is in the middle of the command line. For more information refer to the vim tutorial on page 167. Refer to page 213 for a summary of vim commands.

emacs EDITING MODE

Unlike the vim editor, emacs is modeless. You need not switch between Command mode and Input mode because most emacs commands are control characters (page 231), allowing emacs to distinguish between input and commands. Like vim, the emacs command-line editor provides commands for moving the cursor on the command line and through the command history list and for modifying part or all of a command. However, in a few cases, the emacs command-line editor commands differ from those used in the stand-alone emacs editor.

In emacs you perform cursor movement by using both CONTROL and ESCAPE commands. To move the cursor one character backward on the command line, press CONTROL-B. Press CONTROL-F to move one character forward. As in vim, you can precede these movements with counts. To use a count you must first press ESCAPE; otherwise, the numbers you type will appear on the command line.

Like vim, emacs provides word and line movement commands. To move backward or forward one word on the command line, press ESCAPE **b** or ESCAPE **f**, respectively. To move several words using a count, press ESCAPE followed by the number and the appropriate escape sequence. To move to the beginning of the line, press CONTROL-A; to move to the end of the line, press CONTROL-E; and to move to the next instance of the character *c*, press CONTROL-X CONTROL-F followed by *c*.

You can add text to the command line by moving the cursor to the position you want to enter text and typing. To delete text, move the cursor just to the right of the characters you want to delete and press the erase key (page 29) once for each character you want to delete.

CONTROL-D can terminate your screen session

caution If you want to delete the character directly under the cursor, press CONTROL-D. If you enter CONTROL-D at the beginning of the line, it might terminate your shell session.

If you want to delete the entire command line, press the line kill key (page 30). You can press this key while the cursor is anywhere in the command line. Use CONTROL-K to delete from the cursor to the end of the line. Refer to page 270 for a summary of emacs commands.

READLINE COMPLETION COMMANDS

You can use the TAB key to complete words you are entering on the command line. This facility, called *completion,* works in both vi and emacs editing modes and is similar to the completion facility available in tcsh. Several types of completion are possible, and which one you use depends on which part of a command line you are typing when you press TAB.

COMMAND COMPLETION

If you are typing the name of a command, pressing TAB initiates *command completion,* in which bash looks for a command whose name starts with the part of the word you have typed. If no command starts with the characters you entered, bash beeps. If there is one such command, bash completes the command name. If there is more than one choice, bash does nothing in vi mode and beeps in emacs mode. Pressing TAB a second time causes bash to display a list of commands whose names start with the prefix you typed and allows you to continue typing the command name.

In the following example, the user types **bz** and presses TAB. The shell beeps (the user is in emacs mode) to indicate that several commands start with the letters **bz.** The user enters another TAB to cause the shell to display a list of commands that start with **bz** followed by the command line as the user has entered it so far:

```
$ bz ⇨ TAB (beep) ⇨ TAB
bzcat          bzdiff         bzip2          bzless
bzcmp          bzgrep         bzip2recover   bzmore
$ bz■
```

Next, the user types **c** and presses TAB twice. The shell displays the two commands that start with **bzc.** The user types **a** followed by TAB. At this point the shell completes the command because only one command starts with **bzca.**

```
$ bzc ⇨ TAB (beep) ⇨ TAB
bzcat  bzcmp
$ bzca ⇨ TAB ⇨  t ■
```

PATHNAME COMPLETION

Pathname completion, which also uses TABs, allows you to type a portion of a pathname and have bash supply the rest. If the portion of the pathname you have typed is sufficient to determine a unique pathname, bash displays that pathname. If more than one pathname would match it, bash completes the pathname up to the point where there are choices so that you can type more.

When you are entering a pathname, including a simple filename, and press TAB, the shell beeps (if the shell is in emacs mode—in vi mode there is no beep). It then extends the command line as far as it can.

```
$ cat films/dar ⇨ TAB (beep) cat films/dark_■
```

In the **films** directory every file that starts with **dar** has **k_** as the next characters, so bash cannot extend the line further without making a choice among files. The shell leaves the cursor just past the _ character. At this point you can continue typing the pathname or press TAB twice. In the latter case bash beeps, displays the choices, redisplays the command line, and again leaves the cursor just after the _ character.

```
$ cat films/dark_ ⇨ TAB (beep) ⇨ TAB
dark_passage  dark_victory
$ cat films/dark_█
```

When you add enough information to distinguish between the two possible files and press TAB, bash displays the unique pathname. If you enter **p** followed by TAB after the _ character, the shell completes the command line:

```
$ cat films/dark_p ⇨ TAB ⇨ assage
```

Because there is no further ambiguity, the shell appends a SPACE so you can either finish typing the command line or press RETURN to execute the command. If the complete pathname is that of a directory, bash appends a slash (/) in place of a SPACE.

VARIABLE COMPLETION

When you are typing a variable name, pressing TAB results in *variable completion,* wherein bash attempts to complete the name of the variable. In case of an ambiguity, pressing TAB twice displays a list of choices:

```
$ echo $HO ⇨ TAB (beep) ⇨ TAB
$HOME       $HOSTNAME  $HOSTTYPE
$ echo $HOM ⇨ TAB ⇨ E
```

Pressing RETURN executes the command

caution Pressing RETURN causes the shell to execute the command regardless of where the cursor is on the command line.

.inputrc: CONFIGURING THE READLINE LIBRARY

The Bourne Again Shell and other programs that use the Readline Library read the file specified by the **INPUTRC** environment variable to obtain initialization information. If **INPUTRC** is not set, these programs read the **~/.inputrc** file. They ignore lines of **.inputrc** that are blank or that start with a hashmark (#).

VARIABLES

You can set variables in **.inputrc** to control the behavior of the Readline Library using the syntax:

set variable value

Table 8-11 lists some variables and values you can use. See "Readline Variables" in the bash man or info page for a complete list.

Table 8-11 Readline variables

Variable	Effect
editing-mode	Set to **vi** to start Readline in vi mode. Set to **emacs** to start Readline in emacs mode (the default). Similar to the **set –o vi** and **set –o emacs** shell commands (page 346).
horizontal-scroll-mode	Set to **on** to cause long lines to extend off the right edge of the display area. Moving the cursor to the right when it is at the right edge of the display area shifts the line to the left so you can see more of the line. Shift the line back by moving the cursor back past the left edge. The default value is **off**, which causes long lines to wrap onto multiple lines of the display.
mark-directories	Set to **off** to cause Readline not to place a slash (/) at the end of directory names it completes. The default value is **on**.
mark-modified-lines	Set to **on** to cause Readline to precede modified history lines with an asterisk. The default value is **off**.

KEY BINDINGS

You can map keystroke sequences to Readline commands, changing or extending the default bindings. Like the emacs editor, the Readline Library includes many commands that are not bound to a keystroke sequence. To use an unbound command, you must map it using one of the following forms:

> *keyname: command_name*
> "*keystroke_sequence*" *: command_name*

In the first form, you spell out the name for a single key. For example, CONTROL-U would be written as **control-u**. This form is useful for binding commands to single keys.

In the second form, you specify a string that describes a sequence of keys that will be bound to the command. You can use the emacs-style backslash escape sequences (page 231) to represent the special keys CONTROL (**\C**), META (**\M**), and ESCAPE (**\e**). Specify a backslash by escaping it with another backslash: ****. Similarly, a double or single quotation mark can be escaped with a backslash: **\"** or **\'**.

The **kill-whole-line** command, available in emacs mode only, deletes the current line. Put the following command in **.inputrc** to bind the **kill-whole-line** command (which is unbound by default) to the keystroke sequence CONTROL-R:

```
control-r: kill-whole-line
```

bind Give the command **bind –P** to display a list of all Readline commands. If a command is bound to a key sequence, that sequence is shown. Commands you can use in vi mode start with **vi**. For example, **vi-next-word** and **vi-prev-word** move the cursor to the beginning of the next and previous words, respectively. Commands that do not begin with **vi** are generally available in emacs mode.

Use **bind –q** to determine which key sequence is bound to a command:

```
$ bind -q kill-whole-line
kill-whole-line can be invoked via "\C-r".
```

You can also bind text by enclosing it within double quotation marks (emacs mode only):

```
"QQ": "The Linux Operating System"
```

This command causes bash to insert the string **The Linux Operating System** when you type **QQ** on the command line.

CONDITIONAL CONSTRUCTS

You can conditionally select parts of the **.inputrc** file using the **$if** directive. The syntax of the conditional construct is

$if ***test[=value]***
        commands
    [$else
        commands*]*
$endif

where ***test*** is **mode, term,** or a program name such as **bash.** If ***test*** equals ***value*** (or if ***test*** is *true* when ***value*** is not specified), this structure executes the first set of ***commands.*** If ***test*** does not equal ***value*** (or if ***test*** is *false* when ***value*** is not specified), it executes the second set of ***commands*** if they are present or exits from the structure if they are not present.

The power of the **$if** directive lies in the three types of tests it can perform:

1. You can test to see which mode is currently set.

   ```
   $if mode=vi
   ```

   The preceding test is *true* if the current Readline mode is **vi** and *false* otherwise. You can test for **vi** or **emacs.**

2. You can test the type of terminal.

   ```
   $if term=xterm
   ```

   The preceding test is *true* if the **TERM** variable is set to **xterm.** You can test for any value of **TERM.**

3. You can test the application name.

   ```
   $if bash
   ```

   The preceding test is *true* when you are running bash and not another program that uses the Readline Library. You can test for any application name.

These tests can customize the Readline Library based on the current mode, the type of terminal, and the application you are using. They give you a great deal of power and flexibility when you are using the Readline Library with bash and other programs.

The following commands in **.inputrc** cause CONTROL-Y to move the cursor to the beginning of the next word regardless of whether bash is in vi or emacs mode:

```
$ cat ~/.inputrc
set editing-mode vi
$if mode=vi
        "\C-y": vi-next-word
    $else
        "\C-y": forward-word
$endif
```

Because bash reads the preceding conditional construct when it is started, you must set the editing mode in **.inputrc**. Changing modes interactively using set will not change the binding of CONTROL-Y.

For more information on the Readline Library, open the bash man page and give the command **/^READLINE**, which searches for the word **READLINE** at the beginning of a line.

If Readline commands do not work, log out and log in again

tip The Bourne Again Shell reads **~/.inputrc** when you log in. After you make changes to this file, you must log out and log in again before the changes will take effect.

ALIASES

An *alias* is a (usually short) name that the shell translates into another (usually longer) name or command. Aliases allow you to define new commands by substituting a string for the first token of a simple command. They are typically placed in the **~/.bashrc** (bash) or **~/.tcshrc** (tcsh) startup files so that they are available to interactive subshells.

Under bash the syntax of the alias builtin is

*alias [**name**[=**value**]]*

Under tcsh the syntax is

*alias [**name**[**value**]]*

In the bash syntax no SPACEs are permitted around the equal sign. If ***value*** contains SPACEs or TABs, you must enclose ***value*** within quotation marks. Unlike aliases under tcsh, a bash alias does not accept an argument from the command line in ***value***. Use a bash function (page 356) when you need to use an argument.

An alias does not replace itself, which avoids the possibility of infinite recursion in handling an alias such as the following:

```
$ alias ls='ls -F'
```

You can nest aliases. Aliases are disabled for noninteractive shells (that is, shell scripts). Use the unalias builtin to remove an alias. When you give an alias builtin command without any arguments, the shell displays a list of all defined aliases:

```
$ alias
alias ll='ls -l'
alias l='ls -ltr'
alias ls='ls -F'
alias zap='rm -i'
```

To view the alias for a particular name, enter the command **alias** followed by the name of the alias. Most Linux distributions define at least some aliases. Enter an **alias** command to see which aliases are in effect. You can delete the aliases you do not want from the appropriate startup file.

Single Versus Double Quotation Marks in Aliases

The choice of single or double quotation marks is significant in the alias syntax when the alias includes variables. If you enclose ***value*** within double quotation marks, any variables that appear in ***value*** are expanded when the alias is created. If you enclose ***value*** within single quotation marks, variables are not expanded until the alias is used. The following example illustrates the difference.

The **PWD** keyword variable holds the pathname of the working directory. Max creates two aliases while he is working in his home directory. Because he uses double quotation marks when he creates the **dirA** alias, the shell substitutes the value of the working directory when he creates this alias. The **alias dirA** command displays the **dirA** alias and shows that the substitution has already taken place:

```
$ echo $PWD
/home/max
$ alias dirA="echo Working directory is $PWD"
$ alias dirA
alias dirA='echo Working directory is /home/max'
```

When Max creates the **dirB** alias, he uses single quotation marks, which prevent the shell from expanding the **$PWD** variable. The **alias dirB** command shows that the **dirB** alias still holds the unexpanded **$PWD** variable:

```
$ alias dirB='echo Working directory is $PWD'
$ alias dirB
alias dirB='echo Working directory is $PWD'
```

After creating the **dirA** and **dirB** aliases, Max uses cd to make **cars** his working directory and gives each of the aliases as a command. The alias he created using double quotation marks displays the name of the directory he created the alias in as the working directory (which is wrong). In contrast, the **dirB** alias displays the proper name of the working directory:

```
$ cd cars
$ dirA
Working directory is /home/max
$ dirB
Working directory is /home/max/cars
```

How to prevent the shell from invoking an alias

tip The shell checks only simple, unquoted commands to see if they are aliases. Commands given as relative or absolute pathnames and quoted commands are not checked. When you want to give a command that has an alias but do not want to use the alias, precede the command with a backslash, specify the command's absolute pathname, or give the command as **./*command***.

EXAMPLES OF ALIASES

The following alias allows you to type **r** to repeat the previous command or **r abc** to repeat the last command line that began with **abc**:

```
$ alias r='fc -s'
```

If you use the command **ls –ltr** frequently, you can create an alias that substitutes **ls –ltr** when you give the command **l**:

```
$ alias l='ls -ltr'
$ l
-rw-r-----. 1 max pubs  3089 02-11 16:24 XTerm.ad
-rw-r--r--. 1 max pubs 30015 03-01 14:24 flute.ps
-rw-r--r--. 1 max pubs   641 04-01 08:12 fixtax.icn
-rw-r--r--. 1 max pubs   484 04-09 08:14 maptax.icn
drwxrwxr-x. 2 max pubs  1024 08-09 17:41 Tiger
drwxrwxr-x. 2 max pubs  1024 09-10 11:32 testdir
-rwxr-xr-x. 1 max pubs   485 09-21 08:03 floor
drwxrwxr-x. 2 max pubs  1024 09-27 20:19 Test_Emacs
```

Another common use of aliases is to protect yourself from mistakes. The following example substitutes the interactive version of the rm utility when you enter the command **zap**:

```
$ alias zap='rm -i'
$ zap f*
rm: remove 'fixtax.icn'? n
rm: remove 'flute.ps'? n
rm: remove 'floor'? n
```

The **–i** option causes rm to ask you to verify each file that would be deleted, thereby helping you avoid deleting the wrong file. You can also alias rm with the **rm –i** command: **alias rm='rm –i'**.

The aliases in the next example cause the shell to substitute **ls –l** each time you give an **ll** command and **ls –F** each time you use **ls**. The **–F** option causes ls to print a slash (**/**) at the end of directory names and an asterisk (*) at the end of the names of executable files.

```
$ alias ls='ls -F'
$ alias ll='ls -l'
$ ll
drwxrwxr-x. 2 max pubs  1024 09-27 20:19 Test_Emacs/
drwxrwxr-x. 2 max pubs  1024 08-09 17:41 Tiger/
-rw-r-----. 1 max pubs  3089 02-11 16:24 XTerm.ad
-rw-r--r--. 1 max pubs   641 04-01 08:12 fixtax.icn
-rw-r--r--. 1 max pubs 30015 03-01 14:24 flute.ps
-rwxr-xr-x. 1 max pubs   485 09-21 08:03 floor*
-rw-r--r--. 1 max pubs   484 04-09 08:14 maptax.icn
drwxrwxr-x. 2 max pubs  1024 09-10 11:32 testdir/
```

In this example, the string that replaces the alias **ll** (**ls –l**) itself contains an alias (**ls**). When it replaces an alias with its value, the shell looks at the first word of the replacement string to see whether it is an alias. In the preceding example, the replacement string contains the alias **ls**, so a second substitution occurs to produce the final command **ls –F –l**. (To avoid a *recursive plunge,* the **ls** in the replacement text, although an alias, is not expanded a second time.)

When given a list of aliases without the ***=value*** or ***value*** field, the alias builtin displays the value of each defined alias. The alias builtin reports an error if an alias has not been defined:

```
$ alias ll l ls zap wx
alias ll='ls -l'
alias l='ls -ltr'
alias ls='ls -F'
alias zap='rm -i'
bash: alias: wx: not found
```

You can avoid alias substitution by preceding the aliased command with a backslash (\):

```
$ \ls
Test_Emacs XTerm.ad  flute.ps  maptax.icn
Tiger      fixtax.icn floor     testdir
```

Because the replacement of an alias name with the alias value does not change the rest of the command line, any arguments are still received by the command that is executed:

```
$ ll f*
-rw-r--r--. 1 max pubs   641 04-01 08:12 fixtax.icn
-rw-r--r--. 1 max pubs 30015 03-01 14:24 flute.ps
-rwxr-xr-x. 1 max pubs   485 09-21 08:03 floor*
```

You can remove an alias using the unalias builtin. When the **zap** alias is removed, it is no longer displayed by the alias builtin, and its subsequent use results in an error message:

```
$ unalias zap
$ alias
alias ll='ls -l'
alias l='ls -ltr'
alias ls='ls -F'
$ zap maptax.icn
bash: zap: command not found
```

FUNCTIONS

A shell function (tcsh does not have functions) is similar to a shell script in that it stores a series of commands for execution at a later time. However, because the shell stores a function in the computer's main memory (RAM) instead of in a file on the disk, the shell can access it more quickly than the shell can access a script. The shell also preprocesses (parses) a function so it starts more quickly than a script. Finally the shell executes a shell function in the same shell that called it. If you define too many functions, the overhead of starting a subshell (as when you run a script) can become unacceptable.

You can declare a shell function in the **~/.bash_profile** startup file, in the script that uses it, or directly from the command line. You can remove functions using the unset builtin. The shell does not retain functions after you log out.

Removing variables and functions that have the same name

tip If you have a shell variable and a function that have the same name, using unset removes the shell variable. If you then use unset again with the same name, it removes the function.

The syntax that declares a shell function is

> *[function]* ***function-name*** *() {*
>   ***commands***
> *}*

where the word *function* is optional (and is frequently omitted; it is not portable), ***function-name*** is the name you use to call the function, and ***commands*** comprise the list of commands the function executes when you call it. The ***commands*** can be anything you would include in a shell script, including calls to other functions.

The opening brace ({) can appear on the line following the function name. Aliases and variables are expanded when a function is read, not when it is executed. You can use the **break** statement (page 453) within a function to terminate its execution.

You can declare a function on a single line. Because the closing brace must appear as a separate command, you must place a semicolon before the closing brace when you use this syntax:

```
$ say_hi() { echo "hi" ; }
$ say_hi
hi
```

Shell functions are useful as a shorthand as well as to define special commands. The following function starts a process named **process** in the background, with the output normally displayed by **process** being saved in **.process.out**.

```
start_process() {
process > .process.out 2>&1 &
}
```

The next example creates a simple function that displays the date, a header, and a list of the people who are logged in on the system. This function runs the same commands as the **whoson** script described on page 295. In this example the function is being entered from the keyboard. The greater than (**>**) signs are secondary shell prompts (**PS2**); do not enter them.

```
$ function whoson () {
>   date
>   echo "Users Currently Logged On"
>   who
> }

$ whoson
Thurs Aug 9 15:44:58 PDT 2018
Users Currently Logged On
hls       console      2018-08-08 08:59  (:0)
max       pts/4        2018-08-08 09:33  (0.0)
zach      pts/7        2018-08-08 09:23  (guava)
```

Function local variables You can use the local builtin only within a function. This builtin causes its arguments to be local to the function it is called from and its children. Without local, variables declared in a function are available to the shell that called the function (functions are run in the shell they are called from). The following function demonstrates the use of local:

```
$ demo () {
> x=4
> local y=8
> echo "demo: $x $y"
> }
$ demo
demo: 4 8
$ echo $x
4
$ echo $y

$
```

The **demo** function, which is entered from the keyboard, declares two variables, **x** and **y**, and displays their values. The variable **x** is declared with a normal assignment statement while **y** is declared using local. After running the function, the shell that called the function has access to **x** but knows nothing of **y**. See page 488 for another example of function local variables.

Export a function An **export –f** command places the named function in the environment so it is available to child processes.

Functions in startup files

If you want the **whoson** function to be available without having to enter it each time you log in, put its definition in **~/.bash_profile**. Then run **.bash_profile**, using the . (dot) command to put the changes into effect immediately:

```
$ cat ~/.bash_profile
export TERM=vt100
stty kill '^u'
whoson () {
    date
    echo "Users Currently Logged On"
    who
}

$ . ~/.bash_profile
```

You can specify arguments when you call a function. Within the function these arguments are available as positional parameters (page 470). The following example shows the **arg1** function entered from the keyboard:

```
$ arg1 ( ) { echo "$1" ; }
$ arg1 first_arg
first_arg
```

See the function **switch** () on page 290 for another example of a function.

optional

The following function allows you to place variables in the environment (export them) using tcsh syntax. The env utility lists all environment variables and their values and verifies that **setenv** worked correctly:

```
$ cat .bash_profile
...
# setenv - keep tcsh users happy
setenv() {
    if [ $# -eq 2 ]
        then
            eval $1=$2
            export $1
        else
            echo "Usage: setenv NAME VALUE" 1>&2
    fi
}
$ . ~/.bash_profile
$ setenv TCL_LIBRARY /usr/local/lib/tcl
$ env | grep TCL_LIBRARY
TCL_LIBRARY=/usr/local/lib/tcl
```

eval

The **$#** special parameter (page 475) takes on the value of the number of command-line arguments. This function uses the eval builtin to force bash to scan the command **$1=$2** *twice*. Because **$1=$2** begins with a dollar sign ($), the shell treats the entire string as a single token—a command. With variable substitution performed, the command name becomes **TCL_LIBRARY=/usr/local/lib/tcl**, which results in an error.

With eval, a second scanning splits the string into the three desired tokens, and the correct assignment occurs. See page 500 for more information on eval.

CONTROLLING bash: FEATURES AND OPTIONS

This section explains how to control bash features and options using command-line options and the set and shopt builtins. The shell sets flags to indicate which options are set (on) and expands $– to a list of flags that are set; see page 478 for more information.

bash COMMAND-LINE OPTIONS

You can specify short and long command-line options. Short options consist of a hyphen followed by a letter; long options have two hyphens followed by multiple characters. Long options must appear before short options on a command line that calls bash. Table 8-12 lists some commonly used command-line options.

Table 8-12 bash command-line options

Option	Explanation	Syntax
Help	Displays a usage message.	**––help**
No edit	Prevents users from using the Readline Library (page 345) to edit command lines in an interactive shell.	**––noediting**
No profile	Prevents reading these startup files (page 288): **/etc/profile**, **~/.bash_profile**, **~/.bash_login**, and **~/.profile**.	**––noprofile**
No rc	Prevents reading the **~/.bashrc** startup file (page 289). This option is on by default if the shell is called as **sh**.	**––norc**
POSIX	Runs bash in POSIX mode.	**––posix**
Version	Displays bash version information and exits.	**––version**
Login	Causes bash to run as though it were a login shell.	**–l** (lowercase "l")
shopt	Runs a shell with the ***opt*** shopt option (page 360). A **–O** (uppercase "O") sets the option; **+O** unsets it.	[±]**O** [***opt***]
End of options	On the command line, signals the end of options. Subsequent tokens are treated as arguments even if they begin with a hyphen (**–**).	**––**

SHELL FEATURES

You can control the behavior of the Bourne Again Shell by turning features on and off. Different methods turn different features on and off: The set builtin controls one group of features, and the shopt builtin controls another group. You can also control many features from the command line you use to call bash.

Features, options, variables, attributes?

tip To avoid confusing terminology, this book refers to the various shell behaviors that you can control as *features*. The bash info page refers to them as "options" and "values of variables controlling optional shell behavior." In some places you might see them referred to as *attributes*.

set ±o: TURNS SHELL FEATURES ON AND OFF

The set builtin, when used with the **–o** or **+o** option, enables, disables, and lists certain bash features (the set builtin in tcsh works differently). For example, the following command turns on the **noclobber** feature (page 143):

```
$ set -o noclobber
```

You can turn this feature off (the default) by giving this command:

```
$ set +o noclobber
```

The command **set –o** without an option lists each of the features controlled by set, followed by its state (on or off). The command **set +o** without an option lists the same features in a form you can use as input to the shell. Table 8-13 lists bash features. This table does not list the **–i** option because you cannot set it. The shell sets this option when it is invoked as an interactive shell. See page 472 for a discussion of other uses of set.

shopt: TURNS SHELL FEATURES ON AND OFF

The shopt (shell option) builtin (not in tcsh) enables, disables, and lists certain bash features that control the behavior of the shell. For example, the following command causes bash to include filenames that begin with a period (**.**) when it expands ambiguous file references (the **–s** stands for *set*):

```
$ shopt -s dotglob
```

You can turn this feature off (the default) by giving the following command (where the **–u** stands for *unset*):

```
$ shopt -u dotglob
```

The shell displays how a feature is set if you give the name of the feature as the only argument to shopt:

```
$ shopt dotglob
dotglob         off
```

Without any options or arguments, shopt lists the features it controls and their states. The command **shopt –s** without an argument lists the features controlled by shopt that are set or on. The command **shopt –u** lists the features that are unset or off. Table 8-13 lists bash features.

Setting set ±o features using shopt

tip You can use shopt to set/unset features that are otherwise controlled by **set ±o**. Use the regular shopt syntax using **–s** or **–u** and include the **–o** option. For example, the following command turns on the **noclobber** feature:

```
$ shopt -o -s noclobber
```

Table 8-13 bash features

Feature	Description	Syntax	Alternative syntax
allexport	Automatically places in the environment (exports) all variables and functions you create or modify after giving this command (default is off).	**set –o allexport**	**set –a**
braceexpand	Causes bash to perform brace expansion (default is on; page 366).	**set –o braceexpand**	**set –B**
cdspell	Corrects minor spelling errors in directory names used as arguments to cd (default is off).	**shopt –s cdspell**	
cmdhist	Saves all lines of a multiline command in the same history entry, adding semicolons as needed (default is on).	**shopt –s cmdhist**	
dotglob	Causes shell special characters (wildcards; page 152) in an ambiguous file reference to match a leading period in a filename. By default, special characters do not match a leading period: You must always specify the filenames . and .. explicitly because no pattern ever matches them (default is off).	**shopt –s dotglob**	
emacs	Specifies emacs editing mode for command-line editing (default is on; page 347).	**set –o emacs**	
errexit	Causes bash to exit when a pipeline (page 145), which can be a simple command (page 133; not a control structure), fails (default is off).	**set –o errexit**	**set –e**

Table 8-13 bash features (continued)

Feature	Description	Syntax	Alternative syntax
execfail	Causes a shell script to continue running when it cannot find the file that is given as an argument to exec. By default, a script terminates when exec cannot find the file that is given as its argument (default is off).	**shopt –s execfail**	
expand_aliases	Causes aliases (page 352) to be expanded (default is on for interactive shells and off for noninteractive shells).	**shopt –s expand_aliases**	
hashall	Causes bash to remember where commands it has found using **PATH** (page 318) are located (default is on).	**set –o hashall**	**set –h**
histappend	Causes bash to append the history list to the file named by **HISTFILE** (page 336) when the shell exits (default is off [bash overwrites this file]).	**shopt –s histappend**	
histexpand	Turns on the history mechanism (which uses exclamation points by default; page 341). Turn this feature off to turn off history expansion (default is on).	**set –o histexpand**	**set –H**
history	Enables command history (default is on; page 336).	**set –o history**	
huponexit	Specifies that bash send a SIGHUP signal to all jobs when an interactive login shell exits (default is off).	**shopt –s huponexit**	
ignoreeof	Specifies that bash must receive ten EOF characters before it exits. Useful on noisy dial-up lines (default is off).	**set –o ignoreeof**	
monitor	Enables job control (default is on; page 304).	**set –o monitor**	**set –m**
nocaseglob	Causes ambiguous file references (page 152) to match filenames without regard to case (default is off).	**shopt –s nocaseglob**	
noclobber	Helps prevent overwriting files (default is off; page 143).	**set –o noclobber**	**set –C**
noglob	Disables pathname expansion (default is off; page 152).	**set –o noglob**	**set –f**

Table 8-13 bash features (continued)

Feature	Description	Syntax	Alternative syntax
notify	With job control (page 304) enabled, reports the termination status of background jobs immediately (default is off: bash displays the status just before the next prompt).	**set –o notify**	**set –b**
nounset	Displays an error when the shell tries to expand an unset variable; bash exits from a script but not from an interactive shell (default is off: bash substitutes a null value for an unset variable).	**set –o nounset**	**set –u**
nullglob	Causes bash to substitute a null string for ambiguous file references (page 152) that do not match a filename (default is off: bash passes these file references as is).	**shopt –s nullglob**	
pipefail	Sets the exit status of a pipeline to the exit status of the last (rightmost) simple command that failed (returned a nonzero exit status) in the pipeline; if no command failed, exit status is set to zero (default is off: bash sets the exit status of a pipeline to the exit status of the final command in the pipeline).	**set –o pipefail**	
posix	Runs bash in POSIX mode (default is off).	**set –o posix**	
verbose	Displays each command line after bash reads it but before bash expands it (default is off). See also **xtrace**.	**set –o verbose**	**set –v**
vi	Specifies vi editing mode for command-line editing (default is off; page 346).	**set –o vi**	
xpg_echo	Causes the echo builtin to expand backslash escape sequences without the need for the **–e** option (default is off; page 457).	**shopt –s xpg_echo**	
xtrace	Turns on shell debugging: Displays the value of **PS4** (page 321) followed by each input line after the shell reads and expands it (default is off; see page 442 for a discussion). See also **verbose**.	**set –o xtrace**	**set –x**

PROCESSING THE COMMAND LINE

Whether you are working interactively or running a shell script, bash needs to read a command line before it can start processing it—bash always reads at least one line before processing a command. Some bash builtins, such as **if** and **case**, as well as functions and quoted strings, span multiple lines. When bash recognizes a command that covers more than one line, it reads the entire command before processing it. In interactive sessions, bash prompts with the secondary prompt (**PS2**, **>** by default; page 321) as you type each line of a multiline command until it recognizes the end of the command:

```
$ ps -ef |
> grep emacs
zach      26880 24579  1 14:42 pts/10   00:00:00 emacs notes
zach      26890 24579  0 14:42 pts/10   00:00:00 grep emacs

$ function hello () {
> echo hello there
> }
$
```

For more information refer to "Implicit Command-Line Continuation" on page 512. After reading a command line, bash applies history expansion and alias substitution to the command line.

HISTORY EXPANSION

"Reexecuting and Editing Commands" on page 338 discusses the commands you can give to modify and reexecute command lines from the history list. History expansion is the process bash uses to turn a history command into an executable command line. For example, when you enter the command **!!**, history expansion changes that command line so it is the same as the previous one. History expansion is turned on by default for interactive shells; **set +o histexpand** turns it off. History expansion does not apply to noninteractive shells (shell scripts).

ALIAS SUBSTITUTION

Aliases (page 352) substitute a string for the first word of a simple command. By default, alias substitution is turned on for interactive shells and off for noninteractive shells; **shopt –u expand_aliases** turns it off.

PARSING AND SCANNING THE COMMAND LINE

After processing history commands and aliases, bash does not execute the command immediately. One of the first things the shell does is to *parse* (isolate strings of characters in) the command line into tokens (words). After separating tokens and before executing the command, the shell scans the tokens and performs *command-line expansion.*

COMMAND-LINE EXPANSION

Both interactive and noninteractive shells transform the command line using *command-line expansion* before passing the command line to the program being called. You can use a shell without knowing much about command-line expansion, but you can use what a shell has to offer to a better advantage with an understanding of this topic. This section covers Bourne Again Shell command-line expansion; TC Shell command-line expansion is covered starting on page 384.

The Bourne Again Shell scans each token for the various types of expansion and substitution in the following order. Most of these processes expand a word into a single word. Only brace expansion, word splitting, and pathname expansion can change the number of words in a command (except for the expansion of the variable "$@"—see page 474).

1. Brace expansion (next page)
2. Tilde expansion (page 368)
3. Parameter and variable expansion (page 368)
4. Arithmetic expansion (page 369)
5. Command substitution (page 371)
6. Word splitting (page 372)
7. Pathname expansion (page 372)
8. Process substitution (page 374)
9. Quote removal (page 374)

ORDER OF EXPANSION

The order in which bash carries out these steps affects the interpretation of commands. For example, if you set a variable to a value that looks like the instruction for output redirection and then enter a command that uses the variable's value to perform redirection, you might expect bash to redirect the output.

```
$ SENDIT="> /tmp/saveit"
$ echo xxx $SENDIT
xxx > /tmp/saveit
$ cat /tmp/saveit
cat: /tmp/saveit: No such file or directory
```

In fact, the shell does *not* redirect the output—it recognizes input and output redirection before it evaluates variables. When it executes the command line, the shell checks for redirection and, finding none, evaluates the SENDIT variable. After replacing the variable with **> /tmp/saveit**, bash passes the arguments to echo, which dutifully copies its arguments to standard output. No **/tmp/saveit** file is created.

Quotation marks can alter expansion

tip Double and single quotation marks cause the shell to behave differently when performing expansions. Double quotation marks permit parameter and variable expansion but suppress other types of expansion. Single quotation marks suppress all types of expansion.

BRACE EXPANSION

Brace expansion, which originated in the C Shell, provides a convenient way to specify a series of strings or numbers. Although brace expansion is frequently used to specify filenames, the mechanism can be used to generate arbitrary strings; the shell does not attempt to match the brace notation with the names of existing files. Brace expansion is turned on in interactive and noninteractive shells by default; you can turn it off using **set +o braceexpand**. The shell also uses braces to isolate variable names (page 314).

The following example illustrates how brace expansion works. The ls command does not display any output because there are no files in the working directory. The echo builtin displays the strings the shell generates using brace expansion.

```
$ ls
$ echo chap_{one,two,three}.txt
chap_one.txt chap_two.txt chap_three.txt
```

The shell expands the comma-separated strings inside the braces on the command line into a SPACE-separated list of strings. Each string from the list is prepended with the string **chap_**, called the *preamble,* and appended with the string **.txt**, called the *postscript.* Both the preamble and the postscript are optional. The left-to-right order of the strings within the braces is preserved in the expansion. For the shell to treat the left and right braces specially and for brace expansion to occur, at least one comma must be inside the braces and no unquoted whitespace can appear inside the braces. You can nest brace expansions.

Brace expansion *can* match filenames. This feature is useful when there is a long preamble or postscript. The following example copies four files—**main.c**, **f1.c**, **f2.c**, and **tmp.c**—located in the **/usr/local/src/C** directory to the working directory:

```
$ cp /usr/local/src/C/{main,f1,f2,tmp}.c .
```

You can also use brace expansion to create directories with related names:

```
$ ls -F
file1  file2  file3
$ mkdir vrs{A,B,C,D,E}
$ ls -F
file1  file2  file3  vrsA/  vrsB/  vrsC/  vrsD/  vrsE/
```

The **–F** option causes ls to display a slash (/) after a directory and an asterisk (*) after an executable file. If you tried to use an ambiguous file reference instead of braces to specify the directories, the result would be different (and not what you wanted):

```
$ rmdir vrs*
$ mkdir vrs[A-E]
$ ls -F
file1  file2  file3  vrs[A-E]/
```

An ambiguous file reference matches the names of existing files. In the preceding example, because it found no filenames matching **vrs[A–E]**, bash passed the ambiguous file reference to mkdir, which created a directory with that name. Brackets in ambiguous file references are discussed on page 155.

Sequence expression Under newer versions of bash, brace expansion can include a sequence expression to generate a sequence of characters. It can generate a sequential series of numbers or letters using the following syntax:

{n1..n2[..incr]}

where ***n1*** and ***n2*** are numbers or single letters and ***incr*** is a number. This syntax works on bash version 4.0+; give the command **echo $BASH_VERSION** to see which version you are using. The ***incr*** does not work under macOS. When you specify invalid arguments, bash copies the arguments to standard output. Following are some examples:

```
$ echo {4..8}
4 5 6 7 8
$ echo {8..16..2}
8 10 12 14 16
$ echo {a..m..3}
a d g j m
$ echo {a..m..b}
{a..m..b}
$ echo {2..m}
{2..m}
```

See page 500 for a way to use variables to specify the values used by a sequence expression. Page 444 shows an example in which a sequence expression is used to specify step values in a **for...in** loop.

seq Older versions of bash do not support sequence expressions. Although you can use the seq utility to perform a similar function, seq does not work with letters and displays an error when given invalid arguments. The seq utility uses the following syntax:

*seq **n1** [incr] **n2***

The –s option causes seq to use the specified character to separate its output. Following are some examples:

```
$ seq 4 8
4
5
6
7
8

$ seq -s\  8 2 16
8 10 12 14 16

$ seq a d
seq: invalid floating point argument: a
Try 'seq --help' for more information.
```

TILDE EXPANSION

Chapter 4 introduced a shorthand notation to specify your home directory or the home directory of another user. This section provides a more detailed explanation of *tilde expansion.*

The tilde (~) is a special character when it appears at the start of a token on a command line. When it sees a tilde in this position, bash looks at the following string of characters—up to the first slash (/) or to the end of the word if there is no slash—as a possible username. If this possible username is null (that is, if the tilde appears as a word by itself or if it is immediately followed by a slash), the shell substitutes the value of the **HOME** variable for the tilde. The following example demonstrates this expansion, where the last command copies the file named **letter** from Max's home directory to the working directory:

```
$ echo $HOME
/home/max
$ echo ~
/home/max
$ echo ~/letter
/home/max/letter
$ cp ~/letter .
```

If the string of characters following the tilde forms a valid username, the shell substitutes the path of the home directory associated with that username for the tilde and name. If the string is not null and not a valid username, the shell does not make any substitution:

```
$ echo ~zach
/home/zach
$ echo ~root
/root
$ echo ~xx
~xx
```

Tildes are also used in directory stack manipulation (page 307). In addition, ~+ is a synonym for **PWD** (the name of the working directory), and ~– is a synonym for **OLDPWD** (the name of the previous working directory).

PARAMETER AND VARIABLE EXPANSION

On a command line, a dollar sign ($) that is not followed by an open parenthesis introduces parameter or variable expansion. *Parameters* include both command-line, or positional, parameters (page 470) and special parameters (page 475). *Variables* include both user-created variables (page 312) and keyword variables (page 317). The bash man and info pages do not make this distinction.

The shell does not expand parameters and variables that are enclosed within single quotation marks and those in which the leading dollar sign is escaped (i.e., preceded with a backslash). The shell does expand parameters and variables enclosed within double quotation marks.

ARITHMETIC EXPANSION

The shell performs *arithmetic expansion* by evaluating an arithmetic expression and replacing it with the result. See page 398 for information on arithmetic expansion under tcsh. Under bash the syntax for arithmetic expansion is

$((expression))

The shell evaluates ***expression*** and replaces *$((**expression**))* with the result. This syntax is similar to the syntax used for command substitution [*$(...)*] and performs a parallel function. You can use *$((**expression**))* as an argument to a command or in place of any numeric value on a command line.

The rules for forming ***expression*** are the same as those found in the C programming language; all standard C arithmetic operators are available (see Table 10-8 on page 508). Arithmetic in bash is done using integers. Unless you use variables of type integer (page 316) or actual integers, however, the shell must convert string-valued variables to integers for the purpose of the arithmetic evaluation.

You do not need to precede variable names within ***expression*** with a dollar sign (**$**). In the following example, after read (page 489) assigns the user's response to **age**, an arithmetic expression determines how many years are left until age 100:

```
$ cat age_check
#!/bin/bash
read -p "How old are you? " age
echo "Wow, in $((100-age)) years, you'll be 100!"

$ ./age_check
How old are you? 55
Wow, in 45 years, you'll be 100!
```

You do not need to enclose the ***expression*** within quotation marks because bash does not perform pathname expansion until later. This feature makes it easier for you to use an asterisk (*) for multiplication, as the following example shows:

```
$ echo There are $((60*60*24*365)) seconds in a non-leap year.
There are 31536000 seconds in a non-leap year.
```

The next example uses wc, cut, arithmetic expansion, and command substitution (page 371) to estimate the number of pages required to print the contents of the file **letter.txt**. The output of the wc (word count) utility (page 1027) used with the **–l** option is the number of lines in the file, in columns (character positions) 1 through 4, followed by a SPACE and the name of the file (the first command following). The cut utility (page 784) with the **–c1–4** option extracts the first four columns.

```
$ wc -l letter.txt
351 letter.txt
$ wc -l letter.txt | cut -c1-4
351
```

The dollar sign and single parenthesis instruct the shell to perform command substitution; the dollar sign and double parentheses indicate arithmetic expansion:

```
$ echo $(( $(wc -l letter.txt | cut -c1-4)/66 + 1))
6
```

The preceding example sets up a pipeline that sends standard output from wc to standard input of cut. Because of command substitution, the output of both commands replaces the commands between the $(and the matching) on the command line. Arithmetic expansion then divides this number by 66, the number of lines on a page. A 1 is added because integer division discards remainders.

Fewer dollar signs ($)

tip When you specify variables within **$((** and **))**, the dollar signs that precede individual variable references are optional. This format also allows you to include whitespace around operators, making expressions easier to read.

```
$ x=23 y=37
$ echo $(( 2 * $x + 3 * $y ))
157
$ echo $(( 2 * x + 3 * y ))
157
```

Another way to get the same result without using cut is to redirect the input to wc instead of having wc get its input from a file you name on the command line. When you redirect its input, wc does not display the name of the file:

```
$ wc -l < letter.txt
   351
```

It is common practice to assign the result of arithmetic expansion to a variable:

```
$ numpages=$(( $(wc -l < letter.txt)/66 + 1))
```

let builtin The let builtin (not in tcsh) evaluates arithmetic expressions just as the $(( )) syntax does. The following command is equivalent to the preceding one:

```
$ let "numpages=$(wc -l < letter.txt)/66 + 1"
```

The double quotation marks keep the SPACEs (both those you can see and those that result from the command substitution) from separating the expression into separate arguments to let. The value of the last expression determines the exit status of let. If the value of the last expression is 0, the exit status of let is 1; otherwise, the exit status is 0.

You can supply let with multiple arguments on a single command line:

```
$ let a=5+3 b=7+2
$ echo $a $b
8 9
```

When you refer to variables when doing arithmetic expansion with let or $(( )), the shell does not require a variable name to begin with a dollar sign ($). Nevertheless, it is a good practice to do so for consistency, because in most places you must precede a variable name with a dollar sign.

COMMAND SUBSTITUTION

Command substitution replaces a command with the output of that command. The preferred syntax for command substitution under bash is

$(command)

Under bash you can also use the following, older syntax, which is the only syntax allowed under tcsh:

`command`

The shell executes ***command*** within a subshell and replaces ***command***, along with the surrounding punctuation, with standard output of ***command***. Standard error of ***command*** is not affected.

In the following example, the shell executes pwd and substitutes the output of the command for the command and surrounding punctuation. Then the shell passes the output of the command, which is now an argument, to echo, which displays it.

```
$ echo $(pwd)
/home/max
```

The next script assigns the output of the pwd builtin to the variable **where** and displays a message containing the value of this variable:

```
$ cat where
where=$(pwd)
echo "You are using the $where directory."
$ ./where
You are using the /home/zach directory.
```

Although it illustrates how to assign the output of a command to a variable, this example is not realistic. You can more directly display the output of pwd without using a variable:

```
$ cat where2
echo "You are using the $(pwd) directory."
$ ./where2
You are using the /home/zach directory.
```

The following command uses find to locate files with the name **README** in the directory tree rooted at the working directory. This list of files is standard output of find and becomes the list of arguments to ls.

```
$ ls -l $(find . -name README -print)
```

The next command line shows the older *`command`* syntax:

```
$ ls -l `find . -name README -print`
```

One advantage of the newer syntax is that it avoids the rather arcane rules for token handling, quotation mark handling, and escaped back ticks within the old syntax. Another advantage of the new syntax is that it can be nested, unlike the old syntax. For example, you can produce a long listing of all **README** files whose size exceeds the size of **./README** using the following command:

```
$ ls -l $(find . -name README -size +$(echo $(cat ./README | wc -c)c ) -print )
```

Try giving this command after giving a **set –x** command (page 442) to see how bash expands it. If there is no **README** file, the command displays the output of **ls –l**.

For additional scripts that use command substitution, see pages 439, 458, and 498.

$((versus $(

tip The symbols **$((** constitute a single token. They introduce an arithmetic expression, not a command substitution. Thus, if you want to use a parenthesized subshell (page 302) within **$()**, you must put a SPACE between the **$(** and the following **(**.

WORD SPLITTING

The results of parameter and variable expansion, command substitution, and arithmetic expansion are candidates for word splitting. Using each character of **IFS** (page 321) as a possible delimiter, bash splits these candidates into words or tokens. If **IFS** is unset, bash uses its default value (SPACE-TAB-NEWLINE). If **IFS** is null, bash does not split words.

PATHNAME EXPANSION

Pathname expansion (page 152), also called *filename generation* or *globbing*, is the process of interpreting ambiguous file references and substituting the appropriate list of filenames. Unless **noglob** (page 362) is set, the shell performs this function when it encounters an ambiguous file reference—a token containing any of the unquoted characters *, ?, [, or]. If bash cannot locate any files that match the specified pattern, the token with the ambiguous file reference remains unchanged. The shell does not delete the token or replace it with a null string but rather passes it to the program as is (except see **nullglob** on page 363). The TC Shell generates an error message.

In the first echo command in the following example, the shell expands the ambiguous file reference **tmp*** and passes three tokens (**tmp1**, **tmp2**, and **tmp3**) to echo. The echo builtin displays the three filenames it was passed by the shell. After rm removes the three **tmp*** files, the shell finds no filenames that match **tmp*** when it tries to expand it. It then passes the unexpanded string to the echo builtin, which displays the string it was passed.

```
$ ls
tmp1 tmp2 tmp3
$ echo tmp*
tmp1 tmp2 tmp3
$ rm tmp*
$ echo tmp*
tmp*
```

By default, the same command causes the TC Shell to display an error message:

```
tcsh $ echo tmp*
echo: No match
```

A period that either starts a pathname or follows a slash (/) in a pathname must be matched explicitly unless you have set **dotglob** (page 361). The option **nocaseglob** (page 362) causes ambiguous file references to match filenames without regard to case.

Quotation marks

Putting double quotation marks around an argument causes the shell to suppress pathname and all other kinds of expansion except parameter and variable expansion. Putting single quotation marks around an argument suppresses all types of expansion. The second echo command in the following example shows the variable **$max** between double quotation marks, which allow variable expansion. As a result the shell expands the variable to its value: **sonar**. This expansion does not occur in the third echo command, which uses single quotation marks. Because neither single nor double quotation marks allow pathname expansion, the last two commands display the unexpanded argument **tmp***.

```
$ echo tmp* $max
tmp1 tmp2 tmp3 sonar
$ echo "tmp* $max"
tmp* sonar
$ echo 'tmp* $max'
tmp* $max
```

The shell distinguishes between the value of a variable and a reference to the variable and does not expand ambiguous file references if they occur in the value of a variable. As a consequence you can assign to a variable a value that includes special characters, such as an asterisk (*).

Levels of expansion

In the next example, the working directory has three files whose names begin with **letter**. When you assign the value **letter*** to the variable **var**, the shell does not expand the ambiguous file reference because it occurs in the value of a variable (in the assignment statement for the variable). No quotation marks surround the string **letter***; context alone prevents the expansion. After the assignment the set builtin (with the help of grep) shows the value of **var** to be **letter***.

```
$ ls letter*
letter1  letter2  letter3
$ var=letter*
$ set | grep var
var='letter*'
$ echo '$var'
$var
$ echo "$var"
letter*
$ echo $var
letter1 letter2 letter3
```

The three **echo** commands demonstrate three levels of expansion. When **$var** is quoted with single quotation marks, the shell performs no expansion and passes the character string **$var** to echo, which displays it. With double quotation marks, the shell performs variable expansion only and substitutes the value of the **var** variable for its name, preceded by a dollar sign. No pathname expansion is performed on this command because double quotation marks suppress it. In the final command, the shell, without the limitations of quotation marks, performs variable substitution and then pathname expansion before passing the arguments to echo.

PROCESS SUBSTITUTION

The Bourne Again Shell can replace filename arguments with processes. An argument with the syntax *<(**command**)* causes ***command*** to be executed and the output to be written to a named pipe (FIFO). The shell replaces that argument with the name of the pipe. If that argument is then used as the name of an input file during processing, the output of ***command*** is read. Similarly an argument with the syntax *>(**command**)* is replaced by the name of a pipe that ***command*** reads as standard input.

The following example uses sort (page 969) with the **–m** (merge, which works correctly only if the input files are already sorted) option to combine two word lists into a single list. Each word list is generated by a pipe that extracts words matching a pattern from a file and sorts the words in that list.

```
$ sort -m -f <(grep "[^A-Z]..$" memo1 | sort) <(grep ".*aba.*" memo2 |sort)
```

QUOTE REMOVAL

After bash finishes with the preceding list, it performs *quote removal*. This process removes from the command line single quotation marks, double quotation marks, and backslashes that are not a result of an expansion.

CHAPTER SUMMARY

The shell is both a command interpreter and a programming language. As a command interpreter, it executes commands you enter in response to its prompt. As a programming language, it executes commands from files called shell scripts. When you start a shell, it typically runs one or more startup files.

Running a shell script

When the file holding a shell script is in the working directory, there are three basic ways to execute the shell script from the command line.

1. Type the simple filename of the file that holds the script.
2. Type an absolute or relative pathname, including the simple filename preceded by ./.
3. Type **bash** or **tcsh** followed by the name of the file.

Technique 1 requires the working directory to be in the **PATH** variable. Techniques 1 and 2 require you to have execute and read permission for the file holding the script. Technique 3 requires you to have read permission for the file holding the script.

Job control

A job is another name for a process running a pipeline (which can be a simple command). You can bring a job running in the background into the foreground using the fg builtin. You can put a foreground job into the background using the bg builtin, provided you first suspend the job by pressing the suspend key (typically CONTROL-Z). Use the jobs builtin to display the list of jobs that are running in the background or are suspended.

Variables The shell allows you to define variables. You can declare and initialize a variable by assigning a value to it; you can remove a variable declaration using unset. *Shell variables* are local to the process they are defined in. Environment variables are global and are placed in the environment using the export (bash) or setenv (tcsh) builtin so they are available to child processes. Variables you declare are called *user-created* variables. The shell defines *keyword* variables. Within a shell script you can work with the *positional* (command-line) parameters the script was called with.

Locale Locale specifies the way locale-aware programs display certain kinds of data, such as times and dates, money and other numeric values, telephone numbers, and measurements. It can also specify collating sequence and printer paper size.

Process Each process is the execution of a single command and has a unique identification (PID) number. When you give the shell a command, it forks a new (child) process to execute the command (unless the command is built into the shell). While the child process is running, the shell is in a state called sleep. By ending a command line with an ampersand (&), you can run a child process in the background and bypass the sleep state so the shell prompt returns immediately after you press RETURN. Each command in a shell script forks a separate process, each of which might in turn fork other processes. When a process terminates, it returns its exit status to its parent process. An exit status of zero signifies success; a nonzero value signifies failure.

History The history mechanism maintains a list of recently issued command lines called *events*, that provides a way to reexecute previous commands quickly. There are several ways to work with the history list; one of the easiest is to use a command-line editor.

Command-line editors When using an interactive Bourne Again Shell, you can edit a command line and commands from the history list, using either of the Bourne Again Shell's command-line editors (vim or emacs). When you use the vim command-line editor, you start in Input mode, unlike with the stand-alone version of vim. You can switch between Command and Input modes. The emacs editor is modeless and distinguishes commands from editor input by recognizing control characters as commands.

Aliases An alias is a name the shell translates into another name or command. Aliases allow you to define new commands by substituting a string for the first token of a simple command. The Bourne Again and TC Shells use different syntaxes to define an alias, but aliases in both shells work similarly.

Functions A shell function is a series of commands that, unlike a shell script, is parsed prior to being stored in memory. As a consequence shell functions run faster than shell scripts. Shell scripts are parsed at runtime and are stored on disk. A function can be defined on the command line or within a shell script. If you want the function definition to remain in effect across login sessions, you can define it in a startup file. Like functions in many programming languages, a shell function is called by giving its name followed by any arguments.

Shell features There are several ways to customize the shell's behavior. You can use options on the command line when you call bash. You can also use the bash set and shopt builtins to turn features on and off.

Command-line expansion When it processes a command line, the Bourne Again Shell replaces some words with expanded text. Most types of command-line expansion are invoked by the appearance of a special character within a word (for example, the leading dollar sign that denotes a variable). Table 8-6 on page 325 lists these special characters. The expansions take place in a specific order. Following the history and alias expansions, the common expansions are parameter and variable expansion, command substitution, and pathname expansion. Surrounding a word with double quotation marks suppresses all types of expansion except parameter and variable expansion. Single quotation marks suppress all types of expansion, as does quoting (escaping) a special character by preceding it with a backslash.

EXERCISES

1. Explain the following unexpected result:

```
$ whereis date
date: /bin/date ...
$ echo $PATH
.:/usr/local/bin:/usr/bin:/bin
$ cat > date
echo "This is my own version of date."
$ ./date
Sun May 21 11:45:49 PDT 2017
```

2. What are two ways you can execute a shell script when you do not have execute permission for the file containing the script? Can you execute a shell script if you do not have read permission for the file containing the script?

3. What is the purpose of the **PATH** variable?

   a. Set the **PATH** variable and place it in the environment so it causes the shell to search the following directories in order:

      - **/usr/local/bin**
      - **/usr/bin**
      - **/bin**
      - **/usr/kerberos/bin**
      - The **bin** directory in your home directory
      - The working directory

   b. If there is an executable file named **doit** in **/usr/bin** and another file with the same name in your **~/bin** directory, which one will be executed?

   c. If your **PATH** variable is not set to search the working directory, how can you execute a program located there?

   d. Which command can you use to add the directory **/usr/games** to the end of the list of directories in **PATH**?

4. Assume you have made the following assignment:

```
$ person=zach
```

Give the output of each of the following commands.

a. **echo $person**

b. **echo '$person'**

c. **echo "$person"**

5. The following shell script adds entries to a file named **journal-file** in your home directory. This script helps you keep track of phone conversations and meetings.

```
$ cat journal
# journal: add journal entries to the file
# $HOME/journal-file

file=$HOME/journal-file
date >> $file
echo -n "Enter name of person or group: "
read name
echo "$name" >> $file
echo >> $file
cat >> $file
echo "----------------------------------------------------" >>
$file
echo >> $file
```

a. What do you have to do to the script to be able to execute it?

b. Why does the script use the read builtin the first time it accepts input from the terminal and the cat utility the second time?

6. Assume the **/home/zach/grants/biblios** and **/home/zach/biblios** directories exist. Specify Zach's working directory after he executes each sequence of commands. Explain what happens in each case.

a.
```
$ pwd
/home/zach/grants
$ CDPATH=$(pwd)
$ cd
$ cd biblios
```

b.
```
$ pwd
/home/zach/grants
$ CDPATH=$(pwd)
$ cd $HOME/biblios
```

7. Name two ways you can identify the PID number of the login shell.

8. Enter the following command:

```
$ sleep 30 | cat /etc/services
```

Is there any output from sleep? Where does cat get its input from? What has to happen before the shell will display a prompt?

ADVANCED EXERCISES

9. Write a sequence of commands or a script that demonstrates variable expansion occurs before pathname expansion.
10. Write a shell script that outputs the name of the shell executing it.
11. Explain the behavior of the following shell script:

```
$ cat quote_demo
twoliner="This is line 1.
This is line 2."
echo "$twoliner"
echo $twoliner
```

   a. How many arguments does each echo command see in this script? Explain.

   b. Redefine the **IFS** shell variable so the output of the second echo is the same as the first.

12. Add the exit status of the previous command to your prompt so it behaves similarly to the following:

```
$ [0] ls xxx
ls: xxx: No such file or directory
$ [1]
```

13. The dirname utility treats its argument as a pathname and writes to standard output the path prefix—that is, everything up to but not including the last component:

```
$ dirname a/b/c/d
a/b/c
```

If you give **dirname** a simple filename (no / characters) as an argument, **dirname** writes a **.** to standard output:

```
$ dirname simple
.
```

Implement dirname as a bash function. Make sure it behaves sensibly when given such arguments as **/**.

14. Implement the basename utility, which writes the last component of its pathname argument to standard output, as a bash function. For example, given the pathname **a/b/c/d**, basename writes **d** to standard output:

```
$ basename a/b/c/d
d
```

15. The Linux basename utility has an optional second argument. If you give the command **basename** ***path suffix***, basename removes the ***suffix*** and the prefix from ***path***:

```
$ basename src/shellfiles/prog.bash .bash
prog
$ basename src/shellfiles/prog.bash .c
prog.bash
```

Add this feature to the function you wrote for exercise 14.

9

THE TC SHELL (tcsh)

IN THIS CHAPTER

OBJECTIVES

After reading this chapter you should be able to:

- Identify tcsh startup files
- Explain the function of the **history**, **histfile**, and **savehist** variables
- Set up an alias that uses a command-line argument
- Redirect standard error and standard output of a script to two different files
- Set up and use filename, command, and variable completion
- Correct command-line spelling errors
- Explain and use the @ builtin to work with numeric variables
- Explain the use of the **noclobber** variable
- Use an if structure to evaluate the status of a file
- Describe eight tcsh builtins

The TC Shell (tcsh) performs the same function as the Bourne Again Shell and other shells: It provides an interface between you and the Linux operating system. The TC Shell is an interactive command interpreter as well as a high-level programming language. Although you use only one shell at any given time, you should be able to switch back and forth comfortably between shells as the need arises. In fact, you might want to run different shells in different windows. Chapters 8 and 10 apply to tcsh as well as to bash, so they provide a good background for this chapter. This chapter explains tcsh features that are not found in bash and those that are implemented differently from their bash counterparts.

The TC Shell is an expanded version of the C Shell (csh), which originated on Berkeley UNIX. The "T" in TC Shell comes from the TENEX and TOPS-20 operating systems, which inspired command completion and other features in the TC Shell. A number of features not found in csh are present in tcsh, including file and username completion, command-line editing, and spelling correction. As with csh, you can customize tcsh to make it more tolerant of mistakes and easier to use. By setting the proper shell variables, you can have tcsh warn you when you appear to be accidentally logging out or overwriting a file. Many popular features of the original C Shell are now shared by bash and tcsh.

Assignment statement

Although some of the functionality of tcsh is present in bash, differences arise in the syntax of some commands. For example, the tcsh assignment statement has the following syntax:

set variable = value

Having SPACEs on either side of the equal sign, although illegal in bash, is allowed (but not mandatory) in tcsh. By convention shell variables in tcsh are generally named with lowercase letters, not uppercase (you can use either). If you reference an undeclared variable (one that has had no value assigned to it), tcsh generates an error message, whereas by default bash does not. Finally, the default tcsh prompt is a greater than sign (>), but it is frequently set to a single $ character followed by a SPACE. The examples in this chapter use a prompt of **tcsh $** to avoid confusion with the bash prompt.

Do not use tcsh as a programming language

tip

If you have used UNIX and are comfortable with the C or TC Shell, you might want to use tcsh as your login shell. However, you might find that the TC Shell is not as good a programming language as bash. If you are going to learn only one shell programming language, learn bash. The Bourne Again Shell and dash (page 287), which is a subset of bash, are used throughout Linux to program many system administration scripts.

SHELL SCRIPTS

The TC Shell can execute files containing tcsh commands, just as the Bourne Again Shell can execute files containing bash commands. Although the concepts of writing and executing scripts in the two shells are similar, the methods of declaring and assigning values to variables and the syntax of control structures are different.

You can run bash and tcsh scripts while using any one of the shells as a command interpreter. Various methods exist for selecting the shell that runs a script. Refer to "#! Specifies a Shell" on page 297 for more information.

If the first character of a shell script is a pound sign (#) and the following character is *not* an exclamation point (!), the TC Shell executes the script under tcsh. If the first character is anything other than #, tcsh calls the sh link to dash or bash to execute the script.

echo: getting rid of the RETURN

tip The tcsh echo builtin accepts either a **–n** option or a trailing **\c** to get rid of the RETURN that echo normally displays at the end of a line. The bash echo builtin accepts only the **–n** option (refer to "read: Accepts User Input" on page 489).

Shell game

tip When you are working with an interactive TC Shell, if you run a script in which **#** is *not* the first character of the script and you call the script *directly* (without preceding its name with tcsh), tcsh calls the sh link to dash or bash to run the script. The following script was written to be run under tcsh but, when called from a tcsh command line, is executed by bash. The set builtin (page 472) works differently under bash and tcsh. As a result the following example (from page 401) issues a prompt but does not wait for you to respond:

```
tcsh $ cat user_in
echo -n "Enter input: "
set input_line = "$<"
echo $input_line

tcsh $ user_in
Enter input:
```

Although in each case the examples are run from a tcsh command line, the following one calls tcsh explicitly so that tcsh executes the script and it runs correctly:

```
tcsh $ tcsh user_in
Enter input: here is some input
here is some input
```

Entering and Leaving the TC Shell

chsh You can execute tcsh by giving the command **tcsh**. If you are not sure which shell you are using, use the ps utility to find out. It shows whether you are running tcsh, bash, sh (linked to bash), or possibly another shell. The finger command followed by your username displays the name of your login shell, which is stored in the **/etc/passwd** file. (macOS uses Open Directory [page 1068] in place of this file.) If you want to use tcsh as a matter of course, you can use the chsh (change shell) utility to change your login shell:

```
bash $ chsh
Changing shell for sam.
Password:
New shell [/bin/bash]: /bin/tcsh
```

```
Shell changed.
bash $
```

The shell you specify will remain in effect for your next login and all subsequent logins until you specify a different login shell. The **/etc/passwd** file stores the name of your login shell.

You can leave tcsh in several ways. The approach you choose depends on two factors: whether the shell variable **ignoreeof** is set and whether you are using the shell that you logged in on (your login shell) or another shell that you created after you logged in. If you are not sure how to exit from tcsh, press CONTROL-D on a line by itself with no leading SPACEs, just as you would to terminate standard input to a program. You will either exit or receive instructions on how to exit. If you have not set **ignoreeof** (page 407) and it has not been set for you in a startup file, you can exit from any shell by using CONTROL-D (the same procedure you use to exit from the Bourne Again Shell).

When **ignoreeof** is set, CONTROL-D does not work. The **ignoreeof** variable causes the shell to display a message telling you how to exit. You can always exit from tcsh by giving an **exit** command. A **logout** command allows you to exit from your login shell only.

STARTUP FILES

When you log in on the TC Shell, it automatically executes various startup files. These files are normally executed in the order described in this section, but you can compile tcsh so that it uses a different order. You must have read access to a startup file to execute the commands in it. See page 288 for information on bash startup files and page 1076 for information on startup files under macOS.

/etc/csh.cshrc and /etc/csh.login The shell first executes the commands in **/etc/csh.cshrc** and **/etc/csh.login**. A user working with **root** privileges can set up these files to establish systemwide default characteristics for tcsh users. They contain systemwide configuration information, such as the default **path**, the location to check for mail, and so on.

.tcshrc and .cshrc Next, the shell looks for **~/.tcshrc** or, if it does not exist, **~/.cshrc** (**~/** is shorthand for your home directory; page 91). You can use these files to establish variables and parameters that are specific to your shell. Each time you create a new shell, tcsh reinitializes these variables for the new shell. The following **.tcshrc** file sets several shell variables; establishes two aliases (page 387); and adds two directories to **path**, one at the beginning of the list and one at the end:

```
tcsh $ cat ~/.tcshrc
set noclobber
set dunique
set ignoreeof
set history=256
set path = (~/bin $path /usr/games)
alias h history
alias ll ls -l
```

.history Login shells rebuild the history list from the contents of **~/.history**. If the **histfile** variable exists, tcsh uses the file that **histfile** points to in place of **.history**.

.login Login shells read and execute the commands in **~/.login**. This file contains commands that you want to execute once, at the beginning of each session. You can use setenv (page 396) to declare environment (global) variables here. You can also declare the type of terminal you are using and set some terminal characteristics in your **.login** file.

```
tcsh $ cat ~/.login
setenv history 200
setenv mail /var/spool/mail/$user
if ( -z $DISPLAY ) then
        setenv TERM vt100
    else
        setenv TERM xterm
endif
stty erase '^h' kill '^u' -lcase tab3
date '+Login on %A %B %d at %I:%M %p'
```

The preceding **.login** file establishes the type of terminal you are using by setting the **TERM** variable (the **if** statement [page 409] determines whether you are using a graphical interface and therefore which value should be assigned to **TERM**). It then runs stty (page 987) to set terminal characteristics and date (page 787) to display the time you logged in.

/etc/csh.logout and .logout The TC Shell runs the **/etc/csh.logout** and **~/.logout** files, in that order, when you exit from a login shell. The following sample **.logout** file uses date to display the time you logged out. The sleep command ensures that echo has time to display the message before the system logs you out. The delay might be useful for dial-up lines that take some time to display the message.

```
tcsh $ cat ~/.logout
date '+Logout on %A %B %d at %I:%M %p'
sleep 5
```

FEATURES COMMON TO THE BOURNE AGAIN AND TC SHELLS

Most of the features common to both bash and tcsh are derived from the original C Shell:

- Command-line expansion (also called substitution; next page)
- History (next page)
- Aliases (page 387)
- Job control (page 388)
- Filename substitution (page 388)
- Directory stack manipulation (page 389)
- Command substitution (page 389)

The chapters on bash discuss these features in detail. This section focuses on the differences between the bash and tcsh implementations.

COMMAND-LINE EXPANSION (SUBSTITUTION)

Refer to "Processing the Command Line" on page 364 for an introduction to command-line expansion in the Bourne Again Shell. The tcsh man page uses the term *substitution* instead of *expansion;* the latter is used by bash. The TC Shell scans each token on a command line for possible expansion in the following order:

1. History substitution (below)
2. Alias substitution (page 387)
3. Variable substitution (page 396)
4. Command substitution (page 389)
5. Filename substitution (page 388)
6. Directory stack substitution (page 389)

HISTORY

The TC Shell assigns a sequential *event number* to each command line. You can display this event number as part of the tcsh prompt (refer to "prompt" on page 403). Examples in this section show numbered prompts when they help illustrate the behavior of a command.

THE history BUILTIN

As in bash, the tcsh history builtin displays the events in your history list. The list of events is ordered with the oldest events at the top. The last event in the history list is the **history** command that displayed the list. In the following history list, which is limited to ten lines by the argument of **10** to the **history** command, command 23 modifies the tcsh prompt to display the history event number. The time each command was executed appears to the right of the event number.

```
32 $ history 10
    23  23:59   set prompt = "! $ "
    24  23:59   ls -l
    25  23:59   cat temp
    26  0:00    rm temp
    27  0:00    vim memo
    28  0:00    lpr memo
    29  0:00    vim memo
    30  0:00    lpr memo
    31  0:00    rm memo
    32  0:00    history
```

HISTORY EXPANSION

The same event and word designators work in both shells. For example, **!!** refers to the previous event in tcsh, just as it does in bash. The command **!328** executes event number 328; **!?txt?** executes the most recent event containing the string **txt**. For more information refer to "Using an Exclamation Point (!) to Reference Events" on page 341. Table 9-1 lists the few tcsh word modifiers not found in bash.

Table 9-1 Word modifiers

Modifier	Function
u	Converts the first lowercase letter into uppercase
l	Converts the first uppercase letter into lowercase
a	Applies the next modifier globally within a single word

You can use more than one word modifier in a command. For instance, the **a** modifier, when used in combination with the **u** or **l** modifier, enables you to change the case of an entire word.

```
tcsh $ echo $VERSION
VERSION: Undefined variable.
tcsh $ echo !!:1:al
echo $version
tcsh 6.17.00 (Astron) 2009-07-10 (i386-intel-linux) options wide,nls, ...
```

In addition to using event designators to access the history list, you can use the command-line editor to access, modify, and execute previous commands (page 393).

Variables

The variables you set to control the history list in tcsh are different from those used in bash. Whereas bash uses **HISTSIZE** and **HISTFILESIZE** to determine the number of events that are preserved during and between sessions, respectively, tcsh uses **history** and **savehist** (Table 9-2) for these purposes.

Table 9-2 History variables

Variable	Default	Function
history	100 events	Maximum number of events saved during a session
histfile	~/.history	Location of the history file
savehist	not set	Maximum number of events saved between sessions

history and **savehist** When you exit from a tcsh shell, the most recently executed commands are saved in your **~/.history** file. The next time you start the shell, this file initializes the history list. The value of the **savehist** variable determines the number of lines saved in the **.history** file (not necessarily the same as the **history** variable). If **savehist** is not set, tcsh does not save history information between sessions. The **history** and **savehist** variables must be shell variables (i.e., declared using set, not setenv). The **history** variable holds the number of events remembered during a session and the **savehist** variable holds the number remembered between sessions. See Table 9-2.

If you set the value of **history** too high, it can use too much memory. If it is unset or set to zero, the shell does not save any commands. To establish a history list of the

500 most recent events, give the following command manually or place it in your **~/.tcshrc** startup file:

```
tcsh $ set history = 500
```

The following command causes tcsh to save the 200 most recent events across login sessions:

```
tcsh $ set savehist = 200
```

You can combine these two assignments into a single command:

```
tcsh $ set history=500 savehist=200
```

After you set **savehist**, you can log out and log in again; the 200 most recent events from the previous login sessions will appear in your history list after you log back in. Set **savehist** in your **~/.tcshrc** file if you want to maintain your event list from login to login.

histlit If you set the variable **histlit** (history literal), history displays the commands in the history list exactly as they were typed in, without any shell interpretation. The following example shows the effect of this variable (compare the lines numbered 32):

```
tcsh $ cat /etc/csh.cshrc
...
tcsh $ cp !!:1 ~
cp /etc/csh.cshrc ~
tcsh $ set histlit
tcsh $ history
...
    31  9:35    cat /etc/csh.cshrc
    32  9:35    cp !!:1 ~
    33  9:35    set histlit
    34  9:35    history
tcsh $ unset histlit
tcsh $ history
...
    31  9:35    cat /etc/csh.cshrc
    32  9:35    cp /etc/csh.cshrc ~
    33  9:35    set histlit
    34  9:35    history
    35  9:35    unset histlit
    36  9:36    history
```

optional The bash and tcsh Shells expand history event designators differently. If you give the command **!250w**, bash replaces it with command number 250 with a **w** character appended to it. In contrast, tcsh looks back through your history list for an event that begins with the string **250w** to execute. The reason for the difference: bash interprets the first three characters of **250w** as the number of a command, whereas tcsh interprets those characters as part of the search string **250w**. (If the 250 stands alone, tcsh treats it as a command number.)

If you want to append **w** to command number 250, you can insulate the event number from the **w** by surrounding it with braces:

```
!{250}w
```

ALIASES

The alias/unalias feature in tcsh closely resembles its counterpart in bash (page 352). However, the alias builtin has a slightly different syntax:

alias ***name value***

The following command creates an alias for **ls**:

```
tcsh $ alias ls "ls -lF"
```

The tcsh alias allows you to substitute command-line arguments, whereas bash does not:

```
tcsh $ alias nam "echo Hello, \!^ is my name"
tcsh $ nam Sam
Hello, Sam is my name
```

The string **\!*** within an alias expands to all command-line arguments:

```
tcsh $ alias sortprint "sort \!* | lpr"
```

The next alias displays its second argument:

```
tcsh $ alias n2 "echo \!:2"
```

To display a list of current aliases, give the command **alias**. To display the alias for a particular name, give the command **alias** followed by that name.

SPECIAL ALIASES

Some alias names, called *special aliases,* have special meaning to tcsh. If you define an alias that uses one of these names, tcsh executes it automatically as explained in Table 9-3. Initially, all special aliases are undefined. The following command sets the **cwdcmd** alias so it displays the name of the working directory when you change to a new working directory. The single quotation marks are critical in this example; see page 353.

```
tcsh $ alias cwdcmd 'echo Working directory is now `pwd`'
tcsh $ cd /etc
Working directory is now /etc
tcsh $
```

Table 9-3 Special aliases

Alias	When executed
beepcmd	Whenever the shell would normally ring the terminal bell. Gives you a way to have other visual or audio effects take place at those times.
cwdcmd	Whenever you change to another working directory.
periodic	Periodically, as determined by the number of minutes in the **tperiod** variable. If **tperiod** is unset or has the value 0, **periodic** has no meaning.

Table 9-3 Special aliases (continued)

Alias	When executed
precmd	Just before the shell displays a prompt.
shell	Specifies the absolute pathname of the shell that will run scripts that do not start with **#!** (page 297).

HISTORY SUBSTITUTION IN ALIASES

You can substitute command-line arguments by using the history mechanism, where a single exclamation point represents the command line containing the alias. Modifiers are the same as those used by history (page 341). In the following example, the exclamation points are quoted so the shell does not interpret them when building the aliases:

```
21 $ alias last echo \!:$
22 $ last this is just a test
test
23 $ alias fn2 echo \!:2:t
24 $ fn2 /home/sam/test /home/zach/temp /home/barbara/new
temp
```

Event 21 defines for **last** an alias that displays the last argument. Event 23 defines for **fn2** an alias that displays the simple filename, or tail, of the second argument on the command line.

JOB CONTROL

Job control is similar in both bash (page 304) and tcsh. You can move commands between the foreground and the background, suspend jobs temporarily, and display a list of current jobs. The % character references a job when it is followed by a job number or a string prefix that uniquely identifies the job. You will see a minor difference when you run a multiple-process command line in the background from each shell. Whereas bash displays only the PID number of the last background process in each job, tcsh displays the numbers for all processes belonging to a job. The example from page 304 looks like this under tcsh:

```
tcsh $ find . -print | sort | lpr & grep -l max /tmp/* > maxfiles &
[1] 18839  18840  18841
[2] 18876
```

FILENAME SUBSTITUTION

The TC Shell expands the characters *, ?, and [] in a pathname just as bash does (page 152). The * matches any string of zero or more characters, ? matches any single character, and [ ] defines a character class that matches single characters appearing between the brackets.

The TC Shell expands command-line arguments that start with a tilde (~) into filenames in much the same way that bash does (page 391), with the ~ standing for the user's home directory or the home directory of the user whose name follows the tilde. The bash special expansions ~+ and ~– are not available in tcsh.

Brace expansion (page 366) is available in tcsh. Like tilde expansion, it is regarded as an aspect of filename substitution even though brace expansion can generate strings that are not the names of existing files.

globbing In tcsh and its predecessor csh, the process of using patterns to match filenames is referred to as *globbing* and the pattern itself is called a *globbing pattern*. If tcsh is unable to identify one or more files that match a globbing pattern, it reports an error (unless the pattern contains a brace). Setting the shell variable **noglob** suppresses filename substitution, including both tilde and brace interpretation.

Manipulating the Directory Stack

Directory stack manipulation in tcsh does not differ much from that in bash (page 307). The dirs builtin displays the contents of the stack, and the pushd and popd builtins push directories onto and pop directories off of the stack.

Command Substitution

The $(...) syntax for command substitution is *not* available in tcsh. In its place you must use the original '...' syntax. Otherwise, the implementation in bash and tcsh is identical. Refer to page 371 for more information on command substitution.

Redirecting Standard Error

Both bash and tcsh use a greater than symbol (>) to redirect standard output, but tcsh does *not* use the bash notation 2> to redirect standard error. Under tcsh you use a greater than symbol followed by an ampersand (>&) to combine and redirect standard output and standard error. Although you can use this notation under bash, few people do. The following examples, like the bash examples on page 292, reference file x, which does not exist, and file y, which contains a single line:

```
tcsh $ cat x
cat: x: No such file or directory
tcsh $ cat y
This is y.
tcsh $ cat x y >& hold
tcsh $ cat hold
cat: x: No such file or directory
This is y.
```

With an argument of **y** in the preceding example, cat sends a string to standard output. An argument of **x** causes cat to send an error message to standard error.

Unlike bash, tcsh does not provide a simple way to redirect standard error separately from standard output. A work-around frequently provides a reasonable solution. The following example runs cat with arguments of **x** and **y** in a subshell (the parentheses ensure that the command within them runs in a subshell; page 302). Also within the subshell, a **>** redirects standard output to the file **outfile**. Output sent to standard error is not touched by the subshell but rather is sent to the parent shell, where both it and standard output are sent to **errfile**. Because standard output has already been redirected, **errfile** contains only output sent to standard error.

```
tcsh $ (cat x y > outfile) >& errfile
tcsh $ cat outfile
This is y.
tcsh $ cat errfile
cat: x: No such file or directory
```

It can be useful to combine and redirect output when you want to execute a command that runs slowly in the background and do not want its output cluttering up the screen. For example, because the find utility (page 822) can take a long time to complete, it might be a good idea to run it in the background. The next command finds in the filesystem hierarchy all files that contain the string **biblio** in their name. This command runs in the background and sends its output to the **findout** file. Because the find utility sends to standard error a report of directories that you do not have permission to search, the **findout** file contains a record of any files that are found as well as a record of the directories that could not be searched.

```
tcsh $ find / -name "*biblio*" -print >& findout &
```

In this example, if you did not combine standard error with standard output and redirected only standard output, the error messages would appear on the screen and **findout** would list only files that were found.

While a command that has its output redirected to a file is running in the background, you can look at the output by using tail (page 992) with the **–f** option. The **–f** option causes tail to display new lines as they are written to the file:

```
tcsh $ tail -f findout
```

To terminate the tail command, press the interrupt key (usually CONTROL-C).

WORKING WITH THE COMMAND LINE

This section covers word completion, editing the command line, and correcting spelling.

WORD COMPLETION

The TC Shell completes filenames, commands, and variable names on the command line when you prompt it to do so. The generic term used to refer to all these features under tcsh is *word completion.*

FILENAME COMPLETION

The TC Shell can complete a filename after you specify a unique prefix. Filename completion is similar to filename generation, but the goal of filename completion is to select a single file. Together these capabilities make it practical to use long, descriptive filenames.

To use filename completion when you are entering a filename on the command line, type enough of the name to identify the file uniquely and press TAB; tcsh fills in the name and adds a SPACE, leaving the cursor so you can enter additional arguments or press RETURN. In the following example, the user types the command **cat trig1A** and presses TAB; the system fills in the rest of the filename that begins with **trig1A**:

```
tcsh $ cat trig1A ⇨ TAB ⇨ cat trig1A.302488 ■
```

If two or more filenames match the prefix that you have typed, tcsh cannot complete the filename without obtaining more information. The shell maximizes the length of the prefix by adding characters, if possible, and then beeps to signify that additional input is needed to resolve the ambiguity:

```
tcsh $ ls h*
help.hist  help.trig01  help.txt
tcsh $ cat h ⇨ TAB ⇨ cat help. (beep)
```

You can fill in enough characters to resolve the ambiguity and then press the TAB key again. Alternatively, you can press CONTROL-D to cause tcsh to display a list of matching filenames:

```
tcsh $ cat help. ⇨ CONTROL-D
help.hist    help.trig01  help.txt
tcsh $ cat help.■
```

After displaying the filenames, tcsh redraws the command line so you can disambiguate the filename (and press TAB again) or finish typing the filename manually.

TILDE COMPLETION

The TC Shell parses a tilde (~) appearing as the first character of a word and attempts to expand it to a username when you enter a TAB:

```
tcsh $ cd ~za ⇨ TAB ⇨ cd ~zach/■ ⇨ RETURN
tcsh $ pwd
/home/zach
```

By appending a slash (/), tcsh indicates that the completed word is a directory. The slash also makes it easy to continue specifying a pathname.

COMMAND AND VARIABLE COMPLETION

You can use the same mechanism you use to list and complete filenames with command and variable names. When you specify a simple filename, the shell uses the variable **path** to attempt to complete a command name. The choices tcsh lists might be located in different directories.

```
tcsh $ up ⇨ TAB (beep) ⇨ CONTROL-D
up2date                 updatedb                uptime
up2date-config          update-mime-database
up2date-nox             updmap
tcsh $ up ⇨ t ⇨ TAB ⇨ uptime ■ ⇨ RETURN
9:59am up 31 days, 15:11, 7 users, load average: 0.03, 0.02, 0.00
```

If you set the **autolist** variable as in the following example, the shell lists choices automatically when you invoke completion by pressing TAB. You do not have to press CONTROL-D.

```
tcsh $ set autolist
tcsh $ up ⇨ TAB (beep)
up2date                 updatedb                uptime
up2date-config          update-mime-database
up2date-nox             updmap
tcsh $ up ⇨ t ⇨ TAB ⇨ uptime ■ ⇨ RETURN
10:01am up 31 days, 15:14, 7 users, load average: 0.20, 0.06, 0.02
```

If you set **autolist** to **ambiguous**, the shell lists the choices when you press TAB *only* if the word you enter is the longest prefix of a set of commands. Otherwise, pressing TAB causes the shell to add one or more characters to the word until it is the longest prefix; pressing TAB again then lists the choices:

```
tcsh $ set autolist=ambiguous
tcsh $ echo $h ⇨ TAB (beep)
histfile history home
tcsh $ echo $h■ ⇨ i ⇨ TAB ⇨ echo $hist■ ⇨ TAB
histfile history
tcsh $ echo $hist■ ⇨ o ⇨ TAB ⇨ echo $history ■ ⇨ RETURN
1000
```

The shell must rely on the context of the word within the input line to determine whether it is a filename, a username, a command, or a variable name. The first word on an input line is assumed to be a command name; if a word begins with the special character $, it is viewed as a variable name; and so on. In the following example, the second which command does not work properly: The context of the word **up** makes it look like the beginning of a filename rather than the beginning of a command. The TC Shell supplies which with an argument of **updates** (a nonexecutable file) and which displays an error message:

```
tcsh $ ls up*
updates
tcsh $ which updatedb ups uptime
/usr/bin/updatedb
/usr/local/bin/ups
/usr/bin/uptime

tcsh $ which up ⇨ TAB ⇨ which updates
updates: Command not found.
```

EDITING THE COMMAND LINE

bindkey The tcsh command-line editing feature is similar to that available under bash. You can use either emacs mode commands (default) or vi(m) mode commands. Change to vi(m) mode commands by giving the command **bindkey –v** and to emacs mode commands by giving the command **bindkey –e**. The ARROW keys are bound to the obvious motion commands in both modes, so you can move back and forth (up and down) through the history list as well as left and right on the current command line.

Without an argument, the bindkey builtin displays the current mappings between editor commands and the key sequences you can enter at the keyboard:

```
tcsh $ bindkey
Standard key bindings
"^@"            ->  set-mark-command
"^A"            ->  beginning-of-line
"^B"            ->  backward-char
"^C"            ->  tty-sigintr
"^D"            ->  delete-char-or-list-or-eof
...
Multi-character bindings
"^[[A"          -> up-history
"^[[B"          -> down-history
"^[[C"          -> forward-char
"^[[D"          -> backward-char
"^[[H"          -> beginning-of-line
...
Arrow key bindings
down            -> down-history
up              -> up-history
left            -> backward-char
right           -> forward-char
home            -> beginning-of-line
end             -> end-of-line
```

The ^ indicates a CONTROL character (**^B** = CONTROL-B). The **^[** indicates a META or ALT character; in this case you press and hold the META or ALT key while you press the key for the next character. If this substitution does not work or if the keyboard you are using does not have a META or ALT key, press and release the ESCAPE key and then press the key for the next character. For **^[[F** you would press META-[or ALT-[followed by the **F** key or else ESCAPE [**F**. The **down/up/left/right** indicate ARROW keys, and **home/end** indicate the HOME and END keys on the numeric keypad. See page 231 for more information on the META key.

Under macOS, most keyboards do not have a META or ALT key. See page 1076 for an explanation of how to set up the OPTION key to perform the same functions as the META key on a Macintosh.

The preceding example shows the output from bindkey with the user in emacs mode. Change to vi(m) mode (**bindkey –v**) and give another bindkey command to display the vi(m) key bindings. You can send the output of bindkey through a pipeline to less to make it easier to read.

CORRECTING SPELLING

You can have tcsh attempt to correct the spelling of command names, filenames, and variables (but only using emacs-style key bindings). Spelling correction can take place before and after you press RETURN.

BEFORE YOU PRESS RETURN

For tcsh to correct a word or line before you press RETURN, you must indicate that you want it to do so. The two functions for this purpose are **spell-line** and **spell-word**:

```
$ bindkey | grep spell
"^[$"          -> spell-line
"^[S"          -> spell-word
"^[s"          -> spell-word
```

The output from bindkey shows that **spell-line** is bound to META-$ (ALT-$ or ESCAPE $) and **spell-word** is bound to META-S and META-s (ALT-s or ESCAPE s and ALT-S or ESCAPE S). To correct the spelling of the word to the left of the cursor, press META-s. Pressing META-$ invokes the **spell-line** function, which attempts to correct all words on a command line:

```
tcsh $ ls
bigfile.gz
tcsh $ gunzipp ⇨ META-s ⇨ gunzip bigfele.gz ⇨ META-s ⇨ gunzip bigfile.gz
tcsh $ gunzip bigfele.gz ⇨ META-$ ⇨ gunzip bigfile.gz
tcsh $ ecno $usfr ⇨ META-$ ⇨ echo $user
```

AFTER YOU PRESS RETURN

The variable named **correct** controls what tcsh attempts to correct or complete *after* you press RETURN and before it passes the command line to the command being called. If you do not set **correct**, tcsh will not correct anything:

```
tcsh $ unset correct
tcsh $ ls morning
morning
tcsh $ ecno $usfr morbing
usfr: Undefined variable.
```

The shell reports the error in the variable name and not the command name because it expands variables before it executes the command (page 384). When you give a bad command name without any arguments, the shell reports on the bad command name.

Set **correct** to **cmd** to correct only commands; to **all** to correct commands, variables, and filenames; or to **complete** to complete commands:

```
tcsh $ set correct = cmd
tcsh $ ecno $usfr morbing

CORRECT>echo $usfr morbing (y|n|e|a)? y
usfr: Undefined variable.
tcsh $ set correct = all
tcsh $ echo $usfr morbing

CORRECT>echo $user morning (y|n|e|a)? y
zach morning
```

With **correct** set to **cmd**, tcsh corrects the command name from **ecno** to **echo**. With **correct** set to **all**, tcsh corrects both the command name and the variable. It would also correct a filename if one was present on the command line.

The TC Shell displays a special prompt that lets you enter **y** to accept the modified command line, **n** to reject it, **e** to edit it, or **a** to abort the command. Refer to **prompt3** on page 405 for a discussion of the special prompt used in spelling correction.

In the next example, after setting the **correct** variable the user mistypes the name of the ls command; tcsh then prompts for a correct command name. Because the command that tcsh has offered as a replacement is not ls, the user chooses to edit the command line. The shell leaves the cursor following the command so the user can correct the mistake:

```
tcsh $ set correct=cmd
tcsh $ lx -l ⇨ RETURN (beep)
CORRECT>lex -l (y|n|e|a)? e
tcsh $ lx -l■
```

If you assign the value **complete** to the variable **correct**, tcsh attempts command name completion in the same manner as filename completion (page 391). In the following example, after setting **correct** to **complete** the user enters the command **up**. The shell responds with **Ambiguous command** because several commands start with these two letters but differ in the third letter. The shell then redisplays the command line. The user could press TAB at this point to get a list of commands that start with **up** but decides to enter **t** and press RETURN. The shell completes the command because these three letters uniquely identify the uptime utility:

```
tcsh $ set correct = complete
tcsh $ upRETURN
Ambiguous command
tcsh $ up ⇨ tRETURN ⇨ uptime
4:45pm  up 5 days,  9:54,  5 users,  load average: 1.62, 0.83, 0.33
```

VARIABLES

Although tcsh stores variable values as strings, you can work with these variables as numbers. Expressions in tcsh can use arithmetic, logical, and conditional operators. The @ builtin can evaluate integer arithmetic expressions.

This section uses the term *numeric variable* to describe a string variable that contains a number that tcsh uses in arithmetic or logical arithmetic computations. However, no true numeric variables exist in tcsh.

Variable name A tcsh variable name consists of 1 to 20 characters, which can be letters, digits, and underscores (_). The first character cannot be a digit but can be an underscore.

VARIABLE SUBSTITUTION

Three builtins declare, display, and assign values to variables: set, @, and setenv. The set and setenv builtins both assume nonnumeric string variables. The @ builtin works only with numeric variables. Both set and @ declare shell (local) variables. The setenv builtin declares an environment (global) variable. Using setenv is similar to assigning a value to a variable and then using export in the Bourne Again Shell. See "Environment, Environment Variables, and Inheritance" on page 480 for a discussion of shell and environment variables.

Once the value—or merely the existence—of a variable has been established, tcsh substitutes the value of that variable when the name of the variable, preceded by a dollar sign ($), appears on a command line. If you quote the dollar sign by preceding it with a backslash or enclosing it within single quotation marks, the shell does not perform the substitution. When a variable is within double quotation marks, the substitution occurs even if you quote the dollar sign by preceding it with a backslash.

STRING VARIABLES

The TC Shell treats string variables similarly to the way the Bourne Again Shell does. The major difference lies in their declaration and assignment: tcsh uses an explicit command, set (or setenv), to declare and/or assign a value to a string variable.

```
tcsh $ set name = fred
tcsh $ echo $name
fred
tcsh $ set
argv    ()
```

```
cwd      /home/zach
home     /home/zach
name     fred
path     (/usr/local/bin /bin /usr/bin /usr/X11R6/bin)
prompt   $
shell    /bin/tcsh
status   0
term     vt100
user     zach
```

The first line in the example declares the variable **name** and assigns the string **fred** to it. Unlike bash, tcsh allows—but does not require—SPACEs around the equal sign. The next line displays the value of **name**. When you give a set command without any arguments, it displays a list of all shell (not environment) variables and their values. When you give a set command with the name of a variable and no value, the command sets the value of the variable to the null string.

You can use the unset builtin to remove a variable:

```
tcsh $ set name
tcsh $ echo $name

tcsh $ unset name
tcsh $ echo $name
name: Undefined variable.
```

setenv The setenv builtin declares an environment variable. When using setenv you must separate the variable name from the string being assigned to it by inserting one or more SPACEs and omitting the equal sign. In the following example, the **tcsh** command creates a subshell, echo shows that the variable and its value are known to the subshell, and **exit** returns to the original shell. Try this example, using set in place of setenv:

```
tcsh $ setenv SRCDIR /usr/local/src
tcsh $ tcsh
tcsh $ echo $SRCDIR
/usr/local/src
tcsh $ exit
```

Without arguments, setenv displays a list of the environment (global) variables—variables that are passed to the shell's child processes. By convention, environment variables are named using uppercase letters.

As with set, giving setenv a variable name without a value sets the value of the variable to a null string. Although you can use unset to remove environment and local variables, unsetenv can remove environment variables only.

ARRAYS OF STRING VARIABLES

An *array* is a collection of strings, each of which is identified by its index (1, 2, 3, and so on). Arrays in tcsh use one-based indexing (i.e., the first element of the array has the subscript 1). Before you can access individual elements of an array, you must declare the entire array by assigning a value to each element of the array. The list of values must be enclosed in parentheses and separated by SPACEs:

```
8 $ set colors = (red green blue orange yellow)
9 $ echo $colors
red green blue orange yellow
10 $ echo $colors[3]
blue
11 $ echo $colors[2-4]
green blue orange
12 $ set shapes = ('' '' '' '' '')
13 $ echo $shapes

14 $ set shapes[4] = square
15 $ echo $shapes[4]
square
```

Event 8 declares the array of string variables named **colors** to have five elements and assigns values to each of them. If you do not know the values of the elements at the time you declare an array, you can declare an array containing the necessary number of null elements (event 12).

You can reference an entire array by preceding its name with a dollar sign (event 9). A number in brackets following a reference to the array refers to an element of the array (events 10, 14, and 15). Two numbers in brackets, separated by a hyphen, refer to two or more adjacent elements of the array (event 11). Refer to "Special Variable Forms" on page 401 for more information on arrays.

NUMERIC VARIABLES

The @ builtin assigns the result of a numeric calculation to a numeric variable (as described under "Variables" on page 396, tcsh has no true numeric variables). You can declare single numeric variables using @, just as you can use **set** to declare nonnumeric variables. However, if you give it a nonnumeric argument, @ displays an error message. Just as **set** does, the @ command used without any arguments lists all shell variables.

Many of the expressions that the @ builtin can evaluate and the operators it recognizes are derived from the C programming language. The following syntax shows a declaration or assignment using @ (the SPACE after the @ is required):

@ *variable-name operator expression*

The ***variable-name*** is the name of the variable you are assigning a value to. The ***operator*** is one of the C assignment operators: =, +=, −=, *=, /=, or %=. (See Table 14-4 on page 641 for a description of these operators.) The ***expression*** is an arithmetic expression that can include most C operators (see the next section). You can use parentheses within the expression for clarity or to change the order of evaluation.

Parentheses must surround parts of the expression that contain any of the following characters: <, >, &, or |.

Do not use $ when assigning a value to a variable

tip As with bash, variables having a value assigned to them (those on the left of the operator) must not be preceded by a dollar sign (**$**) in tcsh. Thus,

```
tcsh $ @ $answer = 5 + 5
```

will yield

```
answer: Undefined variable.
```

or, if **answer** is defined,

```
@: Variable name must begin with a letter.
```

whereas

```
tcsh $ @ answer = 5 + 5
```

assigns the value 10 to the variable **answer**.

EXPRESSIONS

An expression can be composed of constants, variables, and most of the bash operators (page 508). Expressions that involve files rather than numeric variables or strings are described in Table 9-8 on page 409.

Expressions follow these rules:

1. The shell evaluates a missing or null argument as 0.
2. All results are decimal numbers.
3. Except for != and ==, the operators act on numeric arguments.
4. You must separate each element of an expression from adjacent elements by a SPACE, unless the adjacent element is &, |, <, >, (, or).

Following are some examples that use @:

```
216 $ @ count = 0
217 $ echo $count
0
218 $ @ count = ( 10 + 4 ) / 2
219 $ echo $count
7
220 $ @ result = ( $count < 5 )
221 $ echo $result
0
222 $ @ count += 5
223 $ echo $count
12
224 $ @ count++
225 $ echo $count
13
```

Event 216 declares the variable **count** and assigns it a value of 0. Event 218 shows the result of an arithmetic operation being assigned to a variable. Event 220 uses the @ symbol to assign the result of a logical operation involving a constant and a variable to **result**. The value of the operation is *false* (= 0) because the variable **count** is not less than 5. Event 222 is a compressed form of the following assignment statement:

```
tcsh $ @ count = $count + 5
```

Event 224 uses a postfix operator to increment **count** by 1.

Postincrement and postdecrement operators

You can use the postincrement (++) and postdecrement (––) operators only in expressions containing a single variable name, as shown in the following example:

```
tcsh $ @ count = 0
tcsh $ @ count++
tcsh $ echo $count
1
tcsh $ @ next = $count++
@: Badly formed number.
```

Unlike in the C programming language and bash, expressions in tcsh cannot use preincrement and predecrement operators.

ARRAYS OF NUMERIC VARIABLES

You must use the set builtin to declare an array of numeric variables before you can use @ to assign values to the elements of that array. The set builtin can assign any values to the elements of a numeric array, including zeros, other numbers, and null strings.

Assigning a value to an element of a numeric array is similar to assigning a value to a simple numeric variable. The only difference is that you must specify the element, or index, of the array. The syntax is

@ *variable-name[index] operator expression*

The ***index*** specifies the element of the array that is being addressed. The first element has an index of 1. The ***index*** cannot be an expression but rather must be either a numeric constant or a variable. In the preceding syntax the brackets around ***index*** are part of the syntax and do not indicate that ***index*** is optional. If you specify an ***index*** that is too large for the array you declared with set, tcsh displays **@: Subscript out of range.**

```
226 $ set ages = (0 0 0 0 0)
227 $ @ ages[2] = 15
228 $ @ ages[3] = ($ages[2] + 4)
229 $ echo $ages[3]
19
230 $ echo $ages
0 15 19 0 0
231 $ set index = 3
232 $ echo $ages[$index]
```

```
19
233 $ echo $ages[6]
ages: Subscript out of range.
```

Elements of a numeric array behave as though they were simple numeric variables. Event 226 declares an array with five elements, each having a value of 0. Events 227 and 228 assign values to elements of the array, and event 229 displays the value of one of the elements. Event 230 displays all the elements of the array, event 232 specifies an element by using a variable, and event 233 demonstrates the out-of-range error message.

BRACES

Like bash, tcsh allows you to use braces to distinguish a variable from the surrounding text without the use of a separator:

```
$ set bb=abc
$ echo $bbdef
bbdef: Undefined variable.
$ echo ${bb}def
abcdef
```

SPECIAL VARIABLE FORMS

The special variable with the following syntax has the value of the number of elements in the ***variable-name*** array:

$#variable-name

You can determine whether ***variable-name*** has been set by looking at the value of the variable with the following syntax:

$?variable-name

This variable has a value of 1 if ***variable-name*** is set and 0 otherwise:

```
tcsh $ set days = (mon tues wed thurs fri)
tcsh $ echo $#days
5
tcsh $ echo $?days
1
tcsh $ unset days
tcsh $ echo $?days
0
```

READING USER INPUT

Within a tcsh shell script, you can use the set builtin to read a line from the terminal and assign it to a variable. The following portion of a shell script prompts the user and reads a line of input into the variable **input_line**:

```
echo -n "Enter input: "
set input_line = "$<"
```

The value of the shell variable **$<** is a line from standard input. The quotation marks around **$<** keep the shell from assigning only the first word of the line of input to the variable **input_line**.

tcsh VARIABLES

TC Shell variables can be set by the shell, inherited by the shell from its parent, or set by the user and used by the shell. Some variables take on significant values (for example, the PID number of a background process). Other variables act as switches: *on* if they are declared and *off* if they are not. Many of the shell variables are often set from a startup file (page 382).

tcsh VARIABLES THAT TAKE ON VALUES

argv Contains the command-line arguments (positional parameters) from the command line that invoked the shell. Like all tcsh arrays, this array uses one-based indexing; **argv[1]** contains the first command-line argument. You can abbreviate references to **$argv[*n*]** as **$*n***. The token **argv[*]** references all the arguments together; you can abbreviate it as **$***. Use **$0** to reference the name of the calling program. Refer to "Positional Parameters" on page 470. The Bourne Again Shell does not use the **argv** form, only the abbreviated form. You cannot assign values to the elements of **argv**.

$#argv *or* **$#** Holds the number of elements in the **argv** array. Refer to "Special Variable Forms" on page 401.

autolist Controls command and variable completion (page 392).

autologout Enables tcsh's automatic logout facility, which logs you out if you leave the shell idle for too long. The value of the variable is the number of minutes of inactivity that tcsh waits before logging you out. The default is 60 minutes except when you are running in a graphical environment, in which case this variable is initially unset.

cdpath Affects the operation of cd in the same way as the **CDPATH** variable does in bash (page 323). The **cdpath** variable is assigned an array of absolute pathnames (see **path**, later in this section) and is usually set in the **~/.login** file with a line such as the following:

```
set cdpath = (/home/zach /home/zach/letters)
```

When you call cd with a simple filename, it searches the working directory for a subdirectory with that name. If one is not found, cd searches the directories listed in **cdpath** for the subdirectory.

correct Set to **cmd** for automatic spelling correction of command names, to **all** to correct the entire command line, and to **complete** for automatic completion of command names. This variable works on corrections that are made after you press RETURN. Refer to "After You Press RETURN" on page 394.

cwd The shell sets this variable to the name of the working directory. When you access a directory through a symbolic link (page 115), tcsh sets **cwd** to the name of the symbolic link.

dirstack The shell keeps the stack of directories used with the pushd, popd, and dirs builtins in this variable. For more information refer to "Manipulating the Directory Stack" on page 307.

fignore Holds an array of suffixes that tcsh ignores during filename completion.

gid The shell sets this variable to your group ID.

histfile Holds the full pathname of the file that saves the history list between login sessions (page 385). The defaults is **~/.history**.

history Specifies the size of the history list. Refer to "History" on page 384.

home *or* **HOME** Holds the pathname of the user's home directory. The cd builtin refers to this variable, as does the filename substitution of ~ (page 368).

mail Specifies files and directories, separated by whitespace, to check for mail. The TC Shell checks for new mail every 10 minutes unless the first word of **mail** is a number, in which case that number specifies how often the shell should check in seconds.

owd The shell keeps the name of your previous (old) working directory in this variable, which is equivalent to ~– in bash.

path *or* **PATH** Holds a list of directories that tcsh searches for executable commands (page 318). If this array is empty or unset, you can execute commands only by giving their pathnames. You can set **path** with a command such as the following:

```
tcsh $ set path = ( /usr/bin /bin /usr/local/bin /usr/bin/X11 ~/bin . )
```

prompt Holds the primary prompt, similar to the bash **PS1** variable (page 319). If it is not set, the prompt is **>**, or **#** when you are working with **root** privileges. The shell expands an exclamation point in the prompt string to the current event number. The following is a typical line from a **.tcshrc** file that sets the value of **prompt**:

```
set prompt = '! $ '
```

Table 9-4 lists some of the formatting sequences you can use in **prompt** to achieve special effects.

Table 9-4 **prompt** formatting sequences

Sequence	Displays in prompt
%/	Value of **cwd** (the working directory)
%~	Same as **%/**, but replaces the path of the user's home directory with a tilde
%! *or* **%h** *or* **!**	Current event number
%d	Day of the week

Table 9-4 **prompt** formatting sequences (continued)

Sequence	Displays in prompt
%D	Day of the month
%m	Hostname without the domain
%M	Full hostname, including the domain
%n	User's username
%t	Time of day through the current minute
%p	Time of day through the current second
%W	Month as **mm**
%y	Year as **yy**
%Y	Year as **yyyy**
%#	A pound sign (**#**) if the user is running with **root** privileges; otherwise, a greater than sign (**>**)
%?	Exit status of the preceding command

prompt2 Holds the secondary prompt, which tcsh uses to indicate it is waiting for additional input. The default value is **%R?**. The TC Shell replaces **%R** with nothing when it is waiting for you to continue an unfinished command, the word **foreach** while iterating through a **foreach** structure (page 414), and the word **while** while iterating through a **while** structure (page 416).

When you press RETURN in the middle of a quoted string on a command line without ending the line with a backslash, tcsh displays an error message regardless of whether you use single or double quotation marks:

```
% echo "Please enter the three values
Unmatched ".
```

In the next example, the first RETURN is quoted (escaped); the shell interprets it literally. Under tcsh, single and double quotation marks produce the same result. The secondary prompt is a question mark (**?**).

```
% echo "Please enter the three values \
? required to complete the transaction."
Please enter the three values
> required to complete the transaction.
```

prompt3 Holds the prompt used during automatic spelling correction. The default value is **CORRECT>%R** (y|n|e|a)?, where **R** is replaced by the corrected string.

savehist Specifies the number of commands saved from the history list when you log out. These events are saved in a file named **~/.history**. The shell uses these events as the initial history list when you log in again, causing your history list to persist across login sessions (page 385).

shell Holds the pathname of the shell you are using.

shlvl Holds the level of the shell. The TC Shell increments this variable each time you start a subshell and decrements it each time you exit a subshell. The TC Shell sets the value to 1 for a login shell.

status Holds the exit status returned by the last command. Similar to $? in bash (page 477).

tcsh Holds the version number of tcsh you are running.

time Provides two functions: automatic timing of commands using the time builtin and the format used by time. You can set this variable to either a single numeric value or an array holding a numeric value and a string. The numeric value is used to control automatic timing; any command that takes more than that number of CPU seconds to run has time display the command statistics when it finishes execution. When set to a value of 0 this results in statistics being displayed after every command. The string controls the formatting of the statistics using formatting sequences, including those listed in Table 9-5.

Table 9-5 time formatting sequences

Sequence	Displays
%U	Time the command spent running user code, in CPU seconds (user mode)
%S	Time the command spent running system code, in CPU seconds (kernel mode)
%E	Wall clock time (total elapsed) taken by the command
%P	Percentage of time the CPU spent on this task during this period, computed as (%U+%S)/%E
%W	Number of times the command's processes were swapped out to disk
%X	Average amount of shared code memory used by the command, in kilobytes
%D	Average amount of data memory used by the command, in kilobytes
%K	Total memory used by the command (as %X+%D), in kilobytes
%M	Maximum amount of memory used by the command, in kilobytes

Table 9-5 time formatting sequences (continued)

Sequence	Displays
%F	Number of major page faults (pages of memory that had to be read from disk)
%I	Number of input operations
%O	Number of output operations

By default the time builtin uses the string

```
"%Uu %Ss %E %P%  %X+%Dk %I+%Oio %Fpf+%Ww"
```

which generates output in the following format:

```
tcsh $ time
0.200u 0.340s 17:32:33.27 0.0%      0+0k 0+0io 1165pf+0w
```

You might want to time commands to check system performance. If commands consistently show many page faults and swaps, the system probably does not have enough memory; you should consider adding more. You can use the information that time reports to compare the performance of various system configurations and program algorithms.

tperiod Controls how often, in minutes, the shell executes the special **periodic** alias (page 387).

user The shell sets this variable to your username.

version The shell sets this variable to contain detailed information about the version of tcsh the system is running.

watch Set to an array of user and terminal pairs to watch for logins and logouts. The word **any** means any user or any terminal, so (**any any**) monitors all logins and logouts on all terminals, whereas (**zach ttyS1 any console $user any**) watches for **zach** on **ttyS1**, any user who accesses the system console, and any logins and logouts that use your account (presumably to catch intruders). By default logins and logouts are checked once every 10 minutes, but you can change this value by beginning the array with a numeric value giving the number of minutes between checks. If you set **watch** to (**1 any console**), logins and logouts by any user on the console will be checked once per minute. Reports are displayed just before a new shell prompt is issued. Also, the log builtin forces an immediate check whenever it is executed. See **who** (next) for information about how you can control the format of the **watch** messages.

who Controls the format of the information displayed in **watch** messages (Table 9-6).

Table 9-6 **who** formatting sequence

Sequence	Displays
%n	Username
%a	Action taken by the user
%l	Terminal on which the action took place

Table 9-6 **who** formatting sequence (continued)

Sequence	Displays
%M	Full hostname of remote host (or **local** if none) from which the action took place
$m	Hostname without domain name

The default string used for watch messages when **who** is unset is **"%n has %a %l from %m"**, which generates the following line:

```
sam has logged on tty2 from local
```

$ As in bash, this variable contains the PID number of the current shell; use it as **$$**.

tcsh VARIABLES THAT ACT AS SWITCHES

The following shell variables act as switches; their values are not significant. If the variable has been declared, the shell takes the specified action. If not, the action is not taken or is negated. You can set these variables in a startup file, in a shell script, or from the command line.

autocorrect Causes the shell to attempt spelling correction automatically, just before each attempt at completion (page 394).

dunique Normally, pushd blindly pushes the new working directory onto the directory stack, meaning that you can end up with many duplicate entries on this stack. Set **dunique** to cause the shell to look for and delete any entries that duplicate the one it is about to push.

echo Causes the shell to display each command before it executes that command. Set **echo** by calling tcsh with the **–x** option or by using set.

filec Enables filename completion (page 391) when running tcsh as csh (and csh is linked to tcsh).

histlit Displays the commands in the history list exactly as entered, without interpretation by the shell (page 386).

ignoreeof Prevents you from using CONTROL-D to exit from a shell so you cannot accidentally log out. When this variable is declared, you must use **exit** or **logout** to leave a shell.

listjobs Causes the shell to list all jobs whenever a job is suspended.

listlinks Causes the ls–F builtin to show the type of file each symbolic link points to instead of marking the symbolic link with an @ symbol.

loginsh Set by the shell if the current shell is running as a login shell.

nobeep Disables all beeping by the shell.

noclobber Prevents you from accidentally overwriting a file when you redirect output and prevents you from creating a file when you attempt to append output to a nonexistent file (Table 9-7). To override **noclobber**, add an exclamation point to the symbol you use for redirecting or appending output (e.g., **>!** and **>>!**). For more information see page 143.

Table 9-7 How **noclobber** works

Command line	noclobber not declared	noclobber declared
x > ***fileout***	Redirects standard output from process **x** to ***fileout***. Overwrites ***fileout*** if it exists.	Redirects standard output from process **x** to ***fileout***. The shell displays an error message if ***fileout*** exists, and does not overwrite the file.
x >> ***fileout***	Redirects standard output from process **x** to ***fileout***. Appends new output to the end of ***fileout*** if it exists. Creates ***fileout*** if it does not exist.	Redirects standard output from process **x** to ***fileout***. Appends new output to the end of ***fileout*** if it exists. The shell displays an error message if ***fileout*** does not exist, and does not create the file.

noglob Prevents the shell from expanding ambiguous filenames. Allows you to use *, ?, ~, and [] literally on the command line or in a shell script without quoting them.

nonomatch Causes the shell to pass an ambiguous file reference that does not match a filename to the command being called. The shell does not expand the file reference. When you do not set **nonomatch**, tcsh generates a **No match** error message and does not execute the command.

```
tcsh $ cat questions?
cat: No match
tcsh $ set nonomatch
tcsh $ cat questions?
cat: questions?: No such file or directory
```

notify When set, tcsh sends a message to the screen immediately whenever a background job completes. Ordinarily tcsh notifies you about job completion just before displaying the next prompt. Refer to "Job Control" on page 304.

pushdtohome Causes a call to pushd without any arguments to change directories to your home directory (equivalent to **pushd –**).

pushdsilent Causes pushd and popd not to display the directory stack.

rmstar Causes the shell to request confirmation when you give an **rm *** command.

verbose Causes the shell to display each command after a history expansion (page 384). Set **verbose** by calling tcsh with the **–v** option or by using **set**.

visiblebell Causes audible beeps to be replaced by flashing the screen.

CONTROL STRUCTURES

The TC Shell uses many of the same control structures as the Bourne Again Shell. In each case the syntax is different, but the effects are the same. This section summarizes the differences between the control structures in the two shells. For more information refer to "Control Structures" on page 430.

if

The syntax of the **if** control structure is

if (expression) simple-command

The **if** control structure works only with simple commands, not with pipelines (page 145) or lists (page 149). You can use the **if...then** control structure (page 413) to execute more complex commands.

```
tcsh $ cat if_1
#!/bin/tcsh
# Routine to show the use of a simple if control structure.
#
if ( $#argv == 0 ) echo "if_1: There are no arguments."
```

The **if_1** script checks whether it was called with zero arguments. If the expression enclosed in parentheses evaluates to *true*—that is, if zero arguments were on the command line—the **if** structure displays a message.

In addition to logical expressions such as the one the **if_1** script uses, you can use expressions that return a value based on the status of a file. The syntax for this type of expression is

–n filename

where ***n*** is one of the values listed in Table 9-8.

If the result of the test is *true,* the expression has a value of 1; if it is *false,* the expression has a value of 0. If the specified file does not exist or is not accessible, tcsh evaluates the expression as 0. The following example checks whether the file specified on the command line is an ordinary or directory file (and not a device or other special file):

```
tcsh $ cat if_2
#!/bin/tcsh
if -f $1 echo "$1 is an ordinary or directory file."
```

Table 9-8 Value of *n*

n	Meaning
b	File is a block special file
c	File is a character special file
d	File is a directory file
e	File exists
f	File is an ordinary or directory file

Table 9-8 Value of *n* (continued)

n	**Meaning**
g	File has the set-group-ID bit set
k	File has the sticky bit (page 1126) set
l	File is a symbolic link
o	File is owned by user
p	File is a named pipe (FIFO)
r	The user has read access to the file
S	File is a socket special file
s	File is not empty (has nonzero size)
t	File descriptor (a single digit replacing ***filename***) is open and connected to the terminal
u	File has the set-user-ID bit set
w	User has write access to the file
X	File is either a builtin or an executable found by searching the directories in **$path**
x	User has execute access to the file
z	File is 0 bytes long

You can combine operators where it makes sense. For example, **–ox filename** is *true* if you own and have execute permission for the file. This expression is equivalent to **–o filename && –x filename**.

Some operators return useful information about a file other than reporting *true* or *false*. They use the same ***–n filename*** syntax, where ***n*** is one of the values shown in Table 9-9.

Table 9-9 Value of *n*

n	**Meaning**
A	The last time the file was accessed.*
A:	The last time the file was accessed displayed in a human-readable format.
M	The last time the file was modified.*
M:	The last time the file was modified displayed in a human-readable format.
C	The last time the file's inode was modified.*

Table 9-9 Value of *n* (continued)

n	**Meaning**
C:	The last time the file's inode was modified displayed in a human-readable format.
D	Device number for the file. This number uniquely identifies the device (a disk partition, for example) on which the file resides.
I	Inode number for the file. The inode number uniquely identifies a file on a particular device.
F	A string of the form **device:inode**. This string uniquely identifies a file anywhere on the system.
N	Number of hard links to the file.
P	The file's permissions, shown in octal, without a leading 0.
U	Numeric user ID of the file's owner.
U:	Username of the file's owner.
G	Numeric ID of the group the file is associated with.
G:	Name of the group the file is associated with.
Z	Number of bytes in the file.

*Time measured in seconds from the *epoch* (usually, the start of January 1, 1970).

You can use only one of these operators in a given test, and it must appear as the last operator in a multiple-operator sequence. Because 0 (zero) can be a valid response from some of these operators (for instance, the number of bytes in a file might be 0), most return –1 on failure instead of the 0 that the logical operators return on failure. The one exception is **F**, which returns a colon if it cannot determine the device and inode for the file.

When you want to use one of these operators outside of a control structure expression, you can use the **filetest** builtin to evaluate a file test and report the result:

```
tcsh $ filetest -z if_1
0
tcsh $ filetest -F if_1
2051:12694
tcsh $ filetest -Z if_1
131
```

goto

The **goto** statement has the following syntax:

goto ***label***

A **goto** builtin transfers control to the statement beginning with ***label:***. The following script fragment demonstrates the use of **goto**:

```
tcsh $ cat goto_1
#!/bin/tcsh
#
# test for 2 arguments
#
if ($#argv == 2) goto goodargs
echo "Usage: $0 arg1 arg2"
exit 1
goodargs:
...
```

The **goto_1** script displays a usage message (page 434) when it is called with more or fewer than two arguments.

INTERRUPT HANDLING

The **onintr** (on interrupt) statement transfers control when you interrupt a shell script. The syntax of an **onintr** statement is

*onintr **label***

When you press the interrupt key during execution of a shell script, the shell transfers control to the statement beginning with ***label:***. This statement allows you to terminate a script gracefully when it is interrupted. For example, you can use it to ensure that when you interrupt a shell script, the script removes temporary files before returning control to the parent shell.

The following script demonstrates the use of **onintr**. It loops continuously until you press the interrupt key, at which time it displays a message and returns control to the shell:

```
tcsh $ cat onintr_1
#!/bin/tcsh
# demonstration of onintr
onintr close
while ( 1 )
    echo "Program is running."
    sleep 2
end
close:
echo "End of program."
```

If a script creates temporary files, you can use **onintr** to remove them.

```
close:
rm -f /tmp/$$*
```

The ambiguous file reference **/tmp/$$*** matches all files in **/tmp** that begin with the PID number of the current shell. Refer to page 476 for a description of this technique for naming temporary files.

if...then...else

The **if...then...else** control structure has three forms. The first form, an extension of the simple **if** structure, executes more complex ***commands*** or a series of ***commands*** if ***expression*** is *true.* This form is still a one-way branch.

```
if (expression) then
    commands
endif
```

The second form is a two-way branch. If ***expression*** is *true,* the first set of ***commands*** is executed. If it is *false,* the set of ***commands*** following **else** is executed.

```
if (expression) then
    commands
else
    commands
endif
```

The third form is similar to the **if...then...elif** structure (page 436). It performs tests until it finds an ***expression*** that is *true* and then executes the corresponding ***commands.***

```
if (expression) then
    commands
else if (expression) then
    commands
. . .
else
    commands
endif
```

The following program assigns a value of 0, 1, 2, or 3 to the variable **class** based on the value of the first command-line argument. The program declares the variable **class** at the beginning for clarity; you do not need to declare it before its first use. Also for clarity, the script assigns the value of the first command-line argument to **number**.

```
tcsh $ cat if_else_1
#!/bin/tcsh
# routine to categorize the first
# command-line argument
set class
set number = $argv[1]
#
```

```
if ($number < 0) then
    @ class = 0
else if (0 <= $number && $number < 100) then
    @ class = 1
else if (100 <= $number && $number < 200) then
    @ class = 2
else
    @ class = 3
endif
#
echo "The number $number is in class $class."
```

The first **if** statement tests whether **number** is less than 0. If it is, the script assigns 0 to **class** and transfers control to the statement following **endif**. If it is not, the second **if** tests whether the number is between 0 and 100. The && Boolean AND operator yields a value of *true* if the expression on each side is *true*. If the number is between 0 and 100, 1 is assigned to **class** and control is transferred to the statement following **endif**. A similar test determines whether the number is between 100 and 200. If it is not, the final **else** assigns 3 to **class**. The **endif** closes the **if** control structure.

foreach

The **foreach** structure parallels the bash **for...in** structure (page 443). The syntax is

*foreach **loop-index** (**argument-list**)*
    commands
end

This structure loops through ***commands***. The first time through the loop, the structure assigns the value of the first argument in ***argument-list*** to ***loop-index***. When control reaches the **end** statement, the shell assigns the value of the next argument from ***argument-list*** to ***loop-index*** and executes the commands again. The shell repeats this procedure until it exhausts ***argument-list***.

The following tcsh script uses a **foreach** structure to loop through the files in the working directory containing a specified string of characters in their filename and to change the string. For example, you can use it to change the string **memo** in filenames to **letter**. Thus, the filenames **memo.1**, **dailymemo**, and **memories** would be changed to **letter.1**, **dailyletter**, and **letterries**, respectively.

This script requires two arguments: the string to be changed (the old string) and the new string. The ***argument-list*** of the **foreach** structure uses an ambiguous file reference to loop through all files in the working directory with filenames that contain the first argument. For each filename that matches the ambiguous file reference, the mv utility changes the filename. The echo and sed commands appear within back ticks (`) that indicate command substitution: Executing the commands within the back ticks replaces the back ticks and everything between them. Refer to "Command Substitution" on page 371 for more information. The sed utility (page 669) substitutes the first argument with the second argument in the filename. The **$1** and **$2** are abbreviated forms of **$argv**[1] and **$argv**[2], respectively.

```
tcsh $ cat ren
#!/bin/tcsh
# Usage:          ren arg1 arg2
#                 changes the string arg1 in the names of files
#                 in the working directory into the string arg2
if ($#argv != 2) goto usage
foreach i ( *$1* )
    mv $i `echo $i | sed -n s/$1/$2/p`
end
exit 0

usage:
echo "Usage: ren arg1 arg2"
exit 1
```

optional The next script uses a **foreach** loop to assign the command-line arguments to the elements of an array named **buffer**:

```
tcsh $ cat foreach_1
#!/bin/tcsh
# routine to zero-fill argv to 20 arguments
#
set buffer = (0 0 0 0 0 0 0 0 0 0 0 0 0 0 0 0 0 0 0 0)
set count = 1
#
if ($#argv > 20) goto toomany
#
foreach argument ($argv[*])
    set buffer[$count] = $argument
    @ count++
end
# REPLACE command ON THE NEXT LINE WITH
# THE PROGRAM YOU WANT TO CALL.
exec command $buffer[*]
#
toomany:
echo "Too many arguments given."
echo "Usage: foreach_1 [up to 20 arguments]"
exit 1
```

The **foreach_1** script calls another program named **command** with a command line guaranteed to contain 20 arguments. If **foreach_1** is called with fewer than 20 arguments, it fills the command line with zeros to complete the 20 arguments for **command**. Providing more than 20 arguments causes it to display a usage message and exit with an error status of 1.

The **foreach** structure loops through the commands one time for each command-line argument. Each time through the loop, **foreach** assigns the value of the next argument from the command line to the variable **argument**. Then the script assigns each of these values to an element of the array **buffer**. The variable **count** maintains the index for the **buffer** array. A postfix operator increments the **count** variable using @ (@ **count++**). The exec builtin (bash and tcsh; page 493) calls **command** so a new process is not initiated. (Once **command** is called, the process running this routine is no longer needed so a new process is not required.)

while

The syntax of the **while** structure is

while (expression)
  commands
end

This structure continues to loop through ***commands*** while ***expression*** is *true*. If ***expression*** is *false* the first time it is evaluated, the structure never executes ***commands***.

```
tcsh $ cat while_1
#!/bin/tcsh
# Demonstration of a while control structure.
# This routine sums the numbers between 1 and n;
# n is the first argument on the command line.
#
set limit = $argv[1]
set index = 1
set sum = 0
#
while ($index <= $limit)
    @ sum += $index
    @ index++
end
#
echo "The sum is $sum"
```

This program computes the sum of all integers up to and including ***n***, where ***n*** is the first argument on the command line. The += operator assigns the value of **sum + index** to **sum**.

break AND continue

You can interrupt a **foreach** or **while** structure with a **break** or **continue** statement. These statements execute the remaining commands on the line before they transfer control. The **break** statement transfers control to the statement after the **end** statement, terminating execution of the loop. The **continue** statement transfers control to the **end** statement, which continues execution of the loop.

switch

The **switch** structure is analogous to the bash **case** structure (page 454):

*switch (**test-string**)*

*case **pattern:***
*   **commands***
breaksw

*case **pattern:***
*   **commands***
breaksw
...
default:
*   **commands***
breaksw

endsw

The **breaksw** statement transfers control to the statement following the **endsw** statement. If you omit **breaksw**, control falls through to the next command. You can use any of the special characters listed in Table 10-2 on page 456 within ***pattern*** except the pipe symbol (|).

```
tcsh $ cat switch_1
#!/bin/tcsh
# Demonstration of a switch control structure.
# This routine tests the first command-line argument
# for yes or no in any combination of uppercase and
# lowercase letters.
#
# test that argv[1] exists
if ($#argv != 1) then
    echo "Usage: $0 [yes|no]"
    exit 1
else
    # argv[1] exists, set up switch based on its value
    switch ($argv[1])
    # case of YES
        case [yY][eE][sS]:
        echo "Argument one is yes."
        breaksw
    #
    # case of NO
        case [nN][oO]:
        echo "Argument one is no."
    breaksw
    #
    # default case
```

```
            default:
            echo "Argument one is not yes or no."
            breaksw
        endsw
    endif
```

BUILTINS

Builtins are commands that are part of (built into) the shell. When you give a simple filename as a command, the shell first checks whether it is the name of a builtin. If it is, the shell executes it as part of the calling process; the shell does not fork a new process to execute the builtin. The shell does not need to search the directory structure for builtin programs because they are immediately available to the shell.

If the simple filename you give as a command is not a builtin, the shell searches the directory structure for the program you want, using the **PATH** variable as a guide. When it finds the program, the shell forks a new process to execute the program.

Although they are not listed in Table 9-10, the control structure keywords (**if**, **foreach**, **endsw**, and so on) are builtins. Table 9-10 describes many of the tcsh builtins, some of which are also built into other shells.

Table 9-10 tcsh builtins

Builtin	Function
% ***job***	A synonym for the fg builtin. The ***job*** is the job number of the job you want to bring to the foreground (page 305).
% ***job*** &	A synonym for the bg builtin. The ***job*** is the number of the job you want to put in the background (page 306).
@	Similar to the set builtin but evaluates numeric expressions. Refer to "Numeric Variables" on page 398.
alias	Creates and displays aliases; tcsh uses a different syntax than bash. Refer to "Aliases" on page 387.
alloc	Displays a report of the amount of free and used memory.
bg	Moves a suspended job into the background (page 306).
bindkey	Controls the mapping of keys to the tcsh command-line editor commands.
bindkey	Without any arguments, bindkey lists all key bindings (page 393).
bindkey –l	Lists all available editor commands and gives a short description of each.
bindkey –e	Puts the command-line editor in emacs mode (page 393).
bindkey –v	Puts the command-line editor in vi(m) mode (page 393).
bindkey ***key command***	Attaches the editor command ***command*** to the key ***key***.

Table 9-10 tcsh builtins (continued)

Builtin	Function
bindkey –b ***key command***	Similar to the previous form but allows you to specify CONTROL keys by using the form C–x (where x is the character you type while you press the CONTROL key), specify META key sequences as M-x (on most keyboards used with Linux, the ALT key is the META key; macOS uses the OPTION key [but you have to set an option in the Terminal utility to use it; see page 1076]), and specify function keys as F-x.
bindkey –c ***key command***	Binds the key ***key*** to the command ***command***. Here the ***command*** is not an editor command but rather a shell builtin or an executable program.
bindkey –s ***key string***	Causes tcsh to substitute ***string*** when you press ***key***.
builtins	Displays a list of all builtins.
cd or chdir	Changes the working directory (page 94).
dirs	Displays the directory stack (page 307).
echo	Displays its arguments. You can prevent echo from displaying a RETURN at the end of a line by using the **–n** option (see "Reading User Input" on page 401) or by using a trailing **\c** (see "read: Accepts User Input" on page 489). The echo builtin is similar to the echo utility (page 812).
eval	Scans and evaluates the command line. When you put eval in front of a command, the command is scanned twice by the shell before it is executed. This feature is useful with a command that is generated through command or variable substitution. Because of the order in which the shell processes a command line, it is sometimes necessary to repeat the scan to achieve the desired result (page 500).
exec	Overlays the program currently being executed with another program in the same shell. The original program is lost. Refer to "exec: Executes a Command or Redirects File Descriptors" on page 493 for more information; also refer to source on page 421.
exit	Exits from a TC Shell. When you follow exit with a numeric argument, tcsh returns that number as the exit status (page 477).
fg	Moves a job into the foreground (page 304).
filetest	Takes one of the file inquiry operators followed by one or more filenames and applies the operator to each filename (page 411). Returns the results as a SPACE-separated list.

Table 9-10 tcsh builtins (continued)

Builtin	Function
glob	Like echo, but does not display SPACEs between its arguments and does not follow its display with a NEWLINE.
hashstat	Reports on the efficiency of tcsh's hash mechanism. The hash mechanism speeds the process of searching through the directories in your search path. See also rehash (page 421) and unhash (page 422).
history	Displays a list of recent commands (page 384).
jobs	Displays a list of jobs (suspended commands and those running in the background).
kill	Terminates a job or process (page 499).
limit	Limits the computer resources that the current process and any processes it creates can use. You can put limits on the number of seconds of CPU time the process can use, the size of files that the process can create, and so forth.
log	Immediately produces the report that the watch shell variable (page 406) would normally cause tcsh to produce every 10 minutes.
login	Logs in a user. Can be followed by a username.
logout	Ends a session if you are using a login shell.
ls–F	Similar to **ls –F** (page 885) but faster. (This builtin is the characters **ls–F** without any SPACEs.)
nice	Lowers the processing priority of a command or a shell. This builtin is useful if you want to run a command that makes large demands on the system and you do not need the output right away. If you are working with **root** privileges, you can use nice to raise the priority of a command. Refer to page 916 for more information on the nice builtin and the nice utility.
nohup	Allows you to log out without terminating processes running in the background. Some systems are set up this way by default. Refer to page 920 for information on the nohup builtin and the nohup utility.
notify	Causes the shell to notify you immediately when the status of one of your jobs changes (page 304).
onintr	Controls the action an interrupt causes within a script (page 412). See "trap: Catches a Signal" on page 496 for information on the equivalent command in bash.
popd	Changes the working directory to the directory on the top of the directory stack and removes that directory from the directory stack (page 307).
printenv	Displays all environment variable names and values.

Table 9-10 tcsh builtins (continued)

Builtin	Function
pushd	Changes the working directory and places the new directory at the top of the directory stack (page 308).
rehash	Re-creates the internal tables used by the hash mechanism. Whenever a new instance of tcsh is invoked, the hash mechanism creates a sorted list of all available commands based on the value of **path**. After you add a command to a directory in **path**, use rehash to re-create the sorted list of commands. If you do not, tcsh might not be able to find the new command. Also refer to hashstat (page 420) and unhash (page 422).
repeat	Takes two arguments—a count and a simple command (no pipelines or lists)—and repeats the command the number of times specified by the count.
sched	Executes a command at a specified time. For example, the following command causes the shell to display the message **Dental appointment.** at 10 AM: `tcsh $ sched 10:00 echo "Dental appointment."` Without any arguments, sched displays the list of scheduled commands. When the time to execute a scheduled command arrives, tcsh executes the command just before it displays a prompt.
set	Declares, initializes, and displays local variables (page 396).
setenv	Declares, initializes, and displays environment variables (page 396).
shift	Analogous to the bash shift builtin (page 473). Without an argument, shift promotes the indexes of the **argv** array. You can use it with an argument of an array name to perform the same operation on that array.
source	Executes the shell script given as its argument: source does not fork another process. It is similar to the bash . (dot) builtin (page 290). The source builtin expects a TC Shell script so no leading **#!** is required in the script. The current shell executes source; thus the script can contain commands, such as set, that affect the current shell. After you make changes to your **.tcshrc** or **.login** file, you can use source to execute it from the shell, thereby putting the changes into effect without logging out and in. You can nest source builtins.
stop	Stops a job or process that is running in the background. The stop builtin accepts multiple arguments.
suspend	Stops the current shell and puts it in the background. It is similar to the suspend key, which stops jobs running in the foreground. This builtin will not suspend a login shell.
time	Executes the command you give it as an argument. It displays a summary of time-related information about the executed command, according to the **time** shell variable (page 405). Without an argument, time displays the times for the current shell and its children.

Table 9-10 tcsh builtins (continued)

Builtin	Function
umask	Identifies or changes the access permissions that tcsh assigns to files you create (page 1021).
unalias	Removes an alias (page 387).
unhash	Turns off the hash mechanism. See also hashstat (page 420) and rehash (page 421).
unlimit	Removes limits (page 420) on the current process.
unset	Removes a variable declaration (page 396).
unsetenv	Removes an environment variable declaration (page 396).
wait	Causes the shell to wait for all child processes to terminate. When you give a wait command in response to a shell prompt, tcsh does not display a prompt until all background processes have finished execution. If you interrupt it with the interrupt key, wait displays a list of background processes before tcsh displays a prompt.
where	When given the name of a command as an argument, locates all occurrences of the command and, for each, tells you whether it is an alias, a builtin, or an executable program in your path.
which	Similar to where but reports on only the command that would be executed, not all occurrences. This builtin is much faster than the which utility and reports on aliases and builtins.

Chapter Summary

Like the Bourne Again Shell, the TC Shell is both a command interpreter and a programming language. The TC Shell, which is based on the C Shell that was developed at the University of California at Berkeley, includes popular features such as history, alias, and job control.

You might prefer to use tcsh as a command interpreter, especially if you are familiar with the C Shell. You can use chsh to change your login shell to tcsh. However, running tcsh as your interactive shell does *not* cause tcsh to run shell scripts; they will continue to be run by bash unless you explicitly specify another shell on the first line of the script or specify the script name as an argument to tcsh. Specifying the shell on the first line of a shell script ensures the behavior you expect.

If you are familiar with bash, you will notice some differences between the two shells. For instance, the syntax you use to assign a value to a variable differs. In addition, tcsh allows SPACEs around the equal sign. Both numeric and nonnumeric variables are created and given values using the set builtin. The @ builtin can evaluate numeric expressions for assignment to numeric variables.

setenv Because there is no export builtin in tcsh, you must use the setenv builtin to create an environment (global) variable. You can also assign a value to the variable with the setenv command. The command unset removes both shell and environment variables, whereas the command unsetenv removes only environment variables.

Aliases The syntax of the tcsh alias builtin is slightly different from that of alias in bash. Unlike bash, the tcsh aliases permit you to substitute command-line arguments using the history mechanism syntax.

Most other tcsh features, such as history, word completion, and command-line editing, closely resemble their bash counterparts. The syntax of the tcsh control structures is slightly different but provides functionality equivalent to that found in bash.

Globbing The term *globbing*, a carryover from the original Bourne Shell, refers to the matching of strings containing special characters (such as * and ?) to filenames. If tcsh is unable to generate a list of filenames matching a globbing pattern, it displays an error message. This behavior contrasts with that of bash, which simply leaves the pattern alone.

Standard input and standard output can be redirected in tcsh, but there is no straightforward way to redirect them independently. Doing so requires the creation of a subshell that redirects standard output to a file while making standard error available to the parent process.

EXERCISES

1. Assume that you are working with the following history list:

```
37  mail zach
38  cd /home/sam/correspondence/business/cheese_co
39  less letter.0321
40  vim letter.0321
41  cp letter.0321 letter.0325
42  grep hansen letter.0325
43  vim letter.0325
44  lpr letter*
45  cd ../milk_co
46  pwd
47  vim wilson.0321 wilson.0329
```

   Using the history mechanism, give commands to

   a. Send mail to Zach.

b. Use vim to edit a file named **wilson.0329**.

c. Send **wilson.0329** to the printer.

d. Send both **wilson.0321** and **wilson.0329** to the printer.

2. a. How can you display the aliases currently in effect?

   b. Write an alias named **homedots** that lists the names (only) of all hidden files in your home directory.

3. a. How can you prevent a command from sending output to the terminal when you start it in the background?

   b. What can you do if you start a command in the foreground and later decide that you want it to run in the background?

4. Which statement can you put in your **~/.tcshrc** file to prevent accidentally overwriting a file when you redirect output? How can you override this feature?

5. Assume that the working directory contains the following files:

```
adams.ltr.03
adams.brief
adams.ltr.07
abelson.09
abelson.brief
anthony.073
anthony.brief
azevedo.99
```

   What happens if you press TAB after typing the following commands?

   a. **less adams.l**

   b. **cat a**

   c. **ls ant**

   d. **file az**

   What happens if you press CONTROL-D after typing the following commands?

   e. **ls ab**

   f. **less a**

6. Write an alias named **backup** that takes a filename as an argument and creates a copy of that file with the same name and a filename extension of **.bak**.

7. Write an alias named **qmake** (quiet make) that runs make with both standard output and standard error redirected to the file named **make.log**. The command **qmake** should accept the same options and arguments as make.

8. How can you make tcsh always display the pathname of the working directory as part of its prompt?

Advanced Exercises

9. Which lines do you need to change in the Bourne Again Shell script **command_menu** (page 456) to turn it into a TC Shell script? Make the changes and verify that the new script works.

10. Users often find rm (and even **rm –i**) too unforgiving because this utility removes files irrevocably. Create an alias named **delete** that moves files specified by its argument(s) into the **~/.trash** directory. Create a second alias named **undelete** that moves a file from the **~/.trash** directory into the working directory. Put the following line in your **~/.logout** file to remove any files that you deleted during the login session:

    ```
    /bin/rm -f $HOME/.trash/* >& /dev/null
    ```

    Explain what could be different if the following line were put in your **~/.logout** file instead:

    ```
    rm $HOME/.trash/*
    ```

11. Modify the **foreach_1** script (page 415) so that it takes the command to exec as an argument.

12. Rewrite the program **while_1** (page 416) so that it runs faster. Use the time builtin to verify the improvement in execution time.

13. Write your own version of find named **myfind** that writes output to the file **findout** but without the clutter of error messages, such as those generated when you do not have permission to search a directory. The **myfind** command should accept the same options and arguments as find. Can you think of a situation in which **myfind** does not work as desired?

14. When the **foreach_1** script (page 415) is supplied with 20 or fewer arguments, why are the commands following **toomany:** not executed? (Why is there no exit command?)

PART IV

Programming Tools

10

Programming the Bourne Again Shell (bash)

In This Chapter

Objectives

After reading this chapter you should be able to:

- Use control structures to implement decision making and repetition in shell scripts
- Handle input to and output from scripts
- Use shell variables (local) and environment variables (global)
- Evaluate the value of numeric variables
- Use bash builtin commands to call other scripts inline, trap signals, and kill processes
- Use arithmetic and logical expressions
- List standard programming practices that result in well-written scripts

Chapter 5 introduced the shells and Chapter 8 went into detail about the Bourne Again Shell. This chapter introduces additional Bourne Again Shell commands, builtins, and concepts that carry shell programming to a point where it can be useful. Although you might make use of shell programming as a system administrator, you do not have to read this chapter to perform system administration tasks. Feel free to skip this chapter and come back to it if and when you like.

The first part of this chapter covers programming control structures, also called control flow constructs. These structures allow you to write scripts that can loop over command-line arguments, make decisions based on the value of a variable, set up menus, and more. The Bourne Again Shell uses the same constructs found in programming languages such as C.

The next part of this chapter discusses parameters and variables, going into detail about array variables, shell versus environment variables, special parameters, and positional parameters. The exploration of builtin commands covers type, which displays information about a command, and read, which allows a shell script to accept user input. The section on the exec builtin demonstrates how to use exec to execute a command efficiently by replacing a process and explains how to use exec to redirect input and output from within a script.

The next section covers the trap builtin, which provides a way to detect and respond to operating system signals (such as the signal generated when you press CONTROL-C). The discussion of builtins concludes with a discussion of kill, which can abort a process, and getopts, which makes it easy to parse options for a shell script. Table 10-6 on page 504 lists some of the more commonly used builtins.

Next, the chapter examines arithmetic and logical expressions as well as the operators that work with them. The final section walks through the design and implementation of two major shell scripts.

This chapter contains many examples of shell programs. Although they illustrate certain concepts, most use information from earlier examples as well. This overlap not only reinforces your overall knowledge of shell programming but also demonstrates how you can combine commands to solve complex tasks. Running, modifying, and experimenting with the examples in this book is a good way to become comfortable with the underlying concepts.

Do not name a shell script test

tip You can unwittingly create a problem if you name a shell script **test** because a bash builtin has the same name. Depending on how you call your script, you might run either your script or the builtin, leading to confusing results.

Control Structures

The *control flow* commands alter the order of execution of commands within a shell script. The TC Shell uses a different syntax for these commands (page 408) than the Bourne Again Shell does. Control structures include the **if...then**, **for...in**, **while**, **until**, and **case** statements. In addition, the **break** and **continue** statements work in conjunction with the control structures to alter the order of execution of commands within a script.

Getting help with control structures — You can use the bash **help** command to display information about bash control structures. See page 39 for more information.

if...then

The **if...then** control structure has the following syntax (see page 409 for tcsh):

> *if* ***test-command***
> *then*
> ***commands***
> *fi*

The ***bold*** words in the syntax description are the items you supply to cause the structure to have the desired effect. The *nonbold* words are the keywords the shell uses to identify the control structure.

test builtin — Figure 10-1 shows that the **if** statement tests the status returned by the ***test-command*** and transfers control based on this status. The end of the **if** structure is marked by a **fi** statement (*if* spelled backward). The following script prompts for two words, reads them, and then uses an **if** structure to execute commands based on the result returned by the test builtin (tcsh uses the test utility) when it compares the two words. (See page 1005 for information on the test utility, which is similar to the test builtin.) The

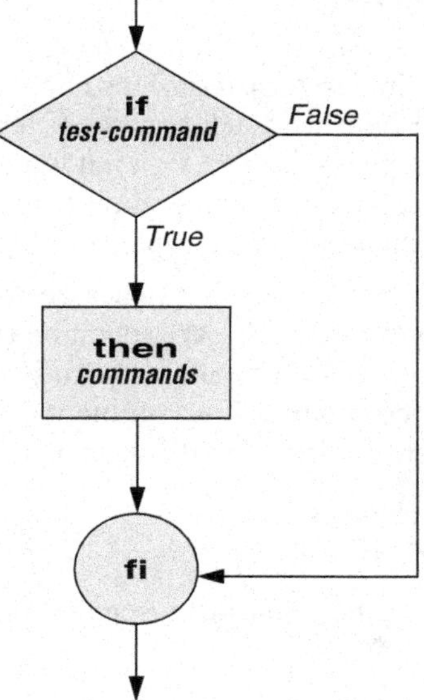

Figure 10-1 An if...then flowchart

test builtin returns a status of *true* if the two words are the same and *false* if they are not. Double quotation marks around **$word1** and **$word2** make sure test works properly if you enter a string that contains a SPACE or other special character.

```
$ cat if1
read -p "word 1:  " word1
read -p "word 2:  " word2

if test "$word1" = "$word2"
    then
        echo "Match"
fi
echo "End of program."

$ ./if1
word 1: peach
word 2: peach
Match
End of program.
```

In the preceding example the ***test-command*** is **test "$word1" = "$word2"**. The test builtin returns a *true* status if its first and third arguments have the relationship specified by its second argument. If this command returns a *true* status (= 0), the shell executes the commands between the **then** and **fi** statements. If the command returns a *false* status (not = 0), the shell passes control to the statement following **fi** without executing the statements between **then** and **fi**. The effect of this **if** statement is to display **Match** if the two words are the same. The script always displays **End of program.**

Builtins In the Bourne Again Shell, test is a builtin—part of the shell. It is also a stand-alone utility kept in **/usr/bin/test**. This chapter discusses and demonstrates many Bourne Again Shell builtins. Each bash builtin might or might not be a builtin in tcsh. The shell will use the builtin version if it is available and the utility if it is not. Each version of a command might vary slightly from one shell to the next and from the utility to any of the shell builtins. See page 489 for more information on shell builtins.

Checking arguments The next program uses an **if** structure at the beginning of a script to confirm that you have supplied at least one argument on the command line. The test –eq criterion compares two integers; the shell expands the **$#** special parameter (page 475) to the number of command-line arguments. This structure displays a message and exits from the script with an exit status of 1 if you do not supply at least one argument.

```
$ cat chkargs
if test $# -eq 0
    then
        echo "You must supply at least one argument."
        exit 1
fi
echo "Program running."
```

```
$ ./chkargs
You must supply at least one argument.
$ ./chkargs abc
Program running.
```

A test like the one shown in **chkargs** is a key component of any script that requires arguments. To prevent the user from receiving meaningless or confusing information from the script, the script needs to check whether the user has supplied the appropriate arguments. Some scripts simply test whether arguments exist (as in **chkargs**); other scripts test for a specific number or specific kinds of arguments.

You can use test to verify the status of a file argument or the relationship between two file arguments. After verifying that at least one argument has been given on the command line, the following script tests whether the argument is the name of an ordinary file (not a directory or other type of file). The test builtin with the **–f** criterion and the first command-line argument (**$1**) checks the file.

```
$ cat is_ordfile
if test $# -eq 0
    then
        echo "You must supply at least one argument."
        exit 1
fi
if test -f "$1"
    then
        echo "$1 is an ordinary file."
    else
        echo "$1 is NOT an ordinary file."
fi
```

You can test many other characteristics of a file using test criteria; see Table 10-1.

Table 10-1 test builtin criteria

Criterion	Tests file to see if it
–d	Exists and is a directory file
–e	Exists
–f	Exists and is an ordinary file (not a directory)
–r	Exists and is readable
–s	Exists and has a size greater than 0 bytes
–w	Exists and is writable
–x	Exists and is executable

Other **test** criteria provide ways to test relationships between two files, such as whether one file is newer than another. Refer to examples later in this chapter and to **test** on page 1005 for more information.

Always test the arguments

tip To keep the examples in this book short and focused on specific concepts, the code to verify arguments is often omitted or abbreviated. It is good practice to test arguments in shell programs that other people will use. Doing so results in scripts that are easier to debug, run, and maintain.

[] is a synonym for test The following example—another version of **chkargs**—checks for arguments in a way that is more traditional for Linux shell scripts. This example uses the bracket ([]) synonym for **test**. Rather than using the word **test** in scripts, you can surround the arguments to **test** with brackets. The brackets must be surrounded by whitespace (SPACEs or TABs).

```
$ cat chkargs2
if [ $# -eq 0 ]
    then
        echo "Usage: chkargs2 argument..." 1>&2
        exit 1
fi
echo "Program running."
exit 0

$ ./chkargs2
Usage: chkargs2 argument...
$ ./chkargs2 abc
Program running.
```

Usage messages The error message that **chkargs2** displays is called a *usage message* and uses the **1>&2** notation to redirect its output to standard error (page 294). After issuing the usage message, **chkargs2** exits with an exit status of 1, indicating an error has occurred. The **exit 0** command at the end of the script causes **chkargs2** to exit with a 0 status after the program runs without an error. The Bourne Again Shell returns the exit status of the last command the script ran if you omit the status code.

The usage message is commonly used to specify the type and number of arguments the script requires. Many Linux utilities provide usage messages similar to the one in **chkargs2**. If you call a utility or other program with the wrong number or wrong kind of arguments, it will often display a usage message. Following is the usage message that **cp** displays when you call it with only one argument:

```
$ cp a
cp: missing destination file operand after 'a'
Try 'cp --help' for more information.
```

if...then...else

The introduction of an **else** statement turns the **if** structure into the two-way branch shown in Figure 10-2. The **if...then...else** control structure (available in tcsh with a slightly different syntax) has the following syntax:

if ***test-command***
    then
        commands
    else
        commands
fi

Because a semicolon (;) ends a command just as a NEWLINE does, you can place **then** on the same line as **if** by preceding it with a semicolon. (Because **if** and **then** are separate builtins, they require a control operator between them; a semicolon and NEWLINE work equally well [page 300].) Some people prefer this notation for aesthetic reasons; others like it because it saves space.

if ***test-command;*** *then*
        commands
    else
        commands
fi

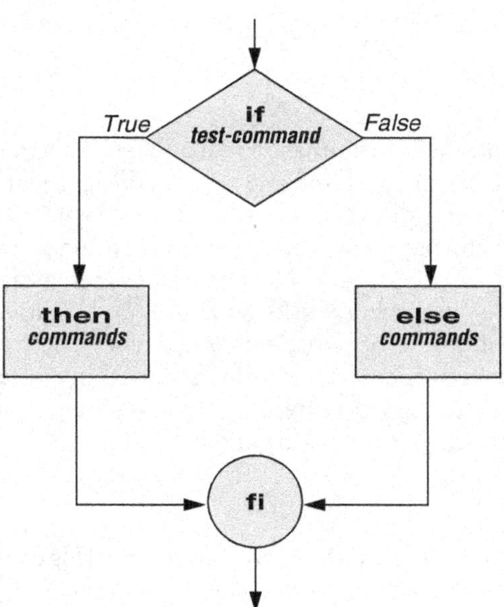

Figure 10-2 An if...then...else flowchart

If the ***test-command*** returns a *true* status, the **if** structure executes the commands between the **then** and **else** statements and then diverts control to the statement following **fi**. If the ***test-command*** returns a *false* status, the **if** structure executes the commands following the **else** statement.

When you run the **out** script with arguments that are filenames, it displays the files on the terminal. If the first argument is **–v** (called an option in this case), **out** uses less (page 53) to display the files one screen at a time. After determining that it was called with at least one argument, **out** tests its first argument to see whether it is **–v**. If the result of the test is *true* (the first argument is **–v**), **out** uses the shift builtin (page 473) to shift the arguments to get rid of the **–v** and displays the files using less. If the result of the test is *false* (the first argument is *not* **–v**), the script uses cat to display the files.

```
$ cat out
if [ $# -eq 0 ]
    then
        echo "Usage: $0 [-v] filenames..." 1>&2
        exit 1
fi

if [ "$1" = "-v" ]
    then
        shift
        less -- "$@"
    else
        cat -- "$@"
fi
```

optional In **out**, the **––** argument to cat and less tells these utilities that no more options follow on the command line and not to consider leading hyphens (**–**) in the following list as indicating options. Thus, **––** allows you to view a file whose name starts with a hyphen (page 133). Although not common, filenames beginning with a hyphen do occasionally occur. (You can create such a file by using the command **cat > –fname**.) The **––** argument works with all Linux utilities that use the getopts builtin (page 501) to parse their options; it does not work with more and a few other utilities. This argument is particularly useful when used in conjunction with rm to remove a file whose name starts with a hyphen (**rm –– –fname**), including any you create while experimenting with the **––** argument.

if...then...elif

The **if...then...elif** control structure (Figure 10-3; not in tcsh) has the following syntax:

*if **test-command***
    then
        commands

```
            elif test-command
                then
                    commands
        . . .
            else
                commands
        fi
```

The **elif** statement combines the **else** statement and the **if** statement and enables you to construct a nested set of **if...then...else** structures (Figure 10-3). The difference between the **else** statement and the **elif** statement is that each **else** statement must be paired with a **fi** statement, whereas multiple nested **elif** statements require only a single closing **fi** statement.

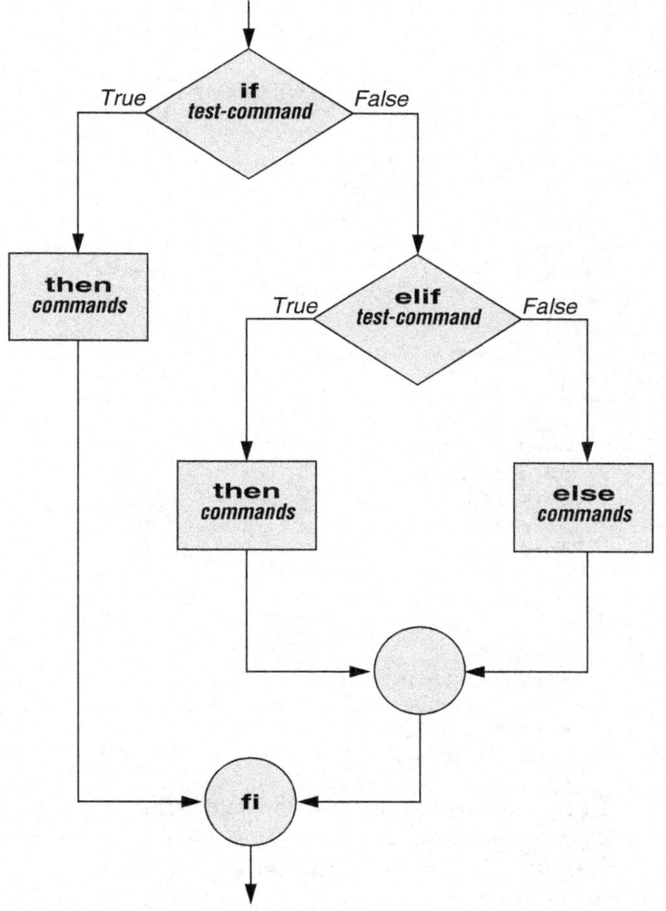

Figure 10-3 An **if...then...elif** flowchart

The following example shows an **if...then...elif** control structure. This shell script compares three words the user enters. The first **if** statement uses the Boolean AND operator (**–a**) as an argument to **test**. The **test** builtin returns a *true* status if the first and second logical comparisons are *true* (that is, **word1** matches **word2** and **word2** matches **word3**). If **test** returns a *true* status, the script executes the command following the next **then** statement, passes control to the statement following **fi**, and terminates.

```
$ cat if3
read -p "word 1: " word1
read -p "word 2: " word2
read -p "word 3: " word3
if [ "$word1" = "$word2" -a "$word2" = "$word3" ]
    then
        echo "Match: words 1, 2, & 3"
    elif [ "$word1" = "$word2" ]
    then
        echo "Match: words 1 & 2"
    elif [ "$word1" = "$word3" ]
    then
        echo "Match: words 1 & 3"
    elif [ "$word2" = "$word3" ]
    then
        echo "Match: words 2 & 3"
    else
        echo "No match"
fi

$ ./if3
word 1: apple
word 2: orange
word 3: pear
No match
$ ./if3
word 1: apple
word 2: orange
word 3: apple
Match: words 1 & 3
$ ./if3
word 1: apple
word 2: apple
word 3: apple
Match: words 1, 2, & 3
```

If the three words are not the same, the structure passes control to the first **elif**, which begins a series of tests to see if any pair of words is the same. As the nesting continues, if any one of the **elif** statements is satisfied, the structure passes control to the next **then** statement and subsequently to the statement following **fi**. Each time an **elif** statement is not satisfied, the structure passes control to the next **elif** statement. The double quotation marks around the arguments to **echo** that contain ampersands (&) prevent the shell from interpreting the ampersands as special characters.

optional THE lnks SCRIPT

The following script, named **lnks**, demonstrates the **if...then** and **if...then...elif** control structures. This script finds hard links to its first argument: a filename. If you provide the name of a directory as the second argument, **lnks** searches for links in the directory hierarchy rooted at that directory. If you do not specify a directory, **lnks** searches the working directory and its subdirectories. This script does not locate symbolic links.

```
$ cat lnks
#!/bin/bash
# Identify links to a file
# Usage: lnks file [directory]

if [ $# -eq 0 -o $# -gt 2 ]; then
    echo "Usage: lnks file [directory]" 1>&2
    exit 1
fi
if [ -d "$1" ]; then
    echo "First argument cannot be a directory." 1>&2
    echo "Usage: lnks file [directory]" 1>&2
    exit 1
else
    file="$1"
fi
if [ $# -eq 1 ]; then
        directory="."
    elif [ -d "$2" ]; then
        directory="$2"
    else
        echo "Optional second argument must be a directory." 1>&2
        echo "Usage: lnks file [directory]" 1>&2
        exit 1
fi

# Check that file exists and is an ordinary file
if [ ! -f "$file" ]; then
    echo "lnks: $file not found or is a special file" 1>&2
    exit 1
fi
# Check link count on file
set -- $(ls -l "$file")

linkcnt=$2
if [ "$linkcnt" -eq 1 ]; then
    echo "lnks: no other hard links to $file" 1>&2
    exit 0
fi

# Get the inode of the given file
set $(ls -i "$file")

inode=$1

# Find and print the files with that inode number
echo "lnks: using find to search for links..." 1>&2
find "$directory" -xdev -inum $inode -print
```

Max has a file named **letter** in his home directory. He wants to find links to this file in his and other users' home directory file hierarchies. In the following example, Max calls **lnks** from his home directory to perform the search. If you are running macOS, substitute **/Users** for **/home**. The second argument to **lnks**, **/home**, is the pathname of the directory where Max wants to start the search. The **lnks** script reports that **/home/max/letter** and **/home/zach/draft** are links to the same file:

```
$ ./lnks letter /home
lnks: using find to search for links...
/home/max/letter
/home/zach/draft
```

In addition to the **if...then...elif** control structure, **lnks** introduces other features that are commonly used in shell programs. The following discussion describes **lnks** section by section.

Specify the shell The first line of the **lnks** script uses **#!** (page 297) to specify the shell that will execute the script:

```
#!/bin/bash
```

In this chapter, the **#!** notation appears only in more complex examples. It ensures that the proper shell executes the script, even when the user is running a different shell or the script is called from a script running a different shell.

Comments The second and third lines of **lnks** are comments; the shell ignores text that follows a hashmark (**#**) up to the next NEWLINE character. These comments in **lnks** briefly identify what the file does and explain how to use it:

```
# Identify links to a file
# Usage: lnks file [directory]
```

Usage messages The first **if** statement tests whether **lnks** was called with zero arguments or more than two arguments:

```
if [ $# -eq 0 -o $# -gt 2 ]; then
    echo "Usage: lnks file [directory]" 1>&2
    exit 1
fi
```

If either of these conditions is *true*, **lnks** sends a usage message to standard error and exits with a status of 1. The double quotation marks around the usage message prevent the shell from interpreting the brackets as special characters. The brackets in the usage message indicate that the **directory** argument is optional.

The second **if** statement tests whether the first command-line argument (**$1**) is a directory (the **–d** argument to test returns *true* if the file exists and is a directory):

```
if [ -d "$1" ]; then
    echo "First argument cannot be a directory." 1>&2
    echo "Usage: lnks file [directory]" 1>&2
    exit 1
else
    file="$1"
fi
```

If the first argument is a directory, **lnks** displays a usage message and exits. If it is not a directory, **lnks** saves the value of **$1** in the **file** variable because later in the script set resets the command-line arguments. If the value of **$1** is not saved before the set command is issued, its value is lost.

Test the arguments

The next section of **lnks** is an **if...then...elif** statement:

```
if [ $# -eq 1 ]; then
        directory="."
    elif [ -d "$2" ]; then
        directory="$2"
    else
        echo "Optional second argument must be a directory." 1>&2
        echo "Usage: lnks file [directory]" 1>&2
        exit 1
fi
```

The first ***test-command*** determines whether the user specified a single argument on the command line. If the ***test-command*** returns 0 (*true*), the **directory** variable is assigned the value of the working directory (.). If the ***test-command*** returns a nonzero value (*false*), the **elif** statement tests whether the second argument is a directory. If it is a directory, the **directory** variable is set equal to the second command-line argument, **$2**. If **$2** is not a directory, **lnks** sends a usage message to standard error and exits with a status of 1.

The next **if** statement in **lnks** tests whether **$file** does not exist. This test keeps **lnks** from wasting time looking for links to a nonexistent file. The test builtin, when called with the three arguments **!**, **–f**, and **$file**, evaluates to *true* if the file **$file** does *not* exist:

```
[ ! -f "$file" ]
```

The **!** operator preceding the **–f** argument to test negates its result, yielding *false* if the file **$file** *does* exist and is an ordinary file.

Next, **lnks** uses set and **ls –l** to check the number of links **$file** has:

```
# Check link count on file
set -- $(ls -l "$file")

linkcnt=$2
if [ "$linkcnt" -eq 1 ]; then
    echo "lnks: no other hard links to $file" 1>&2
    exit 0
fi
```

The set builtin uses command substitution (page 371) to set the positional parameters to the output of **ls –l**. The second field in this output is the link count, so the user-created variable **linkcnt** is set equal to **$2**. The **––** used with set prevents set from interpreting as an option the first argument produced by **ls –l** (the first argument is the access permissions for the file and typically begins with **–**). The **if** statement checks whether **$linkcnt** is equal to 1; if it is, **lnks** displays a message and exits. Although this message is not truly an error message, it is redirected to standard error. The way **lnks** has been written, all informational messages are sent to standard error. Only the final product of **lnks**—the pathnames of links to the specified file—is sent to standard output, so you can redirect the output.

If the link count is greater than 1, **lnks** goes on to identify the *inode* (page 1103) for **$file**. As explained on page 115, comparing the inodes associated with filenames is a good way to determine whether the filenames are links to the same file. The **lnks** script uses set to set the positional parameters to the output of **ls –i**. The first argument to set is the inode number for the file, so the user-created variable named **inode** is assigned the value of **$1**:

```
# Get the inode of the given file
set $(ls -i "$file")

inode=$1
```

Finally, **lnks** uses the find utility (page 822) to search for files having inode numbers that match **$inode**:

```
# Find and print the files with that inode number
echo "lnks: using find to search for links..." 1>&2
find "$directory" -xdev -inum $inode -print
```

The find utility searches the directory hierarchy rooted at the directory specified by its first argument (**$directory**) for files that meet the criteria specified by the remaining arguments. In this example, the remaining arguments send the names of files having inode numbers matching **$inode** to standard output. Because files in different filesystems can have the same inode number yet not be linked, find must search only directories in the same filesystem as **$directory**. The **–xdev** (cross-device) argument prevents find from searching directories on other filesystems. Refer to page 112 for more information about filesystems and links.

The echo command preceding the find command in **lnks**, which tells the user that find is running, is included because find can take a long time to run. Because **lnks** does not include a final exit statement, the exit status of **lnks** is that of the last command it runs: find.

Debugging Shell Scripts

When you are writing a script such as **lnks**, it is easy to make mistakes. You can use the shell's **–x** option to help debug a script. This option causes the shell to display each command after it expands it but before it runs the command. Tracing a script's execution in this way can give you information about where a problem lies.

You can run **lnks** (above) and cause the shell to display each command before it is executed. Either set the **–x** option for the current shell (**set –x**) so all scripts display commands as they are run or use the **–x** option to affect only the shell running the script called by the command line.

```
$ bash -x lnks letter /home
+ '[' 2 -eq 0 -o 2 -gt 2 ']'
+ '[' -d letter ']'
+ file=letter
+ '[' 2 -eq 1 ']'
+ '[' -d /home ']'
+ directory=/home
+ '[' '!' -f letter ']'
...
```

PS4 Each command the script executes is preceded by the value of the **PS4** variable—a plus sign (+) by default—so you can distinguish debugging output from output produced by the script. You must export **PS4** if you set it in the shell that calls the script. The next command sets **PS4** to **>>>>** followed by a SPACE and exports it:

```
$ export PS4='>>>> '
```

You can also set the **–x** option of the shell running the script by putting the following **set** command near the beginning of the script:

```
set -x
```

You can put **set –x** anywhere in the script to turn debugging on starting at that location. Turn debugging off using **set +x**. The **set –o xtrace** and **set +o xtrace** commands do the same things as **set –x** and **set +x**, respectively.

for...in

The **for...in** control structure (tcsh uses **foreach**) has the following syntax:

*for **loop-index** in **argument-list***
do
    commands
done

The **for...in** structure (Figure 10-4) assigns the value of the first argument in the ***argument-list*** to the ***loop-index*** and executes the ***commands*** between the **do** and **done** statements. The **do** and **done** statements mark the beginning and end of the **for** loop, respectively.

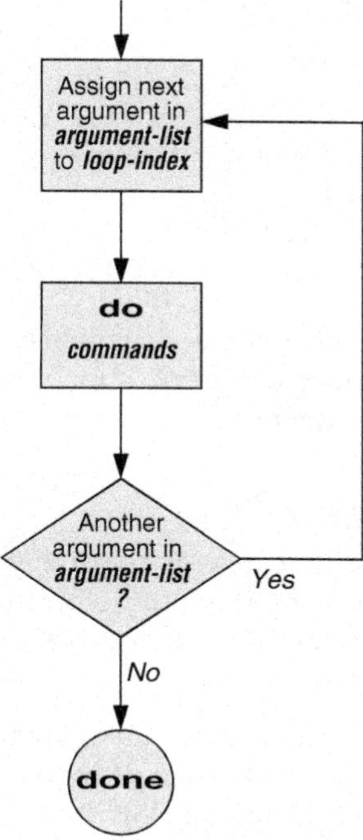

Figure 10-4 A for...in flowchart

After it passes control to the **done** statement, the structure assigns the value of the second argument in the ***argument-list*** to the ***loop-index*** and repeats the ***commands***. It repeats the ***commands*** between the **do** and **done** statements one time for each argument in the ***argument-list***. When the structure exhausts the ***argument-list***, it passes control to the statement following **done**.

The following **for...in** structure assigns **apples** to the user-created variable **fruit** and then displays the value of **fruit**, which is **apples**. Next, the structure assigns **oranges** to **fruit** and repeats the process. When it exhausts the argument list, the structure transfers control to the statement following **done**, which displays a message.

```
$ cat fruit
for fruit in apples oranges pears bananas
do
    echo "$fruit"
done
echo "Task complete."

$ ./fruit
apples
oranges
pears
bananas
Task complete.
```

The next script lists the names of the directory files in the working directory by looping through the files in the working directory and using test to determine which are directory files:

```
$ cat dirfiles
for i in *
do
    if [ -d "$i" ]
        then
            echo "$i"
    fi
done
```

The ambiguous file reference character * matches the names of all files (except hidden files) in the working directory. Prior to executing the **for** loop, the shell will expand the * and then uses the resulting list to assign successive values to the index variable **i**.

optional

STEP VALUES

As an alternative to explicitly specifying values for ***argument-list***, you can specify step values. A **for...in** loop that uses step values assigns an initial value to or increments the ***loop-index***, executes the statements within the loop, and tests a termination condition at the end of the loop.

The following example uses brace expansion with a sequence expression (page 367) to generate the ***argument-list***. This syntax works on bash version 4.0 and above; give the command **echo $BASH_VERSION** to see which version you are using. The increment does not work under macOS. The first time through the loop, bash assigns a value of 0 to **count** (the ***loop-index***) and executes the statement between **do** and **done**. At the bottom of the loop, bash tests whether the termination condition has been met (is **count>10?**). If it has, bash passes control to the statement following **done**; if not, bash increments **count** by the increment value (**2**) and makes another pass through the loop. It repeats this process until the termination condition is met.

```
$ cat step1
for count in {0..10..2}
do
    echo -n "$count "
done
echo

$ ./step1
0 2 4 6 8 10
```

Older versions of bash do not support sequence expressions; you can use the seq utility to perform the same function:

```
$ for count in $(seq 0 2 10); do echo -n "$count "; done; echo
0 2 4 6 8 10
```

The next example uses bash's C-like syntax to specify step values. This syntax gives you more flexibility in specifying the termination condition and the increment value. Using this syntax, the first parameter initializes the ***loop-index***, the second parameter specifies the condition to be tested, and the third parameter specifies the increment.

```
$ cat rand
# $RANDOM evaluates to a random value 0 < x < 32,767
# This program simulates 10 rolls of a pair of dice
for ((x=1; x<=10; x++))
do
   echo -n "Roll #$x: "
   echo -n   $(( $RANDOM % 6 + 1 ))
   echo "   " $(( $RANDOM % 6 + 1 ))
done
```

for

The **for** control structure (not in tcsh) has the following syntax:

for ***loop-index***
do
    commands
done

In the **for** structure, the ***loop-index*** takes on the value of each of the command-line arguments, one at a time. The **for** structure is the same as the **for...in** structure (Figure 10-4, page 443) except in terms of where it gets values for the ***loop-index***. The **for** structure performs a sequence of commands, usually involving each argument in turn.

The following shell script shows a **for** structure displaying each command-line argument. The first line of the script, **for arg**, implies **for arg in "$@"**, where the shell expands **"$@"** into a list of quoted command-line arguments (i.e., **"$1" "$2" "$3"** ...). The balance of the script corresponds to the **for...in** structure.

```
$ cat for_test
for arg
do
    echo "$arg"
done

$ for_test candy gum chocolate
candy
gum
chocolate
```

The next example uses a different syntax. In it, the *loop-index* is named **count** and is set to an initial value of 0. The condition to be tested is **count<=10**: bash continues executing the loop as long as this condition is *true* (as long as **count** is less than or equal to 10; see Table 10-8 on page 508 for a list of operators). Each pass through the loop, bash adds 2 to the value of count (**count+=2**).

```
$ cat step2
for (( count=0; count<=10; count+=2 ))
do
    echo -n "$count "
done
echo

$ ./step2
0 2 4 6 8 10
```

optional

THE whos SCRIPT

The following script, named **whos**, demonstrates the usefulness of the implied **"$@"** in the **for** structure. You give **whos** one or more users' full names or usernames as arguments, and **whos** displays information about the users. The **whos** script gets the information it displays from the first and fifth fields in the **/etc/passwd** file. The first field contains a username, and the fifth field typically contains the user's full name. You can provide a username as an argument to **whos** to display the user's name or provide a name as an argument to display the username. The **whos** script is similar to the finger utility, although **whos** delivers less information. macOS uses Open Directory in place of the **passwd** file; see page 1068 for a similar script that runs under macOS.

```
$ cat whos
#!/bin/bash

if [ $# -eq 0 ]
    then
        echo "Usage: whos id..." 1>&2
        exit 1
fi
```

```
for id
do
    gawk -F: '{print $1, $5}' /etc/passwd |
    grep -i "$id"
done
```

In the next example, **whos** identifies the user whose username is **chas** and the user whose name is **Marilou Smith**:

```
$ ./whos chas "Marilou Smith"
chas Charles Casey
msmith Marilou Smith
```

Use of **"$@"** The **whos** script uses a **for** statement to loop through the command-line arguments. In this script the implied use of "$@" in the **for** loop is particularly beneficial because it causes the **for** loop to treat an argument that contains a SPACE as a single argument. This example encloses **Marilou Smith** in quotation marks, which causes the shell to pass it to the script as a single argument. Then the implied "$@" in the **for** statement causes the shell to regenerate the quoted argument **Marilou Smith** so that it is again treated as a single argument. The double quotation marks in the grep statement perform the same function.

gawk For each command-line argument, **whos** searches the **/etc/passwd** file. Inside the **for** loop, the gawk utility (Chapter 14; awk and mawk work the same way) extracts the first (**$1**) and fifth (**$5**) fields from each line in **/etc/passwd**. The **–F:** option causes gawk to use a colon (:) as a field separator when it reads **/etc/passwd**, allowing it to break each line into fields. The gawk command sets and uses the **$1** and **$5** arguments; they are included within single quotation marks and are not interpreted by the shell. Do not confuse these arguments with positional parameters, which will correspond to command-line arguments. The first and fifth fields are sent to grep (page 853) via a pipeline. The grep utility searches for **$id** (to which the shell has assigned the value of a command-line argument) in its input. The **–i** option causes grep to ignore case as it searches; grep displays each line in its input that contains **$id**.

A pipe symbol (|) at the end of a line Under bash (and not tcsh), a control operator such as a pipe symbol (|) implies continuation: bash "knows" another command must follow it. Therefore, in **whos**, the NEWLINE following the pipe symbol at the end of the line with the gawk command does not have to be quoted. For more information refer to "Implicit Command-Line Continuation" on page 512.

while

The **while** control structure (see page 416 for tcsh) has the following syntax:

while ***test-command***
do
    commands
done

As long as the ***test-command*** (Figure 10-5) returns a *true* exit status, the **while** structure continues to execute the series of ***commands*** delimited by the **do** and **done** statements. Before each loop through the ***commands,*** the structure executes the ***test-command.*** When the exit status of the ***test-command*** is *false,* the structure passes control to the statement after the **done** statement.

test builtin

The following shell script first initializes the **number** variable to zero. The test builtin then determines whether **number** is less than 10. The script uses test with the **–lt** argument to perform a numerical test. For numerical comparisons, you must use **–ne** (not equal), **–eq** (equal), **–gt** (greater than), **–ge** (greater than or equal to), **–lt** (less than), or **–le** (less than or equal to). For string comparisons, use **=** (equal) or **!=** (not equal) when you are working with test. In this example, test has an exit status of 0 (*true*) as long as **number** is less than 10. As long as test returns *true,* the structure executes the commands between the **do** and **done** statements. See page 1005 for information on the test utility, which is very similar to the test builtin.

```
$ cat count
#!/bin/bash
number=0
while [ "$number" -lt 10 ]
    do
        echo -n "$number"
        ((number +=1))
    done
echo
$ ./count
0123456789
$
```

The echo command following **do** displays **number**. The **–n** prevents echo from issuing a NEWLINE following its output. The next command uses arithmetic evaluation [((...)); page 505] to increment the value of **number** by 1. The **done** statement terminates the loop and returns control to the **while** statement to start the loop over again. The final echo causes **count** to send a NEWLINE character to standard output, so the next prompt is displayed at the left edge of the display rather than immediately following the 9.

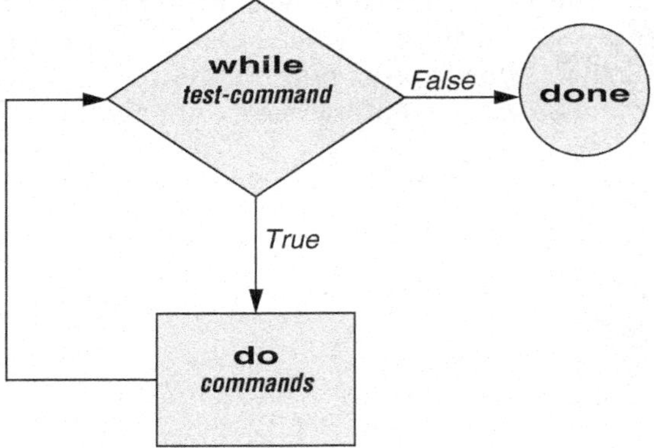

Figure 10-5 A while flowchart

optional The spell_check Script

The aspell utility (page 739; not available under macOS) checks the words in a file against a dictionary of correctly spelled words. With the **list** command, aspell runs in list mode: Input comes from standard input and aspell sends each potentially misspelled word to standard output. The following command produces a list of possible misspellings in the file **letter.txt**:

```
$ aspell list < letter.txt
quikly
portible
frendly
```

The next shell script, named **spell_check**, shows another use of a **while** structure. To find the incorrect spellings in a file, **spell_check** calls aspell to check a file against a system dictionary. But it goes a step further: It enables you to specify a list of correctly spelled words and removes these words from the output of aspell. This script is useful for removing words you use frequently, such as names and technical terms, that do not appear in a standard dictionary. Although you can duplicate the functionality of **spell_check** by using additional aspell dictionaries, the script is included here for its instructive value.

The **spell_check** script requires two filename arguments: the file containing the list of correctly spelled words and the file you want to check. The first **if** statement verifies that the user specified two arguments. The next two **if** statements verify that both arguments are readable files. (The exclamation point negates the sense of the following operator; the **–r** operator causes test to determine whether a file is readable. The result is a test that determines whether a file is *not readable*.)

```
$ cat spell_check
#!/bin/bash
# remove correct spellings from aspell output

if [ $# -ne 2 ]
    then
        echo "Usage: spell_check dictionary filename" 1>&2
        echo "dictionary: list of correct spellings" 1>&2
        echo "filename: file to be checked" 1>&2
        exit 1
fi

if [ ! -r "$1" ]
    then
        echo "spell_check: $1 is not readable" 1>&2
        exit 1
fi
if [ ! -r "$2" ]
    then
        echo "spell_check: $2 is not readable" 1>&2
        exit 1
fi
```

```
aspell list < "$2" |
while read line
do
    if ! grep "^$line$" "$1" > /dev/null
        then
            echo $line
    fi
done
```

The **spell_check** script sends the output from aspell (with the **list** argument, so it produces a list of misspelled words on standard output) through a pipeline to standard input of a **while** structure, which reads one line at a time (each line has one word on it) from standard input. The ***test-command*** (that is, **read line**) returns a *true* exit status as long as it receives a line from standard input.

Inside the **while** loop, an **if** statement monitors the return value of grep, which determines whether the line that was read is in the user's list of correctly spelled words. The pattern grep searches for (the value of **$line**) is preceded and followed by special characters that specify the beginning and end of a line (^ and $, respectively). These special characters ensure that grep finds a match only if the **$line** variable matches an entire line in the file of correctly spelled words. (Otherwise, grep would match a string, such as **paul**, in the output of aspell if the file of correctly spelled words contained the word **paulson**.) These special characters, together with the value of the **$line** variable, form a regular expression (Appendix A).

The output of grep is redirected to **/dev/null** (page 145) because the output is not needed; only the exit code is important. The **if** statement checks the negated exit status of grep (the leading exclamation point negates or changes the sense of the exit status—*true* becomes *false,* and vice versa), which is 0 or *true* (*false* when negated) when a matching line is found. If the exit status is *not* 0 or *false* (*true* when negated), the word was *not* in the file of correctly spelled words. The echo builtin sends a list of words that are not in the file of correctly spelled words to standard output.

Once it detects the EOF (end of file), the read builtin returns a *false* exit status, control passes out of the **while** structure, and the script terminates.

Before you use **spell_check**, create a file of correct spellings containing words that you use frequently but that are not in a standard dictionary. For example, if you work for a company named **Blinkenship and Klimowski, Attorneys,** you would put **Blinkenship** and **Klimowski** in the file. The following example shows how **spell_check** checks the spelling in a file named **memo** and removes **Blinkenship** and **Klimowski** from the output list of incorrectly spelled words:

```
$ aspell list < memo
Blinkenship
Klimowski
targat
hte
$ cat word_list
Blinkenship
Klimowski
$ ./spell_check word_list memo
targat
hte
```

until

The **until** (not in tcsh) and **while** (see page 416 for tcsh) structures are similar, differing only in the sense of the test performed at the top of the loop. Figure 10-6 shows that **until** continues to loop *until* the ***test-command*** returns a *true* exit status. The **while** structure loops *while* the ***test-command*** continues to return a *true* or nonerror condition. The **until** control structure has the following syntax:

until ***test-command***
do
    commands
done

The following script demonstrates an **until** structure that includes read (page 489). When the user enters the correct string of characters, the ***test-command*** is satisfied and the structure passes control out of the loop.

```
$ cat until1
secretname=zach
name=noname
echo "Try to guess the secret name!"
echo
until [ "$name" = "$secretname" ]
do
    read -p "Your guess: " name
done
echo "Very good."

$ ./until1
Try to guess the secret name!

Your guess: helen
Your guess: barbara
Your guess: rachael
Your guess: zach
Very good
```

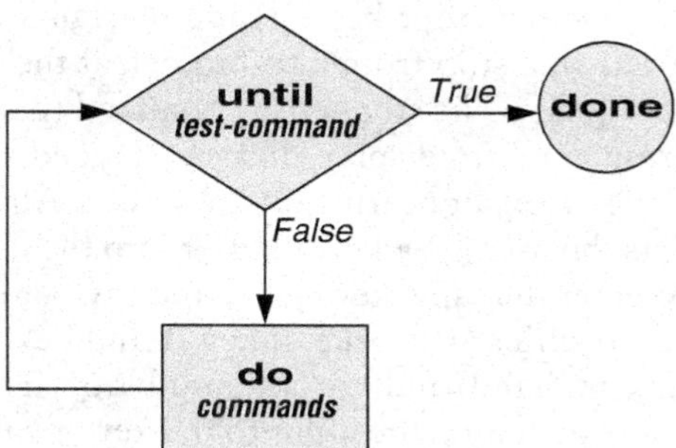

Figure 10-6 An until flowchart

The following **locktty** script is similar to the lock command on Berkeley UNIX and the **Lock Screen** menu selection in GNOME. The script prompts for a key (password) and uses an **until** control structure to lock the terminal. The **until** statement causes the system to ignore any characters typed at the keyboard until the user types the key followed by a RETURN on a line by itself, which unlocks the terminal. The **locktty** script can keep people from using your terminal while you are away from it for short periods of time. It saves you from having to log out if you are concerned about other users using your session.

```
$ cat locktty
#! /bin/bash

trap '' 1 2 3 18
stty -echo
read -p "Key: " key_1
echo
read -p "Again: " key_2
echo
key_3=
if [ "$key_1" = "$key_2" ]
    then
        tput clear
        until [ "$key_3" = "$key_2" ]
        do
            read key_3
        done
    else
        echo "locktty: keys do not match" 1>&2
fi
stty echo
```

Forget your password for locktty?

tip If you forget your key (password), you will need to log in from another (virtual) terminal and give a command to kill the process running **locktty** (e.g., **killall –9 locktty**).

trap builtin

The trap builtin (page 496; not in tcsh) at the beginning of the **locktty** script stops a user from being able to terminate the script by sending it a signal (for example, by pressing the interrupt key). Trapping signal 20 means that no one can use CONTROL-Z (job control, a stop from a tty) to defeat the lock. Table 10-5 on page 496 provides a list of signals. The **stty –echo** command (page 987) turns on keyboard echo (causes the terminal not to display characters typed at the keyboard), preventing the key the user enters from appearing on the screen. After turning off keyboard echo, the script prompts the user for a key, reads it into the user-created variable **key_1**, prompts the user to enter the same key again, and saves it in **key_2**. The statement **key_3=** creates a variable with a NULL value. If **key_1** and **key_2** match, **locktty** clears the screen (with the tput command) and starts an **until** loop. The **until** loop keeps reading from the terminal and assigning the input to the **key_3** variable. Once the user types a string that matches one of the original keys (**key_2**), the **until** loop terminates and keyboard echo is turned on again.

break AND continue

You can interrupt a **for**, **while**, or **until** loop by using a **break** or **continue** statement. The **break** statement transfers control to the statement following the **done** statement, thereby terminating execution of the loop. The **continue** command transfers control to the **done** statement, continuing execution of the loop.

The following script demonstrates the use of these two statements. The **for...in** structure loops through the values 1–10. The first **if** statement executes its commands when the value of the index is less than or equal to 3 (**$index –le 3**). The second **if** statement executes its commands when the value of the index is greater than or equal to 8 (**$index –ge 8**). In between the two **ifs**, echo displays the value of the index. For all values up to and including 3, the first **if** statement displays **continue**, executes a **continue** statement that skips **echo $index** and the second **if** statement, and continues with the next **for** statement. For the value of 8, the second **if** statement displays the word **break** and executes a **break** statement that exits from the **for** loop.

```
$ cat brk
for index in 1 2 3 4 5 6 7 8 9 10
    do
        if [ $index -le 3 ] ; then
            echo "continue"
            continue
        fi
#
    echo $index
#
    if [ $index -ge 8 ] ; then
        echo "break"
        break
    fi
done

$ ./brk
continue
continue
continue
4
5
6
7
8
break
$
```

case

The **case** structure (Figure 10-7; tcsh uses **switch**) is a multiple-branch decision mechanism. The path taken through the structure depends on a match or lack of a match between the ***test-string*** and one of the ***patterns***. When the ***test-string*** matches one of the ***patterns***, the shell transfers control to the ***commands*** following the ***pattern***. The ***commands*** are terminated by a double semicolon (;;) control operator. When control reaches this control operator, the shell transfers control to the command following the esac statement. The **case** control structure has the following syntax:

```
case test-string in
    pattern-1)
        commands-1
        ;;
```

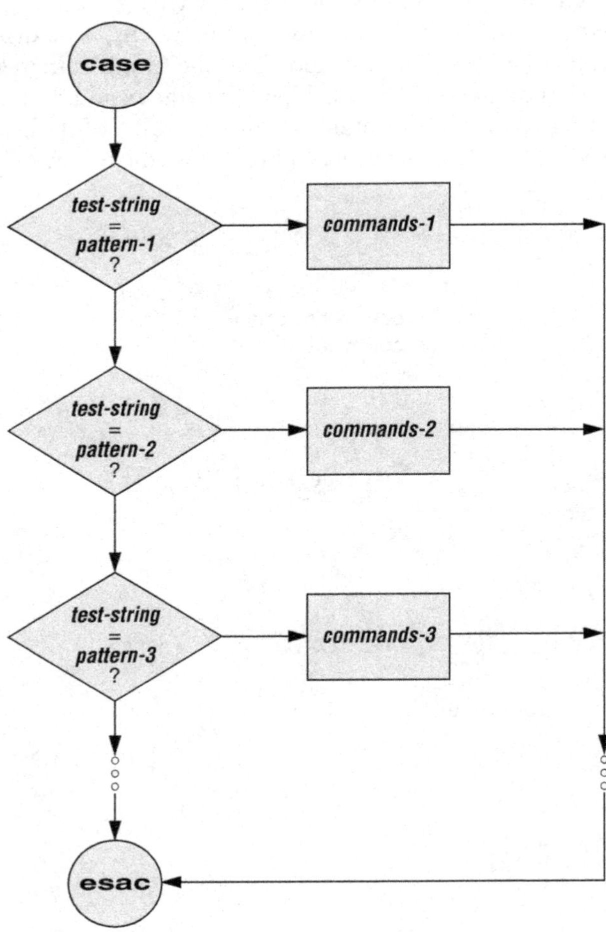

Figure 10-7 A case flowchart

```
        pattern-2)
            commands-2
            ;;
        pattern-3)
            commands-3
            ;;
    . . .
    esac
```

The following **case** structure uses the character the user enters as the ***test-string***. This value is held in the variable **letter**. If the ***test-string*** has a value of **A**, the structure executes the command following the ***pattern*** **A**. The right parenthesis is part of the **case** control structure, not part of the ***pattern***. If the ***test-string*** has a value of **B** or **C**, the structure executes the command following the matching ***pattern***. The asterisk (*) indicates *any string of characters* and serves as a catchall in case there is no match. If no ***pattern*** matches the ***test-string*** and if there is no catchall (*) ***pattern***, control passes to the command following the **esac** statement, without the **case** structure taking any action.

```
$ cat case1
read -p "Enter A, B, or C: " letter
case "$letter" in
    A)
        echo "You entered A"
        ;;
    B)
        echo "You entered B"
        ;;
    C)
        echo "You entered C"
        ;;
    *)
        echo "You did not enter A, B, or C"
        ;;
esac

$ ./case1
Enter A, B, or C: B
You entered B
```

The next execution of **case1** shows the user entering a lowercase **b**. Because the ***test-string*** **b** does not match the uppercase **B** ***pattern*** (or any other ***pattern*** in the **case** statement), the program executes the commands following the catchall ***pattern*** and displays a message:

```
$ ./case1
Enter A, B, or C: b
You did not enter A, B, or C
```

The *pattern* in the **case** structure is a glob (it is analogous to an ambiguous file reference). It can include any special characters and strings shown in Table 10-2.

Table 10-2 Patterns

Pattern	Function
*	Matches any string of characters. Use for the default case.
?	Matches any single character.
[...]	Defines a character class. Any characters enclosed within brackets are tried, one at a time, in an attempt to match a single character. A hyphen between two characters specifies a range of characters.
|	Separates alternative choices that satisfy a particular branch of the **case** structure.

The next script accepts both uppercase and lowercase letters:

```
$ cat case2
read -p "Enter A, B, or C: " letter
case "$letter" in
    a|A)
        echo "You entered A"
        ;;
    b|B)
        echo "You entered B"
        ;;
    c|C)
        echo "You entered C"
        ;;
    *)
        echo "You did not enter A, B, or C"
        ;;
esac

$ ./case2
Enter A, B, or C: b
You entered B
```

optional The following example shows how to use the **case** structure to create a simple menu. The **command_menu** script uses **echo** to present menu items and prompt the user for a selection. (The **select** control structure [page 460] is a much easier way of coding a menu.) The **case** structure then executes the appropriate utility depending on the user's selection.

```
$ cat command_menu
#!/bin/bash
# menu interface to simple commands

echo -e "\n      COMMAND MENU\n"
echo "  a.  Current date and time"
echo "  b.  Users currently logged in"
```

```
echo "  c.  Name of the working directory"
echo -e "  d.  Contents of the working directory\n"
read -p "Enter a, b, c, or d: " answer
echo
#
case "$answer" in
    a)
        date
        ;;
    b)
        who
        ;;
    c)
        pwd
        ;;
    d)
        ls
        ;;
    *)
        echo "There is no selection: $answer"
        ;;
esac

$ ./command_menu

          COMMAND MENU

    a.  Current date and time
    b.  Users currently logged in
    c.  Name of the working directory
    d.  Contents of the working directory

Enter a, b, c, or d: a
Sat Jan  6 12:31:12 PST 2018
```

echo –e The –e option causes echo to interpret **\n** as a NEWLINE character. If you do not include this option, echo does not output the extra blank lines that make the menu easy to read but instead outputs the (literal) two-character sequence **\n**. The –e option causes echo to interpret several other backslash-quoted characters (Table 10-3). Remember to quote (i.e., place double quotation marks around the string) the backslash-quoted character so the shell does not interpret it but rather passes the backslash and the character to echo. See **xpg_echo** (page 363) for a way to avoid using the –e option.

Table 10-3 Special characters in echo (must use **–e**)

Quoted character	echo **displays**
\a	Alert (bell)
\b	BACKSPACE
\c	Suppress trailing NEWLINE

Table 10-3 Special characters in echo (must use **–e**) (continued)

Quoted character	echo **displays**
\f	FORMFEED
\n	NEWLINE
\r	RETURN
\t	Horizontal TAB
\v	Vertical TAB
****	Backslash
nnn	The character with the ASCII octal code ***nnn;*** if ***nnn*** is not valid, echo displays the string literally

You can also use the **case** control structure to take various actions in a script, depending on how many arguments the script is called with. The following script, named **safedit**, uses a **case** structure that branches based on the number of command-line arguments (**$#**). It calls vim and saves a backup copy of a file you are editing.

```
$ cat safedit
#!/bin/bash

PATH=/bin:/usr/bin
script=$(basename $0)
case $# in

    0)
        vim
        exit 0
        ;;

    1)
        if [ ! -f "$1" ]
            then
                vim "$1"
                exit 0
            fi
        if [ ! -r "$1" -o ! -w "$1" ]
            then
                echo "$script: check permissions on $1" 1>&2
                exit 1
            else
                editfile=$1
            fi
        if [ ! -w "." ]
            then
                echo "$script: backup cannot be " \
                    "created in the working directory" 1>&2
                exit 1
            fi
        ;;
```

```
        *)
            echo "Usage: $script [file-to-edit]" 1>&2
            exit 1
            ;;
    esac
    tempfile=/tmp/$$.$script
    cp $editfile $tempfile
    if vim $editfile
        then
            mv $tempfile bak.$(basename $editfile)
            echo "$script: backup file created"
        else
            mv $tempfile editerr
            echo "$script: edit error--copy of " \
                "original file is in editerr" 1>&2
    fi
```

If you call **safedit** without any arguments, the **case** structure executes its first branch and calls vim without a filename argument. Because an existing file is not being edited, **safedit** does not create a backup file. (See the **:w** command on page 179 for an explanation of how to exit from vim when you have called it without a filename.) If you call **safedit** with one argument, it runs the commands in the second branch of the **case** structure and verifies that the file specified by **$1** does not yet exist or is the name of a file for which the user has read and write permission. The **safedit** script also verifies that the user has write permission for the working directory. If the user calls **safedit** with more than one argument, the third branch of the **case** structure presents a usage message and exits with a status of 1.

Set PATH At the beginning of the script, the **PATH** variable is set to search **/bin** and **/usr/bin**. Setting **PATH** in this way ensures that the commands executed by the script are standard utilities, which are kept in those directories. By setting this variable inside a script, you can avoid the problems that might occur if users have set **PATH** to search their own directories first and have scripts or programs with the same names as the utilities the script calls. You can also include absolute pathnames within a script to achieve this end, although this practice can make a script less portable.

Name of the program The next line declares a variable named **script** and initializes it with the simple filename of the script:

```
script=$(basename $0)
```

The basename utility sends the simple filename component of its argument to standard output, which is assigned to the **script** variable, using command substitution. The **$0** holds the command the script was called with (page 470). No matter which of the following commands the user calls the script with, the output of basename is the simple filename **safedit**:

```
$ /home/max/bin/safedit memo
$ ./safedit memo
$ safedit memo
```

After the **script** variable is set, it replaces the filename of the script in usage and error messages. By using a variable that is derived from the command that invoked the script rather than a filename that is hardcoded into the script, you can create links to the script or rename it, and the usage and error messages will still provide accurate information.

Naming temporary files Another feature of **safedit** relates to the use of the **$$** parameter in the name of a temporary file. The statement following the **esac** statement creates and assigns a value to the **tempfile** variable. This variable contains the name of a temporary file that is stored in the **/tmp** directory, as are many temporary files. The temporary filename begins with the PID number of the shell and ends with the name of the script. Using the PID number ensures that the filename is unique. Thus **safedit** will not attempt to overwrite an existing file, as might happen if two people were using **safedit** at the same time. The name of the script is appended so that, should the file be left in **/tmp** for some reason, you can figure out where it came from.

The PID number is used in front of—rather than after—**$script** in the filename because of the 14-character limit placed on filenames by some older versions of UNIX. Linux systems do not have this limitation. Because the PID number ensures the uniqueness of the filename, it is placed first so that it cannot be truncated. (If the **$script** component is truncated, the filename is still unique.) For the same reason, when a backup file is created inside the **if** control structure a few lines down in the script, the filename consists of the string **bak.** followed by the name of the file being edited. On an older system, if **bak** were used as a suffix rather than a prefix and the original filename were 14 characters long, **.bak** might be lost and the original file would be overwritten. The basename utility extracts the simple filename of **$editfile** before it is prefixed with **bak.**.

The **safedit** script uses an unusual ***test-command*** in the **if** structure: **vim $editfile**. The ***test-command*** calls vim to edit **$editfile**. When you finish editing the file and exit from vim, vim returns an exit code. The **if** control structure uses that exit code to determine which branch to take. If the editing session completed successfully, vim returns 0 and the statements following the **then** statement are executed. If vim does not terminate normally (as would occur if the user killed [page 866] the vim process), vim returns a nonzero exit status and the script executes the statements following **else**.

select

The **select** control structure (not in tcsh) is based on the one found in the Korn Shell. It displays a menu, assigns a value to a variable based on the user's choice of items, and executes a series of commands. The **select** control structure has the following syntax:

```
select varname [in arg . . . ]
do
    commands
done
```

The **select** structure displays a menu of the *arg* items. If you omit the keyword **in** and the list of arguments, **select** uses the positional parameters in place of the *arg* items. The menu is formatted with numbers before each item. For example, a **select** structure that begins with

```
select fruit in apple banana blueberry kiwi orange watermelon STOP
```

displays the following menu:

```
1) apple       3) blueberry   5) orange      7) STOP
2) banana      4) kiwi        6) watermelon
```

The **select** structure uses the values of the **LINES** (default is 24) and **COLUMNS** (default is 80) variables to specify the size of the display. With **COLUMNS** set to 20, the menu looks like this:

```
1) apple
2) banana
3) blueberry
4) kiwi
5) orange
6) watermelon
7) STOP
```

PS3 After displaying the menu, **select** displays the value of **PS3**, the **select** prompt. The default value of **PS3** is **?#**, but it is typically set to a more meaningful value. When you enter a valid number (one in the menu range) in response to the **PS3** prompt, **select** sets ***varname*** to the argument corresponding to the number you entered. An invalid entry causes the shell to set ***varname*** to null. Either way, **select** stores your response in the keyword variable **REPLY** and then executes the ***commands*** between **do** and **done**. If you press RETURN without entering a choice, the shell redisplays the menu and the **PS3** prompt.

The **select** structure continues to issue the **PS3** prompt and execute the ***commands*** until something causes it to exit—typically, a **break** or **exit** statement. A **break** statement exits from the loop and an **exit** statement exits from the script.

The following script illustrates the use of **select**:

```
$ cat fruit2
#!/bin/bash
PS3="Choose your favorite fruit from these possibilities: "
select FRUIT in apple banana blueberry kiwi orange watermelon STOP
do
    if [ "$FRUIT" == "" ]; then
        echo -e "Invalid entry.\n"
        continue
    elif [ $FRUIT = STOP ]; then
        echo "Thanks for playing!"
        break
    fi
echo "You chose $FRUIT as your favorite."
echo -e "That is choice number $REPLY.\n"
done
```

```
$ ./fruit2
1) apple        3) blueberry   5) orange       7) STOP
2) banana       4) kiwi        6) watermelon
Choose your favorite fruit from these possibilities: 3
You chose blueberry as your favorite.
That is choice number 3.

Choose your favorite fruit from these possibilities: 99
Invalid entry.

Choose your favorite fruit from these possibilities: 7
Thanks for playing!
```

After setting the **PS3** prompt and establishing the menu with the **select** statement, **fruit2** executes the ***commands*** between **do** and **done**. If the user submits an invalid entry, the shell sets ***varname*** (**$FRUIT**) to a null value. If **$FRUIT** is null, echo displays an error message; **continue** then causes the shell to redisplay the **PS3** prompt. If the entry is valid, the script tests whether the user wants to stop. If so, echo displays an appropriate message and **break** exits from the **select** structure (and from the script). If the user enters a valid response and does not want to stop, the script displays the name and number of the user's response. (See page 457 for information about the echo –e option.)

HERE DOCUMENT

A Here document allows you to redirect input to a shell script from within the shell script itself. A Here document is so named because it is *here*—immediately accessible in the shell script—instead of *there,* perhaps in another file.

The following script, named **birthday**, contains a Here document. The two less than symbols (**<<**) in the first line indicate a Here document follows. One or more characters that delimit the Here document follow the less than symbols—this example uses a plus sign. Whereas the opening delimiter must appear adjacent to the less than symbols, the closing delimiter must be on a line by itself. The shell sends everything between the two delimiters to the process as standard input. In the example it is as though you have redirected standard input to grep from a file, except that the file is embedded in the shell script:

```
$ cat birthday
grep -i "$1" <<+
Max     June 22
Barbara February 3
Darlene May 8
Helen   March 13
Zach    January 23
Nancy   June 26
+
$ ./birthday Zach
Zach    January 23
```

```
$ ./birthday june
Max      June 22
Nancy    June 26
```

When you run **birthday**, it lists all the Here document lines that contain the argument you called it with. In this case the first time **birthday** is run, it displays Zach's birthday because it is called with an argument of **Zach**. The second run displays all the birthdays in June. The **–i** argument causes grep's search not to be case sensitive.

optional The next script, named **bundle**,[1] includes a clever use of a Here document. The **bundle** script is an elegant example of a script that creates a shell archive (**shar**) file. The script creates a file that is itself a shell script containing several other files as well as the code needed to re-create the original files:

```
$ cat bundle
#!/bin/bash
# bundle:  group files into distribution package

echo "# To unbundle, bash this file"
for i
do
    echo "echo $i 1>&2"
    echo "cat >$i <<'End of $i'"
    cat $i
    echo "End of $i"
done
```

Just as the shell does not treat special characters that occur in standard input of a shell script as special, so the shell does not treat the special characters that occur between the delimiters in a Here document as special.

As the following example shows, the output of **bundle** is a shell script, which is redirected to a file named **bothfiles**. It contains the contents of each file given as an argument to **bundle** (**file1** and **file2** in this case) inside a Here document. To extract the original files from **bothfiles**, you simply give it as an argument to a bash command. Before each Here document is a cat command that causes the Here document to be written to a new file when **bothfiles** is run:

```
$ cat file1
This is a file.
It contains two lines.
$ cat file2
This is another file.
It contains
three lines.
```

1. Thanks to Brian W. Kernighan and Rob Pike, *The Unix Programming Environment* (Englewood Cliffs, N.J.: Prentice-Hall, 1984), 98. Reprinted with permission.

```
$ ./bundle file1 file2 > bothfiles
$ cat bothfiles
# To unbundle, bash this file
echo file1 1>&2
cat >file1 <<'End of file1'
This is a file.
It contains two lines.
End of file1
echo file2 1>&2
cat >file2 <<'End of file2'
This is another file.
It contains
three lines.
End of file2
```

In the next example, **file1** and **file2** are removed before **bothfiles** is run. The **bothfiles** script echoes the names of the files it creates as it creates them. The ls command then shows that **bothfiles** has re-created **file1** and **file2**:

```
$ rm file1 file2
$ bash bothfiles
file1
file2
$ ls
bothfiles
file1
file2
```

File Descriptors

As discussed on page 292, before a process can read from or write to a file, it must open that file. When a process opens a file, Linux associates a number (called a *file descriptor*) with the file. A file descriptor is an index into the process's table of open files. Each process has its own set of open files and its own file descriptors. After opening a file, a process reads from and writes to that file by referring to its file descriptor. When it no longer needs the file, the process closes the file, freeing the file descriptor.

A typical Linux process starts with three open files: standard input (file descriptor 0), standard output (file descriptor 1), and standard error (file descriptor 2). Often, these are the only files the process needs. Recall that you redirect standard output with the symbol **>** or the symbol **1>** and that you redirect standard error with the symbol **2>**. Although you can redirect other file descriptors, because file descriptors other than 0, 1, and 2 do not have any special conventional meaning, it is rarely useful to do so. The exception is in programs that you write yourself, in which case you control the meaning of the file descriptors and can take advantage of redirection.

OPENING A FILE DESCRIPTOR

The Bourne Again Shell opens files using the exec builtin with the following syntax:

*exec **n**> **outfile***
*exec **m**< **infile***

The first line opens ***outfile*** for output and holds it open, associating it with file descriptor ***n***. The second line opens ***infile*** for input and holds it open, associating it with file descriptor ***m***.

DUPLICATING A FILE DESCRIPTOR

The <& token duplicates an input file descriptor; >& duplicates an output file descriptor. You can duplicate a file descriptor by making it refer to the same file as another open file descriptor, such as standard input or output. Use the following syntax to open or redirect file descriptor ***n*** as a duplicate of file descriptor ***m***:

*exec **n**<&**m***

Once you have opened a file, you can use it for input and output in two ways. First, you can use I/O redirection on any command line, redirecting standard output to a file descriptor with >&***n*** or redirecting standard input from a file descriptor with <&***n***. Second, you can use the read (page 489) and echo builtins. If you invoke other commands, including functions (page 356), they inherit these open files and file descriptors. When you have finished using a file, you can close it using the following syntax:

*exec **n**<&–*

FILE DESCRIPTOR EXAMPLES

When you call the following **mycp** function with two arguments, it copies the file named by the first argument to the file named by the second argument. If you supply only one argument, the script copies the file named by the argument to standard output. If you invoke **mycp** with no arguments, it copies standard input to standard output.

A function is not a shell script

tip The **mycp** example is a shell function; it will not work as you expect if you execute it as a shell script. (It *will* work: The function will be created in a very short-lived subshell, which is of little use.) You can enter this function from the keyboard. If you put the function in a file, you can run it as an argument to the . (dot) builtin (page 290). You can also put the function in a startup file if you want it to be always available (page 358).

```
function mycp () {
case $# in
    0)
        # Zero arguments
        # File descriptor 3 duplicates standard input
        # File descriptor 4 duplicates standard output
        exec 3<&0 4<&1
        ;;
    1)
        # One argument
        # Open the file named by the argument for input
        # and associate it with file descriptor 3
        # File descriptor 4 duplicates standard output
        exec 3< $1 4<&1
        ;;
    2)
        # Two arguments
        # Open the file named by the first argument for input
        # and associate it with file descriptor 3
        # Open the file named by the second argument for output
        # and associate it with file descriptor 4
        exec 3< $1 4> $2
        ;;
    *)
        echo "Usage: mycp [source [dest]]"
        return 1
        ;;
esac

# Call cat with input coming from file descriptor 3
# and output going to file descriptor 4
cat <&3 >&4

# Close file descriptors 3 and 4
exec 3<&- 4<&-
}
```

The real work of this function is done in the line that begins with cat. The rest of the script arranges for file descriptors 3 and 4, which are the input and output of the cat command, respectively, to be associated with the appropriate files.

optional The next program takes two filenames on the command line, sorts both, and sends the output to temporary files. The program then merges the sorted files to standard output, preceding each line with a number that indicates which file it came from.

```
$ cat sortmerg
#!/bin/bash
usage () {
if [ $# -ne 2 ]; then
    echo "Usage: $0 file1 file2" 2>&1
    exit 1
    fi
}

# Default temporary directory
: ${TEMPDIR:=/tmp}
```

```
# Check argument count
usage "$@"

# Set up temporary files for sorting
file1=$TEMPDIR/$$.file1
file2=$TEMPDIR/$$.file2

# Sort
sort $1 > $file1
sort $2 > $file2

# Open $file1 and $file2 for reading. Use file descriptors 3 and 4.
exec 3<$file1
exec 4<$file2

# Read the first line from each file to figure out how to start.
read Line1 <&3
status1=$?
read Line2 <&4
status2=$?
# Strategy: while there is still input left in both files:
#   Output the line that should come first.
#   Read a new line from the file that line came from.
while [ $status1 -eq 0 -a $status2 -eq 0 ]
    do
        if [[ "$Line2" > "$Line1" ]]; then
            echo -e "1.\t$Line1"
            read -u3 Line1
            status1=$?
        else
            echo -e "2.\t$Line2"
            read -u4 Line2
            status2=$?
        fi
    done

# Now one of the files is at end of file.
# Read from each file until the end.
# First file1:
while [ $status1 -eq 0 ]
    do
        echo -e "1.\t$Line1"
        read Line1 <&3
        status1=$?
    done
# Next file2:
while [[ $status2 -eq 0 ]]
    do
        echo -e "2.\t$Line2"
        read Line2 <&4
        status2=$?
    done

# Close and remove both input files
exec 3<&- 4<&-
rm -f $file1 $file2
exit 0
```

DETERMINING WHETHER A FILE DESCRIPTOR IS ASSOCIATED WITH THE TERMINAL

The test –t criterion takes an argument of a file descriptor and causes test to return a value of 0 (*true*) or not 0 (*false*) based on whether the specified file descriptor is associated with the terminal (screen or keyboard). It is typically used to determine whether standard input, standard output, and/or standard error is coming from/going to the terminal.

In the following example, the **is.term** script uses the test –t criterion ([ ] is a synonym for test; page 1005) to see if file descriptor 1 (initially standard output) of the process running the shell script is associated with the screen. The message the script displays is based on whether test returns *true* (file descriptor 1 is associated with the screen) or *false* (file descriptor 1 is *not* associated with the screen).

```
$ cat is.term
if [ -t 1 ] ; then
        echo "FD 1 (stdout) IS going to the screen"
    else
        echo "FD 1 (stdout) is NOT going to the screen"
fi
```

When you run **is.term** without redirecting standard output, the script displays **FD 1 (stdout) IS going to the screen** because standard output of the **is.term** script has not been redirected:

```
$ ./is.term
FD 1 (stdout) IS going to the screen
```

When you redirect standard output of a program using **>** on the command line, bash closes file descriptor 1 and then reopens it, associating it with the file specified following the redirect symbol.

The next example redirects standard output of the **is.term** script: The newly opened file descriptor 1 associates standard output with the file named **hold**. Now the test command ([–t 1]) fails, returning a value of 1 (*false*), because standard output is not associated with a terminal. The script writes **FD 1 (stdout) is NOT going to the screen** to **hold**:

```
$ ./is.term > hold
$ cat hold
FD 1 (stdout) is NOT going to the screen
```

If you redirect standard error from **is.term**, the script will report **FD 1 (stdout) IS going to the screen** and will write nothing to the file receiving the redirection; standard output has not been redirected. You can use [–t 2] to test if standard error is going to the screen:

```
$ ./is.term 2> hold
FD 1 (stdout) IS going to the screen
```

In a similar manner, if you send standard output of **is.term** through a pipeline, test reports standard output is not associated with a terminal. In this example, cat copies standard input to standard output:

```
$ ./is.term | cat
FD 1 (stdout) is NOT going to the screen
```

optional You can also experiment with test on the command line. This technique allows you to make changes to your experimental code quickly by taking advantage of command history and editing (page 338). To better understand the following examples, first verify that test (called as [ ]) returns a value of 0 (*true*) when file descriptor 1 is associated with the screen and a value other than 0 (*false*) when file descriptor 1 is not associated with the screen. The **$?** special parameter (page 477) holds the exit status of the previous command.

```
$ [ -t 1 ]
$ echo $?
0

$ [ -t 1 ] > hold
$ echo $?
1
```

As explained on page 302, the && (AND) control operator first executes the command preceding it. Only if that command returns a value of 0 (*true*) does && execute the command following it. In the following example, if [–t 1] returns 0, && executes **echo "FD 1 to screen"**. Although the parentheses (page 302) are not required in this example, they are needed in the next one.

```
$ ( [ -t 1 ] && echo "FD 1 to screen" )
FD 1 to screen
```

Next, the output from the same command line is sent through a pipeline to cat, so test returns 1 (*false*) and && does not execute echo.

```
$ ( [ -t 1 ] && echo "FD 1 to screen" ) | cat
$
```

The following example is the same as the previous one, except test checks whether file descriptor 2 is associated with the screen. Because the pipeline redirects only standard output, test returns 0 (*true*) and && executes echo.

```
$ ( [ -t 2 ] && echo "FD 2 to screen" ) | cat
FD 2 to screen
```

In this example, test checks whether file descriptor 2 is associated with the screen(it is) and echo sends its output to file descriptor 1 (which goes through the pipeline to cat).

Parameters

Shell parameters were introduced on page 310. This section goes into more detail about positional parameters and special parameters.

Positional Parameters

Positional parameters comprise the command name and command-line arguments. These parameters are called *positional* because you refer to them by their position on the command line. You cannot use an assignment statement to change the value of a positional parameter. However, the bash set builtin (page 472) enables you to change the value of any positional parameter except the name of the calling program (the command name). The tcsh set builtin does not change the values of positional parameters.

$0: Name of the Calling Program

The shell expands $0 to the name of the calling program (the command you used to call the program—usually, the name of the program you are running). This parameter is numbered zero because it appears before the first argument on the command line:

```
$ cat abc
echo "This script was called by typing $0"
$ ./abc
This script was called by typing ./abc
$ /home/sam/abc
This script was called by typing /home/sam/abc
```

The preceding shell script uses echo to verify the way the script you are executing was called. You can use the basename utility and command substitution to extract the simple filename of the script:

```
$ cat abc2
echo "This script was called by typing $(basename $0)"
$ /home/sam/abc2
This script was called by typing abc2
```

When you call a script through a link, the shell expands $0 to the value of the link. The busybox utility (page 747) takes advantage of this feature so it knows how it was called and which utility to run.

```
$ ln -s abc2 mylink
$ /home/sam/mylink
This script was called by typing mylink
```

When you display the value of $0 from an interactive shell, the shell displays its name because that is the name of the calling program (the program you are running).

```
$ echo $0
bash
```

bash versus –bash

tip On some systems, **echo $0** displays **–bash** while on others it displays **bash**. The former indicates a login shell (page 288); the latter indicates a shell that is not a login shell. In a GUI environment, some terminal emulators launch login shells while others do not.

$1 – $*n*: POSITIONAL PARAMETERS

The shell expands **$1** to the first argument on the command line, **$2** to the second argument, and so on up to **$*n***. These parameters are short for **${1}**, **${2}**, **${3}**, and so on. For values of ***n*** less than or equal to 9, the braces are optional. For values of ***n*** greater than 9, the number must be enclosed within braces. For example, the twelfth positional parameter is represented by **${12}**. The following script displays positional parameters that hold command-line arguments:

```
$ cat display_5args
echo First 5 arguments are $1 $2 $3 $4 $5

$ ./display_5args zach max helen
First 5 arguments are zach max helen
```

The **display_5args** script displays the first five command-line arguments. The shell expands each parameter that represents an argument that is not present on the command line to a null string. Thus, the **$4** and **$5** parameters have null values in this example.

Always quote positional parameters

caution You can "lose" positional parameters if you do not quote them. See the following text for an example.

Enclose references to positional parameters between double quotation marks. The quotation marks are particularly important when you are using positional parameters as arguments to commands. Without double quotation marks, a positional parameter that is not set or that has a null value disappears:

```
$ cat showargs
echo "$0 was called with $# arguments, the first is :$1:."

$ ./showargs a b c
./showargs was called with 3 arguments, the first is :a:.

$ echo $xx

$ ./showargs $xx a b c
./showargs was called with 3 arguments, the first is :a:.
$ ./showargs "$xx" a b c
./showargs was called with 4 arguments, the first is ::.
```

The **showargs** script displays the number of arguments it was called with (**$#**) followed by the value of the first argument between colons. In the preceding example, **showargs** is initially called with three arguments. Next, the echo command shows that the **$xx** variable, which is not set, has a null value. The **$xx** variable is the first argument to the second and third **showargs** commands; it is not quoted in the second command and quoted using double quotation marks in the third command. In the second **showargs** command, the shell expands the arguments to **a b c** and passes **showargs** three arguments. In the third **showargs** command, the shell expands the arguments to "" **a b c**, which results in calling **showargs** with four arguments. The difference in the two calls to **showargs** illustrates a subtle potential problem when using positional parameters that might not be set or that might have a null value.

set: Initializes Positional Parameters

When you call the set builtin with one or more arguments, it assigns the values of the arguments to the positional parameters, starting with **$1** (not in tcsh). The following script uses set to assign values to the positional parameters **$1**, **$2**, and **$3**:

```
$ cat set_it
set this is it
echo $3 $2 $1
$ ./set_it
it is this
```

optional A single hyphen (–) on a set command line marks the end of options and the start of values the shell assigns to positional parameters. A – also turns off the **xtrace** (**–x**) and **verbose** (**–v**) options (Table 8-13 on page 361). The following set command turns on **posix** mode and sets the first two positional parameters as shown by the echo command:

```
$ set -o posix - first.param second.param
$ echo $*
first.param second.param
```

A double hyphen (––) on a set command line without any following arguments unsets the positional parameters; when followed by arguments, –– sets the positional parameters, including those that begin with a hyphen (–).

```
$ set --
$ echo $*

$
```

Combining command substitution (page 371) with the set builtin is a convenient way to alter standard output of a command to a form that can be easily manipulated in a shell script. The following script shows how to use date and set to provide the date in a useful format. The first command shows the output of date. Then cat displays the contents of the **dateset** script. The first command in this script uses command substitution to set the positional parameters to the output of the date utility. The next command, **echo $***, displays all positional parameters resulting from the previous set. Subsequent commands display the values of **$1**, **$2**, **$3**, and **$6**. The final command displays the date in a format you can use in a letter or report.

```
$ date
Tues Aug 15 17:35:29 PDT 2017
$ cat dateset
set $(date)
echo $*
echo
echo "Argument 1: $1"
echo "Argument 2: $2"
echo "Argument 3: $3"
echo "Argument 6: $6"
echo
echo "$2 $3, $6"

$ ./dateset
Tues Aug 15 17:35:34 PDT 2017

Argument 1: Tues
Argument 2: Aug
Argument 3: 15
Argument 6: 2017

Aug 15, 2017
```

You can also use the +*format* argument to date (page 787) to specify the content and format of its output.

set displays shell variables

When called without arguments, set displays a list of the shell variables that are set, including user-created variables and keyword variables. Under bash, this list is the same as that displayed by declare (page 315) when it is called without any arguments.

```
$ set
BASH_VERSION='4.2.24(1)-release'
COLORS=/etc/DIR_COLORS
COLUMNS=89
LESSOPEN='||/usr/bin/lesspipe.sh %s'
LINES=53
LOGNAME=sam
MAIL=/var/spool/mail/sam
MAILCHECK=60
...
```

The bash set builtin can also perform other tasks. For more information refer to "set: Works with Shell Features, Positional Parameters, and Variables" on page 484.

shift: PROMOTES POSITIONAL PARAMETERS

The shift builtin promotes each positional parameter. The first argument (which was represented by **$1**) is discarded. The second argument (which was represented by **$2**) becomes the first argument (now **$1**), the third argument becomes the second, and so on. Because no "unshift" command exists, you cannot bring back arguments that have been discarded. An optional argument to shift specifies the number of positions to shift (and the number of arguments to discard); the default is 1.

The following **demo_shift** script is called with three arguments. Double quotation marks around the arguments to echo preserve the spacing of the output but allow the shell to expand variables. The program displays the arguments and shifts them repeatedly until no arguments are left to shift.

```
$ cat demo_shift
echo "arg1= $1    arg2= $2    arg3= $3"
shift
echo "arg1= $1    arg2= $2    arg3= $3"
shift
echo "arg1= $1    arg2= $2    arg3= $3"
shift
echo "arg1= $1    arg2= $2    arg3= $3"
shift

$ ./demo_shift alice helen zach
arg1= alice    arg2= helen    arg3= zach
arg1= helen    arg2= zach     arg3=
arg1= zach     arg2=    arg3=
arg1=     arg2=    arg3=
```

Repeatedly using shift is a convenient way to loop over all command-line arguments in shell scripts that expect an arbitrary number of arguments. See page 436 for a shell script that uses shift.

$* and $@: Expand to All Positional Parameters

The shell expands the **$*** parameter to all positional parameters, as the **display_all** program demonstrates:

```
$ cat display_all
echo All arguments are $*

$ ./display_all a b c d e f g h i j k l m n o p
All arguments are a b c d e f g h i j k l m n o p
```

"$*" versus "$@"

The **$*** and **$@** parameters work the same way except when they are enclosed within double quotation marks. Using **"$*"** yields a single argument with the first character in **IFS** (page 321; normally a SPACE) between the positional parameters. Using **"$@"** produces a list wherein each positional parameter is a separate argument. This difference typically makes **"$@"** more useful than **"$*"** in shell scripts.

The following scripts help explain the difference between these two parameters. In the second line of both scripts, the single quotation marks keep the shell from interpreting the enclosed special characters, allowing the shell to pass them to echo so echo can display them. The **bb1** script shows that **set "$*"** assigns multiple arguments to the first command-line parameter.

```
$ cat bb1
set "$*"
echo $# parameters with '"$*"'
echo 1: $1
echo 2: $2
echo 3: $3

$ ./bb1 a b c
1 parameters with "$*"
1: a b c
2:
3:
```

The **bb2** script shows that **set "$@"** assigns each argument to a different command-line parameter.

```
$ cat bb2
set "$@"
echo $# parameters with '"$@"'
echo 1: $1
echo 2: $2
echo 3: $3

$ ./bb2 a b c
3 parameters with "$@"
1: a
2: b
3: c
```

SPECIAL PARAMETERS

Special parameters enable you to access useful values pertaining to positional parameters and the execution of shell commands. As with positional parameters, the shell expands a special parameter when it is preceded by a **$**. Also as with positional parameters, you cannot modify the value of a special parameter using an assignment statement.

$#: NUMBER OF POSITIONAL PARAMETERS

The shell expands **$#** to the decimal number of arguments on the command line (positional parameters), not counting the name of the calling program:

```
$ cat num_args
echo "This script was called with $# arguments."
```

```
$ ./num_args sam max zach
This script was called with 3 arguments.
```

The next example shows set initializing four positional parameters and echo displaying the number of parameters set initialized:

```
$ set a b c d; echo $#
4
```

$$: PID Number

The shell expands the $$ parameter to the PID number of the process that is executing it. In the following interaction, echo displays the value of this parameter and the ps utility confirms its value. Both commands show the shell has a PID number of 5209:

```
$ echo $$
5209
$ ps
  PID TTY          TIME CMD
 5209 pts/1    00:00:00 bash
 6015 pts/1    00:00:00 ps
```

Because echo is built into the shell, the shell does not create another process when you give an echo command. However, the results are the same whether echo is a builtin or not, because the shell expands $$ *before* it forks a new process to run a command. Try giving this command using the echo utility (**/bin/echo**), which is run by another process, and see what happens.

Naming temporary files In the following example, the shell substitutes the value of $$ and passes that value to cp as a prefix for a filename:

```
$ echo $$
8232
$ cp memo $$.memo
$ ls
8232.memo memo
```

Incorporating a PID number in a filename is useful for creating unique filenames when the meanings of the names do not matter; this technique is often used in shell scripts for creating names of temporary files. When two people are running the same shell script, having unique filenames keeps the users from inadvertently sharing the same temporary file.

The following example demonstrates that the shell creates a new shell process when it runs a shell script. The **id2** script displays the PID number of the process running it (not the process that called it; the substitution for $$ is performed by the shell that is forked to run **id2**):

```
$ cat id2
echo "$0 PID= $$"
$ echo $$
8232
$ ./id2
```

```
./id2 PID= 8362
$ echo $$
8232
```

The first echo displays the PID number of the interactive shell. Then **id2** displays its name ($0) and the PID number of the subshell it is running in. The last echo shows that the PID number of the interactive shell has not changed.

$!: PID Number of Most Recent Background Process

The shell expands **$!** to the value of the PID number of the most recent process that ran in the background (not in tcsh). The following example executes sleep as a background task and uses echo to display the value of **$!**:

```
$ sleep 60 &
[1] 8376
$ echo $!
8376
```

$?: Exit Status

When a process stops executing for any reason, it returns an *exit status* to its parent process. The exit status is also referred to as a *condition code* or a *return code*. The shell expands the **$?** (**$status** under tcsh) parameter to the exit status of the most recently executed command.

By convention, a nonzero exit status is interpreted as *false* and means the command failed; a zero is interpreted as *true* and indicates the command executed successfully. In the following example, the first ls command succeeds and the second fails; the exit status displayed by echo reflects these outcomes:

```
$ ls es
es
$ echo $?
0
$ ls xxx
ls: xxx: No such file or directory
$ echo $?
1
```

You can specify the exit status a shell script returns by using the exit builtin, followed by a number, to terminate the script. If you do not use exit with a number to terminate a script, the exit status of the script is that of the last command the script ran.

```
$ cat es
echo This program returns an exit status of 7.
exit 7
$ es
This program returns an exit status of 7.
$ echo $?
7
```

```
$ echo $?
0
```

The es shell script displays a message and terminates execution with an exit command that returns an exit status of 7, the user-defined exit status in this script. The first echo then displays the exit status of es. The second echo displays the exit status of the first echo: This value is 0, indicating the first echo executed successfully.

$–: Flags of Options That Are Set

The shell expands the **$–** parameter to a string of one-character bash option flags (not in tcsh). These flags are set by the set or shopt builtins, when bash is invoked, or by bash itself (e.g., –i). For more information refer to "Controlling bash: Features and Options" on page 359. The following command displays typical bash option flags for an interactive shell:

```
$ echo $-
himBH
```

Table 8-13 on page 361 lists each of these flags (except **i**) as options to set in the **Alternative syntax** column. When you start an interactive shell, bash sets the **i** (interactive) option flag. You can use this flag to determine if a shell is being run interactively. In the following example, **display_flags** displays the bash option flags. When run as a script in a subshell, it shows the i option flag is not set; when run using source (page 290), which runs a script in the current shell, it shows the **i** option flag is set.

```
$ cat display_flags
echo $-

$ ./display_flags
hB

$ source ./display_flags
himBH
```

$_: Last Argument of Previously Executed Command

When bash starts, as when you run a shell script, it expands the **$_** parameter to the pathname of the file it is running. After running a command, it expands this parameter to the last argument of the previously executed command.

```
$ cat last_arg
echo $_
echo here I am
echo $_

$ ./last_arg
./last_arg
```

```
here I am
am
```

In the next example, the shell never executes the echo command; it expands $_ to the last argument of the ls command (which it executed, albeit unsuccessfully).

```
$ ls xx && echo hi
ls: cannot access xx: No such file or directory
$ echo $_
xx
```

The tcsh shell expands the $_ parameter to the most recently executed command line.

```
tcsh $ who am i
sam      pts/1        2018-02-28 16:48 (172.16.192.1)
tcsh $ echo $_
who am i
```

VARIABLES

Variables, introduced on page 310, are shell parameters denoted by a name. Variables can have zero or more attributes (page 315; e.g., export, readonly). You, or a shell program, can create and delete variables, and can assign values and attributes to variables. This section adds to the previous coverage with a discussion of the shell variables, environment variables, inheritance, expanding null and unset variables, array variables, and variables in functions.

SHELL VARIABLES

By default, when you create a variable it is available only in the shell you created it in; it is not available in subshells. This type of variable is called a *shell variable*. In the following example, the first command displays the PID number of the interactive shell the user is working in (2802) and the second command initializes the variable **x** to 5. Then a bash command spawns a new shell (PID 29572). This new shell is a child of the shell the user was working in (a subprocess; page 333). The ps –l command shows the PID and PPID (parent PID) numbers of each shell: PID 29572 is a child of PID 2802. The final echo command shows the variable **x** is not set in the spawned (child) shell: It is a shell variable and is local to the shell it was created in.

```
$ echo $$
2802
$ x=5
$ echo $x
5
```

```
$ bash
$ echo $$
29572
$ ps -l
F S   UID   PID  PPID C PRI  NI ADDR SZ WCHAN  TTY          TIME CMD
0 S  1000  2802  2786 0  80   0 -  5374 wait   pts/2    00:00:00 bash
0 S  1000 29572  2802 0  80   0 -  5373 wait   pts/2    00:00:00 bash
0 R  1000 29648 29572 0  80   0 -  1707 -      pts/2    00:00:00 ps
$ echo $x

$
```

Environment, Environment Variables, and Inheritance

This section explains the concepts of the command execution environment and inheritance.

Environment

When the Linux kernel invokes a program, the kernel passes to the program a list comprising an array of strings. This list, called the *command execution environment* or simply the *environment,* holds a series of name-value pairs in the form *name=value.*

Environment Variables

When bash is invoked, it scans its environment and creates parameters for each name-value pair, assigning the corresponding *value* to each *name.* Each of these parameters is an *environment variable;* these variables are in the shell's environment. Environment variables are sometimes referred to as *global variables* or *exported variables.*

Inheritance A child process (a subprocess; see page 333 for more information about the process structure) inherits its environment from its parent. An inherited variable is an environment variable for the child, so its children also inherit the variable: All children and grandchildren, to any level, inherit environment variables from their ancestor. A process can create, remove, and change the value of environment variables, so a child process might not inherit the same environment its parent inherited.

Because of process locality (next), a parent cannot see changes a child makes to an environment variable and a child cannot see changes a parent makes to an environment variable once the child has been spawned (created). Nor can unrelated processes see changes to variables that have the same name in each process, such as commonly inherited environment variables (e.g., **PATH**).

Process Locality: Shell Variables

Variables are *local,* which means they are specific to a process: *Local* means *local to a process.* For example, when you log in on a terminal or open a terminal emulator, you start a process that runs a shell. Assume in that shell the **LANG** environment variable (page 327) is set to **en_US.UTF-8**.

If you then log in on a different terminal or open a second terminal emulator, you start another process that runs a different shell. Assume in that shell the **LANG** environment variable is also set to **en_US.UTF-8**. When you change the value of **LANG** on the second terminal to **de_DE.UTF-8**, the value of **LANG** on the first terminal does not change. It does not change because variables (both names and values) are local to a process and each terminal is running a separate process (even though both processes are running shells).

export: PUTS VARIABLES IN THE ENVIRONMENT

When you run an **export** command with variable names as arguments, the shell places the names (and values, if present) of those variables in the environment. Without arguments, export lists environment (exported) variables.

Under tcsh, setenv (page 396) assigns a value to a variable and places the name (and value) of that variable in the environment. The examples in this section use the bash syntax but the theory applies to both shells.

The following **extest1** shell script assigns the value of **american** to the variable named **cheese** and then displays its name (the shell expands **$0** to the name of the calling program) and the value of **cheese**. The **extest1** script then calls **subtest**, which attempts to display the same information, declares a **cheese** variable by initializing it, displays the value of the variable, and returns control to the parent process, which is executing **extest1**. Finally, **extest1** again displays the value of the original **cheese** variable.

```
$ cat extest1
cheese=american
echo "$0 1: $cheese"
./subtest
echo "$0 2: $cheese"

$ cat subtest
echo "$0 1: $cheese"
cheese=swiss
echo "$0 2: $cheese"

$ ./extest1
./extest1 1: american
./subtest 1:
./subtest 2: swiss
./extest1 2: american
```

The **subtest** script never receives the value of **cheese** from **extest1** (and **extest1** never loses the value): **cheese** is a shell variable, not an environment variable (it is not in the environment of the parent process and therefore is not available in the child process). When a process attempts to display the value of a variable that has not been declared and is not in the environment, as is the case with **subtest**, the process displays nothing; the value of an undeclared variable is that of the null string. The final echo shows the value of **cheese** in **extest1** has not changed: In bash—unlike in the real world—a child can never affect its parent's attributes.

The **extest2** script is the same as **extest1** except it uses export to put **cheese** in the environment of the current process. The result is that **cheese** appears in the environment of the child process running the **subtest** script.

```
$ cat extest2
export cheese=american
echo "$0 1: $cheese"
./subtest
echo "$0 2: $cheese"

$ ./extest2
./extest2 1: american
./subtest 1: american
./subtest 2: swiss
./extest2 2: american
```

Here, the child process inherits the value of **cheese** as **american** and, after displaying this value, changes *its copy* to **swiss**. When control is returned to the parent, the parent's copy of **cheese** retains its original value: **american**.

Alternatively, as the next program shows, you can put a variable in the environment of a child shell without declaring it in the parent shell. See page 134 for more information on this command-line syntax.

```
$ cheese=cheddar ./subtest
./subtest 1: cheddar
./subtest 2: swiss
$ echo $cheese

$
```

You can export a variable without/before assigning a value to it. Also, you do not need to export an already-exported variable after you change its value. For example, you do not usually need to export **PATH** when you assign a value to it in **~/.bash_profile** because it is typically exported in a global startup file.

You can place several export declarations (initializations) on a single line:

```
$ export cheese=swiss coffee=colombian avocados=us
```

Unexport An **export –n** or **declare +x** command removes the export attribute from the named environment variable (unexports the variable), demoting it to become a shell variable while preserving its value.

Export a function An **export –f** command places the named function (page 356) in the environment so it is available to child processes.

printenv: Displays Environment Variable Names and Values

The printenv utility displays environment variable names and values. When called without an argument, it displays all environment variables. When called with the name of an environment variable, it displays the value of that variable. When called with the name of a variable that is not in the environment or has not been declared, it displays nothing. You can also use export (page 481) and env (next page) to display a list of environment variables.

```
$ x=5                    # not in the environment
$ export y=10            # in the environment
$ printenv x
$ printenv y
10
$ printenv
...
SHELL=/bin/bash
TERM=xterm
USER=sam
PWD=/home/sam
y=10
...
```

env: Runs a Program in a Modified Environment

The env utility runs a program as a child of the current shell, allowing you to modify the environment the current shell exports to the newly created process. See page 134 for an easier way to place a variable in the environment of a child process. The env utility has the following syntax:

*env [**options**] [-] [name=value] ... [command-line]*

where ***options*** is one of the following options:

--ignore-environment
–i or –
: Causes ***command-line*** to run in a clean environment; no environment variables are available to the newly created process.

--unset=*name* –u *name*
: Unsets the environment variable named ***name*** so it is not available to the newly created process.

Just as on a bash command line (page 134), zero or more ***name=value*** pairs may be used to set or modify environment variables in the newly created process, except you cannot specify a ***name*** without a ***value***. The env utility evaluates the ***name=value*** pairs from left to right, so if ***name*** appears more than once in this list, the rightmost ***value*** takes precedence.

The ***command-line*** is the command (including any options and arguments) that env executes. The env utility takes its first argument that does not contain an equal sign as the beginning of the command line and, if you specify a command that does not include a slash (i.e., if you specify a simple filename), uses the value of **PATH** (page 318) to locate the command. It does not work with builtin commands.

In the following example, env runs **display_xx**, a script that displays the value of the **xx** variable. On the command line, env initializes the variable **xx** in the environment of the script it calls and echo in the script displays the value of **xx**.

```
$ cat display_xx
echo "Running $0"
echo $xx

$ env xx=remember ./display_xx
Running ./display_xx
remember
```

If you want to declare only environment variables for a program, it is simpler to use the following bash syntax (page 134):

```
$ xx=remember ./display_xx
Running ./display_xx
remember
```

When called without a ***command-line***, env displays a list of environment variables (it behaves similarly to printenv [page 482]):

```
$ env
...
SHELL=/bin/bash
TERM=xterm
USER=sam
PWD=/home/sam
y=10
...
```

set: Works with Shell Features, Positional Parameters, and Variables

The set builtin can perform the following tasks:

- Set or unset shell features (also called attributes; page 360).
- Assign values to positional parameters (page 472).
- Display variables that are available to the current shell. These variables comprise shell variables (variables not in the environment) and environment variables. The set builtin displays variables in a format you can use in a shell script or as input to set to declare and initialize variables. Output is sorted based on the current locale (page 326). You cannot reset readonly variables.

```
$ set
...
BASH=/bin/bash
COLUMNS=70
PWD=/home/sam
SHELL=/bin/bash
```

```
x=5
y=10
...
```

EXPANDING NULL AND UNSET VARIABLES

The expression **${name}** (or just **$name** if it is not ambiguous) expands to the value of the **name** variable. If **name** is null or not set, bash expands **${name}** to a null string. The Bourne Again Shell provides the following alternatives to accepting the null string as the value of the variable:

- Use a default value for the variable.
- Use a default value and assign that value to the variable.
- Display an error.

You can choose one of these alternatives by using a modifier with the variable name. In addition, you can use **set –o nounset** (page 363) to cause bash to display an error message and exit from a script whenever the script references an unset variable.

:– USES A DEFAULT VALUE

The **:–** modifier uses a default value in place of a null or unset variable while allowing a nonnull variable to represent itself:

${name:–default}

The shell interprets **:–** as "If ***name*** is null or unset, expand ***default*** and use the expanded value in place of ***name;*** else, use ***name.***"

The following command lists the contents of the directory named by the **LIT** variable. If **LIT** is null or unset, it lists the contents of **/home/max/literature**:

```
$ ls ${LIT:-/home/max/literature}
```

The shell expands variables in ***default:***

```
$ ls ${LIT:-$HOME/literature}
```

:= ASSIGNS A DEFAULT VALUE

The **:–** modifier does not change the value of a variable. However, you can change the value of a null or unset variable to the expanded value of ***default*** by using the **:=** modifier:

${name:=default}

The shell expands the expression *${**name:=default**}* in the same manner as it expands *${**name:–default**}* but also sets the value of ***name*** to the expanded value of ***default.***

If a script contains a line such as the following and **LIT** is unset or null at the time this line is executed, the shell assigns **LIT** the value **/home/max/literature**:

```
$ ls ${LIT:=/home/max/literature}
```

: (null) builtin Some shell scripts include lines that start with the **:** (null) builtin followed on the same line by the **:=** expansion modifier. This syntax sets variables that are null or unset. The **:** builtin evaluates each token in the remainder of the command line but does not execute any commands.

Use the following syntax to set a default for a null or unset variable in a shell script (a SPACE follows the first colon). Without the leading colon (**:**), the shell would evaluate and attempt to execute the "command" that results from the evaluation.

: *${name:=default}*

When a script needs a directory for temporary files and uses the value of **TEMPDIR** for the name of this directory, the following line assigns to **TEMPDIR** the value **/tmp** if **TEMPDIR** is null:

```
: ${TEMPDIR:=/tmp}
```

:? Sends an Error Message to Standard Error

Sometimes a script needs the value of a variable, but you cannot supply a reasonable default at the time you write the script. In this case you want the script to exit if the variable is not set. If the variable is null or unset, the **:?** modifier causes the script to send an error message to standard error and terminate with an exit status of 1. Interactive shells do not exit when you use **:?**.

${name:?message}

If you omit ***message***, the shell displays **parameter null or not set**. In the following command, **TESTDIR** is not set, so the shell sends to standard error the expanded value of the string following **:?**. In this case the string includes command substitution for date with the %T syntax (page 787), followed by the string **error, variable not set.**

```
cd ${TESTDIR:?$(date +%T) error, variable not set.}
bash: TESTDIR: 16:16:14 error, variable not set.
```

Array Variables

The Bourne Again Shell supports one-dimensional array variables. The subscripts are integers with zero-based indexing (i.e., the first element of the array has the subscript 0). The following syntax declares and assigns values to an array:

name=(element1 element2 ...)

The following example assigns four values to the array **NAMES**:

```
$ NAMES=(max helen sam zach)
```

You reference a single element of an array as follows; the braces are not optional.

```
$ echo ${NAMES[2]}
sam
```

The subscripts [*] and [@] both extract the entire array but work differently when used within double quotation marks. An @ produces an array that is a duplicate of the original array; an * produces a single element of an array (or a plain variable) that holds all the elements of the array separated by the first character in **IFS** (normally a SPACE; page 321). In the following example, the array **A** is filled with the elements of the **NAMES** variable using an *, and **B** is filled using an @. The declare builtin (page 315) with the **–a** option displays the values of the arrays (and reminds you that bash uses zero-based indexing for arrays):

```
$ A=("${NAMES[*]}")
$ B=("${NAMES[@]}")

$ declare -a
declare -a A='([0]="max helen sam zach")'
declare -a B='([0]="max" [1]="helen" [2]="sam" [3]="zach")'
...
declare -a NAMES='([0]="max" [1]="helen" [2]="sam" [3]="zach")'
```

The output of declare shows that **NAMES** and **B** have multiple elements. In contrast, **A**, which was assigned its value with an * within double quotation marks, has only one element: **A** has all its elements enclosed between double quotation marks.

In the next example, echo attempts to display element 1 of array **A**. Nothing is displayed because **A** has only one element and that element has an index of 0. Element 0 of array **A** holds all four names. Element 1 of **B** holds the second item in the array and element 0 holds the first item.

```
$ echo ${A[1]}

$ echo ${A[0]}
max helen sam zach
$ echo ${B[1]}
helen
$ echo ${B[0]}
max
```

The ${#*name*[*]} operator returns the number of elements in an array:

```
$ echo ${#NAMES[*]}
4
```

The same operator, when given the index of an element of an array in place of *, returns the length of the element:

```
$ echo ${#NAMES[1]}
5
```

You can use subscripts on the left side of an assignment statement to replace selected elements of an array:

```
$ NAMES[1]=max
$ echo ${NAMES[*]}
max max sam zach
```

VARIABLES IN FUNCTIONS

Because functions run in the same environment as the shell that calls them, variables are implicitly shared by a shell and a function it calls.

```
$ nam () {
> echo $myname
> myname=zach
> }

$ myname=sam
$ nam
sam
$ echo $myname
zach
```

In the preceding example, the **myname** variable is set to **sam** in the interactive shell. The **nam** function then displays the value of **myname** (**sam**) and sets **myname** to **zach**. The final echo shows that, in the interactive shell, the value of **myname** has been changed to **zach**.

Function local variables

Local variables are helpful in a function written for general use. Because the function is called by many scripts that might be written by different programmers, you need to make sure the names of the variables used within the function do not conflict with (i.e., duplicate) the names of the variables in the programs that call the function. Local variables eliminate this problem. When used within a function, the local builtin declares a variable to be local to the function it is defined in.

The next example shows the use of a local variable in a function. It features two variables named **count**. The first is declared and initialized to 10 in the interactive shell. Its value never changes, as echo verifies after **count_down** is run. The other **count** is declared, using local, to be local to the **count_down** function. Its value, which is unknown outside the function, ranges from 4 to 1, as the echo command within the function confirms.

The following example shows the function being entered from the keyboard; it is not a shell script. See the tip "A function is not a shell script" on page 465.

```
$ count_down () {
> local count
> count=$1
> while [ $count -gt 0 ]
> do
> echo "$count..."
> ((count=count-1))
> sleep 1
> done
> echo "Blast Off."
> }
```

```
$ count=10
$ count_down 4
4...
3...
2...
1...
Blast Off.
$ echo $count
10
```

The **count=count–1** assignment is enclosed between double parentheses, which cause the shell to perform an arithmetic evaluation (page 505). Within the double parentheses you can reference shell variables without the leading dollar sign ($). See page 357 for another example of function local variables.

Builtin Commands

Builtin commands, which were introduced in Chapter 5, do not fork a new process when you execute them. This section discusses the type, read, exec, trap, kill, and getopts builtins. Table 10-6 on page 504 lists many bash builtin commands. See Table 9-10 on page 418 for a list of tcsh builtins.

type: Displays Information About a Command

The type builtin (use which under tcsh) provides information about a command:

```
$ type cat echo who if lt
cat is hashed (/bin/cat)
echo is a shell builtin
who is /usr/bin/who
if is a shell keyword
lt is aliased to 'ls -ltrh | tail'
```

The preceding output shows the files that would be executed if you gave **cat** or **who** as a command. Because cat has already been called from the current shell, it is in the hash table (page 335) and type reports that **cat is hashed**. The output also shows that a call to **echo** runs the echo builtin, **if** is a keyword, and **lt** is an alias.

read: Accepts User Input

A common use for user-created variables is storing information that a user enters in response to a prompt. Using read, scripts can accept input from the user and store that input in variables. See page 401 for information about reading user input under tcsh. The read builtin reads one line from standard input and assigns the words on the line to one or more variables:

```
$ cat read1
echo -n "Go ahead: "
read firstline
echo "You entered: $firstline"
```

```
$ ./read1
Go ahead: This is a line.
You entered: This is a line.
```

The first line of the **read1** script uses echo to prompt for a line of text. The **–n** option suppresses the following NEWLINE, allowing you to enter a line of text on the same line as the prompt. The second line reads the text into the variable **firstline**. The third line verifies the action of read by displaying the value of **firstline**.

The **–p** (prompt) option causes read to send to standard error the argument that follows it; read does not terminate this prompt with a NEWLINE. This feature allows you to both prompt for and read the input from the user on one line:

```
$ cat read1a
read -p "Go ahead: " firstline
echo "You entered: $firstline"

$ ./read1a
Go ahead: My line.
You entered: My line.
```

The variable in the preceding examples is quoted (along with the text string) because you, as the script writer, cannot anticipate which characters the user might enter in response to the prompt. Consider what would happen if the variable were not quoted and the user entered * in response to the prompt:

```
$ cat read1_no_quote
read -p "Go ahead: " firstline
echo You entered: $firstline

$ ./read1_no_quote
Go ahead: *
You entered: read1 read1_no_quote script.1
$ ls
read1   read1_no_quote    script.1
```

The ls command lists the same words as the script, demonstrating that the shell expands the asterisk into a list of files in the working directory. When the variable **$firstline** is surrounded by double quotation marks, the shell does not expand the asterisk. Thus, the **read1** script behaves correctly:

```
$ ./read1
Go ahead: *
You entered: *
```

REPLY When you do not specify a variable to receive read's input, bash puts the input into the variable named **REPLY**. The following **read1b** script performs the same task as **read1**:

```
$ cat read1b
read -p "Go ahead: "
echo "You entered: $REPLY"
```

The **read2** script prompts for a command line, reads the user's response, and assigns it to the variable **cmd**. The script then attempts to execute the command line that results from the expansion of the **cmd** variable:

```
$ cat read2
read -p "Enter a command: " cmd
$cmd
echo "Thanks"
```

In the following example, **read2** reads a command line that calls the echo builtin. The shell executes the command and then displays **Thanks**. Next, **read2** reads a command line that executes the who utility:

```
$ ./read2
Enter a command: echo Please display this message.
Please display this message.
Thanks
$ ./read2
Enter a command: who
max       pts/4         2017-06-17 07:50  (:0.0)
sam       pts/12        2017-06-17 11:54  (guava)
Thanks
```

If **cmd** does not expand into a valid command line, the shell issues an error message:

```
$ ./read2
Enter a command: xxx
./read2: line 2: xxx: command not found
Thanks
```

The **read3** script reads values into three variables. The read builtin assigns one word (a sequence of nonblank characters) to each variable:

```
$ cat read3
read -p "Enter something: " word1 word2 word3
echo "Word 1 is: $word1"
echo "Word 2 is: $word2"
echo "Word 3 is: $word3"
$ ./read3
Enter something: this is something
Word 1 is: this
Word 2 is: is
Word 3 is: something
```

When you enter more words than read has variables, read assigns one word to each variable, assigning all leftover words to the last variable. Both **read1** and **read2** assigned the first word and all leftover words to the one variable the scripts each had to work with. In the following example, read assigns five words to three variables: It assigns the first word to the first variable, the second word to the second variable, and the third through fifth words to the third variable.

```
$ ./read3
Enter something: this is something else, really.
Word 1 is:  this
Word 2 is:  is
Word 3 is:  something else, really.
```

Table 10-4 lists some of the options supported by the read builtin.

Table 10-4 read options

Option	Function
–a *aname*	(array) Assigns each word of input to an element of array ***aname***.
–d *delim*	(delimiter) Uses ***delim*** to terminate the input instead of NEWLINE.
–e	(Readline) If input is coming from a keyboard, uses the Readline Library (page 345) to get input.
–n *num*	(number of characters) Reads ***num*** characters and returns. As soon as the user types ***num*** characters, read returns; there is no need to press RETURN.
–p *prompt*	(prompt) Displays ***prompt*** on standard error without a terminating NEWLINE before reading input. Displays ***prompt*** only when input comes from the keyboard.
–s	(silent) Does not echo characters.
–u*n*	(file descriptor) Uses the integer ***n*** as the file descriptor that read takes its input from. Thus `read -u4 arg1 arg2` is equivalent to `read arg1 arg2 <&4` See "File Descriptors" (page 464) for a discussion of redirection and file descriptors.

The read builtin returns an exit status of 0 if it successfully reads any data. It has a nonzero exit status when it reaches the EOF (end of file).

The following example runs a **while** loop from the command line. It takes its input from the **names** file and terminates after reading the last line from **names**.

```
$ cat names
Alice Jones
Robert Smith
Alice Paulson
John Q. Public

$ while read first rest
> do
> echo $rest, $first
> done < names
Jones, Alice
Smith, Robert
Paulson, Alice
Q. Public, John
$
```

The placement of the redirection symbol (<) for the **while** structure is critical. It is important that you place the redirection symbol at the **done** statement and not at the call to read.

optional Each time you redirect input, the shell opens the input file and repositions the read pointer at the start of the file:

```
$ read line1 < names; echo $line1; read line2 < names; echo $line2
Alice Jones
Alice Jones
```

Here, each read opens **names** and starts at the beginning of the **names** file. In the following example, **names** is opened once, as standard input of the subshell created by the parentheses. Each read then reads successive lines of standard input:

```
$ (read line1; echo $line1; read line2; echo $line2) < names
Alice Jones
Robert Smith
```

Another way to get the same effect is to open the input file with exec and hold it open (refer to "File Descriptors" on page 464):

```
$ exec 3< names
$ read -u3 line1; echo $line1; read -u3 line2; echo $line2
Alice Jones
Robert Smith
$ exec 3<&-
```

exec: EXECUTES A COMMAND OR REDIRECTS FILE DESCRIPTORS

The exec builtin (not in tcsh) has two primary purposes: to run a command without creating a new process and to redirect a file descriptor—including standard input, output, or error—of a shell script from within the script (page 464). When the shell executes a command that is not built into the shell, it typically creates a new process. The new process inherits environment (exported) variables from its parent but does not inherit variables that are not exported by the parent (page 480). In contrast, exec executes a command in place of (overlays) the current process.

exec: EXECUTES A COMMAND

The exec builtin used for running a command has the following syntax:

exec ***command arguments***

exec versus . (dot) Insofar as exec runs a command in the environment of the original process, it is similar to the . (dot) command (page 290). However, unlike the . command, which can run only shell scripts, exec can run both scripts and compiled programs. Also, whereas the . command returns control to the original script when it finishes running, exec does not. Finally, the . command gives the new program access to local variables, whereas exec does not.

exec does not return control

Because the shell does not create a new process when you use **exec**, the command runs more quickly. However, because **exec** does not return control to the original program, it can be used only as the last command in a script. The following script shows that control is not returned to the script:

```
$ cat exec_demo
who
exec date
echo "This line is never displayed."

$ ./exec_demo
zach      pts/7     May 20  7:05 (guava)
hls       pts/1     May 20  6:59 (:0.0)
Wed May 24 11:42:56 PDT 2017
```

The next example, a modified version of the **out** script (page 436), uses **exec** to execute the final command the script runs. Because **out** runs either **cat** or **less** and then terminates, the new version, named **out2**, uses **exec** with both **cat** and **less**:

```
$ cat out2
if [ $# -eq 0 ]
    then
        echo "Usage: out2 [-v] filenames" 1>&2
        exit 1
fi
if [ "$1" = "-v" ]
    then
        shift
        exec less "$@"
    else
        exec cat -- "$@"
fi
```

exec: REDIRECTS INPUT AND OUTPUT

The second major use of **exec** is to redirect a file descriptor—including standard input, output, or error—from within a script. The next command causes all subsequent input to a script that would have come from standard input to come from the file named **infile**:

```
exec < infile
```

Similarly, the following command redirects standard output and standard error to **outfile** and **errfile**, respectively:

```
exec > outfile 2> errfile
```

When you use **exec** in this manner, the current process is not replaced with a new process and **exec** can be followed by other commands in the script.

/dev/tty When you redirect the output from a script to a file, you must make sure the user sees any prompts the script displays. The **/dev/tty** device is a pseudonym for the screen the user is working on; you can use this device to refer to the user's screen without knowing which device it is. (The tty utility displays the name of the device you are using.) By redirecting the output from a script to **/dev/tty**, you ensure that prompts and messages go to the user's terminal, regardless of which terminal the user is logged in on. Messages sent to **/dev/tty** are also not diverted if standard output and standard error from the script are redirected.

The **to_screen1** script sends output to three places: standard output, standard error, and the user's screen. When run with standard output and standard error redirected, **to_screen1** still displays the message sent to **/dev/tty** on the user's screen. The **out** and **err** files hold the output sent to standard output and standard error, respectively.

```
$ cat to_screen1
echo "message to standard output"
echo "message to standard error" 1>&2
echo "message to screen" > /dev/tty

$ ./to_screen1 > out 2> err
message to screen
$ cat out
message to standard output
$ cat err
message to standard error
```

The following command redirects standard output from a script to the user's screen:

```
exec > /dev/tty
```

Putting this command at the beginning of the previous script changes where the output goes. In **to_screen2**, exec redirects standard output to the user's screen so the **> /dev/tty** is superfluous. Following the exec command, all output sent to standard output goes to **/dev/tty** (the screen). Output to standard error is not affected.

```
$ cat to_screen2
exec > /dev/tty
echo "message to standard output"
echo "message to standard error" 1>&2
echo "message to screen" > /dev/tty

$ ./to_screen2 > out 2> err
message to standard output
message to screen
```

One disadvantage of using exec to redirect the output to **/dev/tty** is that all subsequent output is redirected unless you use exec again in the script.

You can also redirect the input to read (standard input) so that it comes from **/dev/tty** (the keyboard):

```
read name < /dev/tty
```

or

```
exec < /dev/tty
```

trap: Catches a Signal

A *signal* is a report to a process about a condition. Linux uses signals to report interrupts generated by the user (for example, pressing the interrupt key) as well as bad system calls, broken pipelines, illegal instructions, and other conditions. The trap builtin (tcsh uses onintr) catches (traps) one or more signals, allowing you to direct the actions a script takes when it receives a specified signal.

This discussion covers six signals that are significant when you work with shell scripts. Table 10-5 lists these signals, the signal numbers that systems often ascribe to them, and the conditions that usually generate each signal. Give the command **kill –l** (lowercase "l"), **trap –l** (lowercase "l"), or **man 7 signal** to display a list of all signal names.

Table 10-5 Signals

Type	Name	Number	Generating condition
Not a real signal	EXIT	0	Exit because of exit command or reaching the end of the program (not an actual signal but useful in trap)
Hang up	SIGHUP or HUP	1	Disconnect the line
Terminal interrupt	SIGINT or INT	2	Press the interrupt key (usually CONTROL-C)
Quit	SIGQUIT or QUIT	3	Press the quit key (usually CONTROL-SHIFT-| or CONTROL-SHIFT-\)
Kill	SIGKILL or KILL	9	The kill builtin with the **–9** option (cannot be trapped; use only as a last resort)
Software termination	SIGTERM or TERM	15	Default of the kill command
Stop	SIGTSTP or TSTP	20	Press the suspend key (usually CONTROL-Z)

Table 10-5 Signals (continued)

Type	Name	Number	Generating condition
Debug	DEBUG		Execute ***commands*** specified in the trap statement after each command (not an actual signal but useful in trap)
Error	ERR		Execute ***commands*** specified in the trap statement after each command that returns a nonzero exit status (not an actual signal but useful in trap)

When it traps a signal, a script takes whatever action you specify: It can remove files or finish other processing as needed, display a message, terminate execution immediately, or ignore the signal. If you do not use trap in a script, any of the six actual signals listed in Table 10-5 (not EXIT, DEBUG, or ERR) will terminate the script. Because a process cannot trap a KILL signal, you can use **kill –KILL** (or **kill –9**) as a last resort to terminate a script or other process. (See page 499 for more information on kill.)

The trap command has the following syntax:

*trap [**'commands'**] [**signal**]*

The optional ***commands*** specifies the commands the shell executes when it catches one of the signals specified by ***signal***. The ***signal*** can be a signal name or number—for example, INT or 2. If ***commands*** is not present, trap resets the trap to its initial condition, which is usually to exit from the script.

Quotation marks The trap builtin does not require single quotation marks around ***commands*** as shown in the preceding syntax but it is a good practice to use them. The single quotation marks cause shell variables within the ***commands*** to be expanded when the signal occurs, rather than when the shell evaluates the arguments to trap. Even if you do not use any shell variables in the ***commands***, you need to enclose any command that takes arguments within either single or double quotation marks. Quoting ***commands*** causes the shell to pass to trap the entire command as a single argument.

After executing the ***commands***, the shell resumes executing the script where it left off. If you want trap to prevent a script from exiting when it receives a signal but not to run any commands explicitly, you can specify a null (empty) ***commands*** string, as shown in the **locktty** script (page 452). The following command traps signal number 15, after which the script continues:

```
trap '' 15
```

The following script demonstrates how the **trap** builtin can catch the terminal interrupt signal (2). You can use SIGINT, INT, or 2 to specify this signal. The script returns an exit status of 1:

```
$ cat inter
#!/bin/bash
trap 'echo PROGRAM INTERRUPTED; exit 1' INT
while true
do
    echo "Program running."
    sleep 1
done
$ ./inter
Program running.
Program running.
Program running.
CONTROL-C
PROGRAM INTERRUPTED
$
```

: (null) builtin

The second line of **inter** sets up a trap for the terminal interrupt signal using INT. When **trap** catches the signal, the shell executes the two commands between the single quotation marks in the **trap** command. The **echo** builtin displays the message **PROGRAM INTERRUPTED**, **exit** terminates the shell running the script, and the parent shell displays a prompt. If **exit** were not there, the shell would return control to the **while** loop after displaying the message. The **while** loop repeats continuously until the script receives a signal because the **true** utility always returns a *true* exit status. In place of **true** you can use the : (null) builtin, which is written as a colon and always returns a 0 (*true*) status.

The **trap** builtin frequently removes temporary files when a script is terminated prematurely, thereby ensuring the files are not left to clutter the filesystem. The following shell script, named **addbanner**, uses two **traps** to remove a temporary file when the script terminates normally or because of a hangup, software interrupt, quit, or software termination signal:

```
$ cat addbanner
#!/bin/bash
script=$(basename $0)

if [ ! -r "$HOME/banner" ]
    then
        echo "$script: need readable $HOME/banner file" 1>&2
        exit 1
fi

trap 'exit 1' 1 2 3 15
trap 'rm /tmp/$$.$script 2> /dev/null' EXIT

for file
do
```

```
    if [ -r "$file" -a -w "$file" ]
        then
            cat $HOME/banner $file > /tmp/$$.$script
            cp /tmp/$$.$script $file
            echo "$script: banner added to $file" 1>&2
        else
            echo "$script: need read and write permission for $file" 1>&2
        fi
done
```

When called with one or more filename arguments, **addbanner** loops through the files, adding a header to the top of each. This script is useful when you use a standard format at the top of your documents, such as a standard layout for memos, or when you want to add a standard header to shell scripts. The header is kept in a file named **~/banner**. Because **addbanner** uses the **HOME** variable, which contains the pathname of the user's home directory, the script can be used by several users without modification. If Max had written the script with **/home/max** in place of **$HOME** and then given the script to Zach, either Zach would have had to change it or **addbanner** would have used Max's **banner** file when Zach ran it (assuming Zach had read permission for the file).

The first trap in **addbanner** causes it to exit with a status of 1 when it receives a hangup, software interrupt (terminal interrupt or quit signal), or software termination signal. The second trap uses **EXIT** in place of **signal-number**, which causes trap to execute its command argument *whenever* the script exits because it receives an exit command or reaches its end. Together, these traps remove a temporary file whether the script terminates normally or prematurely. Standard error of the second trap is sent to **/dev/null** whenever trap attempts to remove a nonexistent temporary file. In those cases rm sends an error message to standard error; because standard error is redirected, the user does not see the message.

See page 452 for another example that uses trap.

kill: Aborts a Process

The kill builtin sends a signal to a process or job. The kill command has the syntax

kill [–signal] PID

where ***signal*** is the signal name or number (for example, INT or 2) and ***PID*** is the process identification number of the process that is to receive the signal. You can specify a job number (page 151) as **%*n*** in place of ***PID***. If you omit ***signal***, kill sends a TERM (software termination, number 15) signal. For more information on signal names and numbers, see Table 10-5 on page 496.

The following command sends the TERM signal to job number 1, regardless of whether it is running or stopped in the background:

```
$ kill -TERM %1
```

Because TERM is the default signal for kill, you can also give this command as **kill %1**. Give the command **kill –l** (lowercase "l") to display a list of signal names.

A program that is interrupted can leave matters in an unpredictable state: Temporary files might be left behind (when they are normally removed), and permissions might be changed. A well-written application traps signals and cleans up before exiting. Most carefully written applications trap the INT, QUIT, and TERM signals.

To terminate a program, first try INT (press CONTROL-C, if the job running is in the foreground). Because an application can be written to ignore this signal, you might need to use the KILL signal, which cannot be trapped or ignored; it is a "sure kill." Refer to page 866 for more information on kill. See also the related utility killall (page 868).

eval: Scans, Evaluates, and Executes a Command Line

The eval builtin scans the command that follows it on the command line. In doing so, eval processes the command line in the same way bash does when it executes a command line (e.g., it expands variables, replacing the name of a variable with its value). For more information refer to "Processing the Command Line" on page 364. After scanning (and expanding) the command line, it passes the resulting command line to bash to execute.

The following example first assigns the value **frog** to the variable **name**. Next, eval scans the command **$name=88** and expands the variable **$name** to **frog**, yielding the command **frog=88**, which it passes to bash to execute. The last command displays the value of **frog**.

```
$ name=frog
$ eval $name=88
$ echo $frog
88
```

Brace expansion with a sequence expression The next example uses eval to cause brace expansion with a sequence expression (page 367) to accept variables, which it does not normally do. The following command demonstrates brace expansion with a sequence expression:

```
$ echo {2..5}
2 3 4 5
```

One of the first things bash does when it processes a command line is to perform brace expansion; later it expands variables (page 364). When you provide an invalid argument in brace expansion, bash does not perform brace expansion; instead, it passes the string to the program being called. In the next example, bash cannot expand **{$m..$n}** during the brace expansion phase because it contains variables, so it continues processing the command line. When it gets to the variable expansion phase, it expands **$m** and **$n** and then passes the string **{2..5}** to echo.

```
$ m=2 n=5
$ echo {$m..$n}
{2..5}
```

When eval scans the same command line, it expands the variables as explained previously and yields the command **echo {2..5}**. It then passes that command to bash, which can now perform brace expansion:

```
$ eval echo {$m..$n}
2 3 4 5
```

getopts: PARSES OPTIONS

The getopts builtin (not in tcsh) parses command-line arguments, making it easier to write programs that follow the Linux argument conventions. The syntax for getopts is

getopts ***optstring varname*** *[arg ...]*

where ***optstring*** is a list of the valid option letters, ***varname*** is the variable that receives the options one at a time, and ***arg*** is the optional list of parameters to be processed. If ***arg*** is not present, getopts processes the command-line arguments. If ***optstring*** starts with a colon (:), the script must take care of generating error messages; otherwise, getopts generates error messages.

The getopts builtin uses the **OPTIND** (option index) and **OPTARG** (option argument) variables to track and store option-related values. When a shell script starts, the value of **OPTIND** is 1. Each time getopts is called and locates an argument, it increments **OPTIND** to the index of the next option to be processed. If the option takes an argument, bash assigns the value of the argument to **OPTARG**.

To indicate that an option takes an argument, follow the corresponding letter in ***optstring*** with a colon (**:**). For example, the ***optstring*** **dxo:lt:r** instructs getopts to search for the **–d**, **–x**, **–o**, **–l**, **–t**, and **–r** options and tells it the **–o** and **–t** options take arguments.

Using getopts as the ***test-command*** in a **while** control structure allows you to loop over the options one at a time. The getopts builtin checks the option list for options that are in ***optstring***. Each time through the loop, getopts stores the option letter it finds in ***varname***.

As an example, assume you want to write a program that can take three options:

1. A **–b** option indicates that the program should ignore whitespace at the start of input lines.
2. A **–t** option followed by the name of a directory indicates that the program should store temporary files in that directory. Otherwise, it should use **/tmp**.

3. A **–u** option indicates that the program should translate all output to uppercase.

In addition, the program should ignore all other options and end option processing when it encounters two hyphens (––).

The problem is to write the portion of the program that determines which options the user has supplied. The following solution does not use getopts:

```
SKIPBLANKS=
TMPDIR=/tmp
CASE=lower
while [[ "$1" = -* ]] # [[ = ]] does pattern match
do
    case $1 in
        -b)     SKIPBLANKS=TRUE ;;
        -t)     if [ -d "$2" ]
                    then
                    TMPDIR=$2
                    shift
                else
                    echo "$0: -t takes a directory argument." >&2
                    exit 1
                fi ;;
        -u)     CASE=upper ;;
        --)     break   ;;      # Stop processing options
        *)      echo "$0: Invalid option $1 ignored." >&2 ;;
        esac
    shift
done
```

This program fragment uses a loop to check and shift arguments while the argument is not ––. As long as the argument is not two hyphens, the program continues to loop through a **case** statement that checks for possible options. The –– **case** label breaks out of the **while** loop. The * **case** label recognizes any option; it appears as the last **case** label to catch any unknown options, displays an error message, and allows processing to continue. On each pass through the loop, the program uses shift so it accesses the next argument on the next pass through the loop. If an option takes an argument, the program uses an extra shift to get past that argument.

The following program fragment processes the same options using getopts:

```
SKIPBLANKS=
TMPDIR=/tmp
CASE=lower

while getopts :bt:u arg
do
    case $arg in
        b)      SKIPBLANKS=TRUE ;;
```

```
        t)      if [ -d "$OPTARG" ]
                    then
                    TMPDIR=$OPTARG
                else
                    echo "$0: $OPTARG is not a directory." >&2
                    exit 1
                fi ;;
        u)      CASE=upper ;;
        :)      echo "$0: Must supply an argument to -$OPTARG." >&2
                exit 1 ;;
        \?)     echo "Invalid option -$OPTARG ignored." >&2 ;;
        esac
done
```

In this version of the code, the **while** structure evaluates the getopts builtin each time control transfers to the top of the loop. The getopts builtin uses the **OPTIND** variable to keep track of the index of the argument it is to process the next time it is called. There is no need to call shift in this example.

In the getopts version of the script, the **case** patterns do not start with a hyphen because the value of **arg** is just the option letter (getopts strips off the hyphen). Also, getopts recognizes -- as the end of the options, so you do not have to specify it explicitly, as in the **case** statement in the first example.

Because you tell getopts which options are valid and which require arguments, it can detect errors in the command line and handle them in two ways. This example uses a leading colon in ***optstring*** to specify that you check for and handle errors in your code; when getopts finds an invalid option, it sets ***varname*** to **?** and **OPTARG** to the option letter. When it finds an option that is missing an argument, getopts sets ***varname*** to **:** and **OPTARG** to the option lacking an argument.

The **\? case** pattern specifies the action to take when getopts detects an invalid option. The **: case** pattern specifies the action to take when getopts detects a missing option argument. In both cases getopts does not write any error message but rather leaves that task to you.

If you omit the leading colon from ***optstring***, both an invalid option and a missing option argument cause ***varname*** to be assigned the string **?**. **OPTARG** is not set and getopts writes its own diagnostic message to standard error. Generally, this method is less desirable because you have less control over what the user sees when an error occurs.

Using getopts will not necessarily make your programs shorter. Its principal advantages are that it provides a uniform programming interface and that it enforces standard option handling.

A Partial List of Builtins

Table 10-6 lists some of the bash builtins. You can use type (page 489) to see if a command runs a builtin. See "Listing bash builtins" on page 158 for instructions on how to display complete lists of builtins.

Table 10-6 bash builtins

Builtin	Function
:	Returns 0 or *true* (the null builtin; pages 486 and 498)
. (dot)	Executes a shell script as part of the current process (page 290)
bg	Puts a suspended job in the background (page 306)
break	Exits from a looping control structure (page 453)
cd	Changes to another working directory (page 94)
continue	Starts with the next iteration of a looping control structure (page 453)
echo	Displays its arguments (page 61)
eval	Scans and evaluates the command line (page 500)
exec	Executes a shell script or program in place of the current process (page 493)
exit	Exits from the current shell (usually the same as CONTROL-D from an interactive shell; page 477)
export	Makes the variable an environment variable (page 481)
fg	Brings a job from the background to the foreground (page 305)
getopts	Parses arguments to a shell script (page 501)
jobs	Displays a list of background jobs (page 305)
kill	Sends a signal to a process or job (page 866)
pwd	Displays the name of the working directory (page 89)
read	Reads a line from standard input (page 489)
readonly	Declares a variable to be readonly (page 315)
set	Sets shell flags or positional parameters; with no argument, lists all variables (pages 360, 396, and 472)
shift	Promotes each positional parameter (page 473)
test	Compares arguments (pages 431 and 1005)
times	Displays total times for the current shell and its children
trap	Traps a signal (page 496)
type	Displays how each argument would be interpreted as a command (page 489)
umask	Sets and displays the file-creation mask (page 1021)
unset	Removes a variable or function (page 314)
wait	Waits for a background process to terminate

Expressions

An expression comprises constants, variables, and operators that the shell can process to return a value. This section covers arithmetic, logical, and conditional expressions as well as operators. Table 10-8 on page 508 lists the bash operators.

Arithmetic Evaluation

The Bourne Again Shell can perform arithmetic assignments and evaluate many different types of arithmetic expressions, all using integers. The shell performs arithmetic assignments in a number of ways. One is with arguments to the let builtin:

```
$ let "VALUE=VALUE * 10 + NEW"
```

In the preceding example, the variables **VALUE** and **NEW** hold integer values. Within a let statement you do not need to use dollar signs ($) in front of variable names. Double quotation marks must enclose a single argument, or expression, that contains SPACEs. Because most expressions contain SPACEs and need to be quoted, bash accepts *((expression))* as a synonym for *let "expression"*, obviating the need for both quotation marks and dollar signs:

```
$ ((VALUE=VALUE * 10 + NEW))
```

You can use either form wherever a command is allowed and can remove the SPACEs. In these examples, the asterisk (*) does not need to be quoted because the shell does not perform pathname expansion on the right side of an assignment (page 313):

```
$ let VALUE=VALUE*10+NEW
```

Because each argument to let is evaluated as a separate expression, you can assign values to more than one variable on a single line:

```
$ let "COUNT = COUNT + 1" VALUE=VALUE*10+NEW
```

You must use commas to separate multiple assignments within a set of double parentheses:

```
$ ((COUNT = COUNT + 1, VALUE=VALUE*10+NEW))
```

Arithmetic evaluation versus arithmetic expansion

tip Arithmetic evaluation differs from arithmetic expansion. As explained on page 369, arithmetic expansion uses the syntax *$((**expression**))*, evaluates ***expression***, and replaces *$((**expression**))* with the result. You can use arithmetic expansion to display the value of an expression or to assign that value to a variable.

Arithmetic evaluation uses the *let **expression*** or *((**expression**))* syntax, evaluates ***expression***, and returns a status code. You can use arithmetic evaluation to perform a logical comparison or an assignment.

Logical expressions You can use the *((expression))* syntax for logical expressions, although that task is frequently left to *[[expression]]* (next). The next example expands the **age_check** script (page 369) to include logical arithmetic evaluation in addition to arithmetic expansion:

```
$ cat age2
#!/bin/bash
read -p "How old are you? " age
if ((30 < age && age < 60)); then
        echo "Wow, in $((60-age)) years, you'll be 60!"
    else
        echo "You are too young or too old to play."
fi

$ ./age2
How old are you? 25
You are too young or too old to play.
```

The ***test-statement*** for the **if** structure evaluates two logical comparisons joined by a Boolean AND and returns 0 (*true*) if they are both *true* or 1 (*false*) otherwise.

LOGICAL EVALUATION (CONDITIONAL EXPRESSIONS)

The syntax of a conditional expression is

*[[**expression**]]*

where ***expression*** is a Boolean (logical) expression. You must precede a variable name with a dollar sign (**$**) within ***expression***. The result of executing this builtin, as with the **test** builtin, is a return status. The ***conditions*** allowed within the brackets are almost a superset of those accepted by **test** (page 1005). Where the **test** builtin uses a **–a** as a Boolean AND operator, *[[**expression**]]* uses **&&**. Similarly, where **test** uses **–o** as a Boolean OR operator, *[[**expression**]]* uses **||**.

To see how conditional expressions work, replace the line that tests **age** in the **age2** script with the following conditional expression. You must surround the [[and]] tokens with whitespace or a command terminator, and place dollar signs before the variables:

```
if [[ 30 < $age && $age < 60 ]]; then
```

You can also use **test**'s relational operators **–gt**, **–ge**, **–lt**, **–le**, **–eq**, and **–ne**:

```
if [[ 30 -lt $age && $age -lt 60 ]]; then
```

String comparisons The **test** builtin tests whether strings are equal. The *[[**expression**]]* syntax adds comparison tests for strings. The **>** and **<** operators compare strings for order (for example, **"aa" < "bbb"**). The **=** operator tests for pattern match, not just equality: *[[**string** = **pattern**]]* is *true* if ***string*** matches ***pattern***. This operator is not symmetrical; the ***pattern*** must appear on the right side of the equal sign. For example, [[**artist = a***]] is *true* (= 0), whereas [[**a* = artist**]] is *false* (= 1):

```
$ [[ artist = a* ]]
$ echo $?
0
$ [[ a* = artist ]]
$ echo $?
1
```

The next example uses a command list that starts with a compound condition. The condition tests whether the directory **bin** and the file **src/myscript.bash** exist. If the result is *true*, cp copies **src/myscript.bash** to **bin/myscript**. If the copy succeeds, chmod makes **myscript** executable. If any of these steps fails, echo displays a message. Implicit command-line continuation (page 512) obviates the need for backslashes at the ends of lines.

```
$ [[ -d bin && -f src/myscript.bash ]] &&
cp src/myscript.bash bin/myscript &&
chmod +x bin/myscript ||
echo "Cannot make executable version of myscript"
```

STRING PATTERN MATCHING

The Bourne Again Shell provides string pattern-matching operators that can manipulate pathnames and other strings. These operators can delete from strings prefixes or suffixes that match patterns. Table 10-7 lists the four operators.

Table 10-7 String operators

Operator	Function
#	Removes minimal matching prefixes
##	Removes maximal matching prefixes
%	Removes minimal matching suffixes
%%	Removes maximal matching suffixes

The syntax for these operators is

${varname op pattern}

where ***op*** is one of the operators listed in Table 10-7 and ***pattern*** is a match pattern similar to that used for filename generation. These operators are commonly used to manipulate pathnames to extract or remove components or to change suffixes:

```
$ SOURCEFILE=/usr/local/src/prog.c
$ echo ${SOURCEFILE#/*/}
local/src/prog.c
$ echo ${SOURCEFILE##/*/}
prog.c
$ echo ${SOURCEFILE%/*}
/usr/local/src
$ echo ${SOURCEFILE%%/*}
```

```
$ echo ${SOURCEFILE%.c}
/usr/local/src/prog
$ CHOPFIRST=${SOURCEFILE#/*/}
$ echo $CHOPFIRST
local/src/prog.c
$ NEXT=${CHOPFIRST%%/*}
$ echo $NEXT
local
```

String length The shell expands ${#*name*} to the number of characters in **name**:

```
$ echo $SOURCEFILE
/usr/local/src/prog.c
$ echo ${#SOURCEFILE}
21
```

ARITHMETIC OPERATORS

Arithmetic expansion and arithmetic evaluation in bash use the same syntax, precedence, and associativity of expressions as the C language. Table 10-8 lists arithmetic operators in order of decreasing precedence (priority of evaluation); each group of operators has equal precedence. Within an expression you can use parentheses to change the order of evaluation.

Table 10-8 Arithmetic operators

Type of operator/operator	Function
Post	
var++	Postincrement
var––	Postdecrement
Pre	
++*var*	Preincrement
––*var*	Predecrement
Unary	
–	Unary minus
+	Unary plus
Negation	
!	Boolean NOT (logical negation)
~	Complement (bitwise negation)
Exponentiation	
**	Exponent

Table 10-8 Arithmetic operators (continued)

Type of operator/operator	Function
Multiplication, division, remainder	
*	Multiplication
/	Division
%	Remainder
Addition, subtraction	
+	Addition
–	Subtraction
Bitwise shifts	
<<	Left bitwise shift
>>	Right bitwise shift
Comparison	
<=	Less than or equal
>=	Greater than or equal
<	Less than
>	Greater than
Equality, inequality	
==	Equality
!=	Inequality
Bitwise	
&	Bitwise AND
^	Bitwise XOR (exclusive OR)
|	Bitwise OR
Boolean (logical)	
&&	Boolean AND
||	Boolean OR
Conditional evaluation	
? :	Ternary operator

Table 10-8 Arithmetic operators (continued)

Type of operator/operator	Function
Assignment	
=, *=, /=, %=, +=, −=, <<=, >>=, &=, ^=, |=	Assignment
Comma	
,	Comma

Pipe symbol The | control operator has higher precedence than arithmetic operators. For example, the command line

```
$ cmd1 | cmd2 || cmd3 | cmd4 && cmd5 | cmd6
```

is interpreted as if you had typed

```
$ ((cmd1 | cmd2) || (cmd3 | cmd4)) && (cmd5 | cmd6)
```

Do not rely on rules of precedence: use parentheses

tip Do not rely on the precedence rules when you use command lists (page 149). Instead, use parentheses to explicitly specify the order in which you want the shell to interpret the commands.

Increment and decrement The postincrement, postdecrement, preincrement, and predecrement operators work with variables. The pre- operators, which appear in front of the variable name (as in **++COUNT** and **––VALUE**), first change the value of the variable (**++** adds 1; **––** subtracts 1) and then provide the result for use in the expression. The post- operators appear after the variable name (as in **COUNT++** and **VALUE––**); they first provide the unchanged value of the variable for use in the expression and then change the value of the variable.

```
$ N=10
$ echo $N
10
$ echo $((--N+3))
12
$ echo $N
9
$ echo $((N++ - 3))
6
$ echo $N
10
```

Remainder The remainder operator (**%**) yields the remainder when its first operand is divided by its second. For example, the expression **$((15%7))** has the value 1.

Ternary The ternary operator, **? :**, decides which of two expressions should be evaluated, based on the value returned by a third expression. The syntax is

expression1 ? expression2 : expression3

If ***expression1*** produces a *false* (0) value, ***expression3*** is evaluated; otherwise, ***expression2*** is evaluated. The value of the entire expression is the value of ***expression2*** or ***expression3***, depending on which is evaluated. If ***expression1*** is *true*, ***expression3*** is not evaluated. If ***expression1*** is *false*, ***expression2*** is not evaluated.

```
$ ((N=10,Z=0,COUNT=1))
$ ((T=N>COUNT?++Z:--Z))
$ echo $T
1
$ echo $Z
1
```

Assignment The assignment operators, such as **+=**, are shorthand notations. For example, **N+=3** is the same as ((**N=N+3**)).

Other bases The following commands use the syntax ***base#n*** to assign base 2 (binary) values. First, **v1** is assigned a value of 0101 (5 decimal) and then **v2** is assigned a value of 0110 (6 decimal). The echo utility verifies the decimal values.

```
$ ((v1=2#0101))
$ ((v2=2#0110))
$ echo "$v1 and $v2"
5 and 6
```

Next, the bitwise AND operator (&) selects the bits that are on in both 5 (0101 binary) and 6 (0110 binary). The result is binary 0100, which is 4 decimal.

```
$ echo $(( v1 & v2 ))
4
```

The Boolean AND operator (&&) produces a result of 1 if both of its operands are nonzero and a result of 0 otherwise. The bitwise inclusive OR operator (|) selects the bits that are on in either 0101 or 0110, resulting in 0111, which is 7 decimal. The Boolean OR operator (||) produces a result of 1 if either of its operands is nonzero and a result of 0 otherwise.

```
$ echo $(( v1 && v2 ))
1
$ echo $(( v1 | v2 ))
7
$ echo $(( v1 || v2 ))
1
```

Next, the bitwise exclusive OR operator (^) selects the bits that are on in either, but not both, of the operands 0101 and 0110, yielding 0011, which is 3 decimal. The Boolean NOT operator (!) produces a result of 1 if its operand is 0 and a result of 0 otherwise. Because the exclamation point in **$((! v1))** is enclosed within double parentheses, it does not need to be escaped to prevent the shell from interpreting the exclamation point as a history event. The comparison operators produce a result of 1 if the comparison is *true* and a result of 0 otherwise.

```
$ echo $(( v1 ^ v2 ))
3
$ echo $(( ! v1 ))
0
$ echo $(( v1 < v2 ))
1
$ echo $(( v1 > v2 ))
0
```

IMPLICIT COMMAND-LINE CONTINUATION

Each of the following control operators (page 299) implies continuation:

```
; ;; | & && |& ||
```

For example, there is no difference between this set of commands

```
cd mydir && rm *.o
```

and this set:

```
cd mydir &&
rm *.o
```

Both sets of commands remove all files with a filename extension of **.o** only if the **cd mydir** command is successful. If you give the second set of commands in an interactive shell, the shell issues a secondary prompt (>; page 321) after you enter the first line and waits for you to complete the command line.

The following commands create the directory named **mydir** if **mydir** does not exist. You can put the commands on one line or two.

```
[ -d mydir ] ||
mkdir mydir
```

Pipe symbol (|) implies continuation

Similarly, the pipe symbol implies continuation:

```
sort names                    |
grep -i '^[a-m]'              |
sed 's/Street/St/'            |
pr --header="Names from A-M"  |
lpr
```

When a command line ends with a pipe symbol, you do *not* need backslashes to indicate continuation.

```
sort names                    | \
grep -i '^[a-m]'              | \
sed 's/Street/St/'            | \
```

```
pr --header="Names from A-M"  | \
lpr
```

Although it will work, the following example is also a poor way to write code because it is hard to read and understand:

```
sort names \
| grep -i '^[a-m]' \
| sed 's/Street/St/' \
| pr --header="Names from A-M" \
| lpr
```

Another way to improve the readability of code you write is to take advantage of implicit command-line continuation to break lines without using backslashes. These commands are easier to read and understand

```
$ [ -e /home/sam/memos/helen.personnel/november ] &&
~sam/report_a november alphaphonics totals
```

than these commands:

```
$ [ -e /home/sam/memos/helen.personnel/november ] && ~sam/report_a \
november alphaphonics totals
```

SHELL PROGRAMS

The Bourne Again Shell has many features that make it a good programming language. The structures that bash provides are not a random assortment, but rather have been chosen to provide most of the structural features found in other procedural languages, such as C and Perl. A procedural language provides the following abilities:

- Declare, assign, and manipulate variables and constant data. The Bourne Again Shell provides both string variables, together with powerful string operators, and integer variables, along with a complete set of arithmetic operators.
- Break large problems into small ones by creating subprograms. The Bourne Again Shell allows you to create functions and call scripts from other scripts. Shell functions can be called recursively; that is, a Bourne Again Shell function can call itself. You might not need to use recursion often, but it might allow you to solve some apparently difficult problems with ease.
- Execute statements conditionally using statements such as **if**.
- Execute statements iteratively using statements such as **while** and **for**.
- Transfer data to and from the program, communicating with both data files and users.

Programming languages implement these capabilities in different ways but with the same ideas in mind. When you want to solve a problem by writing a program, you must first figure out a procedure that leads you to a solution—that is, an *algorithm*. Typically, you can implement the same algorithm in roughly the same way in different programming languages, using the same kinds of constructs in each language.

Chapter 8 and this chapter have introduced numerous bash features, many of which are useful for both interactive use and shell programming. This section develops two complete shell programs, demonstrating how to combine some of these features effectively. The programs are presented as problems for you to solve, with sample solutions provided.

A Recursive Shell Script

A *recursive construct* is one that is defined in terms of itself. Alternatively, you might say that a recursive program is one that can call itself. This concept might seem circular, but it need not be. To avoid circularity, a recursive definition must have a special case that is not self-referential. Recursive ideas occur in everyday life. For example, you can define an ancestor as your mother, your father, or one of their ancestors. This definition is not circular; it specifies unambiguously who your ancestors are: your mother or your father, or your mother's mother or father or your father's mother or father, and so on.

A number of Linux system utilities can operate recursively. See the **–R** option to the chmod (page 759), chown (page 764), and cp (page 772) utilities for examples.

Solve the following problem by using a recursive shell function:

Write a shell function named **makepath** that, given a pathname, creates all components in that pathname as directories. For example, the command **makepath a/b/c/d** should create directories **a**, **a/b**, **a/b/c**, and **a/b/c/d**. (The mkdir –p option creates directories in this manner. Solve the problem without using **mkdir –p**.)

One algorithm for a recursive solution follows:

1. Examine the path argument. If it is a null string or if it names an existing directory, do nothing and return.
2. If the path argument is a simple path component, create it (using mkdir) and return.
3. Otherwise, call **makepath** using the path prefix of the original argument. This step eventually creates all the directories up to the last component, which you can then create using mkdir.

In general, a recursive function must invoke itself with a simpler version of the problem than it was given until it is finally called with a simple case that does not need to call itself. Following is one possible solution based on this algorithm:

makepath

```
# This is a function
# Enter it at the keyboard; do not run it as a shell script
#
```

```
function makepath()
{
    if [[ ${#1} -eq 0 || -d "$1" ]]
        then
            return 0        # Do nothing
    fi
    if [[ "${1%/*}" = "$1" ]]
        then
            mkdir $1
            return $?
    fi
    makepath ${1%/*} || return 1
    mkdir $1
    return $?
}
```

In the test for a simple component (the **if** statement in the middle of the function), the left expression is the argument after the shortest suffix that starts with a **/** character has been stripped away (page 507). If there is no such character (for example, if **$1** is **max**), nothing is stripped off and the two sides are equal. If the argument is a simple filename preceded by a slash, such as **/usr**, the expression **${1%/*}** evaluates to a null string. To make the function work in this case, you must take two precautions: Put the left expression within quotation marks and ensure that the recursive function behaves sensibly when it is passed a null string as an argument. In general, good programs are robust: They should be prepared for borderline, invalid, or meaningless input and behave appropriately in such cases.

By giving the following command from the shell you are working in, you turn on debugging tracing so that you can watch the recursion work:

```
$ set -o xtrace
```

(Give the same command but replace the hyphen with a plus sign [**+**] to turn debugging off.) With debugging turned on, the shell displays each line in its expanded form as it executes the line. A **+** precedes each line of debugging output.

In the following example, the first line that starts with **+** shows the shell calling **makepath**. The **makepath** function is initially called from the command line with arguments of **a/b/c**. It then calls itself with arguments of **a/b** and finally **a**. All the work is done (using mkdir) as each call to **makepath** returns.

```
$ ./makepath a/b/c
+ makepath a/b/c
+ [[ 5 -eq 0 ]]
+ [[ -d a/b/c ]]
+ [[ a/b = \a\/\b\/\c ]]
+ makepath a/b
+ [[ 3 -eq 0 ]]
+ [[ -d a/b ]]
+ [[ a = \a\/\b ]]
+ makepath a
+ [[ 1 -eq 0 ]]
+ [[ -d a ]]
```

```
+ [[ a = \a ]]
+ mkdir a
+ return 0
+ mkdir a/b
+ return 0
+ mkdir a/b/c
+ return 0
```

The function works its way down the recursive path and back up again.

It is instructive to invoke **makepath** with an invalid path and see what happens. The following example, which is run with debugging turned on, tries to create the path **/a/b**. Creating this path requires that you create directory **a** in the root directory. Unless you have permission to write to the root directory, you are not permitted to create this directory.

```
$ ./makepath /a/b
+ makepath /a/b
+ [[ 4 -eq 0 ]]
+ [[ -d /a/b ]]
+ [[ /a = \/\a\/\b ]]
+ makepath /a
+ [[ 2 -eq 0 ]]
+ [[ -d /a ]]
+ [[ '' = \/\a ]]
+ makepath
+ [[ 0 -eq 0 ]]
+ return 0
+ mkdir /a
mkdir: cannot create directory '/a': Permission denied
+ return 1
+ return 1
```

The recursion stops when **makepath** is denied permission to create the **/a** directory. The error returned is passed all the way back, so the original **makepath** exits with nonzero status.

Use local variables with recursive functions

tip The preceding example glossed over a potential problem that you might encounter when you use a recursive function. During the execution of a recursive function, many separate instances of that function might be active simultaneously. All but one of them are waiting for their child invocation to complete.

Because functions run in the same environment as the shell that calls them, variables are implicitly shared by a shell and a function it calls. As a consequence, all instances of the function share a single copy of each variable. Sharing variables can give rise to side effects that are rarely what you want. As a rule, you should use local to make all variables of a recursive function local. See page 488 for more information.

THE quiz SHELL SCRIPT

Solve the following problem using a bash script:

Write a generic multiple-choice quiz program. The program should get its questions from data files, present them to the user, and keep track of the number of correct and incorrect answers. The user must be able to exit from the program at any time and receive a summary of results to that point.

The detailed design of this program and even the detailed description of the problem depend on a number of choices: How will the program know which subjects are available for quizzes? How will the user choose a subject? How will the program know when the quiz is over? Should the program present the same questions (for a given subject) in the same order each time, or should it scramble them?

Of course, you can make many perfectly good choices that implement the specification of the problem. The following details narrow the problem specification:

- Each subject will correspond to a subdirectory of a master quiz directory. This directory will be named in the environment variable **QUIZDIR**, whose default will be **~/quiz**. For example, you could have the following directories correspond to the subjects engineering, art, and politics: **~/quiz/engineering**, **~/quiz/art**, and **~/quiz/politics**. Put the **quiz** directory in **/usr/games** if you want all users to have access to it (requires **root** privileges).

- Each subject can have several questions. Each question is represented by a file in its subject's directory.

- The first line of each file that represents a question holds the text of the question. If it takes more than one line, you must escape the NEWLINE with a backslash. (This setup makes it easy to read a single question with the read builtin.) The second line of the file is an integer that specifies the number of choices. The next lines are the choices themselves. The last line is the correct answer. Following is a sample question file:

  ```
  Who discovered the principle of the lever?
  4
  Euclid
  Archimedes
  Thomas Edison
  The Lever Brothers
  Archimedes
  ```

- The program presents all the questions in a subject directory. At any point the user can interrupt the quiz using CONTROL-C, whereupon the program will summarize the results up to that point and exit. If the user does not interrupt the program, the program summarizes the results and exits when it has asked all questions for the chosen subject.

- The program scrambles the questions related to a subject before presenting them.

Following is a top-level design for this program:

1. Initialize. This involves a number of steps, such as setting the counts of the number of questions asked so far and the number of correct and wrong answers to zero. It also sets up the program to trap CONTROL-C.
2. Present the user with a choice of subjects and get the user's response.
3. Change to the corresponding subject directory.
4. Determine the questions to be asked (that is, the filenames in that directory). Arrange them in random order.
5. Repeatedly present questions and ask for answers until the quiz is over or is interrupted by the user.
6. Present the results and exit.

Clearly, some of these steps (such as step 3) are simple, whereas others (such as step 4) are complex and worthy of analysis on their own. Use shell functions for any complex step, and use the trap builtin to handle a user interrupt.

Here is a skeleton version of the program with empty shell functions:

```
function initialize
{
# Initializes variables.
}

function choose_subj
{
# Writes choice to standard output.
}

function scramble
{
# Stores names of question files, scrambled,
# in an array variable named questions.
}

function ask
{
# Reads a question file, asks the question, and checks the
# answer. Returns 1 if the answer was correct, 0 otherwise. If it
# encounters an invalid question file, exits with status 2.
}

function summarize
{
# Presents the user's score.
}

# Main program
initialize                          # Step 1 in top-level design
```

```
subject=$(choose_subj)              # Step 2
[[ $? -eq 0 ]] || exit 2            # If no valid choice, exit
cd $subject || exit 2               # Step 3
echo                                # Skip a line
scramble                            # Step 4

for ques in ${questions[*]}; do     # Step 5
    ask $ques
    result=$?
    (( num_ques=num_ques+1 ))
    if [[ $result == 1 ]]; then
        (( num_correct += 1 ))
    fi
    echo                            # Skip a line between questions
    sleep ${QUIZDELAY:=1}
done

summarize                           # Step 6
exit 0
```

To make reading the results a bit easier for the user, a sleep call appears inside the question loop. It delays **$QUIZDELAY** seconds (default = 1) between questions.

Now the task is to fill in the missing pieces of the program. In a sense this program is being written backward. The details (the shell functions) come first in the file but come last in the development process. This common programming practice is called top-down design. In top-down design you fill in the broad outline of the program first and supply the details later. In this way you break the problem up into smaller problems, each of which you can work on independently. Shell functions are a great help in using the top-down approach.

One way to write the **initialize** function follows. The cd command causes **QUIZDIR** to be the working directory for the rest of the script and defaults to **~/quiz** if **QUIZDIR** is not set.

```
function initialize ()
{
trap 'summarize ; exit 0' INT       # Handle user interrupts
num_ques=0                          # Number of questions asked so far
num_correct=0                       # Number answered correctly so far
first_time=true                     # true until first question is asked
cd ${QUIZDIR:=~/quiz} || exit 2
}
```

Be prepared for the cd command to fail. The directory might not be searchable or conceivably another user might have removed it. The preceding function exits with a status code of 2 if cd fails.

The next function, **choose_subj**, is a bit more complicated. It displays a menu using a **select** statement:

```
function choose_subj ()
{
subjects=($(ls))
PS3="Choose a subject for the quiz from the preceding list: "
select Subject in ${subjects[*]}; do
    if [[ -z "$Subject" ]]; then
        echo "No subject chosen.  Bye." >&2
        exit 1
    fi
    echo $Subject
    return 0
done
}
```

The function first uses an ls command and command substitution to put a list of subject directories in the **subjects** array. Next, the **select** structure (page 460) presents the user with a list of subjects (the directories found by ls) and assigns the chosen directory name to the **Subject** variable. Finally, the function writes the name of the subject directory to standard output. The main program uses command substitution to assign this value to the **subject** variable [**subject=$(choose_subj)**].

The **scramble** function presents a number of difficulties. In this solution it uses an array variable (**questions**) to hold the names of the questions. It scrambles the entries in an array using the **RANDOM** variable (each time you reference **RANDOM**, it has the value of a [random] integer between 0 and 32767):

```
function scramble ()
{
declare -i index quescount
questions=($(ls))
quescount=${#questions[*]}          # Number of elements
((index=quescount-1))
while [[ $index > 0 ]]; do
    ((target=RANDOM % index))
    exchange $target $index
    ((index -= 1))
done
}
```

This function initializes the array variable **questions** to the list of filenames (questions) in the working directory. The variable **quescount** is set to the number of such files. Then the following algorithm is to be used: Let the variable index count down from **quescount – 1** (the index of the last entry in the array variable). For each value of **index**, the function chooses a random value target between 0 and **index**, inclusive. The command

```
((target=RANDOM % index))
```

produces a random value between 0 and **index – 1** by taking the remainder (using the % operator) when **$RANDOM** is divided by **index**. The function then exchanges the elements of **questions** at positions **target** and **index**. It is convenient to take care of this step in another function named **exchange**:

```
function exchange ()
{
temp_value=${questions[$1]}
questions[$1]=${questions[$2]}
questions[$2]=$temp_value
}
```

The **ask** function also uses the **select** structure. It reads the question file named in its argument and uses the contents of that file to present the question, accept the answer, and determine whether the answer is correct. (See the code that follows.)

The **ask** function uses file descriptor 3 to read successive lines from the question file, whose name was passed as an argument and is represented by **$1** in the function. It reads the question into the **ques** variable and the number of questions into **num_opts**. The function constructs the variable **choices** by initializing it to a null string and successively appending the next choice. Then it sets **PS3** to the value of **ques** and uses a **select** structure to prompt the user with **ques**. The **select** structure places the user's answer in **answer**, and the function then checks that response against the correct answer from the file.

The construction of the **choices** variable is done with an eye toward avoiding a potential problem. Suppose that one answer has some whitespace in it—then it might appear as two or more arguments in **choices**. To avoid this problem, make sure that **choices** is an array variable. The **select** statement does the rest of the work:

quiz

```
$ cat quiz
#!/bin/bash

# remove the # on the following line to turn on debugging
# set -o xtrace

#==================
function initialize ()
{
trap 'summarize ; exit 0' INT      # Handle user interrupts
num_ques=0                         # Number of questions asked so far
num_correct=0                      # Number answered correctly so far
first_time=true                    # true until first question is asked
cd ${QUIZDIR:=~/quiz} || exit 2
}

#==================
function choose_subj ()
{
subjects=($(ls))
PS3="Choose a subject for the quiz from the preceding list: "
select Subject in ${subjects[*]}; do
    if [[ -z "$Subject" ]]; then
        echo "No subject chosen.  Bye." >&2
        exit 1
    fi
    echo $Subject
    return 0
done
}
```

```
#==================
function exchange ()
{
temp_value=${questions[$1]}
questions[$1]=${questions[$2]}
questions[$2]=$temp_value
}

#==================
function scramble ()
{
declare -i index quescount
questions=($(ls))
quescount=${#questions[*]}          # Number of elements
((index=quescount-1))
while [[ $index > 0 ]]; do
    ((target=RANDOM % index))
    exchange $target $index
    ((index -= 1))
done
}

#==================
function ask ()
{
exec 3<$1
read -u3 ques || exit 2
read -u3 num_opts || exit 2

index=0
choices=()
while (( index < num_opts )) ; do
    read -u3 next_choice || exit 2
    choices=("${choices[@]}" "$next_choice")
    ((index += 1))
done
read -u3 correct_answer || exit 2
exec 3<&-

if [[ $first_time = true ]]; then
    first_time=false
    echo -e "You may press the interrupt key at any time to quit.\n"
fi

PS3=$ques"  "                       # Make $ques the prompt for select
                                    # and add some spaces for legibility
select answer in "${choices[@]}"; do
    if [[ -z "$answer" ]]; then
            echo  Not a valid choice. Please choose again.
        elif [[ "$answer" = "$correct_answer" ]]; then
            echo "Correct!"
            return 1
        else
            echo "No, the answer is $correct_answer."
            return 0
    fi
```

```
done
}
#===================
function summarize ()
{
echo                                  # Skip a line
if (( num_ques == 0 )); then
    echo "You did not answer any questions"
    exit 0
fi

(( percent=num_correct*100/num_ques ))
echo "You answered $num_correct questions correctly, out of \
$num_ques total questions."
echo "Your score is $percent percent."
}

#===================
# Main program
initialize                            # Step 1 in top-level design

subject=$(choose_subj)                # Step 2
[[ $? -eq 0 ]] || exit 2              # If no valid choice, exit

cd $subject || exit 2                 # Step 3
echo                                  # Skip a line
scramble                              # Step 4

for ques in ${questions[*]}; do       # Step 5
    ask $ques
    result=$?
    (( num_ques=num_ques+1 ))
    if [[ $result == 1 ]]; then
        (( num_correct += 1 ))
    fi
    echo                              # Skip a line between questions
    sleep ${QUIZDELAY:=1}
done

summarize                             # Step 6
exit 0
```

CHAPTER SUMMARY

The shell is a programming language. Programs written in this language are called shell scripts, or simply scripts. Shell scripts provide the decision and looping control structures present in high-level programming languages while allowing easy access to system utilities and user programs. Shell scripts can use functions to modularize and simplify complex tasks.

Control structures The control structures that use decisions to select alternatives are **if...then**, **if...then...else**, and **if...then...elif**. The **case** control structure provides a multiway branch and can be used when you want to express alternatives using a simple pattern-matching syntax.

The looping control structures are **for...in**, **for**, **until**, and **while**. These structures perform one or more tasks repetitively.

The **break** and **continue** control structures alter control within loops: **break** transfers control out of a loop, and **continue** transfers control immediately to the top of a loop.

The Here document allows input to a command in a shell script to come from within the script itself.

File descriptors The Bourne Again Shell provides the ability to manipulate file descriptors. Coupled with the read and echo builtins, file descriptors allow shell scripts to have as much control over input and output as do programs written in lower-level languages.

Variables By default, variables are local to the process they are declared in; these variables are called *shell variables.* You can use export to cause variables to be *environment variables,* which are available to children of the process they are declared in.

The declare builtin assigns attributes, such as readonly, to bash variables. The Bourne Again Shell provides operators to perform pattern matching on variables, provide default values for variables, and evaluate the length of variables. This shell also supports array variables and local variables for functions and provides built-in integer arithmetic, using the let builtin and an expression syntax similar to that found in the C programming language.

Builtins Bourne Again Shell builtins include type, read, exec, trap, kill, and getopts. The type builtin displays information about a command, including its location; read allows a script to accept user input.

The exec builtin executes a command without creating a new process. The new command overlays the current process, assuming the same environment and PID number of that process. This builtin executes user programs and other Linux commands when it is *not* necessary to return control to the calling process.

The trap builtin catches a signal sent to the process running the script and allows you to specify actions to be taken upon receipt of one or more signals. You can use this builtin to cause a script to ignore the signal that is sent when the user presses the interrupt key.

The kill builtin terminates a running program. The getopts builtin parses command-line arguments, making it easier to write programs that follow standard Linux/macOS conventions for command-line arguments and options.

Utilities in scripts In addition to using control structures, builtins, and functions, shell scripts generally call Linux/macOS utilities. The find utility, for instance, is commonplace in shell scripts that search for files in the system hierarchy and can perform a wide range of tasks.

Expressions There are two basic types of expressions: arithmetic and logical. Arithmetic expressions allow you to do arithmetic on constants and variables, yielding a numeric result. Logical

(Boolean) expressions compare expressions or strings, or test conditions, to yield a *true* or *false* result. As with all decisions within shell scripts, a *true* status is represented by the value 0; *false,* by any nonzero value.

Good programming practices A well-written shell script adheres to standard programming practices, such as specifying the shell to execute the script on the first line of the script, verifying the number and type of arguments that the script is called with, displaying a standard usage message to report command-line errors, and redirecting all informational messages to standard error.

EXERCISES

1. Rewrite the **journal** script of Chapter 8 (exercise 5, page 377) by adding commands to verify that the user has write permission for a file named **journal-file** in the user's home directory, if such a file exists. The script should take appropriate actions if **journal-file** exists and the user does not have write permission to the file. Verify that the modified script works.
2. The special parameter "**$@**" is referenced twice in the **out** script (page 436). Explain what would be different if the parameter "**$***" were used in its place.
3. Write a filter that takes a list of files as input and outputs the basename (page 459) of each file in the list.
4. Write a function that takes a single filename as an argument and adds execute permission to the file for the user.
   a. When might such a function be useful?
   b. Revise the script so it takes one or more filenames as arguments and adds execute permission for the user for each file argument.
   c. What can you do to make the function available every time you log in?
   d. Suppose that, in addition to having the function available on subsequent login sessions, you want to make the function available in your current shell. How would you do so?
5. When might it be necessary or advisable to write a shell script instead of a shell function? Give as many reasons as you can think of.
6. Write a shell script that displays the names of all directory files, but no other types of files, in the working directory.
7. Write a script to display the time every 15 seconds. Read the date man page and display the time, using the **%r** field descriptor. Clear the window (using the clear command) each time before you display the time.

8. Enter the following script named **savefiles**, and give yourself execute permission to the file:

```
$ cat savefiles
#! /bin/bash
echo "Saving files in working directory to the file savethem."
exec > savethem
for i in *
        do
        echo
"==================================================="
        echo "File: $i"
        echo
"==================================================="
        cat "$i"
        done
```

   a. Which error message do you receive when you execute this script? Rewrite the script so that the error does not occur, making sure the output still goes to **savethem**.

   b. What might be a problem with running this script twice in the same directory? Discuss a solution to this problem.

9. Read the bash man or info page, try some experiments, and answer the following questions:

   a. How do you export a function?

   b. What does the hash builtin do?

   c. What happens if the argument to exec is not executable?

10. Using the find utility, perform the following tasks:

   a. List all files in the working directory and all subdirectories that have been modified within the last day.

   b. List all files you have read access to on the system that are larger than 1 megabyte.

   c. Remove all files named **core** from the directory structure rooted at your home directory.

   d. List the inode numbers of all files in the working directory whose filenames end in **.c**.

   e. List all files you have read access to on the root filesystem that have been modified in the last 30 days.

11. Write a short script that tells you whether the permissions for two files, whose names are given as arguments to the script, are identical. If the permissions for the two files are identical, output the common permission field. Otherwise, output each filename followed by its permission field. (*Hint:* Try using the cut utility.)

12. Write a script that takes the name of a directory as an argument and searches the file hierarchy rooted at that directory for zero-length files. Write the names of all zero-length files to standard output. If there is no option on the command line, have the script delete the file after displaying its name, asking the user for confirmation, and receiving positive confirmation. A **–f** (force) option on the command line indicates that the script should display the filename but not ask for confirmation before deleting the file.

ADVANCED EXERCISES

13. Write a script that takes a colon-separated list of items and outputs the items, one per line, to standard output (without the colons).

14. Generalize the script written in exercise 13 so the character separating the list items is given as an argument to the function. If this argument is absent, the separator should default to a colon.

15. Write a function named **funload** that takes as its single argument the name of a file containing other functions. The purpose of **funload** is to make all functions in the named file available in the current shell; that is, **funload** loads the functions from the named file. To locate the file, **funload** searches the colon-separated list of directories given by the environment variable **FUNPATH**. Assume the format of **FUNPATH** is the same as **PATH** and the search of **FUNPATH** is similar to the shell's search of the **PATH** variable.

16. Rewrite **bundle** (page 463) so the script it creates takes an optional list of filenames as arguments. If one or more filenames are given on the command line, only those files should be re-created; otherwise, all files in the shell archive should be re-created. For example, suppose all files with the filename extension **.c** are bundled into an archive named **srcshell**, and you want to unbundle just the files **test1.c** and **test2.c**. The following command will unbundle just these two files:

```
$ bash srcshell test1.c test2.c
```

17. Which kind of links will the **lnks** script (page 439) not find? Why?

18. In principle, recursion is never necessary. It can always be replaced by an iterative construct, such as **while** or **until**. Rewrite **makepath** (page 514) as a nonrecursive function. Which version do you prefer? Why?

19. Lists are commonly stored in environment variables by putting a colon (:) between each of the list elements. (The value of the **PATH** variable is an example.) You can add an element to such a list by catenating the new element to the front of the list, as in

```
PATH=/opt/bin:$PATH
```

If the element you add is already in the list, you now have two copies of it in the list. Write a shell function named **addenv** that takes two arguments: (1) the name of a shell variable and (2) a string to prepend to the list that is the value of the shell variable only if that string is not already an element of the list. For example, the call

```
addenv PATH /opt/bin
```

would add **/opt/bin** to **PATH** only if that pathname is not already in **PATH**. Be sure your solution works even if the shell variable starts out empty. Also make sure you check the list elements carefully. If **/usr/opt/bin** is in **PATH** but **/opt/bin** is not, the example just given should still add **/opt/bin** to **PATH**. (*Hint:* You might find this exercise easier to complete if you first write a function **locate_field** that tells you whether a string is an element in the value of a variable.)

20. Write a function that takes a directory name as an argument and writes to standard output the maximum of the lengths of all filenames in that directory. If the function's argument is not a directory name, write an error message to standard output and exit with nonzero status.

21. Modify the function you wrote for exercise 20 to descend all subdirectories of the named directory recursively and to find the maximum length of any filename in that hierarchy.

22. Write a function that lists the number of ordinary files, directories, block special files, character special files, FIFOs, and symbolic links in the working directory. Do this in two different ways:

    a. Use the first letter of the output of **ls –l** to determine a file's type.

    b. Use the file type condition tests of the *[[**expression**]]* syntax to determine a file's type.

23. Modify the **quiz** program (page 521) so that the choices for a question are randomly arranged.

11

The Perl Scripting Language

In This Chapter

Objectives

After reading this chapter you should be able to:

- Use perldoc to display Perl documentation
- Run a Perl program on the command line and from a file
- Explain the use of the **say** function
- Name and describe the three types of Perl variables
- Write a Perl program that uses each type of variable
- Describe the Perl control structures
- Write programs that read from and write to files
- Use regular expressions in a Perl program
- Write a Perl program that incorporates a CPAN module
- Demonstrate several Perl functions

In 1987 Larry Wall created the Perl (Practical Extraction and Report Language) programming language for working with text. Perl uses syntax and concepts from awk, sed, C, the Bourne Shell, Smalltalk, Lisp, and English. It was designed to scan and extract information from text files and generate reports based on that information. Since its introduction in 1987, Perl has expanded enormously—its documentation growing up with it. Today, in addition to text processing, Perl is used for system administration, software development, and general-purpose programming.

Perl code is portable because Perl has been implemented on many operating systems (see www.cpan.org/ports). Perl is an informal, practical, robust, easy-to-use, efficient, complete, and down-and-dirty language that supports procedural and object-oriented programming. It is not necessarily elegant.

One of the things that distinguishes Perl from many other languages is its linguistic origins. In English you say, "I will buy a car if I win the lottery." Perl allows you to mimic that syntax. Another distinction is that Perl has singular and plural variables, the former holding single values and the latter holding lists of values.

INTRODUCTION TO PERL

A couple of quotes from the manual shed light on Perl's philosophy:

> Many of Perl's syntactic elements are optional. Rather than requiring you to put parentheses around every function call and declare every variable, you can often leave such explicit elements off and Perl will frequently figure out what you meant. This is known as Do What I Mean, abbreviated DWIM. It allows programmers to be lazy and to code in a style with which they are comfortable.
>
> The Perl motto is "There's more than one way to do it." Divining how many more is left as an exercise to the reader.

One of Perl's biggest assets is its support by thousands of third-party modules. The Comprehensive Perl Archive Network (CPAN; www.cpan.org) is a repository for many of the modules and other information related to Perl. See page 568 for information on downloading, installing, and using these modules in Perl programs.

The best way to learn Perl is to work with it. Copy and modify the programs in this chapter until they make sense to you. Many system tools are written in Perl. The first line of most of these tools begins with **#!/usr/bin/perl**, which tells the shell to pass the program to Perl for execution. Most files that contain the string **/usr/bin/perl** are

Perl programs. The following command uses grep to search the **/usr/bin** and **/usr/sbin** directories recursively (**–r**) for files containing the string **/usr/bin/perl**; it lists many local system tools written in Perl:

```
$ grep -r /usr/bin/perl /usr/bin /usr/sbin | head -4
/usr/bin/defoma-user:#! /usr/bin/perl -w
/usr/bin/pod2latex:#!/usr/bin/perl
/usr/bin/pod2latex:    eval 'exec /usr/bin/perl -S $0 ${1+"$@"}'
/usr/bin/splain:#!/usr/bin/perl
```

Review these programs; they demonstrate how Perl is used in the real world. Copy a system program to a directory you own before modifying it. Do not run a system program while running with **root** privileges unless you know what you are doing.

More Information

Local man pages: See the perl and perltoc man pages for lists of Perl man pages

Web Perl home page: www.perl.com
CPAN: www.cpan.org
blog: perlbuzz.com

Book *Programming Perl,* third edition, by Wall, Christiansen, & Orwant, O'Reilly & Associates (July 2000)

Help

Perl is a forgiving language. As such, it is easy to write Perl code that runs but does not perform as you intended. Perl includes many tools that can help you find coding mistakes. The **–w** option and the **use warnings** statement can produce helpful diagnostic messages. The **use strict** statement (see the **perldebtut** man page) can impose order on a program by requiring, among other things, that you declare variables before you use them. When all else fails, you can use Perl's builtin debugger to step through a program. See the **perldebtut** and **perldebug** man pages for more information.

perldoc

You might need to install the perl-doc package before you can use perldoc.

The perldoc utility locates and displays local Perl documentation. It is similar to man (page 33) but specific to Perl. It works with files that include lines of **pod** (plain old documentation), a clean and simple documentation language. When embedded in a Perl program, **pod** enables you to include documentation for the entire program, not just code-level comments.

Following is a simple Perl program that includes **pod**. The two lines following **=cut** are the program; the rest is **pod**-format documentation.

```
$ cat pod.ex1.pl
#!/usr/bin/perl

=head1 A Perl Program to Say I<Hi there.>

This simple Perl program includes documentation in B<pod> format.
The following B<=cut> command tells B<perldoc> that what follows
is not documentation.

=cut
# A Perl program
print "Hi there.\n";

=head1 pod Documentation Resumes with Any pod Command

See the B<perldoc.perl.org/perlpod.html> page for more information
on B<pod> and B<perldoc.perl.org> for complete Perl documentation.
```

You can use Perl to run the program:

```
$ perl pod.ex1.pl
Hi there.
```

Or you can use **perldoc** to display the documentation:

```
$ perldoc pod.ex1.pl
POD.EX1(1)           User Contributed Perl Documentation          POD.EX1(1)


A Perl Program to Say Hi there.
       This simple Perl program includes documentation in pod format.  The
       following =cut command tells perldoc that what follows is not
       documentation.

pod Documentation Resumes with Any pod Command
       See the perldoc.perl.org/perlpod.html page for more information on pod
       and perldoc.perl.org for complete Perl documentation.
```

Most publicly distributed modules and scripts, as well as Perl itself, include embedded **pod**-format documentation. For example, the following command displays information about the Perl **print** function:

```
$ perldoc -f print
    print FILEHANDLE LIST
    print LIST
    print       Prints a string or a list of strings.  Returns true if
                successful.  FILEHANDLE may be a scalar variable containing the
                name of or a reference to the filehandle, thus introducing one
                level of indirection.  (NOTE: If FILEHANDLE is a variable and the
                next token is a term, it may be misinterpreted as an operator
                unless you interpose a "+" or put parentheses around the
...
```

Once you have installed a module (page 568), you can use perldoc to display documentation for that module. The following example shows perldoc displaying information on the locally installed **Timestamp::Simple** module:

```
$ perldoc Timestamp::Simple
Timestamp::Simple(3)  User Contributed Perl Documentation Timestamp::Simple(3)

NAME
       Timestamp::Simple - Simple methods for timestamping

SYNOPSIS
           use Timestamp::Simple qw(stamp);
           print stamp, "\n";
...
```

Give the command **man perldoc** or **perldoc perldoc** to display the perldoc man page and read more about this tool.

Make Perl programs readable

tip Although Perl has many shortcuts that are good choices for one-shot programming, this chapter presents code that is easy to understand and easy to maintain.

TERMINOLOGY

This section defines some of the terms used in this chapter.

Module A Perl *module* is a self-contained chunk of Perl code, frequently containing several functions that work together. A module can be called from another module or from a Perl program. A module must have a unique name. To help ensure unique names, Perl provides a hierarchical *namespace* (page 1111) for modules, separating components of a name with double colons (::). Example module names are **Timestamp::Simple** and **WWW::Mechanize.**

Distribution A Perl *distribution* is a set of one or more modules that perform a task. You can search for distributions and modules at search.cpan.org. Examples of distributions include **Timestamp-Simple** (the **Timestamp-Simple-1.01.tar.gz** archive file contains the **Timestamp::Simple** module only) and **WWW-Mechanize** (**WWW-Mechanize-1.34.tar.gz** contains the **WWW::Mechanize** module, plus supporting modules including **WWW::Mechanize::Link** and **WWW::Mechanize::Image**).

Package A *package* defines a Perl namespace. For example, in the variable with the name **$WWW::Mechanize::ex**, **$ex** is a scalar variable in the **WWW::Mechanize** package, where "package" is used in the sense of a namespace. Using the same name, such as **WWW::Mechanize**, for a distribution, a package, and a module can be confusing.

Block A *block* is zero or more statements, delimited by curly braces ({}), that defines a scope. The shell control structure syntax explanations refer to these elements as ***commands***. See the **if...then** control structure on page 431 for an example.

Package variable A *package variable* is defined within the package it appears in. Other packages can refer to package variables by using the variable's fully qualified name (for example, **$Text::Wrap::columns**). By default, variables are package variables unless you define them as lexical variables.

Lexical variable A *lexical variable*, which is defined by preceding the name of a variable with the keyword **my** (see the tip on page 539), is defined only within the block or file it appears in. Other languages refer to a lexical variable as a local variable. Because Perl 4 used the keyword **local** with a different meaning, Perl 5 uses the keyword **lexical** in its place. When programming using bash, variables that are not exported (page 481) are shell variables and are local to the program they are used in.

List A *list* is a series of zero or more scalars. The following list has three elements—two numbers and a string:

```
(2, 4, 'Zach')
```

Array An *array* is a variable that holds a list of elements in a defined order. In the following line of code, **@a** is an array. See page 541 for more information about array variables.

```
@a = (2, 4, 'Zach')
```

Compound statement A *compound statement* is a statement made up of other statements. For example, the **if** compound statement (page 546) incorporates an **if** statement that normally includes other statements within the block it controls.

RUNNING A PERL PROGRAM

There are several ways you can run a program written in Perl. The **–e** option enables you to enter a program on the command line:

```
$ perl -e 'print "Hi there.\n"'
Hi there.
```

The **–e** option is a good choice for testing Perl syntax and running brief, one-shot programs. This option requires that the Perl program appear as a single argument on the command line. The program must immediately follow this option; it is an argument to this option. An easy way to write this type of program is to enclose the program within single quotation marks.

Because Perl is a member of the class of utilities that take input from a file or standard input (page 142), you can give the command **perl** and enter the program terminated by CONTROL-D (end of file). Perl reads the program from standard input:

```
$ perl
print "Hi there.\n";
CONTROL-D
Hi there.
```

The preceding techniques are useful for quick, one-off command-line programs but are not helpful for running more complex programs. Most of the time, a Perl program is stored in a text file. Although not required, the file typically has a filename extension of **.pl**. Following is the same simple program used in the previous examples stored in a file:

```
$ cat simple.pl
print "Hi there.\n";
```

You can run this program by specifying its name as an argument to Perl:

```
$ perl simple.pl
Hi there.
```

Most commonly and similarly to most shell scripts, the file containing the Perl program is executable. In the following example, chmod (page 295) makes the **simple2.pl** file executable. As explained on page 297, the **#!** at the start of the first line of the file instructs the shell to pass the rest of the file to **/usr/bin/perl** for execution.

```
$ chmod 755 simple2.pl
$ cat simple2.pl
#!/usr/bin/perl -w
print "Hi there.\n";

$ ./simple2.pl
Hi there.
```

In this example, the **simple2.pl** program is executed as **./simple2.pl** because the working directory is not in the user's **PATH** (page 318). The **–w** option tells Perl to issue warning messages when it identifies potential errors in the code.

PERL VERSION 5.22

All examples in this chapter were run under Perl 5.22. Give the following command to see which version of Perl the local system is running:

```
$ perl -v

This is perl 5, version 22, subversion 1 (v5.22.1) built for x86_64-
linux-gnu-thread-multi...
```

use feature 'say' The **say** function is a Perl 6 feature available in Perl 5.22. It works the same way **print** does, except it adds a NEWLINE (**\n**) at the end of each line it outputs. Some versions of Perl require you to tell Perl explicitly that you want to use **say**. The **use** function in the following example tells Perl to enable **say**. Try running this program without the **use** line to see if the local version of Perl requires it.

```
$ cat 5.22.pl
use feature 'say';
say 'Output by say.';
print 'Output by print.';
say 'End.'

$ perl 5.22.pl
Output by say.
Output by print.End.
$
```

Earlier versions of Perl If you are running an earlier version of Perl, you will need to replace **say** in the examples in this chapter with **print** and terminate the **print** statement with a quoted **\n**:

```
$ cat 5.8.pl
print 'Output by print in place of say.', "\n";
print 'Output by print.';
print 'End.', "\n";

$ perl 5.8.pl
Output by print in place of say.
Output by print.End.
```

SYNTAX

This section describes the major components of a Perl program.

Statements A Perl program comprises one or more *statements,* each terminated by a semicolon (;). These statements are free-form with respect to *whitespace* (page 1132), except for whitespace within quoted strings. Multiple statements can appear on a single line, each terminated by a semicolon. The following programs are equivalent. The first occupies two lines, the second only one; look at the differences in the spacing around the equal and plus signs. See **use feature 'say'** (on the previous page) if these programs complain about **say** not being available.

```
$ cat statement1.pl
$n=4;
say "Answer is ", $n + 2;
$ perl statement1.pl
Answer is 6

$ cat statement2.pl
$n = 4; say "Answer is ", $n+2;
$ perl statement2.pl
Answer is 6
```

Expressions The syntax of Perl expressions frequently corresponds to the syntax of C expressions but is not always the same. Perl expressions are covered in examples throughout this chapter.

Quotation marks All character strings must be enclosed within single or double quotation marks. Perl differentiates between the two types of quotation marks in a manner similar to the way the shell does (page 312): Double quotation marks allow Perl to interpolate enclosed variables and interpret special characters such as **\n** (NEWLINE), whereas single quotation marks do not. Table 11-1 lists some of Perl's special characters.

The following example demonstrates how different types of quotation marks, and the absence of quotation marks, affect Perl in converting scalars between numbers and strings. The single quotation marks in the first **print** statement prevent Perl from interpolating the **$string** variable and from interpreting the **\n** special character. The leading **\n** in the second **print** statement forces the output of that statement to appear on a new line.

```
$ cat string1.pl
$string="5";        # $string declared as a string, but it will not matter

print '$string+5\n';    # Perl displays $string+5 literally because of
                        # the single quotation marks
print "\n$string+5\n"; # Perl interpolates the value of $string as a string
                        # because of the double quotation marks
print $string+5, "\n"; # Lack of quotation marks causes Perl to interpret
                        # $string as a numeric variable and to add 5;
                        # the \n must appear between double quotation marks

$ perl string1.pl
$string+5\n
5+5
10
```

Slash By default, regular expressions are delimited by slashes (/). The following example tests whether the string **hours** contains the pattern **our**; see page 563 for more information on regular expression delimiters in Perl.

```
$ perl -e 'if ("hours" =~ /our/) {say "yes";}'
```

The local version of Perl might require **use feature** 'say' (page 535) to work properly:

```
$ perl -e 'use feature "say"; if ("hours" =~ /our/) {say "yes";}'
```

Backslash Within a string enclosed between double quotation marks, a backslash escapes (quotes) another backslash. Thus, Perl displays "\\n" as **\n**. Within a regular expression, Perl does not expand a metacharacter preceded by a backslash. See the **string1.pl** program above.

Comments As in the shell, a comment in Perl begins with a hashmark (#) and ends at the end of the line (just before the NEWLINE character).

Special characters Table 11-1 lists some of the characters that are special within strings in Perl. Perl interpolates these characters when they appear between double quotation marks but not when they appear between single quotation marks. Table 11-3 on page 564 lists metacharacters, which are special within regular expressions.

Table 11-1 Some Perl special characters

Character	When within double quotation marks, interpolated as
\0*xx* (zero)	The ASCII character whose octal value is ***xx***
\a	An alarm (bell or beep) character (ASCII 7)
\e	An ESCAPE character (ASCII 27)
\n	A NEWLINE character (ASCII 10)
\r	A RETURN character (ASCII 13)
\t	A TAB character (ASCII 9)

VARIABLES

Like human languages, Perl distinguishes between singular and plural data. Strings and numbers are singular; lists of strings or numbers are plural. Perl provides three types of variables: *scalar* (singular), *array* (plural), and *hash* (plural; also called *associative arrays*). Perl identifies each type of variable by a special character preceding its name. The name of a scalar variable begins with a dollar sign ($), an array variable begins with an at sign (@), and a hash variable begins with a percent sign (%). As opposed to the way the shell identifies variables, Perl requires the leading character to appear each time you reference a variable, including when you assign a value to the variable:

```
$ name="Zach" ; echo "$name"                    (bash)
Zach

$ perl -e '$name="Zach" ; print "$name\n";'  (perl)
Zach
```

Variable names, which are case sensitive, can include letters, digits, and the underscore character (_). A Perl variable is a package variable (page 533) unless it is preceded by the keyword **my**, in which case it is a lexical variable (page 534) that is defined only within the block or file it appears in. See "Subroutines" on page 559 for a discussion of the locality of Perl variables.

Lexical variables overshadow package variables

caution If a lexical variable and a package variable have the same name, within the block or file in which the lexical variable is defined, the name refers to the lexical variable and not to the package variable.

A Perl variable comes into existence when you assign a value to it; you do not need to define or initialize a variable, although it might make a program more understandable to do so. Normally, Perl does not complain when you reference an uninitialized variable:

```
$ cat variable1.pl
#!/usr/bin/perl
my $name = 'Sam';
print "Hello, $nam, how are you?\n"; # Typo, e left off of name

$ ./variable1.pl
Hello, , how are you?
```

use strict Include **use strict** to cause Perl to require variables to be declared before being assigned values. See the **perldebtut man** page for more information. When you include **use strict** in the preceding program, Perl displays an error message:

```
$ cat variable1b.pl
#!/usr/bin/perl
use strict;
my $name = 'Sam';
print "Hello, $nam, how are you?\n"; # Typo, e left off of name
```

```
$ ./variable1b.pl
Global symbol "$nam" requires explicit package name at ./variable1b.pl line 4.
Execution of ./variable1b.pl aborted due to compilation errors.
```

Using my: lexical versus package variables

tip In **variable1.pl**, **$name** is declared to be lexical by preceding its name with the keyword **my**; its name and value are known within the file **variable1.pl** only. Declaring a variable to be lexical limits its scope to the block or file it is defined in. Although not necessary in this case, declaring variables to be lexical is good practice. This habit becomes especially useful when you write longer programs, subroutines, and packages, where it is harder to keep variable names unique. Declaring all variables to be lexical is mandatory when you write routines that will be used within code written by others. This practice allows those who work with your routines to use whichever variable names they like, without regard to which variable names you used in the code you wrote.

The shell and Perl scope variables differently. In the shell, if you do not **export** a variable to make it an environment variable, it is a shell variable and is local to the routine it is used in (page 480). In Perl, if you do not use **my** to declare a variable to be lexical, it is defined for the package it appears in.

–w and use warnings The **–w** option and the **use warnings** statement perform the same function: They cause Perl to generate an error message when it detects a syntax error. In the following example, Perl displays two warnings. The first tells you that you have used the variable named **$nam** once, on line 3, which probably indicates an error. This message is helpful when you mistype the name of a variable. Under Perl 5.22, the second warning specifies the name of the uninitialized variable. This warning refers to the same problem as the first warning. Although it is not hard to figure out which of the two variables is undefined in this simple program, doing so in a complex program can take a lot of time.

```
$ cat variable1a.pl
#!/usr/bin/perl -w
my $name = 'Sam';
print "Hello, $nam, how are you?\n"; # Prints warning because of typo and -w

$ ./variable1a.pl
Name "main::nam" used only once: possible typo at ./variable1a.pl line 3.
Use of uninitialized value $nam in concatenation (.) or string at ./variable1a.pl line 3.
Hello, , how are you?
```

You can also use **–w** on the command line. If you use **–e** as well, make sure the argument that follows this option is the program you want to execute (e.g., **–e –w** does not work). See the tip on page 562.

```
$ perl -w -e 'my $name = "Sam"; print "Hello, $nam, how are you?\n"'
Name "main::nam" used only once: possible typo at -e line 1.
Use of uninitialized value $nam in concatenation (.) or string at -e line 1.
Hello, , how are you?
```

undef and defined An undefined variable has the special value **undef**, which evaluates to zero (0) in a numeric expression and expands to an empty string ("") when you print it. Use the **defined** function to determine whether a variable has been defined. The following example, which uses constructs explained later in this chapter, calls **defined** with an argument of **$name** and negates the result with an exclamation point (**!**). The result is that the **print** statement is executed if **$name** is *not* defined.

```
$ cat variable2.pl
#!/usr/bin/perl
if (!defined($name)) {
print "The variable '\$name' is not defined.\n"
};

$ ./variable2.pl
The variable '$name' is not defined.
```

Because the **–w** option causes Perl to warn you when you reference an undefined variable, using this option would generate a warning.

SCALAR VARIABLES

A *scalar variable* has a name that begins with a dollar sign (**$**) and holds a single string or number: It is a singular variable. Because Perl converts between the two when necessary, you can use strings and numbers interchangeably. Perl interprets scalar variables as strings when it makes sense to interpret them as strings and as numbers when it makes sense to interpret them as numbers. Perl's judgment in these matters is generally good.

The following example shows some uses of scalar variables. The first two lines of code (lines 3 and 4) assign the string **Sam** to the scalar variable **$name** and the numbers **5** and **2** to the scalar variables **$n1** and **$n2**, respectively. In this example, multiple statements, each terminated with a semicolon (**;**), appear on a single line. See **use feature 'say'** on page 535 if this program complains about **say** not being available.

```
$ cat scalars1.pl
#!/usr/bin/perl -w

$name = "Sam";
$n1 = 5; $n2 = 2;

say "$name $n1 $n2";
say "$n1 + $n2";
say '$name $n1 $n2';
say $n1 + $n2, " ", $n1 * $n2;
say $name + $n1;

$ ./scalars1.pl
Sam 5 2
5 + 2
$name $n1 $n2
7 10
Argument "Sam" isn't numeric in addition (+) at ./scalers1.pl line 11.
5
```

Double quotation marks The first **say** statement sends the string enclosed within double quotation marks to standard output (the screen unless you redirect it). Within double quotation marks,

Perl expands variable names to the value of the named variable. Thus, the first **say** statement displays the values of three variables, separated from each other by SPACEs. The second **say** statement includes a plus sign (**+**). Perl does not recognize operators such as **+** within either type of quotation marks. Thus, Perl displays the plus sign between the values of the two variables.

Single quotation marks

The third **say** statement sends the string enclosed within single quotation marks to standard output. Within single quotation marks, Perl interprets all characters literally, so it displays the string exactly as it appears between the single quotation marks.

In the fourth **say** statement, the operators are not quoted, and Perl performs the addition and multiplication as specified. Without the quoted SPACE, Perl would catenate the two numbers (**710**). The last **say** statement attempts to add a string and a number; the **–w** option causes Perl to display an error message before displaying **5**. The result 5 comes from adding **Sam**, which Perl evaluates as **0** in a numerical context, to the number 5 (0 + 5 = 5).

ARRAY VARIABLES

An *array variable* is an ordered container of scalars whose name begins with an at sign (**@**) and whose first element is numbered zero (zero-based indexing). Because an array can hold zero or more scalars, it is a plural variable. Arrays are ordered; hashes (page 544) are unordered. In Perl, arrays grow as needed. If you reference an uninitialized element of an array, such as an element beyond the end of the array, Perl returns **undef**.

The first statement in the following program assigns the values of two numbers and a string to the array variable named **@arrayvar**. Because Perl uses zero-based indexing, the first **say** statement displays the value of the second element of the array (the element with the index 1). This statement specifies the variable **$arrayvar[1]** as a scalar (singular) because it refers to a single value. The second **say** statement specifies the variable **@arrayvar[1,2]** as a list (plural) because it refers to multiple values (the elements with the indexes 1 and 2).

```
$ cat arrayvar1.pl
#!/usr/bin/perl -w
@arrayvar = (8, 18, "Sam");
say $arrayvar[1];
say "@arrayvar[1,2]";

$ perl arrayvar1.pl
18
18 Sam
```

The next example shows a couple of ways to determine the length of an array and presents more information on using quotation marks within **print** statements. The first assignment statement in **arrayvar2.pl** assigns values to the first six elements of the **@arrayvar2** array. When used in a scalar context, Perl evaluates the name of an array as the length of the array. The second assignment statement assigns the number of elements in **@arrayvar2** to the scalar variable **$num**.

```
$ cat arrayvar2.pl
#!/usr/bin/perl -w
@arrayvar2 = ("apple", "bird", 44, "Tike", "metal", "pike");

$num = @arrayvar2;                    # number of elements in array
print "Elements: ", $num, "\n";       # two equivalent print statements
print "Elements: $num\n";

print "Last: $#arrayvar2\n";          # index of last element in array

$ ./arrayvar2.pl
Elements: 6
Elements: 6
Last: 5
```

The first two **print** statements in **arrayvar2.pl** display the string **Elements:**, a SPACE, the value of **$num**, and a NEWLINE, each using a different syntax. The first of these statements displays three values, using commas to separate them within the **print** statement. The second **print** statement has one argument and demonstrates that Perl expands a variable (replaces the variable with its value) when the variable is enclosed within double quotation marks.

$#array The final **print** statement in **arrayvar2.pl** shows that Perl evaluates the variable **$#*array*** as the index of the last element in the array named ***array***. Because Perl uses zero-based indexing by default, this variable evaluates to one less than the number of elements in the array.

The next example works with elements of an array and uses a dot (**.**; the string catenation operator). The first two lines assign values to four scalar variables. The third line shows that you can assign values to array elements using scalar variables, arithmetic, and catenated strings. The dot operator catenates strings, so Perl evaluates **$va . $vb** as **Sam** catenated with **uel**—that is, as **Samuel** (see the output of the last **print** statement).

```
$ cat arrayvar3.pl
#!/usr/bin/perl -w
$v1 = 5; $v2 = 8;
$va = "Sam"; $vb = "uel";
@arrayvar3 = ($v1, $v1 * 2, $v1 * $v2, "Max", "Zach", $va . $vb);

print $arrayvar3[2], "\n";         # one element of an array is a scalar
print @arrayvar3[2,4], "\n";       # two elements of an array are a list
print @arrayvar3[2..4], "\n\n";    # a slice
```

```
print "@arrayvar3[2,4]", "\n";    # a list, elements separated by SPACEs
print "@arrayvar3[2..4]", "\n\n"; # a slice, elements separated by SPACEs

print "@arrayvar3\n";             # an array, elements separated by SPACEs

$ ./arrayvar3.pl
40
40Zach
40MaxZach

40 Zach
40 Max Zach

5 10 40 Max Zach Samuel
```

The first **print** statement in **arrayvar3.pl** displays the third element (the element with an index of 2) of the **@arrayvar3** array. This statement uses **$** in place of **@** because it refers to a single element of the array. The subsequent **print** statements use the symbol @ because they refer to more than one element. Within the brackets that specify an array subscript, two subscripts separated by a comma specify two elements of an array. The second **print** statement, for example, displays the third and fifth elements of the array.

Array slice When you separate two elements of an array with two dots (**..**; the range operator), Perl substitutes all elements between and including the two specified elements. A portion of an array comprising elements is called a *slice*. The third **print** statement in the preceding example displays the elements with indexes 2, 3, and 4 (the third, fourth, and fifth elements) as specified by **2..4**. Perl puts no SPACEs between the elements it displays.

Within a **print** statement, when you enclose an array variable, including its subscripts, within double quotation marks, Perl puts a SPACE between each of the elements. The fourth and fifth **print** statements in the preceding example illustrate this syntax. The last **print** statement displays the entire array, with elements separated by SPACEs.

shift, **push**, **pop**, and **splice** The next example demonstrates several functions you can use to manipulate arrays. The example uses the **@colors** array, which is initialized to a list of seven colors. The **shift** function returns and removes the first element of an array, **push** adds an element to the end of an array, and **pop** returns and removes the last element of an array. The **splice** function replaces elements of an array with another array; in the example, **splice** inserts the **@ins** array starting at index 1 (the second element), replacing two elements of the array. See **use feature 'say'** on page 535 if this program complains about **say** not being available. See the **perlfunc man** page for more information on the functions described in this paragraph.

```
$ cat ./shift1.pl
#!/usr/bin/perl -w

@colors = ("red", "orange", "yellow", "green", "blue", "indigo", "violet");

say "                            Display array: @colors";
say " Display and remove first element of array: ", shift (@colors);
say "      Display remaining elements of array: @colors";

push (@colors, "WHITE");
say "   Add element to end of array and display: @colors";

say "  Display and remove last element of array: ", pop (@colors);
say "      Display remaining elements of array: @colors";

@ins = ("GRAY", "FERN");
splice (@colors, 1, 2, @ins);
say "Replace second and third elements of array: @colors";

$ ./shift1.pl
                             Display array: red orange yellow green blue indigo violet
 Display and remove first element of array: red
       Display remaining elements of array: orange yellow green blue indigo violet
   Add element to end of array and display: orange yellow green blue indigo violet WHITE
  Display and remove last element of array: WHITE
       Display remaining elements of array: orange yellow green blue indigo violet
Replace second and third elements of array: orange GRAY FERN blue indigo violet
```

HASH VARIABLES

A *hash variable*, sometimes called an *associative array variable*, is a plural data structure that holds an array of key–value pairs. It uses strings as keys (indexes) and is optimized to return a value quickly when given a key. Each key must be a unique scalar. Hashes are unordered; arrays (page 541) are ordered. When you assign a hash to a list, the key–value pairs are preserved, but their order is neither alphabetical nor the order in which they were inserted into the hash; instead, the order is effectively random.

Perl provides two syntaxes to assign values to a hash. The first uses a single assignment statement for each key–value pair:

```
$ cat hash1.pl
#!/usr/bin/perl -w
$hashvar1{boat} = "tuna";
$hashvar1{"number five"} = 5;
$hashvar1{4} = "fish";

@arrayhash1 = %hashvar1;
say "@arrayhash1";

$ ./hash1.pl
boat tuna 4 fish number five 5
```

Within an assignment statement, the key is located within braces to the left of the equal sign; the value is on the right side of the equal sign. As illustrated in the preceding example, keys and values can take on either numeric or string values. You do not need to quote string keys unless they contain SPACEs. This example also shows that you can display the keys and values held by a hash, each separated from the next by a SPACE, by assigning the hash to an array variable and then printing that variable enclosed within double quotation marks.

The next example shows the other way of assigning values to a hash and illustrates how to use the **keys** and **values** functions to extract keys and values from a hash. After assigning values to the **%hash2** hash, **hash2.pl** calls the **keys** function with an argument of **%hash2** and assigns the resulting list of keys to the **@array_keys** array. The program then uses the **values** function to assign values to the **@array_values** array.

```
$ cat hash2.pl
#!/usr/bin/perl -w

%hash2 = (
    boat => "tuna",
    "number five" => 5,
    4 => "fish",
    );

@array_keys = keys(%hash2);
say "  Keys: @array_keys";

@array_values = values(%hash2);
say "Values: @array_values";
$ ./hash2.pl
  Keys: boat 4 number five
Values: tuna fish 5
```

Because Perl automatically quotes a single word appearing to the left of the => operator, you do not need quotation marks around **boat** in the third line of this program. However, removing the quotation marks from around **number five** would generate an error because the string contains a SPACE.

Control Structures

Control flow statements alter the order of execution of statements within a Perl program. Starting on page 430, Chapter 10 discusses bash control structures in detail and includes flow diagrams. Perl control structures perform the same functions as their bash counterparts, although the two languages use different syntaxes. The description of each control structure in this section references the discussion of the same control structure under bash.

In this section, the ***bold italic*** words in the syntax description are the items you supply to cause the structure to have the desired effect, the *nonbold italic* words are the keywords Perl uses to identify the control structure, and *{...}* represents a block (page 533) of statements. Many of these structures use an expression, denoted as ***expr***, to control their execution. See **if/unless** (next) for an example and explanation of a syntax description.

if/unless

The **if** and **unless** control structures are compound statements that have the following syntax:

*if (**expr**) {...}*

*unless (**expr**) {...}*

These structures differ only in the sense of the test they perform. The **if** structure executes the block of statements *if* ***expr*** evaluates to *true*; **unless** executes the block of statements *unless* ***expr*** evaluates to *true* (i.e., if ***expr*** is *false*).

The *if* appears in nonbold type because it is a keyword; it must appear exactly as shown. The ***expr*** is an expression; Perl evaluates it and executes the block (page 533) of statements represented by *{...}* if the expression evaluates as required by the control structure.

File test operators

The ***expr*** in the following example, **–r memo1**, uses the **–r** file test operator to determine if a file named **memo1** exists in the working directory and if the file is readable. Although this operator tests only whether you have read permission for the file, the file must exist for you to have read permission; thus, it implicitly tests that the file is present. (Perl uses the same file test operators as bash; see Table 10-1 on page 433.) If this expression evaluates to *true,* Perl executes the block of statements (in this case one statement) between the braces. If the expression evaluates to *false,* Perl skips the block of statements. In either case, Perl then exits and returns control to the shell.

```
$ cat if1.pl
#!/usr/bin/perl -w
if (-r "memo1") {
    say "The file 'memo1' exists and is readable.";
    }

$ ./if1.pl
The file 'memo1' exists and is readable.
```

Following is the same program written using the postfix **if** syntax. Which syntax you use depends on which part of the statement is more important to someone reading the code.

```
$ cat if1a.pl
#!/usr/bin/perl -w
say "The file 'memo1' exists and is readable." if (-r "memo1");
```

The next example uses a **print** statement to display a prompt on standard output and uses the statement **$entry = <>;** to read a line from standard input and assign the line to the variable **$entry**. Reading from standard input, working with other files, and use of the magic file handle (**<>**) for reading files specified on the command line are covered on page 554.

Comparison operators

Perl uses different operators to compare numbers from those it uses to compare strings. Table 11-2 lists numeric and string comparison operators. In the following example, the expression in the **if** statement uses the **==** numeric comparison operator to compare the value the user entered and the number **28**. This operator performs a numeric comparison, so the user can enter **28**, **28.0**, or **00028** and in all cases the result of the comparison will be *true*. Also, because the comparison is numeric, Perl ignores both the whitespace around and the NEWLINE following the user's entry. Using the **–w** option causes Perl to issue a warning if the user enters a nonnumeric value and the program uses that value in an arithmetic expression; without this option Perl silently evaluates the expression as *false*.

```
$ cat if2.pl
#!/usr/bin/perl -w
print "Enter 28: ";
$entry = <>;
if ($entry == 28) {                    # use == for a numeric comparison
    print "Thank you for entering 28.\n";
    }
print "End.\n";

$ ./if2.pl
Enter 28: 28.0
Thank you for entering 28.
End.
```

Table 11-2 Comparison operators

Numeric operators	String operators	Value returned based on the relationship between the values preceding and following the operator
==	**eq**	*True* if equal
!=	**ne**	*True* if not equal
<	**lt**	*True* if less than
>	**gt**	*True* if greater than
<=	**le**	*True* if less than or equal
>=	**ge**	*True* if greater than or equal
<=>	**cmp**	0 if equal, 1 if greater than, –1 if less than

The next program is similar to the preceding one, except it tests for equality between two strings. The **chomp** function (page 556) removes the trailing NEWLINE from the user's entry; without this function the strings in the comparison would never match. The **eq** comparison operator compares strings. In this example the result of the string comparison is *true* when the user enters the string **five**. Leading or trailing whitespace will yield a result of *false*, as would the string **5**, although none of these entries would generate a warning because they are legitimate strings.

```
$ cat if2a.pl
#!/usr/bin/perl -w
print "Enter the word 'five': ";
$entry = <>;
chomp ($entry);
if ($entry eq "five") {          # use eq for a string comparison
    print "Thank you for entering 'five'.\n";
    }
print "End.\n";

$ ./if2a.pl
Enter the word 'five': five
Thank you for entering 'five'.
End.
```

if...else

The **if...else** control structure is a compound statement that is similar to the bash **if...then...else** control structure (page 435). It implements a two-way branch using the following syntax:

if (expr) {...} else {...}

die The next program prompts the user for two different numbers and stores those numbers in **$num1** and **$num2**. If the user enters the same number twice, an **if** structure executes a **die** function, which sends its argument to standard error and aborts program execution.

If the user enters different numbers, the **if...else** structure reports which number is larger. Because *expr* performs a numeric comparison, the program accepts numbers that include decimal points.

```
$ cat ifelse.pl
#!/usr/bin/perl -w
print "Enter a number: ";
$num1 = <>;
print "Enter another, different number: ";
$num2 = <>;

if ($num1 == $num2) {
    die ("Please enter two different numbers.\n");
    }
if ($num1 > $num2) {
    print "The first number is greater than the second number.\n";
    }
else {
    print "The first number is less than the second number.\n";
    }
```

```
$ ./ifelse.pl
Enter a number: 8
Enter another, different number: 8
Please enter two different numbers.

$ ./ifelse.pl
Enter a number: 5.5
Enter another, different number: 5
The first number is greater than the second number.
```

if...elsif...else

Similar to the bash **if...then...elif** control structure (page 436), the Perl **if...elsif...else** control structure is a compound statement that implements a nested set of **if...else** structures using the following syntax:

if (expr) {...} elsif {...} ... else {...}

The next program implements the functionality of the preceding **ifelse.pl** program using an **if...elsif...else** structure. A **print** statement replaces the **die** statement because the last statement in the program displays the error message; the program terminates after executing this statement anyway. You can use the STDERR handle (page 554) to cause Perl to send this message to standard error instead of standard output.

```
$ cat ifelsif.pl
#!/usr/bin/perl -w
print "Enter a number: ";
$num1 = <>;
print "Enter another, different number: ";
$num2 = <>;
if ($num1 > $num2) {
        print "The first number is greater than the second number.\n";
        }
    elsif ($num1 < $num2) {
        print "The first number is less than the second number.\n";
        }
    else {
        print "Please enter two different numbers.\n";
        }
```

foreach/for

The Perl **foreach** and **for** keywords are synonyms; you can replace one with the other in any context. These structures are compound statements that have two syntaxes. Some programmers use one syntax with **foreach** and the other syntax with the **for**, although there is no need to do so. This book uses **foreach** with both syntaxes.

foreach: SYNTAX 1

The first syntax for the **foreach** structure is similar to the shell's **for...in** structure (page 443)

*foreach|for [**var**] (**list**) {...}*

where ***list*** is a list of expressions or variables. Perl executes the block of statements once for each item in ***list***, sequentially assigning to ***var*** the value of one item in ***list*** on each iteration, starting with the first item. If you do not specify ***var***, Perl assigns values to the $_ variable (page 554).

The following program demonstrates a simple **foreach** structure. On the first pass through the loop, Perl assigns the string **Mo** to the variable **$item** and the **say** statement displays the value of this variable followed by a NEWLINE. On the second and third passes through the loop, **$item** is assigned the value of **Larry** and **Curly**. When there are no items left in the list, Perl continues with the statement following the **foreach** structure. In this case, the program terminates. See **use feature 'say'** on page 535 if this program complains about **say** not being available.

```
$ cat foreach.pl
foreach $item ("Mo", "Larry", "Curly") {
    say "$item says hello.";
    }

$ perl foreach.pl
Mo says hello.
Larry says hello.
Curly says hello.
```

Using **$_** (page 554), you can write this program as follows:

```
$ cat foreacha.pl
foreach ("Mo", "Larry", "Curly") {
    say "$_ says hello.";
    }
```

Following is the program using an array:

```
$ cat foreachb.pl
@stooges = ("Mo", "Larry", "Curly");
foreach (@stooges) {
    say "$_ says hello.";
    }
```

Following is the program using the **foreach** postfix syntax:

```
$ cat foreachc.pl
@stooges = ("Mo", "Larry", "Curly");
say "$_ says hello." foreach @stooges;
```

The loop variable (**$item** and **$_** in the preceding examples) references the elements in the ***list*** within the parentheses. When you modify the loop variable, you modify the element in the list. The **uc** function returns an upshifted version of its argument.

The next example shows that modifying the loop variable **$stooge** modifies the **@stooges** array:

```
$ cat foreachd.pl
@stooges = ("Mo", "Larry", "Curly");
foreach $stooge (@stooges) {
    $stooge = uc $stooge;
    say "$stooge says hello.";
    }
say "$stooges[1] is uppercase"

$ perl foreachd.pl
MO says hello.
LARRY says hello.
CURLY says hello.
LARRY is uppercase
```

See page 557 for an example that loops through command-line arguments.

last AND next

Perl's **last** and **next** statements allow you to interrupt a loop; they are analogous to the Bourne Again Shell's **break** and **continue** statements (page 453). The **last** statement transfers control to the statement following the block of statements controlled by the loop structure, terminating execution of the loop. The **next** statement transfers control to the end of the block of statements, which continues execution of the loop with the next iteration.

In the following program, the **if** structure tests whether **$item** is equal to the string **two**; if it is, the structure executes the **next** command, which skips the **say** statement and continues with the next iteration of the loop. If you replaced **next** with **last**, Perl would exit from the loop and not display **three**. See **use feature 'say'** on page 535 if this program complains about **say** not being available.

```
$ cat foreach1.pl
foreach $item ("one", "two", "three") {
    if ($item eq "two") {
        next;
        }
    say "$item";
    }

$ perl foreach1.pl
one
three
```

foreach: SYNTAX 2

The second syntax for the **foreach** structure is similar to the C **for** structure:

*foreach|for (**expr1**; **expr2**; **expr3**) {...}*

The ***expr1*** initializes the **foreach** loop; Perl evaluates ***expr1*** one time, before it executes the block of statements. The ***expr2*** is the termination condition; Perl evaluates it before each pass through the block of statements and executes the block of statements if ***expr2*** evaluates as *true*. Perl evaluates ***expr3*** after each pass through the block of statements; it typically increments a variable that is part of ***expr2***.

In the next example, the **foreach2.pl** program prompts for three numbers; displays the first number; repeatedly increments this number by the third number, displaying each result until the result would be greater than the second number; and quits. See page 555 for a discussion of the magic file handle (**<>**).

```
$ cat foreach2.pl
#!/usr/bin/perl -w

print "Enter starting number: ";
$start = <>;

print "Enter ending number: ";
$end = <>;

print "Enter increment: ";
$incr = <>;

if ($start >= $end || $incr < 1) {
    die ("The starting number must be less than the ending number\n",
    "and the increment must be greater than zero.\n");
    }

foreach ($count = $start+0; $count <= $end; $count += $incr) {
    say "$count";
    }
$ ./foreach2.pl
Enter starting number: 2
Enter ending number: 10
Enter increment: 3
2
5
8
```

After prompting for three numbers, the preceding program tests whether the starting number is greater than or equal to the ending number or if the increment is less than 1. The || is a Boolean OR operator; the expression within the parentheses following **if** evaluates to *true* if either the expression before or the expression after this operator evaluates to *true*.

The **foreach** statement begins by assigning the value of **$start+0** to **$count**. Adding a 0 (zero) to the string **$start** forces Perl to work in a numeric context, removing the trailing NEWLINE when it performs the assignment. Without this fix, the program would display an extra NEWLINE following the first number it displayed.

while/until

The **while** (page 447) and **until** (page 451) control structures are compound statements that implement conditional loops using the following syntax:

while (expr) {...}

until (expr) {...}

These structures differ only in the sense of their termination conditions. The **while** structure repeatedly executes the block of statements *while* ***expr*** evaluates to *true*; **until** continues *until* ***expr*** evaluates to *true* (i.e., while ***expr*** remains *false*).

The following example demonstrates one technique for reading and processing input until there is no more input. Although this example shows input coming from the user (standard input), the technique works the same way for input coming from a file (see the example on page 556). The user enters CONTROL-D on a line by itself to signal the end of file.

In this example, ***expr*** is **$line = <>**. This statement uses the magic file handle (**<>**; page 555) to read one line from standard input and assigns the string it reads to the **$line** variable. This statement evaluates to *true* as long as it reads data. When it reaches the end of file, the statement evaluates to *false*. The **while** loop continues to execute the block of statements (in this example, only one statement) as long as there is data to read.

```
$ cat while1.pl
#!/usr/bin/perl -w
$count = 0;
while ($line = <>) {
    print ++$count, ". $line";
    }
print "\n$count lines entered.\n";
$ ./while1.pl
Good Morning.
1. Good Morning.
Today is Monday.
2. Today is Monday.
CONTROL-D

2 lines entered.
```

In the preceding example, **$count** keeps track of the number of lines the user enters. Putting the **++** increment operator before a variable (**++$count**; called a preincrement operator) increments the variable before Perl evaluates it. Alternatively, you could initialize **$count** to 1 and increment it with **$count++** (postincrement), but then in the final **print** statement **$count** would equal one more than the number of lines entered.

$. The **$.** variable keeps track of the number of lines of input a program has read. Using **$.** you can rewrite the previous example as follows:

```
$ cat while1a.pl
#!/usr/bin/perl -w
while ($line = <>) {
        print $., ". $line";
        }
print "\n$. lines entered.\n";
```

$_** Frequently, you can simplify Perl code by using the **$_ variable. You can use **$_** many places in a Perl program; think of **$_** as meaning *it,* the object of what you are doing. It is the default operand for many operations. For example, the following section of code processes a line using the **$line** variable. It reads a line into **$line**, removes any trailing NEWLINE from **$line** using **chomp** (page 556), and checks whether a regular expression matches **$line**.

```
while (my $line = <>) {
    chomp $line;
    if ($line =~ /regex/) ...
}
```

You can rewrite this code by using **$_** to replace **$line**:

```
while (my $_ = <>) {
    chomp $_;
    if ($_ =~ /regex/) ...
}
```

Because **$_** is the default operand in these instances, you can omit **$_** altogether:

```
while (<>) {            # read into $_
    chomp;              # chomp $_
    if (/regex/) ...    # if $_ matches regex
}
```

WORKING WITH FILES

Opening a file and assigning a handle A *handle* is a name you can use in a Perl program to refer to a file or process that is open for reading and/or writing. When you are working with the shell, handles are referred to as *file descriptors* (page 464). As when you are working with the shell, the kernel automatically opens handles for standard input (page 137), standard output (page 137), and standard error (page 292) before it runs a program. The kernel closes these descriptors after a program finishes running. The names for these handles are **STDIN**, **STDOUT**, and **STDERR**, respectively. You must manually open handles to read from or write to other files or processes. The syntax of an **open** statement is

*open (**file-handle**, ['**mode**',] "**file-ref**");*

where ***file-handle*** is the name of the handle or a variable you will use in the program to refer to the file or process named by ***file-ref***. If you omit ***mode*** or specify a ***mode*** of **<**, Perl opens the file for input (reading). Specify ***mode*** as **>** to truncate and write to a file or as **>>** to append to a file.

See page 570 for a discussion of reading from and writing to processes.

Writing to a file The **print** function writes output to a file or process. The syntax of a **print** statement is

print [file-handle] "*text*";

where *file-handle* is the name of the handle you specified in an **open** statement and *text* is the information you want to output. The *file-handle* can also be **STDOUT** or **STDERR**, as explained earlier. Except when you send information to standard output, you must specify a handle in a **print** statement. Do not place a comma after *file-handle.* Also, do not enclose arguments to **print** within parentheses because doing so can create problems.

Reading from a file The following expression reads one line, including the NEWLINE (**\n**), from the file or process associated with *file-handle*:

<file-handle>

This expression is typically used in a statement such as

```
$line = <IN>;
```

which reads into the variable **$line** one line from the file or process identified by the handle **IN**.

Magic file handle (**<>**) To facilitate reading from files named on the command line or from standard input, Perl provides the *magic file handle.* This book uses this file handle in most examples. In place of the preceding line, you can use

```
$line = <>;
```

This file handle causes a Perl program to work like many Linux utilities: It reads from standard input unless the program is called with one or more arguments, in which case it reads from the files named by the arguments. See page 142 for an explanation of how this feature works with **cat**.

The **print** statement in the first line in the next example includes the optional handle **STDOUT**; the next **print** statement omits this handle; the final **print** statement uses the **STDERR** file handle, which causes **print**'s output to go to standard error. The first **print** statement prompts the user to enter something. The string that this statement outputs is terminated with a SPACE, not a NEWLINE, so the user can enter information on the same line as the prompt. The second line then uses a magic file handle to read one line from standard input, which it assigns to **$userline**. Because of the magic file handle, if you call **file1.pl** with an argument that is a filename, it reads one line from that file instead of from standard input. The command line that runs **file1.pl** uses **2>** (see "File descriptors" on page 292) to redirect standard error (the output of the third **print** statement) to the **file1.err** file.

```
$ cat file1.pl
print STDOUT "Enter something: ";
$userline = <>;
print "1>>>$userline<<<\n";
chomp ($userline);
```

```
print "2>>>$userline<<<\n";
print STDERR "3. Error message.\n";
$ perl file1.pl 2> file1.err
Enter something: hi there
1>>>hi there
<<<
2>>>hi there<<<

$ cat file1.err
3. Error message.
```

chomp/chop The two **print** statements following the user input in **file1.pl** display the value of **$userline** immediately preceded by greater than signs (**>**) and followed by less than signs (**<**). The first of these statements demonstrates that **$userline** includes a NEWLINE: The less than signs following the string the user entered appear on the line following the string. The **chomp** function removes a trailing NEWLINE, if it exists, from a string. After **chomp** processes **$userline**, the **print** statement shows that this variable no longer contains a NEWLINE. (The **chop** function is similar to **chomp**, except it removes *any* trailing character from a string.)

The next example shows how to read from a file. It uses an **open** statement to assign the lexical file handle **$infile** to the file **/usr/share/dict/words**. Each iteration of the **while** structure evaluates an expression that reads a line from the file represented by **$infile** and assigns the line to **$line**. When **while** reaches the end of file, the expression evaluates to *false;* control then passes out of the **while** structure. The block of one statement displays the line as it was read from the file, including the NEWLINE. This program copies **/usr/share/dict/words** to standard output. A pipe symbol (**|**; page 145) is then used to send the output through head (page 57), which displays the first four lines of the file (the first line is blank).

```
$ cat file2.pl
open (my $infile, "/usr/share/dict/words") or die "Cannot open dictionary: $!\n";
while ($line = <$infile>) {
    print $line;
    }

$ perl file2.pl | head -4

A
A's
AOL
```

$!** The **$! variable holds the last system error. In a numeric context, it holds the system error number; in a string context, it holds the system error string. If the **words** file is not present on the system, **file2.pl** displays the following message:

```
Cannot open dictionary: No such file or directory
```

If you do not have read permission for the file, the program displays this message:

```
Cannot open dictionary: Permission denied
```

Displaying the value of **$!** gives the user more information about what went wrong than simply saying that the program could not open the file.

Always check for an error when opening a file

tip When a Perl program attempts to open a file and fails, the program does not display an error message unless it checks whether **open** returned an error. In **file2.pl**, the **or** operator in the **open** statement causes Perl to execute **die** (page 548) if **open** fails. The **die** statement sends the message **Cannot open the dictionary** followed by the system error string to standard error and terminates the program.

@ARGV The **@ARGV** array holds the arguments from the command line Perl was called with. When you call the following program with a list of filenames, it displays the first line of each file. If the program cannot read a file, **die** (page 548) sends an error message to standard error and quits. The **foreach** structure loops through the command-line arguments, as represented by **@ARGV**, assigning each argument in turn to **$filename**. The **foreach** block starts with an **open** statement. Perl executes the **open** statement that precedes the OR Boolean operator (**or**) or, if that fails, Perl executes the statement following the **or** operator (**die**). The result is that Perl either opens the file named by **$filename** and assigns **IN** as its handle or, if it cannot open that file, executes the **die** statement and quits. The **print** statement displays the name of the file followed by a colon and the first line of the file. When it accepts **$line = <IN>** as an argument to **print**, Perl displays the value of **$line** following the assignment. After reading a line from a file, the program closes the file.

```
$ cat file3.pl
foreach $filename (@ARGV) {
    open (IN, $filename) or die "Cannot open file '$filename': $!\n";
    print "$filename: ", $line = <IN>;
    close (IN);
    }
$ perl file3.pl f1 f2 f3 f4
f1: First line of file f1.
f2: First line of file f2.
Cannot open file 'f3': No such file or directory
```

The next example is similar to the preceding one, except it takes advantage of several Perl features that make the code simpler. It does not quit when it cannot read a file. Instead, Perl displays an error message and continues. The first line of the program uses **my** to declare **$filename** to be a lexical variable. Next, **while** uses the magic file handle to open and read each line of each file named by the command-line arguments; **$ARGV** holds the name of the file. When there are no more files to read, the **while** condition [**(<>)**] is *false*, **while** transfers control outside the **while** block, and the program terminates. Perl takes care of all file opening and closing operations; you do not have to write code to take care of these tasks. Perl also performs error checking.

The program displays the first line of each file named by a command-line argument. Each time through the **while** block, **while** reads another line. When it finishes with one file, it starts reading from the next file. Within the **while** block, **if** tests whether it is processing a new file. If it is, the **if** block displays the name of the file and the (first) line from the file and then assigns the new filename (**$ARGV**) to **$filename**.

```
$ cat file3a.pl
my $filename;
while (<>) {
    if ($ARGV ne $filename) {
        print "$ARGV: $_";
        $filename = $ARGV;
    }
}

$ perl file3a.pl f1 f2 f3 f4
f1: First line of file f1.
f2: First line of file f2.
Can't open f3: No such file or directory at file3a.pl line 3, <> line 3.
f4: First line of file f4.
```

SORT

reverse The **sort** function returns elements of an array ordered numerically or alphabetically, based on the *locale* (page 1107) environment. The **reverse** function is not related to **sort**; it simply returns the elements of an array in reverse order.

The first two lines of the following program assign values to the **@colors** array and display these values. Each of the next two pairs of lines uses **sort** to put the values in the **@colors** array in order, assign the result to **@scolors**, and display **@scolors**. These sorts put uppercase letters before lowercase letters. Observe the positions of **Orange** and **Violet**, both of which begin with an uppercase letter, in the sorted output. The first assignment statement in these two pairs of lines uses the full sort syntax, including the block **{$a cmp $b}** that tells Perl to use the **cmp** subroutine, which compares strings, and to put the result in ascending order. When you omit the block in a **sort** statement, as is the case in the second assignment statement, Perl also performs an ascending textual sort.

```
$ cat sort3.pl
@colors = ("red", "Orange", "yellow", "green", "blue", "indigo", "Violet");

say "@colors";

@scolors = sort {$a cmp $b} @colors;          # ascending sort with
say "@scolors";                               # an explicit block

@scolors = sort @colors;                      # ascending sort with
say "@scolors";                               # an implicit block

@scolors = sort {$b cmp $a} @colors;          # descending sort
```

```
say "@scolors";

@scolors = sort {lc($a) cmp lc($b)} @colors;  # ascending folded sort
say "@scolors";
$ perl sort3.pl
red Orange yellow green blue indigo Violet
Orange Violet blue green indigo red yellow
Orange Violet blue green indigo red yellow
yellow red indigo green blue Violet Orange
blue green indigo Orange red Violet yellow
```

The third sort in the preceding example reverses the positions of **$a** and **$b** in the block to specify a descending sort. The last sort converts the strings to lowercase before comparing them, providing a sort wherein the uppercase letters are folded into the lowercase letters. As a result, **Orange** and **Violet** appear in alphabetical order.

To perform a numerical sort, specify the **<=>** subroutine in place of **cmp**. The following example demonstrates ascending and descending numerical sorts:

```
$ cat sort4.pl
@numbers = (22, 188, 44, 2, 12);

print "@numbers\n";

@snumbers = sort {$a <=> $b} @numbers;
print "@snumbers\n";

@snumbers = sort {$b <=> $a} @numbers;
print "@snumbers\n";
$ perl sort4.pl
22 188 44 2 12
2 12 22 44 188
188 44 22 12 2
```

SUBROUTINES

All variables are package variables (page 533) unless you use the **my** function to define them to be lexical variables (page 534). Lexical variables defined in a subroutine are local to that subroutine.

The following program includes a main part and a subroutine named **add()**. This program uses the variables named **$one**, **$two**, and **$ans**, all of which are package variables: They are available to both the main program and the subroutine. The call to the subroutine does not pass values to the subroutine and the subroutine returns no values. This setup is not typical: It demonstrates that all variables are package variables unless you use **my** to declare them to be lexical variables.

The **subroutine1.pl** program assigns values to two variables and calls a subroutine. The subroutine adds the values of the two variables and assigns the result to another variable. The main part of the program displays the result.

```
$ cat subroutine1.pl
$one = 1;
$two = 2;
add();
print "Answer is $ans\n";

sub add {
    $ans =$one + $two
    }

$ perl subroutine1.pl
Answer is 3
```

The next example is similar to the previous one, except the subroutine takes advantage of a **return** statement to return a value to the main program. The program assigns the value returned by the subroutine to the variable **$ans** and displays that value. Again, all variables are package variables.

```
$ cat subroutine2.pl
$one = 1;
$two = 2;
$ans = add();
print "Answer is $ans\n";

sub add {
    return ($one + $two)
    }

$ perl subroutine2.pl
Answer is 3
```

Keeping variables local to a subroutine is important in many cases. The subroutine in the next example changes the values of variables and insulates the calling program from these changes by declaring and using lexical variables. This setup is more typical.

@_ When you pass values in a call to a subroutine, Perl makes those values available in the array named @_ in the subroutine. Although @_ is local to the subroutine, its elements are aliases for the parameters the subroutine was called with. Changing a value in the @_ array changes the value of the underlying variable, which might not be what you want. The next program avoids this pitfall by assigning the values passed to the subroutine to lexical variables.

The **subroutine3.pl** program calls the **addplusone**() subroutine with two variables as arguments and assigns the value returned by the subroutine to a variable. The first statement in the subroutine declares two lexical variables and assigns to them the values from the @_ array. The **my** function declares these variables to be lexical. (See the caution on lexical and package variables on page 538.) Although you can use **my** without assigning values to the declared variables, the syntax in the example is more commonly used. The next two statements increment the lexical variables **$lcl_one** and **$lcl_two**. The **print** statement displays the value of **$lcl_one** within the subroutine. The **return** statement returns the sum of the two incremented, lexical variables.

```
$ cat subroutine3.pl
$one = 1;
$two = 2;
$ans = addplusone($one, $two);
print "Answer is $ans\n";
print "Value of 'lcl_one' in main: $lcl_one\n";
print "Value of 'one' in main: $one\n";

sub addplusone {
    my ($lcl_one, $lcl_two) = @_;
    $lcl_one++;
    $lcl_two++;
    print "Value of 'lcl_one' in sub: $lcl_one\n";
    return ($lcl_one + $lcl_two)
    }

$ perl subroutine3.pl
Value of 'lcl_one' in sub: 2
Answer is 5
Value of 'lcl_one' in main:
Value of 'one' in main: 1
```

After displaying the result returned by the subroutine, the **print** statements in the main program demonstrate that **$lcl_one** is not defined in the main program (it is local to the subroutine) and that the value of **$one** has not changed.

The next example illustrates another way to work with parameters passed to a subroutine. This subroutine does not use variables other than the **@_** array it was passed and does not change the values of any elements of that array.

```
$ cat subroutine4.pl
$one = 1;
$two = 2;
$ans = addplusone($one, $two);
print "Answer is $ans\n";
sub addplusone {
    return ($_[0] + $_[1] + 2);
    }

$ perl subroutine4.pl
Answer is 5
```

The final example in this section presents a more typical Perl subroutine. The subroutine **max()** can be called with any number of numeric arguments and returns the value of the largest argument. It uses the **shift** function to assign to **$biggest** the value of the first argument the subroutine was called with and to shift the rest of the arguments. After using **shift**, argument number 2 becomes argument number 1 (8), argument 3 becomes argument 2 (64), and argument 4 becomes argument 3 (2). Next, **foreach** loops over the remaining arguments (@_). Each time through the **foreach** block, Perl assigns to $_ the value of each of the arguments, in order. The **$biggest** variable is assigned the value of $_ if $_ is bigger than **$biggest**. When **max**() finishes going through its arguments, **$biggest** holds the maximum value, which **max**() returns.

```
$ cat subroutine5.pl
$ans = max (16, 8, 64, 2);
print "Maximum value is $ans\n";

sub max {
    my $biggest = shift;  # Assign first and shift the rest of the arguments to max()
    foreach (@_) {        # Loop through remaining arguments
    $biggest = $_ if $_ > $biggest;
    }
return ($biggest);
}

$ perl subroutine5.pl
Maximum value is 64
```

REGULAR EXPRESSIONS

Appendix A defines and discusses regular expressions you can use in many Linux utilities. All of the material in Appendix A applies to Perl, except as noted. In addition to the facilities described in Appendix A, Perl offers regular expression features that allow you to perform more complex string processing. This section reviews some of the regular expressions covered in Appendix A and describes some of the additional features of regular expressions available in Perl. It also introduces the syntax Perl uses for working with regular expressions.

SYNTAX AND THE =~ OPERATOR

The –l option The Perl –l option applies **chomp** to each line of input and places **\n** at the end of each line of output. The examples in this section use the Perl –l and –e (page 534) options. Because the program must be specified as a single argument, the examples enclose the Perl programs within single quotation marks. The shell interprets the quotation marks and does not pass them to Perl.

Using other options with –e

tip When you use another option with **–e**, the program must immediately follow the **–e** on the command line. Like many other utilities, Perl allows you to combine options following a single hyphen; if **–e** is one of the combined options, it must appear last in the list of options. Thus, you can use **perl –l –e** or **perl –le** but not **perl –e –l** or **perl –el**.

/ is the default delimiter

By default, Perl delimits a regular expression with slashes (**/**). The first program uses the **=~** operator to search for the pattern **ge** in the string **aged**. You can think of the **=~** operator as meaning "contains." Using different terminology, the **=~** operator determines whether the regular expression **ge** has a match in the string **aged**. The regular expression in this example contains no special characters; the string **ge** is part of the string **aged**. Thus, the expression within the parentheses evaluates to *true* and Perl executes the **print** statement.

```
$ perl -le 'if ("aged" =~ /ge/) {print "true";}'
true
```

You can achieve the same functionality by using a postfix **if** statement:

```
$ perl -le 'print "true" if "aged" =~ /ge/'
true
```

!~

The **!~** operator works in the opposite sense from the **=~** operator. The expression in the next example evaluates to *true* because the regular expression **xy** does *not* match any part of **aged**:

```
$ perl -le 'print "true" if ("aged" !~ /xy/)'
true
```

As explained on page 1039, a period within a regular expression matches any single character, so the regular expression **a..d** matches the string **aged**:

```
$ perl -le 'print "true" if ("aged" =~ /a..d/)'
true
```

You can use a variable to hold a regular expression. The following syntax quotes ***string*** as a regular expression:

*qr/**string**/*

The next example uses this syntax to assign the regular expression **/a..d/** (including the delimiters) to the variable **$re** and then uses that variable as the regular expression:

```
$ perl -le '$re = qr/a..d/; print "true" if ("aged" =~ $re)'
true
```

If you want to include the delimiter within a regular expression, you must quote it. In the next example, the default delimiter, a slash (**/**), appears in the regular expression. To keep Perl from interpreting the **/** in **/usr** as the end of the regular expression, the **/** that is part of the regular expression is quoted by preceding it with a backslash (****). See page 1041 for more information on quoting characters in regular expressions.

```
$ perl -le 'print "true" if ("/usr/doc" =~ /\/usr/)'
true
```

Quoting several characters by preceding each one with a backslash can make a complex regular expression harder to read. Instead, you can precede a delimited regular expression with **m** and use a paired set of characters, such as **{}**, as the delimiters. In the following example, the caret (^) anchors the regular expression to the beginning of the line (page 1040):

```
$ perl -le 'print "true" if ("/usr/doc" =~ m{^/usr})'
true
```

You can use the same syntax when assigning a regular expression to a variable:

```
$ perl -le '$pn = qr{^/usr}; print "true" if ("/usr/doc" =~ $pn)'
true
```

Replacement string and assignment

Perl uses the syntax shown in the next example to substitute a string (the *replacement string*) for a matched regular expression. The syntax is the same as that found in vim and sed. In the second line of the example, an s before the regular expression instructs Perl to substitute the string between the second and third slashes (**worst**; the replacement string) for a match of the regular expression between the first two slashes (**best**). Implicit in this syntax is the notion that the substitution is made in the string held in the variable on the left of the =~ operator.

```
$ cat re10a.pl
$stg = "This is the best!";
$stg =~ s/best/worst/;
print "$stg\n";

$ perl re10a.pl
This is the worst!
```

Table 11-3 lists some of the characters, called *metacharacters*, that are considered special within Perl regular expressions. Give the command **perldoc perlre** for more information.

Table 11-3 Some Perl regular expression metacharacters

Character	Matches
^ (caret)	Anchors a regular expression to the beginning of a line (page 1040)
$ (dollar sign)	Anchors a regular expression to the end of a line (page 1040)
(...)	Brackets a regular expression (page 566)
. (period)	Any single character except NEWLINE (**\n**; page 1039)
****	A backslash (****)
\b	A word boundary (zero-width match)
\B	A nonword boundary (**[^\b]**)
\d	A single decimal digit (**[0–9]**)
\D	A single nondecimal digit (**[^0–9]** or **[^\d]**)

Table 11-3 Some Perl regular expression metacharacters (continued)

Character	Matches
\s (lowercase)	A single whitespace character (SPACE, NEWLINE, RETURN, TAB, FORMFEED)
\S (uppercase)	A single nonwhitespace character (**[^\s]**)
\w (lowercase)	A single word character (a letter or digit; **[a–zA–Z0–9]**)
\W (uppercase)	A single nonword character (**[^\w]**)

GREEDY MATCHES

By default Perl performs *greedy matching,* which means a regular expression matches the longest string possible (page 1041). In the following example, the regular expression /{.*} / matches an opening brace followed by any string of characters, a closing brace, and a SPACE (**{remove me} might have two {keep me}**). Perl substitutes a null string (//) for this match.

```
$ cat 5ha.pl
$string = "A line {remove me} might have two {keep me} pairs of
braces.";
$string =~ s/{.*} //;
print "$string\n";

$ perl 5ha.pl
A line pairs of braces.
```

Nongreedy matches The next example shows the classic way of matching the shorter brace-enclosed string from the previous example. This type of match is called *nongreedy* or *parsimonious matching.* Here, the regular expression matches

1. An opening brace followed by
2. A character belonging to the character class (page 1039) that includes all characters except a closing brace ([^}]) followed by
3. Zero or more occurrences of the preceding character (*) followed by
4. A closing brace followed by
5. A SPACE

(A caret as the first character of a character class specifies the class of all characters that do not match the following characters, so [^}] matches any character that is not a closing brace:

```
$ cat re5b.pl
$string = "A line {remove me} might have two {keep me} pairs of braces.";
$string =~ s/{[^}]*} //;
print "$string\n";

$ perl re5b.pl
A line might have two {keep me} pairs of braces.
```

Perl provides a shortcut that allows you to specify a nongreedy match. In the following example, the question mark in {.*?} causes the regular expression to match the shortest string that starts with an opening brace followed by any string of characters followed by a closing brace.

```
$ cat re5c.pl
$string = "A line {remove me} might have two {keep me} pairs of braces.";
$string =~ s/{.*?} //;
print "$string\n";

$ perl re5c.pl
A line might have two {keep me} pairs of braces.
```

BRACKETING EXPRESSIONS

As explained on page 1042, you can bracket parts of a regular expression and recall those parts in the replacement string. Most Linux utilities use quoted parentheses [i.e., \(and \)] to bracket a regular expression. In Perl regular expressions, parentheses are special characters. Perl omits the backslashes and uses unquoted parentheses to bracket regular expressions. To specify a parenthesis as a regular character within a regular expression in Perl, you must quote it (page 1041).

The next example uses unquoted parentheses in a regular expression to bracket part of the expression. It then assigns the part of the string that the bracketed expression matched to the variable that held the string in which Perl originally searched for the regular expression.

First, the program assigns the string **My name is Sam** to **$stg**. The next statement looks for a match for the regular expression **/My name is (.*)/** in the string held by **$stg**. The part of the regular expression bracketed by parentheses matches **Sam**; the **$1** in the replacement string matches the first (and only in this case) matched bracketed portion of the regular expression. The result is that the string held in **$stg** is replaced by the string **Sam**.

```
$ cat re11.pl
$stg = "My name is Sam";
$stg =~ s/My name is (.*)/$1/;
print "Matched: $stg\n";

$ perl re11.pl
Matched: Sam
```

The next example uses regular expressions to parse a string for numbers. Two variables are initialized to hold a string that contains two numbers. The third line of the program uses a regular expression to isolate the first number in the string. The **\D*** matches a string of zero or more characters that does not include a digit: The **\D** special character matches any single nondigit character. The trailing asterisk makes this part of the regular expression perform a greedy match that does not include a digit (it matches **What is**). The bracketed regular expression **\d+** matches a string of one or more digits. The parentheses do not affect what the regular expression matches;

they allow the **$1** in the replacement string to match what the bracketed regular expression matched. The final **.*** matches the rest of the string. This line assigns the value of the first number in the string to **$string**.

The next line is similar but assigns the second number in the string to **$string2**. The **print** statements display the numbers and the result of subtracting the second number from the first.

```
$ cat re8.pl
$string = "What is 488 minus 78?";
$string2 = $string;
$string =~ s/\D*(\d+).*/$1/;
$string2 =~ s/\D*\d+\D*(\d+).*/$1/;
print "$string\n";
print "$string2\n";
print $string - $string2, "\n";

$ perl re8.pl
488
78
410
```

The next few programs show some of the pitfalls of using unquoted parentheses in regular expressions when you do not intend to bracket part of the regular expression. The first of these programs attempts to match parentheses in a string with unquoted parentheses in a regular expression, but fails. The regular expression **ag(e** matches the same string as the regular expression **age** because the parenthesis is a special character; the regular expression does not match the string **ag(ed)**.

```
$ perl -le 'if ("ag(ed)" =~ /ag(ed)/) {print "true";} else {print "false";}'
false
```

The regular expression in the next example quotes the parentheses by preceding each with a backslash, causing Perl to interpret them as regular characters. The match is successful.

```
$ perl -le 'if ("ag(ed)" =~ /ag\(ed\)/) {print "true";} else {print "false";}'
true
```

Next, Perl finds an unmatched parenthesis in a regular expression:

```
$ perl -le 'if ("ag(ed)" =~ /ag(e/) {print "true";} else {print "false";}'
Unmatched ( in regex; marked by <-- HERE in m/ag( <-- HERE e/ at -e line 1.
```

When you quote the parenthesis, all is well and Perl finds a match:

```
$ perl -le 'if ("ag(ed)" =~ /ag\(e/) {print "true";} else {print "false";}'
true
```

CPAN Modules

CPAN (Comprehensive Perl Archive Network) provides Perl documentation, FAQs, modules (page 533), and scripts on its Web site (www.cpan.org). It holds more than 16,000 distributions (page 533) and provides links, mailing lists, and versions of Perl compiled to run under various operating systems (ports of Perl). One way to locate a module is to visit ww.cpan.org/modules/ and use the search box or click one of the classes of modules listed on that page.

This section explains how to download a module from CPAN and how to install and run the module. Perl provides a hierarchical namespace for modules, separating components of a name with double colons (::). The example in this section uses the module named **Timestamp::Simple**, which you can read about and download from search.cpan.org/dist/Timestamp-Simple. The timestamp is the date and time in the format YYYYMMDDHHMMSS.

To use a Perl module, you first download the file that holds the module. For this example, the search.cpan.org/~shoop/Timestamp-Simple-1.01/Simple.pm Web page has a link on the right side labeled **Download.** Click this link and save the file to the directory you want to work in. You do not need to work as a privileged user until the last step of this procedure, when you install the module.

Most Perl modules come as compressed tar files (page 66). With the downloaded file in the working directory, decompress the file:

```
$ tar xzvf Timestamp-Simple-1.01.tar.gz
Timestamp-Simple-1.01/
Timestamp-Simple-1.01/Simple.pm
Timestamp-Simple-1.01/Makefile.PL
Timestamp-Simple-1.01/README
Timestamp-Simple-1.01/test.pl
Timestamp-Simple-1.01/Changes
Timestamp-Simple-1.01/MANIFEST
Timestamp-Simple-1.01/ARTISTIC
Timestamp-Simple-1.01/GPL
Timestamp-Simple-1.01/META.yml
```

The **README** file in the newly created directory usually provides instructions for building and installing the module. Most modules follow the same steps.

```
$ cd Timestamp-Simple-1.01
$ perl Makefile.PL
Checking if your kit is complete...
Looks good
Writing Makefile for Timestamp::Simple
```

If the module you are building depends on other modules that are not installed on the local system, running **perl Makefile.PL** will display one or more warnings about prerequisites that are not found. This step writes out the makefile even if modules are missing. In this case the next step will fail, and you must build and install missing modules before continuing.

The next step is to run **make** on the makefile you just created. After you run **make**, run **make test** to be sure the module is working.

```
$ make
cp Simple.pm blib/lib/Timestamp/Simple.pm
Manifying blib/man3/Timestamp::Simple.3pm

$ make test
PERL_DL_NONLAZY=1 /usr/bin/perl "-Iblib/lib" "-Iblib/arch" test.pl
1..1
# Running under perl version 5.220000 for linux
# Current time local: Fri Sep  3 18:20:41 2018
# Current time GMT:   Sat Sep  4 01:20:41 2018
# Using Test.pm version 1.25
ok 1
ok 2
ok 3
```

Finally, running with **root** privileges, install the module:

```
# make install
Installing /usr/local/share/perl/5.22.0/Timestamp/Simple.pm
Installing /usr/local/man/man3/Timestamp::Simple.3pm
Writing /usr/local/lib/perl/5.22.0/auto/Timestamp/Simple/.packlist
Appending installation info to /usr/local/lib/perl/5.22.0/perllocal.pod
```

Once you have installed a module, you can use perldoc to display the documentation that tells you how to use the module. See page 531 for an example.

Some modules contain SYNOPSIS sections. If the module you installed includes such a section, you can test the module by putting the code from the SYNOPSIS section in a file and running it as a Perl program:

```
$ cat times.pl
use Timestamp::Simple qw(stamp);
print stamp, "\n";

$ perl times.pl
20180904182627
```

You can then incorporate the module in a Perl program. The following example uses the timestamp module to generate a unique filename:

```
$ cat fn.pl
use Timestamp::Simple qw(stamp);

# Save timestamp in a variable
$ts = stamp, "\n";

# Strip off the year
```

```
$ts =~ s/....(.*)/\1/;

# Create a unique filename
$fn = "myfile." . $ts;

# Open, write to, and close the file
open (OUTFILE, '>', "$fn");
print OUTFILE "Hi there.\n";
close (OUTFILE);

$ perl fn.pl
$ ls myf*
myfile.0905183010
```

substr You can use the **substr** function in place of the regular expression to strip off the year. To do so, replace the line that starts with **$ts =~** with the following line. Here, **substr** takes on the value of the string **$ts** starting at position 4 and continuing to the end of the string:

```
$ts = substr ($ts, 4);
```

Examples

This section provides some sample Perl programs. First, try running these programs as is, and then modify them to learn more about programming with Perl.

The first example runs under Linux and displays the list of groups that the user given as an argument is a member of. Without an argument, it displays the list of groups that the user running the program is a member of. In a Perl program, the **%ENV** hash holds the environment variables from the shell that called Perl. The keys in this hash are the names of environment variables; the values in this hash are the values of the corresponding variables. The first line of the program assigns a username to **$user**. The **shift** function (page 543) takes on the value of the first command-line argument and shifts the rest of the arguments, if any remain. If the user runs the program with an argument, that argument is assigned to **$user**. If no argument appears on the command line, **shift** fails and Perl executes the statement following the Boolean OR (||). This statement extracts the value associated with the **USER** key in **%ENV**, which is the name of the user running the program.

Accepting output from a process The third statement initializes the array **@list**. Although this statement is not required, it is good practice to include it to make the code easier to read. The next statement opens the **$fh** lexical handle. The trailing pipe symbol (|) in the *file-ref* (page 554) portion of this **open** statement tells Perl to pass the command line preceding the pipe symbol to the shell for execution and to accept standard output from the command when the program reads from the file handle. In this case the command uses grep to filter the **/etc/group** file for lines containing the username held in **$user**. (macOS does not use this file; see page 1068 for more information.) The **die** statement displays an error message if Perl cannot open the handle.

```
$ cat groupfind.pl
$user = shift || $ENV{"USER"};
say "User $user belongs to these groups:";
@list = ();
open (my $fh, "grep $user /etc/group |") or die "Error: $!\n";
while ($group = <$fh>) {
    chomp $group;
    $group =~ s/(.*?):.*/$1/;
    push @list, $group;
}
close $fh;
@slist = sort @list;
say "@slist";

$ perl groupfind.pl
User sam belongs to these groups:
adm admin audio cdrom dialout dip floppy kvm lpadmin ...
```

The **while** structure in **groupfind.pl** reads lines from standard output of grep and terminates when grep finishes executing. The name of the group appears first on each line in **/etc/group**, followed by a colon and other information, including the names of the users who belong to the group. Following is a line from this file:

```
sam:x:1000:max,zach,helen
```

The line

```
$group =~ s/(.*?):.*/$1/;
```

uses a regular expression and substitution to remove everything except the name of the group from each line. The regular expression **.*:** would perform a greedy match of zero or more characters followed by a colon; putting a question mark after the asterisk causes the expression to perform a nongreedy match (page 565). Putting parentheses around the part of the expression that matches the string the program needs to display enables Perl to use the string that the regular expression matches in the replacement string. The final **.*** matches the rest of the line. Perl will replace the **$1** in the replacement string with the string the bracketed portion of the regular expression (the part between the parentheses) matched and assigns this value (the name of the group) to **$group**.

The **chomp** statement removes the trailing NEWLINE (the regular expression did not match this character). The **push** statement adds the value of **$group** to the end of the **@list** array. Without **chomp**, each group would appear on a line by itself in the output. After the **while** structure finishes processing input from **grep**, **sort** orders **@list** and assigns the result to **@slist**. The final statement displays the sorted list of groups the user belongs to.

opendir and **readdir** The next example introduces the **opendir** and **readdir** functions. The **opendir** function opens a directory in a manner similar to the way **open** opens an ordinary file. It takes two arguments: the name of the directory handle and the name of the directory to open. The **readdir** function reads the name of a file from an open directory.

In the example, **opendir** opens the working directory (specified by .) using the **$dir** lexical directory handle. If **opendir** fails, Perl executes the statement following the **or** operator: **die** sends an error message to standard error and terminates the program. With the directory opened, **while** loops through the files in the directory, assigning the filename that **readdir** returns to the lexical variable **$entry**. An **if** statement executes **print** only for those files that are directories (**–d**). The **print** function displays the name of the directory unless the directory is named **.** or **..**. When **readdir** has read all files in the working directory, it returns *false* and control passes to the statement following the **while** block. The **closedir** function closes the open directory and **print** displays a NEWLINE following the list of directories the program displayed.

```
$ cat dirs2a.pl
#!/usr/bin/perl
print "The working directory contains these directories:\n";

opendir my $dir, '.' or die "Could not open directory: $!\n";
while (my $entry = readdir $dir) {
    if (-d $entry) {
        print $entry, ' ' unless ($entry eq '.' || $entry eq '..');
    }
}
closedir $dir;
print "\n";

$ ./dirs2a.pl
The working directory contains these directories:
two one
```

split The **split** function divides a string into substrings as specified by a delimiter. The syntax of a call to **split** is

*split (/**re**/, **string**);*

where ***re*** is the delimiter, which is a regular expression (frequently a single regular character), and ***string*** is the string that is to be divided. As the next example shows, you can assign the list that **split** returns to an array variable.

The next program runs under Linux and lists the usernames of users with UIDs greater than or equal to 100 listed in the **/etc/passwd** file. Because macOS uses Open Directory in place of this file, you must modify it before it will run under macOS; see page 1068. It uses a **while** structure to read lines from **passwd** into **$user**, and it uses **split** to break the line into substrings separated by colons. The line that begins with **@row** assigns each of these substrings to an element of the **@row** array. The expression the **if** statement evaluates is *true* if the third substring (the UID) is greater than or equal to 100.

This expression uses the **>=** numeric comparison operator because it compares two numbers; an alphabetic comparison would use the **ge** string comparison operator.

The **print** statement sends the UID number and the associated username to the **$sortout** file handle. The **open** statement for this handle establishes a pipeline that sends its output to **sort –n**. Because the sort utility (page 58) does not display any output until it finishes receiving all of the input, **split3.pl** does not display anything until it closes the **$sortout** handle, which it does when it finishes reading the **passwd** file.

```
$ cat split3.pl
#!/usr/bin/perl -w

open ($pass, "/etc/passwd");
open ($sortout, "| sort -n");
while ($user = <$pass>) {
    @row = split (/:/, $user);
    if ($row[2] >= 100) {
        print $sortout "$row[2] $row[0]\n";
        }
    }
close ($pass);
close ($sortout);
$ ./split3.pl
100 libuuid
101 syslog
102 klog
103 avahi-autoipd
104 pulse
...
```

The next example counts and displays the arguments it was called with, using **@ARGV** (page 557). A **foreach** structure loops through the elements of the **@ARGV** array, which holds the command-line arguments. The **++** preincrement operator increments **$count** before it is displayed.

```
$ cat 10.pl
#!/usr/bin/perl -w

$count = 0;
$num = @ARGV;
print "You entered $num arguments on the command line:\n";
foreach $arg (@ARGV) {
    print ++$count, ". $arg\n";
    }

$ ./10.pl apple pear banana watermelon
You entered 4 arguments on the command line:
1. apple
2. pear
3. banana
4. watermelon
```

CHAPTER SUMMARY

Perl was written by Larry Wall in 1987. Since that time Perl has grown in size and functionality and is now a very popular language used for text processing, system administration, software development, and general-purpose programming. One of Perl's biggest assets is its support by thousands of third-party modules, many of which are stored in the CPAN repository.

The perldoc utility locates and displays local Perl documentation. It also allows you to document a Perl program by displaying lines of **pod** (plain old documentation) that you include in the program.

Perl provides three types of variables: scalar (singular variables that begin with a $), array (plural variables that begin with an @), and hash (also called associative arrays; plural variables that begin with a %). Array and hash variables both hold lists, but arrays are ordered while hashes are unordered. Standard control flow statements allow you to alter the order of execution of statements within a Perl program. In addition, Perl programs can take advantage of subroutines that can include variables local to the subroutines (lexical variables).

Regular expressions are one of Perl's strong points. In addition to the same facilities that are available in many utilities, Perl offers regular expression features that allow you to perform more complex string processing.

EXERCISES

1. What are two different ways to turn on warnings in Perl?
2. What is the difference between an array and a hash?
3. In each example, when would you use a hash and when would you use an array?

   a. Counting the number of occurrences of an IP address in a log file.

   b. Generating a list of users who are over disk quota for use in a report.
4. Write a regular expression to match a quoted string, such as

   ```
   He said, "Go get me the wrench," but I didn't hear him.
   ```
5. Write a regular expression to match an IP address in a log file.
6. Many configuration files contain many comments, including commented-out default configuration directives. Write a program to remove these comments from a configuration file.

ADVANCED EXERCISES

7. Write a program that removes *~ and *.ico files from a directory hierarchy. (*Hint:* Use the **File::Find** module.)
8. Describe a programming mistake that Perl's warnings do not report on.
9. Write a Perl program that counts the number of files in the working directory and the number of bytes in those files, by filename extension.
10. Describe the difference between quoting strings using single quotation marks and using double quotation marks.
11. Write a program that copies all files with a **.ico** filename extension in a directory hierarchy to a directory named **icons** in your home directory. (*Hint:* Use the **File::Find** and **File::Copy** modules.)
12. Write a program that analyzes Apache logs. Display the number of bytes served by each path. Ignore unsuccessful page requests. If there are more than ten paths, display the first ten only.

    Following is a sample line from an Apache access log. The two numbers following the HTTP/1.1 are the response code and the byte count. A response code of 200 means the request was successful. A byte count of – means no data was transferred.

```
__DATA__
92.50.103.52 - - [19/Aug/2018:08:26:43 -0400] "GET /perl/automated-testing/next_active.gif
HTTP/1.1" 200 980 "http://example.com/perl/automated-testing/navigation_bar.htm"
"Mozilla/5.0 (X11; U; Linux x86_64; en-US; rv:1.8.1.6) Gecko/20061201 Firefox/3.0.0.6
(Fedora); Blazer/4.0"
```

12

The Python Programming Language

In This Chapter

Objectives

After reading this chapter you should be able to:

- Give commands using the Python interactive shell
- Write and run a Python program stored in a file
- Demonstrate how to instantiate a list and how to remove elements from and add elements to a list
- Describe a dictionary and give examples of how it can be used
- Describe three Python control structures
- Write a Python program that iterates through a list or dictionary
- Read from and write to a file
- Demonstrate exception processing
- Preserve an object using **pickle**()
- Write a Python program that uses regular expressions
- Define a function and use it in a program

Introduction

Python is a friendly and flexible programming language in widespread use everywhere from Fortune 500 companies to large-scale open-source projects. Python is an interpreted language: It translates code into *bytecode* (page 1087) at runtime and executes the bytecode within the Python virtual machine. Contrast Python with the C language, which is a compiled language. C differs from Python in that the C compiler *compiles* C source code into architecture-specific machine code. Python programs are not compiled; you run a Python program the same way you run a bash or Perl script. Because Python programs are not compiled, they are portable between operating systems and architectures. In other words, the same Python program will run on any system to which the Python virtual machine has been ported.

Object oriented While not required to use the language, Python supports the object-oriented (OO) paradigm. It is possible to use Python with little or no understanding of object-oriented concepts, and this chapter covers OO programming minimally while still explaining Python's important features.

Libraries Python comes with hundreds of prewritten tools that are organized into logical libraries. These libraries are accessible to Python programs, but not loaded into memory at runtime because doing so would significantly increase startup times for Python programs. Entire libraries (or just individual modules) are instead loaded into memory when the program requests them.

Version Python is available in two main development branches: Python 2.x and Python 3.x. This chapter focuses on Python 2.x because the bulk of Python written today uses 2.x. The following commands show that two versions of Python are installed and that the **python** command runs Python 2.7.12:

```
$ whereis python
python: /usr/bin/python /usr/bin/python2.7 /etc/python3.5 /etc/python ...
$ ls -l $(which python)
lrwxrwxrwx 1 root root 9 Dec 20 15:55 /usr/bin/python -> python2.7
$ python -V
Python 2.7.12
```

Invoking Python

This section discusses the methods you can use to run a Python program.

Interactive shell Most of the examples in this chapter use the Python interactive shell because you can use it to debug and execute code one line at a time and see the results immediately. Although this shell is handy for testing, it is not a good choice for running longer, more complex programs. You start a Python interactive shell by calling the python utility (just as you would start a bash shell by calling bash). The primary Python prompt is **>>>**. When Python requires more input to complete a command, it displays its secondary prompt (**...**):

```
$ python
Python 2.7.12 (default, Nov 19 2016, 06:48:10)
[GCC 5.4.0 20160609] on linux2
Type "help", "copyright", "credits" or "license" for more information.
>>>
```

While you are using the Python interactive shell, you can give Python a command by entering the command and pressing RETURN. Use CONTROL-D to exit the shell.

```
>>> print 'Good morning!'
Good morning!
```

Implied display

tip Within the Python interactive shell, Python displays output from any command line that does not have an action. The output is similar to what **print** would display, although it might not be exactly the same. The following examples show explicit **print** and implicit display actions:

```
>>> print 'Good morning!'
Good morning!
>>> 'Good morning!'
'Good morning!'

>>> print 2 + 2
4
>>> 2 + 2
4
```

Implied display allows you to display the value of a variable by typing its name:

```
>>> x = 'Hello'
>>> x
'Hello'
```

Implied display does not work unless you are running the Python interactive shell (i.e., Python does not invoke an implicit display action when it is run from a file).

Program file Most of the time a Python program is stored in a text file. Although not required, the file typically has a filename extension of **.py**. Use chmod (page 759) to make the file executable. As explained on page 297, the **#!** at the start of the first line of the file instructs the shell to pass the rest of the file to **/usr/bin/python** for execution.

```
$ chmod 755 gm.py
$ cat gm.py
#!/usr/bin/python
print 'Good morning!'

$ ./gm.py
Good morning!
```

You can also run a Python program by specifying the name of the program file as an argument or as standard input to python.

```
$ python gm.py
Good morning!

$ python < gm.py
Good morning!

$ cat gm.py | python
Good morning!

$ echo "print 'Good morning! '" | python
Good morning!
```

Because the shell interprets an exclamation point immediately followed by a character other than a SPACE as an event number (page 341), the final command includes a SPACE after the exclamation point.

Command line Using the python –c option, you can run a program from the shell command line. In the preceding and following commands, the double quotation marks keep the shell from removing the single quotation marks from the command line before passing it to Python.

```
$ python -c "print 'Good morning! '"
Good morning!
```

Single and double quotation marks are functionally equivalent

tip You can use single quotation marks and double quotation marks interchangeably in a Python program, and you can use one to quote the other. When Python displays quotation marks around a string it uses single quotation marks.

```
>>> a = "hi"
>>> a
'hi'
>>> print "'hi'"
'hi'
>>> print '"hi"'
"hi"
```

MORE INFORMATION

Local python man page, pydoc program

Python interactive shell From the Python interactive shell give the command **help()** to use the Python **help** feature. When you call it, this utility displays information to help you get started using it. Alternatively, you can give the command **help('*object*')** where ***object*** is the name of an object you have instantiated or the name of a data structure or module such as **list** or **pickle**.

Web Python home page: www.python.org
Documentation: docs.python.org
Index of Python Enhancement Proposals (PEPs): www.python.org/dev/peps
PEP 8 Style Guide for Python Code: www.python.org/dev/peps/pep-0008
PyPI (Python Package Index): pypi.python.org

WRITING TO STANDARD OUTPUT AND READING FROM STANDARD INPUT

raw_input() Python makes it easy to write to standard output and read from standard input, both of which the shell (e.g., bash) connects to the terminal by default. The **raw_input()** function writes to standard output and reads from standard input. It returns the value of the string it reads after stripping the trailing control characters (RETURN-NEWLINE or NEWLINE).

In the following example, **raw_input()** displays its argument (**Enter your name:**) and waits for the user. When the user types something and presses RETURN, Python assigns the value returned by **raw_input()**, which is the string the user entered, to the variable **my_in**.

print Within a **print** statement, a plus sign (+) catenates the strings on either side of it. The **print** statement in the example displays **Hello,** the value of **my_in**, and an exclamation point:

```
>>> my_in = raw_input ('Enter your name: ')
Enter your name: Neo
>>> print 'Hello, ' + my_in + '!'
Hello, Neo!
```

FUNCTIONS AND METHODS

Functions Functions in Python, as in most programming languages, are key to improving code readability, efficiency, and maintenance. Python has a number of builtin functions and functions you can immediately import into a Python program. These functions are available when you install Python. For example, the **int()** function returns the integer (truncated) part of a floating-point number:

```
>>> int(8.999)
8
```

Additional downloadable libraries hold more functions. For more information refer to "Using Libraries" on page 599. Table 12-1 lists a few of the most commonly used functions.

Table 12-1 Commonly used functions

Function	What it does
exit()	Exits from a program
float()	Returns its argument as a floating-point number
help()	Displays help on the object specified by its argument; without an argument opens interactive help (Python interactive shell only; page 580)
int()	Returns the integer (truncated) portion of its argument
len()	Returns the number of elements in a list or dictionary (page 585)
map()	Returns the list that results from applying its first argument (a function) to its remaining arguments (page 603)

Table 12-1 Commonly used functions (continued)

Function	What it does
max()	Returns the maximum value from its argument, which can be a list or other iterable (page 586) data structure (page 603)
open()	Opens the file in the mode specified by its arguments (page 593)
range()	Returns a list of integers between the two values specified by its arguments (page 592)
raw_input()	Prompts with its argument and returns the string the user enters (page 581)
sorted()	Takes a list (or other iterable data structure) as an argument and returns the same type of data structure with its elements in order
type()	Returns the type of its argument (e.g., int, file, method, function)
xrange()	Returns a list of integers between the two values specified by its arguments [more efficient than **range()**; page 592]

Methods Functions and methods are very similar. The difference is that functions stand on their own while methods work on and are specific to objects. You will see the **range()** function used by itself [**range(*args*)**] and the **readall()** method used as an object method [**f.readall(*args*)**, where f is the object (a file) **readall()** is reading from]. Table 12-2 on page 585 and Table 12-4 on page 593 list some methods.

Scalar Variables, Lists, and Dictionaries

This section discusses some of the Python builtin data types. Scalar data types include number and string types. Compound data types include dictionary and list types.

Scalar Variables

As in most programming languages, you declare and initialize a variable using an equal sign. Python does not require the SPACEs around the equal sign, nor does it require you to identify a scalar variable with a prefix (Perl and bash require a leading dollar sign). As explained in the tip on page 579, you can use the **print** function to display the value of a variable or you can just specify the variable name as a command:

```
>>> lunch = 'Lunch time!'
>>> print lunch
Lunch time!
>>> lunch
'Lunch time!'
```

Python performs arithmetic as you might expect:

```
>>> n1 = 5
>>> n2 = 8
>>> n1 + n2
13
```

Floating-point numbers

Whether Python performs floating-point or integer arithmetic depends on the values it is given. If all of the numbers involved in a calculation are integers—that is, if none of the numbers includes a decimal point—Python performs integer arithmetic and will truncate answers that include a fractional part. If at least one of the numbers involved in a calculation is a floating-point number (includes a decimal point), Python performs floating-point arithmetic. Be careful when performing division: If the answer could include a fraction, be sure to include a decimal point in one of the numbers or explicitly specify one of the numbers as a floating-point number:

```
>>> 3/2
1
>>> 3/2.0
1.5
>>> float(3)/2
1.5
```

LISTS

A Python *list* is an object that comprises one or more elements; it is similar to an array in C or Java. Lists are ordered and use zero-based indexing (i.e., the first element of a list is numbered zero). A list is called *iterable* because it can provide successive elements on each iteration through a looping control structure such as **for**; see page 586 for a discussion.

This section shows one way to instantiate (create) a list. The following commands instantiate and display a list named **a** that holds four values:

```
>>> a = ['bb', 'dd', 'zz', 'rr']
>>> a
['bb', 'dd', 'zz', 'rr']
```

Indexes

You can access an element of a list by specifying its index (remember—the first element of a list is numbered zero). The first of the following commands displays the value of the third element of **a**; the next assigns the value of the first element of **a** to **x** and displays the value of **x**.

```
>>> a[2]
'zz'

>>> x = a[0]
>>> x
'bb'
```

When you specify a negative index, Python counts from the end of the array.

```
>>> a[-1]
'rr'

>>> a[-2]
'zz'
```

Replacing an element

You can replace an element of a list by assigning a value to it.

```
>>> a[1] = 'qqqq'
>>> a
['bb', 'qqqq', 'zz', 'rr']
```

Slicing

The next examples show how to access a slice or portion of a list. The first example displays elements 0 up to 2 of the list (elements 0 and 1):

```
>>> a[0:2]
['bb', 'dd']
```

If you omit the number that follows the colon, Python displays from the element with the index specified before the colon through the end of the list. If you omit the number before the colon, Python displays from the beginning of the list up to the element with the number specified after the colon.

```
>>> a[2:]
['zz', 'rr']
>>> a[:2]
['bb', 'dd']
```

You can use negative numbers when slicing a list. The first of the following commands displays element 1 up to the last element of the list (element –1); the second displays from the next-to-last element of the list (element –2) through the end of the list.

```
>>> a[1:-1]
['dd', 'zz']
>>> a[-2:]
['zz', 'rr']
```

remove()

Following Python's object-oriented paradigm, the list data type includes builtin methods. The **remove**(*x*) method removes the first element of a list whose value is *x,* and decreases the length of the list by 1. The following command removes the first element of list **a** whose value is **bb**:

```
>>> a.remove('bb')
>>> a
['dd', 'zz', 'rr']
```

append()

The **append**(*x*) method appends an element whose value is *x* to the list, and increases the length of the list by 1.

```
>>> a.append('mm')
>>> a
['dd', 'zz', 'rr', 'mm']
```

reverse()

The **reverse**() method does not take an argument. It is an efficient method that reverses elements of a list in place, overwriting elements of the list with new values.

```
>>> a.reverse()
>>> a
['mm', 'rr', 'zz', 'dd']
```

sort()

The **sort**() method does not take an argument. It sorts the elements in a list in place, overwriting elements of the list with new values.

```
>>> a.sort()
>>> a
['dd', 'mm', 'rr', 'zz']
```

sorted() If you do not want to alter the contents of the list (or other iterable data structure) you are sorting, use the **sorted**() function. This function returns the sorted list and does not change the original list.

```
>>> b = sorted(a)
>>> a
['mm', 'rr', 'zz', 'dd']
>>> b
['dd', 'mm', 'rr', 'zz']
```

len() The **len**() function returns the number of elements in a list or other iterable data structure.

```
>>> len(a)
4
```

Table 12-2 lists some of the methods that work on lists. The command **help(list)** displays a complete list of methods you can use with a list.

Table 12-2 **list** methods

Method	What it does
append(*x*)	Appends the value ***x*** to the list
count(*x*)	Returns the number of times the value ***x*** occurs in the list
index(*x*)	Returns the index of the first occurrence of ***x*** in the list
remove(*x*)	Removes the first element of a list whose value is ***x***
reverse()	Reverses the order of elements in the list
sort()	Sorts the list in place

WORKING WITH LISTS

Passing a list by reference

Python passes all objects, including lists, by reference. That is, it passes an object by passing a pointer to the object. When you assign one object to another, you are simply creating another name for the object; you are not creating a new object. When you change the object using either name, you can view the change using either name. In the following example, **names** is instantiated as a list that holds the values **sam, max,** and **zach; copy** is set equal to **names**, setting up another name for (reference to) the same list. When the value of the first element of **copy** is changed, displaying **names** shows that its first element has also changed.

```
>>> names = ['sam', 'max', 'zach']
>>> copy = names
>>> names
['sam', 'max', 'zach']
>>> copy[0] = 'helen'
>>> names
['helen', 'max', 'zach']
```

Copying a list When you use the syntax $b = a[:]$ to copy a list, each list remains independent of the other. The next example is the same as the previous one, except **copy2** points to a different location than **names** because the list was copied, not passed by reference: Look at the difference in the values of the first element (zero index) of both lists.

```
>>> names = ['sam', 'max', 'zach']
>>> copy2 = names[:]
>>> copy2[0] = 'helen'
>>> names
['sam', 'max', 'zach']
>>> copy2
['helen', 'max', 'zach']
```

LISTS ARE ITERABLE

An important feature of lists is that they are *iterable,* meaning a control structure such as **for** (page 591) can loop (iterate) through each item in a list. In the following example, the **for** control structure iterates over the list **a**, assigning one element of **a** to **item** each time through the loop. The loop terminates after it has assigned each of the elements of **a** to **item**. The comma at the end of the **print** statement replaces the NEWLINE **print** normally outputs with a SPACE. You must indent lines within a control structure (called a logical block; page 588).

```
>>> a
['bb', 'dd', 'zz', 'rr']
>>> for item in a:
...     print item,
...
bb dd zz rr
```

The next example returns the largest element in a list. In this example, the list is embedded in the code; see page 602 for a similar program that uses random numbers. The program initializes **my_rand_list** as a list holding ten numbers and **largest** as a scalar with a value of –1. The **for** structure retrieves the elements of **my_rand_list** in order, one each time through the loop. It assigns the value it retrieves to **item**. Within the **for** structure, an **if** statement tests to see if **item** is larger than **largest**. If it is, the program assigns the value of **item** to **largest** and displays the new value (so you can see how the program is progressing). When control exits from the **for** structure, the program displays a message and the largest number. Be careful when a logical block (a subblock) appears within another logical block: You must indent the subblock one level more than its superior logical block.

```
$ cat my_max.py
#!/usr/bin/python

my_rand_list = [5, 6, 4, 1, 7, 3, 2, 0, 9, 8]
largest = -1
for item in my_rand_list:
    if (item > largest):
        largest = item
        print largest,
print
print 'largest number is ', largest
```

```
$ ./my_max.py
5 6 7 9
largest number is  9
```

See page 603 for an easier way to find the maximum value in a list.

DICTIONARIES

A Python dictionary holds unordered key–value pairs in which the keys must be unique. Other languages refer to this type of data structure as an associative array, hash, or hashmap. Like lists, dictionaries are iterable. A dictionary provides fast lookups. The class name for dictionary is **dict**; thus, you must type **help(dict)** to display the help page for dictionaries. Use the following syntax to instantiate a dictionary:

dict = { key1 : value1, key2 : value2, key3 : value3 ... }

WORKING WITH DICTIONARIES

The following example instantiates and displays a telephone extension dictionary named **ext**. Because dictionaries are unordered, Python does not display a dictionary in a specific order and usually does not display it in the order it was created.

```
>>> ext = {'sam': 44, 'max': 88, 'zach': 22}
>>> ext
{'max': 88, 'zach': 22, 'sam': 44}
```

keys() and **values()** You can use the **keys()** and **values()** methods to display all keys or values held in a dictionary:

```
>>> ext.keys()
['max', 'zach', 'sam']
>>> ext.values()
[88, 22, 44]
```

You can add a key–value pair:

```
>>> ext['helen'] = 92
>>> ext
{'max': 88, 'zach': 22, 'sam': 44, 'helen': 92}
```

If you assign a value to a key that is already in the dictionary, Python replaces the value (keys must be unique):

```
>>> ext['max'] = 150
>>> ext
{'max': 150, 'zach': 22, 'sam': 44, 'helen': 92}
```

The following example shows how to remove a key–value pair from a dictionary:

```
>>> del ext['max']
>>> ext
{'zach': 22, 'sam': 44, 'helen': 92}
```

You can also query the dictionary. Python returns the value when you supply the key:

```
>>> ext['zach']
22
```

items() The **items()** method returns key–value pairs as a list of tuples (pairs of values). Because a dictionary is unordered, the order of the tuples returned by **items()** can vary from run to run.

```
>>> ext.items()
[('zach', 22), ('sam', 44), ('helen', 92)]
```

Because dictionaries are iterable, you can loop through them using **for**.

```
>>> ext = {'sam': 44, 'max': 88, 'zach': 22}
>>> for i in ext:
...     print i
...
max
zach
sam
```

Using this syntax, the dictionary returns just keys; it is as though you wrote **for i in ext.keys()**. If you want to loop through values, use **for i in ext.values()**.

Keys and values can be of different types within a dictionary:

```
>>> dic = {500: 2, 'bbbb': 'BBBB', 1000: 'big'}
>>> dic
{1000: 'big', 'bbbb': 'BBBB', 500: 2}
```

CONTROL STRUCTURES

Control flow statements alter the order of execution of statements within a program. Starting on page 430, Chapter 10 discusses bash control structures in detail and includes flow diagrams of their operation. Python control structures perform the same functions as their bash counterparts, although the two languages use different syntaxes. The description of each control structure in this section references the discussion of the same control structure under bash.

In this section, the ***bold italic*** words in the syntax description are the items you supply to cause the structure to have the desired effect; the *nonbold italic* words are the keywords Python uses to identify the control structure. Many of these structures use an expression, denoted as ***expr,*** to control their execution. The examples in this chapter delimit ***expr*** using parentheses for clarity and consistency; the parentheses are not always required.

Indenting logical blocks In most programming languages, control structures are delimited by pairs of parentheses, brackets, or braces; bash uses keywords (e.g., **if...fi, do...done**). Python uses a colon (**:**) as the opening token for a control structure. While including SPACEs (or TABs) at the beginning of lines in a control structure is good practice in other languages, Python requires these elements; they indicate a *logical block,* or section of code, that is part of a control structure. The last indented line marks the end of the control structure; the change in indent level is the closing token that matches the opening colon.

if

Similar to the bash **if...then** control structure (page 431), the Python **if** control structure has the following syntax:

if expr:
    ...

As with all Python control structures, the control block, denoted by **...**, must be indented.

In the following example, **my_in != ''** (if **my_in** is not an empty string) evaluates to *true* if the user entered something before pressing RETURN. If ***expr*** evaluates to *true,* Python executes the following indented **print** statement. Python executes any number of indented statements that follow an **if** statement as part of the control structure. If ***expr*** evaluates to *false,* Python skips any number of indented statements following the **if** statement.

```
$ cat if1.py
#!/usr/bin/python
my_in = raw_input('Enter your name: ')
if (my_in != ''):
    print 'Thank you, ' + my_in
print 'Program running, with or without your input.'

$ ./if1.py
Enter your name: Neo
Thank you, Neo.
Program running, with or without your input.
```

if...else

Similar to the bash **if...then...else** control structure (page 435), the **if...else** control structure implements a two-way branch using the following syntax:

if expr:
    ...
else:
    ...

If ***expr*** evaluates to *true,* Python executes the statements in the **if** control block. Otherwise, it executes the statements in the **else** control block. The following example builds on the previous one, displaying an error message and exiting from the program if the user does not enter something.

```
$ cat if2.py
#!/usr/bin/python
my_in = raw_input('Enter your name: ')
if (my_in != ''):
    print 'Thank you, ' + my_in
else:
    print 'Program requires input to continue.'
    exit()
print 'Program running with your input.'
```

```
$ ./if2.py
Enter your name: Neo
Thank you, Neo
Program running with your input.

$ ./if2.py
Enter your name:
Program requires input to continue.
```

if...elif...else

Similar to the bash **if...then...elif** control structure (page 436), the Python **if...elif...else** control structure implements a nested set of **if...else** structures using the following syntax:

if (expr):
  ...
elif (expr)
  ...
else:
  ...

This control structure can include as many **elif** control blocks as necessary. In the following example, the **if** statement evaluates the Boolean expression following it within parentheses and enters the indented logical block below the statement if the expression evaluates to *true*. The **if**, **elif**, and **else** statements are part of one control structure and Python will execute statements in only one of the indented logical blocks.

The **if** and **elif** statements are each followed by a Boolean expression. Python executes each of their corresponding logical blocks only if their expression evaluates to *true*. If none of the expressions evaluates to *true*, control falls through to the **else** logical block.

```
$ cat bignum.py
#!/usr/bin/python
input = raw_input('Please enter a number: ')
if (input == '1'):
    print 'You entered one.'
elif (input == '2'):
    print 'You entered two.'
elif (input == '3'):
    print 'You entered three.'
else:
    print 'You entered a big number...'
print 'End of program.'
```

In the preceding program, even though the user enters an integer/scalar value, Python stores it as a string. Thus, each of the comparisons checks whether this value is equal to a string. You can use **int()** to convert a string to an integer. If you do so, you must remove the quotation marks from around the values:

```
...
input = int(raw_input('Please enter a number: '))
if (input == 1):
    print 'You entered one.'
...
```

while

The **while** control structure (page 447) evaluates a Boolean expression and continues execution while the expression evaluates to *true*. The following program, run using the Python interactive shell, displays 0 through 9. As you enter the command, Python displays its secondary prompt (...) when it requires more input to complete a statement; you must still enter SPACE or TAB characters to indent the logical block.

First, the program initializes **count** to 0. The first time through the loop, the **while** expression evaluates to *true* and Python executes the indented statements that make up the **while** control structure logical block. The comma at the end of the **print** statement causes **print** to output a SPACE instead of a NEWLINE after each string, and the **count += 1** statement increments **count** each time through the loop. When control reaches the bottom of the loop, Python returns control to the **while** statement, where **count** is now 1. The loop continues while **count** is less than or equal to 10. When **count** equals 11, the **while** statement evaluates to *false* and control passes to the first statement after the logical block (the first statement that is not indented; there is none in this example).

```
>>> count = 0
>>> while (count <= 10):
...     print count,
...     count += 1
...
0 1 2 3 4 5 6 7 8 9 10
```

Be careful not to create an infinite loop

tip It is easy to accidentally create an infinite loop using a **while** statement. Ensure that a reachable exit condition exists (e.g., a counter is compared to a finite value *and* the counter is incremented each time through the loop).

for

The **for** control structure (page 445) assigns values from a list, string, or other iterable data structure (page 586) to a loop index variable each time through the loop.

Lists are iterable

In the following example, **lis** is a list that holds the names of four types of animals. The **for** statement iterates through the elements of **lis** in order, starting with **turkey**, and assigning a value to **nam** each time it is called. The **print** statement in the logical block displays the value of **nam** each time through the loop. Python exits from the logical block when it runs out of elements in **lis**.

```
>>> lis = ['turkey', 'pony', 'dog', 'fox']
>>> for nam in lis:
...     print nam
...
turkey
pony
dog
fox
```

Strings are iterable

The next example demonstrates that strings are iterable. The string named **string** holds **My name is Sam.** and the **for** statement iterates through **string**, assigning one character to **char** each time through the loop. The **print** statement displays each character; the comma causes **print** to put a SPACE after each character instead of a NEWLINE.

```
>>> string = 'My name is Sam.'
>>> for char in string:
...     print char,
...
M y   n a m e   i s   S a m .
```

range()

The **range()** function returns a list that holds the integers between the two values specified as its arguments, including the first but excluding the last. An optional third parameter defines a step value.

```
>>> range(1,6)
[1, 2, 3, 4, 5]
>>> range(0,10,3)
[0, 3, 6, 9]
```

The next example shows how to use **range()** in a **for** loop. In this example, **range()** returns a list comprising 0, 3, 6, and 9. The **for** control structure loops over these values, executing the indented statement each time through the loop.

```
>>> for cnt in range(0,10,3):
...     print cnt
...
0
3
6
9
```

optional

xrange()

The **range()** function is useful for generating short lists, but because it stores the list it returns in memory, it takes up a lot of system resources when it generates longer lists. In contrast, **xrange()** has a fixed memory footprint that is independent of the length of the list it returns; as a consequence, it uses fewer system resources than **range()** when working with long lists.

The two functions work differently. Whereas **range()** fills a list with values and stores that list in memory, **xrange()** works only when you iterate through the values it returns: The entire list is never stored in memory.

```
>>> range(1,11)
[1, 2, 3, 4, 5, 6, 7, 8, 9, 10]
>>> xrange(1,11)
xrange(1, 11)

>>> for cnt in xrange(1,11):
...     print cnt,
...
1 2 3 4 5 6 7 8 9 10
```

Reading from and Writing to Files

Python allows you to work with files in many ways. This section explains how to read from and write to text files and how to preserve an object in a file using **pickle**.

File Input and Output

open() The **open()** function opens a file and returns a file object called a *file handle;* it can open a file in one of several modes (Table 12-3). Opening a file in **w** (write) mode truncates the file; use **a** (append) mode if you want to add to a file. The following statement opens the file in Max's home directory named **test_file** in read mode; the file handle is named **f**.

```
f = open('/home/max/test_file', 'r')
```

Table 12-3 File modes

Mode	What it does
r	**Read only** Error if file does not exist.
w	**Write only** File is created if it does not exist. File is truncated if it exists.
r+	**Read and write** File is created if it does not exist.
a	**Append** File is created if it does not exist.
a+	**Append and read** File is created if it does not exist.
b	**Binary** Append to **r** or **w** to work with binary files.

Once the file is opened, you direct input and output using the file handle with one of the methods listed in Table 12-4. When you are finished working with a file, use close() to close it and free the resources the open file is using.

Table 12-4 File object methods

Method	Arguments	Returns or action
close()	None	Closes the file
isatty()	None	Returns *true* if the file is connected to a terminal; *false* otherwise
read()	Maximum number of bytes to read (optional)	Reads until EOF or specified maximum number of bytes; returns file as a string
readline()	Maximum number of bytes to read (optional)	Reads until NEWLINE or specified maximum number of bytes; returns line as a string
readlines()	Maximum number of bytes to read (optional)	Calls **readline()** repeatedly and returns a list of lines (iterable)
write(str)	String to be written	Writes to the file
writelines(strs)	List of strings	Calls **write()** repeatedly, once with each item in the list

The following example reads from **/home/max/test_file**, which holds three lines. It opens this file in read mode and assigns the file handle f to the open file. It uses the **readlines()** method, which reads the entire file into a list and returns that list. Because the list is iterable, Python passes to the **for** control structure one line from **test_file** each time through the loop. The **for** structure assigns the string value of this line to **ln**, which **print** then displays. The **strip()** method removes whitespace and/or a NEWLINE from the end of a line. Without **strip()**, **print** would output two NEWLINEs: the one that terminates the line from the file and the one it automatically appends to each line it outputs. After reading and displaying all lines from the file, the example closes the file.

```
>>> f = open('/home/max/test_file', 'r')
>>> for ln in f.readlines():
...     print ln.strip()
...
This is the first line
and here is the second line
of this file.
>>> f.close()
```

The next example opens the same file in append mode and writes a line to it using **write()**. The **write()** method does not append a NEWLINE to the line it outputs, so you must terminate the string you write to the file with a **\n**.

```
>>> f = open('/home/max/test_file','a')
>>> f.write('Extra line!\n')
>>> f.close()
```

optional In the example that uses **for**, Python does not call the **readlines()** method each time through the **for** loop. Instead, it reads the file into a list the first time **readlines()** is called and then iterates over the list, setting **ln** to the value of the next line in the list each time it is called subsequently. It is the same as if you had written

```
>>> f = open('/home/max/test_file', 'r')
>>> lines = f.readlines()
>>> for ln in lines:
...     print ln.strip()
```

It is more efficient to iterate over the file handle directly because this technique does not store the file in memory.

```
>>> f = open('/home/max/test_file', 'r')
>>> for ln in f:
...     print ln.strip()
```

EXCEPTION HANDLING

An *exception* is an error condition that changes the normal flow of control in a program. Although you can try to account for every problem your code will need to deal with, it is not always possible to do so: Unknown circumstances might arise. What if the file the previous programs opened does not exist? Python raises an IOError (input/output error) number 2 and displays the message **No such file or directory**.

```
>>> f = open('/home/max/test_file', 'r')
Traceback (most recent call last):
  File "<stdin>", line 1, in <module>
IOError: [Errno 2] No such file or directory: '/home/max/test_file'
```

Instead of allowing Python to display what might be an incomprehensible error message and quit, a well-written program handles exceptions like this one gracefully. Good exception handling can help you debug a program and can also provide a nontechnical user with clear information about why the program failed.

The next example wraps the **open** statement that failed with an exception handler in the form of a **try...except** control structure. This structure attempts to execute the **try** block. If execution of the **try** block fails (has an exception), it executes the code in the **except** block. If execution of the **try** block succeeds, it skips the **except** block. Depending on the severity of the error, the **except** block should warn the user that something might not be right or should display an error message and exit from the program.

```
>>> try:
...     f = open('/home/max/test_file', 'r')
... except:
...     print "Error on opening the file."
...
Error on opening the file.
```

You can refine the type of error an **except** block handles. Previously, the **open** statement returned an IOError. The following program tests for an IOError when it attempts to open a file, displays an error message, and exits. If it does not encounter an IOError, it continues normally.

```
$ cat except1.py
#!/usr/bin/python
try:
    f = open('/home/max/test_file', 'r')
except IOError:
    print "Cannot open file."
    exit()
print "Processing file."

$ ./except1.py
Cannot open file.
$
$ touch test_file
$ ./except1.py
Processing file.
```

PICKLE

The **pickle** module allows you to store an object in a file in a standard format for later use by the same or a different program. The object you store can be any type of object as long as it does not require an operating system resource such as a file handle or network socket. The standard **pickle** filename extension is **.p**. For more information visit wiki.python.org/moin/UsingPickle.

Never unpickle data received from an untrusted source

security The **pickle** module is not secure against maliciously constructed data. When you unpickle an object, you are trusting the person who created it. Do not unpickle an object if you do not know or trust its source.

This section discusses two **pickle** methods: **dump()**, which writes an object to disk, and **load()**, which reads an object from disk. The syntax for these methods is

*pickle.dump(**objectname**, open(**filename**, 'wb'))*

*pickle.load(**objectname**, open(**filename**, 'rb'))*

It is critical that you open the file in binary mode (**wb** and **rb**). The **load()** method returns the object; you can assign the object the same name as or a different name from the original object. Before you can use **pickle**, you must import it (page 601).

In the following example, after importing **pickle**, **pickle.dump()** creates a file named **pres.p** in **wb** (write binary) mode with a dump of the **preserves** list, and **exit()** leaves the Python interactive shell:

```
>>> import pickle

>>> preserves = ['apple', 'cherry', 'blackberry', 'apricot']
>>> preserves
['apple', 'cherry', 'blackberry', 'apricot']
>>> pickle.dump(preserves, open('pres.p', 'wb'))
exit()
```

The next example calls the Python interactive shell and **pickle.load()** reads the **pres.p** file in **rb** (read binary) mode. This method returns the object you originally saved using **dump()**. You can give the object any name you like.

```
$ python
...
>>> import pickle

>>> jams = pickle.load(open('pres.p', 'rb'))
>>> jams
['apple', 'cherry', 'blackberry', 'apricot']
```

REGULAR EXPRESSIONS

The Python **re** (regular expression) module handles regular expressions. Python regular expressions follow the rules covered in Appendix A and are similar to Perl regular expressions, which are covered starting on page 562. This section discusses a few of the tools in the Python **re** library. You must give the command **import re** before you can use the **re** methods. To display Python help on the **re** module, give the command **help()** from the Python interactive shell and then type **re**.

findall() One of the simplest **re** methods is **findall()**, which returns a list that holds matches using the syntax

*re.findall(**regex**, **string**)*

where ***regex*** is the regular expression and ***string*** is the string you are looking for a match in.

The ***regex*** in the following example (**hi**) matches the three occurrences of **hi** in the ***string*** (**hi hi hi hello**):

```
>>> import re
>>> a = re.findall('hi', 'hi hi hi hello')
>>> print a
['hi', 'hi', 'hi']
```

Because **findall()** returns a list (it is iterable), you can use it in a **for** statement. The following example uses the period (**.**) special character, which, in a regular expression, matches any character. The ***regex*** (**hi.**) matches the three occurrences of **hi** followed by any character in the ***string***.

```
>>> for mat in re.findall('hi.', 'hit him hid hex'):
...     print mat,
...
hit him hid
```

search() The **search()** re method uses the same syntax as **findall()** and looks through ***string*** for a match to ***regex***. Instead of returning a list if it finds a match, however, it returns a MatchObject. Many **re** methods return a MatchObject (and not a list) when they find a match for the ***regex*** in the ***string***.

```
>>> a = re.search('hi.', 'bye hit him hex')
>>> print a
<_sre.SRE_Match object at 0xb7663a30>
```

bool() The **bool()** function returns *true* or *false* based on its argument. Because you can test the MatchObject directly, **bool()** is not used often in Python programming, but it is included here for its instructional value. A MatchObject evaluates to *true* because it indicates a match. [Although **findall()** does not return a MatchObject, it does evaluate to *true* when it finds a match.]

```
>>> bool(a)
True
```

group() The **group**() method allows you to access the match a MatchObject holds.

```
>>> a.group(0)
'hit'
```

type() When no match exists, **search**() returns a NoneType object [as shown by the **type**() function], which evaluates to **None** or in a Boolean expression evaluates to *false.*

```
>>> a = re.search('xx.', 'bye hit him hex')
>>> type(a)
<type 'NoneType'>
>>> print a
None
>>> bool(a)
False
```

Because a re method in a Boolean context evaluates to *true* or *false,* you can use a **re** method as the expression an **if** statement evaluates. The next example uses **search**() as the expression in an **if** statement; because there is a match, **search**() evaluates as *true,* and Python executes the **print** statement.

```
>>> name = 'sam'
>>> if(re.search(name,'zach max sam helen')):
...     print 'The list includes ' + name
...
The list includes sam
```

match() The **match**() method of the **re** object uses the same syntax as **search**() but looks only at the beginning of ***string*** for a match to ***regex***.

```
>>> name = 'zach'
>>> if(re.match(name,'zach max sam helen')):
...     print 'The list includes ' + name
...
The list includes zach
```

DEFINING A FUNCTION

A Python function definition must be evaluated before the function is called, so it generally appears in the code before the call to the function. The contents of the function, as with other Python logical blocks, must be indented. The syntax of a function definition is

*def my_function(**args**):*
  ...

Python passes lists and other data structures to a function by reference (page 585), meaning that when a function modifies a data structure that was passed to it as an argument, it modifies the original data structure. The following example demonstrates this fact:

```
>>> def add_ab(my_list):
...     my_list.append('a')
...     my_list.append('b')
...
>>> a = [1,2,3]
>>> add_ab(a)
>>> a
[1, 2, 3, 'a', 'b']
```

You can pass arguments to a function in three ways. Assume the function **place_stuff** is defined as follows. The values assigned to the arguments in the function definition are defaults.

```
>>> def place_stuff(x = 10, y = 20, z = 30):
...     return x, y, z
...
```

If you call the function and specify arguments, the function uses those arguments:

```
>>> place_stuff(1,2,3)
(1, 2, 3)
```

If you do not specify arguments, the function uses the defaults:

```
>>> place_stuff()
(10, 20, 30)
```

Alternatively, you can specify values for some or all of the arguments:

```
>>> place_stuff(z=100)
(10, 20, 100)
```

USING LIBRARIES

This section discusses the Python standard library, nonstandard libraries, and Python namespace, as well as how to import and use a function.

STANDARD LIBRARY

The Python standard library, which is usually included in packages installed with Python, provides a wide range of facilities, including functions, constants, string services, data types, file and directory access, cryptographic services, and file formats. Visit docs.python.org/library/index.html for a list of the contents of the standard library.

NONSTANDARD LIBRARIES

In some cases a module you want might be part of a library that is not included with Python. You can usually find what you need in the Python Package Index (PyPI; pypi.python.org), a repository of more than 22,000 Python packages.

You can find lists of modules for the distribution you are using by searching the Web for *distro* **package database**, where *distro* is the name of the Linux distribution you are using, and then searching one of the databases for **python**.

SCIPY AND NUMPY LIBRARIES

Two popular libraries are SciPy and NumPy. The SciPy ("Sigh Pie"; scipy.org) library holds Python modules for mathematics, science, and engineering. It depends on NumPy (numpy.scipy.org), a library of Python modules for scientific computing.

You must download and install the package that holds NumPy before you can use any of its modules. Under Debian/Ubuntu/Mint and openSuSE, the package is named **python-numpy**; under Fedora/RHEL, it is named **numpy**. If you are running macOS, visit www.scipy.org/Installing_SciPy/Mac_OS_X. See Appendix C for instructions on downloading and installing packages. Alternatively, you can obtain the libraries from scipy.org or pypi.python.org. Once you import SciPy (**import scipy**), **help(scipy)** will list the functions you can import individually.

NAMESPACE

A *namespace* comprises a set of names (identifiers) in which all names are unique. For example, the namespace for a program might include an object named **planets**. You might instantiate **planets** as an integer:

```
>>> planets = 5
>>> type(planets)
<type 'int'>
```

Although it is not good programming practice, later on in the program you could assign **planets** a string value. It would then be an object of type string.

```
>>> planets = 'solar system'
>>> type(planets)
<type 'str'>
```

You could make **planets** a function, a list, or another type of object. Regardless, there would always be only one object named **planets** (identifiers in a namespace must be unique).

When you import a module (including a function), Python can merge the namespace of the module with the namespace of your program, creating a conflict. For example, if you import the function named **sample** from the library named **random** and then define a function with the same name, you will no longer be able to access the original function:

```
>>> from random import sample
>>> sample(range(10), 10)
[6, 9, 0, 7, 3, 5, 2, 4, 1, 8]
>>> def sample(a, b):
...     print 'Problem?'
...
```

```
>>> sample(range(10), 10)
Problem?
```

The next section discusses different ways you can import objects from a library and steps you can take to avoid the preceding problem.

IMPORTING A MODULE

You can import a module in one of several ways. How you import the module determines whether Python merges the namespace of the module with that of your program.

The simplest thing to do is to import the whole module. In this case Python does not merge the namespaces but allows you to refer to an object from the module by prefixing its name with the name of the module. The following code imports the **random** module. Using this syntax, the function named **sample** is not defined: You must call it as **random.sample**.

```
>>> import random
>>> sample(range(10), 10)
Traceback (most recent call last):
  File "<stdin>", line 1, in <module>
NameError: name 'sample' is not defined

>>> random.sample(range(10), 10)
[1, 0, 6, 9, 8, 3, 2, 7, 5, 4]
```

This setup allows you to define your own function named **sample**. Because Python has not merged the namespaces from your program and the module named **random**, the two functions can coexist.

```
>>> def sample(a, b):
...     print 'Not a problem.'
...
>>> sample(1, 2)
Not a problem.
>>> random.sample(range(10), 10)
[2, 9, 6, 5, 1, 3, 4, 0, 7, 8]
```

Importing part of a module

Another way to import a module is to specify the module and the object.

```
>>> from random import sample
```

When you import an object using this syntax, you import only the function named **sample**; no other objects from that module will be available. This technique is very efficient. However, Python merges the namespaces from your program and from the object, which can give rise to the type of problem illustrated in the previous section.

You can also use **from *module* import ***. This syntax imports all names from ***module*** into the namespace of your program; it is generally not a good idea to use this technique.

EXAMPLE OF IMPORTING A FUNCTION

The **my_max.py** program on page 586 finds the largest element in a predefined list. The following program works the same way, except at runtime it fills a list with random numbers.

The following command imports the **sample()** function from the standard library module named **random**. You can install an object from a nonstandard library, such as NumPy, the same way.

```
from random import sample
```

After importing this function, the command **help(sample)** displays information about **sample()**. The **sample()** function has the syntax

*sample(**list**, **number**)*

where ***list*** is a list holding the population, or values **sample()** can return, and ***number*** is the number of random numbers in the list **sample()** returns.

```
>>> sample([0, 1, 2, 3, 4, 5, 6, 7, 8, 9], 4)
[7, 1, 2, 5]
>>> sample([0, 1, 2, 3, 4, 5, 6, 7, 8, 9], 6)
[0, 5, 4, 1, 3, 7]
```

The following program uses the **range()** function (page 592), which returns a list holding the numbers from 0 through 1 less than its argument:

```
>>> range(8)
[0, 1, 2, 3, 4, 5, 6, 7]
>>> range(16)
[0, 1, 2, 3, 4, 5, 6, 7, 8, 9, 10, 11, 12, 13, 14, 15]
```

When you combine the two functions, **range()** provides a list of values and **sample()** selects values randomly from that list:

```
>>> sample(range(100),10)
[5, 32, 70, 93, 74, 29, 90, 7, 30, 11]
```

In the following program, **sample** generates a list of random numbers and **for** iterates through them:

```
$ cat my_max2.py
#!/usr/bin/python

from random import sample
my_rand_list = sample(range(100), 10)
print 'Random list of numbers:', my_rand_list
largest = -1
for item in my_rand_list:
        if (item > largest):
                largest = item
                print largest,
print
print 'largest number is ', largest
```

```
$ ./my_max2.py
random list of numbers: [67, 40, 1, 29, 9, 49, 99, 95, 77, 51]
67 99
largest number is  99
$ ./my_max2.py
random list of numbers: [53, 33, 76, 35, 71, 13, 75, 58, 74, 50]
53 76
largest number is  76
```

max() The algorithm used in this example is not the most efficient way of finding the maximum value in a list. It is more efficient to use the **max()** builtin function.

```
>>> from random import sample
>>> max(sample(range(100), 10))
96
```

optional

LAMBDA FUNCTIONS

Python supports *Lambda* functions—functions that might not be bound to a name. You might also see them referred to as *anonymous* functions. Lambda functions are more restrictive than other functions because they can hold only a single expression. In its most basic form, Lambda is another syntax for defining a function. In the following example, the object named **a** is a Lambda function and performs the same task as the function named **add_one**:

```
>>> def add_one(x):
...     return x + 1
...
>>> type (add_one)
<type 'function'>

>>> add_one(2)
3

>>> a = lambda x: x + 1
>>> type(a)
<type 'function'>

>>> a(2)
3
```

map() You can use the Lambda syntax to define a function inline as an argument to a function such as **map()** that expects another function as an argument. The syntax of the **map()** function is

*map(**func**, **seq1**[, **seq2**, ...])*

where ***func*** is a function that is applied to the sequence of arguments represented by ***seq1*** (and ***seq2*** ...). Typically, the sequences that are arguments to **map()** and the object returned by **map()** are lists. The next example first defines a function named **times_two()**:

```
>>> def times_two(x):
...     return x * 2
...
>>> times_two(8)
16
```

Next, the **map()** function applies **times_two()** to a list:

```
>>> map(times_two, [1, 2, 3, 4])
[2, 4, 6, 8]
```

You can define an inline Lambda function as an argument to **map()**. In this example the Lambda function is not bound to a name:

```
>>> map(lambda x: x * 2, [1, 2, 3, 4])
[2, 4, 6, 8]
```

List Comprehensions

List comprehensions apply functions to lists. For example, the following code, which does not use a list comprehension, uses **for** to iterate over items in a list:

```
>>> my_list = []
>>> for x in range(10):
...     my_list.append(x + 10)
...
>>> my_list
[10, 11, 12, 13, 14, 15, 16, 17, 18, 19]
```

You can use a list comprehension to perform the same task neatly and efficiently. The syntax is similar, but a list comprehension is enclosed within square brackets and the operation (**x + 10**) precedes the iteration [**for x in range**(10)].

```
>>> my_list = [x + 10 for x in range(10)]
>>> my_list
[10, 11, 12, 13, 14, 15, 16, 17, 18, 19]
```

The results when using a **for** structure and a list comprehension are the same. The next example uses a list comprehension to fill a list with powers of 2:

```
>>> potwo = [2**x for x in range(1, 13)]
>>> print potwo
[2, 4, 8, 16, 32, 64, 128, 256, 512, 1024, 2048, 4096]
```

The next list comprehension fills a list with even numbers. The **if** clause returns values only if the remainder after dividing a number by 2 is 0 (**if x % 2 == 0**).

```
>>> [x for x in range(1,11) if x % 2 == 0]
[2, 4, 6, 8, 10]
```

The final example shows nested list comprehensions. It nests **for** loops and uses **x + y** to catenate the elements of both lists in all combinations.

```
>>> A = ['a', 'b', 'c']
>>> B = ['1', '2', '3']
>>> all = [x + y for x in A for y in B]
>>> print all
['a1', 'a2', 'a3', 'b1', 'b2', 'b3', 'c1', 'c2', 'c3']
```

CHAPTER SUMMARY

Python is an interpreted language: It translates code into bytecode at runtime and executes the bytecode within the Python virtual machine. You can run a Python program from the Python interactive shell or from a file. The Python interactive shell is handy for development because you can use it to debug and execute code one line at a time and see the results immediately. Within the Python interactive shell, Python displays output from any command line that does not have an action. From this shell you can give the command **help()** to use the Python **help** feature or you can give the command **help('*object*')** to display help on ***object.***

Functions help improve code readability, efficiency, and expandability. Many function are available when you first call Python (builtin functions) and many more are found in libraries that you can download and/or import. Methods are similar to functions except they work on objects whereas functions stand on their own. Python allows you to define both normal functions and nameless functions called Lambda functions.

Python enables you to read from and write to files in many ways. The **open()** function opens a file and returns a file object called a file handle. Once the file is opened, you direct input and output using the file handle. When you are finished working with a file, it is good practice to close it. The **pickle** module allows you to store an object in a file in a standard format for later use by the same or a different program.

A Python list is an object that comprises one or more elements; it is similar to an array in C or Java. An important feature of lists is that they are *iterable,* meaning a control structure such as **for** can loop (iterate) through each item in a list. A Python dictionary holds unordered key–value pairs in which the keys are unique. Like lists, dictionaries are iterable.

Python implements many control structures, including **if...else**, **if...elif...else**, **while**, and **for**. Unlike most languages, Python requires SPACEs (or TABs) at the beginning of lines in a control structure. The indented code marks a *logical block,* or section of code, that is part of the control structure.

Python regular expressions are implemented by the Python **re** (regular expression) module. You must give the command **import re** before you can use the **re** methods.

EXERCISES

1. What is meant by implied display? Is it available in the Python interactive shell or from a program file? Provide a simple example of implied display.
2. Write and run a Python program that you store in a file. The program should demonstrate how to prompt the user for input and display the string the user entered.
3. Using the Python interactive shell, instantiate a list that holds three-letter abbreviations for the first six months of the year and display the list.
4. Using the Python interactive shell, use a **for** control structure to iterate through the elements of the list you instantiated in exercise 3 and display each abbreviated name followed by a period on a line by itself. (*Hint:* The period is a string.)
5. Using the Python interactive shell, put the elements of the list you instantiated in exercise 3 in alphabetical order.
6. Instantiate a dictionary in which the keys are the months in the third quarter of the year and the values are the number of days in the corresponding month. Display the dictionary, the keys, and the values. Add the tenth month of the year to the dictionary and display the value of that month only.
7. What does *iterable* mean? Name two builtin objects that are iterable. Which control structure can you use to loop through an iterable object?
8. Write and demonstrate a Lambda function named **stg()** that appends **.txt** to its argument. What happens when you call the function with an integer?

ADVANCED EXERCISES

9. Define a function named **cents** that returns its argument divided by 100 and truncated to an integer. For example:

```
>>> cents(12345)
123
```

10. Define a function named **cents2** that returns its argument divided by 100 exactly (and includes decimal places if necessary). Make sure your function does not truncate the answer. For example:

```
>>> cents2(12345)
123.45
```

11. Create a list that has four elements. Make a copy of the list and change one of the elements in the copy. Show that the same element in the original list did not change.

12. Why does the following assignment statement generate an error?

```
>>> x.y = 5
Traceback (most recent call last):
  File "<stdin>", line 1, in <module>
NameError: name 'x' is not defined
```

13. Call **map()** with two arguments:
    1. A Lambda function that returns the square of the number it was called with
    2. A list holding the even numbers between 4 and 15; generate the list inline using **range()**

14. Use a list comprehension to display the numbers from 1 through 30 inclusive that are divisible by 3.

15. Write a function that takes an integer, **val,** as an argument. The function asks the user to enter a number. If the number is greater than **val,** the function displays **Too high.** and returns 1; if the number is less than **val,** the function displays **Too low.** and returns –1; if the number equals **val,** the function displays **Got it!** and returns 0. Call the function repeatedly until the user enters the right number.

16. Rewrite exercise 15 to call the function with a random number in between 0 and 10 inclusive. (*Hint:* The **randint** function in the **random** library returns a random number between its two arguments inclusive.)

17. Write a function that counts the characters in a string the user inputs. Then write a routine that calls the function and displays the following output:

```
$ ./count_letters.py
Enter some words: The rain in Spain
The string "The rain in Spain" has  17 characters in it.
```

18. Write a function that counts the vowels (**aeiou**) in a string the user inputs. Make sure it counts upper- and lowercase vowels. Then write a routine that calls the function and displays the following output:

```
$ ./count_vowels.py
Enter some words: Go East young man!
The string "Go East young man!" has  6 vowels in it.
```

19. Write a function that counts all the characters and the vowels in a string the user inputs. Then write a routine that calls the function and displays the following output:

```
$ ./count_all.py
Enter some words: The sun rises in the East and sets in the West.
13 letters in 47 are vowels.
```

13

The MariaDB SQL Database Management System

In This Chapter

Objectives

After reading this chapter you should be able to:

- Explain what SQL is and how it relates to MariaDB
- Explain what a database, table, row, and column are and the relationships among them
- Install a MariaDB server and client on the local system
- Set up MariaDB, including a **~/.my.cnf** file for a user
- Create a database and add a user
- Add data to and retrieve data from the database
- Modify data in the database
- Add a second table and write joins to retrieve data from both tables

HISTORY

MySQL MySQL (My Structured Query Language) is an implementation of SQL. It is the world's most popular open-source RDBMS (relational database management system). MySQL is extremely fast and is used by some of the most frequently visited Web sites on the Internet, including Google, Facebook, Twitter, Yahoo, YouTube, and Wikipedia. Recently, however, some of these companies have moved to MariaDB, which is explained next. Fedora/RHEL has replaced MySQL in its repositories with MariaDB, and Wikipedia has also converted to this variant. Ubuntu provides both versions.

Michael "Monty" Widenius and David Axmark started development of MySQL in 1994. In 2008, Sun Microsystems bought MySQL. Widenius named this RDBMS after his daughter, My.

MariaDB In 2009, not happy with the development process of MySQL under Sun Microsystems, Widenius left Sun and founded a company named Monty Program to work on a fork of MySQL named MariaDB. In 2010, when Oracle Corporation acquired Sun Microsystems, most of the MySQL developers left Sun to join the two MySQL forks MariaDB and Drizzle (www.drizzle.org).

Compatibility Today, MariaDB is a community-developed fork of MySQL that is dedicated to FOSS (free/open source) software (page 2) and released under the GNU GPL (page 6). Currently, MariaDB is a drop-in replacement for MySQL and uses the same commands as MySQL; only the package names differ (but see mariadb.com/kb/en/mariadb-vs-mysql-compatibility). However, MariaDB is planning to introduce significant changes in the next version; at that time there might no longer be compatibility at the feature level. However, one would expect MariaDB to maintain protocol compatibility with MySQL into the future.

MariaDB or MySQL?

tip Because MariaDB is a fork of MySQL, almost all of the code is the same. The places where the code differs do not affect the examples or descriptions in this chapter. The examples in this chapter were tested against MariaDB. If you want to work with MySQL, install the mysql package.

Interfaces Many programming languages provide interfaces and bindings to MariaDB, including C, Python, PHP, and Perl. In addition, you can access a MariaDB database using the industry-standard Open Database Connectivity (ODBC) API. You can also call MariaDB from a shell script or the command line. MariaDB is a core component of the popular LAMP (Linux, Apache, MySQL/MariaDB, PHP/Perl/Python) open-source enterprise software stack.

NOTES

MariaDB has a separate set of users from Linux: Users who have MariaDB accounts might not have Linux accounts on the system, and vice versa. As installed, the name of the MariaDB administrator is **root**. Because the MariaDB **root** user is not the same as the Linux **root** user, it can (and should) have a different password.

MariaDB does not automatically create a database when you create a MariaDB user; users and databases are not rigidly bound.

SQL is free form with respect to whitespace and NEWLINEs.

TERMINOLOGY

This section briefly describes some basic terms used when working with a relational database. See Figure 13-1.

database A structured set of persistent data comprising one or more tables.

row An ordered set of columns in a table. Also *record* or *tuple*.

column A set of one type of values, one per row in a table. Certain columns might be designated as keys. Keys are indexed to speed up access to specific values in the column. Also *field* or *attribute*.

join Two (or more) rows, each from a different table, that are tied together by means of the relationships between values in two (or more) columns. For example, two rows, each from a different table, can be joined based on equal values in two columns.

relational database management system (RDBMS) A database based on the relational model developed by E. F. Codd comprising tables of data. Codd used the term *relations* for what SQL calls tables; thus the name of the database.

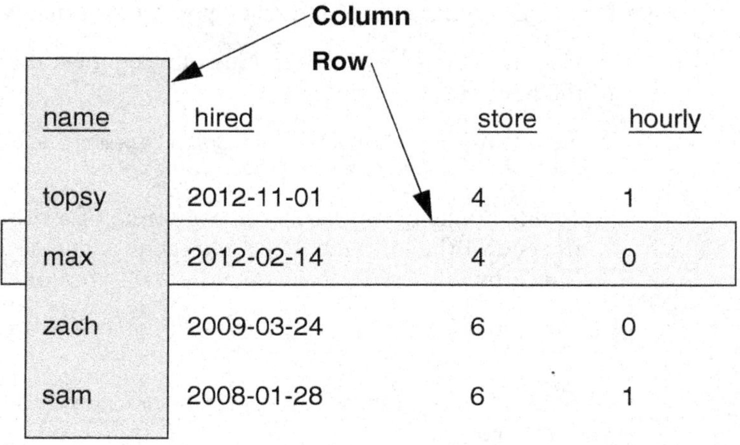

Figure 13-1 A few rows from the **people** table in the **maxdb** database

SQL Structured Query Language. An industry-standard language for creating, updating, and querying relational databases. SQL is not part of the relational model but is often associated with it.

MariaDB A software brand or implementation of SQL.

MariaDB is an implementation of SQL

tip This chapter is about SQL and MariaDB. It explains how to set up a MariaDB server and client. It also shows examples of how to run SQL queries under MariaDB.

table A collection of rows in a relational database. Also *relation*.

SYNTAX AND CONVENTIONS

An SQL program comprises one or more statements, each terminated by a semicolon (;) or **\g**. Although keywords in statements are not case sensitive, this book shows keywords in uppercase letters for clarity. Database and table names are case sensitive; column names are not.

The following example shows a multiline SQL statement (query) that includes both the primary interpreter prompt (**MariaDB [maxdb]>; maxdb** is the name of the selected database) and the secondary interpreter prompt (**–>**). SELECT, FROM, and WHERE are keywords. This statement displays the value of the **name** column from the table named **people** in rows where the value in the **store** column is **4**.

```
MariaDB [maxdb]> SELECT          name
    ->           FROM    people
    ->           WHERE   store = 4;
```

COMMENTS

You can specify a comment in one of three ways in an SQL program. These techniques work in SQL command files and when you are working with MariaDB interactively.

- A hash sign (#) marks the beginning of a comment that continues to the end of the line (the NEWLINE character).

```
# The following line holds an SQL statement and a comment
USE maxdb;    # Use the maxdb database
```

- A double hyphen (--) marks the beginning of a comment that continues to the end of the line (the NEWLINE character). The double hyphen must be followed by whitespace (one or more SPACEs and/or TABs).

```
-- The following line holds an SQL statement and a comment
USE maxdb;    -- Use the maxdb database
```

- As in the C programming language, you can surround a (multiline) comment with /* and */.

```
/* The line following this multiline
comment holds an SQL statement
and a comment */
USE maxdb;    /* Use the maxdb database */
```

DATA TYPES

When you create a table, you specify the name and data type of each column in the table. Each data type is designed to hold a certain kind of data. For example, data type CHAR holds strings of characters, while DATE holds dates. The examples in this section use the following data types, a small sampling of those available under MariaDB.

- **CHAR(*n*)**—Stores a string of up to *n* characters where 0 <= *n* <= 255. You must enclose strings within single or double quotation marks. When you store a string in a type CHAR column, MariaDB right-pads the string with SPACEs to make an *n*-character string. Then, when you retrieve a type CHAR string, MariaDB strips out the trailing SPACEs. Occupies *n* bytes (CHAR has a fixed length). If you omit the length, it defaults to 1. CHAR(0) columns can contain one of two values: an empty string or NULL. Such columns cannot be part of an index. The CONNECT storage engine does not support CHAR(0).
- **VARCHAR(*n*)**—Stores a string of up to *n* characters where 0 <= *n* <= 65,535. You must enclose strings within single or double quotation marks. MariaDB does not pad strings stored in type VARCHAR columns. With a string length of *L*, occupies *L* + 1 bytes if 0 <= *L* <= 255 and *L* + 2 bytes if *L* > 255. (VARCHAR has a variable length.) See page 627 for an example.

VARCHARs might slow large queries

tip MariaDB converts VARCHAR columns to CHAR for operations that generate temporary tables (e.g., sorting, including ORDER BY and GROUP BY). Thus declaring large VARCHAR values [e.g., VARCHAR(255)] for columns that require frequent sorting will result in very large temporary tables that tend to slow queries.

VARCHAR(0) columns can contain one of two values: an empty string or NULL. Such columns cannot be part of an index. The CONNECT storage engine does not support VARCHAR(0).

- **INTEGER**—Stores a 4-byte integer. INTEGER (also INT) supports the attributes UNSIGNED and ZEROFILL.
- **DATE**—Stores a date. MariaDB sets a DATE variable to 0 if you specify an illegal value. Occupies 3 bytes.
- **BOOL**—A synonym for TINYINT. A value of 0 evaluates as *false* and 1–255 evaluate as *true*. Occupies 1 byte. When you specify data type BOOL, MariaDB changes it to a TINYINT.

More Information

Home pages: mariadb.org, www.mysql.com
Documentation: mariadb.com/kb/en/MariaDB, dev.mysql.com/doc
Introduction: mariadb.com/kb/en/mariadb/documentation/getting-started
MariaDB/MySQL compatibility:
mariadb.com/kb/en/mariadb/mariadb-vs-mysql-compatibility
Command syntax: dev.mysql.com/doc/refman/5.6/en/sql-syntax.html
Data types: dev.mysql.com/doc/refman/5.6/en/data-types.html
Joins: blog.codinghorror.com/a-visual-explanation-of-sql-joins
ODBC: dev.mysql.com/downloads/connector/odbc
Security: blog.mariadb.org/tag/security, www.kitebird.com/articles/ins-sec.html (dated)
Backing up databases: webcheatsheet.com/SQL/mysql_backup_restore.php, www.thegeekstuff.com/2008/09/backup-and-restore-mysql-database-using-mysqldump

Installing a MariaDB Server and Client

This section briefly covers installing the MariaDB client and server packages and starting the server running. The steps necessary to set up MariaDB differ by distribution.

You must remove anonymous MariaDB users

tip When you install the MariaDB server, the MariaDB database is set up to allow anonymous users to log in and use MariaDB. The examples in this chapter will not work unless you remove these users from the MariaDB database. See "Removing Anonymous Users" on page 617.

Fedora/RHEL (Red Hat Enterprise Linux)

Install the following packages:

- mariadb
- mariadb-server

Working as a privileged user under Fedora, give the following commands to always start the MariaDB daemon when the system enters multiuser mode and to start the MariaDB daemon immediately:

```
# systemctl enable mariadb.service
# systemctl start mariadb.service
```

Use these commands if you are running RHEL:

```
# chkconfig mariadb on
# service mariadb start
```

Debian/Ubuntu/Mint

Install the following packages:

- **mariadb-client**
- **mariadb-server**

When you install the **mariadb-server** package, the **dpkg** postinst script asks you to provide a password for the MariaDB user named **root**. You will use this password later in this chapter.

openSUSE

Install the following packages:

- **mariadb-cluster-client**
- **mariadb-cluster**

As root, use the following commands to always start the MariaDB daemon when the system enters multiuser mode and to start the MariaDB daemon immediately:

```
# systemctl enable mariadb.service
# systemctl start mariadb.service
```

The first command might display an error message but will work anyway.

macOS

See page 1077 for instructions on how to install MariaDB under macOS.

Client Options

This section describes some of the options you can use on the MariaDB client command line. The options preceded by a single hyphen and those preceded by a double hyphen are equivalent.

––disable-reconnect

Does not attempt to connect to the server again if the connection is dropped. See **––reconnect.**

––host=*hostname*

–h *hostname*

Specifies the address of the MariaDB server as ***hostname***. Without this option MariaDB connects to the server on the local system (127.0.0.1).

––password[=*passwd*]

–p[*passwd*]

Specifies the MariaDB password as ***passwd***. For improved security, do not specify the password on the command line. With this option and no password,

MariaDB prompts for a password. By default MariaDB does not use a password. The short form of this option does not accept a SPACE between the **–p** and ***passwd***.

––reconnect Attempts to connect to the server again if the connection is dropped (default). Disable this behavior using **––disable-reconnect**.

––skip-column-names
Does not display column names in results.

––user=*name* **–u *name***
Specifies the MariaDB user as ***name***. Without this option, ***name*** defaults to the username of the user running the MariaDB command.

––verbose **–v** Increases the amount of information MariaDB displays. Use this option multiple times to increase verbosity. This option displays MariaDB statements as they are executed when running from a command file.

Setting Up MariaDB

You must remove the anonymous users from the MariaDB database before MariaDB will allow you to run commands working as yourself (or as Max if you follow the examples in this section). You can work as the MariaDB user named **root** without removing the anonymous users. To run commands as the MariaDB user named **root** in cases where this user does not have a password, you can either not specify a password or else press RETURN when prompted for a password. In a production environment, as opposed to a testing environment, you can improve security of a MariaDB database by giving a password to the MariaDB user named **root**.

Of the following three steps, only the second, "Removing Anonymous Users," is required. The first step, "Assigning a Password to the MariaDB User Named **root**," makes a database more secure and is a good idea in a production environment.

You can use the third step, "Running the Secure Installation Script," in place of the first two steps. This script removes anonymous users, assigns a password to the MariaDB user named **root**, and takes other actions to make MariaDB more secure.

Assigning a Password to the MariaDB User Named root

The following command, when run as a nonprivileged user, assigns *mysql-password* as the password for the MariaDB user named **root**. If you assigned the MariaDB user named **root** a password when you installed MariaDB, skip this step.

```
$ mysqladmin -u root password 'mysql-password'
```

Removing Anonymous Users

The following commands, which you can run as a nonprivileged user, remove the anonymous users from the MariaDB database, yielding a more secure system. Using the **–u** option causes MariaDB to run as the MariaDB user named **root**. The **–p** option causes MariaDB to prompt for the password (for the MariaDB user named **root**). In response to the prompt, enter the password you assigned to the MariaDB user named **root**.

```
$ mysql -u root -p
Enter password:
...
MariaDB [(none)]> DELETE FROM     mysql.user
MariaDB [(none)]> WHERE   user='';
Query OK, 2 rows affected (0.00 sec)
MariaDB [(none)]> FLUSH PRIVILEGES;
Query OK, 0 rows affected (0.00 sec)

MariaDB [(none)]> quit
Bye
```

Running the Secure Installation Script

As an alternative to the two preceding steps, you can run the following command, which allows you to assign a password to the MariaDB user named **root**, removes anonymous users, disallows remote MariaDB **root** logins, and removes the test database that ships with MariaDB.

```
$ mysql_secure_installation
```

~/.my.cnf: Configures a MariaDB Client

You can use the **~/.my.cnf** file to set MariaDB client options. The following example shows Max's **.my.cnf** file. The [**mysql**] specifies the MariaDB group. The **user** line is useful if your Linux and MariaDB usernames are different. Setting **user** to **max** when Max's Linux username is **max** is not necessary. The **password** line sets Max's MariaDB password to **mpasswd**. With this setup, Max does not have to use **–p** on the command line; MariaDB logs him in automatically. The **database** line specifies the name of the MariaDB database you want to work with; thus you do not need to include a USE statement at the beginning of a MariaDB program or session. Do not add the **database** line to this file until *after* you create the database (next) or you will not be able to use MariaDB.

```
$ cat /home/max/.my.cnf
[mysql]
user="max"
password="mpasswd"
database="maxdb"
```

Because this file can hold a password and other sensitive information, setting permissions on this file so that the user in whose home directory the file resides owns the file and only the owner can read the file makes the MariaDB data more secure.

~/.mysql_history: Stores Your MariaDB History

MariaDB writes each of the statements it executes to a file named **~/.mysql_history**. Because MariaDB can write passwords to this file, setting permissions on this file so that the user in whose home directory the file resides owns the file and only the owner can read the file makes the MariaDB data more secure. If you do not want to store your MariaDB history, delete this file and recreate it as a symbolic link to **/dev/null**.

```
$ rm ~/.mysql_history
$ ln -s /dev/null ~/.mysql_history
```

Creating a Database

If the MariaDB username you add is the same as your Linux username, you will not have to specify a username on the MariaDB command line. In the following example, Max works as the MariaDB user named **root** (**–u root**). Using the **–p** option causes MariaDB to prompt for the password. In response to the **Enter password** prompt, Max supplies the password for the MariaDB user named **root**. If the MariaDB user named **root** does not have a password, press RETURN in response to the prompt.

CREATE DATABASE, SHOW DATABASES

Max uses a CREATE DATABASE statement to create a database named **maxdb** and a SHOW DATABASES statement to display the names of all databases. This command shows the name of the **maxdb** database and several system databases.

```
$ mysql -u root -p
Enter password:
Welcome to the MariaDB monitor.  Commands end with ; or \g.
Your MariaDB connection id is 41
Server version: 10.0.29-0ubuntu0.16.04.1 (Ubuntu)
...
Type 'help;' or '\h' for help. Type '\c' to clear the current input
statement.

MariaDB [(none)]> CREATE DATABASE maxdb;
Query OK, 1 row affected (0.00 sec)

MariaDB [(none)]> SHOW DATABASES;
+--------------------+
| Database           |
+--------------------+
| information_schema |
| maxdb              |
| mysql              |
| performance_schema |
+--------------------+
 rows in set (0.00 sec)
```

If you try to create a database that already exists, MySQL displays an error message.

```
MariaDB [(none)]> CREATE DATABASE maxdb;
ERROR 1007 (HY000): Can't create database 'maxdb'; database exists
```

USE You must tell MariaDB the name of the database you want to work with. If you do not give MariaDB this information, you must prefix the names of tables with the name of the database. For example, you would need to specify the **people** table in the **maxdb** database as **maxdb.people**. When you specify the **maxdb** database in the **~/.my.cnf** file (page 617) or with a USE statement, you can refer to the same table as **people**. In the following example, Max uses a USE statement to specify **maxdb** as the database he is working with:

```
$ mysql
MariaDB [(none)]> USE maxdb;
Database changed
```

ADDING A USER

Before starting to work with the database, create a user so you do not have to work as the MariaDB user named **root**. You must work as the MariaDB user named **root** to create a MariaDB user.

Continuing with his previous MariaDB session, Max adds the MariaDB user named **max** with a password of **mpasswd**. The GRANT statement gives Max the permissions he needs to work (as the user named **max**) with the **maxdb** database. When you are using the MariaDB interpreter, the message **Query OK** indicates that the preceding statement was syntactically correct. Within an SQL statement, you must surround all character and date strings with quotation marks.

```
MariaDB [(none)]> GRANT          ALL PRIVILEGES
    ->         ON      maxdb.* to 'max'
    ->         IDENTIFIED BY 'mpasswd'
    ->         WITH GRANT OPTION;
Query OK, 0 rows affected (0.00 sec)

MariaDB [(none)]> SELECT          user, password
    ->         FROM    mysql.user;
+------+-------------------------------------------+
| user | password                                  |
+------+-------------------------------------------+
| root | *81F5E21E35407D884A6CD4A731AEBFB6AF209E1B |
...
| max  | *34432555DD6C778E7CB4A0EE4551425CE3AC0E16 |
+------+-------------------------------------------+
```

```
7 rows in set (0.00 sec)

MariaDB [(none)]> quit
Bye
```

In the preceding example, after setting up the new user, Max uses a SELECT statement to query the **user** table of the **mysql** database and display the **user** and **password** columns. The **password** column displays encrypted passwords. Two users now exist: **root** and **max**. Max gives the command **quit** to exit from the MariaDB interpreter.

Working as the MariaDB user **max**, Max can now set up a simple database to keep track of people. He does not need to use the **–u** option on the command line because his Linux username and his MariaDB username are the same.

EXAMPLES

This section follows Max as he works with MariaDB. You must first follow the steps described under "Setting Up MariaDB" on page 616 to remove anonymous users and also under "Adding a User" on page 619 to create the **maxdb** database and add the MariaDB user named **max**. If you do not follow these steps, you will not be able to use MariaDB as described in this section.

LOGGING IN

You must log in to MariaDB before you can use it interactively.

You can specify a MariaDB username in **~/.my.cnf** (page 617) or by using the **––user** (**–u**) option on the command line. If you do not specify a user in one of these ways, MariaDB assumes your MariaDB username is the same as your Linux username. The examples in this section assume Max is logging in to MariaDB as **max** (and has not specified a username in the **~/.my.cnf** file).

If a MariaDB account has a password, you must specify that password to log in. You can specify a password in the **~/.my.cnf** file or by using the **––password** (**–p**) option on the command line. Without specifying his password in his **~/.my.cnf** file, Max would log in on the MariaDB interactive interpreter using the following command:

```
$ mysql -p
Enter password: mpasswd
...
```

With his password specified in the **~/.my.cnf** file as shown on page 617, Max can log in without the **–p** option:

```
$ mysql
...
```

CREATING A TABLE

This section assumes Max has specified his password in his **~/.my.cnf** file.

CREATE TABLE Before you can work with a database, you must create a table to hold data. To get started, Max uses the following CREATE TABLE statement to create a table named **people** in the **maxdb** database. This table has four columns. The USE statement specifies the name of the database.

```
$ mysql
MariaDB [(none)]> USE maxdb;
Database changed

MariaDB [(maxdb)]> CREATE TABLE    people (
    ->          name    CHAR(10),
    ->          hired   DATE,
    ->          store   INTEGER,
    ->          hourly  BOOL
    ->          );
Query OK, 0 rows affected (0.04 sec)
```

SQL is free form with respect to whitespace and NEWLINEs. For example, Max could have written the preceding statement as follows:

```
MariaDB [(maxdb)]> CREATE TABLE people (name CHAR(10),
    -> hired DATE, store INTEGER, hourly BOOL);
```

SHOW TABLES After creating the table, Max uses a SHOW TABLES statement to display a list of tables in the **maxdb** database.

```
MariaDB [(maxdb)]> SHOW TABLES;
+-----------------+
| Tables_in_maxdb |
+-----------------+
| people          |
+-----------------+
1 row in set (0.00 sec)
```

DESCRIBE Next, Max uses a DESCRIBE statement to display a description of the table named **people**.

```
MariaDB [(maxdb)]> DESCRIBE people;
+--------+------------+------+-----+---------+-------+
| Field  | Type       | Null | Key | Default | Extra |
+--------+------------+------+-----+---------+-------+
| name   | char(10)   | YES  |     | NULL    |       |
| hired  | date       | YES  |     | NULL    |       |
| store  | int(11)    | YES  |     | NULL    |       |
| hourly | tinyint(1) | YES  |     | NULL    |       |
+--------+------------+------+-----+---------+-------+
4 rows in set (0.00 sec)
```

Figure 13-1 on page 611 shows part of the **people** table after data has been entered in it.

ALTER TABLE Max decides that the **hourly** column should default to *true*. He uses an ALTER TABLE statement to modify the table so he does not have to delete the table and create it again. He then checks his work using a DESCRIBE statement; the output of this statement shows that the **hourly** column now defaults to **1**, which evaluates as *true*.

```
MariaDB [(maxdb)]> ALTER TABLE     people
    ->          MODIFY  hourly BOOL DEFAULT TRUE;
Query OK, 0 rows affected (0.00 sec)
Records: 0  Duplicates: 0  Warnings: 0

MariaDB [(maxdb)]> DESCRIBE people;
+--------+------------+------+-----+---------+-------+
| Field  | Type       | Null | Key | Default | Extra |
+--------+------------+------+-----+---------+-------+
| name   | char(10)   | YES  |     | NULL    |       |
| hired  | date       | YES  |     | NULL    |       |
| store  | int(11)    | YES  |     | NULL    |       |
| hourly | tinyint(1) | YES  |     | 1       |       |
+--------+------------+------+-----+---------+-------+
4 rows in set (0.00 sec)
```

ADDING DATA

This section describes several ways to enter information into a database.

INSERT INTO Max uses an INSERT INTO statement to try to add a row of data to the **people** table. Following the first command, MariaDB displays an error saying it does not know about a column named **topsy**; Max forgot to put quotation marks around the string **topsy** so MariaDB parsed **topsy** as the name of a column. Max includes the quotation marks in the second command.

```
MariaDB [(maxdb)]> INSERT INTO     people
    ->          VALUES ( topsy, '2018/11/01', 4, FALSE);
ERROR 1054 (42S22): Unknown column 'topsy' in 'field list'

MariaDB [(maxdb)]> INSERT INTO     people
    ->          VALUES ( 'topsy', '2018/11/01', 4, FALSE);
Query OK, 1 row affected (0.00 sec)
```

The preceding INSERT INTO statement did not specify which columns the values were to be inserted into; it specified values for all four columns. The next INSERT INTO statement specifies values that are to be added to the **name** and **store** columns; MariaDB sets the other columns in the new rows to their default values.

```
MariaDB [(maxdb)]> INSERT INTO     people (name, store)
    ->          VALUES  ( 'percy', 2 ),
    ->                  ( 'bailey', 2 );
Query OK, 2 rows affected (0.00 sec)
Records: 2  Duplicates: 0  Warnings: 0
```

```
MariaDB [(maxdb)]> QUIT
Bye
```

LOAD DATA LOCAL INFILE The preceding examples showed how to work with MariaDB interactively. The next example shows how to run MariaDB with statements in a command file. At the beginning of the preceding interactive session, Max gave the command **USE maxdb** so MariaDB knew which database the following commands worked with. When you specify commands in a file, you must tell MariaDB which database the commands work with; each file of commands must start with a USE statement or MariaDB will return an error. Alternatively, you can specify the name of the database in your **~/.my.cnf** file (page 617).

The following example adds three rows to the **people** table from a text file named **addfile**. In **addfile**, each line holds data for a single row, with a single TAB separating each column from the next. The **\N** specifies a null value. The file is not terminated with a NEWLINE; if it were, MariaDB would insert a row of NULLs. Unlike in interactive mode, when you run MariaDB from a command file, it does not display a message if everything worked properly. You can use the **–v** (verbose) option to cause MariaDB to display information about the commands it is executing. Multiple **–v** options display more information.

To run SQL commands from a file, enter the command **mysql** and redirect input to come from the command file. The following **mysql** command uses two **–v** options so MariaDB displays statements as it executes them and results of statements after it executes them; input is redirected to come from **load.**

```
$ cat load
USE maxdb;

LOAD DATA LOCAL INFILE '/home/max/addfile'
        INTO TABLE people;

$ cat addfile
max     \N      4       0
zach    09-03-24        6       0
sam     2008-01-28      6       1

$ mysql -vv < load
--------------
LOAD DATA LOCAL INFILE '/home/max/addfile'
        INTO TABLE people
--------------

Query OK, 3 rows affected
Records: 3  Deleted: 0  Skipped: 0  Warnings: 0

Bye
```

RETRIEVING DATA

SELECT The SELECT statement queries the database and displays the data the query returns. Within a SELECT statement, SQL interprets an asterisk (*) to mean all columns in a table. The following interactive query displays all columns of all rows of the **people** table in the **maxdb** database.

```
$ mysql
MariaDB [(none)]> USE maxdb;
MariaDB [(maxdb)]> SELECT       *
    ->          FROM    people;
+--------+------------+-------+--------+
| name   | hired      | store | hourly |
+--------+------------+-------+--------+
| topsy  | 2012-11-01 |     4 |      0 |
| percy  | NULL       |     2 |      1 |
| bailey | NULL       |     2 |      1 |
| max    | NULL       |     4 |      0 |
| zach   | 2009-03-24 |     6 |      0 |
| sam    | 2008-01-28 |     6 |      1 |
+--------+------------+-------+--------+
6 rows in set (0.00 sec)
```

When you run queries from a command file, MariaDB does not line up in columns the data it outputs, but rather simply separates each column from the next using a TAB. This minimal formatting allows you to redirect and format the output as you please. Typically, if you want to redirect the data, you will not specify any **–v** options so MariaDB does not display any messages. The next command includes an ORDER BY clause in the SELECT statement to sort the output. It uses the **sel2** command file and sends the output through tail to strip out the header.

```
$ cat sel2
use maxdb;
SELECT          *
        FROM    people
        ORDER BY name;

$ mysql < sel2 | tail -n +2
bailey  NULL    2       1
max     NULL    4       0
percy   NULL    2       1
sam     2008-01-28      6       1
topsy   2012-11-01      4       0
zach    2009-03-24      6       0
```

WHERE The next example shows a SELECT statement with a WHERE clause. A WHERE clause causes SELECT to return only those rows that match specified criteria. In this example, the WHERE clause causes SELECT to return only rows in which the value in the **store** column is 4. In addition, this SELECT statement returns a single column (**name**). The result is a list of the names of the people who work in store number 4.

```
MariaDB [(maxdb)]> SELECT         name
    ->             FROM    people
    ->             WHERE   store = 4;
+-------+
| name  |
+-------+
| topsy |
| max   |
+-------+
2 rows in set (0.00 sec)
```

The next example shows the use of a relational operator in a WHERE clause. In this case, the SELECT statement returns the names of people who work in stores with numbers greater than 2.

```
MariaDB [(maxdb)]> SELECT         name
    ->             FROM    people
    ->             WHERE   store > 2;
+-------+
| name  |
+-------+
| topsy |
| max   |
| zach  |
| sam   |
+-------+
4 rows in set (0.00 sec)
```

LIKE You can also use the LIKE operator in a WHERE clause. LIKE causes SELECT to return rows in which a column contains a specified string. Within the string that follows LIKE, a percent sign (%) matches any string of zero or more characters and an underscore (_) matches any single character. The following query returns rows in which the **name** column contains the letter **m**.

```
MariaDB [(maxdb)]> SELECT         name,
    ->                     store
    ->             FROM    people
    ->             WHERE   name LIKE '%m%';
+------+-------+
| name | store |
+------+-------+
| max  |     4 |
| sam  |     6 |
+------+-------+
2 rows in set (0.00 sec)
```

BACKING UP A DATABASE

mysqldump The mysqldump utility can back up and restore a database. Backing up a database generates a file of SQL statements that create the tables and load the data. You can then use this file to restore the database from scratch. The next example shows how Max can back up the **maxdb** database to a file named **maxdb.bkup.sql**.

```
$ mysqldump -u max -p maxdb > maxdb.bkup.sql
Enter password:
```

Be careful: The following restore procedure will overwrite an existing database. Before you can restore a database, you must create the database as explained on page 618. After creating the **maxdb** database, Max runs MariaDB with input coming from the file that mysqldump created. When he gives the following command, the **maxdb** database is in the same state it was in when Max backed it up.

```
$ mysql -u max -p maxdb < maxdb.bkup.sql
Enter password:
```

MODIFYING DATA

DELETE FROM The DELETE FROM statement removes one or more rows from a table. The next example deletes the rows from the **people** table where the **name** column holds **bailey** or **percy**.

```
MariaDB [(maxdb)]> DELETE FROM     people
    ->            WHERE   name='bailey'
    ->                    OR name='percy';
Query OK, 2 rows affected (0.00 sec)
```

UPDATE The UPDATE statement changes data in a table. The following example sets the **hourly** column to **TRUE** (**1**) in the rows where the **name** column contains **sam** or **topsy**. The MariaDB messages show the query matched two rows (**sam** and **topsy**) but changed only one row. It changed **hourly** in the row with **topsy**; in the row with **sam**, **hourly** was already set to **TRUE**.

```
MariaDB [(maxdb)]> UPDATE          people
    ->            SET     hourly = TRUE
    ->            WHERE   name = 'sam' OR
    ->                    name = 'topsy';
Query OK, 1 row affected (0.00 sec)
Rows matched: 2  Changed: 1  Warnings: 0
```

CURDATE() The CURDATE() function returns today's date. The next example sets the **hired** column to today's date in the row where **name** contains **max**.

```
MariaDB [(maxdb)]> UPDATE          people
    ->            SET     hired = CURDATE()
    ->            WHERE name = 'max';
Query OK, 1 row affected (0.00 sec)
Rows matched: 1  Changed: 1  Warnings: 0
```

The next query shows the results of the preceding DELETE FROM and UPDATE statements.

```
MariaDB [(maxdb)]> select * from people;
+-------+------------+-------+--------+
| name  | hired      | store | hourly |
+-------+------------+-------+--------+
| topsy | 2012-11-01 |     4 |      1 |
| max   | 2012-02-12 |     4 |      0 |
| zach  | 2009-03-24 |     6 |      0 |
| sam   | 2008-01-28 |     6 |      1 |
+-------+------------+-------+--------+
4 rows in set (0.00 sec)
```

CREATING A SECOND TABLE

The **setup.stores** SQL command file creates, populates, and displays the **stores** table in the **maxdb** database.

```
$ mysql -vv < setup.stores
--------------
CREATE TABLE    stores (
                name VARCHAR(20),
                number INTEGER,
                city VARCHAR(20)
                )
--------------

Query OK, 0 rows affected

--------------
INSERT INTO     stores
        VALUES  ( 'headquarters', 4, 'new york' ),
                ( 'midwest', 5, 'chicago' ),
                ( 'west coast', 6, 'san francisco' )
--------------

Query OK, 3 rows affected
Records: 3  Duplicates: 0  Warnings: 0

--------------
SELECT          *
        FROM    stores
--------------

name    number  city
headquarters    4       new york
midwest 5       chicago
west coast      6       san francisco
3 rows in set
```

VARCHAR The **stores** table contains columns named **name**, **number**, and **city**. The data type for the **name** and **city** columns is VARCHAR. A VARCHAR column stores a variable-length string without the padding required by a CHAR column. In this example, the **name** and **city** columns can store up to 20 characters each.

The size of a VARCHAR is the sum of the length prefix plus the number of characters in the string being stored. The length prefix for a column declared to hold fewer than 255 characters is 1 byte; larger columns have a 2-byte length prefix. In contrast, a CHAR column always occupies the number of characters it was declared to be.

The number in parentheses in a VARCHAR declaration specifies the maximum number of characters any row in the column can hold. In the example, the **city** column is declared to be VARCHAR(20) so a row in that column cannot hold more than 20 characters. The row with **new york** in the **city** column takes up 9 bytes of storage (8 + 1). If the column had been declared to be CHAR(20), each row would occupy 20 bytes, regardless of the length of the string it holds.

JOINS

A join operation combines rows from or across two or more related tables in a database according to some relationship between these tables. (Refer to the discussion of the join utility [page 863] for information on joining text files from the command line.) As an example, consider the **maxdb** database: The **people** table has columns that hold information about employee name, hire date, store at which the employee works, and whether the employee is paid on an hourly basis (as opposed to salaried); the **stores** table has columns that hold information about the store name, number, and city in which it is located. With this setup, you cannot determine which city an employee works in by querying either the **people** or **stores** table alone; you must join the tables to get this information.

You join tables using a SELECT statement that specifies a column in each of the tables and the relationship between those columns. The query that would satisfy the example specifies the **store** column in the **people** table and the **number** column in the **stores** table; the relationship between those columns is equality because both of those columns hold the store number. When you equate like values in these columns, you can display **stores** information for each **name** in the **people** table (or **people** information for each [store] **number** in the **stores** table).

The following query selects rows from the **people** and **stores** tables and joins the rows where the value of **store** in the **people** table equals the value of **number** in the **stores** table (**store = number**). This query uses an implicit join; it does not use the JOIN keyword. The examples following this one use JOIN. Using this keyword makes no difference in the results of the query, but you must use JOIN in certain types of queries.

```
MariaDB [(maxdb)]> SELECT        *
    ->            FROM    people, stores
    ->            WHERE   store = number;
```

```
+-------+------------+-------+--------+--------------+--------+---------------+
| name  | hired      | store | hourly | name         | number | city          |
+-------+------------+-------+--------+--------------+--------+---------------+
| topsy | 2012-11-01 |     4 |      1 | headquarters |      4 | new york      |
| max   | 2012-02-12 |     4 |      0 | headquarters |      4 | new york      |
| zach  | 2009-03-24 |     6 |      0 | west coast   |      6 | san francisco |
| sam   | 2008-01-28 |     6 |      1 | west coast   |      6 | san francisco |
+-------+------------+-------+--------+--------------+--------+---------------+
4 rows in set (0.00 sec)
```

Inner join The preceding query demonstrates an *inner join*. If you like, you can use the keywords INNER JOIN in place of JOIN in this type of query. In each returned row, the value in **people.store** equals the value in **stores.number**. However, the **stores** table has a row with the value of 5 in the **number** column but no row exists in the **people** table with this value in the **store** column. As a result, these queries do not return a row with **people.store** and **stores.number** equal to 5.

Table names When working with a relational database, you can refer to a column in a specific table as **table_name.column_name** (e.g., **stores.name** in the example database). While you are working with a single table, a column name is sufficient to uniquely identify the data you want to work with. When you work with several tables, however, you might need to specify both a table name and a column name to uniquely identify certain data. Specifically, if two columns have the same name in two tables that are being joined, you must specify both the table and the column to disambiguate the columns. The following query demonstrates the problem.

```
MariaDB [(maxdb)]> SELECT         *
    ->          FROM    people, stores
    ->          WHERE   name = 'max';
ERROR 1052 (23000): Column 'name' in where clause is ambiguous
```

In the preceding query, the column **name** is ambiguous: A column named **name** exists in both the **people** and **stores** tables. MariaDB cannot determine which table to use in the WHERE clause. The next query solves this problem. It uses **people.name** in the WHERE clause to specify that MariaDB should use the **name** column from the **people** table.

```
MariaDB [(maxdb)]> SELECT         *
    ->          FROM    people, stores
->          WHERE   people.name = 'max';
+------+------------+-------+--------+--------------+--------+----------+
| name | hired      | store | hourly | name         | number | city     |
+------+------------+-------+--------+--------------+--------+----------+
| max  | 2012-05-01 |     4 |      0 | headquarters |      4 | new york |
+------+------------+-------+--------+--------------+--------+----------+
1 row in set (0.01 sec)
```

Even though it might not be necessary, it can make code and comments clearer to specify both a table and a column as in the following examples.

Table aliases An alias for a table is another, usually shorter, name for the table. Aliases can make a SELECT statement easier to read. You declare table aliases in the FROM clause of a query. For example, the following clause declares **p** to be an alias for the **people** table and **s** to be an alias for the **stores** table.

```
FROM    people p JOIN stores s
```

With these aliases in place, you can refer to the **people** table as **p** and the **stores** table as **s** in the rest of the query.

The next example rewrites an earlier query using aliases and the JOIN keyword. In place of a comma between the table (and alias) names, this syntax uses the keyword JOIN. In place of WHERE, it uses ON. Specifying **p.store** and **s.number** makes it clear that the **store** column of the **people** table (**p.store**) is being joined with the **number** column of the **stores** table (**s.number**). This query returns the same results as the preceding one.

```
SELECT          *
        FROM    people p JOIN stores s
        ON      p.store = s.number;
```

Outer join An *outer join* can return rows in which the common column has a value that does not exist in both tables. You can specify a LEFT OUTER JOIN (or just LEFT JOIN) or a RIGHT OUTER JOIN (or just RIGHT JOIN). Left and right refer to the tables specified on the left and right of the keyword JOIN, respectively.

The next example demonstrates a right outer join. The outer table is **stores**, which has a value in the **number** column that does not have a match in the **store** column of the **people** table. SQL inserts null values in the columns from **people** in the joined row that does not have a match (**stores.number** = 5).

```
MariaDB [(maxdb)]> SELECT          *
    ->             FROM    people p RIGHT JOIN stores s
    ->             ON      p.store = s.number;
+-------+------------+-------+--------+--------------+--------+---------------+
| name  | hired      | store | hourly | name         | number | city          |
+-------+------------+-------+--------+--------------+--------+---------------+
| topsy | 2012-11-01 |     4 |      1 | headquarters |      4 | new york      |
| max   | 2012-02-12 |     4 |      0 | headquarters |      4 | new york      |
| NULL  | NULL       |  NULL |   NULL | midwest      |      5 | chicago       |
| zach  | 2009-03-24 |     6 |      0 | west coast   |      6 | san francisco |
| sam   | 2008-01-28 |     6 |      1 | west coast   |      6 | san francisco |
+-------+------------+-------+--------+--------------+--------+---------------+
5 rows in set (0.00 sec)
```

The following query performs an inner join to list the city in which each person works. A right outer join would show the cities that have no one working in them. A left outer join would show people who are not assigned to a store.

```
MariaDB [(maxdb)]> SELECT          p.name,
    ->                     city
    ->             FROM    people p JOIN stores s
    ->             ON      p.store = s.number;
```

```
+-------+---------------+
| name  | city          |
+-------+---------------+
| topsy | new york      |
| max   | new york      |
| zach  | san francisco |
| sam   | san francisco |
+-------+---------------+
4 rows in set (0.00 sec)
```

Subqueries A subquery is a SELECT statement within the WHERE clause of another SELECT statement. The subquery returns a value or values that restrict the main query.

In the next example, the subquery returns the value of the **number** column from the **stores** table where the **city** column has a value of **new york**. The main query returns the value(s) from the **name** column of the **people** table where the value of the **store** column is equal to the value returned by the subquery. The result is a query that returns the names of people who work in New York.

```
$ cat sel4
use maxdb;

SELECT          name
        FROM    people
        WHERE   store =
       (SELECT          number
                FROM    stores
                WHERE   city = 'new york'
       );

$ mysql < sel4
name
topsy
max
```

The final example is a bash script that queries the MariaDB database created in this chapter. If you have not run the example commands, it will not work. First the script checks that the user knows the database password. Then it displays a list of employees and asks which employee the user is interested in. It queries the database for information about that employee and displays the name of the store the employee works in and the city the store is located in.

```
$ cat employee_info
#! /bin/bash

#
# Script to display employee information
#

# Make sure user is authorized: Get database password
#
echo -n "Enter password for maxdb database: "
stty -echo
read pw
```

```
stty echo
echo
echo

# Check for valid password
#
mysql -u max -p$pw maxdb > /dev/null 2>&1 < /dev/null
if [ $? -ne 0 ]
    then
        echo "Bad password."
        exit 1
fi

# Display list of employees for user to select from
#
echo "The following people are employed by the company:"
mysql -u max -p$pw --skip-column-names maxdb <<+
SELECT name FROM people ORDER BY name;
+
echo
echo -n "Which employee would you like information about? "
read emp

# Query for store name
#
storename=$(mysql -u max -p$pw --skip-column-names maxdb <<+
SELECT stores.name FROM people, stores WHERE store = number AND people.name = "$emp";
+
)

# If null, the user entered a bad employee name
#
if [ "$storename" = "" ]
    then
        echo "Not a valid name."
        exit 1
fi

# Query for city name
#
storecity=$(mysql -u max -p$pw --skip-column-names maxdb <<+
SELECT city FROM people, stores WHERE store = number AND people.name = "$emp";
+
)

# Display report
#
echo
echo $emp works at the $storename store in $storecity
```

Chapter Summary

System administrators are frequently called upon to set up and run MariaDB databases. MariaDB/MySQL is the world's most popular open-source relational database management system (RDBMS). It is extremely fast and is used by some of the most frequently visited Web sites on the Internet. Many programming languages provide interfaces and bindings to MariaDB, including C, PHP, Python, and Perl. You can also call MariaDB directly from a shell script or use it in a pipeline on the command line. MariaDB is a core component of the popular LAMP (Linux, Apache, MariaDB, PHP/Perl/Python) open-source enterprise software stack.

Exercises

1. List two ways you can specify the MariaDB password for a user so as to access MariaDB.
2. Using MariaDB interactively, create a database named **dbsam** that the user named **sam** can modify and grant privileges on. Set up Sam's password to be **porcupine**. The MariaDB user named **root** has the password **five22four**.
3. What is a table? A row? A column?
4. Which commands would you use to set up a table in **dbsam** (created in exercise 2) named **shoplist** with the following columns of the specified types: **day** [DATE], **store** [CHAR(20)], **lettuce** [SMALLINT], **soupkind** [CHAR(20)], **soupnum** [INTEGER], and **misc** [VARCHAR(40)]?
5. Where can you find a list of MariaDB commands you have previously run?
6. List two ways you can specify the name of a specific MariaDB database to work with.
7. What does a join do? When is a join useful?
8. Assume you are working with the **people** table in the **maxdb** database described in this chapter. Write a query that lists the names of all the people and their hire dates sorted by their names.
9. Assume you are working with the **people** and **stores** tables in the **maxdb** database described in this chapter. Write a query that sets up the aliases **q** and **n** for the **people** and **stores** tables, respectively. Have the query join the tables using the **store** column in the **people** table with the **number** column in the **stores** table. From left to right, have the query display the name of the city in which the person works, the name of the person, and the person's hire date. Sort the output by city name.

14

The AWK Pattern Processing Language

In This Chapter

Objectives

After reading this chapter you should be able to:

- Run a gawk program from the command line and from a file
- Select lines from a file using gawk
- Write a report using gawk
- Summarize information in a file using gawk
- Write an interactive shell script that calls gawk

AWK is a pattern-scanning and processing language that searches one or more files for records (usually lines) that match specified patterns. It processes lines by performing actions, such as writing the record to standard output or incrementing a counter, each time it finds a match. Unlike *procedural* languages, AWK is *data driven*: You describe the data you want to work with and tell AWK what to do with the data once it finds it.

You can use AWK to generate reports or filter text. It works equally well with numbers and text; when you mix the two, AWK usually comes up with the right answer. The authors of AWK (Alfred V. Aho, Peter J. Weinberger, and Brian W. Kernighan) designed the language to be easy to use. To achieve this end they sacrificed execution speed in the original implementation.

AWK takes many of its constructs from the C programming language. It includes the following features:

- A flexible format
- Conditional execution
- Looping statements
- Numeric variables
- String variables
- Regular expressions
- Relational expressions
- C's **printf**
- Coprocess execution (gawk only)
- Network data exchange (gawk only)

Syntax

A gawk command line has the following syntax:

*gawk [**options**] [**program**] [**file-list**]*
*gawk [**options**] –f **program-file** [**file-list**]*

The gawk utility takes its input from files you specify on the command line or from standard input. An advanced command, **getline**, gives you more choices about where input comes from and how gawk reads it (page 662). Using a coprocess, gawk can interact with another program or exchange data over a network (page 665; not available under awk or mawk). Output from gawk goes to standard output.

Arguments

In the preceding syntax, ***program*** is a gawk program that you include on the command line. The ***program-file*** is the name of the file that holds a gawk program. Putting the program on the command line allows you to write short gawk programs without having to create a separate ***program-file.*** To prevent the shell from interpreting the gawk commands as shell commands, enclose the ***program*** within single quotation marks. Putting a long or complex program in a file can reduce errors and retyping.

The ***file-list*** contains the pathnames of the ordinary files that gawk processes. These files are the input files. When you do not specify a ***file-list,*** gawk takes input from standard input or as specified by **getline** (page 662) or a coprocess (page 665).

AWK has many implementations

tip The AWK language was originally implemented under UNIX as the awk utility. Most Linux distributions provide gawk (the GNU implementation of awk) or mawk (a faster, stripped-down version of awk). macOS provides awk. This chapter describes gawk. All the examples in this chapter work under awk and mawk except as noted; the exceptions make use of coprocesses (page 665). You can easily install gawk on most Linux distributions. See page 1077 if you want to install gawk on macOS. For a complete list of gawk extensions, see **GNU EXTENSIONS** in the gawk man page or see the gawk info page.

OPTIONS

Options preceded by a double hyphen (––) work under gawk only. They are not available under awk and mawk.

––field-separator *fs*

–F *fs*

Uses *fs* as the value of the input field separator (**FS** variable; page 640).

––file *program-file*

–f *program-file*

Reads the gawk program from the file named ***program-file*** instead of the command line. You can specify this option more than once on a command line. See page 649 for examples.

––help –W help

Summarizes how to use gawk (gawk only).

––lint –W lint

Warns about gawk constructs that might not be correct or portable (gawk only).

––posix –W posix

Runs a POSIX-compliant version of gawk. This option introduces some restrictions; see the gawk man page for details (gawk only).

––traditional –W traditional

Ignores the new GNU features in a gawk program, making the program conform to UNIX awk (gawk only).

––assign *var=value*

–v *var=value*

Assigns ***value*** to the variable ***var.*** The assignment takes place prior to execution of the gawk program and is available within the **BEGIN** pattern (page 639). You can specify this option more than once on a command line.

NOTES

See the tip on the previous page for information on AWK implementations.

For convenience many Linux systems provide a link from **/bin/awk** to **/bin/gawk** or **/bin/mawk**. As a result you can run the program using either name.

LANGUAGE BASICS

A gawk program (from ***program*** on the command line or from ***program-file***) consists of one or more lines containing a ***pattern*** and/or ***action*** in the following syntax:

pattern { action }

The ***pattern*** selects lines from the input. The gawk utility performs the ***action*** on all lines that the ***pattern*** selects. The braces surrounding the ***action*** enable gawk to differentiate it from the ***pattern***. If a program line does not contain a ***pattern***, gawk selects all lines in the input. If a program line does not contain an ***action***, gawk copies the selected lines to standard output.

To start, gawk compares the first line of input (from the ***file-list*** or standard input) with each ***pattern*** in the program. If a ***pattern*** selects the line (if there is a match), gawk takes the ***action*** associated with the ***pattern***. If the line is not selected, gawk does not take the ***action***. When gawk has completed its comparisons for the first line of input, it repeats the process for the next line of input. It continues this process of comparing subsequent lines of input until it has read all of the input.

If several ***patterns*** select the same line, gawk takes the ***actions*** associated with each of the ***patterns*** in the order in which they appear in the program. It is possible for gawk to send a single line from the input to standard output more than once.

PATTERNS

~ and !~ You can use a regular expression (Appendix A), enclosed within slashes, as a ***pattern***. The ~ operator tests whether a field or variable matches a regular expression (examples on page 647). The !~ operator tests for no match. You can perform both numeric and string comparisons using the relational operators listed in Table 14-1. You can combine any of the ***patterns*** using the Boolean operators || (OR) or && (AND).

Table 14-1 Relational operators

Relational operator	Meaning
<	Less than
<=	Less than or equal to
==	Equal to

Table 14-1 Relational operators (continued)

Relational operator	Meaning
!=	Not equal to
>=	Greater than or equal to
>	Greater than

BEGIN and **END** Two unique *patterns*, **BEGIN** and **END**, execute commands before gawk starts processing the input and after it finishes processing the input. The gawk utility executes the *actions* associated with the **BEGIN** *pattern* before, and with the **END** *pattern* after, it processes all the input. See pages 649 and 651 for examples.

, (comma) The comma is the range operator. If you separate two *patterns* with a comma on a single gawk program line, gawk selects a range of lines, beginning with the first line that matches the first *pattern*. The last line selected by gawk is the next subsequent line that matches the second *pattern*. If no line matches the second *pattern*, gawk selects every line through the end of the input. After gawk finds the second *pattern*, it begins the process again by looking for the first *pattern* again. See page 648 for examples.

ACTIONS

The *action* portion of a gawk command causes gawk to take that *action* when it matches a *pattern*. When you do not specify an *action*, gawk performs the default *action*, which is the **print** command (explicitly represented as {**print**}). This *action* copies the record (normally a line; see "Record separators" on page 640) from the input to standard output.

When you follow a **print** command with arguments, gawk displays only the arguments you specify. These arguments can be variables or string constants. You can send the output from a **print** command to a file (use > within the gawk program; page 653), append it to a file (>>), or send it through a pipeline to the input of another program (|). A coprocess (|&) is a two-way pipe that exchanges data with a program running in the background (available under gawk only; page 665).

Unless you separate items in a **print** command with commas, gawk catenates them. Commas cause gawk to separate the items with the output field separator (**OFS**, normally a SPACE; page 640).

You can include several *actions* on one line by separating them with semicolons.

COMMENTS

The gawk utility disregards anything on a program line following a pound sign (#). You can document a gawk program by preceding comments with this symbol.

VARIABLES

Although you do not need to declare gawk variables prior to their use, you can assign initial values to them if you like. Unassigned numeric variables are initialized to 0;

string variables are initialized to the null string. In addition to supporting user variables, gawk maintains program variables. You can use both user and program variables in the *pattern* and *action* portions of a gawk program. Table 14-2 lists a few program variables.

Table 14-2 Variables

Variable	Meaning
$0	The current record (as a single variable)
$1–$*n*	Fields in the current record
FILENAME	Name of the current input file (null for standard input)
FS	Input field separator (default: SPACE or TAB; page 654)
NF	Number of fields in the current record (page 659)
NR	Record number of the current record (page 650)
OFS	Output field separator (default: SPACE; page 652)
ORS	Output record separator (default: NEWLINE; page 659)
RS	Input record separator (default: NEWLINE)

In addition to initializing variables within a program, you can use the **––assign** (**–v**) option to initialize variables on the command line. This feature is useful when the value of a variable changes from one run of gawk to the next.

Record separators By default the input and output record separators are NEWLINE characters. Thus gawk takes each line of input to be a separate record and appends a NEWLINE to the end of each output record. By default the input field separators are SPACEs and TABs; the default output field separator is a SPACE. You can change the value of any of the separators at any time by assigning a new value to its associated variable either from within the program or from the command line by using the **––assign** (**–v**) option.

FUNCTIONS

Table 14-3 lists a few of the functions gawk provides for manipulating numbers and strings.

Table 14-3 Functions

Function	Meaning
length(*str*)	Returns the number of characters in ***str***; without an argument, returns the number of characters in the current record (page 650)
int(*num*)	Returns the integer portion of ***num***
index(*str1*,*str2*)	Returns the index of ***str2*** in ***str1*** or 0 if ***str2*** is not present
split(*str*,*arr*,*del*)	Places elements of ***str***, delimited by ***del***, in the array ***arr***[1]...***arr***[***n***]; returns the number of elements in the array (page 660)

Table 14-3 Functions (continued)

Function	Meaning
sprintf(*fmt,args*)	Formats ***args*** according to ***fmt*** and returns the formatted string; mimics the C programming language function of the same name; see also **printf** on page 642
substr(*str,pos,len*)	Returns the substring of ***str*** that begins at ***pos*** and is ***len*** characters long
tolower(*str*)	Returns a copy of ***str*** in which all uppercase letters are replaced with their lowercase counterparts
toupper(*str*)	Returns a copy of ***str*** in which all lowercase letters are replaced with their uppercase counterparts

ARITHMETIC OPERATORS

The gawk arithmetic operators listed in Table 14-4 are from the C programming language.

Table 14-4 Arithmetic operators

Operator	Meaning
**	Raises the expression preceding the operator to the power of the expression following it
*	Multiplies the expression preceding the operator by the expression following it
/	Divides the expression preceding the operator by the expression following it
%	Takes the remainder after dividing the expression preceding the operator by the expression following it
+	Adds the expression preceding the operator to the expression following it
–	Subtracts the expression following the operator from the expression preceding it
=	Assigns the value of the expression following the operator to the variable preceding it
++	Increments the variable preceding the operator
––	Decrements the variable preceding the operator
+=	Adds the expression following the operator to the variable preceding it and assigns the result to the variable preceding the operator
–=	Subtracts the expression following the operator from the variable preceding it and assigns the result to the variable preceding the operator
*=	Multiplies the variable preceding the operator by the expression following it and assigns the result to the variable preceding the operator
/=	Divides the variable preceding the operator by the expression following it and assigns the result to the variable preceding the operator

Table 14-4 Arithmetic operators

Operator	Meaning
%=	Assigns the remainder, after dividing the variable preceding the operator by the expression following it, to the variable preceding the operator

ASSOCIATIVE ARRAYS

The *associative array* is one of gawk's most powerful features. These arrays use strings as indexes. Using an associative array, you can mimic a traditional array by using numeric strings as indexes. In Perl, an associative array is called a *hash* (page 544).

You assign a value to an element of an associative array using the syntax

array[string] = ***value***

where ***array*** is the name of the array, ***string*** is the index of the element of the array you are assigning a value to, and ***value*** is the value you are assigning to that element.

Using the following syntax, you can use a **for** structure with an associative array:

*for (**elem** in **array**) **action***

where ***elem*** is a variable that takes on the value of each element of the array as the **for** structure loops through them, ***array*** is the name of the array, and ***action*** is the action that gawk takes for each element in the array. You can use the ***elem*** variable in this ***action***.

See page 655 for example programs that use associative arrays.

printf

You can use the **printf** command in place of **print** to control the format of the output gawk generates. See the printf utility on page 942 for more information on using **printf**. (The gawk **printf** requires the commas shown in the following syntax, whereas the printf utility does not allow them.) A **printf** command has the syntax

*printf "**control-string**", **arg1**, **arg2**, ..., **argn***

The ***control-string*** determines how **printf** formats ***arg1***, ***arg2***, ..., ***argn***. These arguments can be variables or other expressions. Within the ***control-string*** you can use **\n** to indicate a NEWLINE and **\t** to indicate a TAB. The ***control-string*** contains conversion specifications, one for each argument. A conversion specification has the syntax

*%[–][x[.y]]**conv***

where – causes **printf** to left-justify the argument, *x* is the minimum field width, and *.y* is the number of places to the right of a decimal point in a number. The ***conv*** indicates the type of numeric conversion and can be selected from the letters in Table 14-5. See page 652 for example programs that use **printf**.

Table 14-5 Numeric conversion

conv	Type of conversion
d	Decimal
e	Exponential notation
f	Floating-point number
conv	**Type of conversion**
g	Use **f** or **e**, whichever is shorter
o	Unsigned octal
s	String of characters
x	Unsigned hexadecimal

CONTROL STRUCTURES

Control (flow) statements alter the order of execution of commands within a gawk program. This section details the **if...else**, **while**, and **for** control structures. In addition, the **break** and **continue** statements work in conjunction with the control structures to alter the order of execution of commands. See page 430 for more information on control structures. You do not need to use braces around ***commands*** when you specify a single, simple command.

if...else

The **if...else** control structure tests the status returned by the ***condition*** and transfers control based on this status. The syntax of an **if...else** structure is shown below. The **else** part is optional.

*if (**condition**)*
*{**commands**}*
[else
*{**commands**}]*

The simple **if** statement shown here does not use braces:

```
if ($5 <= 5000) print $0
```

Next is a gawk program that uses a simple **if...else** structure. Again, there are no braces.

```
$ cat if1
BEGIN   {
        nam="sam"
        if (nam == "max")
                print "nam is max"
            else
                print "nam is not max, it is", nam
        }
$ gawk -f if1
nam is not max, it is sam
```

while

The **while** structure loops through and executes the ***commands*** as long as the ***condition*** is *true*. The syntax of a **while** structure is

> *while* (***condition***)
> {***commands***}

The next gawk program uses a simple **while** structure to display powers of 2. This example uses braces because the **while** loop contains more than one statement. This program does not accept input; all processing takes place when gawk executes the statements associated with the BEGIN pattern.

```
$ cat while1
BEGIN{
    n = 1
    while (n <= 5)
        {
        print "2^" n, 2**n
        n++
        }
    }

$ gawk -f while1
1^2 2
2^2 4
3^2 8
4^2 16
5^2 32
```

for

The syntax of a **for** control structure is

> *for* (***init; condition; increment***)
> {***commands***}

A **for** structure starts by executing the ***init*** statement, which usually sets a counter to 0 or 1. It then loops through the ***commands*** as long as the ***condition*** remains *true*. After each loop it executes the ***increment*** statement. The **for1** gawk program does the same thing as the preceding **while1** program except that it uses a **for** statement, which makes the program simpler:

```
$ cat for1
BEGIN   {
        for (n=1; n <= 5; n++)
        print "2^" n, 2**n
        }

$ gawk -f for1
1^2 2
2^2 4
3^2 8
```

```
4^2 16
5^2 32
```

The gawk utility supports an alternative **for** syntax for working with associative arrays:

> *for (var in array)*
> *{commands}*

This **for** structure loops through elements of the associative array named ***array***, assigning the value of the index of each element of ***array*** to ***var*** each time through the loop. The following line of code (from the program on page 655) demonstrates a **for** structure:

```
END     {for (name in manuf) print name, manuf[name]}
```

break

The **break** statement transfers control out of a **for** or **while** loop, terminating execution of the innermost loop it appears in.

continue

The **continue** statement transfers control to the end of a **for** or **while** loop, causing execution of the innermost loop it appears in to continue with the next iteration.

EXAMPLES

cars data file

Many of the examples in this section work with the **cars** data file. From left to right, the columns in the file contain each car's make, model, year of manufacture, mileage in thousands of miles, and price. All whitespace in this file is composed of single TABs (the file does not contain any SPACEs).

```
$ cat cars
plym    fury    1970    73      2500
chevy   malibu  1999    60      3000
ford    mustang 1965    45      10000
volvo   s80     1998    102     9850
ford    thundbd 2003    15      10500
chevy   malibu  2000    50      3500
bmw     325i    1985    115     450
honda   accord  2001    30      6000
ford    taurus  2004    10      17000
toyota  rav4    2002    180     750
chevy   impala  1985    85      1550
ford    explor  2003    25      9500
```

Missing pattern

A simple gawk program is

```
{ print }
```

This program consists of one program line that is an ***action***. Because the ***pattern*** is missing, gawk selects all lines of input. When used without any arguments the **print** command displays each selected line in its entirety. This program copies the input to standard output:

```
$ gawk '{ print }' cars
plym    fury    1970    73     2500
chevy   malibu  1999    60     3000
ford    mustang 1965    45     10000
volvo   s80     1998    102    9850
...
```

Missing action The next program has a ***pattern*** but no explicit ***action.*** The slashes indicate that **chevy** is a regular expression.

```
/chevy/
```

In this case gawk selects from the input just those lines that contain the string **chevy**. When you do not specify an ***action,*** gawk assumes the ***action*** is **print**. The following example copies to standard output all lines from the input that contain the string **chevy**:

```
$ gawk '/chevy/' cars
chevy   malibu  1999    60     3000
chevy   malibu  2000    50     3500
chevy   impala  1985    85     1550
```

Single quotation marks Although neither gawk nor shell syntax requires single quotation marks on the command line, it is still a good idea to use them because they can prevent problems. If the gawk program you create on the command line includes SPACEs or characters that are special to the shell, you must quote them. Always enclosing the program in single quotation marks is the easiest way to make sure you have quoted any characters that need to be quoted.

Fields The next example selects all lines from the file (it has no ***pattern***). The braces enclose the ***action;*** you must always use braces to delimit the ***action*** so gawk can distinguish it from the ***pattern.*** This example displays the third field (**$3**), a SPACE (the output field separator, indicated by the comma), and the first field (**$1**) of each selected line:

```
$ gawk '{print $3, $1}' cars
1970 plym
1999 chevy
1965 ford
1998 volvo
...
```

The next example, which includes both a ***pattern*** and an ***action,*** selects all lines that contain the string **chevy** and displays the third and first fields from the selected lines:

```
$ gawk '/chevy/ {print $3, $1}' cars
1999 chevy
2000 chevy
1985 chevy
```

In the following example, gawk selects lines that contain a match for the regular expression **h**. Because there is no explicit *action*, gawk displays all the lines it selects.

```
$ gawk '/h/' cars
chevy   malibu  1999    60      3000
ford    thundbd 2003    15      10500
chevy   malibu  2000    50      3500
honda   accord  2001    30      6000
chevy   impala  1985    85      1550
```

~ (matches operator) The next *pattern* uses the matches operator (~) to select all lines that contain the letter **h** in the first field:

```
$ gawk '$1 ~ /h/' cars
chevy   malibu  1999    60      3000
chevy   malibu  2000    50      3500
honda   accord  2001    30      6000
chevy   impala  1985    85      1550
```

The caret (^) in a regular expression forces a match at the beginning of the line (page 1040) or, in this case, at the beginning of the first field:

```
$ gawk '$1 ~ /^h/' cars
honda   accord  2001    30      6000
```

Brackets surround a character class definition (page 1039). In the next example, gawk selects lines that have a second field that begins with **t** or **m** and displays the third and second fields, a dollar sign, and the fifth field. Because there is no comma between the "$" and the $5, gawk does not put a SPACE between them in the output.

```
$ gawk '$2 ~ /^[tm]/ {print $3, $2, "$"  $5}' cars
1999 malibu $3000
1965 mustang $10000
2003 thundbd $10500
2000 malibu $3500
2004 taurus $17000
```

Dollar signs The next example shows three roles a dollar sign can play in a gawk program. First, a dollar sign followed by a number names a field. Second, within a regular expression a dollar sign forces a match at the end of a line or field (5$). Third, within a string a dollar sign represents itself.

```
$ gawk '$3 ~ /5$/ {print $3, $1, "$"  $5}' cars
1965 ford $10000
1985 bmw $450
1985 chevy $1550
```

In the next example, the equal-to relational operator (==) causes gawk to perform a numeric comparison between the third field in each line and the number 1985. The gawk command takes the default *action*, **print**, on each line where the comparison is *true*.

```
$ gawk '$3 == 1985' cars
bmw      325i     1985     115      450
chevy    impala   1985     85       1550
```

The next example finds all cars priced at or less than $3,000:

```
$ gawk '$5 <= 3000' cars
plym     fury     1970     73       2500
chevy    malibu   1999     60       3000
bmw      325i     1985     115      450
toyota   rav4     2002     180      750
chevy    impala   1985     85       1550
```

Textual comparisons When you use double quotation marks, gawk performs textual comparisons by using the ASCII (or other local) collating sequence as the basis of the comparison. In the following example, gawk shows that the *strings* 450 and 750 fall in the range that lies between the *strings* 2000 and 9000, which is probably not the intended result.

```
$ gawk '"2000" <= $5 && $5 < "9000"' cars
plym     fury     1970     73       2500
chevy    malibu   1999     60       3000
chevy    malibu   2000     50       3500
bmw      325i     1985     115      450
honda    accord   2001     30       6000
toyota   rav4     2002     180      750
```

When you need to perform a numeric comparison, do not use quotation marks. The next example gives the intended result. It is the same as the previous example except it omits the double quotation marks.

```
$ gawk '2000 <= $5 && $5 < 9000' cars
plym     fury     1970     73       2500
chevy    malibu   1999     60       3000
chevy    malibu   2000     50       3500
honda    accord   2001     30       6000
```

, (range operator) The range operator (,) selects a group of lines. The first line it selects is the one specified by the ***pattern*** before the comma. The last line is the one selected by the ***pattern*** after the comma. If no line matches the ***pattern*** after the comma, gawk selects every line through the end of the input. The next example selects all lines, starting with the line that contains **volvo** and ending with the line that contains **bmw**:

```
$ gawk '/volvo/ , /bmw/' cars
volvo    s80      1998     102      9850
ford     thundbd  2003     15       10500
chevy    malibu   2000     50       3500
bmw      325i     1985     115      450
```

After the range operator finds its first group of lines, it begins the process again, looking for a line that matches the *pattern* before the comma. In the following example, gawk finds three groups of lines that fall between **chevy** and **ford**. Although the fifth line of input contains **ford**, gawk does not select it because at the time it is processing the fifth line, it is searching for **chevy**.

```
$ gawk '/chevy/ , /ford/' cars
chevy   malibu  1999    60      3000
ford    mustang 1965    45      10000
chevy   malibu  2000    50      3500
bmw     325i    1985    115     450
honda   accord  2001    30      6000
ford    taurus  2004    10      17000
chevy   impala  1985    85      1550
ford    explor  2003    25      9500
```

--file option When you are writing a longer gawk program, it is convenient to put the program in a file and reference the file on the command line. Use the **–f** (**––file**) option followed by the name of the file containing the gawk program.

BEGIN The following gawk program, which is stored in a file named **pr_header**, has two *actions* and uses the **BEGIN** *pattern*. The gawk utility performs the *action* associated with **BEGIN** before processing any lines of the data file: It displays a header. The second *action*, **{print}**, has no *pattern* part and displays all lines from the input.

```
$ cat pr_header
BEGIN   {print "Make    Model   Year    Miles   Price"}
        {print}

$ gawk -f pr_header cars
Make    Model   Year    Miles   Price
plym    fury    1970    73      2500
chevy   malibu  1999    60      3000
ford    mustang 1965    45      10000
volvo   s80     1998    102     9850
...
```

The next example expands the *action* associated with the **BEGIN** *pattern*. In the previous and the following examples, the whitespace in the headers is composed of single TABs, so the titles line up with the columns of data.

```
$ cat pr_header2
BEGIN   {
print "Make     Model   Year    Miles   Price"
print "----------------------------------------"
}
        {print}

$ gawk -f pr_header2 cars
Make    Model   Year    Miles   Price
----------------------------------------
```

```
plym    fury    1970    73      2500
chevy   malibu  1999    60      3000
ford    mustang 1965    45      10000
volvo   s80     1998    102     9850
...
```

length function When you call the **length** function without an argument, it returns the number of characters in the current line, including field separators. The **$0** variable always contains the value of the current line. In the next example, gawk prepends the line length to each line and then a pipeline sends the output from gawk to sort (using the **–n** option specifies a numeric sort; page 969). As a result, the lines of the **cars** file appear in order of line length.

```
$ gawk '{print length, $0}' cars | sort -n
21 bmw  325i    1985    115     450
22 plym fury    1970    73      2500
23 volvo        s80     1998    102     9850
24 ford explor  2003    25      9500
24 toyota       rav4    2002    180     750
25 chevy        impala  1985    85      1550
25 chevy        malibu  1999    60      3000
25 chevy        malibu  2000    50      3500
25 ford taurus  2004    10      17000
25 honda        accord  2001    30      6000
26 ford mustang 1965    45      10000
26 ford thundbd 2003    15      10500
```

The formatting of this report depends on TABs for horizontal alignment. The three extra characters at the beginning of each line throw off the format of several lines; a remedy for this situation is covered shortly.

NR (record number) The **NR** variable contains the record (line) number of the current line. The following ***pattern*** selects all lines that contain more than 24 characters. The ***action*** displays the line number of each of the selected lines.

```
$ gawk 'length > 24 {print NR}' cars
2
3
5
6
8
9
11
```

You can combine the range operator (**,**) and the **NR** variable to display a group of lines of a file based on their line numbers. The next example displays lines 2 through 4:

```
$ gawk 'NR == 2 , NR == 4' cars
chevy   malibu  1999    60      3000
```

```
ford     mustang 1965    45      10000
volvo    s80     1998    102     9850
```

END The END *pattern* works in a manner similar to the BEGIN *pattern*, except gawk takes the *actions* associated with this pattern after processing the last line of input. The following report displays information only after it has processed all the input. The NR variable retains its value after gawk finishes processing the data file, so an *action* associated with an END *pattern* can use it.

```
$ gawk 'END {print NR, "cars for sale." }' cars
12 cars for sale.
```

The next example uses if control structures to expand the abbreviations used in some of the first fields. As long as gawk does not change a record, it leaves the entire record—including any separators—intact. Once it makes a change to a record, gawk changes all separators in that record to the value of the output field separator. The default output field separator is a SPACE.

```
$ cat separ_demo
        {
        if ($1 ~ /ply/)  $1 = "plymouth"
        if ($1 ~ /chev/) $1 = "chevrolet"
        print
        }

$ gawk -f separ_demo cars
plymouth fury 1970 73 2500
chevrolet malibu 1999 60 3000
ford     mustang 1965    45      10000
volvo    s80     1998    102     9850
ford     thundbd 2003    15      10500
chevrolet malibu 2000 50 3500
bmw      325i    1985    115     450
honda    accord  2001    30      6000
ford     taurus  2004    10      17000
toyota   rav4    2002    180     750
chevrolet impala 1985 85 1550
ford     explor  2003    25      9500
```

Stand-alone script Instead of calling gawk from the command line with the –f option and the name of the program you want to run, you can write a script that calls gawk with the commands you want to run. The next example is a stand-alone script that runs the same program as the previous example. The **#!/bin/gawk –f** command (page 297) runs the gawk utility directly. To execute it, you need both read and execute permission to the file holding the script (page 295).

```
$ chmod u+rx separ_demo2
$ cat separ_demo2
#!/bin/gawk -f
        {
        if ($1 ~ /ply/)  $1 = "plymouth"
```

```
        if ($1 ~ /chev/) $1 = "chevrolet"
        print
        }

$ ./separ_demo2 cars
plymouth fury 1970 73 2500
chevrolet malibu 1999 60 3000
ford    mustang 1965    45      10000
...
```

OFS variable You can change the value of the output field separator by assigning a value to the **OFS** variable. The following example assigns a TAB character to **OFS**, using the backslash escape sequence **\t**. This fix improves the appearance of the report but does not line up the columns properly.

```
$ cat ofs_demo
BEGIN   {OFS = "\t"}
        {
        if ($1 ~ /ply/)  $1 = "plymouth"
        if ($1 ~ /chev/) $1 = "chevrolet"
        print
        }

$ gawk -f ofs_demo cars
plymouth        fury    1970    73      2500
chevrolet       malibu  1999    60      3000
ford    mustang 1965    45      10000
volvo   s80     1998    102     9850
ford    thundbd 2003    15      10500
chevrolet       malibu  2000    50      3500
bmw     325i    1985    115     450
honda   accord  2001    30      6000
ford    taurus  2004    10      17000
toyota  rav4    2002    180     750
chevrolet       impala  1985    85      1550
ford    explor  2003    25      9500
```

printf You can use **printf** (page 642) to refine the output format. The following example uses a backslash at the end of two program lines to quote the following NEWLINE. You can use this technique to continue a long line over one or more lines without affecting the outcome of the program.

```
$ cat printf_demo
BEGIN   {
    print "                                         Miles"
    print "Make        Model        Year        (000)        Price"
    print \
    "----------------------------------------------------"
    }
    {
    if ($1 ~ /ply/)  $1 = "plymouth"
```

```
    if ($1 ~ /chev/) $1 = "chevrolet"
    printf "%-10s %-8s    %2d   %5d     $ %8.2f\n",\
        $1, $2, $3, $4, $5
    }
```

```
$ gawk -f printf_demo cars
                                       Miles
Make        Model        Year          (000)         Price
---------------------------------------------------------
plymouth    fury         1970          73     $  2500.00
chevrolet   malibu       1999          60     $  3000.00
ford        mustang      1965          45     $ 10000.00
volvo       s80          1998         102     $  9850.00
ford        thundbd      2003          15     $ 10500.00
chevrolet   malibu       2000          50     $  3500.00
bmw         325i         1985         115     $   450.00
honda       accord       2001          30     $  6000.00
ford        taurus       2004          10     $ 17000.00
toyota      rav4         2002         180     $   750.00
chevrolet   impala       1985          85     $  1550.00
ford        explor       2003          25     $  9500.00
```

Redirecting output The next example creates two files: one with the lines that contain **chevy** and one with the lines that contain **ford**.

```
$ cat redirect_out
/chevy/     {print > "chevfile"}
/ford/      {print > "fordfile"}
END         {print "done."}

$ gawk -f redirect_out cars
done.

$ cat chevfile
chevy   malibu  1999    60      3000
chevy   malibu  2000    50      3500
chevy   impala  1985    85      1550
```

The **summary** program produces a summary report on all cars and newer cars. Although they are not required, the initializations at the beginning of the program represent good programming practice; gawk automatically declares and initializes variables as you use them. After reading all the input data, gawk computes and displays the averages.

```
$ cat summary
BEGIN   {
        yearsum = 0 ; costsum = 0
        newcostsum = 0 ; newcount = 0
        }
        {
        yearsum += $3
```

```
        costsum += $5
        }
$3 > 2000 {newcostsum += $5 ; newcount ++}
END     {
        printf "Average age of cars is %4.1f years\n",\
            2006 - (yearsum/NR)
        printf "Average cost of cars is $%7.2f\n",\
            costsum/NR
            printf "Average cost of newer cars is $%7.2f\n",\
                newcostsum/newcount
        }

$ gawk -f summary cars
Average age of cars is 13.1 years
Average cost of cars is $6216.67
Average cost of newer cars is $8750.00
```

The following gawk command shows the format of a line from a Linux **passwd** file that the next example uses:

```
$ gawk '/mark/ {print}' /etc/passwd
mark:x:107:100:ext 112:/home/mark:/bin/tcsh
```

FS variable The next example demonstrates a technique for finding the largest number in a field. Because it works with a Linux **passwd** file, which delimits fields with colons (**:**), the example changes the input field separator (**FS**) before reading any data. It reads the **passwd** file and determines the next available user ID number (field 3). The numbers do not have to be in order in the **passwd** file for this program to work.

The *pattern* (**$3 > saveit**) causes gawk to select records that contain a user ID number greater than any previous user ID number it has processed. Each time it selects a record, gawk assigns the value of the new user ID number to the **saveit** variable. Then gawk uses the new value of **saveit** to test the user IDs of all subsequent records. Finally, gawk adds 1 to the value of **saveit** and displays the result.

```
$ cat find_uid
BEGIN           {FS = ":"
                saveit = 0}
$3 > saveit     {saveit = $3}
END             {print "Next available UID is " saveit + 1}

$ gawk -f find_uid /etc/passwd
Next available UID is 1092
```

The next example produces another report based on the **cars** file. This report uses nested **if...else** control structures to substitute values based on the contents of the price field. The program has no *pattern* part; it processes every record.

```
$ cat price_range
    {
    if          ($5 <= 5000)                $5 = "inexpensive"
        else if (5000 < $5 && $5 < 10000)   $5 = "please ask"
        else if (10000 <= $5)               $5 = "expensive"
    #
```

```
    printf "%-10s %-8s    %2d    %5d    %-12s\n",\
    $1, $2, $3, $4, $5
    }

$ gawk -f price_range cars
plym        fury        1970       73    inexpensive
chevy       malibu      1999       60    inexpensive
ford        mustang     1965       45    expensive
volvo       s80         1998      102    please ask
ford        thundbd     2003       15    expensive
chevy       malibu      2000       50    inexpensive
bmw         325i        1985      115    inexpensive
honda       accord      2001       30    please ask
ford        taurus      2004       10    expensive
toyota      rav4        2002      180    inexpensive
chevy       impala      1985       85    inexpensive
ford        explor      2003       25    please ask
```

Associative arrays Next, the **manuf** associative array uses the contents of the first field of each record in the **cars** file as an index. The array consists of the elements **manuf[plym]**, **manuf[chevy]**, **manuf[ford]**, and so on. Each new element is initialized to 0 (zero) as it is created. The **++** operator increments the variable it follows.

for structure The *action* following the END *pattern* is a **for** structure, which loops through the elements of an associative array. A pipeline sends the output through sort to produce an alphabetical list of cars and the quantities in stock. Because it is a shell script and not a gawk program file, you must have both read and execute permission to the **manuf** file to execute it as a command.

```
$ cat manuf
gawk '  {manuf[$1]++}
END     {for (name in manuf) print name, manuf[name]}
' cars |
sort

$ ./manuf
bmw 1
chevy 3
ford 4
honda 1
plym 1
toyota 1
volvo 1
```

The next program, **manuf.sh**, is a more general shell script that includes error checking. This script lists and counts the contents of a column in a file, with both the column number and the name of the file specified on the command line.

The first *action* (the one that starts with {**count**}) uses the shell variable **$1** in the middle of the gawk program to specify an array index. Because of the way the single quotation marks are paired, the **$1** that appears to be within single quotation marks is actually not quoted: The two quoted strings in the gawk program surround, but do not include, the **$1**. Because the **$1** is not quoted, and because this is a shell script, the shell substitutes the value of the first command-line argument in place of **$1** (page 471). As a result, the **$1** is interpreted before the gawk command is invoked. The leading dollar sign (the one before the first single quotation mark on that line) causes gawk to interpret what the shell substitutes as a field number.

```
$ cat manuf.sh
if [ $# != 2 ]
    then
        echo "Usage: manuf.sh field file"
        exit 1
fi
gawk < $2 '
        {count[$'$1']++}
END     {for (item in count) printf "%-20s%-20s\n",\
            item, count[item]}' |
sort
$ ./manuf.sh
Usage: manuf.sh field file

$ ./manuf.sh 1 cars
bmw                 1
chevy               3
ford                4
honda               1
plym                1
toyota              1
volvo               1

$ ./manuf.sh 3 cars
1965                1
1970                1
1985                2
1998                1
1999                1
2000                1
2001                1
2002                1
2003                2
2004                1
```

A way around the tricky use of quotation marks that allow parameter expansion within the gawk program is to use the **–v** option on the command line to pass the field number to gawk as a variable. This change makes it easier for someone else to read and debug the script. You call the **manuf2.sh** script the same way you call **manuf.sh**:

```
$ cat manuf2.sh
if [ $# != 2 ]
        then
                echo "Usage: manuf.sh field file"
                exit 1
fi
```

```
gawk -v "field=$1" < $2 '
                {count[$field]++}
END             {for (item in count) printf "%-20s%-20s\n",\
                        item, count[item]}' |
sort
```

The **word_usage** script displays a word usage list for a file you specify on the command line. The tr utility (page 1014) lists the words from standard input, one to a line. The sort utility orders the file, putting the most frequently used words first. The script sorts groups of words that are used the same number of times in alphabetical order.

```
$ cat word_usage
tr -cs 'a-zA-Z' '[\n*]' < $1 |
gawk    '
        {count[$1]++}
END     {for (item in count) printf "%-15s%3s\n", item, count[item]}' |
sort -k 2nr -k 1f,2
$ ./word_usage textfile
the             42
file            29
fsck            27
system          22
you             22
to              21
it              17
SIZE            14
and             13
MODE            13
...
```

Following is a similar program in a different format. The style mimics the style of a C program and might be easier to read and work with for more complex gawk programs.

```
$ cat word_count
tr -cs 'a-zA-Z' '[\n*]' < $1 |
gawk ' {
        count[$1]++
}
END     {
        for (item in count)
            {
            if (count[item] > 4)
                {
                printf "%-15s%3s\n", item, count[item]
                }
        }
} ' |
sort -k 2nr -k 1f
```

The tail utility displays the last ten lines of output, illustrating that words occurring fewer than five times are not listed:

```
$ ./word_count textfile | tail
directories      5
if               5
information      5
INODE            5
more             5
no               5
on               5
response         5
this             5
will             5
```

The next example shows one way to put a date on a report. The first line of input to the gawk program comes from date. The program reads this line as record number 1 (**NR == 1**), processes it accordingly, and processes all subsequent lines with the ***action*** associated with the next ***pattern*** (**NR > 1**).

```
$ cat report
if (test $# = 0) then
    echo "You must supply a filename."
    exit 1
fi
(date; cat $1) |
gawk '
NR == 1    {print "Report for", $1, $2, $3 ", " $6}
NR >  1    {print $5 "\t" $1}'

$ ./report cars
Report for Wed Jan 31, 2018
2500    plym
3000    chevy
10000   ford
9850    volvo
10500   ford
3500    chevy
450     bmw
6000    honda
17000   ford
750     toyota
1550    chevy
9500    ford
```

The next example sums each of the columns in a file you specify on the command line; it takes its input from the **numbers** file. The program performs error checking, reporting on and discarding rows that contain nonnumeric entries. It uses the **next** command (with the comment **skip bad records**) to skip the rest of the commands for the current record if the record contains a nonnumeric entry. At the end of the program, gawk displays a grand total for the file.

```
$ cat numbers
10      20      30.3    40.5
```

```
                    20      30      45.7    66.1
                    30      xyz     50      70
                    40      75      107.2   55.6
                    50      20      30.3    40.5
                    60      30      45.0    66.1
                    70      1134.7  50      70
                    80      75      107.2   55.6
                    90      176     30.3    40.5
                    100     1027.45 45.7    66.1
                    110     123     50      57a.5
                    120     75      107.2   55.6
```

```
$ cat tally
gawk ' BEGIN   {
               ORS = ""
               }

NR == 1 {                                      # first record only
    nfields = NF                               # set nfields to number of
    }                                          # fields in the record (NF)
    {
    if ($0 ~ /[^0-9. \t]/)                     # check each record to see if it contains
        {                                      # any characters that are not numbers,
        print "\nRecord " NR " skipped:\n\t"   # periods, spaces, or TABs
        print $0 "\n"
        next                                   # skip bad records
        }
    else
        {
        for (count = 1; count <= nfields; count++) # for good records loop through fields
            {
            printf "%10.2f", $count > "tally.out"
            sum[count] += $count
            gtotal += $count
            }
        print "\n" > "tally.out"
        }
    }

END     {                                      # after processing last record
    for (count = 1; count <= nfields; count++) # print summary
        {
        print "   -------" > "tally.out"
        }
    print "\n" > "tally.out"
    for (count = 1; count <= nfields; count++)
        {
        printf "%10.2f", sum[count] > "tally.out"
        }
    print "\n\n        Grand Total " gtotal "\n" > "tally.out"
} ' < numbers
```

```
                    $ ./tally
                    Record 3 skipped:
                            30      xyz     50      70
```

```
Record 6 skipped:
        60      30      45.0    66.1

Record 11 skipped:
        110     123     50      57a.5

$ cat tally.out
     10.00      20.00      30.30      40.50
     20.00      30.00      45.70      66.10
     40.00      75.00     107.20      55.60
     50.00      20.00      30.30      40.50
     70.00    1134.70      50.00      70.00
     80.00      75.00     107.20      55.60
     90.00     176.00      30.30      40.50
    100.00    1027.45      45.70      66.10
    120.00      75.00     107.20      55.60
   -------    -------    -------    -------
    580.00    2633.15     553.90     490.50

        Grand Total 4257.55
```

The next example reads the **passwd** file, listing users who do not have passwords and users who have duplicate user ID numbers. (The pwck utility [Linux only] performs similar checks.) Because macOS uses Open Directory (page 1068) and not the **passwd** file, this example will not work under macOS.

```
$ cat /etc/passwd
bill::102:100:ext 123:/home/bill:/bin/bash
roy:x:104:100:ext 475:/home/roy:/bin/bash
tom:x:105:100:ext 476:/home/tom:/bin/bash
lynn:x:166:100:ext 500:/home/lynn:/bin/bash
mark:x:107:100:ext 112:/home/mark:/bin/bash
sales:x:108:100:ext 102:/m/market:/bin/bash
anne:x:109:100:ext 355:/home/anne:/bin/bash
toni::164:100:ext 357:/home/toni:/bin/bash
ginny:x:115:100:ext 109:/home/ginny:/bin/bash
chuck:x:116:100:ext 146:/home/chuck:/bin/bash
neil:x:164:100:ext 159:/home/neil:/bin/bash
rmi:x:118:100:ext 178:/home/rmi:/bin/bash
vern:x:119:100:ext 201:/home/vern:/bin/bash
bob:x:120:100:ext 227:/home/bob:/bin/bash
janet:x:122:100:ext 229:/home/janet:/bin/bash
maggie:x:124:100:ext 244:/home/maggie:/bin/bash
dan::126:100::/home/dan:/bin/bash
dave:x:108:100:ext 427:/home/dave:/bin/bash
mary:x:129:100:ext 303:/home/mary:/bin/bash
```

```
$ cat passwd_check
gawk < /etc/passwd '    BEGIN   {
    uid[void] = ""                          # tell gawk that uid is an array
    }
    {                                       # no pattern indicates process all records
```

```
dup = 0                                     # initialize duplicate flag
split($0, field, ":")                       # split into fields delimited by ":"
if (field[2] == "")                         # check for null password field
    {
    if (field[5] == "")                     # check for null info field
        {
        print field[1] " has no password."
        }
    else
        {
        print field[1] " ("field[5]") has no password."
        }
    }
for (name in uid)                           # loop through uid array
    {
    if (uid[name] == field[3])              # check for second use of UID
        {
        print field[1] " has the same UID as " name " : UID = " uid[name]
        dup = 1                             # set duplicate flag
        }
    }
if (!dup)                                   # same as if (dup == 0)
                                            # assign UID and login name to uid array
    {
    uid[field[1]] = field[3]
    }
}'
```

```
$ ./passwd_check
bill (ext 123) has no password.
toni (ext 357) has no password.
neil has the same UID as toni : UID = 164
dan has no password.
dave has the same UID as sales : UID = 108
```

The next example shows a complete interactive shell script that uses gawk to generate a report on the cars file based on price ranges:

```
$ cat list_cars
trap 'rm -f $$.tem > /dev/null;echo $0 aborted.;exit 1' 1 2 15
read -p "Price range (for example, 5000 7500):" lowrange hirange

echo '
                               Miles
Make       Model       Year    (000)         Price
--------------------------------------------------' > $$.tem
gawk < cars '
$5 >= '$lowrange' && $5 <= '$hirange' {
        if ($1 ~ /ply/)  $1 = "plymouth"
        if ($1 ~ /chev/) $1 = "chevrolet"
        printf "%-10s %-8s    %2d    %5d    $ %8.2f\n", $1, $2, $3, $4,
$5
        }' | sort -n +5 >> $$.tem
```

```
cat $$.tem
rm $$.tem

$ ./list_cars
Price range (for example, 5000 7500):3000 8000

                                    Miles
Make        Model        Year       (000)          Price
--------------------------------------------------------
chevrolet   malibu       1999          60     $  3000.00
chevrolet   malibu       2000          50     $  3500.00
honda       accord       2001          30     $  6000.00

$ ./list_cars
Price range (for example, 5000 7500):0 2000

                                    Miles
Make        Model        Year       (000)          Price
--------------------------------------------------------
bmw         325i         1985         115     $   450.00
toyota      rav4         2002         180     $   750.00
chevrolet   impala       1985          85     $  1550.00

$ ./list_cars
Price range (for example, 5000 7500):15000 100000

                                    Miles
Make        Model        Year       (000)          Price
--------------------------------------------------------
ford        taurus       2004          10     $ 17000.00
```

optional

ADVANCED gawk PROGRAMMING

This section discusses some of the advanced features of AWK. It covers how to control input using the **getline** statement, how to use a coprocess to exchange information between gawk and a program running in the background, and how to use a coprocess to exchange data over a network. Coprocesses are available under gawk only; they are not available under awk and mawk.

getline: CONTROLLING INPUT

Using the **getline** statement gives you more control over the data gawk reads than other methods of input do. When you provide a variable name as an argument to **getline**, **getline** reads data into that variable. The **BEGIN** block of the **g1** program uses **getline** to read one line into the variable **aa** from standard input:

```
$ cat g1
BEGIN   {
        getline aa
        print aa
```

```
        }
$ echo aaaa | gawk -f g1
aaaa
```

The next few examples use the **alpha** file:

```
$ cat alpha
aaaaaaaaa
bbbbbbbbb
ccccccccc
ddddddddd
```

Even when **g1** is given more than one line of input, it processes only the first line:

```
$ gawk -f g1 < alpha
aaaaaaaaa
```

When **getline** is not given an argument, it reads input into **$0** and modifies the field variables (**$1**, **$2**, . . .):

```
$ gawk 'BEGIN {getline;print $1}' < alpha
aaaaaaaaa
```

The **g2** program uses a **while** loop in the **BEGIN** block to loop over the lines in standard input. The **getline** statement reads each line into **holdme** and **print** outputs each value of **holdme**.

```
$ cat g2
BEGIN   {
        while (getline holdme)
            print holdme
        }
$ gawk -f g2 < alpha
aaaaaaaaa
bbbbbbbbb
ccccccccc
ddddddddd
```

The **g3** program demonstrates that gawk automatically reads each line of input into **$0** when it has statements in its body (and not just a **BEGIN** block). This program outputs the record number (**NR**), the string **$0:**, and the value of **$0** (the current record) for each line of input.

```
$ cat g3
        {print NR, "$0:", $0}

$ gawk -f g3 < alpha
1 $0: aaaaaaaaa
2 $0: bbbbbbbbb
3 $0: ccccccccc
4 $0: ddddddddd
```

Next, **g4** demonstrates that **getline** works independently of gawk's automatic reads and **$0**. When **getline** reads data into a variable, it does not modify either **$0** or any of the fields in the current record (**$1**, **$2**, . . .). The first statement in **g4**, which is the same as the statement in **g3**, outputs the line that gawk has automatically read. The **getline** statement reads the next line of input into the variable named **aa.** The third statement outputs the record number, the string **aa:**, and the value of **aa.** The output from **g4** shows that **getline** processes records independently of gawk's automatic reads.

```
$ cat g4
        {
        print NR, "$0:", $0
        getline aa
        print NR, "aa:", aa
        }

$ gawk -f g4 < alpha
1 $0: aaaaaaaaa
2 aa: bbbbbbbbb
3 $0: ccccccccc
4 aa: ddddddddd
```

The **g5** program outputs each line of input except for those lines that begin with the letter **b**. The first **print** statement outputs each line that gawk reads automatically. Next, the **/^b/** ***pattern*** selects all lines that begin with **b** for special processing. The ***action*** uses **getline** to read the next line of input into the variable **hold**, outputs the string **skip this line:** followed by the value of **hold**, and outputs the value of **$1**. The **$1** holds the value of the first field of the record that gawk read automatically, not the record read by **getline**. The final statement displays a string and the value of **NR**, the current record number. Even though **getline** does not change **$0** when it reads data into a variable, gawk increments **NR**.

```
$ cat g5
        # print all lines except those read with getline
        {print "line #", NR, $0}

# if line begins with "b" process it specially
/^b/    {
        # use getline to read the next line into variable named hold
        getline hold

        # print value of hold
        print "skip this line:", hold

        # $0 is not affected when getline reads data into a variable
        # $1 still holds previous value
        print "previous line began with:", $1
        }

        {
        print ">>>> finished processing line #", NR
        print ""
        }

$ gawk -f g5 < alpha
line # 1 aaaaaaaaa
>>>> finished processing line # 1
```

```
line # 2 bbbbbbbbb
skip this line: ccccccccc
previous line began with: bbbbbbbbb
>>>> finished processing line # 3

line # 4 ddddddddd
>>>> finished processing line # 4
```

COPROCESS: TWO-WAY I/O

A *coprocess* is a process that runs in parallel with another process. Starting with version 3.1, gawk can invoke a coprocess to exchange information directly with a background process. A coprocess can be useful when you are working in a client/server environment, setting up an *SQL* (page 1125) front end/back end, or exchanging data with a remote system over a network. The gawk syntax identifies a coprocess by preceding the name of the program that starts the background process with a |& operator.

Only gawk supports coprocesses

tip The awk and mawk utilities do not support coprocesses. Only gawk supports coprocesses.

The coprocess command must be a filter (i.e., it reads from standard input and writes to standard output) and must flush its output whenever it has a complete line rather than accumulating lines for subsequent output. When a command is invoked as a coprocess, it is connected via a two-way pipe to a gawk program so you can read from and write to the coprocess.

to_upper When used alone the tr utility (page 1014) does not flush its output after each line. The **to_upper** shell script is a wrapper for tr that does flush its output; this filter can be run as a coprocess. For each line read, **to_upper** writes the line, translated to uppercase, to standard output. Remove the # before **set –x** if you want **to_upper** to display debugging output.

```
$ cat to_upper
#!/bin/bash
#set -x
while read arg
do
    echo "$arg" | tr '[a-z]' '[A-Z]'
done

$ echo abcdef | ./to_upper
ABCDEF
```

The **g6** program invokes **to_upper** as a coprocess. This gawk program reads standard input or a file specified on the command line, translates the input to uppercase, and writes the translated data to standard output.

```
$ cat g6
    {
    print $0 |& "to_upper"
    "to_upper" |& getline hold
```

```
    print hold
    }

$ gawk -f g6 < alpha
AAAAAAAAA
BBBBBBBBB
CCCCCCCCC
DDDDDDDDD
```

The **g6** program has one compound statement, enclosed within braces, comprising three statements. Because there is no ***pattern***, gawk executes the compound statement once for each line of input.

In the first statement, **print $0** sends the current record to standard output. The **|&** operator redirects standard output to the program named **to_upper**, which is running as a coprocess. The quotation marks around the name of the program are required. The second statement redirects standard output from **to_upper** to a **getline** statement, which copies its standard input to the variable named **hold**. The third statement, **print hold**, sends the contents of the **hold** variable to standard output.

Getting Input from a Network

Building on the concept of a coprocess, gawk can exchange information with a process on another system via an IP network connection. When you specify one of the special filenames that begins with **/inet/**, gawk processes the request using a network connection. The syntax of these special filenames is

/inet/***protocol***/***local-port***/***remote-host***/***remote-port***

where ***protocol*** is usually **tcp** but can be **udp**, ***local-port*** is 0 (zero) if you want gawk to pick a port (otherwise, it is the number of the port you want to use), ***remote-host*** is the *IP address* (page 1104) or *fully qualified domain name* (page 1099) of the remote host, and ***remote-port*** is the port number on the remote host. Instead of a port number in ***local-port*** and ***remote-port***, you can specify a service name such as **http** or **ftp**.

The **g7** program reads the **rfc-retrieval.txt** file from the server at **www.rfc-editor.org**. On **www.rfc-editor.org** the file is located at **/rfc/rfc-retrieval.txt**. The first statement in **g7** assigns the special filename to the **server** variable. The filename specifies a TCP connection, allows the local system to select an appropriate port, and connects to **www.rfc-editor.org** on port 80. You can use **http** in place of **80** to specify the standard HTTP port.

The second statement uses a coprocess to send a **GET** request to the remote server. This request includes the pathname of the file gawk is requesting. A **while** loop uses a coprocess to redirect lines from the server to **getline**. Because **getline** has no variable name as an argument, it saves its input in the current record buffer **$0**.

The final **print** statement sends each record to standard output. Experiment with this script, replacing the final **print** statement with gawk statements that process the file.

```
$ cat g7
BEGIN          {
    # set variable named server
    # to special networking filename
    server = "/inet/tcp/0/www.rfc-editor.org/80"

    # use coprocess to send GET request to remote server
    print "GET /rfc/rfc-retrieval.txt \
    HTTP/1.1\nHost:www.rfc-editor.org\n\n"|& server

    # while loop uses coprocess to redirect
    # output from server to getline
    while (server |& getline)
        print $0
    }

$ gawk -f g7

                   Where and how to get new RFCs
                   =============================

RFCs may be obtained via FTP or HTTP or email from many RFC
repositories.
The official repository for RFCs is:

        http://www.rfc-editor.org/
...
```

Chapter Summary

AWK is a pattern-scanning and processing language that searches one or more files for records (usually lines) that match specified patterns. It processes lines by performing actions, such as writing the record to standard output or incrementing a counter, each time it finds a match. AWK has several implementations, including awk, gawk, and mawk.

An AWK program consists of one or more lines containing a ***pattern*** and/or ***action*** in the following syntax:

> ***pattern*** { ***action*** }

The ***pattern*** selects lines from the input. An AWK program performs the ***action*** on all lines that the ***pattern*** selects. If a ***program*** line does not contain a ***pattern***, AWK selects all lines in the input. If a program line does not contain an ***action,*** AWK copies the selected lines to standard output.

An AWK program can use variables, functions, arithmetic operators, associative arrays, control statements, and C's **printf** statement. Advanced AWK programming takes advantage of **getline** statements to fine-tune input, coprocesses to enable gawk to exchange data with other programs (gawk only), and network connections to exchange data with programs running on remote systems on a network (gawk only).

EXERCISES

1. Write a gawk program that numbers each line in a file and sends its output to standard output.
2. Write a gawk program that displays the number of characters in the first field followed by the first field and sends its output to standard output.
3. Write a gawk program that uses the **cars** file (page 645), displays all cars priced at more than $5,000, and sends its output to standard output.
4. Use gawk to determine how many lines in **/etc/services** contain the string **Mail**. Verify your answer using grep.

ADVANCED EXERCISES

5. Experiment with pgawk (available only with gawk). What does it do? How can it be useful?
6. Write a gawk (not awk or mawk) program named **net_list** that reads from the **rfc-retrieval.txt** file on **www.rfc-editor.org** (see "Getting Input from a Network" on page 666) and displays a the last word on each line in all uppercase letters.
7. Expand the **net_list** program developed in Exercise 6 to use **to_upper** (page 665) as a coprocess to display the list of cars with only the make of the cars in uppercase. The model and subsequent fields on each line should appear as they do in the **cars** file.
8. How can you cause gawk (not awk or mawk) to neatly format—that is, "pretty print"—a gawk program file? (*Hint:* See the gawk man page.)

15

THE sed EDITOR

IN THIS CHAPTER

OBJECTIVES

After reading this chapter you should be able to:

- Use sed to edit a file, replacing words in the file
- Write a sed program that inserts or changes lines in a file
- Change multiple character strings in a file using sed
- Use sed as a filter to modify a file

The sed (stream editor) utility is a batch (noninteractive) editor. It transforms an input stream that can come from a file or standard input. It is frequently used as a filter or in a pipeline. Because it makes only one pass through its input, sed is more efficient than an interactive editor such as ed. Most Linux distributions provide GNU sed; macOS supplies BSD sed. This chapter applies to both versions.

SYNTAX

A sed command line has the following syntax:

sed [–n] ***program*** *[****file-list****]*
sed [–n] –f ***program-file*** *[****file-list****]*

The sed utility takes its input from files you specify on the command line or from standard input. Output from sed goes to standard output.

ARGUMENTS

The ***program*** is a sed program included on the command line. The first syntax allows you to write simple, short sed programs without creating a separate file to hold the sed program. The ***program-file*** in the second syntax is the pathname of a file containing a sed program (see "Editor Basics" on page 671). The ***file-list*** contains pathnames of the ordinary files that sed processes; these are the input files. When you do not specify a ***file-list***, sed takes its input from standard input.

OPTIONS

Options preceded by a double hyphen (––) work under Linux (GNU sed) only. Options named with a single letter and preceded by a single hyphen work under Linux (GNU sed) and macOS (BSD sed).

––file *program-file*
–f ***program-file***
Causes sed to read its program from the file named ***program-file*** instead of from the command line. You can use this option more than once on the command line.

––help
Summarizes how to use sed. LINUX

––in-place[=*suffix*]
–i[***suffix***]
Edits files in place. Without this option sed sends its output to standard output. With this option sed replaces the file it is processing with its output. When you specify a ***suffix***, sed makes a backup of the original file. The backup has

the original filename with ***suffix*** appended. You must include a period in ***suffix*** if you want a period to appear between the original filename and ***suffix***.

--quiet *or* --silent -n Causes sed not to copy lines to standard output except as specified by the Print (p) instruction or flag.

EDITOR BASICS

A sed program consists of one or more lines with the following syntax:

[address[,address]] ***instruction*** *[argument-list]*

The ***address***es are optional. If you omit the ***address,*** sed processes all lines of input. The ***instruction*** is an editing instruction that modifies the text. The ***address***es select the line(s) the ***instruction*** part of the command operates on. The number and kinds of arguments in the ***argument-list*** depend on the ***instruction***. If you want to put several sed commands on one line, separate the commands with semicolons (;).

The sed utility processes input as follows:

1. Reads one line of input from ***file-list*** or standard input.
2. Reads the first instruction from the ***program*** or ***program-file***. If the ***address***(es) select the input line, acts on the input line as the ***instruction*** specifies.
3. Reads the next instruction from the ***program*** or ***program-file***. If the ***address***(es) select the input line, acts on the input line (possibly modified by the previous instruction) as the ***instruction*** specifies.
4. Repeats step 3 until it has executed all instructions in the ***program*** or ***program-file***.
5. Starts over with step 1 if there is another line of input; otherwise, sed is finished.

ADDRESSES

A line number is an address that selects a line. As a special case, the line number that starts with $ represents the last line of input.

A regular expression (Appendix A) is an address that selects those lines containing a string that the regular expression matches. Although slashes are often used to delimit these regular expressions, sed permits you to use any character other than a backslash or NEWLINE for this purpose.

Except as noted, zero, one, or two addresses (either line numbers or regular expressions) can precede an instruction. If you do not specify an address, sed selects all lines, causing the instruction to act on every line of input. Specifying one address causes the instruction to act on each input line the address selects. Specifying two addresses causes the instruction to act on groups of lines. In this case the first address selects the first line in the first group. The second address selects the next subsequent line that it matches; this line is the last line in the first group. If no match for the second address is found, the second address points to the end of the file. After selecting the last line in a group, sed starts the selection process over, looking for the next line the first address matches. This line is the first line in the next group. The sed utility continues this process until it has finished going through the entire file.

INSTRUCTIONS

Pattern space The sed utility has two buffers. The following commands work with the *Pattern space,* which initially holds the line of input that sed just read. The other buffer, the *Hold space,* is discussed on page 674.

a (**append**) The Append instruction appends one or more lines to the currently selected line. If you precede an Append instruction with two addresses, it appends to each line that is selected by the addresses. If you do not precede an Append instruction with an address, it appends to each input line. An Append instruction has the following syntax:

[address[,address]] a
text \
text \
...
text

You must end each line of appended text, except the last, with a backslash, which quotes the following NEWLINE. The appended text concludes with a line that does not end with a backslash. The sed utility *always* writes out appended text, regardless of whether you use a **–n** flag on the command line. It even writes out the text if you delete the line to which you are appending the text.

c (**change**) The Change instruction is similar to Append and Insert except that it changes the selected lines so that they contain the new text. When you specify an address range, Change replaces the range of lines with a single occurrence of the new text.

d (**delete**) The Delete instruction causes sed not to write out the lines it selects and not to finish processing the lines. After sed executes a Delete instruction, it reads the next input line and then begins anew with the first instruction from the ***program*** or ***program-file.***

i (**insert**) The Insert instruction is identical to the Append instruction except that it places the new text *before* the selected line.

N (**next without write**) The Next (**N**) instruction reads the next input line and appends it to the current line. An embedded NEWLINE separates the original line and the new line.

You can use the **N** command to remove NEWLINEs from a file. See the example on page 679.

n (**next**) The Next (**n**) instruction writes out the currently selected line if appropriate, reads the next input line, and starts processing the new line with the next instruction from the ***program*** or ***program-file***.

p (**print**) The Print instruction writes the selected lines to standard output, writing the lines immediately, and does not reflect the effects of subsequent instructions. This instruction overrides the **–n** option on the command line.

q (**quit**) The Quit instruction causes sed to terminate immediately.

r *file* (**read**) The Read instruction reads the contents of the specified file and appends it to the selected line. A single SPACE and the name of the input file must follow a Read instruction.

s (**substitute**) The Substitute instruction in sed is similar to that in vim (page 193). It has the following syntax:

*[address[,address]] s/**pattern**/**replacement-string**/[g][p][w **file**]*

The ***pattern*** is a regular expression (Appendix A) that traditionally is delimited by a slash (/); you can use any character other than a SPACE or NEWLINE. The ***replacement-string*** starts immediately following the second delimiter and must be terminated by the same delimiter. The final (third) delimiter is required. The ***replacement-string*** can contain an ampersand (&), which sed replaces with the matched ***pattern***. Unless you use the **g** flag, the Substitute instruction replaces only the first occurrence of the ***pattern*** on each selected line.

The **g** (global) flag causes the Substitute instruction to replace all nonoverlapping occurrences of the ***pattern*** on the selected lines.

The **p** (print) flag causes sed to send all lines on which it makes substitutions to standard output. This flag overrides the **–n** option on the command line.

The **w** (write) flag is similar to the **p** flag but sends its output to the file specified by ***file***. A single SPACE and the name of the output file must follow a **w** flag.

w *file* (**write**) This instruction is similar to the Print instruction except that it sends the output to the file specified by ***file***. A single SPACE and the name of the output file must follow a Write instruction.

Control Structures

! (**NOT**) Causes sed to apply the following instruction, located on the same line, to each of the lines *not* selected by the address portion of the instruction. For example, **3!d** deletes all lines except line 3 and **$!p** displays all lines except the last.

{ } (**group instructions**) When you enclose a group of instructions within a pair of braces, a single address or address pair selects the lines on which the group of instructions operates. Use semicolons (;) to separate multiple commands appearing on a single line.

Branch instructions The GNU sed info page identifies the branch instructions as "Commands for sed gurus" and suggests that if you need them you might be better off writing your program in awk or Perl.

: *label* Identifies a location within a sed program. The ***label*** is useful as a target for both the **b** and **t** branch instructions.

b [*label*] Unconditionally transfers control to ***label***. Without ***label***, skips the rest of the instructions for the current line of input and reads the next line of input.

t [*label*] Transfers control to ***label*** only if a Substitute instruction has been successful since the most recent line of input was read (conditional branch). Without ***label***, skips the rest of the instructions for the current line of input and reads the next line of input.

THE HOLD SPACE

The commands reviewed up to this point work with the *Pattern space*, a buffer that initially holds the line of input that sed just read. The *Hold space* can hold data while you manipulate data in the Pattern space; it is a temporary buffer. Until you place data in the Hold space, it is empty. This section discusses commands that move data between the Pattern space and the Hold space.

g Copies the contents of the Hold space to the Pattern space. The original contents of the Pattern space is lost.

G Appends a NEWLINE and the contents of the Hold space to the Pattern space.

h Copies the contents of the Pattern space to the Hold space. The original content of the Hold space is lost.

H Appends a NEWLINE and the contents of the Pattern space to the Hold space.

x Exchanges the contents of the Pattern space and the Hold space.

EXAMPLES

lines data file The following examples use the **lines** file for input:

```
$ cat lines
Line one.
The second line.
The third.
This is line four.
Five.
This is the sixth sentence.
This is line seven.
Eighth and last.
```

Unless you instruct it not to, sed sends all lines—selected or not—to standard output. When you use the –n option on the command line, sed sends only certain lines, such as those selected by a Print (p) instruction, to standard output.

The following command line displays all lines in the lines file that contain the word **line** (all lowercase). In addition, because there is no –n option, sed displays all the lines of input. As a result, sed displays the lines that contain the word **line** twice.

```
$ sed '/line/ p' lines
Line one.
The second line.
The second line.
The third.
This is line four.
This is line four.
Five.
This is the sixth sentence.
This is line seven.
This is line seven.
Eighth and last.
```

The preceding command uses the address /line/, a regular expression that is a simple string. The sed utility selects each of the lines that contains a match for that pattern. The Print (p) instruction displays each of the selected lines.

The following command uses the –n option, so sed displays only the selected lines:

```
$ sed -n '/line/ p' lines
The second line.
This is line four.
This is line seven.
```

In the next example, sed displays part of a file based on line numbers. The Print instruction selects and displays lines 3 through 6.

```
$ sed -n '3,6 p' lines
The third.
This is line four.
Five.
This is the sixth sentence.
```

The next command line uses the Quit instruction to cause sed to display only the beginning of a file. In this case sed displays the first five lines of **lines** just as a **head –5 lines** command would.

```
$ sed '5 q' lines
Line one.
The second line.
The third.
This is line four.
Five.
```

program-file When you need to give sed more complex or lengthy instructions, you can use a ***program-file***. The **print3_6** program performs the same function as the command line in the second preceding example. The **–f** option tells sed to read its program from the file named following this option.

```
$ cat print3_6
3,6 p

$ sed -n -f print3_6 lines
The third.
This is line four.
Five.
This is the sixth sentence.
```

Append The next program selects line 2 and uses an Append instruction to append a NEWLINE and the text **AFTER.** to the selected line. Because the command line does not include the **–n** option, sed copies all lines from the input file **lines**.

```
$ cat append_demo
2 a\
AFTER.

$ sed -f append_demo lines
Line one.
The second line.
AFTER.
The third.
This is line four.
Five.
This is the sixth sentence.
This is line seven.
Eighth and last.
```

Insert The **insert_demo** program selects all lines containing the string **This** and inserts a NEWLINE and the text **BEFORE.** before the selected lines.

```
$ cat insert_demo
/This/ i\
BEFORE.

$ sed -f insert_demo lines
Line one.
The second line.
The third.
BEFORE.
This is line four.
Five.
BEFORE.
This is the sixth sentence.
BEFORE.
This is line seven.
Eighth and last.
```

Change The next example demonstrates a Change instruction with an address range. When you specify a range of lines for a Change instruction, it does not change each line within the range but rather changes the block of lines to a single occurrence of the new text.

```
$ cat change_demo
2,4 c\
SED WILL INSERT THESE\
THREE LINES IN PLACE\
OF THE SELECTED LINES.

$ sed -f change_demo lines
Line one.
SED WILL INSERT THESE
THREE LINES IN PLACE
OF THE SELECTED LINES.
Five.
This is the sixth sentence.
This is line seven.
Eighth and last.
```

Substitute The next example demonstrates a Substitute instruction. The sed utility selects all lines because the instruction has no address. On each line **subs_demo** replaces the first occurrence of **line** with **sentence**. The **p** flag displays each line where a substitution occurs. The command line calls sed with the **–n** option, so sed displays only the lines the program explicitly specifies.

```
$ cat subs_demo
s/line/sentence/p

$ sed -n -f subs_demo lines
The second sentence.
This is sentence four.
This is sentence seven.
```

The next example is similar to the preceding one except that a **w** flag and filename (**temp**) at the end of the Substitute instruction cause sed to create the file named **temp**. The command line does not include the **–n** option, so it displays all lines in addition to writing the changed lines to **temp**. The cat utility displays the contents of the file **temp**. The word **Line** (starting with an uppercase L) is not changed.

```
$ cat write_demo1
s/line/sentence/w temp

$ sed -f write_demo1 lines
Line one.
The second sentence.
The third.
This is sentence four.
Five.
This is the sixth sentence.
This is sentence seven.
Eighth and last.
```

```
$ cat temp
The second sentence.
This is sentence four.
This is sentence seven.
```

The following bash script changes all occurrences of **REPORT** to **report, FILE** to **file,** and **PROCESS** to **process** in a group of files. Because it is a shell script and not a sed program file, you must have read and execute permission to the **sub** file to execute it as a command (page 295). The **for** structure (page 445) loops through the list of files on the command line. As it processes each file, the script displays each filename before processing the file with sed. This program uses embedded sed commands that span multiple lines. Because the NEWLINES between the commands are quoted (they appear between single quotation marks), sed accepts multiple commands on a single, extended command line (within the shell script). Each Substitute instruction includes a **g** (global) flag to take care of the case where a string occurs more than once on a line.

```
$ cat sub
for file
do
        echo $file
        mv $file $$.subhld
        sed 's/REPORT/report/g
             s/FILE/file/g
             s/PROCESS/process/g' $$.subhld > $file
done
rm $$.subhld

$ sub file1 file2 file3
file1
file2
file3
```

In the next example, a Write instruction copies part of a file to another file (**temp2**). The line numbers **2** and **4**, separated by a comma, select the range of lines sed is to copy. This program does not alter the lines.

```
$ cat write_demo2
2,4 w temp2

$ sed -n -f write_demo2 lines

$ cat temp2
The second line.
The third.
This is line four.
```

The program **write_demo3** is similar to **write_demo2** but precedes the Write instruction with the NOT operator (**!**), causing sed to write to the file those lines *not* selected by the address.

```
$ cat write_demo3
2,4 !w temp3

$ sed -n -f write_demo3 lines
$ cat temp3
Line one.
Five.
This is the sixth sentence.
This is line seven.
Eighth and last.
```

Next (**n**) The following example demonstrates the Next (**n**) instruction. When it processes the selected line (line 3), sed immediately starts processing the next line without displaying line 3.

```
$ cat next_demo1
3 n
p

$ sed -n -f next_demo1 lines
Line one.
The second line.
This is line four.
Five.
This is the sixth sentence.
This is line seven.
Eighth and last.
```

The next example uses a textual address. The sixth line contains the string **the**, so the Next (**n**) instruction causes sed not to display it.

```
$ cat next_demo2
/the/ n
p

$ sed -n -f next_demo2 lines
Line one.
The second line.
The third.
This is line four.
Five.
This is line seven.
Eighth and last.
```

Next (**N**) The following example is similar to the preceding example except it uses the uppercase Next (**N**) instruction in place of the lowercase Next (**n**) instruction. Here, the Next (**N**) instruction appends the next line to the line that contains the string **the.** In the **lines** file, **sed** appends line 7 to line 6 and embeds a NEWLINE between the two lines. The Substitute command replaces the embedded NEWLINE with a SPACE. The Substitute command does not affect other lines because they do not contain embedded NEWLINEs; rather, they are terminated by NEWLINEs. See page 1068 for an example of the Next (**N**) instruction in a sed script running under macOS.

```
$ cat Next_demo3
/the/ N
s/\n/ /
p
$ sed -n -f Next_demo3 lines
Line one.
The second line.
The third.
This is line four.
Five.
This is the sixth sentence. This is line seven.
Eighth and last.
```

The next set of examples uses the **compound.in** file to demonstrate how sed instructions work together.

```
$ cat compound.in
1. The words on this page...
2. The words on this page...
3. The words on this page...
4. The words on this page...
```

The following example substitutes the string **words** with **text** on lines 1, 2, and 3 and the string **text** with **TEXT** on lines 2, 3, and 4. The example also selects and deletes line 3. The result is **text** on line 1, **TEXT** on line 2, no line 3, and **words** on line 4. The sed utility makes two substitutions on lines 2 and 3: **text** for **words** and **TEXT** for **text**. Then sed deletes line 3.

```
$ cat compound
1,3 s/words/text/
2,4 s/text/TEXT/
3 d

$ sed -f compound compound.in
1. The text on this page...
2. The TEXT on this page...
4. The words on this page...
```

The ordering of instructions within a sed program is critical. Both Substitute instructions are applied to the second line in the following example, as in the previous example, but the order in which the substitutions occur changes the result.

```
$ cat compound2
2,4 s/text/TEXT/
1,3 s/words/text/
3 d

$ sed -f compound2 compound.in
1. The text on this page...
2. The text on this page...
4. The words on this page...
```

In the next example, **compound3** appends two lines to line 2. The sed utility displays all lines from the file once because no **–n** option appears on the command line. The Print instruction at the end of the program file displays line 3 an additional time.

```
$ cat compound3
2 a\
This is line 2a.\
This is line 2b.
3 p

$ sed -f compound3 compound.in
1. The words on this page...
2. The words on this page...
This is line 2a.
This is line 2b.
3. The words on this page...
3. The words on this page...
4. The words on this page...
```

The next example shows that sed always displays appended text. Here, line 2 is deleted but the Append instruction still displays the two lines that were appended to it. Appended lines are displayed even if you use the **–n** option on the command line.

```
$ cat compound4
2 a\
This is line 2a.\
This is line 2b.
2 d

$ sed -f compound4 compound.in
1. The words on this page...
This is line 2a.
This is line 2b.
3. The words on this page...
4. The words on this page...
```

The next example uses a regular expression as the pattern. The regular expression in the following instruction (**^.**) matches one character at the beginning of every line that is not empty. The replacement string (between the second and third slashes) contains a backslash escape sequence that represents a TAB character (**\t**) followed by an ampersand (**&**). The ampersand takes on the value of what the regular expression matched.

```
$ sed 's/^./\t&/' lines
        Line one.
        The second line.
        The third.
...
```

This type of substitution is useful for indenting a file to create a left margin. See Appendix A for more information on regular expressions.

You can also use the simpler form **s/^/\t/** to add TABs to the beginnings of lines. In addition to placing TABs at the beginnings of lines with text on them, this instruction places a TAB at the beginning of every empty line—something the preceding command does not do.

You might want to put the preceding sed instruction into a shell script so you do not have to remember it (and retype it) each time you want to indent a file. The chmod utility gives you read and execute permission to the **ind** file.

```
$ cat ind
sed 's/^./\t&/' $*
$ chmod u+rx ind
$ ind lines
        Line one.
        The second line.
        The third.
...
```

Stand-alone script When you run the preceding shell script, it creates two processes: It calls a shell, which in turn calls sed. You can eliminate the overhead associated with the shell process by putting the line **#!/bin/sed –f** (page 297) at the beginning of the script, which runs the sed utility directly. You need read and execute permission to the file holding the script.

```
$ cat ind2
#!/bin/sed -f
s/^./\t&/
```

In the following sed program, the regular expression (two SPACEs followed by ***$**) matches one or more SPACEs at the end of a line. This program removes trailing SPACEs at the ends of lines, which is useful for cleaning up files you created using vim.

```
$ cat cleanup
sed 's/  *$//' $*
```

The **cleanup2** script runs the same sed command as **cleanup** but stands alone: It calls sed directly with no intermediate shell.

```
$ cat cleanup2
#!/bin/sed -f
s/  *$//
```

Hold space The next sed program makes use of the Hold space to exchange pairs of lines in a file.

```
$ cat s1
h # Copy Pattern space (line just read) to Hold space.
n # Read the next line of input into Pattern space.
p # Output Pattern space.
g # Copy Hold space to Pattern space.
p # Output Pattern space (which now holds the previous line).
```

```
$ sed -nf s1 lines
The second line.
Line one.
This is line four.
The third.
This is the sixth sentence.
Five.
Eighth and last.
This is line seven.
```

The commands in the **s1** program process pairs of input lines. This program reads a line and stores it; reads another line and displays it; and then retrieves the stored line and displays it. After processing a pair of lines, the program starts over with the next pair of lines.

The next sed program adds a blank line after each line in the input file (i.e., it double-spaces a file).

```
$ sed 'G' lines
Line one.

The second line.

The third.

This is line four.

$
```

The **G** instruction appends a NEWLINE and the contents of the Hold space to the Pattern space. Unless you put something in the Hold space, it will be empty. Thus, the **G** instruction appends a NEWLINE to each line of input before sed displays the line(s) from the Pattern space.

The **s2** sed program reverses the order of the lines in a file just as the tac utility does.

```
$ cat s2
2,$G  # On all but the first line, append a NEWLINE and the
      # contents of the Hold space to the Pattern space.
h     # Copy the Pattern space to the Hold space.
$!d   # Delete all except the last line.

$ sed -f s2 lines
Eighth and last.
This is line seven.
This is the sixth sentence.
Five.
This is line four.
The third.
```

```
The second line.
Line one.
```

This program comprises three commands: **2,$G**, **h**, and **$!d**. To understand this script it is important to understand how the address of the last command works: The **$** is the address of the last line of input and the **!** negates the address. The result is an address that selects all lines except the last line of input. In the same fashion you could replace the first command with **1!G**: It would select all lines except the first line for processing; the results would be the same.

Here is what happens as **s2** processes the **lines** file:

1. The sed utility reads the first line of input (**Line one.**) into the Pattern space.

   a. The **2,$G** does not process the first line of input; because of its address the **G** instruction starts processing at the second line.

   b. The **h** copies **Line one.** from the Pattern space to the Hold space.

   c. The **$!d** deletes the contents of the Pattern space. Because there is nothing in the Pattern space, sed does not display anything.

2. The sed utility reads the second line of input (**The second line.**) into the Pattern space.

   a. The **2,$G** adds what is in the Hold space (**Line one.**) to the Pattern space. The Pattern space now contains **The second line.**NEWLINE**Line one.**

   b. The **h** copies what is in the Pattern space to the Hold space.

   c. The **$!d** deletes the second line of input. Because it is deleted, sed does not display it.

3. The sed utility reads the third line of input (**The third.**) into the Pattern space.

   a. The **2,$G** adds what is in the Hold space (**The second line.**NEWLINE**Line one.**) to the Pattern space. The Pattern space now has **The third.**NEWLINE **The second line.**NEWLINE**Line one.**

   b. The **h** copies what is in the Pattern space to the Hold space.

   c. The **$!d** deletes the contents of the Pattern space. Because there is nothing in the Pattern space, sed does not display anything.

   (Repeats for lines 4-7). . .

8. The sed utility reads the eighth (last) line of input into the Pattern space.

   a. The **2,$G** adds what is in the Hold space to the Pattern space. The Pattern space now contains all the lines from **lines** in reverse order.

b. The **h** copies what is in the Pattern space to the Hold space. This step is not necessary for the last line of input but does not alter the program's output.

c. The **$!d** does not process the last line of input. Because of its address the **d** instruction does not delete the last line.

d. The sed utility displays the contents of the Pattern space.

CHAPTER SUMMARY

The sed (stream editor) utility is a batch (noninteractive) editor. It takes its input from files you specify on the command line or from standard input. Unless you redirect the output from sed, it goes to standard output.

A sed program consists of one or more lines with the following syntax:

[address[,address]] ***instruction*** *[argument-list]*

The ***address***es are optional. If you omit the ***address***, sed processes all lines of input. The ***instruction*** is the editing instruction that modifies the text. The ***address***es select the line(s) the ***instruction*** part of the command operates on. The number and kinds of arguments in the ***argument-list*** depend on the ***instruction***.

In addition to basic instructions, sed includes some powerful advanced instructions. One set of these instructions allows sed programs to store data temporarily in a buffer called the Hold space. Other instructions provide unconditional and conditional branching in sed programs.

EXERCISES

1. Write a sed command that copies a file to standard output, removing all lines that begin with the word **Today**.
2. Write a sed command that copies only those lines of a file that begin with the word **Today** to standard output.
3. Write a sed command that copies a file to standard output, removing all blank lines (i.e., lines with no characters on them).
4. Write a sed program named **ins** that copies a file to standard output, changing all occurrences of **cat** to **dog** and preceding each modified line with a line that says **following line is modified:**
5. Write a sed program named **div** that copies a file to standard output, copies the first five lines to a file named **first**, and copies the rest of the file to a file named **last**.

6. Write a sed command that copies a file to standard output, replacing a single SPACE as the first character on a line with a 0 (zero) only if the SPACE is immediately followed by a number (0–9). For example:

```
abc  ⇨ abc
 abc ⇨  abc
 85c ⇨ 085c
55b  ⇨ 55b
 000 ⇨ 0000
```

7. How can you use sed to triple-space (i.e., add two blank lines after each line in) a file?

PART V

SECURE NETWORK UTILITIES

16

The rsync Secure Copy Utility

In This Chapter

Objectives

After reading this chapter you should be able to:

- Copy files and directories using rsync
- Explain why rsync is secure
- Back up files and directories to another system using rsync
- Explain the effect of including a trailing slash on the name of the source directory
- Use rsync options to delete files in the destination that are not in the source, preserve modification times of copied files, and perform a dry run so rsync takes no action

The rsync (remote synchronization) utility copies an ordinary file or directory hierarchy locally or from the local system to or from another system on a network. By default, this utility uses OpenSSH to transfer files and the same authentication mechanism as OpenSSH; it therefore provides the same security as OpenSSH. The rsync utility prompts for a password when it needs one. Alternately, you can use the **rsyncd** daemon as a transfer agent.

SYNTAX

An rsync command line has the following syntax:

rsync [options] [[user@]from-host:]source-file [[user@]to-host:][destination-file]

The rsync utility copies files, including directory hierarchies, on the local system or between the local system and a remote system.

ARGUMENTS

The ***from-host*** is the name of the system you are copying files from; the ***to-host*** is the name of the system you are copying files to. When you do not specify a host, rsync assumes the local system. The ***user*** on either system defaults to the user who is giving the command on the local system; you can specify a different user with ***user@***. Unlike scp, rsync *does not* permit copying between remote systems.

The ***source-file*** is the ordinary or directory file you are copying; the ***destination-file*** is the resulting copy. You can specify files as relative or absolute pathnames. On the local system, relative pathnames are relative to the working directory; on a remote system, relative pathnames are relative to the specified or implicit user's home directory. When the ***source-file*** is a directory, use the **--recursive** or **--archive** option to copy its contents. When the ***destination-file*** is a directory, each of the source files maintains its simple filename. If the ***source-file*** is a single file, you can omit ***destination-file;*** the copied file will have the same simple filename as ***source-file*** (useful only when copying to or from a remote system).

A trailing slash (/) on *source-file* is critical

caution When ***source-file*** is a directory, a trailing slash in ***source-file*** causes rsync to copy the contents of the directory. The slash is equivalent to /*; it tells rsync to ignore the directory itself and copy the files within the directory. Without a trailing slash, rsync copies the directory. See page 694.

Options

The macOS version of rsync accepts long options

tip Options for rsync preceded by a double hyphen (––) work under macOS as well as under Linux.

––acls –A Preserves ACLs (page 106) of copied files.

––archive –a Copies files including dereferenced symbolic links, device files, and special files recursively, preserving ownership, group, permissions, and modification times associated with the files. Using this option is the same as specifying any of the **––devices**, **––specials**, **––group**, **––links**, **––owner**, **––perms**, **––recursive**, and the **––times** options. This option does not include the **––acls**, **––hard-links**, or **––xattrs** options; you must specify these options in addition to **––archive** if you want to use them. See page 694 for an example.

––backup –b Renames files that otherwise would be deleted or overwritten. By default, the rsync utility renames files by appending a tilde (~) to existing filenames. Consider **––backup-dir=*dir*** if you want rsync to put these files in a specified directory instead of renaming them. See also **––link-dest=*dir***.

––backup-dir=*dir* When used with the **––backup** option, moves files that otherwise would be deleted or overwritten to the directory named ***dir***. After moving the older version of the file to ***dir***, rsync copies the newer version of the file from ***source-file*** to ***destination-file***.

The directory named ***dir*** is located on the same system as ***destination-file***. If ***dir*** is a relative pathname, it is relative to ***destination-file***.

––copy-unsafe-links

(**partial dereference**) For each file that is a symbolic link that refers to a file outside the ***source-file*** hierarchy, copies the file the link points to, not the symbolic link itself. Without this option rsync copies all symbolic links, even if it does not copy the file the link refers to. See page 118 for information on dereferencing symbolic links.

–D Same as **––devices ––specials**.

––delete Deletes files in the ***destination-file*** that are not in the ***source-file***. This option can easily remove files you did not intend to remove; see the caution box on page 695.

––devices Copies device files (when working with **root** privileges only).

––dry-run Runs rsync without writing to disk. With the **––verbose** option, this option reports on what rsync would have done had it been run without this option. Useful with the **––delete** option.

--group -g Preserves group associations of copied files.

--hard-links -H Preserves hard links of copied files.

--links -l (lowercase "l"; **no dereference**) For each file that is a symbolic link, copies the symbolic link, not the file the link points to, even if the file the link points to is not in the ***source-file***. See page 118 for information on dereferencing symbolic links.

--link-dest=*dir* If rsync would normally copy a file—that is, if the file exists in ***source-file*** but not in ***destination-file*** or is changed in ***destination-file***—rsync looks in the directory named ***dir*** for the same file. If it finds an exact copy of the file in ***dir***, rsync makes a hard link from the file in ***dir*** to ***destination-file***. If it does not find an exact copy, rsync copies the file to ***destination-file***. See page 698 for an example.

The directory named ***dir*** is located on the same system as ***destination-file***. If ***dir*** is a relative pathname, it is relative to ***destination-file***.

--owner -o Preserves the owner of copied files (when working with **root** privileges only).

-P Same as **--partial** and **--progress**.

--partial Keeps partially copied files. By default rsync deletes partially copied files. See the note on page 693.

--perms -p Preserves the permissions of copied files.

--progress Displays information about the progress of the transfer. Implies **--verbose**.

--recursive -r Recursively descends a directory specified in ***source-file*** and copies all files in the directory hierarchy. See page 693 for an example.

--specials Copies special files.

--times -t Preserves the modification times of copied files. This option also speeds up copying files because it causes rsync not to copy a file that has the same modification time and size in both the ***source-file*** and the ***destination-file***. See page 694 for an example.

--update -u Skips files that are newer in the ***destination-file*** than in the ***source-file***.

--verbose -v Displays information about what rsync is doing. This option is useful with the **--dry-run** option. See page 693 for an example.

--xattrs -X Preserves the extended attributes of copied files. This option is not available with all compilations of rsync.

--compress -z Compresses files while copying them. See "Compression" on page 693.

NOTES

The rsync utility has many options. This chapter describes a few of them; see the rsync man page for a complete list.

OpenSSH By default, rsync copies files to and from a remote system using OpenSSH. The remote system must be running an OpenSSH server. If you can use ssh to log in on the remote system, you can use rsync to copy files to or from that system. If ssh requires you to enter a password, rsync will require a password. See "Copying Files to and from a Remote System" on page 696 for examples. See Chapter 17 for information on setting up and using OpenSSH.

rsyncd daemon If you use a double colon (::) in place of a single colon (:) following the name of a remote system, rsync connects to the **rsyncd** daemon on the remote system (it does not use OpenSSH). See the rsync man page for more information.

Compression The **--compress** option causes rsync to compress files while copying them, which can speed up a transfer. In some cases, when you specify this option in a setup with a fast network connection and a slower CPU, compressing files can slow down the transfer. You typically have this setup when you back up to a NAS (Network Attached Storage device).

Partially copied files The **--partial** option causes rsync to keep partially copied files that result when a transfer is interrupted. By default it deletes these files. Especially with large files, having a partially copied file can speed up a subsequent transfer.

MORE INFORMATION

man page: rsync
rsync home page: www.samba.org/rsync
Backup information: www.mikerubel.org/computers/rsync_snapshots
Backup tools: www.rsnapshot.org, backuppc.sourceforge.net
File synchronization: alliance.seas.upenn.edu/~bcpierce

EXAMPLES

--recursive **--verbose** The first example shows rsync copying a directory while using the **--recursive** and the **--verbose** options. Both the source and destination directories are in the working directory.

```
$ ls -l memos
-rw-r--r--. 1 max pubs 1500 05-14 14:24 0514
-rw-r--r--. 1 max pubs 6001 05-16 16:16 0516

$ rsync --recursive --verbose memos memos.copy
sending incremental file list
created directory memos.copy
memos/
memos/0514
memos/0516

sent 7656 bytes  received 54 bytes  15420.00 bytes/sec
total size is 7501  speedup is 0.97

$ ls -l memos.copy
drwxr-xr-x. 2 max pubs 4096 05-21 14:32 memos
```

In the preceding example, rsync copies the **memos** directory to the **memos.copy** directory. As the following ls command shows, rsync changed the modification times on the copied files to the time it made the copies:

```
$ ls -l memos.copy/memos
-rw-r--r--. 1 max pubs 1500 05-21 14:32 0514
-rw-r--r--. 1 max pubs 6001 05-21 14:32 0516
```

USING A TRAILING SLASH (/) ON *source-file*

Whereas the previous example copied a directory to another directory, you might want to copy the *contents* of a directory to another directory. A trailing slash (/) on the ***source-file*** causes rsync to act as though you had specified a trailing **/*** and causes rsync to copy the contents of the specified directory. A trailing slash on the ***destination-file*** has no effect.

--times The next example makes another copy of the **memos** directory, using **--times** to preserve modification times of the copied files. It uses a trailing slash on **memos** to copy the contents of the **memos** directory—not the directory itself—to **memos.copy2.**

```
$ rsync --recursive --verbose --times memos/ memos.copy2
sending incremental file list
created directory memos.copy2
./
0514
0516

sent 7642 bytes  received 53 bytes  15390.00 bytes/sec
total size is 7501  speedup is 0.97

$ ls -l memos.copy2
-rw-r--r--. 1 max pubs 1500 05-14 14:24 0514
-rw-r--r--. 1 max pubs 6001 05-16 16:16 0516
```

--archive The **--archive** option causes rsync to copy directories recursively, dereferencing symbolic links (copying the files the links point to, not the symbolic links themselves), preserving modification times, ownership, group association of the copied files, and more. This option does not preserve hard links; use the **--hard-links** option for that purpose. See page 691 for more information on **--archive**. The following commands perform the same functions as the previous one:

```
$ rsync --archive --verbose memos/ memos.copy2
$ rsync -av memos/ memos.copy2
```

REMOVING FILES

--delete
--dry-run The **--delete** option causes rsync to delete from ***destination-file*** files that are not in ***source-file***. Together, the **--dry-run** and **--verbose** options report on what an rsync command would do without the **--dry-run** option, without rsync taking any action. With the **--delete** option, the **--dry-run** and **--verbose** options can help you avoid removing files you did not intend to remove. This combination of options marks files

rsync would remove with the word **deleting.** The next example uses these options in addition to the **--archive** option.

```
$ ls -l memos memos.copy3
memos:
-rw-r--r--. 1 max pubs 1500 05-14 14:24 0514
-rw-r--r--. 1 max pubs 6001 05-16 16:16 0516
-rw-r--r--. 1 max pubs 5911 05-18 12:02 0518

memos.copy3:
-rw-r--r--. 1 max pubs 1500 05-14 14:24 0514
-rw-r--r--. 1 max pubs 6001 05-16 16:16 0516
-rw-r--r--. 1 max pubs 5911 05-21 14:36 notes

$ rsync --archive --verbose --delete --dry-run memos/ memos.copy3
sending incremental file list
./
deleting notes
0518

sent 83 bytes  received 18 bytes  202.00 bytes/sec
total size is 13412  speedup is 132.79 (DRY RUN)
```

The rsync utility reports **deleting notes,** indicating which file it would remove if you ran it without the **--dry-run** option. It also reports it would copy the 0518 file.

Test to make sure --delete is going to do what you think it will do

caution The **--delete** option can easily delete an entire directory tree if you omit a needed slash (/) or include an unneeded slash in ***source-file***. Use **--delete** with the **--dry-run** and **--verbose** options to test an rsync command.

If you get tired of using the long versions of options, you can use the single-letter versions. The next rsync command is the same as the previous one (there is no short version of the **--delete** option):

```
$ rsync -avn --delete memos/ memos.copy3
```

The next example runs the same rsync command, omitting the **--dry-run** option. The ls command shows the results of the rsync command: The **--delete** option causes rsync to remove the **notes** file from the ***destination-file*** (**memos.copy3**) because it is not in the ***source-file*** (**memos**). In addition, rsync copies the 0518 file.

```
$ rsync --archive --verbose --delete memos/ memos.copy3
sending incremental file list
./
deleting notes
0518

sent 6034 bytes  received 34 bytes  12136.00 bytes/sec
total size is 13412  speedup is 2.21
```

```
$ ls -l memos memos.copy3
memos:
-rw-r--r--. 1 max pubs 1500 05-14 14:24 0514
-rw-r--r--. 1 max pubs 6001 05-16 16:16 0516
-rw-r--r--. 1 max pubs 5911 05-18 12:02 0518

memos.copy3:
-rw-r--r--. 1 max pubs 1500 05-14 14:24 0514
-rw-r--r--. 1 max pubs 6001 05-16 16:16 0516
-rw-r--r--. 1 max pubs 5911 05-18 12:02 0518
```

Up to this point, the examples have copied files locally, in the working directory. To copy files to other directories, replace the simple filenames with relative or absolute pathnames. On the local system, relative pathnames are relative to the working directory; on a remote system, relative pathnames are relative to the user's home directory. For example, the following command copies the contents of the **memos** directory in the working directory to the **/backup** directory on the local system:

```
$ rsync --archive --verbose --delete memos/ /backup
```

Copying Files to and from a Remote System

To copy files to or from a remote system, that system must be running an OpenSSH server or another transport mechanism rsync can connect to. For more information refer to "Notes" on page 692. To specify a file on a remote system, preface the filename with the name of the remote system and a colon. Relative pathnames on the remote system are relative to the user's home directory. Absolute pathnames are absolute (i.e., they are relative to the root directory). See page 90 for more information on relative and absolute pathnames.

In the next example, Max copies the contents of the **memos** directory in the working directory on the local system to the **holdfiles** directory in his working directory on the remote system named **guava**. The ssh utility runs an ls command on **guava** to show the result of the rsync command. The rsync and ssh utilities do not request a password because Max has set up OpenSSH-based utilities to log in automatically on **guava**.

```
$ rsync --archive memos/ guava:holdfiles

$ ssh guava 'ls -l holdfiles'
-rw-r--r--. 1 max pubs 1500 05-14 14:24 0514
-rw-r--r--. 1 max pubs 6001 05-16 16:16 0516
-rw-r--r--. 1 max pubs 5911 05-18 12:02 0518
```

When copying from a remote system to the local system, place the name of the remote system before *source-file:*

```
$ rsync --archive guava:holdfiles/ ~/memo.copy4
$ rsync --archive guava:holdfiles/ /home/max/memo.copy5
```

Both of these commands copy the contents of the **holdfiles** directory from Max's home directory on **guava** to his home directory on the local system. Under macOS, replace **/home** with **/Users**.

Mirroring a Directory

You can use rsync to maintain a copy of a directory. Because it is an exact copy, this type of copy is called a *mirror*. The mirror directory must be on an OpenSSH server (you must be able to connect to it using an OpenSSH utility such as ssh). If you want to run this script using crontab (page 781), you must set up OpenSSH so you can log in on the remote system automatically (without providing a password).

--compress --update The next example introduces the rsync **--compress** and **--update** options. Using the **--compress** option causes rsync to compress files as it copies them, usually making the transfer go more quickly. See the note on page 693. The **--update** option keeps rsync from overwriting a newer file with an older one.

As with all shell scripts, you must have read and execute access to the **mirror** script. To make it easier to read, each option in this script appears on a line by itself. Each line of each command except the last is terminated with a SPACE and a backslash (\). The SPACE separates one option from the next; the backslash quotes the following NEWLINE so the shell passes all arguments to rsync and does not interpret the NEWLINES as the end of the command.

```
$ cat mirror
rsync \
--archive \
--verbose \
--compress \
--update \
--delete \
~/mirrordir/ guava:mirrordir

$ ./mirror > mirror.out
```

The **mirror** command in the example redirects output to **mirror.out** for review. Remove the **--verbose** option if you do not want the command to produce any output except for errors. The rsync command in **mirror** copies the **mirrordir** directory hierarchy from the user's home directory on the local system to the user's home directory on the remote (server) system. In this example the remote system is named **guava**. Because of use of the **--update** option, rsync will not overwrite newer versions of files on the server with older versions of the same files from the local system. Although this option is not required if files on the server system are never changed manually, it can save you from grief if you accidentally update files on or add files to the server system. The **--delete** option causes rsync to remove files on the server system that are not present on the local system.

Making Backups

After performing an initial full backup, rsync is able to perform subsequent incremental backups efficiently with regard to running time and storage space. By definition, an incremental backup stores only those files that have changed since the last backup; these are the only files that rsync needs to copy. As the following example shows, rsync, without using extra disk space, can make each incremental backup appear to be a full backup by creating hard links between the incremental backup and the unchanged files in the initial full backup.

--link-dest=*dir* The rsync **--link-dest=*dir*** option makes backups easy and efficient. It presents the user and/or system administrator with snapshots that appear to be full backups while taking minimal extra space in addition to the initial backup. The ***dir*** directory is always located on the machine holding the ***destination-file***. If ***dir*** is a relative pathname, the pathname is relative to the ***destination-file***. See page 692 for a description of this option.

Following is a simple rsync command that uses the **--link-dest=*dir*** option:

```
$ rsync --archive --link-dest=../backup source/ destination
```

When you run this command, rsync descends the **source** directory hierarchy, examining each file it finds. For each file in the **source** directory hierarchy, rsync looks in the **destination** directory hierarchy to find an exact copy of the file.

- If it finds an exact copy of the file in the **destination** directory, rsync continues with the next file.
- If it does not find an exact copy of the file in the **destination** directory, rsync looks in the **backup** directory to find an exact copy of the file.
  - If it finds an exact copy of the file in the **backup** directory, rsync makes a hard link from the file in the **backup** directory to the **destination** directory.
  - If it does not find an exact copy of the file in the **backup** directory, rsync copies the file from the **source** directory to the **destination** directory.

Next is a simple example showing how to use rsync to make full and incremental backups using the **--link-dest=*dir*** option. Although the backup files reside on the local system, they could easily be located on a remote system.

As specified by the two arguments to rsync in the **bkup** script, rsync copies the **memos** directory to the **bu.0** directory. The **--link-dest=*dir*** option causes rsync to check whether each file it needs to copy exists in **bu.1**. If it does, rsync creates a link to the **bu.1** file instead of copying it.

The **bkup** script rotates three backup directories named **bu.0**, **bu.1**, and **bu.2** and calls rsync. The script removes **bu.2**, moves **bu.1** to **bu.2**, and moves **bu.0** to **bu.1**. The first time you run the script, rsync copies all the files from **memos** because they do not exist in **bu.0** or **bu.1**.

```
$ cat bkup
rm -rf bu.2
mv bu.1 bu.2
mv bu.0 bu.1
rsync --archive --link-dest=../bu.1 memos/  bu.0
```

Before you run **bkup** for the first time, **bu.0**, **bu.1**, and **bu.2** do not exist. Because of the –f option, rm does not display an error message when it tries to remove the nonexistent **bu.2** directory. Until **bkup** creates **bu.0** and **bu.1**, mv displays error messages saying there is **No such file or directory**.

In the following example, ls shows the **bkup** script and the contents of the **memos** directory. After running **bkup**, ls shows the contents of **memos** and of the new **bu.0** directory; **bu.0** holds exact copies of the files in **memos**. The rsync utility created no links because there were no files in **bu.1**: The directory did not exist.

```
$ ls -l *
-rwxr-xr-x. 1 max pubs   87 05-18 11:24 bkup

memos:
-rw-r--r--. 1 max pubs 1500 05-14 14:24 0514
-rw-r--r--. 1 max pubs 6001 05-16 16:16 0516
-rw-r--r--. 1 max pubs 5911 05-18 12:02 0518

$ ./bkup
mv: cannot stat 'bu.1': No such file or directory
mv: cannot stat 'bu.0': No such file or directory
--link-dest arg does not exist: ../bu.1

$ ls -l *
-rwxr-xr-x. 1 max pubs   87 05-18 11:24 bkup

bu.0:
-rw-r--r--. 1 max pubs 1500 05-14 14:24 0514
-rw-r--r--. 1 max pubs 6001 05-16 16:16 0516
-rw-r--r--. 1 max pubs 5911 05-18 12:02 0518

memos:
-rw-r--r--. 1 max pubs 1500 05-14 14:24 0514
-rw-r--r--. 1 max pubs 6001 05-16 16:16 0516
-rw-r--r--. 1 max pubs 5911 05-18 12:02 0518
```

After working with the files in **memos**, ls shows **0518** has been removed and **newfile** has been added:

```
$ ls -l memos
-rw-r--r--. 1 max pubs 1208 05-21 14:16 0514
-rw-r--r--. 1 max pubs 6001 05-16 16:16 0516
-rw-r--r--. 1 max pubs 7501 05-21 14:16 newfile
```

After running **bkup** again, **bu.0** holds the same files as **memos** and **bu.1** holds the files that **bu.0** held before running **bkup**. The **0516** file has not changed, so rsync, with the **--link-dest=*dir*** option, has not copied it but rather has made a link from the copy in **bu.1** to the copy in **bu.0**, as indicated by the **2** ls displays between the permissions and **max**.

```
$ ./bkup
mv: cannot stat 'bu.1': No such file or directory

$ ls -l bu.0 bu.1
bu.0:
-rw-r--r--. 1 max pubs 1208 05-21 14:16 0514
-rw-r--r--. 2 max pubs 6001 05-16 16:16 0516
-rw-r--r--. 1 max pubs 7501 05-21 14:16 newfile

bu.1:
-rw-r--r--. 1 max pubs 1500 05-14 14:24 0514
-rw-r--r--. 2 max pubs 6001 05-16 16:16 0516
-rw-r--r--. 1 max pubs 5911 05-18 12:02 0518
```

The beauty of this setup is that each incremental backup occupies only the space needed to hold files that have changed. Files that have not changed are stored as links, which take up minimal disk space. Yet users and the system administrator have access to a directory that appears to hold a full backup.

You can run a backup script such as **bkup** once an hour, once a day, or as often as you like. Storage space permitting, you can have as many backup directories as you like. If rsync does not require a password, you can automate this process by using crontab (page 781).

RESTORING A FILE

To restore the most recent copy of a file, list all copies of the file and see which has the most recent date:

```
$ ls -l bu.?/0514
-rw-r--r--. 1 max pubs 1208 05-21 14:16 bu.0/0514
-rw-r--r--. 1 max pubs 1500 05-14 14:24 bu.1/0514
```

Then copy that file to the directory you want to restore it into. Use the **–a** option to keep the same date on the copy of the file as appears on the original file:

```
$ cp -a bu.0/0514 ~max/memos
```

If two copies of (links to) a file show the same time and date it does not matter which you restore from.

CHAPTER SUMMARY

The rsync utility copies an ordinary file or directory hierarchy locally or between the local system and a remote system on a network. By default, this utility uses openSSH to transfer files and the same authentication mechanism as openSSH; therefore, it provides the same security as openSSH. The rsync utility prompts for a password when it needs one.

Exercises

1. List three features of rsync.
2. Write an rsync command that copies the **backmeup** directory from your home directory on the local system to the **/tmp** directory on **guava**, preserving file ownership, permissions, and modification times. Write a command that will copy the same directory to your home directory on **guava**. Do not assume the working directory on the local system is your home directory.
3. You are writing an rsync command that includes the **--delete** option. Which options would you use to test the command without copying or removing any files?
4. What does the **--archive** option do? Why is it useful?
5. When running a script such as **bkup** (page 698) to back up files on a remote system, how could you rotate (rename) files on a remote system?
6. What effect does a trailing slash (**/**) on the ***source-file*** have?

17

The OpenSSH Secure Communication Utilities

In This Chapter

Objectives

After reading this chapter you should be able to:

- Explain the need for encrypted services
- Log in on a remote OpenSSH server system using ssh
- Copy files and directories to and from a remote system securely
- Set up an OpenSSH server
- Configure OpenSSH server options
- Set up a client/server so you do not need to use a password to log in using ssh or scp
- Enable trusted X11 tunneling between a client and an OpenSSH server
- Remove a known host record from the **~/.ssh/known_hosts** file
- Enable trusted X11 forwarding
- List the uses of ssh tunneling (port forwarding)

OpenSSH is a suite of secure network connectivity tools that replaces **telnet/telnetd**, **rcp**, **rsh/rshd**, **rlogin/rlogind**, and **ftp/ftpd**. Unlike the tools they replace, OpenSSH tools encrypt all traffic, including passwords. In this way they can thwart attackers who attempt to eavesdrop, hijack connections, and steal passwords.

This chapter covers the following OpenSSH tools:

- **scp**—Copies files to and from a remote system (page 713)
- **sftp**—Copies files to and from a remote system (a secure replacement for **ftp**; page 715)
- **ssh**—Runs a command on or logs in on a remote system
- **sshd**—The OpenSSH daemon (runs on the server; page 717)
- **ssh-add**—Adds a passphrase for a private key for use by **ssh-agent**.
- **ssh-agent**—Holds your private keys
- **ssh-copy-id**—Appends your public key to **~/.ssh/authorized_keys** on a remote system so you do not need a password to log in (page 719)
- **ssh-keygen**—Creates, manages, and converts RSA or DSA host/user authentication keys (page 718)

INTRODUCTION TO OPENSSH

ssh The **ssh** utility allows you to log in on a remote system over a network. You might choose to use a remote system to access a special-purpose application or to take advantage of a device that is available only on that system, or you might use a remote system because you know it is faster or less busy than the local system. While traveling, many businesspeople use **ssh** on a laptop to log in on a system at company headquarters. From a GUI you can use several systems simultaneously by logging in on each one from a different terminal emulator window.

X11 forwarding When you turn on trusted X11 forwarding on an **ssh** client, it is a simple matter to run a graphical program over an **ssh** connection to a server that has X11 forwarding enabled: Run **ssh** from a terminal emulator running on an X11 server and give an X11 command such as **gnome-calculator**; the graphical output appears on the local display. For more information refer to "Forwarding X11" on page 725.

Security When a client contacts an OpenSSH server, it establishes an encrypted connection and then authenticates the user. When these two tasks are complete, OpenSSH allows the two systems to send information back and forth. The first time an OpenSSH client connects with an OpenSSH server, OpenSSH asks you to verify that the client is connected to the correct server (see "First-time authentication" on page 707). This verification helps prevent an MITM attack (page 1108).

FILES

OpenSSH clients and servers rely on many files. Global files are kept in **/etc/ssh** and user files in **~/.ssh**. In this section, the first word in the description of each file indicates whether the client or the server uses the file. Some of these files are not present on a newly installed system.

rhost authentication is a security risk

security Although OpenSSH can get authentication information from **/etc/hosts.equiv**, **/etc/shosts.equiv**, **~/.rhosts**, and **~/.shosts**, this chapter does not cover the use of these files because they present security risks. The default settings in the **/etc/ssh/sshd_config** configuration file prevent their use.

/etc/ssh: GLOBAL FILES

Global files listed in this section appear in the **/etc/ssh** directory. They affect all users, but a user can override them with files in her **~/.ssh** directory.

moduli **client and server** Contains key exchange information that OpenSSH uses to establish a secure connection. Do not modify this file.

ssh_config **client** The global OpenSSH client configuration file (page 715). Entries here can be overridden by entries in a user's **~/.ssh/config** file.

sshd_config **server** The configuration file for the **sshd** server (page 722).

ssh_host_*xxx*_key
ssh_host_*xxx*_key.pub

server Hold the *xxx* host key pair where *xxx* is **dsa** for DSA keys, **ecdsa** for ECDSA (elliptic curve digital signature algorithm) keys, **ed25519** for ed25519 (a variant ECDSA) keys, or **rsa** for RSA keys. Both files should be owned by **root**. The **ssh_host_*xxx*_key.pub** public file should be readable by anyone but writable only by its owner (644 permissions). The **ssh_host_*xxx*_key** private file should not be readable or writable by anyone except its owner (600 permissions).

ssh_import_id **server** Holds the URL of the keyserver that ssh-import-id obtains public keys from (it uses launchpad.net by default).

ssh_known_hosts

client Holds the public keys of hosts that users on the local system can connect to. This file contains information similar to that found in **~/.ssh/known_hosts** but is set up by the administrator and is available to all users. This file should be owned by **root** and should be readable by anyone but writable only by its owner (644 permissions).

~/.ssh: USER FILES

OpenSSH creates the **~/.ssh** directory and the **known_hosts** file therein automatically when a user connects to a remote system. No one except the owner should have any access to the **~/.ssh** directory.

authorized_keys

server Holds user public keys and enables a user to log in on or copy files to and from another system without supplying a user login password. However, the user might need to supply a passphrase, depending on how a key was set up. No one except the owner should be able to write to this file.

config **client** A user's private OpenSSH configuration file (page 715). Entries here override those in **/etc/ssh/ssh_config**.

environment **server** Contains assignment statements that define environment variables on a server when a user logs in using ssh.

id_*xxx* id_*xxx*.pub **client** Hold the user authentication *xxx* keys generated by ssh-keygen (page 718) where *xxx* is **dsa** for DSA keys, **ecdsa** for ECDSA keys, **ed25519** for ed25519 (a variant ECDSA) keys, or **rsa** for RSA keys. Both files should be owned by the user in whose home directory they appear. The **id_*xxx*.pub** public key file should be readable by anyone but writable only by its owner (644 permissions). The **id_*xxx*** private key file should not be readable or writable by anyone except its owner (600 permissions).

known_hosts **client** Contains public keys of hosts the user has connected to. OpenSSH automatically adds entries each time the user connects to a new server (page 707). If **HashKnownHosts** (page 716) is set to **yes** (default), the hostnames and addresses in this file are hashed to improve security.

More Information

Local man pages: ssh, scp, sftp, ssh-copy-id, ssh-keygen, ssh-agent, ssh-add, ssh_config, sshd, sshd_config

Web OpenSSH home page: www.openssh.com
Search on **ssh** to find various HOWTOs and other documents: tldp.org

Books *Implementing SSH: Strategies for Optimizing the Secure Shell* by Dwivedi; John Wiley & Sons (October 2003)
SSH, The Secure Shell: The Definitive Guide by Barrett, Silverman, & Byrnes; O'Reilly Media (May 2005)

Running the ssh, scp, and sftp OpenSSH Clients

This section covers setting up and using the ssh, scp, and sftp clients.

Prerequisites

Install the following package (installed by default in most Linux distros):

- **openssh**

OpenSSH clients do not run a daemon so there is no service to set up.

JumpStart I: Using ssh and scp to Connect to an OpenSSH Server

The ssh and scp clients do not require setup beyond installing the requisite package, although you can create and edit files that facilitate their use. To run a secure shell on or securely copy a file to or from a remote system, the following criteria must be met: The remote system must be running the OpenSSH daemon (**sshd**), you must have an account on the remote system, and the server must positively identify itself to the client.

ssh The following example shows Zach working on the system named **guava** and using ssh to log in on the remote host named **plum**, running **who am i**, and giving an **exit** command to return to the shell on the local system. The who utility displays the hostname of the system Zach logged in from.

You can omit ***user*@** (**zach@** in the example) from the command line if you want to log in as yourself and if you have the same username on both systems. The first time you connect to a remote OpenSSH server, ssh or scp asks you to confirm that you are connected to the right system. Refer to "First-time authentication" on this page.

scp In the following example, Zach uses scp to copy **ty1** from the working directory on the local system to Zach's home directory on **plum**:

```
zach@guava:~$ scp ty1 zach@plum:
zach@plum's password:
ty1                                  100%  964KB 963.6KB/s   00:00
```

You must follow the name of the remote system with a colon (:). If you omit the colon, scp copies the file locally; in the example you would end up with a copy of **ty1** named **zach@plum**.

Configuring OpenSSH Clients

This section describes how to set up OpenSSH on the client side.

Recommended Settings

X11 forwarding The configuration files provided with most distributions establish a mostly secure system that might or might not meet your needs. One OpenSSH parameter you might want to change is ForwardX11Trusted, which defaults to **yes** in most distros. To increase security, and in some cases reduce usability, set ForwardX11Trusted to **no**. See page 725 for more information on X11 forwarding.

Server Authentication/Known Hosts

Two files list the hosts the local system has connected to and positively identified: **~/.ssh/known_hosts** (user) and **/etc/ssh/ssh_known_hosts** (global). No one except the owner (**root** in the case of the second file) should be able to write to either of these files. No one except the owner should have any access to a **~/.ssh** directory.

First-time authentication When you connect to an OpenSSH server for the first time, the OpenSSH client prompts you to confirm that you are connected to the correct system. This behavior is controlled by **StrictHostKeyChecking** (page 716). This check can help prevent an MITM attack (page 1108):

```
The authenticity of host 'plum (192.168.206.181)' can't be established.
ECDSA key fingerprint is af:18:e5:75:ea:97:f9:49:2b:9e:08:9d:01:f3:7b:d9.
Are you sure you want to continue connecting (yes/no)? yes
Warning: Permanently added 'plum,192.168.206.181' (ECDSA) to the list of
known hosts.
```

Before you respond to the preceding query, make sure you are logging in on the correct system and not on an imposter. If you are not sure, a telephone call to someone who logs in on that system locally can help verify that you are on the intended system. When you answer **yes** (you must spell it out), the client appends the public host key of the server (the single line in the **/etc/ssh/ssh_host_ecdsa_key.pub** or other **.pub** file on the server) to the user's **~/.ssh/known_hosts** file on the local system, creating the **~/.ssh** directory if necessary.

When you subsequently use OpenSSH to connect to that server, the client uses its copy of the public host key of the server to verify it is connected to the correct server.

known_hosts The **~/.ssh/known_hosts** file uses one or two very long lines to identify each host it keeps track of. Each line starts with the hostname and IP address of the system the line corresponds to, followed by the type of encryption being used and the server's public host key. When **HashKnownHosts** (page 716) is set to **yes** (), OpenSSH hashes the system name and IP address to improve security. Because OpenSSH hashes the hostname and IP address separately, OpenSSH puts two lines in **known_hosts** for each host. The following line (logical line wraps on to several physical lines) from **known_hosts** using *ECDSA* (page 1096) encryption:

```
$ cat ~/.ssh/known_hosts
plum,172.16.192.151 ssh-rsa AAAAB3NzaC1yc2EAAAADAQABAAABAQDbhLRVTfI
v9gy7oP+5T3HjZmrKt2q6ydyKmLlHNUjZFXM4hCdkJlpTfJ4wy260UAZBWvrBLP6N9k
...
```

You can use ssh-keygen with the **–R** (remove) option followed by the hostname to remove an entry, even a hashed one. Alternately, you can use a text editor to remove an entry. The ssh-keygen **–F** option displays a line in a **known_hosts** file that corresponds to a specified system, even if the entry is hashed:

ssh_known_hosts As just described, OpenSSH automatically stores public keys from servers it has connected to in user-private files (**~/.ssh/known_hosts**). These files work only for the user whose directory they appear in. Working with **root** privileges and using a text editor, you can copy lines from a user's private list of known hosts to the public list in **/etc/ssh/ssh_known_hosts** to make a server known globally on the local system.

The following example shows Sam putting the hashed entry from his **known_hosts** file into the global **ssh_known_hosts** file. First, working as himself, Sam sends the output of ssh-keygen through tail to strip off the **Host plum found** line and redirects the output to a file named **tmp_known_hosts** in his home directory. Next, working with **root** privileges, Sam appends the contents of the file he just created to **/etc/ssh/ssh_known_hosts**. This command creates this file if it does not exist. Finally, Sam returns to working as himself and removes the temporary file he created.

If, after a remote system's public key is stored in one of the known-hosts files, the remote system supplies a key with a different fingerprint, OpenSSH displays the following message and does not complete the connection:

```
@@@@@@@@@@@@@@@@@@@@@@@@@@@@@@@@@@@@@@@@@@@@@@@@@@@@@@@@@@@
@    WARNING: REMOTE HOST IDENTIFICATION HAS CHANGED!     @
@@@@@@@@@@@@@@@@@@@@@@@@@@@@@@@@@@@@@@@@@@@@@@@@@@@@@@@@@@@
IT IS POSSIBLE THAT SOMEONE IS DOING SOMETHING NASTY!
Someone could be eavesdropping on you right now (man-in-the-middle
attack)!
It is also possible that the RSA host key has just been changed.
The fingerprint for the RSA key sent by the remote host is
f1:6f:ea:87:bb:1b:df:cd:e3:45:24:60:d3:25:b1:0a.
Please contact your system administrator.
Add correct host key in /home/sam/.ssh/known_hosts to get rid of this
message.
Offending key in /home/sam/.ssh/known_hosts:1
RSA host key for plum has changed and you have requested strict
checking.
Host key verification failed.
```

If OpenSSH displays this message, you might be the subject of an MITM attack. More likely, however, something on the remote system changed, causing it to supply a new key. Check with the administrator of the remote system. If all is well, use an editor to remove the offending key from the specified file (the fourth line from the bottom in the preceding message points to the line you need to remove) and try connecting again. Alternately, you can use ssh-keygen with the **–R** option followed by the name of a host to remove an entry. When you reconnect, you will be subject to first-time authentication (page 707) again as OpenSSH verifies you are connecting to the correct system. Follow the same steps as when you initially connected to the remote host.

ssh: Logs in or Executes Commands on a Remote System

The syntax of an ssh command line is

ssh [options] [user@]host [command]

where ***host***, the name of the OpenSSH server (the remote system) you want to connect to, is the only required argument. The ***host*** can be a local system name, the *FQDN* (page 1099) of a system on the Internet, or an IP address.

With the command **ssh *host***, you log in on the remote system ***host*** with the same username you are using on the local system. The remote system displays a shell prompt, and you can run commands on ***host***. Enter the command **exit** to close the connection to ***host*** and return to the local system prompt. Include ***user@*** when you want to log in with a username other than the one you are using on the local system. Depending on how the server is set up, you might need to supply the password you use on the remote system.

When you include ***command***, ssh logs in on ***host***, executes ***command***, closes the connection to ***host***, and returns control to the local system. The remote system never displays a shell prompt.

Opening a remote shell

In the following example, Sam, who is logged in on **guava**, uses ssh to log in on **plum**, gives a **uname** command that shows the name and type of the remote system, and uses **exit** to close the connection to **plum** and return to the local system's prompt:

```
[sam@guava ~]$ ssh plum
sam@plum's password:
[sam@plum ~]$ uname -nm
```

```
plum i686
[sam@plum ~]$ exit
logout
Connection to plum closed.
[sam@guava ~]$
```

Running commands remotely

The following example uses **ls** to list the files in the **memos** directory on the remote system named **plum**. The example assumes the user running the command (Sam) has an account on **plum** and that the **memos** directory is in Sam's home directory on **plum**:

```
$ ssh plum ls memos
sam@plum's password:
memo.0921
memo.draft
$
```

When you run **ssh**, standard output of the command run on the remote system is passed to the local shell as though the command had been run on the local system. As with all shell commands, you must quote special characters that you do not want the local shell to interpret.

In the next example, standard output of the **ls** command, which is run on the remote system, is sent to **ls.out** on the local system.

```
$ ssh plum ls memos > ls.out
sam@plum's password:
$ cat ls.out
memo.0921
memo.draft
```

In the preceding **ssh** command, the redirect symbol (>) is not quoted, so it is interpreted by the local shell and creates the **ls.out** file on the local system.

The next command is similar, but the redirect symbol and the filename are quoted, so the local shell does not interpret them but passes them to the remote shell. The first command creates the **ls.out2** file on the remote system, and the second command displays the file.

```
$ ssh plum 'ls memos > ls.out2'
sam@plum's password:
$ ssh plum cat ls.out2
sam@plum's password:
memo.0921
memo.draft
```

For the next example, assume the working directory on the local system holds a file named **memo.new**. Sam cannot remember whether this file contains certain changes or whether he made these changes to the file named **memo.draft** in the **memos** directory on **plum**. He could copy **memo.draft** to the local system and run **diff** (page 795) on the two files, but then he would have three similar copies of the file spread across two systems. If he is not careful about removing the old copies when he is done, Sam might just become confused again in a few days. Instead of copying the file, you can use **ssh**. This example shows that only the date line differs between the two files:

```
$ ssh plum cat memos/memo.draft | diff memo.new -
sam@plum's password:
1c1
< Thu Jun 14 12:22:14 PDT 2018
---
> Tue Jun 12 17:05:51 PDT 2018
```

In the preceding example, the output of the cat command on **plum** is sent through a pipeline on the local system to diff (running on the local system), which compares the local file **memos.new** to standard input (–). The following command line has the same effect but causes diff to run on the remote system:

```
$ cat memo.new | ssh plum diff - memos/memo.draft
sam@plum's password:
1c1
< Thu Jun 14 12:22:14 PDT 2018
---
> Tue Jun 12 17:05:51 PDT 2018
```

Standard output from diff on the remote system is sent to the local shell, which displays it on the screen (because it is not redirected).

optional Sam now decides to change the password for his **sls** login on **plum**:

```
$ ssh sls@plum passwd
sls@plum's password:
(current) UNIX password: por
```

Sam stops as soon as he sees passwd (running on **plum**) displaying his password: He knows something is wrong. For passwd to work, it must run with a tty (terminal) so it can turn off character echo (**stty –echo**); then it will not display passwords as the user enters them. The **–t** option solves the problem by associating a pseudo-tty with the process running passwd on the remote system:

```
$ ssh -t sls@plum passwd
sls@plum's password:
Changing password for sls.
(current) UNIX password:
Enter new UNIX password:
Retype new UNIX password:
passwd: password updated successfully
Connection to plum closed.
```

The **–t** option is also useful when you are running a program that uses a character-based/pseudographical interface.

Using tar The following example uses tar (page 995) to create an archive file on a remote system containing the contents of the working directory hierarchy on the local system. The **f –** option causes tar to send its output to standard output. A pipeline sends the output of tar running on the local system, via ssh, to dd running on the remote system.

```
$ cat buwd
#! /bin/bash
```

```
# Back up the working directory to the user's
# home directory on the remote system specified
# by $machine

# Remote system:
machine=plum

dir=$(basename $(pwd))
filename=$$.$dir.tar

echo Backing up $(pwd) to your home directory on $machine
tar -cf - . | ssh $machine "dd obs=256k of=$filename"
echo done. Name of file on $machine is $filename

$ ./buwd
Backing up /home/sam to your home directory on plum
10340+0 records in
20+1 records out
5294080 bytes (5.3 MB) copied, 0.243011 s, 21.8 MB/s
done. Name of file on plum is 26537.sam.tar
```

Options

This section describes some of the options you can use with ssh.

–C (**compression**) Enables compression (page 727).

–f (**not foreground**) Sends ssh to the background after asking for a password and before executing the ***command***. Useful when you want to run the ***command*** in the background but must supply a password. Implies **–n**.

–i *filename* (**identity**) Instructs ssh to read the private key from ***filename*** instead of **~/.ssh/id_dsa**, **~/.ssh/id_ecdsa**, **~/.ssh/id_ed25519**, or **~/.ssh/id_rsa** for automatic login.

–L Forwards a port on the local system to a remote system. For more information refer to "Tunneling/Port Forwarding" on page 724.

–l *user* (**login**) Attempts to log in as ***user***.

–n (**null**) Redirects standard input to ssh to come from **/dev/null**. Required when running ssh in the background (**–f** option).

–o *option* (**option**) Specifies ***option*** in the format used in configuration files (page 715).

–p (**port**) Specifies the port on the remote host that the connection is made to. Using the **host** declaration (page 716) in the configuration file, you can specify a different port for each system you connect to.

–R Forwards a port on the remote system to the local client. For more information refer to "Tunneling/Port Forwarding" on page 724.

–t (**tty**) Allocates a pseudo-tty (terminal) to the ssh process on the remote system. Without this option, when you run a command on a remote system, ssh does not allocate a tty (terminal) to the process. Instead, it attaches standard input and standard output of the remote process to the ssh session—which is normally, but not always, what you want. This option forces ssh to allocate a tty on the remote system so programs that require a tty will work.

–v (**verbose**) Displays debugging messages about the connection and transfer. Useful if things are not going as expected. Specify this option up to three times to increase verbosity.

–X (**X11**) Turns on nontrusted X11 forwarding. This option is not necessary if you turn on nontrusted X11 forwarding in the configuration file. For more information refer to "Forwarding X11" on page 725.

–x (**X11**) Turns off X11 forwarding.

–Y (**X11trusted**) Turns on trusted X11 forwarding. This option is not necessary if you turn on trusted X11 forwarding in the configuration file. For more information refer to "Forwarding X11" on page 725.

scp: Copies Files to and from a Remote System

The scp (secure copy) utility copies ordinary and directory files from one system to another over a network; both systems can be remote. This utility uses ssh to transfer files and employs the same authentication mechanism as ssh; thus, it provides the same security as ssh. The scp utility asks for a password when one is required. The format of an scp command is

scp [[user@]from-host:]source-file [[user@]to-host:][destination-file]

where ***from-host*** is the name of the system you are copying files from and ***to-host*** is the system you are copying to. The ***from-host*** and ***to-host*** arguments can be local system names, *FQDNs* (page 1099) of systems on the Internet, or IP addresses. When you do not specify a host, scp assumes the local system. The ***user*** on either system defaults to the user on the local system who is giving the command; you can use ***user*** to specify a different user.

The ***source-file*** is the file you are copying, and the ***destination-file*** is the resulting copy. Make sure you have read permission for the file you are copying and write permission for the directory you are copying it into. You can specify plain or directory files as relative or absolute pathnames. (A relative pathname is relative to the specified directory or to the implicit user's home directory.) When the ***source-file*** is a directory, you must use the **–r** option to copy its contents. When the ***destination-file*** is a directory, each of the source files maintains its simple filename. When the ***destination-file*** is missing, scp assumes the user's home directory.

Suppose Sam has an alternate username, **sls**, on **plum**. In the following example, Sam uses scp to copy **memo.txt** from the home directory of his **sls** account on **plum** to the **allmemos** directory in the working directory on the local system. If **allmemos** were not the name of a directory, **memo.txt** would be copied to a file named **allmemos** in the working directory.

As the transfer progresses, the percentage and number of bytes transferred increase, and the time remaining decreases.

rsync **is much more versatile than** scp

tip The rsync utility is more configurable than scp and uses OpenSSH security by default. It has many options; the most commonly used are **–a** and **–v**. The **–a** option causes rsync to copy ordinary files and directories, preserving the ownership, group, permissions, and modification times associated with the files. It usually does no harm to specify the **–a** option and frequently helps. The **–v** option causes rsync to list files as it copies them. For example, Sam could have given the preceding command as

```
$ rsync -av sls@plum:memo.txt allmemos
sls@plum's password:
receiving incremental file list
memo.txt

sent 30 bytes  received 87495 bytes  19450.00 bytes/sec
total size is 87395  speedup is 1.00
```

The rsync utility is also smarter than scp. If the destination file exists, rsync copies only the parts of the source file that are different from the destination file. This feature can save a lot of time when copying large files with few changes, such as when making backups. The number following **speedup** in the output indicates how much rsync's algorithm has speeded up the process of copying a file. See Chapter 16 for more information on rsync.

In the next example, Sam, while working from **guava**, copies the same file as in the previous example to the directory named **old** in his home directory on **speedy**. For this example to work, Sam must be able to use ssh to log in on **speedy** from **plum** without using a password.

Options

This section describes some of the options you can use with scp.

–C (**compression**) Enables compression (page 727).

–o ***option*** (**option**) Specifies ***option*** in the format used in configuration files (discussed shortly).

–P ***port*** (**port**) Connects to port ***port*** on the remote host. This option is uppercase for scp and in lowercase for ssh.

–p (**preserve**) Preserves the modification and access times as well as the modes of the original file.

–q (**quiet**) Prevents scp from displaying progress information as it copies a file.

–r (**recursive**) Recursively copies a directory hierarchy (follows symbolic links).

–v (**verbose**) Displays debugging messages about the connection and transfer. Useful if things are not going as expected.

sftp: A SECURE FTP CLIENT

OpenSSH provides sftp, a secure alternative to ftp. Functionally the same as ftp, sftp maps ftp commands to OpenSSH commands. You can replace ftp with sftp when you are logging in on a server that is running the OpenSSH daemon, **sshd**. While you are using sftp, enter the command ? to display a list of commands. Refer to the sftp man page for more information.

lftp Alternately, you can use lftp (**lftp** package), which is more sophisticated than sftp and supports sftp. The lftp utility provides a shell-like command syntax that has many features, including support for tab completion and the ability to run jobs in the background. Place the following **.lftprc** file in your home directory to ensure that lftp uses OpenSSH to connect to a server:

```
$ cat ~/.lftprc
set default-protocol sftp
```

With this setup, when you connect to a remote system using lftp, you do not need an FTP server running on the remote system; you only need OpenSSH. You can also use **/etc/lftp.conf** to configure lftp; see the lftp man page for more information.

~/.ssh/config AND /etc/ssh/ssh_config CONFIGURATION FILES

It is rarely necessary to modify OpenSSH client configuration files. For a given user there might be two configuration files: **~/.ssh/config** (user) and **/etc/ssh/ssh_config** (global). These files are read in this order and, for a given parameter, the first one found is the one OpenSSH uses. A user can override a global parameter setting by setting the same parameter in her user configuration file. Parameters given on the ssh or scp command line take precedence over parameters set in either of these files.

For security, a user's **~/.ssh/config** file should be owned by the user in whose home directory it appears and should not be writable by anyone except the owner. This file is typically set to mode 600 as there is no reason for anyone except its owner to be able to read it.

Lines in the configuration files contain declarations. Each of these declarations starts with a keyword that is not case sensitive. Some keywords must be followed by whitespace and one or more case-sensitive arguments. You can use the **Host** keyword to cause declarations to apply to a specific system. A Host declaration applies to all the lines between it and the next Host declaration.

Following are some of the keywords and arguments you can specify. Initial values are underlined.

CheckHostIP **yes** | **no**

Identifies a remote system using the IP address in addition to a hostname from the **known_hosts** file when set to **yes**. Set it to **no** to use a hostname only. Setting CheckHostIP to **yes** can improve system security.

ForwardX11 yes | no

When set to **yes**, automatically forwards X11 connections over a secure channel in nontrusted mode and sets the **DISPLAY** shell variable. Allow this keyword to default to **no** so X11 forwarding is *not* initially enabled. If ForwardX11Trusted is also set to **yes**, the connections are made in trusted mode. Alternately, you can use the **–X** option on the command line to redirect X11 connections in nontrusted mode. For X11 forwarding to work, X11Forwarding must be set to **yes** in the **/etc/ssh/sshd_config** file on the server (default is **no**; page 724). For more information refer to "Forwarding X11" on page 725.

ForwardX11Trusted yes | no

Works in conjunction with ForwardX11, which must be set to **yes** for this keyword to have any effect. When this keyword has a value of **yes** and ForwardX11 is set to **yes**, this keyword gives remote X11 clients full access to the original (server) X11 display. Alternately, you can use the **–Y** option on the command line to redirect X11 connections in trusted mode. For X11 forwarding to work, X11Forwarding must be set to **yes** in the **/etc/ssh/sshd_config** file on the server (default is **no**; page 724). For more information refer to "Forwarding X11" on page 725.

HashKnownHosts yes | no

Causes OpenSSH to hash hostnames and addresses in the **~/.ssh/known_hosts** file (page 708) when set to **yes**. When set to **no**, the hostnames and addresses are written in cleartext.

Host *hostnames* Specifies that the following declarations, until the next Host declaration, apply only to hosts that ***hostnames*** matches. The ***hostnames*** is a whitespace-separated list that can include **?** and ***** wildcards. A single ***** specifies all hosts. Without this keyword, all declarations apply to all hosts.

HostbasedAuthentication yes | no

Tries **rhosts** authentication when set to **yes**. For a more secure system, set to **no**.

HostKeyAlgorithms *algorithms*

The ***algorithms*** is a comma-separated list of algorithms the client uses in order of preference. See the **ssh_config** man page for details.

Port *num* Causes OpenSSH to connect to the remote system on port ***num***. Default is 22.

StrictHostKeyChecking yes | no | ask

Determines whether and how OpenSSH adds host keys to a user's **known_hosts** file (page 708). Set this option to **ask** to ask whether to add a host key when connecting to a new system, **no** to add a host key automatically, or **yes** to require host keys to be added manually. The **yes** and **ask** arguments cause OpenSSH to refuse to connect to a system whose host key has changed. For a more secure system, set to **yes** or **ask**.

TCPKeepAlive yes | no

Periodically checks whether a connection is alive when set to **yes**. Checking causes the ssh or scp connection to be dropped when the server crashes or the connection dies for another reason, even if the interruption is temporary. This option tests the connection at the transport (TCP) layer (page 1128). Setting this parameter to **no** causes the client not to check whether the connection is alive.

This declaration uses the TCP **keepalive** option, which is not encrypted and is susceptible to *IP spoofing* (page 1104). Refer to **ClientAliveInterval** on page 722 for a server-based nonspoofable alternative.

User *name* Specifies a username to use when logging in on a system. You can specify a system with the Host declaration. This option means you do not have to enter a username on the command line when you log in using a username that differs from your username on the local system.

VisualHostKey yes | no
Displays an ASCII art representation (randomart; page 719) of the key of the remote system in addition to the hexadecimal representation (fingerprint) of the key when set to **yes**. When set to **no**, this declaration displays the fingerprint only.

Setting Up an OpenSSH Server (sshd)

This section describes how to set up an OpenSSH server.

Prerequisites

Install the following package:

- **openssh-server**

Note

Firewall An OpenSSH server normally uses TCP port 22.

JumpStart II: Starting an OpenSSH Server

You can display the file or give the command to make sure everything is working properly.

Recommended Settings

The configuration files provided by establish a mostly secure system that might or might not meet your needs. The **/etc/ssh/sshd_config** file turns on X11 forwarding (page 725). It is important to set PermitRootLogin (page 723) to **no**, which prevents a known-name, privileged account from being exposed to the outside world with only password protection.

Authorized Keys: Automatic Login

You can configure OpenSSH so you do not have to enter a password each time you connect to a server (remote system). To set up this feature, you need to generate a key pair on the client (local system), place the public key on the server, and keep the private key on the client. When you connect to the server, it issues a challenge based on the public key. OpenSSH then uses the private key to respond to this challenge. If the client provides the appropriate response, the server logs you in.

The first step in setting up an automatic login is to generate your key pair. First, check whether these authentication keys already exist on the local system by looking in **~/.ssh** for **id_*xxx*** and **id_*xxx*.pub** where *xxx* is **dsa** for DSA keys, **ecdsa** for ECDSA keys, **ed25519** for ed25519 keys, or **rsa** for RSA keys. If one of these pairs of files is present, skip the next step (do not create a new key).

ssh-keygen On the client, the ssh-keygen utility generates a key pair. The key's randomart image is a visual representation of the public key.

```
$ ssh-keygen -t ecdsa
Generating public/private ecdsa key pair.
Enter file in which to save the key (/home/sam/.ssh/id_ecdsa):
Enter passphrase (empty for no passphrase):
Enter same passphrase again:
Your identification has been saved in /home/sam/.ssh/id_ecdsa.
Your public key has been saved in /home/sam/.ssh/id_ecdsa.pub.
The key fingerprint is:
41:f2:6a:06:4e:8c:82:c4:0b:a4:a1:4d:13:ab:d8:6f sam@plum.example.com
The key's randomart image is:
+--[ECDSA  256]---+
|+o+.   . .       |
|*= =    +        |
|* = +    o       |
|.= o . . .       |
|o . . + S        |
|    . o          |
|     E           |
|    .            |
|                 |
+-----------------+
```

Replace **ecdsa** with **dsa** to generate DSA keys, **rsa** for RSA keys, or **ed25519** for ed25519 keys. In this example, the user pressed RETURN in response to each query. You have the option of specifying a passphrase (10–30 characters is a good length) to encrypt the private part of the key. There is no way to recover a lost passphrase. See the "Personal key encryption, passphrase, and ssh-agent" security tip on page 721 for more information on passphrases.

id_ecdsa and **id_ecdsa.pub** In the preceding example, the ssh-keygen utility generates two keys: a private key in **~/.ssh/id_ecdsa** and a public key in **~/.ssh/id_ecdsa.pub**. If you create another type of key, ssh-keygen will put them in appropriately named files. No one except the owner should be able to write to either of these files, and only the owner should be able to read the private key file.

You can use ssh-keygen to display the fingerprint of the public key you just created:

```
$ ssh-keygen -lf ~/.ssh/id_ecdsa.pub
2048 23:8f:99:2e:43:36:93:ed:c6:38:fe:4d:04:61:27:28
/home/sam/.ssh/id_ecdsa.pub (ECDSA)
```

You can also display the key fingerprint of the local server using ssh-keygen:

```
$ ssh-keygen -lf /etc/ssh/ssh_host_ecdsa_key.pub
2048 d1:9d:1b:5b:97:5c:80:e9:4b:41:9a:b7:bc:1a:ea:a1
/etc/ssh/ssh_host_ecdsa_key.pub (ECDSA)
```

ssh-copy-id To log in on or copy files to and from another system without supplying a password, you append your public key (in the example, although ssh-copy-id copies any type of public key) to the file named **~/.ssh/authorized_keys** on the server (remote system). The ssh-copy-id utility creates the **~/.ssh** directory on the server if necessary, appends, and makes sure permissions are correct. The following example shows Sam setting up automatic login on the system named **plum**. You can ignore INFO messages that ssh-copy-id displays.

```
$ ssh-copy-id sam@plum
/usr/bin/ssh-copy-id: INFO: attempting to log in with the new key(s) ...
/usr/bin/ssh-copy-id: INFO: 1 key(s) remain to be installed ...
sam@plum's password:

Number of key(s) added: 1

Now try logging into the machine, with:   "ssh 'sam@plum'"
and check to make sure that only the key(s) you wanted were added.

$ ssh sam@plum
Welcome to Ubuntu 16.04 LTS (GNU/Linux 4.12.0-24-generic i686)
...
```

Sam must supply his password to copy his key file to **plum**. After running ssh-copy-id, Sam can log in on **plum** without providing a password. However, see the tip titled "You must still specify a passphrase." To make the server even more secure, disable password authentication (see the tip titled "Use a personal authentication key instead of a password" on this page). Automatic login will fail (you will have to enter a password) if anyone other than the owner has permission to read from or write to the **~/.ssh** directory on the server.

You must still specify a passphrase

tip If you specified a passphrase when you generated your key pair, you must enter that passphrase each time you log in to the remote machine, even after you set up automatic login. However, you can use ssh-agent to specify your passphrase only once per session.

Use a personal authentication key instead of a password

security Using a key pair to authenticate is more secure than using a password. When you turn off password authentication, brute-force authentication attacks become very unlikely.

Disable password authentication by setting **PasswordAuthentication** to **no** in **/etc/ssh/sshd_config** (remove the **#** from the beginning of the **PasswordAuthentication** line and change the **yes** to **no**; page 723).

RANDOMART IMAGE

The *randomart* image of a system is an OpenSSH ASCII representation of the public key of the host system. This image is displayed by OpenSSH utilities, including ssh, scp, and ssh-keygen. Its display is controlled by the **VisualHostKey** keyword in the **ssh_config** file (page 717) on the client. With this keyword set to **yes**, OpenSSH displays a system's randomart image when you connect:

```
$ ssh sam@plum
Host key fingerprint is af:18:e5:75:ea:97:f9:49:2b:9e:08:9d:01:f3:7b:d9
+--[ECDSA  256]---+
|                 |
|                 |
|        o        |
|         +       |
|        S + .    |
|       o + * o   |
|      . o * ooE  |
|       o + o=o o |
|      . . oooo+  |
+-----------------+
...
```

The randomart image renders a system's host key in a visual format that can be easier to recall than a host key fingerprint (see the preceding example). Making it easier for a user to detect a change in the fingerprint can mean that a user will be aware when he is connecting to a system other than the one he intended to connect to.

ssh-agent: Holds Your Private Keys

When you use ssh-keygen to generate a key pair, you have the option of specifying a passphrase. If you specify a passphrase, you must supply that passphrase each time you use the key. The result is, when you set up a key pair to avoid specifying your password when you log in on a remote system using ssh, you end up supplying the passphrase instead.

If your private key has no passphrase, ssh-agent serves no purpose

tip Using the technique described under "Authorized Keys: Automatic Login" on page 717, you can log in on a remote system without supplying your password. However, if you specified a passphrase when you set up your key pair, you must still supply that passphrase. The ssh-agent utility sets up a session so that you have to supply your passphrase only once, at the beginning of the session. Then, assuming you have set up automatic login, you can log in on a remote system without specifying either the password for the remote system or the passphrase for your private key.

Personal key encryption, passphrase, and ssh-agent

security Your private key is kept in a file that only you can read. When you set up automatic login on a remote system, any user who has access to your account on the local system also has access to your account on the remote system because that user can read your private key. Thus, if an attacker compromises your account or the **root** account on the local system, that attacker has access to your account on the remote system.

Encrypting your private key protects the key and, therefore, restricts access to the remote system should an attacker compromise your local account. However, if you encrypt your private key, you must supply the passphrase you used to encrypt the key each time you use the key, negating the benefit of not having to type a password when logging in on the remote system.

The ssh-agent utility allows you to enter your passphrase once, at the beginning of a session, and remembers it so you do not have to enter it again for the duration of the session.

Storing private keys on a removable medium

security You can store your private keys on a removable medium, such as a USB flash drive, and use your **~/.ssh** directory as the mount point for the filesystem stored on this drive. You might want to encrypt these keys with a passphrase in case you lose the flash drive.

Creating a strong passphrase is critical

security Creating a strong passphrase is critical to prevent unauthorized access.

The ssh-agent utility allows you to use a passphrase with your private key while entering the passphrase only one time, at the beginning of each session. When you log out, ssh-agent forgets the key. Give the following command to enable ssh-agent:

```
$ eval $(ssh-agent -s)
Agent pid 2527
```

ssh-add Once ssh-agent is enabled, use ssh-add to specify the passphrase for your private key:

```
$ ssh-add ~/.ssh/id_ecdsa
Enter passphrase for /home/sam/.ssh/id_ecdsa:
Identity added: /home/sam/.ssh/id_ecdsa (/home/sam/.ssh/id_ecdsa)
```

If you omit the argument to ssh-add, it adds a passphrase for each of the **~/.ssh/id_*** files that exists. With this setup, you can use ssh to work on a remote system without supplying a login password and by supplying your passphrase one time per session.

COMMAND-LINE OPTIONS

Command-line options override declarations in the configuration files. Following are descriptions of some of the more useful **sshd** options.

–D (**noDetach**) Keeps **sshd** in the foreground. Useful for debugging; implied by **–d**.

–d (**debug**) Sets debug mode so that **sshd** sends debugging messages to the system log and the server stays in the foreground (implies –D). Repeat this option up to a total of three times to increase verbosity. See also **–e**. (The ssh client uses **–v** for debugging; page 713.)

–e (**error**) Sends output to standard error, not to the system log. Useful with **–d**.

–f *file* Specifies *file* as the configuration file instead of **/etc/ssh/sshd_config**.

–t (**test**) Checks the configuration file syntax and the sanity of the key files.

/etc/ssh/sshd_config CONFIGURATION FILE

Lines in the **/etc/ssh/sshd_config** configuration file contain declarations. Each of these declarations starts with a keyword that is not case sensitive. Some keywords must be followed by whitespace and one or more case-sensitive arguments. You must reload the **sshd** server before these changes take effect. Following are some of the keywords and arguments you can specify. Initial values are underlined.

AllowUsers *userlist*

The ***userlist*** is a SPACE-separated list of usernames that specifies which users are allowed to log in using **sshd**. This list can include * and ? wildcards. You can specify a user as ***user*** or ***user@host***. If you use the second format, make sure you specify the host as returned by hostname. Without this declaration, any user who can log in locally can log in using an OpenSSH client. Does not work with numeric user IDs.

ClientAliveCountMax *n*

The ***n*** specifies the number of client-alive messages that can be sent without receiving a response before **sshd** disconnects from the client. See **ClientAliveInterval**. Default is 3.

ClientAliveInterval *n*

Sends a message through the encrypted channel after ***n*** seconds of not receiving a message from the client. See **ClientAliveCountMax**. The default is 0, meaning that no messages are sent.

This declaration passes messages over the encrypted channel and is not susceptible to *IP spoofing* (page 1104). It differs from **TCPKeepAlive**, which instead uses the TCP **keepalive** option and is susceptible to IP spoofing.

DenyUsers *userlist*

The ***userlist*** is a SPACE-separated list of usernames that specifies users who are not allowed to log in using **sshd**. This list can include * and ? wildcards. You can specify a user as ***user*** or ***user@host***. If you use the second format, make sure you specify the host as returned by hostname. Does not work with numeric user IDs.

ForceCommand *command*

Executes ***command***, ignoring commands specified by the client and commands in the optional **~/.ssh/ssh/rc** file.

HostbasedAuthentication yes | <u>no</u>

Tries **rhosts** and **/etc/hosts.equiv** authentication when set to **yes**. For a more secure system, set this declaration to **no**.

IgnoreRhosts yes | no
Ignores **.rhosts** and **.shosts** files for authentication. Does not affect the use of **/etc/hosts.equiv** and **/etc/ssh/shosts.equiv** files for authentication. For a more secure system, set this declaration to **yes**.

LoginGraceTime *n*
Waits *n* seconds for a user to log in on the server before disconnecting. Using a value of 0 means there is no time limit. Default is 120 seconds.

LogLevel *val* Specifies how detailed the log messages are. Choose *val* from **QUIET**, **FATAL**, **ERROR**, **INFO**, **VERBOSE**, **DEBUG1**, and **DEBUG3**. Using **DEBUG** levels violates user privacy.

PasswordAuthentication yes | no
Permits a user to use a password for authentication. For a more secure system, set up automatic login and set this declaration to **no**.

PermitEmptyPasswords yes | no
Permits a user to log in on an account that has an empty password.

PermitRootLogin yes | without-password | forced-commands-only | no
Permits **root** to log in using an OpenSSH client. Default is **yes**, but some Linux distributions set PermitRootLogin to **without-password**.

Setting this declaration to **yes** allows a user to log in as a privileged user by suppling the **root** password. This setup allows the **root** password to be sent over the network. Because the password is encrypted, this setting does not present a big security risk. It requires a user connecting as a privileged user to know the **root** password.

Setting this declaration to **no** does not allow **root** to authenticate directly; privilege must come from sudo or su after a user has logged in. Given the number of brute-force attacks on a typical system connected to the Internet, this is a good choice.

Setting this declaration to **without-password** means that the only way for a user to authenticate as **root** directly is by using an authorized key.

Setting this declaration to **forced-commands-only** works with an authorized key but forces a specific command after authentication instead of starting an interactive shell. The command is specified by **ForceCommand** (previous page).

PermitUserEnvironment yes | no
Permits a user to modify the environment he logs in to on the remote system. See **environment** on page 706.

Port *num* Specifies that the **sshd** server listen on port *num*. It might improve security to change *num* to a nonstandard port. Default is 22.

StrictModes yes | no
Checks modes and ownership of the user's home directory and files. Login fails for users other than the owner if the directories and/or files can be written to by anyone other than the owner. For a more secure system, set this declaration to **yes**.

SyslogFacility *val*

Specifies the facility name **sshd** uses when logging messages. Set *val* to DAEMON, USER, AUTH, LOCAL0, LOCAL1, LOCAL2, LOCAL3, LOCAL4, LOCAL5, LOCAL6, or LOCAL7.

TCPKeepAlive yes | no

Periodically checks whether a connection is alive when set to **yes**. Checking causes the ssh or scp connection to be dropped when the client crashes or the connection dies for another reason, even if the interruption is temporary. Setting this parameter to **no** causes the server not to check whether the connection is alive.

This declaration tests the connection at the transport (TCP) layer (page 1128). It uses the TCP **keepalive** option, which is not encrypted and is susceptible to *IP spoofing* (page 1104). Refer to **ClientAliveInterval** (page 722) for a nonspoofable alternative.

X11Forwarding yes | no

Allows X11 forwarding when set to **yes**. For trusted X11 forwarding to work, the ForwardX11Trusted declaration must also be set to **yes** in either the **~/.ssh/config** or **/etc/ssh/ssh_config** configuration file (page 716) on the client. The default is **no**, but sets X11Forwarding to **yes**. For more information refer to "Forwarding X11" on page 725.

Troubleshooting

Log files There are several places to look for clues when you have a problem connecting using ssh or scp. First, look for **sshd** entries in on the server. Following are messages you might see when you are using an **AllowUsers** declaration but have not included the user who is trying to log in (page 722). The message that is marked **PAM** originates with PAM.

Check the configuration file You can use the **sshd –t** option to check the syntax of the server configuration file. The command displays nothing if the syntax of the configuration file is correct.

Debug the client Try connecting with the **–v** option (either ssh or scp—the results should be the same). OpenSSH displays a lot of debugging messages, one of which might help you figure out what the problem is. Repeat this option up to a total of three times to increase verbosity.

Debug the server You can debug from the server side by giving the command **/usr/sbin/sshd –de** while working with **root** privileges. The server will run in the foreground, and its output might help you solve the problem.

Tunneling/Port Forwarding

The ssh utility can forward a port (*port forwarding;* page 1116) through the encrypted connection it establishes. Because the data sent across the forwarded port uses the encrypted ssh connection as its data link layer, the term *tunneling* (page 1130) is applied to this type of connection: "The connection is tunneled through ssh." You can secure protocols—including POP, X, IMAP, VNC, and WWW—by tunneling them through ssh.

Forwarding X11

The ssh utility makes it easy to tunnel the X11 protocol. For X11 tunneling to work, you must enable it on both the server and the client, and the client must be running the X Window System.

Server

On the ssh server, enable X11 forwarding by checking that the X11Forwarding declaration (page 724) is set to **yes** in the **/etc/ssh/sshd_config** file.

Trusted Client

On a client, enable trusted X11 forwarding by setting the ForwardX11 (defaults to **no**; page 716) *and* ForwardX11Trusted (page 716) declarations to **yes** in the **/etc/ssh/ssh_config** or **~/.ssh/config** file. Alternately, you can specify the **–Y** option (page 713) on the command line to start the client in trusted mode.

When you enable X11 forwarding on a client, the client connects as a trusted client, which means the client trusts the server and is given full access to the X11 display. With full access to the X11 display, in some situations a client might be able to modify other clients of the X11 display. Make a trusted connection only when you trust the remote system. (You do not want someone tampering with your client.)

Nontrusted Client

On a client, enable nontrusted X11 forwarding by setting the ForwardX11 (default is **no**; page 716) declaration to **yes** *and* the ForwardX11Trusted (page 716) declaration to **no** in the **/etc/ssh/ssh_config** or **~/.ssh/config** file. Alternately, you can use the **–X** option (page 713) on the command line to start the client in nontrusted mode.

A nontrusted client is given limited access to the X11 display and cannot modify other clients of the X11 display. Few clients work properly when they are run in nontrusted mode. If you are running an X11 client in nontrusted mode and encounter problems, try running in trusted mode (assuming you trust the remote system).

Running ssh

With X11 forwarding turned on, ssh tunnels the X11 protocol, setting the **DISPLAY** environment variable on the system it connects to and forwarding the required port. Typically, you will be running from a GUI, which usually means that you are using ssh in a terminal emulator window to connect to a remote system. When you give an X11 command from an ssh prompt, OpenSSH creates a new secure channel that carries the X11 data, and the graphical output from the X11 program appears on the screen. Typically, you will need to start the client in trusted mode.

By default, ssh uses X Window System display numbers 10 and higher (port numbers 6010 and higher) for forwarded X sessions. After you connect to a remote system using **ssh**, you can give a command (e.g., **gnome-calculator**) to run an X application. The application will then run on the remote system with its display appearing on the local system, such that it appears to run locally.

Port Forwarding

You can forward arbitrary ports using the **–L** and **–R** options. The **–L** option forwards a local port to a remote system, so a program that tries to connect to the forwarded port on the local system transparently connects to the remote system. The **–R** option does the reverse: It forwards remote ports to the local system. Generally, the **–N** option, which prevents ssh from executing remote commands, is used with the **–L** and **–R**. When you specify **–N**, ssh works only as a private network to forward ports. An ssh command line using the **–L** or **–R** option has the format

$ ssh –N –L | –R ***local-port:remote-host:remote-port target***

where ***local-port*** is the number of the local port that is being forwarded to or from ***remote-host***, ***remote-host*** is the name or IP address of the system that ***local-port*** gets forwarded to or from, ***remote-port*** is the number of the port on ***remote-host*** that is being forwarded from or to the local system, and ***target*** is the name or IP address of the system ssh connects to.

For example, assume the POP mail client is on the local system. The POP server is on a remote network, on a system named **pophost**. POP is not a secure protocol; passwords are sent in cleartext each time the client connects to the server. You can make it more secure by tunneling POP through ssh (POP3 connects on port 110; port 1550 is an arbitrary port on the local system):

```
$ ssh -N -L 1550:pophost:110 pophost
```

After giving the preceding command, you can point the POP client at **localhost:1550**. The connection between the client and the server will then be encrypted. (When you set up an account on the POP client, specify the location of the server as **localhost, port 1550**; details vary with different mail clients.)

Firewalls

In the preceding example, ***remote-host*** and ***target*** were the same system. However, the system specified for port forwarding (***remote-host***) does not have to be the same as the destination of the ssh connection (***target***). As an example, assume the POP server is behind a firewall and you cannot connect to it via ssh. If you can connect to the firewall via the Internet using ssh, you can encrypt the part of the connection over the Internet:

```
$ ssh -N -L 1550:pophost:110 firewall
```

Here, ***remote-host*** (the system receiving the port forwarding) is **pophost**, and ***target*** (the system that ssh connects to) is **firewall**.

You can also use ssh when you are behind a firewall (that is running **sshd**) and want to forward a port into your system without modifying the firewall settings:

```
$ ssh -R 1678:localhost:80 firewall
```

The preceding command forwards connections from the outside to port 1678 on the firewall to the local Web server. Forwarding connections in this manner allows you to use a Web browser to connect to port 1678 on the firewall when you connect to the Web server on the local system. This setup would be useful if you ran a Webmail program on the local system because it would allow you to check your mail from anywhere using an Internet connection.

COMPRESSION

Compression, which is enabled using the **–C** option, can speed up communication over a low-bandwidth connection. This option is commonly used with port forwarding. Compression can increase latency to an extent that might not be desirable for an X session forwarded over a high-bandwidth connection.

CHAPTER SUMMARY

OpenSSH is a suite of secure network connectivity tools that encrypts all traffic, including passwords, thereby helping to thwart attackers who might otherwise eavesdrop, hijack connections, and steal passwords. The **sshd** server daemon accepts connections from clients including ssh (runs a command on or logs in on another system), scp (copies files to and from another system), and sftp (securely replaces ftp). Helper programs including ssh-keygen (creates, manages, and converts authentication keys), ssh-agent (manages keys during a session), and ssh-add (works with ssh-agent) create and manage authentication keys.

To ensure secure communications, when an OpenSSH client opens a connection, it verifies that it is connected to the correct server. Then OpenSSH encrypts communication between the systems. Finally, OpenSSH makes sure the user is authorized to log in on or copy files to and from the server. You can secure many protocols—including POP, X, IMAP, VNC, and WWW—by tunneling them through ssh.

When it is properly set up, OpenSSH also enables secure X11 forwarding. With this feature, you can run securely a graphical program on a remote system and have the display appear on the local system.

EXERCISES

1. What is the difference between the scp and sftp utilities?
2. How can you use ssh to find out who is logged in on a remote system named **tiger**?
3. How would you use scp to copy your **~/.bashrc** file from the system named **plum** to the local system?
4. How would you use ssh to run xterm on **plum** and show the display on the local system? Your username on **plum** is **max**.
5. What problem can enabling compression present when you are using ssh to run remote X applications on a local display?
6. When you try to connect to a remote system using an OpenSSH client and OpenSSH displays a message warning you that the remote host identification has changed, what has happened? What should you do?

ADVANCED EXERCISES

7. Which scp command would you use to copy your home directory from **plum** to the local system?
8. Which single command could you give to log in as **max** on the remote system named **plum** and open a **root** shell (on **plum**)? Assume **plum** has remote **root** logins disabled.
9. How could you use ssh to compare the contents of the **~/memos** directories on **plum** and the local system?
10. How would you use rsync along with OpenSSH authentication to copy the **memos12** file from the working directory on the local system to your home directory on **plum**? How would you copy the **memos** directory from the working directory on the local system to your home directory on **plum** and cause rsync to display each file as it copied the file?

PART VI

COMMAND REFERENCE

Command Reference

The following tables list the utilities covered in this part of the book grouped by function and alphabetically within function. Although most of these are true utilities (programs that are separate from the shells), some are built into the shells (shell builtins). The sample utility on page 737 shows the format of the description of each utility in this part of the book.

Utilities That Display and Manipulate Files

aspell	Checks a file for spelling errors—page 739
bzip2	Compresses or decompresses files—page 750
cat	Joins and displays files—page 753
cmp	Compares two files—page 766
comm	Compares sorted files—page 768
cp	Copies files—page 772
cpio	Creates an archive, restores files from an archive, or copies a directory hierarchy—page 776
cut	Selects characters or fields from input lines—page 784
dd	Converts and copies a file—page 790
diff	Displays the differences between two text files—page 795
ditto	Copies files and creates and unpacks archives—page 803 macOS
emacs	Editor—page 221
expand	Converts TABs to SPACEs—page 814
find	Finds files based on criteria—page 822
fmt	Formats text very simply—page 831
grep	Searches for a pattern in files—page 853
gzip	Compresses or decompresses files—page 858
head	Displays the beginning of a file—page 861
join	Joins lines from two files based on a common field—page 863
less	Displays text files, one screen at a time—page 873
ln	Makes a link to a file—page 878
lpr	Sends files to printers—page 881

ls	Displays information about one or more files—page 884
man	Displays documentation for utilities—page 898
mkdir	Creates a directory—page 909
mv	Renames or moves a file—page 914
nl	Numbers lines from a file—page 918
od	Dumps the contents of a file—page 921
open	Opens files, directories, and URLs—page 926 macOS
otool	Displays object, library, and executable files—page 928 macOS
paste	Joins corresponding lines from files—page 930
pax	Creates an archive, restores files from an archive, or copies a directory hierarchy—page 932
plutil	Manipulates property list files—page 938 macOS
pr	Paginates files for printing—page 940
printf	Formats string and numeric data—page 942
rm	Removes a file (deletes a link)—page 953
rmdir	Removes directories—page 955
sed	Edits a file noninteractively—page 669
sort	Sorts and/or merges files—page 969
split	Divides a file into sections—page 978
strings	Displays strings of printable characters from files—page 986
tail	Displays the last part (tail) of a file—page 992
tar	Stores or retrieves files to/from an archive file—page 995
touch	Creates a file or changes a file's access and/or modification time—page 1012
unexpand	Converts SPACEs to TABs—page 814
uniq	Displays unique lines from a file—page 1023
vim	Editor—page 165
wc	Displays the number of lines, words, and bytes in one or more files—page 1027

Network Utilities

curlftpfs	Mounts a directory on an FTP server as a local directory—page 981
ftp	Transfers files over a network—page 838
rsync	Securely copies files and directory hierarchies over a network—page 689

scp	Securely copies one or more files to or from a remote system—pages 713 and 713
ssh	Securely runs a program or opens a shell on a remote system—pages 706 and 709
sshfs	Mounts a directory on an OpenSSH server as a local directory—page 981
telnet	Connects to a remote computer over a network—page 1001

Utilities That Display and Alter Status

cd	Changes to another working directory—page 755
chgrp	Changes the group associated with a file—page 757
chmod	Changes the access mode (permissions) of a file—page 759
chown	Changes the owner of a file and/or the group the file is associated with—page 764
date	Displays or sets the system time and date—page 787
df	Displays disk space usage—page 793
dmesg	Displays kernel messages—page 805
dscl	Displays and manages Directory Service information—page 806 macOS
du	Displays information on disk usage by directory hierarchy and/or file—page 809
file	Displays the classification of a file—page 820
finger	Displays information about users—page 828
GetFileInfo	Displays file attributes—page 851 macOS
kill	Terminates a process by PID—page 866
killall	Terminates a process by name—page 868
nice	Changes the priority of a command—page 916
nohup	Runs a command that keeps running after you log out—page 920
ps	Displays process status—page 946
renice	Changes the priority of a process—page 951
SetFile	Sets file attributes—page 965 macOS
sleep	Creates a process that sleeps for a specified interval—page 967
stat	Displays information about files—page 984
stty	Displays or sets terminal parameters—page 987

sysctl	Displays and alters kernel variables at runtime—page 991
top	Dynamically displays process status—page 1008
umask	Specifies the file-creation permissions mask—page 1021
w	Displays information about local system users—page 1025
which	Shows where in **PATH** a utility is located—page 1028
who	Displays information about logged-in users—page 1030

Utilities That Are Programming Tools

awk	Searches for and processes patterns in a file—page 635
configure	Configures source code automatically—page 770
gawk	Searches for and processes patterns in a file—page 635
gcc	Compiles C and C++ programs—page 846
make	Keeps a set of programs current—page 892
mawk	Searches for and processes patterns in a file—page 635
perl	Scripting language—page 529
python	Programming language—page 577

Miscellaneous Utilities

at	Executes commands at a specified time—page 743
busybox	Implements many standard utilities—page 747
cal	Displays a calendar—page 752
crontab	Maintains crontab files—page 781
diskutil	Checks, modifies, and repairs local volumes—page 800 macOS
echo	Displays a message—page 812
expr	Evaluates an expression—page 816
fsck	Checks and repairs a filesystem—page 833
launchctl	Controls the **launchd** daemon—page 870 macOS
mc	Manages files in a textual environment (aka Midnight Commander)—page 902
mkfs	Creates a filesystem on a device—page 911

screen	Manages several textual windows—page 958
tee	Copies standard input to standard output and one or more files—page 1000
test	Evaluates an expression—page 1005
tr	Replaces specified characters—page 1014
tty	Displays the terminal pathname—page 1017
tune2fs	Changes parameters on an **ext2**, **ext3**, or **ext4** filesystem—page 1018
xargs	Converts standard input to command lines—page 1032

Standard Multiplicative Suffixes

Some utilities allow you to use the suffixes listed in Table VI-1 following a byte count. You can precede a multiplicative suffix with a number that is a multiplier. For example, 5K means 5×2^{10}. The absence of a multiplier indicates that the multiplicative suffix is to be multiplied by 1. This text identifies utilities that accept these suffixes.

Table VI-1 Multiplicative suffixes

Suffix	Multiplicative value	Suffix	Multiplicative value
KB	1,000 (10^3)	PB	10^{15}
K	1,024 (2^{10})	P	2^{50}
MB	1,000,000 (10^6)	EB	10^{18}
M	1,048,576 (2^{20})	E	2^{60}
GB	1,000,000,000 (10^9)	ZB	10^{21}
G	1,073,741,824 (2^{30})	Z	2^{70}
TB	10^{12}	YB	10^{24}
T	2^{40}	Y	2^{80}

For example, the following command uses the dd (page 790) command to create a 2-megabyte (2×10^6 bytes) file of random values. It uses the MB multiplicative suffix following a multiplier of 2 as part of the **count** argument. The ls utility shows the size of the resulting file. It uses the **–h** (human-readable) option (see the tip on page 133) to display a file size of 2.0M instead of the less readable 2000000 (bytes).

```
$ dd if=/dev/urandom of=randf bs=1 count=2MB
2000000+0 records in
2000000+0 records out
2000000 bytes (2.0 MB) copied, 20.5025 s, 97.5 kB/s
$ ls -lh randf
-rw-r--r--. 1 sam pubs 2.0M 04-10 15:42 randf
```

Give the command **info coreutils Block size** for more information.

BLOCKSIZE Under macOS, some utilities use the **BLOCKSIZE** environment variable to set a default block size. You can set **BLOCKSIZE** to a value that is a number of bytes or to a value that uses one of the K, M, or G suffixes. The text identifies utilities that use **BLOCKSIZE**.

Common Options

Several GNU utilities share the options listed in Table VI-2. This text identifies the utilities that accept these options.

Table VI-2 Common command-line options

Option	Effect
–	A single hyphen appearing in place of a filename instructs the utility to accept input from standard input in place of a file.
––	A double hyphen marks the end of the options on a command line. You can follow this option with an argument that begins with a hyphen. Without this option the utility assumes an argument that begins with a hyphen is an option.
––help	Displays a help message for the utility. Some of these messages are quite long; you can use a pipeline to send the output through less to display it one screen at a time. For example, you could give the command **ls ––help | less**. Alternatively, you can send the output through a pipeline to grep if you are looking for specific information. For example, you could give the following command to get information on the **–d** option to ls: **ls ––help | grep –– –d**. See the preceding entry in this table for information on the double hyphen.
––version	Displays version information for the utility.

The sample Utility

The following description of the sample utility shows the format that this part of the book uses to describe the utilities. These descriptions are similar to the man page descriptions (pages 33 and 898); however, most users find the descriptions in this book easier to read and understand. The descriptions emphasize the most useful features of the utilities and often leave out the more obscure features. For information about the less commonly used features, refer to the man and info pages or call the utility with the **––help** option, which works with many utilities.

sample macOS ← *macOS in an oval indicates this utility runs under macOS only.*

Brief description of what the utility does.

sample [options] ***arguments***

Following the syntax line is a description of the utility. The syntax line shows how to run the utility from the command line. Options and arguments enclosed in brackets (*[]*) are not required. Enter words that appear in *this italic typeface* as is. Words that you must replace when you enter the command appear in ***this bold italic typeface.*** Words listed as arguments to a command identify single arguments (for example, ***source-file***) or groups of similar arguments (for example, ***directory-list***). A note here indicates if the utility runs under Linux or macOS only. macOS

Arguments

This section describes the arguments you can use when you run the utility. The argument, as shown in the preceding syntax line, is printed in ***this bold italic typeface.***

Options

This section lists some of the options you can use with the command. Unless otherwise specified, you must precede options with one or two hyphens. Most commands accept a single hyphen before multiple options (page 131). Options in this section are ordered alphabetically by short (single-hyphen) options. If an option has only a long version (two hyphens), it is ordered by its long option. Following are some sample options:

--delimiter=*dchar*
-d *dchar*
This option includes an argument. The argument is set in a ***bold italic typeface*** in both the heading and the description. You substitute another word (filename, string of characters, or other value) for any arguments shown in ***this typeface.*** Type characters that are in **bold type** (such as the **--delimiter** and **-d**) as is.

--make-dirs -m This option has a long and a short version. You can use either option; they are equivalent. This option description ends with **Linux** in a box, indicating it is available under Linux only. Options *not* followed by **Linux** or **macOS** are available under both operating systems. LINUX

-t (**table of contents**) This simple option is preceded by a single hyphen and not followed by arguments. It has no long version. The **table of contents** appearing in parentheses at the beginning of the description is a cue, suggestive of what the option letter stands for. This option description ends with **macOS** in an oval, indicating it is available under macOS only. Options *not* followed by **Linux** or **macOS** are available under both operating systems. macOS

Discussion

This optional section describes how to use the utility and identifies any quirks it might have.

Notes

This section contains miscellaneous notes—some important and others merely interesting.

Examples

This section contains examples illustrating how to use the utility. This section is a tutorial, so it takes a more casual tone than the preceding sections of the description.

aspell

Checks a file for spelling errors

aspell check [options] filename
aspell list [options] < filename
aspell config
aspell help

The aspell utility checks the spelling of words in a file against a standard dictionary. You can use aspell interactively: It displays each misspelled word in context, together with a menu that gives you the choice of accepting the word as is, choosing one of aspell's suggested replacements for the word, inserting the word into your personal dictionary, or replacing the word with one you enter. You can also use aspell in batch mode so it reads from standard input and writes to standard output. The aspell utility is available under Linux only. LINUX

aspell is not like other utilities regarding its input

tip Unlike many utilities, aspell does not accept input from standard input when you do not specify a filename on the command line. Instead, the ***action*** specifies where aspell gets its input.

Actions

You must specify exactly one *action* when you run aspell.

check –c Runs aspell as an interactive spell checker. Input comes from a single file named on the command line. Refer to "Discussion" on page 740.

config Displays aspell's configuration, both default and current values. Send the output through a pipeline to less for easier viewing, or use grep to find the option you are looking for (for example, **aspell config | grep backup**).

help –? Displays an extensive page of help. Send the output through a pipeline to less for easier viewing.

list –l Runs aspell in batch mode (noninteractively) with input coming from standard input and output going to standard output.

Arguments

The *filename* is the name of the file you want to check. The aspell utility accepts this argument only when you use the **check** (**–c**) *action*. With the **list** (**–l**) *action*, input must come from standard input.

Options

The aspell utility has many options. The more commonly used ones are listed in this section; see the aspell man page for a complete list. Default values of many options are determined when aspell is compiled (see the **config** *action*).

You can specify options on the command line, as the value of the **ASPELL_CONF** environment variable, or in your personal configuration file (**~/.aspell.conf**). A user working with **root** privileges can create a global configuration file (**/etc/aspell.conf**). Put one option per line in a configuration file; separate options with a semicolon (;) in **ASPELL_CONF**. Options on the command line override those in **ASPELL_CONF**, which override those in your personal configuration file, which override those in the global configuration file.

This section lists two types of options: Boolean and value. The Boolean options turn a feature on (enable the feature) or off (disable the feature). Precede a Boolean option with **dont–** to turn it off. For example, **––ignore-case** turns the **ignore-case** feature on and **––dont-ignore-case** turns it off.

Value options assign a value to a feature. Follow the option with an equal sign and a value—for example, **––ignore=4**.

For all options in a configuration file or in the **ASPELL_CONF** variable, omit the leading hyphens (**ignore-case** or **dont-ignore-case**).

aspell **options and leading hyphens**

caution The way you specify options differs depending on whether you are specifying them on the command line, by using the **ASPELL_CONF** shell variable, or in a configuration file.

On the command line, prefix long options with two hyphens (for example, **––ignore-case** or **––dont-ignore-case**). In **ASPELL_CONF** and configuration files, omit the leading hyphens (for example, **ignore-case** or **dont-ignore-case**).

––dont-backup Does not create a backup file named *filename*.**bak** (default is **––backup** when *action* is **check**).

––ignore=*n* Ignores words with *n* or fewer characters (default is 1).

––ignore-case Ignores the case of letters in words being checked (default is **––dont-ignore-case**).

––lang=*cc* Specifies the two-letter language code (*cc;* page 327). The language code defaults to the value of **LC_MESSAGES** (page 327).

––mode=*mod* Specifies a filter to use. Select *mod* from **url** (default), **none**, **sgml**, and others. The modes work as follows: **url** skips URLs, hostnames, and email addresses; **none** turns off all filters; and **sgml** skips SGML, HTML, XHTML, and XML commands.

––strip-accents Removes accent marks from all the words in the dictionary before checking words (default is **––dont-strip-accents**).

Discussion

The aspell utility has two modes of operation: batch and interactive. You specify batch mode by using the **list** or **–l** *action*. In batch mode, aspell accepts the document you want to check for spelling errors as standard input and sends the list of potentially misspelled words to standard output.

You specify interactive mode by using the **check** or **–c** ***action***. In interactive mode, aspell displays a screen with the potentially misspelled word highlighted in context and a menu of choices. See "Examples" for an illustration. The menu includes various commands (Table VI-3) as well as some suggestions of similar, correctly spelled words. You either enter one of the numbers from the menu to select a suggested word to replace the word in question or enter a letter to give a command.

Table VI-3 aspell commands

Command	Action
SPACE	Takes no action and goes on to the next misspelled word.
n	Replaces the misspelled word with suggested word number ***n***.
a	Adds the "misspelled" word to your personal dictionary.
b	Aborts aspell; does not save changes.
i *or* **I** (letter "i")	Ignores the misspelled word. **I** (uppercase "I") ignores all occurrences of this word; **i** ignores this occurrence only and has the same effect as SPACE.
l (lowercase "l")	Changes the "misspelled" word to lowercase and adds it to your personal dictionary.
r *or* **R**	Replaces the misspelled word with the word you enter at the bottom of the screen. **R** replaces all occurrences of this word; **r** replaces this occurrence only.
x	Saves the file as corrected so far and exits from aspell.

Notes

For more information refer to the aspell man page, the aspell home page (aspell.net), and the **/usr/share/doc/aspell** directory.

The aspell utility is not a foolproof way of finding spelling errors. It also does not check for misused, properly spelled words (such as *red* instead of *read*).

Spelling from emacs You can make it easy to use aspell from emacs by adding the following line to your **~/.emacs** file (page 266). This line causes emacs' ispell functions to call aspell:

```
(setq-default ispell-program-name "aspell")
```

Spelling from vim Similarly, you can make it easy to use aspell from vim by adding the following line to your **~/.vimrc** file (page 202):

```
map ^T :w!<CR>:!aspell check %<CR>:e! %<CR>
```

When you enter this line in **~/.vimrc** using vim, enter the **^T** as CONTROL-V CONTROL-T (page 186). With this line in **~/.vimrc**, while you are editing a file using vim, CONTROL-T brings up aspell to spell check the file you are editing.

Examples

The following examples use **aspell** to correct the spelling in the **memo.txt** file:

```
$ cat memo.txt
Here's a document for teh aspell utilitey
to check. It obviosly needs proofing
quiet badly.
```

The first example uses **aspell** with the **check** action and no options. The appearance of the screen for the first misspelled word, **teh**, is shown. At the bottom of the screen is the menu of commands and suggested words. Each of the numbered words differs slightly from the misspelled word:

```
$ aspell check memo.txt

Here's a document for teh aspell utilitey
to check. It obviosly needs proofing
quiet badly.

=============================================================
1) the                                  6) th
2) Te                                   7) tea
3) tech                                 8) tee
4) Th                                   9) Ted
5) eh                                   0) tel
i) Ignore                               I) Ignore all
r) Replace                              R) Replace all
a) Add                                  l) Add Lower
b) Abort                                x) Exit
=============================================================
?
```

Enter one of the menu choices in response to the preceding display; **aspell** will do your bidding and move the highlight to the next misspelled word (unless you choose to abort or exit). In this case, entering **1** (one) would change **teh** to **the** in the file.

The next example uses the **list** ***action*** to display a list of misspelled words. The word **quiet** is not in the list; it is not properly used but is properly spelled.

```
$ aspell list < memo.txt
teh
aspell
utilitey
obviosly
```

The last example also uses the **list** action. It shows a quick way to check the spelling of a word or two using a single command. The user gives the **aspell list** command and then enters **seperate temperature** into **aspell**'s standard input (the keyboard). After the user presses RETURN and CONTROL-D (to indicate the EOF or end of file), **aspell** writes the misspelled word to standard output (the screen):

```
$ aspell list
seperate temperatureRETURN
CONTROL-D
seperate
```

at

Executes commands at a specified time

at [options] time [date | +increment]
atq
atrm job-list
batch [options] [time]

The at and batch utilities execute commands at a specified time. They accept commands from standard input or, with the –f option, from a file. Commands are executed in the same environment as the at or batch command. Unless redirected, standard output and standard error from commands are emailed to the user who ran the at or batch command. A *job* is the group of commands that is executed by one call to at. The batch utility differs from at in that it schedules jobs so they run when the CPU load on the system is low.

The atq utility displays a list of queued at jobs; atrm cancels pending at jobs.

Arguments

The ***time*** is the time of day when at runs the job. You can specify the ***time*** as a one-, two-, or four-digit number. One- and two-digit numbers specify an hour, and four-digit numbers specify an hour and minute. You can also give the time in the form **hh:mm**. The at utility assumes a 24-hour clock unless you place **am** or **pm** immediately after the number, in which case it uses a 12-hour clock. You can also specify ***time*** as **now**, **midnight**, **noon**, or **teatime** (4:00 PM).

The ***date*** is the day of the week or day of the month when at runs the job. When you do not specify a day, at executes the job today if the hour you specify in ***time*** is greater than the current hour. If the hour is less than the current hour, at executes the job tomorrow.

You specify a day of the week by spelling it out or abbreviating it to three letters. You can also use the words **today** and **tomorrow**. Use the name of a month followed by the number of the day in the month to specify a date. You can follow the month and day number with a year.

The ***increment*** is a number followed by one of the following (it accepts both plural and singular): **minutes**, **hours**, **days**, or **weeks**. The at utility adds the ***increment*** to ***time***. You cannot specify an increment for a date.

When using atrm, ***job-list*** is a list of one or more at job numbers. You can list job numbers by giving the command **at –l** or **atq**.

Options

The batch utility accepts options under macOS only. The at utility does not accept the **–c**, **–d**, and **–l** options when you initiate a job using at; use these options to determine the status of a job or to cancel a job only.

–c *job-list*
(**cat**) Displays the environment and commands specified by the job numbers in *job-list*.

–d *job-list*
(**delete**) Cancels jobs that you submitted using at. The ***job-list*** is a list of one or more at job numbers to cancel. If you do not remember the job number, use the –l option or run atq to list your jobs and their numbers. Using this option with at has the same effect as running atrm. This option is deprecated under macOS; use the –r option instead.

–f *file*
(**file**) Specifies that commands come from ***file*** instead of standard input. This option is useful for long lists of commands or commands that are executed repeatedly.

–l (**list**) Displays a list of your at jobs. Using this option with at has the same effect as running atq.

–m (**mail**) Sends you email after a job is run, even when nothing is sent to standard output or standard error. When a job generates output, at always emails it to you, regardless of this option.

–r *job-list*
(**remove**) Same as the –d option. macOS

Notes

The at utility uses **/bin/sh** to execute commands. Under Linux, this file is typically a link to bash or dash.

The shell saves the environment variables and the working directory at the time you submit an at job so they are available when at executes commands.

at.allow and **at.deny** A user running with **root** privileges can always use at. The Linux **/etc/at.allow** (macOS uses **/var/at/at.allow**) and Linux **/etc/at.deny** (macOS uses **/var/at/at.deny**) files, which should be readable and writable by **root** only (600 permissions), control which ordinary, local users can use at. When **at.deny** exists and is empty, all users can use at. When **at.deny** does not exist, only those users listed in **at.allow** can use at. Users listed in **at.deny** cannot use at unless they are also listed in **at.allow**.

Under Linux, jobs you submit using at are run by the **atd** daemon. This daemon stores jobs in **/var/spool/at** or **/var/spool/cron/atjobs** and stores their output in **/var/spool/at/spool** or **/var/spool/cron/atspool**. These files are set to mode 700 and owned by the user named **daemon** or the user who ran the job.

Under macOS, jobs you submit using at are run by atrun, which is called every 30 seconds by **launchd**. The atrun utility stores jobs in **/var/at/jobs** and stores their output in **/var/at/spool**, both of which are set to mode 700 and owned by the user named **daemon**.

Under macOS 10.4 and above, the **atrun** daemon is disabled by default. Working with **root** privileges, you can enable and disable **atrun** using the following commands:

```
# launchctl load -w /System/Library/LaunchDaemons/com.apple.atrun.plist
```

```
# launchctl unload -w /System/Library/LaunchDaemons/com.apple.atrun.plist
```

See launchctl (page 870) for more information.

Examples

You can use any of the following techniques to paginate and print **long_file** tomorrow at 2:00 AM. The first example executes the command directly from the command line; the last two examples use the **pr_tonight** file, which contains the necessary command, and execute that command using at. Prompts and output from different versions of at differ.

```
$ at 2am
at> pr long_file | lpr
at>CONTROL-D <EOT>
job 8 at Thu Apr  5 02:00:00 2018

$ cat pr_tonight
#!/bin/bash
pr long_file | lpr

$ at -f pr_tonight 2am
job 9 at Thu Apr  5 02:00:00 2018

$ at 2am < pr_tonight
job 10 at Thu Apr  5 02:00:00 2018
```

If you execute commands directly from the command line, you must indicate the end of the commands by pressing CONTROL-D at the beginning of a line. Press CONTROL-D and at displays a line that begins with **job** followed by the job number and the time at will execute the job.

atq If you run atq after the preceding commands, it displays a list of jobs in its queue:

```
$ atq
8       Thu Apr  5 02:00:00 2018 a sam
9       Thu Apr  5 02:00:00 2018 a sam
10      Thu Apr  5 02:00:00 2018 a sam
```

atrm The following command removes job number 9 from the queue:

```
$ atrm 9
$ atq
8       Thu Apr  5 02:00:00 2018 a sam
10      Thu Apr  5 02:00:00 2018 a sam
```

The next example executes **cmdfile** at 3:30 PM (1530 hours) one week from today:

```
$ at -f cmdfile 1530 +1 week
job 12 at Wed Apr 11 15:30:00 2018
```

The next at command executes a job at 7:00 PM on Thursday. This job uses find to create an intermediate file, redirects the output sent to standard error, and prints the file.

```
$ at 7pm Thursday
at> find / -name "core" -print >report.out 2>report.err
at> lpr report.out
at>CONTROL-D <EOT>
job 13 at Thu Apr  5 19:00:00 2018
```

The final example shows some of the output generated by the –c option when at is queried about the preceding job. Most of the lines show the environment; the last few lines execute the commands as a Here document (page 462):

```
$ at -c 13
#!/bin/sh
# atrun uid=1000 gid=1400
# mail sam 0
umask 22
HOSTNAME=guava; export HOSTNAME
SHELL=/bin/bash; export SHELL
HISTSIZE=1000; export HISTSIZE
USER=sam; export USER
MAIL=/var/spool/mail/sam; export MAIL
PATH=/usr/local/bin:/bin:/usr/bin:/usr/local/sbin:/usr/sbin:/sbin:/hom
/sam/.local/bin:/home/sam/bin; export PATH
PWD=/home/sam; export PWD
...
cd /home/sam || {
         echo 'Execution directory inaccessible' >&2
         exit 1
}
${SHELL:-/bin/sh} << 'marcinDELIMITER3b59900b'
find / -name "core" -print >report.out 2>report.err
lpr report.out

marcinDELIMITER3b59900b
```

busybox

Implements many standard utilities

busybox [applet] [arguments]
busybox --list | --list-full
applet [arguments]

The busybox utility incorporates the functionality of many standard Linux utilities, called *applets* (page 1083), within a single utility.

Arguments

The busybox utility runs ***applet*** with optional ***arguments***. When called without an applet, it displays a usage message that lists the applets it incorporates. See "Notes" for a discussion of typical usage.

Options

The busybox utility accepts two options, each of which displays a list of the applets it incorporates. Most of the applets support a **--help** option that displays a list of options that applet supports.

--list Displays a list of applets you can run from busybox.

--list-full Displays a list of the absolute pathnames of applets you can run from busybox.

Notes

The busybox utility (busybox.net) combines tiny versions of approximately 200 Linux utilities into a single utility. It is called a multicall binary because you can call it many different ways (you can call busybox as any of the utilities it incorporates). In this context, the included utilities are called applets.

Because of the size of busybox, its applets have fewer options than the original GNU utilities. The utility was written to be small, use few resources, and be easily customized. Because running a Linux utility requires several kilobytes of overhead, incorporating many utilities in a single executable file can save disk space and system memory.

With its small size and completeness, busybox is used primarily in embedded systems and as an emergency shell under Linux. When a Linux system cannot boot properly, it will typically drop into busybox so you can repair the system. This utility runs in several environments, including Linux, macOS, Android, and FreeBSD.

Although you can run busybox from a shell, it is typically run as a shell itself. In the latter case, you run a busybox applet by typing the name of the applet and options for that applet (you do not type the word **busybox**).

When busybox is run from a shell, each of the applets it supports is typically linked to busybox so you can type the name of the applet and options for that applet without typing the word **busybox**. With this setup, the **/bin** directory might look like this:

```
$ ls -l /bin
lrwxrwxrwx    1 admin    administ         7 Mar  1 16:34 [ -> busybox
lrwxrwxrwx    1 admin    administ         7 Mar  1 16:34 addgroup -> busybox
lrwxrwxrwx    1 admin    administ         7 Mar  1 16:34 adduser -> busybox
lrwxrwxrwx    1 admin    administ         7 Mar  1 16:34 ash -> busybox
lrwxrwxrwx    1 admin    administ         7 Mar  1 16:34 awk -> busybox
lrwxrwxrwx    1 admin    administ         2 Mar  1 16:34 bash -> sh
-rwxr-xr-x    2 admin    administ    451992 Mar  1 16:18 busybox
lrwxrwxrwx    1 admin    administ         7 Mar  1 16:34 bzcat -> busybox
-rwxr-xr-x    1 admin    administ     95264 Mar  1 16:19 bzip2
lrwxrwxrwx    1 admin    administ         7 Mar  1 16:34 cat -> busybox
...
```

If you install busybox, you will have to enter busybox commands as you would any other commands: beginning with the name of the utility you want to run (busybox).

If busybox has access to the system version of a utility, it will use that version before it uses its internal version. You can use the busybox which (page 69) utility to determine which version of a utility busybox will run. The following example shows that busybox will use its internal version of ls but the system version of cat:

```
$ busybox which ls
$ busybox which cat
/bin/cat
```

The busybox utility is typically set up on an embedded system (e.g., a router) so the name of each utility is a link to busybox. When configured in this manner, you can run the busybox command by simply typing the name of the command you want to run. You can see how this setup works by giving the following commands. The first command links **ls** in the working directory to busybox [**$(which busybox)** uses command substitution to return the absolute pathname of the busybox utility]. The second command executes busybox through the **ls** link, running the busybox version of the ls utility.

```
$ ln -s $(which busybox) ls
$ ./ls
...
```

Examples

When you call busybox without any arguments, it displays information about itself. In the following output, busybox uses the term *function* in place of *applet*:

```
$ busybox
BusyBox v1.22.1 (Ubuntu 1:1.22.0-15ubuntu1) multi-call binary.
BusyBox is copyrighted by many authors between 1998-2012.
Licensed under GPLv2. See source distribution for full notice.

Usage: busybox [function] [arguments]...
   or: busybox --list[-full]
   or: busybox --install [-s] [DIR]
   or: function [arguments]...
```

```
        BusyBox is a multi-call binary that combines many common Unix
        utilities into a single executable.  Most people will create a
        link to busybox for each function they wish to use and BusyBox
        will act like whatever it was invoked as.

Currently defined functions:
        [, [[, acpid, add-shell, addgroup, adduser, adjtimex, ar,
        arp, arping, ash, awk, base64, basename, beep, blkid,
        blockdev, bootchartd, brctl, bunzip2, bzcat, bzip2, cal, cat,
        catv, chat, chattr, chgrp, chmod, chown, chpasswd, chpst,
        chroot, chrt, chvt, cksum, clear, cmp, comm, cp, cpio, crond,
...
```

You can use the **--help** option to display information about most busybox applets:

```
$ busybox ar --help
BusyBox v1.22.1 (Ubuntu 1:1.22.0-15ubuntu1) multi-call binary.

Usage: ar [-o] [-v] [-p] [-t] [-x] ARCHIVE FILES

Extract or list FILES from an ar archive

Options:
        -o      Preserve original dates
        -p      Extract to stdout
        -t      List
        -x      Extract
        -v      Verbose
```

When busybox is installed as a stand-alone utility, a command must start with the word **busybox** followed by the name of the applet you want busybox to run:

```
$ busybox ls -l
-rw-rw-r--    1 sam     sam          8445 Feb  9 17:09 memo1
-rw-rw-r--    1 sam     sam         16890 Feb  9 17:09 memo2
```

If you are running a busybox shell, you can just enter the same commands you would use if you were running bash or tcsh. You can invoke a busybox shell by giving the command **busybox sh**:

```
$ busybox sh

BusyBox v1.22.1 (Ubuntu 1:1.22.0-15ubuntu1) built-in shell (ash)
Enter 'help' for a list of built-in commands.

~ $ ls -l
-rw-rw-r--    1 sam     sam          8445 Feb  9 17:09 memo1
-rw-rw-r--    1 sam     sam         16890 Feb  9 17:09 memo2
```

bzip2

Compresses or decompresses files

*bzip2 [**options**] [**file-list**]*
*bunzip2 [**options**] [**file-list**]*
*bzcat [**options**] [**file-list**]*
*bzip2recover [**file**]*

The bzip2 utility compresses files, bunzip2 restores files compressed using bzip2, and bzcat displays files compressed with bzip2.

Arguments

The ***file-list*** is a list of one or more ordinary files (no directories) that are to be compressed or decompressed. If ***file-list*** is empty or if the special option – is present, bzip2 reads from standard input. The **––stdout** option causes bzip2 to write to standard output.

Options

Under Linux, bzip2, bunzip2, and bzcat accept the common options described on page 736.

The macOS version of bzip2 accepts long options

tip: Options for bzip2 preceded by a double hyphen (––) work under macOS as well as under Linux.

––stdout **–c** Writes the results of compression or decompression to standard output.

––decompress **–d** Decompresses a file that was compressed using bzip2. This option with bzip2 is equivalent to the bunzip2 command.

––fast *or* ––best **–*n*** Sets the block size when compressing a file. The ***n*** is a digit from 1 to 9, where 1 (**––fast**) generates a block size of 100 kilobytes and 9 (**––best**) generates a block size of 900 kilobytes. The default level is 9. The **––fast** and **––best** options are provided for compatibility with gzip and do not necessarily yield the fastest or best compression.

––force **–f** Forces compression even if a file already exists, has multiple links, or comes directly from a terminal. The option has a similar effect with bunzip2.

––keep **–k** Does not delete input files while compressing or decompressing them.

––quiet **–q** Suppresses warning messages; does display critical messages.

––test **–t** Verifies the integrity of a compressed file. Displays nothing if the file is OK.

––verbose **–v** For each file being compressed, displays the name of the file, the compression ratio, the percentage of space saved, and the sizes of the decompressed and compressed files.

Discussion

The bzip2 and bunzip2 utilities work similarly to gzip and gunzip; see the discussion of gzip (page 859) for more information. Normally bzip2 does not overwrite a file; you must use **--force** to overwrite a file during compression or decompression.

Notes

The bzip2 home page is bzip.org.

The bzip2 utility does a better job of compressing files than gzip does.

Use the **--bzip2** modifier with tar (page 996) to compress archive files using bzip2.

See "Compressing and Archiving Files" on page 64 for additional information on and examples of using tar to create and unpack archives.

bzcat *file-list* Works like cat except it uses bunzip2 to decompress ***file-list*** as it copies files to standard output.

bzip2recover Attempts to recover a damaged file that was compressed using bzip2.

Examples

In the following example, bzip2 compresses a file and gives the resulting file the same name with a **.bz2** filename extension. The **–v** option displays statistics about the compression.

```
$ ls -l
-rw-r--r--  1 sam sam 737414 04-03 19:05 bigfile
$ bzip2 -v bigfile
  bigfile: 3.926:1, 2.037 bits/byte, 74.53% saved, 737414 in, 187806 out
$ ls -l
-rw-r--r--  1 sam sam 187806 04-03 19:05 bigfile.bz2
```

Next, touch creates a file with the same name as the original file; bunzip2 refuses to overwrite the file in the process of decompressing **bigfile.bz2**. The **--force** option enables bunzip2 to overwrite the file.

```
$ touch bigfile
$ bunzip2 bigfile.bz2
bunzip2: Output file bigfile already exists.
$ bunzip2 --force bigfile.bz2
$ ls -l
-rw-r--r--  1 sam sam 737414 04-03 19:05 bigfile
```

cal

Displays a calendar

cal [options] [[month] year]

The cal utility displays a calendar.

Arguments

The arguments specify the month and year for which cal displays a calendar. The *month* is a decimal integer from 1 to 12 and the *year* is a decimal integer. Without any arguments, cal displays a calendar for the current month. When you specify a single argument, cal displays a calendar for the year specified by the argument.

Options

–j (**Julian**) Displays Julian days—a calendar that numbers the days consecutively from January 1 (1) through December 31 (365 or 366).

–m (**Monday**) Makes Monday the first day of the week. Without this option, Sunday is the first day of the week. LINUX

–m ***n***
(**month**) Displays a calendar for the *n*th month of the current year. macOS

–y (**year**) Displays a calendar for the current year. LINUX

–3 (**three months**) Displays the previous, current, and next months. LINUX

Notes

Do not abbreviate the year. The year 05 is not the same as 2005.

The ncal (new cal) utility displays a more compact calendar.

Examples

The following command displays a calendar for December 2018:

```
$ cal 12 2018
December 2018
Su Mo Tu We Th Fr Sa
                   1
 2  3  4  5  6  7  8
 9 10 11 12 13 14 15
16 17 18 19 20 21 22
23 24 25 26 27 28 29
30 31
```

Next is a Julian calendar for 1949:

```
$ cal -j 1949
                                     1949

                 January                                 February
 Su  Mo  Tu  We  Th  Fr  Sa      Su  Mo  Tu  We  Th  Fr  Sa
                          1              32  33  34  35  36
  2   3   4   5   6   7   8      37  38  39  40  41  42  43
  9  10  11  12  13  14  15      44  45  46  47  48  49  50
 16  17  18  19  20  21  22      51  52  53  54  55  56  57
 23  24  25  26  27  28  29      58  59
 30  31
...
```

cat

Joins and displays files

cat [options] [file-list]

The cat utility copies files to standard output. You can use cat to display the contents of one or more text files on the screen.

Arguments

The *file-list* is a list of the pathnames of one or more files that cat processes. If you do not specify an argument or if you specify a hyphen (–) in place of a filename, cat reads from standard input.

Options

Under Linux, cat accepts the common options described on page 736. Options preceded by a double hyphen (––) work under Linux only. Except as noted, options named with a single letter and preceded by a single hyphen work under Linux and macOS.

––show-all **–A** Same as **–vET**. LINUX

––number-nonblank
–b Numbers all lines that are not blank as they are written to standard output.

–e (**end**) Same as **–vE**. LINUX macOS

––show-ends **–E** Marks the end of each line with a dollar sign. LINUX

––number **–n** Numbers all lines as they are written to standard output.

––squeeze-blank **–s** Removes extra blank lines so there are never two or more blank lines in a row.

–t (**tab**) Same as **–vT**.

––show-tabs **–T** Displays TABs as **^I**. LINUX

––show-nonprinting
–v Displays CONTROL characters using the caret notation (**^M**) and displays characters that have the high bit set (META characters) using the **M-** notation (page 231). This option does not convert TABs and LINEFEEDs. Use **–T** (**––show-tabs**) if you want to display TABs as **^I**. LINEFEEDs cannot be displayed as anything but themselves; otherwise, the line could be too long.

Notes

See page 138 for a discussion of cat, standard input, and standard output.

Use the od utility (page 921) to display the contents of a file that does not contain text (for example, an executable program file).

Use the tac utility to display lines of a text file in reverse order (Linux only). See the tac info page for more information.

The name cat is derived from one of the functions of this utility, *catenate,* which means to join together sequentially, or end to end.

Set noclobber to avoid overwriting a file

caution Despite cat's warning message, the shell destroys the input file (**letter**) before invoking cat in the following example:

```
$ cat memo letter > letter
cat: letter: input file is output file
```

You can prevent overwriting a file in this situation by setting the **noclobber** variable (pages 143 and 407).

Examples

The following command displays the contents of the **memo** text file on the terminal:

```
$ cat memo
...
```

The next example catenates three text files and redirects the output to the file named **all**:

```
$ cat page1 letter memo > all
```

You can use cat to create short text files without using an editor. Enter the following command line, type the text you want in the file, and press CONTROL-D on a line by itself:

```
$ cat > new_file
...
(text)
...
CONTROL-D
```

In this case cat takes input from standard input (the keyboard) and the shell redirects standard output (a copy of the input) to the file you specify. The CONTROL-D indicates the EOF (end of file) and causes cat to return control to the shell.

In the next example, a pipeline sends the output from who to standard input of cat. The shell redirects cat's output to the file named **output**; after the commands have finished executing, **output** contains the contents of the **header** file, the output of who, and the contents of **footer**. The hyphen on the command line causes cat to read standard input after reading **header** and before reading **footer**.

```
$ who | cat header - footer > output
```

cd

Changes to another working directory

cd [options] [directory]

The cd builtin makes ***directory*** the working directory.

Arguments

The ***directory*** is the pathname of the directory you want to be the new working directory. Without an argument, cd makes your home directory the working directory. Using a hyphen in place of ***directory*** changes to the previous working directory.

Options

The following options are available under bash and dash only.

–L (**no dereference**) If ***directory*** is a symbolic link, cd makes the symbolic link the working directory (default). See page 118 for information on dereferencing symbolic links.

–P (**dereference**) If ***directory*** is a symbolic link, cd makes the directory the symbolic link points to the working directory. See page 118 for information on dereferencing symbolic links.

Notes

The cd command is a bash, dash, and tcsh builtin.

See page 94 for a discussion of cd.

Without an argument, cd makes your home directory the working directory; it uses the value of the **HOME** (bash; page 317) or **home** (tcsh; page 403) variable to determine the pathname of your home directory.

With an argument of a hyphen, cd makes the previous working directory the working directory. It uses the value of the **OLDPWD** (bash) or **owd** (tcsh) variable to determine the pathname of the previous working directory.

The **CDPATH** (bash; page 323) or **cdpath** (tcsh; page 402) variable contains a colon-separated list of directories that cd searches. Within this list, a null directory name (::) or a period (:.:) represents the working directory. If **CDPATH** or **cdpath** is not set, cd searches only the working directory for ***directory***. If this variable is set and ***directory*** is not an absolute pathname (does not begin with a slash), cd searches the directories in the list; if the search fails, cd searches the working directory. See page 323 for a discussion of **CDPATH**.

Examples

A cd command without an argument makes a user's home directory the working directory. In the following example, cd makes Max's home directory the working directory and the pwd builtin verifies the change:

```
$ pwd
/home/max/literature
$ cd
$ pwd
/home/max
```

Under macOS, home directories are stored in **/Users**, not **/home**.

The next command uses an absolute pathname to make the **/home/max/literature** directory the working directory:

```
$ cd /home/max/literature
$ pwd
/home/max/literature
```

Next, the cd utility uses a relative pathname to make a subdirectory of the current working directory the new working directory:

```
$ cd memos
$ pwd
/home/max/literature/memos
```

Finally, cd uses the .. reference to the parent of the working directory (page 95) to make the parent of the current working directory the new working directory:

```
$ cd ..
$ pwd
/home/max/literature
```

chgrp

Changes the group associated with a file

chgrp [options] group file-list
chgrp [options] --reference=rfile file-list LINUX

The chgrp utility changes the group associated with one or more files. The second syntax works under Linux only.

Arguments

The ***group*** is the name or numeric group ID of the new group. The ***file-list*** is a list of the pathnames of the files whose group association is to be changed. The ***rfile*** is the pathname of a file whose group is to become the new group associated with ***file-list***.

Options

Options preceded by a double hyphen (--) work under Linux only. Except as noted, options named with a single letter and preceded by a single hyphen work under Linux and macOS.

--changes **-c** Displays a message for each file whose group is changed. LINUX

--dereference For each file that is a symbolic link, changes the group of the file the link points to, not the symbolic link itself. Under Linux, this option is the default. See page 118 for information on dereferencing symbolic links. LINUX

--quiet *or* **--silent** **-f** Suppresses warning messages about files whose permissions prevent you from changing their group IDs.

--no-dereference **-h** For each file that is a symbolic link, changes the group of the symbolic link, not the file the link points to. See page 118 for information on dereferencing symbolic links.

-H (**partial dereference**) For each file that is a symbolic link, changes the group of the file the link points to, not the symbolic link itself. This option affects files specified on the command line; it does not affect files found while descending a directory hierarchy. This option treats files that are not symbolic links normally and works with **-R** only. See page 118 for information on dereferencing symbolic links.

-L (**dereference**) For each file that is a symbolic link, changes the group of the file the link points to, not the symbolic link itself. This option affects all files, treats files that are not symbolic links normally, and works with **-R** only. See page 118 for information on dereferencing symbolic links.

-P (**no dereference**) For each file that is a symbolic link, changes the group of the symbolic link, not the file the link points to (default). This option affects all files, treats files that are not symbolic links normally, and works with **-R** only. See page 118 for information on dereferencing symbolic links.

--recursive –R Recursively descends a directory specified in ***file-list*** and changes the group ID on all files in the directory hierarchy.

--reference=*rfile* Changes the group of the files in ***file-list*** to that of ***rfile***. LINUX

--verbose –v For each file, displays a message saying whether its group was retained or changed.

Notes

Only the owner of a file or a user working with **root** privileges can change the group association of a file.

Unless you are working with **root** privileges, you must belong to the specified ***group*** to change the group ID of a file to that ***group***.

See page 764 for information on how to use chown to change the group associated with and/or the owner of a file.

Examples

See "Dereferencing Symbolic Links Using chgrp" on page 120 for examples that use the **–H**, **–L**, and **–P** options.

The following command changes the group that the **manuals** file is associated with; the new group is **pubs**:

```
$ chgrp pubs manuals
```

The next example uses the **–v** option to cause chgrp to report on each file it is called with:

```
$ chgrp -v pubs *
changed group of 'mixture' to pubs
group of 'memo' retained as pubs
```

chmod

Changes the access mode (permissions) of a file

chmod [options] who operator permission file-list symbolic
chmod [options] mode file-list absolute
chmod [options] --reference=rfile file-list referential LINUX

The chmod utility changes the ways in which a file can be accessed by the owner of the file, the group the file is associated with, and/or all other users. You can specify the new access mode absolutely or symbolically. Under Linux, you can also specify the mode referentially (third syntax). Under macOS, you can use chmod to modify ACLs (page 1074).

Arguments

Arguments specify which files are to have their modes changed in which ways. The *rfile* is the pathname of a file whose permissions are to become the new permissions of the files in *file-list*.

Symbolic

You can specify multiple sets of symbolic modes (*who operator permission*) by separating each set from the next with a comma.

The chmod utility changes the access permission for the class of users specified by *who*. The class of users is designated by one or more of the letters specified in the *who* column of Table VI-4.

Table VI-4 Symbolic mode user class specification

who	User class	Meaning
u	User	Owner of the file
g	Group	Group the file is associated with
o	Other	All other users
a	All	Use in place of **ugo**

Table VI-5 lists the symbolic mode *operators*.

Table VI-5 Symbolic mode operators

operator	Meaning
+	Adds the permission for the specified user class
–	Removes the permission for the specified user class
=	Sets the permission for the specified user class; resets all other permissions for that user class

The access ***permission*** is specified by one or more of the letters listed in Table VI-6.

Table VI-6 Symbolic mode permissions

permission	Meaning
r	Sets read permission
w	Sets write permission
x	Sets execute permission
s	Sets the user ID or group ID (depending on the ***who*** argument) to that of the owner of the file while the file is being executed (for more information see page 104)
t	Sets the sticky bit (only a user working with **root** privileges can set the sticky bit, and it can be used only with **u**; see page 1126)
X	Makes the file executable only if it is a directory or if another user class has execute permission
u	Sets the specified permissions to those of the owner
g	Sets the specified permissions to those of the group
o	Sets the specified permissions to those of others

Absolute

You can use an octal number to specify the access mode. Construct the number by ORing the appropriate values from Table VI-7. To OR two or more octal numbers from this table, just add them. (Refer to Table VI-8 on the next page for examples.)

Table VI-7 Absolute mode specifications

mode	Meaning
4000	Sets the user ID when the program is executed (page 104)
2000	Sets the group ID when the program is executed (page 104)
1000	Sticky bit (page 1126)
0400	Owner can read the file
0200	Owner can write to the file
0100	Owner can execute the file
0040	Group can read the file
0020	Group can write to the file

Table VI-7 Absolute mode specifications (continued)

mode	**Meaning**
0010	Group can execute the file
0004	Others can read the file
0002	Others can write to the file
0001	Others can execute the file

Table VI-8 lists some typical modes.

Table VI-8 Examples of absolute mode specifications

Mode	**Meaning**
0777	Owner, group, and others can read, write, and execute the file
0755	Owner can read, write, and execute the file; group and others can read and execute the file
0711	Owner can read, write, and execute the file; group and others can execute the file
0644	Owner can read and write the file; group and others can read the file
0640	Owner can read and write the file, group can read the file, and others cannot access the file

Options

Options preceded by a double hyphen (--) work under Linux only. Except as noted, options named with a single letter and preceded by a single hyphen work under Linux and macOS.

--changes **–c** Displays a message for each file whose permissions are changed. LINUX

--quiet *or* --silent **–f** Suppresses warning messages about files whose ownership prevents chmod from changing the permissions of the file.

–H (**partial dereference**) For each file that is a symbolic link, changes permissions of the file the link points to, not the symbolic link itself. This option affects files specified on the command line; it does not affect files found while descending a directory hierarchy. This option treats files that are not symbolic links normally and works with **–R** only. See page 118 for information on dereferencing symbolic links. macOS

–L (**dereference**) For each file that is a symbolic link, changes permissions of the file the link points to, not the symbolic link itself. This option affects all files, treats files that are not symbolic links normally, and works with **–R** only. See page 118 for information on dereferencing symbolic links. macOS

–P (**no dereference**) For each file that is a symbolic link, changes permissions of the symbolic link, not the file the link points to. This option affects all files, treats files that are not symbolic links normally, and works with **–R** only. See page 118 for information on dereferencing symbolic links. macOS

––recursive **–R** Recursively descends a directory specified in ***file-list*** and changes the permissions on all files in the directory hierarchy.

––reference=*rfile* Changes the permissions of the files in ***file-list*** to that of ***rfile***. LINUX

––verbose **–v** For each file, displays a message saying that its permissions were changed (even if they were not changed) and specifying the permissions. Use **––changes** to display messages only when permissions are actually changed.

Notes

Only the owner of a file or a user working with **root** privileges can change the access mode, or permissions, of a file.

When you use symbolic arguments, you can omit the ***permission*** from the command line when the ***operator*** is =. This omission takes away all permissions for the specified user class. See the second example in the next section.

Under Linux, chmod never changes the permissions of symbolic links.

Under Linux, chmod dereferences symbolic links found on the command line. In other words, chmod changes the permissions of files that symbolic links found on the command line point to; chmod does not affect files found while descending a directory hierarchy. This behavior mimics the behavior of the macOS **–H** option.

A big difference between absolute chmod commands and symbolic chmod commands is that, when using a symbolic command, you use the + or – operators to modify existing permissions of a file or you use the = operator to set permissions to a specified value. When using absolute commands, you can only set permissions to a specified value.

See page 102 for another discussion of chmod.

Examples

See page 1074 for examples of using chmod to change ACLs under macOS.

The following examples show how to use the chmod utility to change the permissions of the file named **temp**. The initial access mode of **temp** is shown by ls. See "Discussion" on page 887 for information about the ls display.

```
$ ls -l temp
-rw-rw-r-- 1 max pubs 57 07-12 16:47 temp
```

When you do not follow an equal sign with a permission, chmod removes all permissions for the specified user class. The following command removes all access permissions for the group and all other users so only the owner has access to the file:

```
$ chmod go= temp
$ ls -l temp
-rw------- 1 max pubs 57 07-12 16:47 temp
```

The next command changes the access modes for all users (owner, group, and others) to read and write. Now anyone can read from or write to the file.

```
$ chmod a=rw temp
$ ls -l temp
-rw-rw-rw- 1 max pubs 57 07-12 16:47 temp
```

Using an absolute argument, **a=rw** becomes **666**. The next command performs the same function as the preceding one:

```
$ chmod 666 temp
```

The next command removes write access permission for other users. As a result, members of the **pubs** group can read from and write to the file, but other users can only read from the file:

```
$ chmod o-w temp
$ ls -l temp
-rw-rw-r-- 1 max pubs 57 07-12 16:47 temp
```

The following command yields the same result, using an absolute argument:

```
$ chmod 664 temp
```

The next command adds execute access permission for all users:

```
$ chmod a+x temp
$ ls -l temp
-rwxrwxr-x 1 max pubs 57 07-12 16:47 temp
```

If **temp** is a shell script or other executable file, all users can now execute it. (The operating system requires read and execute access to execute a shell script but only execute access to execute a binary file.) The absolute command that yields the same result is

```
$ chmod 775 temp
```

The final command uses symbolic arguments and the = operator to achieve the same result as the preceding command. It sets permissions to read, write, and execute for the owner and the group, and to read and execute for other users. A comma separates the sets of symbolic modes.

```
$ chmod ug=rwx,o=rx temp
```

chown

Changes the owner of a file and/or the group the file is associated with

chown [options] owner file-list
chown [options] owner:group file-list
chown [options] owner: file-list
chown [options] :group file-list
chown [options] --reference=rfile file-list LINUX

The chown utility changes the owner of a file and/or the group the file is associated with. Only a user working with **root** privileges can change the owner of a file. Only a user working with **root** privileges or the owner of a file who belongs to the new group can change the group a file is associated with. The last syntax works under Linux only.

Arguments

The *owner* is the username or numeric user ID of the new owner. The *group* is the group name or numeric group ID of the new group the file is to be associated with. The *file-list* is a list of the pathnames of the files whose ownership and/or group association you want to change. The *rfile* is the pathname of a file whose owner and/or group association is to become the new owner and/or group association of *file-list*. Table VI-9 shows the ways you can specify the new *owner* and/or *group*.

Table VI-9 Specifying the new owner and/or group

Argument	Meaning
owner	The new owner of *file-list*; the group is not changed
owner:group	The new owner of and new group associated with *file-list*
owner:	The new owner of *file-list*; the group associated with *file-list* is changed to the new owner's login group
:group	The new group associated with *file-list*; the owner is not changed

Options

Under Linux, chown accepts the common options described on page 736. Options preceded by a double hyphen (--) work under Linux only. Except as noted, options named with a single letter and preceded by a single hyphen work under Linux and macOS.

--changes -c Displays a message for each file whose ownership/group is changed. LINUX

--dereference Changes the ownership/group of the files symbolic links point to, not the symbolic links themselves. Under Linux, this option is the default. See page 118 for information on dereferencing symbolic links. LINUX

--quiet *or* **--silent -f** Suppresses error messages about files whose ownership and/or group association chown cannot change.

-H (**partial dereference**) For each file that is a symbolic link, changes the owner and/or group association of the file the link points to, not the symbolic link itself.

This option affects files specified on the command line; it does not affect files found while descending a directory hierarchy. This option treats files that are not symbolic links normally and works with **–R** only. See page 118 for information on dereferencing symbolic links.

--no-dereference **–h** For each file that is a symbolic link, changes the owner and/or group association of the symbolic link, not the file the link points to. See page 118 for information on dereferencing symbolic links.

–L (**dereference**) For each file that is a symbolic link, changes the owner and/or group association of the file the link points to, not the symbolic link itself. This option affects all files, treats files that are not symbolic links normally, and works with **–R** only. See page 118 for information on dereferencing symbolic links.

–P (**no dereference**) For each file that is a symbolic link, changes the owner and/or group association of the symbolic link, not the file the link points to. This option affects all files, treats files that are not symbolic links normally, and works with **–R** only. See page 118 for information on dereferencing symbolic links.

--recursive **–R** When you include directories in the ***file-list,*** this option descends the directory hierarchy, setting the specified owner and/or group association for all files in the hierarchy.

--reference=*rfile* Changes the owner and/or group association of the files in the ***file-list*** to that of ***rfile.*** LINUX

--verbose **–v** For each file, displays a message saying whether its owner and/or group association was retained or changed.

Notes

The chown utility clears setuid and setgid bits when it changes the owner of a file.

Examples

The following command changes the owner of the **chapter1** file in the **manuals** directory; the new owner is Sam:

```
# chown sam manuals/chapter1
```

The following command makes Max the owner of, and Max's login group the group associated with, all files in the **/home/max/literature** directory and in all its subdirectories:

```
# chown -R max: /home/max/literature
```

Under macOS, home directories are stored in **/Users**, not **/home**.

The next command changes the ownership of the files in **literature** to **max** and the group associated with these files to **pubs**:

```
# chown max:pubs /home/max/literature/*
```

The final example changes the group association of the files in **manuals** to **pubs** without altering their ownership. The owner of the files, who is executing this command, must belong to the **pubs** group.

```
$ chown :pubs manuals/*
```

cmp

Compares two files

cmp [options] file1 [file2 [skip1 [skip2]]]

The cmp utility displays the differences between two files on a byte-by-byte basis. If the files are the same, cmp is silent. If the files differ, cmp displays the byte and line number of the first difference.

Arguments

The *file1* and *file2* arguments are the pathnames of the files that cmp compares. If *file2* is omitted, cmp uses standard input instead. Using a hyphen (–) in place of *file1* or *file2* causes cmp to read standard input instead of that file.

The ***skip1*** and ***skip2*** arguments are decimal numbers indicating the number of bytes to skip in each file before beginning the comparison. You can use the standard multiplicative suffixes after ***skip1*** and ***skip2***; see Table VI-1 on page 735.

Options

Under Linux *and* macOS, cmp accepts the common options described on page 736.

The macOS version of cmp accepts long options

tip: Options for cmp preceded by a double hyphen (––) work under macOS as well as under Linux.

––print–bytes –b Displays more information, including filenames, byte and line numbers, and the octal and ASCII values of the first differing byte.

––ignore–initial=*n1*[:*n2*]
–i *n1*[:*n2*]
Without ***n2***, skips the first ***n1*** bytes in both files before beginning the comparison. With ***n1*** and ***n2***, skips the first ***n1*** bytes in ***file1*** and skips the first ***n2*** bytes in ***file2*** before beginning the comparison. You can follow ***n1*** and/or ***n2*** with one of the multiplicative suffixes listed in Table VI-1 on page 735.

––verbose –l (lowercase "l") Instead of stopping at the first byte that differs, continues comparing the two files and displays both the location and the value of each byte that differs. Locations are displayed as decimal byte count offsets from the beginning of the files; byte values are displayed in octal. The comparison terminates when an EOF is encountered on either file.

––silent –s Suppresses output from cmp; only sets the exit status (see "Notes"). You may also use --quiet.

Notes

Byte and line numbering start at 1.

The cmp utility does not display a message if the files are identical; it only sets the exit status. This utility returns an exit status of 0 if the files are the same and an exit status of 1 if they are different. An exit status greater than 1 means an error occurred.

When you use ***skip1*** (and ***skip2***), the offset values cmp displays are based on the byte where the comparison began.

Under macOS, cmp compares data forks (page 1071) of a file only.

Unlike diff (page 795), cmp works with binary as well as ASCII files.

Examples

The examples use the files named **a** and **b**. These files have two differences. The first difference is that the word **lazy** in file **a** is replaced by **lasy** in file **b**. The second difference is subtler: A TAB character appears just before the NEWLINE character in file **b**.

```
$ cat a
The quick brown fox jumped over the lazy dog.
$ cat b
The quick brown fox jumped over the lasy dog.TAB
```

The first example uses cmp without any options to compare the two files. The cmp utility reports that the files are different and identifies the offset from the beginning of the files where the first difference is found:

```
$ cmp a b
a b differ: char 39, line 1
```

You can display the octal ASCII values of the bytes and the characters at that location by adding the **–b** (**––print–bytes**) option:

```
$ cmp --print-bytes a b
a b differ: char 39, line 1 is 172 z 163 s
```

The **–l** option displays all bytes that differ between the two files. Because this option creates a lot of output if the files have many differences, you might want to redirect the output to a file. The following example shows the two differences between files **a** and **b**. The **–b** option displays the values for the bytes as well. Where file **a** has a CONTROL-J (NEWLINE), file **b** has a CONTROL-I (TAB). The message saying that the EOF on file **a** has been reached indicates that file **b** is longer than file **a**.

```
$ cmp -lb a b
39 172 z    163 s
46  12 ^J    11 ^I
cmp: EOF on a
```

In the next example, the **––ignore–initial** option causes cmp to ignore 39 bytes, skipping over the first difference in the files. The cmp utility now reports on the second difference. The difference is put at character 7, which is the 46th character in the original file **b** (7 characters past the ignored 39 characters).

```
$ cmp --ignore-initial=39 a b
a b differ: char 7, line 1
```

You can use ***skip1*** and ***skip2*** in place of the **––ignore–initial** option used in the preceding example:

```
$ cmp a b 39 39
a b differ: char 7, line 1
```

comm

Compares sorted files

comm [options] file1 file2

The comm utility displays a line-by-line comparison of two sorted files. The first of the three columns it displays lists the lines found only in *file1*, the second column lists the lines found only in *file2*, and the third lists the lines common to both files.

Arguments

The *file1* and *file2* arguments are pathnames of the files that comm compares. Using a hyphen (–) in place of *file1* or *file2* causes comm to read standard input instead of that file.

Options

You can combine the options. With no options, comm produces three-column output.

–1 Does not display column 1 (does not display lines found only in **file1**).

–2 Does not display column 2 (does not display lines found only in **file2**).

–3 Does not display column 3 (does not display lines found in both files).

Notes

If the files have not been sorted, comm will not work properly.

Lines in the second column are preceded by one TAB, and those in the third column are preceded by two TABs.

The exit status indicates whether comm completed normally (0) or abnormally (not 0).

Examples

The following examples use files named **c** and **d**. The files have already been sorted:

```
$ cat c
bbbbb
ccccc
ddddd
eeeee
fffff
$ cat d
aaaaa
ddddd
eeeee
ggggg
hhhhh
```

Refer to sort on page 969 for information on sorting files.

The following example calls comm without any options, so it displays three columns. The first column lists those lines found only in file **c**, the second column lists those found in **d**, and the third lists the lines found in both **c** and **d**:

```
$ comm c d
        aaaaa
bbbbb
ccccc
                ddddd
                eeeee
fffff
        ggggg
        hhhhh
```

The next example uses options to prevent comm from displaying columns 1 and 2. The result is column 3, a list of the lines common to files **c** and **d**:

```
$ comm -12 c d
ddddd
eeeee
```

configure

Configures source code automatically

*./configure [**options**]*

The configure script is part of the GNU Configure and Build System. Software developers who supply source code for their products face the problem of making it easy for relatively naive users to build and install their software packages on a wide variety of machine architectures, operating systems, and system software. To facilitate this process many software developers supply a shell script named configure with their source code.

When you run configure, it determines the capabilities of the local system. The data collected by configure is used to build the makefiles with which make (page 892) builds the executables and libraries. You can adjust the behavior of configure by specifying command-line options and environment variables.

Options

The macOS version of configure accepts long options

tip Options for configure preceded by a double hyphen (--) work under macOS as well as under Linux.

--disable-*feature* Works in the same manner as *--enable-feature* except it disables support for *feature*.

--enable-*feature* The *feature* is the name of a feature that can be supported by the software being configured. For example, configuring the Z Shell source code with the command **configure --enable-zsh-mem** configures the source code to use the special memory allocation routines provided with zsh instead of using the system memory allocation routines. Check the **README** file supplied with the software distribution to see the choices available for *feature*.

--help Displays a detailed list of all options available for use with configure. The contents of this list depends on the software you are installing.

--prefix=*directory*

By default configure builds makefiles that install software in the **/usr/local** directory hierarchy (when you give the command **make install**). To install software into a different directory, replace *directory* with the absolute pathname of the desired directory.

--with-*package* The *package* is the name of an optional package that can be included with the software you are configuring. For example, if you configure the source code for the Windows emulator wine with the command **configure --with-dll**, the source code is configured to build a shared library of Windows emulation support. Check the **README** file supplied with the software you are installing to see the choices available for ***package***. The command **configure --help** usually displays the choices available for ***package***.

Discussion

The GNU Configure and Build System allows software developers to distribute software that can configure itself to be built on a variety of systems. It builds a shell script named configure, which prepares the software distribution to be built and installed on a local system. The configure script searches the local system to find the dependencies for the software distribution and constructs the appropriate makefiles. Once you have run configure, you can build the software using a **make** command and install the software using a **make install** command.

The configure script determines which C compiler to use (usually gcc) and specifies a set of flags to pass to that compiler. You can set the environment **CC** and **CFLAGS** variables to override these values. See the "Examples" section.

Notes

Each package that uses the GNU autoconfiguration utility provides its own custom copy of configure, which the software developer created using the GNU autoconf utility (www.gnu.org/software/autoconf). Read the **README** and **INSTALL** files that are provided with the software you are installing for information about the available options.

The configure scripts are self-contained and run correctly on a wide variety of systems. You do not need any special system resources to use configure.

The configure utility will exit with an error message if a dependency is not installed.

Examples

The simplest way to call configure is to cd to the base directory for the software you are installing and run the following command:

```
$ ./configure
```

The **./** is prepended to the command name to ensure you are running the configure script supplied with the software you are installing. For example, to cause configure to build makefiles that pass the flags **–Wall** and **–O2** to gcc, give the following command from bash:

```
$ CFLAGS="-Wall -O2" ./configure
```

If you are using tcsh, give the following command:

```
tcsh $ env CFLAGS="-Wall -O2" ./configure
```

cp

Copies files

cp [options] source-file destination-file
cp [options] source-file-list destination-directory

The cp utility copies one or more files. It can either make a copy of a single file (first syntax) or copy one or more files to a directory (second syntax). With the **–R** option, cp can copy directory hierarchies.

Arguments

The ***source-file*** is the pathname of the file that cp makes a copy of. The ***destination-file*** is the pathname cp assigns to the resulting copy of the file.

The ***source-file-list*** is a list of one or more pathnames of files that cp makes copies of. The ***destination-directory*** is the pathname of the directory in which cp places the copied files. With this syntax, cp gives each copied file the same simple filename as its ***source-file***.

The **–R** option enables cp to copy directory hierarchies recursively from the ***source-file-list*** into the ***destination-directory***.

Options

Under Linux, cp accepts the common options described on page 736. Options preceded by a double hyphen (––) work under Linux only. Except as noted, options named with a single letter and preceded by a single hyphen work under Linux and macOS.

––archive **–a** Attempts to preserve the owner, group, permissions, access date, and modification date of source file(s) while copying recursively without dereferencing symbolic links. Same as **–dpR**.

––backup **–b** If copying a file would remove or overwrite an existing file, this option makes a backup copy of the file that would be overwritten. The backup copy has the same name as the ***destination-file*** with a tilde (~) appended to it. When you use both **––backup** and **––force**, cp makes a backup copy when you try to copy a file over itself. For more backup options, search for **Backup options** in the **core utils** info page. LINUX

–d For each file that is a symbolic link, copies the symbolic link, not the file the link points to. Also preserves hard links in ***destination-files*** that exist between corresponding ***source-files***. This option is equivalent to **––no-dereference** and **––preserve=links**. See page 118 for information on dereferencing symbolic links. LINUX

––force **–f** When the ***destination-file*** exists but cannot be opened for writing, causes cp to try to remove ***destination-file*** before copying ***source-file***. This option is useful when the user copying a file does not have write permission to an existing ***destination-file*** but does have write permission to the directory containing the ***destination-file***. Use this option with **–b** to back up a destination file before removing or overwriting it.

–H (**partial dereference**) For each file that is a symbolic link, copies the file the link points to, not the symbolic link itself. This option affects files specified on the command line; it does not affect files found while descending a directory hierarchy. This option treats files that are not symbolic links normally. Under macOS, works with **–R** only. See page 118 for information on dereferencing symbolic links.

––interactive –i Prompts you whenever cp would overwrite a file. If you respond with a string that starts with **y** or **Y**, cp copies the file. If you enter anything else, cp does not copy the file.

––dereference –L (**dereference**) For each file that is a symbolic link, copies the file the link points to, not the symbolic link itself. This option affects all files and treats files that are not symbolic links normally. Under macOS, works with **–R** only. See page 118 for information on dereferencing symbolic links.

––no-dereference –P (**no dereference**) For each file that is a symbolic link, copies the symbolic link, not the file the link points to. This option affects all files and treats files that are not symbolic links normally. Under macOS, works with **–R** only. See page 118 for information on dereferencing symbolic links.

––preserve[=*attr*] –p Creates a ***destination-file*** with the same owner, group, permissions, access date, modification date, and ACLs as the ***source-file***. The **–p** option does not take an argument.

Without ***attr***, **––preserve** works as described above. The ***attr*** is a comma-separated list that can include **mode** (permissions), **ownership** (owner and group), **timestamps** (access and modification dates), **links** (hard links), and **all** (all attributes).

––parents Copies a relative pathname to a directory, creating directories as needed. See the "Examples" section. LINUX

––recursive –R *or* **–r**

Recursively copies directory hierarchies including ordinary files. Under Linux, the **––no-dereference** (**–d**) option is implied: With the **–R**, **–r**, or **––recursive** option, cp copies the links (not the files the links point to). The **–r** and **––recursive** options are available under Linux only.

––update –u Copies only when the ***destination-file*** does not exist or when it is older than the ***source-file*** (i.e., this option will not overwrite a newer destination file). LINUX

––verbose –v Displays the name of each file as cp copies it.

–X Do not copy extended attributes (page 1070). macOS

Notes

Under Linux, cp dereferences symbolic links unless you also use one or more of the **–R**, **–r**, **––recursive**, **–P**, **–d**, or **––no-dereference** options. As explained on the previous page, under Linux the **–H** option dereferences only symbolic links listed on the command line. Under macOS, without the **–R** option, cp always dereferences symbolic links; with the **–R** option, cp does not dereference symbolic links (**–P** is the default) unless you specify **–H** or **–L**.

Many options are available for cp under Linux. See the **coreutils** info page for a complete list.

If the ***destination-file*** exists before you execute a cp command, cp overwrites the file, destroying its contents but leaving the access privileges, owner, and group associated with the file as they were.

If the ***destination-file*** does not exist, cp uses the access privileges of the ***source-file***. The user who copies the file becomes the owner of the ***destination-file*** and the user's login group becomes the group associated with the ***destination-file***.

Using the **–p** option (or **––preserve** without an argument) causes cp to attempt to set the owner, group, permissions, access date, and modification date to match those of the ***source-file***.

Unlike with the ln utility (page 878), the ***destination-file*** that cp creates is independent of its ***source-file***.

Under macOS version 10.4 and above, cp copies extended attributes (page 1070). The **–X** option causes cp not to copy extended attributes.

Examples

The first command makes a copy of the file **letter** in the working directory. The name of the copy is **letter.sav**.

```
$ cp letter letter.sav
```

The next command copies all files with a filename extension of **.c** to the **archives** directory, which is a subdirectory of the working directory. Each copied file retains its simple filename but has a new absolute pathname. The **–p** (**––preserve**) option causes the copied files in **archives** to have the same owner, group, permissions, access date, and modification date as the source files.

```
$ cp -p *.c archives
```

The next example copies **memo** from Sam's home directory to the working directory:

```
$ cp ~sam/memo .
```

The next example runs under Linux and uses the **––parents** option to copy the file **memo/thursday/max** to the **dir** directory as **dir/memo/thursday/max**. The find utility shows the newly created directory hierarchy.

```
$ cp --parents memo/thursday/max dir
$ find dir
dir
dir/memo
dir/memo/thursday
dir/memo/thursday/max
```

The following command copies the files named **memo** and **letter** into another directory. The copies have the same simple filenames as the source files (**memo** and **letter**) but have different absolute pathnames. The absolute pathnames of the copied files are **/home/sam/memo** and **/home/sam/letter**, respectively.

```
$ cp memo letter /home/sam
```

The final command demonstrates one use of the **–f** (**––force**) option. Max owns the working directory and tries unsuccessfully to copy **one** over another file (**me**) that he does not have write permission for. Because he has write permission to the directory that holds **me**, Max can remove the file but cannot write to it. The **–f** (**––force**) option unlinks, or removes, **me** and then copies **one** to the new file named **me**.

```
$ ls -ld
drwxrwxr-x    2 max max 4096 10-16 22:55 .
$ ls -l
-rw-r--r--    1 root root 3555 10-16 22:54 me
-rw-rw-r--    1 max max 1222 10-16 22:55 one
$ cp one me
cp: cannot create regular file 'me': Permission denied
$ cp -f one me
$ ls -l
-rw-r--r--    1 max max 1222 10-16 22:58 me
-rw-rw-r--    1 max max 1222 10-16 22:55 one
```

If Max had used the **–b** (**––backup**) option in addition to **–f** (**––force**), **cp** would have created a backup of **me** named **me~**. Refer to "Directory Access Permissions" on page 105 for more information.

cpio

Creates an archive, restores files from an archive, or copies a directory hierarchy

*cpio --create|–o [**options**]*
*cpio --extract|–i [**options**] [**pattern-list**]*
*cpio --pass-through|–p [**options**] **destination-directory***

The cpio utility has three modes of operation: Create (copy-out) mode places multiple files into a single archive file, extract (copy-in) mode restores files from an archive, and pass-through (copy-pass) mode copies a directory hierarchy. The archive file cpio creates can be saved on disk, tape, other removable media, or a remote system.

Create mode reads a list of names of ordinary or directory files from standard input and writes the resulting archive file to standard output. You can use this mode to create an archive. Extract mode reads an archive from standard input and extracts files from that archive. You can restore all files from the archive or only those files whose names match a pattern. Pass-through mode reads a list of names of ordinary or directory files from standard input and copies the files to a specified directory.

Arguments

In create mode, cpio constructs an archive from the files named on standard input.

By default cpio in extract mode extracts all files found in the archive. You can choose to extract files selectively by supplying a ***pattern-list***. If the name of a file in the archive matches one of the patterns in ***pattern-list***, cpio extracts that file; otherwise, it ignores the file. The patterns in a cpio ***pattern-list*** are similar to shell wildcards (page 152) except that ***pattern-list*** match slashes (**/**) and a leading period (**.**) in a filename.

In pass-through mode you must supply the name of the ***destination-directory*** as an argument to cpio.

Options

A major option specifies the mode in which cpio operates: create, extract, or pass-through.

Major Options

You must include exactly one of these options. Options preceded by a double hyphen (––) work under Linux only. Options named with a single letter and preceded by a single hyphen work under Linux and macOS.

--extract –i (**copy-in mode**) Reads the archive from standard input and extracts files. Without a ***pattern-list***, cpio extracts all files from the archive. With a ***pattern-list***, cpio extracts only files with names that match one of the patterns in ***pattern-list***. The following example extracts from the device mounted on **/dev/sde1** only those files whose names end in **.c**:

```
$ cpio -i \*.c < /dev/sde1
```

The backslash prevents the shell from expanding the * before it passes the argument to cpio.

--create -o (**copy-out mode**) Constructs an archive from the files named on standard input. These files, which can be ordinary or directory files, must each appear on a separate line. The archive is written to standard output as it is built. The find utility frequently generates the filenames that cpio uses. The following command builds an archive of the **/home** filesystem and writes it to the device mounted on **/dev/sde1**:

```
# find /home -depth -print | cpio -o > /dev/sde1
```

The **–depth** option causes find to search for files in a depth-first search, thereby reducing the likelihood of permissions problems when you restore the files from the archive. See the discussion of this option on page 779.

--pass-through -p (**copy-pass mode**) Copies files from one place on the system to another. Instead of constructing an archive file containing the files named on standard input, cpio copies them to the ***destination-directory*** (the last argument on the cpio command line). The effect is the same as if you had created an archive with copy-out mode and then extracted the files with copy-in mode, except using pass-through mode avoids creating an archive. The following example copies the files in the working directory and all subdirectories into **~max/code**:

```
$ find . -depth -print | cpio -pdm ~max/code
```

Other Options

The following options alter the behavior of cpio. These options work with one or more of the preceding major options.

Except as noted, options preceded by a double hyphen (--) work under Linux only. Except as noted, options named with a single letter and preceded by a single hyphen work under Linux and macOS.

--reset-access-time

-a Resets the access times of source files after copying them so they have the same access time after copying as they did before.

-B (**block**) Sets the block size to 5,120 bytes instead of the default 512 bytes. Under Linux this option affects input and output block sizes; under macOS it affects only output block sizes.

--block-size=*n* Sets the block size used for input and output to ***n*** 512-byte blocks. LINUX

-c (**compatible**) Writes header information in ASCII so older (incompatible) cpio utilities on other systems can read the file. This option is rarely needed.

--make-directories

-d Creates directories as needed when copying files. For example, you need this option when you are extracting files from an archive with a file list generated by find with the **–depth** option. This option can be used only in conjunction with the **–i** (**--extract**) and **–p** (**--pass-through**) options.

--pattern-file=*filename*

-E *filename*

Reads ***pattern-list*** from ***filename,*** one ***pattern*** per line. Additionally, you can specify ***pattern-list*** on the command line.

--file=*archive* -F *archive*

Uses ***archive*** as the name of the archive file. In extract mode, reads from ***archive*** instead of standard input. In create mode, writes to ***archive*** instead of standard output. You can use this option to access a device on another system on a network; see the **-f** (**--file**) option to tar (page 996) for more information.

--format *fmt*

In create mode, writes the archive in ***fmt*** format, as shown in Table VI-10. If you do not specify a format, cpio writes a POSIX format file (**odc** in the table). macOS

Table VI-10 cpio archive formats

format	Description
cpio	The same as odc
newc	The format used for cpio archives under UNIX System V, release 4
odc	The historical POSIX portable octet-oriented cpio format (default)
pax	The POSIX pax format
ustar	The POSIX tar format

--nonmatching -f (**flip**) Reverses the sense of the test performed on ***pattern-list*** when extracting files from an archive. Files are extracted from the archive only if they do *not* match any of the patterns in the ***pattern-list.***

--help Displays a list of options. LINUX macOS

--dereference -L For each file that is a symbolic link, copies the file the link points to (not the symbolic link itself). This option treats files that are not symbolic links normally. See page 118 for information on dereferencing symbolic links.

--link -l When possible, links files instead of copying them.

--preserve-modification-time

-m Preserves the modification times of files that are extracted from an archive. Without this option the files show the time they were extracted. With this option the created files show the time they had when they were copied into the archive.

--no-absolute-filenames

In extract mode, creates all filenames relative to the working directory—even files that were archived using absolute pathnames. LINUX

--quiet Suppresses most messages. LINUX macOS

--rename -r Allows you to rename files as cpio copies them. When cpio prompts you with the name of a file, you respond with the new name. The file is then copied with the new name. If you press RETURN without entering a filename, cpio does not copy the file.

--list	-t	(**table of contents**) Displays a table of contents of the archive. This option works only with the **-i** (**--extract**) option, although no files are actually extracted from the archive. With the **-v** (**--verbose**) option, it displays a detailed table of contents in a format similar to that displayed by **ls -l**.
--unconditional	-u	Overwrites existing files regardless of their modification times. Without this option cpio will not overwrite a more recently modified file with an older one; it displays a warning message.
--verbose	-v	Lists files as they are processed. With the **-t** (**--list**) option, it displays a detailed table of contents in a format similar to that displayed by **ls -l**.

Discussion

Without the **-u** (**--unconditional**) option, cpio will not overwrite a more recently modified file with an older file.

You can use both ordinary and directory filenames as input when you create an archive. If the name of an ordinary file appears in the input list before the name of its parent directory, the ordinary file appears before its parent directory in the archive as well. This order can lead to an avoidable error: When you extract files from the archive, the child has nowhere to go in the file structure if its parent has not yet been extracted.

Making sure that files appear after their parent directories in the archive is not always a solution. One problem occurs if the **-m** (**--preserve-modification-time**) option is used when extracting files. Because the modification time of a parent directory is updated whenever a file is created within it, the original modification time of the parent directory is lost when the first file is written to it.

The solution to this potential problem is to ensure that all files appear *before* their parent directories when creating an archive *and* to create directories as needed when extracting files from an archive. When you use this technique, directories are extracted only after all files have been written to them and their modification times are preserved.

With the **-depth** option, find generates a list of files, with all children appearing in the list before their parent directories. If you use this list to create an archive, the files are in the proper order. (Refer to the first example in the next section.) When extracting files from an archive, the **-d** (**--make-directories**) option causes cpio to create parent directories as needed and the **-m** (**--preserve-modification-time**) option does just what its name says. Using this combination of utilities and options preserves directory modification times through a create/extract sequence.

This strategy also solves another potential problem. Sometimes a parent directory might not have permissions set so that you can extract files into it. When cpio automatically creates the directory with **-d** (**--make-directories**), you can be assured that you have write permission to the directory. When the directory is extracted from the archive (after all the files are written into the directory), it is extracted with its original permissions.

Examples

The first example creates an archive of the files in Sam's home directory, writing the archive to a USB flash drive mounted at **/dev/sde1**:

```
$ find /home/sam -depth -print | cpio -oB >/dev/sde1
```

The find utility produces the filenames that cpio uses to build the archive. The **–depth** option causes all entries in a directory to be listed before listing the directory name itself, making it possible for cpio to preserve the original modification times of directories (see the preceding "Discussion" section). Use the **–d** (**––make-directories**) and **–m** (**––preserve-modification-time**) options when you extract files from this archive (see the following examples). The **–B** option sets the block size to 5,120 bytes.

Under macOS, home directories are stored in **/Users**, not **/home**.

To check the contents of the archive file and display a detailed listing of the files it contains, give the following command:

```
$ cpio -itv < /dev/sde1
```

The following command restores the files that formerly were in the **memo** subdirectory of Sam's home directory:

```
$ cpio -idm /home/sam/memo/\* < /dev/sde1
```

The **–d** (**––make-directories**) option ensures that any subdirectories that were in the **memo** directory are re-created as needed. The **–m** (**––preserve-modification-time**) option preserves the modification times of files and directories. The asterisk in the regular expression is escaped to keep the shell from expanding it.

The next command is the same as the preceding command except that it uses the Linux **––no-absolute-filenames** option to re-create the **memo** directory in the working directory, which is named **memocopy**. The pattern does not start with the slash that represents the root directory, allowing cpio to create the files with relative pathnames.

```
$ pwd
/home/sam/memocopy
$ cpio -idm --no-absolute-filenames home/sam/memo/\* < /dev/sde1
```

The final example uses the **–f** option to restore all files in the archive except those that were formerly in the **memo** subdirectory:

```
$ cpio -ivmdf /home/sam/memo/\* < /dev/sde1
```

The **–v** option lists the extracted files as cpio processes the archive, verifying that the expected files have been extracted.

crontab

Maintains crontab files

*crontab [–u **user-name**] **filename***
*crontab [–u **user-name**] **option***

A crontab file associates periodic times (such as 14:00 on Wednesdays) with commands. The **cron/crond** daemon executes each command at the specified time. When you are working as yourself, the crontab utility installs, removes, lists, and allows you to edit your crontab file. A user working with **root** privileges can work with any user's crontab file.

Arguments

The first syntax copies the contents of ***filename*** (which contains crontab commands) into the crontab file of the user who runs the command or that of ***username***. When the user does not have a crontab file, this process creates a new one; when the user has a crontab file, this process overwrites the file. When you replace ***filename*** with a hyphen (–), crontab reads commands from standard input.

The second syntax lists, removes, or allows you to edit the crontab file, depending on which option you specify.

Options

Choose only one of the **–e**, **–l**, or **–r** options. A user working with **root** privileges can use **–u** with one of these options.

–e (**edit**) Runs the text editor specified by the **VISUAL** or **EDITOR** environment variable on the crontab file, enabling you to add, change, or delete entries. This option installs the modified crontab file when you exit from the editor.

–l (**list**) Displays the contents of the crontab file.

–r (**remove**) Deletes the crontab file.

–u *username*
(**user**) Works on ***username***'s crontab file. Only a user working with **root** privileges can use this option.

Notes

This section covers the versions of crontab and crontab files that were written by Paul Vixie; hence this version of cron is called *Vixie cron*. These versions are POSIX compliant and differ from an earlier version of Vixie cron as well as from the classic SVR3 syntax.

User crontab files are kept in the **/var/spool/cron** or **/var/spool/cron/crontabs** directory. Each file is named with the username of the user to whom it belongs.

The daemon named **cron/crond** reads the crontab files and runs the commands. If a command line in a crontab file does not redirect its output, all output sent to standard output and standard error is mailed to the user unless you set the **MAILTO** variable within the crontab file to a different username.

Crontab files do not inherit variables set in startup files. For this reason, you might want to put the assignment **export BASH_ENV=~/.bashrc** near the top of crontab files you write.

Crontab directories

To make the system administrator's job easier, the directories named **/etc/cron.hourly**, **/etc/cron.daily**, **/etc/cron.weekly**, and **/etc/cron.monthly** hold crontab files that, on most systems, are run by run-parts, which in turn are run by the **/etc/crontab** file. Each of these directories contains files that execute system tasks at the interval named by the directory. A user working with **root** privileges can add files to these directories instead of adding lines to **root**'s crontab file. A typical **/etc/crontab** file looks like this:

```
$ cat /etc/crontab
SHELL=/bin/bash
PATH=/sbin:/bin:/usr/sbin:/usr/bin
MAILTO=root
HOME=/

# run-parts
01 * * * * root run-parts /etc/cron.hourly
02 4 * * * root run-parts /etc/cron.daily
22 4 * * 0 root run-parts /etc/cron.weekly
42 4 1 * * root run-parts /etc/cron.monthly
```

Each entry in a crontab file begins with five fields that specify when the command is to be run (minute, hour, day of the month, month, and day of the week). An asterisk appearing in place of a number is a wildcard representing all possible values. In the day-of-the-week field, you can use either 7 or 0 to represent Sunday.

It is a good practice to start **cron/crond** jobs a variable number of minutes before or after the hour, half-hour, or quarter-hour. When you start jobs at these times, it becomes less likely that many processes will start at the same time, thereby potentially overloading the system.

When **cron/crond** starts (usually when the system is booted), it reads all crontab files into memory. Once a minute, the **cron/crond** daemon reviews all crontab entries it has stored in memory and runs whichever jobs are due to be run at that time.

Special time specifications

You can use the special time specifications shown in Table VI-11 in place of the initial five fields described above.

Table VI-11 crontab special time specifications

Specification	Meaning	Replaces
@reboot	Run when the system boots	
@yearly	Run on January 1	0 0 1 1 *
@monthly	Run on the first day of each month	0 0 1 * *
@weekly	Run every Sunday	0 0 * * 0
@daily	Run once a day	0 0 * * *
@hourly	Run once an hour	0 * * * *

cron.allow, cron.deny By creating, editing, and removing the **cron.allow** and **cron.deny** files, a user working with **root** privileges determines which users can run **cron/crond** jobs. Under Linux these files are kept in the **/etc** directory; under macOS they are kept in **/var/at** (which has a symbolic link at **/usr/lib/cron**). When you create a **cron.deny** file with no entries and no **cron.allow** file exists, everyone can use crontab. When the **cron.allow** file exists, only users listed in that file can use crontab, regardless of the presence and contents of **cron.deny**. Otherwise, you can list in the **cron.allow** file those users who are allowed to use crontab and in **cron.deny** those users who are not allowed to use it. (Listing a user in **cron.deny** is not strictly necessary because, if a **cron.allow** file exists and the user is not listed in it, the user will not be able to use crontab anyway.)

Examples

In the following example, Sam uses **crontab –l** to list the contents of his crontab file (**/var/spool/cron/sam**). All the scripts that Sam runs are in his **~/bin** directory. The first line sets the **MAILTO** variable to **max** so Max gets the output from commands run from Sam's crontab file that is not redirected. The **sat.job** script runs every Saturday (day 6) at 2:05 AM; **twice.week** runs at 12:02 AM on Sunday and Thursday (days 0 and 4); and **twice.day** runs twice a day, every day, at 10:05 AM and 4:05 PM.

```
$ who am i
sam

$ crontab -l
MAILTO=max
05 02 * * 6         $HOME/bin/sat.job
00 02 * * 0,4       $HOME/bin/twice.week
05 10,16 * * *      $HOME/bin/twice.day
```

To add an entry to your crontab file, run the crontab utility with the **–e** (edit) option. Some Linux systems use a version of crontab that does not support the **–e** option. If the local system runs such a version, you need to make a copy of your existing **crontab** file, edit it, and then resubmit it, as in the following example. The **–l** (list) option displays a copy of your **crontab** file.

```
$ crontab -l > newcron
$ vim newcron
...
$ crontab newcron
```

cut

cut

Selects characters or fields from input lines

cut [options] [file-list]

The cut utility selects characters or fields from lines of input and writes them to standard output. Character and field numbering start with 1.

Arguments

The *file-list* is a list of ordinary files. If you do not specify an argument or if you specify a hyphen (–) in place of a filename, cut reads from standard input.

Options

Under Linux, cut accepts the common options described on page 736. Options preceded by a double hyphen (––) work under Linux only. Options named with a single letter and preceded by a single hyphen work under Linux and macOS.

––characters=*clist*
–c *clist*
: Selects the characters given by the column numbers in ***clist***. The value of ***clist*** is one or more comma-separated column numbers or column ranges. A range is specified by two column numbers separated by a hyphen. A range of ***–n*** means columns **1** through ***n***; ***n*–** means columns ***n*** through the end of the line.

––delimiter=*dchar*
–d *dchar*
: Specifies ***dchar*** as the input field delimiter. Also specifies ***dchar*** as the output field delimiter unless you use the **––output-delimiter** option. The default delimiter is a TAB character. Quote ***dchar*** as necessary to protect it from shell expansion.

––fields=*flist* –f *flist*
: Selects the fields specified in ***flist***. The value of ***flist*** is one or more comma-separated field numbers or field ranges. A range is specified by two field numbers separated by a hyphen. A range of ***–n*** means fields **1** through ***n***; ***n*–** means fields ***n*** through the last field. The field delimiter is a TAB character unless you are using the **–d** (**––delimiter**) option to change it.

––output-delimiter=*ochar*
: Specifies ***ochar*** as the output field delimiter. The default delimiter is the TAB character. You can specify a different delimiter by using the **––delimiter** option. Quote ***ochar*** as necessary to protect it from shell expansion.

--only-delimited –s
: Copies only lines containing delimiters. Without this option, cut copies—but does not modify—lines that do not contain delimiters. This works only with the **–d** (**––delimiter**) option.

Notes

Although limited in functionality, cut is easy to learn and use, and is a good choice when columns and fields can be selected without using pattern matching. Sometimes cut is used with paste (page 930).

Examples

For the next two examples, assume that an ls –l command produces the following output:

```
$ ls -l
total 2944
-rwxr-xr-x  1 zach pubs     259 02-01 00:12 countout
-rw-rw-r--  1 zach pubs    9453 02-04 23:17 headers
-rw-rw-r--  1 zach pubs 1474828 01-14 14:15 memo
-rw-rw-r--  1 zach pubs 1474828 01-14 14:33 memos_save
-rw-rw-r--  1 zach pubs    7134 02-04 23:18 tmp1
-rw-rw-r--  1 zach pubs    4770 02-04 23:26 tmp2
-rw-rw-r--  1 zach pubs   13580 11-07 08:01 typescript
```

The following command outputs the permissions of the files in the working directory. The cut utility with the **–c** option selects characters 2 through 10 from each input line. The characters in this range are written to standard output.

```
$ ls -l | cut -c2-10
otal 2944
rwxr-xr-x
rw-rw-r--
rw-rw-r--
rw-rw-r--
rw-rw-r--
rw-rw-r--
rw-rw-r--
```

The next command outputs the size and name of each file in the working directory. The **–f** option selects the fifth and ninth fields from the input lines. The **–d** option tells cut to use SPACEs, not TABs, as delimiters. The tr utility (page 1014) with the **–s** option changes sequences of more than one SPACE character into a single SPACE; otherwise, cut counts the extra SPACE characters as separate fields.

```
$ ls -l | tr -s '  ' ' ' | cut -f5,9 -d' '

259 countout
9453 headers
1474828 memo
1474828 memos_save
7134 tmp1
4770 tmp2
13580 typescript
```

The last example displays a list of full names as stored in the fifth field of the **/etc/passwd** file. The **–d** option specifies that the colon character be used as the field delimiter. Although this example works under macOS, be aware that **/etc/passwd** does not contain information about most users; see “Open Directory” on page 1068 for more information.

```
$ cat /etc/passwd
root:x:0:0:Root:/:/bin/sh
sam:x:401:50:Sam the Great:/home/sam:/bin/zsh
max:x:402:50:Max Wild:/home/max:/bin/bash
zach:x:504:500:Zach Brill:/home/zach:/bin/tcsh
hls:x:505:500:Helen Simpson:/home/hls:/bin/bash
sage:x:402:50:Wise Sage:/home/sage:/bin/bash
sedona:x:402:50:Sedona Pink:/home/sedona:/bin/bash
philip:x:402:50:Philip Gamemaster:/home/philip:/bin/bash
evan:x:402:50:Evan Swordsman:/home/evan:/bin/bash

$ cut -d: -f5 /etc/passwd
Root
Sam the Great
Max Wild
Zach Brill
Helen Simpson
Wise Sage
Sedona Pink
Philip Gamemaster
Evan Swordsman
```

date

Displays or sets the system time and date

date [options] [+format]
date [options] [newdate]

The date utility displays the time and date known to the system. A user working with **root** privileges can use date to change the system clock.

Arguments

The *+format* argument specifies the format for the output of date. The format string, which consists of field descriptors and text, follows a plus sign (+). The field descriptors are preceded by percent signs, and date replaces each one with its value in the output. Table VI-12 lists some of the field descriptors.

Table VI-12 Selected field descriptors

Descriptor	Meaning
%A	Unabbreviated weekday—Sunday to Saturday
%a	Abbreviated weekday—Sun to Sat
%B	Unabbreviated month—January to December
%b	Abbreviated month—Jan to Dec
%c	Date and time in default format used by date
%D	Date in mm/dd/yy format
%d	Day of the month—01 to 31
%H	Hour—00 to 23
%I	Hour—00 to 12
%j	Julian date (day of the year—001 to 366)
%M	Minutes—00 to 59
%m	Month of the year—01 to 12
%n	NEWLINE character
%P	AM or PM
%r	Time in AM/PM notation
%S	Seconds—00 to 60 (the 60 accommodates leap seconds)
%s	Number of seconds since the beginning of January 1, 1970

Table VI-12 Selected field descriptors (continued)

Descriptor	Meaning
%T	Time in HH:MM:SS format
%t	TAB character
%w	Day of the week—0 to 6 (0 = Sunday)
%Y	Year in four-digit format (for example, 2018)
%y	Last two digits of the year—00 to 99
%Z	Time zone (for example, PDT)

By default date zero fills numeric fields. Placing an underscore (_) immediately following the percent sign (%) for a field causes date to blank fill the field. Placing a hyphen (–) following the percent sign causes date not to fill the field—that is, to left-justify the field.

The date utility assumes that, in a format string, any character that is not a percent sign, an underscore or a hyphen following the percent sign, or a field descriptor is ordinary text and copies it to standard output. You can use ordinary text to add punctuation to the date and to add labels (for example, you can put the word **DATE:** in front of the date). Surround the ***format*** argument with single quotation marks if it contains SPACEs or other characters that have a special meaning to the shell.

Setting the system clock

When a user working with **root** privileges specifies ***newdate,*** the system changes the system clock to reflect the new date. The ***newdate*** argument has the syntax

nnddhhmm[[cc]yy][.ss]

where ***nn*** is the number of the month (01–12), ***dd*** is the day of the month (01–31), ***hh*** is the hour based on a 24-hour clock (00–23), and ***mm*** is the minutes (00–59). When you change the date, you must specify at least these fields.

The optional ***cc*** specifies the first two digits of the year (the value of the century minus 1), and ***yy*** specifies the last two digits of the year. You can specify ***yy*** or ***ccyy*** following ***mm***. When you do not specify a year, date assumes that the year has not changed.

You can specify the number of seconds past the start of the minute using ***.ss***.

Options

Under Linux, date accepts the common options described on page 736. Options preceded by a double hyphen (––) work under Linux only. Except as noted, options named with a single letter and preceded by a single hyphen work under Linux and macOS.

––date=*datestring*

–d *datestring*

Displays the date specified by ***datestring,*** not the current date. According to the date man page, "the ***datestring*** is a mostly free-format date string" such as **2pm next thursday**. See **Date input formats** in the date info page for details about the syntax of ***datestring.*** This option does not change the system clock. LINUX

--reference=*file* –r *file*
Displays the modification date and time of ***file*** in place of the current date and time. LINUX

--utc –u Displays or sets the time and date using Universal Coordinated Time (*UTC;* page 1131). UTC is also called Greenwich Mean Time (GMT). You can also use **--universal.**

Notes

If you set up a locale database, date uses that database to substitute terms appropriate to your locale. For more information refer to "Locale" on page 326.

Examples

The first example shows how to set the date to 2:07:30 PM on August 19 without changing the year:

```
# date 08191407.30
Sat Aug 19 14:07:30 PDT 2017
```

The next example shows the ***format*** argument, which causes date to display the date in a commonly used format:

```
$ date '+Today is %h %d, %Y'
Today is Aug 19, 2017
```

dd

Converts and copies a file

dd [arguments]

The dd (device-to-device copy) utility converts and copies a file. The primary use of dd is to copy files to and from hard disk files and removable media. It can operate on hard disk partitions and create block-for-block identical disk images. Often dd can handle the transfer of information to and from other operating systems when other methods fail. Its rich set of arguments gives you precise control over the characteristics of the transfer.

Arguments

Under Linux, dd accepts the common options described on page 736. By default dd copies standard input to standard output.

bs=*n* (**block size**) Reads and writes ***n*** bytes at a time. This argument overrides the **ibs** and **obs** arguments.

cbs=*n* (**conversion block size**) When performing data conversion during the copy, converts ***n*** bytes at a time.

conv=*type[,type...]*

By applying conversion ***types*** in the order given on the command line, converts the data being copied. The ***types*** must be separated by commas with no SPACEs. Table VI-13 lists the types of conversions.

count=*numblocks* Restricts to ***numblocks*** the number of blocks of input that dd copies. The size of each block is the number of bytes specified by the **bs** or **ibs** argument.

ibs=*n* (**input block size**) Reads ***n*** bytes at a time.

if=*filename* (**input file**) Reads from ***filename*** instead of from standard input. You can specify a device name for ***filename*** to read from that device.

obs=*n* (**output block size**) Writes ***n*** bytes at a time.

of=*filename* (**output file**) Writes to ***filename*** instead of to standard output. You can specify a device name for ***filename*** to write to that device.

seek=*numblocks* Skips ***numblocks*** blocks of output before writing any output. The size of each block is the number of bytes specified by the **bs** or **obs** argument.

skip=*numblocks* Skips ***numblocks*** blocks of input before starting to copy. The size of each block is the number of bytes specified by the **bs** or **ibs** argument.

Table VI-13 Conversion types

type	**Meaning**
ascii	Converts EBCDIC-encoded characters to ASCII, allowing you to read tapes written on IBM mainframe and similar computers.

Table VI-13 Conversion types (continued)

type	Meaning
block	Each time dd reads a line of input (i.e., a sequence of characters terminated by a NEWLINE), dd outputs a block of text and pads it with SPACEs until it is the size given by the **bs** or **obs** argument. It then outputs the NEWLINE that ends the line of output.
ebcdic	Converts ASCII-encoded characters to EBCDIC, allowing you to write tapes for use on IBM mainframe and similar computers.
lcase	Converts uppercase letters to lowercase while copying data.
noerror	If a read error occurs, dd normally terminates. This conversion allows dd to continue processing data and is useful when you are trying to recover data from bad media.
notrunc	Does not truncate the output file before writing to it.
ucase	Converts lowercase letters to uppercase while copying data.
unblock	Performs the opposite of the block conversion.

Notes

Under Linux, you can use the standard multiplicative suffixes to make it easier to specify large block sizes. See Table VI-1 on page 735. Under macOS, you can use some of the standard multiplicative suffixes; however, macOS uses lowercase letters in place of the uppercase letters shown in the table. In addition, under macOS, dd supports **b** (block; multiply by 512) and **w** (word; multiply by the number of bytes in an integer).

Examples

You can use dd to create a file filled with pseudorandom bytes:

```
$ dd if=/dev/urandom of=randfile2 bs=1 count=100
```

The preceding command reads from the **/dev/urandom** file (an interface to the kernel's random number generator) and writes to the file named **randfile**. Here, the block size is 1 and the count is 100, so **randfile** is 100 bytes long. For bytes that are more random, you can read from **/dev/random**. See the **urandom** and **random** man pages for more information. Under macOS, **urandom** and **random** behave identically.

Copying a partition

You can also use dd to make an exact copy of a disk partition. Be careful, however; the following command wipes out anything that was on the **/dev/sdb1** partition:

```
# dd if=/dev/sda1 of=/dev/sdb1
```

Backing up a partition

The following command copies the partition named **/dev/sda2** to a file named **boot.img**. Under macOS, hdiutil might do a better job of copying a partition.

```
# dd if=/dev/sda2 of=boot.img
1024000+0 records in
1024000+0 records out
524288000 bytes (524 MB) copied, 14.4193 s, 36.4 MB/s
```

Be careful if you copy the image file to a partition: You will overwrite the information in the partition. Unmount the partition and reverse the **if** and **of** parameters to copy the image file to the partition. Mount the partition once dd has copied the image file.

```
# umount /dev/sda2
# dd if=boot.img of=/dev/sda2
1024000+0 records in
1024000+0 records out
524288000 bytes (524 MB) copied, 15.7692 s, 33.2 MB/s
# mount /dev/sda2
```

You can compress a partition image file just as you can compress most files:

```
# ls -lh boot.img
-rw-r--r--. 1 root root 500M 04-03 15:27 boot.img
# bzip2 boot.img
# ls -lh boot.img.bz2
-rw-r--r--. 1 root root 97M 04-03 15:27 boot.img.bz2
```

Wiping a file You can use a similar technique to wipe data from a file before deleting it, making it almost impossible to recover data from the deleted file. You might want to wipe a file for security reasons; wipe a file several times for added security.

In the following example, ls shows the size of the file named **secret**; dd, with a block size of 1 and a count corresponding to the number of bytes in **secret**, then wipes the file. The **conv=notrunc** argument ensures that dd writes over the data in the file and not another place on the disk.

```
$ ls -l secret
-rw-rw-r--  1 max max 2494 02-06 00:56 secret
$ dd if=/dev/urandom of=secret bs=1 count=2494 conv=notrunc
2494+0 records in
2494+0 records out
$ rm secret
```

You can also use the shred (Linux) or srm (macOS) utility to securely delete files.

df

Displays disk space usage

df [options] [filesystem-list]

The df (disk free) utility reports on the total space and the free space on each mounted device.

Arguments

When you call df without an argument, it reports on the free space on each of the devices mounted on the local system.

The ***filesystem-list*** is an optional list of one or more pathnames that specify the filesystems you want the report to cover. This argument works on macOS and some Linux systems. You can refer to a mounted filesystem by its device pathname or by the pathname of the directory it is mounted on.

Options

Options preceded by a double hyphen (––) work under Linux only. Except as noted, options named with a single letter and preceded by a single hyphen work under Linux and macOS.

––all **–a** Reports on filesystems with a size of 0 blocks, such as **/dev/proc**. Normally df does not report on these filesystems.

––block-size=*sz* **–B *sz***
The *sz* specifies the units the report uses (the default is 1-kilobyte blocks). The *sz* is a multiplicative suffix from Table VI-1 on page 735. See also the **–H** (**––si**) and **–h** (**––human-readable**) options. LINUX

–g (**gigabyte**) Displays sizes in 1-gigabyte blocks. macOS

––si **–H** Displays sizes in K (kilobyte), M (megabyte), and G (gigabyte) blocks, as is appropriate. Uses powers of 1,000.

––human-readable
–h Displays sizes in K (kilobyte), M (megabyte), and G (gigabyte) blocks, as is appropriate. Uses powers of 1,024.

––inodes **–i** Reports the number of *inodes* (page 1103) that are used and free instead of reporting on blocks.

–k (**kilobyte**) Displays sizes in 1-kilobyte blocks.

––local **–l** Displays local filesystems only.

–m (**megabyte**) Displays sizes in 1-megabyte blocks. macOS

––type=*fstype* **–t *fstype***
Reports information only about the filesystems of type ***fstype***, such as DOS or NFS. Repeat this option to report on several types of filesystems. LINUX

–T *fstype*
Reports information only about the filesystems of type ***fstype***, such as DOS or NFS. Separate multiple filesystem types with commas. macOS

--exclude-type=*fstype*
–x *fstype*
Reports information only about the filesystems *not* of type ***fstype***. LINUX

Notes

Under macOS, the df utility supports the **BLOCKSIZE** environment variable (page 736) and ignores block sizes smaller than 512 bytes or larger than 1 gigabyte.

Under macOS, the count of used and free inodes (**–i** option) is meaningless on HFS+ filesystems. On these filesystems, new files can be created as long as free space is available in the filesystem.

Examples

In the following example, df displays information about all mounted filesystems on the local system:

```
$ df
Filesystem          1k-blocks      Used Available Use% Mounted on
/dev/sda12            1517920     53264   1387548   4% /
/dev/sda1               15522      4846      9875  33% /boot
/dev/sda8             1011928    110268    850256  11% /free1
/dev/sda9             1011928     30624    929900   3% /free2
/dev/sda10            1130540     78992    994120   7% /free3
/dev/sda5             4032092   1988080   1839188  52% /home
/dev/sda7             1011928        60    960464   0% /tmp
/dev/sda6             2522048    824084   1569848  34% /usr
zach:/c               2096160   1811392    284768  86% /zach_c
zach:/d               2096450   1935097    161353  92% /zach_d
```

Next, df is called with the **–l** and **–h** options, generating a human-readable list of local filesystems. The sizes in this listing are given in terms of megabytes and gigabytes.

```
$ df -lh
Filesystem            Size  Used Avail Use% Mounted on
/dev/sda12            1.4G   52M  1.3G   4% /
/dev/sda1              15M  4.7M  9.6M  33% /boot
/dev/sda8             988M  108M  830M  11% /free1
/dev/sda9             988M   30M  908M   3% /free2
/dev/sda10            1.1G   77M  971M   7% /free3
/dev/sda5             3.8G  1.9G  1.8G  52% /home
/dev/sda7             988M   60k  938M   0% /tmp
/dev/sda6             2.4G  805M  1.5G  34% /usr
```

The next example, which runs under Linux only, displays information about the **/free2** partition in megabyte units:

```
$ df -BM /free2
Filesystem          1M-blocks      Used Available Use% Mounted on
/dev/sda9                 988        30       908   3% /free2
```

The final example, which runs under Linux only, displays information about NFS filesystems in human-readable terms:

```
$ df -ht nfs
Filesystem            Size  Used Avail Use% Mounted on
zach:/c               2.0G  1.7G  278M  86% /zach_c6
zach:/d               2.0G  1.8G  157M  92% /zach_d
```

diff

Displays the differences between two text files

diff [options] file1 file2
diff [options] file1 directory
diff [options] directory file2
diff [options] directory1 directory2

The diff utility displays line-by-line differences between two text files. By default diff displays the differences as instructions, which you can use to edit one of the files to make it the same as the other.

Arguments

The *file1* and *file2* are pathnames of ordinary text files that diff works on. When the *directory* argument is used in place of *file2*, diff looks for a file in *directory* with the same name as *file1*. It works similarly when *directory* replaces *file1*. When you specify two directory arguments, diff compares the files in *directory1* with the files that have the same simple filenames in *directory2*.

Options

The diff utility accepts the common options described on page 736, with one exception: When one of the arguments is a directory and the other is an ordinary file, you cannot compare to standard input.

The macOS version of diff accepts long options

tip Options for diff preceded by a double hyphen (––) work under macOS as well as under Linux.

––ignore-blank-lines
–B Ignores differences that involve only blank lines.

––ignore-space-change
–b Ignores whitespace (SPACEs and TABs) at the ends of lines and considers other strings of whitespace to be equal.

––context[=*lines*] **–C [*lines*]**
Displays the sections of the two files that differ, including ***lines*** lines (the default is 3) around each line that differs to show the context. Each line in *file1* that is missing from *file2* is preceded by a hyphen (–); each extra line in *file2* is preceded by a plus sign (+); and lines that have different versions in the two files are preceded by an exclamation point (!). When lines that differ are within ***lines*** lines of each other, they are grouped together in the output.

––ed **–e** Creates and sends to standard output a script for the ed editor, which will edit *file1* to make it the same as *file2*. You must add **w** (Write) and **q** (Quit) instructions to the end of the script if you plan to redirect input to ed from the script. When you use **––ed**, diff displays the changes in reverse order: Changes to the end of the file are listed before changes to the top, preventing early changes from affecting later changes when the script is used as input to ed. For example, if a line near the top were deleted, subsequent line numbers in the script would be wrong.

--ignore-case **–i** Ignores differences in case when comparing files.

--new-file **–N** When comparing directories, when a file is present in one of the directories only, considers it to be present and empty in the other directory.

--show-c-function
–p Shows which C function, bash control structure, Perl subroutine, and so forth is affected by each change.

--brief **–q** Does not display the differences between lines in the files. Instead, diff reports only that the files differ.

--recursive **–r** When using diff to compare the files in two directories, causes the comparisons to descend through the directory hierarchies.

--unified[=*lines*] **–U *lines*** *or* **–u**
Uses the easier-to-read unified output format. See the discussion of diff on page 59 for more detail and an example. The ***lines*** argument is the number of lines of context; the default is three. The **–u** option does not take an argument and provides three lines of context.

--width=*n* **–W *n***
Sets the width of the columns that diff uses to display the output to ***n*** characters. This option is useful with the **--side-by-side** option. The sdiff utility (see the "Notes" section) uses a lowercase **w** to perform the same function: **–w *n*.**

--ignore-all-space
–w (**whitespace**) Ignores whitespace when comparing lines.

--side-by-side **–y** Displays the output in a side-by-side format. This option generates the same output as sdiff. Use the **–W** (**--width**) option with this option.

Discussion

When you use diff without any options, it produces a series of lines containing Add (**a**), Delete (**d**), and Change (**c**) instructions. Each of these lines is followed by the lines from the file you need to add to, delete from, or change, respectively, to make the files the same. A less than symbol (**<**) precedes lines from ***file1***. A greater than symbol (**>**) precedes lines from ***file2***. The diff output appears in the format shown in Table VI-14. A pair of line numbers separated by a comma represents a range of lines; a single line number represents a single line.

The diff utility assumes you will convert ***file1*** to ***file2***. The line numbers to the left of each of the **a**, **c**, or **d** instructions always pertain to ***file1***; the line numbers to the right of the instructions apply to ***file2***. To convert ***file2*** to ***file1***, run diff again, reversing the order of the arguments.

Notes

The sdiff utility is similar to diff but its output can be easier to read. The diff **--side-by-side** option produces the same output as sdiff. See the "Examples" section and refer to the diff and sdiff man and info pages for more information.

Use the diff3 utility to compare three files.

Use cmp (page 766) to compare nontext (binary) files.

Table VI-14 diff output

Instruction	Meaning (to change file1 to file2)
`line1 a line2,line3` `> lines from file2`	Append line2 through line3 from **file2** after line1 in **file1**
`line1,line2 d line3` `< lines from file1`	Delete line1 through line2 from **file1**

`line1,line2 c line3,line4`
`< lines from file1`
`---`
`> lines from file 2`
	Change line1 through line2 in **file1** to line3 through line4 from **file2**

Examples

The first example shows how diff displays the differences between two short, similar files:

```
$ cat m
aaaaa
bbbbb
ccccc

$ cat n
aaaaa
ccccc

$ diff m n
2d1
< bbbbb
```

The difference between files **m** and **n** is that the second line of file **m** (**bbbbb**) is missing from file **n**. The first line that diff displays (**2d1**) indicates that you need to delete the second line from *file1* (**m**) to make it the same as *file2* (**n**). The next line diff displays starts with a less than symbol (**<**), indicating that this line of text is from **file1**. In this example, you do not need this information; all you need to know is the line number so that you can delete the line.

The **––side-by-side** option and the sdiff utility, when both have the output width set to 30 characters, display the same output. In the output, a less than symbol points to the extra line in file **m**; diff/sdiff leaves a blank line in file **n** where the extra line would go to make the files the same.

```
$ diff --side-by-side --width=30 m n
aaaaa            aaaaa
bbbbb          <
ccccc            ccccc

$ sdiff -w 30 m n
aaaaa            aaaaa
bbbbb          <
ccccc            ccccc
```

The next example uses the same **m** file and a new file, **p**, to show diff issuing an **a** (Append) instruction:

```
$ cat p
aaaaa
bbbbb
rrrrr
ccccc

$ diff m p
2a3
> rrrrr
```

In the preceding example, diff issues the instruction **2a3** to indicate you must append a line to file **m**, after line 2, to make it the same as file **p**. The second line diff displays indicates the line is from file **p** (the line begins with **>**, indicating **file2**). In this example, you need the information on this line; the appended line must contain the text **rrrrr**.

The next example uses file **m** again, this time with file **r**, to show how diff indicates a line that needs to be changed:

```
$ cat r
aaaaa
-q
ccccc

$ diff m r
2c2
< bbbbb
---
> -q
```

The difference between the two files appears in line 2: File **m** contains **bbbbb**, and file **r** contains **–q**. The diff utility displays **2c2** to indicate that you need to change line 2. After indicating a change is needed, diff shows you must change line 2 in file **m** (**bbbbb**) to line 2 in file **r** (**–q**) to make the files the same. The three hyphens indicate the end of the text in file **m** that needs to be changed and the beginning of the text in file **r** that is to replace it.

Comparing the same files using the side-by-side and width options (**–y** and **–W**) yields an easier-to-read result. The pipe symbol (|) indicates the line on one side must replace the line on the other side to make the files the same:

```
$ diff -y -W 30 m r
aaaaa           aaaaa
bbbbb         | -q
ccccc           ccccc
```

The next examples compare the two files **q** and **v**:

```
$ cat q         $ cat v
Monday          Monday
Tuesday         Wednesday
Wednesday       Thursday
Thursday        Thursday
Saturday        Friday
Sunday          Saturday
                Sundae
```

Running in side-by-side mode, diff shows **Tuesday** is missing from file **v**, there is only one **Thursday** in file **q** (there are two in file **v**), and **Friday** is missing from file **q**. The last line is **Sunday** in file **q** and **Sundae** in file **v**: diff indicates these lines are different. You can change file **q** to be the same as file **v** by removing **Tuesday**, adding one **Thursday** and **Friday**, and substituting **Sundae** from file **v** for **Sunday** from file **q**. Alternatively, you can change file **v** to be the same as file **q** by adding **Tuesday**, removing one **Thursday** and **Friday**, and substituting **Sunday** from file **q** for **Sundae** from file **v**.

```
$ diff -y -W 30 q v
Monday          Monday
Tuesday       <
Wednesday       Wednesday
Thursday        Thursday
              > Thursday
              > Friday
Saturday        Saturday
Sunday        | Sundae
```

Context diff With the **--context** option (called a *context diff*), diff displays output that tells you how to turn the first file into the second file. The top two lines identify the files and show that **q** is represented by asterisks, whereas **v** is represented by hyphens. Following a row of asterisks that indicates the beginning of a hunk of text is a row of asterisks with the numbers **1,6** in the middle. This line indicates that the instructions in the first section tell you what to remove from or change in file **q**—specifically, lines 1 through 6 (that is, all the lines of file **q**; in a longer file it would mark the first hunk). The hyphen on the second subsequent line indicates you need to remove the line with **Tuesday**. The line with an exclamation point indicates you need to replace the line with **Sunday** with the corresponding line from file **v**. The row of hyphens with the numbers **1,7** in the middle indicates that the next section tells you which lines from file **v**—lines 1 through 7—you need to add or change in file **q**. You need to add a second line with **Thursday** and a line with **Friday**, and you need to change **Sunday** in file **q** to **Sundae** (from file **v**).

```
$ diff --context q v
*** q   Mon Aug 27 18:26:45 2018
--- v   Mon Aug 27 18:27:55 2018
***************
*** 1,6 ****
  Monday
- Tuesday
  Wednesday
  Thursday
  Saturday
! Sunday
--- 1,7 ----
  Monday
  Wednesday
  Thursday
+ Thursday
+ Friday
  Saturday
! Sundae
```

diskutil macOS

Checks, modifies, and repairs local volumes

diskutil action [arguments]

The diskutil utility mounts, unmounts, and displays information about disks and partitions (volumes). It can also format and repair filesystems and divide a disk into partitions. The diskutil utility is available under macOS only. macOS

Arguments

The *action* specifies what diskutil is to do. Table VI-15 lists common *actions* along with the argument each takes.

Table VI-15 diskutil actions

Action	Argument	Description
eraseVolume	***type name device***	Reformats ***device*** using the format ***type*** and the label ***name***. The ***name*** specifies the name of the volume; alphanumeric names are the easiest to work with. The filesystem ***type*** is typically HFS+ but can also be UFS or MS-DOS. You can specify additional options as part of the ***type***. For example, a FAT32 filesystem (as used in Windows 98 and above) would have a type of MS-DOS FAT32. A journaled, case-sensitive, HFS+ filesystem would have a ***type*** of Case-sensitive Journaled HFS+.
info	***device***	Displays information about ***device***. Does not require ownership of ***device***.
list	***[device]***	Lists partitions on ***device***. Without ***device*** lists partitions on all devices. Does not require ownership of ***device***.
mount	***device***	Mounts ***device***.
mountDisk	***device***	Mounts all devices on the disk containing ***device***.
reformat	***device***	Reformats ***device*** using its current name and format.
repairVolume	***device***	Repairs the filesystem on ***device***.
unmount	***device***	Unmounts ***device***.
unmountDisk	***device***	Unmounts all devices on the disk containing ***device***.
verifyVolume	***device***	Verifies the filesystem on ***device***. Does not require ownership of ***device***.

Notes

The diskutil utility provides access to the Disk Management framework, the support code used by the Disk Utility application. It allows some choices that are not supported from the graphical interface.

You must own ***device***, or be working with **root** privileges, when you specify an ***action*** that modifies or changes the state of a volume.

fsck The diskutil **verifyVolume** and **repairVolume** actions are analogous to the fsck utility on Linux systems. Under macOS, the fsck utility is deprecated except when the system is in single-user mode.

disktool Some of the functions performed by diskutil were handled by disktool in the past.

Examples

The first example displays a list of disk devices and volumes available on the local system:

```
$ diskutil list
/dev/disk0
   #:                       type name               size      identifier
   0: Apple_partition_scheme                        *152.7 GB disk0
   1:    Apple_partition_map                        31.5 KB   disk0s1
   2:              Apple_HFS Eva01                  30.7 GB   disk0s3
   3:              Apple_HFS Users                  121.7 GB  disk0s5
/dev/disk1
   #:                       type name               size      identifier
   0: Apple_partition_scheme                        *232.9 GB disk1
   1:    Apple_partition_map                        31.5 KB   disk1s1
   2:         Apple_Driver43                        28.0 KB   disk1s2
   3:         Apple_Driver43                        28.0 KB   disk1s3
   4:       Apple_Driver_ATA                        28.0 KB   disk1s4
   5:       Apple_Driver_ATA                        28.0 KB   disk1s5
   6:         Apple_FWDriver                        256.0 KB  disk1s6
   7:     Apple_Driver_IOKit                        256.0 KB  disk1s7
   8:          Apple_Patches                        256.0 KB  disk1s8
   9:              Apple_HFS Spare                  48.8 GB   disk1s9
  10:              Apple_HFS House                  184.1 GB  disk1s10
```

The next example displays information about one of the mounted volumes:

```
$ diskutil info disk1s9
   Device Node:        /dev/disk1s9
   Device Identifier:  disk1s9
   Mount Point:        /Volumes/Spare
   Volume Name:        Spare

   File System:        HFS+
   Owners:             Enabled
   Partition Type:     Apple_HFS
   Bootable:           Is bootable
   Media Type:         Generic
   Protocol:           FireWire
   SMART Status:       Not Supported
   UUID:               C77BB3DC-EFBB-30B0-B191-DE7E01D8A563

   Total Size:         48.8 GB
   Free Space:         48.8 GB

   Read Only:          No
   Ejectable:          Yes
```

The next example formats the partition at **/dev/disk1s8** as an HFS+ Extended (HFSX) filesystem and labels it **Spare2**. This command erases all data on the partition:

```
# diskutil eraseVolume 'Case-sensitive HFS+' Spare2 disk1s8
Started erase on disk disk1s10
Erasing
Mounting Disk
Finished erase on disk disk1s10
```

The final example shows the output of a successful **verifyVolume** operation:

```
$ diskutil verifyVolume disk1s9
Started verify/repair on volume disk1s9 Spare
Checking HFS Plus volume.
Checking Extents Overflow file.
Checking Catalog file.
Checking Catalog hierarchy.
Checking volume bitmap.
Checking volume information.
The volume Spare appears to be OK.
Mounting Disk
Verify/repair finished on volume disk1s9 Spare
```

ditto macOS

Copies files and creates and unpacks archives

ditto [options] source-file destination-file
ditto [options] source-file-list destination-directory
ditto –c [options] source-directory destination-archive
ditto –x [options] source-archive-list destination-directory

The ditto utility copies files and their ownership, timestamps, and other attributes, including extended attributes (page 1070). It can copy to and from cpio and zip archive files, as well as copy ordinary files and directories. The ditto utility is available under macOS only. macOS

Arguments

The ***source-file*** is the pathname of the file that ditto is to make a copy of. The ***destination-file*** is the pathname that ditto assigns to the resulting copy of the file.

The ***source-file-list*** specifies one or more pathnames of files and directories that ditto makes copies of. The ***destination-directory*** is the pathname of the directory that ditto copies the files and directories into. When you specify a ***destination-directory***, ditto gives each of the copied files the same simple filename as its ***source-file***.

The ***source-directory*** is a single directory that ditto copies into the ***destination-archive***. The resulting archive holds copies of the contents of ***source-directory*** but not the directory itself.

The ***source-archive-list*** specifies one or more pathnames of archives that ditto extracts into ***destination-directory***.

Using a hyphen (–) in place of a filename or a directory name causes ditto to read from standard input or write to standard output instead of reading from or writing to that file or directory.

Options

You cannot use the **–c** and **–x** options together.

–c (**create archive**) Creates an archive file.

––help Displays a help message.

–k (**pkzip**) Uses the zip format, instead of the default cpio (page 776) format, to create or extract archives. For more information on zip, see the tip on page 64.

––norsrc (**no resource**) Ignores extended attributes. This option causes ditto to copy only data forks (the default behavior under macOS 10.3 and earlier).

––rsrc (**resource**) Copies extended attributes, including resource forks (the default behavior under macOS 10.4 and above). Also **–rsrc** and **–rsrcFork**.

–V (**very verbose**) Sends a line to standard error for each file, symbolic link, and device node copied by ditto.

–v (**verbose**) Sends a line to standard error for each directory copied by ditto.

–X (**exclude**) Prevents ditto from searching directories in filesystems other than the filesystems that hold the files it was explicitly told to copy.

–x (**extract archive**) Extracts files from an archive file.

–z (**compress**) Uses gzip (page 858) or gunzip to compress or decompress cpio archives.

Notes

The ditto utility does not copy the locked attribute flag (page 1072). The utility also does not copy ACLs.

By default ditto creates and reads *archives* (page 1083) in the cpio (page 776) format.

The ditto utility cannot list the contents of archive files; it can only create or extract files from archives. Use pax or cpio to list the contents of cpio archives, and use unzip with the –l option to list the contents of zip files.

Examples

The following examples show three ways to back up a user's home directory, including extended attributes (except as mentioned in "Notes"), while preserving timestamps and permissions. The first example copies Zach's home directory to the volume (filesystem) named **Backups**; the copy is a new directory named **zach.0228**:

```
$ ditto /Users/zach /Volumes/Backups/zach.0228
```

The next example copies Zach's home directory into a single cpio-format archive file on the volume named **Backups**:

```
$ ditto -c /Users/zach /Volumes/Backups/zach.0228.cpio
```

The next example copies Zach's home directory into a zip archive:

```
$ ditto -c -k /Users/zach /Volumes/Backups/zach.0228.zip
```

Each of the next three examples restores the corresponding backup archive into Zach's home directory, overwriting any files that are already there:

```
$ ditto /Volumes/Backups/zach.0228 /Users/zach
$ ditto -x /Volumes/Backups/zach.0228.cpio /Users/zach
$ ditto -x -k /Volumes/Backups/zach.0228.zip /Users/zach
```

The following example copies the **Scripts** directory to a directory named **ScriptsBackups** on the remote host **plum**. It uses an argument of a hyphen in place of *source-directory* locally to write to standard output and in place of *destination-directory* on the remote system to read from standard input:

```
$ ditto -c Scripts - | ssh plum ditto -x - ScriptsBackups
```

The final example copies the local startup disk (the root filesystem) to the volume named **Backups.root**. Because some of the files can be read only by **root**, the script must be run by a user with **root** privileges. The –X option keeps ditto from trying to copy other volumes (filesystems) that are mounted under **/**.

```
# ditto -X / /Volumes/Backups.root
```

dmesg

Displays kernel messages

dmesg [options]

The dmesg utility displays messages stored in the kernel ring buffer.

Options

–c Clears the kernel ring buffer after running dmesg. LINUX

–M ***core***
The ***core*** is the name of the (core dump) file to process (defaults to **/dev/kmem**). macOS

–N ***kernel***
The ***kernel*** is the pathname of a kernel file (defaults to **/mach**). If you are displaying information about a core dump, ***kernel*** should be the kernel that was running at the time the core file was created. macOS

Discussion

When the system boots, the kernel fills its ring buffer with messages regarding hardware and module initialization. Messages in the kernel ring buffer are often useful for diagnosing system problems.

Notes

Under macOS, you must run this utility while working with **root** privileges.

As a ring buffer, the kernel message buffer keeps the most recent messages it receives, discarding the oldest messages once it fills up. To save a list of kernel boot messages, give the following command immediately after booting the system and logging in:

```
$ dmesg > dmesg.boot
```

This command saves the kernel messages in the **dmesg.boot** file. This list can be educational and quite useful when you are having a problem with the boot process.

Under most Linux systems, after the system boots, the system records much of the same information as dmesg displays in **/var/log/messages** or a similar file.

Examples

The following command displays kernel messages in the ring buffer with the string **serial** in them, regardless of case:

```
$ dmesg | grep -i serial
[    1.304433] Serial: 8250/16550 driver, 4 ports, IRQ sharing enabled
[    1.329978] serial8250: ttyS0 at I/O 0x3f8 (irq = 4) is a 16550A
[    1.354473] serial8250: ttyS1 at I/O 0x2f8 (irq = 3) is a 16550A
[    1.411213] usb usb1: New USB device strings: Mfr=3, Product=2, SerialNumber=1
[    1.411221] usb usb1: SerialNumber: 0000:02:03.0
...
```

dscl macOS

Displays and manages Directory Service information

dscl [options] [datasource [command]]

The dscl (Directory Service command line) utility enables you to work with Directory Service directory nodes. When you call dscl without arguments, it runs interactively. The dscl utility is available under macOS only. macOS

Arguments

The ***datasource*** is a node name or a macOS Server host specified by a hostname or IP address. A period (**.**) specifies the local domain.

Options

–p (**prompt**) Prompts for a password as needed.

–q (**quiet**) Does not prompt.

–u ***user***
Authenticates as ***user***.

Commands

Refer to the "Notes" section for definitions of some of the terms used here.

The hyphen (**–**) before a command is optional.

–list *path [key]* (also **–ls**) Lists subdirectories in ***path***, one per line. If you specify ***key***, this command lists subdirectories that match ***key***.

–read *[path [key]]*
(also **–cat** and **.**) Displays a directory, one property per line.

–readall *[path [key]]*
Displays properties with a given key.

–search ***path key value***
Displays properties where ***key*** matches ***value***.

Notes

When discussing Directory Service, the term *directory* refers to a collection of data (a database), not to a filesystem directory. Each directory holds one or more properties. Each property comprises a key–value pair, where there might be more than one value for a given key. In general, dscl displays a property with the key first, followed by a colon, and then the value. If there is more than one value, the values are separated by SPACEs. If a value contains SPACEs, dscl displays the value on the line following the key.

Under macOS and macOS Server, Open Directory stores information for the local system in key–value-formatted XML files in the **/var/db/dslocal** directory hierarchy.

The dscl utility is the command-line equivalent of NetInfo Manager (available on versions of macOS prior to 10.5) or of Workgroup Manager on macOS Server.

Examples

The dscl –list command displays a list of top-level directories when you specify a path of /:

```
$ dscl . -list /
AFPServer
AFPUserAliases
Aliases
AppleMetaRecord
Augments
Automount
...
SharePoints
SMBServer
Users
WebServer
```

The period as the first argument to dscl specifies the local domain as the data source. The next command displays a list of **Users** directories:

```
$ dscl . -list /Users
_amavisd
_appowner
_appserver
_ard
...
_www
_xgridagent
_xgridcontroller
daemon
max
nobody
root
```

You can use the dscl **–read** command to display information about a specific user:

```
$ dscl . -read /Users/root
AppleMetaNodeLocation: /Local/Default
GeneratedUID: FFFFEEEE-DDDD-CCCC-BBBB-AAAA00000000
NFSHomeDirectory: /var/root
Password: *
PrimaryGroupID: 0
RealName:
 System Administrator
RecordName: root
RecordType: dsRecTypeStandard:Users
UniqueID: 0
UserShell: /bin/sh
```

The following dscl **–readall** command lists all usernames and user IDs on the local system. The command looks for the **RecordName** and **UniqueID** keys in the **/Users** directory and displays the associated values. The dscl utility separates multiple values with SPACEs. See page 1068 for an example of a shell script that calls dscl while using the **–readall** command.

```
$ dscl . -readall /Users RecordName UniqueID
RecordName: _amavisd amavisd
UniqueID: 83
-
RecordName: _appowner appowner
UniqueID: 87
-
...
RecordName: daemon
UniqueID: 1
-
RecordName: sam
UniqueID: 501
-
RecordName: nobody
UniqueID: -2
-
RecordName: root
UniqueID: 0
```

The following example uses the dscl **–search** command to display all properties where the key **RecordName** equals **sam**:

```
$ dscl . -search / RecordName sam
Users/sam               RecordName = (
    sam
)
```

du

Displays information on disk usage by directory hierarchy and/or file

du [options] [path-list]

The du (disk usage) utility reports how much disk space is occupied by a directory hierarchy or a file. By default du displays the number of 1,024-byte blocks occupied by the directory hierarchy or file.

Arguments

Without any arguments, du displays information about the working directory and its subdirectories. The ***path-list*** specifies the directories and files du displays information about.

Options

Options preceded by a double hyphen (––) work under Linux only. Except as noted, options named with a single letter and preceded by a single hyphen work under Linux and macOS.

Without any options, du displays the total storage used for each argument in ***path-list***. For directories, du displays this total after recursively listing the totals for each subdirectory.

––all **–a** Displays the space used by all ordinary files along with the total for each directory.

––block-size=*sz* **–B *sz***
The *sz* argument specifies the units the report uses. It is a multiplicative suffix from Table VI-1 on page 735. See also the **–H** (**––si**) and **–h** (**––human-readable**) options. LINUX

––total **–c** Displays a grand total at the end of the output.

––dereference-args
–D (**partial dereference**) For each file that is a symbolic link, reports on the file the link points to, not the symbolic link itself. This option affects files specified on the command line; it does not affect files found while descending a directory hierarchy. This option treats files that are not symbolic links normally. See page 118 for information on dereferencing symbolic links. LINUX

–d *depth*
Displays information for subdirectories to a level of *depth* directories. macOS

––si (**human readable**) Displays sizes in K (kilobyte), M (megabyte), and G (gigabyte) blocks, as appropriate. Uses powers of 1,000. LINUX

–H (**partial dereference**) For each file that is a symbolic link, reports on the file the link points to, not the symbolic link itself. This option affects files specified on the command line; it does not affect files found while descending a directory hierarchy. This option treats files that are not symbolic links normally. See page 118 for information on dereferencing symbolic links. macOS

--human-readable
–h Displays sizes in K (kilobyte), M (megabyte), and G (gigabyte) blocks, as appropriate. Uses powers of 1,024.

–k Displays sizes in 1-kilobyte blocks.

--dereference **–L** For each file that is a symbolic link, reports on the file the link points to, not the symbolic link itself. This option affects all files and treats files that are not symbolic links normally. The default is **–P** (**--no-dereference**). See page 118 for information on dereferencing symbolic links.

–m Displays sizes in 1-megabyte blocks.

--no-dereference **–P** For each file that is a symbolic link, reports on the symbolic link, not the file the link points to. This option affects all files and treats files that are not symbolic links normally. This behavior is the default. See page 118 for information on dereferencing symbolic links.

--summarize **–s** Displays only the total size for each directory or file you specify on the command line; subdirectory totals are not displayed.

--one-file-system **–x** Reports only on files and directories on the same filesystem as that of the argument being processed.

Examples

In the first example, du displays size information about subdirectories in the working directory. The last line contains the total for the working directory and its subdirectories.

```
$ du
26      ./Postscript
4       ./RCS
47      ./XIcon
4       ./Printer/RCS
12      ./Printer
105     .
```

The total (105) is the number of blocks occupied by all plain files and directories under the working directory. All files are counted, even though du displays only the sizes of directories.

If you do not have read permission for a file or directory that du encounters, then du sends a warning to standard error and skips that file or directory. Next, using the **–s** (summarize) option, du displays the total for each of the directories in **/usr** but does not display information for subdirectories:

```
$ du -s /usr/*
4       /usr/X11R6
260292  /usr/bin
10052   /usr/games
7772    /usr/include
1720468 /usr/lib
105240  /usr/lib32
0       /usr/lib64
```

```
du: cannot read directory `/usr/local/lost+found': Permission denied
...
130696  /usr/src
```

When you add the **–c** (total) option to the preceding example, du displays the same listing with a total at the end:

```
$ du -sc /usr/*
4       /usr/X11R6
260292  /usr/bin
...
130696  /usr/src
3931436 total
```

The following example uses the **–s** (summarize), **–h** (human-readable), and **–c** (total) options:

```
$ du -shc /usr/*
4.0K    /usr/X11R6
255M    /usr/bin
9.9M    /usr/games
7.6M    /usr/include
1.7G    /usr/lib
103M    /usr/lib32
...
128M    /usr/src
3.8G    total
```

The final example displays, in human-readable format, the total size of all files the user can read in the **/usr** filesystem. Redirecting standard error to **/dev/null** discards all warnings about files and directories that are unreadable.

```
$ du -hs /usr 2>/dev/null
3.8G    /usr
```

echo

Displays a message

echo [options] message

The echo utility copies its arguments, followed by a NEWLINE, to standard output. Both the Bourne Again and TC Shells have their own echo builtin that works similarly to the echo utility.

Arguments

The ***message*** consists of one or more arguments, which can include quoted strings, ambiguous file references, and shell variables. A SPACE separates each argument from the next. The shell recognizes unquoted special characters in the arguments. For example, the shell expands an asterisk into a list of filenames in the working directory.

Options

You can configure the tcsh echo builtin to treat backslash escape sequences and the **–n** option in different ways. Refer to **echo_style** in the tcsh man page. The typical tcsh configuration recognizes the **–n** option, enables backslash escape sequences, and ignores the **–E** and **–e** options.

–E Suppresses the interpretation of backslash escape sequences such as **\n**. Available with the bash builtin version of echo only.

–e Enables the interpretation of backslash escape sequences such as **\n**. Available with the bash builtin version of echo only.

––help Gives a short summary of how to use echo. The summary includes a list of the backslash escape sequences interpreted by echo. This option works only with the echo utility; it does not work with the echo builtins. LINUX

–n Suppresses the NEWLINE terminating the ***message.***

Notes

Suppressing the interpretation of backslash escape sequences is the default behavior of the bash builtin version of echo and of the echo utility.

You can use echo to send messages to the screen from a shell script. See page 154 for a discussion of how to use echo to display filenames using wildcard characters.

The echo utility and builtins provide an escape notation to represent certain nonprinting characters in ***message*** (Table VI-16). You must use the **–e** option for these backslash escape sequences to work with the echo utility and the bash echo builtin. Typically, you do not need the **–e** option with the tcsh echo builtin.

Table VI-16 Backslash escape sequences

Sequence	Meaning
\a	Bell
\c	Suppress trailing NEWLINE

Table VI-16 Backslash escape sequences (continued)

Sequence	Meaning
\n	NEWLINE
\t	HORIZONTAL TAB
\v	VERTICAL TAB
\\	BACKSLASH

Examples

Following are some echo commands. These commands will work with the echo utility (/bin/echo) and the bash and tcsh echo builtins except for the last, which might not need the –e option under tcsh.

```
$ echo "This command displays a string."
This command displays a string.
$ echo -n "This displayed string is not followed by a NEWLINE."
This displayed string is not followed by a NEWLINE.$ echo hi
hi
$ echo -e "This message contains\v a vertical tab."
This message contains
                      a vertical tab.
$
```

The following examples contain messages with the backslash escape sequence \c. In the first example, the shell processes the arguments before calling echo. When the shell sees the \c, it replaces the \c with the character c. The next three examples show how to quote the \c so that the shell passes it to echo, which then does not append a NEWLINE to the end of the message. The first four examples are run under bash and require the –e option. The final example runs under tcsh, which might not need this option.

```
$ echo -e There is a newline after this line.\c
There is a newline after this line.c

$ echo -e 'There is no newline after this line.\c'
There is no newline after this line.$

$ echo -e "There is no newline after this line.\c"
There is no newline after this line.$

$ echo -e There is no newline after this line.\\c
There is no newline after this line.$

$ tcsh
tcsh $ echo -e 'There is no newline after this line.\c'
There is no newline after this line.$
```

You can use the –n option in place of –e and \c.

expand/unexpand

Converts TABs to SPACEs and SPACEs to TABs

expand [option] [file-list]
unexpand [option] [file-list]

The expand utility converts TABs to SPACEs and the unexpand utility converts SPACEs to TABs.

Arguments

The expand utility reads files from ***file-list*** and converts all TABs on each line to SPACEs, assuming TAB stops are eight spaces apart.

The unexpand utility reads files from ***file-list*** and converts all SPACEs at the beginning of each line to TABs. It stops converting for a line when it reads the first character on a line that is not a SPACE or a TAB.

If you do not specify a filename or if you specify a hyphen (–) in place of a filename, expand/unexpand reads from standard input.

Options

The expand/unexpand utilities accept the common options described on page 736.

––all **–a** On each line, converts all SPACEs and TABs, not just the initial ones (unexpand only).

––first-only On each line, stops converting SPACEs after reading the first character that is not a SPACE or a TAB (unexpand only). Overrides the **––all** option.

––initial **–i** On each line, stops converting TABs after reading the first character that is not a SPACE or a TAB (expand only).

––tabs=*num* | *list*
–t *num* | *list*
Specifies ***num*** as the number of SPACEs per TAB stop. With ***list***, specifies each TAB stop as the number of characters from the left margin. By default TAB stops are eight characters apart. With unexpand, implies the **––all** option.

Examples

The following examples show how expand works. All blanks in the **tabs.only** file are single TABs. The **––show-tabs** option causes cat to display TABs as **^I** and SPACEs as SPACEs.

```
$ cat tabs.only
>>	>>	>>	>>	x

$ cat --show-tabs tabs.only
>>^I>>^I>>^I>>^Ix
```

The expand **––tabs=2** option specifies two SPACEs per TAB stop; **––tabs=20,24,30,36** specifies TAB stops at columns 20, 24, 30, and 36.

```
$ expand --tabs=2 tabs.only | cat --show-tabs
>>  >>  >>  >>  x

$ expand --tabs=20,24,30,36 tabs.only | cat --show-tabs
>>                  >>  >>    >>    x
```

Next, unexpand converts each group of eight SPACEs to a TAB. All blanks in the **spaces.only** file are multiple SPACEs. Because unexpand converts TABs the same way the terminal driver does (TAB stops every eight characters), the output from cat and from unexpand with the –a option appear the same.

```
$ cat spaces.only
                  >>                        >>  >>    >> x

$ unexpand -a spaces.only
                  >>                        >>  >>    >> x
```

When you send the output of unexpand with the –a option through a pipeline to cat with the **––show-tabs** option, you can see where unexpand put the TABs.

```
$ unexpand -a spaces.only | cat --show-tabs
^I^I  >>^I^I      >>  >>^I>> x
```

expr

Evaluates an expression

expr expression

The expr utility evaluates an expression and sends the result to standard output. It evaluates character strings that represent either numeric or nonnumeric values. Operators are used with the strings to form expressions.

Arguments

The *expression* is composed of strings interspersed with operators. Each string and operator constitute a distinct argument that you must separate from other arguments with a SPACE. You must quote operators that have special meanings to the shell (for example, the multiplication operator, *).

The following list of expr operators is given in order of decreasing precedence. Each operator within a group of operators has the same precedence. You can change the order of evaluation by using parentheses.

: (**comparison**) Compares two strings, starting with the first character in each string and ending with the last character in the second string. The second string is a regular expression with an implied caret (^) as its first character. If expr finds a match, it displays the number of characters in the second string. If expr does not find a match, it displays a zero.

* (**multiplication**)
/ (**division**)
% (**remainder**)
Work only on strings that contain the numerals 0 through 9 and optionally a leading minus sign. Convert strings to integer numbers, perform the specified arithmetic operation on numbers, and convert the result back to a string before sending it to standard output.

\+ (**addition**)
\- (**subtraction**)
Function in the same manner as the preceding group of operators.

< (**less than**)
<= (**less than or equal to**)
= *or* == (**equal to**)
!= (**not equal to**)
>= (**greater than or equal to**)
> (**greater than**)
Relational operators work on both numeric and nonnumeric arguments. If one or both of the arguments are nonnumeric, the comparison is nonnumeric, using the machine collating sequence (typically ASCII). If both arguments are numeric, the comparison is numeric. The expr utility displays a 1 (one) if the comparison is *true* and a 0 (zero) if it is *false*.

& (AND) Evaluates both of its arguments. If neither is 0 or a null string, expr displays the value of the first argument. Otherwise, it displays a 0 (zero). You must quote this operator.

| (OR) Evaluates the first argument. If it is neither 0 nor a null string, expr displays the value of the first argument. Otherwise, it displays the value of the second argument. You must quote this operator.

Notes

The expr utility returns an exit status of 0 (zero) if the expression evaluates to anything other than a null string or the number 0, a status of 1 if the expression is null or 0, and a status of 2 if the expression is invalid.

Although expr and this discussion distinguish between numeric and nonnumeric arguments, all arguments to expr are nonnumeric (character strings). When applicable, expr attempts to convert an argument to a number (for example, when using the + operator). If a string contains characters other than 0 through 9 and optionally a leading minus sign, expr cannot convert it. Specifically, if a string contains a plus sign or a decimal point, expr considers it to be nonnumeric. If both arguments are numeric, the comparison is numeric. If one is nonnumeric, the comparison is lexicographic.

Examples

In the following examples, expr evaluates constants. You can also use expr to evaluate variables in a shell script. The fourth command displays an error message because of the illegal decimal point in 5.3:

```
$ expr 17 + 40
57
$ expr 10 - 24
-14
$ expr -17 + 20
3
$ expr 5.3 + 4
expr: non-numeric argument
```

The multiplication (*), division (/), and remainder (%) operators provide additional arithmetic power. You must quote the multiplication operator (precede it with a backslash) so that the shell will not treat it as a special character (an ambiguous file reference). You cannot put quotation marks around the entire expression because each string and operator must be a separate argument.

```
$ expr 5 \* 4
20
$ expr 21 / 7
3
$ expr 23 % 7
2
```

The next two examples show how parentheses change the order of evaluation. You must quote each parenthesis and surround the backslash/parenthesis combination with SPACEs:

```
$ expr 2 \* 3 + 4
10
$ expr 2 \* \( 3 + 4 \)
14
```

You can use relational operators to determine the relationship between numeric or nonnumeric arguments. The following commands compare two strings to see if they are equal; expr displays a 0 when the relationship is *false* and a 1 when it is *true*.

```
$ expr fred == sam
0
$ expr sam == sam
1
```

In the following examples, the relational operators, which must be quoted, establish order between numeric or nonnumeric arguments. Again, if a relationship is *true*, expr displays a 1.

```
$ expr fred \> sam
0
$ expr fred \< sam
1
$ expr 5 \< 7
1
```

The next command compares **5** with **m**. When one of the arguments expr is comparing with a relational operator is nonnumeric, expr considers the other to be nonnumeric. In this case, because **m** is nonnumeric, expr treats **5** as a nonnumeric argument. The comparison is between the ASCII (on many systems) values of **m** and **5**. The ASCII value of **m** is 109 and that of **5** is 53, so expr evaluates the relationship as *true*.

```
$ expr 5 \< m
1
```

In the next example, the matching operator determines that the four characters in the second string match the first four characters in the first string. The expr utility displays the number of matching characters (4).

```
$ expr abcdefghijkl : abcd
4
```

The & operator displays a 0 if one or both of its arguments are 0 or a null string; otherwise, it displays the first argument.

```
$ expr '' \& book
0

$ expr magazine \& book
magazine
```

```
$ expr 5 \& 0
0

$ expr 5 \& 6
5
```

The | operator displays the first argument if it is not 0 or a null string; otherwise, it displays the second argument.

```
$ expr '' \| book
book

$ expr magazine \| book
magazine

$ expr 5 \| 0
5

$ expr 0 \| 5
5

$ expr 5 \| 6
5
```

file

Displays the classification of a file

file [option] file-list

The file utility classifies files according to their contents.

Arguments

The ***file-list*** is a list of the pathnames of one or more files that file classifies. You can specify any kind of file, including ordinary, directory, and special files, in the ***file-list***.

Options

The macOS version of file accepts long options

tip Options for file preceded by a double hyphen (––) work under macOS as well as under Linux.

––files-from=*file* –f *file*
Takes the names of files to be examined from ***file*** rather than from ***file-list*** on the command line. The names of the files must be listed one per line in ***file***.

––no-dereference –h For each file that is a symbolic link, this reports on the symbolic link, not the file the link points to. This option treats files that are not symbolic links normally. This behavior is the default on systems where the environment variable **POSIXLY_CORRECT** is not defined (typical). See page 118 for information on dereferencing symbolic links.

––help Displays a help message.

––mime –I Displays *MIME* (page 1110) type strings. macOS

––mime –i Displays *MIME* (page 1110) type strings. LINUX

–i (**ignore**) Does not display regular files. macOS

––dereference –L For each file that is a symbolic link, this reports on the file the link points to, not the symbolic link itself. This option treats files that are not symbolic links normally. This behavior is the default on systems where the environment variable **POSIXLY_CORRECT** is defined. See page 118 for information on dereferencing symbolic links.

––uncompress –z (**zip**) Attempts to classify files within a compressed file.

Notes

The file utility can classify more than 5,000 file types. Some of the more common file types found on Linux systems, as displayed by file, follow:

```
archive
ascii text
c program text
commands text
core file
cpio archive
data
directory
ELF 32-bit LSB executable
empty
English text
executable
```

The file utility uses a maximum of three tests in its attempt to classify a file: filesystem, magic number, and language tests. When file identifies the type of a file, it ceases testing. The filesystem test examines the value returned by a **stat**() system call to see whether the file is empty or a special file. The *magic number* (page 1108) test looks for data in particular fixed formats near the beginning of the file. The language test, if needed, determines whether the file is a text file, which encoding it uses, and which language it is written in. Refer to the file man page for a more detailed description of how file works. The results of file are not always correct.

Examples

Some examples of file identification follow:

```
/etc/Muttrc:                     ASCII English text
/etc/Muttrc.d:                   directory
/etc/adjtime:                    ASCII text
/etc/aliases.db:                 Berkeley DB (Hash, version 9, native byte-order)
/etc/at.deny:                    writable, regular file, no read permission
/etc/bash_completion:            UTF-8 Unicode English text, with very long lines
/etc/blkid.tab.old:              Non-ISO extended-ASCII text, with CR,
                                 LF line terminators
/etc/brltty.conf:                UTF-8 Unicode C++ program text
/etc/chatscripts:                setgid directory
/etc/magic:                      magic text file for file(1) cmd
/etc/motd:                       symbolic link to '/var/run/motd'
/etc/qemu-ifup:                  POSIX shell script text executable
/usr/bin/4xml:                   a python script text executable
/usr/bin/Xorg:                   setuid executable, regular file, no read permission
/usr/bin/debconf:                a /usr/bin/perl -w script text executable
/usr/bin/locate:                 symbolic link to '/etc/alternatives/locate'
/usr/share/man/man7/term.7.gz:   gzip compressed data, from Unix, max compression
```

find

find

Finds files based on criteria

find [directory-list] [option] [expression]

The find utility selects files that are located in specified directory hierarchies and that meet specified criteria.

Arguments

The ***directory-list*** specifies the directory hierarchies that find is to search. When you do not specify a ***directory-list,*** find searches the working directory hierarchy.

The ***option*** controls whether find dereferences symbolic links as it descends directory hierarchies. By default find does not dereference symbolic links (it works with the symbolic link, not the file the link points to). Under macOS, you can use the **–x** option to prevent find from searching directories in filesystems other than those specified in ***directory-list.*** Under Linux, the **–xdev** criterion performs the same function.

The ***expression*** contains criteria, as described in the "Criteria" section. The find utility tests each of the files in each of the directories in the ***directory-list*** to see whether it meets the criteria described by the ***expression.*** When you do not specify an ***expression,*** the ***expression*** defaults to **–print**.

A SPACE separating two criteria is a Boolean AND operator: The file must meet *both* criteria to be selected. A **–or** or **–o** separating the criteria is a Boolean OR operator: The file must meet one or the other (or both) of the criteria to be selected.

You can negate any criterion by preceding it with an exclamation point. The find utility evaluates criteria from left to right unless you group them using parentheses.

Within the ***expression*** you must quote special characters so the shell does not interpret them but rather passes them to find. Special characters that are frequently used with find include parentheses, brackets, question marks, and asterisks.

Each element within the ***expression*** is a separate argument. You must separate arguments with SPACEs. A SPACE must appear on both sides of each parenthesis, exclamation point, criterion, or other element.

Options

–H (**partial dereference**) For each file that is a symbolic link, works with the file the link points to, not the symbolic link itself. This option affects files specified on the command line; it does not affect files found while descending a directory hierarchy. This option treats files that are not symbolic links normally. See page 118 for information on dereferencing symbolic links.

–L (**dereference**) For each file that is a symbolic link, works with the file the link points to, not the symbolic link itself. This option affects all files and treats files that are not symbolic links normally. See page 118 for information on dereferencing symbolic links.

–P (**no dereference**) For each file that is a symbolic link, works with the symbolic link, not the file the link points to. This option affects all files and treats files that are not symbolic links normally. This behavior is the default. See page 118 for information on dereferencing symbolic links.

–x Causes find not to search directories in filesystems other than the one(s) specified by ***directory-list.*** macOS

––xdev Causes find not to search directories in filesystems other than the one(s) specified by ***directory-list.*** LINUX

Criteria

You can use the following criteria within the ***expression.*** As used in this list, **±*n*** is a decimal integer that can be expressed as **+*n*** (more than ***n***), **–*n*** (fewer than ***n***), or ***n*** (exactly ***n***).

–anewer ***filename***

(**accessed newer**) The file being evaluated meets this criterion if it was accessed more recently than ***filename.***

–atime ±***n***

(**access time**) The file being evaluated meets this criterion if it was last accessed **±*n*** days ago. When you use this option, find changes the access times of directories it searches.

–depth

The file being evaluated always meets this action criterion. It causes find to take action on entries in a directory before it acts on the directory itself. When you use find to send files to the cpio utility, the **–depth** criterion enables cpio to preserve the modification times of directories when you restore files (assuming you use the **––preserve–modification–time** option to cpio). See the "Discussion" and "Examples" sections under cpio on pages 779 and 780.

–exec ***command*** \;

The file being evaluated meets this action criterion if the ***command*** returns a 0 (zero [*true*]) exit status. You must terminate the ***command*** with a quoted semicolon. The find utility replaces a pair of braces ({}) within the ***command*** with the name of the file being evaluated. You can use the **–exec** action criterion at the end of a group of other criteria to execute the ***command*** if the preceding criteria are met. Refer to the following "Discussion" section for more information. See the section on xargs on page 1032 for a more efficient way of doing what this option does.

–group ***name***

The file being evaluated meets this criterion if it is associated with the group named ***name.*** You can use a numeric group ID in place of ***name.***

–inum ***n***

The file being evaluated meets this criterion if its inode number is ***n.***

–links ±***n***

The file being evaluated meets this criterion if it has **±*n*** links.

–mtime ±***n***

(**modify time**) The file being evaluated meets this criterion if it was last modified **±*n*** days ago.

–name *filename*
The file being evaluated meets this criterion if the pattern *filename* matches its name. The *filename* can include wildcard characters (*, ?, and []) but these characters must be quoted.

–newer *filename*
The file being evaluated meets this criterion if it was modified more recently than *filename.*

–nogroup
The file being evaluated meets this criterion if it does not belong to a group known on the local system.

–nouser
The file being evaluated meets this criterion if it does not belong to a user known on the local system.

–ok *command* \;
This action criterion is the same as **–exec** except that it displays each *command* to be executed enclosed in angle brackets as a prompt and executes the *command* only if it receives a response that starts with a **y** or **Y** from standard input.

–perm [±]*mode*
The file being evaluated meets this criterion if it has the access permissions given by *mode.* If *mode* is preceded by a minus sign (–), the file access permissions must include all the bits in *mode.* For example, if *mode* is 644, then a file with 755 permissions will meet this criterion. If *mode* is preceded by a plus sign (+), the file access permissions must include at least one of the bits in *mode.* If no plus or minus sign precedes *mode,* the mode of the file must exactly match *mode.* You may use either a symbolic or octal representation for *mode* (see chmod on page 759).

–print
The file being evaluated always meets this action criterion. When evaluation of the *expression* reaches this criterion, find displays the pathname of the file it is evaluating. If **–print** is the only criterion in the *expression,* find displays the names of all files in the *directory-list.* If this criterion appears with other criteria, find displays the name only if the preceding criteria are met. If no action criteria appear in the *expression,* **–print** is assumed. (Refer to the following "Discussion" and "Notes" sections.)

–size ±*n*[c|k|M|G]
The file being evaluated meets this criterion if it is the size specified by **±*n*,** measured in 512-byte blocks. Follow *n* with the letter **c** to measure files in characters, **k** to measure files in kilobytes, **M** to measure files in megabytes, or **G** to measure files in gigabytes.

–type *filetype*
The file being evaluated meets this criterion if its file type is specified by *filetype.* Select a *filetype* from the following list:

b Block special file
c Character special file
d Directory file
f Ordinary file
l Symbolic link
p FIFO (named pipe)
s Socket

–user ***name***
The file being evaluated meets this criterion if it belongs to the user with the username ***name***. You can use a numeric user ID in place of ***name***.

–xdev
The file being evaluated always meets this action criterion. It prevents find from searching directories in filesystems other than the one specified by ***directory-list***. Also **–mount**. LINUX

–x The file being evaluated always meets this action criterion. It prevents find from searching directories in filesystems other than the one specified by ***directory-list***. Also **–mount**. macOS

Discussion

Assume **x** and **y** are criteria. The following command line never tests whether the file meets criterion **y** if it does not meet criterion **x**. Because the criteria are separated by a SPACE (the Boolean AND operator), once find determines that criterion **x** is not met, the file cannot meet the criteria, so find does not continue testing. You can read the expression as "(test to see whether) the file meets criterion **x** *and* [SPACE means *and*] criterion **y**."

```
$ find dir x y
```

The next command line tests the file against criterion **y** if criterion **x** is not met. The file can still meet the criteria, so find continues the evaluation. You can read the expression as "(test to see whether) the file meets criterion **x** *or* criterion **y**." If the file meets criterion **x**, find does not evaluate criterion **y** as there is no need to do so.

```
$ find dir x -or y
```

Action criteria

Certain "criteria" do not select files but rather cause find to take action. The action is triggered when find evaluates one of these *action criteria*. Therefore, the position of an action criterion on the command line—not the result of its evaluation—determines whether find takes the action.

The **–print** action criterion causes find to display the pathname of the file it is testing. The following command line displays the names of *all* files in the **dir** directory (and all its subdirectories), regardless of how many links they have:

```
$ find dir -print -links +1
```

The following command line displays the names of only those files in the **dir** directory that have more than one link:

```
$ find dir -links +1 -print
```

This use of **–print** after the testing criteria is the default action criterion. The following command line generates the same output as the preceding one:

```
$ find dir -links +1
```

Notes

You can use the **–a** (or **–and**) operator between criteria to improve clarity. This operator is a Boolean AND operator, just as the SPACE is.

You might want to consider using pax (page 932) in place of cpio. macOS users might want to use ditto (page 803).

Examples

The simplest find command has no arguments and lists the files in the working directory and all subdirectories:

```
$ find
...
```

The following command finds and displays the pathnames of files in the working directory and subdirectories that have filenames beginning with **a**. The command uses a period to designate the working directory. To prevent the shell from interpreting the **a*** as an ambiguous file reference, it is enclosed within single quotation marks.

```
$ find . -name 'a*' -print
```

If you omit the ***directory-list*** argument, find searches the working directory. The next command performs the same function as the preceding one without explicitly specifying the working directory or the **–print** criterion:

```
$ find -name 'a*'
```

The next command sends a list of selected filenames to the cpio utility, which writes them to the device mounted on **/dev/sde1**. The first part of the command line ends with a pipe symbol, so the shell expects another command to follow and displays a secondary prompt (**>**) before accepting the rest of the command line. You can read this find command as "find, in the root directory and all subdirectories (**/**), ordinary files (**–type f**) that have been modified within the past day (**–mtime –1**), with the exception of files whose names are suffixed with **.o** (**! –name '*.o'**)." (An object file carries a **.o** suffix and usually does not need to be preserved because it can be re-created from the corresponding source file.)

```
$ find / -type f -mtime -1 ! -name '*.o' -print |
> cpio -oB > /dev/sde1
```

The following command finds, displays the filenames of, and deletes the files named **core** or **junk** in the working directory and its subdirectories:

```
$ find . \( -name core -o -name junk \) -print -exec rm {} \;
...
```

The parentheses and the semicolon following **–exec** are quoted so the shell does not treat them as special characters. SPACEs separate the quoted parentheses from other elements on the command line. Read this find command as "find, in the working directory and subdirectories (**.**), files named **core** (**–name core**) *or* (**–o**) **junk** (**–name**

junk) [if a file meets these criteria, continue] *and* (SPACE) then print the name of the file (**–print**) *and* (SPACE) then delete the file (**–exec rm {}**)."

The following shell script uses find in conjunction with grep to identify files that contain a particular string. This script enables you to look for a file when you remember its contents but cannot remember its filename. The **finder** script locates files in the working directory and subdirectories that contain the string specified on the command line. The **–type f** criterion causes find to pass to grep only the names of ordinary files, not directory files.

```
$ cat finder
find . -type f -exec grep -l "$1" {} \;

$ finder "Executive Meeting"
 ./january/memo.0102
 ./april/memo.0415
```

When called with the string **Executive Meeting, finder** locates two files containing that string: **./january/memo.0102** and **./april/memo.0415**. The period (.) in the pathnames represents the working directory; **january** and **april** are subdirectories of the working directory. The **grep** utility with the **––recursive** option performs the same function as the **finder** script.

The next command looks in two user directories for files that are larger than 100 blocks (**–size +100**) and have been accessed only more than five days ago—that is, files that have not been accessed within the past five days (**–atime +5**). This find command then asks whether you want to delete the file (**–ok rm {}**). You must respond to each query with **y** (for *yes*) or **n** (for *no*). The rm command works only if you have write and execute access permissions to the directory holding the file.

```
$ find /home/max /home/hls -size +100 -atime +5 -ok rm {} \;
< rm ... /home/max/notes >? y
< rm ... /home/max/letter >? n
...
```

In the next example, **/home/sam/track/memos** is a symbolic link to the directory named **/home/sam/memos.** When you use the **–L** option, find dereferences (follows) the symbolic link and searches that directory.

```
$ ls -l /home/sam/track
lrwxrwxrwx. 1 sam pubs    15 04-12 10:35 memos -> /home/sam/memos
-rw-r--r--. 1 sam pubs 12753 04-12 10:34 report

$ find /home/sam/track
/home/sam/track
/home/sam/track/memos
/home/sam/track/report

$ find -L /home/sam/track
/home/sam/track
/home/sam/track/memos
/home/sam/track/memos/memo.710
/home/sam/track/memos/memo.817
/home/sam/track/report
```

finger

Displays information about users

*finger [**options**] [**user-list**]*

The finger utility displays the usernames of users, together with their full names, terminal device numbers, times they logged in, and other information. The ***options*** control how much information finger displays, and the ***user-list*** specifies which users finger displays information about. The finger utility can retrieve information from both local and remote systems.

Arguments

Without any arguments, finger provides a short (**–s**) report on users who are logged in on the local system. When you specify a ***user-list***, finger provides a long (**–l**) report on each user in the ***user-list***. Names in the ***user-list*** are not case sensitive.

If the name includes an at sign (@), the finger utility interprets the name following the @ as the name of a remote host to contact over the network. If a username appears in front of the @, finger provides information about that user on the remote system.

Options

–l (**long**) Displays detailed information (the default display when you specify ***user-list***).

–m (**match**) If a ***user-list*** is specified, displays entries only for those users whose username matches one of the names in ***user-list***. Without this option the ***user-list*** names match usernames and full names.

–p (**no plan, project, or pgpkey**) Does not display the contents of **.plan**, **.project**, and **.pgpkey** files for users. Because these files might contain backslash escape sequences that can change the behavior of the screen, you might not wish to view them. Normally, the long listing displays the contents of these files if they exist in the user's home directory.

–s (**short**) Provides a short report for each user (the default display when you do not specify ***user-list***).

Discussion

The long report provided by the finger utility includes the user's username, full name, home directory location, and login shell, plus information about when the user last logged in and how long it has been since the user last typed on the keyboard and read her email. After extracting this information from system files, finger displays the contents of the **~/.plan**, **~/.project**, and **~/.pgpkey** files in the user's home directory. It is up to each user to create and maintain these files, which usually provide more information about the user (such as telephone number, postal mail address, schedule, interests, and PGP key).

The short report generated by finger is similar to that provided by the w utility; it includes the user's username, his full name, the device number of the user's terminal, the amount of time that has elapsed since the user last typed on the terminal keyboard, the time the user logged in, and the location of the user's terminal. If the user logged in over the network, finger displays the name of the remote system.

Notes

Not all Linux distributions install finger by default.

When you specify a network address, the finger utility queries a standard network service that runs on the remote system. Although this service is supplied with most Linux systems, some administrators choose not to run it (to minimize the load on their systems, eliminate possible security risks, or simply maintain privacy). If you try to use finger to get information on someone at such a site, the result might be an error message or nothing at all. The remote system determines how much information to share with the local system and in which format. As a result the report displayed for any given system might differ from the examples shown in this section. See also "finger: Lists Users on the System" on page 72.

A file named **~/.nofinger** causes finger to deny the existence of the person in whose home directory it appears. For this subterfuge to work, the finger query must originate from a system other than the local host and the **fingerd** daemon must be able to see the **.nofinger** file (generally, the home directory must have its execute bit for other users set).

Examples

The first example displays information on the users logged in on the local system:

```
$ finger
Login     Name               Tty     Idle  Login  Time  Office  Office Phone
max       Max Wild           tty1    13:29 Jun 25 21:03
hls       Helen Simpson      *pts/1  13:29 Jun 25 21:02 (:0)
sam       Sam the Great      pts/2         Jun 26 07:47 (plum.example.com)
```

The asterisk (*) in front of the name of Helen's terminal (TTY) line indicates she has blocked others from sending messages directly to her terminal (see mesg on page 76). A long report displays the string **messages off** for users who have disabled messages.

The next two examples cause finger to contact the remote system named **guava** over the network for information:

```
$ finger @guava
[guava]
Login     Name               Tty     Idle  Login Time   Office  Office Phone
max       Max Wild           tty1    23:15 Jun 25 11:22
roy       Roy Wong           pts/2         Jun 25 11:22

$ finger max@guava
[guava]
Login: max                               Name: Max Wild
Directory: /home/max                     Shell: /bin/zsh
On since Sat Jun 23 11:22 (PDT) on tty1,  idle 23:22
Last login Sun Jun 24 06:20 (PDT) on ttyp2 from speedy
Mail last read Thu Jun 21 08:10 2018 (PDT)
```

```
Plan:
For appointments contact Sam the Great, x1963.
```

fmt

Formats text very simply

fmt [option] [file-list]

The fmt utility performs simple text formatting by attempting to make all nonblank lines nearly the same length.

Arguments

The fmt utility reads the files in ***file-list*** and sends a formatted version of their contents to standard output. If you do not specify a filename or if you specify a hyphen (–) in place of a filename, fmt reads from standard input.

Options

Options preceded by a double hyphen (––) work under Linux only. Except as noted, options named with a single letter and preceded by a single hyphen work under Linux and macOS.

––split-only **–s** Splits long lines but does not fill short lines. LINUX

–s Replaces whitespace (multiple adjacent SPACE and/or TAB characters) with a single SPACE. macOS

––tagged-paragraph
–t Indents all but the first line of each paragraph. LINUX

–t *n*
Specifies ***n*** as the number of SPACEs per TAB stop. The default is eight. macOS

––uniform-spacing
–u Changes the formatted output so that one SPACE appears between words and two SPACEs appear between sentences. LINUX

––width=*n* **–w *n***
Changes the output line length to ***n*** characters. Without this option, fmt keeps output lines close to 75 characters wide. You can also specify this option as **–*n***.

Notes

The fmt utility works by moving NEWLINE characters. The indention of lines, as well as the spacing between words, is left intact.

You can use fmt to format text while you are using an editor, such as vim. For example, you can format a paragraph with the vim editor in command mode by positioning the cursor at the top of the paragraph and then entering **!}fmt –60**. This command replaces the paragraph with the output generated by feeding it through fmt, specifying a width of 60 characters. Type **u** immediately if you want to undo the formatting.

Examples

The following example shows how fmt attempts to make all lines the same length. The **–w** 50 option gives a target line length of 50 characters.

```
$ cat memo
One factor that is important to remember while administering the dietary
intake of Charcharodon carcharias is that there is, at least from
the point of view of the subject,
very little
differentiating the prepared morsels being proffered from your digits.

In other words, don't feed the sharks!

$ fmt -w 50 memo
One factor that is important to remember while
administering the dietary intake of Charcharodon
carcharias is that there is, at least from the
point of view of the subject, very little
differentiating the prepared morsels being
proffered from your digits.

In other words, don't feed the sharks!
```

The next example demonstrates the **––split-only** option. Long lines are broken so that none is longer than 50 characters; this option prevents fmt from filling short lines.

```
$ fmt -w 50 --split-only memo
One factor that is important to remember while
administering the dietary
intake of Charcharodon carcharias is that there
is, at least from
the point of view of the subject,
very little
differentiating the prepared morsels being
proffered from your digits.

In other words, don't feed the sharks!
```

fsck

Checks and repairs a filesystem

fsck [options] [filesystem-list]

The fsck utility verifies the integrity of a filesystem and reports on and optionally repairs problems it finds. It is a front end for filesystem checkers, each of which is specific to a filesystem type. Although fsck is present on a Macintosh, the diskutil front end is typically used to call it; see "Notes." LINUX

Arguments

Without the –A option and with no ***filesystem-list***, fsck checks the filesystems listed in the **/etc/fstab** file one at a time (serially). With the **–A** option and with no ***filesystem-list***, fsck checks the filesystems listed in the **/etc/fstab** file in parallel if possible. See the **–s** option for a discussion of checking filesystems in parallel.

The ***filesystem-list*** specifies the filesystems to be checked. It can either specify the name of the device that holds the filesystem (e.g., **/dev/sda2**) or, if the filesystem appears in **/etc/fstab**, specify the mount point (e.g., **/usr**) for the filesystem. The ***filesystem-list*** can also specify the label for the filesystem from **/etc/fstab** (e.g., **LABEL=home**) or the UUID specifier (e.g., **UUID=397df592-6e...**).

Options

When you run fsck, you can specify both global options and options specific to the filesystem type that fsck is checking (e.g., **ext2/ext3/ext4, msdos, vfat**). Global options must precede type-specific options.

Global Options

–A (**all**) Processes all filesystems listed in the **/etc/fstab** file, in parallel if possible. See the **–s** option for a discussion of checking filesystems in parallel. Do not specify a ***filesystem-list*** when you use this option; you can specify filesystem types to be checked with the **–t** option. Use this option with either the **–a**, **–p**, or **–n** option so fsck does not attempt to process filesystems in parallel *interactively* (in which case you would have no way of responding to its multiple prompts).

–N (**no**) Assumes a *no* response to any questions that arise while processing a filesystem. This option generates the messages you would normally see but causes fsck to take no action.

–R (**root-skip**) With the **–A** option, does not check the root filesystem. This option is useful when the system boots, because the root filesystem might be mounted with read-write access.

–s (**serial**) Causes fsck to process filesystems one at a time. Without this option, fsck processes multiple filesystems that reside on separate physical disk drives in parallel. Parallel processing enables fsck to process multiple filesystems more quickly. This option is required if you want to process filesystems interactively. See one of the **–a**, **–p**, or **–N** (or **–n**, on some filesystems) options to turn off interactive processing.

–T (**title**) Causes fsck not to display its title.

–t *fstype*
(**filesystem type**) A comma-separated list that specifies the filesystem type(s) to process. With the **–A** option, fsck processes all the filesystems in **/etc/fstab** that are of type *fstype*. Common filesystem types are **ext2/ext3/ext4**, **msdos**, and **vfat**. You do not typically check remote NFS filesystems.

–V (**verbose**) Displays more output, including filesystem type-specific commands.

Filesystem Type-Specific Options

The following command lists the filesystem checking utilities available on the local system. Files with the same inode numbers are linked (page 115).

```
$ ls -i /sbin/*fsck*
 9961 /sbin/btrfsck      21955 /sbin/fsck.ext2      8646 /sbin/fsck.ntfs
 3452 /sbin/dosfsck      21955 /sbin/fsck.ext3      3502 /sbin/fsck.vfat
21955 /sbin/e2fsck       21955 /sbin/fsck.ext4      3804 /sbin/fsck.xfs
 8471 /sbin/fsck         21955 /sbin/fsck.ext4dev
 6489 /sbin/fsck.cramfs   8173 /sbin/fsck.msdos
```

Review the man page or give the pathname of the filesystem checking utility to determine which options the utility accepts:

```
$ /sbin/fsck.ext4
Usage: /sbin/fsck.ext4 [-panyrcdfvstDFSV] [-b superblock] [-B blocksize]
                [-I inode_buffer_blocks] [-P process_inode_size]
                [-l|-L bad_blocks_file] [-C fd] [-j ext-journal]
                [-E extended-options] device

Emergency help:
 -p                   Automatic repair (no questions)
 -n                   Make no changes to the filesystem
 -y                   Assume "yes" to all questions
 -c                   Check for bad blocks and add them to the badblock list
 -f                   Force checking even if filesystem is marked clean
...
```

The following options apply to many filesystem types, including **ext2/ext3/ext4**:

–a (**automatic**) Same as the **–p** option; kept for backward compatibility.

–f (**force**) Forces fsck to check filesystems even if they are clean. A *clean* filesystem is one that was just successfully checked with fsck or was successfully unmounted and has not been mounted since then. Clean filesystems are skipped by fsck, which greatly speeds up system booting under normal conditions. For information on setting up periodic, automatic filesystem checking on **ext2/ext3/ext4** filesystems, see tune2fs on page 1018.

–n (**no**) Same as the **–N** global option. Does not work on all filesystems.

–p (**preen**) Attempts to repair all minor inconsistencies it finds when processing a filesystem. If any problems are not repaired, fsck terminates with a nonzero exit status. This option runs fsck in batch mode; as a consequence, it does not ask whether to correct each problem it finds. The **–p** option is commonly used with the **–A** option when checking filesystems while booting Linux.

–r (**interactive**) Asks whether to correct or ignore each problem that is found. For many filesystem types, this behavior is the default. This option is not available on all filesystems.

–y (**yes**) Assumes a *yes* response to any questions that fsck asks while processing a filesystem. Use this option with caution, as it gives fsck free rein to do what it thinks is best to clean a filesystem.

Notes

Apple suggests using diskutil (page 800) in place of fsck unless you are working in an environment where diskutil is not available (e.g., single-user mode). For more information see support.apple.com/en-us/HT203176.

You can run fsck from a live or rescue CD/DVD.

When a filesystem is consistent, fsck displays a report such as the following:

```
# fsck -f /dev/sdb1
fsck from util-linux 2.29
e2fsck 1.43.4 (31-Jan-2017)
Pass 1: Checking inodes, blocks, and sizes
Pass 2: Checking directory structure
Pass 3: Checking directory connectivity
Pass 4: Checking reference counts
Pass 5: Checking group summary information
/dev/sdb1: 710/4153408 files (10.1% non-contiguous), 455813/8303589 blocks
```

Interactive mode — You can run fsck either interactively or in batch mode. For many filesystems, unless you use one of the **–a**, **–p**, **–y**, or **–n** options, fsck runs in interactive mode. In interactive mode, if fsck finds a problem with a filesystem, it reports the problem and allows you to choose whether to repair or ignore it. If you repair a problem you might lose some data; however, that is often the most reasonable alternative.

Although it is technically feasible to repair files that are damaged and that fsck says you should remove, this action is rarely practical. The best insurance against significant loss of data is to make frequent backups.

Order of checking — The fsck utility looks at the sixth column in the **/etc/fstab** file to determine if, and in which order, it should check filesystems. A **0** (zero) in this position indicates the filesystem should not be checked. A **1** (one) indicates it should be checked first; this status is usually reserved for the root filesystem. A **2** (two) indicates the filesystem should be checked after those marked with a **1**.

fsck is a front end — Similar to mkfs (page 911), fsck is a front end that calls other utilities to handle various types of filesystems. For example, fsck calls e2fsck to check the widely used **ext2**/**ext3**/**ext4** filesystems. Refer to the e2fsck man page for more information. Other utilities that fsck calls are typically named **fsck.*type***, where ***type*** is the filesystem type. By splitting fsck in this manner, filesystem developers can provide programs to check their filesystems without affecting the development of other filesystems or changing how system administrators use fsck.

Boot time Run fsck on filesystems that are unmounted or are mounted readonly. When Linux is booting, the root filesystem is first mounted readonly to allow it to be processed by fsck. If fsck finds no problems with the root filesystem, it is then remounted (using the **remount** option to the mount utility) read-write and fsck is typically run with the **–A**, **–R**, and **–p** options.

lost+found When it encounters a file that has lost its link to its filename, fsck asks whether to reconnect it. If you choose to reconnect it, fsck puts the file in a directory named **lost+found** in the root directory of the filesystem in which it found the file. The reconnected file is given its inode number as a name. For fsck to restore files in this way, a **lost+found** directory must be present in the root directory of each filesystem. For example, if a system uses the **/**, **/usr**, and **/home** filesystems, you should have these three **lost+found** directories: **/lost+found**, **/usr/lost+found**, and **/home/lost+found.** Each **lost+found** directory must have unused entries in which fsck can store the inode numbers for files that have lost their links. When you create an **ext2/ext3/ext4** filesystem, mkfs (page 911) creates a **lost+found** directory with the required unused entries. Alternatively, you can use the mklost+found utility to create this directory in **ext2/ext3/ext4** filesystems if needed. On other types of filesystems, you can create the unused entries by adding many files to the directory and then removing them: Use touch (page 1012) to create 500 entries in the **lost+found** directory and then use rm to delete them.

Messages

Table VI-17 lists fsck's common messages. In general fsck suggests the most logical way of dealing with a problem in the file structure. Unless you have information that suggests another response, respond to the prompts with **yes**. Use the system backup tapes or disks to restore data that is lost as a result of this process.

Table VI-17 Common fsck messages

Phase (message)	What fsck checks
Phase 1 - Checking inodes, blocks, and sizes	Checks inode information.
Phase 2 - Checking directory structure	Looks for directories that point to bad inodes that fsck found in Phase 1.
Phase 3 - Checking directory connectivity	Looks for unreferenced directories and a nonexistent or full **lost+found** directory.
Phase 4 - Checking reference counts	Checks for unreferenced files, a nonexistent or full **lost+found** directory, bad link counts, bad blocks, duplicated blocks, and incorrect inode counts.
Phase 5 - Checking group summary information	Checks whether the free list and other filesystem structures are OK. If any problems are found with the free list, Phase 6 is run.
Phase 6 - Salvage free list	If Phase 5 found any problems with the free list, Phase 6 fixes them.

Cleanup

Once it has repaired the filesystem, fsck informs you about the status of the filesystem. The fsck utility displays the following message after it repairs a filesystem:

```
*****File System Was Modified*****
```

On ext2/ext3/ext4 filesystems, fsck displays the following message when it has finished checking a filesystem:

*filesys: **used/maximum** files (**percent** non-contiguous), **used/maximum** blocks*

This message tells you how many files and disk blocks are in use as well as how many files and disk blocks the filesystem can hold. The ***percent*** *non-contiguous* tells you how fragmented the disk is.

ftp

Transfers files over a network

ftp [options] [remote-system]

The ftp utility is a user interface to the standard File Transfer Protocol (FTP), which transfers files between systems that can communicate over a network. To establish an FTP connection, you must have access to an account (personal, guest, or anonymous) on the remote system.

Use FTP only to download public information

security FTP is not a secure protocol. The ftp utility sends your password over the network as cleartext, which is not a secure practice. You can use sftp (page 715) as a secure replacement for ftp if the server is running OpenSSH. You can also use scp (page 713) for many FTP functions other than allowing anonymous users to download information. Because scp uses an encrypted connection, user passwords and data cannot be sniffed.

Arguments

The *remote-system* is the name or IP address of the server, running an FTP daemon (e.g., **ftpd, vsftpd,** or **sshd**), you want to exchange files with.

Options

–i (**interactive**) Turns off prompts during file transfers with **mget** and **mput**. See also **prompt** (next page).

–n (**no automatic login**) Disables automatic logins.

–p (**passive mode**) Starts ftp in passive mode (page 840).

–v (**verbose**) Tells you more about how ftp is working. Displays responses from the *remote-system* and reports transfer times and speeds.

Commands

The ftp utility is interactive. After you start it, ftp prompts you to enter commands to set parameters and transfer files. Following are some of the commands you can use in response to the **ftp>** prompt.

!*[command]* Escapes to (spawns) a shell on the local system; use CONTROL-D or **exit** to return to ftp when you are finished using the local shell. Follow the exclamation point with a command to execute that command only; ftp returns to the **ftp>** prompt when the command completes executing. Because the shell that ftp spawns with this command is a child of the shell that is running ftp, no changes you make in this shell are preserved when you return to ftp. Specifically, when you want to copy files to a local directory other than the directory that you started ftp from, you need to use the ftp **lcd** command to change the local working directory: Issuing a **cd** command in the spawned shell will not make the change you desire. See page 843 for an example.

ascii Sets the file transfer type to ASCII. This command allows you to transfer text files from systems that end lines with a RETURN/LINEFEED combination and automatically strip off the RETURN. Such a transfer is useful when the remote computer is a DOS or MS Windows machine. The **cr** command must be ON for **ascii** to work.

binary Sets the file transfer type to binary. This command allows you to transfer correctly files that contain non-ASCII (unprintable) characters. It also works for ASCII files that do not require changes to the ends of lines.

bye Closes the connection to a remote system and terminates ftp. Same as **quit**.

cd ***remote-directory***
Changes to the working directory named ***remote-directory*** on the remote system.

close Closes the connection with the remote system without exiting from ftp.

cr (**carriage return**) Toggles RETURN stripping when you retrieve files in ASCII mode. See **ascii**.

dir *[directory [file]]*
Displays a listing of the directory named ***directory*** from the remote system. When you do not specify ***directory***, the working directory is displayed. When you specify a ***file***, the listing is saved on the local system in a file named ***file***.

get ***remote-file*** *[local-file]*
Copies ***remote-file*** to the local system under the name ***local-file***. Without ***local-file***, ftp uses ***remote-file*** as the filename on the local system. The ***remote-file*** and ***local-file*** can be pathnames.

glob Toggles filename expansion for the **mget** and **mput** commands and displays the current state (**Globbing on** or **Globbing off**).

help Displays a list of commands recognized by the ftp utility on the local system.

lcd *[local_directory]*
(**local change directory**) Changes your working directory on the local system to ***local_directory***. Without an argument, this command changes the working directory on the local system to your home directory (just as cd does without an argument).

ls *[directory [file]]*
Similar to **dir** but produces a more concise listing on some remote systems.

mget ***remote-file-list***
(**multiple get**) Unlike the **get** command, allows you to retrieve multiple files from the remote system. You can name the remote files literally or use wildcards (see **glob**). See also **prompt**.

mput ***local-file-list***
(**multiple put**) The **mput** command allows you to copy multiple files from the local system to the remote system. You can name the local files literally or use wildcards (see **glob**). See also **prompt**.

open Interactively specifies the name of the remote system. This command is useful if you did not specify a remote system on the command line or if the attempt to connect to the remote system failed.

passive Toggles between the active (PORT—the default) and passive (PASV) transfer modes and displays the transfer mode. See "Passive versus active connections" under the "Notes" section.

prompt When using **mget** or **mput** to receive or send multiple files, ftp asks for verification (by default) before transferring each file. This command toggles that behavior and displays the current state (**Interactive mode off** or **Interactive mode on**).

put *local-file [remote-file]*
Copies ***local-file*** to the remote system under the name ***remote-file.*** Without ***remote-file,*** ftp uses ***local-file*** as the filename on the remote system. The ***remote-file*** and ***local-file*** can be pathnames.

pwd Causes ftp to display the pathname of the remote working directory. Use **!pwd** to display the name of the local working directory.

quit Closes the connection to a remote system and terminates ftp. Same as **bye**.

reget *remote-file* Attempts to resume an aborted transfer. This command is similar to **get**, but instead of overwriting an existing local file, ftp appends new data to it. Not all servers support **reget**.

user *[username]* If the ftp utility did not log you in automatically, you can specify your account name as ***username***. If you omit ***username,*** ftp prompts for a username.

Notes

A Linux or macOS system running ftp can exchange files with any of the many operating systems that support the FTP protocol. Many sites offer archives of free information on an FTP server, although many of these FTP sites are merely alternatives to an easier-to-access Web site (for example, ftp://ftp.ibiblio.org/pub/Linux and http://www.ibiblio.org/software/linux). Most browsers can connect to and download files from FTP servers.

The ftp utility makes no assumptions about filesystem naming or structure because you can use ftp to exchange files with non-UNIX/Linux systems (whose filename conventions might be different).

See page 981 for information on using curlftpfs to mount an FTP directory on the local system without needing **root** privileges.

Anonymous FTP Many systems—most notably those from which you can download free software—allow you to log in as **anonymous**. Most systems that support anonymous logins accept the name **ftp** as an easier-to-spell and quicker-to-enter synonym for **anonymous**. An anonymous user is usually restricted to a portion of a filesystem set aside to hold files shared with remote users. When you log in as an anonymous user, the server prompts you to enter a password. Although any password might be accepted, by convention you are expected to supply your email address. Many systems that permit anonymous access store interesting files in the **pub** directory.

Passive versus active connections A client can ask an FTP server to establish either a PASV (passive—the default) or PORT (active) connection for data transfer. Some servers are limited to one type of connection. The difference between passive and active FTP connections lies in whether the client or server initiates the data connection. In passive mode, the client initiates the data connection to the server (on port 20 by default); in active mode, the server initiates the data connection (there is no default port). Neither type of connection is inherently more secure. Passive connections are more common because a client behind a *NAT* (page 1111) firewall can connect to a passive server and because it is simpler to program a scalable passive server.

Automatic login You can store server-specific FTP username and password information so you do not have to enter it each time you visit an FTP site. Each line of the **~/.netrc** file identifies a server. When you connect to an FTP server, ftp reads **~/.netrc** to determine whether you have an automatic login set up for that server. The syntax of a line in **~/.netrc** is

machine ***server*** *login* ***username*** *password* ***passwd***

where ***server*** is the name of the server, ***username*** is your username, and ***passwd*** is your password on ***server***. Replace *machine* with **default** on the last line of the file to specify a username and password for systems not listed in **~/.netrc**. The **default** line is useful for logging in on anonymous servers. A sample **~/.netrc** file follows:

```
$ cat ~/.netrc
machine plum login max password mypassword
default login anonymous password max@example.com
```

To protect the account information in **.netrc**, make it readable by only the user in whose home directory it appears. Refer to the **netrc** man page for more information.

Examples

Following are two ftp sessions wherein Max transfers files from and to an FTP server named **plum**. When Max gives the command **ftp plum**, the local ftp client connects to the server, which asks for a username and a password. Because he is logged in on his local system as **max**, ftp suggests that he log in on **plum** as **max**. To log in as **max**, Max could just press RETURN. His username on **plum** is **watson**, however, so he types **watson** in response to the **Name (plum:max):** prompt. Max responds to the **Password:** prompt with his normal (remote) system password, and the FTP server greets him and informs him that it is **Using binary mode to transfer files.** With ftp in binary mode, Max can transfer ASCII and binary files.

Connect and log in

```
$ ftp plum
Connected to plum (172.16.192.151).
220 (vsFTPd 2.3.4)
Name (plum:max): watson
331 Please specify the password.
Password:
230 Login successful.
Remote system type is UNIX.
Using binary mode to transfer files.
ftp>
```

After logging in, Max uses the ftp **ls** command to display the contents of his remote working directory, which is his home directory on **plum**. Then he cds to the **memos** directory and displays the files there.

ls and **cd**

```
ftp> ls
227 Entering Passive Mode (172,16,192,151,222,168)
150 Here comes the directory listing.
drwxr-xr-x    2 500      500          4096 Oct 10 23:52 expenses
drwxr-xr-x    2 500      500          4096 Oct 10 23:59 memos
drwxrwxr-x   22 500      500          4096 Oct 10 23:32 tech
226 Directory send OK.

ftp> cd memos
250 Directory successfully changed.
```

```
ftp> ls
227 Entering Passive Mode (172,16,192,151,226,0)
150 Here comes the directory listing.
-rw-r--r--    1 500      500          4770 Oct 10 23:58 memo.0514
-rw-r--r--    1 500      500          7134 Oct 10 23:58 memo.0628
-rw-r--r--    1 500      500          9453 Oct 10 23:58 memo.0905
-rw-r--r--    1 500      500          3466 Oct 10 23:59 memo.0921
-rw-r--r--    1 500      500          1945 Oct 10 23:59 memo.1102
226 Directory send OK.
```

Next, Max uses the ftp **get** command to copy **memo.1102** from the server to the local system. His use of binary mode ensures that he will get a good copy of the file regardless of whether it is in binary or ASCII format. The server confirms the file was copied successfully and notes the size of the file and the time it took to copy. Max then copies the local file **memo.1114** to the remote system. The file is copied into his remote working directory, **memos**.

get and **put**

```
ftp> get memo.1102
local: memo.1102 remote: memo.1102
227 Entering Passive Mode (172,16,192,151,74,78)
150 Opening BINARY mode data connection for memo.1102 (1945 bytes).
226 Transfer complete.
1945 bytes received in 7.1e-05 secs (2.7e+04 Kbytes/sec)

ftp> put memo.1114
local: memo.1114 remote: memo.1114
227 Entering Passive Mode (172,16,192,151,214,181)
150 Ok to send data.
226 Transfer complete.
1945 bytes sent in 2.8e-05 secs (6.8e+04 Kbytes/sec)
```

After a while Max decides he wants to copy all the files in the **memos** directory on **plum** to a new directory on the local system. He gives an **ls** command to make sure he is going to copy the right files, but ftp has timed out. Instead of exiting from ftp and giving another ftp command from the shell, Max gives ftp an **open plum** command to reconnect to the server. After logging in, he uses the ftp **cd** command to change directories to **memos** on the server.

Timeout and **open**

```
ftp> ls
No control connection for command: Success
Passive mode refused.
ftp> open plum
Connected to plum (172.16.192.151).
220 (vsFTPd 2.3.4)
...
ftp> cd memos
250 Directory successfully changed.
```

At this point, Max realizes he has not created the new directory to hold the files he wants to download. Giving an ftp **mkdir** command would create a new directory on the server, but Max wants a new directory on the local system. He uses an exclamation point (**!**) followed by a **mkdir memos.hold** command to invoke a shell and run mkdir on the local system, thereby creating a directory named **memos.hold** in his working directory on the local system. (You can display the name of your working directory on the local system using **!pwd**.) Next, because he wants to copy files from the server to the **memos.hold** directory on the local system, Max has to change his working directory on the local system. Giving the command **!cd memos.hold** will not accomplish what Max wants to do because the exclamation point spawns a new shell on the local system and the **cd** command would be effective only in the new shell, which is not the shell that ftp is running under. For this situation, ftp provides the **lcd** (local cd) command, which changes the working directory for ftp and reports on the new local working directory.

lcd (local cd)

```
ftp> !mkdir memos.hold

ftp> lcd memos.hold
Local directory now /home/max/memos.hold
```

Max uses the ftp **mget** (multiple get) command followed by the asterisk (*) wildcard to copy all the files from the remote **memos** directory to the **memos.hold** directory on the local system. When ftp prompts him for the first file, he realizes that he forgot to turn off the prompts, so he responds with **n** and presses CONTROL-C to stop copying files in response to the second prompt. The server checks whether he wants to continue with his **mget** command.

Next, Max gives the ftp **prompt** command, which toggles the prompt action (turns it *off* if it is *on* and turns it *on* if it is *off*). Now when he gives an **mget *** command, ftp copies all the files without prompting him.

After getting the files he wants, Max gives a **quit** command to close the connection with the server, exit from ftp, and return to the local shell prompt.

mget and **prompt**

```
ftp> mget *
mget memo.0514? n
mget memo.0628? CONTROL-C
Continue with mget? n

ftp> prompt
Interactive mode off.
ftp> mget *
local: memo.0514 remote: memo.0514
227 Entering Passive Mode (172,16,192,151,153,231)
150 Opening BINARY mode data connection for memo.0514 (4770 bytes).
226 Transfer complete.
4770 bytes received in 8.8e-05 secs (5.3e+04 Kbytes/sec)
local: memo.0628 remote: memo.0628
227 Entering Passive Mode (172,16,192,151,20,35)
150 Opening BINARY mode data connection for memo.0628 (7134 bytes).
226 Transfer complete.
...
150 Opening BINARY mode data connection for memo.1114 (1945 bytes).
226 Transfer complete.
1945 bytes received in 3.9e-05 secs (4.9e+04 Kbytes/sec)
```

```
ftp> quit
221 Goodbye.
```

gawk

Searches for and processes patterns in a file

gawk [options] [program] [file-list]
gawk [options] –f program-file [file-list]

AWK is a pattern-scanning and processing language that searches one or more files for records (usually lines) that match specified patterns. It processes lines by performing actions, such as writing the record to standard output or incrementing a counter, each time it finds a match. As opposed to *procedural* languages, AWK is *data driven*: You describe the data you want to work with and tell AWK what to do with the data once it finds it.

See Chapter 14 for information on gawk

tip See Chapter 14 starting on page 635 for information on the awk, gawk, and mawk implementations of the AWK language.

gcc

Compiles C and C++ programs

gcc [options] file-list [–larg]
g++ [options] file-list [–larg]

The Linux and macOS operating systems use the GNU C compiler, gcc, to preprocess, compile, assemble, and link C language source files. The same compiler with a different front end, g++, processes C++ source code. The gcc and g++ compilers can also assemble and link assembly language source files, link object files only, or build object files for use in shared libraries.

These compilers take input from files you specify on the command line. Unless you use the **–o** option, they save the executable program in a file named **a.out**.

The gcc and g++ compilers are part of GCC, the *GNU Compiler Collection,* which includes front ends for C, C++, Objective C, Fortran, Go, and Ada as well as libraries for these languages. Visit gcc.gnu.org for more information.

gcc and g++

tip Although this section specifies the gcc compiler, most of the information applies to g++ as well.

Arguments

The *file-list* is a list of files gcc is to process.

Options

Without any options gcc accepts C language source files, assembly language files, object files, and other files described in Table VI-18 on page 848. The gcc utility preprocesses, compiles, assembles, and links these files as appropriate, producing an executable file named **a.out**. When you create object files without linking them to produce an executable file, gcc names each object file by adding the extension **.o** to the basename of the corresponding source file. When you create an executable file, gcc deletes the object files after linking.

Some of the most commonly used options are listed here. When certain filename extensions are associated with an option, you can assume gcc adds the extension to the basename of the source file.

–c (**compile**) Suppresses the linking step of compilation. Compiles and/or assembles source code files and leaves the object code in files with the extension **.o**.

–D*name*[=*value*]
Usually, **#define** preprocessor directives are given in header, or include, files. You can use this option to define symbolic names on the command line instead. For example, **–DLinux** is equivalent to placing the line **#define Linux** in an include file; **–DMACH=i586** is the same as **#define MACH i586**.

–E (**everything**) For source code files, suppresses all steps of compilation *except* preprocessing and writes the result to standard output. By convention the extension **.i** is used for preprocessed C source and **.ii** for preprocessed C++ source.

–fpic

Causes gcc to produce *position-independent* code, which is suitable for installing in a shared library.

–fwritable-strings

By default the GNU C compiler places string constants into *protected memory,* where they cannot be changed. Some (usually older) programs assume you can modify string constants. This option changes the behavior of gcc so that string constants can be modified.

–g (**gdb**) Embeds diagnostic information in the object files. This information is used by symbolic debuggers, such as gdb. Although this option is necessary only if you later use a debugger, it is a good practice to include it as a matter of course.

–I*directory*

Looks for include files in ***directory*** before looking in the standard locations. Give this option multiple times to look in more than one directory.

–l*arg*

(lowercase "l") Searches the directories **/lib** and **/usr/lib** for a library file named **lib*arg*.a**. If the file is found, gcc then searches this library for any required functions. Replace ***arg*** with the name of the library you want to search. For example, the **–lm** option normally links the standard math library **libm.a**. The position of this option is significant: It generally needs to appear at the end of the command line but can be repeated multiple times to search different libraries. Libraries are searched in the order in which they appear on the command line. The linker uses the library only to resolve undefined symbols from modules that *precede* the library option on the command line. You can add other library paths to search for **lib*arg*.a** using the **–L** option.

–L*directory*

Adds ***directory*** to the list of directories to search for libraries specified using the **–l** option. Directories that are added to the list with **–L** are searched before gcc looks in the standard locations for libraries.

–o *file*

(**output**) Names the executable program that results from linking ***file*** instead of **a.out**.

–O*n*

(**optimize**) Attempts to improve (optimize) the object code produced by the compiler. The value of ***n*** might be **0**, **1**, **2**, or **3** (or **06** if you are compiling code for the Linux kernel). The default value of ***n*** is **1**. Larger values of ***n*** result in better optimization but might increase both the size of the object file and the time it takes gcc to run. Specify **–O0** to turn off optimization. Many related options control precisely the types of optimizations attempted by gcc when you use **–O**. Refer to the gcc info page for details.

–pedantic
The C language accepted by the GNU C compiler includes features that are not part of the ANSI standard for the C language. Using this option forces gcc to reject these language extensions and accept only standard C programming language features.

–Q Displays the names of functions as gcc compiles them. This option also displays statistics about each pass.

–S (**suppress**) Suppresses the assembling and linking steps of compilation on source code files. The resulting assembly language files have **.s** filename extensions.

–traditional
Causes gcc to accept only C programming language features that existed in the traditional Kernighan and Ritchie C programming language. With this option, older programs written using the traditional C language (which existed before the ANSI standard C language was defined) can be compiled correctly.

–Wall
Causes gcc to warn you about questionable code in the source code files. Many related options control warning messages more precisely.

Notes

The preceding list of options represents only a small fraction of the full set of options available with the GNU C compiler. See the gcc info page for a complete list.

Although the **–o** option is generally used to specify a filename in which to save object code, this option also allows you to name files resulting from other compilation steps. In the following example, the **–o** option causes the assembly language produced by the gcc command to be stored in the file **acode** instead of **pgm.s**, the default:

```
$ gcc -S -o acode pgm.c
```

The lint utility found in many UNIX systems is not available on Linux or macOS. However, the **–Wall** option performs many of the same checks and can be used in place of lint.

Table VI-18 summarizes the conventions used by the C compiler for assigning filename extensions.

Table VI-18 Filename extensions

Extension	Type of file
.a	Library of object modules
.c	C language source file

Table VI-18 Filename extensions (continued)

Extension	Type of file
.C, **.cc**, *or* **.cxx**	C++ language source file
.i	Preprocessed C language source file
.ii	Preprocessed C++ language source file
.m	Objective C
.mm	Objective C++
.o	Object file
.s	Assembly language source file
.S	Assembly language source file that needs preprocessing

macOS/clang Apple has not shipped a new version of gcc in a long time. It uses the LLVM compiler suite (www.llvm.org)—in particular, the clang front end for C/C++ and Objective C (clang.llvm.org). The command-line arguments for clang are compatible with gcc. Both clang and gcc are part of the optional Xcode package.

Examples

The first example compiles, assembles, and links a single C program, **compute.c**. The executable output is saved in **a.out**. The gcc utility deletes the object file.

```
$ gcc compute.c
```

The next example compiles the same program using the C optimizer (**–O** option, level 2). It assembles and links the optimized code. The **–o** option causes gcc to store the executable output in **compute**.

```
$ gcc -O2 -o compute compute.c
```

Next, a C source file, an assembly language file, and an object file are compiled, assembled, and linked. The executable output is stored in **progo**.

```
$ gcc -o progo procom.c profast.s proout.o
```

In the next example, gcc searches the standard math library found at **/lib/libm.a** when it is linking the **himath** program and stores the executable output in **a.out**:

```
$ gcc himath.c -lm
```

In the following example, the C compiler compiles **topo.c** with options that check the code for questionable source code practices (**–Wall** option) and violations of the ANSI C standard (**–pedantic** option). The **–g** option embeds debugging support in the executable file, which is saved in **topo** with the **–o topo** option. Full optimization is enabled with the **–O3** option.

The warnings produced by the C compiler are sent to standard output. In this example the first and last warnings result from the **–pedantic** option; the other warnings result from the **–Wall** option.

```
$ gcc -Wall -g -O3 -pedantic -o topo topo.c
In file included from topo.c:2:
/usr/include/ctype.h:65: warning: comma at end of enumerator list
topo.c:13: warning: return-type defaults to 'int'
topo.c: In function 'main':
topo.c:14: warning: unused variable 'c'
topo.c: In function 'getline':
topo.c:44: warning: 'c' might be used uninitialized in this function
```

When compiling programs that rely on the X11 include files and libraries, you might need to use the **–I** and **–L** options to tell gcc where to locate those include files and libraries. The next example uses those options and instructs gcc to link the program with the basic X11 library:

```
$ gcc -I/usr/X11R6/include plot.c -L/usr/X11R6/lib -lX11
```

GetFileInfo macOS

Displays file attributes

GetFileInfo [option] file

The GetFileInfo utility displays file attributes (page 1072), including the file's type and creator code, creation and last modification times, and attribute flags such as the invisible and locked flags. The GetFileInfo utility is available under macOS only. macOS

Arguments

The *file* specifies a single file or a directory that GetFileInfo displays information about.

Options

The options for GetFileInfo correspond to the options for SetFile (page 965).

Without an option, GetFileInfo reports on the metadata of *file*, indicating the flags that are set, the file's type and creator codes, and its creation and modification dates. Missing data is omitted. When you specify an option, GetFileInfo displays the information specified by that option only. This utility accepts a single option; it silently ignores additional options.

–a*flag*
(**attribute**) Reports the status of the single attribute flag named *flag*. This option displays **1** if *flag* is set and 0 if *flag* is not set. The *flag* must follow the **–a** immediately, without any intervening SPACEs. See Table D-2 on page 1072 for a list of attribute flags.

–c (**creator**) Displays the creator code of *file*. If *file* is a directory and has no creator code, this option displays an error message.

–d (**date**) Displays the creation date of *file* as **mm/dd/yyyy hh:mm:ss**, using a 24-hour clock.

–m (**modification**) Displays the modification date of *file* as **mm/dd/yyyy hh:mm:ss**, using a 24-hour clock.

–P (**no dereference**) For each file that is a symbolic link, displays information about the symbolic link, not the file the link points to. This option affects all files and treats files that are not symbolic links normally. See page 118 for information on dereferencing symbolic links.

–t (**type**) Displays the type code of *file*. If *file* is a directory and has no type code, this option displays an error message.

Discussion

Without an option, GetFileInfo displays flags as the string **avbstclinmedz**, with uppercase letters denoting which flags are set. See page 1072 for a discussion of attribute flags.

Notes

You can use the SetFile utility (page 965) to set file attributes. You can set macOS permissions and ownership (page 100) using chmod (page 759) or chown (page 764), and you can display this information using ls (page 884) or stat (page 984).

Directories do not have type or creator codes, and they might not have all flags. The GetFileInfo utility cannot read special files such as device files.

Examples

The first example shows the output from GetFileInfo when you call it without an option:

```
$ GetFileInfo picture.jpg
file: "/private/tmp/picture.jpg"
type: "JPEG"
creator: "GKON"
attributes: avbstClinmedz
created: 07/18/2018 15:15:26
modified: 07/18/2018 15:15:26
```

The only uppercase letter on the **attributes** line is C, indicating that this flag is set. The **c** flag tells the Finder to look for a custom icon for this file. See Table D-2 on page 1072 for a list of flags.

The next example uses the **–a** flag to display the attribute flags for a file:

```
$ GetFileInfo -a /Applications/Games/Alchemy/Alchemy
avBstclInmedz
```

The output shows that the **b** and **i** flags are set.

The GetFileInfo utility can process only one file each time you call it. The following multiline bash command uses a **for** loop (page 443) to display the creator codes of multiple files. The echo command displays the name of the file being examined because GetFileInfo does not always display the name of the file:

```
$ for i in *
> do echo -n "$i: "; GetFileInfo -c "$i"
> done
Desktop: Desktop is a directory and has no creator
Documents: Documents is a directory and has no creator
...
aa: ""
ab: ""
...
```

grep

Searches for a pattern in files

grep [options] pattern [file-list]

The grep utility searches one or more text files for the ***pattern***, which can be a simple string or another form of a regular expression. The grep utility takes various actions, specified by options, each time it finds a line that contains a match for the ***pattern***. This utility takes its input either from files you specify on the command line or from standard input.

Arguments

The ***pattern*** is a regular expression, as defined in Appendix A. You must quote regular expressions that contain special characters, SPACEs, or TABs. An easy way to quote these characters is to enclose the entire expression within single quotation marks.

The ***file-list*** is a list of the pathnames of ordinary text files that grep searches. With the **–r** option, ***file-list*** can contain directories; grep searches the files in these directory hierarchies.

Options

Without any options grep sends lines that contain a match for ***pattern*** to standard output. When you specify more than one file on the command line, grep precedes each line it displays with the name of the file it came from, followed by a colon.

Major Options

You can use only one of the following three options at a time. Normally you do not need to use any of these options, because grep defaults to **–G**, which is regular grep.

–E (**extended**) Interprets ***pattern*** as an extended regular expression (page 1120). The command **grep –E** is the same as egrep. See the "Notes" section.

–F (**fixed**) Interprets ***pattern*** as a fixed string of characters. The command **grep –F** is the same as fgrep.

–G (**grep**) Interprets ***pattern*** as a basic regular expression (default).

Other Options

The grep utility accepts the common options described on page 736.

The macOS version of grep accepts long options

tip: Options for grep preceded by a double hyphen (**––**) work under macOS as well as under Linux.

––count **–c** Displays only the number of lines that contain a match in each file.

––context=*n* **–C *n***
Displays ***n*** lines of context around each matching line.

--file=*file* –f *file*
Reads ***file***, which contains one pattern per line, and finds lines in the input that match each of the patterns.

--no-filename –h Does not display the filename at the beginning of each line when searching multiple files.

--ignore-case –i Causes lowercase letters in the pattern to match uppercase letters in the file, and vice versa. Use this option when you are searching for a word that might appear at the beginning of a sentence (that is, the word might or might not start with an uppercase letter).

--files-with-matches
–l (lowercase "l"; **list**) Displays only the name of each file that contains one or more matches. A filename is displayed only once, even if the file contains more than one match.

--max-count=*n* –m *n*
Stops reading each file, or standard input, after displaying ***n*** lines containing matches.

--line-number –n Precedes each line with its line number in the file. The file does not need to contain line numbers.

--quiet –q Does not write anything to standard output; only sets the exit code. You can also use **--silent**.

--recursive –r *or* –R
Recursively descends directories in the ***file-list*** and processes files within these directories.

--no-messages –s (**silent**) Does not display an error message if a file in the ***file-list*** does not exist or is not readable.

--invert-match –v Causes lines *not* containing a match to satisfy the search. When you use this option by itself, grep displays all lines that do *not* contain a match for the ***pattern***.

--word-regexp –w With this option, the ***pattern*** must match a whole word. This option is helpful if you are searching for a specific word that might also appear as a substring of another word in the file.

--line-regexp –x The ***pattern*** matches whole lines only.

Notes

The grep utility returns an exit status of 0 if it finds a match, 1 if it does not find a match, and 2 if the file is not accessible or the grep command contains a syntax error.

egrep and fgrep Two utilities perform functions similar to that of grep. The egrep utility (same as **grep –E**) allows you to use *extended regular expressions* (page 1120), which include a different set of special characters than basic regular expressions (page 1120). The fgrep utility (same as **grep –F**) is fast and compact but processes only simple strings, not regular expressions.

GNU grep, which runs under Linux and macOS, uses extended regular expressions in place of regular expressions. Thus, egrep is virtually the same as grep. Refer to the grep info page for a minimal distinction.

Examples

The following examples assume the working directory contains three files: **testa**, **testb**, and **testc**.

File testa	File testb	File testc
aaabb	aaaaa	AAAAA
bbbcc	bbbbb	BBBBB
ff-ff	ccccc	CCCCC
cccdd	ddddd	DDDDD
dddaa		

The grep utility can search for a pattern that is a simple string of characters. The following command line searches **testa** and displays each line that contains the string **bb**:

```
$ grep bb testa
aaabb
bbbcc
```

The **–v** option reverses the sense of the test. The following example displays the lines in **testa** that do *not* contain the string **bb**:

```
$ grep -v bb testa
ff-ff
cccdd
dddaa
```

The **–n** option displays the line number of each displayed line:

```
$ grep -n bb testa
1:aaabb
2:bbbcc
```

The grep utility can search through more than one file. Here, it searches through each file in the working directory. The name of the file containing the string precedes each line of output.

```
$ grep bb *
testa:aaabb
testa:bbbcc
testb:bbbbb
```

When you include the **–w** option in the search for the string **bb**, grep produces no output because none of the files contains the string **bb** as a separate word:

```
$ grep -w bb *
$
```

The search **grep** performs is case sensitive. Because the previous examples specified lowercase **bb**, **grep** did not find the uppercase string **BBBBB** in **testc**. The **–i** option causes both uppercase *and* lowercase letters to match either case of letter in the pattern:

```
$ grep -i bb *
testa:aaabb
testa:bbbcc
testb:bbbbb
testc:BBBBB
$ grep -i BB *
testa:aaabb
testa:bbbcc
testb:bbbbb
testc:BBBBB
```

The **–c** option displays the number of lines in each file that contain a match:

```
$ grep -c bb *
testa:2
testb:1
testc:0
```

The **–f** option finds matches for each pattern in a file of patterns. In the next example, **gfile** holds two patterns, one per line, and **grep** searches for matches to the patterns in **gfile**:

```
$ cat gfile
aaa
bbb
$ grep -f gfile test*
testa:aaabb
testa:bbbcc
testb:aaaaa
testb:bbbbb
```

The following command line searches **text2** and displays lines that contain a string of characters starting with **st**, followed by zero or more characters (**.*** represents zero or more characters in a regular expression; see Appendix A), and ending in **ing**:

```
$ grep 'st.*ing' text2
...
```

The ^ regular expression matches the beginning of a line and, by itself, matches every line in a file. Together with the **–n** option, ^ displays each line in a file preceded by its line number:

```
$ grep -n '^' testa
1:aaabb
2:bbbcc
3:ff-ff
4:cccdd
5:dddaa
```

The next command line counts the number of times **#include** statements appear in C source files in the working directory. The **–h** option causes grep to suppress the filenames from its output. The input to sort consists of all lines from ***.c** that match **#include**. The output from sort is an ordered list of lines that contains many duplicates. When uniq with the **–c** option processes this sorted list, it outputs repeated lines only once, along with a count of the number of repetitions of each repeated line in its input.

```
$ grep -h '#include' *.c | sort | uniq -c
9 #include "buff.h"
2 #include "poly.h"
1 #include "screen.h"
6 #include "window.h"
2 #include "x2.h"
2 #include "x3.h"
2 #include <math.h>
3 #include <stdio.h>
```

The final command calls the vim editor with a list of files in the working directory that contain the string **Sampson**. The **$(...)** command substitution construct (page 371) causes the shell to execute grep in place and supply vim with a list of filenames to edit:

```
$ vim $(grep -l 'Sampson' *)
...
```

The single quotation marks are not necessary in this example, but they are required if the regular expression contains special characters or SPACEs. It is a good habit to quote the pattern so the shell does not interpret special characters the pattern might contain.

gzip

Compresses or decompresses files

*gzip [**options**] [**file-list**]*
*gunzip [**options**] [**file-list**]*
*zcat [**file-list**]*

The gzip utility compresses files, the gunzip utility restores files compressed with gzip, and the zcat utility displays files compressed with gzip.

Arguments

The ***file-list*** is a list of the names of one or more files that are to be compressed or decompressed. If a directory appears in ***file-list*** with no **--recursive** option, gzip/gunzip issues an error message and ignores the directory. With the **--recursive** option, gzip/gunzip recursively compresses/decompresses files within the directory hierarchy.

If ***file-list*** is empty or if the special option – (hyphen) is present, gzip reads from standard input. The **--stdout** option causes gzip and gunzip to write to standard output.

The information in this section also applies to gunzip, a link to gzip.

Options

The gzip, gunzip, and zcat utilities accept the common options described on page 736.

The macOS versions of gzip, gunzip, and zcat accept long options

tip Options for gzip, gunzip, and zcat preceded by a double hyphen (--) work under macOS as well as under Linux.

--stdout **–c** Writes the results of compression or decompression to standard output instead of to ***filename**.gz* or ***filename***, respectively.

--decompress *or* **--uncompress** **–d** Decompresses a file compressed with gzip. This option with gzip is equivalent to the gunzip command.

--force **–f** Overwrites an existing output file on compression/decompression.

--list **–l** For each compressed file in ***file-list***, displays the file's compressed and decompressed sizes, the compression ratio, and the name of the file before compression. Use this option with **--verbose** to display additional information.

--fast *or* **--best** ***–n*** Controls the tradeoff between the speed of compression and the amount of compression. The ***n*** argument is a digit from 1 to 9; level 1 is the fastest (least) compression and level 9 is the best (slowest and most) compression. The default level is 6. The options **--fast** and **--best** are synonyms for –1 and –9, respectively.

--quiet **–q** Suppresses warning messages.

--recursive –r Recursively descends directories in ***file-list*** and compresses/decompresses files within these directories.

--test –t Verifies the integrity of a compressed file. This option displays nothing if the file is OK.

--verbose –v During compression, displays the name of the file, the name of the compressed file, and the amount of compression as each file is processed.

Discussion

Compressing files reduces disk space requirements and shortens the time needed to transmit files between systems. When gzip compresses a file, it adds the extension **.gz** to the filename. For example, compressing the file **fname** creates the file **fname.gz** and, unless you use the **--stdout** (**–c**) option, deletes the original file. To restore **fname**, use the command **gunzip** with the argument **fname.gz**.

Almost all files become much smaller when compressed with gzip. On rare occasions a file will become larger, but only by a slight amount. The type of a file and its contents (as well as the ***–n*** option) determine how much smaller a file becomes; text files are often reduced by 60 to 70 percent.

The attributes of a file, such as its owner, permissions, and modification and access times, are left intact when gzip compresses and gunzip decompresses a file.

If the compressed version of a file already exists, gzip reports that fact and asks for your confirmation before overwriting the existing file. If a file has multiple links to it, gzip issues an error message and exits. The **--force** option overrides the default behavior in both of these situations.

Notes

The bzip2 utility (page 750) compresses files more efficiently than does gzip.

Without the **--stdout** (**–c**) option, gzip removes the files in ***file-list.***

In addition to the gzip format, gunzip recognizes several other compression formats, enabling gunzip to decompress files compressed with compress.

To see an example of a file that becomes larger when compressed with gzip, compare the size of a file that has been compressed once with the same file compressed with gzip again. Because gzip complains when you give it an argument with the extension **.gz**, you need to rename the file before compressing it a second time.

The tar utility with the **–z** modifier (page 997) calls gzip.

You can catenate files by catenating their gzip'd versions. In the following example, gzip first compresses the file named **aa** and, by means of the **--stdout** option, sends the output to **cc.gzip**; then it compresses **bb** appending the output to **cc.gzip**. The final command shows zcat decompressing **cc.gzip**, which contains the contents of both files.

```
$ gzip --stdout aa > cc.gzip
$ gzip --stdout bb >> cc.gzip
```

```
$ zcat cc.gzip
This is file aa.
This is file bb.
```

The following related utilities display and manipulate compressed files. None of these utilities changes the files it works on.

zcat *file-list* Works like cat except it uses gunzip to decompress *file-list* as it copies files to standard output.

zdiff [*options*] *file1* [*file2*]
Works like diff (page 795) except *file1* and *file2* are decompressed with gunzip as needed. The zdiff utility accepts the same options as diff. If you omit *file2*, zdiff compares *file1* with the compressed version of *file1*.

zless *file-list* Works like less except that it uses gunzip to decompress *file-list* as it displays files.

Examples

In the first example, gzip compresses two files. Next, gunzip decompresses one of the files. When a file is compressed and decompressed, its size changes but its modification time remains the same.

```
$ ls -l
-rw-rw-r-- 1 max group 33557 07-20 17:32 patch-2.0.7
-rw-rw-r-- 1 max group 143258 07-20 17:32 patch-2.0.8

$ gzip *
$ ls -l
-rw-rw-r-- 1 max group 9693 07-20 17:32 patch-2.0.7.gz
-rw-rw-r-- 1 max group 40426 07-20 17:32 patch-2.0.8.gz

$ gunzip patch-2.0.7.gz
$ ls -l
-rw-rw-r-- 1 max group 33557 07-20 17:32 patch-2.0.7
-rw-rw-r-- 1 max group 40426 07-20 17:32 patch-2.0.8.gz
```

In the next example, the files in Sam's home directory are archived using cpio (page 776). The archive is compressed with gzip before it is written to the device mounted on /dev/sde1.

```
$ find ~sam -depth -print | cpio -oBm | gzip >/dev/sde1
```

head

Displays the beginning of a file

head [options] [file-list]

The head utility displays the beginning of a file. This utility takes its input either from one or more files you specify on the command line or from standard input.

Arguments

The *file-list* is a list of the pathnames of the files that head displays. When you specify more than one file, head displays the filename before displaying the first few lines of each file. When you do not specify a file, head takes its input from standard input.

Options

Under Linux, head accepts the common options described on page 736. Options preceded by a double hyphen (––) work under Linux only. Except as noted, options named with a single letter and preceded by a single hyphen work under Linux and macOS.

––bytes=*n[u]* **–c *n[u]***
Displays the first ***n*** bytes (characters) of a file. Under Linux only, the ***u*** argument is an optional multiplicative suffix as described on page 735, except that head uses a lowercase **k** for kilobyte (1,024-byte blocks) and accepts **b** for 512-byte blocks. If you include a multiplicative suffix, head counts by this unit instead of by bytes.

––lines=*n* **–n *n***
Displays the first ***n*** lines of a file. You can use *–**n*** to specify ***n*** lines without using the **lines** keyword or the **–n** option. If you specify a negative value for ***n***, head displays all but the last ***n*** lines of the file.

––quiet **–q** Suppresses header information when you specify more than one filename on the command line. LINUX

Notes

The head utility displays the first ten lines of a file by default.

Examples

The examples in this section are based on the following file:

```
$ cat eleven
line one
line two
line three
line four
line five
line six
line seven
line eight
line nine
line ten
line eleven
```

Without any arguments head displays the first ten lines of a file:

```
$ head eleven
line one
line two
line three
line four
line five
line six
line seven
line eight
line nine
line ten
```

The next example displays the first three lines (**–n 3**) of the file:

```
$ head -n 3 eleven
line one
line two
line three
```

The following example is equivalent to the preceding one:

```
$ head -3 eleven
line one
line two
line three
```

The next example displays the first six characters (**–c 6**) in the file:

```
$ head -c 6 eleven
line o$
```

The final example displays all but the last seven lines of the file:

```
$ head -n -7 eleven
line one
line two
line three
line four
```

join

Joins lines from two files based on a common field

join [options] file1 file2

The join utility displays a single line for each pair of lines from ***file1*** and ***file2*** that have the same value in a common field called the join field. Both files must be sorted on the join field or join will not display the correct output.

Arguments

The join utility reads lines from ***file1*** and ***file2*** and, for each pair of lines, compares the specified join field from both lines. If you do not specify a join field, join takes the first field as the join field. If the join fields are the same, join copies the join field along with the rest of the lines from both files to standard output. You can specify a hyphen (–) in place of either filename (but not both) to cause join to read from standard input.

Options

The join utility accepts the **––help** and **––version** options described on page 736.

–1 *field*
Specifies field number ***field*** as the join field in ***file1***. The first field on a line is field number 1.

–2 *field*
Specifies field number ***field*** as the join field in ***file2***. The first field on a line is field number 1.

–a 1 | 2
Displays lines from ***file1*** (if you specify **1**) or ***file2*** (if you specify **2**) whose join field does not match the join field from the other file. Also displays normal output of join (lines with join fields that match). See also the **–v** option.

––ignore-case **–i** Matches uppercase letters to lowercase letters, and vice versa.

–j *field*
Specifies field number ***field*** as the join field in both ***file1*** and ***file2***. The first field on a line is field number 1.

–t *char*
Specifies ***char*** as the input and output field separator and causes join to include blanks (SPACEs and/or TABs) as part of the fields.

–v 1 | 2
Displays lines from ***file1*** (if you specify **1**) or ***file2*** (if you specify **2**) whose join field does not match the join field from the other file. Suppresses the normal output of join (lines with join fields that match). See also the **–a** option.

––check-order Makes sure ***file1*** and ***file2*** are both sorted on the join field and displays an error message if they are not. Default is **––nocheck-order**.

Notes

The concept of a join comes from relational databases; see page 628 for information on joins under SQL.

By default join does the following:

- Uses the first field on each line as the common field it joins on.
- Uses one or more blanks (SPACEs and/or TABs) as field separators and ignores leading blanks. The **–t** option causes join to include blanks as part of the fields and to use the specified character as the input and output field separator.
- Separates output fields with a single SPACE.
- Outputs for each pair of joined lines the common join field followed by the remaining fields from ***file1*** and then the remaining fields from ***file2***.
- Does not check if input files are sorted on the common field that is the basis for the join. See the **––check-order** option.

Examples

The examples in this section use the following files:

```
$ cat one
9999 first line file one.
aaaa second line file one.
cccc third line file one.

$ cat two
aaaa FIRST line file two.
bbbb SECOND line file two.
cccc THIRD line file two.
```

The first example shows the simplest use of join. The files named **one** and **two** are joined based, by default, on the first field in each line of both files. Both files are in sorted order based on the join field. The join fields on two pairs of lines match and join displays those lines.

```
$ join one two
aaaa second line file one. FIRST line file two.
cccc third line file one. THIRD line file two.
```

You can use the **––check-order** option to see if both files are properly sorted. In the following example, sort (page 969) with the **–r** option sorts **one** in reverse alphabetical order and sends the output through a pipeline to join. The shell replaces the written – argument to join with the standard input to join, which comes from the pipeline; join displays an error message.

```
$ sort -r one | join --check-order - two
join: file 1 is not in sorted order
```

Next, the **–a** option with an argument of **1** causes join to display, in addition to its normal output, lines from the first file (**one**) that do not have a matching join field.

```
$ join -a 1 one two
9999 first line file one.
aaaa second line file one. FIRST line file two.
cccc third line file one. THIRD line file two.
```

Use **–v** in place of **–a** to prevent join from displaying those lines it normally displays (those that have a matching join field).

```
$ join -v 1 one two
9999 first line file one.
```

The final example uses **onea** as the first file and specifies the third field of the first file (**–1 3**) as the match field. The second file (**two**) uses the default (first) field for matching.

```
$ cat onea
first line aaaa file one.
second line 1111 file one.
third line cccc file one.

$ join -1 3 onea two
aaaa first line file one. FIRST line file two.
cccc third line file one. THIRD line file two.
```

kill

Terminates a process by PID

kill [option] PID-list
kill –l [signal-name | signal-number]

The kill utility sends a signal to one or more processes. Typically, this signal terminates the processes. For kill to work, the processes must belong to the user executing kill. However, a user working with **root** privileges can terminate any process. The –l (lowercase "l") option lists information about signals.

Arguments

The ***PID-list*** is a list of process identification (PID) numbers of processes that kill is to terminate.

Options

–l (list) Without an argument, displays a list of signals. With an argument of a ***signal-name***, displays the corresponding ***signal-number***. With an argument of a ***signal-number***, displays the corresponding ***signal-name***.

–signal-name | –signal-number
Sends the signal specified by ***signal-name*** or ***signal-number*** to ***PID-list***. You can specify a ***signal-name*** preceded by SIG or not (e.g., SIGKILL or KILL). Without this option, kill sends a software termination signal (SIGTERM; signal number 15).

Notes

See also killall on page 868 and "kill: Aborting a Background Job" on page 152.

Table 10-5 on page 496 lists some signals. The command **kill –l** displays a complete list of signal numbers and names.

In addition to the kill utility, a kill builtin is available in the Bourne Again and TC Shells. The builtins work similarly to the utility described here. Give the command **/bin/kill** to use the kill utility and the command **kill** to use the builtin. It does not usually matter which version you use.

The shell displays the PID number of a background process when you initiate the process. You can also use the ps utility (page 946) to determine PID numbers.

If the software termination signal does not terminate a process, try sending a KILL signal (signal number 9). A process can choose to ignore any signal except KILL.

root: Do not run kill with arguments of –9 0 *or* KILL 0

caution If you run the command **kill –9 0** while you are working with **root** privileges, you will bring the system down.

The kill utility/builtin accepts job identifiers in place of the ***PID-list***. Job identifiers consist of a percent sign (%) followed by either a job number or a string that uniquely identifies the job.

To terminate all processes that the current login process initiated and have the operating system log you out, give the command **kill –9 0**.

Examples

The first example shows a command line executing the file **compute** as a background process and kill terminating that process:

```
$ compute &
[2] 259
$ kill 259
$ RETURN
[2]+  Terminated                    compute
```

The next example shows the ps utility determining the PID number of the background process running a program named **xprog** and the kill utility terminating **xprog** with the TERM signal:

```
$ ps
PID TTY          TIME CMD
 7525 pts/1    00:00:00 bash
14668 pts/1    00:00:00 xprog
14699 pts/1    00:00:00 ps

$ kill -TERM 14668
$
```

The final example shows kill terminating a background process using a job number. As explained on page 152, the jobs builtin lists the numbers of all jobs controlled by the terminal the command is given from.

```
$ sleep 60 &
[1] 24280
$ kill %1
$ RETURN
[1]+  Terminated                    sleep 60
$
```

killall

Terminates a process by name

killall [option] name-list

The killall utility sends a signal to one or more processes executing specified commands. Typically, this signal terminates the processes. For killall to work, the processes must belong to the user executing killall. However, a user working with **root** privileges can terminate any process.

Arguments

The ***name-list*** is a SPACE-separated list of names of programs that are to receive signals.

Options

Options preceded by a double hyphen (––) work under Linux only. Except as noted, options named with a single letter and preceded by a single hyphen work under Linux and macOS.

––interactive –i Prompts for confirmation before killing a process. LINUX

––list –l Displays a list of signals (but **kill –l** displays a better list). With this option killall does not accept a ***name-list.***

––quiet –q Does not display a message if killall fails to terminate a process. LINUX

–signal-name* | *–signal-number

Sends the signal specified by ***signal-name*** or ***signal-number*** to ***name-list.*** You can specify a ***signal-name*** preceded by SIG or not (e.g., **SIGKILL** or **KILL**). Without this option, kill sends a software termination signal (**SIGTERM**; signal number 15).

Notes

See also kill on page 866.

Table 10-5 on page 496 lists some signals. The command **kill –l** displays a complete list of signal numbers and names.

If the software termination signal does not terminate the process, try sending a KILL signal (signal number 9). A process can choose to ignore any signal except KILL.

You can use ps (page 946) to determine the name of the program you want to terminate.

Examples

You can give the following commands to experiment with killall:

```
$ sleep 60 &
[1] 23274
$ sleep 50 &
[2] 23275
$ sleep 40 &
[3] 23276
$ sleep 120 &
```

```
[4] 23277
$ killall sleep
$ RETURN
[1]   Terminated              sleep 60
[2]   Terminated              sleep 50
[3]-  Terminated              sleep 40
[4]+  Terminated              sleep 120
```

The next command, run by a user with **root** privileges, terminates all instances of the Firefox browser:

```
# killall firefox
```

launchctl macOS

Controls the **launchd** daemon

*launchctl [**command** [**options**] [**arguments**]]*

The launchctl utility controls the **launchd** daemon. The launchctl utility is available under macOS only. macOS

Arguments

The ***command*** is the command that launchctl sends to **launchd.** Table VI-19 lists some of the ***commands*** and the options and arguments each ***command*** accepts. Without a ***command,*** launchctl reads commands, options, and arguments from standard input, one set per line. Without a ***command,*** when standard input comes from the keyboard, launchctl runs interactively.

Table VI-19 launchctl commands

Command	Argument	Description
help	None	Displays a help message
list	None	Lists jobs loaded into **launchd**
load [–w]	Job configuration file	Loads the job named by the argument
shutdown	None	Prepares for shutdown by removing all jobs
start	Job name	Starts the job named by the argument
stop	Job name	Stops the job named by the argument
unload [–w]	Job configuration file	Unloads the job named by the argument

Option

Only the **load** and **unload** ***commands*** take an option.

–w (**write**) When loading a file, removes the **Disabled** key and saves the modified configuration file. When unloading a file, adds the **Disabled** key and saves the modified configuration file.

Discussion

The launchctl utility is the user interface to **launchd,** which manages system daemons and background tasks (called jobs). Each job is described by a job configuration file, which is a property list file in the format defined by the **launchd.plist** man page.

For security reasons, users not working with **root** privileges cannot communicate with the system's primary **launchd** process, PID 1. When such a user loads jobs, macOS creates a new instance of **launchd** for that user. When all its jobs are unloaded, that instance of **launchd** quits.

Notes

The launchctl utility and **launchd** daemon were introduced in macOS version 10.4. Under version 10.3 and earlier, system jobs were managed by **init**, **xinetd**, and **cron**.

Examples

The first example, which is run by a user with **root** privileges, uses the **list** command to list **launchd** jobs running on the local system:

```
# launchctl list
PID     Status  Label
51479   -       0x109490.launchctl
50515   -       0x10a780.bash
50514   -       0x10a680.sshd
50511   -       0x108d20.sshd
22      -       0x108bc0.securityd
-       0       com.apple.launchctl.StandardIO
37057   -       [0x0-0x4e84e8].com.apple.ScreenSaver.Engine
27860   -       0x10a4e0.DiskManagementTo
27859   -       [0x0-0x3a23a2].com.apple.SoftwareUpdate
...
```

The next example enables the **ntalk** service. Looking at the **ntalk.plist** file before and after the launchctl command is executed shows that launchctl has modified the file by removing the **Disabled** key.

```
# cat /System/Library/LaunchDaemons/ntalk.plist
...
<dict>
        <key>Disabled</key>
        <true/>
        <key>Label</key>
        <string>com.apple.ntalkd</string>
...
# launchctl load -w /System/Library/LaunchDaemons/ntalk.plist
# cat /System/Library/LaunchDaemons/ntalk.plist
...
<dict>
        <key>Label</key>
        <string>com.apple.ntalkd</string>
...
```

Without any arguments, launchctl prompts for commands on standard input. Give a **quit** command or press CONTROL-D to exit from launchctl. In the last example, a user running with **root** privileges causes launchctl to display a list of jobs and then to stop the job that would launch **airportd**:

```
# launchctl
launchd% list
PID     Status  Label
8659    -       0x10ba10.cron
1       -       0x10c760.launchd
...
-       0       com.apple.airport.updateprefs
-       0       com.apple.airportd
-       0       com.apple.AirPort.wps
-       0       0x100670.dashboardadvisoryd
```

```
-       0       com.apple.launchctl.System
launchd% stop com.apple.airportd
launchd% quit
```

less

Displays text files, one screen at a time

less [options] [file-list]

The less utility displays text files, one screen at a time.

Arguments

The ***file-list*** is the list of files you want to view. If there is no ***file-list***, less reads from standard input.

Options

The less utility accepts the common options described on page 736.

The macOS version of less accepts long options

tip Options for less preceded by a double hyphen (––) work under macOS as well as under Linux.

––clear-screen **–c** Repaints the screen from the top line down instead of scrolling.

––QUIT-AT-EOF **–E** (exit) Normally, less requires you to enter **q** to terminate. This option exits automatically the *first* time less reads the end of file.

––quit-at-eof **–e** (exit) Similar to **–E**, except that less exits automatically the *second* time it reads the end of file.

––quit-if-one-screen
–F Displays the file and quits if the file can be displayed on a single screen.

––ignore-case **–i** Causes a search for a string of lowercase letters to match both uppercase and lowercase letters. This option is ignored if you specify a pattern that includes uppercase letters.

––IGNORE-CASE
–I Causes a search for a string of letters of any case to match both uppercase and lowercase letters, regardless of the case of the search pattern.

––long-prompt **–m** Each prompt reports the percentage of the file less has displayed. It reports byte numbers when less reads from standard input because less has no way of determining the size of the input file.

––LINE-NUMBERS
–N Displays a line number at the beginning of each line.

––prompt=*prompt*
–P*prompt*
Changes the short prompt string (the prompt that appears at the bottom of each screen of output) to ***prompt***. Enclose ***prompt*** in quotation marks if it contains SPACEs. The less utility replaces special symbols in ***prompt*** with other values when it displays the prompt. For example, less displays the current filename in place of

%f. See the less info page for a list of these special symbols and descriptions of other prompts. Custom prompts are useful if you are running less from within another program and want to give instructions or information to the person using the program. The default prompt is the name of the file displayed in reverse video.

--squeeze-blank-lines

–s Displays multiple, adjacent blank lines as a single blank line. When you use less to display text that has been formatted for printing with blank space at the top and bottom of each page, this option shortens these headers and footers to a single line.

--tabs=*n* –x*n*

Sets tab stops *n* characters apart. The default is eight characters.

--window=*n* –[z]*n*

Sets the scrolling size to *n* lines. The default is the height of the display in lines. Each time you move forward or backward a page, you move *n* lines. The z part of the option maintains compatibility with more and can be omitted.

+*command*

Any command you can give less while it is running can also be given as an option by preceding it with a plus sign (+) on the command line. See the "Commands" section. A command preceded by a plus sign on the command line is executed as soon as less starts and applies to the first file only.

++*command*

Similar to +*command* except that *command* is applied to every file in *file-list*, not just the first file.

Notes

The phrase "less is more" explains the origin of the name of this utility. The more utility is the original Berkeley UNIX pager (also available under Linux). The less utility is similar to more but includes many enhancements. (Under macOS, less and more are copies of the same file.) After displaying a screen of text, less displays a prompt and waits for you to enter a command. You can skip forward and backward in the file, invoke an editor, search for a pattern, or perform a number of other tasks.

See the v command in the next section for information on how you can edit the file you are viewing.

You can set the options to less either from the command line when you call less or by setting the **LESS** environment variable. For example, the following bash command causes less to run with the –x4 and –s options:

```
$ export LESS="-x4 -s"
```

Normally, you would set **LESS** in **~/.bash_profile** if you are using bash or in **~/.login** if you are using tcsh. Once you have set the **LESS** variable, less is invoked with the specified options each time you call it. Any options you give on the command line override the settings in the **LESS** variable. The **LESS** variable is used both when you call less from the command line and when less is invoked by another program, such as man. To specify less as the pager to use with man and other programs, set the environment variable **PAGER** to **less**; under bash you can add the following line to **~/.bash_profile:**

```
export PAGER=less
```

Commands

Whenever less pauses, you can enter any of a large number of commands. This section describes some commonly used commands. Refer to the less info page and also the **less --help** command for more information. The optional numeric argument ***n*** defaults to 1, except as noted. You do not need to follow these commands with a RETURN.

n*b *or* *n*CONTROL-B** (**backward**) Scrolls backward ***n lines. The default value of ***n*** is the height of the screen in lines.

n*d *or* *n*CONTROL-D** (**down**) Scrolls forward ***n lines. The default value of ***n*** is one-half the height of the screen in lines. When you specify ***n***, it becomes the new default value for this command.

F (**forward**) Scrolls forward. If the end of the input is reached, this command waits for more input and then continues scrolling. This command allows you to use less in a manner similar to **tail –f** (page 992), except that less paginates the output as it appears.

n*g** (**go**) Goes to line number ***n. This command might not work if the file is read from standard input and you have moved too far into the file. The default value of ***n*** is 1.

h *or* H (**help**) Displays a summary of all available commands. The summary is displayed using less, as the list of commands is quite long.

n*RETURN *or* *n*j** (**jump**) Scrolls forward ***n lines. The default value of ***n*** is 1.

q *or* :q Terminates less.

n*u *or* *n*CONTROL-U** (**up**) Scrolls backward ***n lines. The default value of ***n*** is one-half the height of the screen in lines. When you specify ***n***, it becomes the default value for this command.

v Brings the current file into an editor with the cursor on the current line. The less utility uses the editor specified by the **EDITOR** environment variable. If **EDITOR** is not set, less uses vi (which is typically linked to vim).

n*w** Scrolls backward like ***n*b**, except that the value of ***n becomes the new default value for this command.

n*y *or* *n*k** Scrolls backward ***n lines. The default value of ***n*** is 1.

n*z** Displays the next ***n lines like ***n*SPACE** except that the value of ***n***, if present, becomes the new default value for the **z** and SPACE commands.

n*SPACE** Displays the next ***n lines. Pressing the SPACE bar by itself displays the next screen of text.

/regular-expression

Skips forward in the file, looking for lines that contain a match for ***regular-expression***. If you begin ***regular-expression*** with an exclamation point (**!**), this command looks for lines that do *not* contain a match for ***regular-expression***. If ***regular-expression*** begins with an asterisk (*), this command continues the search through ***file-list.*** (A normal search stops at the end of the current file.) If ***regular-expression*** begins with an at sign (@), this command begins the search at the beginning of ***file-list*** and continues to the end of ***file-list.***

?regular-expression
This command is similar to the preceding one except it searches backward through the file (and ***file-list***). An asterisk (*) as the first character in ***regular-expression*** causes the search to continue backward through ***file-list*** to the beginning of the first file. An at sign (@) causes the search to start with the last line of the last file in ***file-list*** and progress toward the first line of the first file.

{ *or* (*or* [If one of these characters appears in the top line of the display, this command scrolls forward to the matching right brace, parenthesis, or bracket. For example, typing { causes less to move the cursor forward to the matching }.

} *or*) *or*] Similar to the preceding commands, these commands move the cursor backward to the matching left brace, parenthesis, or bracket.

CONTROL-L Redraws the screen. This command is useful if the text on the screen has become garbled.

[n]:n Skips to the next file in ***file-list.*** If ***n*** is given, skips to the ***n***th next file in ***file-list.***

!*[command line]* Executes ***command line*** under the shell specified by the **SHELL** environment variable or under sh (usually linked to or a copy of bash or dash) by default. A percent sign (%) in ***command line*** is replaced by the name of the current file. If you omit ***command line,*** less starts an interactive shell.

Examples

The following example displays the file **memo.txt**. To see more of the file, the user presses the SPACE bar in response to the less prompt at the lower-left corner of the screen:

```
$ less memo.txt
...
memo.txt SPACE
...
```

In the next example, the user changes the prompt to a more meaningful message and uses the **–N** option to display line numbers. The command line also instructs less to skip forward to the first line containing the string **procedure**.

```
$ less -Ps"Press SPACE to continue, q to quit" -N +/procedure ncut.icn
     28  procedure main(args)
     29      local filelist, arg, fields, delim
     30
     31      filelist:=[]
...
     45      # Check for real field list
     46      #
     47      if /fields then stop("-fFIELD_LIST is required.")
     48
```

```
    49       # Process the files and output the fields
Press SPACE to continue, q to quit
```

ln

Makes a link to a file

ln [options] existing-file [new-link]
ln [options] existing-file-list directory

The ln utility creates hard or symbolic links to one or more files. You can create a symbolic link, but not a hard link, to a directory.

Arguments

In the first syntax the ***existing-file*** is the pathname of the file you want to create a link to. The ***new-link*** is the pathname of the new link. When you are creating a symbolic link, the ***existing-file*** can be a directory. If you omit ***new-link***, ln creates a link to ***existing-file*** in the working directory, using the same simple filename as ***existing-file***.

In the second syntax the ***existing-file-list*** is a list of the pathnames of the ordinary files you want to create links to. The ln utility establishes the new links in the ***directory***. The simple filenames of the entries in the ***directory*** are the same as the simple filenames of the files in the ***existing-file-list***.

Options

Options preceded by a double hyphen (––) work under Linux only. Except as noted, options named with a single letter and preceded by a single hyphen work under Linux and macOS.

––backup **–b** If the ln utility will remove a file, this option makes a backup by appending a tilde (~) to the filename. This option works only with **––force**. LINUX

––force **–f** Normally, ln does not create the link if ***new-link*** already exists. This option removes ***new-link*** before creating the link. When you use **––force** and **––backup** together (Linux only), ln makes a copy of ***new-link*** before removing it.

––interactive **–i** If ***new-link*** already exists, this option prompts you before removing ***new-link***. If you enter **y** or **yes**, ln removes ***new-link*** before creating the link. If you answer **n** or **no**, ln does not remove ***new-link*** and does not make a new link.

––symbolic **–s** Creates a symbolic link. When you use this option, the ***existing-file*** and the ***new-link*** might be directories and might reside on different filesystems. Refer to "Symbolic Links" on page 115.

Notes

For more information refer to "Links" on page 112. The ls utility with the **–l** option displays the number of hard links to a file (Figure 4-12; page 98).

Hard links By default ln creates *hard links*. A hard link to a file is indistinguishable from the original file. All hard links to a file must be in the same filesystem. For more information refer to "ln: Creates a Hard Link" on page 113.

Symbolic links You can also use ln to create *symbolic links*. Unlike a hard link, a symbolic link can exist in a different filesystem from the linked-to file. Also, a symbolic link can point to a directory. For more information refer to "Symbolic Links" on page 115.

If ***new-link*** is the name of an existing file, ln does not create the link unless you use the **––force** option (Linux only) or answer **yes** when using the **–i** (**––interactive**) option.

Examples

The following command creates a link between **memo2** in the **literature** subdirectory of Zach's home directory and the working directory. The file appears as **memo2** (the simple filename of the existing file) in the working directory:

```
$ ln ~zach/literature/memo2 .
```

You can omit the period that represents the working directory from the preceding command. When you give a single argument to ln, it creates a link in the working directory.

The next command creates a link to the same file. This time the file appears as **new_memo** in the working directory:

```
$ ln ~zach/literature/memo2 new_memo
```

The following command creates a link that causes the file to appear in Sam's home directory:

```
$ ln ~zach/literature/memo2 ~sam/new_memo
```

You must have write and execute access permissions to the other user's directory for this command to work. If you own the file, you can use chmod to give the other user write access permission to the file.

The next command creates a symbolic link to a directory. The **ls –ld** command shows the link:

```
$ ln -s /usr/local/bin bin
$ ls -ld bin
lrwxrwxrwx  1 zach zach 14 Feb 10 13:26 bin -> /usr/local/bin
```

The final example attempts to create a symbolic link named **memo1** to the file **memo2**. Because the file **memo1** exists, ln refuses to make the link. When you use the **–i** (**––interactive**) option, ln asks whether you want to replace the existing **memo1** file with the symbolic link. If you enter **y** or **yes**, ln creates the link and the old **memo1** disappears.

```
$ ls -l memo?
-rw-rw-r--   1 zach group 224 07-31 14:48 memo1
-rw-rw-r--   1 zach group 753 07-31 14:49 memo2
$ ln -s memo2 memo1
ln: memo1: File exists
$ ln -si memo2 memo1
ln: replace 'memo1'? y
```

```
$ ls -l memo?
lrwxrwxrwx   1 zach group 5 07-31 14:49 memo1 -> memo2
-rw-rw-r--   1 zach group 753 07-31 14:49 memo2
```

Under Linux you can also use the **--force** option to cause ln to overwrite a file.

lpr

Sends files to printers

lpr [options] [file-list]
lpq [options] [job-identifiers]
lprm [options] [job-identifiers]

The lpr utility places one or more files into a print queue, providing orderly access to printers for several users or processes. This utility can work with printers attached to remote systems. You can use the lprm utility to remove files from the print queues and the lpq utility to check the status of files in the queues. Refer to "Notes" later in this section.

Arguments

The ***file-list*** is a list of one or more filenames for lpr to print. Often these files are text files, but many systems are configured so lpr can accept and properly print a variety of file types, including PostScript and PDF files. Without a ***file-list,*** lpr accepts input from standard input.

The ***job-identifiers*** is a list of job numbers or usernames. If you do not know the job number, use lpq to display a list of print jobs.

Options

Some of the following options depend on which type of file is being printed as well as on how the system is configured for printing.

–h (**no header**) Suppresses printing of the header (burst) page. This page is useful for identifying the owner of the output in a multiuser setup, but printing it is a waste of paper when this identification is not needed.

–l (lowercase "l") Specifies that lpr should not preprocess (filter) the file being printed. Use this option when the file is already formatted for the printer.

–P ***printer***

Routes the print jobs to the queue for the printer named ***printer.*** If you do not use this option, print jobs are routed to the default printer for the local system. The acceptable values for ***printer*** are found in the Linux file **/etc/printcap** and can be displayed by an **lpstat –t** command. These values vary from system to system.

–r (**remove**) Deletes the files in ***file-list*** after calling lpr.

–# ***n***

Prints ***n*** copies of each file. Depending on which shell you are using, you might need to escape the # by preceding it with a backslash to keep the shell from interpreting it as a special character.

Discussion

The lpr utility takes input either from files you specify on the command line or from standard input; it adds these files to the print queue as *print jobs*. The utility assigns a unique identification number to each print job. The lpq utility displays the job numbers of the print jobs that lpr has set up; you can use the lprm utility to remove a job from the print queue.

lpq The lpq utility displays information about jobs in a print queue. When called without any arguments, lpq lists all print jobs queued for the default printer. Use lpr's **–P *printer*** option with lpq to look at other print queues—even those for printers connected to remote systems. With the **–l** option, lpq displays more information about each job. If you give a username as an argument, lpq displays only the printer jobs belonging to that user.

lprm One item displayed by lpq is the job number for each print job in the queue. To remove a job from the print queue, give the job number as an argument to lprm. Unless you are working with **root** privileges, you can remove only your own jobs. Even a user working with **root** privileges might not be able to remove a job from a queue for a remote printer. If you do not give any arguments to lprm, it removes the active printer job (that is, the job that is now printing) from the queue, if you own that job.

Notes

If you normally use a printer other than the system default printer, you can set up lpr to use another printer as your personal default by assigning the name of this printer to the environment variable **PRINTER**. For example, if you use bash, you can add the following line to **~/.bash_profile** to set your default printer to the printer named **ps**:

```
export PRINTER=ps
```

LPD and LPR Traditionally, UNIX had two printing systems: the BSD Line Printer Daemon (LPD) and the System V Line Printer system (LPR). Linux adopted those systems at first, and both UNIX and Linux have seen modifications to and replacements for these systems. Today CUPS is the default printing system under Linux and macOS.

CUPS CUPS is a cross-platform print server built around the Internet Printing Protocol (IPP), which is based on HTTP. CUPS provides a number of printer drivers and can print different types of files, including PostScript files. CUPS provides System V and BSD command-line interfaces and, in addition to IPP, supports LPD/LPR, HTTP, SMB, and JetDirect (socket) protocols, among others.

This section describes the LPD command-line interface that runs under CUPS and also in native mode on older systems.

Examples

The first command sends the file named **memo2** to the default printer:

```
$ lpr memo2
```

Next, a pipeline sends the output of ls to the printer named **deskjet**:

```
$ ls | lpr -Pdeskjet
```

The next example paginates and sends the file **memo** to the printer:

```
$ pr -h "Today's memo" memo | lpr
```

The next example shows a number of print jobs queued for the default printer. Max owns all the jobs, and the first one is being printed (it is active). Jobs 635 and 639 were created by sending input to lpr's standard input; job 638 was created by giving **ncut.icn** as an argument to the lpr command. The last column gives the size of each print job.

```
$ lpq
deskjet is ready and printing
Rank   Owner     Job  Files                              Total Size
active max       635  (stdin)                           38128 bytes
1st    max       638  ncut.icn                           3587 bytes
2nd    max       639  (stdin)                            3960 bytes
```

The next command removes job 638 from the default print queue:

```
$ lprm 638
```

ls

ls

Displays information about one or more files

ls [options] [file-list]

The ls utility displays information about one or more files. It lists the information alphabetically by filename unless you use an option that changes the order.

Arguments

When you do not provide an argument, ls displays the names of the visible files (those with filenames that do not begin with a period) in the working directory.

The ***file-list*** is a list of one or more pathnames of any ordinary, directory, or device files. It can include ambiguous file references.

When the ***file-list*** includes a directory, ls displays the contents of the directory. It displays the name of the directory only when needed to avoid ambiguity, such as when the listing includes more than one directory. When you specify an ordinary file, ls displays information about that one file.

Options

Options preceded by a double hyphen (––) work under Linux only. Except as noted, options named with a single letter and preceded by a single hyphen work under Linux and macOS.

The options determine the type of information ls displays, the manner in which it displays the information, and the order in which the information is displayed. When you do not use an option, ls displays a short list that contains just the names of files, in alphabetical order.

––almost-all –A The same as –a but does not list the . and .. directory entries.

––all –a Includes hidden filenames (those filenames that begin with a period; page 88) in the listing. Without this option ls does not list information about files with hidden filenames unless you include the name of a hidden file in the ***file-list***. The * ambiguous file reference does not match a leading period in a filename, so you must use this option or explicitly specify a filename (ambiguous or not) that begins with a period to display files with hidden filenames.

––escape –b Displays nonprinting characters in a filename, using backslash escape sequences similar to those used in C language strings (Table VI-20). Other nonprinting characters are displayed as a backslash followed by an octal number.

Table VI-20 Backslash escape sequences

Sequence	Meaning
\b	BACKSPACE
\n	NEWLINE

Table VI-20 Backslash escape sequences (continued)

Sequence	Meaning
\r	RETURN
\t	HORIZONTAL TAB
\v	VERTICAL TAB
\\	BACKSLASH

--color[=*when*] The ls utility can display various types of files in different colors but normally does not use colors (the same result as when you specify ***when*** as **none**). If you do not specify ***when*** or if you specify ***when*** as **always,** ls uses colors. When you specify ***when*** as **auto,** ls uses colors only when the output goes to a screen. See the "Notes" section for more information. LINUX

--directory **–d** Displays directories without displaying their contents. This option does not dereference symbolic links; that is, for each file that is a symbolic link, this option lists the symbolic link, not the file the link points to.

–e Displays ACLs (page 1074). macOS

--classify **–F** Displays a slash (/) after each directory, an asterisk (*) after each executable file, and an at sign (@) after a symbolic link.

--format=*word* By default ls displays files sorted vertically. This option sorts files based on ***word:*** **across** or **horizontal** (also **–x**), separated by **commas** (also **–m**), **long** (also **–l**), or **single-column** (also **–1**). LINUX

--dereference-command-line

–H (**partial dereference**) For each file that is a symbolic link, lists the file the link points to, not the symbolic link itself. This option affects files specified on the command line; it does not affect files found while descending a directory hierarchy. This option treats files that are not symbolic links normally. See page 118 for information on dereferencing symbolic links.

--human-readable

–h With the **–l** option, displays sizes in K (kilobyte), M (megabyte), and G (gigabyte) blocks, as appropriate. This option works with the **–l** option only. It displays powers of 1,024. Under macOS, it displays B (bytes) in addition to the preceding suffixes. See also **--si.**

--inode **–i** Displays the inode number of each file. With the **–l** option, this option displays the inode number in column 1 and shifts other items one column to the right.

--dereference **–L** (**dereference**) For each file that is a symbolic link, lists the file the link points to, not the symbolic link itself. This option affects all files and treats files that are not symbolic links normally. See page 118 for information on dereferencing symbolic links.

--format=long **–l** (lowercase "l") Lists more information about each file. This option does not dereference symbolic links; that is, for each file that is a symbolic link, this option lists the symbolic link, not the file the link points to. If standard output for a directory listing is sent to the screen, this option displays the number of blocks used by all files in the listing on a line before the listing. Use this option with **–h** to make file sizes more readable. See the "Discussion" section for more information.

--format=commas
–m Displays a comma-separated list of files that fills the width of the screen.

–P (**no dereference**) For each file that is a symbolic link, lists the symbolic link, not the file the link points to. This option affects all files and treats files that are not symbolic links normally. See page 118 for information on dereferencing symbolic links. macOS

--hide-control-chars
–q Displays nonprinting characters in a filename as question marks. When standard output is sent to the screen, this behavior is the default. Without this option, when standard output is sent to a filter or a file, nonprinting characters are output as themselves.

--recursive **–R** Recursively lists directory hierarchies.

--reverse **–r** Displays the list of filenames in reverse sorted order.

--size **–s** Displays the number of 1,024-byte (Linux) or 512-byte (macOS) blocks allocated to the file. The size precedes the filename. With the **–l** option, this option displays the size in column 1 and shifts other items one column to the right. If standard output for a directory listing is sent to the screen, this option displays the number of blocks used by all files in the listing on a line before the listing. You can include the **–h** option to make the file sizes easier to read.

Under macOS, you can use the **BLOCKSIZE** environment variable (page 736) to change the size of the blocks this option reports on.

--si With the **–l** option, displays sizes in K (kilobyte), M (megabyte), and G (gigabyte) blocks, as appropriate. This option works with the **–l** option only. This option displays powers of 1,000. See also **--human-readable.** LINUX

--sort=time **–t** Displays files sorted by the time they were last modified.

--sort=*word* By default ls displays files in ASCII order. This option sorts files based on ***word:*** filename **extension** (**–X**; Linux only), **none** (**–U**; Linux only), file **size** (**–S**), **access** time (**–u**), or modification **time** (**–t**). See **--time** for an exception. LINUX

--time=*word* By default ls with the **–l** option displays the modification time of a file. Set ***word*** to **atime** (**–u**) to display the access time or set to to **ctime** (**–t**) to display the modification time. The list will be sorted by ***word*** when you also give the **--sort=time** option. LINUX

--sort=access –u Displays files sorted by the time they were last accessed.

--format=extension

–X Displays files sorted by filename extension. Files with no filename extension are listed first. LINUX

--format=across –x Displays files sorted by lines (the default display is sorted by columns).

--format=single-column

–1 (one) Displays one file per line. This type of display is the default when you redirect the output from ls.

Discussion

The ls long listing (–l or **--format=long** options) displays the columns shown in Figure 4-12 on page 98. The first column, which contains 10 or 11 characters, is divided as described in the following paragraphs. The character in the first position describes the type of file, as shown in Table VI-21.

Table VI-21 First character in a long ls display

Character	Meaning
–	Ordinary
b	Block device
c	Character device
d	Directory
p	FIFO (named pipe)
l	Symbolic link

The next nine characters of the first column describe the access permissions associated with the file. These characters are divided into three sets of three characters each.

The first three characters represent the owner's access permissions. If the owner has read access permission to the file, **r** appears in the first character position. If the owner is not permitted to read the file, a hyphen appears in this position. The next two positions represent the owner's write and execute access permissions. If **w** appears in the second position, the owner is permitted to write to the file; if **x** appears in the third position, the owner is permitted to execute the file. An **s** in the third position indicates that the file has both setuid and execute permissions. An **S** in the third position indicates that setuid permission without execute permission. A hyphen indicates that the owner does not have the access permission associated with the character position.

In a similar manner the second set of three characters represents the access permissions for the group the file is associated with. An **s** in the third position indicates the file has setgid permission with execute permission, and an **S** indicates setgid permission with no execute permission.

The third set of three characters represents the access permissions for other users. A t in the third position indicates that the file has the *sticky bit* (page 1126) set.

Refer to chmod on page 759 for information on changing access permissions.

If ACLs (page 106) are enabled and a listed file has an ACL, **ls –l** displays a plus sign (+) following the third set of three characters.

Still referring to Figure 4-12 on page 101, the second column indicates the number of hard links to the file. Refer to page 112 for more information on links.

The third and fourth columns display the name of the owner of the file and the name of the group the file is associated with, respectively.

The fifth column indicates the size of the file in bytes or, if information about a device file is being displayed, the major and minor device numbers. In the case of a directory, this number is the size of the directory file, not the size of the files that are entries within the directory. (Use du [page 809] to display the sum of the sizes of all files in a directory.) Use the **–h** option to display the size of files in kilobytes, megabytes, or gigabytes.

The last two columns display the date and time the file was last modified and the filename.

Notes

By default ls does not dereference symbolic links: For each file that is a symbolic link, ls lists the symbolic link, not the file the link points to. Use the **–L** or **–H** option to dereference symbolic links. For more information refer to "Dereferencing Symbolic Links Using ls" on page 119.

For other than long listings (displayed by the **–l** option), when standard output goes to the screen, ls displays output in columns based on the width of the screen. When you redirect standard output to a filter or file, ls displays a single column.

Refer to page 152 for examples of using ls with ambiguous file references.

Set the **LANG** locale variable to **C** if ls output is sorted in a way you would not expect. See the tip titled "The C locale" on page 328 for more information.

With the **––color** option, ls displays the filenames of various types of files in different colors. By default executable files are green, directory files are blue, symbolic links are cyan, archives and compressed files are red, and ordinary text files are black. The manner in which ls colors the various file types is specified in the **/etc/DIR_COLORS** file. If this file does not exist on the local system, ls will not color filenames. You can modify **/etc/DIR_COLORS** to alter the default color/filetype mappings on a systemwide basis. For your personal use, you can copy **/etc/DIR_COLORS** to the **~/.dir_colors** file in your home directory and modify it. For your login, **~/.dir_colors** overrides the systemwide colors established in **/etc/DIR_COLORS**. Refer to the **dir_colors** and dircolors man pages for more information.

Examples

See "Dereferencing Symbolic Links Using ls" on page 119 for examples that use the –H and –L options.

The first example shows ls, without any options or arguments, listing the names of the files in the working directory in alphabetical order. The list is sorted in columns (vertically):

```
$ ls
bin  calendar  letters
c    execute   shell
```

The next example shows the ls utility with the –x option, which sorts the files horizontally:

```
$ ls -x
bin      c        calendar
execute  letters  shell
```

The –F option appends a slash (/) to files that are directories, an asterisk to files that are executable, and an at sign (@) to files that are symbolic links:

```
$ ls -Fx
bin/      c/        calendar
execute*  letters/  shell@
```

Next, the –l (**long**) option displays a long list. The files are still in alphabetical order:

```
$ ls -l
drwxr-xr-x 2 sam pubs 4096 05-20 09:17 bin
drwxr-xr-x 2 sam pubs 4096 03-26 11:59 c
-rw-r--r-- 1 sam pubs  104 01-09 14:44 calendar
-rwxr-xr-x 1 sam pubs   85 05-06 08:27 execute
drwxr-xr-x 2 sam pubs 4096 04-04 18:56 letters
lrwxrwxrwx 1 sam sam     9 05-21 11:35 shell -> /bin/bash
```

The –a (**all**) option lists all files, including those with hidden names:

```
$ ls -a
.         bin       execute
..        c         letters
.profile  calendar  shell
```

Combining the –a and –l options displays a long listing of all files, including those with hidden filenames (page 88), in the working directory. This list is still in alphabetical order:

```
$ ls -al
drwxr-xr-x 5 sam sam  4096 05-21 11:50 .
drwxrwxrwx 3 sam sam  4096 05-21 11:50 ..
-rw-r--r-- 1 sam sam   160 05-21 11:45 .profile
drwxr-xr-x 2 sam pubs 4096 05-20 09:17 bin
drwxr-xr-x 2 sam pubs 4096 03-26 11:59 c
-rw-r--r-- 1 sam pubs  104 01-09 14:44 calendar
-rwxr-xr-x 1 sam pubs   85 05-06 08:27 execute
drwxr-xr-x 2 sam pubs 4096 04-04 18:56 letters
lrwxrwxrwx 1 sam sam     9 05-21 11:35 shell -> /bin/bash
```

When you add the **–r** (reverse) option to the command line, ls produces a list in reverse alphabetical order:

```
$ ls -ral
lrwxrwxrwx 1 sam sam      9 05-21 11:35 shell -> /bin/bash
drwxr-xr-x 2 sam pubs 4096 04-04 18:56 letters
-rwxr-xr-x 1 sam pubs   85 05-06 08:27 execute
-rw-r--r-- 1 sam pubs  104 01-09 14:44 calendar
drwxr-xr-x 2 sam pubs 4096 03-26 11:59 c
drwxr-xr-x 2 sam pubs 4096 05-20 09:17 bin
-rw-r--r-- 1 sam sam   160 05-21 11:45 .profile
drwxrwxrwx 3 sam sam  4096 05-21 11:50 ..
drwxr-xr-x 5 sam sam  4096 05-21 11:50 .
```

Use the **–t** and **–l** options to list files so the *most recently* modified file appears at the top of the list:

```
$ ls -tl
lrwxrwxrwx 1 sam sam      9 05-21 11:35 shell -> /bin/bash
drwxr-xr-x 2 sam pubs 4096 05-20 09:17 bin
-rwxr-xr-x 1 sam pubs   85 05-06 08:27 execute
drwxr-xr-x 2 sam pubs 4096 04-04 18:56 letters
drwxr-xr-x 2 sam pubs 4096 03-26 11:59 c
-rw-r--r-- 1 sam pubs  104 01-09 14:44 calendar
```

Together, the **–r** and **–t** options cause the file you modified *least recently* to appear at the top of the list:

```
$ ls -trl
-rw-r--r-- 1 sam pubs  104 01-09 14:44 calendar
drwxr-xr-x 2 sam pubs 4096 03-26 11:59 c
drwxr-xr-x 2 sam pubs 4096 04-04 18:56 letters
-rwxr-xr-x 1 sam pubs   85 05-06 08:27 execute
drwxr-xr-x 2 sam pubs 4096 05-20 09:17 bin
lrwxrwxrwx 1 sam sam      9 05-21 11:35 shell -> /bin/bash
```

The next example shows ls with a directory filename as an argument. The ls utility lists the contents of the directory in alphabetical order:

```
$ ls bin
c  e  lsdir
```

To display information about the directory file itself, use the **–d** (directory) option. This option lists information about the directory only:

```
$ ls -dl bin
drwxr-xr-x 2 sam pubs 4096 05-20 09:17 bin
```

You can use the following command to display a list of all files that have hidden filenames (filenames that start with a period) in your home directory. It is a convenient way to list the startup (initialization) files in your home directory.

```
$ ls -d ~/.*
/home/sam/.
/home/sam/..
/home/sam/.AbiSuite
/home/sam/.Azureus
/home/sam/.BitTornado
...
```

A plus sign (+) to the right of the permissions in a long listing denotes the presence of an ACL for a file:

```
$ ls -l memo
-rw-r--r--+ 1 sam pubs 19 07-19 21:59 memo
```

Under macOS you can use the –le option to display an ACL:

```
$ ls -le memo
-rw-r--r-- + 1 sam pubs 19 07-19 21:59 memo
 0: user:jenny allow read
```

See page 1074 for more examples of using ls under macOS to display ACLs.

make

Keeps a set of programs current

make [options] [target-files] [arguments]

The GNU make utility keeps a set of executable programs (or other files) current, based on differences in the modification times of the programs and the source files that each program is dependent on.

Arguments

The ***target-files*** refer to targets on dependency lines in the makefile. When you do not specify a ***target-file***, make updates the target on the first dependency line in the makefile. Command-line ***arguments*** of the form ***name=value*** set the variable ***name*** to ***value*** inside the makefile. See the "Discussion" section for more information.

Options

If you do not use the –f option, make takes its input from a file named **GNUmakefile**, **makefile**, or **Makefile** (in that order) in the working directory. In this section, this input file is referred to as **makefile**. Many users prefer to use the name **Makefile** because it shows up earlier in directory listings.

The macOS version of make accepts long options

tip Options for make preceded by a double hyphen (––) work under macOS as well as under Linux.

––directory=*dir* –C *dir*
Changes directories to *dir* before starting.

––debug –d Displays information about how make decides what to do.

––file=*file* –f *file*
(**input file**) Uses *file* as input instead of **makefile**.

––jobs[=*n*] –j [*n*]
Runs up to ***n*** commands at the same time instead of the default of one command. Running multiple commands simultaneously is especially effective if you are working on a multiprocessor system. If you omit ***n***, make does not limit the number of simultaneous jobs.

––keep-going –k Continues with the next file from the list of ***target-files*** instead of quitting when a construction command fails.

––just-print –n (**no execution**) Displays, but does not execute, the commands that make would execute to bring the ***target-files*** up-to-date. You can also use **--dry-run**.

––silent –s Does not display the names of the commands being executed. You can also use **--quiet**.

––touch –t Updates the modification times of target files but does not execute any construction commands. Refer to touch on page 1012.

Discussion

The make utility bases its actions on the modification times of the programs and the source files that each program depends on. Each of the executable programs, or ***target-files,*** depends on one or more prerequisite files. The relationships between ***target-files*** and prerequisites are specified on *dependency lines* in a makefile. Construction commands follow the dependency line, specifying how make can update the ***target-files.*** See page 895 for examples of makefiles.

Documentation Refer to www.gnu.org/software/make/manual/make.html and to the make info page for more information about make and makefiles.

Although the most common use of make is to build programs from source code, this general-purpose build utility is suitable for a wide range of applications. Anywhere you can define a set of dependencies to get from one state to another represents a candidate for using make.

Much of make's power derives from the features you can set up in a makefile. For example, you can define variables using the same syntax found in the Bourne Again Shell. *Always* define the variable **SHELL** in a makefile; set it to the pathname of the shell you want to use when running construction commands. To define the variable and assign it a value, place the following line near the top of a makefile:

```
SHELL=/bin/sh
```

Assigning the value **/bin/sh** to **SHELL** allows you to use a makefile on other computer systems. On Linux systems, **/bin/sh** is generally linked to **/bin/bash** or **/bin/dash**. Under macOS, **/bin/sh** is a copy of bash that attempts to emulate the original Bourne Shell. The make utility uses the value of the environment variable **SHELL** if you do not set **SHELL** in a makefile. If **SHELL** does not hold the path of the shell you intended to use and if you do not set **SHELL** in a makefile, the construction commands might fail.

Following is a list of additional make features.

- You can run specific construction commands silently by preceding them with an at sign (@). For example, the following lines will display a short help message when you run the command **make help**:

  ```
  help:
      @echo "You can make the following:"
      @echo " "
      @echo "libbuf.a         -- the buffer library"
      @echo "Bufdisplay       -- display any-format buffer"
      @echo "Buf2ppm          -- convert buffer to pixmap"
  ```

  Without the @s in the preceding example, make would display each of the echo commands before executing it. This way of displaying a message works because no file is named **help** in the working directory. As a result make runs the construction commands in an attempt to build this file. Because the construction commands display messages but do not build the file **help**, you can run **make help** repeatedly with the same result.

- You can cause make to ignore the exit status of a command by preceding the command with a hyphen (–). For example, the following line allows make to continue regardless of whether the call to **/bin/rm** is successful (the call to **/bin/rm** fails if **libbuf.a** does not exist):

```
-/bin/rm libbuf.a
```

- You can use special variables to refer to information that might change from one use of make to the next. Such information might include files that need updating, files that are newer than the target, and files that match a pattern. For example, you can use the variable **$?** in a construction command to identify all prerequisite files that are newer than the target file. This variable allows you to print any files that have changed since the last time you printed those files:

```
list:       .list
.list:      Makefile buf.h xtbuff_ad.h buff.c buf_print.c xtbuff.c
pr $? | lpr
date >.list
```

The target list depends on the source files that might be printed. The construction command **pr $? | lpr** prints only those source files that are newer than the file **.list**. The line **date > .list** modifies the **.list** file so it is newer than any of the source files. The next time you run the command **make list**, only the files that have been changed are printed.

- You can include other makefiles as if they were part of the current makefile. The following line causes make to read **Make.config** and treat the content of that file as though it were part of the current makefile, allowing you to put information common to more than one makefile in a single place:

```
include Make.config
```

Note

Under macOS, the make utility is part of the optional Xcode package.

Examples

The first example causes make to bring the ***target-file*** named **analysis** up-to-date by issuing three **cc** commands. It uses a makefile named **GNUmakefile**, **makefile**, or **Makefile** in the working directory.

```
$ make analysis
cc -c analy.c
cc -c stats.c
cc -o analysis analy.o stats.o
```

The following example also updates **analysis** but uses a makefile named **analysis.mk** in the working directory:

```
$ make -f analysis.mk analysis
'analysis' is up to date.
```

The next example lists the commands make would execute to bring the ***target-file*** named **credit** up-to-date. Because of the **–n** option, make does not execute the commands.

```
$ make -n credit
cc -c -O credit.c
cc -c -O accounts.c
cc -c -O terms.c
cc -o credit credit.c accounts.c terms.c
```

The next example uses the **–t** option to update the modification time of the ***target-file*** named **credit**. After you use this option, make thinks that **credit** is up-to-date.

```
$ make -t credit
$ make credit
'credit' is up to date.
```

Example makefiles

Following is a very simple makefile named **Makefile**. This makefile compiles a program named **morning** (the target file). The first line is a dependency line that shows **morning** depends on **morning.c**. The next line is the construction line: It shows how to create **morning** using the gcc C compiler. The construction line must be indented using a TAB, not SPACEs.

```
$ cat Makefile
morning: morning.c
TAB gcc -o morning morning.c
```

When you give the command **make**, make compiles **morning.c** if it has been modified more recently than **morning**.

The next example is a simple makefile for building a utility named ff. Because the cc command needed to build ff is complex, using a makefile allows you to rebuild ff easily, without having to remember and retype the cc command.

```
$ cat Makefile
# Build the ff command from the fastfind.c source
SHELL=/bin/sh

ff:
gcc -traditional -O2 -g -DBIG=5120 -o ff fastfind.c myClib.a

$ make ff
gcc -traditional -O2 -g -DBIG=5120 -o ff fastfind.c myClib.a
```

In the next example, a makefile keeps the file named **compute** up-to-date. The make utility ignores comment lines (lines that begin with a hashmark [#]); the first three lines of the following makefile are comment lines. The first dependency line shows that **compute** depends on two object files: **compute.o** and **calc.o**. The corresponding construction line gives the command make needs to produce **compute**. The second dependency line shows that **compute.o** depends not only on its C source file but also on the **compute.h** header file. The construction line here for **compute.o** uses the C compiler optimizer (**–O3** option). The third set of dependency and construction lines is not required. In their absence, make infers that **calc.o** depends on **calc.c** and produces the command line needed for the compilation.

```
$ cat Makefile
#
# Makefile for compute
#
compute: compute.o calc.o
        gcc -o compute compute.o calc.o

compute.o: compute.c compute.h
        gcc -c -O3 compute.c

calc.o: calc.c
        gcc -c calc.c

clean:
    rm *.o *core* *~
```

There are no prerequisites for **clean**, the last target. This target is often used to remove extraneous files that might be out-of-date or no longer needed, such as **.o** files.

The next example shows a much more sophisticated makefile that uses features not discussed in this section. Refer to the sources cited under "Documentation" on page 893 for information about these and other advanced features.

```
$ cat Makefile
############################################################
## build and maintain the buffer library
############################################################
SHELL=/bin/sh

############################################################
## Flags and libraries for compiling. The XLDLIBS are needed
#   whenever you build a program using the library. The CCFLAGS
#   give maximum optimization.
CC=gcc
CCFLAGS=-O2 $(CFLAGS)
XLDLIBS= -lXaw3d -lXt -lXmu -lXext -lX11 -lm
BUFLIB=libbuf.a

############################################################
## Miscellaneous
INCLUDES=buf.h
XINCLUDES=xtbuff_ad.h
OBJS=buff.o buf_print.o xtbuff.o

############################################################
## Just a 'make' generates a help message
help:   Help
        @echo "You can make the following:"
        @echo " "
        @echo " libbuf.a        -- the buffer library"
```

```
        @echo " bufdisplay      -- display any-format buffer"
        @echo " buf2ppm         -- convert buffer to pixmap"
############################################################
## The main target is the library
libbuf.a:  $(OBJS)
    -/bin/rm libbuf.a

    ar rv libbuf.a $(OBJS)
    ranlib libbuf.a
############################################################
## Secondary targets -- utilities built from the library
bufdisplay: bufdisplay.c libbuf.a
    $(CC) $(CCFLAGS) bufdisplay.c -o bufdisplay $(BUFLIB) $(XLDLIBS)

buf2ppm: buf2ppm.c libbuf.a
    $(CC) $(CCFLAGS) buf2ppm.c -o buf2ppm $(BUFLIB)


############################################################
## Build the individual object units
buff.o: $(INCLUDES) buff.c
    $(CC) -c $(CCFLAGS) buff.c

buf_print.o:$(INCLUDES) buf_print.c
    $(CC) -c $(CCFLAGS) buf_print.c

xtbuff.o: $(INCLUDES) $(XINCLUDES) xtbuff.c
    $(CC) -c $(CCFLAGS) xtbuff.c
```

The make utility can be used for tasks other than compiling code. As a final example, assume you have a database that lists IP addresses and the corresponding hostnames in two columns; also assume the database dumps these values to a file named **hosts.tab**. You need to extract only the hostnames from this file and generate a Web page named **hosts.html** containing these names. The following makefile is a simple report writer:

```
$ cat makefile
#
SHELL=/bin/bash
#
hosts.html: hosts.tab
        @echo "<HTML><BODY>" > hosts.html
        @awk '{print $$2, "<br>"}' hosts.tab >> hosts.html
        @echo "</BODY></HTML>" >> hosts.html
```

man

Displays documentation for utilities

man [options] [section] command
man –k keyword

The man (manual) utility provides online documentation for Linux and macOS utilities. In addition to utilities, documentation is available for many system commands and details that relate to Linux and macOS. Because many Linux and macOS utilities come from GNU, the GNU info utility (page 36) frequently provides more complete information about them.

A one-line header is associated with each manual page. This header consists of a utility name, the section of the manual in which the command is found, and a brief description of what the utility does. These headers are stored in a database, enabling you to perform quick searches on keywords associated with each man page.

Arguments

The ***section*** argument tells man to limit its search to the specified section of the manual (see page 34 for a listing of manual sections). Without this argument man searches the sections in numerical order and displays the first man page it finds. In the second form of the man command, the **–k** option searches for the ***keyword*** in the database of man page headers; man displays a list of headers that contain the ***keyword***. A **man –k** command performs the same function as apropos (page 35).

Options

Options preceded by a double hyphen (––) work under Linux only. Not all options preceded by a double hyphen work under all Linux distributions. Options named with a single letter and preceded by a single hyphen work under Linux and macOS.

––all **–a** Displays man pages for all sections of the manual. Without this option man displays only the first page it finds. Use this option when you are not sure which section contains the desired information.

–K *keyword*
Searches for ***keyword*** in all man pages. This option can take a long time to run. It is not available under some Linux distributions.

––apropos **–k *keyword***
Displays manual page headers that contain the string ***keyword***. You can scan this list for commands of interest. This option is equivalent to the apropos command (page 35).

––manpath=*path* **–M *path***
Searches the directories in ***path*** for man pages, where ***path*** is a colon-separated list of directories. See "Discussion."

––troff **–t** Formats the page for printing on a PostScript printer. The output goes to standard output.

Discussion

The manual pages are organized into sections, each pertaining to a separate aspect of the Linux system. Section 1 contains user-callable utilities and is the section most likely to be accessed by users who are not system administrators or programmers. Other sections of the manual describe system calls, library functions, and commands used by system administrators. See page 34 for a listing of the manual sections.

Pager The man utility uses less (page 873) to display manual pages that fill more than one screen. To use another pager, set the environment variable **PAGER** to the pathname of that pager. For example, adding the following line to the **~/.bash_profile** file sets up a bash user to use more instead of less:

```
export PAGER=$(which more)
```

This statement assigns the pathname of the more utility [**$(which more)** returns the absolute pathname of the more utility] to the environment variable **PAGER**. Under macOS, less and more are copies of the same file. Because of the way each is called, they work slightly differently.

MANPATH You can tell man where to look for man pages by setting the environment variable **MANPATH** to a colon-separated list of directories. For example, bash users running Linux can add the following line to **~/.bash_profile** to cause man to search the **/usr/man**, **/usr/local/man**, and **/usr/local/share/man** directories:

```
export MANPATH=/usr/man:/usr/local/man:/usr/local/share/man
```

Working as a privileged user, you can edit **/etc/manpath.config** or **/etc/man.config** (Linux) or **/etc/man.conf** (macOS) to further configure man. Refer to the man man page for more information.

Notes

See page 33 for another discussion of man.

The argument to man does not have to be the name of a utility. For example, the command **man ascii** lists the ASCII characters and their various representations; the command **man –k postscript** lists man pages that pertain to PostScript.

The man pages are commonly stored in an unformatted, compressed form. When you request a man page, it has to be decompressed and formatted before being displayed. To speed up subsequent requests for that man page, man attempts to save the formatted version of the page.

Some utilities described in the manual pages have the same name as shell builtin commands. The behavior of the shell builtin might differ slightly from the behavior of the utility as described in the manual page. For information about shell builtins, see the man page for **builtin** or the man page for a specific shell.

References to man pages frequently use section numbers in parentheses. For example, **write(2)** refers to the man page for **write** in section 2 of the manual (page 34).

The first of the following commands uses the col utility to generate a simple text man page that does not include bold or underlined text. The second command generates a PostScript version of the man page.

```
$ man ls | col -b > ls.txt
$ man -t ls > ls.ps
```

Under Linux you can use ps2pdf to convert the PostScript file to a PDF file.

Examples

The following example uses man to display the documentation for the write utility, which sends messages to another user's terminal:

```
$ man write
WRITE(1)                    User Commands                   WRITE(1)

NAME
       write - send a message to another user

SYNOPSIS
       write user [ttyname]

DESCRIPTION
       Write  allows you to communicate with other users, by copying
       lines from your terminal to theirs.

       When you run the write command, the user you are  writing  to
       gets a message of the form:

              Message from yourname@yourhost on yourtty at hh:mm ...
...
```

The next example displays the man page for another utility—the man utility itself, which is a good starting place for someone learning about the system:

```
$ man man
MAN(1)                   Manual pager utils                   MAN(1)

NAME
       man - an interface to the on-line reference manuals

SYNOPSIS
       man [-C file] [-d] [-D] [--warnings[=warnings]] [-R encoding]
       [-L locale] [-m system[,...]] [-M path] [-S list] [-e  exten-
       sion]  [-i|-I]  [--regex|--wildcard] [--names-only] [-a] [-u]
       [--no-subpages] [-P pager] [-r  prompt]  [-7]  [-E  encoding]
       ...

DESCRIPTION
       man is the system's manual pager. Each page argument given to
       man  is  normally the name of a program, utility or function.
```

```
The manual page associated with each of  these  arguments  is
...
```

You can also use the man utility to find the man pages that pertain to a topic. In the next example, **man –k** displays man page headers containing the string **latex**. The apropos utility functions similarly to **man –k**.

```
$ man -k latex
elatex (1) [latex]    - structured text formatting and typesetting
latex (1)             - structured text formatting and typesetting
mkindex (1)           - script to process LaTeX index and glossary files
pdflatex (1)          - PDF output from TeX
pod2latex (1)         - convert pod documentation to latex format
Pod::LaTeX (3pm)      - Convert Pod data to formatted Latex
...
```

The search for the keyword entered with the **–k** option is not case sensitive. Although the keyword entered on the command line is all lowercase, it matches the last header, which contains the string **LaTeX** (uppercase and lowercase). The **3pm** entry on the last line indicates the man page is from Section 3 (Subroutines) of the Linux System Manual and comes from the *Perl Programmers Reference Guide* (it is a Perl subroutine; see Chapter 11 for more information on the Perl programming language).

mc

Manages files in a textual environment (aka Midnight Commander)

mc [options] [dirL [dirR]]

Midnight Commander is a full-screen textual user shell that includes a comprehensive file manager; a simple editor; and FTP, SSH, and Samba clients.

Arguments

The *dirL* and *dirR* are the names of the directories Midnight Commander displays in the left and right panels, respectively. When called without arguments, Midnight Commander displays in both panels the working directory of the shell it was called from.

Options

This section describes a few of the many options Midnight Commander accepts. See the mc man page for a complete list. You can set many options from the Options menu on the menubar (page 905).

––stickcars **–a** Disables the display of graphical characters for drawing lines.

––nocolor **–b** Displays Midnight Commander in black and white.

––color **–c** Displays Midnight Commander in color if the device it is running on is capable of displaying color.

––nomouse **–d** Disables support for the mouse.

––version **–V** Displays version and build information.

Notes

Midnight Commander (www.midnight-commander.org) was written in 1994 by Miguel de Icaza. It has a comprehensive man page (mc). Current versions of Midnight Commander accept mouse input (which this section does not discuss).

The Midnight Commander input lines approximate standard emacs commands and the Midnight Commander documentation uses the same key notation as emacs; see page 231 for more information.

By default Midnight Commander uses its internal editor. Select **Options⇨Configuration** to display the Configure options window (Figure VI-5; page 906) and remove the tick from the check box labeled **Use internal edit** to use a different editor. When Midnight Commander does not use its internal editor, it uses the editor specified by the **EDITOR** environment variable. If **EDITOR** is not set, it uses vi (which is typically linked to vim).

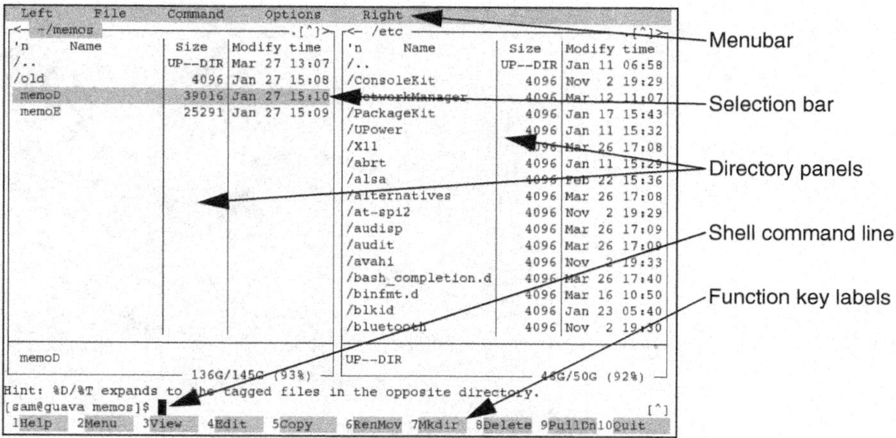

Figure VI-1 The basic Midnight Commander screen

The Display

As shown in Figure VI-1, the Midnight Commander screen is divided into four sections, the two largest occupied by the directory panels. The top line holds the menubar; if it is not visible, press F9. The next-to-bottom line holds the shell command line and the bottom line holds the function key labels. Function key labels change depending on context.

The current directory panel holds the selection bar (the highlight that runs the width of the panel), which specifies the current file. Most commands work on the current file; some commands, such as those that copy or move a file, use the directory displayed in the second panel as the target.

Moving the Cursor

This section describes some of the ways you can move the cursor from the directory panel and the menubar.

In the current directory panel

- UP ARROW (or CONTROL-P) and DOWN ARROW (or CONTROL-N) keys move the selection bar up and down, respectively.
- TAB moves the selection bar to the second panel and makes the second panel the current panel.
- F1 displays the Help window (Figure VI-2). Exactly what F1 displays depends on the context in which it is used.
- F2 displays the User menu (Figure VI-3).
- F9 moves the cursor to the menubar (Figure VI-4; page 905).
- F10 exits from Midnight Commander or closes a window if one is open.
- Typing a command enters the command on the shell command line.

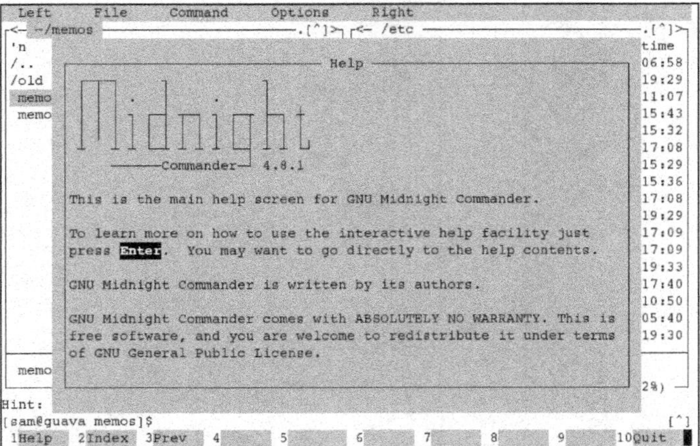

Figure VI-2 The Help window (F1)

- Other function keys open windows as specified on the bottom line.

With an entry on the menubar highlighted (after pressing F9)

- RIGHT ARROW and LEFT ARROW keys move the cursor from menu to menu.
- With no drop-down menu displayed, the DOWN ARROW or RETURN key opens the highlighted drop-down menu. Alternatively, you can type the initial letter of the menu to open it.

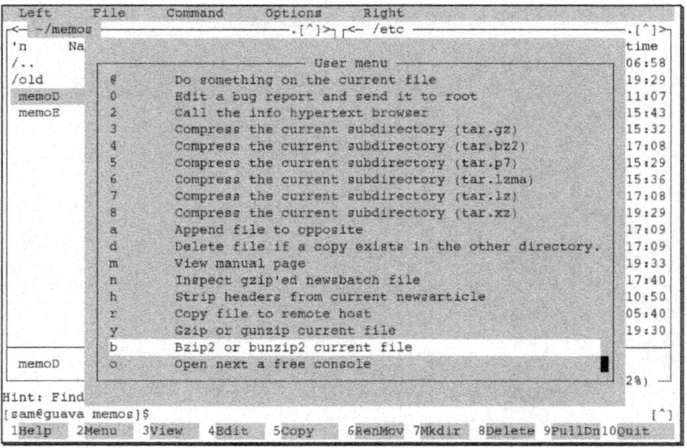

Figure VI-3 The User menu (F2)

- With a drop-down menu displayed, UP ARROW and DOWN ARROW keys move the highlight from menu item to menu item and RETURN selects the highlighted item. Alternatively, you can type the highlighted letter in an item to select it.

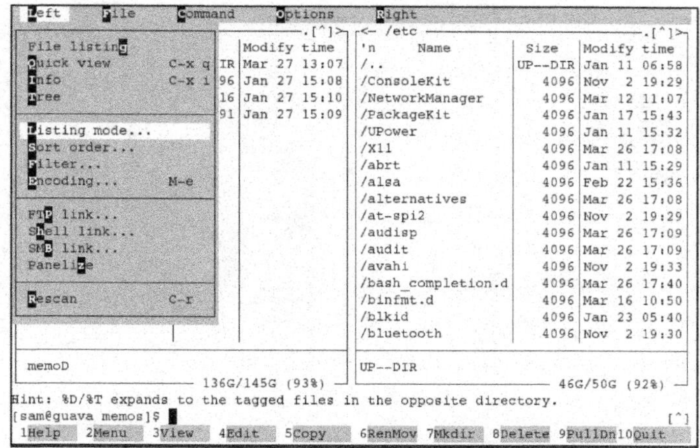

Figure VI-4 The menubar and the Left drop-down menu

Commands

This section describes giving commands by selecting menu items. You can also give commands by typing emacs-like commands at the shell command line. For example, CONTROL-X c (**C-x c** in emacs notation; page 231) runs chmod on the current file. See the mc man page for a complete list of Midnight Commander commands.

Menubar

The menubar, shown in Figure VI-4, holds five drop-down menus.

- **Left**—Changes the display and organization of the left directory panel, allowing you to control which information about each file is listed, the order in which the listed files are displayed, and more. This menu also enables you to open an FTP, OpenSSH, or Samba site.
- **File**—Allows you to view, edit, copy, move, link, rename, and delete the current file. Also allows you to change the mode (chmod), group, or owner of the current file. The function keys are shortcuts to many items on this menu.
- **Command**—Enables you to find, compress, compare, and list files in many ways.
- **Options**—Displays windows that allow you to configure Midnight Commander. One of the most useful is the Configure options window (Figure VI-5).
- **Right**—Performs the same functions as the Left menu except it works on the right directory panel.

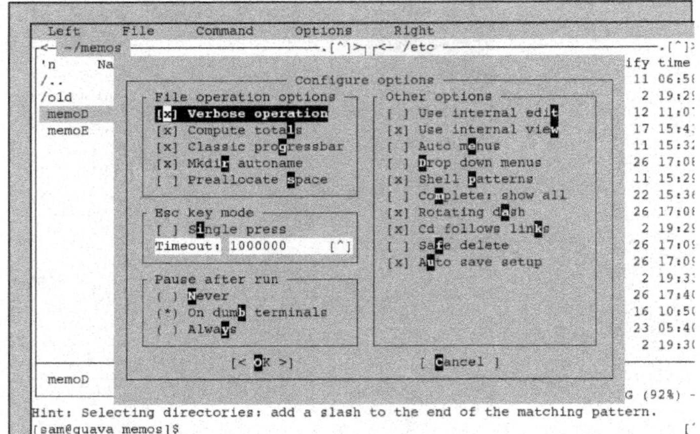

Figure VI-5 The Configure options window

Tutorial

This tutorial follows Sam as he works with Midnight Commander.

Changing directories Sam starts Midnight Commander from his home directory by giving the command **mc.** Midnight Commander displays a screen similar to the one shown in Figure VI-1 on page 903, except it shows his home directory in both directory panels; the selection bar is at the top of the left panel, over the **..** entry (page 95). Sam wants to display a list of the files in the **memos** subdirectory of his home directory, so he presses the DOWN ARROW key several times until the selection bar is over **memos**. Then he presses RETURN to display the contents of the **memos** directory in the left panel. Midnight Commander displays the name of the directory it is displaying (**~/memos**) at the upper-left corner of the panel.

Viewing a file Next, Sam wants to look at the contents of the **memoD** file in the **memos** directory; he uses the DOWN ARROW key to move the selection bar until it is over **memoD** and presses F3 (View). Because it is a long text file, Sam uses the SPACE bar to scroll through the file; Midnight Commander displays information about which part of the file it is displaying at the top of the screen. The function key labels on the last line change to tasks that are useful while viewing a file (e.g., edit, hex, save). When Sam is done viewing the file, he presses F10 (Quit) to close the view window and redisplay the panels.

Copying a file Sam wants to copy **memoD**, but he is not sure which directory he wants to copy it to. He makes the right directory panel the active panel by pressing TAB; the selection bar moves to the right panel, which is still displaying his home directory. Sam moves the selection bar until it is over the name of the directory he wants to examine and presses RETURN. When he is satisfied that this directory is the one he wants to copy **memoD** to, he presses TAB again to move the selection bar back to the left panel, where it is once again over **memoD**. Next, he presses F5 (Copy) to display the Copy window (Figure VI-6) and presses RETURN to copy the file.

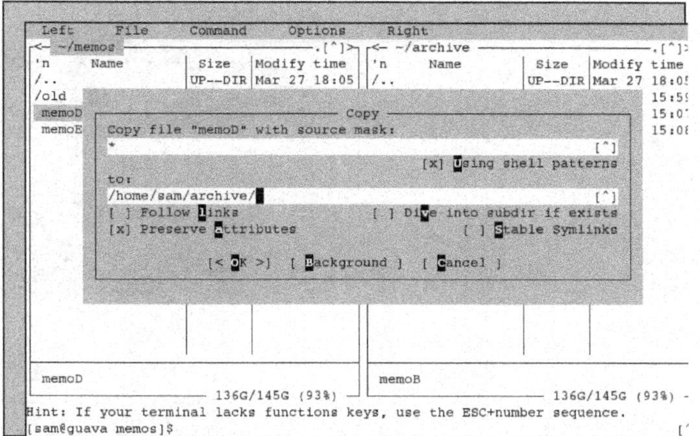

Figure VI-6 The Copy window

Using FTP Next, Sam wants to look at some files on the ftp.kernel.org FTP site, so he presses F9 (PullDn) to move the cursor to the menubar; Midnight Commander highlights Left on the menubar. Sam presses RETURN to display the Left drop-down menu. Using the DOWN ARROW key, he moves the highlight down to the FTP link and presses RETURN; Midnight Commander displays the FTP to machine window (Figure VI-7). Sam presses RETURN to display the top level of the ftp.kernel.org site in the left directory panel. Now he can work with the files at this site as though they were local, copying files to the local system as needed.

The hotlist Because Sam visits ftp.kernel.org frequently, he decides to add it to his hotlist. You can add any directory, local or remote, to your hotlist. With ftp.kernel.org displayed in the left panel, Sam enters CONTROL-\ to open the Directory hotlist window and presses **A** to add the current directory to the hotlist. Midnight Commander displays a small Add to hotlist window and Sam presses RETURN to confirm he wants to add the directory to his hotlist. Now ftp.kernel.org is in the hotlist; Sam presses F10 (Quit) to close the Directory hotlist window.

Because Sam is done working with ftp.kernel.org, he types **cd** (followed by a RETURN); the command appears on the shell command line and the left panel displays his home directory. When Sam wants to display the files at ftp.kernel.org, he can give the command CONTROL-\ to display the Directory hotlist window, move the highlight until it is over ftp.kernel.org, and press RETURN.

This tutorial covers a very small selection of Midnight Commander commands. Use the Midnight Commander help key (F1) and the mc man page to learn about other commands.

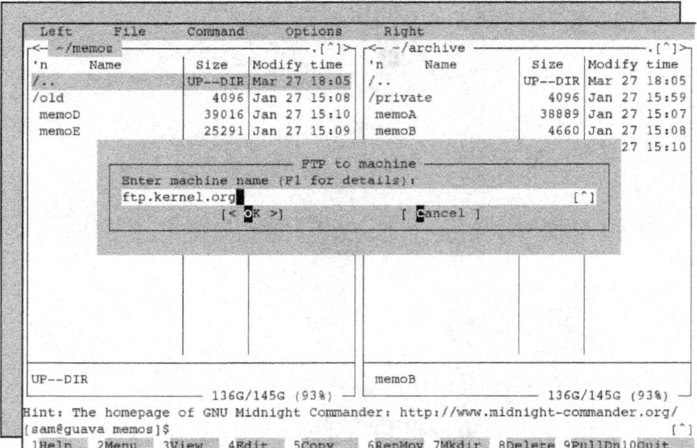

Figure 6-7 The FTP to machine window

mkdir

Creates a directory

mkdir [options] directory-list

The mkdir utility creates one or more directories.

Arguments

The ***directory-list*** is a list of pathnames of directories that mkdir creates.

Options

Under Linux, mkdir accepts the common options described on page 736. Options preceded by a double hyphen (––) work under Linux only. Options named with a single letter and preceded by a single hyphen work under Linux and macOS.

––mode=*mode* **–m *mode***
Sets the permission to ***mode***. You can represent the ***mode*** absolutely using an octal number (Table VI-7 on page 760) or symbolically (Table VI-4 on page 759).

––parents **–p** Creates directories that do not exist in the path to the directory you wish to create.

––verbose **–v** Displays the name of each directory created. This option is helpful when used with the –p option.

Notes

You must have permission to write to and search (execute permission) the parent directory of the directory you are creating. The mkdir utility creates directories that contain the standard hidden entries (. and ..).

Examples

The following command creates the **accounts** directory as a subdirectory of the working directory and the **prospective** directory as a subdirectory of **accounts**:

```
$ mkdir -p accounts/prospective
```

Without changing working directories, the same user now creates another subdirectory within the **accounts** directory:

```
$ mkdir accounts/existing
```

Next, the user changes the working directory to the **accounts** directory and creates one more subdirectory:

```
$ cd accounts
$ mkdir closed
```

The last example shows the user creating another subdirectory. This time the **--mode** option removes all access permissions for the group and others:

```
$ mkdir -m go= accounts/past_due
```

mkfs

Creates a filesystem on a device

mkfs [options] device

The mkfs utility creates a filesystem on a device such as a flash drive or a partition of a hard disk. It acts as a front end for programs that create filesystems, each specific to a filesystem type. The mkfs utility is available under Linux only. LINUX

mkfs destroys all data on a device

caution Be careful when using mkfs: It destroys all data on a device or partition.

Arguments

The *device* is the name of the device that you want to create the filesystem on. If the device name is in **/etc/fstab**, you can use the mount point of the device instead of the device name (e.g., **/home** in place of **/dev/sda2**).

Options

When you run mkfs, you can specify both global options and options specific to the filesystem type that mkfs is creating (e.g., **ext2**, **ext3**, **ext4**, **msdos**, **reiserfs**). Global options must precede type-specific options.

Global Options

–t *fstype*

(type) The *fstype* is the type of filesystem you want to create—for example, **ext3**, **ext4**, **msdos**, or **reiserfs**. The default filesystem varies.

–v (verbose) Displays more output. Use **–V** for filesystem-specific information.

Filesystem Type-Specific Options

The options described in this section apply to many common filesystem types, including **ext2/ext3/ext4**. The following command lists the filesystem creation utilities available on the local system:

```
$ ls /sbin/mkfs.*
/sbin/mkfs.btrfs   /sbin/mkfs.ext3     /sbin/mkfs.msdos  /sbin/mkfs.xfs
/sbin/mkfs.cramfs  /sbin/mkfs.ext4     /sbin/mkfs.ntfs
/sbin/mkfs.ext2    /sbin/mkfs.ext4dev  /sbin/mkfs.vfat
```

There is frequently a link to **/sbin/mkfs.ext2** at **/sbin/mke2fs**. Review the man page or give the pathname of the filesystem creation utility to determine which options the utility accepts.

```
$ /sbin/mkfs.ext4
Usage: mkfs.ext4 [-c|-l filename] [-b block-size] [-f fragment-size]
        [-i bytes-per-inode] [-I inode-size] [-J journal-options]
        [-G meta group size] [-N number-of-inodes]
        [-m reserved-blocks-percentage] [-o creator-os]
        [-g blocks-per-group] [-L volume-label] [-M last-mounted-directory]
```

```
[-O feature[,...]] [-r fs-revision] [-E extended-option[,...]]
[-T fs-type] [-U UUID] [-jnqvFKSV] device [blocks-count]
```

–b ***size***
(**block**) Specifies the size of blocks in bytes. On **ext2**, **ext3**, and **ext4** filesystems, valid block sizes are 1,024, 2,048, and 4,096 bytes.

–c (**check**) Checks for bad blocks on the device before creating a filesystem. Specify this option twice to perform a slow, destructive, read-write test.

Discussion

Before you can write to and read from a hard disk or other device in the usual fashion, there must be a filesystem on it. Typically, a hard disk is divided into *partitions* (page 1115), each with a separate filesystem. A flash drive normally holds a single filesystem. Refer to Chapter 4 for more information on filesystems.

Notes

Under macOS, use diskutil (page 800) to create a filesystem.

You can use tune2fs (page 1018) with the –j option to change an existing **ext2** filesystem into a *journaling filesystem* (page 1105) of type **ext3**. (See the "Examples" section.) You can also use tune2fs to change how often fsck (page 833) checks a filesystem.

mkfs is a front end Much like fsck, mkfs is a front end that calls other utilities to handle various types of filesystems. For example, mkfs calls mke2fs (which is typically linked to mkfs.ext2, mkfs.ext3, and mkfs.ext4) to create the widely used **ext2/ext3/ext4** filesystems. Refer to the mke2fs man page for more information. Other utilities that mkfs calls are typically named **mkfs.*type***, where ***type*** is the filesystem type. By splitting mkfs in this manner, filesystem developers can provide programs to create their filesystems without affecting the development of other filesystems or changing how system administrators use mkfs.

Examples

In the following example, mkfs creates a default filesystem on the device at **/dev/sda2**:

```
# mkfs /dev/sda2
mke2fs 1.43.4 (31-Jan-2017)
Filesystem label=
OS type: Linux
Block size=1024 (log=0)
Fragment size=1024 (log=0)
Stride=0 blocks, Stripe width=0 blocks
128016 inodes, 512000 blocks
25600 blocks (5.00%) reserved for the super user
First data block=1
Maximum filesystem blocks=67633152
63 block groups
8192 blocks per group, 8192 fragments per group
2032 inodes per group
Superblock backups stored on blocks:
        8193, 24577, 40961, 57345, 73729, 204801, 221185, 401409

Writing inode tables: done
Writing superblocks and filesystem accounting information: done
```

```
This filesystem will be automatically checked every 22 mounts or
180 days, whichever comes first.  Use tune2fs -c or -i to override.
```

The next command writes a VFAT filesystem to a USB flash drive at **/dev/sdb1**:

```
# mkfs -t vfat /dev/sdb1
mkfs.vfat 4.1 (2017-01-24)
```

See page 1020 for an example that uses tune2fs to convert an **ext2** filesystem to an **ext3** journaling filesystem.

mv

Renames or moves a file

mv [options] existing-file new-filename
mv [options] existing-file-list directory
mv [options] existing-directory new-directory

The mv utility, which renames or moves one or more files, has three formats. The first renames a single file with a new filename that you supply. The second renames one or more files so that they appear in a specified directory. The third renames a directory. The mv utility physically moves (copies and deletes) the original file if it is not possible to rename it (that is, if you move the file from one filesystem to another).

Arguments

In the first form, the ***existing-file*** is a pathname of the ordinary file you want to rename. The ***new-filename*** is the new pathname of the file.

In the second form, the ***existing-file-list*** is a list of the pathnames of the files you want to rename and the ***directory*** specifies the new parent directory for the files. The files you rename will have the same simple filenames as each of the files in the ***existing-file-list*** but new absolute pathnames.

The third form renames the ***existing-directory*** with the ***new-directory*** name. This form works only when the ***new-directory*** does not exist.

Options

Under Linux, mv accepts the common options described on page 736. Options preceded by a double hyphen (––) work under Linux only. Except as noted, options named with a single letter and preceded by a single hyphen work under Linux and macOS.

––backup **–b** Makes a backup copy (by appending ~ to the filename) of any file that would be overwritten. LINUX

––force **–f** Causes mv *not* to prompt you if a move would overwrite an existing file that you do not have write permission for. You must have write permission for the directory holding the existing file.

––interactive **–i** Prompts for confirmation if mv would overwrite a file. If your response begins with a y or Y, mv overwrites the file; otherwise, mv does not move the file.

––update **–u** If a move would overwrite an existing file—not a directory—this option causes mv to compare the modification times of the source and target files. If the target file has a more recent modification time (the target is newer than the source), mv does not replace it. LINUX

––verbose **–v** Lists files as they are moved.

Notes

When GNU mv copies a file from one filesystem to another, mv is implemented as cp (with the –a option) and rm: It first copies the ***existing-file*** to the ***new-file*** and then deletes the ***existing-file***. If the ***new-file*** already exists, mv might delete it before copying.

As with rm, you must have write and execute access permissions to the parent directory of the ***existing-file***, but you do not need read or write access permission to the file itself. If the move would overwrite a file that you do not have write permission for, mv displays the file's access permissions and waits for a response. If you enter y or Y, mv overwrites the file; otherwise, it does not move the file. If you use the –f option, mv does not prompt you for a response but simply overwrites the file.

Although earlier versions of mv could move only ordinary files between filesystems, mv can now move any type of file, including directories and device files.

Examples

The first command renames **letter**, a file in the working directory, as **letter.1201**:

```
$ mv letter letter.1201
```

The next command renames the file so it appears with the same simple filename in the user's **~/archives** directory:

```
$ mv letter.1201 ~/archives
```

The following command moves all files in the working directory whose names begin with **memo** so they appear in the **/p04/backup** directory:

```
$ mv memo* /p04/backup
```

Using the **–u** option prevents mv from replacing a newer file with an older one. After the **mv –u** command shown below is executed, the newer file (**memo2**) has not been overwritten. The **mv** command without the **–u** option overwrites the newer file (**memo2**'s modification time and size have changed to those of **memo1**).

```
$ ls -l
-rw-rw-r--  1 sam sam 22 03-25 23:34 memo1
-rw-rw-r--  1 sam sam 19 03-25 23:40 memo2
$ mv -u memo1 memo2
$ ls -l
-rw-rw-r--  1 sam sam 22 03-25 23:34 memo1
-rw-rw-r--  1 sam sam 19 03-25 23:40 memo2
$ mv memo1 memo2
$ ls -l
-rw-rw-r--  1 sam sam 22 03-25 23:34 memo2
```

nice

Changes the priority of a command

nice [option] [command-line]

The nice utility reports the priority of the shell or alters the priority of a command. An ordinary user can decrease the priority of a command, but only a user working with **root** privileges can increase the priority of a command. The nice builtin in the TC Shell uses a different syntax. Refer to the "Notes" section for more information.

Arguments

The ***command-line*** is the command line you want to execute at a different priority. Without any options or arguments, nice displays the priority of the shell running nice.

Options

Without an option, nice defaults to an adjustment of 10, lowering the priority of the command by 10—typically from 0 to 10. As you raise the priority value, the command runs at a lower priority.

The option preceded by a double hyphen (––) works under Linux only. The option named with a single letter and preceded by a single hyphen works under Linux and macOS.

––adjustment=*value*

–n *value*

Changes the priority by the increment (or decrement) specified by ***value***. The priorities range from –20 (the highest priority) to 19 (the lowest priority). A positive ***value*** lowers the priority, whereas a negative ***value*** raises the priority. Only a user working with **root** privileges can specify a negative ***value***. When you specify a value outside this range, the priority is set to the limit of the range.

Notes

You can use renice (page 951) or top's r command (page 1010) to change the priority of a running process.

Higher (more positive) priority values mean that the kernel schedules a job less often. Lower (more negative) values cause the job to be scheduled more often.

When a user working with **root** privileges schedules a job to run at the highest priority, this change can affect the performance of the system for all other jobs, including the operating system itself. For this reason you should be careful when using nice with negative values.

The TC Shell includes a nice builtin. Under tcsh, use the following syntax to change the priority at which ***command-line*** is run. The default priority is 4. You must include the plus sign for positive values.

*nice [±**value**] **command line***

The tcsh nice builtin works differently from the nice utility: When you use the builtin, **nice –5** decrements the priority at which ***command-line*** is run. When you use the utility, **nice –n –5** increments the priority at which ***command-line*** is run.

Examples

The following command executes find in the background at the lowest possible priority. The ps –l command displays the nice value of the command in the **NI** column:

```
# nice -n 19 find / -name core -print > corefiles.out &
[1] 422
# ps -l
F S   UID   PID  PPID  C PRI  NI ADDR SZ WCHAN  TTY          TIME CMD
4 R     0   389  8657  0  80   0 -  4408 -      pts/4    00:00:00 bash
4 D     0   422   389 28  99  19 -  1009 -      pts/4    00:00:04 find
0 R     0   433   389  0  80   0 -  1591 -      pts/4    00:00:00 ps
```

The next command finds very large files and runs at a high priority (–15):

```
# nice -n -15 find / -size +50000k
```

nl

Numbers lines from a file

nl [options] file-list

The nl utility reads files and sequentially numbers some or all of the lines before sending them to standard output. It does not change the files it reads.

Arguments

The ***file-list*** is a list of the pathnames of one or more files that nl reads. If you do not specify an argument or if you specify a hyphen (–) in place of a filename, nl reads from standard input.

Options

Under Linux, nl accepts the common options described on page 736. Options preceded by a double hyphen (––) work under Linux only. Except as noted, options named with a single letter and preceded by a single hyphen work under Linux and macOS.

––body-numbering=a | p*RE*
–b a | p*RE*
Specifies which lines nl numbers; use **a** to number all lines or **p** followed by a basic regular expression (Appendix A) to number lines that match that regular expression. By default nl numbers nonblank lines only.

––number-format=ln | rn | rz
–n ln | rn | rz
Specifies the line number style; use **ln** to left-justify line numbers without leading zeros (no fill), **rn** to right-justify line numbers without leading zeros (default), or **rz** to right-justify line numbers with leading zeros (zero fill).

––number-separator=*stg*
–s *stg*
Separates line numbers from the text using the characters in ***stg***. Default separator is a TAB.

––number-width=*num*
–w *num*
Sets the width of the line number field to ***num*** characters. Default is 6 characters.

Notes

The nl utility has many options including ones that can start renumbering at the top of each page and ones that can number headers, footers, and the body of a document separately. Give the command **info coreutils 'nl invocation'** for more information.

Examples

When called without options, nl numbers all nonblank lines.

```
$ nl lines
     1  He was not candid. He lacked a certain warmth so that you

     2  always felt chilled and uncomfortable in his presence.
```

With the **–b** (**––body-numbering**) option set to **a,** nl numbers all lines.

```
$ nl -b a lines
     1  He was not candid. He lacked a certain warmth so that you
     2
     3  always felt chilled and uncomfortable in his presence.
```

With the **–n** (**––number-format**) option set to **ln,** nl left-justifies numbers.

```
$ nl -n ln lines
1       He was not candid. He lacked a certain warmth so that you

2       always felt chilled and uncomfortable in his presence.
```

You can combine options. The following example right-justifies and zero-fills (**–n rz**) within a field of three characters (**–w** 3) all lines (**–b a**) and separates the numbers from the lines using two SPACEs (**–s** ' ').

```
$ nl -n rz -w 3 -b a -s '  ' lines
001  He was not candid. He lacked a certain warmth so that you
002
003  always felt chilled and uncomfortable in his presence.
```

The final example numbers lines that contain the word **and.** Within a regular expression (Appendix A), **\<** forces a match to the beginning of a word and **\>** forces a match to the end of a word so the regular expression **\<and\>** matches only the word **and** and does not match the string **and** within the word **candid.**

```
$ nl -b p'\<and\>' lines
       He was not candid. He lacked a certain warmth so that you

     1  always felt chilled and uncomfortable in his presence.
```

nohup

Runs a command that keeps running after you log out

nohup command line

The nohup utility executes a command line such that the command keeps running after you log out. In other words, nohup causes a process to ignore a SIGHUP signal. Depending on how the local shell is configured, a process started without nohup and running in the background might be killed when you log out. The TC Shell includes a nohup builtin. Refer to the "Notes" section for more information.

Arguments

The ***command line*** is the command line you want to execute.

Notes

Under Linux, nohup accepts the common options described on page 736.

If you do not redirect the output from a command you execute using nohup, both standard output *and* standard error are sent to the file named **nohup.out** in the working directory. If you do not have write permission for the working directory, nohup sends output to **~/nohup.out**.

Unlike the nohup utility, the TC Shell's nohup builtin does not send output to **nohup.out**. Background jobs started from tcsh continue to run after you log out.

Examples

The following command executes find in the background, using nohup:

```
$ nohup find / -name core -print > corefiles.out &
[1] 14235
```

od

Dumps the contents of a file

od [options] [file-list]

The od (octal dump) utility dumps the contents of a file. The dump is useful for viewing executable (object) files and text files with embedded nonprinting characters. This utility takes its input from the file you specify on the command line or from standard input.

Arguments

The *file-list* specifies the pathnames of the files that od displays. When you do not specify a *file-list*, od reads from standard input.

Options

The od utility accepts the common options described on page 736. Options preceded by a double hyphen (––) work under Linux only. Options named with a single letter and preceded by a single hyphen work under Linux and macOS.

––address-radix=*base*
–A *base*
Specifies the base used when displaying the offsets shown for positions in the file. By default offsets are given in octal. Possible values for *base* are **d** (decimal), **o** (octal), **x** (hexadecimal), and **n** (no offsets displayed).

––skip-bytes=*n* **–j *n***
Skips *n* bytes before displaying data.

––read-bytes=*n* **–N *n***
Reads a maximum of *n* bytes and then quits.

––strings=*n* **–S *n***
Outputs from the file only those bytes that contain runs of *n* or more printable ASCII characters that are terminated by a NULL byte.

––format=*type[n]*
–t *type[n]*
Specifies the output format for displaying data from a file. You can repeat this option with different format *types* to see the file in several different formats. Table VI-22 lists the possible values for *type*. Table VI-23 lists the output format backslash escape sequences with type c.

By default od dumps a file as 2-byte octal numbers. You can specify the number of bytes od uses to compose each number by specifying a length indicator, *n*. You can specify a length indicator for all types except **a** and **c**. Table VI-24 (next page) lists the possible values of *n*.

Table VI-22 Output formats

type	**Type of output**
a	Named character: displays nonprinting control characters using their official ASCII names; for example, FORMFEED is displayed as ff
c	ASCII character: displays nonprinting control characters as backslash escape sequences (Table VI-23) or three-digit octal numbers
d	Signed decimal
f	Floating point
o	Octal (default)
u	Unsigned decimal
x	Hexadecimal

Table VI-23 Output format type **c** backslash escape sequences

Sequence	**Meaning**
\0	NULL
\a	BELL
\b	BACKSPACE
\f	FORMFEED
\n	NEWLINE
\r	RETURN
\t	HORIZONTAL TAB
\v	VERTICAL TAB

Table VI-24 Length indicators

n	**Number of bytes to use**
Integers (types d, o, u, and x)	
C (character)	Uses single characters for each decimal value
S (short integer)	Uses 2 bytes
I (integer)	Uses 4 bytes

Table VI-24 Length indicators (continued)

L (long)	Uses 4 bytes on 32-bit machines and 8 bytes on 64-bit machines
Floating point (type f)	
F (float)	Uses 4 bytes
D (double)	Uses 8 bytes
L (long double)	Typically uses 8 bytes

Notes

To retain backward compatibility with older, non-POSIX versions of od, the od utility includes the options listed in Table VI-25 as shorthand versions of many of the preceding options.

Table VI-25 Shorthand format specifications

Shorthand	Equivalent specification
–a	–t a
–b	–t oC
–c	–t c
–d	–t u2
–f	–t fF
–h	–t x2
–i	–t d2
–l	–t d4
–o	–t o2
–x	–t x2

Examples

The file ac, which is used in the following examples, contains all of the ASCII characters. In the first example, the bytes in this file are displayed as named characters. The first column shows the offset of the first byte on each line of output from the start of the file. The offsets are displayed as octal values.

```
$ od -t a ac
0000000 nul soh stx etx eot enq ack bel bs ht nl vt ff cr so si
0000020 dle dc1 dc2 dc3 dc4 nak syn etb can em sub esc fs gs rs us
0000040 sp ! " # $ % & ' ( ) * + , - . /
0000060 0 1 2 3 4 5 6 7 8 9 : ; < = > ?
0000100 @ A B C D E F G H I J K L M N O
0000120 P Q R S T U V W X Y Z [ \ ] ^ _
0000140 ` a b c d e f g h i j k l m n o
```

```
0000160 p q r s t u v w x y z { | } ~ del
0000200 nul soh stx etx eot enq ack bel bs ht nl vt ff cr so si
0000220 dle dc1 dc2 dc3 dc4 nak syn etb can em sub esc fs gs rs us
0000240 sp ! " # $ % & ' ( ) * + , - . /
0000260 0 1 2 3 4 5 6 7 8 9 : ; < = > ?
0000300 @ A B C D E F G H I J K L M N O
0000320 P Q R S T U V W X Y Z [ \ ] ^ _
0000340 ` a b c d e f g h i j k l m n o
0000360 p q r s t u v w x y z { | } ~ del
0000400 nl
0000401
```

In the next example, the bytes are displayed as octal numbers, ASCII characters, or printing characters preceded by a backslash (refer to Table VI-23 on page 922):

```
$ od -t c ac
0000000 \0 001 002 003 004 005 006 \a \b \t \n \v \f \r 016 017
0000020 020 021 022 023 024 025 026 027 030 031 032 033 034 035 036 037
0000040 ! " # $ % & ' ( ) * + , - . /
0000060 0 1 2 3 4 5 6 7 8 9 : ; < = > ?
0000100 @ A B C D E F G H I J K L M N O
0000120 P Q R S T U V W X Y Z [ \ ] ^ _
0000140 ` a b c d e f g h i j k l m n o
0000160 p q r s t u v w x y z { | } ~ 177
0000200 200 201 202 203 204 205 206 207 210 211 212 213 214 215 216 217
0000220 220 221 222 223 224 225 226 227 230 231 232 233 234 235 236 237
0000240 240 241 242 243 244 245 246 247 250 251 252 253 254 255 256 257
0000260 260 261 262 263 264 265 266 267 270 271 272 273 274 275 276 277
0000300 300 301 302 303 304 305 306 307 310 311 312 313 314 315 316 317
0000320 320 321 322 323 324 325 326 327 330 331 332 333 334 335 336 337
0000340 340 341 342 343 344 345 346 347 350 351 352 353 354 355 356 357
0000360 360 361 362 363 364 365 366 367 370 371 372 373 374 375 376 377
0000400 \n
0000401
```

The final example finds in the file **/usr/bin/who** all strings that are at least three characters long (the default) and are terminated by a null byte. See strings on page 986 for another way of displaying a similar list. The offset positions are given as decimal offsets.

```
$ od -A d -S 3 /usr/bin/who
...
0035151 GNU coreutils
0035165 en_
0035169 /usr/share/locale
0035187 Michael Stone
0035201 David MacKenzie
0035217 Joseph Arceneaux
0035234 who
0035238 abdlmpqrstuwHT
0035253 %Y-%m-%d %H:%M
0035268 %b %e %H:%M
0035280 extra operand %s
0035297 all
0035301 count
0035307 dead
```

```
0035312 heading
0035320 login
0035326 lookup
0035333 message
...
```

open macOS

Opens files, directories, and URLs

open [option] [file-list]

The open utility opens one or more files, directories, or URLs. The open utility is available under macOS only. macOS

Arguments

The *file-list* specifies the pathnames of the files, directories, or URLs that open is to open.

Options

Without any options, open opens the files in *file-list* as though you had double-clicked each of the files' icons in the Finder.

–a *application*
: Opens *file-list* using *application*. This option is equivalent to dragging *file-list* to the *application*'s icon in the Finder.

–b *bundle*
: Opens *file-list* using the application with bundle identifier *bundle*. A bundle identifier is a string, registered with the system, that identifies an application that can open files. For example, the bundle identifier **com.apple.TextEdit** specifies the TextEdit editor.

–e (**edit**) Opens *file-list* using the TextEdit application.

–F (**fresh**) Does not attempt to restore application windows that were open the last time you launched the application.

–f (**file**) Opens standard input as a file in the default text editor. This option does not accept *file-list*.

–g (**background**) Allows the application to run in the background.

–h (**header**) Finds and opens a header matching *file-list* using Xcode. Prompts if more than one header matches.

–n (**new**) Opens a new instance of the application even if one is already open.

–R (**reveal**) Shows the file in the Finder instead of opening the associated application.

–t (**text**) Opens *file-list* using the default text editor (see the "Discussion" section).

–W (**wait**) Does not display the shell prompt until you quit the application.

Discussion

Opening a file brings up the application associated with that file. For example, opening a disk image file mounts it. The open utility returns immediately, without waiting for the application to launch.

LaunchServices is a system framework that identifies applications that can open files. It maintains lists of available applications and user preferences about which application to use for each file type. LaunchServices also keeps track of the default text editor used by the **–t** and **–f** options.

Notes

When a file will be opened by a GUI application, you must run open from Terminal or another terminal emulator that is running under a GUI. Otherwise, the operation will fail.

Examples

The first example mounts the disk image file **backups.dmg**. The disk is mounted in **/Volumes**, using the name it was formatted with.

```
$ ls /Volumes
House   Spare   Lion
$ open backups.dmg
$ ls /Volumes
Backups   House     Spare     Lion
```

The next command opens the file **picture.jpg**. You must run this and the following example from a textual window within a GUI (e.g., Terminal). The application selected depends on the file attributes. If the file's type and creator code specify a particular application, open opens the file using that application. Otherwise, open uses the system's default program for handling **.jpg** files.

```
$ open picture.jpg
```

The next example opens the **/usr/bin** directory in the Finder. The **/usr** directory is normally hidden from the Finder because its **invisible** file attribute flag (page 1072) is set. However, the open utility can open any file you can access from the shell, even if it is not normally accessible from the Finder.

```
$ open /usr/bin
```

The next command opens **/usr/include/c++/4.2.1/tr1/stdio.h** in Xcode:

```
$ open -h stdio.h
```

When more than one header matches the argument you give with the **–h** option, open prompts to determine which you want to open:

```
$ open -h stdio
stdio?
[0]     cancel
[1]     all

[2]     /usr/include/c++/4.2.1/cstdio
[3]     /usr/include/c++/4.2.1/ext/stdio_filebuf.h
...
Which header(s) for "stdio"?
```

otool macOS

Displays object, library, and executable files

*otool **options file-list***

The otool utility displays information about, or part of, object, library, and executable files. The otool utility is available under macOS only. macOS

Arguments

The ***file-list*** specifies the pathnames of files that otool is to display.

Options

You must use at least one of the **–L**, **–M**, **–t**, or **–T** options to specify which part of each file in ***file-list*** otool is to display.

–L (**libraries**) Displays the names and version numbers of the shared libraries an object file uses.

–M (**module**) Displays the module table of a shared library.

–p ***name***
(**print**) Begins output at the symbol named ***name***. This option requires the **–t** option and either the **–v** or **–V** option.

–T (**table of contents**) Displays the table of contents of a shared library.

–t (**text**) Displays the TEXT section of an object file.

–V (**very verbose**) Displays even more data (than the **–v** option) symbolically. When displaying code, this option causes otool to display the names of called routines instead of their addresses.

–v (**verbose**) Displays data symbolically. When displaying code, this option causes otool to display the names of instructions instead of numeric codes.

Discussion

The otool utility displays information about the contents and dependencies of object files. This information can be helpful when you are debugging a program. For example, when you are setting up a chroot jail, otool can report which libraries are needed to run a given program.

Some options are useful only with certain types of object modules. For example, the –T option does not report anything for a typical executable file.

Notes

The otool utility is part of the Developer Tools optional install.

An **otool –L** command performs a function similar to the ldd utility on systems using the ELF binary format.

Examples

The examples in this section use the compiled version of the following C program:

```
$ cat myname.c
#include <stdio.h>
int main(void) {
    printf("My name is Sam.\n");
    return 0;
}
```

In the first example, otool displays the libraries the program is linked with:

```
$ otool -L myname
myname:
        /usr/lib/libmx.A.dylib (compatibility version 1.0.0, current version 92.0.0)
        /usr/lib/libSystem.B.dylib (compatibility version 1.0.0, current version 88.0.0)
```

In some cases, a library used by a program will depend on other libraries. You can use **otool –L** on a library to see whether it uses other libraries:

```
$ otool -L /usr/lib/libmx.A.dylib /usr/lib/libSystem.B.dylib
/usr/lib/libmx.A.dylib:
        /usr/lib/libmx.A.dylib (compatibility version 1.0.0, current version 92.0.0)
        /usr/lib/libSystem.B.dylib (compatibility version 1.0.0, current version 88.0.0)
/usr/lib/libSystem.B.dylib:
        /usr/lib/libSystem.B.dylib (compatibility version 1.0.0, current version 88.0.0)
        /usr/lib/system/libmathCommon.A.dylib (compatibility version 1.0.0, current ...
```

The next example disassembles the code for the **main** function. When compiling programs, the compiler sometimes modifies symbol names. The compiler gives functions, such as **main**, a leading underscore; thus, the symbol name is **_main**.

```
$ otool -Vt -p _main myname
myname:
(__TEXT,__text) section
_main:
00002ac0        mfspr   r0,lr
00002ac4        stmw    r30,0xfff8(r1)
00002ac8        stw     r0,0x8(r1)
00002acc        stwu    r1,0xffb0(r1)
00002ad0        or      r30,r1,r1
00002ad4        bcl     20,31,0x2ad8
00002ad8        mfspr   r31,lr
00002adc        addis   r2,r31,0x0
00002ae0        addi    r3,r2,0x4b8
00002ae4        bl      _printf$LDBLStub
00002ae8        li      r0,0x0
00002aec        or      r3,r0,r0
00002af0        lwz     r1,0x0(r1)
00002af4        lwz     r0,0x8(r1)
00002af8        mtspr   lr,r0
00002afc        lmw     r30,0xfff8(r1)
00002b00        blr
...
```

paste

Joins corresponding lines from files

paste [option] [file-list]

The paste utility reads lines from the ***file-list*** and joins corresponding lines in its output. By default output lines are separated by a TAB character.

Arguments

The ***file-list*** is a list of ordinary files. When you specify a hyphen (–) instead of a filename, paste reads from standard input.

Options

Under Linux, paste accepts the common options described on page 736. Options preceded by a double hyphen (––) work under Linux only. Options named with a single letter and preceded by a single hyphen work under Linux and macOS.

––delimiter=*dlist* –d *dlist*
: The ***dlist*** is a list of characters used to separate output fields. If ***dlist*** contains a single character, paste uses that character instead of the default TAB character to separate fields. If ***dlist*** contains more than one character, the characters are used in turn to separate fields and are then reused from the beginning of the list as necessary.

––serial –s
: Processes one file at a time; pastes horizontally. See the "Examples" section.

Notes

The paste utility is often used to rearrange the columns of a table. A utility, such as cut, can place the desired columns in separate files, and then paste can join them in any order.

Examples

The following example uses the files **fnames** and **acctinfo**. You can create these files using cut (page 784) and the **/etc/passwd** file. The paste command puts the full-name field first, followed by the remaining user account information. A TAB character separates the two output fields. Although this example works under macOS, **/etc/passwd** does not contain information about most users; see "Open Directory" on page 1068 for more information.

```
$ cat fnames
Sam the Great
Max Wild
Zach Brill
Helen Simpson

$ cat acctinfo
sam:x:401:50:/home/sam:/bin/zsh
max:x:402:50:/home/max:/bin/bash
zach:x:504:500:/home/zach:/bin/tcsh
hls:x:505:500:/home/hls:/bin/bash
```

```
$ paste fnames acctinfo
Sam the Great   sam:x:401:50:/home/sam:/bin/zsh
Max Wild        max:x:402:50:/home/max:/bin/bash
Zach Brill      zach:x:504:500:/home/zach:/bin/tcsh
Helen Simpson   hls:x:505:500:/home/hls:/bin/bash
```

The next examples use the files **p1**, **p2**, **p3**, and **p4**. In the last example in this group, the **–d** option gives paste a list of characters to use to separate output fields:

```
$ cat p1
1
one
ONE
$ cat p2
2
two
TWO
extra
$ cat p3
3
three
THREE
$ cat p4
4
four
FOUR

$ paste p4 p3 p2 p1
4       3       2       1
four    three   two     one
FOUR    THREE   TWO     ONE
                extra

$ paste -d="+-=" p3 p2 p1 p4
3+2-1=4
three+two-one=four
THREE+TWO-ONE=FOUR
+extra-=
```

The final example uses the **––serial** option to paste the files one at a time:

```
$ paste --serial p1 p2 p3 p4
1       one     ONE
2       two     TWO     extra
3       three   THREE
4       four    FOUR
```

pax

pax

Creates an archive, restores files from an archive, or copies a directory hierarchy

pax [options] [pattern-list]
pax –w [options] [source-files]
pax –r [options] [pattern-list]
pax –rw [options] [source-files] destination-directory

The pax utility has four modes of operation: List mode displays the list of files in an archive, create mode places multiple files into a single archive file, extract mode restores files from an archive, and copy mode copies a directory hierarchy. The archive files created by pax can be saved on disk, removable media, or a remote system.

List mode (absence of a major option) reads an archive from standard input and displays a list of files stored in the archive. Create mode (**–w** for *write*) reads a list of ordinary or directory filenames from the command line or standard input and writes the resulting archive file to standard output. Extract mode (**–r** for *read*) reads an archive from standard input and extracts files from that archive; you can restore all files from the archive or only those files whose names match a pattern. Copy mode (**–rw**) reads a list of ordinary or directory filenames from the command line or standard input and copies the files to an existing directory.

Arguments

In create mode, pax reads the names of files that will be included in the archive from ***source-files*** on the command line. If ***source-files*** is not present, pax reads the names from standard input, one filename per line.

By default, in extract mode pax extracts, and in list mode pax displays the names of, all files in the archive it reads from standard input. You can choose to extract or display the names of files selectively by supplying a ***pattern-list.*** If the name of a file in the archive matches a pattern in the ***pattern-list,*** pax extracts that file or displays that filename; otherwise, it ignores the file. The pax patterns are similar to shell wildcards (page 152) except they match slashes (/) and a leading period (.) in a filename. See the fnmatch man page for more information about pax patterns (macOS only).

In copy mode, pax does not create ***destination-directory.*** Thus ***destination-directory*** must exist before you give pax a copy mode command.

Options

A major option specifies the mode in which pax operates: create, extract, or copy.

Major Options

Three options determine the mode in which pax operates. You must include zero or one of these options. Without a major option, pax runs in list mode.

–r (**read**) Reads the archive from standard input and extracts files. Without a ***pattern-list*** on the command line, pax extracts all files from the archive. With a *pattern-list*, pax extracts only those files whose names match one of the patterns in the *pattern-list*. The following example extracts from the **root.pax** archive file on an external drive only those files whose names end in **.c**:

```
$ pax -r \*.c < /Volumes/Backups/root.pax
```

The backslash prevents the shell from expanding the * before it passes the argument to pax.

–rw (**copy**) Copies files named on the command line or standard input from one place on the system to another. Instead of constructing an archive file containing the files named on standard input, pax copies them to the ***destination-directory*** (the last argument on the pax command line). The effect is the same as if you had created an archive in create mode and then extracted the files in extract mode, except using copy mode avoids creating an archive.

The following example copies the working directory hierarchy to the **/Users/max/code** directory. The **code** directory must exist before you give this command. Make sure that **~max/code** is not a subdirectory of the working directory or you will perform a recursive copy.

```
$ pax -rw . ~max/code
```

–w (**write**) Constructs an archive from the files named on the command line or standard input. These files might be ordinary or directory files. When the files come from standard input, each must appear on a separate line. The archive is written to standard output. The find utility frequently generates the filenames that pax uses. The following command builds an archive of the **/Users** directory and writes it to the archive file named **Users.pax** on **/Volumes/Backups**:

```
# find -d /Users -print | pax -w > /Volumes/Backups/Users.pax
```

The **–d** option causes find to search for files in a depth-first manner, reducing the likelihood of permissions problems when you restore the files from the archive. See the discussion of this find option on page 779.

Other Options

The following options alter the behavior of pax. These options work with one or more of the major options.

–c (**complement**) Reverses the sense of the test performed on ***pattern-list***. Files are listed or put in the archive only if they do *not* match any of the patterns in ***pattern-list***.

–f ***archive***
(**file**) Uses ***archive*** as the name of the archive file. In list and extract modes, this option reads from ***archive*** instead of standard input. In create mode, it writes to ***archive*** instead of standard output. You can use this option to access a device on another system on a network; see the **––file** option to tar (page 996) for more information.

–H (**partial dereference**) For each file that is a symbolic link, copies the file the link points to, not the symbolic link itself. This option affects files specified on the command line; it does not affect files found while descending a directory hierarchy. This option treats files that are not symbolic links normally. See page 118 for information on dereferencing symbolic links.

–L (**dereference**) For each file that is a symbolic link, copies the file the link points to, not the symbolic link itself. This option affects all files and treats files that are not symbolic links normally. See page 118 for information on dereferencing symbolic links.

–l (**link**) In copy mode, when possible, makes hard links instead of copying files.

–P (**no dereference**) For each file that is a symbolic link, copies the symbolic link, not the file the link points to. This option affects all files and treats files that are not symbolic links normally. This behavior is the default for pax. See page 118 for information on dereferencing symbolic links.

–p *preserve-list*
Preserves or discards the file attributes specified by ***preserve-list***. The ***preserve-list*** is a string of one or more letters as shown in Table VI-26. By default pax preserves file access and modification times but does not preserve ownership or file permissions. This option works in extract and copy modes only.

Table VI-26 Preserve flags

Letter	Meaning
a	Discard the access time
e	Preserve everything
m	Discard the modification time
o	Preserve ownership
p	Preserve permissions

–s *subcmd*
Executes ***subcmd***, a substitution command, on filenames while storing them in any of the modes. The ***subcmd*** has the following syntax:

s/search-string/replacement-string/[gp]

The pax utility replaces occurrences of the regular expression ***search-string*** with ***replacement-string***. A trailing **g** indicates a global replacement; without it pax replaces only the first instance of ***search-string*** in each filename. A trailing **p** (for print) causes pax to display each substitution it makes. The ***subcmd*** is similar to vim's search and replace feature described on page 194, except it lacks an address.

–v (**verbose**) In list mode, displays output similar to that produced by **ls –l**. In other modes, displays a list of files being processed.

–X In copy and create modes, prevents pax from searching (descending into) directories in filesystems other than those holding ***source-files***.

–x *format*
In create mode, writes the archive in ***format*** format, as shown in Table VI-27. If you do not specify a format, pax writes a (POSIX) tar format file (**ustar** in the table).

–z (gzip) In create mode, compresses archives using gzip. In extract mode, decompresses archives using gunzip.

Table VI-27 pax archive formats

format	Description
cpio	The format specified for cpio archives in POSIX
sv4cpio	The format used for cpio archives under UNIX System V, release 4
tar	The historical Berkeley tar format
ustar	The POSIX tar format (default)

Discussion

The pax utility is a general replacement for tar, cpio, and other archive programs.

In create and copy modes, pax processes specified directories recursively. In list and extract modes, if a pattern in the ***pattern-list*** matches a directory name, pax lists or extracts the files from the named directory.

Notes

There is no native pax format. Instead, the pax utility can read and write archives in a number of formats. By default it creates POSIX tar format archives. See Table VI-27 for the list of formats pax supports.

The pax utility determines the format of an archive file; it does not allow you to specify an archive format (**–x** option) in list or extract mode.

Under macOS version 10.4 and above, pax copies extended attributes (page 1070).

Examples

In the first example, pax creates an archive named **corres.0901.pax**. This archive stores the contents of the **corres** directory.

```
$ pax -w corres > corres.0901.pax
```

The **–w** option puts pax in create mode, where the list of files to be put in an archive is supplied by command-line arguments (**corres** in the preceding example) or from standard input. The pax utility sends the archive to standard output. The preceding example redirects that output to a file named **corres.0901.pax**.

Next, without any options, pax displays a list of files in the archive it reads from standard input:

```
$ pax < corres.0901.pax
corres
corres/hls
corres/max
corres/max/0823
corres/max/0828
corres/max/0901
corres/memo1
corres/notes
```

The following command uses the –f option to name the input file and performs the same function as the preceding command:

```
$ pax -f corres.0901.pax
```

When pax reads an archive file, as in the previous examples, it determines the format of the file. You do not have to (nor are you allowed to) specify the format.

The next example, run under macOS, attempts to create an archive of the **/etc** directory hierarchy in the default tar format. In this case pax is run by a user with **root** privileges because some of the files in this hierarchy cannot be read by ordinary users. Because pax does not follow (dereference) symbolic links by default, and because under macOS **/etc** is a symbolic link, pax copies the link and not the directory the link points to. The first command creates the archive, the second command shows the link in the archive, and the third command uses the **–v** option to show that it is a link:

```
# pax -w -f /tmp/etc.tar /etc
# pax -f /tmp/etc.tar
/etc
# pax -v -f /tmp/etc.tar
lrwxr-xr-x  1 root     admin          0 May 21 01:48 /etc => private/etc
pax: ustar vol 1, 1 files, 10240 bytes read, 0 bytes written.
```

The **–L** option follows (dereferences) links. In the next example, pax creates the desired archive of **/etc**:

```
# pax -wLf /tmp/etc.tar /etc
# pax -f /tmp/etc.tar
/etc
/etc/6to4.conf
/etc/AFP.conf
/etc/afpovertcp.cfg
/etc/aliases
/etc/aliases.db
/etc/amavisd.conf
/etc/amavisd.conf.personal
/etc/appletalk.cfg
...
```

The next example uses pax to create a backup of the **memos** directory, preserving ownership and file permissions. The destination directory must exist before you give pax a copy mode command.

```
$ mkdir memos.0625
$ pax -rw -p e memos memos.0625
$ ls memos.0625
memos
```

The preceding example copies the **memos** directory into the destination directory. You can use pax to make a copy of a directory in the working directory without putting it in a subdirectory. In the next example, the –s option causes pax to replace the name of the **memos** directory with the name **.** (the name of the working directory) as it writes files to the **memos.0625** directory:

```
$ pax -rw -p e -s /memos/./ memos memos.0625
```

The following example uses find to build a list of files that begin with the string **memo** and that are located in the working directory hierarchy. The pax utility writes these files to an archive in cpio format. The output from pax goes to standard output, which is sent through a pipeline to bzip2, which compresses it before writing it to the archive file.

```
$ find . -type f -name "memo*" | pax -w -x cpio | bzip2 > memos.cpio.bz2
```

The final example extracts files from an archive, removing leading slashes (using the ^ forces the match to the beginning of the line) to prevent overwriting existing system files. The replacement string uses **!** as a separator so that a forward slash can be in one of the strings.

```
$ pax -r -f archive.pax -s '!^/!!p'
```

plutil macOS

Manipulates property list files

plutil [options] file-list

The plutil utility converts property list files between formats and checks their syntax. The plutil utility is available under macOS only. macOS

Arguments

The *file-list* specifies the pathnames of one or more files that plutil is to manipulate.

Options

–convert *format*
: Converts *file-list* to *format*, which must be either **xml1** or **binary1**.

–e *extension*
: Gives output files a filename extension of ***extension***.

–help
: Displays a help message.

–lint
: Checks the syntax of files (default).

–o *file*
: (**output**) Names the converted file *file*.

–s
: (**silent**) Does not display any messages for successfully converted files.

Discussion

The plutil utility converts files from the XML property list format to binary format, and vice versa. The plutil utility can read—but not write—the older plain-text property list format.

Notes

The plutil utility accepts a double hyphen (––) to mark the end of the options on the command line. For more information refer to "Common Options" on page 736.

Examples

The following example checks the syntax of the file named **java.plist**:

```
$ plutil java.plist
java.plist: OK
```

The next example shows the output of plutil as it checks a damaged property list file:

```
$ plutil broken.plist
broken.plist:
XML parser error:
        Encountered unexpected element at line 2 (plist can only include one object)
```

```
Old-style plist parser error:
        Malformed data byte group at line 1; invalid hex
```

The next example converts the file **StartupParameters.plist** to binary format, overwriting the original file:

```
$ plutil -convert binary1 StartupParameters.plist
```

The final example converts the binary format property list file **loginwindow.plist** in the working directory to XML format and, because of the **–o** option, puts the converted file in **/tmp/lw.p**:

```
$ plutil -convert xml1 -o /tmp/lw.p loginwindow.plist
```

pr

pr

Paginates files for printing

pr [options] [file-list]

The pr utility breaks files into pages, usually in preparation for printing. Each page has a header with the name of the file, date, time, and page number.

The pr utility takes its input from files you specify on the command line or from standard input. The output from pr goes to standard output and is frequently redirected through a pipeline to a printer.

Arguments

The ***file-list*** is a list of the pathnames of text files that you want pr to paginate. When you omit the ***file-list***, pr reads from standard input.

Options

Under Linux, pr accepts the common options described on page 736. Options preceded by a double hyphen (--) work under Linux only. Except as noted, options named with a single letter and preceded by a single hyphen work under Linux and macOS.

You can embed options within the ***file-list***. An embedded option affects only those files following it on the command line.

--show-control-chars
–c Displays control characters with a caret (^; for example, **^H**). Displays other nonprinting characters as octal numbers preceded by a backslash. LINUX

--columns=*col* **–*col***
Displays output in ***col*** columns with a default of one. This option might truncate lines and cannot be used with the **–m** (**--merge**) option.

--double-space **–d** Double-spaces the output.

--form-feed **–F** Uses a FORMFEED character to skip to the next page rather than filling the current page with NEWLINE characters.

--header=*head* **–h *head***
Replaces the filename at the top of each page with ***head***. If ***head*** contains SPACEs, you must enclose it within quotation marks.

--length=*lines* **–l *lines***
Sets the page length to ***lines*** lines. The default is 66 lines.

--merge **–m** Displays all specified files simultaneously in multiple columns. This option cannot be used with the **–*col*** (**--columns**) option.

--number-lines=*[c[num]]*
–n*[c[num]]*
Numbers the lines of output. The pr utility appends the character ***c*** to the number to separate it from the contents of the file (the default is a TAB). The ***num*** specifies the number of digits in each line number (the default is 5).

--indent=*spaces* –o *spaces*
Indents the output by ***spaces*** characters (specifies the left margin).

--separator=*c* –s[*c*]
Separates columns with the single character ***c*** (defaults to TAB when you omit ***c***). By default pr uses TABs as separation characters to align columns unless you use the **–w** option, in which case nothing separates the columns.

--omit-header –t Causes pr not to display its five-line page header and trailer. The header that pr normally displays includes the name of the file, the date, time, and page number. The trailer is five blank lines.

--width=*num* –w *num*
Sets the page width to ***num*** columns. This option is effective only with multi-column output (the **–m** [**--merge**] or ***–col*** [**--columns**] option).

--pages=*firstpage[:lastpage]*
+*firstpage[:lastpage]*
Output begins with the page numbered ***firstpage*** and ends with ***lastpage***. Without ***lastpage***, pr outputs through the last page of the document. The short version of this option begins with a plus sign, not a hyphen. macOS does not accept the ***lastpage*** argument; printing always continues through the end of the document.

Notes

When you use the ***–col*** (**--columns**) option to display the output in multiple columns, pr displays the same number of lines in each column (with the possible exception of the last column).

Examples

The first command shows pr paginating a file named **memo** and sending its output through a pipeline to lpr for printing:

```
$ pr memo | lpr
```

Next, **memo** is sent to the printer again, this time with a special heading at the top of each page. The job is run in the background.

```
$ pr -h 'MEMO RE: BOOK' memo | lpr &
[1] 4904
```

Finally, pr displays the **memo** file on the screen, without any header, starting with page 3:

```
$ pr -t +3 memo
...
```

printf

Formats string and numeric data

printf format-string [data-list]

The printf utility formats a list of arguments. Many shells (e.g., bash, tcsh, busybox) and some utilities (e.g., gawk) have their own printf builtins that work similarly to the printf utility.

Arguments

The printf utility reads *data-list* and sends it to standard output based on *format-string*. The *format-string* features presented in this section are not complete; see a C **printf**() function reference for more details. However, the printf utility is not a complete implementation of the C **printf**() function, so not all features of that function work in the printf utility.

The *format-string* holds three types of objects: characters, escape sequences, and format specifications. The printf utility copies characters from *format-string* to standard output without modification; it converts escape sequences before copying them. For each format specification, printf reads one element from *data-list*, formats that element according to the specification, and sends the result to standard output.

Some of the more commonly used escape sequences are **\n** (NEWLINE), **\t** (TAB), \" ("), and \\ (\).

Each format specification in *format-string* has the syntax

% [flag][min-width][.precision][spec-letter]

where

% introduces the format specification.

flag is **–** (left justify; printf right-justifies by default), **0** (pad with zeros; printf pads with SPACEs by default), or **+** (precede positive numbers with a plus sign; printf does not precede positive numbers with a plus sign by default).

min-width is the minimum width of the number or string printf outputs.

.precision specifies the number of digits to the right of the decimal (floating-point numbers), the number of digits (integer/decimal numbers), or the length of the string (strings; longer strings are truncated to this length).

spec-letter is one of the values listed in Table VI-28.

Table VI-28 printf *spec-letters*

spec-letter	Type of data	Notes
c	Character	Single character; use **s** for strings
d	Decimal	Width defaults to width of number

Table VI-28 printf *spec-letters* (continued)

spec-letter	Type of data	Notes
e	Floating point	Exponential notation (e.g., 1.20e+01)
f	Floating point	Includes decimal point; defaults to eight decimal places
g	Floating point	Same as **f**, unless exponent is less than –4, then same as **e**
o	Octal	Converts to octal
s	String	Width defaults to width of string
X	Uppercase hexadecimal	Converts to hexadecimal
x	Lowercase hexadecimal	Converts to hexadecimal

Option

The printf utility has no options. The bash printf builtin accepts the following option:

–v *var*

Assigns the output of printf to the variable named ***var*** instead of sending it to standard output (bash printf builtin only).

Notes

The printf utility and the bash printf builtin do not accept commas following ***format-string*** and between each of the elements of ***data-list***. The gawk version of printf requires commas in these locations.

If ***data-list*** has more elements than ***format-string*** specifies, printf reuses ***format-string*** as many times as necessary to process all elements in ***data-list***. If ***data-list*** has fewer elements than ***format-string*** specifies, printf assumes zero (for numbers) or null (for characters and strings) values for the nonexistent elements.

Examples

The examples in this section use the bash printf builtin. Using the printf utility yields the same results.

By itself, the %s ***format-string*** element causes printf to copy an item from ***data-list*** to standard output. It does not terminate its output with a NEWLINE.

```
$ printf %s Hi
Hi$
```

You can specify a NEWLINE (as the **\n** escape sequence) at the end of ***format-string*** to cause the shell prompt to appear on the line following the output. Because the backslash is a special shell character, you must quote it by preceding it with another backslash or by putting it within single or double quotation marks.

```
$ printf "%s\n" Hi
Hi
$
```

When you specify more than one element in the *data-list* but have only a single format specification in the *format-string*, printf reuses the format specification as many times as necessary:

```
$ printf "%s\n" Hi how are you?
Hi
how
are
you?
```

When you enclose the *data-list* within quotation marks, the shell passes the *data-list* to printf as a single argument; the *data-list* has a single element and it is processed in one pass by the single format specification.

```
$ printf "%s\n" "Hi how are you?"
Hi how are you?
```

%c The c *spec-letter* processes a single character of a *data-list* element. It discards extra characters. Use s for processing strings.

```
$ printf "%c\n" abcd
a
```

%d The d *spec-letter* processes a decimal number. By default the width occupied by the number is the number of characters in the number. In the next example, the text within the *format-string* (other than %d) consists of characters; printf copies these without modifying them.

```
$ printf "Number is %d end\n" 1234
Number is 1234 end
```

You can specify *min-width* to cause a number to occupy more space. The next example shows a four-digit number occupying ten SPACEs:

```
$ printf "Number is %10d end\n" 1234
Number is       1234 end
```

You can use the 0 flag to zero-fill the number or the – flag to left-justify it.

```
$ printf "Number is %010d end\n" 1234
Number is 0000001234 end
$ printf "Number is %-10d end\n" 1234
Number is 1234       end
```

%f The f *spec-letter* processes a floating-point number so it appears as a number with a decimal point. The **amt.left** shell script calls printf with the f *spec-letter*, a *min-width* of four characters, and a precision of two decimal places.

This example assigns a value to the **dols** variable and places it in the environment of the **amt.left** script. When given a value of 102.442, printf displays a six-character value with two places to the right of the decimal point.

```
$ cat amt.left
printf "I have $%4.2f dollars left.\n" $dols
$ dols=102.442 ./amt.left
I have $102.44 dollars left.
```

If you use e in place of f, printf displays a floating-point number with an exponent:

```
$ printf "We have %e miles to go.\n" 4216.7829
We have 4.216783e+03 miles to go.
```

%X The **X** *spec-letter* converts a decimal number to hexadecimal:

```
$ cat hex
read -p "Enter a number to convert to hex: " x
printf "The converted value is %X\n" $x

$ ./hex
Enter a number to convert to hex: 255
The converted value is FF
```

ps

Displays process status

ps [options] [process-list]

The ps utility displays status information about processes running on the local system.

Arguments

The ***process-list*** is a comma- or SPACE-separated list of PID numbers. When you specify a ***process-list***, ps reports on just the processes in that list.

Options

Under Linux, the ps utility accepts three types of options, each preceded by a different prefix. You can intermix the options. See the ps man page for details.

Two hyphens:	GNU (long) options
One hyphen:	UNIX98 (short) options
No hyphens:	BSD options

Options preceded by a double hyphen (––) work under Linux only. Options named with a single letter and preceded by no hyphen or a single hyphen work under Linux and macOS.

–A (**all**) Reports on all processes. Also **–e**.

–e (**everything**) Reports on all processes. Also **–A**.

–f (**full**) Displays a listing with more columns of information.

––forest **f** Displays the process tree (no hyphen before the **f**). LINUX

–l (**long**) Produces a long listing showing more information about each process. See the "Discussion" section for a description of the columns this option displays.

––no-headers Omits the header. This option is useful if you are sending the output to another program. LINUX

––user *usernames* **–u*usernames***
Reports on processes being run by ***usernames***, a comma-separated list of the names or UIDs of one or more users on the local system.

–w (**wide**) Without this option ps truncates output lines at the right side of the screen. This option extends the display to 132 columns; it wraps around one more line, if needed. Use this option twice to extend the display to an unlimited number of columns, which is the default when you redirect the output of ps.

Discussion

Without any options ps displays the statuses of all active processes controlled by your terminal or screen. Table VI-29 (next page) lists the heading and content of each of the four columns ps displays.

Table VI-29 Column headings I

Heading	Meaning
PID	The process identification number.
TTY (terminal)	The name of the terminal that controls the process.
TIME	The number of hours, minutes, and seconds the process has been running.
CMD	The command line the process was called with. The command is truncated to fit on one line. Use the **–w** option to see more of the command line.

The columns that ps displays depend on your choice of options. Table VI-30 lists the headings and contents of the most common columns; the column titles differ, depending on the type of option you use. Table VI-30 shows the headings for UNIX98 (one-hyphen) options.

Table VI-30 Column headings II

Heading	Meaning
%CPU	The percentage of total CPU time the process is using. Because of the way Linux handles process accounting, this figure is approximate, and the total of **%CPU** values for all processes might exceed 100%.
%MEM (memory)	The percentage of RAM the process is using.
COMMAND *or* **CMD**	The command line the process was called with. The command is truncated to fit on one line. Use the **–w** option to see more of the command line. This column is always displayed last on a line.
F (flags)	The flags associated with the process.
NI (nice)	The nice value of the process (page 916).
PID	The process identification number.
PPID (parent PID)	The process identification number of the parent process.
PRI (priority)	The priority of the process.
RSS (resident set size)	The number of blocks of memory the process is using.
SIZE *or* **SZ**	The size, in blocks, of the core image of the process.

Table VI-30 Column headings II (continued)

Heading	Meaning
STAT *or* **S** (status)	The status of the process as specified by one or more letters from the following list: **<** High priority **D** Sleeping and cannot be interrupted **L** Pages locked in memory (real-time and custom I/O) **N** Low priority **R** Available for execution (in the run queue) **S** Sleeping **T** Either stopped or being traced **W** Has no pages resident in RAM **X** Dead **Z** Zombie process that is waiting for its child processes to terminate before it terminates
STIME *or* **START**	The date the process started.
TIME	The number of minutes and seconds that the process has been running.
TTY (terminal)	The name of the terminal controlling the process.
USER *or* **UID**	The username of the user who owns the process.
WCHAN (wait channel)	If the process is waiting for an event, the address of the kernel function that caused the process to wait. This value is 0 for processes that are not waiting or sleeping.

Notes

Use top (page 1008) to display process status information dynamically.

Examples

The first example shows ps, without any options, displaying the user's active processes. The first process is the shell (bash), and the second is the process executing the ps utility.

```
$ ps
  PID TTY          TIME CMD
 2697 pts/0    00:00:02 bash
 3299 pts/0    00:00:00 ps
```

With the –l (long) option, ps displays more information about the processes:

```
$ ps -l
  F S   UID   PID  PPID  C PRI  NI ADDR    SZ WCHAN  TTY          TIME CMD
000 S   500  2697  2696  0  75   0    -   639 wait4  pts/0    00:00:02 bash
000 R   500  3300  2697  0  76   0    -   744 -      pts/0    00:00:00 ps
```

The –u option shows information about the specified user:

```
$ ps -u root
  PID TTY          TIME CMD
    1 ?        00:00:01 init
    2 ?        00:00:00 kthreadd
    3 ?        00:00:00 migration/0
    4 ?        00:00:01 ksoftirqd/0
    5 ?        00:00:00 watchdog/0
...
```

The ––forest option causes ps to display what the man page describes as an "ASCII art process tree." Processes that are children of other processes appear indented under their parents, making the process hierarchy, or tree, easier to see.

```
$ ps -ef --forest
UID        PID  PPID  C STIME TTY          TIME CMD
root         1     0  0 Jul22 ?        00:00:03 init
root         2     1  0 Jul22 ?        00:00:00 [keventd]
...
root       785     1  0 Jul22 ?        00:00:00 /usr/sbin/apmd -p 10 -w 5 -W -P
root       839     1  0 Jul22 ?        00:00:01 /usr/sbin/sshd
root      3305   839  0 Aug01 ?        00:00:00  \_ /usr/sbin/sshd
max       3307  3305  0 Aug01 ?        00:00:00      \_ /usr/sbin/sshd
max       3308  3307  0 Aug01 pts/1    00:00:00          \_ -bash
max       3774  3308  0 Aug01 pts/1    00:00:00              \_ ps -ef --forest
...
root      1040     1  0 Jul22 ?        00:00:00 login -- root
root      3351  1040  0 Aug01 tty2     00:00:00  \_ -bash
root      3402  3351  0 Aug01 tty2     00:00:00      \_ make modules
root      3416  3402  0 Aug01 tty2     00:00:00          \_ make -C drivers CFLA
root      3764  3416  0 Aug01 tty2     00:00:00              \_ make -C scsi mod
root      3773  3764  0 Aug01 tty2     00:00:00                  \_ ld -m elf_i3
```

ps and kill The next sequence of commands shows how to use ps to determine the PID number of a process running in the background and how to terminate that process using kill. In this case it is not necessary to use ps because the shell displays the PID number of the background processes. The ps utility verifies the PID number.

The first command executes find in the background. The shell displays the job and PID numbers of the process, followed by a prompt.

```
$ find ~ -name memo -print > memo.out &
[1] 3343
```

Next, ps confirms the PID number of the background task. If you did not already know this number, using ps would be the only way to obtain it.

```
$ ps
  PID TTY          TIME CMD
 3308 pts/1    00:00:00 bash
 3343 pts/1    00:00:00 find
 3344 pts/1    00:00:00 ps
```

Finally, kill (page 866) terminates the process:

```
$ kill 3343
$ RETURN
[1]+  Terminated                find ~ -name memo -print >memo.out
$
```

renice

Changes the priority of a process

*renice **priority** [option] **process-list***
*renice **–n increment** [option] **process-list***

The renice utility alters the priority of a running process. An ordinary user can decrease the priority of a process that he owns. Only a user running with **root** privileges can increase the priority of a process or alter the priority of another user's process.

Arguments

The *process-list* specifies the PID numbers of the processes that are to have their priorities altered. Each process has its priority set to ***priority*** or, using the second format, has its priority incremented by a value of ***increment*** (which can be negative).

Options

The options, which you can specify throughout the ***process-list***, change the interpretation of the arguments that follow them on the command line.

–p (**process**) Interprets the following arguments as process ID (PID) numbers (default).

–u (**user**) Interprets the following arguments as usernames or user ID numbers.

Notes

The range of priorities is from –20 (the highest priority) to +20 (the lowest priority). Higher (more positive) priority values mean the kernel schedules a job less often. Lower (more negative) values cause the job to be scheduled more often.

When a user running with **root** privileges schedules a job to run at the highest priority, this change can affect the performance of the system for all other jobs, including the operating system itself. For this reason you should be careful when using renice with negative values.

See nice (page 916) if you want to start a process with a nondefault priority.

Examples

The first example decreases the priority of all tasks owned by Zach:

```
$ renice -n 5 -u zach
```

In the following example, a user running with **root** privileges uses ps to check the priority of the process running find. The **NI** (nice) column shows a value of 19 and the administrator decides to increase the priority by 5:

```
# ps -l
UID    PID  PPID CPU PRI NI    VSZ    RSS WCHAN  STAT  TT       TIME COMMAND
501   9705  9701   0  31  0  27792    856 -      Ss    p1    0:00.15 -bash
```

```
501 10548  9705    0  12 19  27252    516 -      RN    p1    0:00.62 find /
# renice -n -5 10548
```

rm

Removes a file (deletes a link)

rm [options] file-list

The rm utility removes hard and/or symbolic links to one or more files. When you remove the last hard link to a file, the file is deleted.

caution

Be careful when you use rm with wildcards

Because this utility enables you to remove a large number of files with a single command, use rm cautiously, especially when you are working with ambiguous file references. If you have any doubts about the effect of an rm command with an ambiguous file reference, first use echo with the same file reference and evaluate the list of files the reference generates. Alternatively, you can use the rm **–i** (**––interactive**) option.

Arguments

The *file-list* is a list of the files whose links rm will remove. Removing the only hard link to a file deletes the file. Removing a symbolic link deletes the symbolic link only.

Options

Under Linux, rm accepts the common options described on page 736. Options preceded by a double hyphen (––) work under Linux only. Options named with a single letter and preceded by a single hyphen work under Linux and macOS.

––force **–f** Without asking for your consent, removes files for which you do not have write access permission. This option also suppresses informative messages if a file does not exist.

––interactive **–i** Asks before removing each file. If you use **––recursive** with this option, rm also asks you before examining each directory.

–P Overwrites the files three times before removing them.

––recursive **–r** Deletes the contents of the specified directory, including all its subdirectories, and the directory itself. Use this option with caution.

––verbose **–v** Displays the name of each file as it is removed.

Notes

To delete a file, you must have execute and write access permission to the parent directory of the file, but you do not need read or write access permission to the file itself. If you are running rm interactively (that is, if rm's standard input is coming from the keyboard) and you do not have write access permission to the file, rm displays your access permission and waits for you to respond. If your response starts with a y or Y, rm deletes the file; otherwise, it takes no action. If standard input is not coming from a keyboard, rm deletes the file without querying you.

Refer to page 113 for information on hard links and page 115 for information on symbolic links. Page 118 includes a discussion about removing links. You can use rm with the –r option or rmdir (page 955) to remove an empty directory.

When you want to remove a file that begins with a hyphen, you must prevent rm from interpreting the filename as an option. One way to do so is to give the special option –– (double hyphen) before the name of the file. This option tells rm that no more options follow: Any arguments that come after it are filenames, even if they look like options.

Use shred to remove a file securely

security Using rm does not securely delete a file; it is possible to recover a file that has been deleted using rm. Use the shred utility to delete files more securely. See the example "Wiping a file" on page 792 for another method of securely deleting files.

Examples

The following commands delete files both in the working directory and in another directory:

```
$ rm memo
$ rm letter memo1 memo2
$ rm /home/sam/temp
```

The next example asks the user before removing each file in the working directory and its subdirectories:

```
$ rm -ir *
```

This command is useful for removing filenames that contain special characters, especially SPACEs, TABs, and NEWLINEs. (You should not create filenames containing these characters on purpose, but it might happen accidentally.)

rmdir

Removes directories

rmdir ***directory-list***

The rmdir utility deletes empty directories.

Arguments

The ***directory-list*** is a list of pathnames of empty directories that rmdir removes.

Options

Under Linux, rmdir accepts the common options described on page 736. Options preceded by a double hyphen (––) work under Linux only. Except as noted, options named with a single letter and preceded by a single hyphen work under Linux and macOS.

––ignore-fail-on-non-empty
: Suppresses the message rmdir normally displays when it fails because a directory is not empty. With the **––parents** option, rmdir does not quit when it finds a directory that is not empty. LINUX

––parents –p
: Removes a hierarchy of empty directories.

––verbose –v
: Displays the names of directories as they are removed. LINUX

Notes

Use the rm utility with the **–r** option if you need to remove directories that are not empty, together with their contents.

Examples

The following command deletes the empty **literature** directory from the working directory:

```
$ rmdir literature
```

The next command removes the **letters** directory, using an absolute pathname:

```
$ rmdir /home/sam/letters
```

The final command removes the **letters**, **march**, and 05 directories, assuming the directories are empty except for other directories named in the path:

```
$ rmdir -p letters/march/05
```

rsync

Securely copies files and directory hierarchies over a network

rsync [options] [[user@]from-host:]source-file [[user@]to-host:][destination-file]

The rsync (remote synchronization) utility copies an ordinary file or directory hierarchy locally or from the local system to or from another system on a network. By default this utility uses OpenSSH to transfer files and the same authentication mechanism as OpenSSH; as a consequence, it provides the same security as OpenSSH. The rsync utility prompts for a password when it needs one. Alternatively, you can use the **rsyncd** daemon as a transfer agent.

See Chapter 16 for information on rsync

tip See Chapter 16 starting on page 689 for information on rsync.

scp

Securely copies one or more files to or from a remote system

scp [[user@]from-host:]source-file [[user@]to-host:][destination-file]

The scp (secure copy) utility copies an ordinary or directory file from one system to another on a network. This utility uses OpenSSH to transfer files and the same authentication mechanism as OpenSSH; as a consequence, it provides the same security as OpenSSH. The scp utility prompts for a password when it needs one.

See Chapter 17 for information on scp

tip See the sections of Chapter 17 starting on page 713 for information on the scp secure copy utility, one of the OpenSSH secure communication utilities.

screen

screen

Manages several textual windows

screen [options] [program]

The screen utility (screen package) is a full-screen textual window manager. A single session run on one physical or virtual terminal allows you to work in one of several windows, each of which typically runs a shell. It allows you to detach from and attach to a session and can help prevent you from losing data when a connection drops.

Arguments

The ***program*** is the name of the program screen runs initially in the windows it opens. If you do not specify ***program***, screen runs the shell specified by the **SHELL** environment variable. If **SHELL** is not set, it runs sh, which is typically linked to bash or dash.

Options

This section describes a few of the many options screen accepts. See the screen man page for a complete list. When you call screen you can specify options to perform tasks. While you are working in a screen session you can use commands (next) to perform many of the same tasks.

–d [***pid.tty.host***]

(**detach**) Detaches the screen session specified by ***pid.tty.host***. Does not start screen. Equivalent to typing CONTROL-A **D** from a screen session.

–L Turns on logging for all windows in the session you are starting.

–ls (**list**) Displays a list of screen sessions including identification strings (i.e., ***pid.tty.host***) you can use to attach to a session. Does not start screen.

–r [***pid.tty.host***]

(**resume**) Attaches to the screen session specified by ***pid.tty.host*** or simply ***pid***. You do not need to specify ***pid.tty.host*** if only a single screen session is running. Does not start a new screen session.

–S [***session***]

Specifies ***session*** as the name of the session you are starting.

–t [***title***]

Specifies ***title*** as the name of all windows in the session you are starting. If you do not specify a ***title*** or if you do not use this option, the ***title*** defaults to the name of the program the window is running, typically bash.

Do not hold the SHIFT key while typing a CONTROL character

tip This book uses the common convention of showing an uppercase letter following the CONTROL key. However, all control characters are entered as lowercase characters. *Do not hold down the* SHIFT *key while entering a* CONTROL *character.* In no case is a CONTROL character typed as an uppercase letter.

Commands

Table VI-31 lists a few of the many commands screen accepts; see the screen man page for a complete list. You must give these commands from an active window (while you are running screen). By default all commands start with CONTROL-A.

Table VI-31 screen commands

Command	What it does
CONTROL-A **?**	(**help**) Displays a list of screen commands (key bindings).
CONTROL-A **"**	Displays a list of windows in the current session. You can select a new active window from this list.
CONTROL-A **1**, **2**, ... **9**	Makes window number 1, 2, ..., 9 the active window.
CONTROL-A **A**	(**annotate**) Prompts for a window title. Use the erase key (typically BACKSPACE) to back up over the current title before entering a new title.
CONTROL-A **c**	(**create**) Opens a new window and makes that window the active window.
CONTROL-A **d**	Detaches from the screen session.
CONTROL-A **H**	Toggles logging for the active window.
CONTROL-A **m**	(**message**) Redisplays the most recent message.
CONTROL-A **N**	(**number**) Displays the title and number of the active window.
CONTROL-A **n**	(**next**) Makes the window with the next higher number the active window. The window with the highest number wraps to the window with the lowest number.
CONTROL-A **p**	(**previous**) Makes the window with the next lower number the active window. The window with the lowest number wraps to the window with the highest number.

Notes

You might want to look at one of the other tools that does the same work as screen: tmux (github.com/tmux), byobu (launchpad.net/byobu), Terminator (GUI; code.google.com/archive/p/jessies/wikis/Terminator.wiki), or Guake (GUI; guake.org).

Discussion

Terminology **Session** When you run screen from the command line, you start a screen *session*. One session can have many windows. A session name has the format *pid.tty.host*. A session comprises one or more windows. You can attach to and detach from a session without interrupting the work you are doing in the windows. Also *terminal*.

Window When used with reference to screen, the term *window* refers to a textual window, not a graphical one. Typically, a screen window occupies the entire physical or virtual screen. Within a session, you can identify a window by its window number. Also *screen.*

Active window The *active window* is the window screen is displaying (and you are working with).

How it works When you call screen without naming a ***program*** on the command line, it opens a window running a shell. This window looks identical to your login screen but it is not running a login shell and might display information on its status (last) line. From this screen window you can use screen commands to open additional windows and display other windows (switch to a different active window).

Summary You call screen once to start a session and then open windows as needed. You can detach from and attach to a session at will.

Logging By default screen log files are written to the user's home directory and are named **screenlog.*no***, where ***no*** is the number of the screen whose log the file holds.

emacs If you are running emacs in a screen session, use CONTROL-A **a** in place of the normal CONTROL-A to move the cursor to the beginning of a line.

Starting screen with the **–L** option turns logging on for all windows in the session; pressing CONTROL-A **H** from a screen window turns logging on for that (the active) window if logging is off and turns it off if it is on. When you turn logging on and a log file for the active window exists, screen appends to that file.

~/.screenrc The screen startup file is named **.screenrc** and is located in the user's home directory. You can put many commands in this file; this section briefly discusses how to set up a window's status line. The first line in the following file turns the status line on (it is on by default). The second line pertains to terminals that do not have a status line: It makes the last line of the terminal the status line. The third line specifies what screen is to display on the status line.

```
$ cat ~/.screenrc
hardstatus on
hardstatus alwayslastline
hardstatus string "%{Rb} Host %H %= Title %t %= Number %n %= Session %S %= %D %c "
```

Within the **hardstatus** string, the **%** sign is the escape mechanism that tells screen the next character has a special meaning. Braces enclose multiple special characters; string displays any character not preceded by **%** as itself; **%=** causes screen to pad the status line with SPACEs. From left to right, **%{Rb}** causes screen to display the status line with a bright red foreground and a blue background; screen replaces **%H** with the hostname, **%t** with the title of the window, **%n** with the window number, **%S** with the name of the session, **%D** with the day of the week, and **%c** with the time based on a 24-hour clock. See **STRING ESCAPES** in the screen man page for a complete list of escapes you can use in the **hardstatus** string.

Tutorial

This tutorial follows Sam as he works with screen. Sam has some work to do on a remote system he connects to using ssh (Chapter 17). The connection Sam uses is not reliable and he does not want to lose his work if he gets disconnected. Also, it is late in the day, and Sam wants to be able to disconnect from the remote system, go home, and reconnect without losing track of what he is doing.

Working from the system named **guava**, Sam uses ssh to connect to **plum**, the remote system he wants to work on:

```
[sam@guava ~]$ ssh plum
Last login: Fri Feb 23 11:48:33 2018 from 172.16.192.1
[sam@plum ~]$
```

Next, he gives the command **screen** without any options or arguments. Sam's **~/.screenrc** on **plum** is the same as the one shown on the preceding page. The screen utility opens a new window and starts a shell that displays a prompt. Sam's terminal looks the same as it did when he first logged in except for the status line at the bottom of the screen:

```
Host plum    Title bash    Number 0    Session pts-1.plum    Tue 10:59
```

The status line shows Sam is working on the system named **plum** in window number 0. Initially the title of the window is the name of the program running in the window; in this case it is **bash**. Sam wants to make the status line reflect the work he is doing in the window. He is compiling a program, and wants to change the title to **Compile**. He gives a CONTROL-A **A** command to change the window title; screen responds by prompting him on the message line (just above the status line):

```
Set window's title to: bash
```

Before he can enter a new title, Sam must use the erase key (typically BACKSPACE) to back up over **bash**. Then he enters **Compile** and presses RETURN. Now the status line looks like this:

```
Host plum   Title Compile    Number 0    Session pts-1.plum    Tue 11:01
```

Sam wants to keep track of the work he does in this window so he enters CONTROL-A **H** to turn logging on; screen confirms the creation of the log file on the status line:

```
Creating logfile "screenlog.0".
```

If there had been a file named **screenlog.0**, screen would have reported it was appending to the file.

Sam wants to work on two more tasks: reading reports and writing a letter. He gives a CONTROL-A **c** command to open a new window; the status bar reports this window is number **1**. Then he changes the title of the window to **Report** using CONTROL-A **A** as before. He repeats the process, opening window number 2 and giving it the title **Letter**. When he gives a CONTROL-A **"** (CONTROL-A followed by a double quotation mark) command, screen displays information about the three windows Sam has set up:

```
 Num Name                                                      Flags

   0 Compile                                                   $(L)
   1 Report                                                       $
   2 Letter                                                       $
...
Host plum     Title      Number -      Session pts-1.plum      Tue 11:14
```

The output from this command shows the window numbers, titles (under the heading **Name**), and the flags associated with each window. The **L** flag on the Compile window indicates logging has been turned on for that window. On the status line, the window number is a hyphen, indicating this window is an informational window.

Sam can select a different active window from this informational window by using the UP ARROW and DOWN ARROW keys to move the highlight between the listed windows and pressing RETURN when the highlight is over the window he wants to use. He highlights the Compile window and presses RETURN; screen closes the informational window and displays the Compile window. Sam gives the commands to start the compilation with the output from the compilation going to the screen.

Next, Sam wants to work on the letter, and because he knows it is in window number 2, he uses a different technique to select the Letter window. He presses CONTROL-A **2** and screen displays window number 2. As he is working on the letter, he realizes he needs some information from a report. He is using window number 2 and he remembers the reports are in window number 1. He presses CONTROL-A **p** to display the previous window (the window with the next lowest number); screen displays window number 1, which is the Report window, and Sam starts looking for the information he needs.

All of a sudden Sam sees his prompt from **guava**; the connection failed. Undaunted, he uses ssh to reconnect to **plum** and gives a **screen –ls** command to list screen sessions that are running on **plum**:

```
[sam@guava ~]$ ssh plum
Last login: Tue May  1 10:55:53 2018 from guava
[sam@plum ~]$ screen -ls
There is a screen on:
        2041.pts-1.plum (Detached)
1 Socket in /var/run/screen/S-sam.
```

All Sam needs to do is attach to the detached screen session and he will be back where he was with his work. Because only one screen session exists, he could simply give a **screen –r** command to attach to it; he chooses to give a command that includes the name of the session he wants to attach to:

```
[sam@plum ~]$ screen -r 2041.pts-1.plum
```

The screen utility displays the Report window, which still shows the same information as it did when Sam got disconnected.

Sam works for a while longer, periodically checking on the compilation, and decides it is time to go home. This time Sam detaches from the screen session on purpose by giving a CONTROL-A **d** command. He sees the original command he used to start screen followed by a message from screen saying he has detached from the session and giving the session number. Then he logs out of **plum**, and **guava** displays a prompt.

```
$ screen
[detached from 2041.pts-1.plum]
[sam@plum ~]$ exit
logout
Connection to plum closed.
[sam@guava ~]$
```

Sam goes home and eats dinner. When he is ready to work again, he uses ssh to log in on **plum** from his computer at home. He attaches to his screen session as he did after the connection failed and displays window 0, the Compile window, to see how the compilation is doing. The window holds the last lines of the compilation that show it was successful, so he types **exit** to close the window; screen displays the previous active window. Now CONTROL-A " would list two windows.

After working on the letter for a while, Sam starts worrying about which commands he gave to compile his program—so he opens the log file from the old window 0 (**screenlog.0**) and checks. In that file he sees all the commands he gave after he turned logging on, together with the shell prompts and other output that appeared on the screen. All is well.

Sam is done so he exits from each of the two remaining windows. Now **plum** displays its prompt preceded by the commands he gave before he started running screen. Sam logs off of **plum** and he is done.

You do not have to run screen on a remote system. This utility can be useful on the local system when you want to work with several windows at the same time. If you are running several virtual machines or working with several local or remote systems, you can run one local screen session with several windows, each logged in on a different system.

sed

sed

Edits a file noninteractively

sed [–n] ***program*** *[file-list]*
sed [–n] –f ***program-file*** *[file-list]*

The sed (stream editor) utility is a batch (noninteractive) editor. It transforms an input stream that can come from a file or standard input. It is frequently used as a filter or in a pipeline. Because it makes only one pass through its input, sed is more efficient than an interactive editor such as ed. Most Linux distributions provide GNU sed; macOS supplies BSD sed. Chapter 15 applies to both versions.

See Chapter 15 for information on sed

tip See Chapter 15 starting on page 669 for information on sed.

SetFile macOS

Sets file attributes

SetFile [options] file-list

The SetFile utility sets file attributes (page 1072), including the file's type and creator codes, creation and last modification times, and attribute flags such as the invisible and locked flags. The SetFile utility is available under macOS only. macOS

Arguments

The *file-list* specifies the pathnames of one or more files that SetFile works on.

Options

The options for SetFile correspond to the options for GetFileInfo (page 851).

–a *flags*
: (**attribute**) Sets the attribute flags specified by ***flags***. An uppercase letter for a flag sets that flag and a lowercase letter unsets the flag. The values of unspecified flags are not changed. See Table D-2 on page 1072 or the SetFile man page for a list of attribute flags.

–c *creator*
: Sets the creator code to ***creator***.

–d *date*
: Sets the creation date to ***date***. The format of the ***date*** is **mm/dd/[yy]yy [hh:mm:[:ss] [AM | PM]]**. If you do not specify **AM** or **PM**, SetFile assumes a 24-hour clock. You must enclose a ***date*** string that contains SPACEs within quotation marks.

–m *date*
: (**modification**) Sets the modification date to ***date***. The format of ***date*** is the same as that used with the **–d** option.

–P (**no dereference**) For each file that is a symbolic link, sets information about the symbolic link, not the file the link points to. This option affects all files and treats files that are not symbolic links normally. See page 118 for information on dereferencing symbolic links. By default SetFile dereferences symbolic links.

–t *type*
: Sets the type code to ***type***.

Notes

The SetFile utility is part of the optional Xcode package.

The options to SetFile and the corresponding options to GetFileInfo have minor differences. For example, you can specify multiple attribute flags with the **–a** option to SetFile but only a single flag with GetFileInfo. Also, SetFile requires a SPACE between the **–a** option and the list of flags; GetFileInfo does not allow a SPACE there.

Examples

The first example sets the type and creator codes of the file named **arch** to **SIT5** and **SIT!**, respectively, indicating that it is a StuffIt archive. The GetFileInfo utility displays these codes.

```
$ SetFile -t SIT5 -c SIT! arch
$ GetFileInfo -c arch
"SIT!"
$ GetFileInfo -t arch
"SIT5"
```

The next example marks the file named **secret** as invisible and locked. The file will not be visible in the Finder, and most macOS applications will be unable to overwrite it.

```
$ SetFile -a VL secret
```

The final example clears the invisible attribute flag from every file (but not files with hidden filenames [page 88]) in the working directory:

```
$ SetFile -a v *
```

sleep

Creates a process that sleeps for a specified interval

*sleep **time***
*sleep **time-list*** LINUX

The sleep utility causes the process executing it to go to sleep for the time specified.

Arguments

By itself, the ***time*** denotes a number of seconds; the ***time*** can be an integer or a decimal fraction. Under Linux you can append a unit specification to ***time:*** **s** (seconds), **m** (minutes), **h** (hours), or **d** (days).

Under Linux you can construct a ***time-list*** by including several times on the command line: The total time the process sleeps is the sum of these times. For example, if you specify **1h 30m 100s**, the process will sleep for 91 minutes and 40 seconds.

Examples

You can use sleep from the command line to execute a command after a period of time. The following example executes in the background a process that reminds you to make a phone call in 20 minutes (1,200 seconds):

```
$ (sleep 1200; echo "Remember to make call.") &
[1] 4660
```

Alternatively, under Linux, you could give the following command to get the same reminder:

```
$ (sleep 20m; echo "Remember to make call.") &
[2] 4667
```

You can also use sleep within a shell script to execute a command at regular intervals. For example, the **per** shell script executes a program named **update** every 90 seconds:

```
$ cat per
#!/bin/bash
while true
do
    update
    sleep 90
done
```

If you execute a shell script such as **per** in the background, you can terminate it only by using kill.

The final shell script accepts the name of a file as an argument and waits for that file to appear on the disk. If the file does not exist, the script sleeps for 1 minute and 45 seconds before checking for the file again.

```
$ cat wait_for_file
#!/bin/bash

if [ $# != 1 ]; then
    echo "Usage: wait_for_file filename"
    exit 1
fi

while true
do
    if [ -f "$1" ]; then
        echo "$1 is here now"
        exit 0
    fi
    sleep 1m 45s
done
```

Under macOS, replace **1m 45s** with **105**.

sort

Sorts and/or merges files

sort [options] [file-list]

The sort utility sorts and/or merges one or more text files.

Arguments

The *file-list* is a list of pathnames of one or more ordinary files that contain the text to be sorted. If the *file-list* is omitted, sort takes its input from standard input. Without the **–o** option, sort sends its output to standard output. This utility sorts and merges files unless you use the **–m** (merge only) or **–c** (check only) option.

Options

The sort utility orders the file using the collating sequence set by the **LC_COLLATE** locale variable (page 327). Without a **––key** option, sort orders a file based on full lines. Use **––key** to specify sort fields within a line. You can follow a **––key** option with additional options without a leading hyphen; see the "Discussion" section for more information.

The macOS version of sort accepts long options

tip Options for sort preceded by a double hyphen (**––**) work under macOS as well as under Linux.

––ignore-leading-blanks

–b Blanks (TAB and SPACE characters) normally mark the beginning of fields in the input file. Without this option, sort considers leading blanks to be part of the field they precede. This option ignores leading blanks within a field, so sort does not consider these characters in sort comparisons.

––check **–c** Checks whether the file is properly sorted. The sort utility does not display anything if everything is in order. It displays a message if the file is not in sorted order and returns an exit status of 1.

––dictionary-order

–d Ignores all characters that are not alphanumeric characters or blanks. For example, sort does not consider punctuation with this option. Using the **LC_CTYPE** locale variable (page 327) affects the outcome when you specify this option.

––ignore-case **–f** (**fold**) Considers all lowercase letters to be uppercase letters. Use this option when you are sorting a file that contains both uppercase and lowercase letters.

--ignore-nonprinting

-i Ignores nonprinting characters. This option is overridden by the **--dictionary-order** option. The **LC_CTYPE** locale variable (page 327) affects the outcome when you specify this option.

--key=*start[,stop]*

-k *start[,stop]*

Specifies a sort field within a line. Without this option sort orders a file based on full lines. The sort field starts at the position on the line specified by ***start*** and ends at ***stop***, or the end of the line if ***stop*** is omitted. The ***start*** and ***stop*** positions are in the format *f[.c]*, where *f* is the field number and *c* is the optional character within the field. Numbering starts with 1. When *c* is omitted from ***start***, it defaults to the first character in the field; when *c* is omitted from ***stop***, it defaults to the last character in the field. See the "Discussion" section for further explanation of sort fields and the "Examples" section for illustrations of their use.

--merge -m Assumes that each of the multiple input files is in sorted order and merges them without verifying they are sorted.

--numeric-sort -n Sorts in arithmetic sequence; does not order lines or sort fields in the machine collating sequence. With this option, minus signs and decimal points take on their arithmetic meaning.

--output=*filename*

-o *filename*

Sends output to ***filename*** instead of standard output; ***filename*** can be the same as one of the names in the ***file-list***.

--reverse -r Reverses the sense of the sort (for example, **z** precedes **a**).

--field-separator=*x*

-t *x*

Specifies *x* as the field separator. See the "Discussion" section for more information on field separators.

--unique -u Outputs repeated lines only once. When you use this option with **--check**, sort displays a message if the same line appears more than once in the input file, even if the file is in sorted order.

Discussion

Without any options, sort bases its ordering on full lines.

Sort order The way locale is set affects the way sort orders a file. For traditional ordering, set **LC_ALL** to **C** before running sort.

Field In the following description, a *field* is a sequence of characters in a line of input. Without the **--field-separator** option, fields are bounded by the empty string preceding a group of one or more blanks (TAB and SPACE characters). You cannot see the empty string that delimits the fields; it is an imaginary point between two fields. Fields are also bounded by the beginning and end of the line. The line shown in Figure VI-8

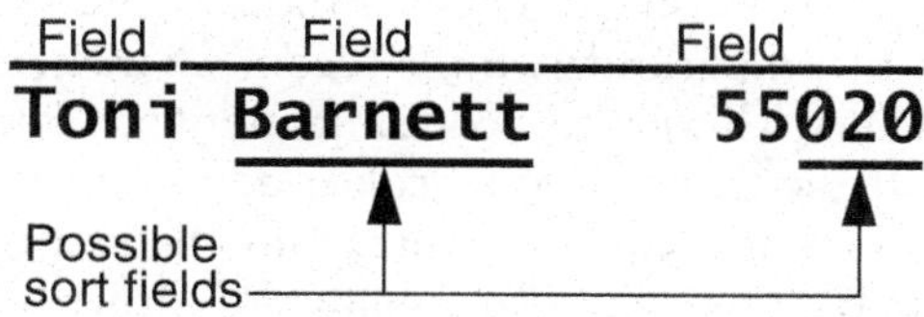

Figure VI-8 Fields and sort fields

holds the fields **Toni**, SPACE**Barnett**, and SPACESPACESPACESPACE**55020**. These fields define sort fields. Sometimes fields and sort fields are the same.

Sort field A *sort field* is a sequence of characters that sort uses to put lines in order. A sort field can contain all or part of one or more fields (Figure VI-8).

The **--key** option specifies pairs of pointers that define subsections of each line (sort fields) for comparison. See the **--key** option (page 970) for details.

Leading blanks The **–b** option causes sort to ignore leading blanks in a sort field. If you do not use this option, sort considers each leading blank to be a character in the sort field and includes it in the sort comparison.

Options You can specify options that pertain only to a given sort field by immediately following the ***stop*** pointer (or the ***start*** pointer if there is no ***stop*** pointer) with one of the options **b**, **d**, **f**, **i**, **n**, or **r**. In this case you must *not* precede the option with a hyphen.

Multiple sort fields When you specify more than one sort field, sort examines them in the order you specify them on the command line. If the first sort field of two lines is the same, sort examines the second sort field. If these are again the same, sort looks at the third field. This process continues for all the sort fields you specify. If all the sort fields are the same, sort examines the entire line.

Examples

The examples in this section demonstrate some of the features and uses of the sort utility. The examples assume **LC_ALL** is set to **C** and the following file named **list** is in the working directory:

```
$ cat list
Tom Winstrom         94201
Janet Dempsey        94111
Alice MacLeod        94114
David Mack           94114
Toni Barnett         95020
Jack Cooper          94072
Richard MacDonald    95510
```

This file contains a list of names and ZIP codes. Each line of the file contains three fields: the first name field, the last name field, and the ZIP code field. For the examples to work, the blanks in the file must be SPACEs, and not TABs.

The first example demonstrates sort without any options; the only argument is the name of the input file. In this case sort orders the file on a line-by-line basis. If the first characters on two lines are the same, sort looks at the second characters to determine the proper order. If the second characters are the same, sort looks at the third characters. This process continues until sort finds a character that differs between the lines. If the lines are identical, it does not matter which one sort puts first. In this example, sort needs to examine only the first three characters (at most) of each line. It displays a list that is in alphabetical order by first name.

```
$ sort list
Alice MacLeod         94114
David Mack            94114
Jack Cooper           94072
Janet Dempsey         94111
Richard MacDonald     95510
Tom Winstrom          94201
Toni Barnett          95020
```

You can instruct sort to skip any number of fields and characters on a line before beginning its comparison. Blanks normally mark the beginning of a field. The next example sorts the same list by last name, the second field: The **--key=2** argument instructs sort to begin its comparison with this field. Because there is no second pointer, the sort field extends to the end of the line. Now the list is almost in last-name order, but there is a problem with **Mac**.

```
$ sort --key=2 list
Toni Barnett          95020
Jack Cooper           94072
Janet Dempsey         94111
Richard MacDonald     95510
Alice MacLeod         94114
David Mack            94114
Tom Winstrom          94201
```

In the preceding example, **MacLeod** comes before **Mack**. After finding that the sort fields of these two lines were the same through the third letter (**Mac**), sort put **L** before **k** because it arranges lines based on the value of **LC_COLLATE**, which is assumed to be set to **C**, which specifies that uppercase letters come before lowercase ones.

The **--ignore-case** option makes sort treat uppercase and lowercase letters as equals and fixes the problem with **MacLeod** and **Mack**:

```
$ sort --ignore-case --key=2 list
Toni Barnett          95020
Jack Cooper           94072
Janet Dempsey         94111
Richard MacDonald     95510
David Mack            94114
Alice MacLeod         94114
Tom Winstrom          94201
```

The next example attempts to sort **list** on the third field, the ZIP code. In this case sort does not put the numbers in order but rather puts the shortest name first in the sorted list and the longest name last. The **--key=3** argument instructs sort to begin its comparison with the third field, the ZIP code. A field starts with a blank and includes subsequent blanks. In the case of the **list** file, the blanks are SPACEs. The ASCII value of a SPACE character is less than that of any other printable character, so sort puts the ZIP code that is preceded by the most SPACEs first and the ZIP code that is preceded by the fewest SPACEs last.

```
$ sort --key=3 list
David Mack              94114
Jack Cooper             94072
Tom Winstrom            94201
Toni Barnett            95020
Janet Dempsey           94111
Alice MacLeod           94114
Richard MacDonald       95510
```

The **–b** (**--ignore-leading-blanks**) option causes sort to ignore leading SPACEs within a field. With this option, the ZIP codes come out in the proper order. When sort determines that **MacLeod** and **Mack** have the same ZIP codes, it compares the entire lines, putting **Alice MacLeod** before **David Mack** (because **A** comes before **D**).

```
$ sort -b --key=3 list
Jack Cooper             94072
Janet Dempsey           94111
Alice MacLeod           94114
David Mack              94114
Tom Winstrom            94201
Toni Barnett            95020
Richard MacDonald       95510
```

To sort alphabetically by last name when ZIP codes are the same, sort needs to make a second pass that sorts on the last name field. The next example shows how to make this second pass by specifying a second sort field and uses the **–f** (**--ignore-case**) option to keep the **Mack/MacLeod** problem from cropping up again:

```
$ sort -b -f --key=3 --key=2 list
Jack Cooper             94072
Janet Dempsey           94111
David Mack              94114
Alice MacLeod           94114
Tom Winstrom            94201
Toni Barnett            95020
Richard MacDonald       95510
```

The next example shows a **sort** command that skips not only fields but also characters. The **–k 3.4** option (equivalent to **--key=3.4**) causes sort to start its comparison with the fourth character of the third field. Because the command does not define an end to the sort field, it defaults to the end of the line. The sort field is the last two digits in the ZIP code.

```
$ sort -fb -k 3.4 list
Tom Winstrom            94201
```

```
Richard MacDonald     95510
Janet Dempsey         94111
Alice MacLeod         94114
David Mack            94114
Toni Barnett          95020
Jack Cooper           94072
```

The problem of how to sort by last name within the last two digits of the ZIP code is solved by a second pass covering the last name field. The f option following **–k 2** affects the second pass, which orders lines by last name only.

```
$ sort -b -k 3.4 -k 2f list
Tom Winstrom          94201
Richard MacDonald     95510
Janet Dempsey         94111
David Mack            94114
Alice MacLeod         94114
Toni Barnett          95020
Jack Cooper           94072
```

The next set of examples uses the **cars** data file. All blanks in this file are TABs; it contains no SPACEs. From left to right, the columns in this file contain each car's make, model, year of manufacture, mileage, and price:

```
$ cat cars
plym    fury    1970    73      2500
chevy   malibu  1999    60      3000
ford    mustang 1965    45      10000
volvo   s80     1998    102     9850
ford    thundbd 2003    15      10500
chevy   malibu  2000    50      3500
bmw     325i    1985    115     450
honda   accord  2001    30      6000
ford    taurus  2004    10      17000
toyota  rav4    2002    180     750
chevy   impala  1985    85      1550
ford    explor  2003    25      9500
```

Without any options sort displays a sorted copy of the file:

```
$ sort cars
bmw     325i    1985    115     450
chevy   impala  1985    85      1550
chevy   malibu  1999    60      3000
chevy   malibu  2000    50      3500
ford    explor  2003    25      9500
ford    mustang 1965    45      10000
ford    taurus  2004    10      17000
ford    thundbd 2003    15      10500
honda   accord  2001    30      6000
plym    fury    1970    73      2500
toyota  rav4    2002    180     750
volvo   s80     1998    102     9850
```

The objective of the next example is to sort by manufacturer and by price within manufacturer. Unless you specify otherwise, a sort field extends to the end of the line. The **–k 1** sort field specifier sorts from the beginning of the line. The command line instructs sort to sort on the entire line and then make a second pass, sorting on the fifth field all lines whose first-pass sort fields were the same (**–k 5**):

```
$ sort -k 1 -k 5 cars
bmw      325i    1985    115     450
chevy    impala  1985    85      1550
chevy    malibu  1999    60      3000
chevy    malibu  2000    50      3500
ford     explor  2003    25      9500
ford     mustang 1965    45      10000
ford     taurus  2004    10      17000
ford     thundbd 2003    15      10500
honda    accord  2001    30      6000
plym     fury    1970    73      2500
toyota   rav4    2002    180     750
volvo    s80     1998    102     9850
```

Because no two lines are the same, sort makes only one pass, sorting on each entire line. (If two lines differed only in the fifth field, they would be sorted properly on the first pass anyway, so the second pass would be unnecessary.) Look at the lines containing **taurus** and **thundbd**. They are sorted by the second field rather than by the fifth field, demonstrating that sort never made a second pass and so never sorted on the fifth field.

The next example forces the first-pass sort to stop at the end of the first field. The shown **–k 1,1** option specifies a ***start*** pointer of the first character of the first field and a ***stop*** pointer of the last character of the first field. When you do not specify a character within a ***start*** pointer, it defaults to the first character; when you do not specify a character within a ***stop*** pointer, it defaults to the last character. Now **taurus** and **thundbd** are properly sorted by price. But look at **explor**: It is less expensive than the other Fords, but sort has it positioned as the most expensive. The sort utility put the list in ASCII collating sequence order, not in numeric order: 9500 comes after 10000 because 9 comes after 1.

```
$ sort -k 1,1 -k 5 cars
bmw      325i    1985    115     450
chevy    impala  1985    85      1550
chevy    malibu  1999    60      3000
chevy    malibu  2000    50      3500
ford     mustang 1965    45      10000
ford     thundbd 2003    15      10500
ford     taurus  2004    10      17000
ford     explor  2003    25      9500
honda    accord  2001    30      6000
plym     fury    1970    73      2500
toyota   rav4    2002    180     750
volvo    s80     1998    102     9850
```

The **–n** (numeric) option on the second pass puts the list in the proper order:

```
$ sort -k 1,1 -k 5n cars
bmw     325i    1985    115     450
chevy   impala  1985    85      1550
chevy   malibu  1999    60      3000
chevy   malibu  2000    50      3500
ford    explor  2003    25      9500
ford    mustang 1965    45      10000
ford    thundbd 2003    15      10500
ford    taurus  2004    10      17000
honda   accord  2001    30      6000
plym    fury    1970    73      2500
toyota  rav4    2002    180     750
volvo   s80     1998    102     9850
```

The next example again demonstrates that, unless you instruct it otherwise, sort orders a file starting with the field you specify and continuing to the end of the line. It does not make a second pass unless two of the first sort fields are the same. Because there is no ***stop*** pointer on the first sort field specifier, the sort field for the first pass includes the third field through the end of the line. Although this example sorts the cars by years, it does not sort the cars by model within manufacturer within years (**ford thundbd** comes before **ford explor**, so these lines should be reversed).

```
$ sort -k 3 -k 1 cars
ford    mustang 1965    45      10000
plym    fury    1970    73      2500
bmw     325i    1985    115     450
chevy   impala  1985    85      1550
volvo   s80     1998    102     9850
chevy   malibu  1999    60      3000
chevy   malibu  2000    50      3500
honda   accord  2001    30      6000
toyota  rav4    2002    180     750
ford    thundbd 2003    15      10500
ford    explor  2003    25      9500
ford    taurus  2004    10      17000
```

Specifying an end to the sort field for the first pass allows sort to perform its secondary sort properly:

```
$ sort -k 3,3 -k 1 cars
ford    mustang 1965    45      10000
plym    fury    1970    73      2500
bmw     325i    1985    115     450
chevy   impala  1985    85      1550
volvo   s80     1998    102     9850
chevy   malibu  1999    60      3000
chevy   malibu  2000    50      3500
honda   accord  2001    30      6000
toyota  rav4    2002    180     750
ford    explor  2003    25      9500
ford    thundbd 2003    15      10500
ford    taurus  2004    10      17000
```

The next examples demonstrate important sorting techniques: putting a list in alphabetical order, merging uppercase and lowercase entries, and eliminating duplicates. The unsorted list follows:

```
$ cat short
Pear
Pear
apple
pear
Apple
```

Following is a plain sort:

```
$ sort short
Apple
Pear
Pear
apple
pear
```

The following folded sort is a good start, but it does not eliminate duplicates:

```
$ sort -f short
Apple
apple
Pear
Pear
pear
```

The **–u** (unique) option eliminates duplicates but without the **–f** the uppercase entries come first:

```
$ sort -u short
Apple
Pear
apple
pear
```

When you attempt to use both **–u** and **–f**, some of the entries get lost:

```
$ sort -uf short
apple
Pear
```

Two passes is the answer. Both passes are unique sorts, and the first folds lowercase letters onto uppercase ones:

```
$ sort -u -k 1f -k 1 short
Apple
apple
Pear
pear
```

split

Divides a file into sections

split [options] [filename [prefix]]

The split utility breaks its input into 1,000-line sections named **xaa, xab, xac,** and so on. The last section might be shorter. Options can change the sizes of the sections and lengths of the names.

Arguments

The *filename* is the pathname of the file that split processes. If you do not specify an argument or if you specify a hyphen (–) instead of the *filename*, split reads from standard input. The *prefix* is one or more characters that split uses to prefix the names of the files it creates; the default is **x**.

Options

Under Linux, split accepts the common options described on page 736. Options preceded by a double hyphen (––) work under Linux only. Options named with a single letter and preceded by a single hyphen work under Linux and macOS.

––suffix-length=*len*
–a *len*
Specifies that the filename suffix is *len* characters long (the default is 2).

––bytes=*n[u]* **–b *n*[*u*]**
Breaks the input into files that are *n* bytes long. The *u* is an optional unit of measure that can be **k** (kilobyte or 1,024-byte blocks) or **m** (megabyte or 1,048,576-byte blocks). If you include the unit of measure, split counts by this unit instead of by bytes. Under Linux, *u* can be **b** (512-byte blocks) or any of the suffixes listed in Table VI-1 on page 735.

––numeric-suffixes
–d Specifies numeric suffixes instead of alphabetic suffixes.

––lines=*num* **–l *num***
Breaks the input into files that are *num* lines long (the default is 1,000).

Discussion

By default split names the first file it creates **xaa**. The **x** is the default prefix. You can change the prefix by using the *prefix* argument on the command line. You can change the number of characters in each filename following the prefix by using the **––suffix-length** option.

Examples

By default split breaks a file into 1,000-line sections with the names **xaa, xab, xac,** and so on. The wc utility with the **–l** option shows the number of lines in each file. The last file, **xar,** is smaller than the rest.

```
$ split /usr/share/dict/words
$ wc -l *
  1000 xaa
  1000 xab
  1000 xac
...
  1000 xdt
   569 xdu
 98569 total
```

The next example uses the ***prefix*** argument to specify a filename prefix of **SEC** and uses **–c** (**––suffix-length**) to change the number of letters in the filename suffix to 3:

```
$ split -a 3 /usr/share/dict/words SEC
$ ls
SECaaa  SECaak  SECaau  SECabe  SECabo  SECaby  SECaci  SECacs  SECadc  SECadm
SECaab  SECaal  SECaav  SECabf  SECabp  SECabz  SECacj  SECact  SECadd  SECadn
...
SECaaj  SECaat  SECabd  SECabn  SECabx  SECach  SECacr  SECadb  SECadl
```

ssh

Securely runs a program or opens a shell on a remote system

ssh [option] [user@]host [command-line]

The ssh utility logs in on a remote system and starts a shell. Optionally, ssh executes a command on the remote system and logs out. The ssh utility provides secure, encrypted communication between two systems over an unsecure network.

See Chapter 17 for information on ssh

tip See the sections of Chapter 17 starting on pages 704 and 706 for information on the ssh utility, one of the OpenSSH secure communication utilities.

sshfs/curlftpfs

Mounts a directory on an OpenSSH or FTP server as a local directory

sshfs [options] [user@]host:[remote-directory] mount-point
curlftpfs [options] host mount-point
fusermount –u mount-point

The sshfs and curlftpfs utilities enable a nonprivileged user to mount a directory hierarchy on an OpenSSH or FTP host as a local directory.

Arguments

The ***user*** is the optional username sshfs logs in as. The ***user*** defaults to the username of the user running the command on the local system. The ***host*** is the server running the OpenSSH or FTP daemon.

The ***remote-directory*** is the directory to be mounted and defaults to the home directory of the user sshfs logs in as. A relative pathname specifies a directory relative to the user's home directory; an absolute pathname specifies the absolute pathname of a directory.

The ***mount-point*** is the (empty) local directory where the remote directory is mounted. Unless ssh/ftp is set up to log in automatically, curlftpfs prompts for a username and sshfs and curlftpfs prompt for a password. See page 717 (ssh) and page 840 (ftp) for information on setting up automatic logins.

Options

The sshfs and curlftpfs utilities have many options; see their respective man pages for complete lists.

–o allow_other

Grants access to the ***mount-point*** to users other than the user who ran the sshfs/curlftpfs command, including a privileged user. By default only the user who ran the command (and not a privileged user) can access the ***mount-point*** regardless of directory permissions. You must uncomment the **user_allow_other** line in **/etc/fuse.conf** for this option to work (see "Notes," following).

–o allow_root

Grants access to the ***mount-point*** to a privileged user. By default only the user who ran the sshfs/curlftpfs command can access the ***mount-point***. You must uncomment the **user_allow_other** line in **/etc/fuse.conf** for this option to work (see "Notes," following).

–o debug –d Displays FUSE debugging information. Implies –f.

–f Runs sshfs/curlftpfs in the foreground.

–p *port*

Connects to port ***port*** on the remote system (sshfs only).

Discussion

The sshfs and curlftpfs utilities are based on the FUSE (Filesystems in USErspace; github.com/libfuse) kernel module. FUSE enables users to mount remote directories they have access to without working as a privileged user (which is required when giving a mount command) and without the remote system exporting the directory hierarchy (required when running NFS). The mounted directory can be in a location that is convenient to the user, typically in the user's home directory hierarchy. If the user can mount the directory without entering a username and password, the process can be automated by putting commands in one of the user's startup files.

Notes

You might need to install the **sshfs** or **curlftpfs** package before you can run sshfs, curlftpfs, or fusermount. See Appendix C for details.

The sshfs and curlftpfs utilities depend on the FUSE kernel module. The following command checks whether this module is loaded:

```
$ lsmod | grep fuse
fuse                     71167  3
```

The documentation recommends running sshfs and curlftpfs as a nonprivileged user. Without the **–o allow_other** option, only the user who gives the sshfs or curlftpfs command can access the mounted directory, regardless of permissions. Not even a privileged user can access it. You can use the **–o allow_other** option to give other users access to the mounted directory and **–o allow_root** to give a privileged user access. For these options to work, you must work as a privileged user to uncomment the **user_allow_other** line in the **/etc/fuse.conf** file. This line must appear exactly as shown, with nothing else on the line.

```
$ cat /etc/fuse.conf
# mount_max = 1000
user_allow_other
```

The **mount_max** line specifies the maximum number of simultaneous mounts. If you uncomment this line, the syntax must be exactly as shown.

Examples

sshfs

To use sshfs to mount a remote directory, you must be able to use ssh to list that directory. Sam has set up ssh so he does not need a password to run commands on the remote system named **plum**. See page 717 for information on setting up ssh so it does not require a password. If ssh requires you to supply a password, sshfs will also require a password.

```
$ ssh plum ls
letter.0505
memos
pix
```

After Sam checks that he can use ssh to run commands on **plum**, he creates the **sam.plum.fs** directory and mounts his home directory from **plum** on that directory.

An **ls** command shows that Sam's files on **plum** are now available in the **sam.plum.fs** directory.

```
$ mkdir sam.plum.fs
$ sshfs plum: sam.plum.fs
$ ls sam.plum.fs
letter.0505  memos  pix
```

When he is done using the files, Sam unmounts the remote directory using fusermount with the **–u** option:

```
$ fusermount -u sam.plum.fs
$ ls sam.plum.fs
```

Next, Sam mounts his **memos** directory from **plum** so anyone on his local system can access the files in that directory. First, working as a privileged user, he creates a directory under the root directory and gives himself ownership of that directory.

```
# mkdir /sam.memos ; chown sam:sam /sam.memos
# ls -ld /sam.memos
drwxr-xr-x. 2 sam sam 4096 02-23 15:55 /sam.memos
```

Again working with **root** privileges, he edits the **/etc/fuse.conf** file and uncomments the **user_allow_other** line so other users will be able to access the mounted directory. Then, working as himself, Sam uses sshfs with the **–o allow_other** option to mount his **plum memos** directory on the local system as **/sam.memos**. The df utility (page 793) shows the mounted directory.

```
$ sshfs -o allow_other plum:memos /sam.memos
$ ls /sam.memos
0602  0603  0604

$ df -h /sam.memos
Filesystem      Size  Used Avail Use% Mounted on
plum:memos      146G  2.3G  136G   2% /sam.memos
```

Now any user on the system can access Sam's **memos** directory from **plum** as **/sam.memos** on the local system.

curlftpfs The next example shows how to mount an anonymous FTP server as a local directory. See page 840 for information about setting up a **.netrc** file so you do not have to supply a password on the command line.

In the following example, Sam creates the **kernel.org** directory and then runs curlftpfs to mount the FTP directory at **mirrors.kernel.org** as **kernel.org**. Here, he is using the **–o user=ftp** option to specify a username and enters his email address in response to the password prompt. Use **fusermount –u** to unmount the remote directory.

```
$ mkdir kernel.org
$ curlftpfs -o user=ftp mirrors.kernel.org kernel.org
Enter host password for user 'ftp':
$ ls -l kernel.org | head -4
dr-xr-xr-x.  18 root root  4096 01-14 19:13 archlinux
drwxrwxr-x.  30 root root  4096 12-21 09:33 centos
drwxrwxr-x.  12 root root  4096 2018-02-23  cpan
```

stat

Displays information about files

stat [options] [file-list]

The stat utility displays information about files.

Arguments

The *file-list* specifies the pathnames of one or more files that stat displays information about. Without a *file-list,* stat displays information about standard input.

Options

Options preceded by a double hyphen (––) work under Linux only. Except as noted, options named with a single letter and preceded by a single hyphen work under Linux and macOS.

Without any options, stat displays all available information about each file it processes.

––format=*fmt* –c *fmt*
: Formats output using *fmt.* See the stat man page for more information. LINUX

–F
: (**file type**) Displays a slash (/) after each directory, an asterisk (*) after each executable file, an at sign (@) after a symbolic link, an equal sign (=) after a socket, and a pipe symbol (|) after a FIFO. macOS

–f
: (**filesystem**) Displays filesystem information instead of file information. LINUX

–f *fmt*
: Formats output using *fmt.* The *fmt* string is similar to that used by printf (page 942). See the stat man page for more information. macOS

––dereference –L
: For each file that is a symbolic link, displays information about the file the link points to, not the symbolic link itself. This option treats files that are not symbolic links normally. See page 118 for information on dereferencing symbolic links.

–l
: (**long**) Uses the same format as **ls –l** (page 100). macOS

––printf=*fmt*
: Formats output using *fmt.* The *fmt* string is similar to that used by printf (page 942). See the stat man page for more information.

–q
: (**quiet**) Suppresses error messages. macOS

–s
: (**shell**) Displays information in a format that can be used to initialize shell variables. macOS

–x
: (**Linux**) Displays a more verbose format that is compatible with the version of stat found on Linux. macOS

Examples

The Linux and macOS versions of stat display different information. The examples show the output from the Linux version.

The first example displays information about the **/bin/bash** file:

```
$ stat /bin/bash
  File: '/bin/bash'
  Size: 893964          Blocks: 1752       IO Block: 4096   regular file
Device: fd01h/64769d    Inode: 22183       Links: 1
Access: (0755/-rwxr-xr-x)  Uid: (    0/    root)   Gid: (    0/    root)
Context: system_u:object_r:shell_exec_t:s0
Access: 2018-05-02 03:12:22.065940944 -0700
Modify: 2018-03-13 08:53:35.000000000 -0700
Change: 2018-05-02 03:12:16.675941400 -0700
 Birth: -
```

The next example displays information about the root filesystem:

```
$ stat -f /
  File: "/"
    ID: 491003435dced81d Namelen: 255     Type: ext2/ext3
Block size: 4096       Fundamental block size: 4096
Blocks: Total: 13092026    Free: 12171215   Available: 12040183
Inodes: Total: 3276800     Free: 3177256
```

strings

strings

Displays strings of printable characters from files

strings [options] file-list

The strings utility displays strings of printable characters from object and other nontext files.

Arguments

The *file-list* is a list of files that strings processes.

Options

Options preceded by a double hyphen (––) work under Linux only. Except as noted, options named with a single letter and preceded by a single hyphen work under Linux and macOS.

––all –a Processes whole files. Without this option strings processes only the initialized and loaded parts of an object file.

––print-file-name –f Precedes each string with the name of the file that the string comes from. LINUX

––bytes=*min* –*min*
Displays strings of characters that are at least ***min*** characters long (the default is 4).

Discussion

The strings utility can help you determine the contents of nontext files. One notable application for strings is determining the owner of files in a **lost+found** directory.

Examples

The following example displays strings of four or more printable characters in the executable file for the man utility. If you did not know what this file was, these strings could help you determine that it was the man executable.

```
$ strings /usr/bin/man
...
--Man-- next: %s [ view (return) | skip (Ctrl-D) | quit (Ctrl-C) ]
format: %d, save_cat: %d, found: %d
cannot write to %s in catman mode
creating temporary cat for %s
can't write to temporary cat for %s
can't create temporary cat for %s
cat-saver exited with status %d
found ultimate source file %s
...
```

stty

Displays or sets terminal parameters

stty [options] [arguments]

Without any arguments, stty displays parameters that affect the operation of the terminal or terminal emulator. For a list of some of these parameters and an explanation of each, see the "Arguments" section. The arguments establish or change parameters.

Options

Under Linux, stty accepts the common options described on page 736. Options preceded by a double hyphen (--) work under Linux only. Except as noted, options named with a single letter and preceded by a single hyphen work under Linux and macOS.

--all **-a** Reports on all parameters. This option does not accept arguments.

--file=*device* **-F *device***
Affects ***device***. Without this option stty affects the device attached to standard input. You can change the characteristics of a device only if you own its device file or if you are working with **root** privileges. LINUX

-f *device*
Affects ***device***. Performs the same function as **-F**. macOS

--save **-g** Generates a report of the current settings in a format you can use as arguments to another stty command. This option does not accept arguments.

Arguments

The arguments to stty specify which terminal parameters stty is to alter. To turn on each of the parameters that is preceded by an optional hyphen (indicated in the following list as [–]), specify the parameter without the hyphen. To turn it off, use the hyphen. Unless specified otherwise, this section describes the parameters in their *on* states.

Special Keys and Characteristics

columns *n* Sets the line width to ***n*** columns.

ek (**erase kill**) Sets the erase and line kill keys to their default values. Many systems use DELETE and CONTROL-U, respectively, as the defaults.

erase *x* Sets the erase key to ***x***. To specify a control character, precede ***x*** with CONTROL-V (for example, use CONTROL-V CONTROL-H to indicate CONTROL-H) or use the notation **^h**, where **^** is a caret (SHIFT-6 on most keyboards).

intr *x* Sets the interrupt key to ***x***. See **erase *x*** for conventions.

kill *x* Sets the line kill key to ***x***. See **erase *x*** for conventions.

rows *n* Sets the number of screen rows to ***n***.

sane Sets the terminal parameters to values that are usually acceptable. The **sane** argument is useful when several stty parameters have changed, making it difficult to use the terminal to run stty to set things right. If **sane** does not appear to work, try entering the following characters:

CONTROL-J **stty sane** CONTROL-J

susp *x* (**suspend**) Sets the suspend (terminal stop) key to *x*. See **erase *x*** for conventions.

werase *x* (**word erase**) Sets the word erase key to *x*. See **erase *x*** for conventions.

Modes of Data Transmission

[–]cooked See **raw**. LINUX

cooked See **sane**. macOS

[–]cstopb (**stop bits**) Selects two stop bits (**–cstopb** specifies one stop bit).

[–]parenb (**parity enable**) Enables parity on input and output. When you specify **–parenb**, the system does not use or expect a parity bit when communicating with the terminal.

[–]parodd (**parity odd**) Selects odd parity (**–parodd** selects even parity).

[–]raw The normal state is **–raw**. When the system reads input in its raw form, it does not interpret the following special characters: erase (usually DELETE), line kill (usually CONTROL-U), interrupt execution (CONTROL-C), and EOF (CONTROL-D). In addition, the system does not use parity bits. Reflecting the humor that is typical of Linux's heritage, under Linux you can also specify **–raw** as **cooked**.

Treatment of Characters

[–]echo Echoes characters as they are typed (full-duplex operation). If a terminal is half-duplex and displays two characters for each one it should display, turn the **echo** parameter off (**–echo**). Use **–echo** when the user is entering passwords.

[–]echoe (**echo erase**) The normal setting is **echoe**, which causes the kernel to echo the character sequence BACKSPACE SPACE BACKSPACE when you use the erase key to delete a character. The effect is to move the cursor backward across the line, removing characters as you delete them.

[–]echoke (**echo kill erase**) The normal setting is **echoke**. When you use the kill character to delete a line while this option is set, all characters back to the prompt are erased on the current line. When this option is negated, pressing the kill key moves the cursor to the beginning of the next line.

[–]echoprt (**echo print**) The normal setting is **–echoprt**, which causes characters to disappear as you erase them. When you set **echoprt**, characters you erase are displayed between a backslash (\) and a slash (/). For example, if you type the word **sort** and then erase it by pressing BACKSPACE four times, Linux displays **sort\tros/** when **echoprt** is set. If you use the kill character to delete the entire line, having **echoprt** set causes the entire line to be displayed as if you had BACKSPACEd to the beginning of the line.

[–]lcase For uppercase-only terminals, translates all uppercase characters into lowercase as they are entered (also [–]**LCASE**). LINUX

[–]nl Accepts only a NEWLINE character as a line terminator. With **–nl** in effect, the system accepts a RETURN character from the terminal as a NEWLINE but sends a RETURN followed by a NEWLINE to the terminal in place of a NEWLINE.

[–]tabs Transmits each TAB character to the terminal as a TAB character. When **tabs** is turned off (**–tabs**), the kernel translates each TAB character into the appropriate number of SPACEs and transmits them to the terminal (also [–]**tab3**).

Job Control Parameters

[–]tostop Stops background jobs if they attempt to send output to the terminal (**–tostop** allows background jobs to send output to the terminal).

Notes

The name stty is an abbreviation for *set teletypewriter,* or *set tty* (page 1017), the first terminal UNIX was run on. Today stty is commonly thought of as meaning *set terminal.*

The shells retain some control over standard input when you use them interactively. As a consequence, a number of the options available with stty appear to have no effect. For example, the command **stty –echo** appears to have no effect under tcsh:

```
tcsh $ stty -echo
tcsh $ date
Mon May 28 16:53:01 PDT 2018
```

While **stty –echo** does work when you are using bash interactively, **stty –echoe** does not. However, you can still use these options to affect shell scripts and other utilities.

```
$ cat testit
#!/bin/bash
stty -echo
read -p "Enter a value: " a
echo
echo "You entered: $a"
stty echo

$ ./testit
Enter a value:
You entered: 77
```

The preceding example does not display the user's response to the **Enter a value:** prompt. The value is retained by the **a** variable and is displayed by the **echo "You entered: $a"** statement.

Examples

The first example shows that stty without any arguments displays several terminal operation parameters. (The local system might display more or different parameters.) The character following the **erase =** is the erase key. A ^ preceding a character indicates a CONTROL key. In the example the erase key is set to CONTROL-H. If stty does not display the erase character, it is set to its default value of DELETE. If it does not display a kill character, it is set to its default of ^U.

```
$ stty
speed 38400 baud; line = 0;
erase = ^H;
```

Next, the ek argument returns the erase and line kill keys to their default values:

```
$ stty ek
```

The next display verifies the change. The stty utility does not display either the erase character or the line kill character, indicating both are set to their default values:

```
$ stty
speed 38400 baud; line = 0;
```

The next example sets the erase key to CONTROL-H. The CONTROL-V quotes the CONTROL-H so the shell does not interpret it and passes it to stty unchanged:

```
$ stty erase CONTROL-V CONTROL-H
$ stty
speed 38400 baud; line = 0;
erase = ^H;
```

Next, stty sets the line kill key to CONTROL-X. This time the user enters a caret (^) followed by an **x** to represent CONTROL-X. You can use either a lowercase or uppercase letter.

```
$ stty kill ^X
$ stty
speed 38400 baud; line = 0;
erase = ^H; kill = ^X;
```

Now stty changes the interrupt key to CONTROL-C:

```
$ stty intr CONTROL-VCONTROL-C
```

In the following example, stty turns off TABs so the appropriate number of SPACEs is sent to the terminal in place of a TAB. Use this command if a terminal does not automatically expand TABs.

```
$ stty -tabs
```

If you log in under Linux and everything appears on the terminal in uppercase letters, give the following command and then check the CAPS LOCK key. If it is set, turn it off.

```
$ STTY -LCASE
```

Turn on lcase if you are using a very old terminal that cannot display lowercase characters. Although no one usually changes the suspend key from its default of CONTROL-Z, you can. Give the following command to change the suspend key to CONTROL-T:

```
$ stty susp ^T
```

sysctl

Displays and alters kernel variables at runtime

sysctl [options] [variable-list]
sysctl [options] **–w** *[var=value ...]*

The sysctl utility displays and alters kernel variables, including kernel tuning parameters, at runtime.

Arguments

The ***variable-list*** is a list of kernel variables whose values sysctl displays. In the second syntax, each ***value*** is assigned to the variable named ***var***.

Options

–a (**all**) Displays all kernel variables.

–b (**binary**) Displays kernel variables as binary data without terminating NEWLINEs. macOS

–n (**no label**) Displays variables without labels.

Discussion

The sysctl utility provides access to a number of kernel variables, including the maximum number of processes the kernel will run at one time, the filename used for core files, and the system security level. Some variables cannot be altered or can be altered only in certain ways. For example, you can never lower the security level.

Examples

The sysctl utility is commonly used for tuning the kernel. The process limits can be displayed by anyone, but can be altered only by a user who is working with **root** privileges. The following example shows a user displaying and changing the maximum number of threads:

```
$ sysctl kernel.threads-max
kernel.threads-max = 32015
...
# sysctl -w kernel.threads-max=20000
kernel.threads-max = 20000
```

tail

Displays the last part (tail) of a file

tail [options] [file-list]

The tail utility displays the last part, or end, of a file.

Arguments

The ***file-list*** is a list of pathnames of the files that tail displays. When you specify more than one file, tail displays the filename of each file before displaying lines from that file. If you do not specify an argument or, under Linux, if you specify a hyphen (–) instead of a filename, tail reads from standard input.

Options

Under Linux, tail accepts the common options dcribed on page 736. Options preceded by a double hyphen (––) work under Linux only. Except as noted, options named with a single letter and preceded by a single hyphen work under Linux and macOS.

–b *[+]**n***
: Counts by 512-byte blocks instead of lines. The ***n*** argument is an integer that specifies the number of blocks. Thus, the command **tail –b 5** displays the last five blocks of a file. See the note about using a plus sign (+) in the next option. macOS

––bytes=*[+]n[u]* **–c** *[+]**n**[**u**]*
: Counts by bytes (characters) instead of lines. The ***n*** argument is an integer that specifies the number of bytes. Thus, the command **tail –c 5** displays the last five bytes of a file. Under Linux only, the ***u*** is an optional multiplicative suffix as described on page 735, except that tail uses a lowercase **k** for kilobyte (1,024-byte blocks). If you include a multiplicative suffix, tail counts by this unit instead of by bytes.

  If you put a plus sign (+) in front of ***n***, tail counts from the start of the file instead of the end. The tail utility still *displays characters through the end* of the file, even though it *starts counting* from the beginning. Thus, **tail –c +5** causes tail to display from the fifth character through the end of the file.

––follow **–f**
: After copying the last line of the file, tail enters an endless loop, waiting and copying additional lines from the file if the file grows. If you specify multiple files in ***file-list*** with this option, tail includes a new header each time it displays output from a different file so you know which file is being added to. This option is useful for tracking the progress of a process that is running in the background and sending its output to a file. The tail utility continues to wait indefinitely, so you must use the interrupt key to terminate it. See also the **–s** option.

--lines=*[+]n[u]* -n *[+]n[u]*
Counts by lines (the default). The ***n*** argument is an integer that specifies the number of lines. Under Linux, the ***u*** is an optional unit of measure; see the **-c** (**--bytes**) option for an explanation of its use. Although it is not documented, you can use **±*n*** to specify a number of lines without using this option.

If you put a plus sign (+) in front of ***n***, tail counts from the start of the file instead of the end. The tail utility still *displays lines through the end* of the file, even though it *starts counting* from the beginning. Thus, **tail -n +5** causes tail to display from the fifth line through the last line of the file.

--quiet -q Suppresses header information when you specify multiple files in ***file-list***. LINUX

--sleep-interval=*n* -s *n*
When used with **-f**, causes tail to sleep for ***n*** seconds between checks for additional output. LINUX

Notes

The tail utility displays the last ten lines of its input by default.

Examples

The examples are based on the **eleven** file:

```
$ cat eleven
line one
line two
line three
line four
line five
line six
line seven
line eight
line nine
line ten
line eleven
```

First, tail displays the last ten lines of the **eleven** file (no options):

```
$ tail eleven
line two
line three
line four
line five
line six
line seven
line eight
line nine
line ten
line eleven
```

Next, it displays the last three lines (**-n 3** or **--lines 3**) of the file:

```
$ tail -n 3 eleven
line nine
line ten
line eleven
```

The following example displays the file starting at line 8 (**+8**):

```
$ tail -n +8 eleven
line eight
line nine
line ten
line eleven
```

The next example displays the last six characters in the file (**–c 6** or **––bytes 6**). Only five characters are evident (**leven**); the sixth is a NEWLINE.

```
$ tail -c 6 eleven
leven
```

Monitor output The final example demonstrates the **–f** option. Here, tail monitors the output of a make command, which is being sent to the file **accounts.out**:

```
$ make accounts > accounts.out &
$ tail -f accounts.out
        cc -c trans.c
        cc -c reports.c
...
CONTROL-C
$
```

In the preceding example, running tail with **–f** displays the same information as running make in the foreground and not redirecting its output to a file. However, using tail offers some advantages. First, the output of make is saved in a file. (The output would not be saved if you did not redirect its output.) Second, if you decide to do something else while make is running, you can kill tail and the screen will be free for you to use while make continues running in the background. When you are running a large job such as compiling a large program, you can use tail with the **–f** option to check on its progress periodically.

tar

Stores or retrieves files to/from an archive file

tar option [modifiers] [file-list]

The tar (tape archive) utility creates, adds to, lists, and retrieves files from an archive file.

Arguments

The ***file-list*** is a list of pathnames of the files that tar archives or extracts.

Options

Use only one of the following options to indicate which action you want tar to take. You can alter the action of the option by following it with one or more ***modifiers***.

The macOS version of tar accepts long options

tip: Options for tar preceded by a double hyphen (––) work under macOS as well as under Linux.

––create **–c** Creates an archive. This option stores the files named in ***file-list*** in a new archive. If the archive already exists, tar destroys it before creating the new archive. If a ***file-list*** argument is a directory, tar copies the directory hierarchy into the archive. Without the **––file** option, tar writes the archive to standard output.

––compare **–d** Compares an archive with the corresponding disk files and reports on the differences. You can also use **--diff**.

––help Displays a list of options and modifiers, along with short descriptions of each.

––append **–r** Writes the files named in ***file-list*** to the end of the archive. This option leaves files that are already in the archive intact, so duplicate copies of files might appear in the archive. When tar extracts the files, the last version of a file read from the archive is the one that ends up on the disk.

––list **–t** (**table of contents**) Without a ***file-list,*** this option produces a table of contents listing all files in an archive. With a ***file-list,*** it displays the name of each file in the ***file-list*** each time it occurs in the archive. You can use this option with the **––verbose** option to display detailed information about files in an archive.

––update **–u** Adds the files from ***file-list*** if they are not already in the archive or if they have been modified since they were last written to the archive. Because of the additional checking required, tar runs more slowly when you specify this option.

––extract **–x** Extracts ***file-list*** from the archive and writes it to the disk, overwriting existing files with the same names. Without a ***file-list,*** this option extracts all files from the archive. If the ***file-list*** includes a directory, tar extracts the directory hierarchy. The tar utility attempts to keep the owner, modification time, and access privileges the same as those of the original file. If tar reads the same file more than once, the last version read will appear on the disk when tar is finished.

Modifiers

--blocking-factor *n*

-b *n*

Uses ***n*** as the blocking factor for creating an archive. Use this option only when tar is creating an archive directly to removable media. (When tar reads an archive, it automatically determines the blocking factor.) The value of ***n*** is the number of 512-byte blocks to write as a single block on the removable medium.

--directory *dir* -C *dir*

Changes the working directory to ***dir*** before processing.

--checkpoint

Displays periodic messages. This option lets you know tar is running without forcing you to view all the messages displayed by **--verbose**.

--exclude=*file*

Does not process the file named ***file***. If ***file*** is a directory, no files or directories in that directory hierarchy are processed. The ***file*** can be an ambiguous file reference; quote special characters as needed.

--file *filename* -f *filename*

Uses ***filename*** as the name of the file the archive is created in or extracted from. The ***filename*** can be the name of an ordinary file or a device (e.g., a DVD or USB flash drive). You can use a hyphen (–) instead of the ***filename*** to refer to standard input when creating an archive and to standard output when extracting files from an archive. The following two commands are equivalent ways of creating a compressed archive of the files in the **/home** directory hierarchy on **/dev/sde1**:

```
$ tar -zcf /dev/sde1 /home
$ tar -cf - /home | gzip > /dev/sde1
```

--dereference -h

For each file that is a symbolic link, archives the file the link points to, not the symbolic link itself. See page 118 for information on dereferencing symbolic links.

--ignore-failed-read

When creating an archive, tar normally quits with a nonzero exit status if any of the files in ***file-list*** is unreadable. This option causes tar to continue processing, skipping unreadable files.

--bzip2 -j

Uses bzip2 (pages 64 and 750) to compress/decompress files when creating an archive and extracting files from an archive.

--tape-length *n* -L *n*

Asks for a new medium after writing ***n*** *1,024 bytes to the current medium. This feature is useful when you are building archives that are too big to fit on a single USB flash drive, partition, DVD, or other storage device.

--touch -m

Sets the modification time of the extracted files to the time of extraction. Without this option tar attempts to maintain the modification time of the original file.

--one-file-system When a directory name appears in ***file-list*** while it is creating an archive, tar recursively processes the files and directories in the named directory hierarchy. With this option tar stays in the filesystem that contains the named directory and does not process directories in other filesystems. Under macOS, you can use **-l** (lowercase "l") in place of **--one-file-system**. Under Linux, **-l** is used for a different purpose.

--absolute-names -P The default behavior of tar is to force all pathnames to be relative by stripping leading slashes from them. This option disables this feature, so absolute pathnames remain absolute.

--sparse -S Linux allows you to create *sparse files* (large, mostly empty files). The empty sections of sparse files do not take up disk space. When tar extracts a sparse file from an archive, it normally expands the file to its full size. As a result, when you restore a sparse file from a tar backup, the file takes up its full space and might no longer fit in the same disk space as the original. This option causes tar to handle sparse files efficiently so they do not take up unnecessary space either in the archive or when they are extracted.

--verbose -v Lists each file as tar reads or writes it. When combined with the **-t** option, **-v** causes tar to display a more detailed listing of the files in the archive, showing their ownership, permissions, size, and other information.

--interactive -w Asks you for confirmation before reading or writing each file. Respond with **y** if you want tar to take the action. Any other response causes tar not to take the action.

--exclude-from *filename*
-X *filename*
Similar to the **--exclude** option, except ***filename*** specifies a file that contains a list of files to exclude from processing. Each file listed in ***filename*** must appear on a separate line.

--compress *or* **--uncompress -Z** Uses compress when creating an archive and uncompress when extracting files from an archive.

--gzip *or* **--gunzip -z** Uses gzip when creating an archive and gunzip when extracting files from an archive. This option also works to extract files from archives that have been compressed with the compress utility.

Notes

The **--help** option displays all tar options and modifiers; the **--usage** option provides a brief summary of the same information. The info page on tar provides extensive information, including a tutorial for this utility.

You can use ambiguous file references in ***file-list*** when you create an archive but not when you extract files from an archive.

The name of a directory file within the ***file-list*** references the directory hierarchy (all files and directories within that directory).

The file that tar sends its output to by default is compilation specific; typically, it goes to standard output. Use the **–f** option to specify a different filename or device to hold the archive.

When you create an archive using a simple filename in ***file-list,*** the file appears in the working directory when you extract it. If you use a relative pathname when you create an archive, the file appears with that relative pathname, starting from the working directory when you extract it. If you use the **–P** option and an absolute pathname when you create an archive, and if you use the **–P** option when you extract files from the archive, tar extracts the file with the same pathname and might overwrite the original files.

See page 711 for an example of using ssh with tar to create an archive file on a remote system of the contents of the working directory hierarchy.

Leading hyphens The tar utility does not require leading hyphens on options and modifiers. However, it behaves slightly differently with regard to the order of options and modifiers it requires with and without the hyphen.

You can specify one or more modifiers following an option. With a leading hyphen, the following tar command generates an error:

```
$ tar -cbf 10 /dev/sde1 memos
tar: f: Invalid blocking factor
Try 'tar --help' or 'tar --usage' for more information.
```

The error occurs because the **–b** modifier takes an argument but is not the last modifier in a group. The same command works correctly if you omit the leading hyphen.

You must use leading hyphens if you separate options:

```
$ tar -cb 10 -f /dev/sde1 memos
```

Examples

The following example makes a copy of the **/home/max** directory hierarchy on a USB flash drive mounted at **/dev/sde1**. The **v** modifier causes the command to list the files it writes to the device. This command erases anything that was already on the device. The message from tar explains that the default action is to store all pathnames as relative paths instead of absolute paths, thereby allowing you to extract the files into a different directory on the disk.

```
$ tar -cvf /dev/sde1 /home/max
tar: Removing leading '/' from member names.
/home/max/
/home/max/.bash_history
/home/max/.bash_profile
...
```

In the next example, the same directory is saved on the device mounted on **/dev/sde1** with a blocking factor of 100. Without the v modifier, tar does not display the list of files it is writing to the device. The command runs in the background and displays any messages after the shell issues a new prompt.

```
$ tar -cb 100 -f /dev/sde1 /home/max &
[1] 4298
$ tar: Removing leading '/' from member names.
```

The next command displays the table of contents of the archive on the device mounted on **/dev/sde1**:

```
$ tar -tvf /dev/sde1
drwxrwxrwx max/group         0 Jun 30 21:39 2018 home/max/
-rw-r--r-- max/group       678 Aug  6 14:12 2018 home/max/.bash_history
-rw-r--r-- max/group       571 Aug  6 14:06 2018 home/max/.bash_profile
drwx------ max/group         0 Nov  6 22:34 2018 home/max/mail/
-rw------- max/group      2799 Nov  6 22:34 2018 home/max/mail/sent-mail
...
```

Next, Max creates a gzipped tar archive in **/tmp/max.tgz**. This approach is a popular way to bundle files that you want to transfer over a network or otherwise share with others. Ending a filename with **.tgz** is one convention for identifying gzipped tar archives. Another convention is to end the filename with **.tar.gz**.

```
$ tar -czf /tmp/max.tgz literature
```

The final command lists the files in the compressed archive **max.tgz**:

```
$ tar -tzvf /tmp/max.tgz
...
```

tee

Copies standard input to standard output and one or more files

tee [options] file-list

The tee utility copies standard input to standard output *and* to one or more files.

Arguments

The *file-list* is a list of the pathnames of files that receive output from tee. If a file in *file-list* does not exist, tee creates it.

Options

Options preceded by a double hyphen (––) work under Linux only. Options named with a single letter and preceded by a single hyphen work under Linux and macOS. Without any options, tee overwrites the output files if they exist and responds to interrupts.

––append –a Appends output to existing files rather than overwriting them.

–i Causes tee not to respond to the **SIGINT** interrupt. macOS

––ignore-interrupts
–i Causes tee not to respond to interrupts. LINUX

Examples

In the following example, a pipeline sends the output from make to tee, which copies that information to standard output and to the file **accounts.out**. The copy that goes to standard output appears on the screen. The cat utility displays the copy that was sent to the file.

```
$ make accounts | tee accounts.out
        cc -c trans.c
        cc -c reports.c
...
$ cat accounts.out
        cc -c trans.c
        cc -c reports.c
...
```

Refer to page 994 for a similar example that uses **tail –f** rather than tee.

telnet

Connects to a remote computer over a network

telnet [options] [remote-system]

The telnet utility implements the TELNET protocol to connect to a remote computer over a network.

telnet is not secure

security The telnet utility is not secure. It sends your username and password over the network in cleartext, which is not a secure practice. Use ssh (pages 703 and 704) when it is available.

Arguments

The ***remote-system*** is the name or IP address of the remote system that telnet connects to. When you do not specify a ***remote-system,*** telnet works interactively and prompts you to enter one of the commands described in this section.

Options

–a Initiates automatic login (the default behavior under macOS).

–e *c*
(**escape**) Changes the escape character from CONTROL-] to the character ***c***.

–K Prevents automatic login. This option is available under macOS and some Linux distributions (it is the default behavior under Linux).

–l *username*
Attempts an automatic login on the remote system using ***username***. If the remote system understands how to handle automatic login with telnet, it prompts for a password.

Discussion

After telnet connects to a remote system, you can put telnet into command mode by typing the escape character (usually CONTROL-]). The remote system typically reports the escape character it recognizes. To leave command mode, type RETURN on a line by itself.

In command mode, telnet displays the **telnet>** prompt. You can use the following commands in command mode:

? (**help**) Displays a list of commands recognized by the telnet utility on the local system.

close Closes the connection to the remote system. If you specified the name of a system on the command line when you started telnet, **close** has the same effect as **quit:** The telnet program quits, and the shell displays a prompt. If you used the **open** command instead of specifying a remote system on the command line, **close** returns telnet to command mode.

logout Logs you out of the remote system; similar to **close**.

open *remote-computer*
If you did not specify a remote system on the command line or if the attempt to connect to the system failed, you can specify the name or IP address of a remote system interactively using this command.

quit Quits the telnet session.

z Suspends the telnet session. When you suspend a session, you return to the login shell on the local system. To resume the suspended telnet session, type **fg** (page 151) at a shell prompt.

Notes

Under Linux, telnet does not attempt to log in automatically. Under macOS, telnet attempts to log in automatically. When telnet attempts to log in automatically, it uses your username on the local system unless you specify a different name with the **–l** option.

The telnet utility (**telnet** package), a user interface to the TELNET protocol, is older than ssh and is not secure. Nevertheless, it might work where ssh (page 703) is not available (there is more non-UNIX support for TELNET access than for ssh access). In addition, some legacy devices, such as terminal servers, facilities infrastructure, and network devices, still do not support ssh.

telnet versus ssh When you connect to a remote UNIX or Linux system, telnet presents a textual **login:** prompt. Because telnet is designed to work with non-UNIX and non-Linux systems, it does not assume your remote username is the same as your local username (ssh does make this assumption). In some cases, telnet requires no login credentials.

In addition, telnet allows you to configure special parameters, such as how RETURNs or interrupts are processed (ssh does not give you this option). When using telnet between UNIX and/or Linux systems, you rarely need to change any parameters.

Examples

In the following example, Sam connects to the remote system named **plum**. After running a few commands on **plum**, he types CONTROL-] to escape to command mode and types **help** to display a list of telnet commands. Next, he uses the **z** command to suspend the telnet session so he can run a few commands on the local system. He then gives an **fg** command to the shell to resume using telnet; he has to press RETURN to display the prompt on **plum**. The **logout** command on the remote system ends the telnet session, and the local shell displays a prompt.

```
[sam@guava ~]$ telnet plum
Trying 172.16.192.151...
Connected to plum.
Escape character is '^]'.
Fedora release 16 (Verne)
Kernel 3.3.0-4.fc16.i686 on an i686 (1)
login: sam
Password:
Last login: Tue Apr 10 10:28:19 from guava
...
```

```
[sam@plum ~]$ CONTROL-]
telnet> help
Commands may be abbreviated.  Commands are:

close           close current connection
logout          forcibly logout remote user and close the connection
display         display operating parameters
mode            try to enter line or character mode ('mode ?' for more)
...
telnet> z

[1]+  Stopped                  telnet plum
...
[sam@guava ~]$ fg
telnet plum
RETURN
[sam@plum ~]$ logout
Connection closed by foreign host.
[sam@guava ~]$
```

Using telnet to connect to other ports

By default telnet connects to port 23, which is used for remote logins. However, you can use telnet to connect to other services by specifying a port number. In addition to standard services, many of the special remote services available on the Internet use unallocated port numbers. Unlike the port numbers for standard protocols, these port numbers can be picked arbitrarily by the administrator of the service.

Although telnet is no longer commonly employed to log in on remote systems, it is still used extensively as a debugging tool by allowing you to communicate directly with a TCP server. Some standard protocols are simple enough that an experienced user can debug problems by connecting to a remote service directly using telnet. If you are having a problem with a network server, a good first step is to try to connect to it using telnet.

If you use telnet to connect to port 25 on a host, you can interact with SMTP. In addition, port 110 connects to the POP protocol, port 80 connects with a WWW server, and port 143 connects to IMAP. All of these are ASCII protocols and are documented in *RFCs* (page 1120). You can read the RFCs or search the Web for examples of how to use them interactively.

In the following example, a system administrator who is debugging a problem with email delivery uses telnet to connect to the SMTP port (port 25) on the server at **example.com** to see why it is bouncing mail from the **spammer.com** domain. The first line of output indicates which IP address telnet is trying to connect to. After telnet displays the **Connected to smtpsrv.example.com** message, the user emulates an SMTP dialog, following the standard SMTP protocol. The first line, which starts with **helo**, begins the session and identifies the local system. After the SMTP server identifies itself, the user enters a line that identifies the mail sender as **user@spammer.com**. The SMTP server's response explains why the message is bouncing, so the user ends the session with **quit**.

```
$ telnet smtpsrv 25
Trying 192.168.1.1...
Connected to smtpsrv.example.com.
Escape character is '^]'.
helo example.com
220 smtpsrv.example.com ESMTP Sendmail 8.13.1/8.13.1; Wed, 2 May 2018 00:13:43 -0500 (CDT)
250 smtpsrv.example.com Hello desktop.example.com [192.168.1.97], pleased to meet you
mail from:user@spammer.com
571 5.0.0 Domain banned for spamming
quit
221 2.0.0 smtpsrv.example.com closing connection
```

The telnet utility allows you to use any protocol you want, as long as you know it well enough to type commands manually.

test

Evaluates an expression

test expression
[expression]

The **test** utility evaluates an expression and returns a condition code indicating the expression is either *true* (0) or *false* (not 0). You can place brackets ([]) around the expression instead of using the word **test** (second syntax).

Arguments

The *expression* contains one or more criteria (see the following list) that **test** evaluates. A **–a** separating two criteria is a Boolean AND operator: Both criteria must be *true* for **test** to return a condition code of *true*. A **–o** is a Boolean OR operator. When **–o** separates two criteria, one or the other (or both) of the criteria must be *true* for **test** to return a condition code of *true*.

You can negate any criterion by preceding it with an exclamation point (**!**). You can group criteria using parentheses. If there are no parentheses, **–a** takes precedence over **–o**, and **test** evaluates operators of equal precedence from left to right.

Within the *expression* you must quote special characters, such as parentheses, so the shell does not interpret them but rather passes them to **test** unchanged.

Because each element, such as a criterion, string, or variable within the **expression**, is a separate argument, you must separate each element from other elements using a SPACE. Table VI-32 lists the criteria you can use within the *expression*. Table VI-33 on page 1007 lists **test**'s relational operators.

Table VI-32 Criteria

Criterion	Meaning
string	*True* if ***string*** has a length greater than zero. LINUX *True* if ***string*** is not a null string. macOS
–n *string*	*True* if ***string*** has a length greater than zero.
–z *string*	*True* if ***string*** has a length of zero.
string1* = *string2	*True* if ***string1*** is equal to ***string2***.
string1* != *string2	*True* if ***string1*** is not equal to ***string2***.
int1 relop int2	*True* if integer ***int1*** has the specified algebraic relationship to integer ***int2***. The ***relop*** is a relational operator from Table VI-33 on page 1007. As a special case, **–l *string***, which returns the length of ***string***, may be used for ***int1*** or ***int2***.
file1* –ef *file2	*True* if ***file1*** and ***file2*** have the same device and inode numbers.

Table VI-32 Criteria (continued)

Criterion	Meaning
file1* –nt *file2	*True* if ***file1*** was modified after ***file2*** (the modification time of ***file1*** is **n**ewer **t**han that of ***file2***).
file1* –ot *file2	*True* if ***file1*** was modified before ***file2*** (the modification time of ***file1*** is **o**lder **t**han that of ***file2***).
–b *filename*	*True* if the file named ***filename*** exists and is a block special file.
–c *filename*	*True* if the file named ***filename*** exists and is a character special file.
–d *filename*	*True* if the file named ***filename*** exists and is a directory.
–e *filename*	*True* if the file named ***filename*** exists.
–f *filename*	*True* if the file named ***filename*** exists and is an ordinary file.
–g *filename*	*True* if the file named ***filename*** exists and its setgid bit (page 104) is set.
–G *filename*	*True* if the file named ***filename*** exists and is associated with the group that is the primary group of the user running the command (same effective group ID).
–k *filename*	*True* if the file named ***filename*** exists and its sticky bit (page 1126) is set.
–L *filename*	*True* if the file named ***filename*** exists and is a symbolic link.
–O *filename*	*True* if the file named ***filename*** exists and is owned by the user running the command (same effective user ID).
–p *filename*	*True* if the file named ***filename*** exists and is a named pipe.
–r *filename*	*True* if the file named ***filename*** exists and the user running the command has read permission for it.
–s *filename*	*True* if the file named ***filename*** exists and contains information (has a size greater than 0 bytes).
–t *file-descriptor*	*True* if ***file-descriptor*** is open and associated with the screen or keyboard. The ***file-descriptor*** for standard input is 0, for standard output is 1, and for standard error is 2. See page 468 for more information.
–u *filename*	*True* if the file named ***filename*** exists and its setuid bit (page 104) is set.
–w *filename*	*True* if the file named ***filename*** exists and you have write permission for it.
–x *filename*	*True* if the file named ***filename*** exists and the user running **test** has execute/search permission for it.

Table VI-33 Relational operators

Relational operator	Meaning
–eq	Equal to
–ge	Greater than or equal to
–gt	Greater than
–le	Less than or equal to
–lt	Less than
–ne	Not equal to

Notes

The **test** command is built into the Bourne Again and TC Shells.

Examples

See page 468 for examples that use the **–t** criterion to check whether a file descriptor from the process running **test** is associated with the terminal.

The following examples demonstrate the use of the **test** utility in Bourne Again Shell scripts. Although **test** works from a command line, it is more commonly employed in shell scripts to test input or verify access to a file.

The first example prompts the user, reads a line of input into a variable, and uses the synonym for **test**, **[]**, to see whether the user entered **yes**:

```
$ cat user_in
read -p "Input yes or no: " user_input
if [ "$user_input" = "yes" ]
    then
        echo "You input yes."
fi
```

The next example prompts for a filename and then uses the synonym for **test**, **[]**, to see whether the user has read access permission (**–r**) for the file *and* (**–a**) whether the file contains information (**–s**):

```
$ cat validate
read -p "Enter filename: " filename
if [ -r "$filename" -a -s "$filename" ]
    then
        echo "File $filename exists and contains information."
        echo "You have read access permission to the file."
fi
```

top

Dynamically displays process status

*top [**options**]*

The top utility displays information about the status of the local system, including information about current processes.

Options

Although top does not require the use of hyphens with options, it is a good idea to include them for clarity and consistency with other utilities. You can cause top to run as though you had specified any of the options by giving commands to the utility while it is running. See the "Discussion" section for more information.

–ca Causes top to run in accumulative mode. In this mode, times and events are counted cumulatively since top started. See the top man page if you want to use the **–c** option to run top in another mode. macOS

–d *ss.tt*
(**delay**) Specifies ***ss.tt*** as the number of seconds and tenths of seconds of delay from one display update to the next. The default is 3 seconds. LINUX

–i Ignores idle and *zombie processes* (processes without a parent). LINUX

–n ***n***
(**number**) Specifies the number of iterations: top updates the display ***n*** times and exits. LINUX

–p ***n***
(**PID**) Monitors the process with a PID of ***n***. You can use this option up to 20 times on a command line or specify ***n*** as a comma-separated list of up to 20 PID numbers. LINUX

–S (**sum**) Causes top to run in cumulative mode. In cumulative mode, the CPU times reported for processes include forked processes and CPU times accumulated by child processes that are now dead. LINUX

–s (**secure**) Runs top in secure mode, restricting the commands you can use while top is running to those that pose less of a security risk. LINUX

–s ***ss***
(**seconds**) Specifies ***ss*** as the number of seconds of delay from one display update to the next. The default is 1 second. macOS

Discussion

The first few lines top displays summarize the status of the local system. You can turn each of these lines on or off with the toggle switches (interactive command keys) specified in the following descriptions. The first line is the same as the output of the uptime utility (page 73) and shows the current time, the amount of time the local system has been running since it was last booted, the number of users logged in, and the load averages from the last 1, 5, and 15 minutes (toggle **l** [lowercase "l"]). The second line indicates the number of running processes (toggle **t**). Next is one or more lines, one for each CPU/core (also toggle **t**) followed by a line for memory (toggle **m**) and one for swap space (also toggle **m**).

The rest of the display reports on individual processes, which are listed in order by descending CPU usage (i.e., the most CPU-intensive process is listed first). By default top displays the number of processes that fit on the screen.

Table VI-34 describes the meanings of the fields displayed for each process.

Table VI-34 Field names

Name	Meaning
PID	Process identification number
USER	Username of the owner of the process
PR	Priority of the process
NI	nice value (page 916)
VIRT	Number of kilobytes of virtual memory used by the process
RES	Number of kilobytes of physical (nonswapped) memory used by the process
SHR	Number of kilobytes of shared memory used by the process
S	Status of the process (see **STAT** on page 948)
%CPU	Percentage of the total CPU time the process is using
%MEM	Percentage of physical memory the process is using
TIME[+]	Total CPU time used by the process
COMMAND	Command line that started the process or name of the program (toggle with **c**)

While top is running, you can issue the following commands to modify its behavior:

h (**help**) Displays a summary of the commands you can use while top is running. LINUX

? (**help**) Displays a summary of the commands you can use while top is running. macOS

k (**kill**) Allows you to kill a process. Unless you are working with **root** privileges, you can kill only processes you own. When you use this command, top prompts you for the PID of the process and the signal to send to the process. You can enter either a signal number or a name. (See Table 10-5 on page 496 for a list of signals.) This command is disabled when you are working in secure mode. LINUX

n (**number**) When you give this command, top asks you to enter the number of processes you want it to display. If you enter 0 (the default), top shows as many processes as fit on the screen.

q (**quit**) Terminates top.

r (**renice**) Changes the priority of a running process (refer to renice on page 951). Unless you are working with **root** privileges, you can change the priority of only your own processes and only to lower the priority by entering a positive value. A user working with **root** privileges can enter a negative value, increasing the priority of the process. This command is disabled when you are working in secure mode. LINUX

S (**sum**) Toggles top between cumulative mode and regular mode. See the **–S** option for details. LINUX

s (**seconds**) Prompts for the number of seconds to delay between updates to the display (3 is the default). You may enter an integer, a fraction, or 0 (for continuous updates). Under Linux, this command is disabled when you are working in secure mode.

W (**write**) Writes top's current configuration to your personal configuration file (**~/.toprc**). LINUX

SPACE
Refreshes the screen.

Notes

The Linux and macOS versions of top are very different. Although it applies to both versions, this coverage of top is oriented toward the Linux version. Refer to the macOS top man page for more information about the macOS version.

The top utility is similar to ps but periodically updates the display, enabling you to monitor the behavior of the local system over time.

This utility shows only as much of the command line for each process as fits on a line. If a process is swapped out, top replaces the command line with the name of the command in parentheses.

Under Linux, the top utility uses the **proc** filesystem. When **proc** is not mounted, top does not work.

Requesting continuous updates is almost always a mistake. The display is updated too quickly and the system load increases dramatically.

Example

The following display is the result of a typical execution of top on a system that has a CPU with four cores:

```
top - 15:58:38 up 8 days,  5:25,  1 user,  load average: 0.54, 0.70, 0.71
Tasks: 295 total,   1 running, 293 sleeping,   0 stopped,   1 zombie
Cpu0  :  2.0%us,  2.3%sy,  0.0%ni, 95.7%id,  0.0%wa,  0.0%hi,  0.0%si,  0.0%st
Cpu1  :  3.5%us,  5.4%sy,  0.0%ni, 90.8%id,  0.0%wa,  0.0%hi,  0.3%si,  0.0%st
Cpu2  :  7.1%us,  1.0%sy,  0.0%ni, 91.9%id,  0.0%wa,  0.0%hi,  0.0%si,  0.0%st
Cpu3  :  5.4%us, 10.9%sy,  0.0%ni, 83.4%id,  0.0%wa,  0.3%hi,  0.0%si,  0.0%st
Mem:  16466476k total, 16275772k used,   190704k free,   370208k buffers
Swap: 58589160k total,      108k used, 58589052k free, 12858064k cached

  PID USER      PR  NI  VIRT  RES  SHR S %CPU %MEM    TIME+  COMMAND
 1530 root      20   0  267m 175m  38m S   12  1.1 216:19.29 Xorg
  942 zach      20   0 3937m 3.2g 3.0g S    7 20.4 171:19.46 vmware-vmx
 3354 zach      20   0  790m  86m  34m S    7  0.5 321:18.92 kwin
19166 zach      20   0  586m 122m  28m S    3  0.8   4:13.05 plugin-containe
19126 zach      20   0 1178m 658m  33m S    1  4.1  13:56.39 firefox
 7867 zach      20   0 2567m 1.6g 1.5g S    1 10.0  18:15.98 vmware-vmx
 7919 zach      20   0 2635m 2.1g 2.0g S    1 13.2  43:57.29 vmware-vmx
12234 zach      20   0 2692m 1.4g 1.4g S    1  9.1  14:09.21 vmware-vmx
21269 zach      20   0 19356 1564 1064 R    1  0.0   0:00.56 top
 3617 zach      20   0  762m 108m  21m S    0  0.7   9:59.94 plasma-desktop
 4867 zach      20   0  463m  40m  16m S    0  0.3   0:55.99 konsole
 5223 zach      20   0  474m 216m  22m S    0  1.3  21:35.01 vmware
21277 root      20   0     0    0    0 S    0  0.0   0:00.01 vmware-rtc
    1 root      20   0 23844 2000 1220 S    0  0.0   0:01.21 init
    2 root      20   0     0    0    0 S    0  0.0   0:00.06 kthreadd
    3 root      RT   0     0    0    0 S    0  0.0   0:00.02 migration/0
...
```

touch

Creates a file or changes a file's access and/or modification time

touch [options] file-list

The touch utility changes the access and/or modification time of a file to the current time or a time you specify. You can also use touch to create a file.

Arguments

The ***file-list*** is a list of the pathnames of the files that touch will create or update.

Options

Under Linux, touch accepts the common options described on page 736. Options preceded by a double hyphen (--) work under Linux only. Except as noted, options named with a single letter and preceded by a single hyphen work under Linux and macOS. Without any options, touch changes the access and modification times to the current time. When you do not specify the **-c** (**--no-create**) option, touch creates files that do not exist.

-a Updates the access time only, leaving the modification time unchanged.

--no-create **-c** Does not create files that do not exist.

--date=*datestring* **-d** ***datestring***

Updates times using the date specified by ***datestring***. Most familiar formats are permitted for ***datestring***. Components of the date and time not included in ***datestring*** are assumed to be the current date and time. This option may not be used with **-t**. LINUX

-m Updates the modification time only, leaving the access time unchanged.

--reference=*file* **-r** ***file***

Updates times with the times of ***file***.

-t [[*cc*]*yy*]*nnddhhmm*[*.ss*]

Changes times to the date specified by the argument. The ***nn*** argument is the number of the month (01–12), ***dd*** is the day of the month (01–31), ***hh*** is the hour based on a 24-hour clock (00–23), and ***mm*** is the minutes (00–59). You must specify at least these fields. You can specify the number of seconds past the start of the minute with *.ss*.

The optional ***cc*** specifies the first two digits of the year (the value of the century minus 1), and ***yy*** specifies the last two digits of the year. When you do not specify a year, touch assumes the current year. When you do not specify ***cc,*** touch assumes 20 for ***yy*** in the range 0–68 and 19 for ***yy*** in the range 69–99.

This option may not be used with **-d**.

Examples

The first three commands show touch updating an existing file. The ls utility with the –l option displays the modification time of the file. The last three commands show touch creating a file.

```
$ ls -l program.c
-rw-r--r--. 1 sam pubs 17481 03-13 16:22 program.c
$ touch program.c
$ ls -l program.c
-rw-r--r--. 1 sam pubs 17481 05-02 11:30 program.c

$ ls -l read.c
ls: cannot access read.c: No such file or directory
$ touch read.c
$ ls -l read.c
-rw-r--r--. 1 sam pubs 0 05-02 11:31 read.c
```

The first of the following ls commands displays the file *modification* times; the second ls (with the **–lu** options) displays the file *access* times:

```
$ ls -l
-rw-r--r--. 1 sam pubs  466 01-10 19:44 cases
-rw-r--r--. 1 sam pubs 1398 04-18 04:24 excerpts

$ ls -lu
-rw-r--r--. 1 sam pubs  466 05-02 11:34 cases
-rw-r--r--. 1 sam pubs 1398 05-02 11:34 excerpts
```

The next example works on the two files shown above and demonstrates the use of the **–a** option to change the access time only and the **–t** option to specify a date for touch to use instead of the current date and time. After the touch command is executed, ls shows that the access times of the files **cases** and **excerpts** have been updated but the modification times remain the same.

```
$ touch -at 02040608 cases excerpts
$ ls -l
-rw-r--r--. 1 sam pubs  466 01-10 19:44 cases
-rw-r--r--. 1 sam pubs 1398 04-18 04:24 excerpts

$ ls -lu
-rw-r--r--. 1 sam pubs  466 02-04 06:08 cases
-rw-r--r--. 1 sam pubs 1398 02-04 06:08 excerpts
```

tr

tr

Replaces specified characters

tr [options] string1 [string2]

The tr utility reads standard input and, for each input character, either maps it to an alternate character, deletes the character, or leaves the character as is. This utility reads from standard input and writes to standard output.

Arguments

The tr utility is typically used with two arguments, ***string1*** and ***string2***. The position of each character in the two strings is important: Each time tr finds a character from ***string1*** in its input, it replaces that character with the corresponding character from ***string2***.

With one argument, ***string1***, and the **–d** (**––delete**) option, tr deletes the characters specified in ***string1***. The option **–s** (**––squeeze-repeats**) replaces multiple sequential occurrences of characters in ***string1*** with single occurrences (for example, **abbc** becomes **abc**).

Ranges

A range of characters is similar in function to a character class within a regular expression (page 1120). GNU tr does not support ranges (character classes) enclosed within brackets. You can specify a range of characters by following the character that appears earlier in the collating sequence with a hyphen and the character that comes later in the collating sequence. For example, **1–6** expands to **123456**. Although the range A–Z expands as you would expect in ASCII, this approach does not work when you use the EBCDIC collating sequence, as these characters are not sequential in EBCDIC. See "Character Classes" for a solution to this issue.

Character Classes

A tr character class is not the same as the character class described elsewhere in this book. (GNU documentation uses the term *list operator* for what this book calls a *character class*.) You specify a character class as '***[:class:]***', where ***class*** is one of the character classes from Table VI-35. You must specify a character class in ***string1*** (and not ***string2***) unless you are performing case conversion (see the "Examples" section) or you use the **–d** and **–s** options together.

Table VI-35 Character classes

Class	Meaning
alnum	Letters and digits
alpha	Letters
blank	Whitespace

Table VI-35 Character classes (continued)

Class	Meaning
cntrl	CONTROL characters
digit	Digits
graph	Printable characters but not SPACEs
lower	Lowercase letters
print	Printable characters including SPACEs
punct	Punctuation characters
space	Horizontal or vertical whitespace
upper	Uppercase letters
xdigit	Hexadecimal digits

Options

Options preceded by a double hyphen (––) work under Linux only. Except as noted, options named with a single letter and preceded by a single hyphen work under Linux and macOS.

––complement **–c** Complements ***string1***, causing tr to match all characters *except* those in ***string1***.

––delete **–d** Deletes characters that match those specified in ***string1***. If you use this option with the **–s** (**––squeeze-repeats**) option, you must specify both ***string1*** and ***string2*** (see "Notes").

––help Summarizes how to use tr, including the special symbols you can use in ***string1*** and ***string2***. LINUX

––squeeze-repeats **–s** Replaces multiple sequential occurrences of a character in ***string1*** with a single occurrence of the character when you call tr with only one string argument. If you use both ***string1*** and ***string2***, the tr utility first translates the characters in ***string1*** to those in ***string2***; it then replaces multiple sequential occurrences of a character in ***string2*** with a single occurrence of the character.

––truncate-set1 **–t** Truncates ***string1*** so it is the same length as ***string2*** before processing input. LINUX

Notes

When ***string1*** is longer than ***string2***, the initial portion of ***string1*** (equal in length to ***string2***) is used in the translation. When ***string1*** is shorter than ***string2***, tr repeats the last character of ***string1*** to extend ***string1*** to the length of ***string2***. In this case tr departs from the POSIX standard, which does not define a result.

If you use the **–d** (**––delete**) and **–s** (**––squeeze-repeats**) options at the same time, tr first deletes the characters in ***string1*** and then replaces multiple sequential occurrences of a character in ***string2*** with a single occurrence of the character.

Examples

You can use a hyphen to represent a range of characters in *string1* or *string2*. The two command lines in the following example produce the same result:

```
$ echo abcdef | tr  'abcdef' 'xyzabc'
xyzabc
$ echo abcdef | tr  'a-f' 'x-za-c'
xyzabc
```

The next example demonstrates a popular method for disguising text, often called ROT13 (rotate 13) because it replaces the first letter of the alphabet with the thirteenth, the second with the fourteenth, and so forth. The first line ends with a pipe symbol that implicitly continues the line (see the optional section on page 148) and causes bash to start the next line with a secondary prompt (page 321).

```
$ echo The punchline of the joke is ... |
> tr 'A-M N-Z a-m n-z' 'N-Z A-M n-z a-m'
Gur chapuyvar bs gur wbxr vf ...
```

To make the text intelligible again, reverse the order of the arguments to tr:

```
$ echo Gur chapuyvar bs gur wbxr vf ... |
> tr 'N-Z A-M n-z a-m' 'A-M N-Z a-m n-z'
The punchline of the joke is ...
```

The **--delete** option causes tr to delete selected characters:

```
$ echo If you can read this, you can spot the missing vowels! |
> tr --delete 'aeiou'
If y cn rd ths, y cn spt th mssng vwls!
```

In the following example, tr replaces characters and reduces pairs of identical characters to single characters:

```
$ echo tennessee | tr -s 'tnse' 'srne'
serene
```

The next example replaces each sequence of nonalphabetic characters (the complement of all the alphabetic characters as specified by the character class **alpha**) in the file **draft1** with a single NEWLINE character. The output is a list of words, one per line.

```
$ tr -c -s '[:alpha:]' '\n' < draft1
```

The next example uses character classes to upshift the string **hi there**:

```
$ echo hi there | tr '[:lower:]' '[:upper:]'
HI THERE
```

tty

Displays the terminal pathname

tty [option]

The tty utility displays the pathname of standard input if it is a terminal and displays **not a tty** if it is not a terminal. The exit status is 0 if standard input is a terminal and 1 if it is not.

Options

Under Linux, tty accepts the common options described on page 736. The option preceded by a double hyphen (--) works under Linux only. The option named with a single letter and preceded by a single hyphen works under Linux and macOS.

--silent *or* **--quiet** **-s** Causes tty not to print anything. The tty utility sets its exit status. See "Examples" for another way to determine if standard input is coming from a terminal.

Notes

The term *tty* is short for *teletypewriter,* the terminal device on which UNIX was first run. This command appears in UNIX, and Linux has kept it for the sake of consistency and tradition.

Examples

The following example illustrates the use of tty:

```
$ tty
/dev/pts/11
$ echo $?
0
$ tty < memo
not a tty
$ echo $?
1
```

You can use test (or [ ]; page 1005) with the **-t** option in place of tty with the **-s** option to determine if file descriptor 0 (normally standard input) is associated with the terminal.

```
$ [ -t 0 ]
$ echo $?
0
$ [ -t 0 ] < /dev/null
$ echo $?
1
```

See "Determining Whether a File Descriptor Is Associated with the Terminal" on page 468 for more information on using test with the **-t** option.

tune2fs

Changes parameters on an **ext2**, **ext3**, or **ext4** filesystem

tune2fs [options] device

The tune2fs utility displays and modifies filesystem parameters on **ext2**, **ext3**, and **ext4** filesystems. This utility can also set up journaling on an **ext2** filesystem, turning it into an **ext3** filesystem. With typical filesystem permissions, tune2fs must be run by a user working with **root** privileges. The tune2fs utility is available under Linux only. LINUX

Arguments

The ***device*** is the name of the device, such as **/dev/sda8**, that holds the filesystem whose parameters you want to display or modify.

Options

–C *n*
: (**count**) Sets the number of times the filesystem has been mounted without being checked to ***n***. This option is useful for staggering filesystem checks (see "Discussion") and for forcing a check the next time the system boots.

–c *n*
: (**max count**) Sets the maximum number of times the filesystem can be mounted between filesystem checks to ***n***. Set ***n*** to 0 (zero) to disregard this parameter.

–e *behavior*
: (**error**) Specifies what the kernel will do when it detects an error. Set ***behavior*** to **continue** (continues execution), **remount-ro** (remounts the filesystem readonly), or **panic** (causes a kernel panic). Regardless of how you set this option, an error will cause fsck to check the filesystem the next time the system boots.

–i *n[u]*
: (**interval**) Sets the maximum time between filesystem checks to ***n*** time periods. Without ***u*** or with ***u*** set to **d**, the time period is days. Set ***u*** to **w** to set the time period to weeks; use **m** for months. Set ***n*** to 0 (zero) to disregard this parameter. Because a filesystem check is forced only when the system is booted, the time specified by this option might be exceeded.

–j (**journal**) Adds an **ext3** journal to an **ext2** filesystem. For more information on journaling filesystems, see page 1105.

–l (**list**) Lists information about the filesystem.

–T *date*
: (**time**) Sets the time the filesystem was last checked to ***date***. The ***date*** is the time and date in the format ***yyyynndd[hh[mm]ss]]]***. Here, ***yyyy*** is the year, ***nn*** is the number of the month (01–12), and ***dd*** is the day of the month (01–31). You must specify at least these fields. The ***hh*** is the hour based on a 24-hour clock

(00–23), ***mm*** is the minutes (00–59), and ***.ss*** is the number of seconds past the start of the minute. You can also specify ***date*** as **now**.

Discussion

Checking a large filesystem can take a long time. When all filesystem checks occur at the same time, the system might boot slowly. Use the **–C** and/or **–T** options to stagger filesystem checks so they do not all happen at the same time.

Examples

Following is the output of **tune2fs** run with the **–l** option on a typical **ext3** filesystem:

```
# /sbin/tune2fs -l /dev/sda1
tune2fs 1.42.13 (17-May-2015)
Filesystem volume name:   <none>
Last mounted on:          <not available>
Filesystem UUID:          b6d9714e-ed5d-45b8-8023-716a669c16d8
Filesystem magic number:  0xEF53
Filesystem revision #:    1 (dynamic)
Filesystem features:      has_journal ext_attr resize_inode dir_index
    filetype needs_recovery sparse_super large_file
Filesystem flags:         signed_directory_hash
Default mount options:    (none)
Filesystem state:         clean
Errors behavior:          Continue
Filesystem OS type:       Linux
Inode count:              624624
Block count:              2498099
Reserved block count:     124904
Free blocks:              1868063
Free inodes:              509355
First block:              0
Block size:               4096
Fragment size:            4096
Reserved GDT blocks:      609
Blocks per group:         32768
Fragments per group:      32768
Inodes per group:         8112
Inode blocks per group:   507
Filesystem created:       Tue Dec 20 09:41:43 2016
Last mount time:          Wed May  3 03:54:59 2017
Last write time:          Wed May  3 03:54:59 2017
Mount count:              4
Maximum mount count:      31
Last checked:             Tue Dec 20 09:41:43 2016
Check interval:           15552000 (6 months)
Next check after:         Fri May 5 09:41:43 2017
Reserved blocks uid:      0 (user root)
Reserved blocks gid:      0 (group root)
First inode:              11
Inode size:               256
Required extra isize:     28
Desired extra isize:      28
Journal inode:            8
```

```
First orphan inode:       308701
Default directory hash:   half_md4
Directory Hash Seed:      bceae349-a46f-4d45-a8f1-a21b1ae8d2bd
Journal backup:           inode blocks
```

Next, the administrator uses tune2fs to convert an ext2 filesystem to an ext3 journaling filesystem:

```
# /sbin/tune2fs -j /dev/sda5
tune2fs 1.42.13 (17-May-2015)
Creating journal inode: done
This filesystem will be automatically checked every 30 mounts or
180 days, whichever comes first.  Use tune2fs -c or -i to override.
```

umask

Specifies the file-creation permissions mask

umask [option] [mask]

The umask builtin specifies the mask the system uses to set up access permissions when it creates a file. This builtin works slightly differently in each of the shells.

Arguments

The ***mask*** can be a three- or four-digit octal number (bash and tcsh) or a symbolic value (bash) such as you would use with chmod (page 759).

Without any arguments, umask displays the file-creation permissions mask.

Option

–S (**symbolic**) Displays the file-creation permissions mask symbolically.

Discussion

A ***mask*** that you specify using symbolic values specifies the permissions that *are* allowed. A ***mask*** that you specify using octal numbers specifies the permissions that are *not* allowed; the digits correspond to the permissions for the owner of the file, members of the group the file is associated with, and everyone else.

Because the resulting file creation mask specifies the permissions that are *not* allowed, the system uses binary arithmetic to subtract each of the three digits from 7 when you create a file. If the file is an ordinary file (and not a directory file), the system then removes execute permissions from the file. The result is three or four octal numbers that specify the access permissions for the file (the numbers you would use with chmod).

An octal value of 1 (001 binary) represents execute permission, 2 (010 binary) write permission, and 4 (100 binary) read permission (for a file).

You must use binary or octal arithmetic when performing permissions calculations. To calculate file permissions given a umask value, subtract the umask value from octal 777.

For example, assume a umask value of 003:

```
 777    Starting permissions for calculation
-003    Subtract umask value
 774    Resulting permissions for a directory
 111    Remove execute permissions
 664    Resulting permissions for an ordinary file
```

To calculate permissions for a directory, umask subtracts the umask value from 777: In the example where umask has a value of 003, octal 7 minus octal 0 equals octal 7 (for two positions). Octal 7 minus octal 3 equals octal 4—or, using binary arithmetic,

111 – 011 = 100. The result is that the system sets permissions of 774 (**rwxrwxr––**) to a directory.

To calculate permissions for an ordinary file, the system changes the execute bit (001 binary) to 0 for each position. If the execute bit is not set, the system does not change the execute bit. In the example, removing the execute bit from octal 7 yields octal 6 (removing 001 from 111 yields 110; two positions). Octal 4 remains octal 4 because the execute bit is not set (the 001 bit is not set in 100, so it remains 100). The result is that the system gives permissions of 664 (**rw–rw–r––**) to an ordinary file.

Notes

Most utilities and applications do not attempt to create files with execute permissions, regardless of the value of ***mask;*** they assume you do not want an executable file. As a result, when a utility or application such as touch creates a file, the system subtracts each of the digits in ***mask*** from 6. An exception occurs with mkdir, which does assume that you want the execute (access in the case of a directory) bit set. See the "Examples" section.

The umask program is a builtin in bash and tcsh and generally goes in the initialization file for your shell (**~/.bash_profile** [bash] or **~/.login** [tcsh]).

Under bash, the argument **u=rwx,go=r** turns *off* all bits in the ***mask*** for the owner and turns *off* the read bit in the ***mask*** for groups and other users (the mask is 0033), causing those bits to be *on* in file permissions (744 or 644). Refer to chmod on page 759 for more information about symbolic permissions.

Examples

The following commands set the file-creation mask and display the mask and its effect when you create a file and a directory. The mask of 022, when subtracted from 777, gives permissions of 755 (**rwxr–xr–x**) for a directory. For an ordinary file, the system subtracts execute permissions from 755, yielding permissions of 644 (**rw–r––r––**).

```
$ umask 022
$ umask
0022
$ touch afile
$ mkdir adirectory
$ ls -ld afile adirectory
drwxr-xr-x. 2 sam pubs 4096 12-31 12:42 adirectory
-rw-r--r--. 1 sam pubs    0 12-31 12:42 afile
```

The next example sets the same mask using symbolic values. The –S option displays the mask symbolically:

```
$ umask u=rwx,g=rx,o=rx
$ umask
0022
$ umask -S
u=rwx,g=rx,o=rx
```

uniq

Displays unique lines from a file

uniq [options] [input-file] [output-file]

The uniq utility displays its input, removing all but one copy of successive repeated lines. If the file has been sorted (see sort on page 969), uniq ensures that no two lines it displays are the same.

Arguments

When you do not specify the ***input-file***, uniq reads from standard input. When you do not specify the ***output-file***, uniq writes to standard output.

Options

Under Linux, uniq accepts the common options described on page 736. Options preceded by a double hyphen (––) work under Linux only. Except as noted, options named with a single letter and preceded by a single hyphen work under Linux and macOS. A *field* is a sequence of characters bounded by SPACEs, TABs, NEWLINEs, or a combination of these characters.

––count **–c** Precedes each line with the number of occurrences of the line in the input file.

––repeated **–d** Displays one copy of lines that are repeated; does not display lines that are not repeated.

––skip-fields=*nfield*
–f *nfield*
Ignores the first ***nfield*** blank-separated fields of each line. The uniq utility bases its comparison on the remainder of the line, including the leading blanks of the next field on the line (see the **–s** [**––skip-chars**] option).

––ignore-case **–i** Ignores case when comparing lines.

––skip-chars=*nchar*
–s *nchar*
Ignores the first ***nchar*** characters of each line. If you also use the **–f** (**––skip-fields**) option, uniq ignores the first ***nfield*** fields followed by ***nchar*** characters. You can use this option to skip over leading blanks of a field.

––unique **–u** Displays only lines that are *not* repeated.

––check-chars=*nchar*
–w *nchar*
Compares up to ***nchars*** characters on a line after honoring the **–f** (**––skip-fields**) and **–s** (**––skip-chars**) options. By default uniq compares the entire line. LINUX

Examples

These examples assume the file named **test** in the working directory contains the following text:

```
$ cat test
boy took bat home
boy took bat home
girl took bat home
dog brought hat home
dog brought hat home
dog brought hat home
```

Without any options, uniq displays only one copy of successive repeated lines:

```
$ uniq test
boy took bat home
girl took bat home
dog brought hat home
```

The **–c** (**––count**) option displays the number of consecutive occurrences of each line in the file:

```
$ uniq -c test
   2 boy took bat home
   1 girl took bat home
   3 dog brought hat home
```

The **–d** (**––repeated**) option displays only lines that are consecutively repeated in the file:

```
$ uniq -d test
boy took bat home
dog brought hat home
```

The **–u** (**––unique**) option displays only lines that are *not* consecutively repeated in the file:

```
$ uniq -u test
girl took bat home
```

In the next example, the **–f** (**––skip-fields**) option skips the first field in each line, causing the lines that begin with **boy** and the one that begins with **girl** to appear to be consecutive repeated lines. The uniq utility displays only one occurrence of these lines:

```
$ uniq -f 1 test
boy took bat home
dog brought hat home
```

The next example uses both the **–f** (**––skip-fields**) and **–s** (**––skip-chars**) arguments first to skip two fields and then to skip two characters. The two characters this command skips include the SPACE that separates the second and third fields and the first character of the third field. Ignoring these characters, all the lines appear to be consecutive repeated lines containing the string **at home**. The uniq utility displays only the first of these lines:

```
$ uniq -f 2 -s 2 test
boy took bat home
```

w

Displays information about local system users

w [options] [username]

The w utility displays the names of users logged in on the local system, together with their terminal device numbers, the times they logged in, the commands they are running, and other information.

Arguments

The ***username*** restricts the display to information about that user. Under macOS you can specify several usernames separated by SPACEs.

Options

–f (**from**) Removes the **FROM** column. For users who are directly connected, this field contains a hyphen. LINUX

–h (**no header**) Suppresses the header line.

–i (**idle**) Sorts output by idle time. macOS

–s (**short**) Displays less information: username, terminal device, idle time, and command. LINUX

Discussion

The first line w displays is the same as that displayed by uptime (page 73). This line includes the time of day, how long the system has been running (in days, hours, and minutes), how many users are logged in, and how busy the system is (load average). From left to right, the load averages indicate the number of processes that have been waiting to run in the past 1 minute, 5 minutes, and 15 minutes.

The columns of information that w displays have the following headings:

```
USER TTY FROM LOGIN@ IDLE JCPU PCPU WHAT
```

The **USER** is the username of the user. The **TTY** is the device name for the line the user logged in on. The **FROM** is the system name a remote user is logged in from; it is a hyphen for a local user. The **LOGIN@** gives the date and time the user logged in. The **IDLE** indicates how many minutes have elapsed since the user last used the keyboard. The **JCPU** is the CPU time used by all processes attached to the user's tty, not including completed background jobs. The **PCPU** is the time used by the process named in the **WHAT** column. The **WHAT** is the command the user is running.

Examples

The first example shows the full list produced by the w utility:

```
$ w
 10:26am  up 1 day, 55 min,  6 users,  load average: 0.15, 0.03, 0.01
USER     TTY      FROM             LOGIN@   IDLE   JCPU   PCPU  WHAT
max      tty1     -                Fri 9am 20:39m  0.22s  0.01s  vim td
max      tty2     -                Fri 5pm 17:16m  0.07s  0.07s  -bash
```

```
root      pts/1    -                 Fri 4pm 14:28m  0.20s  0.07s  -bash
sam       pts/2    -                 Fri 5pm  3:23   0.08s  0.08s  /bin/bash
hls       pts/3    potato            10:07am  0.00s  0.08s  0.02s  w
```

In the next example, the –s option produces an abbreviated listing:

```
$ w -s
 10:30am  up 1 day, 58 min,  6 users,  load average: 0.15, 0.03, 0.01
USER      TTY      FROM                 IDLE  WHAT
max       tty1     -                  20:43m  vim td
max       tty2     -                  17:19m  -bash
root      pts/1    -                  14:31m  -bash
sam       pts/2    -                   0.20s  vim memo.030125
hls       pts/3    potato              0.00s  w -s
```

The final example requests information only about Max:

```
$ w max
 10:35am  up 1 day,  1:04,  6 users,  load average: 0.06, 0.01, 0.00
USER      TTY      FROM                  LOGIN@   IDLE   JCPU   PCPU  WHAT
max      tty1     -                  Fri 9am 20:48m  0.22s  0.01s  vim td
max      tty2     -                  Fri 5pm 17:25m  0.07s  0.07s  -bash
```

wc

Displays the number of lines, words, and bytes in one or more files

wc [options] [file-list]

The wc utility displays the number of lines, words, and bytes in one or more files. When you specify more than one file on the command line, wc displays totals for each file as well as totals for all files.

Arguments

The *file-list* is a list of the pathnames of one or more files that wc analyzes. When you omit *file-list*, wc takes its input from standard input.

Options

Under Linux, wc accepts the common options described on page 736. Options preceded by a double hyphen (––) work under Linux only. Except as noted, options named with a single letter and preceded by a single hyphen work under Linux and macOS.

––bytes –c Displays only the number of bytes in the input.

––max-line-length –L Displays the length of the longest line in the input. LINUX

––lines –l (lowercase "l") Displays only the number of lines (that is, NEWLINE characters) in the input.

––chars –m Displays only the number of characters in the input.

––words –w Displays only the number of words in the input.

Notes

A *word* is a sequence of characters bounded by SPACEs, TABs, NEWLINEs, or a combination of these characters.

When you redirect its input, wc does not display the name of the file.

Examples

The following command analyzes the file named **memo**. The numbers in the output represent the number of lines, words, and bytes in the file.

```
$ wc memo
       5      31     146 memo
```

The next command displays the number of lines and words in three files. The line at the bottom, with the word **total** in the right column, contains the sum of each column.

```
$ wc -lw memo1 memo2 memo3
      10      62 memo1
      12      74 memo2
      12      68 memo3
      34     204 total
```

which

which

Shows where in **PATH** a utility is located

*which **utility-list***

For each utility in ***utility-list***, the which utility searches the directories in the **PATH** variable (page 318) and displays the absolute pathname of the first file it finds whose simple filename is the same as the utility.

Arguments

The ***utility-list*** is a list of one or more utilities (commands) that which searches for. For each utility, which searches the directories listed in the **PATH** environment variable, in order, and displays the full pathname of the first utility (executable file) it finds. If which does not locate a utility, it displays a message.

Options

Options preceded by a double hyphen (––) work under Linux only; not all of these options are available under all Linux distributions. Except as noted, options named with a single letter and preceded by a single hyphen work under Linux and macOS.

––all **–a** Displays all matching executable files in **PATH**, not just the first.

––read-alias **–i** Reads aliases from standard input and reports on matching aliases in addition to executable files in **PATH** (turn off with **––skip-alias**). LINUX

––read-functions Reads shell functions from standard input and reports on matching functions in addition to executable files in **PATH** (turn off with **––skip-functions**). LINUX

––show-dot Displays **./** in place of the absolute pathname when a directory in **PATH** starts with a period and a matching executable file is in that directory (turn off with **––skip-dot**). LINUX

––show-tilde Displays a tilde (~) in place of the absolute pathname of the user's home directory where appropriate. This option is ignored when a user working with **root** privileges runs which. LINUX

––tty-only Does not process more options (to the right of this option) if the process running which is not attached to a terminal. LINUX

Notes

Some distributions define an alias for which such as the following:

```
$ alias which
alias which='alias | /usr/bin/which --tty-only --read-alias --show-dot --show-tilde'
```

If which is not behaving as you would expect, verify that you are not running using an alias. The preceding alias causes which to be effective only when it is run interactively (**––tty-only**) and to display aliases, display the working directory as a period when appropriate, and display the name of the user's home directory as a tilde.

The TC Shell includes a which builtin (see the tcsh man page) that works slightly differently from the which utility (**/usr/bin/which**). Without any options, the which utility does not locate aliases, functions, and shell builtins because these do not appear in **PATH.** In contrast, the tcsh which builtin locates aliases, functions, and shell builtins.

Examples

The first example quotes the first letter of the utility (**\which**) to prevent the shell from invoking the alias (page 354) for which:

```
$ \which vim dir which
/usr/bin/vim
/bin/dir
/usr/bin/which
```

The next example, which works on some Linux systems only, is the same as the first but uses the alias for which (which it displays):

```
$ which vim dir which
alias which='alias | /usr/bin/which --tty-only --read-alias --show-dot --show-tilde'
        /usr/bin/which
/usr/bin/vim
/usr/bin/dir
```

The final example is the same as the preceding one except it is run from tcsh. The tcsh which builtin is used instead of the which utility:

```
tcsh $ which vim dir which
/usr/bin/vim
/bin/dir
which: shell built-in command.
```

who

Displays information about logged-in users

*who [**options**]*
who am i

The who utility displays information about users who are logged in on the local system. This information includes each user's username, terminal device, login time, and, if applicable, the hostname of the remote system the user is logged in from.

Arguments

When given two arguments (traditionally, **am i**), who displays information about the user giving the command. If applicable, the username is preceded by the hostname of the system the user is logged in from (e.g., **plum!max**).

Options

Under Linux, who accepts the common options described on page 736. Options preceded by a double hyphen (––) work under Linux only. Except as noted, options named with a single letter and preceded by a single hyphen work under Linux and macOS.

––all **–a** Displays a lot of information. LINUX

––boot **–b** Displays the date and time the system was last booted. LINUX

––heading **–H** Displays a header.

––login **–l** (lowercase "l") Lists devices waiting for a user to log in. LINUX

––count **–q** (**quick**) Lists the usernames only, followed by the number of users logged in on the system.

––mesg **–T** Appends after each user's username a character that shows whether that user has messages enabled. A plus sign (**+**) means that messages are enabled, and a hyphen (**–**) means that they are disabled, and a question mark (**?**) indicates that who cannot find the device. If messages are enabled, you can use write to communicate with the user. Refer to "mesg: Denies or Accepts Messages" on page 76.

––users **–u** Includes each user's idle time in the display. If the user has typed on her terminal in the past minute, a period (**.**) appears in this field. If no input has occurred for more than a day, the word **old** appears. In addition, this option displays the PID number and comment fields. See the "Discussion" section.

Discussion

The line who displays has the following syntax:

user [messages] line login-time [idle] [PID] comment

The ***user*** is the username of the user. The ***messages*** argument indicates whether messages are enabled or disabled (see the **–T** [**––mesg**] option). The ***line*** is the device name associated with the line the user is logged in on. The ***login-time*** is the date and time when the user logged in. The ***idle*** argument is the length of time since the terminal was last used (the *idle time;* see the **–u** [**––users**] option). ***PID*** is the process identification number. The ***comment*** is the name of the remote system the user is logged in from (it is blank for local users).

Notes

The finger utility (pages 72 and 828) provides information similar to that given by who.

Examples

The following examples demonstrate the use of the who utility:

```
$ who
max        tty2         2017-05-01 10:42 (:0)
sam        pts/1        2017-05-01 10:39 (plum)
zach       tty3         2017-05-01 10:43 (:1)

$ who am i
sam        pts/1        2017-05-01 10:39 (plum)

$ who -HTu
NAME       LINE          TIME                IDLE          PID COMMENT
max        + tty2        2017-05-01 10:42 00:08           1825 (:0)
sam        + pts/1       2017-05-01 10:39   .             1611 (plum)
zach       - tty3        2017-05-01 10:43 00:08           2259 (:1)
```

xargs

xargs

Converts standard input to command lines

xargs [options] [command]

The xargs utility is a convenient, efficient way to convert standard output of one command into arguments for another command. This utility reads from standard input, keeps track of the maximum allowable length of a command line, and avoids exceeding that limit by repeating ***command*** as needed. Finally, xargs executes the constructed command line(s).

Arguments

The ***command*** is the command line you want xargs to use as a base for the command it constructs. If you omit ***command***, it defaults to echo. The xargs utility appends to ***command*** the arguments it receives from standard input. If any arguments should precede the arguments from standard input, you must include them as part of ***command***.

Options

Options preceded by a double hyphen (––) work under Linux only. Except as noted, options named with a single letter and preceded by a single hyphen work under Linux and macOS.

–I *[marker]*
(**replace**) Allows you to place arguments from standard input anywhere within ***command***. All occurrences of ***marker*** in ***command*** for xargs are replaced by the arguments generated from standard input of xargs. With this option, xargs executes ***command*** for each input line. The **–l** (**––max-lines**) option is ignored when you use this option.

––max-lines*[=num]*
–l *[num]*
(lowercase "l") Executes ***command*** once for every ***num*** lines of input (***num*** defaults to 1). LINUX

––max-args=*num* **–n *num***
Executes ***command*** once for every ***num*** arguments in the input line.

––max-procs=*num*
–P *num*
Allows xargs to run up to ***maxprocs*** instances of ***command*** simultaneously. (The default is 1, which runs ***commands*** sequentially.) This option might improve the throughput if xargs is running on a multiprocessor system.

––interactive **–p** Prompts prior to each execution of ***command***.

--no-run-if-empty

-r Causes xargs not to execute ***command*** if standard input is empty. Ordinarily, xargs executes ***command*** at least once, even if standard input includes only blanks (SPACEs and TABs). LINUX

Discussion

The xargs utility reads arguments to ***command*** from standard input, interpreting each whitespace-delimited string as a separate argument. It then constructs a command line from ***command*** and a series of arguments. When the maximum command line length would be exceeded by adding another argument, xargs runs the command line it has built. If there is more input, xargs repeats the process of building a command line and running it. This process continues until all input has been read.

Notes

The xargs utility is often used as an efficient alternative to the **-exec** option of find (page 823). If you call find with the **-exec** option to run a command, it runs the command once for each file it processes. Each execution of the command creates a new process, which can drain system resources when you are processing many files. By accumulating as many arguments as possible, xargs can greatly reduce the number of processes needed. The first example in the "Examples" section shows how to use xargs with find.

Examples

To locate and remove all files with names ending in **.o** from the working directory and its subdirectories, you can use the find **-exec** option:

```
$ find . -name \*.o -exec rm --force {} \;
```

This approach calls the rm utility once for each **.o** file that find locates. Each invocation of rm requires a new process. If a lot of **.o** files exist, the system must spend a significant amount of time creating, starting, and then cleaning up these processes. You can reduce the number of processes by allowing xargs to accumulate as many filenames as possible before calling rm:

```
$ find . -name \*.o -print | xargs rm --force
```

In the next example, the content of all ***.txt** files located by find is searched for lines containing the word **login**. All filenames that contain **login** are displayed by grep.

```
$ find . -name \*.txt -print | xargs grep -w -l login
```

The next example shows how to use the **-I** option to cause xargs to embed standard input within ***command*** instead of appending it to ***command***. This option also causes ***command*** to be executed each time a NEWLINE character is encountered in standard input; **-l** (**--max-lines**) does not override this behavior.

```
$ cat names
Tom,
Dick,
and Harry
```

```
$ xargs echo "Hello," < names
Hello, Tom, Dick, and Harry

$ xargs -I xxx echo "Hello xxx. Join me for lunch?" < names
Hello Tom,. Join me for lunch?
Hello Dick,. Join me for lunch?
Hello and Harry. Join me for lunch?
```

The final example uses the same input file as the previous examples, adding the two –n (––max-args) and –l (––max-lines) options:

```
$ xargs -n 1 echo "Hi there" < names
Hi there Tom,
Hi there Dick,
Hi there and
Hi there Harry

$ xargs -l 2 echo "Hi there" < names
Hi there Tom, Dick,
Hi there and Harry
```

PART VII

APPENDIXES

A

Regular Expressions

In This Appendix

A *regular expression* defines a set of one or more strings of characters. A simple string of characters is a regular expression that defines one string of characters: itself. A more complex regular expression uses letters, numbers, and special characters to define many different strings of characters. A regular expression is said to *match* any string it defines.

This appendix describes the regular expressions used by ed, vim, emacs, grep, mawk/gawk, sed, Perl, and many other utilities. Refer to page 562 for more information on Perl regular expressions. The regular expressions used in shell ambiguous file references are different and are described in "Filename Generation/Pathname Expansion" on page 152.

CHARACTERS

As used in this appendix, a *character* is any character *except* a NEWLINE. Most characters represent themselves within a regular expression. A *special character,* also called a *metacharacter,* is one that does not represent itself. If you need to use a special character to represent itself, you must quote it as explained on page 1041.

DELIMITERS

A character called a *delimiter* usually marks the beginning and end of a regular expression. The delimiter is always a special character for the regular expression it delimits (that is, it does not represent itself but marks the beginning and end of the expression). Although vim permits the use of other characters as a delimiter and grep does not use delimiters at all, the regular expressions in this appendix use a forward slash (/) as a delimiter. In some unambiguous cases, the second delimiter is not required. For example, you can sometimes omit the second delimiter when it would be followed immediately by RETURN.

SIMPLE STRINGS

The most basic regular expression is a simple string that contains no special characters except the delimiters. A simple string matches only itself (Table A-1). In the examples in this appendix, the strings that are matched are underlined and look like this.

Table A-1 Simple strings

Regular expression	Matches	Examples
/ring/	ring	ring, spring, ringing, stringing
/Thursday/	Thursday	Thursday, Thursday's
/or not/	or not	or not, poor nothing

SPECIAL CHARACTERS

You can use special characters within a regular expression to cause the regular expression to match more than one string. When a regular expression also includes a special character it always matches the longest possible string, starting as far toward the beginning (left) of the line as possible.

PERIODS

A period (.) matches any character (Table A-2).

Table A-2 Periods

Regular expression	Matches	Examples
/ .alk/	All strings consisting of a SPACE followed by any character followed by alk	will talk, might balk
/.ing/	All strings consisting of any character preceding ing	sing song, ping, before inglenook

BRACKETS

Brackets ([]) define a *character class*[1] that will match any single character within the brackets (Table A-3). If the first character following the left bracket is a caret (^), the brackets define a character class that matches any single character not within the brackets. You can use a hyphen to indicate a range of characters. Within a character-class definition, backslashes and asterisks (described in the following sections) lose their special meanings. A right bracket (appearing as a member of the character class) can appear only as the first character following the left bracket. A caret is special only if it is the first character following the left bracket. A dollar sign is special only if it is followed immediately by the right bracket.

Table A-3 Brackets

Regular expression	Matches	Examples
/[bB]ill/	Member of the character class b and B followed by ill	bill, Bill, billed
/t[aeiou].k/	t followed by a lowercase vowel, any character, and a k	talkative, stink, teak, tanker
/# [6–9]/	# followed by a SPACE and a member of the character class 6 through 9	# 60, # 8:, get # 9
/[^a–zA–Z]/	Any character that is not a letter (ASCII character set only)	1, 7, @, ., }, Stop!

1. GNU documentation and POSIX call these List Operators and defines Character Class operators as expressions that match a predefined group of characters, such as all numbers (see Table VI-35 on page 1014).

ASTERISKS

An asterisk can follow a regular expression that represents a single character (Table A-4). The asterisk represents *zero* or more occurrences of a match of the regular expression. An asterisk following a period matches any string of characters. (A period matches any character, and an asterisk matches zero or more occurrences of the preceding regular expression.) A character-class definition followed by an asterisk matches any string of characters that are members of the character class.

Table A-4 Asterisks

Regular expression	Matches	Examples
/ab*c/	a followed by zero or more b's followed by a c	ac, abc, abbc, debbcaabbbc
/ab.*c/	ab followed by zero or more characters followed by c	abc, abxc, ab45c, xab 756.345 x cat
/t.*ing/	t followed by zero or more characters followed by ing	thing, ting, I thought of going
/[a–zA–Z]*/	A string composed only of letters and SPACEs	1. any string without numbers or punctuation!
/(.*)/	As long a string as possible between (and)	Get (this) and (that);
/([^)]*)/	The shortest string possible that starts with (and ends with)	(this), Get (this and that)

CARETS AND DOLLAR SIGNS

A regular expression that begins with a caret (^) can match a string only at the beginning of a line. In a similar manner, a dollar sign ($) at the end of a regular expression matches the end of a line. The caret and dollar sign are called anchors because they force (anchor) a match to the beginning or end of a line (Table A-5).

Table A-5 Carets and dollar signs

Regular expression	Matches	Examples
/^T/	A T at the beginning of a line	This line..., That Time..., In Time
/^+[0–9]/	A plus sign followed by a digit at the beginning of a line	+5 +45.72, +759 Keep this...
/:$/	A colon that ends a line	...below:

QUOTING SPECIAL CHARACTERS

You can quote any special character (but not parentheses [except in Perl; page 566] or a digit) by preceding it with a backslash (Table A-6). Quoting a special character makes it represent itself.

Table A-6 Quoted special characters

Regular expression	Matches	Examples
/end\./	All strings that contain end followed by a period	The end., send., pretend.mail
/\\/	A single backslash	\
/*/	An asterisk	*.c, an asterisk (*)
/\[5\]/	[5]	it was five [5]
/and\/or/	and/or	and/or

RULES

The following rules govern the application of regular expressions.

LONGEST MATCH POSSIBLE

A regular expression always matches the longest possible string, starting as far toward the beginning (left end) of the line as possible. Perl calls this type of match a *greedy match* (page 565). For example, given the string

```
This (rug) is not what it once was (a long time ago), is it?
```

the expression **/Th.*is/** matches

```
This (rug) is not what it once was (a long time ago), is
```

and /(.*)/ matches

```
(rug) is not what it once was (a long time ago)
```

However, /([^)]*)/ matches

```
(rug)
```

Given the string

```
singing songs, singing more and more
```

the expression **/s.*ing/** matches

```
singing songs, singing
```

and **/s.*ing song/** matches

```
singing song
```

Empty Regular Expressions

Within some utilities, such as vim and less (but not grep), an empty regular expression represents the last regular expression you used. For example, suppose you give vim the following Substitute command:

```
:s/mike/robert/
```

If you then want to make the same substitution again, you can use the following command:

```
:s//robert/
```

Alternatively, you can use the following commands to search for the string **mike** and then make the substitution

```
/mike/
:s//robert/
```

The empty regular expression (**//**) represents the last regular expression you used (**/mike/**).

Bracketing Expressions

You can use quoted parentheses, \(and \), to *bracket* a regular expression. (However, Perl uses unquoted parentheses to bracket regular expressions; page 566.) The string the bracketed regular expression matches can be recalled, as explained in "Quoted Digit" on page 1043. A regular expression does not attempt to match quoted parentheses. Thus, a regular expression enclosed within quoted parentheses matches what the same regular expression without the parentheses would match. The expression **/\(rexp\)/** matches what **/rexp/** would match; **/a\(b*\)c/** matches what **/ab*c/** would match.

You can nest quoted parentheses. The bracketed expressions are identified only by the opening \(, so no ambiguity arises in identifying them. The example expression **/\([a–z]\([A–Z]*\)x\)/** consists of two bracketed expressions, one nested within the other. In the string **3 t dMNORx7 l u**, the preceding regular expression matches **dMNORx**, with the first bracketed expression matching **dMNORx** and the second matching **MNOR**.

The Replacement String

The vim and sed editors use regular expressions as search strings within Substitute commands. You can use the ampersand (&) and quoted digits (*n*) special characters to represent the matched strings within the corresponding replacement string.

Ampersand

Within a replacement string, an ampersand (&) takes on the value of the string that the search string (regular expression) matched. For example, the following vim Substitute command surrounds a string of one or more digits with **NN**. The ampersand in the replacement string matches whatever string of digits the regular expression (search string) matched:

```
:s/[0-9][0-9]*/NN&NN/
```

Two character-class definitions are required because the regular expression [0–9]* matches *zero* or more occurrences of a digit, and *any* character string constitutes zero or more occurrences of a digit.

Quoted Digit

Within the search string, a bracketed regular expression, **\(xxx\)** [**(xxx)** in Perl], matches what the regular expression would have matched without the quoted parentheses, **xxx**. Within the replacement string, a quoted digit, **\n**, represents the string that the bracketed regular expression (portion of the search string) beginning with the *n*th \(matched. Perl accepts a quoted digit for this purpose, but the preferred style is to precede the digit with a dollar sign (**$n**; page 566). For example, you can take a list of people in the form

```
last-name, first-name initial
```

and put it in the form

```
first-name initial last-name
```

with the following vim command:

```
:1,$s/\([^,]*\), \(.*\)/\2 \1/
```

This command addresses all the lines in the file (**1,$**). The Substitute command (**s**) uses a search string and a replacement string delimited by forward slashes. The first bracketed regular expression within the search string, \([^,]*\), matches what the same unbracketed regular expression, [^,]*, would match: zero or more characters not containing a comma (the **last-name**). Following the first bracketed regular expression are a comma and a SPACE that match themselves. The second bracketed expression, \(.*\), matches any string of characters (the **first-name** and **initial**).

The replacement string consists of what the second bracketed regular expression matched (\2), followed by a SPACE and what the first bracketed regular expression matched (\1).

Extended Regular Expressions

This section covers patterns that use an extended set of special characters. These patterns are called *full regular expressions* or *extended regular expressions*. In addition to ordinary regular expressions, Perl and vim provide extended regular expressions. The three utilities egrep, grep when run with the –E option (similar to egrep), and mawk/gawk provide all the special characters included in ordinary regular expressions, except for \(and \), as well those included in extended regular expressions.

Two of the additional special characters are the plus sign (+) and the question mark (?). They are similar to *, which matches *zero* or more occurrences of the previous character. The plus sign matches *one* or more occurrences of the previous character, whereas the question mark matches *zero* or *one* occurrence. You can use any one of the special characters *, +, and ? following parentheses, causing the special character to apply to the string surrounded by the parentheses. Unlike the parentheses in bracketed regular expressions, these parentheses are not quoted (Table A-7).

Table A-7 Extended regular expressions

Regular expression	Matches	Examples
/ab+c/	a followed by one or more b's followed by a c	yabcw, abbc57
/ab?c/	a followed by zero or one b followed by c	back, abcdef
/(ab)+c/	One or more occurrences of the string ab followed by c	zabcd, ababc!
/(ab)?c/	Zero or one occurrence of the string ab followed by c	xc, abcc

In full regular expressions, the vertical bar (|) special character is a Boolean OR operator. Within vim, you must quote the vertical bar by preceding it with a backslash to make it special (\|). A vertical bar between two regular expressions causes a match with strings that match the first expression, the second expression, or both. You can use the vertical bar with parentheses to separate from the rest of the regular expression the two expressions that are being ORed (Table A-8).

Table A-8 Full regular expressions

Regular expression	Meaning	Examples
/ab|ac/	Either ab or ac	ab, ac, abac *(**abac** is two matches of the regular expression)*
/^Exit|^Quit/	Lines that begin with Exit or Quit	Exit, Quit, No Exit
/(D|N)\. Jones/	D. Jones or N. Jones	P.D. Jones, N. Jones

APPENDIX SUMMARY

A regular expression defines a set of one or more strings of characters. A regular expression is said to match any string it defines.

In a regular expression, a special character is one that does not represent itself. Table A-9 lists special characters.

Table A-9 Special characters

Character	Meaning
.	Matches any single character
*	Matches zero or more occurrences of a match of the preceding character
^	Forces a match to the beginning of a line
$	A match to the end of a line
\	Quotes special characters
\<	Forces a match to the beginning of a word
\>	Forces a match to the end of a word

Table A-10 lists ways of representing character classes and bracketed regular expressions.

Table A-10 Character classes and bracketed regular expressions

Class	Defines
[*xyz*]	Defines a character class that matches ***x***, ***y***, or ***z***
[^*xyz*]	Defines a character class that matches any character except ***x***, ***y***, or ***z***
[*x*–*z*]	Defines a character class that matches any character ***x*** through ***z*** inclusive
\\(*xyz*\\)	Matches what ***xyz*** matches (a bracketed regular expression; not Perl)
(*xyz*)	Matches what ***xyz*** matches (a bracketed regular expression; Perl only)

In addition to the preceding special characters and strings (excluding quoted parentheses, except in vim), the characters in Table A-11 are special within full, or extended, regular expressions.

Table A-11 Extended regular expressions

Expression	Matches
+	Matches one or more occurrences of the preceding character
?	Matches zero or one occurrence of the preceding character

Table A-11 Extended regular expressions (continued)

Expression	Matches
(*xyz*)+	Matches one or more occurrences of what ***xyz*** matches
(*xyz*)?	Matches zero or one occurrence of what ***xyz*** matches
(*xyz*)*	Matches zero or more occurrences of what ***xyz*** matches
xyz*|*abc	Matches either what ***xyz*** or what ***abc*** matches (use \\| in vim)
(*xy*|*ab*)*c*	Matches either what ***xyc*** or what ***abc*** matches (use \\| in vim)

Table A-12 lists characters that are special within a replacement string in sed and vim.

Table A-12 Replacement strings

String	Represents
&	Represents what the regular expression (search string) matched
n	A quoted number, ***n***, represents what the ***n***th bracketed regular expression in the search string matched
$*n*	A number preceded by a dollar sign, ***n***, represents what the ***n***th bracketed regular expression in the search string matched (Perl only)

B

HELP

IN THIS APPENDIX

You need not be alone as a user or system administrator in isolation. A large community of Linux and macOS experts is willing to assist you in learning about, helping you solve problems with, and getting the most out of a Linux or macOS system. Before you ask for help, however, make sure you have done everything you can to solve the problem yourself. No doubt someone has experienced the same problem before you and the answer to your question exists somewhere on the Internet. Your job is to find it. This appendix lists resources and describes methods that can help you in that task.

Solving a Problem

Following is a list of steps that can help you solve a problem without asking someone for help. Depending on your understanding of and experience with the hardware and software involved, these steps might lead to a solution.

1. Most Linux and macOS distributions come with extensive documentation. Read the documentation on the specific hardware or software you are having a problem with. If it is a GNU product, use info; otherwise, use man to find local information. Also look in **/usr/share/doc** for documentation on specific tools. For more information refer to "Where to Find Documentation" on page 33.
2. When the problem involves some type of error or other message, use a search engine, such as Google (www.google.com) or Google Groups (groups.google.com), to look up the message on the Internet. If the message is long, pick a unique part of the message to search for; 10 to 20 characters should be enough. Enclose the search string within double quotation marks. See "Using the Internet to Get Help" on page 40 for an example of this kind of search.
3. Check whether the Linux Documentation Project (www.tldp.org) has a HOWTO or mini-HOWTO on the subject in question. Search its site for keywords that relate directly to the product and problem. Read the FAQs.
4. GNU manuals are available at www.gnu.org/manual. In addition, you can visit the GNU home page (www.gnu.org) to obtain other documentation and GNU resources. Many of the GNU pages and resources are available in a variety of languages.
5. Use Google or Google Groups to search on keywords that relate directly to the product and problem.
6. When all else fails (or perhaps before you try anything else), examine the system logs in **/var/log**. First, look at the end of the **messages** (Linux) or **system.log** (macOS) file using one of the following commands:

   ```
   # tail -20 /var/log/messages
   # tail -20 /var/log/system.log
   ```

   If **messages** or **system.log** contains nothing useful, run the following command. It displays the names of the log files in chronological order, with the most recently modified files appearing at the bottom of the list.

   ```
   $ ls -ltr /var/log
   ```

   Look at the files at the bottom of the list first. If the problem involves a network connection, review the **secure** or **auth.log** file (some systems might use a different name) on the local and remote systems. Also look at **messages** or **system.log** on the remote system.

7. The **/var/spool** directory contains subdirectories with useful information: **cups** holds the print queues; **postfix, mail,** or **exim4** holds the user's mail files; and so on.

If you are unable to solve a problem yourself, a thoughtful question to an appropriate newsgroup or mailing list (page 1049) can elicit useful information. When you send or post a question, make sure you describe the problem and identify the local system carefully. Include the version numbers of the operating system and any software packages that relate to the problem. Describe the hardware, if appropriate. There is an etiquette to posting questions—see www.catb.org/~esr/faqs/smart-questions.html for a good paper by Eric S. Raymond and Rick Moen titled "How To Ask Questions the Smart Way."

FINDING LINUX AND MACOS RELATED INFORMATION

Linux and macOS distributions come with reference pages stored online. You can read these documents by using the man or info (page 36) utility. You can read man and info pages to get more information about specific topics while reading this book or to determine which features are available with Linux or macOS. To search for topics, use apropos (see page 35 or give the command **man apropos**). The Apple support site (www.apple.com/support) has many useful macOS links.

MAILING LISTS

Subscribing to a mailing list allows you to participate in an electronic discussion. With most lists, you can send and receive email dedicated to a specific topic to and from a group of users. Moderated lists do not tend to stray as much as unmoderated lists, assuming the list has a good moderator. The disadvantage of a moderated list is that some discussions might be cut off when they get interesting if the moderator deems that the discussion has gone on for too long. Mailing lists described as bulletins are strictly unidirectional: You cannot post information to these lists but can only receive periodic bulletins. If you have the subscription address for a mailing list but are not sure how to subscribe, put the word **help** in the body and/or header of email you send to the address. You will usually receive instructions via return email. You can also use a search engine to search for **mailing list linux** or **mailing list macos**.

You can find Red Hat and Fedora mailing lists at www.redhat.com/mailman/listinfo, Ubuntu mailing lists at www.ubuntu.com/support/community/mailinglists, and Debian mailing lists at www.debian.org/MailingLists/subscribe.

Apple supports many mailing lists. Visit www.lists.apple.com/mailman/listinfo to display a list of macOS mailing lists; click on the name of a list to display subscription information.

SPECIFYING A TERMINAL

Because vim, emacs, and other textual and pseudographical programs take advantage of features specific to various kinds of terminals and terminal emulators, you must tell these programs the name of the terminal you are using or the terminal your terminal emulator is emulating. Most of the time the terminal name is set for you. If the terminal name is not specified or is not specified correctly, the characters on the screen will be garbled or, when you start a program, the program will ask which type of terminal you are using.

Terminal names describe the functional characteristics of a terminal or terminal emulator to programs that require this information. Although terminal names are referred to as either Terminfo or Termcap names, the difference relates to the method each system uses to store the terminal characteristics internally—not to the manner in which you specify the name of a terminal. Terminal names that are often used with Linux terminal emulators and with graphical monitors while they are run in textual mode include **ansi**, **linux**, **vt100**, **vt102**, **vt220**, and **xterm**.

When you are running a terminal emulator, you can specify the type of terminal you want to emulate. Set the emulator to either **vt100** or **vt220**, and set **TERM** to the same value.

When you log in, you might be prompted to identify the type of terminal you are using:

```
TERM = (vt100)
```

You can respond to this prompt in one of two ways. First, you can press RETURN to set your terminal type to the name in parentheses. If that name does not describe the terminal you are using, you can enter the correct name and then press RETURN.

```
TERM = (vt100) ansi
```

You might also receive the following prompt:

```
TERM = (unknown)
```

This prompt indicates that the system does not know which type of terminal you are using. If you plan to run programs that require this information, enter the name of the terminal or terminal emulator you are using before you press RETURN.

TERM If you do not receive a prompt, you can give the following command to display the value of the **TERM** variable and check whether the terminal type has been set:

```
$ echo $TERM
```

If the system responds with the wrong name, a blank line, or an error message, set or change the terminal name. From the Bourne Again Shell (bash), enter a command similar to the following to set the **TERM** variable so the system knows which type of terminal you are using:

*export TERM=**name***

Replace ***name*** with the terminal name for the terminal you are using, making sure you do not put a SPACE before or after the equal sign. If you always use the same type of terminal, you can place this command in your **~/.bashrc** file (page 288), causing the shell to set the terminal type each time you log in. For example, give the following command to set your terminal name to **vt100**:

```
$ export TERM=vt100
```

Use the following syntax under the TC Shell (tcsh):

*setenv TERM **name***

Again, replace ***name*** with the terminal name for the terminal you are using. Under tcsh you can place this command in your **~/.login** file (page 382). For example, under tcsh you can give this command to set your terminal name to **vt100**:

```
$ setenv TERM vt100
```

LANG For some programs to display information correctly, you might need to set the **LANG** variable (page 324). Frequently, you can set this variable to **C**. Under bash use the command

```
$ export LANG=C
```

and under tcsh use

```
$ setenv LANG C
```

C

Keeping the System Up-to-Date

In This Appendix

The apt-get and dnf utilities both fill the same role: They install and update software packages. Both utilities compare the files in a repository (generally on the Internet) with those on the local system and update the files on the local system according to your instructions. Both utilities automatically install and update any additional files that a package depends on (dependencies). Most Linux distributions come with apt-get or dnf. Debian-based systems such as Ubuntu and Mint are set up to use apt-get, which works with **deb** packages. Red Hat Enterprise Linux and Fedora use dnf, which works with **rpm** packages. There are also versions of apt-get that work with **rpm** packages. On a macOS system it is easiest to use the software update GUI to keep the system up-to-date.

To facilitate the update process, apt-get and dnf keep a local list of packages that are held in each of the repositories they use. Any software you want to install or update must reside in a repository.

When you give apt-get or dnf a command to install a package, they look for the package in a local package list. If the package appears in the list, apt-get or dnf fetches both that package and any packages the package you are installing depends on and installs the packages.

The dnf examples in this section are from a Fedora system and the apt-get examples are from an Ubuntu system. Although the files, input, and output on the local system might look different, how you use the tools—and the results—will be the same.

In contrast to apt-get and dnf, BitTorrent efficiently distributes large amounts of static data, such as installation ISO images. It does not examine files on the local system and does not check for dependencies.

Using dnf

Early releases of Linux did not include a tool for managing updates. Although the rpm utility could install or upgrade individual software packages, it was up to the user to locate a package and any packages it depended on. When Terra Soft produced its Red Hat–based Linux distribution for the PowerPC, named Yellow Dog, the company created the Yellow Dog Updater to fill this gap. This program has since been ported to other architectures and distributions. The result is named Yellow Dog Updater, Modified (yum; yum.baseurl.org). Over time, the need to improve **yum** gave birth to Dandified Yum (dnf). For most users, the change is superficial and involves replacing **yum** with **dnf** in commands. By comparison, the improvements in performance, memory usage, and package dependency resolution are quite significant. You can read more about the changes in the dnf CLI compared to yum at dnf.readthedocs.io/en/latest/cli_vs_yum.html.

rpm packages The dnf utility works with **rpm** packages. When dnf installs or upgrades a software package, it also installs or upgrades packages that the package depends on.

Repositories The dnf utility downloads package headers and packages from servers called repositories. Frequently, dnf is set up to use copies of repositories kept on mirror sites. See "Configuring dnf" on page 1058 for information on selecting a repository.

Using dnf to Install, Remove, and Update Packages

Installing packages The behavior of dnf depends on which options you specify. To install a new package together with the packages it depends on, while working with **root** privileges give the command **dnf install**, followed by the name of the package. After dnf determines what it needs to do, it asks for confirmation. The next example installs the **tcsh** package:

```
# dnf install tcsh
Last metadata expiration check: 0:0:53 ago on Fri Jun 2 10:11:21 2017.
Dependencies resolved.

==============================================================================
 Package           Arch             Version                Repository      Size
==============================================================================
Installing:
 tcsh              x86_64           6.19.00-17.fc25        updates        446 k

Transaction Summary
==============================================================================
```

```
Install  1 Package

Total download size: 446 k
Installed size: 1.2 M
Is this ok [y/N]: y
Downloading Packages:
tcsh-6.19.00-17.fc25.x86_64.rpm                                  | 446 kB     00:05
------------------------------------------------------------------------------------
Total                                                            | 446 kB     00:05
Running transaction check
Transaction check succeeded
Running transaction test
Transaction test succeeded
Running Transaction
  Installing : tcsh-6.19.00-17.fc25.x86_64.rpm                                  1/1
  Verifying  : tcsh-6.19.00-17.fc25.x86_64.rpm                                  1/1

Installed:
  tcsh.x86_64 6.19.00-17.fc25

Complete!
```

Removing packages

You can also use dnf to remove packages, using a similar syntax. The following example removes the **tcsh** package:

```
# dnf remove tcsh
Dependencies Resolved
====================================================================================
 Package          Arch             Version                    Repository       Size
====================================================================================
Removing:
 tcsh             x86_64           6.19.00-17.fc25            @updates        1.2 M

Transaction Summary
====================================================================================
Remove  1 Package

Installed size: 1.2 M
Is this ok [y/N]: y
Running transaction check
Transaction check succeeded
Running transaction test
Transaction test succeeded
Running Transaction
  Erasing    : tcsh-6.19.00-17.fc25.x86_64                                      1/1
  Verifying  : tcsh-6.19.00-17.fc25.x86_64                                      1/1

Removed:
  tcsh.x86_64 6.19.00-17.fc25

Complete!
```

Updating packages

The **update** option, without additional parameters, updates all installed packages. It downloads summary files that hold information about package headers for installed packages, determines which packages need to be updated, prompts to continue, and downloads and installs the updated packages. Unlike the situation with apt-get, the dnf **upgrade** command is very similar to dnf **update**.

In the following example, dnf determines that two packages, **acl** and **firefox**, need to be updated and checks dependencies. Once it has determined what it needs to do, dnf advises you of the action(s) it will take, prompts with **Is this ok [y/N]**, and, if you approve, downloads and installs the packages.

```
# dnf update
Last metadata expiration check: 0:21:39 ago on Fri Jun 2 10:11:21 2017.

Dependencies Resolved
================================================================================
 Package           Arch            Version                Repository       Size
================================================================================
Updating:
 acl               x86_64          2.2.52-12.fc25         updates          76 k
 firefox           x86_64          53.0.3-1.fc25          updates          84 M

Transaction Summary
================================================================================
Upgrade  2 Packages

Total download size: 84 M
Is this ok [y/N]: y
Downloading Packages:
(1/2): acl-2.2.52-12.fc25.x86_64.rpm                    | 76 kB      00:00
(2/2): firefox-53.0.3-1.fc25.x86_64.rpm                 | 84 M      01:24
[DPRM] acl-2.2.52-12.fc25.x86_64.drpm: done
[DPRM] firefox-53.0.3-1.fc25.x86_64.drpm: done
--------------------------------------------------------------------------------
Total                                                     84 M      01:24
Running transaction check
Transaction check succeeded
Running transaction test
Transaction test succeeded
Running Transaction
Upgrading   : acl-2.2.52-12.fc25.x86_64
Upgrading   : firefox-53.0.3-1.fc25.x86_64
Cleanup     : acl-2.2.52-12.fc25.x86_64
Cleanup     : firefox-53.0.3-1.fc25.x86_64
Verifying   : acl-2.2.52-12.fc25.x86_64
Verifying   : firefox-53.0.3-1.fc25.x86_64

Upgraded:
  acl-2.2.52-12.fc25.x86_64
  firefox-53.0.3-1.fc25.x86_64

Complete!
```

You can update individual packages by specifying the names of the packages on the command line following the word **update**.

OTHER dnf COMMANDS

Many dnf commands and options are available. A few of the more useful commands are described here. The dnf man page contains a complete list.

check-update Lists packages installed on the local system that have updates available in the dnf repositories.

clean Removes header files that dnf uses for resolving dependencies. Also removes cached packages—dnf does not automatically remove packages once they have been downloaded and installed, unless you set **keepcache** (page 1058) to 0.

help (command) Displays the help text for all commands, or for a specific command if specified.

info Lists description and summary information about installed and available packages.

list Lists all packages that can be installed from the dnf repositories.

search *word* Searches for ***word*** in the package description, summary, packager, and name.

dnf GROUPS

In addition to working with single packages, dnf can work with groups of packages. The next example shows how to display a list of installed and available package groups:

```
$ dnf group list
Installed Groups:
   Administration Tools
   Design Suite
   GNOME Desktop Environment
...
Installed Language Groups:
   Arabic Support [ar]
   Armenian Support [hy]
   Assamese Support [as]
...
Available Groups:
   Authoring and Publishing
   Base
   Books and Guides
   DNS Name Server
...
Available Language Groups:
   Afrikaans Support [af]
   Akan Support [ak]
   Albanian Support [sq]
...
Done
```

The command **dnf group info** followed by the name of a group displays information about the group, including a description of the group and a list of mandatory, default, and optional packages. The next example displays information about the DNS Name Server group of packages. If the name of the package includes a SPACE, you must quote it.

```
$ dnf group info "DNS Name Server"
Group: DNS Name Server
 Description: This package group allows you to run a DNS name server
(BIND) on the system.
 Default Packages:
   bind-chroot
 Optional Packages:
   bind
   dnsperf
   ldns
   nsd
   pdns
   pdns-recursor
   rbldnsd
   unbound
```

To install a group of packages, give the command **dnf group install** followed by the name of the group.

Downloading rpm Package Files Using dnf download

The dnf download utility is a plugin that locates and downloads—but does not install—**rpm** package files. Plugins are **yum** utilities that have been ported over to DNF. For more information about plugins, see dnf.readthedocs.io/en/latest.To use dnf download, you may need to install the **dnf-plugins-core** package.

The following example downloads the **samba rpm** file to the working directory:

```
$ dnf download samba
Fedora 25 - x86_64 - Updates                     5.1 MB/s | 23 MB      00:04
Fedora 25 - x86_64                               4.5 MB/s | 50 MB      00:11
Last metadata expiration check: 0:21:39 ago on Fri Jun 2 10:11:21 2017.
samba-4.5.10-0.fc25.x86_64.rpm                   1.3 MB/s | 638 kB     00:23
```

Downloading source files You can use dnf download with the **--source** option to download **rpm** source package files. The dnf download utility automatically enables the necessary source repositories. The following example downloads in the working directory the **rpm** file for the latest version of the kernel source code for the installed release:

```
$ dnf download --source kernel
enabling updates-source repository
enabling fedora-source repository
Fedora 25 - Updates Source                       5.1 MB/s | 23 MB      00:04
Fedora 25 - Source                               4.5 MB/s | 50 MB      00:11
Last metadata expiration check: 0:21:39 ago on Fri Jun 2 10:11:21 2017.
kernel-4.11.3-200.fc25.src                                | 64 MB     02:09
```

Without the **--source** option, dnf download downloads the executable kernel **rpm** file.

Configuring dnf

dnf.conf Most Linux distributions that use dnf for updating files come with dnf ready to use; you do not need to configure it. This section describes the dnf configuration files for those users who want to modify them. The primary configuration file, **/etc/dnf/dnf.conf**, holds global settings. The first example shows a typical **dnf.conf** file:

```
$ cat /etc/dnf/dnf.conf
[main]
gpgcheck=1
installonly_limit=3
clean_requirements_on_remove=True
```

The section labeled **[main]** defines global configuration options. When **gpgcheck** is set to **1**, dnf checks the GPG (GNU Privacy Guard; GnuPG.org) signatures on packages it installs. This check verifies the authenticity of the packages. The **installonlypkgs** parameter (not shown) specifies packages that dnf is to install but never upgrade, such as a kernel. The **installonly_limit** specifies the number of package versions of a given

installonlypkgs package that are to be installed at one time.

dnf.repos.d As noted in the comment at the end of the file, dnf repository information is kept in files in the **/etc/yum.repos.d** directory. A parameter set in a repository section overrides the same parameter set in the **[main]** section. Following is a sample listing for a **yum.repos.d** directory on a Fedora system:

```
$ ls /etc/yum.repos.d

fedora-cisco-openh264.repo  fedora.repo
fedora-updates.repo         fedora-updates-testing.repo
```

Each of these files contains a header, such as **[fedora]**, which provides a unique name for the repository. The name of the file is generally similar to the repository name, with the addition of a **fedora-** (or similar) prefix and a **.repo** filename extension. On a Fedora system, commonly used repositories include **fedora** (held in the **fedora.repo** file), which contains the packages found on the installation DVD; **updates** (held in the **fedora-updates.repo** file), which contains updated versions of the stable packages; and **updates-testing** (held in the **fedora-updates-testing.repo** file), which contains updates that are not ready for release. The last two repositories are not enabled; do not enable either of these repositories unless you are testing unstable packages. Never enable them on a production system.

Each *.repo file can specify several repositories

tip Each ***.repo** file includes specifications for several related repositories, which are usually disabled. For example, the **fedora.repo** file holds **[fedora-debuginfo]** and **[fedora-source]** in addition to **[fedora]**.

You cannot download source files using dnf. Instead, use the dnf download plugin (page 1058) for this task.

The next example shows part of the **fedora.repo** file that specifies the parameters for the **fedora** repository:

```
$ cat /etc/yum.repos.d/fedora.repo
[fedora]
name=Fedora $releasever - $basearch
failovermethod=priority
#baseurl=http://download.fedoraproject.org/pub/fedora/linux/releases/$releasever/Everything/$basearch/os/
metalink=https://mirrors.fedoraproject.org/metalink?repo=fedora-$releasever&arch=$basearch
enabled=1
metadata_expire=7d
gpgcheck=1
gpgkey=file:///etc/pki/rpm-gpg/RPM-GPG-KEY-fedora-$basearch
skip_if_available=False

...
```

Repository specification Each repository specification contains the name of the repository enclosed in brackets ([]), a **name**, a **failovermethod**, a **baseurl**, and a **metalink**. The **name** provides an informal name for the repository that dnf displays. The **failovermethod** determines the order in which dnf contacts an initial mirror site and additional mirror sites if the first one fails; **priority** selects the sites in the order in which they appear and **round-robin** selects sites randomly. The **baseurl** indicates the location of the main repository; it is normally commented out. The **metalink** specifies the URL of a file that holds a list of **baseurls**, or mirrors of the main repository. The mirror list server uses geoip (geolocation; www.geoiptool.com) to attempt to return the nearest mirrors for dnf to try. You can only use either **baseurl** or **metalink** at one time, not both. These definitions use two variables: dnf sets **$basearch** to the architecture of the system and **$releasever** to the version of the release (such as **25** for Fedora 25).

The repository described by the file is enabled (dnf will use it) if **enabled** is set to **1** and is disabled if **enabled** is set to 0. As described earlier, **gpgcheck** determines whether dnf checks GPG signatures on files it downloads. The **gpgkey** specifies the location of the GPG key. Refer to the **dnf.conf** man page for more options.

USING apt-get

APT (Advanced Package Tool) is a collection of utilities that download, install, remove, upgrade, and report on software packages. APT utilities download packages and call **dpkg** utilities to manipulate the packages once they are on the local system. For more information refer to www.debian.org/doc/manuals/apt-howto.

Updating the package list

The primary APT command is apt-get; its arguments determine what the command does. Working with **root** privileges, give the command **apt-get update** to update the local package list:

```
# apt-get update
Get:1 http://extras.ubuntu.com xenial InRelease [72 B]
Get:2 http://security.ubuntu.com xenial-security InRelease [198 B]
Hit http://extras.ubuntu.com xenial InRelease
Get:3 http://security.ubuntu.com xenial-security InRelease [49.6 kB]
Hit http://extras.ubuntu.com xenial/main Sources
Get:4 http://us.archive.ubuntu.com xenial InRelease [198 B]
Hit http://extras.ubuntu.com xenial/main amd64 Packages
Get:5 http://us.archive.ubuntu.com xenial-updates InRelease [198 B]
Get:6 http://us.archive.ubuntu.com xenial-backports InRelease [198 B]
Get:7 http://us.archive.ubuntu.com xenial InRelease [49.6 kB]
Get:8 http://security.ubuntu.com xenial-security/main Sources [22.5 kB]
Get:9 http://security.ubuntu.com xenial-security/restricted Sources [14 B]
...
Fetched 13.4 MB in 2min 20s (95.4 kB/s)
Reading package lists... Done
```

Check the dependency tree

The apt-get utility does not tolerate a broken dependency tree. To check the status of the local dependency tree, give the command **apt-get check**:

```
# apt-get check
Reading package lists... Done
Building dependency tree
Reading state information... Done
```

The easiest way to fix errors that apt-get reveals is to remove the offending packages and then reinstall them using apt-get.

USING apt-get TO INSTALL, REMOVE, AND UPDATE PACKAGES

Installing packages

The following command uses apt-get to install the **zsh** package:

```
# apt-get install zsh
Reading package lists... Done
Building dependency tree
Reading state information... Done
Suggested packages:
  zsh-doc
The following NEW packages will be installed:
  zsh
0 upgraded, 1 newly installed, 0 to remove and 2 not upgraded.
Need to get 0 B/4,667 kB of archives.
After this operation, 11.5 MB of additional disk space will be used.
Selecting previously unselected package zsh.
(Reading database ... 166307 files and directories currently installed.)
Unpacking zsh (from .../zsh_4.3.17-1ubuntu1_i386.deb) ...
Processing triggers for man-db ...
Setting up zsh (4.3.17-1ubuntu1) ...
update-alternatives: using /bin/zsh4 to provide /bin/zsh (zsh) in auto mode.
update-alternatives: using /bin/zsh4 to provide /bin/rzsh (rzsh) in auto mode.
update-alternatives: using /bin/zsh4 to provide /bin/ksh (ksh) in auto mode.
```

Removing packages

Remove a package the same way you install a package, substituting **remove** for **install**:

```
# apt-get remove zsh
Reading package lists... Done
Building dependency tree
Reading state information... Done
The following packages will be REMOVED:
  zsh
0 upgraded, 0 newly installed, 1 to remove and 2 not upgraded.
After this operation, 11.5 MB disk space will be freed.
Do you want to continue [Y/n]? y
(Reading database ... 167467 files and directories currently installed.)
Removing zsh ...
Processing triggers for man-db ...
```

To ensure you can later reinstall a package with the same configuration, the apt-get **remove** command does not remove configuration files from the /etc directory hierarchy. Although it is not recommended, you can use the **purge** command instead of **remove** to remove all the package files, including configuration files. Alternatively, you can move these files to an archive so you can restore them later if necessary.

Using apt-get to Upgrade the System

Two arguments cause apt-get to upgrade all packages on the system: **upgrade** upgrades all packages on the system that do not require new packages to be installed and **dist-upgrade** upgrades all packages on the system, installing new packages as needed; this argument will install a new version of the operating system if one is available.

The following command updates all packages on the system that depend only on installed packages:

```
# apt-get upgrade
Reading package lists... Done
Building dependency tree
Reading state information... Done
The following packages will be upgraded:
  eog libtiff4
2 upgraded, 0 newly installed, 0 to remove and 0 not upgraded.
Need to get 906 kB of archives.
After this operation, 20.5 kB disk space will be freed.
Do you want to continue [Y/n]? y
Get:1 http://us.archive.ubuntu.com/ubuntu/ xenial-updates/main libtiff4 i386 3.9.5-2ubuntu1.1 [142 kB]
Get:2 http://us.archive.ubuntu.com/ubuntu/ xenial-updates/main eog i386 3.4.2-0ubuntu1 [763 kB]
Fetched 906 kB in 2s (378 kB/s)
(Reading database ... 167468 files and directories currently installed.)
Preparing to replace libtiff4 3.9.5-2ubuntu1 (using .../libtiff4_3.9.5-2ubuntu1.1_i386.deb) ...
Unpacking replacement libtiff4 ...
Preparing to replace eog 3.4.1-0ubuntu1 (using .../eog_3.4.2-0ubuntu1_i386.deb) ...
Unpacking replacement eog ...
Processing triggers for libglib2.0-0 ...
Processing triggers for man-db ...
Processing triggers for gconf2 ...
Processing triggers for hicolor-icon-theme ...
Processing triggers for bamfdaemon ...
Rebuilding /usr/share/applications/bamf.index...
Processing triggers for desktop-file-utils ...
Processing triggers for gnome-menus ...
Setting up libtiff4 (3.9.5-2ubuntu1.1) ...
Setting up eog (3.4.2-0ubuntu1) ...
Processing triggers for libc-bin ...
ldconfig deferred processing now taking place
```

When apt-get asks if you want to continue, enter **Y** to upgrade the listed packages; otherwise, enter **N**. Packages that are not upgraded because they depend on packages that are not already installed are listed as **kept back**.

Use **dist-upgrade** to upgrade all packages, including packages that depend on packages that are not installed. This command also installs dependencies.

Other apt-get Commands

autoclean Removes old archive files.

check Checks for broken dependencies.

clean Removes archive files.

dist-upgrade Upgrades packages on the system, installing new packages as needed. If a new version of the operating system is available, this option upgrades to the new version.

purge Removes a package and all its configuration files.

source Downloads source files.

update Retrieves new lists of packages.

upgrade Upgrades all packages on the system that do not require new packages to be installed.

USING apt COMMANDS

Debian and its derivatives, including Ubuntu, are in the process of updating apt-get and creating a new tool named apt. This change is similar to the change from yum to dnf in the RPM world. As with that change, in most cases the only difference is entering **apt** in commands instead of **apt-get**. Not all of the commands have been ported over yet, but those that have also include a few visible upgrades such as colored text and progress indicators.

REPOSITORIES

Repositories hold collections of software packages and related information, including headers that describe each package and provide information on other packages the package depends on. Typically, a Linux distribution maintains repositories for each of its releases.

Software package categories — Software packages are frequently divided into several categories. Ubuntu uses the following categories:

- **main**—Ubuntu-supported open-source software
- **universe**—Community-maintained open-source software
- **multiverse**—Software restricted by copyright or legal issues
- **restricted**—Proprietary device drivers
- **backports**—Packages from later releases of Ubuntu that are not available for an earlier release

The apt-get utility selects packages from repositories it searches based on the categories specified in the **sources.list** file.

sources.list: SPECIFIES REPOSITORIES FOR apt-get TO SEARCH

The **/etc/apt/sources.list** file specifies the repositories apt-get searches when you ask it to find or install a package. You must modify the **sources.list** file to enable apt-get to download software from nondefault repositories. Typically, you do not need to configure apt-get to install supported software.

Each line in **sources.list** describes one repository and has the following syntax:

type URI repository category-list

where *type* is **deb** for packages of executable files and **deb-src** for packages of source files; *URI* is the location of the repository, usually **cdrom** or an Internet address that starts with **http://**; *repository* is the name of the repository apt-get is to search; and *category-list* is a SPACE-separated list of categories apt-get selects packages from. Comments begin with a pound sign (#) anywhere on a line and end at the end of the line.

The following line from **sources.list** on an Ubuntu system causes apt-get to search the **Xenial** archive located at us.archive.ubuntu.com/ubuntu for **deb** packages that contain executable files. It accepts packages that are categorized as **main, restricted,** and **multiverse:**

```
deb http://us.archive.ubuntu.com/ubuntu/ xenial main restricted multiverse
```

Replace **deb** with **deb-src** to search for packages of source files in the same manner. Use the **apt-get source** command to download source packages.

Default repositories The default **sources.list** file on an Ubuntu system includes repositories such as **xenial, xenial-updates** (major bug fixes after the release of xenial), **xenial-security** (critical security-related updates), and **xenial-backports** (newer, less-tested software that is not reviewed by the Ubuntu security team). Some repositories in **sources.list** might be commented out. Remove the leading pound sign (#) on the lines of the repositories you want to enable. After you modify **sources.list**, give the command **apt-get update** (page 1060) to update the local package indexes.

The next line, which was added to **sources.list,** enables apt-get to search a third-party repository (but see the following security tip):

```
deb http://download.skype.com/linux/repos/debian/ stable non-free
```

In this case, the repository is named **stable** and the category is **non-free**. Although the code is compiled for Debian, it runs on Ubuntu, as is frequently the case.

Use repositories you trust

security There are many repositories of software packages. Be selective in which repositories you add to **sources.list**: When you add a repository, you are trusting the person who runs the repository not to put malicious software in packages you might download. In addition, unsupported packages might conflict with other packages or cause upgrades to fail.

BITTORRENT

The easiest way to download a BitTorrent file is to click the torrent file object in a Web browser or in the Nautilus File Browser; this action opens a GUI. This section describes how BitTorrent works and explains how to download a BitTorrent file from the command line.

The BitTorrent protocol implements a hybrid client/server and *P2P* (page 1114) file transfer mechanism. BitTorrent efficiently distributes large amounts of static data, such as the Fedora/RHEL installation ISO images. It can replace protocols such as anonymous FTP, where client authentication is not required. Each BitTorrent client that downloads a file provides additional bandwidth for uploading the file, thereby reducing the load on the initial source. In general, BitTorrent downloads proceed faster than FTP downloads. Unlike protocols such as FTP, BitTorrent groups multiple files into a single package; that is, a BitTorrent file.

Tracker, peer, seed, and swarm

BitTorrent, like other P2P systems, does not use a dedicated server. Instead, the functions of a server are performed by the tracker, peers, and seeds. The *tracker* is a server that allows clients to communicate with each other. Each client—called a *peer* when it has downloaded part of the BitTorrent file and a *seed* after it has downloaded the entire BitTorrent file—acts as an additional source for the BitTorrent file. Peers and seeds are collectively called a *swarm*. As with a P2P network, a member of a swarm uploads to other clients the sections of the BitTorrent file it has already downloaded. There is nothing special about a seed: It can be removed at any time after the torrent is available for download from other seeds.

The torrent

The first step in downloading a BitTorrent file is to locate or acquire the *torrent*, a file with the filename extension of **.torrent**. A torrent contains pertinent information (metadata) about the BitTorrent file to be downloaded, such as its size and the location of the tracker. You can obtain a torrent by accessing its URI, or you can acquire it via the Web, an email attachment, or other means. The BitTorrent client can then connect to the tracker to learn the locations of other members of the swarm it can download the BitTorrent file from.

Manners

After you have downloaded a BitTorrent file (the local system has become a seed), it is good manners to allow the local BitTorrent client to continue to run so peers (clients that have not downloaded the entire BitTorrent file) can upload *at least* as much information as you have downloaded.

Prerequisites

If necessary, use dnf (page 1054) or apt-get (page 1061) to install the **rtorrent** package.

Using BitTorrent

The rtorrent utility is a textual BitTorrent client that provides a pseudographical interface. When you have a torrent, enter a command such as the following, substituting the name of the torrent you want to download for the Fedora torrent in the example:

```
$ rtorrent Fedora-Workstation-Live-x86_64-26.torrent
```

A torrent can download one or more files; the torrent specifies the filename(s) for the downloaded file(s) and, in the case of a multifile torrent, a directory to hold the files. The torrent in the preceding command saves the BitTorrent files in the **Fedora-17-i686-Live-Desktop** directory in the working directory.

The following example shows rtorrent running. Depending on the speed of the Internet connection and the number of seeds, downloading a large BitTorrent file can take from hours to days.

```
*** rTorrent 0.8.9/0.12.9 - guava:7739 ***
[View: main]
   Fedora-Workstation-Live-x86_64-26
```

```
                479.9 /  646.0 MB Rate:   0.0 / 1187.6 KB Uploaded:
...
[Throttle off/off KB] [Rate  2.2/1193.5 KB] [Port: 6977] [U 0/0]
```

You can abort the download by pressing CONTROL-Q. The download will automatically resume from where it left off when you download the same torrent to the same location again.

Make sure you have enough room to download the torrent

caution Some torrents are huge. Make sure the partition you are working in has enough room to hold the BitTorrent file you are downloading.

Enter the command **rtorrent --help** for a list of options. Visit libtorrent.rakshasa.no/wiki/RTorrentUserGuide for more complete documentation. One of the most useful options is **–o upload_rate**, which limits how much bandwidth in kilobytes per second the swarm can use while downloading the torrent *from the local system* (upstream bandwidth). By default, there is no limit to the bandwidth the swarm can use. The following command prevents BitTorrent from using more than 100 kilobytes per second of upstream bandwidth:

```
$ rtorrent -o upload_rate=100 Fedora-Workstation-Live-x86_64-26.torrent
```

BitTorrent usually allows higher download rates for members of the swarm that upload more data, so it is to your advantage to increase this value if you have spare bandwidth. You need to leave enough free upstream bandwidth for the acknowledgment packets from your download to get through or the download will be very slow.

The value assigned to **max_uploads** specifies the number of concurrent uploads that rtorrent will permit. By default, there is no limit. If you are downloading over a very slow connection, try setting **upload_rate=3** and **max_uploads=2**.

The name of the file or directory in which BitTorrent saves a file or files is specified by the torrent. You can specify a different file or directory name by using the **directory=*directory*** option.

D

macOS Notes

In This Appendix

This appendix is a brief guide to macOS features that differ from those of Linux. See Chapter 1 for a history of UNIX, Linux, and macOS.

The material here is based on the operating system that was called *Mac OS X* in 2001–2012, *OS X* in 2012–2016, and macOS today. This appendix will use *macOS* throughout. For clarity, version numbers and *Mac OS* are used when referring to the older, classic operating system that existed prior to 2001, which was not UNIX-based.

Open Directory

Open Directory replaced the monolithic NetInfo database in macOS version 10.5. The ni* utilities, including nireport and nidump, were replaced by dscl (page 806). The work the **lookupd** daemon did is now done by the **DirectoryService** daemon.

To obtain information on the local system, macOS now uses a hierarchy of small ***.plist** XML files called *nodes*, which are stored in the **/var/db/dslocal** hierarchy. Many of these files are human readable. On macOS Server, a networkwide Open Directory is based on OpenLDAP, Kerberos, and the SASL-based Password Server.

/etc/passwd macOS uses the **/etc/passwd** file only when it boots into single-user mode. Because macOS does not use the user information stored in the **/etc/passwd** file while it is in multiuser mode, examples in this book that use this file do not run under macOS. In most cases you must use dscl to extract information from the **passwd** database. As an example, the **whos2** program discussed next is a version of **whos** (page 446) that runs under macOS 10.5 and above.

whos2 For each command-line argument, **whos2** searches the **passwd** database. Inside the **for** loop, the dscl (page 806) **–readall** command lists all usernames and user IDs on the local system. The command looks for the **RealName** keys in the **/Users** directory and displays the associated values. The four-line sed (page 669) command deletes lines containing only a dash (**/^–$/ d**), finds lines containing only **RealName:** (**/^RealName:$/**), reads and appends the next line (**N**; page 672), and substitutes a semicolon for the NEWLINE (**s/\n/; /**). Finally grep (page 853) selects lines containing the ID the program was called with.

```
$ cat whos2
#!/bin/bash

if [ $# -eq 0 ]
    then
        echo "Usage: whos id..." 1>&2
        exit 1
fi

for id
do
    dscl . -readall /Users RealName |
    sed '/^-$/ d
        /^RealName:$/N;s/\n//
        N
        s/\n/; /'                   |
    grep -i "$id"
done
```

/etc/group *Groups* (page 1100) allow users to share files or programs without allowing all system users access to them. This scheme is useful if several users are working with files that are not public. In a Linux system, the **/etc/group** file associates one or more usernames with each group (number). macOS 10.5 and above rely on Open Directory (page 1068) to provide group information. macOS 10.4 and below use NetInfo for this task.

FILESYSTEMS

macOS supports several types of filesystems. The most commonly used is the default HFS+ (Hierarchical File System Plus). Introduced under Mac OS 8.1 to support larger disks, HFS+ is an enhanced version of the original HFS filesystem. When it was introduced in OS 3.0 in 1986, HFS stood in contrast to the then-standard MFS (Macintosh File System). Some applications will not run correctly under filesystems other than HFS+.

HFS+ is different from Linux filesystems, but because Linux offers a standardized filesystem interface, the differences are generally transparent to the user. The most significant differences are the following:

- HFS+ is case preserving but not case sensitive (discussed later in this section).
- HFS+ allows a user working with **root** privileges to create hard links to directories.
- HFS+ files have extended attributes (discussed later in this appendix).

macOS also supports Linux filesystems such as UFS (UNIX File System), which it inherited from Berkeley UNIX. Other supported filesystems include FAT16 and FAT32, which were originally used in DOS and Windows. These filesystems are typically used on removable media, such as digital camera storage cards. macOS also supports NTFS (Windows), exFAT (USB flash drives), ISO9660 (CD-ROMs), and UDF (DVDs).

NONDISK FILESYSTEMS

macOS supports filesystems that do not correspond to a physical volume such as a partition on a hard disk or a CD-ROM. A **.dmg** (disk image) file is one example (to mount a disk image file so you can access the files it holds, double-click it in the Finder). Another example is a virtual filesystem in which the filenames represent kernel functionality. For example, the **/Network** virtual filesystem holds a directory tree representing the local network; most network filesystem protocols use this filesystem. Also, you can use the Disk Utility to create encrypted or password-protected **.iso** (*ISO9660;* page 1105) image files you can mount. Finally you can use hdiutil to mount and manipulate disk images.

Case Sensitivity

The default macOS filesystem, HFS+, is, by default, case preserving but not case sensitive. *Case preserving* means the filesystem remembers which capitalization you used when you created a file and displays the filename with that capitalization, but accepts any capitalization to refer to the file. Thus, under HFS+, files named **JANUARY**, **January**, and **january** refer to the same file. You can set up an HFS+ filesystem to be case sensitive.

/Volumes

Startup disk Each physical hard disk in a macOS system is typically divided into one or more logical sections (partitions or volumes). Each macOS system has a volume, called the *startup disk*, that the system boots from. By default, the startup disk is named **Macintosh HD**. When the system boots, **Macintosh HD** is mounted as the root directory (/).

The root directory always has a subdirectory named **Volumes**. For historical reasons, every volume other than the startup disk is mounted in the **/Volumes** directory. For example, the pathname of a disk labeled **MyPhotos** is **/Volumes/MyPhotos**.

To simplify access, **/Volumes** holds a symbolic link (page 115) to the startup disk (the root directory). Assuming that the startup disk is named **Macintosh HD**, **/Volumes/Macintosh HD** is a symbolic link to /.

```
$ ls -ld '/Volumes/Macintosh HD'
lrwxr-xr-x   1 root  admin  1 Jul 12 19:03 /Volumes/Macintosh HD -> /
```

The system automatically mounts all volumes in **/Volumes**. The desktop presented by the Finder contains an icon for each mounted disk and for files in the user's **Desktop** directory, making the **/Volumes** directory the effective root (top level or /) for the Finder and other applications. The Finder presents the pre-UNIX Mac OS view of the filesystem.

Extended Attributes

macOS files have *extended attributes* that include file forks (e.g., data, resource), file attributes, and access control lists (ACLs). Not all utilities recognize extended attributes.

Resource forks and file attributes are native to the HFS+ filesystem. macOS emulates resource forks and file attributes on other types of filesystems. These features are not found on Linux filesystems.

Some utilities do not process extended attributes

caution Some third-party programs and most utilities under macOS 10.3 and below do not support extended attributes. Some utilities require options to process extended attributes.

See also the tip "Redirection does not support resource forks" on the next page.

File Forks

Forks are segments of a single file, each holding different content. macOS has supported file forks since its inception. The most widely used are the *data fork* and the *resource fork*.

Data forks The data fork is equivalent to a Linux file. It consists of an unstructured stream of bytes. Many files have only a data fork.

Resource forks The resource fork holds a database that allows random access to resources, each of which has a type and identifier number. Modifying, adding, or deleting one resource has no effect on the other resources. Resource forks can store different types of information—some critical and some merely useful. For example, a macOS graphics program might save a smaller copy of an image (a preview or thumbnail) in a resource fork. Also, text files created with the BBEdit text editor store display size and tab stop information in the file's resource fork. Because this program is a text editor and not a word processor, this type of information cannot be stored in the data fork. Losing a resource fork that holds a thumbnail or display information is at most an inconvenience because, for example, the thumbnail can be regenerated from the original image. Other programs store more important data in the resource fork or create files that contain only a resource fork, which holds all the file's information. In this case, losing the resource fork is just as bad as losing the data fork. It might even be worse: You might not notice a resource fork is missing because the data fork is still there. You might notice the loss only when you try to use the file.

Linux utilities might not preserve resource forks A Linux filesystem associates each filename with a single stream of bytes. Forks do not fit this model. As a result, many Linux utilities do not process resource forks, but instead process only data forks. Most of the file utilities provided with macOS 10.4 and above support resource forks. Many third-party utilities do not support resource forks.

Pipelines do not work with resource forks

caution Pipelines work with the data fork of a file only; they do not work with resource forks.

Redirection does not support resource forks

caution When you redirect input to or output from a utility (page 140), only the information in the data fork is redirected. Information in the resource fork is not redirected. For example, the following command copies the data fork of **song.ogg** only:

```
$ cat song.ogg > song.bak.ogg
```

If you are unsure whether a program supports resource forks, test it before relying on this functionality. Make a backup copy using the Finder, ditto, or, under version 10.4 and above, cp. Then check whether the copied file works correctly.

Table D-1 lists utilities that manipulate resource forks. These utilities are installed with the Developer Tools package. Consult the respective man pages for detailed descriptions.

Table D-1 Utilities that manipulate resource forks

Utility	Function
Rez	Creates a resource fork from a resource description file
DeRez	Creates a resource description file from a resource fork
RezWack	Converts a file with forks to a single flat file that holds all the forks
Utility	**Function**
UnRezWack	Converts a flat file that holds forks to a file with forks
SplitForks	Converts a file with forks to multiple files, each holding a fork

File Attributes

A file contains data. Information about the file is called *metadata.* Examples of metadata include ownership information and permissions for a file. macOS stores more metadata than Linux stores. This section discusses *file attributes,* the metadata stored by macOS.

File attributes include the following:

- Attribute flags
- Type codes
- Creator codes

The same caveats apply to file attributes as apply to resource forks: Some utilities might not preserve them when copying or manipulating files, and many utilities do not recognize attribute flags. Loss of file attributes is particularly common when you move files to non-Macintosh systems.

Attribute Flags

Attribute flags (Table D-2) hold information that is distinct from Linux permissions. Two especially notable attribute flags are the invisible flag (which keeps a file from being displayed in file dialogs and in the Finder) and the locked flag (which keeps a file from being modified). Flags are generally ignored by command-line utilities and affect only GUI applications. The ls utility lists files that have the invisible flag set. See GetFileInfo on page 851 and SetFile on page 965 for information on displaying, setting, and clearing attribute flags.

Table D-2 Attribute flags

Flag	Can the flag be set on a directory?	Description
a	No	Alias file

Table D-2 Attribute flags (continued)

Flag	Can the flag be set on a directory?	Description
b	No	Has bundle
c	Yes	Custom icon
l	No	Locked
t	No	Stationery pad file
v	Yes	Invisible

CREATOR CODES AND TYPE CODES

Type codes and creator codes are 32-bit integers, generally displayed as 4-character words, that specify the type and creator of a file. The creator code specifies the application that created a document, not the user who created it. An application can typically open documents that have the same creator code as the application, but cannot open documents with other creator codes.

Creator codes Creator codes generally correspond to vendors or product lines. The operating system—and in particular the Finder—uses creator codes to group related files. For example, the AppleWorks application file and its document files have the creator code **BOBO**. In the file browser in an application's open file dialog box, grayed-out files generally indicate files that have a different creator code from the application and that the application cannot open. The open utility (page 926) also looks at creator codes when it opens a file.

Type codes Type codes indicate how a file is used. The type code **APPL** indicates an application—a program used to open other files. For example, an AppleWorks word processor document has the type code **CWWP**, a mnemonic for Claris Works Word Processor (AppleWorks used to be named Claris Works). While a few type codes, such as the application type, are standardized, vendors are free to invent new type codes for their programs. A single application might support several document types. For example, AppleWorks supports spreadsheet files (**CWSS**), word processor documents (**CWWP**), and drawings (**CWGR**). Similarly a graphics program will typically support many document types. Data files used by an application might also have the same creator code as the application, even though they cannot be opened as documents. For example, the dictionary used by a spell checker cannot be opened as a document but typically uses the same creator code as the spell checker.

Filename extensions Filename extensions (page 87) can substitute for type and creator codes. For example, an AppleWorks word processor document is saved with an extension of **.cwk**. Also, if open cannot determine which application to use to open a file using the file's creator code, it reverts to using the file's filename extension.

ACLs

ACLs (access control lists) are discussed on page 106. This section discusses how to enable and work with ACLs under macOS.

chmod: Working with ACLs

Under macOS, you can use chmod (page 759) to create, modify, and delete ACL rules. A chmod command used for this purpose has the following syntax:

*chmod **option[# n]** "**who** allow|deny **permission-list**" **file-list***

where ***option*** is **+a** (add rule), **–a** (remove rule), or **=a** (change rule); ***n*** is an optional rule number; ***who*** is a username, user ID number, group name, or group ID number; ***permission-list*** is one or more comma-separated file access permissions selected from **read, write, append**, and **execute**; and ***file-list*** is the list of files the rule is applied to. The quotation marks are required. In the first example, Sam adds a rule that grants Helen read and write access to the **memo** file:

```
$ chmod +a "helen allow read,write" memo
```

The chmod utility displays an error message if you forget the quotation marks:

```
$ chmod +a max deny write memo
chmod: Invalid entry format -- expected allow or deny
```

ls –l An ls –l command displays a plus sign (+) following the permissions for a file that has an ACL (see also Figure 4-12 on page 101):

```
$ ls -l memo
-rw-r--r--+ 1 sam  staff  1680 May 12 13:30 memo
```

ls –le Under macOS, the ls –e option displays ACL rules:

```
$ ls -le memo
-rw-r--r--+ 1 sam  staff  1680 May 12 13:30 memo
 0: user:helen allow read,write
```

For each rule, the **–e** option displays from left to right the rule number followed by a colon, **user:** or **group:** followed by the name of the user or group the rule pertains to, **allow** or **deny** depending on whether the rule grants or denies permissions, and a list of the permissions that are granted or denied.

The kernel processes multiple rules in an ACL in rule number order but does not necessarily number rules in the order you enter them. In general, rules denying permissions come before rules granting permissions. You can override the default order by assigning a number to a rule using the **+a# *n*** syntax. The following command bumps rule 0 from the previous example to rule 1 and replaces it with a rule that denies Max write access to **memo**:

```
$ chmod +a# 0 "max deny write" memo
$ ls -le memo
-rw-r--r--+ 1 sam  staff  1680 May 12 13:30 memo
```

```
0: user:max deny write
1: user:helen allow read,write
```

There are two ways to remove access rules. First, you can specify a rule by using its number:

```
$ chmod -a# 1 memo
$ ls -le memo
-rw-r--r--+ 1 sam  staff  1680 May 12 13:30 memo
 0: user:max deny write
```

Second, you can specify a rule by giving the string you used when you added it:

```
$ chmod -a "max deny write" memo
$ ls -le memo
-rw-r--r--  1 sam  staff  1680 May 12 13:30 memo
```

After you remove the last rule, **memo** does not have an ACL. (There is no **+** in the line **ls –le** displays.) When you specify an ACL operation that chmod cannot complete, it displays an error message:

```
$ chmod -a# 0 memo
chmod: No ACL present
```

In the next example, Sam restores Helen's read and write permissions to **memo**:

```
$ chmod +a "helen allow read,write" memo
$ ls -le memo
-rw-r--r--+ 1 sam  staff  1680 May 12 13:30 memo
 0: user:helen allow read,write
```

Sam then removes the write permissions he just gave Helen. When you remove one of several access permissions from a rule, the other permissions remain unchanged:

```
$ chmod -a "helen allow write" memo
$ ls -le memo
-rw-r--r--+ 1 sam  staff  1680 May 12 13:30 memo
 0: user:helen allow read
```

The next example shows that chmod inserts rules in an ACL in a default order. Even though Sam added the **allow** rule before the **deny** rule, the **allow** rule appears first. The rule controlling permission for Helen, which was added before either of the other rules, appears last.

```
$ chmod +a "max allow read" memo
$ chmod +a "max deny read" memo

$ ls -le memo
-rw-r--r--+ 1 sam  staff  1680 May 12 13:30 memo
 0: user:max deny read
 1: user:max allow read
 2: user:helen allow read
```

You can replace a rule using the **=a** syntax. In the following example, Sam changes rule 2 to grant Helen read and write permissions to **memo**:

```
$ chmod =a# 2 "helen allow read,write" memo
$ ls -le memo
-rw-r--r--+ 1 sam  staff  1680 May 12 13:30 memo
 0: user:max deny read
 1: user:max allow read
 2: user:helen allow read,write
```

Activating the Terminal META Key

Using the macOS Terminal utility, you can make the OPTION (or ALT) key work as the META key. From the Terminal utility's **File** menu, select **Window Settings** to display the Terminal Inspector window. This window provides a drop-down menu of properties you can change. Select **Keyboard,** check the box labeled **Use option key as meta key,** and click **Use Settings as Defaults.** This procedure causes the OPTION key (on Mac keyboards) or the ALT key (on PC keyboards) to function as the META key *while you are using the* Terminal *utility.*

Startup Files

Both macOS and application documentation refer to startup files as *configuration files* or *preference files*. Many macOS applications store startup files in the **Library** and **Library/Preferences** subdirectories of a user's home directory, which are created when an account is set up. Most of these files do not have invisible filenames. Use launchctl (page 870) to modify these files.

Remote Logins

By default, macOS does not allow remote logins. You can enable remote logins via ssh by enabling remote login in the **Services** tab of the Sharing pane of the Preferences window. macOS does not support telnet logins.

Many Utilities Do Not Respect Apple Human Interface Guidelines

By default, rm under macOS does not act according to the Apple Human Interface Guidelines, which state that an operation should either be reversible or ask for confirmation. In general, macOS command-line utilities do not ask whether you are sure of what you are doing.

INSTALLING XCODE AND MACPORTS

Xcode is free software supplied by Apple. See developer.apple.com/xcode for more information. To download and install Xcode, open the App Store, search for and click **xcode**, and then follow the instructions for installation. Once you have installed Xcode, you might want to install Command Line Tools; you must install this package if you want to use MacPorts (discussed next). To install Command Line Tools, select Xcode Preferences, click **Downloads**, and click **Install** adjacent to Command Line Tools.

The MacPorts (www.macports.org) project is an "open-source community initiative to design an easy-to-use system for compiling, installing, and upgrading either command-line, X11, or Aqua-based open-source software on the macOS operating system." MacPorts includes more than 14,000 tools; see www.macports.org/ports.php for a list.

To work with MacPorts on a Macintosh, you must first install Xcode as explained earlier. You can then install MacPorts by visiting www.macports.org/install.php and following the instructions in the section titled **macOS Package (.pkg) Installer**.

Installing gawk Once you have installed MacPorts, you can install individual packages using the port utility. For example, you can install gawk using the following command:

```
$ sudo port install gawk
--->  Computing dependencies for gawk
--->  Fetching archive for gawk
...
--->  No broken files found.
```

Installing MySQL Once you have installed MacPorts, you can install MySQL using the following command:

```
$ sudo port install mysql51
--->  Dependencies to be installed: mysql_select zlib
--->  Fetching archive for mysql_select
...
--->  No broken files found.
```

Alternatively, you can visit www.mysql.com/downloads/mysql (the MySQL Community Server), select **macOS** as your platform, and download the appropriate DMG Archive or Compressed TAR Archive file. These files include a **launchd** startup item and a System Preferences pane for MySQL; see the MySQL documentation at dev.mysql.com/doc/refman/5.6/en/macosx-installation.html.

MACOS IMPLEMENTATION OF LINUX FEATURES

Table D-3 explains how some Linux features are implemented under macOS.

Table D-3 macOS implementation of Linux features

Linux feature	macOS implementation
/bin/sh	The **/bin/sh** file is a copy of bash (**/bin/bash**); it is not a link to **/bin/bash**, as it is on most Linux systems. The original Bourne Shell does not exist under macOS. When you call bash using the command **sh**, bash tries to mimic the behavior of the original Bourne Shell as closely as possible.
Core files	By default, macOS does not save core files. When core files are saved, they are kept in **/cores**, not in the working directory.
Developer tools	The Developer Tools package is not installed by default.
Development APIs	macOS uses two software development APIs: Cocoa and BSD UNIX.
Dynamic linker ld.so	The macOS dynamic linker is dyld, not ld.so.
ELF and **a.out** binary formats	The primary binary format under macOS is Mach-O, not ELF or **a.out**.
/etc/group	macOS uses Open Directory (page 1068), not **/etc/group**, to store group information.
/etc/passwd	macOS uses Open Directory (page 1068), not **/etc/passwd**, to store user accounts.
Filesystem structure **/etc/fstab**	Instead of filesystems being mounted according to settings in **/etc/fstab**, filesystems are automatically mounted in the **/Volumes** directory (page 1070).
finger	By default, macOS disables remote finger support.
LD_LIBRARY_PATH	The variable used to control the dynamic linker is **DYLD_LIBRARY_PATH**, not **LD_LIBRARY_PATH**.
Shared libraries ***.so**	macOS shared library files are named ***.dylib**, not ***.so**. They are typically distributed in **.framework** bundles that include resources and headers.

Table D-3 macOS implementation of Linux features (continued)

Linux feature	macOS implementation
System databases	Some system databases, such as **passwd** and **group**, are stored by Open Directory (page 1068), not in the **/etc** directory (page 99). You can work with Open Directory databases using the dscl utility (page 806).
vi editor	As with many Linux distributions, when you call the vi editor, macOS 10.3 and above run vim (page 165) because the file **/usr/bin/vi** is a link to **/usr/bin/vim**.

Glossary

All entries marked with FOLDOC are based on definitions in the Free On-Line Dictionary of Computing (foldoc.org), Denis Howe, editor. Used with permission.

10.0.0.0 See *private address space* on page 1117.

172.16.0.0 See *private address space* on page 1117.

192.168.0.0 See *private address space* on page 1117.

802.11 A family of specifications developed by IEEE for wireless LAN technology, including 802.11 (1–2 megabits per second), 802.11a (54 megabits per second), 802.11b (11 megabits per second), and 802.11g (54 megabits per second).

absolute pathname A pathname that starts with the root directory (represented by /). An absolute pathname locates a file without regard to the working directory.

access In computer jargon, a verb meaning to use, read from, or write to. To access a file means to read from or write to the file.

Access Control List See *ACL*.

access permissions Permission to read from, write to, or execute a file. If you have write access permission to a file (usually just called *write permission*), you can write to the file. Also *access privilege*.

ACL Access Control List. A system that performs a function similar to file permissions but with much finer-grain control.

active window On a desktop, the window that receives the characters you type on the keyboard. Same as *focus, desktop* (page 1098).

address mask See *network mask* on page 1112.

alias A mechanism of a shell that enables you to define new commands.

alphanumeric character One of the characters, either uppercase or lowercase, from A to Z and 0 to 9, inclusive.

ambiguous file reference A reference to a file that does not necessarily specify any one file but can be used to specify a group of files. The shell expands an ambiguous file reference into a list of filenames. Special characters represent single characters (?), strings of zero or more characters (*), and character classes ([]) within ambiguous file references. An ambiguous file reference is a type of *regular expression* (page 1120).

angle bracket A left angle bracket (<) and a right angle bracket (>). The shell uses < to redirect a command's standard input to come from a file and > to redirect the standard output. The shell uses the characters << to signify the start of a Here document and >> to append output to a file.

animate When referring to a window action, means that the action is slowed down so the user can view it. For example, when you minimize a window, it can disappear all at once (not animated), or it can slowly telescope into the panel so you can get a visual feel for what is happening (animated).

anti-aliasing Adding gray pixels at the edge of a diagonal line to get rid of the jagged appearance and thereby make the line look smoother. Anti-aliasing sometimes makes type on a screen look better and sometimes worse; it works best on small and large fonts and is less effective on fonts from 8 to 15 points. See also *subpixel hinting* (page 1126).

API Application program interface. The interface (calling conventions) by which an application program accesses an operating system and other services. An API is defined at the source code level and provides a level of abstraction between the application and the kernel (or other privileged utilities) to ensure the portability of the code.FOLDOC

append To add something to the end of something else. To append text to a file means to add the text to the end of the file. The shell uses >> to append a command's output to a file.

applet A small program that runs within a larger program. Examples are Java applets that run in a browser and panel applets that run from a desktop panel.

APT Advanced Package Tool. This package manager checks dependencies and updates software on DEB systems.

archive A file that contains a group of smaller, typically related, files. Also, to create such a file. The tar and cpio utilities can create and read archives.

argument A number, letter, filename, or another string that gives some information to a command and is passed to the command when it is called. A command-line argument is anything on a command line following the command name that is passed to the command. An option is a kind of argument.

arithmetic expression A group of numbers, operators, and parentheses that can be evaluated. When you evaluate an arithmetic expression, you end up with a number. The Bourne Again Shell uses the expr command to evaluate arithmetic expressions; the TC Shell uses @, and the Z Shell uses let.

ARP Address Resolution Protocol. A method for finding a host's *MAC address* (page 1108; also Ethernet address) from its IP address. ARP allows the IP address to be independent of the MAC address.FOLDOC

array An arrangement of elements (numbers or strings of characters) in one or more dimensions. The Bourne Again, TC, and Z Shells and awk/mawk/gawk can store and process arrays.

ASCII American Standard Code for Information Interchange. A code that uses seven bits to represent both graphic (letters, numbers, and punctuation) and CONTROL characters. You can represent textual information, including program source code and English text, in ASCII code. Because ASCII is a standard, it is frequently used when exchanging information between computers. See the file **/usr/pub/ascii** or give the command **man ascii** to see a list of ASCII codes.

Extensions of the ASCII character set use eight bits. The seven-bit set is common; the eight-bit extensions are still coming into popular use. The eighth bit is sometimes referred to as the *metabit*.

ASCII terminal A textual terminal. Contrast with *graphical display* (page 1100).

ASP Application service provider. A company that provides applications over the Internet.

asynchronous event An event that does not occur regularly or synchronously with another event. Linux system signals are asynchronous; they can occur at any time because they can be initiated by any number of nonregular events.

attachment A file that is attached to, but is not part of, a piece of email. Attachments are frequently opened by programs (including your Internet browser) that are called by your mail program, so you might not be aware that they are not an integral part of an email message.

authentication The verification of the identity of a person or process. In a communication system, authentication verifies that a message really comes from its stated source, like the signature on a (paper) letter. The most common form of authentication is typing a user name (which might be widely known or easily guessable) and a corresponding password that is presumed to be known only to the individual being authenticated. Other methods of authentication on a Linux system include the **/etc/passwd** and **/etc/shadow** files, LDAP, biometrics, Kerberos 5, and SMB.[FOLDOC]

automatic mounting A way of demand mounting directories from remote hosts without having them hard-configured into **/etc/fstab**. Also called *automounting*.

avoided An object, such as a panel, that should not normally be covered by another object, such as a window.

back door A security hole deliberately left in place by the designers or maintainers of a system. The motivation for creating such holes is not always sinister; some operating systems, for example, come out of the box with privileged accounts intended for use by field service technicians or the vendor's maintenance programmers.

Ken Thompson's 1983 Turing Award lecture to the ACM revealed the existence, in early UNIX versions, of a back door that might be the most fiendishly clever security hack of all time. The C compiler contained code that would recognize when the **login** command was being recompiled and would insert some code recognizing a password chosen by Thompson, giving him entry to the system whether or not an account had been created for him.

Normally, such a back door could be removed by removing it from the source code for the compiler and recompiling the compiler. But to recompile the compiler, you have to *use* the compiler, so Thompson arranged that the compiler would *recognize when it was compiling a version of itself*. It would insert into the recompiled compiler the code to insert into the recompiled **login** the code to allow Thompson entry, and, of course, the code to recognize itself and do the whole thing again the next time around. Having done this once, he was then able to recompile the compiler from the original sources; the hack perpetuated itself invisibly, leaving the back door in place and active but with no trace in the sources.

Sometimes called a wormhole. Also *trap door*.FOLDOC

background process A process that is not run in the foreground. Also called a *detached process*, a background process is initiated by a command line that ends with an ampersand (&) control operator. You do not have to wait for a background process to run to completion before giving the shell additional commands. If you have job control, you can move background processes to the foreground, and vice versa.

basename The name of a file that, in contrast with a pathname, does not mention any of the directories containing the file (and therefore does not contain any slashes [/]). For example, **hosts** is the basename of **/etc/hosts**.FOLDOC

baud The maximum information-carrying capacity of a communication channel in symbols (state transitions or level transitions) per second. It coincides with bits per second only for two-level modulation with no framing or stop bits. A symbol is a unique state of the communication channel, distinguishable by the receiver from all other possible states. For example, it might be one of two voltage levels on a wire for a direct digital connection, or it might be the phase or frequency of a carrier.FOLDOC

Baud is often mistakenly used as a synonym for bits per second.

baud rate Transmission speed. Usually used to measure terminal or modem speed. Common baud rates range from 110 to 38,400 baud. See *baud*.

Berkeley UNIX One of the two major versions of the UNIX operating system. Berkeley UNIX was developed at the University of California at Berkeley by the Computer Systems Research Group and is often referred to as *BSD* (Berkeley Software Distribution).

beta release Evaluation, pre-release software that is potentially unreliable. Beta software is made available to selected users (beta testers) before it is released to the general public. Beta testing aims to discover bugs that occur only in certain environments or under certain patterns of use, while reducing the volume of feedback to a manageable level. The testers benefit by having earlier access to new products, features, and fixes. The term derives from early 1960s terminology for product cycle checkpoints, first used at IBM but later made standard throughout the industry. Contrast with *stable release* (page 1125).FOLDOC

BIND Berkeley Internet Name Domain. An implementation of a *DNS* (page 1095) server developed and distributed by the University of California at Berkeley.

BIOS Basic Input/Output System. On PCs, *EEPROM*-based (page 1096) system software that provides the lowest-level interface to peripheral devices and controls the first stage of the *bootstrap* (page 1086) process, which loads the operating system. The BIOS can be stored in different types of memory. The memory must be nonvolatile so that it remembers the system settings even when the system is turned off. Also BIOS ROM.

bit The smallest piece of information a computer can handle. A *bit* is a binary digit: either 1 or 0 (*on* or *off*).

bit depth Same as *color depth* (page 1090).

bit-mapped display A graphical display device in which each pixel on the screen is controlled by an underlying representation of zeros and ones.

blank character Either a SPACE or a TAB character, also called *whitespace* (page 1132). In some contexts, NEWLINEs are considered blank characters.

block A section of a disk or tape (usually 1,024 bytes long but shorter or longer on some systems) that is written at one time.

block device A disk or tape drive. A block device stores information in blocks of characters and is represented by a block device (block special) file. Contrast with *character device* (page 1089).

block number Disk and tape *blocks* are numbered so that Linux can keep track of the data on the device.

blocking factor The number of logical blocks that make up a physical block on a tape or disk. When you write 1K logical blocks to a tape with a physical block size of 30K, the blocking factor is 30.

Boolean The type of an expression with two possible values: *true* and *false*. Also, a variable of Boolean type or a function with Boolean arguments or result. The most common Boolean functions are AND, OR, and NOT.[FOLDOC]

boot See *bootstrap*.

boot loader A very small program that takes its place in the *bootstrap* process that brings a computer from off or reset to a fully functional state.

bootstrap Derived from "Pull oneself up by one's own bootstraps," the incremental process of loading an operating system kernel into memory and starting it running without any outside assistance. Frequently shortened to *boot*.

Bourne Again Shell bash. GNU's command interpreter for UNIX, bash is a POSIX-compliant shell with full Bourne Shell syntax and some C Shell commands built in. The Bourne Again Shell supports emacs-style command-line editing, job control, functions, and online help.[FOLDOC]

Bourne Shell sh. This UNIX command processor was developed by Steve Bourne at AT&T Bell Laboratories.

brace A left brace ({) and a right brace (}). Braces have special meanings to the shell.

bracket A *square bracket* (page 1125) or an *angle bracket* (page 1082).

branch In a tree structure, a branch connects nodes, leaves, and the root. The Linux filesystem hierarchy is often conceptualized as an upside-down tree. The branches connect files and directories. In a source code control system, such as SCCS or RCS, a branch occurs when a revision is made to a file and is not included in subsequent revisions to the file.

bridge Typically, a two-port device originally used for extending networks at layer 2 (data link) of the Internet Protocol model.

broadcast A transmission to multiple, unspecified recipients. On Ethernet, a broadcast packet is a special type of *multicast* (page 1111) packet; it has a special address indicating that all devices that receive it should process it. Broadcast traffic exists at several layers of the network stack, including Ethernet and IP. Broadcast traffic has one source but indeterminate destinations (all hosts on the local network).

broadcast address The last address on a subnet (usually 255), reserved as shorthand to mean all hosts.

broadcast network A type of network, such as Ethernet, in which any system can transmit information at any time, and all systems receive every message.

BSD See *Berkeley UNIX* on page 1085.

buffer An area of memory that stores data until it can be used. When you write information to a file on a disk, Linux stores the information in a disk buffer until there is enough to write to the disk or until the disk is ready to receive the information.

bug An unwanted and unintended program property, especially one that causes the program to malfunction.[FOLDOC]

builtin (command) A command that is built into a shell. Each of the three major shells—the Bourne Again, TC, and Z Shells—has its own set of builtins.

byte A component in the machine data hierarchy, usually larger than a bit and smaller than a word; now most often eight bits and the smallest addressable unit of storage. A byte typically holds one character.[FOLDOC]

bytecode A binary file containing an executable program consisting of a sequence of (op code, data) pairs. A bytecode program is interpreted by a bytecode interpreter; Python uses the Python virtual machine. The advantage of bytecode is that it can be run on any processor for which there is a bytecode interpreter. Compiled code (machine code) can run only on the processor for which it was compiled.[FOLDOC]

C programming language A modern systems language that has high-level features for efficient, modular programming as well as lower-level features that make it suitable for use as a systems programming language. It is machine independent so that carefully written C programs can be easily transported to run on different machines. Most of the Linux operating system is written in C, and Linux provides an ideal environment for programming in C.

C Shell csh. The C Shell command processor was developed by Bill Joy for BSD UNIX. It was named for the C programming language because its programming constructs are similar to those of C. See *shell* on page 1123.

CA Certificate Authority (trusted third party). An entity (typically, a company) that issues digital certificates to other entities (organizations or individuals) that allow them to prove their identity to others. A CA might be an external company such as VeriSign that offers digital certificate services or an internal organization such as a corporate MIS department. The primary function of a CA is to verify the identity of entities and issue digital certificates attesting to that identity.[FOLDOC]

cable modem A type of modem that allows you to access the Internet by using your cable television connection.

cache Holding recently accessed data, a small, fast memory designed to speed up subsequent access to the same data. Most often applied to processor-memory access but also used for a local copy of data accessible over a network, from a hard disk, and so on.[FOLDOC]

calling environment A list of variables and their values that is made available to a called program. Refer to "Executing a Command" on page 335.

cascading stylesheet See *CSS* on page 1092.

cascading windows An arrangement of windows such that they overlap, generally with at least part of the title bar visible. Opposite of *tiled windows* (page 1128).

case sensitive Able to distinguish between uppercase and lowercase characters. Unless you set the **ignorecase** parameter, vim performs case-sensitive searches. The grep utility performs case-sensitive searches unless you use the **–i** option.

catenate To join sequentially, or end to end. The Linux cat utility catenates files: It displays them one after the other. Also *concatenate.*

Certificate Authority See *CA.*

chain loading The technique used by a boot loader to load unsupported operating systems. Used for loading such operating systems as DOS or Windows, it works by loading another boot loader.

character-based A program, utility, or interface that works only with *ASCII* (page 1083) characters. This set of characters includes some simple graphics, such as lines and corners, and can display colored characters. It cannot display true graphics. Contrast with *GUI* (page 1100).

character-based terminal A terminal that displays only characters and very limited graphics. See *character-based.*

character class In a regular expression, a group of characters that defines which characters can occupy a single character position. A character-class definition is usually surrounded by square brackets. The character class defined by [**abcr**] represents a character position that can be occupied by **a**, **b**, **c**, or **r**. Also *list operator*.

In GNU documentation and POSIX, used to refer to sets of characters with a common characteristic, denoted by the notation [:*class*:]; for example, [:upper:] denotes the set of uppercase letters.

This book uses the term character class as explained under "Brackets" on page 1039.

character device A terminal, printer, or modem. A character device stores or displays characters one at a time. A character device is represented by a character device (character special) file. Contrast with *block device* (page 1086).

check box A GUI widget, usually the outline of a square box with an adjacent caption, that a user can click to display or remove a *tick* (page 1128). When the box holds a tick, the option described by the caption is on or *true*. Also *tick box*.

checksum A computed value that depends on the contents of a block of data and is transmitted or stored along with the data to detect corruption of the data. The receiving system recomputes the checksum based on the received data and compares this value with the one sent with the data. If the two values are the same, the receiver has some confidence that the data was received correctly.

The checksum might be 8, 16, or 32 bits, or some other size. It is computed by summing the bytes or words of the data block, ignoring overflow. The checksum might be negated so that the total of the data words plus the checksum is zero.

Internet packets use a 32-bit checksum.[FOLDOC]

child process A process that is created by another process, the parent process. Every process is a child process except for the first process, which is started when Linux begins execution. When you run a command from the shell, the shell spawns a child process to run the command. See *process* on page 1117.

CIDR Classless Inter-Domain Routing. A scheme that allocates blocks of Internet addresses in a way that allows summarization into a smaller number of routing table entries. A CIDR block is a block of Internet addresses assigned to an ISP by the Internic.[FOLDOC]

CIFS Common Internet File System. An Internet filesystem protocol based on *SMB* (page 1123). CIFS runs on top of TCP/IP, uses DNS, and is optimized to support slower dial-up Internet connections. SMB and CIFS are used interchangeably.[FOLDOC]

CIPE Crypto IP *Encapsulation* (page 1096). This *protocol* (page 1117) *tunnels* (page 1130) IP packets within encrypted *UDP* (page 1130) packets; is lightweight and simple; and works over dynamic addresses, *NAT* (page 1111), and *SOCKS* (page 1124) *proxies* (page 1118).

cipher (cypher) The core algorithm that transforms *plaintext* (page 1116) to *ciphertext*. The encryption algorithm includes the cipher and the (usually complex) technique that is used to apply the cipher to the message.

ciphertext Text that has been processed by a *cipher* (is encrypted). Contrast with *plaintext* (page 1116).

Classless Inter-Domain Routing See *CIDR* on page 1089.

cleartext Text that is not encrypted. Also *plaintext*. Contrast with *ciphertext*.

CLI Command-line interface. See also *character-based* (page 1088). Also *textual interface*.

client A computer or program that requests one or more services from a server.

cloud A system that provides access via a network (typically, the Internet) to hardware and/or software computing resources, often via a Web browser.

CODEC Coder/decoder or compressor/decompressor. A hardware and/or software technology that codes and decodes data. MPEG is a popular CODEC for computer video.

color depth The number of bits used to generate a pixel—usually 8, 16, 24, or 32. The color depth is directly related to the number of colors that can be generated. The number of colors that can be generated is 2 raised to the color-depth power. Thus, a 24-bit video adapter can generate about 16.7 million colors.

color quality See *color depth*.

combo box A combination of a *drop-down list* (page 1096) and *text box* (page 1128). You can enter text in a combo box. Or you can click a combo box, cause it to expand and display a static list of selections for you to choose among.

command What you give the shell in response to a prompt. When you give the shell a command, it executes a utility, another program, a builtin command, or a shell script. Utilities are often referred to as commands. When you are using an interactive utility, such as vim or mail, you use commands that are appropriate to that utility.

command line A line containing instructions and arguments that executes a command. This term usually refers to a line you enter in response to a shell prompt on a character-based terminal or terminal emulator.

command substitution Replacing a command with its output. The shells perform command substitution when you enclose a command between $(and) or between a pair of back ticks (` `), also called grave accent marks.

component architecture A notion in object-oriented programming where "components" of a program are completely generic. Instead of having a specialized set of methods and fields, they have generic methods through which the component can advertise the functionality it supports to the system into which it is loaded. This strategy enables completely dynamic loading of objects. JavaBeans is an example of a component architecture.[FOLDOC]

concatenate See *catenate* on page 1088.

condition code See *exit status* on page 1097.

connection-oriented protocol A type of transport layer data communication service that allows a host to send data in a continuous stream to another host. The transport service guarantees that all data will be delivered to the other end in the same order as sent and without duplication. Communication proceeds through three well-defined phases: connection establishment, data transfer, and connection release. The most common example is *TCP* (page 1128).

Also called connection-based protocol and stream-oriented protocol. Contrast with *connectionless protocol* and *datagram* (page 1093).[FOLDOC]

connectionless protocol The data communication method in which communication occurs between hosts with no previous setup. Packets sent between two hosts might take different routes. There is no guarantee that packets will arrive as transmitted or even that they will arrive at the destination at all. *UDP* (page 1130) is a connectionless protocol. Also called packet switching. Contrast with circuit switching and *connection-oriented protocol.*[FOLDOC]

console The main system terminal, usually directly connected to the computer and the one that receives system error messages. Also *system console* and *console terminal.*

console terminal See *console.*

control character A character that is not a graphic character, such as a letter, number, or punctuation mark. Such characters are called control characters because they frequently act to control a peripheral device. RETURN and FORMFEED are control characters that control a terminal or printer.

The word CONTROL is shown in this book in THIS FONT because it is a key that appears on most terminal keyboards. Control characters are represented by ASCII codes less than 32 (decimal). See also *nonprinting character* on page 1113.

control operator A token that performs a control function. The Bourne Again Shell uses the following symbols as control operators: ||, &, &&, ;, ;;, (,), |, |&, and RETURN.

control structure A statement used to change the order of execution of commands in a shell script or other program. Each shell provides control structures (for example, **if** and **while**) as well as other commands that alter the order of execution (for example, exec). Also *control flow commands.*

cookie Data stored on a client system by a server. The client system browser sends the cookie back to the server each time it accesses that server. For example, a catalog shopping service might store a cookie on your system when you place your first order. When you return to the site, it knows who you are and can supply your name and address for subsequent orders. You might consider cookies to be an invasion of privacy.

CPU Central processing unit. The part of a computer that controls all the other parts. The CPU includes the control unit and the arithmetic and logic unit (ALU). The control unit fetches instructions from memory and decodes them to produce signals that control the other parts of the computer. These signals can cause data to be transferred between memory and ALU or peripherals to perform input or output. A CPU that is housed on a single chip is called a microprocessor. Also *processor* and *central processor*.

cracker An individual who attempts to gain unauthorized access to a computer system. These individuals are often malicious and have many means at their disposal for breaking into a system. Contrast with *hacker* (page 1100).FOLDOC

crash The system suddenly and unexpectedly stops or fails. Derived from the action of the hard disk heads on the surface of the disk when the air gap between the two collapses.

Creative Commons (creativecommons.org) Creative Commons is a nonprofit organization that provides copyright licenses that enable you to share and use creativity and knowledge. The licenses give the public permission to share and use your creative work while reserving some rights.

cryptography The practice and study of encryption and decryption—encoding data so that only a specific individual or machine can decode it. A system for encrypting and decrypting data is a cryptosystem. Such systems usually rely on an algorithm for combining the original data (plaintext) with one or more keys—numbers or strings of characters known only to the sender and/or recipient. The resulting output is called *ciphertext* (page 1090). Contrast with *plaintext* (page 1116).

The security of a cryptosystem usually depends on the secrecy of keys rather than on the supposed secrecy of an algorithm. Because a strong cryptosystem has a large range of keys, it is not possible to try all of them. Ciphertext appears random to standard statistical tests and resists known methods for breaking codes.FOLDOC

.cshrc file In your home directory, a file that the TC Shell executes each time you invoke a new TC Shell. You can use this file to establish variables and aliases.

CSS Cascading stylesheet. Describes how documents are presented on screen and in print. Attaching a stylesheet to a structured document can affect the way it looks without adding new HTML (or other) tags and without giving up device independence. Also *stylesheet*.

current (process, line, character, directory, event, and so on) The item that is immediately available, working, or being used. The current process is the program you are running, the current line or character is the one the cursor is on, and the current directory is the working directory.

cursor A small lighted rectangle, underscore, or vertical bar that appears on a terminal screen and indicates where the next character will appear. Differs from the *mouse pointer* (page 1110).

daemon A program that is not invoked explicitly but lies dormant, waiting for some condition(s) to occur. The perpetrator of the condition need not be aware that a daemon is lurking (although often a program will commit an action only because it knows that it will implicitly invoke a daemon). From the mythological meaning, later rationalized as the acronym Disk And Execution MONitor.[FOLDOC]

data structure A particular format for storing, organizing, working with, and retrieving data. Frequently, data structures are designed to work with specific algorithms that facilitate these tasks. Common data structures include trees, files, records, tables, and arrays.

datagram A self-contained, independent entity of data carrying sufficient information to be routed from the source to the destination computer without reliance on earlier exchanges between this source and destination computer and the transporting network. *UDP* (page 1130) uses datagrams; *IP* (page 1104) uses *packets* (page 1114). Packets are indivisible at the network layer; datagrams are not.[FOLDOC] See also *frame* (page 1099).

dataless A computer, usually a workstation, that uses a local disk to boot a copy of the operating system and access system files but does not use a local disk to store user files.

dbm A standard, simple database manager. Implemented as **gdbm** (GNU database manager), it uses hashes to speed searching. The most common versions of the **dbm** database are **dbm**, **ndbm**, and **gdbm**.

DDoS attack Distributed denial of service attack. A *DoS attack* (page 1095) from many systems that do not belong to the perpetrator of the attack.

DEB The default software packaging format for Debian and Debian-derived distributions.

debug To correct a program by removing its bugs (that is, errors).

default Something that is selected without being explicitly specified. For example, when used without an argument, ls displays a list of the files in the working directory by default.

delta A set of changes made to a file that has been encoded by the Source Code Control System (SCCS).

denial of service *See DoS attack* on page 1095.

dereference To access the thing to which a pointer points—that is, to follow the pointer. At first sight the word *dereference* might be thought to mean "to cause to stop referring," but its meaning is well established in jargon. See page 118.[FOLDOC]

When speaking of symbolic links, dereference means to follow the link rather than working with the reference to the link. For example, the **–L** or **––dereference** option causes **ls** to list the entry that a symbolic link points to rather than the symbolic link (the reference) itself.

desktop A collection of windows, toolbars, icons, and buttons, some or all of which appear on your display. A desktop comprises one or more *workspaces* (page 1133).

desktop manager An icon- and menu-based user interface to system services that allows you to run applications and use the filesystem without using the system's command-line interface.

detached process See *background process* on page 1085.

device A disk drive, printer, terminal, plotter, or other input/output unit that can be attached to the computer. Short for *peripheral device*.

device driver Part of the Linux kernel that controls a device, such as a terminal, disk drive, or printer.

device file A file that represents a device. Also *special file*.

device filename The pathname of a device file. All Linux systems have two kinds of device files: block and character device files. Linux also has FIFOs (named pipes) and sockets. Device files are traditionally located in the **/dev** directory.

device number See *major device number* (page 1108) and *minor device number* (page 1110).

DHCP Dynamic Host Configuration Protocol. A protocol that dynamically allocates IP addresses to computers on a LAN.[FOLDOC]

dialog box In a GUI, a special window, usually without a titlebar, that displays information. Some dialog boxes accept a response from the user.

directory Short for *directory file*. A file that contains a list of other files.

directory hierarchy A directory, called the root of the directory hierarchy, and all the directory and ordinary files below it (its children).

directory service A structured repository of information on people and resources within an organization, facilitating management and communication.[FOLDOC]

disk partition See *partition* on page 1115.

diskless A computer, usually a workstation, that has no disk and must contact another computer (a server) to boot a copy of the operating system and access the necessary system files.

distributed computing A style of computing in which tasks or services are performed by a network of cooperating systems, some of which might be specialized.

DMZ Demilitarized zone. A host or small network that is a neutral zone between a LAN and the Internet. It can serve Web pages and other data to the Internet and allow local systems access to the Internet while preventing LAN access to unauthorized Internet users. Even if a DMZ is compromised, it holds no data that is private and none that cannot be easily reproduced.

DNF Dandified YUM. This package manager is the replacement for YUM and checks dependencies and updates software on RPM systems.

DNS Domain Name Service. A distributed service that manages the correspondence of full hostnames (those that include a domain name) to IP addresses and other system characteristics.See *domain name.*

document object model See *DOM.*

DOM Document Object Model. A platform-/language-independent interface that enables a program to update the content, structure, and style of a document dynamically. The changes can then be made part of the displayed document. Go to www.w3.org/DOM for more information.

domain name A name associated with an organization, or part of an organization, to help identify systems uniquely. Technically, the part of the *FQDN* (page 1099) to the right of the leftmost period. Domain names are assigned hierarchically. The domain berkeley.edu refers to the University of California at Berkeley, for example; it is part of the top-level edu (education) domain. Also *DNS domain name.* Different from *NIS domain name* (page 1113).

Domain Name Service See *DNS.*

door An evolving filesystem-based *RPC* (page 1121) mechanism.

DoS attack Denial of service attack. An attack that attempts to make the target host or network unusable by flooding it with spurious traffic.

DPMS Display Power Management Signaling. A standard that can extend the life of CRT monitors and conserve energy. DPMS supports four modes for a monitor: Normal, Standby (power supply on, monitor ready to come to display images almost instantly), Suspend (power supply off, monitor takes up to ten seconds to display an image), and Off.

drag The motion part of *drag-and-drop.*

drag-and-drop To move an object from one position or application to another within a GUI. To drag an object, the user clicks a mouse button (typically the left one) while the mouse pointer *hovers* (page 1102) over the object. Then, without releasing the mouse button, the user drags the object, which stays attached to the mouse pointer, to a different location. The user can then drop the object at the new location by releasing the mouse button.

drop-down list A *widget* (page 1132) that displays a static list for a user to choose from. When the list is not active, it appears as text in a box, displaying the single selected entry. When a user clicks the box, a list appears; the user can move the mouse cursor to select an entry from the list. Different from a *list box* (page 1107).

druid In role-playing games, a character that represents a magical user. Fedora/RHEL uses the term *druid* at the ends of names of programs that guide you through a task-driven chain of steps. Other operating systems call these types of programs *wizards*.

DSA Digital Signature Algorithm. A public key cipher used to generate digital signatures.

DSL Digital Subscriber Line/Loop. Provides high-speed digital communication over a specialized, conditioned telephone line. See also *xDSL* (page 1133).

Dynamic Host Configuration Protocol See *DHCP* on page 1094.

ECDSA Elliptic Curve Digital Signature Algorithm. A public key encryption algorithm that iuses a variant of *DSA* that uses ECC (elliptic curve cryptography). A much shorter ECDSA key can provide the same security level as a longer DSA key.

editor A utility, such as vim or emacs, that creates and modifies text files.

EEPROM Electrically erasable, programmable, readonly memory. A *PROM* (page 1117) that can be written to.

effective UID The UID (user ID) that a process appears to have; usually the same as the *real UID* (page 1119). For example, while you are running a setuid program, the effective UID of the process running the program is that of the owner of the program, frequently **root**, while the real UID remains your UID. Refer to "Directory Files and Ordinary Files" on page 85.

element One thing; usually, a basic part of a group of things. An element of a numeric array is one of the numbers stored in the array.

emoticon See *smiley* on page 1124.

encapsulation See *tunneling* on page 1130.

encryption A procedure used in cryptography to convert *plaintext* (page 1116) into *ciphertext* (page 1090).

entropy A measure of the disorder of a system. Systems tend to go from a state of order (low entropy) to a state of maximum disorder (high entropy).[FOLDOC]

environment See *calling environment* on page 1088.

environment variable (shell) A variable that was in the environment the shell was called with or a variable that has been marked for export via the environment. An environment variable is available to children of the shell; also called a global variable. As explained on page 315, you can use the export builtin, or the **–x** option to the declare builtin, to mark a variable for export via the environment.

EOF End of file.

EPROM Erasable programmable readonly memory. A *PROM* (page 1117) that can be written to by applying a higher than normal voltage.

escape See *quote* on page 1118.

Ethernet A type of *LAN* (page 1106) capable of transfer rates as high as 1,000 megabits per second.

Ethernet address See *MAC address* on page 1108.

event An occurrence, or happening, of significance to a task or program—for example, the completion of an asynchronous input/output operation, such as a keypress or mouse click.[FOLDOC]

exabyte 2^{60} bytes or about 10^{18} bytes. See also *large number* (page 1106).

exit status The status returned by a process; either successful (usually 0) or unsuccessful (usually 1).

exploit A security hole or an instance of taking advantage of a security hole.[FOLDOC]

expression See *logical expression* (page 1108) and *arithmetic expression* (page 1083).

extranet A network extension for a subset of users (such as students at a particular school or engineers working for the same company). An extranet limits access to private information even though it travels on the public Internet.

failsafe session A session that allows you to log in on a minimal desktop in case your standard login does not work well enough to allow you to log in to fix a login problem.

FDDI Fiber Distributed Data Interface. A type of *LAN* (page 1106) designed to transport data at the rate of 100 million bits per second over fiberoptic cable.

file A collection of related information referred to with a *filename* and frequently stored on a disk. Text files typically contain memos, reports, messages, program source code, lists, or manuscripts. Binary or executable files contain utilities or programs that you can run. Refer to "Directory Files and Ordinary Files" on page 85.

filename The name of a file. A filename refers to a file.

filename completion Automatic completion of a filename after you specify a unique prefix.

filename extension The part of a filename following a period.

filename generation What occurs when the shell expands ambiguous file references. See *ambiguous file reference* on page 1082.

filesystem A *data structure* (page 1093) that usually resides on part of a disk. All Linux systems have a root filesystem, and many have other filesystems. Each filesystem is composed of some number of blocks, depending on the size of the disk partition that has been assigned to the filesystem. Each filesystem has a control block, named the superblock, that contains information about the filesystem. The other blocks in a filesystem are inodes, which contain control information about individual files, and data blocks, which contain the information in the files.

filling A variant of maximizing in which window edges are pushed out as far as they can go without overlapping another window.

filter A command that can take its input from standard input and send its output to standard output. A filter transforms the input stream of data and sends it to standard output. A pipe symbol (|) usually connects a filter's input to standard output of one command, and a second pipe symbol connects the filter's output to standard input of another command. The grep and sort utilities are commonly used as filters.

firewall A device for policy-based traffic management used to keep a network secure. A firewall can be implemented in a single router that filters out unwanted packets, or it can rely on a combination of routers, proxy servers, and other devices. Firewalls are widely used to give users access to the Internet in a secure fashion and to separate a company's public WWW server from its internal network. They are also employed to keep internal network segments more secure.

Recently, the term has come to be defined more loosely to include a simple packet filter running on an endpoint machine.

See also *proxy server* on page 1118.

firmware Software built into a computer, often in *ROM* (page 1121). Might be used as part of the *bootstrap* (page 1086) procedure.

focus, desktop On a desktop, the window that is active. The window with the desktop focus receives the characters you type on the keyboard. Same as *active window* (page 1082).

footer The part of a format that goes at the bottom (or foot) of a page. Contrast with *header* (page 1101).

foreground process When you run a command in the foreground, the shell waits for the command to finish before giving you another prompt. You must wait for a foreground process to run to completion before you can give the shell a subsequent command. If you have job control, you can move background processes to the foreground, and vice versa. See *job control* on page 1105. Contrast with *background process* (page 1085).

fork To create a process. When one process creates another process, it forks a process. Also *spawn*.

FQDN Fully qualified domain name. The full name of a system, consisting of its hostname and its domain name, including the top-level domain. Technically, the name that **gethostbyname**(2) returns for the host named by **gethostname**(2). For example, **speedy** is a hostname and **speedy.example.com** is an FQDN. An FQDN is sufficient to determine a unique Internet address for a machine on the Internet.FOLDOC

frame A data link layer packet that contains, in addition to data, the header and trailer information required by the physical medium. Network layer packets are encapsulated to become frames.FOLDOC See also *datagram* (page 1093) and *packet* (page 1114).

free list In a filesystem, the list of blocks that are available for use. Information about the free list is kept in the superblock of the filesystem.

free space The portion of a hard disk that is not within a partition. A new hard disk has no partitions and contains all free space.

full duplex The ability to receive and transmit data simultaneously. A *network switch* (page 1112) is typically a full-duplex device. Contrast with *half-duplex* (page 1100).

fully qualified domain name See *FQDN*.

function See *shell function* on page 1123.

gateway A generic term for a computer or a special device connected to more than one dissimilar type of network to pass data between them. Unlike a router, a gateway often must convert the information into a different format before passing it on. The historical usage of gateway to designate a router is deprecated.

GCOS See *GECOS*.

GECOS General Electric Comprehensive Operating System. For historical reasons, the user information field in the **/etc/passwd** file is called the GECOS field. Also *GCOS*.

gibibyte Giga binary byte. A unit of storage equal to 2^{30} bytes = 1,073,741,824 bytes = 1024 *mebibytes* (page 1109). Abbreviated as GiB. Contrast with *gigabyte*.

gigabyte A unit of storage equal to 10^9 bytes. Sometimes used in place of *gibibyte*. Abbreviated as GB. See also *large number* on page 1106.

global variable (shell) See *environment variable (shell)* on page 1097.

glyph A symbol that communicates a specific piece of information nonverbally. A *smiley* (page 1124) is a glyph.

GMT Greenwich Mean Time. See *UTC* on page 1131.

graphical display A bitmapped monitor that can display graphical images. Contrast with *ASCII terminal* (page 1084).

graphical user interface See *GUI.*

group (of users) A collection of users. Groups are used as a basis for determining file access permissions. If you are not the owner of a file and you belong to the group the file is assigned to, you are subject to the group access permissions for the file. A user can simultaneously belong to several groups.

group (of windows) A way to identify similar windows so they can be displayed and acted on similarly. Typically, windows started by a given application belong to the same group.

group ID A unique number that identifies a set of users. It is stored in the password and group databases (**/etc/passwd** and **/etc/group** files or their NIS equivalents). The group database associates group IDs with group names. Also *GID.*

GUI Graphical user interface. A GUI provides a way to interact with a computer system by choosing items from menus or manipulating pictures drawn on a display screen instead of by typing command lines. Under Linux, the X Window System provides a graphical display and mouse/keyboard input. GNOME and KDE are two popular desktop managers that run under X. Contrast with *character-based* (page 1088).

hacker A person who enjoys exploring the details of programmable systems and learning how to stretch their capabilities, as opposed to users, who prefer to learn only the minimum necessary. One who programs enthusiastically (even obsessively) or who enjoys programming rather than just theorizing about programming.[FOLDOC] Contrast with *cracker* (page 1092).

half-duplex A half-duplex device can only receive or transmit at a given moment; it cannot do both. A *hub* (page 1102) is typically a half-duplex device. Contrast with *full duplex* (page 1099).

hard link A directory entry that contains the filename and inode number for a file. The inode number identifies the location of control information for the file on the disk, which in turn identifies the location of the file's contents on the disk. Every file has at least one hard link, which locates the file in a directory. When you remove the last hard link to a file, you can no longer access the file. See *link* (page 1107) and *symbolic link* (page 1127).

hash A string that is generated from another string. See *one-way hash function* on page 1113. When used for security, a hash can prove, almost to a certainty, that a message has not been tampered with during transmission: The sender generates a hash of a message, encrypts the message and hash, and sends the encrypted message and hash to the recipient. The recipient decrypts the message and hash, generates a second hash from the message, and compares the hash that the sender generated to the new hash. When they are the same, the message has probably not been tampered with. Hashed versions of passwords can be used to authenticate users. A hash can also be used to create an index called a *hash table*. Also *hash value*.

hash table An index created from hashes of the items to be indexed. The hash function makes it highly unlikely that two items will create the same hash. To look up an item in the index, create a hash of the item and search for the hash. Because the hash is typically shorter than the item, the search is more efficient.

header When you are formatting a document, the header goes at the top, or head, of a page. In electronic mail the header identifies who sent the message, when it was sent, what the subject of the message is, and so forth.

Here document A shell script that takes its input from the file that contains the script.

hesiod The nameserver of project Athena. Hesiod is a name service library that is derived from *BIND* (page 1085) and leverages a DNS infrastructure.

heterogeneous Consisting of different parts. A heterogeneous network includes systems produced by different manufacturers and/or running different operating systems.

hexadecimal number A base 16 number. Hexadecimal (or *hex*) numbers are composed of the hexadecimal digits 0–9 and A–F. Computers use *bits* (page 1086) to represent data. A set of 4 bits represents 16 possible values, 0 through F. A hexadecimal digit provides a convenient way to represent a group of 4 bits. See Table G-1.

hidden filename A filename that starts with a period. These filenames are called hidden because the ls utility does not normally list them. Use the –a option of ls to list all files, including those with hidden filenames. The shell does not expand a leading asterisk (*) in an ambiguous file reference to match files with hidden filenames. Also *hidden file, invisible file*.

hierarchy An organization with a few things, or thing—one at the top—and with several things below each other thing. An inverted tree structure. Examples in computing include a file tree where each directory might contain files or other directories, a hierarchical network, and a class hierarchy in object-oriented programming.[FOLDOC] Refer to "The Hierarchical Filesystem" on page 84.

Table G-1 Decimal, octal, and hexadecimal numbers

Decimal	Octal	Hex	Decimal	Octal	Hex
1	1	1	17	21	11
2	2	2	18	22	12
3	3	3	19	23	13
4	4	4	20	24	14
5	5	5	21	25	15

Table G-1 Decimal, octal, and hexadecimal numbers (continued)

Decimal	Octal	Hex	Decimal	Octal	Hex
6	6	6	31	37	1F
7	7	7	32	40	20
8	10	8	33	41	21
9	11	9	64	100	40
10	12	A	96	140	60
11	13	B	100	144	64
12	14	C	128	200	80
13	15	D	254	376	FE
14	16	E	255	377	FF
15	17	F	256	400	100
16	20	10	257	401	101

history A shell mechanism that enables you to modify and reexecute recent commands.

home directory The directory that is the working directory when you first log in. The pathname of this directory is stored in the **HOME** shell variable.

hover To leave the mouse pointer stationary for a moment over an object. In many cases hovering displays a *tooltip* (page 1129).

HTML Hypertext Markup Language. A *hypertext* document format used on the World Wide Web. Tags, which are embedded in the text, consist of a less than sign (<), a directive, zero or more parameters, and a greater than sign (>). Matched pairs of directives, such as <TITLE> and </TITLE>, delimit text that is to appear in a special place or style.[FOLDOC] For more information on HTML, visit www.htmlhelp.com/faq/ html/all.html.

HTTP Hypertext Transfer Protocol. The client/server TCP/IP protocol used on the World Wide Web for the exchange of *HTML* documents.

hub A multiport repeater. A hub rebroadcasts all packets it receives on all ports. This term is frequently used to refer to small hubs and switches, regardless of the device's intelligence. It is a generic term for a layer 2 shared-media networking device. Today, the term *hub* is sometimes used to refer to small intelligent devices, although that was not its original meaning. Contrast with *network switch* (page 1112).

hypertext A collection of documents/nodes containing (usually highlighted or underlined) cross-references or links, which, with the aid of an interactive browser program, allow the reader to move easily from one document to another.[FOLDOC]

Hypertext Markup Language See *HTML*.

Hypertext Transfer Protocol See *HTTP*.

i18n Internationalization. An abbreviation of the word *internationalization* uses the letter *i* followed by 18 letters (*nternationalizatio*) followed by the letter *n*.

i/o device Input/output device. See *device* on page 1094.

IANA Internet Assigned Numbers Authority. A group that maintains a database of all permanent, registered system services (www.iana.org).

ICMP Internet Control Message Protocol. A type of network packet that carries only messages, no data. The most common ICMP packet is the echo request which is sent by the ping utility.

icon In a GUI, a small picture representing a file, directory, action, program, and so on. When you click an icon, an action, such as opening a window and starting a program or displaying a directory or Web site, takes place. From miniature religious statues.FOLDOC

iconify To change a window into an *icon*. Contrast with *restore* (page 1120).

ignored window A state in which a window has no decoration and therefore no buttons or titlebar to control it with.

indentation See *indention*.

indention The blank space between the margin and the beginning of a line that is set in from the margin.

inode A *data structure* (page 1093) that contains information about a file. An inode for a file contains the file's length, the times the file was last accessed and modified, the time the inode was last modified, owner and group IDs, access privileges, number of links, and pointers to the data blocks that contain the file itself. Each directory entry associates a filename with an inode. Although a single file might have several filenames (one for each link), it has only one inode.

input Information that is fed to a program from a terminal or other file. See *standard input* on page 1125.

installation A computer at a specific location. Some aspects of the Linux system are installation dependent. Also *site*.

interactive A program that allows ongoing dialog with the user. When you give commands in response to shell prompts, you are using the shell interactively. Also, when you give commands to utilities, such as vim and mail, you are using the utilities interactively.

interface The meeting point of two subsystems. When two programs work together, their interface includes every aspect of either program that the other deals with. The *user interface* (page 1130) of a program includes every program aspect the user comes into contact with: the syntax and semantics involved in invoking the program, the input and output of the program, and its error and informational messages. The shell and each of the utilities and built-in commands have a user interface.

International Organization for Standardization See *ISO*.

internet A large network that encompasses other, smaller networks.

Internet The largest internet in the world. The Internet (uppercase "I") is a multilevel hierarchy composed of backbone networks (ARPANET, NSFNET, MILNET, and others), midlevel networks, and stub networks. These include commercial (**.com** or **.co**), university (**.ac** or **.edu**), research (**.org** or **.net**), and military (**.mil**) networks and span many different physical networks around the world with various protocols, including the Internet Protocol (IP). Outside the United States, country code domains are popular (**.us**, **.es**, **.mx**, **.de**, and so forth), although you will see them used within the United States as well.

Internet Protocol See *IP*.

Internet service provider See *ISP*.

intranet An in-house network designed to serve a group of people such as a corporation or school. The general public on the Internet does not have access to an intranet.

invisible file See *hidden filename* on page 1101.

IP Internet Protocol. The network layer for TCP/IP. IP is a best-effort, packet-switching, *connectionless protocol* (page 1091) that provides packet routing, fragmentation, and reassembly through the data link layer. *IPv4* is slowly giving way to *IPv6*.[FOLDOC]

IP address Internet Protocol address. A four-part address associated with a particular network connection for a system using the Internet Protocol (IP). A system that is attached to multiple networks that use the IP will have a different IP address for each network interface.

IP multicast See *multicast* on page 1111.

IP spoofing A technique used to gain unauthorized access to a computer. The would-be intruder sends messages to the target machine. These messages contain an IP address indicating that the messages are coming from a trusted host. The target machine responds to the messages, giving the intruder (privileged) access to the target.

IPC Interprocess communication. A method to communicate specific information between programs.

IPv4 *IP* version 4. See *IP* and *IPv6*.

IPv6 *IP* version 6. The next generation of Internet Protocol, which provides a much larger address space (2^{128} bits versus 2^{32} bits for IPv4) that is designed to accommodate the rapidly growing number of Internet addressable devices. IPv6 also has built-in autoconfiguration, enhanced security, better multicast support, and many other features.

iSCSI Internet Small Computer System Interface. A network storage protocol that encapsulates SCSI data into TCP packets. You can use this protocol to connect a system to a storage array using an Ethernet connection.

ISDN Integrated Services Digital Network. A set of communications standards that allows a single pair of digital or standard telephone wires to carry voice, data, and video at a rate of 64 kilobits per second.

ISO International Organization for Standardization. A voluntary, nontreaty organization founded in 1946. It is responsible for creating international standards in many areas, including computers and communications. Its members are the national standards organizations of 89 countries, including the American National Standards Institute.[FOLDOC]

ISO9660 The *ISO* standard defining a filesystem for CD-ROMs.

ISP Internet service provider. Provides Internet access to its customers.

job control A facility that enables you to move commands from the foreground to the background, and vice versa. Job control enables you to stop commands temporarily.

journaling filesystem A filesystem that maintains a noncached log file, or journal, which records all transactions involving the filesystem. When a transaction is complete, it is marked as complete in the log file.

The log file results in greatly reduced time spent recovering a filesystem after a crash, making it particularly valuable in systems where high availability is an issue.

JPEG Joint Photographic Experts Group. This committee designed the JPEG standard image-compression algorithm. JPEG is intended for compressing either full-color or gray-scale digital images of natural, real-world scenes and does not work as well on nonrealistic images, such as cartoons or line drawings. Filename extensions: **.jpg**, **.jpeg**.[FOLDOC]

justify To expand a line of type in the process of formatting text. A justified line has even margins. A line is justified by increasing the space between words and sometimes between letters on the line.

Kerberos An MIT-developed security system that authenticates users and machines. It does not provide authorization to services or databases; it establishes identity at logon, which is used throughout the session. Once you are authenticated, you can open as many terminals, windows, services, or other network accesses as you like until your session expires.

kernel The part of the operating system that allocates machine resources, including memory, disk space, and *CPU* (page 1092) cycles, to all other programs that run on a computer. The kernel includes the low-level hardware interfaces (drivers) and manages *processes* (page 1117), the means by which Linux executes programs. The kernel is the part of the Linux system that Linus Torvalds originally wrote (see the beginning of Chapter 1).

kernelspace The part of memory (RAM) where the kernel resides. Code running in kernelspace has full access to hardware and all other processes in memory. See the *KernelAnalysis-HOWTO*.

key binding A *keyboard* key is said to be bound to the action that results from pressing it. Typically, keys are bound to the letters that appear on the keycaps: When you press **A**, an **A** appears on the screen. Key binding usually refers to what happens when you press a combination of keys, one of which is CONTROL, ALT, META, or SHIFT, or when you press a series of keys, the first of which is typically ESCAPE.

keyboard A hardware input device consisting of a number of mechanical buttons (keys) that the user presses to input characters to a computer. By default a keyboard is connected to standard input of a shell.[FOLDOC]

kilo- In the binary system, the prefix *kilo-* multiplies by 2^{10} (i.e., 1,024). Kilobit and kilobyte are common uses of this prefix. Abbreviated as *k*.

Korn Shell ksh. A command processor, developed by David Korn at AT&T Bell Laboratories, that is compatible with the Bourne Shell but includes many extensions. See also *shell* on page 1123.

l10n Localization. An abbreviation of the word *localization* uses the letter *l* followed by 10 letters (*ocalizatio*) followed by the letter *n*.

LAN Local area network. A network that connects computers within a localized area (such as a single site, building, or department).

large number Visit mathworld.wolfram.com/LargeNumber.html for a comprehensive list.

LDAP Lightweight Directory Access Protocol. A simple protocol for accessing online directory services. LDAP is a lightweight alternative to the X.500 Directory Access Protocol (DAP). It can be used to access information about people, system users, network devices, email directories, and systems. In some cases, it can be used as an alternative for services such as NIS. Given a name, many mail clients can use LDAP to discover the corresponding email address. See *directory service* on page 1094.

leaf In a tree structure, the end of a branch that cannot support other branches. When the Linux filesystem hierarchy is conceptualized as a tree, files that are not directories are leaves. See *node* on page 1113.

least privilege, concept of Mistakes made by a user working with **root** privileges can be much more devastating than those made by an ordinary user. Therefore, when you are working on computer system, especially when you are working as the system administrator, always perform any task using the least privilege possible. If you can perform a task logged in as an ordinary user, do so. If you must work with **root** privileges, do as much as you can as an ordinary user, log in as **root** or give an su or sudo command so you are working with **root** privileges, do as much of the task that has to be done with **root** privileges, and revert to being an ordinary user as soon as you can.

Because you are more likely to make a mistake when you are rushing, this concept becomes more important when you have less time to apply it.

library Software library. A collection of subroutines and functions stored in one or more files, usually in compiled form, for linking with other programs. Libraries are often supplied by the operating system or software development environment developer to be used in many different programs. Libraries are linked with a user's program to form an executable.[FOLDOC]

Lightweight Directory Access Protocol See *LDAP*.

link A pointer to a file. Two kinds of links exist: *hard links* (page 1100) and *symbolic links* (page 1127) also called *soft links*. A hard link associates a filename with a place on the disk where the content of the file is located. A symbolic link associates a filename with the pathname of a hard link to a file.

Linux-PAM See *PAM* on page 1115.

Linux-Pluggable Authentication Modules See *PAM* on page 1115.

list box A *widget* (page 1132) that displays a static list for a user to choose from. The list appears as multiple lines with a *scrollbar* (page 1122) if needed. The user can scroll the list and select an entry. Different from a *drop-down list* (page 1096).

loadable kernel module See *loadable module*.

loadable module A portion of the operating system that controls a special device and that can be loaded automatically into a running kernel as needed to access that device.

local area network See *LAN*.

locale The language; date, time, and currency formats; character sets; and so forth that pertain to a geopolitical place or area. For example, en_US specifies English as spoken in the United States and dollars; en_UK specifies English as spoken in the United Kingdom and pounds. See the locale man page in section 5 of the system manual for more information. Also the locale utility.

log in To gain access to a computer system by responding correctly to the **login:** and **Password:** prompts. Also *log on, login.*

log out To end your session by exiting from your login shell. Also *log off.*

logical expression A collection of strings separated by logical operators (**>**, **>=**, **=**, **!=**, **<=**, and **<**) that can be evaluated as *true* or *false*. Also *Boolean* (page 1086) *expression.*

.login file A file in a user's home directory that the TC Shell executes when you log in. You can use this file to set environment variables and to run commands that you want executed at the beginning of each session.

login name See *username* on page 1131.

login shell The shell you are using when you log in. The login shell can fork other processes that can run other shells, utilities, and programs. See page 288.

.logout file A file in a user's home directory that the TC Shell executes when you log out, assuming that the TC Shell is your login shell. You can put in the **.logout** file commands that you want run each time you log out.

MAC address Media Access Control address. The unique hardware address of a device connected to a shared network medium. Each network adapter has a globally unique MAC address that it stores in ROM. MAC addresses are 6 bytes long, enabling 256^6 (about 300 trillion) possible addresses or 65,536 addresses for each possible IPv4 address.

A MAC address performs the same role for Ethernet that an IP address performs for TCP/IP: It provides a unique way to identify a host. Also called an Ethernet address.

machine collating sequence The sequence in which the computer orders characters. The machine collating sequence affects the outcome of sorts and other procedures that put lists in alphabetical order. Many computers use ASCII codes so their machine collating sequences correspond to the ordering of the ASCII codes for characters.

macro A single instruction that a program replaces by several (usually more complex) instructions. The C compiler recognizes macros, which are defined using a #define instruction to the preprocessor.

magic number A magic number, which occurs in the first 512 bytes of a binary file, is a 1-, 2-, or 4-byte numeric value or character string that uniquely identifies the type of file (much like a DOS 3-character filename extension). See **/usr/share/magic** and the **magic** man page for more information.

main memory Random access memory (RAM), an integral part of the computer. Although disk storage is sometimes referred to as memory, it is never referred to as main memory.

major device number A number assigned to a class of devices, such as terminals, printers, or disk drives. Using the ls utility with the **–l** option to list the contents of the **/dev** directory displays the major and minor device numbers of many devices (as major, minor).

MAN Metropolitan area network. A network that connects computers and *LANs* (page 1106) at multiple sites in a small regional area, such as a city.

man-in-the-middle attack A security attack wherein the attacker interposes himself between two subjects. For example, if Max and Zach try to carry on a secure email exchange over a network, Max first sends Zach his public key. However, suppose Mr. X sits between Max and Zach on the network and intercepts Max's public key. Mr. X then sends *his* public key to Zach. Zach then sends his public key to Max, but once again Mr. X intercepts it and substitutes *his* public key and sends that to Max. Without some kind of active protection (a piece of shared information), Mr. X, the *man-in-the-middle,* can decrypt all traffic between Max and Zach, reencrypt it, and send it on to the other party. Also called MTM attack.

masquerade To appear to come from one domain or IP address when actually coming from another. Said of a packet (iptables) or message (**sendmail/exim4**). See also *NAT* on page 1111.

MD5 Message Digest 5. A *one-way hash function* (page 1113). MD5 is no longer considered secure; use *SHA2* (page 1123) in its place.

MDA Mail delivery agent. One of the three components of a mail system; the other two are the *MTA* (page 1111) and *MUA* (page 1111). An MDA accepts inbound mail from an MTA and delivers it to a local user.

mebibyte Mega binary byte. A unit of storage equal to 2^{20} bytes = 1,048,576 bytes = 1,024 kibibytes. Abbreviated as MiB. Contrast with *megabyte.*

megabyte A unit of storage equal to 10^6 bytes. Sometimes used in place of *mebibyte.* Abbreviated as MB.

memory See *RAM* on page 1118.

menu A list from which the user might select an operation to be performed. This selection is often made with a mouse or other pointing device under a GUI but might also be controlled from the keyboard. Very convenient for beginners, menus show which commands are available and facilitate experimenting with a new program, often reducing the need for user documentation. Experienced users usually prefer keyboard commands, especially for frequently used operations, because they are faster to use.[FOLDOC]

merge To combine two ordered lists so that the resulting list is still in order. The sort utility can merge files.

META key On the keyboard, a key that is labeled META or ALT. Use this key as you would the SHIFT key. While holding it down, press another key. The emacs editor makes extensive use of the META key.

metacharacter A character that has a special meaning to the shell or another program in a particular context. Metacharacters are used in the ambiguous file references recognized by the shell and in the regular expressions recognized by several utilities. You must quote a metacharacter if you want to use it without invoking its special meaning. See *regular character* (page 1119) and *special character* (page 1125).

metadata Data about data. In data processing, metadata is definitional data that provides information about, or documentation of, other data managed within an application or environment.

For example, metadata can document data about data elements or attributes (name, size, data type, and so on), records or *data structures* (page 1093) (length, fields, columns, and so on), and data itself (where it is located, how it is associated, who owns it, and so on). Metadata can include descriptive information about the context, quality and condition, or characteristics of the data.[FOLDOC]

metropolitan area network See *MAN* on page 1108.

MIME Multipurpose Internet Mail Extension. Originally used to describe how specific types of files that were attached to email were to be handled. Today, MIME types describe how a file is to be opened or worked with, based on its contents, determined by its *magic number* (page 1108), and filename extension. An example of a MIME *type* is **image/jpeg**: The MIME *group* is **image** and the MIME *subtype* is **jpeg**. Many MIME groups exist, including application, audio, image, inode, message, text, and video.

minimize See *iconify* on page 1103.

minor device number A number assigned to a specific device within a class of devices. See *major device number* on page 1108.

modem Modulator/demodulator. A peripheral device that modulates digital data into analog data for transmission over a voice-grade telephone line. Another modem demodulates the data at the other end.

module See *loadable module* on page 1107.

motherboard The main printed circuit board in a personal computer. It contains the bus, the microprocessor, and integrated circuits used for controlling any built-in peripherals such as the keyboard, display, serial and parallel ports, joystick, and mouse interfaces. Most motherboards contain sockets that accept additional boards. Also mobo.[FOLDOC]

mount To make a filesystem accessible to system users. When a filesystem is not mounted, you cannot read from or write to files it contains.

mount point A directory that you mount a local or remote filesystem on.

mouse A device you use to point to a particular location on a display screen, typically so you can choose a menu item, draw a line, or highlight some text. You control a pointer on the screen by sliding a mouse around on a flat surface; the position of the pointer moves relative to the movement of the mouse. You select items by pressing one or more buttons on the mouse.

mouse pointer In a GUI, a marker that moves in correspondence with the mouse. It is usually a small black **x** with a white border or an arrow. Differs from the *cursor* (page 1093).

mouseover The action of passing the mouse pointer over an object on the screen.

MTA Mail transfer agent. One of the three components of a mail system; the other two are the *MDA* and *MUA*. An MTA accepts mail from users and MTAs.

MTM attack See *man-in-the-middle attack* on page 1109.

MUA Mail user agent. One of the three components of a mail system; the other two are the *MDA* (page 1109) and *MTA*. An MUA is an end-user mail program such as KMail, mutt, or Outlook.

multiboot specification Specifies an interface between a boot loader and an operating system. With compliant boot loaders and operating systems, any boot loader should be able to load any operating system. The object of this specification is to ensure that different operating systems will work on a single machine. For more information, go to odin-os.sourceforge.net/guides/multiboot.html.

multicast A multicast packet has one source and multiple destinations. In multicast, source hosts register at a special address to transmit data. Destination hosts register at the same address to receive data. In contrast to *broadcast* (page 1087), which is LAN-based, multicast traffic is designed to work across routed networks on a subscription basis. Multicast reduces network traffic by transmitting a packet one time, with the router at the end of the path breaking it apart as needed for multiple recipients.

multitasking A computer system that allows a user to run more than one job at a time. A multitasking system, such as Linux, allows you to run a job in the background while running a job in the foreground.

multiuser system A computer system that can be used by more than one person at a time. Linux is a multiuser operating system. Contrast with *single-user system* (page 1123).

namespace A set of names (identifiers) in which all names are unique.[FOLDOC]

NAS Network Attached Storage. A system of fixed disks, *RAID* (page 1118) arrays, and magnetic tape drives connected directly to a *SAN* (page 1122) or other direct network connection. Contrast with a file server where the peripherals are connected to the network via a computer (the server).[FOLDOC]

NAT Network Address Translation. A scheme that enables a LAN to use one set of IP addresses internally and a different set externally. The internal set is for LAN (private) use. The external set is typically used on the Internet and is Internet unique. NAT provides some privacy by hiding internal IP addresses and allows multiple internal addresses to connect to the Internet through a single external IP address. See also *masquerade* on page 1109.

NBT NetBIOS over TCP/IP. A protocol that supports NetBIOS services in a TCP/IP environment. Also NetBT.

negative caching Storing the knowledge that something does not exist. A cache normally stores information about something that exists. A negative cache stores the information that something, such as a record, does not exist.

NetBIOS Network Basic Input/Output System. An *API* (page 1083) for writing network-aware applications.

netboot To boot a computer over the network (as opposed to booting from a local disk).

netiquette The conventions of etiquette—that is, polite behavior—recognized on Usenet and in mailing lists, such as not (cross-)posting to inappropriate groups and refraining from commercial advertising outside the business groups.

The most important rule of netiquette is "Think before you post." If what you intend to post will not make a positive contribution to the newsgroup and be of interest to several readers, do not post it. Personal messages to one or two individuals should not be posted to newsgroups; use private email instead.[FOLDOC]

network address The network portion (**netid**) of an IP address. For a class A network, it is the first byte, or segment, of the IP address; for a class B network, it is the first two bytes; and for a class C network, it is the first three bytes. In each case the balance of the IP address is the host address (**hostid**). Assigned network addresses are globally unique within the Internet. Also *network number*.

Network Filesystem See *NFS*.

Network Information Service See *NIS*.

network mask A bit mask used to identify which bits in an IP address correspond to the network address and subnet portions of the address. Called a network mask because the network portion of the address is determined by the number of bits that are set in the mask. The network mask has ones in positions corresponding to the network and subnet numbers and zeros in the host number positions. Also *subnet mask* or *mask*.

network number See *network address*.

network segment A part of an Ethernet or other network on which all message traffic is common to all nodes; that is, it is broadcast from one node on the segment and received by all others. This commonality normally occurs because the segment is a single continuous conductor. Communication between nodes on different segments is via one or more routers.[FOLDOC]

network switch A connecting device in networks. Switches are increasingly replacing shared media hubs in an effort to increase bandwidth. For example, a 16-port 10BaseT hub shares the total 10 megabits-per-second bandwidth among all 16 attached nodes. By replacing the hub with a switch, both the sender and receiver can take advantage of the full

10 megabits-per-second capacity. Each port on the switch can give full bandwidth to a single server or client station or to a hub with several stations. Network switch refers to a device with intelligence. Contrast with *hub* (page 1102).

Network Time Protocol See *NTP* on page 1113.

NFS Network Filesystem. A remote filesystem designed by Sun Microsystems, available on computers from most UNIX system vendors.

NIC Network interface card (or controller). An adapter circuit board installed in a computer to provide a physical connection to a network. Each NIC has a unique *MAC address* (page 1108).FOLDOC

NIS Network Information Service. A distributed service built on a shared database to manage system-independent information (such as usernames and passwords).

NIS domain name A name that describes a group of systems that share a set of NIS files. Different from *domain name* (page 1095).

NNTP Network News Transfer Protocol.

node In a tree structure, the end of a branch that can support other branches. When the Linux filesystem hierarchy is conceptualized as a tree, directories are nodes. See *leaf* on page 1106.

nonprinting character See *control character* on page 1091. Also *nonprintable character*.

nonvolatile storage A storage device whose content is preserved when its power is off. Also NVS and persistent storage. Some examples are CD-ROM, paper punch tape, hard disk, *ROM* (page 1121), *PROM* (page 1117), *EPROM* (page 1097), and *EEPROM* (page 1096). Contrast with *RAM* (page 1118).

NTP Network Time Protocol. Built on top of TCP/IP, NTP maintains accurate local time by referring to known accurate clocks on the Internet.

null string A string that could contain characters but does not. A string of zero length.

octal number A base 8 number. Octal numbers are composed of the digits 0–7, inclusive. Refer to Table G-1 on page 1101.

one-way hash function A one-way function that takes a variable-length message and produces a fixed-length hash. Given the hash, it is computationally infeasible to find a message with that hash; in fact, you cannot determine any usable information about a message with that hash. Also *message digest function*. See also *hash* (page 1100).

open source A method and philosophy for software licensing and distribution designed to encourage use and improvement of software written by volunteers by ensuring that anyone can copy the source code and modify it freely.

The term *open source* is now more widely used than the earlier term *free software* (promoted by the Free Software Foundation; www.fsf.org) but has broadly the same meaning—free of distribution restrictions, not necessarily free of charge.

OpenSSH A free version of the SSH (secure shell) protocol suite that replaces TELNET, rlogin, and more with secure programs that encrypt all communication—even passwords—over a network. Refer to "The OpenSSH Secure Communication Utilities" on page 703.

operating system A control program for a computer that allocates computer resources, schedules tasks, and provides the user with a way to access resources.

optical drive A disk drive that uses light to read data from and write data to optical media. CD-ROMs and DVDs are types of optical media. See also *ISO9660* (page 1105).

option A command-line argument that modifies the effects of a command. Options are usually preceded by hyphens on the command line and traditionally have single-character names (such as **–h** or **–n**). Some commands allow you to group options following a single hyphen (for example, **–hn**). GNU utilities frequently have two arguments that do the same thing: a single-character argument and a longer, more descriptive argument; the longer version is then preceded by two hyphens (such as **––show-all** and **––invert-match**).

ordinary file A file that is used to store a program, text, or other user data. See *directory* (page 1094) and *device file* (page 1094).

output Information that a program sends to the terminal or another file. See *standard output* on page 1125.

P2P Peer-to-Peer. A network that does not divide nodes into clients and servers. Each computer on a P2P network can fulfill the roles of client and server. In the context of a file-sharing network, this ability means that once a node has downloaded (part of) a file, it can act as a server. BitTorrent implements a P2P network.

packet A unit of data sent across a network. *Packet* is a generic term used to describe a unit of data at any layer of the OSI protocol stack, but it is most correctly used to describe network or application layer data units ("application protocol data unit," APDU).[FOLDOC] See also *frame* (page 1099) and *datagram* (page 1093).

packet filtering A technique used to block network traffic based on specified criteria, such as the origin, destination, or type of each packet. See also *firewall* (page 1098).

packet sniffer A program or device that monitors packets on a network. See *sniff* on page 1124.

pager A utility that allows you to view a file one screen at a time (for example, less and more).

paging The process by which virtual memory is maintained by the operating system. The content of process memory is moved (paged out) to the *swap space* (page 1127) as needed to make room for other processes.

PAM Linux-PAM or Linux-Pluggable Authentication Modules. These modules allow a system administrator to determine how various applications authenticate users.

parent process A process that forks other processes. See *process* (page 1117) and *child process* (page 1089).

partition A section of a (hard) disk that has a name so you can address it separately from other sections. A disk partition can hold a filesystem or another structure, such as the swap area. Under DOS and Windows, partitions (and sometimes whole disks) are labeled **C:**, **D:**, and so on. Also *disk partition* and *slice.*

passive FTP Allows FTP to work through a firewall by allowing the flow of data to be initiated and controlled by the client FTP program instead of the server. Also called PASV FTP because it uses the FTP PASV command.

passphrase A string of words and characters that you type in to authenticate yourself. A passphrase differs from a *password* only in length. A password is usually short—around 6 to 10 characters. A passphrase is usually much longer—up to 100 characters or more. The greater length makes a passphrase harder to guess or reproduce than a password and therefore more secure.[FOLDOC]

password To prevent unauthorized access to a user's account, an arbitrary string of characters chosen by the user or system administrator and used to authenticate the user when attempting to log in.[FOLDOC] See also *passphrase.*

PASV FTP See *passive FTP.*

pathname A list of directories separated by slashes (/) and ending with the name of a file, which can be a directory. A pathname is used to trace a path through the file structure to locate or identify a file.

pathname, last element of a The part of a pathname following the final slash (/), or the whole filename if there is no /. A simple filename. Same as *basename* (page 1085).

pathname element One of the filenames that forms a pathname.

peripheral device See *device* on page 1094.

persistent Data that is stored on nonvolatile media, such as a hard disk.

phish An attempt to trick users into revealing or sharing private information, especially passwords or financial information. The most common form is email purporting to be from a bank or vendor that requests that a user fill out a form to "update" an account on a phony Web site disguised to appear legitimate. Generally sent as *spam* (page 1124).

physical device A tangible device, such as a disk drive, that is physically separate from other, similar devices.

PID Process identification, usually followed by the word *number*. Linux assigns a unique PID number as each process is initiated.

pipeline One or more simple commands. If a pipeline comprises two or more commands, the commands are connected such that standard output of one command is connected by a pipe symbol (|; a control operator) to standard input of the next.

pixel The smallest element of a picture—typically a single dot on a display screen.

PKI Public Key Infrastructure. A system of public key encryption that manages digital certificates that can authenticate each party in an electronic transaction.

plaintext Text that is not encrypted. Also *cleartext*. Contrast with *ciphertext* (page 1090).

Pluggable Authentication Modules See *PAM* on page 1115.

point-to-point link A connection limited to two endpoints, such as the connection between a pair of modems.

port A logical channel or channel endpoint in a communications system. The *TCP* (page 1128) and *UDP* (page 1130) transport layer protocols used on Ethernet use port numbers to distinguish between different logical channels on the same network interface on the same computer.

The **/etc/services** file (see the beginning of this file for more information) or the *NIS* (page 1113) **services** database specifies a unique port number for each application program. The number links incoming data to the correct service (program). Standard, well-known ports are used by everyone: Port 80 is used for HTTP (Web) traffic. Some protocols, such as TELNET and HTTP (which is a special form of TELNET), have default ports specified as mentioned earlier but can use other ports as well.[FOLDOC]

port forwarding The process by which a network *port* on one computer is transparently connected to a port on another computer. If port X is forwarded from system A to system B, any data sent to port X on system A is sent to system B automatically. The connection can be between different ports on the two systems. See also *tunneling* (page 1130).

portmapper A server that converts TCP/IP port numbers into *RPC* (page 1121) program numbers.

power supply An electronic module that converts high-voltage (110 or 240 VAC) alternating current mains electricity into smoothed direct current at the various different voltages required by the motherboard, internal peripheral devices, and external connections such as USB.[FOLDOC]

printable character One of the graphic characters: a letter, number, or punctuation mark. Contrast with a nonprintable, or CONTROL, character. Also *printing character*.

private address space *IANA* (page 1103) has reserved three blocks of IP addresses for private internets or LANs:

```
10.0.0.0 - 10.255.255.255
172.16.0.0 - 172.31.255.255
192.168.0.0 - 192.168.255.255
```

You can use these addresses without coordinating with anyone outside of your LAN (you do not have to register the system name or address). Systems using these IP addresses cannot communicate directly with hosts using the global address space but must go through a gateway. Because private addresses have no global meaning, routing information is not stored by DNSs and most ISPs reject privately addressed packets. Make sure that your router is set up not to forward these packets onto the Internet.

privileged port A *port* (page 1116) with a number less than 1,024. On Linux and other UNIX-like systems, only a process running with **root** privileges can bind to a privileged port. Any user on Windows 98 and earlier Windows systems can bind to any port. Also *reserved port.*

procedure A sequence of instructions for performing a particular task. Most programming languages, including machine languages, enable a programmer to define procedures that allow the procedure code to be called from multiple places. Also *subroutine.*FOLDOC

process The execution of a command by Linux. See "Processes" on page 333.

.profile file A startup file in a user's home directory that the Bourne Again or Z Shell executes when you log in. The TC Shell executes **.login** instead. You can use the **.profile** file to run commands, set variables, and define functions.

program A sequence of executable computer instructions contained in a file. Linux utilities, applications, and shell scripts are all programs. Whenever you run a command that is not built into a shell, you are executing a program.

PROM Programmable readonly memory. A kind of nonvolatile storage. *ROM* (page 1121) that can be written to using a PROM programmer.

prompt A cue from a program, usually displayed on the screen, indicating that it is waiting for input. The shell displays a prompt, as do some of the interactive utilities, such as mail. By default the Bourne Again and Z Shells use a dollar sign (**$**) as a prompt, and the TC Shell uses a percent sign (**%**).

protocol A set of formal rules describing how to transmit data, especially across a network. Low-level protocols define the electrical and physical standards, bit and byte ordering, and transmission, error detection, and correction of the bit stream. High-level protocols deal with data formatting, including message syntax, terminal-to-computer dialog, character sets, and sequencing of messages.FOLDOC

proxy A service that is authorized to act for a system while not being part of that system. See also *proxy gateway* and *proxy server*.

proxy gateway A computer that separates clients (such as browsers) from the Internet, working as a trusted agent that accesses the Internet on their behalf. A proxy gateway passes a request for data from an Internet service, such as HTTP from a browser/client, to a remote server. The data that the server returns goes back through the proxy gateway to the requesting service. A proxy gateway should be transparent to the user.

A proxy gateway often runs on a *firewall* (page 1098) system and acts as a barrier to malicious users. It hides the IP addresses of the local computers inside the firewall from Internet users outside the firewall.

You can configure browsers, such as Mozilla/Firefox and Netscape, to use a different proxy gateway or to use no proxy for each URL access method including FTP, netnews, SNMP, HTTPS, and HTTP. See also *proxy*.

proxy server A *proxy gateway* that usually includes a *cache* (page 1088) that holds frequently used Web pages so that the next request for that page is available locally (and therefore more quickly). The terms *proxy server* and *proxy gateway* are frequently interchanged so that the use of cache does not rest exclusively with the proxy server. See also *proxy*.

Python A simple, high-level, interpreted, object-oriented, interactive language that bridges the gap between C and shell programming. Suitable for rapid prototyping or as an extension language for C applications, Python supports packages, modules, classes, user-defined exceptions, a good C interface, and dynamic loading of C modules. It has no arbitrary restrictions. See Chapter 12.[FOLDOC]

quote When you quote a character, you take away any special meaning that it has in the current context. You can quote a character by preceding it with a backslash. When you are interacting with the shell, you can also quote a character by surrounding it with single quotation marks. For example, the command **echo *** or **echo '*'** displays *. The command **echo *** displays a list of the files in the working directory. See *ambiguous file reference* (page 1082), *metacharacter* (page 1109), *regular character* (page 1119), *regular expression* (page 1120), and *special character* (page 1125). See also *escape* on page 1097.

radio button In a GUI, one of a group of buttons similar to those used to select the station on a car radio. Radio buttons within a group are mutually exclusive; only one button can be selected at a time.

RAID Redundant array of inexpensive/independent disks. Two or more (hard) disk drives used in combination to improve fault tolerance and performance. RAID can be implemented in hardware or software.

RAM Random access memory. A kind of volatile storage. A data storage device for which the order of access to different locations does not affect the speed of access. Contrast with a hard disk or tape drive, which provides quicker access to sequential data because accessing a nonsequential location requires physical movement of the storage medium and/or read/write head rather than just electronic switching. Contrast with *nonvolatile storage* (page 1113). Also *memory*.FOLDOC

RAM disk *RAM* that is made to look like a floppy diskette or hard disk. A RAM disk is frequently used as part of the *boot* (page 1086) process.

RAS Remote access server. In a network, a computer that provides access to remote users via analog modem or ISDN connections. RAS includes the dial-up protocols and access control (authentication). It might be a regular fileserver with remote access software or a proprietary system, such as Shiva's LANRover. The modems might be internal or external to the device.

RDF Resource Description Framework. Being developed by W3C (the main standards body for the World Wide Web), a standard that specifies a mechanism for encoding and transferring *metadata* (page 1110). RDF does not specify what the metadata should or can be. It can integrate many kinds of applications and data, using XML as an interchange syntax. Examples of the data that can be integrated include library catalogs and worldwide directories; syndication and aggregation of news, software, and content; and collections of music and photographs. Visit www.w3.org/RDF for more information.

real UID The UID (user ID) that a user logs in with as defined in **/etc/passwd**. Differentiated from *effective UID* (page 1096). See also *UID* on page 1130.

redirection The process of directing standard input for a program to come from a file rather than from the keyboard. Also, directing standard output or standard error to go to a file rather than to the screen.

reentrant Code that can have multiple simultaneous, interleaved, or nested invocations that do not interfere with one another. Noninterference is important for parallel processing, recursive programming, and interrupt handling.

It is usually easy to arrange for multiple invocations (that is, calls to a subroutine) to share one copy of the code and any readonly data. For the code to be reentrant, however, each invocation must use its own copy of any modifiable data (or synchronized access to shared data). This goal is most often achieved by using a stack and allocating local variables in a new stack frame for each invocation. Alternatively, the caller might pass in a pointer to a block of memory that that invocation can use (usually for output), or the code might allocate some memory on a heap, especially if the data must survive after the routine returns.

Reentrant code is often found in system software, such as operating systems and teleprocessing monitors. It is also a crucial component of multithreaded programs, where the term *thread-safe* is often used instead of reentrant.FOLDOC

regular character A character that always represents itself in an ambiguous file reference or another type of regular expression. Contrast with *special character*.

regular expression A string—composed of letters, numbers, and special symbols—that defines one or more strings. See Appendix A.

relative pathname A pathname that starts from the working directory. Contrast with *absolute pathname* (page 1082).

remote access server See *RAS* on page 1119.

remote filesystem A filesystem on a remote computer that has been set up so that you can access (usually over a network) its files as though they were stored on your local computer's disks. An example of a remote filesystem is NFS.

remote procedure call See *RPC* on page 1121.

resolver The TCP/IP library software that formats requests to be sent to the *DNS* (page 1095) for hostname-to-Internet address conversion.[FOLDOC]

Resource Description Framework See *RDF* on page 1119.

restore The process of turning an icon into a window. Contrast with *iconify* (page 1103).

return code See *exit status* on page 1097.

RFC Request for comments. Begun in 1969, one of a series of numbered Internet informational documents and standards widely followed by commercial software and freeware in the Internet and UNIX/Linux communities. Few RFCs are standards, but all Internet standards are recorded in RFCs. Perhaps the single most influential RFC has been RFC 822, the Internet electronic mail format standard.

The RFCs are unusual in that they are floated by technical experts acting on their own initiative and reviewed by the Internet at large rather than being formally promulgated through an institution such as ANSI. For this reason they remain known as RFCs, even after they are adopted as standards. The RFC tradition of pragmatic, experience-driven, after-the-fact standard writing done by individuals or small working groups has important advantages over the more formal, committee-driven process typical of ANSI or ISO. For a complete list of RFCs, go to www.rfc-editor.org.[FOLDOC]

RPM The default software packaging format for Fedora and other RPM-based distributions.

roam To move a computer between *wireless access points* (page 1133) on a wireless network without the user or applications being aware of the transition. Moving between access points typically results in some packet loss, although this loss is transparent to programs that use TCP.

ROM Readonly memory. A kind of nonvolatile storage. A data storage device that is manufactured with fixed contents. In general, ROM describes any storage system whose contents cannot be altered, such as a phonograph record or printed book. When used in reference to electronics and computers, ROM describes semiconductor integrated circuit memories, of which several types exist, and CD-ROM.

ROM is nonvolatile storage; it retains its contents even after power has been removed. ROM is often used to hold programs for embedded systems, as these usually have a fixed purpose. ROM is also used for storage of the *BIOS* (page 1085) in a computer. Contrast with *RAM* (page 1118).FOLDOC

root directory The ancestor of all directories and the start of all absolute pathnames. The root directory has no name and is represented by **/** standing alone or at the left end of a pathname.

root filesystem The filesystem that is available when the system is brought up in single-user/recovery mode. This filesystem is always represented by **/**. You cannot unmount or mount the root filesystem. You can remount root to change its mount options.

root login Usually, the username of *Superuser* (page 1127).

root (user) Another name for *Superuser* (page 1127).

root window Any place on the desktop not covered by a window, object, or panel.

rootkit Software that provides a user with **root** privileges while hiding its presence.

rotate When a file, such as a log file, gets indefinitely larger, you must keep it from taking up too much space on the disk. Because you might need to refer to the information in the log files in the near future, it is generally not a good idea to delete the contents of the file until it has aged. Instead, you can periodically save the current log file under a new name and create a new, empty file as the current log file. You can keep a series of these files, renaming each as a new one is saved. You will then *rotate* the files. For example, you might remove **xyzlog.4**, **xyzlog.3**⇨**xyzlog.4**, **xyzlog.2**⇨**xyzlog.3**, **xyzlog.1**⇨ **xyzlog.2**, and **xyzlog**⇨**xyzlog.1**, and create a new **xyzlog** file. By the time you remove **xyzlog.4**, it will not contain any information more recent than you want to remove.

round-robin A scheduling algorithm in which processes are activated in a fixed cyclic order.FOLDOC

router A device (often a computer) that is connected to more than one similar type of network to pass data between them. See *gateway* on page 1099.

RPC Remote procedure call. A call to a *procedure* (page 1117) that acts transparently across a network. The procedure itself is responsible for accessing and using the network. The RPC libraries make sure that network access is transparent to the application. RPC runs on top of TCP/IP or UDP/IP.

RSA A public key encryption technology that is based on the lack of an efficient way to factor very large numbers. Because of this lack, it takes an extraordinary amount of computer processing time and power to deduce an RSA key. The RSA algorithm is the de facto standard for data sent over the Internet.

run To execute a program.

runlevel Before the introduction of the systemd/Upstart **init** daemon, runlevels specified the state of the system, including single-user/recovery and multiuser.

Samba A free suite of programs that implement the Server Message Block (SMB) protocol. See *SMB* (page 1123).

SAN Storage Area Network. A high-speed subnetwork of shared storage devices wherein all storage devices are available to all servers on a LAN or WAN. This setup offloads disk I/O overhead from the servers, allowing them to give more resources to the applications they are running. It also allows disk space to be added without altering individual machines.

SASL Simple Authentication and Security Layer. SASL is a framework for authentication and data security in Internet protocols.

schema Within a GUI, a pattern that helps you see and interpret the information that is presented in a window, making it easier to understand new information that is presented using the same schema.

scroll To move lines on a terminal or window up and down or left and right.

scrollbar A *widget* (page 1132) found in graphical user interfaces that controls (scrolls) which part of a document is visible in the window. A window can have a horizontal scrollbar, a vertical scrollbar (more common), or both.[FOLDOC]

server A powerful centralized computer (or program) designed to provide information to clients (smaller computers or programs) on request.

session The lifetime of a user login process. For a desktop, this refers to the lifetime of the desktop session manager. For a character-based terminal, it is the lifetime of user's login shell process. In KDE, it is launched by kdeinit. A session might also be the sequence of events between when you start using a program, such as an editor, and when you finish.

setgid When you execute a file that has setgid (set group ID) permission, the process executing the file takes on the privileges of the group the file belongs to. The ls utility shows setgid permission as an **s** in the group's executable position. See also *setuid*.

setuid When you execute a file that has setuid (set user ID) permission, the process executing the file takes on the privileges of the owner of the file. As an example, if you run a setuid program that removes all the files in a directory, you can remove files in any of the file owner's directories, even if you do not normally have permission to do so. When the program is owned by **root**, you can remove files in any directory that a user working with **root** privileges can remove files from. The ls utility shows setuid permission as an s in the owner's executable position. See also *setgid.*

sexillion In the British system, 10^{36}. In the American system, this number is named *undecillion.* See also *large number* (page 1106).

SHA1 Secure Hash Algorithm 1. The SHA family is a set of cryptographic *hash* (page 1100) algorithms that were designed by the National Security Agency (NSA). The second member of this family is SHA1, a successor to *MD5* (page 1109). See also *cryptography* on page 1092.

SHA2 Secure Hash Algorithm 2. The third member of the SHA family (see *SHA1*), SHA2 is a set of four cryptographic hash functions named SHA-224, SHA-256, SHA-384, and SHA-512, with digests that are 224, 256, 384, and 512 bits, respectively.

share A filesystem hierarchy that is shared with another system using *SMB* (page 1123). Also *Windows share* (page 1132).

shared network topology A network, such as Ethernet, in which each packet might be seen by systems other than its destination system. *Shared* means that the network bandwidth is shared by all users.

shell A Linux system command processor. The three major shells are the *Bourne Again Shell* (page 1086), the *TC Shell* (page 1127), and the *Z Shell* (page 1134).

shell function A series of commands that the shell stores for execution at a later time. Shell functions are like shell scripts but run more quickly because they are stored in the computer's main memory rather than in files. Also, a shell function is run in the shell that calls it (unlike a shell script, which is typically run in a subshell).

shell script An ASCII file containing shell commands. Also shell program.

signal A very brief message that the UNIX system can send to a process, apart from the process's standard input. Refer to "trap: Catches a Signal" on page 496.

simple filename A single filename containing no slashes (/). A simple filename is the simplest form of pathname. Also the last element of a pathname. Also *basename* (page 1085).

single-user system A computer system that only one person can use at a time. Contrast with *multiuser system* (page 1111).

slider A *widget* (page 1132) that allows a user to set a value by dragging an indicator along a line. Many sliders allow the user also to click on the line to move the indicator. Differs from a *scrollbar* (page 1122) in that moving the indicator does not change other parts of the display.

SMB Server Message Block. Developed in the early 1980s by Intel, Microsoft, and IBM, SMB is a client/server protocol that is the native method of file and printer sharing for Windows. In addition, SMB can share serial ports and communications abstractions, such as named pipes and mail slots. SMB is similar to a remote procedure call

(*RPC,* page 1121) that has been customized for filesystem access. Also *Microsoft Networking* or *CIFS* (page 1089).FOLDOC

SMP Symmetric multiprocessing. Two or more similar processors connected via a high-bandwidth link and managed by one operating system, where each processor has equal access to I/O devices. The processors are treated more or less equally, with application programs able to run on any or all processors interchangeably, at the discretion of the operating system.FOLDOC

smiley A character-based *glyph* (page 1099), typically used in email, that conveys an emotion. The characters :-) in a message portray a smiley face (look at it sideways). Because it can be difficult to tell when the writer of an electronic message is saying something in jest or in seriousness, email users often use :-) to indicate humor. The two original smileys, designed by Scott Fahlman, were :-) and :-(. Also *emoticon, smileys,* and *smilies.* For more information search on **smiley** on the Internet.

smilies See *smiley.*

SMTP Simple Mail Transfer Protocol. A protocol used to transfer electronic mail between computers. It is a server-to-server protocol, so other protocols are used to access the messages. The SMTP dialogue usually happens in the background under the control of a message transport system such as **sendmail/exim4**.FOLDOC

snap (windows) As you drag a window toward another window or edge of the workspace, it can move suddenly so that it is adjacent to the other window/edge. Thus, the window *snaps* into position.

sneakernet Using hand-carried magnetic media to transfer files between machines.

sniff To monitor packets on a network. A system administrator can legitimately sniff packets, and a malicious user can sniff packets to obtain information such as usernames and passwords. See also *packet sniffer* (page 1114).

SOCKS A networking proxy protocol embodied in a SOCKS server, which performs the same functions as a *proxy gateway* (page 1118) or *proxy server* (page 1118). SOCKS works at the application level, requiring that an application be modified to work with the SOCKS protocol, whereas a *proxy* (page 1118) makes no demands on the application.

SOCKSv4 does not support authentication or UDP proxy. SOCKSv5 supports a variety of authentication methods and UDP proxy.

sort To put in a specified order, usually alphabetic or numeric.

SPACE **character** A character that appears as the absence of a visible character. Even though you cannot see it, a SPACE is a printable character. It is represented by the ASCII code 32 (decimal). A SPACE character is considered a *blank* or *whitespace* (page 1132).

spam Posting irrelevant or inappropriate messages to one or more Usenet newsgroups or mailing lists in deliberate or accidental violation of *netiquette* (page 1112). Also sending large amounts of unsolicited email indiscriminately. This email usually promotes a product or service. Another common purpose of spam is to *phish* (page 1115). Spam is the electronic equivalent of junk mail. From the Monty Python "Spam" song.[FOLDOC]

sparse file A file that is large but takes up little disk space. The data in a sparse file is not dense (thus its name). Examples of sparse files are core files and dbm files.

spawn See *fork* on page 1099.

special character A character that has a special meaning when it occurs in an ambiguous file reference or another type of regular expression, unless it is quoted. The special characters most commonly used with the shell are * and ?. Also *metacharacter* (page 1109) and *wildcard*.

special file See *device file* on page 1094.

spin box In a GUI, a type of *text box* (page 1128) that holds a number you can change by typing over it or using the up and down arrows at the end of the box. Also *spinner*.

spinner See *spin box*.

spoofing See *IP spoofing* on page 1104.

spool To place items in a queue, each waiting its turn for some action. Often used when speaking about printers. Also used to describe the queue.

SQL Structured Query Language. A language that provides a user interface to relational database management systems (RDBMS). SQL, the de facto standard, is also an ISO and ANSI standard and is often embedded in other programming languages.[FOLDOC]

square bracket A left square bracket ([) or a right square bracket (]). These special characters define character classes in ambiguous file references and other regular expressions.

stable release A fully tested, reliable software release that is typically available to the general public. Contrast with *beta release* (page 1085).

standard error A file to which a program can send output. Usually, only error messages are sent to this file. Unless you instruct the shell otherwise, it directs this output to the screen (that is, to the device file that represents the screen).

standard input A file from which a program can receive input. Unless you instruct the shell otherwise, it directs this input so that it comes from the keyboard (that is, from the device file that represents the keyboard).

standard output A file to which a program can send output. Unless you instruct the shell otherwise, it directs this output to the screen (that is, to the device file that represents the screen).

startup file A file that the login shell runs when you log in. The Bourne Again and Z Shells run **.profile**, and the TC Shell runs **.login**. The TC Shell also runs **.cshrc** whenever a new

TC Shell or a subshell is invoked. The Z Shell runs an analogous file whose name is identified by the **ENV** variable.

status line The bottom (usually the twenty-fourth) line of the terminal. The vim editor uses the status line to display information about what is happening during an editing session.

sticky bit Originally, an access permission bit that caused an executable program to remain on the swap area of the disk. Today, Linux and macOS kernels do not use the sticky bit for this purpose but rather use it to control who can remove files from a directory. In this new capacity, the sticky bit is called the *restricted deletion flag.* If this bit is set on a directory, a file in the directory can be removed or renamed only by a user who is working with **root** privileges or by a user who has write permission for the directory *and* who owns the file or the directory.

streaming tape A tape that moves at a constant speed past the read/write heads rather than speeding up and slowing down, which can slow the process of writing to or reading from the tape. A proper blocking factor helps ensure that the tape device will be kept streaming.

streams See *connection-oriented protocol* on page 1091.

string A sequence of characters.

stylesheet See *CSS* on page 1092.

subdirectory A directory that is located within another directory. Every directory except the root directory is a subdirectory.

subnet Subnetwork. A portion of a network, which might be a physically independent network segment, that shares a network address with other portions of the network and is distinguished by a subnet number. A subnet is to a network as a network is to an internet.[FOLDOC]

subnet address The subnet portion of an IP address. In a subnetted network, the host portion of an IP address is split into a subnet portion and a host portion using a network mask (also subnet mask). See also *subnet number.*

subnet mask See *network mask* on page 1112.

subnet number The subnet portion of an IP address. In a subnetted network, the host portion of an IP address is split into a subnet portion and a host portion using a *network mask.* Also *subnet mask.* See also *subnet address.*

subpixel hinting Similar to *anti-aliasing* (page 1083) but takes advantage of colors to do the anti-aliasing. Particularly useful on LCD screens.

subroutine See *procedure* on page 1117.

subshell A shell that is forked as a duplicate of its parent shell. When you run an executable file that contains a shell script by using its filename on the command line, the shell forks a subshell to run the script. Also, commands surrounded with parentheses are run in a subshell.

superblock A block that contains control information for a filesystem. The superblock contains housekeeping information, such as the number of inodes in the filesystem and free list information.

superserver The extended Internet services daemon (**xinetd**; deprecated).

Superuser A user working with **root** privileges. This user has access to anything any other system user has access to and more. The system administrator must be able to become Superuser (work with **root** privileges) to establish new accounts, change passwords, and perform other administrative tasks. The username of Superuser is usually **root**. Also *root* or *root user*.

swap The operating system moving a process from main memory to a disk, or vice versa. Swapping a process to the disk allows another process to begin or continue execution.

swap space An area of a disk (that is, a swap file) used to store the portion of a process's memory that has been paged out. Under a virtual memory system, the amount of swap space—rather than the amount of physical memory—determines the maximum size of a single process and the maximum total size of all active processes. Also *swap area* or *swapping area*.FOLDOC

switch 1. A GUI *widget* (page 1132) that allows a user to select one of two options, typically On and Off.

2. See *network switch* on page 1112.

symbolic link A directory entry that points to the pathname of another file. In most cases a symbolic link to a file can be used in the same ways a hard link can be used. Unlike a hard link, a symbolic link can span filesystems and can connect to a directory.

system administrator The person responsible for the upkeep of the system. The system administrator has the ability to log in as **root** or use sudo to work with **root** privileges. See also *Superuser*.

system console See *console* on page 1091.

system mode The designation for the state of the system while it is doing system work. Some examples are making system calls, running NFS and autofs, processing network traffic, and performing kernel operations on behalf of the system. Contrast with *user mode* (page 1131).

System V One of the two major versions of the UNIX system.

TC Shell tcsh. An enhanced but completely compatible version of the BSD UNIX C shell, csh.

TCP Transmission Control Protocol. The most common transport layer protocol used on the Internet. This connection-oriented protocol is built on top of *IP* (page 1104) and is nearly always seen in the combination TCP/IP (TCP over *IP*). TCP adds reliable communication, sequencing, and flow control and provides full-duplex, process-to-process connections. *UDP* (page 1130), although connectionless, is the other protocol that runs on top of *IP*.FOLDOC

tera- In the binary system, the prefix *tera-* multiplies by 2^{40} (1,099,511,627,776). Terabyte is a common use of this prefix. Abbreviated as *T*. See also *large number* on page 1106.

termcap Terminal capability. On older systems, the **/etc/termcap** file contained a list of various types of terminals and their characteristics. *System V* replaced the function of this file with the *terminfo* system.

terminal Differentiated from a *workstation* (page 1133) by its lack of intelligence, a terminal connects to a computer that runs Linux. A workstation runs Linux on itself.

terminfo Terminal information. The **/usr/lib/terminfo** directory contains many subdirectories, each containing several files. Each of those files is named for and holds a summary of the functional characteristics of a particular terminal. Visually oriented textual programs, such as vim, use these files. An alternative to the **termcap** file.

text box A GUI *widget* (page 1132) that allows a user to enter text.

theme Defined as an implicit or recurrent idea, *theme* is used in a GUI to describe a look that is consistent for all elements of a desktop.

thicknet A type of coaxial cable (thick) used for an Ethernet network. Devices are attached to thicknet by tapping the cable at fixed points.

thinnet A type of coaxial cable (thin) used for an Ethernet network. Thinnet cable is smaller in diameter and more flexible than *thicknet* cable. Each device is typically attached to two separate cable segments by using a T-shaped connector; one segment leads to the device ahead of it on the network and one to the device that follows it.

thread-safe See *reentrant* on page 1119.

thumb The movable button in the *scrollbar* (page 1122) that positions the image in the window. The size of the thumb reflects the amount of information in the buffer. Also *bubble*.

tick A mark, usually in a *check box* (page 1089), that indicates a positive response. The mark can be a check mark (✔) or an **x**. Also *check mark* or *check*.

TIFF Tagged Image File Format. A file format used for still-image bitmaps, stored in tagged fields. Application programs can use the tags to accept or ignore fields, depending on their capabilities.FOLDOC

tiled windows An arrangement of windows such that no window overlaps another. The opposite of *cascading windows* (page 1088).

time to live See *TTL*.

toggle To switch between one of two positions. For example, the ftp **glob** command toggles the **glob** feature: Give the command once, and it turns the feature on or off; give the command again, and it sets the feature back to its original state.

token A basic, grammatically indivisible unit of a language, such as a keyword, operator, or identifier.[FOLDOC]

token ring A type of *LAN* (page 1106) in which computers are attached to a ring of cable. A token packet circulates continuously around the ring. A computer can transmit information only when it holds the token.

tooltip A minicontext help system that a user activates by allowing the mouse pointer to *hover* (page 1102) over an object (such as those on a panel).

transient window A dialog or other window that is displayed for only a short time.

Transmission Control Protocol See *TCP* on page 1128.

Trojan horse A program that does something destructive or disruptive to your system. Its action is not documented, and the system administrator would not approve of it if she were aware of it.

The term *Trojan horse* was coined by MIT-hacker-turned-NSA-spook Dan Edwards. It refers to a malicious security-breaking program that is disguised as something benign, such as a directory lister, archive utility, game, or (in one notorious 1990 case on the Mac) a program to find and destroy viruses. Similar to *back door* (page 1084).[FOLDOC]

TTL Time to live.

1. All DNS records specify how long they are good for—usually, up to a week at most. This time is called the record's *time to live*. When a DNS server or an application stores this record in *cache* (page 1088), it decrements the TTL value and removes the record from cache when the value reaches zero. A DNS server passes a cached record to another server with the current (decremented) TTL guaranteeing the proper TTL, no matter how many servers the record passes through.
2. In the IP header, a field that indicates how many more hops the packet should be allowed to make before being discarded or returned.

TTY Teletypewriter. The terminal device that UNIX was first run from. Today, TTY refers to the screen (or window, in the case of a terminal emulator), keyboard, and mouse that are connected to a computer. This term appears in UNIX, and Linux has kept the term for the sake of consistency and tradition.

tunneling Encapsulation of protocol A within packets carried by protocol B such that A treats B as though it were a data link layer. Tunneling is used to transfer data between administrative domains that use a protocol not supported by the internet connecting those domains. It can also be used to encrypt data sent over a public internet, as when you use ssh to tunnel a protocol over the Internet.[FOLDOC] See also *VPN* (page 1132) and *port forwarding* (page 1116).

UDP User Datagram Protocol. The Internet standard transport layer protocol that provides simple but unreliable datagram services. UDP is a *connectionless protocol* (page 1091) that, like *TCP* (page 1128), is layered on top of *IP* (page 1104).

Unlike *TCP*, UDP neither guarantees delivery nor requires a connection. As a result it is lightweight and efficient, but the application program must handle all error processing and retransmission. UDP is often used for sending time-sensitive data that is not particularly sensitive to minor loss, such as audio and video data.[FOLDOC]

UID User ID. A number that the **passwd** database associates with a username. See also *effective UID* (page 1096) and *real UID* (page 1119).

undecillion In the American system, 10^{36}. In the British system, this number is named *sexillion.* See also *large number* (page 1106).

unicast A packet sent from one host to another host. Unicast means one source and one destination.

Unicode A character encoding standard that was designed to cover all major modern written languages with each character having exactly one encoding and being represented by a fixed number of bits.

unmanaged window See *ignored window* on page 1103.

URI Universal Resource Identifier. The generic set of all names and addresses that are short strings referring to objects (typically on the Internet). The most common kinds of URIs are *URLs.*[FOLDOC]

URL Uniform (was Universal) Resource Locator. A standard way of specifying the location of an object, typically a Web page, on the Internet. URLs are a subset of *URIs.*

usage message A message displayed by a command when you call the command using incorrect command-line arguments.

User Datagram Protocol See *UDP.*

User ID See *UID.*

user interface See *interface* on page 1103.

user mode The designation for the state of the system while it is doing user work, such as running a user program (but not the system calls made by the program). Contrast with *system mode* (page 1127).

username The name you enter in response to the **login:** prompt. Other users use your username when they send you mail or write to you. Each username has a corresponding user ID, which is the numeric identifier for the user. Both the username and the user ID are stored in the **passwd** database (**/etc/passwd** or the NIS equivalent). Also *login name*.

userspace The part of memory (RAM) where applications reside. Code running in userspace cannot access hardware directly and cannot access memory allocated to other applications. Also *userland*. See the *KernelAnalysis-HOWTO*.

UTC Coordinated Universal Time. UTC is the equivalent to the mean solar time at the prime meridian (0 degrees longitude). Also called Zulu time (Z stands for longitude zero) and GMT (Greenwich Mean Time).

UTF-8 An encoding that allows *Unicode* (previous page) characters to be represented using sequences of 8-bit bytes.

utility A program included as a standard part of Linux. You typically invoke a utility either by giving a command in response to a shell prompt or by calling it from within a shell script. Utilities are often referred to as commands. Contrast with *builtin (command)* (page 1087).

UUID Universally Unique Identifier. A 128-bit number that uniquely identifies an object on the Internet. Frequently used on Linux systems to identify an **ext2**, **ext3**, or **ext4** disk partition.

variable A name and an associated value. The shell allows you to create variables and use them in the interactive shell and in shell scripts. Also, the shell inherits variables when it is invoked (environment variables; page 480). Some shell variables establish characteristics of the shell; others have values that reflect different aspects of your ongoing interaction with the shell.

viewport Same as *workspace* (page 1133).

virtual console Additional consoles, or displays, that you can view on the system, or physical, console.

virtual machine See *VM*.

virus A *cracker* (page 1092) program that searches out other programs and "infects" them by embedding a copy of itself in them so that they become *Trojan horses* (page 1129). When these programs are executed, the embedded virus is executed as well, propagating the "infection," usually without the user's knowledge. By analogy with biological viruses.[FOLDOC]

VLAN Virtual LAN. A logical grouping of two or more nodes that are not necessarily on the same physical network segment but that share the same network number. A VLAN is often associated with switched Ethernet.[FOLDOC]

VM Virtual machine. A software/hardware emulation of a physical computing environment (i.e., a computer). A virtual machine executes programs just as a physical machine would.

VPN Virtual private network. A private network that exists on a public network, such as the Internet. A VPN is a less expensive substitute for company-owned/leased lines and uses encryption to ensure privacy. A nice side effect is that you can send non-Internet protocols, such as AppleTalk, IPX, or *NetBIOS* (page 1112), over the VPN connection by *tunneling* (page 1130) them through the VPN IP stream.

W2K Windows 2000 Professional or Server.

W3C World Wide Web Consortium (www.w3.org).

WAN Wide area network. A network that interconnects *LANs* (page 1106) and *MANs* (page 1108), spanning a large geographic area (typically states or countries).

WAP Wireless access point. A bridge or router between wired and wireless networks. WAPs typically support some form of access control to prevent unauthorized clients from connecting to the network.

Web ring A collection of Web sites that provide information on a single topic or group of related topics. Each home page that is part of the Web ring has a series of links that let you go from site to site.

whitespace A collective name for SPACEs and/or TABs and occasionally NEWLINEs. Also *white space*.

wide area network See *WAN*.

widget The basic objects of a graphical user interface. A button, *combo box* (page 1090), and *scrollbar* (page 1122) are examples of widgets.

wildcard See *metacharacter* on page 1109.

Wi-Fi Wireless Fidelity. A generic term that refers to any type of *802.11* (page 1082) wireless network.

window On a display screen, a region that runs or is controlled by a particular program.

window manager A program that controls how windows appear on a display screen and how you manipulate them.

Windows share See *share* on page 1123.

WINS Windows Internet Naming Service. The service responsible for mapping NetBIOS names to IP addresses. WINS has the same relationship to NetBIOS names that DNS has to Internet domain names.

WINS server The program responsible for handling WINS requests. This program caches name information about hosts on a local network and resolves them to IP addresses.

wireless access point See *WAP*.

word A sequence of one or more nonblank characters separated from other words by TABs, SPACEs, or NEWLINEs. Used to refer to individual command-line arguments. In vim, a word is similar to a word in the English language—a string of one or more characters bounded by a punctuation mark, a numeral, a TAB, a SPACE, or a NEWLINE.

Work buffer A location where vim stores text while it is being edited. The information in the Work buffer is not written to the file on the disk until you give the editor a command to write it.

working directory The directory that you are associated with at any given time. The relative pathnames you use are *relative to* the working directory. Also *current directory*.

workspace A subdivision of a *desktop* (page 1094) that occupies the entire display.

workstation A small computer, typically designed to fit in an office and be used by one person, and usually equipped with a bit-mapped graphical display, keyboard, and mouse. Differentiated from a *terminal* (page 1128) by its intelligence. A workstation runs Linux on itself while a terminal connects to a computer that runs Linux.

worm A program that propagates itself over a network, reproducing itself as it goes. Today, the term has negative connotations, as it is assumed that only *crackers* (page 1092) write worms. Compare to *virus* (page 1131) and *Trojan horse* (page 1129). From Tapeworm in John Brunner's novel *The Shockwave Rider* (Ballantine Books, 1990) (via XEROX PARC).[FOLDOC]

WYSIWYG What You See Is What You Get. A graphical application, such as a word processor, whose display is similar to its printed output.

X server The X server is the part of the *X Window System* that runs the mouse, keyboard, and display. (The application program is the client.)

X terminal A graphics terminal designed to run the X Window System.

X Window System A design and set of tools for writing flexible, portable windowing applications, created jointly by researchers at MIT and several leading computer manufacturers.

XDMCP X Display Manager Control Protocol. XDMCP allows the login server to accept requests from network displays. XDMCP is built into many X terminals.

***x*DSL** Different types of *DSL* (page 1096) are identified by a prefix—for example, ADSL, HDSL, SDSL, and VDSL.

Xinerama An extension to X.org. Xinerama allows window managers and applications to use the two or more physical displays as one large virtual display. Refer to the Xinerama-HOWTO.

XML Extensible Markup Language. A universal format for structured documents and data on the Web. Developed by *W3C* (page 1132), XML is a pared-down version of SGML. See www.w3.org/XML.

XSM X Session Manager. This program allows you to create a session that includes certain applications. While the session is running, you can perform a *checkpoint* (saves the application state) or a *shutdown* (saves the state and exits from the session). When you log back in, you can load your session so that everything in your session is running just as it was when you logged off.

YUM Yellow Dog Updater, Modified. This package manager checks dependencies and updates software on RPM systems. It has been replaced by DNF.

Z Shell zsh. A *shell* (page 1123) that incorporates many of the features of the *Bourne Again Shell* (page 1086), *Korn Shell* (page 1106), and *TC Shell* (page 1127), as well as many original features.

Zulu time See *UTC* on page 1131.

File Tree Index

A light page number such as 456 indicates a brief mention.

Symbols

Utility Index

A light page number such as 456 indicates a brief mention. Page numbers followed by the letter t refer to tables.

Symbols

A

B

C

L

M

N

O

P

R

S

MAIN INDEX

An italic page number such as *123* indicates a definition. A light page number such as 456 indicates a brief mention. Page numbers followed by the letter t refer to tables. Only variables that must always appear with a leading dollar sign are indexed with a leading dollar sign. Other variables are indexed without a leading dollar sign.

SYMBOLS

NUMERICS

A

B

C

D

E

F

N

Q

R

T

U

W